June 27–29, 2011
Darmstadt, Germany

II0131988

**Association for
Computing Machinery**

Advancing Computing as a Science & Profession

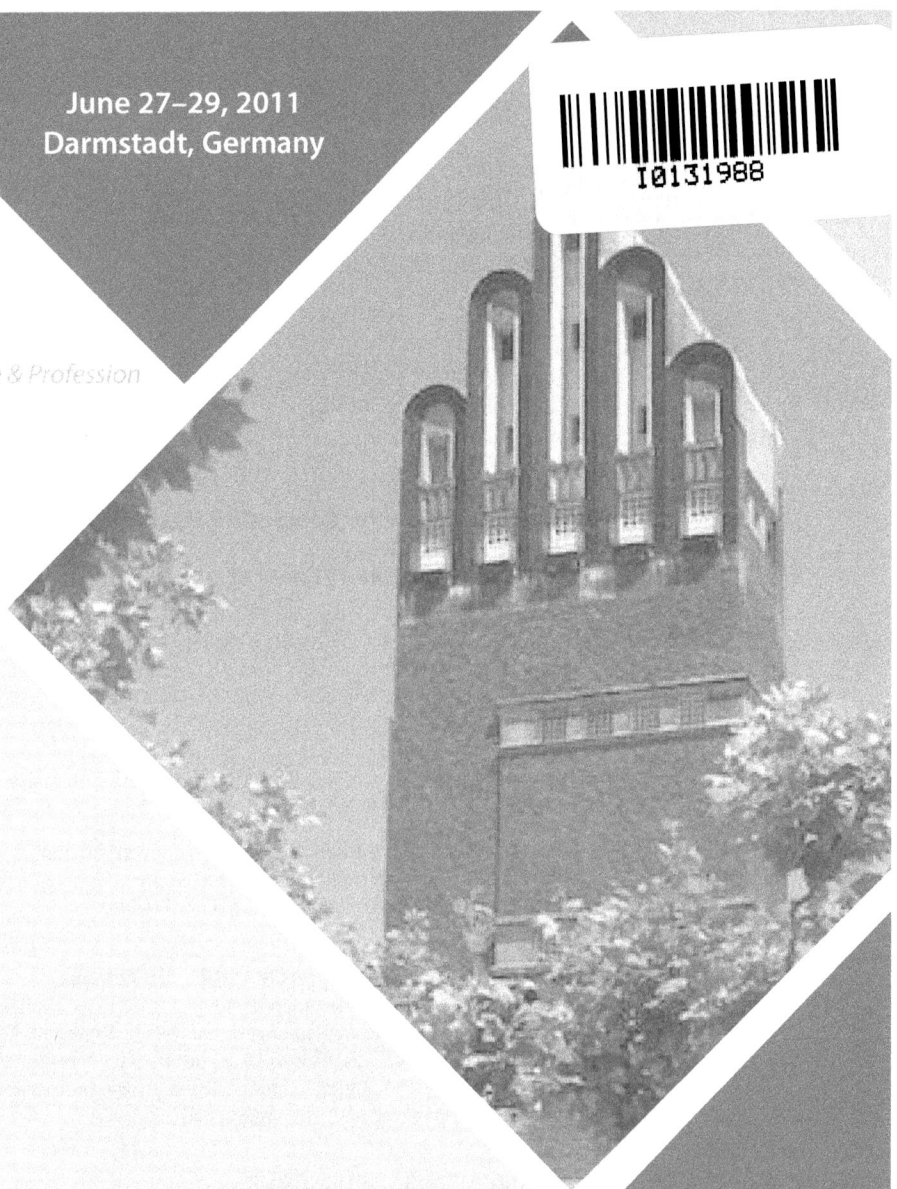

ITiCSE'11

Proceedings of the 16th Annual Conference on
Innovation and Technology in Computer Science

Sponsored by:
ACM SIGCSE

Supported by:
**TU Darmstadt, Intel, BlackBerry, GK E-Learning, SoftwareAG,
Carlo und Karin Giersch-Stiftung, and Sparkasse Darmstradt**

Association for Computing Machinery

Advancing Computing as a Science & Profession

The Association for Computing Machinery
2 Penn Plaza, Suite 701
New York, New York 10121-0701

ISBN: 978-1-4503-0887-8

Additional copies may be ordered prepaid from:

ACM Order Department
PO Box 30777
New York, NY 10087-0777, USA

Phone: 1-800-342-6626 (USA and Canada)
+1-212-626-0500 (Global)
Fax: +1-212-944-1318
E-mail: acmhelp@acm.org
Hours of Operation: 8:30 am – 4:30 pm ET

Printed in the USA

Foreword

Welcome to Darmstadt, Germany ...

Darmstadt is a small town well-placed in the infrastructural center of Germany, roughly half-way between Frankfurt with its large international airport and banking center, and Heidelberg with its many cultural offerings. Both Darmstadt and the TU Darmstadt look back on a long history where they played larger or smaller roles in history or science.

We are proud that the 16th ACM Innovation and Technology in Computer Science Education (ITiCSE) conference has chosen Darmstadt and the TU Darmstadt as their host. This is the first time the conference is held in Germany, and we are sure that Darmstadt will prove to have been a great choice for this!

ITiCSE 2011 welcomes all researchers and professionals interested in the use of technology in support of learning and teaching in the computing field including the practice of teaching and research. The program consists of invited keynotes, working groups, exhibits, and technical sessions featuring papers, panels, posters, demonstrations, tips, techniques, and student posters. Keynote speakers include Prof. Dr. Ulrik Schroeder from the RWTH Aachen (Germany) and Prof. Mark Guzdial, Georgia Institute of Technology and winner of the 2010 Karl V. Karlstrom Outstanding Educator Award.

The conference offers a variety of opportunities to learn from and interact with computing colleagues from around the world. The conference opens with a plenary presentation by an invited speaker and includes three parallel tracks with paper presentations, invited panels, working groups and special project presentations. We accepted 66 excellent papers for presentation from among the 169 submitted—an acceptance rate of 39%. Each paper received at least four reviews. We could easily have filled another conference day with very good paper submissions if we had had the time! Additionally, 52 posters and 16 tips, techniques, or courseware presentations were accepted, possibly setting a new record for this category.

Working groups start on Saturday and will work in earnest throughout the conference, with a presentation of their preliminary results on Monday. The conference itself will start with a keynote, followed by parallel paper sessions, a panel and the Working Group reports.

Tuesday afternoon and evening is kept free to allow participants to join one of the two excursions, to explore the city on their own, to mingle with colleagues on city tours or simply to relax. The conference will end with a great conference dinner in the ruins of a nearby castle. The conference is also framed by the FIFA Women's World Cup, with Germany facing Nigeria on the evening following the conference, and the Darmstadt City "Heinerfest" festival.

We would like to thank our reviewers and conference committee members.

Guido Rößling
ITiCSE 2011 Conference Chair

Tom Naps, Christian Spannagel
ITiCSE 2011 Program Co-chairs

Table of Contents

Keynote Talks

Session 1: Coding Skills

Session 2: Web Development

Session 3: Understanding OO

Session 4: Activities for Hardware Courses

Session 5: Attracting K-12 Students to CS

Session 6: Enhancing CS Lectures

Session 7: Environments for Motivating Students

Session 8: Tool Support for Upper-Level Courses

Session 9: Integrating Web-Based Technologies into Courses

Tips, Techniques & Courseware Session III: Tools and APIs

Tips, Techniques & Courseware Session IV: Supporting Novice Programmers

Panel

Posters

ITiCSE 2011 Conference Organization

Conference Chair: Guido Rößling *(TU Darmstadt, Germany)*

Program Co-Chairs: Tom Naps *(University of Wisconsin Oshkosh, USA)*
Christian Spannagel *(PH Heidelberg, Germany)*

Treasurer and Registrar: Cary Laxer *(Rose-Hulman Institute of Technology, USA)*

Working Groups Co-Coordinators: Elizabeth S. Adams *(James Madison University, USA)*
Jürgen Börstler *(Blekinge Institute of Technology, Sweden)*

Panels and Faculty Posters: Myles McNally *(Alma College, USA)*

Student Posters: Torsten Brinda *(Universität Erlangen, Germany)*

Tips, Techniques and Courseware: Steve Cunningham *(Brown Cunningham Associates, USA)*
Rainer Oechsle *(FH Trier, Germany)*

Proceedings: Michael Goldweber *(Xavier University, USA)*

Student Activities: Stephen Cooper *(Stanford University, USA)*
Fabian Rothmann *(TU Darmstadt, Germany)*

Evaluations: Michael E. Caspersen *(Aarhus University, Denmark)*

ITiCSE 2011 Working Groups

Working Group 1: Motivating All Our Students?

Leader: Janet Carter (*University of Kent at Canterbury*)

Participants: Dennis Bouvier (*Southern Illinois University*)
                Rachel Cardell-Oliver (*University of Western Australia*)
                Stan Kurkovsky (*Central Connecticut State*)
                Stefanie Markham (*Georgia State University*)
                Bill McClung (*Nebraska Weseleyan University*)
                Roger McDermott (*Robert Gordon University*)
                Chuck Riedesel (*University of Nebraska – Lincoln*)
                Jian Shi (*University of Southhampton*)
                Su White (*University of Southampton*)
                Malcolm Wieck (*Christchurch Polytechnic Institute of Technology*)

Working Group 2: Informatics in Secondary Education

Co-Leaders: Peter Hubwieser (*TU München*)
              Torsten Brinda (*University of Erlangen-Nuremberg*)
              Johannes Magenheim (*University of Paderborn*)
              Sigrid Schubert (*University of Siegen*)

Participants: Michal Armoni (*Weizmann Institute of Science*)
                Valentina Dagiene (*Vilnius University*)
                Ira Diethelm (*Carl von Ossietzky Universität Oldenburg*)
                Michail N. Giannakos (*Ionian University*)
                Maria Knobelsdorf (*Universität Potsdam*)
                Roland Mittermeir (*Alpen-Adria Universität Klagenfurt*)

Working Group 3: Information Assurance Education in Two- and Four-Year Institutions

Co-Leaders: Lance Pérez (*University of Nebraska – Lincoln*)
              Stephen Cooper (*Stanford University*)
              Elizabeth K. Hawthorne (*Union County College*)
              Susanne Wetzel (*Stevens Institute of Technology*)

Participants: Joel Brynielsson (*Royal Institute of Technology*)
                Asım Gençer Gökce (*TÜBİTAK / UEKAE*)
                John Impagliazzo (*Qatar University*)
                Margaret Leary (*Northern Virginia Community College*)
                Kara Nance (*University of Alaska, Fairbanks*)
                Amelia Phillips (*Highline Community College*)
                Norbert Pohlmann (*University of Applied Science, Gelsenkirchen*)
                Blair Taylor (*Towson University*)
                Shambhu Upadhyaya (*University of Buffalo*)

ITiCSE 2011 Reviewers

Raman Adaikkalavan, *Indiana University South Bend*

Elizabeth S. Adams, *James Madison University*

Rajeev Agrawal, *North Carolina A&T State University*

Tuukka Ahoniemi, *Tampere University of Technology and Digia Plc*

Carl Alphonce, *University at Buffalo, The State University of New York*

Ruth Anderson, *University of Washington*

Barbara Anthony, *Southwestern University*

Michal Armoni, *Weizmann Institute of Science*

John Aycock, *University of Calgary*

David Barnes, *University of Kent*

Lewis Barnett, *University of Richmond*

John Barr, *Ithaca College*

Valerie Barr, *Union College*

Tim Bell, *University of Canterbury*

Mordechai Ben-Ari, *Weizmann Institute of Science*

Mikael Berndtsson, *University of Skovde*

Stefan Brandle, *Taylor University*

Torsten Brinda, *University of Erlangen-Nuremberg*

Kim Bruce, *Pomona College*

Dennis Brylow, *Marquette University*

David Bunde, *Knox College*

Barry Burd, *Drew University*

Andre Paul Calitz, *Nelson Mandela Metropolitan University*

Daniel Canas, *Wake Forest University*

Lillian N. Cassel, *Villanova University*

Maiga Chang, *Athabasca University*

Mahesh Chaudhari, *Arizona State University*

Peng-Wen Chen, *Oriental Institute of Technology*

Ping Chen, *University of Houston-Downtown*

Li-hsiang Cheo, *William Paterson University of New Jersey*

Jayan Kurian Chirayath, *Royal Melbourne Institute of Technology*

Radhouane Chouchane, *Columbus State University*

Vincent Cicirello, *Richard Stockton College*

John Cigas, *Park University*

Peter Clarke, *Florida International University*

Tony Clear, *Auckland University of Technology*

Joe Clifton, *University of Wisconsin, Platteville*

Stephen Cooper, *Purdue University*

Michelle Craig, *University of Toronto*

Mark Crouch, *Angelo State University*

Joyce Blair Crowell, *Belmont University*

Jose Cunha, *New University of Lisbon*

Steve Cunningham, *Stanford University*

Quintin Cutts, *University of Glasgow*

Nell Dale, *University of Texas at Austin*

Andrew Dalton, *Western Carolina University*

Douglas Dankel, *University of Florida*

Lawrence D'Antonio, *Ramapo College of New Jersey*

Stephen Davies, *University of Mary Washington*

Renzo Davoli, *University of Bologna*

Adrienne Decker, *University at Buffalo SUNY*

Katherine Deibel, *University of Washington-Seattle*

Rafael del Vado, *Universidad Complutense de Madrid*

Dorothy Deremer, *Montclair State University*

Molisa Derk, *Dickinson State University*

Kamyar Dezhgosha, *University of Illinois at Springfield*

Michele Di Santo, *University of Sannio*

Suzanne W. Dietrich, *Arizona State University*

William Doane, *Bennington College*

Zachary Dodds, *Harvey Mudd College*

John Dooley, *Knox College*

Brian Dorn, *University of Hartford*

Maureen Doyle, *Northern Kentucky University*

Peter Drexel, *Plymouth State University*

J. Philip East, *University of Northern Iowa*

Mary Anne Egan, *Siena College*

Joseph Ekstrom, *Brigham Young University*

Stephanie Elzer, *Millersville University*

Barbara Ericson, *Georgia Tech*

Daniel Ernst, *The University of Wisconsin - Eau Claire*

Henry Etlinger, *Rochester Institute of Technology*

Alan Fekete, *University of Sydney*

Maria Feldgen, *Universidad de Buenos Aires*

Ernest Ferguson, *Northwest Missouri State University*

Samantha Foley, *Oak Ridge National Laboratory*

Edward Fox, *Virginia Tech*

Alessio Gaspar, *University of South Florida Polytechnic*

Paul Gestwicki, *Ball State University*

Michael Goldweber, *Xavier University*

Jean Goulet, *Universite de Sherbrooke*

Mary Granger, *George Washington University*

Simon Gray, *College of Wooster*

Mark Guzdial, *Georgia Institute of Technology*

Bruria Haberman, *Holon Inst. of Technology and The Weizmann Inst. of Science*

John Hamer, *University of Auckland*

Brian Hanks, *Amazon.com*

Stuart Hansen, *University of Wisconsin - Parkside*

Michael Hartle, *TU Darmstadt*

Christopher Haynes, *Indiana University*

Orit Hazzan, *Technion – Israel Institute of Technology*

Sarah Heckman, *North Carolina State University*

David Hemmendinger, *Union College*

Katherine Herbert, *Montclair State University*

Matthew Hertz, *Canisius College*

Curtis Hill, *Valley City State University*

Lewis Hitchner, *Cal Poly State University*

William Hochstettler, *Franklin*

Kai Hoever, *TU Darmstadt*

Jesper Holck, *Copenhagen Business School*

William Hooper, *Belmont University*

Cay Horstmann, *San Jose State University*

David Hovemeyer, *York College of Pennsylvania*

Janet Hughes, *University of Dundee*

Frances Hunt, *Educational Testing Service*

Steven Huss-Lederman, *Beloit College*

Michelle Hutton, *The Girls' Middle School/CSTA*

Jorge Eduardo Ibarra-Esquer, *Universidad Autonoma de Baja California*

Richard James, *Rollins College*

David John, *Wake Forest University*

Colin Johnson, *University of Kent at Canterbury*

Julie Johnson, *Vanderbilt University*

Mark Johnson, *Central College*

Anthony Joseph, *Pace University*

Daniel Joyce, *Villanova University*

Edward Jung, *Southern Polytechnic State University*

Ville Karavirta, *Aalto University*

David Kauchak, *Pomona College*

David G. Kay, *University of California, Irvine*

Jennifer Kay, *Rowan University*

Andreas Kerren, *Linnaeus University*

Nancy Kinnersley, *University of Kansas*

Carsten Kleiner, *University of Applied Sciences & Arts Hannover*

Michael Kolling, *University of Kent*

Janet Kourik, *Webster University*

Joan Krone, *Denison University*

Stan Kurkovsky, *Central Connecticut State University*

Zachary Kurmas, *Grand Valley State University*

Lynn Lambert, *Christopher Newport University*

Catherine Lang, *Swinburne University of Technology*

Eric Larson, *Seattle University*

Mary Last, *self-employed*

Deirdre Lawless, *Dublin Institute of Technology*

Cary Laxer, *Rose-Hulman Institute of Technology*

Alina Lazar, *Youngstown State University*

Arthur Lee, *Claremont McKenna College*

Byong Lee, *Bennett College*

Gilliean Lee, *Lander University*

Ming-Han Lee, *TU Darmstadt*

Weidong Liao, *Shepherd University*

Raymond Lister, *University of Technology*

Jigang Liu, *Metropolitan State University*

Sergio F. Lopes, *University of Minho*

Antonio M. Lopez, *Retired*

Joan Lucas, *State University of New York, College At Brockport*

Andrew Luxton-Reilly, *The University of Auckland*

Bonnie MacKellar, *St John's University*

Michael Main, *University of Colorado at Boulder*

Lauri Malmi, *Aalto University*

Yannis Manolopoulos, *Aristotle University of Thessaloniki*

Dave Mason, *Ryerson Polytechnic University*

Lester McCann, *The University of Arizona*

O. William McClung, *Nebraska Wesleyan University*

Jeffrey McConnell, *Canisius College*

Chris McDonald, *The University of Western Australia*

Scott McElfresh, *Wake Forest University*

Pedro Medeiros, *Universidade Nova de Lisboa*

Antonio Jose Mendes, *University of Coimbra*

Jose Carlos Metrolho, *Polytechnic Institute of Castelo Branco*

Gail Miles, *Lenoir-Rhyne College*

Joe Miro, *Universitat de les Illes Balears*

David Moffat, *Glasgow Caledonian University*

Patricia Morreale, *Kean University*

Michael Murphy, *Concordia University Texas*

Robert Neufeld, *McPherson College - Emeritus*

Robert Noonan, *College of William and Mary*

Rainer Oechsle, *FH Trier*

Amos Olagunju, *St. Cloud State University*

Simon Olberding, *TU Darmstadt*

Lawrence Osborne, *Lamar University*

Barbara Owens, *Southwestern University*

Katherine Panciera, *University of Minnesota*

Iraklis Paraskakis, *City College*

Abelardo Pardo, *Carlos III University of Madrid*

David Parker, *Salisbury University*

James Paterson, *Glasgow Caledonian University*

Laurie Patterson, *University of North Carolina Wilmington*

Arnold Pears, *Uppsala University*

Teresa Peterman, *Grand Valley State University*

Andrew Petersen, *University of Toronto Mississauga*

Vreda Pieterse, *University of Pretoria*

Paul Piwowarski, *University of Kentucky*

Wayne Pollock, *Hillsborough Community College*

Irene Polycarpou, *Colorado School of Mines*

John-Paul Pretti, *University of Waterloo*

Philip Prins, *Seattle Pacific University*

Atanas Radenski, *Chapman University*

John Rager, *Amherst College*

Noa Ragonis, *Beit Berl College*

Bina Ramamurthy, *University at Buffalo*

Samuel Rebelsky, *Grinnell College*

Charles Riedesel, *University of Nebraska - Lincoln*

Suzanne Rivoire, *Sonoma State University*

Christian Roberson, *Plymouth State University*

Eric Roberts, *Stanford University*

Stefan Robila, *Montclair State University*

Susan H. Rodger, *Duke University*

Guido Roessling, *Technische Universitaet Darmstadt*

Constantine Roussos, *Lynchburg College*

Ingrid Russell, *University of Hartford*

Adrian Rusu, *Rowan University*

Mihaela Sabin, *University of New Hampshire*

Mehran Sahami, *Stanford University*

Ian Sanders, *University of the Witwatersrand*

Otto Seppala, *Helsinki University of Technology*

Behrooz Seyed-Abbassi, *University of North Florida*

Judy Sheard, *Monash University*

Ching-Kuang Shene, *Michigan Technological University*

Mark Sherriff, *University of Virginia*

Yasuto Shirai, *Shizuoka University*

Charles Shub, *University of Colorado at Colorado Springs*

Peter Smith, *California State University - Channel Islands*

Raja Sooriamurthi, *Carnegie Mellon University*

Barry Soroka, *Cal Poly Pomona*

Christian Spannagel, *PH Heidelberg*

Carol Spradling, *Northwest Missouri State University*

Jeffrey Stone, *Pennsylvania State University*

Fred Strickland, *South University*

Dario Suarez Gracia, *Universidad de Zaragoza*

Jorma Tarhio, *Helsinki University of Technology*

James Teresco, *Siena College*

Allison Elliott Tew, *Georgia Institute of Technology*

William Thacker, *Winthrop University*

Megan Thomas, *California State University Stanislaus*

Rebecca Thomas, *Bard College*

Errol Thompson, *University of Birmingham*

John Thompson, *Buffalo State College*

Deborah Trytten, *University of Oklahoma*

Shengru Tu, *University of New Orleans*

William Turner, *Wabash College*

Guenter Tusch, *Grand Valley State University*

Hakan Tuzun, *Hacettepe University*

Suleyman Uludag, *The University of Michigan - Flint*

Jaime Urquiza-Fuentes, *Rey Juan Carlos University/Lecturer*

Ian Utting, *University of Kent at Canterbury*

Jan Vahrenhold, *Technische Universität Dortmund*

Tammy VanDeGrift, *University of Portland*

Troy Vasiga, *University of Waterloo*

Steven Vegdahl, *University of Portland*

J. Angel Velazquez-Iturbide, *Universidad Rey Juan Carlos*

Tamar Vilner, *The Open University of Israel*

David Voorhees, *Le Moyne College*

Sally Wahba, *Clemson University*

Gursimran Walia, *North Dakota State University*

Henry Walker, *Grinnell College*

Thomas Way, *Villanova University*

Howard Whitston, *University of South Alabama*

Linda Wilkens, *Providence College*

Craig Wills, *Worcester Polytechnic Institute*

Gary Ka Wai Wong, *the Community College at Lingnan University*

Arthur Yanushka, *Christian Brothers University*

Juang Yih-Ruey, *Jinwen University of Science & Technology*

ITiCSE 2011 Sponsor & Supporters

Sponsor:

Supporters:

 TECHNISCHE UNIVERSITÄT DARMSTADT

 GRADUIERTENKOLLEG E-LEARNING

Carlo und Karin Giersch-Stiftung

Keynote Talk

A Bouquet of Measures to Promote Computer Science in Middle & High Schools

Ulrik Schroeder
RWTH Aachen University
schroeder@informatik.rwth-aachen.de

Abstract

Computer science faces the same problem worldwide: too few women in computing, low enrollment and high failure rates in university programs. There is growing consciousness which has led to various ideas and programs to deal with these problems. My talk will introduce a set of measures which we have implemented at RWTH Aachen University to tackle the problem on different levels. Therefore, I will present our successful program go4IT! of robotic courses for girls in 5th and 6th grade and some empirical results of how these influence their interest in STEM topics. Currently we are developing follow-up measures based on Android and GUI programming on smartphones. These measures cumulate into our newly founded Computer Science Junior Academy InfoSphere as out-of-school educational lab. There we offer a variety of learning modules which can last between two hours and a few days. Complete school classes can book InfoSphere modules or interested pupils of different ages can collaborate on self-organized projects. We have implemented various learning programs for multi-modal devices such as multi-touch tables and smartphones in order to introduce different topics of computer science. Our vision for these educational labs is the enhancement to different disciplines which bring together learners of all ages from K-12, students, researchers and professionals for life-long learning and vocational training.

Categories and Subject Descriptors: K.3.2 [**Computers and Education**]: Computer and Information Science Education – *Computer Science Education*

General Terms: Design, Experimentation

Bio

Dr. Schroeder received his Diploma in Computer Science from the Technische Universität (TU) Darmstadt. He stayed at the TU Darmstadt receiving his Ph.D. there as well. His teaching focus lies in software engineering, CS1, and computer science dducation. After leaving the TU Darmstadt, he took on a professorship at the PH Ludwigsburg in the Didactics of computer science, and then changed to a full professorship at the RWTH Aachen, where he now heads the I9 research group focussing on e-learning and computer science education research. He is active in the GI, the German sister of the ACM, where is plays a leading role in several areas touching on e-learning or computer science education.

Keynote Talk

Technology for Teaching the Rest of Us

Mark Guzdial

Georgia Institute of Technology

guzdial@cc.gatech.edu

Abstract

The motivated student is easy to teach. You facilitate learning and get out of the way. It's much more challenging to teach the student who is less motivated, or who needs knowledge to support their main interest. Think of the graphics designer who chooses to learn scripting to make their job easier, but doesn't want to learn to "program" and whose many (simple) mistakes cost valuable time. Think of the secondary-school business teacher who wants to teach computer science, but who doesn't want to learn to be a professional programmer. The number of people who need some knowledge of a domain may be much greater than those who need expertise in that domain. Providing learning opportunities tailored to the needs and interests of the learner, potentially motivating that interest where necessary, is a great and important challenge in an increasingly technological society. My talk will describe characteristics of these challenges and suggest where computing technologies and computing education research insights may provide solutions.

Categories and Subject Descriptors: K.3.2 [**Computers and Education**]: Computer and Information Science Education – *Computer Science Education*

General Terms: Design, Experimentation

Bio

Mark Guzdial is a Professor in the School of Interactive Computing in the College of Computing at Georgia Institute of Technology. His research focuses on learning sciences and technology, specifically, computing education research. He has published several books on the use of media as a context for learning computing. He was the original developer of the "Swiki" which was the first wiki designed for educational use. He received the Ph.D. degree in Education and Computer Science from the University of Michigan in 1993. He serves on the both ACM's Education Board and the Special Interest Group in CS Education (SIGCSE) Board, and is on the editorial boards of the "Journal of the Learning Sciences," "ACM Transactions on Computing Education," and "Communications of the ACM." Dr. Guzdial, along with his wife and colleague, Barbara Ericson, were the recipients of the 2010 ACM Karl V. Karlstrom Outstanding Educator award.

Security Injections: Modules to Help Students Remember, Understand, and Apply Secure Coding Techniques

Blair Taylor
Towson University
7800 York Rd., Towson, MD, USA, 21252
410-704-4560
btaylor@towson.edu

Siddharth Kaza
Towson University
7800 York Rd., Towson, MD, USA, 21252
410-704-2633
skaza@towson.edu

ABSTRACT

With our global reliance on software, secure and robust programming has never been more important. Yet academic institutions have been slow to add secure coding to the curriculum. We present a model using checklist-based security injection modules to increase student awareness and ability to apply secure coding principles, specifically - identify, understand, and correct key security issues in code. The model is evaluated by mapping assessment questions to the cognitive dimension of the revised Bloom's taxonomy. Experiments with students in four sections of CS0 and CS1 show that students using our modules perform significantly better at remembering, understanding and applying secure coding concepts. Students exposed to the modules also show increased ability to write code to address specific security issues.

Categories and Subject Descriptors

K3.2 [**Computers and Education**]: Computer and Information Science Education - *computer science education, curriculum, information systems education.*

General Terms

Security

Keywords

Security Education, Computer Science Curriculum, Information Security Curriculum Development, Secure Coding, Checklists

1. INTRODUCTION

With the advent of 2011, secure coding is more important than ever. Globally, we are increasingly reliant on software in all fields, including military, medical, financial, and critical infrastructure systems. At the same time, increased connectivity means more malicious attacks. The net effect sets up the scenario for the perfect storm in cybersecurity. The costs are already staggering – the U.S. economy loses one trillion dollars a year to cyber-attacks [8] and the human costs in terms of loss-of-life and health risks are escalating [21].

Security education is a crucial component in addressing the current cybersecurity crisis [4, 7]. However, while many colleges and universities have added security tracks and security courses,

the Computer Science (CS) academic community has been slow to incorporate security and secure coding as part of the entire curriculum [12, 16]. The challenges are significant - faculty that are untrained in security, an academic culture that fails to recognize the consequence of software vulnerabilities, a lack of resources, and courses that are overcrowded with difficult topics and struggling students.

For the past four years, we have been developing and implementing checklist-based security injection modules for the introductory courses towards the goal of increasing students' security awareness and ability to apply security principles. To address the challenges of teaching secure coding we have adapted the following tenets: 1) create a security mindset, 2) start early, and 3) use active learning components.

Our previous publications in this area [5, 14, 15] have focused on student awareness. In this paper we present the results of assessing, not just awareness, but also the ability to apply the concepts learned. In doing so, we map our assessment questions to the revised Bloom's taxonomy [1] and present results on how well students remembered, understood, applied, and created knowledge related with secure coding in four CS0 and CS1 classes.

2. BACKGROUND

In the past decade, both two and four year institutions have responded to the security crisis by adding security tracks and security electives, which may or may not include secure coding, to the CS curriculum. At our own institution, while the number of students in the security track is increasing, the majority of students do not opt for the track. The problem with electives is that they are a) optional and b) offered late in the curriculum, after students have established programming skills. The end result is that most CS students graduate with inadequate secure coding skills.

2.1 Security in the CS Curriculum

To ensure that all computing graduates are armed with the necessary security skills, including secure coding, the next step is comprehensive security integration throughout the CS curriculum [11,14]. There is evidence of progress in this direction [3] including government initiatives calling for a larger role of education in cybersecurity [20]. The 2008 changes made by the ACM and IEEE to the CS curriculum guidelines include the word "secure" or "security" 136 times [1, 12] which will shape future course development. Based on our research and experience, the strategies for successful security integration include:

Creating a 'security mindset'. Many secure coding experts agree that the most critical issue in security education is encouraging 'a security mindset'. The first step is getting faculty and students to recognize the importance of software vulnerabilities and writing secure and robust code.

Security Checklist		
Vulnerability:Buffer Overflow **Course:** CS1		
Task - Check each line of code		Completed
1. Finding Arrays:		
1.1 Underline each array declaration		
1.2 For each array, underline all subsequent references		
2. Index Variables - legal range for an array of size n is o <= i < n		
2.1 For each underlined access that uses a variable as an index, write the legal range next to it.		
2.2 For each index marked in 2.1, underline all occurrences of that variable.		
2.3. Mark with a V any assignments, inputs or operations that may modify these index variables.		
3. Loops that modify index variables		
3.1 Find loops that modify variables used to index arrays. For any index that occurs as part of a loop conditional, underline the loop limit. For example, if *i < max* is the conditional in a for *loop*, underline *max*		
3.2. Write the legal range of the array index next to the loop limit as you did in step 2.1. Mark with a V if the loop limit could exceed the legal range of the array index. Watch out for loop that go until *i <=max* , as the largest valid index is *max-1*		
3.3 If the upper or lower loop limit is a variable, it must be checked just as indices are checked in Step 2		
Highlighted areas indicate vulnerabilities!		

Figure 1. An example checklist for buffer overflow from the CS1 security injection

Starting early. Secure coding education must begin in the first courses required of CS students - Computer Science I (CS1) and Computer Science 2 (CS2) and the prerequisite logic course Computer Science 0 (CS0), if applicable. Teaching secure coding concepts in parallel with programming fundamentals ensures that students establish robust programming skills. One of the fundamental principles of security is to "build security in" and not treat security as an afterthought.

Using active learning. Most college professors, including Computer Science educators, have no formal background in education. As a result, Computer Science and Information Security curriculum is often constructed with little consideration to learning sciences. Niekerk recommends "adherence to sound pedagogical principles when constructing information security campaigns, could improve the efficiency of such campaigns" [10]. In many courses, security concepts are relegated to a sidebar in the textbook. Computer science students have been found to be active learners [9, 17] and we need to ensure that we are using techniques that allow students to assimilate secure coding concepts.

2.2 The Security Injections Project

For the past four years, we have worked with instructors across five institutions to incorporate secure coding concepts into the CS curriculum [5, 13, 14,15,19]. Employing the adage, *start early*, we have focused primarily on the introductory programming courses required of all CS majors: Computer Science I (CS1) and Computer Science II (CS2), and the preparatory course in programming logic (CS0). Our project goals include:

1) Increase faculty awareness of secure coding concepts
2) Increase students' awareness of secure coding issues
3) Increase students' ability to apply secure coding principles

Towards this end, we have developed and implemented a series of self-contained security injection modules that target key security concepts including integer overflow, buffer overflow, and input validation. Modules are available in different languages, including C++ and Java and are located at http://triton.towson.edu/~cssecinj.

Our project goal of increasing faculty awareness goes hand in hand towards *creating a security mindset*. We have conducted on-site workshops at each institution to introduce faculty to our modules and discuss the importance of this effort. Currently, we have reached over 60 faculty. Faculty surveys show that instructors felt more comfortable with the concepts after using the modules.

To reach our project goal of increasing students' security awareness and at the same time *create a security mindset,* each module addresses a key security concept and provides real life examples, to drive home the significance of security vulnerabilities. To ensure that student have fully inculcated these concepts and can apply secure coding principles, we have designed our modules with *active learning* in mind. The modules were created to ensure that learning progresses at various levels of the Cognitive dimension of the Bloom's taxonomy with its six categories – remembering, understanding, applying, analyzing, evaluating, and creating [2].They are modeled on the labs used in the traditional sciences which include background information to create a framework for learning, a hands-on lab activity, and reflective questions.

Another component of our modules and a primary example of the way we employ active learning is the security checklist [13].Checklists have long been used in aviation for pre-flight checks and more recently have grabbed headlines for their use in healthcare for error reduction and adherence to best practices in clinical care. The security checklist is not "a substitute for analysis" [2], but serves primarily as a learning tool to help reinforce key security principles. Each checklist targets one concept, such as the CS1 buffer overflow example in **Figure 1**. The self-check process or evaluation required by the checklist requires higher order skills in the learning taxonomy and helps students fully synthesize the targeted skill.

In this paper, we report on results to assess student ability to apply the secure coding concepts. We do this by mapping our assessment questions to the Bloom's taxonomy and using a quasi-experimental design with four sections of CS0 and CS1.

3. ASSESSMENT DESIGN

The assessment was done using two tools - a pre/post survey and a code-check exercise at the end of the semester. The survey contained three kinds of questions:

1. general security awareness: assessed familiarity with common security concerns including phishing, firewalls, and encryption
2. secure coding specific: assessed knowledge on buffer overflow, input validation, and integer error as targeted in the modules
3. demographic and interest in security

The code check exercise included a small code sample (shown in Table 1 followed by three questions (shown later in the section). The intent of the code-check was to test student ability to apply the concepts learned in the modules.

Table 1. Code check exercise used in CS0

```
#include <iostream>
using namespace std;
int main()
{
    int roomLength;
    int roomWidth;
    int area;
    int arr[10];
    int i;

    cout << "Enter room length and width";
    cin >> roomLength;
    cin >> roomWidth;

    area = roomLength * roomWidth;
    cout << "room area is " << area << endl;

    cout << "Enter which element you want?";
    cin >> i;
    cout << arr[i];

    return 0;
}
```

We used the guidelines suggested by Thompson et al. [18] to map our assessment tools to the revised Bloom's taxonomy. Table 2 shows the mapping of the pre and post vulnerability-specific survey questions.

Table 2. Classification of the pre/post survey questions within the cognitive process dimension of the Bloom's taxonomy

Question	Classi-fication
Integer overflow occurs when ...	R
Integer overflow is caused by:	U
Which of the following should your well-designed program do before processing user input?	R
Invalid input can come from the...	U
Which programming mistake is one of the major vulnerabilities in today's applications?	R

Note: The categories are marked as Remembering (R) and Understanding (U)

Similarly, the questions in the code-check results were also classified into the taxonomy. As Thompson et al. [18] suggest, classifying questions related to coding into one category is not easy or appropriate. The first two questions in the code-check were:

1. *Review the above code. Mark with a 'V' each line of code that has a potential vulnerability.*
2. *Next to the 'V', list whether it is a possible:*
   a. *Buffer overflow*
   b. *Integer overflow*
   c. *Input validation error*

We classified both of these as questions in the 'Remembering' and the 'Applying' category. The applying category was appropriate as both questions required 'carrying out or using a procedure in a given situation' [18]. The procedure in this case was the use of the security checklist to identify the lines in the code where the vulnerability was present. However, to do that, students needed to recall the appropriate checklist for each vulnerability thus classifying them into the remembering category.

The third question was:

3. *Next to each 'V', write the appropriate code or describe the steps to avoid the vulnerability.*

This question was classified into the 'Creating' category as it required the students to construct a code segment through the application of known techniques. For instance, our injection modules had guidelines on the procedures to write code to prevent a buffer overflow, however, they did not provide explicit code examples to do the same. Thus, even though the students knew the procedure, they were creating the new code.

The survey and the code check were given to two sections of CS1 and two sections of CS0. Two of the sections were 'experimental' sections that explicitly used the three security modules and two were control sections. All sections were taught by the same instructor. No special effort was made to not introduce the security vulnerabilities in the control section and the instructor was encouraged to include her usual content when discussing input validation, integer errors and buffer overflows.

In this study, we only focused on the results of the vulnerability specific questions (type 2) in the survey and the code-check exercise. The following hypotheses were tested:

H1: The post-survey scores of the experimental sections will be significantly higher than the post-survey scores of control sections.

> H1a: The pre-survey scores of both sections will show no significant difference (this will imply that initial student knowledge in both groups was the same).

H2: Students in the experimental sections will be better at locating potential security vulnerabilities in a given code segment.

H3: Students in the experimental sections will be better at identifying potential security vulnerabilities in a given code segment.

H4: Students in experimental sections will be better at fixing security vulnerabilities in a given code segment.

4. RESULTS

A total of 109 students provided valid responses to the survey and 93 students completed the code-check exercise over two semesters.

4.1 Comparison of survey scores

The score of each survey was calculated by counting the number of correct answers (we report on just the secure coding related questions here). We picked the Mann-Whitney non-parametric test to compare the mean rank of the scores in the two groups (experiment and control). This was done for three primary reasons – 1) the n for the groups is different, 2) the Kolmogorov-Smirnov and Shapiro-Wilk test showed that the scores were not normally distributed, and 3) the two groups were independent samples. Figure 2 summarizes the results. As can be seen, for CS0 sections (first two bars in the figure), it was found that the difference between the average post-survey scores of the control (n = 32) and the experimental sections (n = 26) was statistically significant ($p < 0.001$). We also found that there was no statistically significant difference in the pre-survey scores of both sections, thus implying that students started at the same level of knowledge. For CS1, there was no significant difference in the post-survey scores between the sections (n = 15 for control and n = 17 for experiment) at the $p < 0.01$ level, though the difference was significant at the $p < 0.10$ level (which we are considering as mildly significant). However, we also found that in the pre-survey, the control section was significantly higher than the experimental section, implying that the students already knew more about the vulnerabilities than the experimental section at the start of the semester. Thus, even though both sections improved at the end of the semester and the experiment section scored higher, the difference between the two in the post-tests was only significant at $p < 0.10$. Since the n was small in CS1, drawing strong conclusions is difficult.

Overall, these results look promising and H1 was strongly supported in the CS0 sections. Since the survey questions were all in the remembering and understanding category of the revised Bloom's taxonomy, this implies that the security modules allow students to remember and understand the common vulnerabilities better.

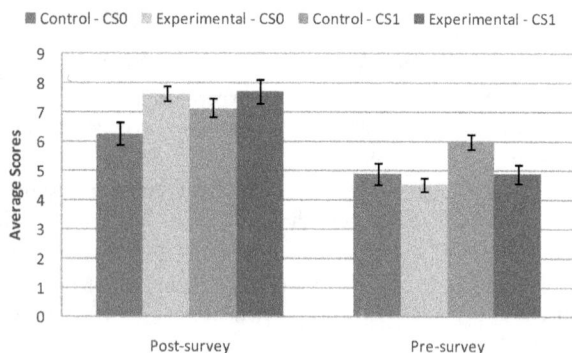

Figure 2. Pre and post survey scores in the control and experimental sections of CS0 and CS1

4.2 Comparison of Code-check results

Scoring the code-check presented a different challenge since students used different techniques to fix security vulnerabilities.

We first came up with an answer sheet that was used by two independent graders to grade the exercise. The scores of each question were tallied and the Cohen's Kappa statistic was used to compare the agreement in the scores assigned by both graders. During the first round, a low level of agreement was found and we revised the answer sheet to be more specific with respect to the point deduction strategy. For the first question - locating vulnerabilities in code - students were scored from 0-5, specifically 0-2 for identifying potential integer errors, 0-3 for identifying the need for input validation, and 0/1 for identifying potential buffer overflows. For the second question, which entailed mitigating the vulnerabilities, a score of 0-2 was assigned for doing the correct input validation and 0-2 for checking and preventing the buffer overflow (in this question students could write code or describe in plain English how to address it). A second round grading led to an agreement of 89.00% in the grade for locating vulnerabilities (across both semesters), 76.70% for identifying vulnerabilities, and 84.90% for fixing vulnerabilities. As suggested in the literature [6], these are considered substantial levels of agreement. Since the levels of agreement were high, we selected one of the rates randomly for further analysis. The results (shown in Figure 3) are based on combining the two control sections (CS0 and CS1) and experimental sections for clarity.

We found that students in experimental sections (n = 35) performed significantly better ($p < 0.05$) than students in the control sections (n = 48) at locating the potential vulnerabilities in code. This supports H2 and provides further evidence that the modules (and specifically the security checklists) allow students in the experimental sections to remember and better apply the security concepts they learned.

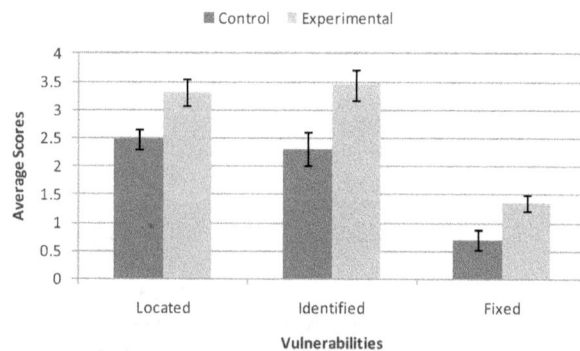

Figure 3. Average scores for control and experimental sections in exercise to locate, identify, and fix vulnerabilities in code

There was also a significant difference in the total scores for identifying the vulnerabilities in code among the two sections (with the experimental section scoring higher). On closer examination, it was found that there was a significant difference in identifying input validation and buffer overflow vulnerabilities (the experimental section scored more) though scores in integer overflow were similar. This may be due to the fact that it is easier to locate integer overflow as its name gives clues on where to find it in code. This supports H3 and points to the advantage of using the modules to introduce the vulnerabilities.

As can be seen in the figure, although both sections scored low in fixing errors, the experimental section scored significantly better. Even though this supports H4, the results show that there is significant work to be done in teaching CS0 and CS1 students the techniques to prevent buffer overflows in code. We found that most students in the experimental sections recognized and attempted to mitigate the buffer overflow, however, most attempts were incomplete.

5. CONCLUSIONS

We present a model using checklist-based security injection modules to increase student awareness and ability to apply secure coding principles, specifically - identify, understand, and correct key security issues in code. Experiments with students in four sections of CS0 and CS1 show that students using the modules are significantly better at remembering, understanding and applying secure coding concepts. Students exposed to the modules also show increased ability to write code to address specific security issues.

While previous studies [5,13-15] demonstrated improved security awareness in students across five institutions, the most recent study, which assesses students' ability to apply secure coding techniques, was limited to one instructor and two split (one control and one experimental) sections in both CS0 and CS1. This assessment is particularly challenging due to the laborious nature of the grading, but further studies are in progress to validate the generalizability of these results.

6. ACKNOWLEDGMENTS

This project is supported by the NSF Course Curriculum and Laboratory Improvement (CLLI) grant number DUE-0817267. We greatly appreciate our colleagues and partners at Towson University, Bowie State University, Harford County Community College, Community College of Baltimore County, and Anne Arundel Community College. In particular, we are grateful to Harry Hochheiser, Mike O'Leary, Shiva Azadegan, AC Chaplin, Patricia Gregory, Jack McLaughlin for their contributions.

7. REFERENCES

[1] ACM/IEEE. 2008. *Computer Science Curriculum 2008: An Interim Revision of CS 2001.*

[2] Bellovin, S. 2008. Security by Checklist. *Security & Privacy, IEEE*, 6, 2, 88-88.

[3] Bishop, M. and Frincke, D. A. 2008. Information Assurance Education: A Work In Progress. *Security and Privacy, IEEE*, 6, 5, 54-57.

[4] Clinton, L. 2009. Education's Critical Role in Cybersecurity. *EDUCAUSE Review*, 44, 5, 60-61.

[5] Kaza, S., Taylor, B., Hochheiser, H., Azadegan, S., O'Leary, M. and Turner, C. F. 2010. Injecting Security in the Curriculum – Experiences in Effective Dissemination and Assessment Design. In *Proceedings of the The Colloquium for Information Systems Security Education (CISSE)* (Baltimore, MD, 2010).

[6] Landis, J. R. and Koch, G. G. 1977. The measurement of observer agreement for categorical data. *Biometrics*, 33, 1, 159-174.

[7] Maughan, D. 2010. The Need for a National Cybersecurity Research and Development Agenda. *Communications of the Acm*, 53, 2 (Feb), 29-31.

[8] McAfee. 2009. *Unsecured Economies : Protecting Vital Information Contributors.*

[9] McConnell, J. 1996. Active learning and its use in computer science. In *Proceedings of the ACM Special Interest Group on Computer Uses in Education (SIGCUE)* (New York, NY, 1996).

[10] Niekerk, J. V. and Solms, R. V. 2008. Bloom's Taxonomy for Information Security Education. In *Proceedings of the International Federation for Information Processing (IFIP)* (South Africa, 2008). IEEE.

[11] Perrone, L., Aburdene, M. and Meng, X. 2005. Approaches to undergraduate instruction in computer security. In *Proceedings of the Annual Conference of the American Society of Engineering Education (ASEE)* (2005).

[12] Redwine, S. T. 2010. Fitting Software Assurance into Higher Education. *Computer*, 43, 9 (Sep), 41-46.

[13] Taylor, B. and Azadegan, S. 2007. Using Security Checklists and Scorecards in CS Curriculum. In *Proceedings of the Colloquium for Information Systems Security Education (CISSE)* (Seattle, WA, 2007).

[14] Taylor, B. and Azadegan, S. 2008. Moving beyond security tracks: integrating security in cs0 and cs1. In *Proceedings of the 39th SIGCSE technical symposium on Computer science education* (Portland, OR, USA, 2008). ACM.

[15] Taylor, B., Hochheiser, H., Azadegan, S. and Leary, M. O. 2009. Cross-site Security Integration : Preliminary Experiences across Curricula and Institutions. In *Proceedings of the Colloquium for Information Systems Security Education(CISSE)* (2009).

[16] Taylor, C. and Shumba, R. 2008. Security education: a roadmap to the future. In *Proceedings of the 39th SIGCSE technical symposium on Computer science education* (Portland, OR, USA, 2008). ACM.

[17] Thomas, L., Ratcliffe, M., Woodbury, J. and Jarman, E. 2002. Learning Styles and Performance in the Introductory Programming Sequence. In *Proceedings of the Technical Symposium on Computer Science Education (SIGCSE)* (2002). ACM.

[18] Thompson, E., Luxton-Reilly, A., Whalley, J. L., Hu, M. and Robbins, P. 2008. Bloom's taxonomy for CS assessment. In *Proceedings of the Tenth Conference on Australasian computing education (ACE)* (2008).

[19] Turner, C., Hochheiser, H., Feng, J., Taylor, B. and Lazar, J. 2009. Cooperative Information Assurance Capacity Building. In *Proceedings of the Colloquium for Information Systems Security Education (CISSE)* (2009).

[20] U.S. Department of Homeland Security. 2009. *A Roadmap for Cybersecurity Research.*

[21] Zhivich, M. and Cunningham, R. K. 2009. The Real Cost of Software Errors. *IEEE Security & Privacy*, 7, 2, 87-90.

The Design and Coding of Greedy Algorithms Revisited

J. Ángel Velázquez-Iturbide
Departamento de Lenguajes y Sistemas Informáticos I
Escuela Técnica Superior de Ingeniería Informática
Universidad Rey Juan Carlos
C/ Tulipán s/n, 28933 Móstoles, Madrid, Spain
angel.velazquez@urjc.es

ABSTRACT

In this paper we argue that the most typical instruction method used to teach greedy algorithms is inadequate at achieving certain learning goals and we present several contributions to alleviate this situation. Our first group of contributions highlights the role of selection functions and proposes separate treatment in their discovery and proof of optimality. For discovery, we outline some interesting cases of selection functions and for proofs, we examine the role of counterexamples. Furthermore, we argue that their separation provides more opportunities for instructional activities. Our second group of contributions concerns coding greedy algorithms. We discuss the role and adequacy of the template in current use, and also the role of sorting candidates and how to implement sorting.

Categories and Subject Descriptors

K.3.2 [**Computers and Education**]: Computer and Information Science Education – *computer science education*.

General Terms

Algorithms, Design, Theory, Verification.

Keywords

Computer Science Education, Algorithms, Greedy Algorithms.

1. INTRODUCTION

Algorithms can be taught in many ways. For instance, David Ginat has dealt extensively with the creative design of algorithms [6]. His approach fosters both creativity and rigor by devoting about 20% of course time to problem-solving activities. Our concern in this paper is the remaining 80% of course time, where the core course material is taught and practiced. In particular, we are concerned with the teaching and learning of greedy algorithms, one of the basic algorithm design techniques. We refer to textbooks for a definition (e.g. [3][4][8]).

The learning aims of greedy algorithms can be stated in terms of Bloom's taxonomy [2], therefore the student should be able to:

- Understand the technique basics (comprehension level).

- Understand classic greedy algorithms, e.g. Dijkstra's algorithm (comprehension level).
- State a selection function for a given problem and prove its optimality (application or synthesis level).
- Implement a greedy algorithm based on a selection function (application or synthesis level).

The first two learning goals refer to a general but shallow understanding of greedy algorithms, whereas the last two goals are concerned with a deeper understanding. In this paper, it is this second group of more demanding objectives which interest us. Our claim is that at present they are not adequately supported, as we elaborate below.

If we leaf through a textbook on algorithms, we notice that the chapter on the greedy technique typically starts with a description of the technique, followed by a number of problems. Each problem has the following structure: description, optimal function selection, proof of optimality, coding, and complexity analysis.

This presentation of problems reads like a recipe and leaves little scope for inquiry. It is difficult for the teacher to design and propose not only interesting problems, but also drill-and-practice exercises. Anderson et al. [1] might argue that there is no alignment between learning objectives and instructional activities.

For instance, consider the design of an optimal selection function. The only two problems where we have detected a discussion on alternatives are the knapsack problem (e.g. [7]) and the minimum-cost spanning tree (e.g. [3][4][8]). In the first case, three strategies are commonly considered, namely increasing order of weight, decreasing order of benefit, and decreasing order of benefit/weight (which is the optimal one). In the second case, several optimal selection functions are identified, leading to the well-known Prim's and Kruskal's algorithms, in addition to Sollin's (e.g. [8]) and Barůvka's (e.g. [7]). However, alternative, non-optimal selection functions are not discussed. Notice also the lack of instructional activities involving the design process that leads to optimal selection functions.

This paper tries to enhance quality in the teaching of greedy algorithms by presenting alternative ways of organizing chapter contents. As a consequence, the theory is covered more comprehensively and consistently and, additionally, new didactic activities can be proposed. In the section 2, we address the design and proof of selection function optimality, while section 3 deals with coding greedy algorithms. Finally, section 4 contains our conclusions and a short discussion.

2. SELECTION FUNCTIONS

The third learning goal stated in our introduction consists in discovering a selection function for a given problem and proving its optimality. This is easy for simple problems (e.g. the coin changing problem), but it is much more demanding for others (e.g. the single-source shortest paths problem). To illustrate this point more clearly, we could argue that it is unrealistic to expect a student to discover an algorithm such as Dijkstra's for the single-source shortest paths problem. Consequently, the effort necessary to discover an optimal selection function must commonly be placed at the synthesis level of Bloom's taxonomy.

The learning goal is simpler to achieve if it is split into its two constituent parts: discovery of the selection function and proof of optimality. In this section we propose devoting independent attention to these two subgoals. In subsection 2.1 we discuss how to go deeper into the study and practice of selection functions. In subsection 2.2 we address the search for counterexamples to prove non-optimality of selection functions. In subsection 2.3 we discuss the benefits of separate treatment.

2.1 Selection Functions

The first step in solving optimization problems consists in organizing a multistage process to incrementally construct an optimal solution from available candidates. This process takes different forms in different design techniques. Greedy algorithms share the common feature that at each step only one candidate is taken into consideration by a selection function. In other design techniques, such as dynamic programming or backtracking, several candidates must be taken into consideration at each step.

Explicit discussion of selection functions smoothes their learning curve and provides opportunities for a wider range of activities, as outlined in the four points below.

Firstly, some optimal selection functions require considerable effort and are not immediately obvious. For instance, it is evident to us, the teachers, that decreasing order of benefit/weight is the optimal selection function for the knapsack problem. However, this may not be such an obvious conclusion for a novice student.

Secondly, some selection functions can be stated in different, yet equivalent ways. For instance, Cormen et al. identify increasing order of activity finishing times as the optimal selection function for the activity selection problem [4]. We denote this selection function as $F\uparrow$. An equivalent selection function is decreasing order of start time (denoted $S\downarrow$). Their equivalence is easy to prove by symmetry. We lack the space here to give full details, but we can illustrate the point informally with an example.

Consider the set of five activities displayed in Figure 1, indexed top-down from 0 to 4. The application of the $F\uparrow$ selection function results in successively selecting activities 2 and 1, successively discarding activities 3 and 4, and selecting activity 0. (The order of selection is highlighted by the use of tones, the darker tones corresponding to the activities that are selected first.) Figure 2 illustrates a symmetric order of selection, according to the $S\downarrow$ selection function. As overlapping among activities is invariant, the two selection functions yield the same result.

Thirdly, reasonable selection functions for some problems are non-optimal and to prove this, students must find a counter-example. The search for a counterexample requires the student to demonstrate a deeper understanding of the problem.

Consider again the activity selection problem. A selection function which is promising for most students is increasing order of duration (we denote it $D\uparrow$). It is non-optimal but it is a nearly-optimal greedy heuristic, as it computes an optimal schedule in more than 96% of the cases. We may find a counterexample composed of three activities (see Figure 3), where this selection function only yields one activity (then second one).

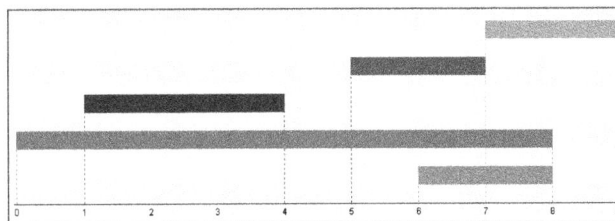

Figure 1. Five activities selected in order $F\uparrow$

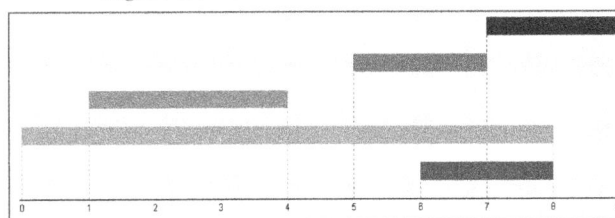

Figure 2. Five activities selected in order $S\downarrow$

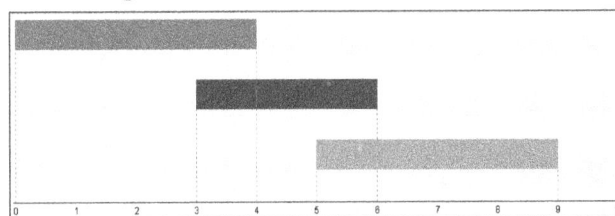

Figure 3. Three activities selected in order $D\uparrow$

Fourthly, being familiar with finding counterexamples helps students to obtain evidence that there is no optimal selection function for many problems, e.g. the knapsack 0/1 problem.

2.2 The Role of Counterexamples

Once a selection function has been stated, it must be proven for optimality. Proving formulas is a demanding task for most students. However, many selection functions are non-optimal, so it is enough to find a counterexample. Here, we advocate reinforcing the study of counterexamples. In subsection 2.1, we have referred twice to counterexamples.

Searching for counterexamples requires detailed analysis, allowing students to become familiar with the problem and to gain insight into its properties. Furthermore, it is simpler than constructing a proof. Not surprisingly, Wing [10] identifies it as a part of computational thinking and this emphasis on counterexamples can also be seen as a different way of going from the concrete to the abstract in instruction [5].

2.3 Instructional Activities

Separating the discovery of selection functions and their proof, as well as fostering the search for counterexamples, permits the design of a greater number of instructional activities, including drill-and-practice exercises. For instance, the teacher can propose just the discovery of reasonable (not necessarily optimal) selection functions for a given problem.

A second advantage is that the search for counterexamples is common to a wider range of problems to be studied. In effect, nearly-optimal selection functions open a door to the study of approximation algorithms and heuristics. Furthermore, problems that are typically solved using other techniques, such as dynamic programming, can also be studied. In summary, the study of selection functions provides a unifying theme and methodology for the initial phases in the study of other techniques.

3. CODING GREEDY ALGORITHMS

The fourth learning goal given in our introduction consists in coding a greedy algorithm. The greedy technique is usually characterized in abstract terms, but it may also be formalized as a code template. For instance, see Brassard and Bratley [3]:

```
function greedy (C: set): set
  {C is the set of candidates}
  S ← ∅ {We build the solution in set S}
  while C≠∅ and not solution(S) do
    x ← select(C)
    C ← C\{x}
    if feasible(S∪{x}) then S ← S∪{x}
  if solution(S) then return S
  else return «there are no solutions»
```

This template is very clear and is extremely useful for ensuring that the elements of greedy algorithms are understood. However, using it effectively to code a greedy algorithm is not straightforward. Therefore, the effort necessary to code a given greedy algorithm must often be placed at Bloom's synthesis level.

In the rest of this section we address different issues related to the coding of greedy algorithms.

3.1 A High-Level Template

If we analyze the greedy algorithms found in textbooks, we see that they do not resemble the template given above. For instance, consider one of the simplest problems used to illustrate the greedy technique, namely the coin-changing problem. We include below an algorithm which solves it, also by Brassard and Bratley [3]:

```
function coin-changing (n): set of coins
{It changes n units using the smallest
possible number of coins. The constant C
specifies the coins available}
  const C = {100, 25, 10, 5, 1}
  S ← ∅ {We build the solution in set S}
  s ← 0 {s is the sum of elements in S}
  while s≠n do
    x ← the largest element in C
        such that s+x ≤ n
    if that element does not exist then
      return «I cannot find the solution»
    S ← S∪{one coin of value x}
    s ← s + x
  return S
```

The code is similar to the template, but it also exhibits a number of minor syntactic and organizational differences: the loop control, the relative placement of if-then and return sentences, etc.

These differences between the template and the code become more marked as the algorithm becomes more complex. After studying a number of cases, we concluded that the template shown above must be considered as a high-level template which is used to illustrate greedy algorithms behavior. This differentiates

such a template from the templates frequently found in textbooks, which are directly instantiated into code. For instance, we find code templates for divide-and-conquer algorithms (e.g. [3]).

The role of this high-level template is to capture the essence of greedy algorithm behavior. We may call this kind of template a "semantic" template. Templates that can be applied directly to code an algorithm may be called "syntactic". The corollary for the teaching of greedy algorithms is that the template cannot be used directly by the student to code. Consequently, any other guide will be valuable for her, as we show in the next two subsections.

3.2 Sorting Candidates and Generalization of the Template

The degree to which some algorithms deviate from the template given above is much greater than in the case of the coin-changing problem. This is because they contain an initial sorting phase. Such a phase is not considered in the description of the technique: it obviously is an optimization for selecting the candidates efficiently. In these cases, the candidates are sorted at the beginning, so the selection of the next candidate is reduced to selecting the next element in a sorted data structure.

Why do some greedy algorithms not include such an optimizing, sorting phase? In order to answer this question, we performed a study of five problems that can be optimally solved with greedy algorithms: coin changing, knapsack, activity selection, minimum-cost spanning tree, and single-source shortest paths. For each problem, we proposed coding it in two different ways: with a sorting phase and with a specific selection function.

We succeeded in coding the first three algorithms in both ways, but we were unable to code the last algorithm with a sorting phase. The fourth problem (minimum-cost spanning tree) was coded in both ways with some selection functions (e.g. Kruskal's algorithm) but not with others (e.g. Prim's algorithm).

Finally, we came to a conclusion that we had not found in any textbook: for some greedy algorithms, the set of candidates is constant and known at the beginning of their execution, but for other algorithms, the set of candidates varies along their execution. Algorithms of the first kind are the four aforementioned: coin changing, knapsack, activity selection, and Kruskal's algorithm. Algorithms of the second kind are the remaining two: Prim's and Dijkstra's algorithms.

An example may illustrate this point more clearly. For instance, consider Prim's algorithm for the minimum-cost spanning tree (MST) problem. Figure 4(a) shows the initial state, where node 1 is the only one in the MST. Notice that three arc candidates, highlighted in red, leave node 1. Figure 4(b) shows that the arc included in the MST is arc 1-2, which is the shortest of the three. Figure 4(c) displays in red the list of candidates updated for the next step of the greedy algorithm. Now, the list of candidates contains arcs 1-4 and 1-7, which were already present in the initial candidate list, but it also contains arcs 2-3 and 2-5.

A consequence of the distinction stated above is that a template that assumes that the set of candidates is initially known, can only be applied to the first kind of greedy algorithms.

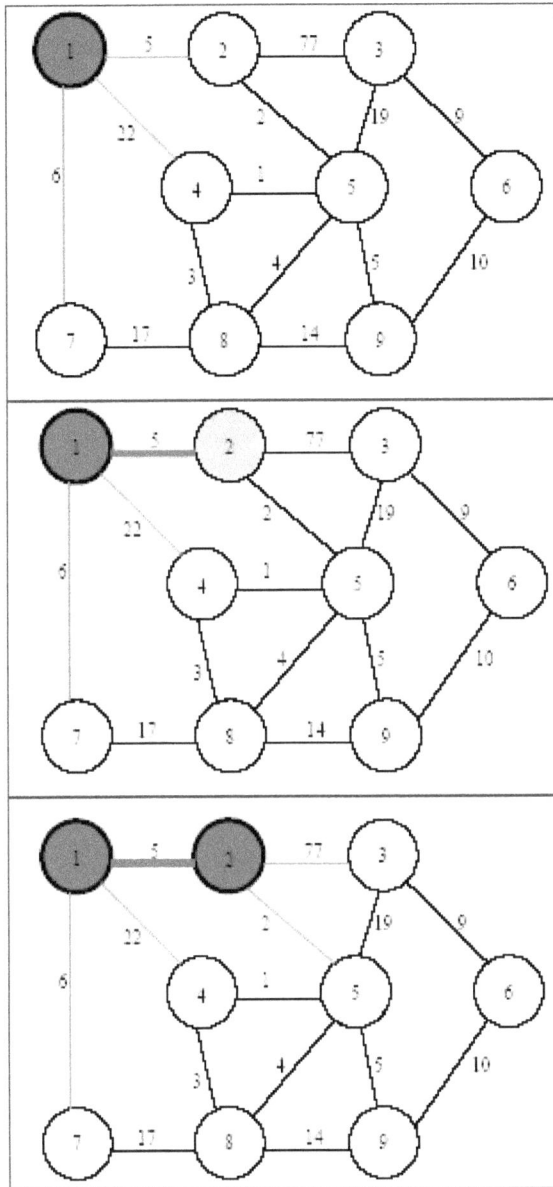

Figure 4. Three successive states of Prim's algorithm: (a) arc candidates from node 1, (b) selection of node 1-2, and (c) arc candidates from nodes 1 and 2

If we want to present a "general" template to students, it must also consider the second kind of algorithms. A minor generalization of the template that achieves this is as follows.

```
function greedy (P: set): set
  {P is the problem}
  {C is the set of candidates}
  C ← initialize(P)
  S ← ∅ {We build the solution in set S}
  while C≠∅ and not solution(S) do
    x ← select(C)
    C ← C\{x}
    if feasible(S∪{x}) then
      S ← S∪{x}
      update (C, x, P)
```

```
  if solution(S) then return S
  else return «there are no solutions»
```

The new template differs from the original one in the handling of the set C of candidates. Firstly, C is initialized with a subset of the problem P. After selecting a candidate x and removing it from the set C of candidates, C is updated with new elements that depend on the candidate x and the problem P.

3.3 How to Sort Candidates

There is something interesting to note in the treatment given in textbooks to the first kind of algorithms identified above (namely, algorithms where the set of candidates is constant and known from the beginning). They are commonly treated in one of the following ways:

- The set of candidates is assumed to be sorted.
- The set of candidates is sorted in a first phase of the algorithm, according to the selection criterion.

The first method is unrealistic. The problem is well-defined on any valid input data, therefore in general the candidates are not sorted. This means that the algorithm, as specified in textbooks, is only a part of the complete, working algorithm. Not making this partial nature explicit may lead to misunderstandings.

The second method is more realistic. However, sorting in place the set of candidates leads to a modification of the original data structure. It is bad design style to develop a method that produces side-effects, such as a modification of its input parameters. Such sorting should be performed without affecting the original input data. The treatment given in textbooks is again incomplete.

Before discussing an alternative treatment, it is worth noting a second point: a complete solution to an optimization problem must contain not only an optimal value, but also the decisions that lead to that value. When we develop a first version of the algorithm, it is better to ignore the computation of decisions because they make the algorithm more obscure. However, they must be explicitly computed afterwards.

Let us turn back to our original problem, namely how to sort the candidates in order to obtain a realistic algorithm in good style. A third method consists in copying the candidates into an auxiliary data structure, which is then sorted. Let us consider now how to compute the decisions. If we want them to be meaningful to the method caller, such decisions must refer to the original placement of the candidates. Consequently, if the algorithm sorts the candidates at the beginning, their original positions must be restored at the end to make the decisions meaningful.

Let us analyze this point with an example. Consider the knapsack problem with 6 objects of weight {26,68,64,53,53,66} and benefits {81,40,9,5,54,24}. Sorting the objects in decreasing order of benefit/weight results in selecting the objects in order 0,4,1,5,2,3 (using Java criterion for array indices). If we sort the weight and profit arrays according to this criterion, their new values are {26,53,68,66,64,53} and {81,54,40,24,9,5}, respectively. Now we could use them to fill the knapsack. For instance, for a knapsack of capacity 180, we could introduce the first three objects in total, and half the fourth object. The benefit gained is 81+54+40+12=187. However, we do not know the original indices of the objects introduced.

A fourth, good-style method which obtains these original indices consists in indirectly sorting the candidates. The array of candidates is not sorted explicitly, but we build an auxiliary array storing the index of each candidate in the ideal, sorted array. Thus, we know the position that corresponds to each object in the ideal, sorted array while at the same time keeping the original array. Due to lack of space, we are unable to include the code of the algorithm here, but we illustrate it with an example below.

Consider the knapsack problem with the same data, namely $w=\{26,68,64,53,53,66\}$, $b=\{81,40,9,5,54,24\}$, and capacity 180. If the sorting phase produces an array of indices $i=\{0,4,1,5,2,3\}$, we have the following sequence of decisions: (1) Introduce object 0 complete, leaving $180-w[0]=180-26=154$ spare capacity; (2) Introduce object 4 complete, leaving $154-w[4]=154-53=101$ spare capacity; (3) Introduce object 1 complete, leaving $101-w[1]=101-68=33$ spare capacity; (4) Introduce half the object 5, given that its weight is $w[5]=66$ and free space is 33; and (5) Objects 2 and 3 are discarded as there is no free space. The total benefit obtained is: $b[i[0]]+b[i[4]]+b[i[1]]+0.5\cdot b[i[5]] = 187$.

4. CONCLUSIONS AND DISCUSSION

We have presented two classes of contributions regarding the teaching of greedy algorithms. The first class of contributions is related to design, and the second class concerns coding. Each set of contributions plays a different role. The former class emphasizes the central role of selection functions in greedy algorithms, and provides more opportunities for instructional activities with greedy algorithms. It is expected that students will gain a greater understanding of the foundations of greedy algorithms. In addition, it provides a unifying theme for the initial phases in the study of other design techniques. The goal of the latter class of contributions is to make the role of some elements of the technique clearer, to make several coding issues more explicit and to discuss alternative solutions. It is expected that this will assist students in better structuring coding decisions.

In the introduction, we cited David Ginat's work on the creative design of algorithms [6] His approach is very different from ours, but it does share certain elements (use of counterexamples) and observations (students' lack of rigor). Our contributions are complementary since they fit with a more traditional chapter organization, where basic concepts are given and later practiced in closed laboratories.

The two classes of contributions must be dealt with at different moments in a chapter on greedy algorithms. Firstly, the design of selection functions is at the core of greedy algorithms, so it should be addressed at an early stage. Secondly, coding issues may be addressed in a more progressive way. The template must be provided early on. Addressing the existence of two kinds of problems (depending on the variability of the set of candidates) is more useful later in the chapter, when several greedy algorithms have been studied. Issues on implementing decisions and on the sorting of candidates must also be addressed later in the chapter.

The contributions proposed here can be integrated into a course naturally. Selection functions for greedy algorithms can be addressed at little cost in terms of teaching time, and at no cost for non-optimal and nearly-optimal ones (they are usually studied in chapters on dynamic programming and approximate algorithms, respectively). Addressing the coding issues requires extra time, but this time pays dividends because students would ask these questions as they code. The impact of computing the sequence of decisions can also be covered in a minimum amount of extra time because a simplified version of an algorithm can be given in class, leaving the more realistic version available at the course web site. Alternatively, it may form part of a programming assignment.

Our emphasis has been one of completeness and consistency in the instructional design and study of greedy algorithms and we have presented our contributions with relative independence of the pedagogical approach of the course. However, we would like to point out that the study of selection functions is suitable for studying and experimenting with the scientific method [9], as well as for promoting learning by discovery.

5. ACKNOWLEDGMENTS

This work was supported by research grant TIN2008-04103 of the Spanish Ministry of Science and Innovation.

6. REFERENCES

[1] Anderson, L.W., Krathwohl, D.R., Airasian, P.W., Cruikshank, K.A., Pintrich, P.R., Raths, J., and Wittrock, M.C. 2001. A Taxonomy for Learning, Teaching and Assessing: A Revision of Bloom's Taxonomy of Educational Objectives. Longman.

[2] Bloom, B., Furst, E., Hill, W., and Krathwohl, D. R. 1956. Taxonomy of Educational Objectives: Handbook I, The Cognitive Domain. Addison-Wesley.

[3] Brassard, G., and Bratley, P. 1996. Fundamentals of Algorithmics. Prentice-Hall.

[4] Cormen, T. H., Leiserson, C. E., Rivest. R. L., and Stein, C. 2009. Introduction to Algorithms. The MIT Press, 3rd ed.

[5] Dann, W., and Cooper, S. 2009. Alice 3: Concrete to abstract. Comm. ACM 52, 8 (Aug. 2009), 27-29. DOI= 10.1145/1536616.1536628

[6] Ginat, D. 2008. Learning from wrong and creative algorithm design. In Proceedings of the 39th SIGCSE Technical Symposium on Computer Science Education (Portland, OR, USA, March 12 - 15, 2008). SIGCSE'08. ACM Press, New York, NY, 26-30. DOI= 10.1145/1352135.1352148

[7] Horowitz, E., and Sahni, S. 1978. Fundamentals of Computer Algorithms. Pitman.

[8] Sahni, S. 2004. Data Structures, Algorithms, and Applications in Java. Silicon Press, 2nd ed.

[9] Velázquez-Iturbide, J. Á., and Pérez-Carrasco, A. 2009. Active learning of greedy algorithms by means of interactive experimentation. In Proceedings of the 14th Annual Conference on Innovation and Technology in Computer Science Education (Paris, France, July 06 - 09, 2009). ITiCSE'09. ACM Press, New York, NY, 119-123. DOI= 10.1145/1562877.1562917

[10] Wing, J. M. 2006. Computational thinking. Com. ACM 49, 3 (Mar. 2006), 33-35. DOI= 10.1145/1118178.1118215

Measuring Static Quality of Student Code

Dennis Breuker
Hogeschool van Amsterdam
Duivendrechtsekade 36-38
1096 AH Amsterdam NL
+31 20 595 1645

d.m.breuker@hva.nl

Jan Derriks
Hogeschool van Amsterdam
Duivendrechtsekade 36-38
1096 AH Amsterdam NL
+31 20 595 1674

j.derriks@hva.nl

Jacob Brunekreef
Fontys Hogeschool
Rachelsmolen 1
5612 MA Eindhoven NL
+31 6 5535 8860

j.brunekreef@fontys.nl

ABSTRACT

In this paper we report about a large-scale measurement programme concerning the static quality of student-written Java code. The goal of the programme is two-fold: we investigate what metrics are useful for measuring static quality in an educational setting, and we investigate what conclusions can be drawn from the measurement results.

Categories and Subject Descriptors

D.2.8 [**Software Engineering**]: Metrics – *product metrics.*

General Terms

Measurement, Experimentation.

Keywords

Software quality, software metrics, measurement programme.

1. INTRODUCTION

In the first two years of their education as a computer science bachelor, students at the Hogeschool van Amsterdam (Amsterdam University of Applied Sciences) work half of their time on team assignments (projects). In these student projects many lines of code are produced. In an assessment of the project results, often the focus is on functional (*dynamic*) aspects of the delivered product. Does the program work as expected? Is the usability of the GUI OK? Is the performance OK? In this paper we look at the *static* quality of the student code. Static code quality includes properties like code structure, code layout, statement quality, etc. In our experience this is an underexposed subject in many CS curricula (including ours).

We do not expect novice students to write quality code from the beginning. So, measuring static code quality on an absolute scale would not make much sense. However, we would like to see improvements when looking at student code produced by second year teams. Second year students have had more training and have

more programming experience. Therefore, we have formulated the following research question:

Do second year students produce code with better static quality properties than first year students?

In the search for an answer on this question we first have selected a set of characteristics that tell something about the static quality of the inspected code. For each of these characteristics we have designated one or more concrete code properties. Quality characteristics and code properties are presented in Section 2. In Section 3 we define a set of hypotheses related to our research question and the code properties.

We have tested the hypotheses on a large code base with Java code from many student projects. The construction of the code base is explained in Section 4. In this section we also describe how we have measured (most of) the identified code properties.

In Section 5 we present the measurement results and the statistical processing of the hypotheses we have defined, resulting in acceptance or rejection.

Finally, in Section 6 we draw our conclusions, and we elaborate on future research.

In the remainder of this section we briefly discuss related work. We have found not too much in literature about measuring static code quality in an educational setting. Gresse von Wangenheim *et al.* observe that in software engineering curricula only little attention is paid to software measurement anyhow ([1]). In [5] McCracken *et al.* describe a big inquiry to programming skills of students. Writing code that meets static quality standards does not seem to be an issue. Only marginal attention is paid to programming style. Huffman Hayes reports about a small experiment concerning measuring software quality ([5]). Part of this experiment concerns measuring static code properties. Patton and McGill ([9]) present a longitudinal study concerning student portfolios and software quality metrics in computer science education. Counsell *et al.* ([2]) describe a small empirical study concerning measuring class cohesion in an educational setting.

2. CODE QUALITY

A rich set of quality characteristics can be found in literature, when examining the static quality of source code. One of the most well-known software product quality standards is the ISO/IEC 9126 standard ([6]). In this standard more than twenty quality characteristics are defined, grouped in six sections. Not all characteristics deal with static code quality and not all characteristics are meaningful in an educational context. At the end of a student project a software product is delivered that (exceptions aside) will not be deployed somewhere else. So, focusing on aspects like *reliability* or *portability* is not realistic (unless these features are explicitly part of the requirements in the project). We have decided to focus on quality characteristics that directly contribute to the *static* quality of the software product at the end of a project. We have formulated seven code characteristics that, in our opinion, cover most of the quality aspects we would like to address in student-written code. We expect student code

- to be *size-balanced*,
- to be *readable*,
- to be *understandable*,
- to have a good *structure*,
- to have a low *complexity*,
- to contain a minimum of *code duplicates*,
- to contain a minimum of *ill-formed statements*.

With size-balanced we mean that there is a good balance in the size of various code components: not all code in a single class, not too many methods in a single class, and no methods with thousands of lines of code. Examples of ill-formed statements are assignments in an if- or while-condition, switch statements without default clause, a break outside a switch.

For our quality measurement project we have made a translation from the code characteristics listed above to a set of 22 concrete code properties. We have selected these properties from literature (e.g., Fenton [3], McConnell [7]), from metrics tools and from our own experiences with software measurement in an educational setting.

Size-balanced:
P1. The number of classes in a package
P2. The number of methods in a class
P3. The number of lines of code in a class
P4. The number of lines of code in a method

Readable:
P5. The percentage of blank lines
P6. The percentage of (too) long lines

Understandable:
P7. The percentage of comment lines
P8. The usage of multiple languages in identifier naming
P9. The percentage of short identifiers

Structure:
P10. The maximum depth of inheritance in a class tree
P11. The percentage of static variables
P12. The percentage of static methods
P13. The percentage of non-private attributes in a class

Complexity:
P14. The maximum cyclomatic complexity at method level
P15. The maximum level of statement nesting at method level

Code duplicates:
P16. The number of code duplicates
P17. The maximum size of code duplicates

Ill-formed statements:
P18. The number of assignments in an if- or while-condition

P19. The number of switch statements without default
P20. The number of breaks outside a switch statement
P21. The number of methods with multiple returns
P22. The number of hard-coded constants in expressions

We do not claim that these properties are the only ones that should be used when looking at static code quality in an educational context. But, in our experience these properties can easily be explained to students by presenting examples of good code and bad code. And they can be used for classroom discussions about questions like "what is a good number of classes in a package?", or "how bad is it when you use breaks outside a switch statement?"

Most of the properties can be directly measured by counting: lines, classes, static methods, etc. Some properties require some more elaboration. The usage of a single natural language in identifier naming (no mixed English and Dutch language) requires visual inspection. The detection of code duplicates requires some kind of parsing of the code. The same holds for the detection of breaks outside a switch statement.

In our measurement programme we deal with a large code base with more than a million lines of code. It is clear that measuring properties of such a large code base requires automatic, tool-based measuring. We are aware of the fact that for some code properties automatic measuring will be hard, if not impossible. We will return to this in Section 4.

3. HYPOTHESES

As mentioned in Section 1, our quality measurement programme is focused on finding differences between the static quality of code produced by first year student teams and code produced by second year student teams. In order to get an answer to our research question we have stated 22 hypotheses. In each hypothesis we compare the measured values for a specific quality property of all first year projects to the measured values for the same property of all second year projects. All hypotheses are stated as null hypotheses and reflect the reverse of what we would expect. In general we expect that second year teams perform different (better) than first year teams. So, for instance, the null hypothesis for the first code property is stated as follows:

H1. The number of classes in a package in second year projects is not significantly different from the number of classes in a package in first year projects.

(We expect a smaller number of classes in a package for second year projects, as second year students know better how to spread functionality over different packages.)

In the same way we have formulated the hypotheses H2 up to H22, each comparing measurement results from first year projects with measurement results from second year projects with respect to a particular property. We do not list all these hypotheses here in full text.

In order to be able to test the hypotheses we need to extract the Java source code and measure the code properties. This is described in the next section.

4. MEASUREMENT PROCESS

Starting from 2007, student teams at the Hogeschool van Amsterdam are required to use Subversion (SVN) as version management system in their projects. Each team gets its own repository at the beginning of a project. At the end the results have to be delivered in this repository. Most (not all) of the code produced by students is Java code. The input for our measurement process consisted of 252 team repositories, filled with project results over three academic years, from 2007-2008 up to and including 2009-2010. These repositories contained over 28,000 Java files. In order to obtain a code base suited for our quality measurements we executed two steps:

1. extract all Java code from each team repository,

2. clean up the code: remove imported Java files, generated Java files, preliminary versions, duplicate files.

Step 1 was rather easy. After this step it appeared that 45 team repositories did not contain any substantial Java code at all. We removed these repositories from our measurement programme.

The second step took some effort. Student teams now and then use third-party utilities. Sometimes they import the Java code of such a utility. The quality of this code is of no interest for our research question, so it had to be removed. The same holds for generated code: sometimes students use tools that generate code (e.g., NetBeans GUI Builder). We do not want to measure the quality of this code. Finally, in some team repositories we found different versions of the code in different folders. Apparently, some teams were not very experienced in using a version management tool. We have cleaned up the code by inspection at "folder level": when a certain folder clearly only contained imported code, generated code or a different version of the code, then the complete folder has been removed. As we have not inspected each separate file, some non-student-written code may be present in the code base we have used for measuring. Visually inspecting all individual Java files was no option. Duplicate files have been removed by using the tool DupFinder ([10]). After these operations we were left with a code base with 207 team repositories, containing about 8,400 Java files with in total about 1.3 million (physical) lines of code.

No single metrics tool is capable of measuring all the desired code properties. We have selected different tools. RSM ([12]) has been used for code size, comments, blank lines, complexity, and statement quality. SourceMonitor ([14]) has been used for block depth. PMD ([14]) has been used for the detection of duplicate code. A home-made tool, created with ANTLR ([15]) and a Java grammar, has been used for identifying static variables and methods, for identifying non-private attributes and for the extraction of identifiers.

With these tools not all code properties could be measured. As can be imagined, for the property concerning naming of identifiers (P8) automated tool-based measurement is hard. As our code base is way too big for visual inspection, we have no measurement results for the hypothesis related to this code property. Furthermore, no tool could measure the number of hard-coded constants in expressions (P22). We leave these two properties open for future work.

Note. In previous work we have shown that metrics tools are not very reliable ([1]) Using different tools for measuring a particular

code property often yields different results. In the research project described in this paper we have used one tool per property. We know that the values we have obtained may not always be correct. However, in our hypotheses we only compare values with each other, making the absolute correctness of the values less important.

5. RESULTS AND ANALYSIS

Each metrics tool that we have used has a command-line interface from which it can be activated. We have written scripts that feed the Java code repositories to these tools. We collected the output in spreadsheets. For further processing we have aggregated the measured values to project level. E.g., for code property P1 (the number of classes in a package) we have taken the average value for a student project: the number of packages in the project divided by the number of classes in the project. Some measurements required more processing before statistical analysis could be performed. As stated in Section 1, we want to compare the results of novice (first year) project teams with the results of more experienced second year project teams. In general second year projects are bigger. So, for code properties representing absolute numbers (e.g., the number of static variables, the number of code duplicates) it does not make sense to compare the measurement results. In these cases we have related the number of occurrences to the size of a project, producing relative numbers. For instance, for property P12 we take the number of static methods and divide it by the total number of methods. In this way we guarantee that a few static methods in a big project result in a different quality profile than the same number of static methods in a small project.

We have performed a statistical analysis on the measurement results, using the statistical package SPSS ([17]) For each hypothesis we have tried to find a statistically significant difference (with a level of confidence of 95%) between two datasets, one obtained from first year project teams, one obtained from second year project teams. As the datasets have no normal distribution, we have used a Mann-Whittney test to check whether the two datasets differ or not. We refer to SPSS help documentation for further explanation.

When a statistically relevant difference was found, we identified the nature of the difference (second year teams scoring higher or lower numbers). The results are listed below.

For the following ten code properties we found no statistically significant difference between the measurement results concerning first year projects and second year projects:

*   the average number of methods in a class (P2),
*   the average number of lines of code in a class (P3),
*   the percentage of blank lines (P5),
*   the percentage of (too) long lines (P6),
*   the percentage of comment lines (P7),
*   the percentage of static variables (P11),
*   the percentage of non-private attributes in a class (P13),
*   the number of code duplicates (P16),
*   the maximum size of code duplicates (P17),
*   the number of switch statements without default (P19).

For the following ten code properties we found that second year teams performed different from first year teams:

- the number of classes in a package (P1) was bigger,
- the number of lines of code in a method (P4) was lower,
- the percentage of short identifiers (P9) was lower,
- the maximum depth of inheritance in a class tree (P10) was bigger,
- the percentage of static methods (P12) was lower,
- the maximum cyclomatic complexity at method level (P14) was higher,
- the maximum level of statement nesting at method level (P15) was higher,
- the number of assignments in an if- or while statement (P18) was lower,
- the number of breaks outside a switch statement (P20) was higher,
- the number of methods with multiple returns (P21) was higher.

The statistical results can be illustrated by box plots, showing the distribution of the measurement values for first year teams and second year teams in one plot. These box plots can also be generated with the SPSS package. Figure 1 shows the box plot related to P1.

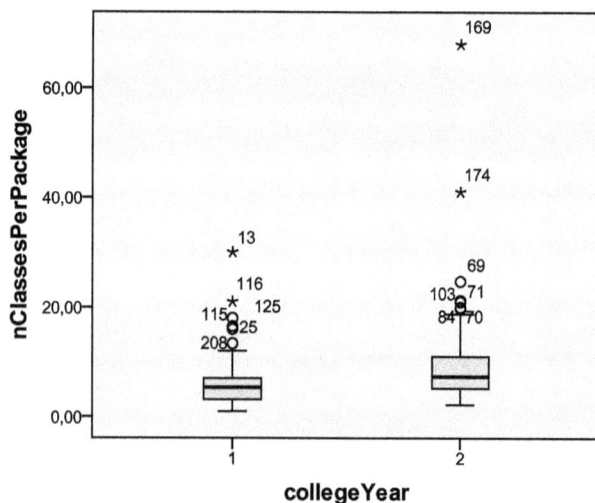

Figure 1. Box plot P1 – Number of classes in a package.

From this box plot it can directly be observed that second year teams have more classes in a package than first year teams.

So, for half of the code properties that we have identified for measuring the static code quality, second year project teams did not perform significantly different from first year project teams. In most of these cases the measured values were "OK". However, we observed that in many cases the spread in the measured values was much bigger for first year projects. The box plot presented in Figure 2 serves as an illustration of this observation.

For some properties, e.g., P14, P15, P20, P21, second year teams perform worse, probably due to the increased complexity of their projects. For some other properties (P1, P10) the difference can be explained by the size of the projects. Second year projects are larger than first year projects and hence have more classes,

resulting in more classes in a package and a bigger class tree with greater depth. After all there are four properties where second year projects perform better than first year projects: the average number of lines of code in a method (P4), the percentage of short identifiers (P9), the percentage of static methods (P12) and the number of assignments in an if- or while statement (P18) were all lower.

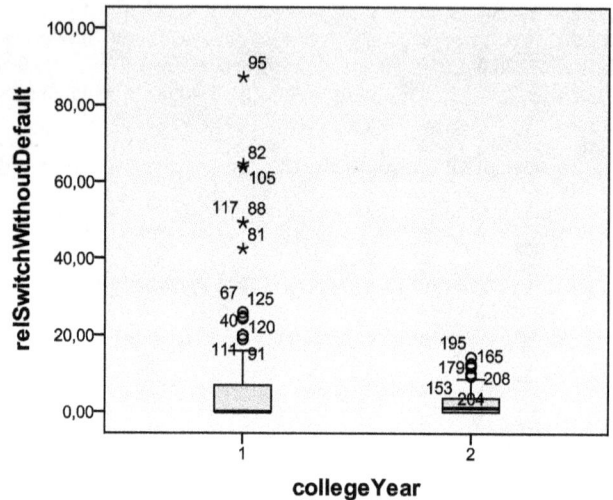

Figure 2. Box plot P19 – Relative number of switch statements without default.

The results presented in this section imply that our research question stated in Section 1 ("Do second year students produce code with better static quality properties than first year students?") has to be answered negatively.

6. CONCLUSIONS AND FUTURE WORK

Measuring the static quality of code written by student teams is a hard job producing interesting results. First of all it is a hard job, because it is difficult to separate student written code from imported code or generated code, and to remove copies of (part of) a product. It is also a hard job because no tool exists that produces a set of measurement results that covers more or less the wide spectrum of code properties that one is interested in when looking at static code quality. And, finally, not all interesting code characteristics *can* be measured by tools.

As stated in Section 2, we do not claim universal validity with respect to the set of quality characteristics and code properties that we have used. We are still working on improvements. We welcome comments of other researchers / teachers.

The measurement results that we have obtained show that, in many cases, there is no clear difference between the static quality of code produced by students in different years of study. A first cause of this result is that second year projects are bigger and more complex than first year projects. So, there are more opportunities for producing low quality code. However, we feel that the main causes of this result is that in programming courses and in project assessments little attention is paid to static code quality. Students are not trained in this subject, and, apparently, they do not produce quality code by themselves. The results of this lack of training can be experienced in the outside world every day: software that can only be maintained at high risks and high costs. In our opinion it is important to train students from the beginning in writing code that is not only working, but that also meets static quality standards. And, with more attention to this subject, we may also hope for a more extensive toolset for measuring static code quality.

For this research we examined the results of first and second year students. It would be very interesting to see how the results compare to third and fourth year students. Unfortunately, as of now, we do not have the data to investigate this.

Currently, little or no emphasis is put on teaching quality code. It would be interesting to hear how the results change after more attention is paid to this in first and second year courses. It would then be interesting to follow those students as they go into industry to see what difference, if any, this makes to their career tracks.

We will keep working on improvement of the set of code properties that we have identified, both for introducing the subject of static quality in the classroom, and for an improvement of our measurement program. The measurement results can also be used for a more fine-grained statistical analysis, e.g., concerning differences between first year teams or second year teams in subsequent academic years. And, we definitely need better tooling. At this moment we are not able to measure all desired code properties automatically. Currently we are working on our own 'generic' metrics tool using ANTLR technology. The first results are promising. We will continue with the development of this tool. We will also investigate the incorporation of other well-known tools for measuring static code quality, like CheckStyle ([10]) and FindBugs ([12]).

7. ACKNOWLEDGMENTS

We thank Ahmed Nait Aicha (Hogeschool van Amsterdam) for his help in mastering SPSS.

8. REFERENCES

[1] Breuker, D., Brunekreef, J., Derriks, J., Nait Aicha, A. (2009). Reliability of software metrics tools. In Proceedings IWSM, Industrial Track Papers. November 2009, 10-22.

[2] Counsell, S., Swift, S., Tucker, A. 2006. Object Oriented Cohesion Subjectivity amongst Experienced and Novice Developers: an Empirical Study, *ACM SIGSOFT Software Engineering Notes,* 31(5), 1-10.

[3] Fenton, N.E, Pfleeger, S.L., 1997. *Software Metrics, a Rigorous & Practical Approach.* Boston: PWS Publishing Company, 1997.

[4] Gresse von Wangenheim, C, Thiry, M, Kochanski, D. 2009. Empirical evaluation of an educational game on software measurement, *Empir Software Eng* (2009) 14:418–452.

[5] Huffman Hayes, J. Energizing Software Engineering Education through Real-World Projects as Experimental Studies, *Proceedings of the 15th Conference on Software Engineering Education and Training CSEET* (Covington, KY, February 2002, 192-206)

[6] ISO/IEC 9126-1 2001. Software Engineering- Product Quality – Part 1: Quality Model. Geneva, 2001.

[7] McConnell, S. 2004. *Code Complete.* Redmond: Microsoft Press, 2004.

[8] McCracken et al, 2001. Assessment of Programming Skills of First-year CS Students (Report by the ITiCSE 2001 Working Group on Assessment of Programming Skills of First-year CS Students), ITiCSE 2001, 125-180.

[9] Patton, A., McGill, M. 2006. Student Portfolios and Software Quality Metrics in Computer Science Education, *Consortium for Computing Sciences in Colleges.*

[10] http://checkstyle.sourceforge.net/

[11] http://download.cnet.com/DupFinder/3000-2206_4-10800512.html

[12] http://findbugs.sourceforge.net/

[13] http://msquaredtechnologies.com/m2rsm/.

[14] http://pmd.sourceforge.net/cpd.html.

[15] http://www.antlr.org

[16] http://www.campwoodsw.com/sourcemonitor.html.

[17] http://www.spss.com.

Awakening Rip Van Winkle: Modernizing the Computer Science Web Curriculum

Randy Connolly
Dept. Computer Science & Information
Systems
Mount Royal University
4825 Mount Royal Gate SW, Calgary,
AB, Canada T3E 6K6
403-440-6061

rconnolly@mtroyal.ca

ABSTRACT

The world of web development has experienced a great deal of change over the past decade. The importance and complexity of web development is currently not adequately reflected in the ACM Computer Science 2008 Curriculum, nor in most reported computer science programs. This paper examines published literature on teaching the web since 2001 and argues that the computer science curriculum needs to be woken up and modernized in regards to the importance of web development. The paper critiques the approach of teaching web development topics within a single course. It articulates a wide variety of web development topics that need to be covered in any contemporary computer science program and which are often absent in other published accounts of this course. The paper concludes by arguing that a multi-course stream in web development can help the students integrate the discrete pieces of knowledge garnered during their undergraduate education.

Categories and Subject Descriptors

K.3.2 [Computers and Education]: Computer & Information Science Education – computer science education.

General Terms

Design, Experimentation.

Keywords

CS Education, Web Development, Pedagogy.

1. INTRODUCTION

One of the earliest and most well-known characters in American literature is that of Rip Van Winkle, who appeared in Washington's Irving's *Sketch Book* of 1819. In the story, Rip, a bit of a lazy vagabond, drinks some dubious home brew up in the hills, falls asleep, awakens twenty years later, and is utterly astounded by the transformation of his colonial village of Sleepy Hollow into a bustling commerce-driven republican town. If like

Rip, we were to have slept, but only for the ten years since 2000, we also might be amazed at the transformations in how people experience the web. Back in 1999 people used the web for occasional online shopping at home and examining stock prices or breaking news on their desktop computers. While this kind of usage is still important, the type of web sites being accessed, the user experience while using these sites, and the devices we use to do it has changed quite a bit in the intervening ten years. In this decade, the web has transformed into an ever-present information retrieval mechanism as well as the principal platform for hosting software applications [25]. Somewhat inexplicably, however, while the web has experienced this remarkable transformation, there has been a certain dormancy to the way that the web is being taught in the computer science curriculum.

While web topics are certainly a recommended component of a variety of ACM curricula reports, it still very much appears as a peripheral topic within computer science. In the CS 2008 curriculum, for instance, almost all of the topics recognizable as pertaining to the field of web development are marked as elective topics [1]. Similarly, there is a relative dearth of research in the computer education literature which is somewhat surprising given the ostensive importance of web technology in the real world of software development. Each year SIGCSE and ITiCSE have multiple papers on teaching beginning programming, databases, and other curricula areas, but only fairly rarely will a paper on teaching web development appear.

In fact, looking at all the papers presented at SIGCSE and ITiCSE in the last decade, only about 1.5% of them have pertained at all to the teaching of web topics. Since 2005 the percentage is even lower; there have been only 17 papers during that time about web topics – and many of those were only peripherally focused on teaching web development. As a point of comparison, in the same five-year time span, there were 65 papers on game-related topics in those two conferences. While clearly this represents the discipline's interest in trying to increase enrollments in computer science via the appeal of games, it certainly is not at all indicative of the job market computer science graduates will face, one in which arguably a majority of software development jobs are broadly within the web context [21]. One can verify this by examining an employment website such as monster.com or simplyhired.com. For instance, on two different three-day time periods in October and November 2010, there were roughly twice as many web-related development job postings as non-web ones on those two job sites.

Now it is quite possible that the reason why there have been so few papers on teaching web topics is because the professors teaching these courses are too busy adapting to new web technologies to publish their experiences. This is certainly the impression one gets from reading many of these papers (for instance, [2], [19], and [40]). These papers invariably agree with Treu's designation of the web application course as the "Unteachable Class" [34].

This paper is going to argue that the computer science curricula needs to be woken up and modernized in regards to the importance of web development, and will argue that a two- or a three-course stream in web development can acquaint students with the real world of web application development in a significantly less "unteachable" manner. The paper will describe a variety of web development topics that should be covered in a web stream, and yet which are almost always absent in published accounts of web courses. Its perspective is informed by the author's experience teaching these topics since 1998, by his on-going experiences as a professional web developer for a wide variety of international clients, and by his experiences writing a book in this field. The paper will conclude by arguing that such a series of courses can also address one of the key problems in the education of our students: namely, how to integrate the discrete pieces of knowledge that they have gathered during their progress through their computer science education.

2. HOW THE WEB IS BEING TAUGHT

Most computer science educators would no doubt agree that there is a lot of material that needs to be shoe-horned into a typical four-year computer science program. The ACM curriculum for computer science [1] articulates the very broad body of knowledge in computer science; it consists of recommended mandatory learning outcomes as well as additional optional outcomes. The web topics, subsumed under the banner of Net-centric computing, include only a very small number of mandatory core topic outcomes, mainly of the awareness variety. There are also a number of elective topics that conceivably could be covered by a single optional course on web development. Tellingly, despite a decade of transformation in the real world of web development, the Net-centric topic list in the CS 2008 report is essentially unchanged from the 2001 version [17].

Yet it appears that despite the (limited) mandate of the ACM curriculum and despite the importance of web technology to the student's own lives, to their job prospects, and also to the research efforts of many computer science professors, not every computer science program includes a course in these topics. In 2003, Lee noted that "there is a surprisingly small number of universities that offer a serious web programming course for the advanced computer science student" [19]. Six years later, Stepp in 2009 noted that most universities still don't cover web development in their computer science programs, but do so in their IS or IT ones. [33].

Given the unruly and shifting number of web standards and practices, it is not surprising that "there does not seem to be a consensus about where in the curriculum, and at what detail, to introduce this material" [33]. Surveying the literature that does exist on teaching web topics, one can see the most common teaching approaches in Table 1. As is apparent from the number of references, by far the most common way of teaching the web

course in the reported literature is to try to fit all the material within a single upper-level course. Not coincidentally, it is in these papers that one finds most of the complaints about the difficulty of teaching the web course.

Table 1. Summary of CS web education papers

Course Approach	#	References
Teach the material as a CS0 course or as non-major elective.	4	12, 16, 26, 27
Use Javascript in the CS1/CS2 course or teach web topics in a CS 1.5 course.	3	16, 29, 33
An intermediate to advanced single web course which sometimes serves as a capstone course.	14	2, 3, 4, 10, 14, 19, 22, 23, 29, 32, 34, 36, 37, 40
A two (or more) course stream on web development.	3	13, 16, 24

3. WEB TOPICS TO BE TAUGHT

Given the oft-stated worries about the breadth of material needing to be taught in a web course, this author strongly believes that the All-the-Web-in-One-Course (AWOC) approach very much needs to be retired. Back in the late 1960s/early 1970s, a math program might have had a single course in programming in Fortran or a business program might have a single course on data processing in Cobol, but eventually it was recognized that a body of knowledge as complex as programming requires multiple courses to teach the material properly. Web development should by now be in a similar state.

The principal reason why the AWOC approach is no longer appropriate is due to the peculiar combination of change and persistence that characterizes the web development world. As noted by many of the authors cited in this paper, the web environment is one very much characterized by flux. It is this author's belief that the web environment experiences something analogous to paradigm shifts, in that web development experiences cycles of short periods of substantial change followed by periods of relative stability (see Table 2). The key point is that these are not exactly paradigm shifts in the Kuhnean sense since a previous web technology isn't always being displaced and replaced (though, for instance, with CGI and ASP it was); more often the next set of important technologies or approaches are being used "on top" of, or in addition to, the previous ones, meaning that knowledge and expertise in the previous paradigm is still required.

Table 2. Web development paradigms

Principal technology context/layer	Approx. Year
HTML + CGI	1995-1998
CSS (simple) + Javascript (simple) + ASP/JSP	1999-2002
Semantic Web Standards + PHP/ASP.NET	2003-2006
AJAX + REST/JSON services	2006-2009
Frameworks + Platforms (WordPress,JQuery,Sharepoint,etc)	2009-

There are indications that the web development environment is currently at the start of a new cycle of change and, as such, new topics need to be integrated into how we teach the web. For those stuck in an AWOC model, it will become increasingly difficult to keep those courses comprehensive and relevant. As the title of another paper with a similar theme suggests, those courses will increasingly seem like they are "partying like it's 1999" [5].

So what needs to continue to be taught in any web course and what new topics need to be added in? The remainder of this section describes those web topics divided into two subcategories: material that is proscribed, however briefly, in the ACM CS 2008, and material that is not mentioned in the ACM report, but which, nonetheless, needs to be covered in contemporary and future web courses.

3.1 Web Topics in CS 2008

The obvious beginning point of any web stream is with the way the web works (e.g., the various protocols, the hardware infrastructure, etc) and with HTML itself. While HTML is relatively trivial to learn, it is important to cover it in a way that is consonant with contemporary best practice usage. For reasons of accessibility [27], maintainability, content management system (CMS) integration, and search-engine optimization (SEO), HTML markup today is semantically-structured so as to separate content from presentation [41].

For these same reasons, CSS is now an essential part of web development. CSS coverage in reported AWOC courses is often quite minimal [2,22,36]. While basic text formatting in CSS is indeed quite straightforward, real world CSS, which is commonly used as well for positioning and layout, is notoriously difficult to master due to browser bugs, incompatibilities, and non-obvious CSS box model interactions [41]. To complicate matters further, the CSS landscape is undergoing a period of transition, with both CSS3 and CSS frameworks like 960 adding to the layers of CSS knowledge necessary for contemporary and future practitioners.

Javascript is another key web development technology. The type of Javascript that can be covered in just a few lectures (rollovers, form data validation, browser sniffing) was reasonably close to what was needed professionally in the late 1990s. Since the "discovery" of XmlHttpRequest and the subsequent flourishing of new user interface coding and asynchronous communication with web services, Javascript coding has become simultaneously crucial to contemporary web development and significantly more complicated. Analogous to the case with CSS, this type of Javascript programming is very difficult to learn due to browser differences, the untyped nature of the language, the lack of a cross-browser debugging environment, and the general conceptual complexity of working with callback functions.

Another key part of learning real-world web development is the server-side environment. Potentially this is a very large topic and has its own difficulties from a teaching perspective. There are a number of different competing technologies (PHP, ASP.NET, JSP, Ruby on Rails) which all accomplish the same thing: interacting with server resources and programmatically generating HTML, CSS, and Javascript that is returned to the browser. Server-side development also has a number of substantial additional topics, such as the HTTP protocol, SQL and database-access APIs, replicating database changes across data servers,

local and distributed transactions, maintaining state (via cookies, sessions, querystrings, and form elements) across requests (and, in a web farm, across processes), internationalization, architecting web infrastructures for scalability, and enterprise design patterns, which are almost impossible to fit into a AWOC course.

Digital media and information architecture and usability is another vital area of real-world web practice. This area is often under-represented in most reported web courses. Usability in general is a very large topic and will likely be covered in a computer science program's HCI courses. Nonetheless, usability in the web context does require its own unique topics which may not make it into the typical HCI course. These topics include: the unique factors affecting web site usability, the different ways of organizing and structuring web content, the development and articulation of web conventions, designing web navigation systems, and an overview of visual design principles. These usability topics rarely make it into an AWOC course. Of all the papers examined for this article, only [27], [31], and [39] included usability or digital media in its reported topic lists.

Web vulnerabilities/security is another vital web topic that can be difficult to comprehensively cover using the AWOC approach (see [22] for an exception). Security in general is a very large topic, and many of the more important general issues and concepts are likely to be covered in a dedicated networking course. Web security does have its own unique problems and concerns. For instance, cross-site scripting, SQL injection attacks and other common web vulnerabilities are unique to the web context and as a consequence are often not covered in a standard network security course. Interestingly, none of the current web textbooks [7,18,30] examined for this paper contained any substantial material on web security.

3.2 Web Topics Not in CS 2008

While most of the reported web courses cover some portion of the preceding topics, the remaining topics that need to be taught in any future web courses are almost never covered. The first of these topics is that of web frameworks and APIs. One of the key features of the contemporary web landscape is that many organizations are no longer creating their web infrastructure from scratch but are using single (or integrating multiple) already existing open-source and/or proprietary web frameworks [11, 35]. Complex content management systems such as Drupal, Joomla, DotNetNuke, or Microsoft SharePoint, blogging systems such as WordPress or Blogger, web forums such as phpBB or vBulletin, e-commerce systems such osCommerce or Magento, and common business practice portals and services such as SugarCRM, Salesforce, or Exact are often used as the main framework for an organization's public or private web presence.

In other words, the platform for current and future web development is expanding significantly beyond LAMP (Linux, Apache, MySQL, and PHP) or WISA (Windows, IIS, SQL Server, and ASP.NET). Contemporary web development is increasingly more about building new solutions that involve customizing or leveraging APIs and/or extension frameworks (which may themselves be built on LAMP or WISA, so knowledge of them is still required), such as the Facebook API, Sharepoint, Drupal, WordPress, Zend, JQuery, and ASP.NET MVC. The scale of something like the Facebook API usage (over a million developers and over half a million applications [9]) or the number of sites built on WordPress (perhaps as many as 10% of all significant sites on the entire web [11]) is often invisible to the end user, but is something that needs to be made completely visible to our computer science students. For the students, it is important to learn about the existence of these existing frameworks because the future of web systems will increasingly lie in their use, integration, and customization.

Another important part of the web systems knowledge area that is generally missing from computer science education is that of hosting and deployment. For practical reasons, students generally learn web development using their own computer or a lab computer as if it was a web server. Ultimately, however, a web site needs to be deployed on a public web server. Students thus need to learn about the advantages and disadvantages of the main web server platforms as well as third-party hosting environments. Hosting topics such as web gardens, web farms, load balancing, data center redundancy and replication, as well as server configurations for scalability also need to be covered if a computer science graduate is going to have a realistic sense of the contemporary web world.

Finally, it is important for students to learn about web service consumption and integration, especially RESTful services (though SOAP services should be taught as well). With the broad interest in the asynchronous consumption of server data at the browser using Javascript (generally referred to as AJAX) and due to the relatively easy availability of a wide-range of RESTful services, a new style of web development known as the mashup has become increasingly common [10,14]. Consuming these services typically involves learning XML parsing, XPath search expressions, as well as more conceptual issues such as mediation techniques between heterogeneous data sources [6].

4. SAMPLE WEB COURSES

The previous section described a range of topics that should be covered in our web courses. Below is one sample way to split this material across three hypothetical semester courses. It should be mentioned that this list is not completely hypothetical in that it is the way this author's department teaches the web. It may be possible to reduce some of the coverage in order to fit it into just two courses or to fit it into three quarter-style courses.

4.1 Web 1

This course covers the concepts and practice necessary for creating an effective web site at the introductory level. Topics include: how the web works, XHTML (with an emphasis on web standards, accessibility, and semantic markup), CSS (not just styling but also positioning and layout), digital media, information architecture and usability, a very brief introduction to Javascript, and a brief introduction to server-side development.

4.2 Web 2

This course covers the concepts and technologies needed to design and develop server-side applications. Its main focus would be on how server-side technology works and on developing with server-side technology. Complicated web development environments such as JSP or ASP.NET have a substantial learning curve. A fair percentage of this type of course must be devoted to teaching the practicalities of developing within it. Other topics

would include accessing databases in web applications, software design in web applications, designing for scalability and reliability, mechanisms for maintaining state, consuming REST and SOAP web services, and designing and implementing web security (though these last two could move to the Web 3 course).

4.3 Web 3

This course expands on the foundation client, server, and database topics. The course covers: intermediate Javascript development, asynchronous consumption of web services in Javascript, using Javascript frameworks and web APIs, web application deployment and hosting, and issues in adapting web sites for differing locales and cultures.

5. CONCLUSION

It is this author's strong belief that teaching web topics can play a vital role in the development of a computer science student. Adams has noted that one of the key limitations with computer science education and the many specialized knowledge competencies it tries to engender is that "students struggle to put all the pieces together" [2]. Humphrey similarly noted this lacuna not just in undergraduate but in graduate computer science students as well; even graduate students "usually have little or no experiences in designing, implementing, and evaluating, large-scale software systems for complex, dynamic, and heterogeneous environments" [14]. That is, it is not enough to teach each technology and concept in isolation; "students must understand how these technologies relate to each other" [2]. This theme has also been raised by a number of other authors in their reflections on what needs to be improved in the way computer science is taught [8,28].

One of the key benefits to teaching web development in two or three serious web courses is that it can provide the students with a taste of that needed integration and complexity. Kazmerik [15] reported in an undergraduate student's perspective on just such a series of two web courses that the experience was akin to finally getting to play the guitar. In Kazmerik's analogy, all the prior computer courses were about understanding or making some small component pieces of the guitar, such as the strings, the pickups, or the frets. This, according to Kazmerik, frustrates the students because they decided to take a computer degree because of their desire to the guitar – that is, many took computer science because of their desire to create a finished, complex and inspiring software system such as a real game or a real web application. A multi-course web stream can provide that much-desired integration for the upper-level students. It can provide an experience that White and Weinberg have called for: core integration at the end of the CS curriculum that helps "clarify the manner in which the core areas [of the computer science curriculum] are interdependent" [38].

6. ACKNOWLEDGMENTS

The author would like to thank Amber Settle for her very diligent reading and insightful feedback on earlier drafts of this paper.

7. REFERENCES

[1] ACM Interim Review Task Force. (2008). *Computer Science Curriculum 2008: An Interim Revision of CS 2001*.

http://www.acm.org/education/curricula/ComputerScience2008.pdf.

[2] Adams, D. R. (2007). Integration early: a new approach to teaching web application development. *Journal of Computing Sciences in College.* 23 (1): 97-104.

[3] Bloss, A. (2001). Teaching fundamentals for web programming and e-commerce in a liberal arts computer science curriculum. *Journal of Computing Sciences in Colleges* 16 (2).

[4] Coffman, J. and Weaver, A.C. (2010). Electronic Commerce Virtual Laboratory. In *SIGCSE '10.*

[5] Connolly, R. (2009). No Longer Partying Like It's 1999: Designing a Modern Web Stream Using the IT2008 Curriculum Guidelines. In *SIGITE '09.*

[6] Connolly, R (2010). Small service is true service while it lasts: integrating web services into IT education. *In SIGITE '10.*

[7] Deitel, H., Deitel, P. (2008). *Internet & World Wide Web: How to Program, Fourth Edition.* Prentice Hall.

[8] Denning, P. and McGettrick, A. (2005). Recentering Computer Science. *Communications of the ACM* 48 (11).

[9] Facebook. (2010). Press Room. http://www.facebook.com/press/info.php?statistics.

[10] Frydenberg, M. (2008). Slickr: A Multi-Tiered Web Development Capstone Project Using Databases, Web Services, and AJAX. *Information Systems Education Journal* 6 (37).

[11] Gelbmann, M. (2010). The amazing dominance of WordPress as CMS. http://w3techs.com/blog.

[12] Gousie, M.B. (2006). A Robust Web Programming and Graphics Course for Non-Majors. In *SIGCSE '06.*

[13] Hufford, K.D. (2001). CS265 web network and web site management development of a core course in the Internet technology minor curriculum. *Journal of Computing Science in Colleges* 16 (4).

[14] Humphrey, Marty. (2004). Web Services as the Foundation for Learning Complex Software System Development. In *SIGCSE '04.*

[15] Kazmerik, R. W. (2010). Who cares about web services?: a student perspective on web technology education. In *SIGITE '10.*

[16] Knuckles, C. D. (2002). A net-centric curricular focus. *Journal of Computing Sciences in Colleges* 17 (6).

[17] Joint Task Force on Computing Curricula. (2001). Computing Curricula 2001 Computer Science.

[18] Lecky-Thompson, G.W. (2008). *Just Enough Web Programming with XHTML, PHP, and MySQL.* Course Technology.

[19] Lee, A. H. (2003). A manageable web software architecture: searching for simplicity. In *SIGCSE '03.*

[20] Lim, B., Hosack, B, and Vogt, P. (2010). A web service-oriented approach to teaching CS/IS1. In *SIGCSE '10.*

[21] Monster.com. (2009). Winter 2009-10 IT Job Market Report. http://media.monster.com/a/i/intelligence.

[22] Noonan, R.E. (2007). A course in web programming. *Journal of Computing Sciences in Colleges* 22 (3).

[23] Olan, M. (2009). Web applications: a test bed for advanced topics. *Journal of Computing Sciences in Colleges* 24 (3).

[24] Phillips, J., et al (2002). Design of a two-course sequence in web programming and e-commerce. *Journal of Computing Sciences in Colleges* 19 (2).

[25] Pirolli, P. (2007). *Information Foraging Theory: Adaptive Interaction with Information.* Oxford University Press.

[26] Reed, D. (2001). Rethinking CS0 with JavaScript. In *SIGCSE '01.*

[27] Rosmaita, B.J. (2006). Accessibility first!: a new approach to web design. In *SIGCSE '06.*

[28] Sahami, M., Aiken, A., and Zelenski, J. (2010). Expanding the frontiers of computer science: designing a curriculum to reflect a diverse field. In *SIGCSE '10.*

[29] Scott, T., Ursyn, A. (2006). A web design course team taught by professors in art and computer science. *Journal of Computing Sciences in Colleges* 22 (1).

[30] Sebesta, R. W. (2009). *Programming the World-Wide Web, Fifth Edition.* Addison-Wesley.

[31] Sharda, N. (2007). Creating innovative new media programs: need, challenges, and development framework. In *Emme '07.*

[32] Silverman, R. (2007). Ecommerce systems design course using Java servlets. *Journal of Computing Sciences in Colleges* 23 (1).

[33] Stepp, M., Miller, J., and Kirst, V. (2009). A 'CS 1.5' Introduction to Web Programming. In *SIGCSE '09.*

[34] Treu, K. (2002). To teach the unteachable class: an experimental course in web-based application design. In *SIGCSE '02.*

[35] W3techs .com. (2010). Historical trends in the usage of content management systems for websites. http://w3techs.com/technologies/history_overview.

[36] Wang, X. (2006). A practical way to teach web programming in computer science. *Journal of Computing Sciences in Colleges* 22 (1).

[37] Weaver, A.C. Electronic Commerce Software Laboratory. (2004). In *SIGCSE '04.*

[38] White, W. W. and Weinberg, J. B. (2009). Breadth-last technical electives: integrating the CS core via computer games and mobile robotics. In *SIGCSE '09.*

[39] Wong, Y.L., Burg, J., and Strokanova, V. (2004). Digital media in computer science curricula. In *SIGCSE '04.*

[40] Yue, K.B., Ding, W. (2004). Design and evolution of an undergraduate course on web application development. In *ITiCSE '04.*

[41] Zeldman, J. (2003). *Designing with Web Standards.* New Riders

Experiences in Implementing a Studio Component into a Course for Novice Web Developers

Rebecca Grasser
Information Technology and Computer Science Department
Lakeland Community College
Kirtland, Ohio
bgrasser@lakelandcc.edu

ABSTRACT

This paper discusses an educational experience aimed at producing better computer-based projects by including in the assessment process an art appreciation-like critique component. We tested this idea at a medium-size Community College offering many degrees in various applied areas of computing (such as web programming). In a way that at times parallels the constructive criticism of work done by art students we asked our participants to critique their classmates as well as themselves. New elements of assessment such as aesthetics, user-engagement, naturalness, completeness, and unrealized potential of the projects appeared in the discourse. In our opinion, the assessment of computer code as just being correct or incorrect is enriched when designers look at their artifacts as pieces to be shown to others (technical and non-technical viewers) in a studio-like environment. Although it is very early to extrapolate results, our conclusion is that a noticeable improvement of the overall quality of the final products as well as a higher level of collaboration, participation, and student satisfaction resulted from this approach.

Categories and Subject Descriptors

K.3 [**Computer and Information Science Education**]: Self-assessment; J.5 [**Arts And Humanities**]: Arts, fine and performing

General Terms

Design, Experimentation, Human Factors.

Keywords

Studio-based learning and instruction, Design crits, web programming, novice programmers.

1. INTRODUCTION

In introductory programming courses, students tend to view their program's output as right or wrong. In more advanced application design courses, they still use the same thought process: does the application work or not?

In contrast, art students understand the need for critique as part of the learning process. Art creations are not necessarily right or wrong. The elements of judgment are particular to each discipline but in general incorporate notions such as aesthetics, value, function, usage, beauty, color, shape, motion, composition, balance, contrast, repetition, and so forth. The particular items that appear in the critique are usually discussed in the studio component of each course. "While the art students are well accustomed to this format, the computer science students need some adjustment to this process. This is probably due to the fact that, despite Knuth's teachings, Computer Science students often think in terms of a correct or incorrect program, and rarely in terms of programming elegance."[15] Interestingly, many computer scientists are trained in the arts, yet still view their applications in black and white or right and wrong.[12]

The use of the *studio component* is not a new idea, many programs such as those described in [8, 9, 13, 15] have some form of a studio component as part of the curriculum. We have not, in our readings, found an active curriculum that contains the studio component in programming classes at the two-year college level.

We chose to implement a studio component after hearing from employers, our academic advisory committee, and other faculty that graduating students have weak soft skills in that they cannot discuss their work with technical and non-technical professionals. Our plan to incorporate more of those soft skills started by encouraging our students to provide more presentations and defense of their work.

Generally, programming courses include a phase in which actual code is reviewed, one idea after the next. In our program, the student rarely experiences one of those review sessions. We want to expose the student to the code review process in a supportive environment that involves all the students and allows the presenter to learn from the experience.

The next step was to create measurable learning objectives for these concepts. In looking at the ACM Two Year College Curricular reports [1], we used the following language: "Students will be exposed to techniques of critical analysis."

Our next task was to define what we meant by critical analysis. In reviewing past courses, it was determined that our students were not academically mature enough to complete the formal code review processes. We chose to look at the critique process used in the studio arts. It was our opinion that this process would provide a supportive environment while still pointing out challenges in the code and application design. "The critique is the primary vehicle through which students get feedback on their work. Improvement in image making is almost always based upon the reactions we get from others after they look at and consider our work. Few of us could survive in the art world if we lived in a critical vacuum. We gain an important kind of objectivity in relation to our work when we listen to what others have to say about it. The kind of criticism we do in our classes is applied criticism - as opposed to theoretical criticism. Students are supposed to use the feedback to improve their work. We are trying to affect changes in their process of making images." [5]

This framework highlighting critical judgment was strongly emphasized and insisted upon as integral part of the assessment process. The message delivered to the students was that evaluation of a piece includes input from the instructor, the creator, the peers, and external viewers.

2. BACKGROUND

Lakeland Community College (LCC) is a medium-sized two-year college located in Northeast Ohio. The Information Technology & Computer Science (IT & CS) department is part of the Business Technologies Division and offers eight degree concentrations as part of the Associate of Applied Business and sixteen certificates for students seeking a specific skill set. We offer concentrations in both Internet Programming (designed for those with an interest in application development) and Web Content Developer (designed for those with an interest in graphics and basic user interaction). In any given section in the IT & CS department, we can roughly divide the age ranges as [16 - 22], [23 - 35], and [35 - 75]. The average age, college-wide, is 31. Many of our students are first generation college students and/or coming to us to learn a new skill to keep or obtain employment. The region has a heavy manufacturing base, with a significant proportion of our students having never been out of the local area.

All of the courses in the IT & CS department are structured using a lecture/lab format. The majority of these courses have a one to three or one to four ratio of lecture to lab classroom (contact) hours every week. By way of an example, the second course in web programming is a three credit (semester hour), five contact hours course: 1 contact hour for lecture and four for the lab component. Courses are delivered in various ways including a traditional face-to-face setting, an online/distance learning setting (using a vendor supplied course management system), and a hybrid format (50% of the contact time is in the classroom, the remaining 50% is online). The lecture/lab format is a strength of our program as students have a structured period in which to explore topics from the course while the instructor is present.

These degree programs are designed to be completed in four semesters. At the end of the four semesters, students have been exposed to a number of technologies, languages, and commercial platforms including XHTML, PHP, Ruby, Java, .NET, JavaScript, Adobe Flash & ActionScript, and the Oracle and MySQL database systems.

3. METHODOLOGY

Each of the courses in the program has a required lecture

Figure 1: Questions discussed as a group

1. Is the project presented in a professional format? Explain.

2. What worked and worked really well? Why?

3. Where did you see some problems or concerns? Explain

4. What is the next logical step for making the application work better or become that much cooler?

Please note that comments like "Wow that is cool!" will require further clarification and use of the vocabulary and concepts discussed. Now is the time to practice.

and lab component. In the hybrid offering of these courses, the online portion of the course was to be used by the student to read the assigned sections of the text and other ancillary material, meet with classmates and do outside research on the problem, and complete the lab assignments. The in-class portion of the course was used to discuss material not in the text and as guided skill practice in the computer lab. The studio component was created by shortening the contact time of the lab portion (the guided skill practice). The critique and extended discussions took place during the studio component of the class.

We looked at one third-semester course (JavaScript Programming) to see if adding in a studio and critique component helped improve student confidence in their ability to discuss technical projects in a non-technical fashion as well as giving oral presentations in general.

In this course, students have a ten lab assignments, a final project, and three written exams. They were asked to present at least four labs and their final project during the studio period. As a result, they have four or more opportunities to practice their presentation skills and ten or more opportunities to practice in-class critiquing. The prerequisites for this course include a computer literacy class and a basic logic course.

Before the studio portion of the class for the first lab, students were given an overview of the process, vocabulary, etiquette, and behavior expected during a critique (drawn from [3, 10, 17]) Shneiderman's Golden Rules [16], and a set of terms and concepts dealing with aesthetics (much of this information was drawn from [4]). Every student presented their first lab and the rest of the class, using an analysis worksheet (based on [6, 7, 11]) critiqued both the presentation and the product (See Tables 1, 2, and Figure 1). This presentation and critique session was graded as satisfactory/unsatisfactory so students could see their strong points and where they needed to improve. During this time, we discussed why this process was important not only in the classroom, but as they developed their own projects (self-critique) and in the workforce. We also discussed what is and is not a critique. As noted by Cline [5] "The classroom critique presents us with important learning opportunities but also with certain challenges.[...] In our culture, the term "criticism" has acquired negative connotations. It has become synonymous with ridicule and denigration for many people. So, it's no wonder many students experience apprehension about having their images critiqued. To mitigate

Table 1: Table based on E. J. Mirielli. *Using peer-evaluation in a website design course.* J. Comput. Small Coll., 22(4):14-21, 2007.

Web Site Evaluation Criteria	
For each of the items below, rate the web site presented by each individual on a scale of 1 to 5, with 1 being a low rating and 5 being a high rating of the quality assessed	
Planning and Design For Specified Audience	1-5
Clearly identifies the audience/consumer of the web site content	
Clearly states the goals of the consumer/user	
Clearly discusses user needs analysis	
Content Organization	1-5
Content is organized around clearly identifiable user and or task analysis goals	
Content organization ascribes to clearly stated organizational schema and structure	
Visual Organization	1-5
Web site effectively uses proximity to enhance visual organization	
Web site effectively uses alignment to enhance visual organization	
Web site effectively uses consistency to enhance visual organization	
Web site effectively uses contrast to enhance visual organization	
Aesthetics	1-5
Web site provides consistency in use of color and fonts	
Colors chosen are aesthetically pleasing	
Content is easy to read	
Images and graphics enhance the look of the web site	
Overall the web site is aesthetically pleasing	

Table 2: Based on D. D. Dankel, II and J. Ohlrich. **Students teaching students: incorporating presentations into a course.** In *SIGCSE '07: Proceedings of the 38th SIGCSE technical symposium on Computer science education*, pages 96-99, New York, NY, USA, 2007. ACM.

Presentation Evaluation Form (Check the appropriate box)	Excellent	Very Good	Good	Ave	Fair	Poor	NA
Understanding of material							
Coverage							
Organization of presentation							
Layout of slides							
Coverage of material							
Good examples							
Discussion							
Style							
Eye contact							
Pace (speed)							
Speaking volume							
Nervous							
If the speaker is NOT obviously nervous, rate as Excellent or very good							
Understandability							
Body language							

these fears, we need to make clear to our students - and to ourselves - what we mean by "criticism."" We spent part of each classroom period for the next several weeks reminding students that the critique provided a model for improvement - it was to help their classmates (and by extension, themselves) improve in both creating and crafting web applications as well as discussing those artifacts during class.

For the second and subsequent lab assignments, a portion of the class presented their work and the critique sessions were student-led. As the course sections are small (less than 18 students), all students participated in each of the sessions. We found that small group sessions (where the remainder of the class worked on their projects as in Reimer and Douglas [14]) did not work well with these groups. Each non-presenting student filled out an analysis worksheet on each of the presenting students. After the class session, worksheets were collected and the data cleaned and returned to the student in the form of average scores for each component and comments from their classmates. Participation in the critique and the completed worksheet formed part of the presentation grade.

4. RESULTS

Students presented between five and seven lab assignments during the semester, and these presentations were formative and counted very little towards their final grades. During the last week of the course, several faculty and the division academic dean were invited to the students' presentation of their final project. This presentation was summative and the critiques were provided by our guests. The students in the class were, by this time, very comfortable with presenting their work, and the dean and faculty had both constructive criticism and very positive comments for the students.

On the first day of class, a survey was distributed to the students. With a response rate of 70%, students reported that 42% had completed a traditional studio arts course and 85% completed a speech course at the post-secondary level. We asked the students if they were comfortable giving oral presentations and 28% said they agreed with the statement and 52% neither agreed nor disagreed with the statement (20% declined to answer). At the end of the course, we asked the same question and 25% strongly agreed and 75% agreed with the statement.

The positive gains in the presentation comfort level were not the only item noted. The online portion of the class had a discussion board environment that was optional, but available to the students as a place to ask and answer questions during times when the class was not in session. In traditional online courses, where students have no in-person contact with each other, we typically would see between twenty and one hundred postings in an academic semester. During the experimental course, we saw over seven hundred posts in the same time period. This is with a group of students that saw each other at least once per week. We attribute this to the increased comfort level of the students with respect to working with each other on solving a common set of problems and having to do so in a very public fashion.

5. CONCLUSIONS

In our limited experience with this course, we have found that the students were much more outgoing with each other and arguably created more interesting projects than past students who did not use the studio learning strategy. We believe we have realized at least some of the potential noted by Bergin et al., "Studio Based Learning, whether adopted in whole or in part, has potential to change the relationship of students to instructors, each other, and the university. It presents a more fulfilling, humane, educational experience for the student and so may have implications for issues of broader interest such as student recruitment, retention, and long-term satisfaction with their educational experience." [2]

Our preliminary results are encouraging. We intend on requiring a similar studio component in all future offerings of courses designed for novice web developers. It is our plan to survey students before and after these courses and then monitor their progress in the program's capstone course to see if there is an improvement in the ability to present their work to both peers and invited faculty and administrators. We feel that even the modest gains seen in the presenters' comfort level will help our graduates gain an advantage over their peers when pursuing their first job.

6. ACKNOWLEDGMENTS

We would like to thank Bruce Cline and Frank Prpic of the Photography Department at Lakeland Community College for their help on this project.

7. REFERENCES

[1] 2000 acm guidelines for associate-degree programs to support computing in a networked environment. *http://www.acmtyc.org/WebReports/ITreport/*.

[2] J. Bergin, R. Mercer, D. West, R. C. Duvall, E. Wallingford, P. M. Rostal, and R. P. Gabriel. A snapshot of studio based learning: code reviews as a means of community building. In *OOPSLA Companion '08: Companion to the 23rd ACM SIGPLAN conference on Object-oriented programming systems languages and applications*, pages 887–888, New York, NY, USA, 2008. ACM.

[3] R. Carter. Teaching visual design principles for computer science students. *Computer Science Education*, 13(1):67, 2003.

[4] B. Cline. *Critiquing Student Photographs in the College Classroom*. PhD thesis, Ohio University, 1994.

[5] B. Cline. Evaluating student work. *Interactive Design Forum*, (4), October 1999. http://www.awdsgn.com/HTML/EduClineCrit.html Accessed 25 June 2010.

[6] J. L. Colwell, J. Whittington, and J. Higley. Assessment measures and outcomes for computer graphics programs. *Engineering Design Graphics Journal*, 2005.

[7] D. D. Dankel, II and J. Ohlrich. Students teaching students: incorporating presentations into a course. In *SIGCSE '07: Proceedings of the 38th SIGCSE technical symposium on Computer science education*, pages 96–99, New York, NY, USA, 2007. ACM.

[8] E. DeBartolo and R. Robinson. A freshman engineering curriculum integrating design and experimentation. *International Journal of Mechanical Engineering Education*, 35(2):91 – 107, 2007.

[9] D. Hendrix, L. Myneni, H. Narayanan, and M. Ross. Implementing studio-based learning in cs2. In *SIGCSE*

'10: Proceedings of the 41st ACM technical symposium on Computer science education, pages 505–509, New York, NY, USA, 2010. ACM.

[10] R. Kosara. Visualization criticism — the missing link between information visualization and art. In *Proceedings of the 11th International Conference on Information Visualisation (IV)*.

[11] E. J. Mirielli. Using peer-evaluation in a website design course. *J. Comput. Small Coll.*, 22(4):14–21, 2007.

[12] J. Parker. Games and animation: collaborations between the arts and computer science. In *Information Technology: Coding and Computing, 2004. Proceedings. ITCC 2004. International Conference on*, volume 1, pages 164 – 168 Vol.1, 5-7 2004.

[13] R. Pausch and D. Marinelli. Carnegie mellon's entertainment technology center: combining the left and right brain. *Commun. ACM*, 50(7):50–57, 2007.

[14] Y. J. Reimer and S. A. Douglas. Teaching hci design with the studio approach. *Computer Science Education*, 13(3):191, 2003.

[15] N. Ribner and P. T. Metaxas. The art and science of multimedia: an interdisciplinary approach to teaching multimedia at a liberal arts college. In *SIGGRAPH '98: ACM SIGGRAPH 98 Conference abstracts and applications*, pages 46–51, New York, NY, USA, 1998. ACM.

[16] B. Shneiderman. *Designing the User Interface*. Addison-Wesley, 1987.

[17] J. Whittington. The process of effective critiques. *Computers & Graphics*, 28(3):401 – 407, 2004.

A Tool to Support the Web Accessibility Evaluation Process for Novices

Dr. Elaine Pearson
Teesside University
Accessibility Research Centre
School of Computing
Middlesbrough, TS1 3BA, UK.
+44 (0)1642 342656
e.pearson@tees.ac.uk

Christopher Bailey
Teesside University
Accessibility Research Centre
School of Computing
Middlesbrough, TS1 3BA, UK.
+44 (0)1642 384648
c.p.bailey@tees.ac.uk

Dr. Steve Green
Teesside University
Accessibility Research Centre
School of Computing
Middlesbrough, TS1 3BA, UK.
+44 (0)1642 342670
s.j.green@tees.ac.uk

ABSTRACT

The Accessibility Evaluation Assistant (AEA) is designed to assist novice auditors in the process of an accessibility evaluation of websites. The tool has been incorporated into an undergraduate computing module in Accessibility and Adaptive Technologies. It takes a structured walkthrough approach to guide the novice through a series of checks for established web accessibility principles with the goal of conducting a comprehensive accessibility evaluation. An initial evaluation of the AEA with 38 students confirms its potential for supporting the development of skills in auditing of websites for accessibility.

Categories and Subject Descriptors

H.5.2 [**Information Interfaces and Presentation**]: User Interfaces – *Evaluation/methodology.* K.3.2 [**Computers and Education**]: Computer and Information Science Education – *Curriculum.* K.4.2 [**Computers and Society**]: Social Issues – *Assistive Technologies for persons with disabilities.*

General Terms

Measurement, Human Factors, Verification.

Keywords

Web Accessibility Evaluation, Web Accessibility Guidelines, Accessibility Education.

1. INTRODUCTION

The study of accessibility is included in the required body of knowledge for the ACM curricula of Computer Science (CS2008), Information Systems (IS2010) and Information Technology (IT2008) [2]. This reflects the recognition that digital products and services must be inclusive and meet the needs of all users. The need to make the Internet accessible to the widest range of users, including those with disabilities is also recognised in ACM policy [18] and a plethora of laws, guidelines [20], [21] and standards [11]. Yet the incidence of inaccessible websites persists. One of the contributing factors is a lack of knowledge and understanding on the part of designers and developers and insufficient implementation of techniques to support accessibility

[17]. Limited exposure to accessibility during training of I.T. professionals and computing graduates [12] has also been identified as an issue. Computing departments are beginning to address this by integrating accessibility topics throughout the undergraduate curriculum [19], however such examples remain exceptions. Unless accessibility is specifically included in the curriculum, computing students will have limited knowledge and understanding of disability and accessibility issues.

As part of their Undergraduate curriculum, computing students within our Institution design and develop rich internet applications and websites. Our students often carry out authentic projects for 'live' clients. Testing and evaluating their work for accessibility can be a significant issue. Students lack knowledge and understanding of accessibility guidelines, have problems interpreting the results of automated evaluation tools, have limited access to disabled end users, may not have access to expert reviewers and have little time to dedicate to accessibility in the wider context of their assignments.

Projects involving accessibility requirements or working with disabled users have been shown to significantly increase awareness of designing to meet the needs of a diverse population, and students become aware that considering accessibility helps to produce a more usable product for everyone [19]. Undergraduate and postgraduate students increasingly need skills in accessible design to prepare them for work placement projects and employment. They need to understand accessibility beyond the basics, and to apply it in real-world situations, such as developing specific content and solutions for different audiences.

This paper focuses on the evaluation of an educational web accessibility knowledge management tool which aims to support novice evaluators. It is developed specifically for undergraduate computing students and incorporates a structured walkthrough method to guide the novice auditor through the process of an accessibility evaluation. The prototype Accessibility Evaluation Assistant (AEA) [5] has been incorporated into a final year module: Accessibility and Adaptive Technologies. This is a final year elective module for students studying a range of computing degrees, (Computing, Web Development, Creative Digital Media, Web Design).

The primary function of the tool is to guide the novice auditor through the process of an accessibility evaluation, and provide a template for the production of their own evaluation report. Research has identified accessibility evaluation reports as having a positive educational and motivational effect on those who do not have expertise in web accessibility [17]. An evaluation technique should incorporate a set of easily digestible, specific expert recommendations, tailored to the resource being assessed [16]; this is of particular importance when working with novice auditors. The over-riding aim of any accessibility evaluation should be to provide information that is clear, logical and comprehensible [15]. It follows that any tool assisting the process should also be easy to use, self-explanatory and relevant to the context of the site.

Evaluation of the AEA was conducted with 38 final year undergraduate students registered on the Accessible and Adaptive Technologies module. The first element of the module assessment (worth 50% of the total mark) required the students to perform a website accessibility evaluation.

2. BACKGROUND AND RELATED WORK

The Web Content Accessibility Guidelines (WCAG) [20], [21] remain the de facto standard against which the accessibility of websites is measured. Despite their limitations [17], the guidelines provide an accepted point of reference. Conformance review against the WCAG 2.0 Guidelines can be too complex for a novice auditor. The guidelines need to be applied with informed judgement and the results of any tool used to assist the evaluation need to be interpreted correctly.

The W3C consider checkpoints to be reliably testable if 80% of knowledgeable evaluators would agree on the conclusion. Brajnik [9] evaluated 21 checkpoints taken from WCAG 1.0 and 2.0 with 35 inexperienced evaluators and found that neither of the guideline sets have checkpoints whose reliability is definitely higher than the W3C recommended threshold.

A study examining the testability of the 25 highest priority level 'A' success criteria using manual evaluation techniques found that only 8 could be considered reliably human testable when the auditors were novices [4]. These finding are supported by Brajnik [10] whose evaluation of WCAG 2.0 with non-experts showed that they missed 49% of the true accessibility problems. In an evaluation of the Barrier Walkthrough method with experts and non-experts [22], it was concluded that the auditor's level of expertise is an important factor in the quality and accuracy of an accessibility evaluation.

A number of evaluation tools have been developed, although they are all designed to support expert evaluators in the professional domain. Baguma et al. [6] propose a framework for filtering and presenting web accessibility guidelines according to different contexts of use. MAGENTA [13] is a semi-automatic evaluation tool which checks a website against a specified set of guidelines. The evaluator is able to select from a range of pre-defined guideline sets, and can select the individual guidelines within a set. The Accessibility Guidelines Management Framework [3], is a repository of different sets of guidelines including general web accessibility, as well as those for different application types and different end-users. OceanAcc integrates an automated evaluation tool with accessibility metrics [14] to simplify and quicken the evaluation process. User intervention is required to filter false positives and results which are not applicable to the context of the website.

While the AEA shares some of the same concepts with these tools (context of use and filtering recommendations by user group), it is designed specifically to support novice auditors. The AEA aims to remove some of the complexity inherent in web site evaluation. It simplifies the process for those without in-depth knowledge of accessibility guidelines yet remains comprehensive.

3. THE ACCESSIBILITY EVALUATION ASSISTANT

The 48 separate accessibility checks are based on established accessibility principles taken from a range of accessibility guidelines, evaluation methodologies proposed by accessibility practitioners and the authors' expertise through consultancy projects in website evaluation. The AEA is not an automated evaluation tool, but does utilise existing resources where appropriate. The AEA [1] supports three types of evaluation: by Check Categories, by User Group and by Site Features.

3.1 Check Categories

The Check Categories function supports a comprehensive accessibility evaluation incorporating all 48 checks. To make the process more manageable for novices, the checks are broken down into a further five categories:

- *Design Checks*: 11 checks are concerned with aspects of visual presentation, the use of text and colour and the layout and positioning of items. Design Checks are generally conducted by a visual examination of the website.

- *User Checks:* 15 checks that cannot be completed with automated tools. The auditor must interact with the website in order to conduct these checks.

- *Structural Checks*: 11 checks to ascertain that semantic information about the content of a webpage is provided and implemented correctly.

- *Technical Checks:* 5 checks concerned with coding elements such as validating the HTML and CSS mark-up used to produce a webpage.

- *Global Checks:* 6 checks which apply to the entire website. Checks that refer to specific content and functionality can sometimes be verified by examining a single page (usually the home page) and need only be conducted once.

3.2 User Group

The Check by User Group function currently allows the auditor to prioritise checks based on the needs of 10 different disability groups. Accessibility issues may have a greater impact on one user group when compared to another. By enabling the novice auditor to filter and prioritise the accessibility checks - according to the needs of different user groups they become familiar with the common principles of accessible design, identify specific exceptions and learn about the needs of diverse user groups.

3.3 Site Features

In WCAG 2.0, accessibility guidelines for a single element or site feature (e.g. forms) can be spread across two or three different priority levels. This could be confusing for a novice evaluator and makes the evaluation process overly complex. The Site Features function allows the auditor to filter the checks based on specific elements of a website (Forms, Images, Cascading Style Sheets,

Links, Multimedia, Semantic HTML, Tables). This feature was not included in this particular trial.

3.4 The Structured Walkthrough Approach

The AEA provides a step-by-step walkthrough for each check based on the Barrier Walkthrough method [8]. The auditor is given support on the accessibility principle they are checking for; the user group(s) affected; the nature of the barrier or problem and a procedure for checking and verifying the issue. This procedure may be manual, automatic or a combination of both. A step by step guide accompanied by a video demonstration helps the novice to interpret the results; this is a key element of the AEA as an 'expert system'. For each check the user must select one of four options; Met, Not Met, Partly Met or Not Applicable and enter comments to justify the decision.

4. EVALUATION

The AEA was trialled with a group of 38 final year undergraduate students studying a range of computing degrees. The students had limited previous knowledge of web accessibility and none had conducted an accessibility evaluation. The module introduced a range of topics related to accessibility, including types of disability, disability legislation and legal case studies, WCAG Guidelines, assistive technology, inclusive design, standards and evaluation methods and tools. The students were introduced to the AEA before they received the assignment during which they would use the tool.

The students were instructed to carry out an accessibility evaluation of a given website using the Check Categories function of the AEA; assess those features which support accessibility; and identify potential accessibility barriers. Four websites were used for this study, and each student was assigned one from:

- Vancouver 2010 Winter Olympics website: http://www.vancouver2010.com

- CNN: http://www.cnn.com/

- The F.A. Premier League: http://www.premierleague.com/

- WalMart: http://www.walmart.com/

The websites were chosen for their size, complexity and diverse range of content. The students were required to evaluate the home page and two other pages which together must contain multimedia content; multiple photographs, images or graphics; form elements; navigation menu items; and table elements. Each check required a judgement of Met, Not Met, Partly Met or Not Applicable and a short justification for the decision.

The second part of the assignment assessed the students understanding of accessibility in relation to specific user groups. We developed six personas describing the needs and requirements of hypothetical users, from which each student was given two. Each persona was not necessarily related to a single user group. Personas are hypothetical archetypes of actual users defined with significant rigour and precision. They are increasingly used in accessibility research to reflect data obtained from research with real people. The aim is to enable developers, designers, managers and other stakeholders to develop empathy for their end-users, to think from the user's perspective and to put into context the application of guidelines [7].

The students used the AEA User Group function to consider the Critical and Important checks for their personas and produce a short reflective piece identifying the extent to which the website met the needs and requirements of their two personas. An expert auditor also conducted an evaluation of each site and those results were compared with that of the novices. Validity was measured according to the extent to which the novices accurately identified the accessibility barriers [9].

5. RESULTS

For the purpose of this paper, only the home page is considered as this was common to all student evaluations.

5.1 Consensus Analysis

A consensus analysis was carried out to determine the extent of agreement between the novice auditors for each check. The results are summarised in Table 1 below.

Table 1: Novice Consensus Summary

Home Page	Consensus Agreement of Each Check		
	>50%	>60%	>70%
Vancouver Olympics	96% (46/48)	79% (38/48)	60% (29/48)
CNN	83% (40/48)	66% (32/48)	50% (24/48)
F.A. Premier League	71% (34/48)	58% (32/48)	45% (22/48)
WalMart	79% (38/48)	67% (32/48)	56% (27/48)
Combined results of all 4 home pages	82%	68%	53%

These figures do not meet the reliability level of 80% required by the W3C for knowledgeable evaluators. However, in all cases except the Premier League home page, there was more than 70% agreement in a majority of the checks (53% overall). Given that the auditors were accessibility novices and this was their first evaluation, we consider these figures promising.

5.2 Expert Comparison

The second analysis involved a comparison of the decisions made by the novice auditors with that of the expert evaluator. Table 2 shows that 60% of the novice decisions for all homes pages matched that of the auditor. This compares to a figure of 51% of average validity in a similar investigation of the testability of WCAG 2 guidelines by novices in a study reported by Brajnik et al. [10]. This suggests that novices using the AEA tool are able to achieve a higher level of validity, although this requires further investigation.

Table 2: Comparison of Novice Results with Expert Audit

Home Page	Total of Novice Decisions matching Expert Decision (%)	Checks with majority novice/expert agreement
Vancouver Olympics	65%	36/48 checks
CNN	60%	31/48
Premier League	56%	25/48
WalMart	58%	29/48
Combined Results	60%	124/192

Taking the Vancouver site as an example, we analysed the novice agreement with the expert evaluation for each check category to determine which checks were most and least likely to be correctly evaluated by the novices. The results are shown in Table 3 below:

Table 3: Novice agreement with expert by check category

Check category	Novice agreement with expert
Design Checks	59%
User Checks	49%
Structural Checks:	68%
Technical Checks	76%
Global Checks	85%

These results confirm that those checks which can largely be carried out using automated tools returned the most accurate results, while those that require a high degree of judgement by the evaluator (Design and User checks) returned a lower level of agreement with the expert auditor.

6. DISCUSSION OF RESULTS

By examining the students' justification of their decision, we are able to draw some conclusions as to why there were inconsistencies. Some of these explanations are similar to the study conducted by Alonso et al [4] who found that knowledge, effort and comprehension affected their decisions when evaluating against WCAG 2.0 Guidelines. For many individual checks there are more than one criterion, for example, a site map should be provided and the link to it placed in a prominent position on the page. If the website meets one of these requirements, but not the other, then the auditor could reasonably justify a judgement of met, partly met or not met. The expert, however, will highlight specific examples of instances of accessibility barriers, and record a result of 'partly met'.

There were also examples of the evaluator effect, as discussed by Brajnik [9]. Based on experience, the expert auditor might ignore isolated incidents of very minor accessibility problems. For example, a commonly used acronym (e.g. U.S.A.) that was not expanded using HTML elements the expert would regard Met, whereas the novices selected Not Met or Partly Met. This was also evident when examining a rotating Flash Banner on the Vancouver website. This caused many students to judge the Moving Elements check as Not Met, as technically there was a moving element on the page, however the expert judged it as met - the user had control over which part of the banner was displayed.

Some checks were misinterpreted. For example, the Use of Colour check refers to using colour as a sole means of identifying information and a Colour Contrast check features separately. Some students considered these checks as one.

Students used Not Applicable and Met to signify that there was no accessibility barrier, for example, if there were no moving elements on a page, the student would make a decision of Not Applicable while the expert classed as Met. Both judgements and justifications were correct, but this issue requires review.

Some of the AEA examples were taken too literally, e.g. the Supplementary Images check suggested that a flag could be used to signify that the site was available in different languages, and said the check was Not Met if this was not present. In other cases the novice was simply incorrect e.g. a check referring to the accessibility of Flash elements was recorded as Met, because Flash content was present on the page.

Some checks are subjective and open to interpretation e.g. judging when instructional information is required or whether navigation links are big enough. This could be considered a limitation of the tool if clearer guidance could be provided.

6.1 Student Feedback

Although the tool is organised by types of check, some students' indicated they would prefer it if similar checks were grouped together. Although such a grouping exists in the Site Feature function of the tool, this was not evaluated by the students. It may be beneficial to repeat sub-groups of categories within the main Check Categories. The students commented that the evaluation process was well explained, the progression through the checks was clear and the AEA used language they could understand.

"This was the first time I have completed an accessibility evaluation and I found it opened my eyes to a lot of issues that I wouldn't have considered before. I found the whole process simple to follow using the AEA tool and it made it very simple when unsure about how to evaluate a certain point."

They found the video tutorials useful as it showed them examples on live websites. Students found making judgements about some checks such as colour contrast and text alternatives difficult and suggested they needed to conduct more evaluations to gain experience.

"I did not know there were so many considerations when developing a website – the AEA made me realise that there is more than just producing valid code."

There was evidence that the tool increased the students' understanding of the needs of different user groups.

"From evaluating using the personas it really shows that you have to consider a lot of user groups that will expect certain requirements to be met. I thought that the AEA was a great application to use as it guided me through the evaluation process – I will certainly use this method again."

"Carrying out the accessibility evaluation really helped me understand the importance of web accessibility. Before I carried out the evaluation..... I didn't know what checks to carry out."

7. CONCLUSION

This study has highlighted the potential of the AEA as a learning application. Although initial results are presented here, a deeper analysis will explore further those aspects of checking best supported. The AEA is successful as a means to encourage students to articulate and justify their decision, consider the accessibility implications of each check in more detail and assist the tutor in giving feedback about erroneous decisions.

In terms of evaluating the validity of the method, the next stage is to compare the results with audits conducted by expert evaluators. However, this first trial indicates that some of this expertise can be incorporated into the AEA and student feedback suggests that incorporating the tool into the teaching of accessibility will contribute to the preparation of graduates as accessibility professionals.

8. REFERENCES

[1] Accessibility Evaluation Assistant. *Accessibility Research Centre*. http://arc.tees.ac.uk/aea/. Accessed: 27/11/10.

[2] ACM. Current Curricula. Available Online: http://www.acm.org/education/curricula/. Accessed: 14/11/11.

[3] Arrue, M., Vigo, M., Aizpurua, A. and Abascal, J. 2007. Accessibility Guidelines Management Framework. *In C. Stephanidis (Ed.). Universal Access in HCI, Part III, HCI International 2007* (Beijing, China, July 22-27, 2007). LNCS 4556, 3--10, Springer, 2007.

[4] Alonso, F., Fuertes, J.L., Gonzalez, L.A. and Martinez, L. 2010. On the testability of WCAG 2.0 for beginners. In *Proceedings of the 2010 International Cross Disciplinary Conference on Web Accessibility (W4A)* (W4A '10). ACM, New York, NY, USA. DOI= http://doi.acm.org/10.1145/1805986.1806000

[5] Bailey, C., and Pearson, E. 2010. An educational tool to support the accessibility evaluation process. In *Proceedings of the 2010 International Cross Disciplinary Conference on Web Accessibility (W4A)* (W4A '10). ACM, New York, NY, USA. DOI=http://doi.acm.org/10.1145/1805986.1806003

[6] Baguma, R., Stone, R. G., Lugega, J. T., and van der Weide, T. P. 2009. A framework for filtering web accessibility guidelines. In *Proceedings of the 2009 international Cross-Disciplinary Conference on Web Accessibililty (W4a)* (Madrid, Spain, April 20 - 21, 2009). W4A '09. ACM, New York, NY, 46-49. DOI= http://doi.acm.org/10.1145/1535654.1535663

[7] Baguma, R., Stone, G., Lubega, J., and van der Weide, T. 2009. Integrating accessibility and functional requirements. *Lecture Notes in Computer Science*, Springer Berlin / Heidelberg, Vol. 5616. 2009, 635-644.

[8] Brajnik, G. 2008. A comparative test of web accessibility evaluation methods. In *Proceedings of the 10th international ACM SIGACCESS Conference on Computers and Accessibility* (Halifax, Nova Scotia, Canada, October 13 - 15, 2008). Assets '08. ACM, New York, NY, 113-120. DOI= http://doi.acm.org/10.1145/1414471.1414494

[9] Brajnik, G. 2009. Validity and reliability of web accessibility guidelines. In *Proceedings of the 11th international ACM SIGACCESS conference on Computers and accessibility* (Assets '09). ACM, New York, NY, USA, 131-138. DOI=http://doi.acm.org/10.1145/1639642.1639666

[10] Brajnik, G., Yesilada, Y. and Harper, S. 2010. Testability and validity of WCAG 2.0: the expertise effect. In *Proceedings of the 12th international ACM SIGACCESS conference on Computers and accessibility* (ASSETS '10). ACM, New York, NY, USA, 43-50. DOI= http://doi.acm.org/10.1145/1878803.1878813

[11] Dublin Core. Available Online: http://dublincore.org/accessibilitywiki/AccessForAllApplicationProfile. Accessed: 14/1/11.

[12] Law, C., Jacko, J., and Edwards, P. 2005. Programmer-focused website accessibility evaluations. In *Proceedings of the 7th international ACM SIGACCESS Conference on Computers and Accessibility* (Baltimore, MD, USA, October 09 - 12, 2005). Assets '05. ACM, New York, NY, 20-27. DOI= http://doi.acm.org/10.1145/1090785.1090792

[13] Leporini, B., Paternò, F., Scorcia, A. 2006. Flexible tool support for accessibility evaluation, *Interacting with Computers*, v.18 n.5, p.869-890, September, 2006 DOI=10.1016/j.intcom.2006.03.001

[14] Naftali, M. 2010. Analysis and integration of web accessibility metrics. In *Proceedings of the 2010 International Cross Disciplinary Conference on Web Accessibility (W4A)* (W4A '10). ACM, New York, NY, USA. DOI=http://doi.acm.org/10.1145/1805986.1805996

[15] Sloan, D., Gregor, P., Rowan, M,. and Booth, P. 2000. Accessible accessibility. In *Proceedings on the 2000 conference on Universal Usability* (CUU '00). ACM, New York, NY, USA, 96-101. DOI=http://doi.acm.org/10.1145/355460.355480

[16] Sloan, D. 2002. Auditing accessibility of UK Higher Education web sites. *Interacting with computers 14 (2002).* 313-325.

[17] Sloan, D. 2006. The Effectiveness of the Web Accessibility Audit as a Motivational and Educational Tool in Inclusive Web Design. Ph.D. Thesis, University of Dundee, Scotland. June, 2006.

[18] USACM. 2008. Policy Statement in Internet Accessibility. Available Online: http://www.acm.org/public-policy/accessibility. Accessed: 14/11/11.

[19] Waller, A., Hanson, V., and Sloan, D. 2009. Including accessibility within and beyond undergraduate computing courses. In *Proceedings of the 11th international ACM SIGACCESS conference on Computers and accessibility* (ASSETS '09). ACM, New York, NY, USA, 155-162. DOI= http://doi.acm.org/10.1145/1639642.1639670

[20] W3C. 1999. Web Content Accessibility Guidelines Version 1.0. Retrieved January 20th 2010: http://www.w3.org/TR/WCAG10/

[21] W3C. 2008. Web Content Accessibility Guidelines Version 2.0. Retrieved January 20th 2010: http://www.w3.org/TR/WCAG20/

[22] Yesilada, Y. Brajnik, G. and Harper, S. 2009. How much does expertise matter?: a barrier walkthrough study with experts and non-experts. In *Proceedings of the 11th international ACM SIGACCESS conference on Computers and accessibility* (Assets '09). ACM, New York, NY, USA, 203-210. DOI=http://doi.acm.org/10.1145/1639642.1639678

Relationship Between Text and Action Conceptions of Programming:
A Phenomenographic and Quantitative Perspective

Anna Eckerdal
Uppsala University
Department of Information
Technology
Uppsala Sweden
+46 18 4717893
Anna.Eckerdal@
it.uu.se

Mikko-Jussi Laakso
University of Turku
Department of Information
Technology
20014 Turun yliopisto
Finland
+358 2 333 51
milaak@utu.fi

Mike Lopez
Manukau Institute of
Technology
Private Bag 94006
Manukau 2241
New Zealand
+64 9 968 8000
mike.lopez@
manukau.ac.nz

Amitrajit Sarkar
Christchurch Polytechnic
Institute of Technology
PO Box 540
Christchurch 8140
New Zealand
+64 3 940 8495
SarkarA@cpit.ac.nz

ABSTRACT

Phenomenographic research studies have identified different understandings of the concepts *class* and *object* by novice programmers. Aspects of understanding include a focus on artefacts of text, syntax and structure (text), as active agents in a program (action) and as models of an external reality (model). We explore the hypothesis that these aspects of conceptual understanding form a hierarchy in which mastery of the text aspect is a necessary precondition for understanding objects as active agents and the action aspect is a precondition for model understandings. We use empirical data from the final examination of an introductory programming course to test the relationship between the text and action aspects. Our findings do not support the hypothesis of a hierarchy but rather suggest that text and action understandings develop in parallel.

Categories and Subject Descriptors

K.3.2 [**Computers and Education**]: Computers and Information Science Education - *Computer Science Education*

General Terms

Languages, Theory

Keywords

novice programming, phenomenographic outcome space, critical aspects, text and action, hierarchy

1. INTRODUCTION

Learning to program is a challenging task for novice learners. Already in the late 1980s, du Boulay [1] identified five sub fields of programming skills that novices need to handle efficiently: understanding what programming is about and what computers can do, how a program is executed in a computer (i.e. notional machine), knowledge of a programming language, knowledge of programming principles (schemas), knowledge of using tools such as compilers, editors, debuggers etc. Looking at this extensive list,

it is not surprising that many wide scale studies have found that novices are struggling in the early stages of this learning process.

Previous research has studied students' learning of skills [9, 14, 19] as well as concepts [2, 7]. The present research takes its starting point from a phenomenographic study on novice students' understanding of the concepts *object* and *class* [4]. While the BRACElet project [20], of which the present study is a part, hypothesizes a hierarchy of skills, we hypothesize a hierarchy in how students learn aspects of concepts.

Literature in mathematics education research suggests a hierarchy in how students learn concepts [17]. We believe that it is of interest to the Computing Education community to study potential hierarchies in students' learning of programming concepts. The existence or otherwise of such hierarchies may inform curriculum design and approaches to teaching and learning.

Our study sought to test the support for a hypothesized hierarchy against empirical assessment data from the final examination in an introductory programming course. To what extent would this data support or disconfirm the hypothesized hierarchy?

The remainder of this paper is organized as follows. Section 1.1 describes the BRACElet project. Section 2 presents background and related work for this study. The setup of the study is presented is section 3 and the results are presented in Section 4. Finally, discussion and conclusions are drawn in section 5.

1.1 BRACElet

BRACElet is a multi-institutional multi-national project in Computer Science Education [20]. It began as an investigation into the reading and comprehension skills of novice programmers and was motivated by the fact that worldwide failure rates in introductory programming subjects are among the worst in universities. The difficulties that lead to failure appear to begin from the very first day of a student's introductory programming course. First year programming is the start of a rollercoaster journey for most students and while novices in every discipline make a similar journey, we continue to wonder why the journey is so much more fraught with danger for programming students.

A 2001 ITiCSE working group assessed the programming ability of an international student population from several universities [14]. Students were tested on a common set of program-writing problems and the majority of students performed more poorly than expected. It was not clear why the students struggled to write the required programs. In 2004, another ITiCSE working group (the "Leeds group") attempted to investigate some of the reasons why students find programming difficult [9]. The working group set out to benchmark the program-reading skills of novice programmers. They found that many students could not answer program reading problems, "suggesting that such students have a fragile grasp of skills that are a pre-requisite for problem-solving".

The BRACElet project aimed to extend the work of the Leeds group. The intention was to add to the existing Leeds toolkit new research instruments that would assess program comprehension (reading) and writing skills, enabling comparisons to be made between them.

The purpose of the final workshop was to extend the work on theory initiated at the Paris ITiCSE Working group in 2009 [10] and to launch an ongoing programme of research through the Software Engineering Research Laboratory at Auckland University of Technology into the novice to expert programmer continuum. This scope of this project (titled "NExpertise") would extend from "programming in the small" to "programming in the large" and the work of professional programmers. Thus the project has the goal of contributing to broader and deeper understandings and impacting practice for both educators and software practitioners. The workshop brought together twelve academics from New Zealand, Australia, Finland and Sweden, who are interested to build theory on how learners acquire programming knowledge. Potential research questions arising from previous BRACElet work were discussed in depth. Subsequently the workshop participants formed into groups that focused on three questions. Our group focused on this particular question.

> Is there a hierarchical relationship between the TEXT, ACTION and MODEL aspects of the concepts object and class in novice students' learning?

The work of our group led to the current study which is described in section 3 in detail.

2. BACKGROUND

2.1 Related Work

There is a vast literature on novice students' learning to program. The starting point of the present research was critical aspects related to different understandings of concepts in object-oriented programming, and we will thus focus on similar literature. These critical aspects were identified in a phenomenographic study [11].

Phenomenography is a research approach that aims at describing the qualitatively different understandings of some phenomenon expressed by a group of people. The data are often, as in the present case, semi-structured, individual interviews which are transcribed and analyzed in an iterative way. The result is an outcome space with categories that describe the different understandings identified in the analysis, excerpts from the interviews to illustrate these understandings, and a discussion that explains the categories and the relation between them.

Examples of phenomenographic studies from computing education that discuss students' understanding of concepts are: Berglund [3] who discussed senior students' understanding of concepts within computer systems; Boustedt [2] who studied senior students' understanding of some advanced object-oriented concepts; and Sorva [18] who discussed introductory programming students' understandings of variables.

An example of other research on conceptual understanding is Sanders et al. [16] who used concept maps to investigate what novice students see as the most important concepts and their relationships in object-oriented programming. One result from the investigation was that "few students see modelling as one of the most important OO concepts", which is in line with Eckerdal and Thuné's [4] finding where the MODEL aspect related to the most advanced way to understand the concepts.

It can be argued that some misconceptions reflect critical aspects of understandings. Sorva [18] discusses misconceptions in relation to a phenomenographic outcome space. There is an extensive body of research that focuses on misconceptions in computing education. Examples of this are Holland et al. [8] who identified several misconceptions beginners have on objects, and Fleury [7] who found that students construct their own understanding of concepts, which is not always correct. Ragonis and Ben-Ari [15] performed a longitudinal study on high-school students' learning of object-oriented concepts. The results are presented as categories that reflect important findings in the data, for example object vs. class with subcategories like object creation, and the connection between objects and classes. Each subcategory is further described in terms of difficulties and misconceptions identified, e.g. difficulties in understanding the static aspect of a class definition. This seems to be close to the TEXT aspect discussed in the present study, see Section 2.2. Another category is Program Flow with subcategories like Understanding execution of methods and Understanding data flow. Student questions that relate to this category are e.g. "What actions are carried out?" when a program is executed, and "What triggers the action?" (p. 214). This category seems to be close to the critical aspect ACTION.

2.2 Phenomenographic Outcome Space

Eckerdal and Thuné [4] performed a phenomenographic study [11] on the understandings of the concepts *object* and *class by* novice programming students who had just finished their first programming course in Java. Their analysis showed three qualitatively different categories of understandings. The analysis further revealed the different foci of the understandings identified. Since both concepts are closely related, a summary of the analysis can be presented in one outcome space [5, 6]. Table 1 below shows a summary of parts of the outcome spaces that are presented in [5].

Eckerdal [6] further discusses the critical aspects [12] that relate to each of the categories of understanding in the outcome space. A critical aspect is an aspect of the concept that is critical from an educational point of view. If a student does not discern and understand this aspect of a phenomenon, an important part of the learning goal is missing, and the student might have problems with his or her further learning. The critical aspects are related to the focus of each category of understanding. In the first category, the aspect in focus is the textual representation of the concepts and the corresponding critical aspect is labelled TEXT. In the second category, an additional aspect is the active behaviour of the program when it is executed and the corresponding critical aspect is labelled ACTION. The new aspect in the third category is the modelling aspects of the concepts, which is labelled MODEL.

Table 1: The phenomenographic outcome space.

Different understandings of the concepts *object* and *class*	The focus of each understanding
1. Object is experienced as a piece of program text. Class is experienced as an entity of the program that structures the code and describes the object.	Focus on the program text and the syntax rules of the programming language. Focus on the structure of the program.
2. As above and in addition class is experienced as a description of properties and behaviour of objects, and objects as something that is active when the program is executed.	As above and in addition focus on the objects that the program creates and events happening at execution of the program.
3. As above and in addition object is a model of some real world phenomenon.	As above and in addition focus on the reality the class depicts.

The categories that emerged from Eckerdal and Thuné's study [5] were inclusive; the latter categories include the understandings in the former. It is not clear whether this reflects the way that the learning and teaching unfolded for their students or whether there is a universal hierarchy or order of how students learn.

3. THE STUDY

Our study attempted to find empirical evidence to support or disconfirm the hypothesis of a hierarchy. We were not able to explore the MODEL aspect from the data available so we decided to focus on the relation between the TEXT and ACTION aspects.

We carried out a quantitative post-analysis study in which we analyzed data from the final examination of an introductory programming course. The course was a typical introductory course with an object-first approach including topics like objects, classes, variables, conditional statements, repetition, arrays, methods, etc. There were 13 weeks in the course's curriculum with two hours of lectures and two hours of tutorials each week. The final examination comprised 9 questions.

The participants were first year university students and most of the students were studying computing or mathematical sciences. We analyzed the examination scripts from the 108 students who gave consent for the research.

3.1 Text and Action

The TEXT aspect was mapped to two questions in the examination. The first question presented the student with sample code which had various program parts and key words highlighted and annotated with identifying letters. The student was asked to match these letters to a given list of terms. This required the student to discern main parts of a program, read code and recognize key words. The second question presented the student with sample code and a set of errors produced by the compiler. The student was asked to correct the errors. Both of these questions relate to a focus on the program text, syntax rules and structure of the program.

The ACTION aspect was mapped to one question in the exam. This asked the student to identify the state of a variable after a specified sequence of method calls. The method calls involved assignment, addition, subtraction and a single if statement. The student was required to read code and understand what will happen when the instructions are executed. The focus was on the program execution at run time.

4. RESULTS

A non-parametric approach to analysis was taken. Threshold marks were set at 4 for the ACTION aspect question and 10 for the sum of marks of two TEXT aspect questions. Marks of these thresholds or higher were considered to represent "can do" of the appropriate aspects.

Setting appropriate thresholds is not essential for the logic of the analysis but helps with the interpretation of any findings. From this perspective, the choice of threshold for the ACTION aspect is reasonably straightforward. The threshold was set at full marks (4). With this threshold, 54 of the 108 students (50%) were classified as "can do".

The choice of threshold for TEXT is more problematic. If this is set at 11 (full marks), then only 27 students would be classified as "can do" and the proposition that TEXT is a prerequisite for ACTION can be immediately rejected.

Accordingly, the threshold was set at 10 for the discussion below. However, for completeness, the analysis was carried out for each plausible threshold level and this is discussed subsequently. Based on these thresholds of 4 and 10, the contingency table shown in Table 2 was prepared.

Table 2: Observed classification of students

Observed counts	Text=0	Text=1	Total
Action=1	19	35	54
Action=0	31	23	54
Total	50	58	108

Under an assumption of independence, neither aspect should give information about the other; thus the same odds ratios should apply to each row and each column. This leads to the expected values shown in Table 3.

Table 3: Expected classification if independent

Expected counts	Text=0	Text=1	Total
Action=1	25	29	54
Action=0	25	29	54
Total	50	58	108

A chi-squared test of independence gives a χ^2 value of 5.36. Thus it is unlikely (p=0.0206) that this is just a result of expected sample variation and it can be concluded that ACTION and TEXT are positively correlated (φ=0.223).

There are three main possible explanations for this correlation: a) TEXT might be a prerequisite of ACTION; b) ACTION might be a prerequisite of TEXT or c) some other underlying factor might contribute to both TEXT and ACTION. In case a, we would expect the count in the cell text=0, action=1 to be close to zero. In case b, we would expect the count in the cell text=1, action=0 to be close to zero. In case c, we would expect the ratio between these two cells to be close to 25:29.

To test this objectively, a binomial test was carried out to establish the likelihood of observing the data under assumption c. This gave a significance of 0.5084. The standard error of the binomial for the observed data is 3.23. For case a, the observed count of 19 differs from the expected zero by 5.89 standard errors (p<.0001). For case b, the observed count of 23 differs from zero by 7.13 standard errors (p<.0001).

Thus we can conclude that the data are consistent with case c but neither case a, nor case b is likely. To explore the sensitivity of these results to the threshold value chosen for the TEXT aspect, the analysis was repeated for each plausible threshold value. Threshold values of 8 or less were not considered plausible because 90% or more of students would be classified as "can do" and there would be insufficient variability for any valid statistical conclusions to be drawn. The results are presented in Table 4.

Table 4: Sensitivity to thresholds

Threshold	Pr (case = a)	Pr (case = b)	Pr (case = c)	"Can do"
11	<0.0001	0.0018	0.9170	25%
10	<0.0001	<0.0001	0.5084	54%
9	0.0021	<0.0001	0.2814	81%

For each of these thresholds, the same conclusions can be drawn. It is unlikely that TEXT is a prerequisite of ACTION; it is unlikely that ACTION is a prerequisite of TEXT; it is likely that both TEXT and ACTION depend on some underlying factor. This in turn suggests that awareness of both TEXT and ACTION aspects develops independently as students pursue their learning journey.

In summary, intuitively it seems plausible that mastery of the TEXT aspect of a program might be a necessary pre-requisite to understanding of the ACTION aspect. Our findings tend to disconfirm this proposition. Although we have studied the examination performance of students in only one course at one university, this leads us to believe that such a pre-requisite relationship, if it exists at all, is neither universal nor necessary.

5. DISCUSSION

Eckerdal [6] also discusses critical aspects that relate to different programming skills. The analysis showed that the three aspects TEXT, ACTION, and MODEL relate to activities students do in the lab when they read, write, and debug and test code. Since the present research discusses the TEXT and ACTION aspects, we discuss activities related to them. In Table 5 below are some examples of activities that represent the focus of these skills.

When performing activities shown in the TEXT column, students need only focus on the textual representation of the code. When performing those in the TEXT and ACTION column, students need to focus not only on the textual representation of the code, but also on the ACTION aspect and on how the two relate.

The activities are at different levels of proficiency. To read, write, or debug and test code thus require different levels of proficiency depending on which activity is performed. To be able to discern the meaning embedded in an activity, the students need to discern the critical aspects that are related to the activity. The critical aspects that are discussed in the present research are interesting

since they relate to both activities and concept. These aspects can act as bridges between learning theory and learning practice. If a student discerns an aspect, this can help the student to understand both related theory and the meaning of related activities.

Table 5: Activities and related foci by skill

Skill	TEXT	TEXT and ACTION
Read	Reading code and recognizing key words	Reading code and understanding what will happen when it is executed
Write	Using an editor to emphasis the structure of a program by means of indents, empty lines etc.	Designing a short algorithm.
Test and debug	Using a compiler to find and correct minor syntax errors like adding and removing curly brackets without necessarily understanding the semantics.	Debugging code by hand execution or "tracing"

In this way the findings from the present study are closely related to the BRACElet project and to some extent can explain some of the previous findings. The critical aspects discussed in the present research relate to all the skills discussed in the BRACElet project. When a critical aspect is discerned this can thus open the door to a deeper understanding and learning of any or all of the skills to read, write, or debug and test code. Our results suggest there is no hierarchy between the aspects we have studied. The presented findings show that students can learn aspects of concepts and activities in different and individual order. Our results thus tell against a hierarchy of aspects of concepts *and* skills. This is in line with the previous findings within the BRACElet project. Lister et al. [10] discuss Sfard's work [17]:

> While we acknowledge the notion of conceptual hierarchies as proposed in the mathematics education literature, the true extent to which they apply to computing education remains open to question. (p. 6)

The present findings verify this previous discussion. This does not imply that there are no hierarchies of concepts in computer science, but rather that this is not as prominent as Sfard proposes in mathematics education.

The present research shows that both TEXT and ACTION aspects may develop independently in students' learning. The results thus offer some empirical evidence in the discussion on how to teach programming to novices, supporting the idea of different and individual learning trajectories.

The existence of hierarchies or prerequisites would suggest that learning always progresses in a linear manner, leading to a notion of a single best way to sequence the work. Absence of such relationships suggests that there may be more than one effective way to approach the sequencing of learning and teaching.

What is important, however, is that educators offer a learning environment that helps students discern critical aspects of concepts as well as of activities in the lab. Marton and Tsui discuss how combining variation and invariance in systematic ways can help students to discern such aspects [12]. A future study could be to video record students in the laboratory in order to catch moments when a misconception is discovered by a student, or the "aha" moments when a critical aspect is discerned. Such a study could provide evidence of critical aspects, and insights in the complex process of learning to program.

6. ACKNOWLEDGMENTS

The authors would like to thank Auckland University of Technology (AUT) for making a meeting place and resources available and Umeå University for providing an electronic meeting place. We would especially like to thank the students at AUT for giving us permission to study their examination scripts.

7. REFERENCES

[1] du Boulay, D. Some difficulties of learning to program. In E. Soloway and J. Spohrer, editors, *Studying the Novice Programmer*, pages 283–299. Lawrence Erlbaum, 1989

[2] Boustedt, J. (2010) *On the Road to a Software Profession: Students' Experiences of Concepts and Thresholds.* Digital Comprehensive Summaries of Uppsala Dissertations from the Faculty of Science and Technology, ISSN 1651-6214; 734

[3] Berglund, A. (2005) *Learning computer systems in a distributed project course. The what, why, how and where.* Number 62 in Uppsala Dissertations from the Faculty of Science and Technology. Acta Universitatis Upsaliensis, Uppsala Sweden.

[4] Eckerdal, A., and Thuné, M. (2005) Novice java programmers conceptions of "object" and "class" and variation theory. *SIGCSE Bull.* 37, 3:89-93.

[5] Eckerdal, A. (2006) *Novice Students' Learning of Object-Oriented Programming.* Licentiate thesis, Uppsala University, Uppsala Sweden.

[6] Eckerdal, A. (2009) *Novice Programming Students' Learning of Concepts and Practise.* Digital Comprehensive Summaries of Uppsala Dissertations from the Faculty of Science and Technology 600. ISBN 978-91-554-7406-5.

[7] Fleury, A. 2000. (2000) Programming in Java: student-constructed rules. *SIGCSE Bull.* 32, 1:197-201.

[8] Holland, S., Griffiths, R., and Woodman, M. (1997). Avoiding object misconceptions. In *Proceedings of the twenty-eighth SIGCSE technical symposium on Computer science education*, pages 131–134.

[9] Lister, R., Adams, E. S., Fitzgerald, S., Fone, W., Hamer, J., Lindholm, M., McCartney, R., Moström, J. E., Sanders, K., Seppälä, O., Simon, B., and Thomas, L. (2004). A multi-national study of reading and tracing skills in novice programmers. *SIGCSE Bull.* 36(4):119–150.

[10] Lister, R., Clear, T., Simon, Bouvier, D. J., Carter, P., Eckerdal, A., Jackova', J., Lopez, M., McCartney, R., Robbins, P., Seppälä, O. and Thompson, E. (2009) Naturally occurring data as research instrument: analyzing examination responses to study the novice programmer. *SIGCSE Bull.* 41(4).

[11] Marton, F. and Booth, S. (1997) *Learning and Awareness.* Lawrence Erlbaum Ass., Mahwah, NJ.

[12] Marton, F. and Tsui, A. (2004) *Classroom Discourse and the Space of Learning.* Lawrence Erlbaum Ass., Mahwah, NJ.

[13] Mead, J., Gray, S., Hamer, J., James, R., Sorva, J., St. Clair, C. and Thomas, L. (2006). A cognitive approach to identifying measurable milestones for programming skill acquisition. *SIGCSE Bull.* 38, 4, 182-194.

[14] McCracken, M., Almstrum, V., Diaz, D., Guzdial, M., Hagan, D., Ben-David Kolikant, Y., Laxer, C., Thomas, L., Utting, I., and Wilusz, T. (2001). A multinational, multi-institutional study of assessment of programming skills of first-year cs students. *SIGCSE Bull.* 33(4):125–180.

[15] Ragonis, N. and Ben-Ari, M. (2005). A long-term investigation of the comprehension of OOP concepts. *Computer Science Education*, 15(3):203–221.

[16] Sanders, K., Boustedt, J., Eckerdal, A., McCartney, R., Moström, J., Thomas, L., Zander, C. (2008). Student Understanding of Object-Oriented Programming as Expressed in Concept Maps. In *Proceedings of the SIGCSE 2008 Technical Symposium on Computer Science Education*.

[17] Sfard, A. (1991). On the dual nature of mathematical conceptions: Reflections on processes and objects as different sides of the same coin. *Educational Studies in Mathematics.* 22: 1-36.

[18] Sorva, J. (2008). The same but different students' understandings of primitive and object variables. In *Proceedings of the 8th International Conference on Computing Education Research* (Koli '08). ACM, New York, NY, USA, 5-15.

[19] Tenenberg, J., Fincher, S., Blaha, K., Bouvier, D., Chen, T.-Y., Chinn, D., Cooper, S., Eckerdal, A., John-son, H., McCartney, R. and Monge, A. (2005). Students designing software: a multi-national, multi-institutional study. *Informatics in Education*, 4(1), 143-162.

[20] Whalley, J., Clear, T. & Lister, R. (2007). The Many Ways of the BRACElet Project. *Bulletin of Applied Computing and Information Technology* Vol. 5, Issue 1.

Automated Checks on UML Diagrams

Michael Striewe
Paluno – The Ruhr Insitute for Software
Technology
University of Duisburg-Essen
Essen, Germany
michael.striewe@paluno.uni-due.de

Michael Goedicke
Paluno – The Ruhr Insitute for Software
Technology
University of Duisburg-Essen
Essen, Germany
michael.goedicke@paluno.uni-due.de

ABSTRACT

Automated checks for software artefacts like UML diagrams used in automated assessment or tutoring systems do often rely on direct comparisons between a solution and a sample solution. This approach has drawbacks regarding flexibility in face of different possible solutions which are quite common in modeling tasks. This paper presents an alternative technique for checking UML class diagrams based on graph queries which promises to be more flexible.

Categories and Subject Descriptors

D.2.1 [**Software Engineering**]: Requirements/Specifications—*Languages*; K.3.1 [**Computers and Education**]: Computer Uses in Education—*Computer-assisted instruction (CAI)*

General Terms

Verification

Keywords

Intelligent Tutoring Systems, Automated Tutoring, Diagram Analysis

1. INTRODUCTION

It is not unusual to use automated tutoring systems in computer science courses. The earliest systems concerned with programming exercises date back to the 1960s. Since then, software engineering has become more and more complex and modeling languages are of the same value as programming languages nowadays. Modeling languages like UML are often already taught in introductory courses in computer science, possibly with hundreds of participants. In this scenario, manual inspection of exercise solutions consumes much time for the teachers. Thus it is appealing to offer automated tutoring or assessment not only for programming exercises, but also for modeling exercises. There

exist some systems concerned with this task since the 2000s (e.g. [9, 8, 3]), but in comparison to automated systems for programming they are far less common. These systems use comparisons between a sample solution and the solution submitted by students to generate feedback. Three problems can be noticed with this approach: First, generation of sample solutions may be too expensive, if there are many different ways to solve the given exercise. Second, checks based on this technique will never be able to accept an alternative solution that is correct, but does not match any of the given sample solutions completely. Third, for a solution that is half the way the same as one sample solution and half the way the same as an alternative sample solution, it will be hard to generate feedback that does not contradict one of the sample solutions.

The first two problems are especially hard, since modeling exercises tend to be less restricted than programming exercises and thus allow more than just one possible solution. The problem of several equally valid sample solutions with slightly differing, mutually exclusive, features is known for some years [2], but still not solved. In addition, checking diagrams is not just a matter of right and wrong, but also a matter of quality of the solution. In pure comparisons with sample solutions it is not directly visible whether using a different element is just lower quality but still right, or really wrong.

This paper discusses an alternative approach, which does not use complete sample solutions, but rule-based checks instead. In this approach, each rule represents a desirable or undesirable feature of a correct solution and triggers feedback when this feature is not found or found, respectively. This approach tries to automated the process of grading diagrams in a straightforward manner. It assumes that human tutors would check a solution by asking themselfes questions like "Does the solution contain an element representing X?" or "Is there a directed association between the elements representing X and Y, where Y has cardinality 1..*?". Depending on the answers to these questions they mark elements in the diagram as right or wrong or give a sketch of missing elements.

The expected benefit of this approach is to get a much finer granularity in feedback by decomposing the expected solution into a set of rules. Rules are designed in a way that allows for boolean connectors between them, allowing representation of a large space of possible solutions by a small set of different rules in different combinations. Moreover, each rule can produce individual feedback, i.e. providing information whether this rule is about correctness or quality

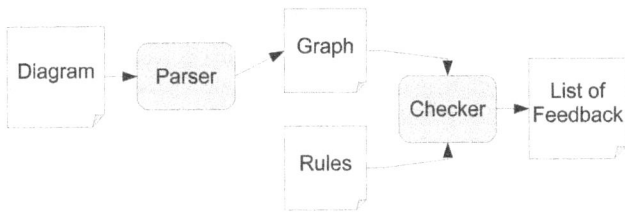

Figure 1: Overview about the diagram checking process.

of the solution. If overall grades are to be given, each rule can get individual scores, reducing the impact of rules concerned with quality in comparison to those concerned with correctness.

The remainder of this paper is organized as follows: Section 2 explains the technical details on how rule-based checks for UML class diagrams can be implemented using a graph query language. Section 3 provides an example from a bachelor-degree course on UML modeling, in which exercise solutions created by students were checked automatically. The impact of the approach is evaluated by this example. Section 4 describes related work and section 5 wraps up the paper with conclusions and future work.

2. ENABLING GRAPH QUERIES ON DIAGRAMS

The basis of the approach discussed in this paper is to consider UML class diagrams as graphs and to formalize the questions sketched in the introduction by using a formal graph query language. More precisely, it is not the UML class diagrams that are queried directly, but the graphs that represent their abstract syntax. Thus the approach consists of two steps: First, the solution submitted by a student has to be parsed to a suitable data format for abstract syntax graphs. Second, graph queries have to be applied to this representation. Each result of a query may produce feedback messages, which are collected in a result file. The overall process and its artefacts is illustrated in figure 1.

2.1 From UML Diagrams to their Abstract Syntax Graphs

Almost every diagramming tool uses its own proprietary data format for saving diagrams. To allow for model exchange between different tools, the XMI standard based on XML files has been developed. The current version is XMI 2.1.1 [5]. Many diagramming tools allow exporting projects in this format, so that it is considered sufficient to base work on a diagram checking tool on this format. However, both the ease of use of XMI exports and the accuracy of adherence to the XMI specification varies from tool to tool. Moreover, some tool do not offer XMI 2.1 export, but other versions of the standard. These limitations and possible resulting problems have to be taken into account when bringing an automated tutoring system for diagrams to productive use. Possible consequences on course design are discussed in section 3.4.

Despite these format issues, handling diagrams is easy. Models in XMI format can be parsed by a XML parser to a data structure that can be represented as a graph. The XMI schema for UML is already a direct representation of the

diagram's abstract syntax, thus in the resulting graph each relevant diagram element is represented as a node. Nodes have types and attributes, while arcs connecting these node just have types. For fast handling of graphs of this kind, the library JGraLab [1] is used with Java as programming language.

2.2 Using a Graph Query Engine

Besides efficient handling of graphs, JGraLab also offers a query language named GReQL for creating reports on graphs [1]. This language is somewhat similar to SQL and well suited to implement rule-based checks. Queries in this language allow searching for elements of certain type that are connected in a certain way and own certain attributes. This allows for basic graph queries of the following types:

- Existence of diagram elements based on their type (in UML class diagrams i.e. classes, interfaces, properties, operations, parameters, associations, and generalizations).

- Existence of diagram elements based on the value of their attributes, e.g. their names or cardinalities.

- Existence of tuples of elements based on the connections between them, e.g. a class having an operation that takes another class as parameter type.

Executing queries of this types via the graph query engine returns either a list of found elements matching the specified condition or an empty list.

2.3 Designing Checking Rules

To get rules usable for checking diagrams in automated tutoring systems, queries have to be enriched with additional information. First, it has to be defined by the author of the rules whether the query specifies a desired or undesired element or element tuple, respectively. Depending on this definition, the result of the query is interpret differently: In case the query specifies desired elements, an error has to be reported if the result list is empty. Contrary, in case the query specifies undesired elements an error has to be reported if the result list is not empty. Consequently, there is a difference in the meaning of "matching query" and "matching rule" in the remainder of this paper: A "matching query" is a graph query in GReQL that reports at least one element. A "matching rule" is a checking rule in which either a desired element is found or an undesired element is not found.

Second, it may be necessary to combine different graph queries by logical operators to allow for alternatives. In the simplest case two or more different spellings of an element name may be allowed. Then a rule should report all elements using any of these spellings. This can be achieved trivially by combining several query expressions, each for one spelling, by using the logical OR.

Finally, scores and feedback messages have to be assigned to each rule. Scores can be handled differently in optimistic and pessimistic approaches: In an optimistic approach, each solution gets full credit initially and any checking rule that does not match reduces this credit by the given score. In a pessimistic approach, a solution gets 0 credit initially and every matching rule increases this credit by the given score. Independent of these two models, textual feedback messages are displayed for any checking rule that does not match.

[1] http://userpages.uni-koblenz.de/~ist/JGraLab

3. EXAMPLE

The technique discussed in the previous section has been used in a bachelor-degree course on UML modeling in winter term 2010/2011 at the University of Duisburg-Essen. It was no introductory course, so mass validation of solutions was not truely required in this particular course. Consequently, this example focusses on functional and practical issues and handles time effectiveness as a minor aspect. Using the same system with larger cohorts of students remains future work.

Two exercises concerned with UML class diagrams were given to the students who had to solve it in teams of two. The student teams were asked to submit their solutions as XMI files in XMI 2 format. These files were feed into a software component for automated checks manually by the authors of this paper. The software component is implemented as an extension of the automated tutoring system JACK [6] and can thus be accessed by students via the web for productive use.

Figure 2 shows one of the solutions for the first exercise submitted by one of six student teams. The task (which was originally given in German and has been translated for this paper) was to model customers that get invoices for using telecommunication services. Each invoice is composed of several parts, possibly from different phone companies. Each part consists of several items, each related to a tariff that was offered by a phone company and used by the customer. A correct solution does not only involve to create a sufficient number of classes with reasonable naming, but also to use cardinalities, names, and directions for associations. The exercise description also contained some attribute names, so their correct usage had to be checked, too.

A total set of 17 rules has been written initially to describe the teacher's requirements for a correct solution. The checking process was based on a pessimistic approach, starting with 0 credit for an unchecked solution and giving credit for each matching rule. The set of rules can be subdivided into two subsets: One contains rules specific for this task, e.g. using element names taken from the task description. Another subset contains generic rules, that are concerned with general features of correct UML class diagrams, e.g. directions for named associations. Both subsets are explained by examples in the following subsections.

3.1 Task Specific Rules

The set of task specific rules contains 12 rules. Seven of these rules are concerned with attributes and simple relations between elements as shown in listing 1 by example: This graph query checks for classes named "Tariff", having an attribute called "Name" or "Identifier" (which was considered to be an acceptable synonym for "Name"), ignoring the case of the first letter for the attribute. Having this class with the respective attribute is a desired feature of a correct solution, so credit is given if this query matches.

```
from x : V{Class}, y : V{Property}
with x --> y and x.name="Tariff" and
    (capitalizeFirst(y.name)="Name" or
     capitalizeFirst(y.name)="Identifier")
report x.name, y.name end
```

Listing 1: Graph query for checking a class and its attribute

The task description given to the students contained not only necessary information, but also some narrative context, i.e. introducing a phone company named "Pink Panther". Students were expected to be able to identify this name as an instance name and to not include a class with this name in their diagrams. The graph query used to check this is shown in listing 2. The corresponding rule defines to give credit if and only if this query does not match. Hence only solutions having no element named "Pink Panther" got the credit defined for this rule.

```
from x : V{Class}
with x.name="PinkPanther" or x.name="Pink Panther"
    or x.name="Pink_Panther"
report x.name end
```

Listing 2: Graph query for checking for an element with a given name. This element is not desired in correct solutions, so an error is reported if this query matches

Note that several possible spellings are used in the query. Elements with completely different spellings will not be detected by the query. This may cause the rule to match, although a student tried to model "Pink Panther" in some way. At least this is no specific problem in checking UML diagrams, but a common issue in any string-based pattern matching problem. However, this problem can be solved to some extend with JGraLab. The library allows to extend the query language by user defined functions. The function "capitalizeFirst" used in listing 1 is a predefined function, that changes the first letter of a string to upper case. In the same manner additional functions can be defined, e.g. for comparing strings while ignoring whitespaces. This shortens the query given in listing 2 and makes writing rules easier.

The remaining five task specific checking rules are concerned with more complex relations involving at least three elements as shown in listing 3 by example: This graph query checks for two classes x and y named "Customer" and "Invoice", respectively. These classes are expected to be connected by an association. Note that this query does not care about the direction of the association, because correct solutions can be designed for both directions. As above, having an association between these elements in general is a desired feature of a correct solution and thus credit is given if this query matches.

```
from x,y : V{Class}
with x <-- V{Property} <-- V{Association} --> V{Property} --> y
    and x.name="Customer" and y.name="Invoice"
report x.name, y.name end
```

Listing 3: Graph query for checking two classes and their association

3.2 Generic Checking Rules

The set of generic checking rules, which are not specific to the given task, contains five rules. Four of them check for missing names, roles, cardinalities, or directions of associations. The fifth one (see listing 4) checks if the diagram contains attribute names staring with a lower case letter and others starting with an upper case letter. This is a stylistic feature, hence it does not check the correctness of the

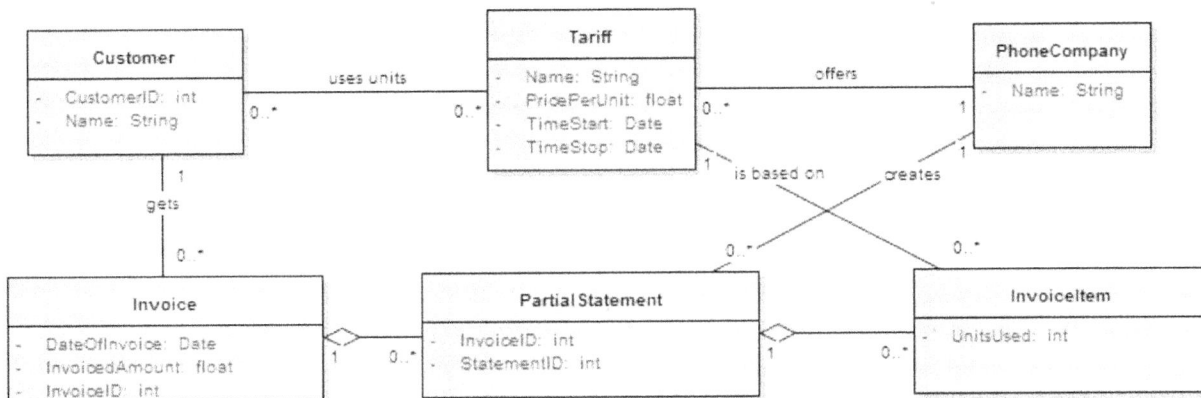

Figure 2: Solution submitted by a student team for the exercise discussed in section 3.

solution, but the quality. Credit is only given if either all attributes start with lower case letters or all attributes start with upper case letters.

```
from x,y : V{Property}
with not isNull(x.name) and not isNull(y.name) and x.name=
    capitalizeFirst(x.name) and not (y.name=capitalizeFirst(y
    .name))
report x.name, y.name end
```

Listing 4: Graph query for checking upper and lower case letters in attribute names

3.3 Results and Evaluation

As mentioned at the beginning of this section, six student teams submitted solutions for the given task. All six solutions could be checked with the rule set described above. The best solution was graded with 91 out of 100 points, the worst solution with 67 out of 100. This was within the same range as the marks given by an additional human teacher, who graded the solutions without knowing the rule set used for automatic grading. The solution shown in figure 2 is the one that got the best grade. Only three generic rules did not match for this solution, because there are missing roles, names, and directions at some associations in this diagram.

Despite these good results it turned out that the rule set did not cover all aspects that could be taken into account during grading. This is not a technical problem but a problem in writing the rule set without knowing the submitted solutions. A human teacher can easily react to unexpected features in the solutions, but fully automated checks with a fixed rule set cannot do this. Thus it is necessary to adjust the rule set if it turns out to be inappropriate and to rerun the checks for the solutions checked so far.

This drawback does not limit the technical soundness of the approach, but limits the time efficiency for small sets of solutions. However, two factors can be identified that decrease the time needed for defining checks: First, a large and field-tested set of generic rules can be reused and will provide substantional feedback without time investments for each new exercise. Second, in the same way an experienced teacher gets faster in grading solutions manually, he or she will also get faster in writing rules. Moreover, writing rules is a way of externalizing and codifying teachers knowledge

on typical flaws, which will grow with every unexpected solution a teacher sees. In contrast to a teacher's personal knowledge, rules can easily be shared alongside tasks and exercises, when they are stored in repositories or used in textbooks.

3.4 Additional Observations

As expected it turned out to be a major obstacle for the students to provide their solutions in the necessary data format. Although there was an appropriate version of an UML tool available in the computer pools used by the course, only one of six student teams managed to provide correct data. All others provided their solution in XMI 1 instead of XMI 2. These were opened manually in an appropiate UML tool by the authors of this paper and reexported as XMI 2. During this process, it could be noticed that some of the solutions contained obviously useless extra folders, packages or classes with default names (like NewClass1, NewClass2 and so on), which may stem from a lack of experience or confidence in handling the tool used by the students.

This raises the question how much tool handling has to be taught in courses on modeling languages. On the one hand, correctness of a model does not depend on the tool used for drawing, even if this tool is pen and paper and not a technical aid at all. On the other hand, modeling is more than drawing, but using formal languages which are intended to be readable both for humans and machines in most cases. Consequently, the problem of wrong data formats has to be tackled from both ends: On the one hand, students must be taught that using diagramming tools is more than drawing on a sketchpad. On the other hand, tools must be able to gently handle typical, tool specific data format issues and problems in model organization.

4. RELATED WORK

Using graph queries is not the only possible way to check UML diagrams. As already mentioned in the introduction, diagram checking by comparison of sample solutions and student diagrams has been developed since the early 2000s [9, 8] for single diagram types. It has been extended to UML diagrams by the system DUESIE which compares diagrams to a minimal sample solution to determine conformance, missing parts and superflous parts [3]. The drawbacks of this approaches have already been discussed in the introduction.

The work from [8] has recently been extended with focus on reading imprecise diagrams from raster images [7]. Although the concept of "minimal meaningful units" (MMUs) used in that work is somewhat similar to defining small queries, there is a major difference: MMUs are used to read diagrams and identify elements by finding a best match for them. Grades are given based on this matching in a second step. However, finding a match can be ambiguous and thus grades may be less comprehensible. Our approach avoids the problem to find a best match by using rules that either match or not match.

Rule-based checks using graph patterns have also been explored for static checks of source code with graph transformation tools [4]. However, graph transformation tools are reported to be relatively slow, while the graph query engine in this paper is specialized for efficient storing and querying of graphs.

5. CONCLUSIONS AND FUTURE WORK

This paper introduced a concept of diagram checks based on graph queries for automated assessment and tutoring systems. It has been shown that it is possible to define a set of rules that express both desired and undesired features of solutions. It has also been shown that this rule-based approach allows differentiation between correctness and quality of solutions.

Issues to be solved by future work are especially related to string analysis. Covering different spellings of the same term currently needs tedious lists of alternative strings. More sophisticated functions for covering different spellings, e.g. by using regular expressions or string tokenizers may improve the system. Moreover, natural language processing may allow checking the correct direction of associations based on their names. Both features can neatly be integrated into the presented approach by defining custom functions for GReQL.

As depicted in figure 1, the output of the checking process currently is a list of feedback. Since this is a textual artefact it is different from the input, which is (the XMI representation of) a graphical artefact. Consequently another future step can be to include feedback directly in the submitted diagrams.

The use of graph queries is obviously not limited to UML class diagrams. Thus it is an important next step to explore the possibilities of rule-based checks for other diagram types. It is also not necessary to stick to UML, but to apply the same technique to any other language that can be parsed to a graph-based representation of its abstract syntax, which includes in particular virtually all programming languages, as visible from the original use cases of GReQL [1].

Acknowledgments: The authors would like to thank Eric Schmieders for providing exercises and solutions from the bachelor-degree course and Don Ho for carefully comparing the automated results with the manual feedback. In addition, we are deeply grateful for all the detailed comments provided by the anonymous reviewers.

6. REFERENCES

[1] D. Bildhauer and J. Ebert. Querying Software Abstraction Graphs. In *Working Session on Query Technologies and Applications for Program Comprehension (QTAPC 2008), collocated with ICPC 2008*, 2008.

[2] C. A. Higgins and B. Bligh. Formative computer based assessment in diagram based domains. In *Proceedings of the 11th annual SIGCSE conference on Innovation and technology in computer science education*, ITICSE '06, pages 98–102, New York, NY, USA, 2006. ACM.

[3] A. Hoffmann, A. Quast, and R. Wismüller. Online-Übungssystem für die Programmierausbildung zur Einführung in die Informatik. In S. Seehusen, U. Lucke, and S. Fischer, editors, *DeLFI 2008, 6. e-Learning Fachtagung Informatik*, volume 132 of *LNI*, pages 173–184. GI, 2008.

[4] C. Köllmann and M. Goedicke. Automation of Java Code Analysis for Programming Exercises. In *Proceedings of the Third International Workshop on Graph Based Tools*, volume 1 of *Electronic Communications of the EASST*, 2006.

[5] OMG. MOF 2.0 / XML Metadata Interchange (XMI), v2.1.1 specification, 2007. http://www.omg.org/spec/XMI/2.1.1/.

[6] M. Striewe, M. Balz, and M. Goedicke. A flexible and modular software architecture for computer aided assessments and automated marking. In *Proceedings of the First International Conference on Computer Supported Eductation (CSEDU), 23 - 26 March 2009, Lisboa, Portugal*, volume 2, pages 54–61. INSTICC, 2009.

[7] P. Thomas, N. Smith, and K. Waugh. Automatically assessing graph-based diagrams. *Learning, Media and Technology*, 33(3):249–267, 2008.

[8] P. Thomas, K. Waugh, and N. Smith. Experiments in the automatic marking of ER-diagrams. In *ITiCSE '05: Proceedings of the 10th annual SIGCSE conference on Innovation and technology in computer science education*, pages 158–162, New York, NY, USA, 2005. ACM.

[9] A. Tsintsifas. *A Framework for the Computer Based Assessment of Diagram Based Coursework*. PhD thesis, University of Nottingham, School of Computer Science and Information Technology, 2002.

AGUIA/J: A Tool for Interactive Experimentation of Objects

André L. Santos[*†]
andre.santos@iscte.pt

[*]Faculty of Sciences, University of Lisbon
LASIGE, Bloco C6, Piso 3, Campo Grande
1749-016 Lisboa, Portugal

[†]Instituto Universitário de Lisboa (ISCTE-IUL)
Av. das Forças Armadas, Edifício II
1649-026 Lisboa, Portugal

ABSTRACT

Learning and teaching object-oriented programming are still perceived as being difficult tasks. This paper presents AGUIA/J, a pedagogical tool for interactive experimentation and visualization of object-oriented Java programs. The approach is based on having a graphical environment for experimenting a set of user-developed classes where objects of such classes can be created and controlled interactively. The main innovative aspects of the tool comprise the visualization of objects in widgets that take different forms according to their classes and state, a mechanism to address the query-command separation principle, and the capability of runtime adaptation of the objects in the workbench to new versions of their classes. An experiment using AGUIA/J as courseware in pilot lab classes has resulted in higher approval rates for the involved students, as well as significantly lower drop-out rates.

Categories and Subject Descriptors

K.3.2 [**Computers and Education**]: Computer and Information Science Education; D.1.5 [**Programming Techniques**]: Object-oriented Programming

General Terms

Design, Human Factors

1. INTRODUCTION

Programming is a complex activity that involves mental models that apprentices struggle to develop during introductory programming courses. In particular, object-oriented programming is often considered more problematic, given that its concepts are tightly interrelated and cannot be easily taught and learned in isolation [1].

In this paper, we present a tool consisting of an interactive environment for experimenting object-oriented Java programs that we refer to as AGUIA/J[1]. Such a tool is an adaptive application that takes as input classes developed by the user and adapts itself according to those classes, providing a graphical user interface to create and control objects of those classes. Within the tool, the objects

---

[1]Adaptive and Generic User Interface Application (for Java)

"gain life" in their own widgets, which a user may interact with by invoking operations and observe how the objects' state evolve. When recompiling the classes, the user may request the system to adapt at runtime, implying the existing objects to instantly morph according to the new versions of the classes.

Our approach is centered on having programming language features metaphorically represented by the GUI elements of the tool's user interface. The object widgets take different forms according to their structural members and state. For instance, operations are mapped to buttons and are invoked when the button is pressed, different data types have different kinds of widgets exhibiting them (e.g. a boolean is represented as a check box, while an enum type is represented as a set of radio buttons), private class members are not displayed, etc.

We have conducted an experiment using AGUIA/J in an introduction to programming course. The experiment was based on having pilot lab class groups using AGUIA/J as courseware. The results have shown that the lab groups where AGUIA/J was used registered significantly higher approval rates and lower drop-out rates.

This paper proceeds as follows. Section 2 briefly presents the philosophy underlying the proposed tool and the requirements that drove its elaboration. Section 3 presents the AGUIA/J tool resorting to concrete usage examples. Section 4 presents the evaluation of the tool, detailing the experiment and discussing its results. Section 5 situates our approach regarding related work, and finally, Section 6 concludes the paper.

2. APPROACH

Nowadays it is common to adopt an object-oriented language in introductory programming courses. However, these courses typically suffer from high drop-out and failures rates. Our approach consists of a new tactic for understanding object orientation backed up by tool support. We aimed at a tool that was adequate as courseware of an introductory programming course where Java is taught. We chose the Java language given its widespread use in teaching.

Our approach is strongly based on drawing *conceptual metaphors* from the source domain of GUI elements to the target domain of object-oriented concepts. A conceptual metaphor is a metaphor in which one concept is understood in terms of another concept. The conceptual domain from which metaphors are drawn to understand another conceptual domain is known as the *source domain*, whereas the conceptual domain that is understood in this way is the *target domain*. Conceptual metaphors typically employ more abstract concepts as their targets and more concrete concepts as their sources.

In our approach, the metaphors serve the purpose of illustrating object-oriented concepts within a graphical environment. The ad-

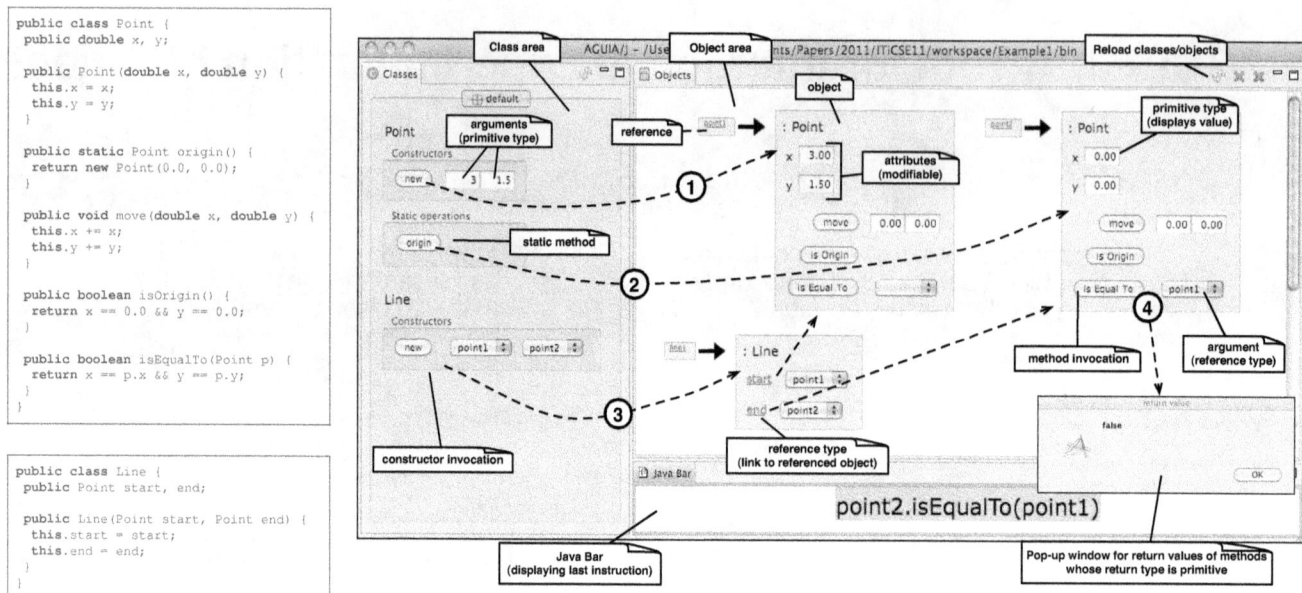

```java
public class Point {
  public double x, y;

  public Point(double x, double y) {
    this.x = x;
    this.y = y;
  }

  public static Point origin() {
    return new Point(0.0, 0.0);
  }

  public void move(double x, double y) {
    this.x += x;
    this.y += y;
  }

  public boolean isOrigin() {
    return x == 0.0 && y == 0.0;
  }

  public boolean isEqualTo(Point p) {
    return x == p.x && y == p.y;
  }
}
```

```java
public class Line {
  public Point start, end;

  public Line(Point start, Point end) {
    this.start = start;
    this.end = end;
  }
}
```

Figure 1: Objects and references in AGUIA/J.

vantage of using a source domain of GUI elements for the metaphors is that it is very well-known, simple, and with a visual representation. A central metaphor that we represent in the tool is "object as machine", inspired on [5] (Figure 7.5). The idea is to shape apprentices' perception of objects as machines with several displays (properties) that may change when interacting with the machine by pressing its buttons (operations).

The machine is like a black box that only shows the external interface of the object. The user is allowed to interact with the objects according to what could be done programmatically through its public interface. This issue is closely related with the perception of encapsulation, and we believe this to be a powerful metaphor for grasping such a concept.

As argued in [3], we believe that starting to exemplify Java with its "main" method is pedagogically incorrect. The reason is that the "main" method has nothing to do with object orientation, and thus, we are starting with an exception to the rule. Moreover, early introduction of language features related to I/O can be considered harmful. The reason is that it detracts apprentices from the essential concepts and forces teachers to "hand wave" when addressing necessary language features that involve more advanced topics (e.g. exceptions). These issues drove the design of the BlueJ environment [2]. Our approach follows this philosophy, enabling apprentices to exercise the several object-oriented concepts without resorting to the "main" method or any language features related to I/O.

In order to achieve enhanced usability and interactivity, it was our goal to support the capability of runtime adaptation upon recompilation of user classes. This means that a user may be experimenting some objects and on request morph the existing objects according to the new version of their classes. This enables an agile switching between concept explanation and exemplification. Changing the type of attributes, introducing new methods, changing methods to static, or changing access modifiers, are examples of modifications that can be performed on the classes and after which the objects in the environment adapt according to such changes.

3. AGUIA/J

This section presents AGUIA/J, a tool we have developed according to the philosophy and goals described in the previous section. AGUIA/J is a stand-alone GUI application built using Java SWT that looks as shown in the right-hand side of Figure 1.

The AGUIA/J window is divided into a class area (left) and an object area (right). The class area adapts itself according to the set of classes and their constructors, whereas the object area is populated as the user interacts with the application. The object area displays widgets that represent "objects as machines", which may be controlled by the user. On the bottom part we can find the Java Bar, which displays the Java instructions that are equivalent to the user actions performed through the user interface (e.g. object creation, method invocation). Alternatively to controlling the objects directly, the user may type Java instructions to create and invoke operations on the objects.

In order to use the tool, the user develops simple classes without any instantiation code (i.e. the "main" method) or additional configurations, and further launches the tool passing the working directory where the compiled class files are located. The tool will adapt itself according to the classes (and packages) found at the given directory. On request, the user may reload the environment with new versions of the classes without having to restart execution. The existing objects that were created remain on the environment and morph according to the new versions of their classes.

AGUIA/J executes user code in a "sandbox" so that runtime errors and infinite cycle bugs are captured and presented to the user in a friendly manner. In case of a runtime exception caused by user code (e.g. NullPointerException, ArrayOutOfBoundsException), an error dialog will pop-up, containing a more apprentice-friendly error message that indicates the exception (in contrast to a stack trace), as well as the location in the code where it occurred. With respect to infinite cycle bugs, AGUIA/J has a configurable time-out parameter that sets the number of seconds that the execution of a method/constructor is allowed to last, until execution is interrupted and a warning message informing about a possible infinite cycle bug is displayed.

```
public class Point {
  private double x, y;

  public Point(double x, double y) {
    this.x = x;
    this.y = y;
  }

  public String toString() {
    return "(" + x + ", " + y + ")";
  }

  public boolean isOrigin() {
    return x == 0.0 && y == 0.0;
  }

  public double getAbscissa() {
    return x;
  }

  public double getOrdinate() {
    return y;
  }
}
```

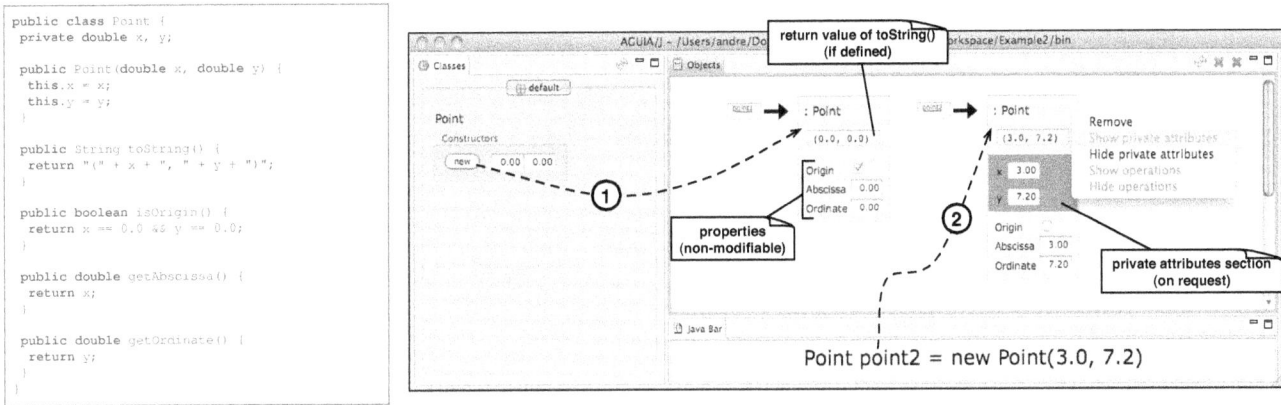

Figure 2: Encapsulation and properties in AGUIA/J.

The next subsections illustrate AGUIA/J's features with examples. AGUIA/J covers many other features that are not illustrated in this paper due to space constraints. With respect to object-oriented concepts, these features essentially comprise inheritance, polymorphism, and enumerations.

3.1 Objects and references

As explained, the tool adapts itself to a set of classes. The first step of such adaptation is related to the class area on the left-hand side of the application window (see Figure 1). This area will contain a section for each class defined according to the different ways of creating objects of such class. These are determined by the existing public constructors. For each constructor there will be a button for creating an object using that constructor. The created objects will appear in the object area on the right-hand side of the application window.

After being created, each object is displayed in a widget with several sections. In the objects of Figure 1 we can see a header with the object's type, a section with the public attributes, and a section with the public operations for that object. An object widget enables interaction with the object through its external interface, as if the object would be used programmatically. Both static methods and static attributes of a class appear on the left-hand area rather than on each object, in order to give the intuition that they are not associated to any particular object.

Figure 1 presents two simple classes, Point and Line, whose members are all public. The screenshot of the tool is annotated with the interaction steps that were taken before the reaching the shown execution state. Although having non-private attributes is not a best-practice in Java, enabling attributes to be visualized is useful to transmit the basic notion that objects have state. We believe it is beneficial to be able to delay the use of access modifiers until the concept of encapsulation is introduced.

On step one, a Point object was created by typing the necessary arguments in the constructor widget and clicking the "new" button. Upon doing so the newly created object appears on the object area, as well as a reference to it. Reference names are given automatically by the tool. This decision favored usability over functionality, given that asking an identifier to the user upon the creation of each object would slightly slow down interaction. However, if using the Java Bar the user may choose which reference names to use. On step two, the static method Point.origin() was invoked. Because the method returned an object, such object was placed on the object area. On step three, a Line object was created passing refer-

ences point1 and point2 (which were assigned to the previously created Point objects). Arguments of a reference type will have a drop-down list from which an existing compatible reference can be selected. References are represented by links, on which a user may click to obtain a new reference to the referenced object. The state of the objects is always kept updated with the current value of the objects' attributes. Operations may be invoked on an object by clicking on its buttons. For instance, on step four, the operation isEqualTo(Point) was invoked. Since its return value is of a primitive type, a dialog window pops-up displaying the returned value.

3.2 Encapsulation and properties

Encapsulation is an important concept in object orientation that often apprentices fail to grasp. In Java, encapsulation is achieved using access modifiers (i.e. public, protected, default, and private). In AGUIA/J, the possible interactions with the objects are determined by their external interface. In this way, the "machine" that represents the object only enables the user to visualize and interact with the public members of the object. Therefore, non-public attributes are not displayed and non-public operations are not available for invocation, just as if the object was being used programmatically. We believe that this mechanism is useful to help on developing the intuition that encapsulation is a means to control how an object can be used and to separate interface from implementation. For debug purposes, the user may activate a section of the object that displays its private attributes (see Figure 2).

The *command query separation* principle [5] states that a method should either implement a *query* that does not change the object's state or a *command* that possibly changes the object's state, not both simultaneously. The return values of query methods that require no arguments can be thought of as being object *properties*, which are either calculated or directly given by attribute values. Based on the method signatures and on the widely-used naming conventions (*get**, *is**), AGUIA/J detects which methods are representing property accessors. In this way, for each method considered as a property accessor there will be a field showing its return value at every moment of execution (see Figure 2). Naturally, the fields that exhibit properties are non-modifiable. In case a method detected as a property accessor modifies the object's state, the tool displays a warning. Although what described is the default tool behavior, it is possible to customize the property detection policy (or disable it).

Finally, if a class overrides Java's toString() method, its return value is handled as a special property, appearing in a dedicated section on the top of the object widget (see Figure 2).

3.3 Arrays

AGUIA/J features array visualization and interaction, representing them as objects with a field for each array position. Figure 3 illustrates arrays resorting to the class Point given previously. On step one, an array of type Point was created using the JavaBar. On step two, a Point object was created. On step three, the Point object was assigned to the first position of the array through the drop-down list (which includes the references with a compatible type). Finally on step four, the Point object is obtained by clicking on the link of the first position of the array.

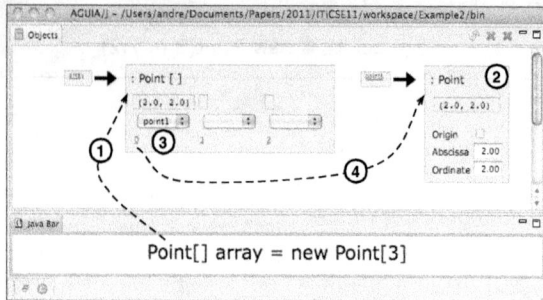

Figure 3: Arrays in AGUIA/J.

4. EVALUATION

In order to evaluate AGUIA/J we have conducted an experiment involving the introductory programming course taught at our department. This section details such an experiment and presents its results concerning drop-out and approval rates.

4.1 Context

The introduction to programming course duration is 12 weeks, each one having a lecture of 1,5 hour and a lab class of 3 hours. On a given week, the lecture covers certain topics, whereas the lab class is based on a set of exercises related to those topics. Lab classes are designed to have an initial summary, where the teacher addresses the class, but, during the remainder of the class the teacher helps each student individually. University policy requires every class (both lectures and lab classes) to have a record of attendance.

During a semester there are several lab class groups working separately. The number of students in a lab group is typically between 20 and 30. In order to obtain approval in the course, a student has to perform the final exam. Attending the final exam requires the student to obtain prior approval in the lab classes, by means of tests and assignments.

The course has roughly 3 stages, which are summarized in Table 1. In past course editions, records show a considerably high drop-out between the end of Stage 2 and the beginning of Stage 3. Typically, if a student reaches Stage 3 with no reasonable skills regarding the previous topics, either gives up the course or proceeds but fails to obtain approval. In this course, a drop-out rate of more than 30% is often common.

Table 1: Introduction to programming course stages.

Stage	Weeks	Topics
1	4	Variables, loops, selection statements
2	4	Arrays, references, functions/procedures
3	4	Classes, encapsulation, enumerations

4.2 Experiment

The experiment involved two of the degrees where the course is taught, namely *Computer Science and Engineering* (CSE) and *Informatics and Management* (IM). On the semester when the experiment was carried out, each of the degrees had 4 lab groups, totalizing 8 lab groups. The lab groups registered an initial number of students of approximately 85 in CSE and 110 in IM. The experiment took place in 2 out of the 8 lab groups, having one pilot lab group from each degree. The other 6 lab groups had the role of control groups in this study. The distribution of students by the lab groups was performed by the university in the normal manner, without our intervention. The author of this paper was the teacher in the 2 pilot lab groups, while the other 6 control lab groups were taught by 5 different teachers. The author was neither involved in the elaboration of the final exam nor on its grading.

The experiment consisted of providing the pilot groups with AGUIA/J, so that the students would perform the lab exercises using it. The lab exercises for the pilot groups were the same as in the control groups (i.e. the regular course exercises). The students had approximately 8 hours of contact with the tool, spanned across 4 lab classes on the Stage 3 of the course. We are aware that some of these students have used the tool outside the class, but we have no concrete data for quantifying this factor.

Slightly after the middle of the semester (on week 8) there was a small compulsory test that every student had to do in the lab class as part of the course evaluation. Given that this test took place just before the experiment of using AGUIA/J has started, it was a good indicator of how the student population was distributed among control and pilot groups. Table 2 presents information about the test, namely attendance distribution among pitot and control groups (*dist*), average score (*avg*), and standard deviation of scores (*std*). We can see that in CSE the scores are similar, while in IM the average score is a little lower, but with less disperse scores. In CSE the number of students of the pilot group that performed the test was a quarter of the total (25%), whereas in IM the pilot group represented slightly over a quarter of the total (28%).

Table 2: Mid-semester test: pilot and control group results.

Group	CSE			IM		
	dist.	avg.	std.	dist.	avg.	std.
Pilot (1)	20 (25%)	73%	20%	28 (28%)	63%	18%
Control (3)	59 (75%)	73%	25%	72 (72%)	69%	27%

4.3 Results

With respect to exam attendance (see Figure 4), which was only possible for students that succeed in the lab class evaluation, we observed that, for both degrees, the proportion of pilot group students was higher than the proportion of pilot group students that attended the mid-semester test. This means that the pilot groups as a whole were more successful in reaching the exam than the control groups. Moreover, the proportion of pilot group students that obtained approval in the course was higher than the proportion of pilot group students that attended the exam. This means that the pilot groups as a whole were more successful in the exam than the control groups. Figure 4 also presents a chart with the exam success rates, according to degree. Here it is only considered the students that have made it to the exam, thus excluding drop-outs.

We believe that these results provide evidence that the usage of AGUIA/J as courseware was effective. However, as a threat to validity, we acknowledge that the fact of having different teachers on pilot and control groups could have influenced the results. On the other hand, the fact that the teacher of the pilot groups was not in-

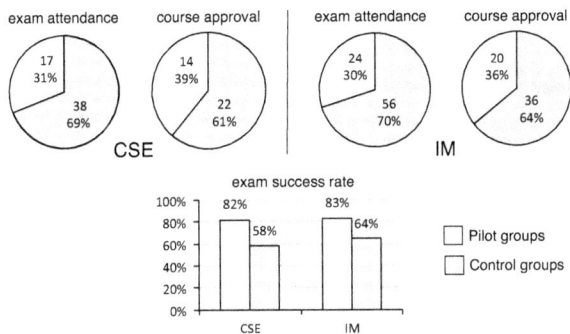

Figure 4: Exam attendance and course approvals.

volved in exam elaboration and grading strengthens the impartial nature of the measurements that determined the results.

Finally, we have analyzed the records of student attendance in the lab classes. Having the initial number of students that was attending a certain lab class and the number of students that remained until the last week, we calculated the drop-out rate for each lab group. Figure 5 presents a chart with the course drop-out rates, according to degree. We can observe considerably lower drop-out rates in the pilot groups of both degrees. The higher success of the pilot groups in reaching the exam is in principle related with this indicator, given that if more students remain in the course, there will probably be more students reaching the exam.

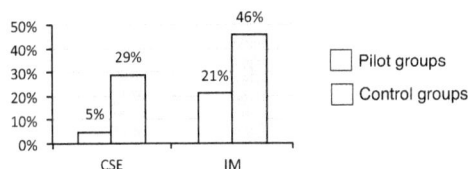

Figure 5: Drop-out rates.

5. RELATED WORK

BlueJ [2] is an established and popular environment for teaching and learning object orientation using Java. AGUIA/J has several aspects in common with BlueJ. Both tools have a code pad where users may type in instructions to create and interact with objects. Another common aspect is the fact that apprentices neither need to develop I/O code nor to develop the "main" method in order to instantiate object classes. Despite the similarities with BlueJ, AGUIA/J has some fundamental differences with respect to the representation of objects, interaction style, and tool usability.

A fundamental difference pertains to the fact that in BlueJ the object fields are displayed homogeneously in a textbox using their textual value, while in AGUIA/J the fields assume different widgets according to their type, access modifiers, and state. Moreover, AGUIA/J features a graphical metaphor for encapsulation, whereas for instance in BlueJ the difference between the representation of a private and a public attribute is solely textual.

Upon the creation of an object, BlueJ displays on its object bench a red block that represents a reference to the created object. In AGUIA/J, the user is always faced with the actual created object, which later on might have several references pointing to it. This multiple-to-one relationship is not made explicit in BlueJ, since

distinct reference red blocks do not provide any graphical hint in case they are pointing to a same object.

Finally, AGUIA/J is capable of readapting itself on request to new class versions, enabling the user to see the existing objects in the environment morphing according to the version of the classes. While in AGUIA/J the user may continue interacting with the existing objects, in BlueJ the existing objects in the environment disappear upon recompilation of their classes.

DrJava [6] is a pedagogical programming environment where apprentices develop Java classes and input Java expressions in an interactive console for experimenting objects based on a "read-eval-print loop". As in AGUIA/J, and BlueJ, DrJava also relieves apprentices of dealing with I/O. In contrast to AGUIA/J, DrJava does not attempt to draw graphical conceptual metaphors for understanding object orientation.

Jeliot [4] is a pedagogical animation system for Java programs. Such a system is capable of animating a Java program from beginning to end in a friendly and intuitive environment. However, Jeliot does not allow interactive experimentation of objects as in AGUIA/J, BlueJ, or DrJava. Therefore, despite the fact that apprentices may visualize their programs in Jeliot, the tool is not the best choice for students to develop lab class exercises, as suggested by its authors. Moreover, given that in Jeliot all classes have to be given in a single file and that every object creation is visualized, the tool usage does not scale well for large examples.

6. CONCLUSION

In this paper we proposed a tool (AGUIA/J) that exploits graphical conceptual metaphors based on GUI elements for addressing the problem of understanding of object orientation. The approach was evaluated by accessing approval and drop-out rates of pilot lab groups that were using AGUIA/J as courseware. The main innovative aspects of the tool comprise (a) representing "objects as machines" according to its structural members and state, (b) a mechanism for addressing the query-command separation principle based on object properties, and (c) the capability of runtime adaption to new class versions.

7. ACKNOWLEDGMENTS

I would like to thank Luís Nunes for his valuable comments. This work was partially supported by FCT through LASIGE (U.408) Multiannual Funding.

8. REFERENCES

[1] J. Bennedsen, M. E. Caspersen, and M. Kölling. *Reflections on the Teaching of Programming: Methods and Implementations.* Springer Publishing Company, Incorporated, 2008.

[2] M. Kölling, B. Quig, A. Patterson, and J. Rosenberg. The BlueJ system and its pedagogy. *Journal of Computer Science Education, Special issue on Learning and Teaching Object Technology,* 13(4):249–268, December 2003.

[3] M. Kölling and J. Rosenberg. Guidelines for teaching object orientation with java. In *ITiCSE '01: Proceedings of the 6th annual conference on Innovation and technology in computer science education,* pages 33–36, New York, NY, USA, 2001.

[4] R. B.-B. Levy, M. Ben-Ari, and P. A. Uronen. The Jeliot 2000 program animation system. *Comput. Educ.,* 40(1):1–15, 2003.

[5] B. Meyer. *Object-Oriented Software Construction.* Prentice-Hall, Inc., Upper Saddle River, NJ, USA, 1988.

[6] E. A. Robert, R. Cartwright, and B. Stoler. Drjava: A lightweight pedagogic environment for java. In *SIGCSE Bulletin and Proceedings,* pages 137–141. ACM Press, 2002.

Intelligent Systems Development in a Non Engineering Curriculum

Emily A. Brand
Loyola University Chicago
Department of Computer Science
Chicago, Illinois 60611 USA
+1.512.609.0338

eabrand@gmail.com

William L. Honig
Loyola University Chicago
Department of Computer Science
Chicago, Illinois 60611 USA
+1.312.915.7988

whonig@luc.edu

Matthew Wojtowicz
Loyola University Chicago
Department of Computer Science
Chicago, Illinois 60611 USA
+1.312.915.7989

mattu16@gmail.com

ABSTRACT

Much of computer system development today is programming in the large–systems of millions of lines of code distributed across servers and the web. At the same time, microcontrollers have also become pervasive in everyday products, economical to manufacture, and represent a different level of learning about system development. Real world systems at this level require integrated development of custom hardware and software.

How can academic institutions give students a view of this other extreme–programming on small microcontrollers with specialized hardware? Full scale system development including custom hardware and software is expensive, beyond the range of any but the larger engineering oriented universities, and hard to fit into a typical length course. The course described here is a solution using microcontroller programming in high level language, small hardware components, and the Arduino open source microcontroller. The results of the hands-on course show that student programmers with limited hardware knowledge are able to build custom devices, handle the complexity of basic hardware design, and learn to appreciate the differences between large and small scale programming.

Categories and Subject Descriptors

C.3 [**Computer Systems Organization**]: Special-Purpose and Application-Based Systems – *microprocessor/microcomputer applications, real-time and embedded systems;* I.2.9 [**Artificial Intelligence**]: Robotics – *propelling mechanisms, sensors;* K.3.2 [**Computers and Education**]: Computer and Information Science Education – *curriculum.*

General Terms

Design, Economics, Experimentation.

Keywords

Arduino course, microcontroller course, embedded systems

1. INTRODUCTION

This paper presents the approach used in an experimental course to offer small scale microcontroller system development to computer science students. The results show that experienced student programmers (both advanced undergraduates and graduate students) are able to learn how to construct combined hardware and software systems. Further, the course successfully introduces smaller scale microcontroller development which they may not otherwise have an opportunity to learn.

This experimental course addressing small scale embedded programming fits in the ACM Computer Science Curriculum 2008 as the Intelligent System / Robotics knowledge area [4]. It was conceived to limit the amount and expense of customized hardware development but still allow students to gain exposure to advanced intelligent systems using sensors and robotics.

The original goal was to use a small microcontroller to provide students access to hardware control and software interactions in a participative and "tinkering" course (similar to [5,10]). Having experience with LEGO Mindstorms robots [13] which allow only a few simple plug-in sensors of fixed types, we sought a more open-ended and expandable platform. After an investigation of various microcontrollers, the Arduino microcontroller board was selected. Although there have been some earlier courses using the Arduino [2] many of these have focused on the small, flexible, wearable LilyPad variant of the Arduino controller [3,7].

2. MOTIVATION AND BACKGROUND

2.1 Small Embedded System Development

The Microsoft Windows XP operating system is 45 million lines of code [9]. A military operating system, for specialized surveillance computers, is 50 million lines of code [6]. Courses in Rapid Application Development using architectures and tools such as Service Oriented Architecture (SOA) or .NET allow students to quickly generate large complex systems with database management systems, network access, and web interfaces.

There is another kind of development: small, often real time systems never destined to run on a personal computer or the Internet. Instead of visible computers the software runs on microcontrollers; a microcontroller is a single semiconductor chip including a small 8 or 16-bit processor, timing circuitry, and volatile and static memory. Microcontrollers are inside other objects (automobiles, toasters, traffic monitors) and often a key part of providing the user's features. In this world the software has two major differences. First, the application is more intimately tied to the physical world and hardware (sensors, controls, many kinds of analog or digital inputs). Second, the software running on a small microcontroller is fully in charge of the device without the need to timeshare with other applications for the user. Microcontrollers have limited memory and often much less processor speed than today's personal computers.

This smaller scale system development is becoming more visible and a focus in the popular press [11]. Computer Science students need to have opportunities to understand the differences from the large applications world, acquire skills for developing small intelligent systems, and be able to make informed decisions about their career directions.

2.2 Open Source Microcontroller

The technical heart of the experimental course is the Arduino microcontroller board. The Arduino Duemilanove model used in class [1, 12] is a 6.8 by 5.3cm printed circuit board and includes an ATmega microprocessor, connecting pins for digital and analog input and output, several powering options, a boot loader, and 32K bytes of memory. Thus, it is a ready-made piece part for small projects including a variety of inputs and outputs. Students are able to use the board without needing to learn and build the lowest level of hardware including timing and power supply regulation.

The Arduino hardware and software are both covered with open source licenses. The hardware design is available to interested users under a Creative Commons Attribution Share-Alike license. Although not important to the class described here, the hardware design may be freely modified and incorporated into products and shared with the same license.

3. COURSE STRUCTURE

3.1 Student Preparation

The course was designed for experienced programmers but did not require specific electronics or hardware preparation. Students had previously completed a minimum of three software development courses, with emphasis on object oriented development in Java. Some students had considerably more experience in distributed systems, server based software, and mobile application development. Students included both advanced undergraduates and masters degree seeking students.

3.2 Instruction Topics

The course covered a combination of hardware and systems / software topics with the goal of preparing students to undertake an individually designed project in the latter part of the 15 week semester. Topics included:

- Introduction to Arduino microcontroller hardware and system development (hands-on implementation of first circuit and software)

- Electronics tutorial (amps, volts, ohms, and circuit diagrams), building basic breadboard circuits, and dangers of Electro Static Discharge (ESD)

- Physical world input and output (light and temperature sensor, LED, speaker, and motor control)

- Real time software strategy without an operating system

- Designing interactive real time systems using Structured Analysis and Design Technique (SADT) [8].

Figure 1 is an example early project used to expose students to the basics steps of hardware and system design. The Arduino board at the rear of the figure is connected to a circuit of multiple lights on a solderless breadboard (front of figure). The project explores real time performance by increasing the rate of blinking each light and detecting when all processor time is consumed.

Figure 1. Example real time performance project.

Students completed this lab with multiple blinking LEDs with and without using the microcontroller's delay() function for real time control. Then they moved onto adding buzzers and other outside sensors to create a more complicated system with light and temperature sensors, other input buttons, sound output, and small motors and servo controls.

The course was structured as a seminar class with emphasis on student prototyping or "tinkering". There were no formal examinations. Student's grades were partially based on peer evaluation of their projects and class contributions by students.

3.3 Course Equipment

The course was new and the university had not previously taught similar classes. The physical meeting space for the course was a departmental research and project laboratory with limited space. The department acquired Arduino controller boards, wireless breadboards, electronics parts, switches, joysticks, sensors, and robotics kits for the class and from which the student's built their final class projects.

The course equipment cost US$2500 of which US$500 was for hand tools, soldering equipment, and storage cases for parts (supporting 12 students, the limit imposed by lab space). A single Arduino Duemilanove microcontroller board, fully assembled, costs less than US$40. Much of the equipment survived the course unharmed and will be used in future course offerings.

3.4 Student Projects

After working on initial simple systems with a few LED lights or sensors, students spent about half of the course developing their projects (some individually, others on two person teams). Student projects included:

- Airplane glider control to maintain a heading (Figure 2)

- Tracked robot rover with wireless interface

- Memory testing game similar to SIMON

- Guitar sound modification system

- Music / speech sound generation system

- Wearable environmental sensing clothing

Figure 2. Microcomputer autonomous glider

4. COURSE FINDINGS AND LEARNING OUTCOMES

The course was conducted as an experiment to determine both the feasibility of teaching more hardware intensive courses and to see if students would learn the differences between developing large and small scale computer based systems.

4.1 Learning Small Microcontroller Programming

The Arduino development environment forced students to confront the differences of large and small scale programming. First, there is no operating system beyond a basic loader and a suggested division of the software into initialization code and a repeated main processing loop. The standard Arduino delay() function simply loops the processor for a number of cycles to use up time. Student software needs to decide what to do with all of the processor time and how to divide time between different parts of the system.

Second, unlike most programs, a controller system usually runs forever (or until a reset button is pressed or power is removed). While running, the microcontroller code needs to accommodate the differences between internal processor time and the connected real world components. For example, it does not work to test the state of a push button switch every millisecond (possible with the Arduino's processor speed of 16Mhz). Too rapid checking of the switch state (typically as a current flow across an Arduino pin) can result in many false inputs during the time the button is being pressed and the contacts begin to conduct electricity. Students learned to do "debouncing" to compare and time inputs to determine when to act upon them.

As a result, students were forced to consider the key differences between large and small scale programming. Although none of the students had developed small systems in the past, the course end survey (Figure 3) showed they believed they understood this key distinction.

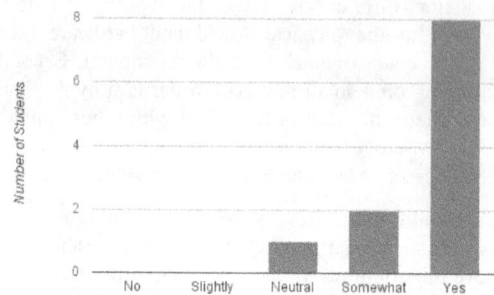

Figure 3. Do you understand the difference between programming microcontrollers and higher level programming(i.e., Java)?

The instructor concurred and saw further evidence in student's projects. For example, several projects dealt with large differences in real time demands between different parts of their systems (e.g. checking for inputs and driving output displays and generating sound).

4.2 Using SADT for Design and Communication

Microcontroller based systems are different from the computers students normally use in classes and projects. Instead of a keyboard, mouse, display and network connections, the microcontroller can connect to a number of specialized input and outputs depending on its intended function.

This combination of hardware and software thinking was a common problem students had to overcome. Once projects began to increase in complexity, students had trouble describing their projects to the class. The essence of the problem was clearly separating their software logic and hardware logic. Students looking at a peer's project had trouble understanding the system just from looking at the hardware and the source code.

The solution to these problems was using a high level analysis technique, Structured Analysis and Design Technique (SADT) diagrams [8]. SADT gave students a common diagramming paradigm that had the capabilities to describe both the system's hardware and software design on multiple levels. Design techniques such as UML and use case diagrams, due to their software focus, failed in comparison to SADT diagrams.

Figure 4 is a high level template SADT for student projects. The course used SADT diagrams to clearly define the actions of the software in response to physical world inputs. In this approach actions are the main components (boxes) with inputs coming into the action from the left and outputs leaving to the right. Data not manipulated by the system (i.e., state setting, control bits) are depicted as arrows coming into the top of the action. Software logic (debouncing, data manipulation, routing, real time control) is represented within the action or by decomposing it into another diagram. Arrows to the bottom of an action box are the mechanisms or tools used by the action.

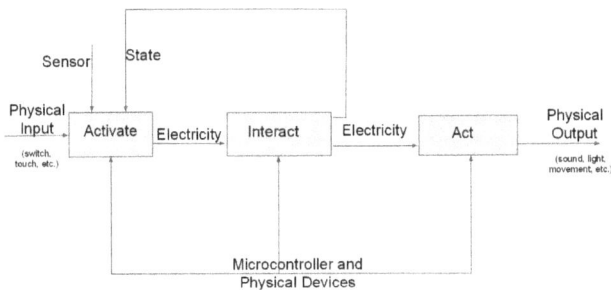

Figure 4. Generic SADT diagram for project analysis

All of the inward arrows coming together cause the action to occur and the output to be created. Students' systems typically consisted of a sensor listener to initiate actions, cause a physical manifestation using other devices, and possibly cause other actions to take place immediately or after some time.

SADT diagrams allowed students to coherently present and critique other students' projects. With the ability to communicate their projects, all students were able to receive quick and useful feedback. The diagrams also allowed students to pen and paper prototype before going through all the hardware set-up, allowing for instructors to catch problems early and prevent later frustration.

4.3 Running a Seminar Class with Tinkering

The course was structured as a hands-on seminar with laboratory workshops. This informal setting with only a few formal lectures allowed students to fully understand how microcontrollers work; it also enabled class discussions about the labs since every student was working on the lab at the same time. The students with more background were able to refresh and solidify their understanding of software or electricity and share it quickly with others. Less experienced students could delve in with a safety net since the professor, teaching assistants, and peers were all able to be of assistance when a problem arose.

The most interesting aspect of small intelligent systems is the hands-on capability and the ability to make mistakes without major consequences. Because of the relatively inexpensive cost of the equipment and no concern about affecting the wider network and servers, students were able to tinker and play with their creations. Sometimes students would simply try different circuits and make wiring changes to see what happened and try to explain the results. Outside of class time, students took their projects with them and worked on them as they wished.

The authors believe that forcing a more structured class could drain the students' ambition, interest in microcontrollers, and low-level programming. Keeping class lectures and exams to a minimum allows students to take advantage of and challenge their creativity and current skill-set. Pushing students to alter the labs to use their own desired inputs and outputs encourages creativity and discussion, two key features of this course.

As part of the course structure, students were asked to evaluate other students' work. Figure 5 summarizes the peer evaluation results for the final projects at the end of the class. While students do rate each other highly (above 7 on a 1 to 10 scale) they did show a reasonable distribution between the best and the worst work.

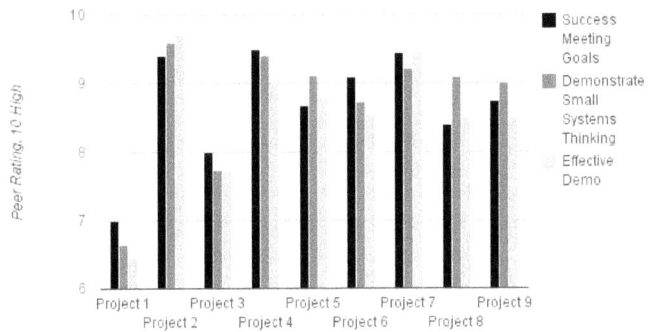

Figure 5. Average Peer Rankings of Final Projects

4.4 Other Findings

In addition, the student course end survey and feedback produced some other points of interest to those planning similar courses:

- Students enjoyed and appreciated the opportunity to learn and practice soldering of electrical parts; 100% rated soldering "useful" in the course end survey. Not all construction was possible using the solderless breadboard and jumper wires.

- Students indicated they would be willing to pay a laboratory fee for the class. Such a fee could be used to replace and expand the hardware components and tools used in the class.

- Students who attempted sound generation projects such as synthesizers had difficulties and were unsuccessful multiple times. These topics require more preparation and more sophisticated hardware components.

5. NEXT STEPS AND FURTHER COURSES

Future courses in similar topics can benefit from using a similar approach and considering several possible improvements.

5.1 Speeding up the Basics

One of the most difficult aspects for the students to grasp at the beginning of the course was electrical knowledge and understanding. Theoretical exploration of the topic in two lectures proved to cause more confusion than clarification. The best approach was to lead the students through a series of hands-on workshops that demonstrated resistance, electrical flow, and other relevant aspects. Students at the end of the course requested that next time there be more of these workshops in order to solidify their foundations in electrical know how.

In order to provide students with a solid base to begin their own project the authors suggest taking time to walk through the following labs for students without prior electronics training:

- A light on/off switch to introduce basic electric principles (using meters, not the microcontroller).
- A button on/off switch to teach debouncing and introduce microcontroller sensor interaction.
- An incremental on off switch that steps up LED brightness with each press of a button. This exercise will introduce topics such as state in a microcontroller

and analog output using Pulse Width Modulation (PWM).

5.2 Interest in Machine Learning and Robotics

When asked what topic they would most wish to continue in future classes, the students were split between an advanced microcontrollers class and a machine learning class. A possible solution, while still using resources economically, is a robotics class. This would allow for both groups to continue in their areas of interest without the need for two classes.

A suitable robotics class can expand on the real time and control knowledge and also allow more focus on learning and decision making algorithms. One of the first topics that can be addressed is communicating with other microcontrollers that control separate, multiple motors. Another aspect of small scale programming that robotics emphasizes is the importance of real time. Students will be pushed to handle real time events and program for responsiveness possibly with many inputs at once. Students would have to handle failures due to time constraints and learn how to minimize the loss such an error causes. Both of these topics could prove valuable for future students.

5.3 Possible Assembly Language Option

The Arduino microcontroller provides an excellent tool for students to get into smaller scale programming. The class used the open source Arduino development environment and the C programming language. Specific processor bits and flags can be accessed and manipulated from the C language directly (e.g. the processor library defines hardware timer number one's data as TCCR1B and makes it available to the C program as a variable).

However, the C language still comes between the student and direct control of the machine. The Arduino environment allows linkage to assembly language programs or inline assembly language instructions for the ATmega processor of the microcontroller.

For further and more precise planning and control of real time response or greater understanding of the performance limits of the microcontroller, it is reasonable to add assembly language programming. This lower level of programming may be usefully applied to a small device interface via the Arduino input and output pins or to better control time delays. Future versions of the course, or follow-on courses, will develop small projects in these areas.

6. SUMMARY

The course was successful in accomplishing its major goals. Institutions such as ours that have focused on purely software courses and are without major engineering facilities should not hesitate to bring more hardware based courses into the computing curriculum. Open source hardware and software such as the Arduino microcontroller make such a course both economical and practical; it possible to effectively teach a microcontroller course without a heavy financial cost. Students no longer need to think that all software runs on a personal computer and a web server.

7. REFERENCES

[1] Banzi, M. 2008. *Getting Started with Arduino*. Maker Media, San Rafael, CA.

[2] Brock, J. D., Bruce, R. F., and Reiser, S. L. 2009. Using Arduino for introductory programming courses. Tutorial Presentation. *Journal of Computing Sciences in Colleges*. 25,2 (Dec. 2009), 129-130.

[3] Buechley, L., Eisenberg, M. Catchen, J. and Crockett, A. 2008. The LilyPad Arduino: using computational textiles to investigate engagement, aesthetics, and diversity in computer science education. In *Proceedings of the twenty-sixth annual SIGCHI conference on Human factors in computing systems* (CHI '08), ACM, New York, NY, 423-432. DOI= http://doi.acm.org/10.1145/1357054.1357123.

[4] CS Review Task Force 2008. Computer Science Curriculum 2008: An Interim Revision of CS 2001. Association of Computing Machinery, IEEE Computer Society. http://www.acm.org//education/curricula/ComputerScience2008.pdf Retrieved Jan. 10, 2011.

[5] Gehringer, E. F., and Miller, Carolyn S. 2009. Student-generated active-learning exercises. In *Proceedings of the 40th ACM technical symposium on computer science education* (SIGCSE '09), ACM, New York, NY, 81-85. DOI= http://doi.acm.org/10.1145/1508865.1508897

[6] Hersh, S.M. 2010. The online threat: should we be worried about a cyber war? *The New Yorker* (Nov. 2010).

[7] Lau, W. W. Y., Ngai, G., Chan, S. C. F., and Cheung, J. C. Y. 2009. Learning programming through fashion and design: a pilot summer course in wearable computing for middle school students. In *Proceedings of the 40th ACM technical symposium on Computer science education* (SIGCSE '09), ACM, New York, NY, 504-508. DOI= http://doi.acm.org/10.1145/1539024.1509041.

[8] Marca, D. A. and McGowan, C. L. 1987. *SADT: Structured Analysis and Design Technique*. McGraw-Hill, New York, NY.

[9] Microsoft Corp. 2010. A history of Windows. http://windows.microsoft.com/en-US/windows/history Retrieved Jan. 10, 2011.

[10] Qian, K., Liu, J., and Tao, L. 2009. Teach real-time embedded system online with real hands-on labs. Poster. In *Proceedings of the 14th annual ACM SIGCSE conference on Innovation and technology in computer science education* (ITiCSE '09), ACM, New York, NY, 367-367. DOI= http://doi.acm.org/10.1145/1595496.1563009.

[11] Siegele, L. 2010. It's a smart world, a special report on smart systems. *The Economist* (6 Nov. 2010), 3-18.

[12] Russell, D. 2010. *Introduction to Embedded Systems: Using ANSI C and the Arduino Development Environment*. Morgan and Claypool, Sebastopol, CA.

[13] Williams, A.B. 2003. The qualitative impact of using LEGO MINDSTORMS robots to teach computer engineering. *IEEE Transactions on Education*. 46,1 (Feb. 2003), 206. DOI= http://10.1109/TE.2002.808260.

Design of Innovative Integrated Circuits in Education

André Schäfer
Institute of Microsystem Technology
University of Siegen
andre.schaefer@uni-siegen.de

Matthias Mielke
Institute of Microsystem Technology
University of Siegen
matthias.mielke@uni-siegen.de

Rainer Brück
Institute of Microsystem Technology
University of Siegen
rainer.brueck@uni-siegen.de

ABSTRACT

Teaching practical ASIC design, one faces a lot of problems, such as high manufacturing costs, long workflow, and heterogeneous previous knowledge of the students. On one hand, it is difficult to find topics that motivate students and, at the same time, are not too complex. On the other hand, the industry requires students who are trained not only theoretically, but also have practical experience in team work and project management. We regard these problems as a challenge and are going to create a concept of a project-oriented ASIC design course that focuses on teaching hard and soft skills.

In this paper, we describe our concept for a student project work, which leaves to the students a lot of degrees of freedom in the design process and offers the possibility to realize an own idea as integrated circuit.

Categories and Subject Descriptors

K.3.2 [**Computer and Education**]: Computer and Information Science Education - *Computer science education, Curriculum*

General Terms

Management, Design, Experimentation, Human Factors

Keywords

IC Design, Education, Motivation, Project work

1. INTRODUCTION

The understanding of hardware is important, even for students of the computer science. Bouldin reports in [3] that he supports direct contact with hardware in particular to computer science students, so that they overcome their fear of the technical base and understand the specific features of hardware.

Results of the research and own experiences with students from electrical engineering and computer science have shown that very effective course forms are laboratories and comparable project work for undergraduate engineering [6], [11]. In [6] 13 fundamental objectives of engineering instructional laboratories are described. Among these fundamental objectives are hard skills or knowledge-oriented objectives, and soft skills like teamwork.

In the literature, different universities presented laboratories for teaching integrated circuit design. Most of the reported courses have several properties in common:

1. Mostly a bottom-up approach is used. The resulting circuits are of relative low complexity.

2. The concrete design and the path towards realization are guided by detailed instructions.

3. The designs developed by the students were not fabricated due to the high fabrication costs. Thus, they stay at a "theoretical" level.

The first and the second properties are consequences of the complexity and the high effort in time. The third property is a result of the aforementioned high fabrication costs. Besides the numerous university courses without fabrication (e.g. [7], [9], [1]), only few universities are known to the authors, where students have the possibility for a complete chip development ([2], [8], [12]).

All these projects are subject to strict constraints. The task is precisely defined, the tools are fixed, and the design flow is also predefined. Even the time frames for the design steps are given. While these projects provide a good understanding of IC design, they are only partly able to teach soft skills such as teamwork, communication, self-organization, sense of responsibility, time management, project management, and presentation skills due to the strict constraints. Additionally, they do not stimulate the student's creativity.

In the following, the authors will present a concept for a so called *project group* (PG) which provides to the students a lot of freedom in the design process and offers the possibility to implement an own idea as an IC at the same time. On this occasion, objectives were to promote not only subjects of chip design, but also soft skills. The concept was already tested once and currently is in the second round.

This paper is organized in five sections. Chapter two describes the concept of a project group. Chapter three shows the design flow and management of the previous project groups. In chapter four we briefly present the topic and the projects of the last two groups. Finally, conclusions are given in the last chapter.

2. THE CONCEPT

This chapter describes what project group is and how we planned, managed and financed them.

2.1 A Project Group

At the University of Siegen, a project group is a major activity in the course of studies for students of electrical engineering and computer science. Dependent on the field of study of the individual student, the intended effort is between 300 and 900 hours. A project group consists of six to twelve students, dealing with a developmental and scientific task applying technical and scientific methods. Besides the training of the technical and professional skills, the training of soft skills or objectives, such as teamwork, (self-) organization, independent work, creativity, time management, project management, and presentation skills, is a major goal.

2.2 Previous Knowledge of the Students

The previous knowledge of individual students is very different because the participants of a project group come from different courses of studies (electrical engineering and computer science) and have reached a different level in their studies. However, we experienced that the previous knowledge of the computer science and electrical engineering students complemented each other very well. In the past projects, the groups had basic theoretical knowledge about electrical engineering, computer science, microelectronics, high-level design, physical design, PCB design, and semiconductor technology. Nevertheless, this previous knowledge was distributed very unequally among the individual students.

2.3 Main Concept

The concept was developed at the Department of Electrical Engineering and Computer Science at the University of Siegen. To create an industry-oriented, realistic scenario, the PG is treated as an independent design team. The institute acts as the customer for the developed microchip. At the beginning of the project, project group and customer develop an idea for the concrete microchip. Based on that idea, the project group develops the specification, concepts for realization, and the design. The project group is responsible for scheduling, cost and personnel planning, and management of the development process. In addition, the group, represented by a student group leader, has to account their decisions in monthly management reports and discussions with the customer. The time frame for the project is one year.

Two research assistants of the institute are available as contact persons for questions concerning the concept and realization of the chip and the management of the project work.

2.4 Project Timetable

The concept defines little constraints to give the students maximal space for creative ideas, but the following constraints and milestones are important:

1. The first important appointment for the student is the *kick off meeting*. Every student must give a talk at this meeting on a subject relevant for the work. The subjects were predefined by the customer and enclosed the essential elements of a design-flow (e.g.: electronic system level design, high-level design, physical design, PCB design, verification, and test). In addition, one subject is predefined, focusing on organization and documentation of projects. The *kick-off meeting* lasts two days. In the first part, the talks are given, while in the second part the first working steps are planned by the students. To improve the feeling for the group and to give the students the possibility to get to know each other, the first day is usually finished in a pub.

2. The second important date for the project group is the *tape-out*. The date of the tape-out is timed by the foundry. The decision whether at this date the design is released for manufacturing is decided by the customer one week before this date. For this decision, the design and the present work of the PG are analyzed. If the PG does not manage to deliver a design in time and qualified for tape-out, the remaining course of the project changes

strongly. In this case, no ASIC will be fabricated. The PG must validate and finish their design in detail and write the documentation. A test of their design implemented on an FPGA would be possible, as well as detailed simulations of their design at the electrical level. Nevertheless, in both recent projects the PG could deliver a design qualified for *tape-out*. After *tape-out* the group has the task to write the project documentation and to build a test board for the tests of the ICs. The PG has two months of time to test after delivery of the chips produced.

3. The last defined date for the PG is the *project end*. For this date the PG has to finish the documentation and present their work and results in a public presentation.

Beside these fixed key dates, many more dates must be defined in arrangement with the PG (e.g. for the completion of the specification or the monthly reports).

2.5 Financial Conditions

To keep the costs for manufacturing as low as possible, the designs were manufactured as part of an MPW run by EURO-PRACTICE [5]. A 0.35µm technology with four metal-layers from austriamicrosystems *AG* was chosen in the first project. For the second project we chose LFoundry GmbH's 0.15µm low-power CMOS process. The costs for the manufacturing could be financed to a large extent by German tuition fees (dedicated to improve the education).

For the IC design, the PGs have access to tools from the EURO-PRACTICE Cadence portfolio and to Modelsim from Mentor Graphics, because both tool suites are also used in other courses in the department.

For the test of the ICs, a test board has to be developed by the PG. The PGs had access to different FPGA boards, but also the opportunity to develop a new test board. In total, each PG has an amount of maximum 100€ for the construction of a test board.

3. CHIP DESIGN BY A PROJECT GROUP

At the beginning of the project, the design flow was generated based on the selected technology and the available tools. The design flow was developed mainly by the PGs themselves and differs in a lot of details. Hence, the general part of the design flow which was same in both PGs is described hereinafter. In chapter 3.2 we describe how the PGs manage themselves and which problems arise hereby.

3.1 Design Flow

At the beginning of the project, the algorithms were programmed and tested in a high-level programming language (like C++, Delphi, Java, or Matlab). After this proof of concept the behavioral descriptions of the algorithms were implemented in VHDL and simulated. For the simulation Mentor Graphics's Modelsim was used. When the system showed the desired behavior, Cadence's Encounter RTL Compiler was used for the synthesis of the VHDL code. On this occasion, the standard-cell libraries of the technology were integrated. The result was exported to First Encounter, where place and route was executed.

The placed and routed design was imported into the design Framework II (DFII). In DFII, the padring design and final assembly were carried out. Finally, the Design Rule Check (DRC) and the Layout Versus Schematic (LVS) were carried out in DFII. The completed design was tested for design rule violations by

Assura DRC. When the DRC showed no violations, layout and schematic were compared by Assura LVS. After finishing the design, crucial parts were simulated more in detail using electrical simulation. Different transient and DC analyses were performed with Cadence's simulator Spectre. Simulations at the electrical level were only performed for certain aspects of the design.

After manufacturing, the functionality of the chips was tested on a developed board under laboratory conditions.

3.2 Management of the Project Group

Besides the training of the technical and professional skills, the training of social and management skills was a major goal in the planning of the project group.

At the beginning of the project, the students were urged to orientate themselves for the project work on a procedure model. Besides, both present PGs decided on a management model, too. Thus every student was responsible for well-defined parts and areas of the project.

The students were responsible for distributing the work among themselves on their own and had to provide a schedule and a cost evaluation. It was required that the students scored weekly how many hours they invested in the project. It turned out quickly, that these time reports were necessary for the later time management and the allocation of duties. One significant problem was the job management; students from different courses had to invest different time in the PG (between 300h and 900h) and had different foreknowledge, so that not everyone could do any job in the project equally well. Also absence time for examinations and holidays had to be taken into consideration for the time planning.

The PG itself was responsible for the whole management of the project work. For this, the PG had to choose a manager who represented its interests at monthly meetings with the customer, where the PG manager presented the works of the last month. The head of the institute, the research assistants, and the appointed manager (and vice-manager) of the PG took part at these meetings. For these meetings a monthly report was prepared by the PG and submitted to the customer three days before the meeting.

The weekly meeting of all participants took place for the allocation of duties and the project management. The PG manager planned and managed these meetings. A protocol was generated for each meeting. The research assistants took part in these meetings, but remained, however, passive. Hence, the research assistants had a good overview about the topical works and could draw the attention of the PG early to upcoming problems.

4. PROJECTS

The concept of this kind of project group was already tested once in the first PG and a second run is now ongoing. Both projects are briefly presented in the following.

4.1 Automatic Siren Detection

In the first project, a group of seven students developed a system called *Automatic Siren Detection* (ASD) that is able to detect acoustic emergency signals of German ambulance, police, and fire department cars from the ambient noise. The idea to the chip was developed by a student of the group. The ASD-chip can be used as a driver assistance system to generate a warning signal for the driver or to reduce the car radio volume, which results in the earlier recognition of the emergency vehicle. The chip was realized in a 0.35µm technology with four metal layers from austriamicrosystems AG. A photograph of the die is shown in Figure 1.

First tests revealed some flaws in the fabricated devices that influence the recognition negatively. However, functional tests showed that the chip is able to detect emergency signals in the usual ambient noise of a car [10].

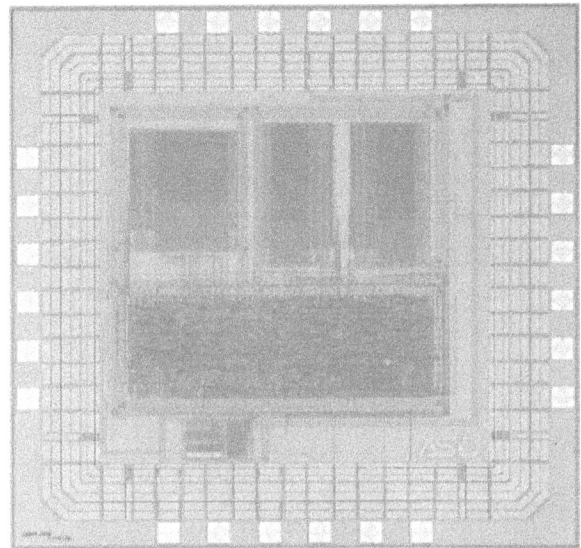

Figure 1. Microphotograph of the microchip

The ASD-project went from April, 2009 to April, 2010. At the end of the projects, the students presented their chip to a professional audience within the scope of the University Booth on the DATE 2010 (see Figure 2). Two of the students started their diploma thesis at austriamicrosystems AG due to their successful work in the PG. They designed a chip for automotive applications, mostly relying on their own experience.

Figure 2. The PG presents its work at the University Booth of the DATE

4.2 Chip with Lowpass filtering Image Pyramid

The aim of the second project is the development of a microchip which processes in real time a continuous picture data stream. The system is called *Chip with Lowpass filtering Image Pyramid* (CLIP). The chip generates a pyramid-like set of images with decreasing resolution with a low-pass filtering and scaling in real-time. The algorithm itself is not new and is described in [4]. This pyramid is often used in the digital image processing and is an important preprocessing step of the incoming data.

Six students work on the CLIP-project. They have handed over their design (see Figure 3) to the Fab at the end of 2010. The chip will be fabricated using the 0.15µm-process LF150 of LFoundry GmbH. At the moment, the test board is developed by the PG. Probably at the end of February the tests will begin.

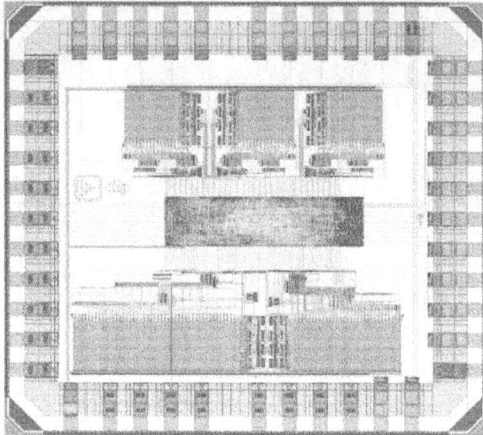

Figure 3. The design of the CLIP project.

5. Conclusion

In this paper we present the concept for a project group (PG) for chip design in education. Participating in the PG, the students learn all steps of a design flow and get important experiences from most aspects of complex chip design. The students have the opportunity to make mistakes and learn from them.

The concept was already tested with large success. It was shown, that the students were prepared very well by their experiences from the PG for their future professional life. Thus two of the students of the PG ASD immediately have accomplished their diploma thesis at austriamicrosystems AG very successfully after the project work. Within their diploma thesis they have developed mainly autonomously a chip in the industrial sphere. Without the experiences gained in the PG this work would not have been possible, according to the students.

The project work improves not only the students' knowledge of chip design, but also their social skills by giving them the responsibilities for organization, planning, and management for the project. The students learned to resolve conflicts originating from teamwork.

Our plan is to start a chip design PG every year. On account of the expected discontinuation of the tuition fees in North Rhine-Westphalia we must plan the financing of the PG anew. Beside the described concept of the PG, we work on a reworking of a

laboratory which accompanies the lecture series on micro system design. In parallel to the lecture, we will also design a small ASIC in this laboratory.

Acknowledgements

Special thanks to Johanna Schirmacher and Michael Wahl for their support.

6. REFERENCES

[1] Andersson, M., Wernehag, J., Axholt, A., and Sjöland, H. 2007. Teaching Top Down Design of Analog/Mixed Signal ICs Through Design Projects. In 37th Annual Frontiers in Education Conference. IEEE Press, Milwaukee, United States, 40–43.

[2] Blaikie, R., Alkaisi, M., Durbin, S., and Cumming, D. 2002. Teaching integrated circuit and semiconductor device design in New Zealand: the University of Canterbury approach. In Proceedings of the First IEEE International Workshop on Electronic Design, Test and Applications, 223–229.

[3] Bouldin, D. 2004. Impacting Education Using FPGAs. In Parallel and Distributed Processing Symposium. IEEE Computer Society, Los Alamitos, Calif, 142–147.

[4] Burt, P. and Adelson, E. 1983. The Laplacian Pyramid as a Compact Image Code. IEEE Trans. Commun 31, 4, 532–540.

[5] EUROPRACTICE. http: // www.europractice.com/.

[6] Feisel, L. D. and Rosa, A. J. 2005. The Role of the Laboratory in Undergraduate Engineering Education. In Journal of Engineering Education 94, 121–130.

[7] Ghazali, A. and Azlee Hamid, F. 2009. Teaching introductory level VLSI Design course to UNITEN undergraduate students. In International Conference on Engineering Education, Kuala Lumpur, Malaysia, 40–44.

[8] Hedberg, H., Rodrigues, J. N., Kristensen, F., Svensson, H., Kamuf, M., and Owall, V. 2005. Teaching digital ASIC design to students with heterogeneous previous knowledge. In Proceedings. IEEE Computer Society, Los Alamitos, Calif, 236–243.

[9] Lyons, E., Ganti, V., Goldman, R., Melikyan, V., and Mahmoodi, H. 2009. Full-custom design project for digital VLSI and IC design courses using Synopsys' generic 90nm CMOS library. In International Conference on Microelectronic Systems Education, San Francisco, CA, USA, 45–48.

[10] Mielke, M., Schäfer, A., and Brück, R. 2010. A Mixed Signal ASIC for Detection of Acoustic Emergency Signals in Road Traffic. In International Journal of Microelectronics and Computer Science 2, Łódź, Poland, 105–111.

[11] Nooshabadi, S. and Garside, J. 2006. Modernization of Teaching in Embedded Systems Design—An International Collaborative Project. IEEE Trans. Educ 49, 2, 254–262.

[12] Payá-Vayá, G., Jambor, T., Septinus, K., Hesselbarth, S., Flatt, H., Freisfeld, M., and Pirsch, P. 2007. Chipdesign - from theory to real world. In Proceedings of the 2007 workshop on Computer architecture education. ACM, San Diego, CA.

Preparing Students for Future Architectures with an Exploration of Multi- and Many-Core Performance

Daniel J. Ernst
Department of Computer Science
University of Wisconsin – Eau Claire
Eau Claire, WI 54702-4004

ernstdj@uwec.edu

ABSTRACT

The recent progression of modern computer architectures from serial to multi-core to many-core has raised numerous questions about the placement of parallel computing topics in undergraduate computer science curricula. While several papers have explored how programming and algorithms courses might introduce parallel programming topics, there has been very little discussion of the changes needed in computer organization and architecture coursework to help students understand key issues about the behavior of these platforms.

To increase the relevance of these courses and to tackle more modern architectural issues, we propose extending the performance coverage of a traditional computer organization course to include an exploration of the quantitative characterization of a program's performance on a variety of architectural platforms, including modern GPU hardware.

In this paper, we outline the changes made to the Computer Organization and Design course at University of Wisconsin – Eau Claire. These modifications included a 3 week unit on the basics of parallel and GPU architectures, along with a tiered project on program optimization.

Categories and Subject Descriptors

K.3.2 [**Computers and Education**]: Computer and Information Science Education – *Curriculum*

General Terms: Design, Experimentation

Keywords: computer organization, GPGPU, curriculum design

1. INTRODUCTION

Although Moore's Law continues to provide a quickly growing number of transistors, processor manufacturers are now focusing their use on increasing the core count on modern CPUs, instead of manufacturing single-core chips with faster clocks. Traditional sequential applications will not currently take advantage of these new hardware capabilities, and will therefore not benefit from any future hardware developments.

In recent years, educators have begun to wrestle with the challenge of training students for a world where parallelism is ubiquitous. [2, 9] The discussion has been spirited, creative, and has largely focused on the challenges programmers face with the current state of parallel algorithms and programming techniques.

While current multicore architectures have quickly brought attention to parallelism issues, our current transition to many-core architectures is bringing about another change that isn't getting as much attention. Global shared-memory architectures, which modern multi-cores use to great effectiveness, do not perform well as the number of cores increases much past the teens. As a result, current [1][6] (and future [5]) many-core processors will have more complicated memory hierarchies with an increasing number of levels of software managed memories. On these types of platforms, keeping working set data arranged correctly carries an enormous amount of weight in getting good performance. It can be generally said that, on future processors, *computation* will be essentially free, while the amount a program needs to *move data* will likely determine most of that program's runtime. This is a massive shift in how we reason about the performance of programs.

Ironically, there has been very little discussion of how computer organization and architecture courses should present either of these platform changes to students. Previous coverage of parallel architectures in these courses has been limited largely to the basic classification of systems (MIMD vs. SIMD and/or shared vs. distributed memory) with very little coverage of the trade-offs involved. Further, current and upcoming many-core architectures do not fit into these classifications very easily.

As complex (and uncertain) as the technological road map may be, though, it is a certainty that unless students and, consequently, the academic curriculum begin to address the changes now, there will be a prohibitive barrier to adaptation once a new steady state is reached. Due to the large flux in the development of these systems (and their software ecosystems), we cannot simply teach students a single tool, concept, architecture, or language since it is very likely any particular path will undergo rapid shifts. We believe that the interim and long term solution, therefore, revolves around the conveying to students an understanding of the relationship between a program and its hardware resources, which we broadly classify as *application characterization*. This concept is discussed further in Section 2.

Pedagogically, to grant students meaningful insights into the consequences of programming decisions in this space, two issues need to be addressed:

- They must see significant changes in performance to motivate time spent on optimization, and

- They must see these changes on realistic pieces of code, instead of simple short assembly examples.

With the exception of a few very specific caching tricks, traditional CPUs do not fulfill this role very well. In fact, one of the reasons that programming for performance has fallen out of pedagogical (and industrial) favor is because, in the era of massive microprocessor performance gains, small benefits from optimization were clearly not worth the time spent.

As will be discussed in Section 3, GPGPU programming (in our case, using nVidia's CUDA) fulfills both requirements extremely well. The performance difference between baseline CUDA code and optimized CUDA applications is often over an order of magnitude, usually with only a small amount of code modification.

Section 4 will present a course module designed for a computer organization class, but which could be adapted to other systems classes. The module content includes an exploration of the basic tradeoffs involved in parallel architectures from shared-memory multicores to massively parallel GPUs. The module also includes a project that takes students through the implementation of a basic particle simulation code on several architectures, both serial and parallel. Section 4 also includes some qualitative observations by both instructor and students from during and after the project.

2. APPLICATION CHARACTERIZATION

What is the role of a computer organization class? This can change drastically based on the department(s) that use it. Universities with a Computer Engineering department and major often focus more on the implementation of microarchitectural features such as pipelining and often require digital logic as a prerequisite [8]. The same course, taught in the context of an independent Computer Science department, often spends much less time on implementation details, but adds in more treatment of assembly programming issues and the operating systems interface [7]. One topic that both approaches typically address is basic performance evaluation, including the concept of speedup, the components of execution time, and Amdahl's Law. These concepts are typically taught in the context of microarchitectural changes in the datapath [8]. At the University of Wisconsin – Eau Claire, our Computer Science department has traditionally taken a "middle of the road" approach, as a vast majority of our students are future software developers, but with a very small minority pursuing a special Computer Engineering "emphasis" built to serve local industry.

In either case, the perspective of the performance coverage in these courses is typically "hardware-up", meaning that techniques are used to evaluate how changes in hardware affect the performance of a given program. While this perspective is certainly needed in the CPU design process to motivate and justify changes, it loses relevance very quickly in parallel environments and architectures with explicit memory management. In these cases, it isn't possible to easily evaluate effects on program performance as the program must change to take advantage of the hardware.

The approach we have taken at University of Wisconsin – Eau Claire is to additionally work with a "software-down" perspective. This process, which we call *application characterization*, focuses on the exploration of an application's demands on parallelism, memory, and/or energy consumption with respect to a class of computer architectures. Broadly speaking, this process involves the identification of parallelism within an application, the general access patterns of its data, and the trade-offs and overheads involved in mapping the application to different types of architectures.

While this perspective can initially seem as if programming techniques are invading hardware courses, the lessons learned largely emphasize the need to know the parameters of various computer organizations. Using just a few examples, the concept that programming choices can have significant performance ramifications due to a hardware configuration can be reinforced very strongly.

3. MAKING PROGRAMMING CHOICES COUNT WITH CUDA

3.1 Application Characterization on CPUs

In the past, exploring program performance behavior was largely limited to a few different code optimizations with fairly low impacts, such as loop unrolling, pre-fetching, and cache blocking/tiling. On traditional CPUs, these techniques typically increase performance by no more than 40-50%, and often far less.

To properly motivate time spent on program changes, programmers need to see that any optimizations made had a significant impact on program behavior. In the software development industry, the choice of how much to optimize is a cost-benefit analysis. In an era of quickly increasing raw hardware performance, spending developer money on these types of optimizations very rarely was deemed worthwhile.

Modern multi-core CPUs provide a more interesting platform for optimization. If the application has easily exploitable parallelism, making changes to use multiple cores can show some very compelling speedups.

3.2 Application Characterization on GPUs

Historically, graphics processor units (GPUs) have been very specialized hardware, allowing only very specific operations having to do with known graphics techniques. This allowed them to optimize quite heavily for computational throughput. In recent years, GPUs have been getting more flexible (and programmable) as graphics techniques have evolved. Around 10 years ago, researchers began exploring the use of GPUs for accelerating throughput-oriented general purpose applications. While programming their computations using OpenGL was certainly difficult, the results these studies obtained were quite striking.[10]

In 2007, nVidia released the first CUDA (Compute Unified Device Architecture) SDK, a tool chain for general purpose programming on their devices. Programming these devices is done through simple extensions to the C language. Additionally, wrappers now exist for using CUDA in many other popular languages, such as Java and Python.

The organization of modern GPUs provides an excellent glimpse at how the challenges of coordinating many cores can be tackled. As can been seen with the CUDA architecture in Figure 1, these chips include a large number of loosely associated groups of cores, along with a small centralized control area. When invoking a GPU computational kernel, a massive collection of threads, each of which does a small portion of an application's work, is sent to this dispatch element, which coarsely distributes these threads on a demand basis to the computational elements.

All of the GPU cores have access to the global GPU DRAM, but there are essentially no synchronization primitives. In terms of latency, accessing this DRAM is expensive, costing roughly 200 clock cycles. CPUs address this problem by using hardware managed caches to keep the most frequently used data in much faster SRAMs.

Most GPU architectures do not use this approach. Instead, each small group of CUDA cores (called a Streaming Multiprocessor, or SM) has its own software-managed SRAM (labeled "shared mem" in Figure 1). This SRAM can be used much like a cache; however moving data in and out of this space must usually be done *explicitly* – meaning that the programmer must perform the copy in their code. For applications with any data re-use, this copy pays large dividends, as the latency of these SRAMs is essentially only one clock cycle.

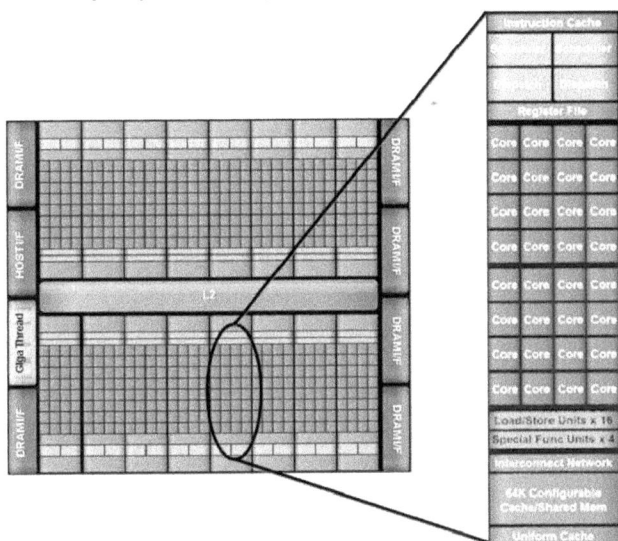

Figure 1. Block diagram of nVidia's "Fermi" GPU Architecture. One "Streaming Multiprocessor (SM) is highlighted. Each SM has its own fast Shared Memory SRAMs, which is only accessible by its local threads.

In CUDA training materials, a commonly used example [3] of an application using these memories is matrix-matrix multiplication. While a basic matrix multiplication kernel (like the one shown in Figure 2) performs quite well on a GPU when compared to a basic CPU implementation, it can be shown with some simple back-of-the-envelope math that the application is being slowed down significantly by the constant access requests to the global DRAM. By modifying the code to make a blocked move of data to shared memory, the number of global address requests is reduced by a factor of 16, allowing for much higher performance. In Figure 3, I show a run of a program that performs a 2048 x 2048 matrix-matrix multiplication 3 different ways: on the CPU, with the basic GPU version shown in Figure 2, and with the fully optimized cuBLAS library (which uses the SRAM shared memories). The performance differences are extremely large.

Modern GPU architectures, therefore, contain all of the essential elements we require for the illustration of application characterization; they are highly parallel, they have a software-managed memory hierarchy, and they can show very significant performance differences based on an application's mapping to the architecture. They also have the added bonus of using one of the hardware (and software) models that will likely see significant use as throughput-oriented many-core architectures become more common.

4. CURRICULAR MODULE

The material discussed here is designed to be presented in a roughly 3 week (9 class hour) time frame of a class on computer organization. Based on experience, courses in our department tend to have somewhat aggressive schedules compared to other institutions, so this material could easily be stretched to accommodate a slower pace. In our course, this material was placed at the end of the semester, and was directly preceded by fairly deep coverage of cache structures and policies. While there are places in the presented material where that content is used (specifically, for a blocking optimization step in the project), the module can still be taught, with small modifications, without having covered it. Students will need, however, to have a basic understanding of the reasons for, and organization of, a standard memory hierarchy.

To make room for this module, we removed one week of old parallel architecture coverage, roughly one week of pipelining implementation details, a pipelining simulator project, and a small amount of digital logic material that was deemed to be a duplication of material covered in our discrete mathematics course. As the material in organization and architecture courses at different universities can vary widely, this information is only provided as an example of our thought processes and is not meant to be a strict recommendation.

Figure 2. A general matrix-matrix multiplication kernel in CUDA C. This *kernel* is invoked once for each spawned thread in a CUDA *grid*. In this implementation, each thread will do the computations for one element of the output matrix. (Code from [3])

```
__global__ void MMKernel(float *Md, float *Nd, float *Pd, int Width) {
    int Row = blockIdx.y*BLOCK_SIZE + threadIdx.y;  // calculate the row and column
    int Col = blockIdx.x*BLOCK_SIZE + threadIdx.x;  // based on thread indexes
    float Pvalue = 0;
    // each thread computes one element of the result matrix
    for (int k = 0; k < Width; k++)
        Pvalue += Md[Row*Width+k] * Nd[k*Width+Col];
    Pd[Row*Width + Col] = Pvalue;
}
```

```
-bash-3.2$ ./mmult -n 2048
CPU time: 394.849
threadDim: 16  blockDim: 128
naive kernel time: 0.772124
cublas time: 0.0487702
```

Figure 3. A runtime comparison of three different implementations of matrix-matrix multiplication.

4.1 Material Covered

In the first week of the module, students are given a few motivating examples of application optimization, along with a basic introduction to the concept of parallelism. Because our class had just finished coverage of caching, the first example we used to show how programs are affected by hardware was the poorly designed nested for loop listed in Figure 4. In class, we walked through the memory access pattern of the code and determined that it missed the cache 100% of the time. By simply reversing the order of the i and j loops, the code runs more than 10x faster, depending on the architecture. To further emphasize the topic, a basic one-dimensional cache blocking optimization was also shown. To introduce the concept of parallelism, students were presented with examples of instruction-level, data-level, and thread-level parallelism [8].

The second week of the module introduced students to a variety of parallel architectures, with an emphasis on the cost differences for certain operations and access patterns on each. These concepts were initially presented using the "Jigsaw Puzzle Analogy" [4], which demonstrates the basics of parallelism, contrasts shared memory parallelism with distributed parallelism, depicts parallel overhead (specifically contention and communication costs), and illustrates simple load balancing. The week concludes with a very basic coverage of OpenMP, which, given a properly structured environment, makes basic parallelization possible in very few lines of code. (The emphasis was not on teaching them OpenMP deeply, but on using it as a tool to explore application performance for a varying number of threads.)

The last four class periods (end of week 2 and all of week 3) of the module is devoted to covering CUDA as an example of GPU programming. The terminology involved in GPU programming can get confusing quickly (*i.e.* grid, block, thread, warp, etc.), but the actual code is typically quite concise and readable. An effort was made to simplify the model parameters, when possible, and to use a lot of code examples. Showing simple conversions of CPU loops into GPU grids is a straightforward way of illustrating the fundamental idea behind the approach.

There are many optimization techniques for CUDA, but the simplest and most important is to make use of the fast block-shared SRAMS. For this module, the instructor ran the matrix-matrix multiplication program (from Section 3) to show the performance benefits of using the user-controlled fast memories. Instead of showing them code from that program, however, a simple one-dimensional example was used to illustrate the necessary changes, which amount to roughly 4-5 lines of code.

```
float m[MSIZE][MSIZE];
…
for(j=0;j<MSIZE;j++)
    for(i=0;i<MSIZE;i++)
        m[i][j] = 2*m[i][j];
```

Figure 4. Array traversal with bad cache performance. Because the array is laid out in row-major order, this traversal does not make use of cache-provided spatial locality, giving it a 0% hit rate. Simply re-ordering the loops results in a more than 10x speedup.

4.2 Characterization Project

Alongside this module's classroom material, a project was assigned that asks students to analyze the behavior of an application, and then progressively optimize it using the technologies and techniques described in class. The final deliverables for the project, other than code, are a spreadsheet containing timing measurements and analysis of speedups and a document containing answers to a few reflection questions.

We offered computational resources to the students in the form of a small compute cluster, where one node had a Tesla C2050 GPU card. At other institutions, it may also be feasible for students to use campus lab computers, provided they had multicore processors and GPUs with CUDA (or OpenCL) compute capability.

4.2.1 The Problem

The code that students are given is a simplistic 2-D particle simulation application. This program uses an algorithm that can be applied to a number of science simulations, including the motion of stars and galaxies, fluids, or molecules. The algorithm, at its core, calculates an interaction force between each pair of particles at each time step. Because it involves calculations between all pairs, it is a $O(n^2)$ approach – meaning that using it on a large number of particles requires either a different algorithm, or a lot of compute horsepower. The code has an option to dump particle locations to a file. Students can use a provided visualization program to easily check their output for correctness.

Students were first asked to run a parameter sweep of the program observing (and graphing) its runtime versus the number of particles and number of time steps, with a bounding time limit of 10 minutes per run. This step was used both as a chance to work through any platform or compiling issues and also as a way to highlight which portion of the algorithm the students should be optimizing in the next steps.

4.2.2 CPU Optimizations

The first change students are asked to make is a simple blocking optimization to improve cache performance. The code change amounts to about 3 lines of modification, and mimics what is demonstrated in class. In their spreadsheet, they are asked to graph run time against block size to choose an optimal parameter, and then to calculate the speedup versus the baseline code.

The second change students implement is to use OpenMP to spread the particle force calculations out across multiple CPU cores. Done correctly, this optimization consists of only one line of code. In their spreadsheet, they are asked to graph program runtime versus the number of active threads and then to calculate the speedup versus the baseline code.

4.2.3 GPU Implementation and Optimization

The next step in the project is for students to convert the force calculations in the code to run on a CUDA-capable GPU. The translation to a simple GPU kernel is quite straightforward – once students write the function wrapper, all that is required is to remove the outer loop of the calculation and instead spawn that many threads. This is the same approach demonstrated by the examples in class.

When their GPU implementation is complete, students are asked to graph program runtime versus the number of threads per block in their CUDA grid, and then graph the speedup over the baseline code versus the number of particles simulated.

Finally, students are asked to change their GPU solutions to use fast shared SRAMs. The coding modifications somewhat mirror the earlier blocking optimization with an additional explicit copy to fast shared SRAM. Students are asked to graph the speedup over the baseline GPU code versus the number of particles simulated. The speedup for this step, if done correctly, is usually between 10-30x, depending on the card.

At this point, students have taken the code and modified its layout to map onto several different hardware configurations. The project follows the content in the module directly, so students are advised to work on the project progressively as the content is covered. (Checkpoints could be enforced if desired)

4.3 Experiences and Feedback

This module and project were first used at the end of the 2010 Fall Semester. Due to some unusual circumstances that resulted in a shorter semester than normal, the amount of time available for this module was just over two weeks instead of the desired three. As a result, there were a couple of modifications made to the project to compensate. Specifically, the students were given the baseline GPU code, in addition to the baseline CPU code, so that they could still run and characterize on that hardware, while focusing their efforts on the optimization steps.

The classroom lectures and activities were well received. Based on their feedback, students were particularly engaged for at least one of two reasons:

- They could see real interactions between the code they may be writing in their careers and the hardware they would be running on.
- They enjoyed learning about new and "up-to-date" technologies, like multi-cores and GPGPU programming.

The project work students turned in reflected their enthusiasm, as very few of them failed to complete the required optimizations. There were a few cases where optimized code was not validated correctly and so speedups were erroneously reported for a broken program. Due to this, further emphasis will be made on validating their results for the next offering of the module.

In their reflection questions, students seemed to "get" the lesson about application characterization – even though I hadn't discussed the concept directly in any depth. As an example, one student stated:

"I have learned that you can get a HUGE speed up by laying code out on different processors. [...] By comparing CPU and GPU baselines, it is obvious what kind of an advantage GPU's have, and I can understand this is why the future of supercomputing is headed in this direction. The most surprising thing was how little code was required to create these vast improvements in performance. I definitely believe that programmers should attempt the coding/performance boost tradeoff whenever the situation could benefit from it."

5. CONCLUSIONS

The goal of our curriculum changes is to provide our students with the skills they will need to succeed in their professional careers. By giving them a clear understanding of the performance interactions between their programs and hardware, we enable them to learn about and use the future platforms that they will undoubtedly be exposed to, as well as make intelligent choices in their programs and their hardware purchases. Both multi-core and GPU/throughput architectures will continue to grow and develop. The integration of these topics into a standard computer organization course updates them to cover modern systems and hardware techniques, but also updates the skills taught to be more relevant for our students' careers.

6. REFERENCES

[1] Anand Lal Shimpi, "Intel's Sandy Bridge Architecture Exposed," *Anandtech*, Sept. 2010. [Online] Available: http://www.anandtech.com/show/3922/intels-sandy-bridge-architecture-exposed

[2] Daniel J. Ernst and Daniel E. Stevenson. "Concurrent CS: Preparing Students for a Multicore World". Appears in *the 13th Annual Conference on Innovation and Technology in Computer Science* (ITiCSE '08), 2008.

[3] David Kirk and Wen-mei W. Hwu, *Programming Massively Parallel Processors*, Morgan Kaufmann, 2010.

[4] H. Neeman, L. Lee, J. Mullen, G. Newman, 2006: "Analogies for Teaching Parallel Computing to Inexperienced Programmers." *inroads: SIGCSE Bulletin*, 38 (4), 64-67D.

[5] "NVIDIA Announces 'Project Denver' to Build Custom CPU Cores Based on ARM Architecture, Targeting Personal Computers to Supercomputers", NVIDIA press release.

[6] NVIDIA Corporation, "NVIDIA CUDA: Compute unified device architecture," NVidia CUDA Documentation, June 2008.[Online].Available: http://developer.download.nvidia.com/compute/cuda/2_0/docs/NVIDIA_CUDA_Programming_Guide_2.0.pdf

[7] Yale Patt and Sanjay Patel, *Introduction to Computing Systems: From Bits and Gates to C and Beyond*, 2/e, McGraw-Hill, 2004.

[8] David A Patterson and John L Hennessy, *Computer Organization and Design: The Hardware/Software Interface*, 4th Ed., Morgan Kaufmann, 2008.

[9] Suzanne Rivoire, "A Breadth-First Course in Multicore and Manycore Programming," Proceedings of *the 41st ACM Technical Symposium on Computer Science Education* (SIGCSE '10), Milwaukee, WI, March 2010.

[10] Chris J. Thompson, Sangyun Hahn, and Mark Oskin. "Using Modern Graphics Architectures for General-Purpose Computing: A Framework and Analysis," *International Symposium on Microarchitecture* (MICRO), Turkey, Nov. 2002.

A Study in Engaging Female Students in Computer Science Using Role Models

Jonathan Black
Queen Mary University of London
Mile End Road,
London. E1 4NS
+44 20 7882 7559
jonathanb@
eecs.qmul.ac.uk

Paul Curzon
Queen Mary University of London
Mile End Road,
London. E1 4NS
+44 20 7882 5212
pc@eecs.qmul.ac.uk

Chrystie Myketiak
Queen Mary University of London
Mile End Road,
London. E1 4NS
+44 20 7882 7559
chrystie@
eecs.qmul.ac.uk

Peter W. McOwan
Queen Mary University of London
Mile End Road,
London. E1 4NS
+44 20 7882 5224
pmco@
eecs.qmul.ac.uk

ABSTRACT

An effective approach to engaging young women to take computing in higher education is to provide examples of successful female computer scientists. Can a print publication that combines core computing concepts with inspiring stories of women in the field be effective? In this paper, we describe a campaign that distributed a 60-page booklet on women in computing to UK secondary schools. We analyse the initial response from teachers, and draw some general conclusions from the project. Teachers expressed strong enthusiasm for the booklet, and also report the desire for recruitment and retention of girls in their computing programmes. They had confidence in the potential for this booklet to inspire young women to take computing.

Categories and Subject Descriptors

K.3.2 [Computers and Education]: Computer and Information Science Education – Computer Science Education

General Terms

Human Factors.

Keywords

Public engagement, outreach, recruitment, gender issues, K-12, teachers, girls, representation, diversity, cs4fn.

1. INTRODUCTION

The often forgotten story of women in computing is rich and diverse, and reaches back to the very beginning of the field itself. It is also, unfortunately, a story in which women have mostly been a minority within the field. In recent years more attention has been drawn to the imbalance between the genders in computing, and many excellent initiatives are attempting to change this imbalance

[6,9,12]. One commonly used strategy is to call attention to successful women in computing, to act as role models for female students.

In this paper, we describe our recent contribution to these efforts – a 60-page 'fun' booklet, published in May 2010, aimed at secondary school students (ages 14-18). The booklet tells the stories of contributions made by women in computing, and gives some examples of the research accomplishments made by contemporary women who have devoted their careers to computing. We look quantitatively and qualitatively at the initial responses from UK teachers to this initiative. In our future work, we will examine additional feedback from both students and teachers.

2. BACKGROUND ON CS4FN

Our booklet was part of a larger campaign, Computer Science For Fun (cs4fn) [3]. The cs4fn project is a widening participation scheme aimed at young people (10+), which gives them a taste of current research and deep principles in computing, presented in a style that is engaging and straightforward. It began in 2005 at Queen Mary, University of London. A 2006 review by the UK's Engineering and Physical Sciences Research Council (EPSRC) named cs4fn an example of good practice. In 2008 the EPSRC awarded cs4fn major funding enabling the project to expand on an assured financial footing, and in the same year Google added its financial support as part of its CS4HS programme for Europe, the Middle East and Africa. In 2011, cs4fn has a global audience and university partners across the UK, Europe and North America.

The cornerstone of the cs4fn campaign is a twice-yearly 20-page magazine, aimed primarily at secondary school students. It is distributed, free of charge, to ICT teachers at UK secondary schools, and is available for anyone in the world to subscribe, also for free, via a form on our website. The stories in the magazine are usually taken from specific research projects, but sometimes the subject is a core topic of computing (e.g. binary numbers, NP-completeness) or a story drawn from the history of computing. In each case, we find an engaging real-life basis for the story and explain the computing in those terms. We show that computing can be a vehicle for accomplishing amazing things and solving interesting problems in whatever field excites the reader (e.g. robotics, mathematics, art, language, biology, sport). We have documented the success of this general approach elsewhere [3,4,5].

As part of our EPSRC funding, we produce annual compendiums of stories from the cs4fn magazine. The first such edition simply collected the first three issues of cs4fn, but for the second edition we believed that it would be worthwhile to collect stories from the entire history of cs4fn in which research by women was featured, as well as writing new content by and about women in computing. It is the early evaluation of this initiative on which we report here.

3. CONTEXT AND RELATED WORK

3.1 Female engagement with computing

For more than two decades, computer science has been battling the decline of female student interest and self-confidence in computing, especially as girls get older [18]. Unfortunately for computer science enrolment figures, this decline coincides with the age when students begin to make career decisions. As a consequence, female enrolment in CS degree courses is declining in many countries [13], with no change to the trend in sight [1].

The pervasive stereotype is that computing as a domain is somehow essentially male. This has measurable effects on young women's confidence in computing: Moorman and Johnson showed that female students rated their abilities less highly than their male counterparts, despite achieving higher average marks [14]. Meanwhile, Fisher and Margolis cite a drop in confidence as a precursor to declining interest [8]. Therefore, employing strategies to maintain and enhance female students' initial confidence may be a useful way of retaining their interest.

3.2 How role models can help

One common approach to raising female confidence in computer science is by increasing the visibility of female role models in the field [10]. Calling attention to successful females in computing shows young women that the unwelcoming stereotype is wrong and can be subverted. In addition, it shows girls that women are present and making significant contributions to the field. This, in turn, may inspire girls themselves. Many initiatives that aim to inspire girls do so by having students meet real computer scientists, like Microsoft's Digigirlz [6], Carnegie Mellon's Women@SCS Roadshows [9] and The Digital Divas programme in Victoria, Australia [12]. Other programmes do not rely on the role models actually being present – using video for example [16,17] – this experience, though more remote, is more easily scaled and disseminated. Still additional research shows that changing objects in a computer science classroom or laboratory from being stereotypically computer science-like (i.e., interpreted as male; such as Star Trek posters and video games) to more neutral items (e.g., nature posters) raised female students' interest in computer science to levels comparable to that of male students [2]. A project that places its emphasis on women's contributions to computing, and could be distributed relatively easily and cheaply, should be a useful contribution to help inspire female students who might be feeling the effects of the negative stereotypes of women in computing.

3.3 A cs4fn approach to inspiring students

We postulated that a booklet in the cs4fn style about women in computing would fit the above criteria. We write the cs4fn magazine in such a way that researchers and their findings are given prominence and made relevant to students' everyday life contexts, thereby providing the potential for the reader to cast the researchers as role models. Comments from teachers tell us that they appreciate the regular cs4fn magazine as an effective tool for consistently inspiring their students. For example, one American teacher requested copies of a different issue of cs4fn magazine for her class, framing her request in terms of inspiration: "My goal is to give them skills and inspire them to think deeper, to explore and create."

4. THE BOOKLET

4.1 Look and feel

The finished booklet itself comprises sixty glossy, full-colour A4 pages with a paperback-style binding. The design and layout are magazine-style with bold colours and lots of images, designed by the publications department at our university. We publish all our materials this way; readers get a rich, good-quality physical impression from the aesthetic experience of the booklet as well as from the text. In short, we aim to ensure the materials will be as attractive and fun to read as a mainstream publication for young adults.

4.2 Content

4.2.1 Stories about current female researchers

The great majority of the 44 articles in the book are about original research done by women. Some of these examples are current research, for example Anje-Margriet Neutel's work on biosphere complexity for the British Antarctic Survey, and others are on work that has become a cornerstone of CS, such as Fran Allen's development of compilers. In all of the articles on research, the science and its context is in the foreground – reading the two articles mentioned will teach a student why understanding the complex rules that govern an ecosystem can help the organisms in it survive, and how an optimising compiler helps a program run faster than the unoptimized code. However, these stories also tell the story of the scientist doing the work. In the case of the article on Allen's work, the story mentions how she won the Turing Prize, showing how women have risen to the top of the computing profession. In the story on Neutel, we explain that her background is in linguistics rather than ecology, which introduces readers to the interdisciplinary nature of CS, and how it rewards rather than hinders diverse interests in its practitioners.

4.2.2 Stories about history and gender

Other articles are about historical women in computing, like Ada Lovelace and Florence Nightingale, showing that women were pioneers in computing and the visualisation of data. Other article topics deal with gender issues more explicitly: for example, about women as portrayed in films about technology, female entrepreneurs in technology, organisations for female computer scientists and what we call "a gendered timeline of technology": a timeline that runs through the booklet, providing mini-histories of technology with a focus on gender issues.

4.2.3 Stories about students

It was important for us to tell the stories of aspiring female computer scientists too; the steps on the ladder to international success and groundbreaking work must be made explicit. There are numerous stories about students in the booklet, such as a secondary school student who won a computer animation competition with a short film about the Iberian lynx. We also talk about student groups like Women@SCS at Carnegie Mellon University, who have set up a mentoring and support network for students and graduates, and the Nerd Girls, a group based at Tufts University who created alternative energy systems for an island off the east coast of the USA. These stories show readers that it is possible to create innovative work in CS at any age.

4.2.4 Stories by women

In this special issue of cs4fn we also invited female researchers to write articles about their own work and experience. Whereas most of the articles in the booklet are unsigned and written in the third person (following the style for cs4fn articles in general), these particular articles are written in the first person and attributed to their authors. In this way we (as three men and one woman producing the booklet) seek to make sure that the 'voices' in it are either female or gender-neutral.

In summary, we hoped that anyone reading the booklet would find inspiration and encouragement inside. It was also essential that teachers immediately see the potential for inspiring students, as they choose how to use and distribute the booklet within their schools.

5. PRINTING AND DISTRIBUTION

In order to achieve the widest possible readership for the booklet, we printed 15,000 copies and sent them by post to both our regular UK teacher subscribers and unsolicited to ICT teachers and librarians in UK secondary schools. Our first round of distribution was an unsolicited mailing to UK secondary schools. Each school on our list received two separate copies, one addressed to the subject leader for ICT (as computing classes are known in the UK) and another to the library/LRC manager. In our second round of distribution, we sent copies to the teachers in the UK who have subscribed to the cs4fn magazine via our website, for themselves and/or to distribute to their classes. We allocated roughly 20% of our total printing to send to teachers who requested more, and for our own use as giveaways when visiting schools and festivals during our normal outreach activities.

We also distribute the booklet online. A PDF version of the booklet is available for free on our website at http://www.cs4fn.org/annual/cs4fnannual2.pdf. In this paper we focus exclusively on the response to the printed booklet, but the PDF version has proven popular: from April 2010 to January 2011 it had been downloaded 9420 times.

6. THE RESPONSE

6.1 Requests for more copies

The first responses to the unsolicited mailing came about four days after the mailing began. Almost all the responses to the mailing came within five working days of each other, and within nine working days of the mailing.

In total we received 74 requests for extra copies from teachers, amounting to 1838 copies. The mean number of copies requested was around 24 copies, and the mode of the requests was 30 – larger than the average secondary class in England and Wales [10]. Comparing data from the previous three mailings of the standard cs4fn magazine, sent to a comparable number of teachers, the women's edition garnered roughly three times the response.

Of the 74 requests, 72 were sent to teachers in the UK, four copies were sent to Scotland, two to Wales and one copy to Northern Ireland. Five requests for the magazine were sent to the teachers'

individual homes. We can break down details of the 69 schools remaining. Of these schools, 50 were secondary/6th form schools (meaning students attend them from the ages of 11-18). Eight were 6th form only (education from 16-18), seven were secondary only (from 11-16), one school was primary/secondary (from 5-16) and three offered education for all age groups from 5-18. There were 62 state schools and seven were independent. Mixed gender schools accounted for 59 schools, while eight were girls' schools, one was a girls' school with a mixed 6th form, and one was a boys' school with a mixed 6th form.

6.2 Teacher comments

We also provided a space on the web subscription form for teachers to write comments about why they were ordering extra copies. Of the 74 requests for additional copies of the magazine, 66 teachers left comments. In future work we will conduct a more detailed analysis of the responses from teachers. Here we present a preliminary analysis of themes that emerged from the requests we received.

6.2.1 Comments about the booklet

The comments were overwhelmingly positive about the booklet itself. Teachers reported not only that they found the booklet interesting and informative, but also appreciated the fact that the stories spanned different subjects within computing and across the arts & sciences. A few specifically appreciated a computing book that emphasised fun. One thought that having the magazine in her library might make the library 'cool'.

Some teachers made comments that suggested our belief about the importance of the physical look and feel are substantiated. For example, a teacher wrote: "I showed it to some of my pupils who enjoyed its content and loved the layout of the topics." Another praised the format: "For some reason, glossy mags attract our students much more that a PDF – sorry about the trees."

6.2.2 Comments about inspiring girls in computing

Teachers' comments focused on two distinct but associated themes relating to inspiring their female students. For some, the main attraction of the magazine is simply the 'wow factor', which they hope excites girls in a positive way. One teacher mentioned the effect on their students: "Girls were enthralled by the copy [of the booklet] that you kindly sent us." Another wanted "as many multiple copies as it is possible to receive to inspire our students."

Other teachers linked the idea of inspiring students to gender imbalance. Teachers reported difficulty in inspiring girls to take ICT/computing classes, and saw the magazine as a significant resource in motivating them. Some teachers had watched an almost equal balance between genders in younger years become more disparate in upper years. As one teacher states: "This is just the motivation we need to promote Computing Science to girls in school. In middle school the divide is even but in upper school the tendency is for boys to continue studying and the girls to drop out of this field". Some teachers said that their female students viewed computing as a subject more suited to males, and they thought that the magazine would help change that perception. For example one wrote: "Girls in our school view ICT as a 'boys' subject' therefore it would be great to have some positive material to promote the subjects for girls."

7. DISCUSSION

Our focus in this paper has been on teacher responses to the booklet for a number of important reasons. Teachers will act as the gatekeepers for any outreach project that incorporates school students. Securing their enthusiasm is therefore essential to success. The interest we have received from teachers over an extended period, as well as their positive comments, demonstrates that they believe the cs4fn model for inspiring and encouraging students is right for the job. It is important that teachers have been so enthusiastic, and believe along with us that the booklet will engage young women with computer science.

7.1.1 Which teachers responded?

The requests for copies were divided between state (free-to-student) schools and independent (fee-paying) schools in a way that reflected current schooling provision in the UK: the percentage of requests from independent schools (11.3%) was close to the actual percentage of independent schools in England (9.1% in 2007) [7]. This suggests that female engagement with computing is seen as an important issue throughout the UK educational sector, and that our magazine fits the requirements of both state and independent teachers. In terms of widening participation, this also means that our booklets are getting into the hands of traditionally harder-to-reach audiences in state-funded schools. Most of the teacher requests came from mixed-gender schools, which means boys will be exposed to the booklet as well – especially those in schools that have ordered copies for all their computing students. Sosik and Goldshalk assert that males may derive more benefit from cross-gender role models than females [15]; therefore there may be a bonus role model benefit to males as well, even though they are not the primary audience for the booklet.

7.1.2 Teacher comments

Teachers commented on the design and layout of the magazine, finding it eye-catching and exciting. In addition to comments about the aesthetics of the magazine, teachers were overwhelmingly positive about the content. They reported that the booklet would be flexible enough to benefit current female computing students, to motivate and retain them, and also to attract new female students to take a subject that they may have felt excluded from before.

Teacher responses also indicate that they share our desire for girls to be better represented in computing, as indicated by their positive response to a booklet that puts the issue right on the cover, supported by the tendency for comments to mention the difficulty in recruiting girls to computing. We seem to have tapped into a shared priority in computing education. The fact that the response to a booklet featuring this particular topic was so much larger than other cs4fn issues can be taken to indicate that teachers are specifically looking out for computing material for girls, perhaps more so than material about computing in general.

7.1.3 Initial lessons from the cs4fn approach

Though our formal evaluation will appear at the completion of the cs4fn project grant in 2013, there are informal lessons from the production and distribution of the booklet that we would like to note. First of all, as reported elsewhere, the fact that cs4fn is free seems to be important to its success [5]. In the specific case of the 'women in computing' booklet we are working to achieve what might be seen as a 'soft' goal – increasing participation of a particular group, rather than a 'hard' curriculum-based goal like trying to teach a particular programming language. For that reason a free resource may be much easier to take up, as there is no need for a teacher to justify the expense, or take up valuable time going through a school's procedure for ordering and payment.

The success of the response from teachers may owe much to the booklet's cover design which made its topic and purpose clear. The design and layout of the booklet have been shown to help attract teachers, and teachers in turn believe that students will be attracted by it as well. This is evidenced not only by the number of requests for class sets to give to students, but also their comments that specifically refer to expected student response.

8. CONCLUSIONS

By almost any measure, the response to the cs4fn 'women in computing' booklet was extremely positive. We received around three times as many teacher requests for the booklet as we had for a typical issue of cs4fn magazine (based on an average of the last three issues). We also received positive comments from almost every teacher who responded. They enthused about the booklet's content and appearance, and thought that it would help encourage more girls to take up (and stick with) computing, as we had hoped it would.

There is clearly further evaluation work to be done on student responses to the booklet, and the question of how it can impact on female uptake of computing. Student responses may be different to teachers' expectations. We have recently started to collect data from university students about the effect of the cs4fn magazine on their enrollment in computer science courses with initial data suggesting that cs4fn has encouraged both male and female students to take the subject at university. What we can say about our results from teachers is that teachers share many of the same concerns we do. They too are interested in inspiring students, particularly young women, and felt that a booklet such as ours was extremely useful to help them achieve their aims. We will continue to monitor and analyse feedback – and are planning a deeper, grounded theory-based analysis of the teacher responses to extract more information from this corpus.

We created the booklet in order to inspire female students, and teacher response suggests our approach has struck a significant chord. Women have been under-represented in computer science and teachers are seeking resources to help combat this problem. Telling the stories of women in computing may help to enthrall, inspire and attract more to the field in the future.

9. ACKNOWLEDGMENTS

We are grateful to our funders including EPSRC (EP/F032641/1), the Westfield Trust, Google, ARM and Microsoft. We are also grateful to Karen Shoop of the School of Electronic Engineering and Computer Science at Queen Mary, University of London.

10. REFERENCES

[1] Becerra-Fernandez, I., Elam, J., and Clemmons, S. 2010. Reversing the landslide in computer-related degree programs. Commun. ACM 53, 2 (Feb. 2010), 127-133. DOI= http://doi.acm.org/10.1145/1646353.1646387

[2] Cheryan, S., Plaut, V. C., Davies, P.G., and Steele, C.M. Ambient belonging: How stereotypical cures impact gender

participation in computer science. Journal of Personality and Social Psychology 97, 4 1045-1060.

[3] Curzon, P. 2007. Serious fun in computer science, ACM SIGCSE Bulletin 39(3) p1. Invited keynote at ITiCSE07. DOI= http://doi.acm.org/10.1145/1269900.1268785

[4] Curzon, P., Peckham, J., Taylor, H., Settle, A., and Roberts, E. 2009. Computational thinking (CT): on weaving it in. SIGCSE Bull. 41, 3 (Aug. 2009), 201-202. DOI= http://doi.acm.org/10.1145/1595496.1562941

[5] Curzon, P., Black, J., Meagher, L. R., and McOwan, P. W. 2009. cs4fn.org: Enthusing Students about Computer Science. In Proceedings of Informatics Education Europe IV, Hermann, C, Lauer, T., Ottmann, T. and Welte. M. Eds., (Freiburg, Germany, November 5 - 6, 2009), 73-80.

[6] Digigirlz Programs: Digigirlz Day, 2009. Retrieved 22 August 2010, from Microsoft: http://www.microsoft.com/about/diversity/programs/digigirlz/digigirlzday.aspx

[7] DCSF (Department for Children, Schools and Families) (2007a) Schools and pupils in England, January 2007 (final), London: DfES. Retrieved 22 August 2010, from the DfES: www.dfes.gov.uk/rsgateway/DB/SFR/s000744/index.shtml

[8] Fisher, A. and Margolis, J. 2002. Unlocking the clubhouse: the Carnegie Mellon experience. SIGCSE Bull. 34, 2 (Jun. 2002), 79-83. DOI= http://doi.acm.org/10.1145/543812.543836

[9] Frieze, C. 2005. Diversifying the images of computer science: undergraduate women take on the challenge!. SIGCSE Bull. 37, 1 (Feb. 2005), 397-400. DOI= http://doi.acm.org/10.1145/1047124.1047476

[10] Gürer, D., and Camp, T. 2002. Investigating the Incredible Shrinking Pipeline for Women in Computer Science. Final Report, NSF Project 9812016.

[11] Hansard HC vol 498 cols 220W (25 Nov 2009).

[12] Lang, C., Craig, A., Fisher, J., and Forgasz, H. 2010. Creating digital divas: scaffolding perception change through secondary school and university alliances. In Proceedings of the Fifteenth Annual Conference on innovation and Technology in Computer Science Education (Bilkent, Ankara, Turkey, June 26 - 30, 2010). ITiCSE '10. ACM, New York, NY, 38-42. DOI= http://doi.acm.org/10.1145/1822090.1822103

[13] Millar, J., and Jagger, N. 2001. *Women in ITEC courses and careers*. London, Department of Education and Skills, Department for Employment. The Women's Unit: 156.

[14] Moorman, P. and Johnson, E. 2003. Still a stranger here: attitudes among secondary school students towards computer science. In Proceedings of the 8th Annual Conference on innovation and Technology in Computer Science Education (Thessaloniki, Greece, June 30 - July 02, 2003). D. Finkel, Ed. ITiCSE '03. ACM, New York, NY, 193-197. DOI= http://doi.acm.org/10.1145/961511.961564

[15] Sosik, J. J., Godshalk, V. 2000. The Role of Gender in Mentoring: Implications for Diversified and Homogenous Mentoring Relationships. Journal of Vocational Behavior. 57, 1 (August 2000) 102-122, DOI= http://dx.doi.org/10.1006/jvbe.1999.1734.

[16] Teague, J. 2002. Women in computing: what brings them to it, what keeps them in it?. SIGCSE Bull. 34, 2 (Jun. 2002), 147-158. DOI= http://doi.acm.org/10.1145/543812.543849

[17] Townsend, G. C. 1996. Viewing video-taped role models improves female attitudes toward computer science. In Proceedings of the Twenty-Seventh SIGCSE Technical Symposium on Computer Science Education (Philadelphia, Pennsylvania, United States, February 15 - 17, 1996). K. J. Klee, Ed. SIGCSE '96. ACM, New York, NY, 42-46. DOI= http://doi.acm.org/10.1145/236452.236491

[18] Volman, M., and van Eck, E. 2001. Gender Equity and Information Technology in Education: The Second Decade. Review of Educational Research 71, 4 (Dec 2001) 613-634. DOI= 10.3102/00346543071004613

Kinesthetic Learning of Computing via "Off-beat" Activities

Ursula Wolz
Computer Science
The College of New Jersey
Ewing, NJ 08528
+1 609 771 2766
wolz@tcnj.edu

Michael Milazzo
g8four
36 B Church St.
Mountain Brook, AL, 35205
+1 866 899 4889
michael.milazzo@g8four.com

Meredith Stone
Computer Science
The College of New Jersey
Ewing, NJ 08528
+1 609 771 2286
MeredithKStone@aol.com

ABSTRACT

To broaden participation in computing requires exposing students to a variety of experiences. CS Unplugged promotes learning through kinesthetic activities. This paper identifies three types of learning (1) problem solving, (2) creative construction, and (3) open-ended invention, that lend themselves to activities that engage middle school students in physical movement to learn computing. Via surveys and a personality traits activity "True Colors" we examined whether self-identified personality types were predisposed to particular kinesthetic learning activities. Our results suggest that personality type as defined by True Colors does not predict selection of an activity type. Furthermore, the students in our summer Interactive Journalism Institute were significantly more predisposed to pick open-ended invention. These results suggest directions in which K-12 computing curriculum should take to reach the broadest constituency.

Categories and Subject Descriptors

K.3.2 [**Computing Milieux**] Computer and Information Science Education
K. 4.0 Computers and Society

General Terms

Human Factors

Keywords

Computational Thinking, Kinesthetic Learning, CS Unplugged, Scratch, Interactive Journalism, Broadening Participation in CS

1. INTRODUCTION

The CS Unplugged initiative (csunplugged.org) promotes alternative activities to engage young people in computer science[3] via both formal and informal learning environments. Simultaneously the CSTA (csta.acm.org) is promoting curriculum in the US for kindergarten through grade 12. The presumption is that a large variety of experiences can reach a diverse constituency. Yet there has been little formal research on what computing concepts and activities are age appropriate, what sorts of learners they engage, and whether that learning transfers to formal coursework in computer science.

This paper describes kinesthetic "Off-beat" activities presented to middle school students as a means to "burn off energy" during a computing intensive 5-day Interactive Journalism Institute [5,6] held in July 2010. The activities were "problem solving," "creative construction", and "open-ended invention." Students were exposed to each type of activity in the first three days. On the fourth and fifth day they were given the choice of activity. The students overwhelmingly picked "open-ended invention." This suggests that pre-high school curricular efforts, especially those of a kinesthetic nature, focus on invention, over computing concept mastery, or even directed problem solving with known algorithmic solution (e.g. Towers of Hanoi).

As part of our program we do a diversity equity exercise called "True Colors" (www.true-colors.com) through which students become aware of their personality traits and learning style. This exercise is intended to reinforce that you don't have to be a "math geek" to be good at computer science. We were curious to see if there was any correlation between self-identified personality type and kinesthetic activity selection. Although the sample size (43) is small, the results confirmed our past experience that our program attracts a diverse group of young people who are not particularly predisposed to math and science. We were however, delightfully surprised to see that the students wanted to be inventive, regardless of personality type.

These results suggest that current assumptions about personality traits, gender, and cultural/ethnic/racial background should be carefully examined when predictions are made regarding students' motivation to engage in learning about computing. Rather than study predilection toward a particular content area (e.g. robots, game programming, storytelling), we believe that the computer science community needs to identify the degree of individual choice, creativity and inventiveness required. Furthermore, these results suggest that developing predictors of success in computing, such as math, may be intractable. If the goal is to cast a wide net to engage students in computing, then a rich variety of activities, rather than a rigid curriculum, may best serve the goal to ensure computing fluency in the next generation.

2. RATIONALE AND BACKGROUND

Jane Margolis et. al. [1] speak eloquently to the absence of access to computing in US schools. Creating formal curriculum, providing professional development for teachers, and establishing state and national standards is daunting. As initiatives to address this move forward, there are philosophical and pedagogical goals that raise important questions:

- What content is developmentally appropriate for students, for example at what age can children learn functions?

- Is it necessary to teach programming to teach computing: are off computer activities (e.g. CS unplugged) sufficient?

- What modalities work best with particular constituencies? For example the Scratch community promotes a constructivist pedagogy where children "imagine, program, share." (scratch.mit.edu)

- It has been argued that computational thinking is intricately related to problem solving [2]. Can computing be taught in a didactic fashion?

The conflict for computing curriculum developers and policy-makers is that we cannot wait for research-based answers to these questions. We need to engage students now because of the overall lack of engagement in K-12 classrooms. This suggests treading lightly, and promoting multiple modalities.

The three types of activities identified here illustrate the potential range of activities for reaching students. All three are kinesthetic. They differ in pedagogic style and degree to which students can express their individual creativity. We posit, but do not show, that these types could also be computer-based activities.

The over-arching goals for expanding instruction in computing must be considered. One goal is workforce preparedness: how to encourage more young people to pursue computing careers. This suggests a need to be able to predict success in computing. A second goal is to diversify the computing workforce. The rationale given is that inviting in a broader constituency will provide more diverse styles of problem solving, and a consequently broader potential for innovation and creativity. A third goal is the need for a computing fluent citizenry to support democracy. Every citizen needs to be an informed consumer, understanding both the potential and limitations of computing technology.

Our summer program is primarily focused on the second goal: to encourage a broader constituency of computing professionals. We are also committed to the third goal, to develop a computing fluent citizenry. We see the focus on the first goal as problematic. Beyond a need to be a flexible, life-long learner, there are no predictors for success in future, as yet undefined computing careers. Exposing young people to a wide variety of activities that empower them as thinkers and learners is therefore critical.

Our week-long summer program introduces computing through interactive journalism. The students spend most of their day on the computer creating an interactive on-line magazine. This collaborative environment provides a rich model of interdisciplinary work. Besides writing prose, students shoot video and create procedural animations in Scratch to support their news stories. By using Scratch, our program empowers students to become confident programmers. We directly address the stereotype that to program you have to be "good at math." [5,6]. The True Colors exercise helps reaffirm that "non-geeks" can do computer science too.

True Colors is a visual and kinesthetic activity to self-identify personality traits and learning style. It focuses on expressing the "individual character" of the participant to help them recognize their particular strengths and the strengths of others. The activity, which involves movement, multi-media and active verbal and physical interaction fits naturally into our program's interaction dynamic, reinforcing teamwork and mutual respect. The True Colors activity explicitly reinforces the agenda that many types of people contribute to a media effort that is based in computational

thinking. Through the exercise participants come to understand that we all have a mix of traits, although one or two might dominate. An intended outcome is to develop respect for those who "don't think and act like us."

The shared kinesthetic emphasis of True Colors and Off-beat activities suggests that any correlation in the data collected from them will be more accurate than correlating Off-beat with text-based personality tests. A typical, written learning style test is at a disadvantage because it lacks any kinesthetic engagement, making the physical activity an independent variable.

3. Off Beat Activities

The workday for our summer students is intense as they collaborate on their "news beats" from 8:30 AM to 4:30 PM. They are rising 8th graders (13 - 14 years). At lunch, their energy level is measured in decibels. To burn it off, they participate in 45 minutes of "off beat" activities that require them to be physically active outside, weather permitting. We borrowed heavily from CS Unplugged to create developmentally appropriate group activities that required them to move, but through which they would continue to learn about computer science.

3.1 Problem Solving

Problem solving is a traditional structured approach to teaching computational thinking via puzzles with known solutions. Students are exposed to concepts and techniques that require them to design a solution based on classic methods defined by Polya [4]. The activities reinforce the process of inventing a procedural solution. Although it is most directly applied to programming, creating an innovative sequence of steps to achieve an outcome is equally important to video editing and media construction. Algorithms as well as the process of inventing algorithms are taught. The common assumption is that students who enjoy this activity will enjoy computing.

Our problem solving activities were based on classic problems: (1) Towers of Hanoi, (2) Dining Philosophers, (3) Missionaries and Cannibals – renamed Lions and Gazelles to mitigate the racial offensiveness of the traditional problem statement. Using large props, small groups of students were given the problem and asked to find a solution by moving boxes (Towers), tossing balls to each other (Dining), or acting out moving across a river (Lions).

This activity required the students to follow explicit instructions and to try to reach a well-defined goal. Adult teachers were primarily responsible for keeping the students on task and motivating them to continue to problem solve. The teachers were explicitly discouraged from guiding the students to a solution.

3.2 Creative Construction

Creative construction refers to the aspect of computer science in which designers create a constrained, but not necessarily precise solution using the tools at hand. These types of problems typically do not have a "known" solution. Programmers engage in this by using the constructs of a language (e.g loops, variables, objects). These skills are also used by media designers using tools such as Adobe CS4 for website development or Final Cut for video production. The intended goal may evolve as the process evolves. It is essential to balance creativity and methodology, and to have a degree of competence in the requisite building blocks.

Our program as a whole demonstrates how creating a news story fits into this mold. In the newsroom students learn an iterative refinement process to produce text, video and procedural animations to research and tell a story. During the Off-beat activities dance choreography reinforced this process.

One of the authors (Milazzo) is a swing dance instructor. He taught basic steps and asked participants to create their own dance. Supervising adults were responsible for encouraging the students to participate and worked with individuals as needed.

3.3 Open-ended Invention

Open-ended invention stimulates innovation and engineering creativity. Designers are given a constrained set of resources and the freedom to create their solution to a loosely defined problem. These kinds of activities are promoted in environments like Scratch where students are not assigned a problem, but encouraged to follow their own agenda. This activity correlates well with news reporting where a reporter pitches a story rather than taking an assignment. The story is constructed from the collected artifacts (notes, pictures, video.) It has been argued that this is a critical skill for computational thinking [2].

Our Off-beat open-ended invention activity involved giving teams of students a bucket of toys and novelty items. Literally. The bucket contained approximately $15 worth of random plastic objects collected at a local dollar store.[1] It included balls, toy rakes and shovels, stuffed animals, scrubbing brushes, various small thought provoking toys, plastic mats, and toy traffic cones. The students were challenged to invent a physical game and demonstrate how it was played.

The teachers were responsible for keeping the students on task. The teachers were explicitly discouraged from taking a lead in defining the game, but were given permission to guide the communication process to negotiate the game rules.

4. HYPOTHESIS AND METHODOLOGY

Contrary to stereotypical assumptions, our experience with middle school enrichment programs prior to July 2010 led to the hypothesis that personality traits would not impact choice of activity. Assuming a broad range of personalities, this should result in an even distribution of activity choice.

The Interactive Journalism Institute runs Monday to Friday. The Off-beat activities are scheduled for 45 minutes immediately following lunch. All students participated in the same activity on the first three days: "Lions and Gazelles" on the first day, "Swing Dancing" on the second, and "game design" on the third. The order of activities was chosen to reflect an increasing emphasis on individual choice, and decreasing specificity of instructions. Loosing constraints each day facilitated establishing responsible and cooperative behavior.

After the third day Off-beat activity, students were asked to sign up for the fourth day. They could change their mind the next morning. After the fourth day activity, they signed up for the fifth day. They could switch the following morning.

On all five days the students were also asked to rate the Off-beat activities on a scale of 1 – 10 from "Hated it" to "Loved it." At the end of each day all students were asked to complete a survey that tracked their attitudes about their experience thus far. Two questions addressed the Off-beat activities:

- What was the most interesting thing about today's "Off-beat" activity and why?

- What was the least interesting thing about today's "Off-beat" activity and why?

Answering the surveys was strictly voluntary. Students could decline to participate in any of the activities throughout the day including Off-beat and True Colors.

4.1 Off-beat Activities

Day 1: Problem Solving
The 43 students were split into two groups, each with two adult facilitators. Each group was given six tags to identify a "lion," six to identify a "gazelle," and a tag for the boat pilot. Paper instructions and background information were reviewed verbally. The boat could hold no more than two guests and the pilot. There could not be more lions than gazelles on either shore.

Day 2: Creative Construction
The whole group was taught solo, unpartnered jazz dance vernacular moves that are short and simple enough for students to feel confident in their ability to perform. The students were lined up in three rows and taught a simple one minute routine on an eight count that was a variable sequence of steps: step-together, cross over (a shim sham variation), turn, walk, pirate, knee slap and walk back. Experienced adult dancers assisted individuals.

Day 3: Creative Construction
The students were divided into three groups and given a 2 foot high, 2 foot diameter plastic bucket with a variety of plastic toys, kitchen and bath implements. All teams received some of the same items (balls, rakes, shovels, cones), as well as some unique things (e.g. oven mitt, scrub brush, sponge, spatula). The written instructions, reviewed verbally, were to create a game and demonstrate it. Each group had an adult facilitator.

Days 4 and 5: Student Choice
Based on personal choice students participated in one of the following on the fourth day with adult facilitators for each group:

1) "The Orange Game" from CS Unplugged, a variation of the "Dining Philosophers." The students were given a set of five colored name tags, pairs of balls colored red, green, blue, and orange and a single white ball. Written instructions were reviewed verbally with the adult facilitator.

2) Swing dance. Students reviewed dance steps and were shown a video of choreographies to facilitate discussion of what makes a good dance. They began to design their own dance.

3) Game design. Students were set loose to either refine their game from the previous day or design a new one.

On the fifth day the following options were available, each with at least one adult facilitator per group:

1) Written instructions for "Towers of Hanoi" were reviewed verbally. The students were given six cardboard boxes (cubes) ranging in size from three feet to six inches on a side.

2) The Swing dancers designed, rehearsed and performed their own original choreography.

3) The game design groups refined or created a new game.

4.2 True Colors

The True Colors program is an active means for illustrating how temperament impacts group dynamics. We use it to create awareness of how gender, racial, and ethnic stereotypes impact

---

[1] A Dollar store is a US phenomenon where everything in the store is priced at one dollar.

productive group work. In particular we address the assumptions about who is "good at" programming, art and storytelling, the three essential components of interactive journalism.

True colors defines four types: gold, green, blue, and orange. For coding purposes we identify "gold" as "yellow" (y), to prevent confusion with "green" (g). Students participate in reflective activities through which they rank the influence of various colors on their actions and attitudes. For example, one of the authors is primarily green, then blue, then orange, with only a bit of yellow. In the broadest terms the colors represent:

- Yellow (gold) personalities are loyal, dependable, and responsible. They plan ahead, come prepared and are procedurally oriented. The archetype is the "good student."

- Green personalities are analytic, creative and fair. They rely on research rather than intuition. The archetype of the scientist is green. This is the "brain" in the class.

- Blue personalities value balance and harmony. They are loving, peaceful, sympathetic and nurturing. The archetype is a teacher or nurse. This is the sweet kid in the class.

- Orange personalities are spontaneous, and fun. They live in the moment, are competitive and enterprising. The archetype is the sports hero. This is the kid who can't sit still.

We must stress that we use True Colors, not to identify which kids are which type, but rather to assert that it takes all kinds in a collaborative setting like a newsroom, video game or software company. We emphasize to the students that they are a mix of personality types, not an archetype, and that success in computing is not tied to one type. Further, the language used here to summarize the types was not used with the students, in particular identifying archetypes. We use these descriptions here to highlight stereotypes typically invoked in computing education: people who succeed in math (and thus computing) are primarily green/yellow. Girls are stereotypically assumed to be more blue/orange.

This pedagogic emphasis did not preclude looking at which types chose which activities on days four and five. As part of the True colors exercise the students placed colored dots on their nametags as they ranked their color preferences. Adults supervised the process to ensure accurate labeling. Because we collected nametags each day, we were able to reliably capture this data.

4.3 Cohort Demographics
Our cohort was assembled through recommendations from the language arts teachers who have worked in our program for three years. The cohort naturally selected to 2/1 female/male (from a school population that is 1/1 female/male). The cohort also reflected the school demographics with approximately half white/Asian and half black/Hispanic. It was also scholastically representative of the rising 8th grade, and included some of the most and least successful students. The school is an "urban rim" school, with a middle class/working class population. The district takes pride in stabilizing diversity ten years ago and preventing "white flight." Gender, ethnicity and race are intentionally omitted from our data analysis.

5. RESULTS
Table 1 provides a summary of the personality types. The best conclusion we can draw is that our students represented a full range of personality types.

Tables 2-6 present individual color combinations organized by activity selection. All students who selected dance remained with dance both days. Twenty-six of thirty-one students who selected games on the fourth day, chose it again on the fifth. Four switched to problem solving. Four of six who chose problem solving on the fourth day, remained, while two switched to game design. Statistically, the overwhelming selection of "games" did not occur by chance. This must be an indication of an overall preference for open-ended activities. 72% chose games on the fourth day and 65% chose it on the fifth.

Interesting clusters did occur within each group. Within the dance group, the majority of the students were primarily green or blue; no primarily yellows chose the activity and only one primarily orange did. This orange was also one of the few wholly unique color patterns in the entire group. No student in the dance group had orange as their least pronounced personality type, contrasting the lack of yellows in the first position. In the game design group, we noted that there were a large number of redundant color patterns, particularly among those primarily orange or green. Among those who were primarily yellow though, there were no repeated color patterns. This group also contained less unique color patterns, or patterns that did not appear in any other participants. The second largest group, the puzzle group (including those who switched in or out), contained no repeated color patterns. They were primarily yellow – those who like to follow directions.

Table 7 summarizes the student rating of the Off-beat activities. The students became more enthusiastic once they were given a choice. The standard deviation for dance raises some interesting questions that we are not prepared to answer. The short answer questions posed on the first through third day corroborate the selection of game design on day four. The majority of responses to both the best and worst of the puzzle experience on the first day was that it was "challenging", and "difficult." On the second day students thought the best thing was that it was dance, but that the worst was that it was "boring" and hot. Temperatures reached 100F. On the third day they overwhelmingly said the best thing was that they could create something themselves. In response to what was worst, half said "nothing."

5.1 ANALYSIS AND SUMMARY
Our hypothesis regarding personality types proved correct. There was no significant match between self-identified personality traits and selection of activity type. However, it is an understatement to say we were surprised that the overwhelming majority of students selected the open-ended games activity on the fourth and fifth day. The surveys told us why: they wanted to make something that was their own creation. Yet the dance instruction, intended as creative construction, was the least well received. In retrospect we realized, that despite the heat, this activity most closely models the type of instruction typically given in a computing class. The teacher presents essential skills and then gives an assignment to demonstrate those skills. Given the intensity of the entire day, it stands to reason that the students wanted some "down time" after lunch. Problem solving was "hard but fun." Creative construction required paying attention despite being kinesthetic. Making a game, using their imagination, was simply fun.

There is a cultural bias, at least in the US, that to "do computing" you need to be a green/yellow type. Further, the challenge of solving problems such as Towers of Hanoi would suggest that "green" types would migrate to this activity. Our results do not support this. Similarly one would expect the systematic learning of new skills (e.g. the dance group) to be populated with "yellows" who like things with structure. It wasn't. Of most significance to us, the build game group was dominated by "oranges" the spontaneous type, that look to have fun.

The results described here point toward a constructivist approach to teaching computing concepts that maximizes individual freedom to be creative. This requires a tool kit that is accessible, and does not require extensive instruction. The kids didn't have the patience to learn the dance steps. They liked inventing new uses for existing tools in the buckets.

Our overall conclusion is that the computer science education community needs to know more about personality styles and how they articulate with particular activities both on and off the computer. Further we need to be cautious about predicting computing career success based on these types, success in particular subject areas (e.g. math/science), or learning styles. For example identifying the "green/yellows" may exclude creative people who can make significant contributions to the field.

In developing curricula to rebuild a pipeline into computing we need to stop focusing on "sets" of people, but instead take the opportunity both on and off the computer to create a diverse variety of experiences for young people to become enamored of computing, whether through puzzles, games, storytelling, dance, or the simple joy of inventing something new.

6. ACKNOWLEDGMENTS

This work is supported by NFS CNS 0739173 and reflects the opinions of the authors.

7. REFERENCES

[1] Margolis, J., Estrella, R., Goode, J., Holme, J. J., Nao, K. 2008, *Stuck in the Shallow End: Education, Race, and Computing*, The MIT Press, Cambridge, MA.

[2] National Research Council (NRC) Committee for the Workshops on Computational Thinking, 2010, *Report of a Workshop on The Scope and Nature of Computational Thinking.* Washington, DC, The National Academies Press.

[3] Nishida, T., Kanemune, S., Idosaka, Y., Namiki, M., Bell, T., Kuno. Y. 2009. A CS unplugged design pattern, *Proceedings of the 40th ACM technical symposium on Computer science education,* , 231-235

[4] Polya, G. 1945 *How to Solve It.* Princeton University Press.

[5] Wolz, U., Stone, M., Pulimood, M., Pearson, K. 2010, Computational Thinking via Interactive Journalism in Middle School *Proceedings of the 41st technical symposium on computer science education,* , pp 239 – 243

[6] Wolz, U., K. Pearson, S.M. Pulimood, M. Stone, M. Switzer 2011, Computational Thinking and Expository Writing in the Middle School: A novel approach to broadening participation in computing", to appear in the *Transactions on Computing Education,* anticipated June 2011.

Table 1. Totals of Personality Types

Rank	1	2	3	4
Yellow (Gold)	7	10	17	9
Green	12	8	9	14
Blue	8	14	7	14
Orange	16	11	10	6

Table 2. Profile for Dance Both Days

B	G	O	Y
B	O	Y	G
B	Y	O	G
G	B	O	Y
G	Y	O	B
O	B	G	Y

Table 3. Profile for Puzzle Both Days

Y	B	G	O
Y	O	G	B
G	Y	O	B

Table 4. Profile for Puzzle to Games

B	O	Y	G
G	O	B	Y

Table 5. Profile for Games to Puzzle

O	B	Y	G
G	O	Y	B
G	B	Y	O
O	G	Y	B
Y	B	O	G

Table 6. Profile for Games Both Days

B	O	Y	G
B	O	Y	G
B	Y	O	G
G	B	O	Y
G	B	Y	O
G	B	Y	O
G	O	Y	B
G	O	Y	B
G	Y	O	B
O	B	Y	G
O	B	Y	G
O	B	Y	G
O	G	B	Y
O	G	B	Y
O	G	B	Y
O	G	B	Y
O	G	Y	B
O	G	Y	B
O	Y	B	G
O	Y	G	B
O	Y	G	B
O	Y	G	B
Y	B	G	O
Y	B	O	G
Y	O	B	G
Y	O	G	B

Table 7. Ratings of Off-beat Activities

Day	Average Rating	Stand Deviation
1: Puzzle	5.23	2.69
2: Dance	4.07	6.68
3. Game	6.68	2.91
4. Choice	7.67	2.54
5. Choice	8.09	2.39

A Technology-Assisted Scavenger Hunt for Introducing K-12 Students to Sensor Networks

Sally K. Wahba, Yvon Feaster, and Jason O. Hallstrom
School of Computing, Clemson University, Clemson, SC 29634-0974
{sallyw, yfeaste, jasonoh}@cs.clemson.edu

ABSTRACT

Sensor networks serve as a powerful recruiting vehicle to excite and engage students in socially-relevant applications of computing. In this paper, we describe a technology-assisted scavenger hunt for introducing young learners —from grade school through high school— to sensor networks and computer science. The desired outcome is to expand students' content knowledge and positively impact their impressions of the discipline. We describe the outreach program and present promising evaluation results across three pilots involving 5th graders, 7th graders, and 11th graders.

Categories and Subject Descriptors

K.3.2 [**Computers and Education**]: Computer and Info. Science Education—*Comp. sci. education, Curriculum*

General Terms

Experimentation, Human Factors

Keywords

Sensor networks, computer science outreach, high school curriculum, experimental evaluation

1. INTRODUCTION

In 2008, only 1.0% of prospective college students in the U.S. indicated computer science as a probable field of study, as compared to 11.5%, 9.3%, and 9.4% for the social sciences, biological sciences, and engineering, respectively [18]. Indeed, even at its peak in 2000, computer science garnered only 3.7% of the student vote. With a 24% projected increase in U.S. demand for computer scientists over the next decade [4], the potential labor market shortfall is troubling.

For educators, the lagging interest is perplexing. Computer science lies at the heart of virtually every major discovery and innovation within the past two decades — from genomics and proteomics to music and cinema. We begin with the supposition that the connections between computer science and its myriad applications are not being reinforced during the formative years of students' academic careers.

With this in mind, we developed a new outreach module designed to introduce K-12 students to some of the exciting applications of computer science, while highlighting key technical concepts underlying those applications. Although the module is readily adaptable to other application domains, we focus on *wireless sensor networks*.

Wireless sensor networks (WSNs) comprise tiny wireless computers that sense, process, and communicate environmental stimuli (e.g., temperature, light, vibration). When embedded within a host environment (e.g., a forest, a river), these networks enable in situ measurement at unprecedented scales. Representative applications include habitat monitoring [8], roadway management [11], intruder detection [1], and social networking [9], noting only a few. With the breadth of application possibilities these networks afford, the topic area is an ideal candidate for engaging students in exciting, socially-relevant applications of computer science.

In this paper, we describe a sensor-assisted scavenger hunt for introducing K-12 students to key applications and concepts associated with sensor networks. To assess the impact of the module on student attitudes and content understanding, we administer a post-pilot content quiz and Likert-style attitudinal survey. Informal interviews with students and their university leaders are also used to provide anecdotal data. We piloted the module in three separate outreach programs (a total of four student groups) during the summer of 2010. The groups included 5th grade, 7th grade, and 11th grade students. The evaluation results were uniformly positive across the groups.

Paper Organization. Section 2 surveys similar scavenger hunt outreach modules. Section 3 describes the structure and content of our module. Section 4 presents the results of our evaluation. Finally, Section 5 concludes with a brief summary and pointers to future work.

2. RELATED WORK

Outreach is essential for the continued growth of computer science. There have been a number of successful programs. Some of the most popular are based on CS Unplugged [7], Scratch [10], and Alice [5]. These programs are in use with primary through first-year college students, as well as K-12 educators. CS Unplugged comprises interactive learning modules designed to teach computer science concepts without the use of computers [2, 3]. Scratch is a programming language that uses a drag-and-drop format that allows students to create interactive programs [3, 15, 20]. Alice is a drag-and-drop 3D programming environment that students can use to create animated stories, games, and videos [5].

Scavenger hunts are another popular outreach activity, in

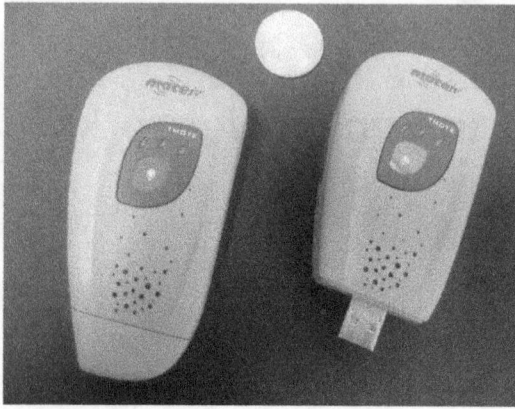

Figure 1: Tmote Invent (Telos-based)

and outside of computer science. For example, Pennsylvania College of Technology provides a career scavenger hunt for K-12 students [14]. The hunt starts when students are asked to choose a career they find interesting. Using the Internet, the students are then directed to research and answer a list of questions about the chosen career.

Washington State University hosts a program for middle school students to participate in an all-day scavenger hunt that takes them to various locations across the university [20]. The event allows students to interact with professors and college students, giving them an opportunity to gain "real-life" experience on a university campus.

The University of Illinois at Urbana-Champaign conducts a scavenger hunt during orientation for incoming freshmen in the Department of Computer Science [17]. Handheld computers aid students in exploring the university campus. One goal of this program is to increase enrollment and retention rates. The authors found that 54% of students indicated that they made friends during the activity and felt a connection to the department. The authors identified the lack of social networks as a contributing factor in many cases where students transferred out of the department. The authors conclude that the hunt had a positive impact on student retention, which was 4.6% higher than the previous five-year historical average.

We take this observation as our point of departure: Scavenger hunt activities have been effective across a range of programs in engaging students, initiating social connections, and improving student retention. By enhancing this simple, yet fun activity with new technology and meaningful technical content, the benefits can be amplified even further.

3. WSN SCAVENGER HUNT

We use the scavenger hunt concept to introduce students to WSNs. In this section, we describe the structure and content of our module, followed by a brief overview of each pilot group.

3.1 Module Description

The scavenger hunt begins with an introduction to sensor devices by passing around a Telos *mote* [12,13], (popular in academic research) and briefly explaining its functionality. Students are tasked with hunting for 10 Telos devices hidden across 3 floors of the computer science building. Along with each mote, an envelope is hidden containing multiple copies of a short fact about wireless sensor networks. These motes serve as beacons, periodically broadcasting radio messages.

Each student (or pair of students) is provided with a mote that acts as a receiver. (Figure 1 shows a sample receiver mote [12].) As students walk through the building, their motes receive messages sent by each beacon and blink an appropriate LED indicating their proximity to the hidden mote. As students approach a hidden device, the color of the blinking LED changes, guiding the explorers until the mote is found. Students then collect a copy of the associated fact, leaving the beacon in place for others to find. Students typically spend 10 minutes trying to find as many motes as they can.

After the allocated 10 minutes are over, students receive, as an incentive, a piece of candy for every notecard they collected. The students are then given a survey to complete. (Survey results are discussed in Section 4.) Upon completion of the survey, students are given the facts they were unable to collect. Next, they spend 10 minutes reading the facts, and 10 minutes answering a short quiz based on the facts. (Quiz results are also discussed in Section 4.) Finally, as we discuss the solutions with the students, they grade their own quizzes. As a reward, students receive additional candy equivalent to the number of correct answers.

After the module is complete, university leaders (referred to as *teachers* hereafter) are asked to complete a survey about how they think their students enjoyed the hunt, what the students learned during the game, and how the module can be further improved.

3.2 Facts

The scavenger hunt is designed to introduce students to WSNs. Here we summarize the facts used in the hunt.

Fact 1: Factors Affecting Reception. Two factors that affect wireless reception are distance and interference. Specifically, as distance or interference increases, the quality of communication decreases.

Fact 2: Resource Limitations. Motes possess less resource capacity than a typical computer. Key areas affected by resource limitations are: (*i*) energy, (*ii*) storage, and (*iii*) radio connectivity. Specifically, motes have limited energy, little space to save data, and a radio that can reach limited distances.

Fact 3: Information Relay. Motes usually relay information to a distant receiver. They typically achieve this by forming a chain, where one mote sends data to another until the data reaches the destination mote.

Fact 4: Hardware. The main hardware constituents of a mote are: (*i*) a microcontroller, (*ii*) a radio, (*iii*) program storage, (*iv*) data storage, (*v*) a battery, and (*vi*) sensors.

Fact 5: Time Synchronization. Time synchronization is an important concept in the absence of a shared global clock. Motes rely on specialized coordination algorithms to synchronize their local time.

Fact 6: Applications. Two canonical applications of wireless sensor networks are habitat monitoring and precision agriculture. For example, sensor networks are used to monitor the behavior of endangered species, as well as measure the content of the soil for better crop yield.

Fact 7: Programming a Mote. A program written on a desktop computer is transferred through a USB port to the mote's microcontroller and stored in program memory.

Fact 8: Common Sensors. Some of the common sensors available on motes include (*i*) motion, (*ii*) temperature, (*iii*) accelerometers, and (*iv*) light. These sensors are widely used in security systems, thermostats, video game controllers, and phones, respectively.

Fact 9: RSSI - Received Signal Strength Indicator. RSSI concerns a relatively low-level technical detail. RSSI is calculated by the radio to determine the reception strength of a signal.

Fact 10: Fun Fact. A mote is more powerful than the computer used in the first Apollo shuttle that traveled to the moon.

The facts described above consist of only a summary of the actual facts presented during the scavenger hunt.

3.3 Scavenger Hunt Pilots

We used the scavenger hunt module with four groups of various ages participating in three outreach workshops. Here we provide a brief overview of the workshops the students participated in.

3.3.1 STEM-ICT 3D

Science, Technology, Engineering, and Math – Information Communications Technologies 3D (STEM-ICT) [16] is a project funded by the NSF's Innovative Technology Experiences for Students and Teachers (ITEST) program. The goal of this project is to motivate underrepresented middle school students to study and pursue careers in one of the STEM disciplines. Identified during the sixth grade, participating students attend a two-week summer academy where they learn to design, build, and use a 3D virtual environment. During the second week, working together with their teachers, they create virtual environments that will be used in the classroom to teach STEM curriculum.

We piloted the scavenger hunt module with a group of 11 rising seventh grade students. Each student was given a receiver mote during the scavenger hunt.

3.3.2 Emerging Scholars Program

Emerging Scholars [6] is a nationally recognized outreach program that targets students from rural counties with significant economic and educational barriers with respect to technology. These barriers make the transition from high school to higher education more difficult. Locally, the Emerging Scholars program addresses this issue by working with high schools to identify students with the potential to succeed in higher education, but who need additional support. These students are identified during their freshman year of high school and enter the program as rising sophomores. They can continue in the program through their senior year.

We piloted the scavenger hunt module with two groups of Emerging Scholars in their junior year. The first group consisted of 14 students; the second group consisted of 15 students. During the scavenger hunt, each pair of students was given a receiver mote due to the limited number of available motes.

3.3.3 Girl Scouts

To introduce young girls to the field of computer science and the careers computer science has to offer, we invited a Girl Scouts troop and 3 other girls who previously expressed an interest in attending the computer science workshop. In this workshop, we introduced the students to basic programming through MIT's Scratch tool [10]. The girls were also taught basic computer science concepts, such as networking and sorting using CS Unplugged activities [7].

We piloted the scavenger hunt module with 5 student participants – 2 rising fifth graders and 3 rising eighth graders. During the hunt, each student was given a receiver mote.

4. EVALUATION

4.1 Instruments

After the students participated in the scavenger hunt module, they were given a survey consisting of 10 Likert-style attitudinal statements, as shown in Listing 1. For each statement, students were asked to rate their level of agreement. Available ratings were *strongly disagree*, *disagree*, *neither agree nor disagree*, *agree*, and *strongly agree*. We assigned values to each rating from 1 to 5, corresponding to strongly disagree and strongly agree, respectively.

After completing the survey, we gave each student the notecards she was missing. Students were given 10 minutes to read through the notecards, and 10 minutes to answer a quiz based on the facts they learned about wireless sensor networks. The quiz consisted of 7 true/false questions and 3 short answer questions, as shown in Listing 2.

```
1.   Scavenger hunts are fun
2.   Computer Science is fun.
3.   WSNs are fun.
4.   WSNs are important.
5.   I enjoyed learning about WSNs.
6.   College is fun.
7.   Professors are easy to communicate with.
8.   I want to learn more about WSNs.
9.   CS is a good major of study in college.
10.  The scavenger hunt using WSNs was not just
     fun, but educational.
```

Listing 1: Student Survey

```
1.   (T/F) As the distance between motes increases,
     the quality of communication becomes better
     since the radio signal is not as powerful.
2.   (T/F) Information relay can be used to allow
     communication between distant motes.
3.   (T/F) Motes can form a chain to send
     information to a desktop computer.
4.   (T/F) Motes use time synchronization to adjust
     for the time difference between motes since
     one mote might be awake, while another
     might be asleep.
5.   (T/F) WSNs can be used in agriculture.
6.   (T/F) If we write a program on a computer, we
     cannot transfer that program to a mote.
7.   (T/F) If we relate RSSI to our cell phone, it
     tells us the remaining battery life left on
     the phone.
8.   List two types of sensors you learned about.
9.   Mention two limitations that WSNs present
     that desktop computers do not.
10.  Mention two components of a mote's hardware.
```

Listing 2: Student Quiz

Upon completion of the module, we asked each group's teacher to fill out the survey shown in Listing 3. The survey consisted of 4 attitudinal statements. Again, teachers were asked to rate their level of agreement. For the fifth question, teachers were given the options of *elementary school*, *middle school*, *high school*, *elementary and middle school*, *middle and high school*, and *all grades*. Finally, in the last question, we asked the teachers to suggest improvements to the activity. It is worth noting that we do not have completed surveys for teachers of the STEM-ICT 3D group as they were not present during the activity. We gathered one survey for each of the other three groups, from two teachers.

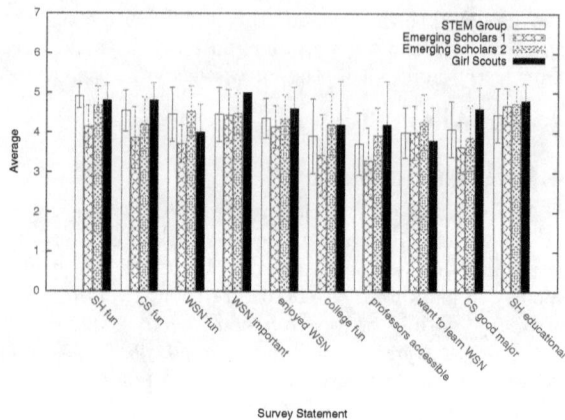

Figure 2: Student Survey Results

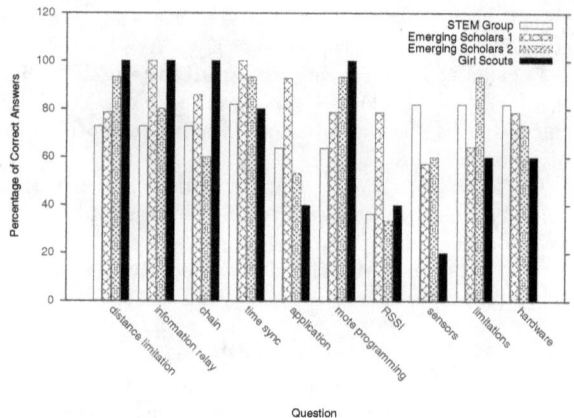

Figure 3: Student Quiz Results

---

1. The students seem to have enjoyed the
   wireless sensor scavenger hunt.
2. The students appear to have learned
   about WSNs.
3. The scavenger hunt using WSNs is an
   activity I would like to have my
   other classes participate in.
4. The students had prior knowledge
   of wireless sensor networks.
5. What age group do you think is most
   appropriate for this activity?
6. How can this activity be further improved?

Listing 3: Teacher Survey

4.2 Results

4.2.1 Student Survey

Figure 2 summarizes the student survey results. The x-axis shows the survey statement; the y-axis shows the average and standard deviation of the student ratings. For the first statement, the STEM-ICT 3D group had the highest rating. We attribute this to the fact that they were looking forward to playing the game after hearing about it from their friends who played it the year before. (We used the module the previous year with other groups; however, no data was collected.) The Girl Scouts had the next highest rating. We attribute this to their young age, as scavenger hunts are likely to be more appealing to this age group.

The first Emerging Scholars group had the lowest rating for 9 statements. We attribute this to a comment from their teacher that the students are inactive since their session is early in the morning, just after breakfast. Accordingly, the students seem to have enjoyed the game less than the other groups as it involved a lot of movement inside the building.

The second Emerging Scholars group had the highest rating for statements 3 (WSNs are fun) and 8 (I want to learn more about WSNs). We attribute this to the initial interest of the students, who asked a lot of questions before the game about what the motes are and what they do. Also, this group tied with the Girl Scouts group in statement 6 (College is fun). This is an interesting observation considering the age difference between the groups.

The Girl Scouts group, followed by the STEM-ICT 3D group (the youngest groups), had the highest ratings for statements 2 (CS is fun), 4 (WSNs are important), 5 (I enjoyed learning about WSNs), 7 (Professors are accessible), 9 (CS is a good major), and 10 (Scavenger hunt is educational). This observation raises an important question:

Should computer science outreach efforts target students at an earlier age? Further, the first Emerging Scholars group scored the lowest on these statements (except for statement 10). This also raises an important issue of whether starting computer science outreach efforts at the high school level may be too late to recruit students to computer science.

The average for each survey statement is 4.6, 4.2, 4.2, 4.5, 4.3, 3.9, 3.7, 4.1, 3.9, and 4.6 for statements 1 through 10, respectively. The lowest average among these statements was 3.7, for statement 7 (professors are easy to communicate with). We attribute this to the fact that students may not have had a chance to interact with more computer science professors while participating in the summer workshops.

The average standard deviation is 0.64, 0.65, 0.64, and 0.61 for the STEM-ICT 3D, first Emerging Scholars, second Emerging Scholars, and Girl Scouts groups, respectively. Statement 6 (college is fun) had the highest standard deviation across most groups. The standard deviation was 0.94, 1.02, 0.77 (second highest), 1.09, for the STEM-ICT 3D, first and second Emerging Scholars, and Girl Scouts groups, respectively. We believe the students may not have had enough time to determine if college was fun.

Overall, note that even the relative differences discussed in the preceding paragraphs are minor – the results are uniformly positive. This is evident from the consistently low standard deviation values.

Threats to Validity. It is worth emphasizing that a number of experimental factors were outside of our control. For example, the effect of other activities within the same outreach program on how students perceive computer science (i.e., questions 2, 6, 7, and 9) needs to be addressed. Further, as with many outreach projects, the long-lasting effect of the activity could be assessed in the future to evaluate whether the results we obtained were short-term.

4.2.2 Quiz

The percentage of students in each group who answered the quiz questions correctly is shown in Figure 3. The x-axis shows the quiz questions; the y-axis shows the percentage of students who answered the questions correctly. It is surprising that even though the second Emerging Scholars group showed the highest interest in the material, their performance was not the best overall. The average of the quiz grades was 7.1, 8.1, 7.4, and 7 for the STEM-ICT 3D group, first and second Emerging Scholars group, and Girl Scouts group, respectively.

Another interesting observation is that the youngest group (Girl Scouts) scored the highest in 40% of the questions. They tied with the oldest group (first group of Emerging Scholars), as opposed to the STEM-ICT 3D group (20%) and the second group of Emerging Scholars (10%). From this, as well as the previous results, we think there is an opportunity to target students at an earlier age and capture their enthusiasm in the subject.

The Girl Scouts group scored the lowest on the short answer questions. We attribute this to the noticeably increased level of anxiety the girls showed when trying to answer these questions. We attribute this anxiety to their age based on the hypothesis that the girls may not have been confident about their vocabulary choice when answering the short answer questions.

Finally, question 7 (RSSI) had the lowest percentage overall. We believe that this is because this question was associated with the most technical fact; many students appear to have had a difficult time understanding RSSI.

4.2.3 Teacher Evaluation

We had two teachers complete three surveys, both from our institution. (The two Emerging Scholars groups had the same teacher, who filled out a survey for each group.) Teachers for the STEM-ICT 3D group were not available during the activity and therefore did not complete a survey. Although the data is only anecdotal, the overall teacher survey results were positive. The average for the first four questions was 4.67, 4, 4.67, and 2.3, while the standard deviation for the same questions was 0.58, 0, 0.58, and 1.53, respectively. The fourth question had a low average, as teachers generally did not agree that students had prior knowledge of WSNs. For the fifth question, two surveys indicated that the activity was appropriate for all age groups, while the third indicated it was more appropriate for elementary and middle school students. From the consistently positive student evaluations and high quiz scores, we think the module is appropriate for all age groups. For the last question, one of the teachers suggested the inclusion of a video about WSNs before the game. Finally, another teacher suggested modifying the game such that finding the next hidden mote required understanding concepts learned during the game. This is an excellent idea that we intend to explore.

5. CONCLUSION

Created long before the first computer was even conceptualized, the intent of the classic 1930s scavenger hunt game was simple — to occupy party guests with an engaging, highly-social, and fun activity [19]. Given that these are precisely the characteristics that educators look for in designing classroom and outreach activities, the scavenger hunt serves as a natural outreach vehicle. Beginning from this observation, we described a technology-assisted scavenger hunt for introducing K-12 students to wireless sensor network technology. The evaluation data from four independent pilots indicates a uniformly positive impact on student attitudes toward computer science and content understanding.

The main goal of this paper is to document an effective outreach activity so that it may find application at other institutions. An important secondary goal is to encourage other educators to document their experiences —both positive and negative— conducting K-12 outreach programs at a variety of institutions. One exciting possible outcome is the formation of a *Nifty Outreach* community analogous to the increasingly popular *Nifty Assignments* group. While maintaining the interest of our students is critical, we must first attract them to the discipline.

Acknowledgments

This work is supported by the National Science Foundation through awards CNS-0745846, DUE-1022941, and DUE-0633506. Yvon Feaster is an NSF Graduate Research Fellow. We would also like to thank Hao Jiang for developing the scavenger hunt software.

6. REFERENCES

[1] A. Arora et al. ExScal: Elements of an extreme scale wireless sensor network. In *Proceedings of the 11th IEEE International Conference on Embedded and Real-Time Computing Systems and Applications*, pages 102–108, Los Alamitos, CA USA, August 2005. IEEE Computer Society.

[2] T. Bell et al. Computer science without computers: new outreach methods from old tricks. In *Proceedings of the 21st Annual Conference of National Advisory Committee on Computing Qualifications*, pages 127–133, Rotorua, New Zealand, July 2008. NACCQ.

[3] L. Blum and T. Cortina. CS4HS: an outreach program for high school CS teachers. In *Proceedings of the 38th Technical Symposium on Computer Science Education*, pages 19–23, New York, NY USA, March 2007. ACM.

[4] Bureau of Labor Statistics, U.S. Department of Labor. Occupational outlook handbook, 2010-11 edition, computer scientists. www.bls.gov/oco/ocos304.htm, 2010. (*date of last access*).

[5] Carnegie Mellon University. Alice. http://www.alice.org/, 2010. (*date of last access*).

[6] Clemson University Emerging Scholars. Emerging Scholars. http://www.clemson.edu/academics/programs/emerging-scholars/, 2010. (*date of last access*).

[7] Computer Science Unplugged. Computer science unplugged. csunplugged.org/, 2010. (*date of last access*).

[8] A. Mainwaring et al. Wireless sensor networks for habitat monitoring. In *Proceedings of the 1st ACM International Workshop on Wireless Sensor Networks and Applications*, pages 88–97, New York, NY USA, September 2002. ACM.

[9] E. Miluzzo et al. CenceMe injecting sensing presence into social networking applications. In *Smart Sensing and Context*, volume 4793, pages 1–28. Springer, Berlin, Germany, 2007.

[10] MIT. Scratch: Imagine, program, share. http://scratch.mit.edu, 2010. (*date of last access*).

[11] P. Mohan et al. Nericell: Rich monitoring of road and traffic conditions using mobile smartphones. In *Proceedings of the 6th ACM Conference on Embedded Network Sensor Systems*, pages 323–336, New York, NY USA, November 2008. ACM.

[12] Moteiv Corporation. Tmote Invent. http://moteiv.com, 2010. (*date of last access*).

[13] Moteiv Corporation. Tmote Sky. http://www.moteiv.com/community/Tmote_Sky_Downloads, 2010. (*date of last access*).

[14] Pennsylvania College of Technology. Outreach for k-12, career scavenger hunt. http://www.pct.edu/k12/careerday-scavenger.htm, 2010.

[15] P. Sivilotti and S. Laugel. Scratching the surface of advanced topics in software engineering: A workshop module for middle school students. In *Proceedings of the 39th Technical Symposium on Computer Science Education*, pages 291–295, New York, NY USA, March 2008. ACM.

[16] STEM-ICT 3D. STEM-ICT 3D. http://www.stem-ict-3d.org/research.php, 2010. (*date of last access*).

[17] J. Talton et al. Scavenger hunt: Computer science retention through orientation. In *Proceedings of the 39th Technical Symposium on Computer Science Education*, pages 443–447, New York, NY USA, March 2006. ACM.

[18] The Higher Education Research Institute. The american freshman: National norms (annual). heri.ucla.edu/publicationstore.php, 2009.

[19] Time Magazine. The press: Elsa at war. *Time Magazine*, November 1944.

[20] Washington State University. Finley 7th graders bleed crimson. http://www.earlyoutreach.wsu.edu/flame/index.php?option=com_content&task=view&id=519&Itemid=188, 2009.

Does Lecture Capture Make a Difference for Students in Traditional Classrooms?

Amber Settle
DePaul University
243 S. Wabash Avenue
Chicago, IL 60604
(312) 362-5324

asettle@cdm.depaul.edu

Lucia Dettori
DePaul University
243 S. Wabash Avenue
Chicago, IL 60604
(312) 362-8243

lucia@cdm.depaul.edu

Mary Jo Davidson
DePaul University
243 S. Wabash Avenue
Chicago, IL 60604
(312) 362-8239

mdavidson@cdm.depaul.edu

ABSTRACT

The College of Computing and Digital Media (CDM) at DePaul University has recorded thousands of courses using an in-house system called Course Online (COL) since 2001. These recordings are available not only to students enrolled in online CDM courses, but also to students in traditional classrooms at CDM. In this study we analyzed survey responses and grade data to determine whether traditional students found COL recordings to be a valuable substitutional tool and whether the recordings had any impact on student performance. We found that a large majority of traditional CDM students find the recordings useful and believe that they improve performance. Somewhat counter to the students' perceptions, we found that there were no large differences in performance prior to the introduction of COL recordings and after COL recordings began to be available.

Categories and Subject Descriptors

K.3.1 [**Computing Milieux**]: Computer Uses in Education – computer assisted instruction.

General Terms

Design, performance

Keywords

Lecture capture systems, student performance, student perception, retention

1. INTRODUCTION

Like many other institutions DePaul University, and its College of Computing and Digital Media (CDM) in particular, has actively worked to provide online education for students [10]. As early as the mid 1990s, CDM offered students the option to view class sessions remotely, although the technologies used were not scalable. When online learning was introduced in a broad way in 2001, the goal was to provide a large variety of online courses while minimizing the impact on the faculty and the regular sections of courses [7]. To do so, an in-house hardware and software system called Course Online (COL) was developed. COL simultaneously captures audio, video, the instructor's notes written on the whiteboard, and material displayed on the instructor's computer screen. All components are synchronized and presented to students using an in-house course management system. The technology needed to support COL was deployed in all of the CDM-controlled classrooms and many general DePaul classrooms. Hundreds of in-class courses are recorded each quarter, and many of these classes have an associated online section where the students participate in the class by viewing the recordings. The students in the in-class sections have a traditional classroom experience, whether that means a lecture, discussion, or other learning activity, but have access also to COL recordings and the associated course management system.

The impact of some form of lecture capture system on in-class students has been widely studied. One of the motivations to do so is to gauge the impact of such systems on attendance since many institutions provide lecture capture for undergraduates as a value-added feature and do not wish to diminish the experience in the classroom as a result [1, 4, 6, 9, 11, 12]. There have been some mixed results regarding the issue of in-class attendance, with some authors suggesting that attendance is negatively impacted by the availability of lecture recordings [9] while others have found little or no impact on attendance [4, 5, 11, 12]. The impact on the in-class experience is certainly influenced by the ways the students use the recordings, and McGarr has suggested [8] that there are three main uses for recordings (in the case of his work, podcasts): substitutional use (for review and revision), supplementary use (to provide additional information beyond the classroom experience), and creative use (student-generated recordings). There is some literature that suggests substitutional use can change in-class activity in a positive way by allowing students to concentrate on present activities knowing that the recording will allow them to review the details of the class at a later point [1, 4]. There is evidence that both substitutional and supplementary use can improve retention [2, 11] although there is also evidence that the use of lecture capture does not have any impact on student performance [5] and cannot be used to predict scholastic achievement [12]. The type of course that is recorded has an impact on the value of the recordings for students. McKinlay has suggested [9] that a recording of a typical lecture may be superior to the live experience since listeners can pace themselves. He further suggests that a recording of a more interactive classroom experience may be diminished since the deeper learning that such an experience can bring will only be duplicated when students watching or listening to the recording have the ability to communicate in the same way that the students who are present do. The perceived value of the recordings is important since students are more likely to view or listen to the recordings when they perceive that the recordings have value

[12], and one thing that many studies of the impact of lecture capture find is that students believe the availability of recordings to be valuable [4, 6, 10, 11].

Despite having provided lecture recordings to in-class students since 2001, there had never been a study of the impact of lecture recording availability on in-class students at CDM. This study focuses on three main questions: whether in-class CDM students utilize course recording as a substitutional tool to review challenging material or catch up if they missed a class; whether the availability of COL recordings has produced any impact on student performance; and whether students perceive the availability of COL recordings as valuable.

2. STUDY LOGISTICS

We now provide a more detailed overview of the Course Online lecture capture system (COL) used at CDM and discuss the courses that were selected for inclusion.

2.1 Course Online (COL)

As mentioned previously, the in-house hardware and software system, COL, simultaneously captures audio, video, the instructor's notes written on the whiteboard, and the images displayed on the instructor's computer screen. The capture of the information is done automatically, and although the equipment is monitored remotely, there is no technical support staff in the classroom when the recording is done. All the captured components are synchronized, and made available to students registered in the class by the following morning. The recordings can be viewed in several formats, including streaming video, Flash recordings, and when the instructor enables it, podcasts. The recordings are a part of an integrated course management system that allows faculty to post course information such as the syllabus, assignments, class notes, and grades and includes a homework submission system. More technology intensive than labor intensive, this form of lecture capture system was unique when it was introduced [7] although there have been a number of similar systems introduced subsequently [3, 10, 11].

2.2 Courses in the Study

Our assumption in approaching this study was that students taking traditional, in-person classes would find lecture recording most valuable when the course had a stronger emphasis on technically- or mathematically-challenging material. We also believed, as McKinlay suggests [9], that reviewing COL recordings from traditional lectures would be the most rewarding for students and provide them with the most motivation for substitutional use. Since one of the goals of the study was to determine the impact of COL on grade distributions, we considered courses between the 1980s and 2009. While course numbers and titles changed over time, they can be grouped by the following broad categories:

- First Quarter Programming (in Java or C++)
- Foundations of Computer Science
- Algorithms
- Database Design and Technology
- Data Analysis
- Object Oriented Software Development
- User Interface Development
- Web Development
- Analysis and Design Techniques

3. THE SURVEYS

COL provides no way to track statistics about student usage. To gather information about how in-class students are using COL recordings, we conducted two surveys during each quarter (Fall, Winter and Spring) of the 2008 – 2009 academic year. The surveys were also used to gather information about the perceived value of using COL. The "pre-quarter survey" was conducted during the first days of the quarter and the "end-of-quarter survey" during the last week of the quarter.

3.1 Survey Questions

The questions and the possible answers for the pre-quarter Fall 2008 survey were as follows:

1. Sex: female, male, prefer not to specify
2. I am: an undergraduate, a graduate student, a student at large
3. If you are an undergraduate, you are a: freshman (1st year), sophomore (2nd year), junior (3rd year), senior (4th year+)
4. If you are a graduate student, indicate how many quarters you have been a graduate student at DePaul:
5. I have taken a CDM class prior to this quarter: Y/N
6. I have taken a COL-recorded CDM class prior to this quarter: Y/N
7. I have watched at least one COL recording prior to this quarter: Y/N
8. (*Added in Winter 2009*) How many times have you watched COL recordings prior to this quarter: 0, 1, 2, 3, 4, more
9. I found the COL recordings to be a helpful resource when I missed classes: Y/N/I never missed classes (This was to be answered only if the answer to question 7 was yes since otherwise the student had no experience with COL recordings during the class)
10. I found the COL recordings to be a helpful resource for reviewing class material: Y/N/I never used COL for reviewing (This was to be answered only if the answer to question 7 was yes for the reason given above)

The questions and the possible answers for the mid-quarter and end-of-quarter Fall 2008 surveys were the same for the first four questions listed above. We provide the different questions below:

5. I have watched at least one COL recording for this class: Y/N.
6. If you watched at least one COL recording this quarter, indicate all the reasons you watched the recording(s): I missed class; I wanted to review material in preparation for the homework, quizzes, or exams; I wanted to review material to improve my understanding; Other (please indicate your reasons in the box below)
7. Which of the following best describes the frequency with which you watch COL recordings? Mark as many as are applicable for you: Parts of all the recordings this quarter; The entire recording for a particular class; All of the recordings for all of the classes
8. If you watched a COL recording for a particular class, indicate which one(s):
9. What is the overall percentage of the COL recordings that you have watched (1-100%)?
10. How useful was watching the COL recordings? 4 = very useful, 3 = somewhat useful, 2 = not very useful, 1 = not useful at all

11. What grade do you expect to earn in the class: A, B, C, D, F, do not know
12. (*Added in Winter 2009*) Do you think COL has helped you improve your performance: significantly, somewhat, not really

3.2 Analysis of Survey Data

All of the surveys were completed online by students who were solicited by e-mail. The surveys were anonymous, and students who were taking multiple CDM courses covered by the study were sent only a single e-mail request but were given the ability to discuss all of their COL-recorded courses on the survey. Ideally we would have liked to obtain data from classes that did not have COL recordings available as controls, but that is unfortunately not possible. In the vast majority of cases either all of the sections of the class or none of the sections of the class have COL recordings available. Recall as stated before that only those students in traditional or in-person sections, that is, non-online students were solicited for this study.

Table 1 shows the number of solicited students for each quarter. Since some students were taking multiple courses, the number of unique students solicited is less than the total number of students in the courses.

Table 1: Students surveyed

	F08	W09	S09
Total students	625	659	52
Distinct students	546	472	47
Pre-quarter responses/ rates	91 (16.67%)	154 (32.63%)	16 (34.0%)
End-of-quarter responses / rates	50 (9.16%)	108 (25.29%)	10 (21.28%)

The improvement in the response rate in Winter and Spring 2009 resulted from instructors encouraging their students to complete the survey. Instructors were not, however, involved in the collection or analysis of data.

To avoid duplication of the data gathered during the previous two quarters, the Spring 2009 survey was targeted at first-quarter students who would not have been counted in previous quarters. This explains why only 47 students were solicited.

3.2.1 Survey responses

Across the three quarters there were a total of 261 responses for the pre-quarter surveys and 168 responses for the end-of-quarter surveys. Table 2 summarizes responses and rates for basic demographic information, status at DePaul, and expected grade. Targeting only first quarter students in the Spring surveys resulted in some variations in the mix of students in that quarter. Almost all respondents were graduate students, approximately only 25% had taken a CDM course and only 12.5% had taken a prior COL course. Table 3 shows pre-quarter survey responses to the most critical questions.

In addition, 7 (2.7%) indicated that COL recordings were not helpful for missed classes, and 57 (21.8%) indicated that they never missed class. 23 (8.8%) never used COL for review, and 9 (3.4%) did not find COL recordings helpful for review.

Table 4 shows end-of-quarter survey responses to the most critical questions. Note that students were not required to answer each question and were allowed to provide multiple answers to some questions so that the percentages may not sum to 100%.

Table 2: Demographics, Status and expected grade

	Pre-quarter	End-of-quarter
Male	195 (74.7%)	133 (79.2)
Female	62 (23.8%)	28 (16.7)
Not Specified	3 (1.1%)	7 (4.2)
Undergraduate	133 (51%)	72 (42.9)
Graduate	123 (47.1%)	91 (54.2)
Took a CDM class	204 (78.2%)	N/A
Took a COL class	172 (65.9%)	N/A
Expect A	N/A	108 (64.3%)
Expect B	N/A	46 (27.4%)
Expect C or D	N/A	3 (1.8)
Don't know	N/A	11 (6.5%)

Table 3: Pre-quarter survey: Reason for watching lectures

Watched lectures in previous year	
At least once	184 (70.5%)
Reason for watching	
Missed classed	157 (60.2%)
Review	186 (71.3%)

Table 4: End-of-quarter survey responses

Watched lectures	
At least once	148 (88.1%)
How much did they watch	
Parts of some recordings	96 (57.1%)
At least one entire recording	60 (35.7%)
All recordings	20 (11.9%)
Reason for watching	
Missed classed	102 (60.7%)
Prep for class	120 (71.4%)
Review	100 (59.5%)
Percentage of watched recordings	
25% of recordings	37 (22.0%)
25%-50% of recordings	34 (20.2%)
50%-100%	16 (9.5%)
Recordings were useful	
Very	124 (73.8%)
Somewhat	21 (12.5%)
Not useful	31(1.8%)
Recordings improved my performance	
Significantly	68 (40.5%)
Somewhat	39 (23.2%)
Did not improve	11 (6.5%)

3.2.2 Some conclusions

A majority of students in traditional classrooms at CDM actively watched the COL recordings, with 88.1% of respondents indicating that they watched at least one recording during the quarter. The most frequently cited reason for doing so was to prepare for class (71.4%) followed closely by missing class (60.7%) and reviewing for understanding (59.5%). This is consistent with other studies of student use of lecture recordings [4, 10, 11]. It is interesting that missing class is not the most frequent reason for watching the recordings, supporting other studies that have suggested that the availability of lecture recordings does not negatively impact attendance [4, 5, 11, 12]. Approximately a third of the students watched the entire recording, with most choosing to watch parts of all the recordings. This is consistent with their reported use of the recordings for class preparation and review. Students in the traditional course overwhelmingly found the recordings useful, with 86.3% of respondents indicating this, even if only 63.7% of the students believed that it improved performance, a result that is again consistent with previous work [4, 11]. This is the most surprising result of the survey, since one might assume that students would only find the recordings beneficial if they believe that they would improve performance. And yet there is a gap of 22 percentage points between the number of students who find the recordings useful and the number of students who believe they improve performance. Other studies have suggested that students appreciate the safety net provided by having lecture recordings available [4, 5, 6]. Unfortunately the survey questions did not capture what it was about the recordings that the students found useful.

4. GRADE DATA

To better understand the performance trends of the years before and after COL recordings were available, we gathered and analyzed grade data from the CDM courses included in this study. We will call the data from the period 1982 – 2000 "pre-COL" since COL recordings began in 2001. The data from the period 2001 - 2008 will be referred to as "COL". All grade data available in our systems was included, producing an overall data set of 12550 individual grades (6086 pre-COL grades, and 6464 grades earned during COL).

It is useful to consider the standard "satisfactory" (grades at or above C-) and "unsatisfactory" (grades below C-) grade classification in the context of this study. In total, students in the period 1982 – 2009 earned 9162 (73%) satisfactory and 2100 (16.7%) unsatisfactory grades. Missing grades, withdrawals and administrative grades were excluded from our analysis, which is why the totals do not sum to 100.

4.1 Analysis of Grade Data

To begin to understand whether the COL recordings had an impact on the courses in the study, we ran a chi-squared analysis on the satisfactory grades versus the unsatisfactory grades earned in each type of course. The analysis showed seven groupings of courses with statistically significant differences between the number of satisfactory and unsatisfactory grades earned pre-COL and during COL (see Table 5). In all cases there were more satisfactory grades earned during the pre-COL period. This is an interesting result, as it appears on the surface to contradict the

impression on the part of the students that the availability of the COL recordings had a positive impact on their grades.

Table 5: Courses with statistically-significant pre COL /COL

Course grouping	Chi-squared	Likelihood ratio	N
First-quarter programming	30.514	30.113	10445
Database technology	44.846	45.405	5493
Database design	16.634	17.153	1568
Algorithms	32.146	30.392	3196
Data analysis	50.645	49.467	5906
User-interface development	93.246	107.674	1509
Object-oriented software development	54.710	76.932	2266

To gain some insight on whether the availability of recordings was a key contributor to the consistently greater percentage of satisfactory grades pre-COL, further divided the data for the statistically significant courses by 5-year time periods.

Table 6: Percentage of satisfactory grades for statistically-significant courses by 5-year time periods

Course grouping	Pre 86-90	Pre 91-95	Pre 96-00	COL 01-05	COL 06-09
First-quarter programming	76%	86%	84%	82%	82%
Database technology	93%	100%	89%	86%	94%
Database design	92%	97%	96%	87%	86%
Algorithms	83%	94%	92%	87%	87%
Data analysis	81%	87%	84%	84%	80%
User-interface development	N/A	N/A	90%	79%	80%
Object-oriented software development	N/A	N/A	100%	90%	92%

The distribution in Table 6 suggests that there are confounding factors that make it difficult to conclude that the availability of recordings is the only factor in the grade differences. A discussion of a specific example will help illustrate the confounding factors. Consider the first-quarter programming grouping. Prior to 2001, the language taught was C++. In 2001 C++ was phased out, and Java began to be taught under a different course number, In 2004 several majors required the reintroduction of C++. While each of these courses has been taught by a fairly consistent set of instructors (for example there have been only 9 instructors for the 42 sections of C++ taught since 2004), the grades for First Quarter Programming relate to different languages over the time periods. This course grouping is further complicated by the dot-com boom that occurred in the late 1990s and early 2000s which drew a broader population of students to take technical courses. The first-quarter programming classes are required in the prerequisite phase of many Masters degrees at CDM, and those courses often serve as a barrier to further progress for some students. Finally, COL recordings were introduced once online programs became available at CDM, but because of the purpose of the study grades from the online sections were not considered in the analysis. Online courses have a tendency to attract students who are more organized and mature, and it may be that the post-COL period therefore has a different mix of students in the introductory programming classes than the pre-COL period. That there is less than a 5% difference between the pre- and post-COL time periods is somewhat surprising given all of these factors.

5. CONCLUSIONS AND FUTURE WORK

A large majority of students in traditional classrooms at CDM report actively watching COL recordings. Students report doing so to prepare for class and improve understanding as well as to make up for missed classes. They also find the recordings useful and believe that they improve performance, although there is a 20 percentage point gap between the students who find them useful and those who believe they improve performance. Most students indicate that they are watching only parts of the COL recordings.

The study of grade data is somewhat counter to the students' impressions. When there are statistically significant differences among the grades, the courses for which COL recordings were available have a lower percentage of satisfactory grades. However, there are a number of confounding factors such as the changing content of courses over time, the instructors assigned to the courses, the degree programs in which the courses are required, fluctuations in the student population due to increasing and waning interest in technology programs, and the change of the mix of traditional students after the introduction of online programs. We are not able to conclude that the availability of COL recordings of courses for traditional students is the sole factor in the grade differences for the courses in the study.

Clearly, however, students find value in COL recordings. It would be interesting to develop a new survey to determine more clearly what it is that students find useful about either watching the recordings or having the recordings available for watching. It would also be useful to gather more information about what parts of the recordings the students are watching and whether students are reviewing the recordings as frequently as they self report. While COL does not have mechanisms to track student access of recordings, DePaul University is moving to the Desire2Learn course management system which does have mechanisms that allow for more precise monitoring of student activity. The integration of lecture capture recordings into the Desire2Learn system would provide an opportunity to do a more precise study of student behavior with respect to course recordings.

6. REFERENCES

[1] Balfour, J. 2006. Audio Recordings of Lectures as an E-Learning Resource. In the *Built Environment Education Annual Conference* (*BEECON 2006*), September 2006, London, U.K., http://www.cebe.heacademy.ac.uk/news/events/beecon2006/pdf/P24_Jim_Balfour.pdf, accessed August 2010.

[2] Briggs, L. 2007. Can Classroom Capture Boost Retention Rates*? Campus Technology*. http://campustechnology.com/articles/2007/10/can-classroom-capture-boost-retention-rates.aspx, accessed August 2010.

[3] Brotherton, J. and Abowd, G. 2004. Lessons Learned From eClass: Assessing Automated Capture and Access in the Classroom. In *ACM Transactions on Computer-Human Interaction*, 11:2, pp. 121-155.

[4] Davis, S., Connolly, A, and Linfield, E. 2009. Lecture Capture: Making the Most of Face-to-face Learning. In *Engineering Education: Journal of the Higher Education Academy Engineering Subject Centre*, 4:2.

[5] Deal, A. 2007. A Teaching with Technology White Paper: Podcasting. Available from http://192.231.233.6/IDlab/CMU_Podcasting_Jun07.pdf, accessed August 2010.

[6] Guertin, L., Bodek, M., Zappe, S., and Heeyoung, K. 2007. Questioning the Student Use of and Desire for Lecture Podcasts. In *the Journal of Online Learning and Teaching*, 3:2.

[7] Knight, L. , Steinbach, T., and White J. 2002. An Alternative Approach to Web-based Education: Technology-intensive, Not Labor-Intensive. In the *Proceedings of the Information Systems Education Conference*, San Antonio, Texas.

[8] McGarr, O. 2009. A Review of Podcasting in Higher Education: Its Influence on the Traditional Lecture. In the *Australasian Journal of Educational Technology*, 25:3, pp. 309-321.

[9] McKinlay, N. 2007. The Vanishing Student Trick – The Trouble with Recording Lectures. In *the 6th Teaching Matters Conference: Showcasing Innovation*, University of Tasmania.

[10] Nagel, D. 2008. Lecture Capture: No Longer Optional? http://campustechnology.com/articles/2008/09/lecture-capture-no-longer-optional.aspx, accessed August 2010.

[11] Toppin, I. 2010. Video Lecture Capture (VLC) system: A Comparison of Student versus Faculty Perceptions. In *Education and Information Technologies*, Volume 15.

[12] Von Konsky, B., Ivins, J., and Gribble, S. 2009. Lecture Attendance and Web Based Lecture Technologies: A Comparison of Student Perceptions and Usage Patterns. In the *Australasian Journal of Educational Technology*, 24:4, pp. 581-595.

Impact of an e-learning Platform on CSE Lectures

Guillaume Jourjon
NICTA
Alexandria, NSW 1435
Australia
guillaume.jourjon@nic-ta.com.au

Salil Kanhere
UNSW
Sydney,
Australia
salilk@csw.unsw.edu.au

Jun Yao
UNSW
Sydney,
Australia
jyao@csw.unsw.edu.au

ABSTRACT

This article presents a comprehensive summary and recommendations towards the use of IREEL, an e-learning platform designed for network studies in CSE courses, based on our hands-on experience in a large hybrid undergraduate/postgraduate course at the UNSW. We found that the tool was well received by the students for understanding key concepts, especially when compared to legacy tools used in labs. Furthermore we show that our tool was able to handle a very large number of experiments in a relatively short amount of time.

Categories and Subject Descriptors

K.3.2 [**Computers and Education**]: Computer and Information Science Education

General Terms

Experimentation, Performance

Keywords

CSE lecture, e-learning, Networking

1. INTRODUCTION

During the last decade, general knowledge of networking and internetworking in particular has become a basic component of the many engineering courses, ranging from pure CS courses to aeronautical engineering through electrical engineering. In this context, when teaching introductory or advanced networking subjects, lecturers face the difficulty of illustrating both the concepts and technologies, and assessing students from various backgrounds. This illustration phase is usually implemented in the form of laboratory classes, where students use a variety of software tools to experiment on various networking scenarios and observe the protocols studied in the lectures in action. While different solutions may be used for different course levels, it is desirable that such tools allow the experimentations of both basic and advanced networking scenarios. This would offer a degree of consistency and ease the learning curve across a 3–4 year engineering degree. Similarly, the tools used in the assessment phase need to allow the fair evaluation of students in the presented key concepts. For example, the classical client server based programming assignment from most introductory network courses [10] might not be suitable for students with limited programming skills (*e.g.* some undergraduate engineering programs do not have compulsory programming courses).

In order to address student diversity, lecturers have often developed tools and labs based on research tools. Among these tools, two kinds of approaches may be identified; simulation-based such as ns-3 or OPNET [1, 5] and real measurement-based in closed lab settings such as tcpdump or wireshark [4]. The first offers a large panel of experiments but suffers from the models on which the studied protocols are based. The latter method allows students to get a more realistic experience but the associated labs are difficult to maintain and cannot be repeated once the lab is finished. Lately, a third option has been made available through the development of large-scale testbeds and in particular with PlanetLab [2]. Nevertheless, this kind of approach does not offer a general enough abstraction to be used by students with little knowledge in programming as demonstrated by the implementation in Plush [6] and Seattle testbed [3].

In [7] and its second version in [8], we have proposed a novel approach for teaching networking in undergraduate and postgraduatecourses called IREEL[1]. This solution originally provided an e-learning platform where students followed labs' description that recalls the lecture and then had to configure experiments to answer related questions. The originality of IREEL consists in offering the ability to run real experiments whilst conserving an easy to use interface. While the two versions of IREEL provide the same basic functionality to the student, the second version [8] offers more flexibility to the instructor. Indeed, we have integrated a state of the art testbed control and management framework called OMF [12] and its companion measurement library OML [13].

During the second semester of 2010, we used IREEL for an hybrid undergraduate/postgraduate introductory course on networking at the University of New South Wales, Australia. In this course, the IREEL platform has been used during two labs whilst the remainder of the lab set used the

---

[1]The current platform is available on `http://ireel.npc.nitca.com.au/`

Wireshark packet analyser. At the end of the course the students were asked to give an evaluation of both the UI and the teaching capabilities of the tool. The analysis of the students' use of this tool shows that it was able to reach a very high robustness. Furthermore, the evaluation forms showed that the tool was very well rated in terms of overall understanding of lectures key concepts and when compared to the Wireshark labs.

The remainder of this paper is organised as follows. Section 2 presents the methodology used in our study and in particular the details about the students and the course material. Section 3 gives comprehensive statistical analysis of the potential benefit of IREEL as seen by the students and also provides an overview of qualitative measurements of the e-learning platform. In Section 4, we discuss the implications of these results in terms of usability of the platform in an introductory course to networking and as a stand alone tool. Finally, Section 5 concludes this paper and presents some potential future works.

2. METHOD

We used the IREEL platform in a hybrid postgraduate/ undergraduate course offered by the School of Computer Science and Engineering at the University of NSW, Sydney during the second semester of 2010. This course, entitled "COMP 3331/9331, Computer Networks and Applications", provides an in-depth overview of computer networks and the Internet. This is a core course for the Software Engineering and Computer Engineering Undergraduate programs and also for the Internetworking major under the Master of IT postgraduate program.

However, students from various Engineering programs including Computer Science, Bioinformatics, Electrical and Telecommunications Engineering, Mechanical Engineering and Information Technology also enrol in this course. This course has an assessable lab component which makes up approximately 10% of the total course mark. The labs were designed such that students could get a hands-on understanding of the various protocols discussed during the lectures. There were a total of seven lab exercises of which five labs used the Wireshark sniffer [4] to observe pre-recorded packet traces. The remaining 2 lab exercises used the IREEL platform [8]. The aim of the first IREEL lab was to illustrate the behaviour and the evolution of the HTTP protocol. The second lab focused on explaining the basics of reliable data transfer over the network. At the end of the semester, after the conclusion of all lab exercises, students were asked to fill in a written questionnaire to provide feedback on the UI and effectiveness of IREEL as a learning tool.

2.1 Participants

A total of 103 undergraduate and 59 postgraduate students were enrolled in COMP 3331/9331 during semester 2, 2010. Out of these students, a total of 63 students consisting of 41 undergraduates and 18 postgraduates completed the evaluation questionnaire. The students in the sample ranged from 19 to 30 years of age of whom 7 were female and 52 male.

The students were divided into 10 lab classes each containing approximately 16 students. Students worked on the labs in pairs. Each lab class lasted for 2 hours. Six labs took place on Tuesday in 2 hour slots from 12pm–8pm. Two parallel labs were held from 12pm–2pm and 2pm–4pm. Four

labs were held on Wednesday with two sessions in parallel running form 12pm–2pm and 2pm–4pm. The answers to the lab questions were only due in the following week. Thus students could run experiments outside lab hours via the IREEL web interface, which was always accessible.

During IREEL labs, students were teamed in pairs to address questions based on both theoretical background and live experiments. After receiving their marks on the two IREEL labs, the students answered the evaluation forms during a non-compulsory lab session.

2.2 Materials

2.2.1 IREEL Labs Description

The lecture was following a top-down approach [10] and therefore we decided to use our platform to illustrate two fundamental concepts from the lectures; the evolution of HTTP, referred to in the following of the document as the first lab, and the illustration of Reliable Data Transfer, referred to as the second lab in the remainder of this article.

During the first lab, students, after a reminder of the lecture, were asked to analyse the difference in the performance of the two versions of HTTP (1.0 and 1.1). The experiments consisted of downloading several HTML pages with a varying number of embedded objects using the two versions of HTTP and comparing the total end-to-end delay. Overall, in this lab, students had to configure and analyse the results of 13 experiments.

In the second lab, students analysed the performance of different reliable data transfer; Stop and Wait, Go-back-N and Selective Repeat. In this lab, the students were able to analyse the effect of the retransmission time-out based on the end-to-end delay and the effect of the packet loss rate in the transmission of a stream of packets. During this lab, students had to configure more than 30 experiments. However, due to the randomness of the packet loss rate the number of experiments was expected to be greater.

2.2.2 Student Feedback Forms

After the two IREEL labs, students gave us feedback on the newly introduced tool. This feedback consisted of 11 questions rated using a likert-type scale [11] divided in two categories, "UI appreciation" and "learning capability and its comparison with other tool"[2].

In the first category, the students rated IREEL in terms of user interface, description of labs and questions and general navigation through the website.

In the second category, the students rated IREEL as an e-leaning tool, in particular, for concept understanding, related lecture understanding, and whether it was an effective self-learning tool. Students were also asked to compare it to other labs in which they had used Wireshark [4].

3. RESULTS

In this section, we first present the quantitative analysis of the use of IREEL during the two aforementioned labs. Then we present the statistical analysis of the feedback forms.

3.1 Quantitative Factors

During the month IREEL was used, more than seven thousand experiments were configured.

[2]This form is accessible on `http://guillaume.jourjon.name/ireel.pdf`

If we compare this number with the average number of experiments run on the actual Orbit-lab testbed, we have, during a single month, run more experiments than what is usually conducted using OMF in the Orbit-lab in an entire year. This large number demonstrate the scalability of the the platform.

Table 1 presents the experiment success rate summary, where an experiment is considered successful if the student received all the associated results.

Table 1: Quantitative data

	Total Experiment	Success Rate
1st lab	1,959	100.0%
2nd lab	5,434	97.9%
Total	7,393	98.4%

The previous table shows that the robustness of the platform is very high despite some error in the second lab. Furthermore we can verify that the students ran more than twice the number of experiments for the 2nd lab as compared to the first. As discussed earlier, the higher ratio is because of the requisite number of experiments to be done to answer all the questions. It is indeed higher than expected because of the reconfiguration of the failed experiments and the fact that some experiments were configured several times in order to obtain the correct packet loss rate.

Table 2 presents the average number of experiments done by each group of student as well as the standard deviation.

Table 2: Number of experiments

	Average	Standard Deviation
1st lab	20.97	5.30
2nd lab	60.14	14.84

As expected the number of experiments in the second lab was higher than for the first one. Overall, the average number of experiments for both was higher than the required number. This is explained by two factors; the failed experiment as shown in the previous Table and the fact that even if students were paired, we did not put any restriction on whether one or both students could configure experiments.

3.2 Qualitative Factors

In this section, we provide results from students' feedback rating. These results have been reformatted to be centred on 0 with a scale going from −2 to 2 with 2 being in favour of IREEL and −2 against it.

Figure 1 presents the first, second and third quartile of the eleven normalised likert-type scales [11]. On these normalised scales positive values are in favour of IREEL. For example, if the value is 11 in the case of *norm_spe_concept_vs* it means that the student rated IREEL as a better tool to understand specific concept compared to Wireshark [4].

Overall, the appreciation of IREEL is positive except for the self-learning components. In particular, the user interface components, with the exception of the overall interface, have a median value of 1 and three have a first quartile of 0.

Concerning the e-learning perception, students considered IREEL as an efficient e-leaning tool by itself and compared

to Wireshark for teaching general and specific concept but did not find it as good a self-learning tool. This result is surprising especially as Wireshark is only accessible in labs whereas IREEL is available from anywhere, allowing students to go further and configure a larger range of experiments.

3.2.1 User Interface Factor

In Table 3, we present the mean values and the standard deviations of the user interface factors.

Table 3: UI appreciation

	Average	Std Dev
Result Analysis	.60	.834
Experiment Configuration	.27	1.066
Lab Description	.79	.919
Question Description	.75	.861
General UI	.02	1.198

Overall, IREEL received mainly positive UI appreciations. Nevertheless, students gave lower ratings to the general interface than to the other components.

3.2.2 Learning Perception

In Table 4, we present mean values and the standard deviations of the learning capability of IREEL.

Table 4: UI appreciation

	Average	Std Dev
General Concept	.41	1.186
Specific Concept	.60	1.238
Self Learning Tool	−.17	1.498
General Concept vs Wireshark	.41	1.433
Specific Concept vs Wireshark	.54	1.216
Self Learning Tool vs Wireshark	−.10	1.316

This table shows that, with the exception of its self-learning capacities, IREEL has been perceived as an effective tool to promote the student understanding of the general and specific concepts presented previously in lectures. In addition, this table shows that the students agreed less in their perception of the knowledge transmission faculty of IREEL than they did about IREEL's UI impression as confirmed by the larger values of the standard deviation.

3.2.3 Impact of the UI on the learning perception

In Table 5, we present the different correlations between the students' UI perception and their e-learning experience.

These results show a significant correlation between the general UI perception and the three comparisons to the Wireshark's labs and the self learning tool perception. Table 5 also shows that there is significant correlation between the lab description and the understanding of general and specific concepts when compared to the Wireshark's lab. On the contrary, no significant correlation was found between the perception of both experiment configuration and result analysis when compared to the e-learning perception.

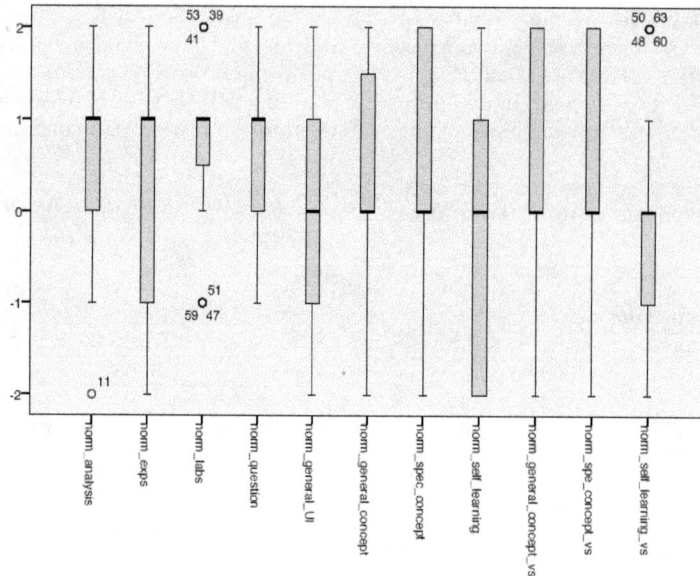

Figure 1: Overall quartiles of the different likert scales from the evaluation forms

Table 5: Correlation of Learning perception vs UI appreciation. (** Correlation is significant at the 0.01 level (2-tailed). *. Correlation is significant at the 0.05 level (2-tailed)).

		Analysis	Experiment	Lab Description	Question Description	General UI
General	Pearson Correlation	.103	.102	.257*	.136	.188
Concept	Sig. (2-tailed)	.422	.427	.042	.288	.140
Specific	Pearson Correlation	.032	-.003	.310*	.252*	.243
Concept	Sig. (2-tailed)	.800	.981	.014	.046	.054
Self Learning	Pearson Correlation	.060	.202	.208	.253*	.361**
Tool	Sig. (2-tailed)	.641	.113	.102	.046	.004
General Concept	Pearson Correlation	.004	.063	.360**	.348**	.353**
vs Wireshark	Sig. (2-tailed)	.973	.623	.004	.005	.005
Specific Concept	Pearson Correlation	.199	.185	.419**	.272*	.371**
vs Wireshark	Sig. (2-tailed)	.118	.148	.001	.031	.003
Self Learning Tool	Pearson Correlation	.200	.295*	.250*	.220	.420**
vs Wireshark	Sig. (2-tailed)	.116	.019	.048	.083	.001

4. DISCUSSION

4.1 On the quantitative metrics

The quantitative metrics, as shown in Section 3.1, indicate the robustness of the platform. Nevertheless, the few failed experiments may have contributed to some of the lower ratings in the evaluation. These weaknesses have been identified in the new version of IREEL and addressed accordingly. They were mainly due to a stack overflow error in the measurement server. This error only appeared in the second lab, as the results in the first lab consisted as a separated file and therefore the measurement server was not in use.

This error in the measurement server has been magnified due to the concentration of the labs. Indeed, as explained in Section 2.2, the ten labs being concentrated in the time span of two afternoons and the experiments not being prerecorded, students in late afternoon labs suffered some delays when retrieving their experiment results.

These delays did not occur in the first lab mainly for two reasons. The first reason being the lower number of experiments required for the first lab (as shown in Table 2). The second and main reason is the natural learning curve of the students exposed to a new tool. Indeed, we found that when students were using IREEL for the first time, they spent a substantial amount of time reading through the entire description of the lab exercise before starting the experiments During their first experiments, students waited to get results prior to configuring new ones. Therefore the experiment queue was rarely over ten experiments (*i.e.* about three minutes). During the second lab, students did not take the same approach and very quickly started configuring experiments after only briefly glancing through the lab description. Therefore, when the next lab started, the platform was still processing the queue of the previous lab.

In order to solve this problem, we recommend the lab instructors to limit the number of experiments to only fifteen per group as it seems to be efficient in the first lab. Another solution to this problem would be the introduction of reservation following the schema developed for OMF [9]. Finally, based on our experience, we do not recommend to use this platform with such a concentrated schedule unless the lecturer is able to expand the computation resources available beyond the default configuration of a single client and server.

4.2 On the evaluation forms

The evaluation forms gave us some important indications about IREEL. The main finding of these forms is the students' perception of the teaching capabilities of this newly introduced tool. As expected, students gave high ratings to our e-learning platform for concept understanding as a whole and when compared to the Wireshark's labs. In the comparison cases, it seems, based on the correlations with the lab and question descriptions, that the organisation of the lab on a single web page has been well received and helped the students to identify the concepts the labs were meant to emphasise.

The most surprising finding of the forms concerns ratings of our platform as a self-learning tool. Indeed, since our platform is a web-based e-learning platform which is accessible anytime and from anywhere thus providing students a longer hands-on time and more flexibility with the tool, we expected to receive good feedback for the self-learning aspect.

In order to explain this finding, we propose two hypotheses. The first is linked to the correlation between the general UI interface and the self-learning tool ratings. As shown in Table 5, there is a significant correlation between these ratings, which could be due to a lack of separate IREEL manual instead of online documentations and online how-to.

The second hypothesis to explain students' self-learning appreciation is related to the way students marked our platform when compared to Wireshark labs and can be called a "Google effect". This proposed effect concerns the tendency whereby students may not read online document or manual but go directly to Google or other search engines to find similar labs to answer the questions. Indeed, even if we consider Wirreshark as a good teaching tool, we may not also consider it as a effective self-learning tool as students usually cannot modify the underlying network topology nor redo the experiment once the lab is finished. The main difference between the two tools resides in the large community of Wireshark users and therefore it was considered more beneficial for the student to compare what they were asked to do with what other students or researchers did using this tool.

In order to improve the self learning aspect of our platform, one solution, in addition to provide an off-line manual, might be to allow more modularities to the student. For example, we could not specify all the parameters they need to configure and instead give them a range for each of them.

5. CONCLUDING REMARKS

Based on both quantitative and student-opinion based metrics, we have presented a comprehensive, and exhaustive, study of the IREEL e-learning platform. Based on the quantitative data we obtained, we found that our platform is robust even when stressed to a very high degree, for example we conducted nearly 5500 experiments in less than a week. We have also been able to better quantify the number of experiments to configure in a span of 2 hours in order to give a better quality of experience to the students and thus avoid multiple configurations of the same experiment.

The analysis of the evaluation forms was very positive overall, as the students rated that our platform was more effective to promote the understanding of specific and general concept than Wireshark-based labs. Nevertheless, students did not rate it as highly for a self-learning platform. We hypothesised that students might have found Wireshark to be a better self-learning experiences because they were able to compare their experience with this tool with other Internet users.

We plan to reuse this tool in the second semester of 2011 in a similar class environment. This would provide further support for the proposed "Google effect" hypothesis. Furthermore, we plan to use this platform in a more advanced course where the students will have to develop their own protocols and test them through the web interface using the next generation of IREEL based on the OMF portal [9].

6. REFERENCES

[1] NS3 Network Simulator. *at:* `http://www.nsnam.org/`.

[2] PlanetLab Testbed. `http://www.planet-lab.org/`.

[3] Seattle, Open Peer-to-Peer computing. `https://seattle.cs.washington.edu/html/`.

[4] Tcpdump/libpcap public repository. `http://tcpdump.org`.

[5] The OPNET Network Simulator. *at:* `http://www.opnet.com/`.

[6] J. Albrecht, C. Tuttle, A. C. Snoeren, and A. Vahdat. PlanetLab Application Management Using Plush. In *ACM Operating Systems Review*, 2006.

[7] L. Dairaine, G. Jourjon, E. Lochin, and S. Ardon. IREEL: Remote Experimentation with Real Protocols and Applications over Emulated Network. *Inroads, the SIGCSE Bulletin*, 39(2):92–96, June 2007.

[8] G. Jourjon, T. Rakotoarivelo, and M. Ott. From Learning to Researching, Ease the Shift through Testbeds. In *Proc. of TridentCom 2010,*, volume 46 of *LNICST*, pages 496–505, Berlin Heidelberg, May 2010. Springer-Verlag.

[9] G. Jourjon, T. Rakotoarivelo, and M. Ott. A Portal to Support Rigorous Experimental Methodology in Networking Research. In *Proc. of TridentCom 2011*, 2011.

[10] J. F. Kurose and K. W. Ross. *Computer Networking: A Top-Down Approach, 4th Edition*. Addison-Wesley, 2008.

[11] R. Likert. A Technique for the Measurement of Attitudes. *Archives of Psychology*, 22(140):1–55, 1932.

[12] T. Rakotoarivelo, M. Ott, I. Seskar, and G. Jourjon. OMF: a control and management framework for networking testbeds. In *SOSP Workshop on Real Overlays and Distributed Systems (ROADS '09)*, page 6, Big Sky, USA, Oct. 2009.

[13] J. White, G. Jourjon, T. Rakotoarivelo, and M. Ott. Measurement architectures for network experiments with disconnected mobile nodes. In *Proc. of TridentCom 2010*, volume 46 of *LNICST*, pages 350–365, Berlin Heidelberg, May 2010. Springer-Verlag.

Evaluating How Students would use a Collaborative Linked Learning Space

Kai Michael Höver
hoever@acm.org

Michael Hartle
mhartle@tk.informatik.tu-darmstadt.de

Guido Rößling
roessling@acm.org

Max Mühlhäuser
Max.Muehlhaeuser@acm.org
Dept. of Computer Science
TU Darmstadt
64289 Darmstadt, Germany

ABSTRACT

Personal interaction with learning materials, (re-)arranging learning resources in a semantically meaningful way is important for comprehension and personal knowledge construction. Current learning systems only enable learners to add simple digital ink or text notes. How would users work with a system for collaboratively augmenting and semantically connecting learning materials with related knowledge resources? This paper presents user studies conducted with both students and educators to elicit users' acceptance, needs and preferences regarding such a learning system.

Categories and Subject Descriptors

K.3.1 [**Computer Uses in Education**]: Collaborative learning; K.3.2 [**Computer and Information Science Education**]: Computer science education

General Terms

Design, Experimentation

Keywords

CLLS, Collaborative Learning, Study, User Requirements, Web-based Learning

1. INTRODUCTION

Besides learning materials provided by educators, students create and search for additional learning resources, especially in the World Wide Web [9]. This may be due to various reasons, e.g., if students do not have sufficient prior knowledge to understand the content, or if learning materials do not satisfy individual learning preferences. Due to these reasons, students implicitly augment provided learning material. Augmentations typically include content and state-

ments about the relationship between learning resources. For example, a figure in a PDF exemplifies the content of a slide, or a paragraph of a website contradicts a section of a lecture video.

Active learning with the provided learning materials is an important part of learning processes for transferring provided information to personal knowledge. Iske underlines the importance of the creation of connections, the correlation and meaningful arranging of information and putting knowledge in context [8]. Empirical studies in the field of Adaptive Hypermedia showed the positive effect of link annotation to guide students [6]. By sharing learning resources with other learners and explicitly naming the relationship between the resources

- students can see the relationships between different learning resources as an orientation aid,
- other students can benefit from the augmentations added by fellow students,
- educators can see how students are interacting with the learning material,
- educators can benefit from the students' augmentation, e.g., to see which parts have been difficult to understand, and to find additional or better presentations for their lectures.

In this paper, we present the results of a study examing how students and educators accept and would use a system that enables users to add learning resources to lecture recordings, and to connect various information resources. With this evaluation, we underline theoretical considerations by eliciting the needs and acceptance of both students and educators for such a system. We begin with an overview of related learning systems, introduce a working prototype used for evaluation, explain the evaluation design and present its results. Finally, we provide a summary and an outlook on future work.

2. STATE OF THE ART

Many systems exist for presenting lecture materials and enabling users to add annotations to lecture materials. Systems such as AOF [11], and We-LCoME [5] enable students to replay lecture recordings and to add text notes to slides. eMargo [12] allows students to add text notes to the document margin. Other systems such as Livenotes [10], and WriteOn [4] support the addition of ink notes. Some others allow students to add both text and digital ink notes, for example Classroom Presenter [1] and CoScribe [13]. MRAS [2] enables users to add audio annotations to lecture videos. CoScribe [13] also links paper-based notes with web-based resources. However, none of these learning systems allows users to explicitly name the semantic relationship between two learning resources in a machine processable form.

This brief overview shows that many systems limit the augmentations of learning materials for both educators and students. Due to these limitations, learners can hardly augment the provided learning material with other learning resources, either found or created by themselves, and describe the semantic relationships between them.

In addition, most of the above systems are desktop applications for Windows. Some support a wider range of operating systems (OSs) as they are Java- or Flash-based, but require additional installations. Those systems also do not support iOS-based devices, such as the iPhone and the iPad. Therefore, learners are restricted to particular OSs and devices when learning. This is a problem for supporting both traditional and mobile learning scenarios.

To sum up, the discussed systems offer no or only limited support for:

- augmenting the provided learning materials for both students and instructors regarding various media types,
- arranging different learning resources and describing the connection between them,
- using a wide range of different devices including laptops, mobile devices, and tablet PCs and computers,
- exchanging learning resources between lecturers and students, and between students.

In the next section, we introduce a system that addresses these problems. We then present studies that examine the acceptance and preferences of both students and educators.

3. THE CLLS SYSTEM

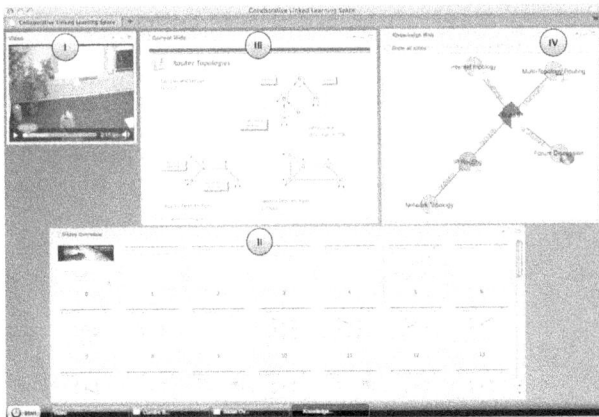

Figure 1: Graphical User Interface of CLLS

Collaborative Linked Learning Space (CLLS) is a web-based application. Users interact with the system with their browsers. Figure 1 depicts the user interface of CLLS. It shows a lecture recording and the corresponding knowledge graph that is collaboratively created by the users. The lecture replay functionality provides a video of the lecturer (I), a slides overview (II), and the currently selected slide (III). The knowledge graph window (IV) shows a graphical rep-

resentation of the collaboratively created knowledge graph. Nodes represent learning resources such as slides, PDF documents, or images; edges represent the relationship between the learning resources, e.g., "illustrates", "contradicts", or "exemplifies". Users can for example link a slide with a figure by simply dragging and dropping an image onto the slide or the corresponding node in the knowledge graph. In principle, all information resources can be linked with each other as long as they have an Uniform Resource Identifier (URI). After the user has chosen the label for the relationship, the knowledge graph automatically updates, and the new information are distributed if the added resource is shared. A more detailed description of the system can be found in [7].

4. USER INTERVIEWS

We conducted interviews with both computer science students and educators. In this section, we describe the goals of the study, the chosen methodology, and the results.

4.1 Goals and methodology

We interviewed *students* about the following aspects:

- How do students assess the opportunity to link learning resources with other material with a semantical description, and how would they use this?
- How do students assess the usability of CLLS?
- Do students see a benefit in using CLLS and how would they use it?

Educators were interviewed about similar aspects:

- How do educators assess the opportunity to link learning resources with each other and how would they use this?
- Would educators use such a system for their courses?
- Which pros and cons are seen by educators?

The methodology consisted of semi-structured interviews. A common structure with key questions ensured consistency between the interviews. To enhance the interviewees' understanding and to contextualize the questions, the interviewees had the opportunity to use the system. We also demonstrated the system at the beginning of each interview.

A 5-point Likert scale was used when we asked for an interviewee's assessment. 1 always meant "strongly disagree" or "not helpful", and 5 was "strongly agree" or "very helpful", depending on the type of question. For these questions, the arithmetic mean (AM) and the standard deviation (SD) were computed. One-sample t-tests on the 0.05 level were conducted to investigate whether the ratings were significantly higher or lower than the midpoint of the Likert scale. If yes, values are printed italic. Frequency and statistical analyses of the consolidated interview data were carried out to reach a comprehensive and in-depth understanding of users' views.

The interviews were conducted with two groups: 14 computer science students and 6 computer science lecturers from different research fields including P2P networks, HCI, computer networks, and e-learning. On average, each interview took 1.5 hour. Partly, both groups had the same or similar questions. Due to different foci of the interviews, there were also differences in questions. We also performed an acceptance study with students. They could use the system in advance and were thus familiar with the system. Educators received a demonstration of the system at the beginning of the interviews.

Semantic description	Students AM (SD)	Educators AM (SD)
explains	4.86 (0.36)	4.83 (0.41)
example for	4.57 (0.76)	5.0 (0.0)
illustrates	4.14 (1.29)	4.0 (1.10)
extends	3.86 (1.03)	4.6 (0.55)
contradicts	3.79 (1.37)	3.4 (0.89)
agrees	2.57 (1.16)	2.8 (1.3)

Table 1: Ratings of the helpfulness of semantic descriptions

4.2 Results

In the following, we present the results of the interviews. Where students and educators had the same question, we compare their answers.

4.2.1 Usability

We tested the usability of the system by conducting a System Usability Scale (SUS) test [3] with the students. SUS scores have a range of 0 to 100. The average score was 88. Thus, students assess the system as very easy to use. This includes an easy navigation through lecture recordings and connecting two learning resources by drag and drop.

4.2.2 Linking learning resources

Students assessed the possibility of linking different learning resources as very helpful (AM=4.71, SD=0.47). They also welcomed the possibility to describe the semantic meaning of such a link (AM=4.57, SD=0.65). Educators agreed with this appraisal. In their opinions, this is very helpful for themselves (AM=4.5, SD=0.84) and students (AM=4.83, SD=0.41). They also thought that a semantic description of the connections between learning resources is helpful for themselves (AM=3.67, SD=0.52) and especially for students in their learning processes (AM=4.20, SD=0.84).

An open question asked both students and educators which semantic descriptions they would use with the system. Both groups suggested "explains", "example for", and "illustrates". Students added "question to" to this list, while educators added structural terms like "prerequisite for", "before" and "after" referring to the didactical design of a course.

We also provided a list of semantic descriptions and asked both groups to rate each element. Table 1 shows the ratings of both groups. The ratings are quite similar except for "extends". Educators found this helpful to connect additional learning material for further reading.

Both students and educators were asked in an open question what types of learning resources they would link with each other. Both groups listed "website", "figure", "PDF document", "video", "animation", and "source code". In addition, they rated the importance of presented types of learning resources (see Table 2). Although the ratings of both groups are similar, there are some interesting differences. For example, educators rate Web 2.0 applications like forums, blogs, and Wikipedia higher than students.

Apart from connecting whole documents with each other, it is conceivable to make selections on a more fine-grained level. The interviewees were asked which level they would use. For text documents, the majority would reference to paragraphs as well as single words for linking them with definitions for instance. Timestamps and period of time are

Type of learning resource	Students AM (SD)	Educators AM (SD)
Slide	5.0 (0.0)	5.0 (0.0)
PDF document	4.93 (0.27)	4.8 (0.45)
website	4.57 (0.85)	4.8 (0.45)
figure, diagram	4.5 (0.76)	4.4 (0.89)
Wikipedia article	4.07 (1.0)	4.6 (0.89)
forum post	3.64 (1.28)	5.0 (0.0)
video	3.57 (1.02)	4.8 (0.45)
word proc. document	3.5 (1.02)	3.2 (1.1)
pen note (digital pen)	3.36 (1.55)	4.0 (0.71)
spreadsheet document	3.14 (1.1)	3.2 (1.64)
chat message	2.79 (1.05)	3.8 (1.1)
blog post	2.64 (1.01)	4.6 (0.89)

Table 2: Ratings of learning resources

important referencing a video. Educators also suggested referencing code snippets.

4.2.3 Sharing learning resources

All interviewed students said they share knowledge resources they have created or found with fellow students. Usually, they use eMail (86%), Web storage (71%), and Instant Messaging software (71%) for the exchange of learning resources. The majority of the interviewees thinks that it is very helpful be able to share learning resources with a system such as CLLS (AM=4.71, SD=0.47). They welcome seeing the semantic relationships added by other learners when those added a learning resource (AM=4.29, SD=0.61). In this way, they can better understand why someone else has connected two learning resources.

Although most students would share learning resources found or created by themselves with fellow students, it is also important for some to be able to make private additions (AM=2.93, SD=1.49), e.g., for notes or private documents. However, the opinions are divided for this question. Some students vote for an open system sharing every linked resource with all other users.

All educators indicated that they often need to pass additional learning material or exercises to students after a lecture. Usually, they do this via eMail, or publish the material on the course website or forum.

All interviewed lectures appreciated the possibility of the system to add additional learning material to the slides of their lectures and to share it with their students. The educators also welcomed that students can augment the provided learning materials. For themselves, they agree that this a good opportunity to recognise problems students have with the learning materials (AM=4.67, SD=0.82), and to see alternative representations of the learning material (AM=4.60, SD=0.89). Thereby they receive feedback to their lectures and can improve their learning materials (AM=4.2, SD=0.84).

4.2.4 Assessing shared learning resources

Students said they think rating learning resources added by other learners and seeing their average rating is very helpful (AM=4.29, SD=0.73), because it could give an orientation which learning resource to access first. Students do not think that there is a benefit to see the rating of a certain person (AM=3.00, SD=0.96) except for the educator. 93% find it helpful to see how the educator has rated certain resources. Educators agreed with this. They also thought

Filter criteria	AM	SD
learning resources added by the educator	5.0	0.0
type of learning resource	4.50	0.76
semantic relationship	4.36	0.74
average rating	4.14	0.86
learning resources added by a certain group	3.21	1.05
period of time	3.0	1.52

Table 3: Students' rating of filter criteria

that it is important students can see their assessment of a resource (AM=4.83, SD=0.41). However, a student remarked that this could discourage students to add learning resources, because they might be afraid of receiving a bad rating for linked materials. Thus, the possibility to make anonymous posting would lower this barrier to participate. 29% find seeing the average rating of a learning group interesting, 14% the one of a specific student.

4.2.5 Filtering shared learning resources

If learning materials are constantly augmented by both instructors and students, the amount of linked learning resources can be very confusing. Therefore, it is important to be able to set filters to fade out uninteresting items and highlight important ones. We asked students which filter criteria they would use. They prefer filtering for certain semantic relationships, e.g., "show all learning resources that provide an example for this slide", and for certain types, e.g., "all images". Students also want to filter learning resources with particular ratings. After this open question, students were asked to rate the filter criteria of a given list (see Table 3). Again, the type and the semantic relation are highly rated, but most important is a filter for the learning resources that were added by the educator. This shows that an educator's resources have a special position. According to the students, this is because these resources are more important and their correctness is more reliable than resources added by students.

In addition to single filter criteria, a filter may consist of several filters logically connected with each other. Students welcome such a feature (AM=4.36, SD=0.93), because it allows making more detailed queries. Here, most students want to query for a certain type of learning resource that has a certain relationship to another, e.g., "all figures that provide an example for this slide". They ideally expect a logical combination of all single filters.

4.2.6 Visualization

We wanted to find out how both students and educators assess using a graph to represent resources and their connections (figure 1). Most students believe that this is very helpful (AM=4.0, SD=0.88). The educators shared this view. They assessed a graphical representation of the created knowledge graph to be helpful for both themselves (AM=3.8, SD=0.84) and students (AM=4.0, SD=1.0). However, some interviewees stated that such a representation could be confusing or they would simply prefer a non-visual presentation. Instead, a simple table could be a better representation. Many interviewees also felt that a visual feedback after connecting two learning resources is important as well as being able to see connected learning resources directly on the slide. Some interviewed educators commented that a

simple graph as presented is helpful but not sufficient. Such a graphical representation should make it easy to navigate through the graph and to find information. This is especially challenging when many students contribute and a knowledge graph is growing over a long period of time.

An open question asked the interviewees what a good visualization would be from their point of view. One idea was the combination of different colors and shapes for distinguishing different learning types and their importance. To visualize the rating of a resource, it was suggested to arrange more important resources closer to the corresponding node, or to visualize the different ratings of resource by different color intensities or node sizes. It was also suggested to use clusters in the visualization for an easier navigation.

4.2.7 Archiving linked learning resources

From an educator's perspective, it can be valuable to be able to save a certain version or state of a knowledge graph including the connected learning resources such as slides, documents, websites, and videos. On average, the educators assessed such an option to be very helpful (AM=4.6, SD=0.55). With this opportunity it is possible to create a final version for the students at the end of a term containing all learning resources. Such a version (maybe edited by the teaching staff) can also be a starting point for students of the lecture in a subsequent term. In addition, saving a knowledge graph could be used for offline usage of CLLS.

Although students did not assess preserving a knowledge graph as high as educators did (AM=3.79, SD=1.19), they saw a benefit in preserving Web resources for removal (100%) and modification (79%). Just under one half of the students want to have a personal final version of the learning resources and their links after a lecture. Instead, the majority would prefer a preservation of the whole resources in combination with filtering mechanisms.

4.2.8 General usage

Both students and educators welcome that the system runs in a Web browser without any plugins, so they do not need to install any extra software. Nevertheless, the majority of the interviewees would like to be able to work both online and offline. Only few students said that they prefer pure online learning. An educator commented that although the system runs on different devices, a different presentation for different device classes would be necessary, due to differences in screen sizes and interaction techniques between devices.

Most students also like the flexible user interface that allows them to arrange it as they like (AM=4.57, SD=0.51). However, almost all students request the presence of layout presets (AM=3.57, SD=1.5).

All interviewed students own a laptop, but would use the system on different devices, especially with laptops (100%), tablet computers such as the iPad (93%), and PCs (70%). Many students said they would like to access CLLS with a smartphone, but are concerned about the small screen size.

In a final question, we asked the interview participants to share their views on the system regarding benefits and disadvantages, and in comparison to known learning systems. The majority assess the integration of different learning resources as the greatest benefit. Students welcome that, in contrast to LMSs and lecture recording players, they can actively link learning resources by themselves directly with the learning materials. They like the easy usability of the system and the sharing opportunities of information resources. However, some students saw a potential danger of low quality resources added by some students. In summary, the students felt that they would learn effectively with such a system (AM=*4.14*, SD=0.77).

The overall feedback from all educators was also very positive. They stated that such a system could support students in active learning with learning materials, especially due to the possibility to add learning resources and to make semantic connections between them. For some educators this was a big advantage in comparison with LMSs. They also saw a benefit that students have an integrated view of learning materials and social presence of co-learners.

5. SUMMARY AND OUTLOOK

In this paper, we have presented user studies regarding a system that facilitates users to collaboratively link learning resources with each other and to describe these relationships. In order to elicit the acceptance and preferences of both students and educators for such a system we have built a working prototype and conducted interviews with users. The interview results showed that both groups say a system like CLLS could effectively support students in their learning processes. Students welcome the easy usability of the system. They especially welcome the opportunity to connect information resources, which they have created or found in the WWW, with the provided lecture materials. They also support the exchange of information resources with fellow students, because they could benefit from the learning resources added by others and vice versa. Students appreciate the integrative character of CLLS collecting all learning resources in one place. The interviewed educators underlined these statements. Each educator would use such a system for their lectures. Due to student augmentations, educators receive feedback to improve their teaching materials.

Besides the advantages of the system, new requirements and concerns emerged during the interviews. Although a browser-based system has advantages such as a wide support of different devices, the majority of students demands both an online and offline use. Another challenge is the visualization and interaction with a huge knowledge graph collaboratively created by many users over a long period of time.

The reactions of both students and educators have been very motivating for us. The small deviation of the answers makes it unlikely that the positive reactions are partially due to a wish to make us happy. We plan to conduct a long term study to examine how the system is used over a long period of time by both educators and students with a particular focus on collaborative learning activities. We also plan to integrate collaboration tools like chat, discussion forum, and social networks in order to facilitate interaction and to support the semantic connection of such tools. Furthermore, we plan to perform user studies with different visualizations of the knowledge graph, and interactions techniques. Whereas computer science lectures are often slide-based, other subjects like philosophy are more text-based. Thus, we want to support users to link various types of information resources with fine-grained selectors for different types of media.

6. REFERENCES

[1] R. Anderson, R. Anderson, P. Davis, N. Linnell, C. Prince, V. Razmov, and F. Videon. Classroom Presenter: Enhancing Interactive Education with Digital Ink. *Computer*, 40(9):56–61, 2007.

[2] D. Bargeron, J. Grudin, A. Gupta, E. Sanocki, F. Li, and S. Leetiernan. Asynchronous Collaboration Around Multimedia Applied to On-Demand Education. *Journal of Management Information Systems*, 18(4):117–145, 2002.

[3] J. Brooke. SUS - A quick and dirty usability scale. *Usability evaluation in industry*, pages 189–194, 1996.

[4] S. Chandrasekar, J. G. Tront, and J. C. Prey. WriteOn1.0: a tablet PC-based tool for effective classroom instruction. In *ITiCSE '09: Proceedings of the 14th annual ACM SIGCSE conference on Innovation and Technology in Computer Science Education*, pages 323–327, New York, NY, USA, 2009. ACM.

[5] S. Ferretti, S. Mirri, L. A. Muratori, M. Roccetti, and P. Salomoni. E-learning 2.0: you are We-LCoME! In *W4A '08: Proceedings of the 2008 International cross-disciplinary Conference on Web Accessibility*, pages 116–125, New York, NY, USA, 2008. ACM.

[6] I.-H. Hsiao, P. Brusilovsky, M. Yudelson, and A. Ortigosa. The value of adaptive link annotation in e-learning: a study of a portal-based approach. In *Proceedings of the 21st ACM conference on Hypertext and hypermedia*, HT '10, pages 223–228, New York, NY, USA, 2010. ACM.

[7] K. M. Höver, M. Hartle, and G. Rößling. A Collaborative Linked Learning Space. In *ITiCSE '11: Proceedings of the 16th annual ACM SIGCSE Conference on Innovation and Technology in Computer Science Education (in press)*, 2011.

[8] S. Iske. *Vernetztes Wissen: Hypertext-Strategien im Internet*. Wilhelm Bertelsmann Verlag, Bielefeld, 2002.

[9] S. Iske, A. Klein, N. Kutscher, and H.-U. Otto. Young people's Internet use and its significance for informal education and social participation. *Technology, Pedagogy and Education*, 17(2):131–141, 2008.

[10] M. Kam, J. Wang, A. Iles, E. Tse, J. Chiu, D. Glaser, O. Tarshish, and J. Canny. Livenotes: A System for Cooperative and Augmented Note-Taking in Lectures. In *CHI '05: Proceedings of the SIGCHI conference on Human factors in computing systems*, pages 531–540, New York, NY, USA, 2005. ACM.

[11] R. Müller and T. Ottmann. The "Authoring on the Fly" system for automated recording and replay of (tele)presentations. *Multimedia Systems*, 8(3):158–176, 10 2000.

[12] G. Rößling and A. Kothe. Extending Moodle to Better Support Computing Education. In *ITiCSE '09: Proceedings of the 14th annual ACM SIGCSE Conference on Innovation and Technology in Computer Science Education*, pages 146–150, New York, NY, USA, 2009. ACM.

[13] J. Steimle, O. Brdiczka, and M. Mühlhäuser. CoScribe: Integrating Paper and Digital Documents for Collaborative Knowledge Work. *IEEE Transactions on Learning Technologies*, 2(3):174–188, 7 2009.

Efficient and Playful Tools to Teach Unix to New Students

Matthieu Moy
Grenoble-INP (Ensimag), Verimag UMR 5104
Grenoble, F-38041, France
Matthieu.Moy@grenoble-inp.fr

ABSTRACT

Teaching Unix to new students is a common tasks in many higher schools. This paper presents an approach to such course where the students progress autonomously with the help of the teacher. The traditional textbook is complemented with a wiki, and the main thread of the course is a game, in the form of a *treasure hunt*. The course finishes with a *lab exam*, where students have to perform practical manipulations similar to the ones performed during the treasure hunt. The exam is graded fully automatically.

This paper discusses the motivations and advantages of the approach, and gives an overall view of the tools we developed. The tools are available from the web, and open-source, hence re-usable outside the Ensimag.

Categories and Subject Descriptors

K.3.2 [**Computers and Education**]: Computer and Information Science Education; D.4.m [**Operating Systems**]: Miscellaneous

General Terms

Human Factors

Keywords

Unix, Education, Exam, Treasure Hunt

1. INTRODUCTION

Ensimag is a french engineering school of computer science and applied mathematics. The computing environment is essentially based on Unix (servers and workstations), which the students have to learn when they enter the school. The students therefore follow a quick unix-learning course at the beginning of the first year.

While this introduction to Unix has sometimes been considered as an unimportant course, we believe it is a fundamental mistake to underestimate its importance: the few hours taken at the beginning of the year to learn and train with the basics influence the students' productivity for the next 3 years, and even if learning Unix is not a goal in itself, it conditions the success of further courses. This paper discusses the challenges and solutions set up in the Ensimag the last few years to reconsider the introduction to Unix as an important course, to motivate the students and teach them as efficiently as possible.

After detailing the context and our motivations in section 2, we give a quick overview of the course and training material in section 3. The main contributions of this paper are two tools used in the course:

- A set of exercises in the form of a *treasure hunt*, used by the students to train autonomously during the course (presented is section 4).
- A *lab exam* that allows grading the students at the end of the course, with practical manipulations (presented in section 5).

Both tools are published as open-source software, and could be re-used and adapted by other teachers/schools.

2. PARTICULARITIES OF THE UNIX INTRODUCTION AND MOTIVATIONS

One challenging aspect of teaching Unix to beginners is the heterogeneity of students. All of them have used a computer prior to entering the school, but around half never used Unix before. On the other hand, a number of them had some exposure to user-friendly Linux distributions, and a small number are already command-line gurus. The difficulty is to let the course be effective to total beginners, while remaining interesting to the other students.

Our way to tackle heterogeneity is twofold. First, we designed the course to let the students learn at their own pace, with a maximum degree of autonomy. This is not hard since we teach them practical aspects first: all the classes are done in the computer rooms, one student per machine. The students essentially follow a textbook plus some on-line exercises, and teachers provide advices and answers to questions. Since the goal of the introduction is really to teach *practice*, we do not enforce team work like in e.g. [3], but ask each student to work individually. Mutual help is appreciated and encouraged, but we do not want a situation where one student holds the keyboard, and another watches without practicing.

We provide the students teaching material containing all the basics, but extensively use remarks targeted to more advance users. For the most advanced users, we provide additional documentations on various topics and pointers to external documentations, so that they can start learning concepts that they would otherwise miss, or learn a few months later.

A common example of advanced topic is revision control-system. Most users won't understand the need for one immediately, and we wait for some time before imposing them one. Still, encouraging a handful of students to start using it spreads the knowledge with a network effect: these students will encourage (or force!) their co-workers to use it. In short: teaching useful advanced concepts to advanced users also help beginners in the long run. Another subtle advantage of giving material to advanced users is that it helps keeping them in the machine rooms (as opposed to missing classes they don't need), indirectly promoting mutual help.

The other challenging aspect is the students motivation. Most students come from so-called "classes preparatoires" in the french system, with a huge exam pressure, and many of them expect the engineering school to be easy enough to pass exams without working.

Another issue with students' motivation is the desire to learn Unix and the command-line, as opposed to another operating system (like Windows or the graphical part of Mac OS). We do believe in the pedagogical qualities of Unix and the command-line, since they somehow *force* the user to understand what s/he's doing, but the students often don't understand the need to re-learn the computer basics (file manipulation, launching applications, ...), since they already know it with other paradigms on other platforms. The vast majority of students have a personal laptop with either Windows or Mac OS installed, and some of them wouldn't use Unix at all unless we find the right arguments.

In addition, the organization of the school does not leave room for a lot of teaching hours for this course. We have just 10 hours to teach them all this. For the slowest students, this is far below what would be needed, so we need to convince them to complement the classes with their personal work.

We therefore needed to work a lot on students motivation. The first thing we did was to start with very simple manipulation in a graphical environment, to avoid scaring new students at the first contact. The message perceive by students should be more like "look, you can still do the kind of things you're used to, *but you can also do many others*" than "forget all you know, and then learn". Unix and the command-line should not be the new things to be *scared* of, but the friendly companion which will help them to learn new things. For example, we show them how to surf the web, read their mail, and use a word processor before diving into the command-line. Also, changing the recommended text editor from `vi` to `emacs`, we noticed that students started to actually use the editor we recommended them (at the time when `vi` was recommended, the majority of students was using `nedit`!).

After avoiding to scare students during the first contact, a lot is still to be done to maintain their motivation during the course. One tool for this is the "treasure hunt" game described in section 4, that the students follow all along the course. The basic idea is a sequence of levels, designed such that accessing level $n+1$ requires performing a manipulation described at level n. This creates a little (sane) competition between students, and many of them really have fun while learning.

After setting up this treasure hunt and rewriting the textbook, we had very positive feedback from students and all

of those who completed the game were even thankful for the fun they had. However, less than half of the students did complete the game. Based on this observation, it was clear that we had to complement the course with the other side of students motivation: exams and grading. We therefore designed an exam, essentially based on the same manipulations as the treasure hunt, but for which the questions are independent. We will describe it in details in section 5.

3. BASIC TEACHING MATERIAL

Before detailing the main contributions of the paper, we give an overview of the course, and the teaching material. The teachers do not provide any lecture and only occasionally talks to the whole students group: to give the instructions, and to show a few demos for technical aspects that are better explained live than on a textbook or webpage.

3.1 Textbook

The course starts with the distribution of a textbook ([2], french only). The textbook is made to be read linearly. It was designed to allow multiple levels of reading: remarks for advanced users are identified visually (technically, using LaTeX macros). Each notion taught by the textbook is illustrated immediately with a small exercise (also marked visually to draw the attention of students).

While previous versions of the textbook used to try being independent from the school, we decided to adapt it deliberately to the school and the course, making frequent references to the school's intranet, the particular configurations of the machines they are using... While this requires more effort from the teachers to maintain the book up to date, we believe this gives a real added value over a random Unix introduction found on the Internet.

Having the textbook in paper form makes reading long text more comfortable than on-screen reading, and the linear structure ensures everybody goes through all the important points.

3.2 EnsiWiki: Students' and Teachers' Wiki

In complement to the textbook, a wiki called EnsiWiki [5]is provided to the students. Historically, it is a merge of a wiki launched by the school and an independent initiative carried out by students. We try to maintain the equilibrium between teachers' and students' contributions (both having full write access).

As opposed to the textbook, the wiki is not meant to be linear. It doesn't have a beginning and an end, but is basically a set of pages with hyperlinks (plus a classification using the category system of MediaWiki). Students read pages that are of interest to them in the order they wish, and of course, add and improve pages as they wish: it's a wiki! Unlike the textbook, the wiki is not just a starting point, but will really accompany the students throughout their studies. It is public, and indexed by web search engines, so searching for information is usually relatively easy.

The duality between the textbook and the wiki can be summarized as follows: as a beginner, the textbook tells the students what they have to learn, but when the students know what they are looking for, the wiki should be able to provide them the information needed.

A positive side-effect of the wiki is that it increases the visibility of the school on the web. Some of the articles are of great quality (including many articles written by students!), and are very well ranked on popular search engines.

4. TREASURE HUNT

4.1 Principle

As discussed above, the real challenge in this course is not to provide content to students, but to motivate them, and to make sure they work autonomously but efficiently. One tool we developed to accomplish this goal is the *treasure hunt* (called "jeu de piste" in its original version, since the course is in french).

The principle is simple, basically an electronic version of the children's game: the first level contains instructions to reach the second, which itself contains instructions to get to the third, and so on. It contains 28 levels (plus 7 bonus levels to make sure the geekest students—and teachers—to have fun too!).It can be seen as a Unix-ish, pedagogical version of ouverture-facile [1].

In theory, this is similar to a set of unrelated exercises, but in practice, this makes a real difference, with at least the following advantages: *The students cannot mistakenly think they completed the exercise.* Either they solved the level, and know it, or they didn't, without half-measure. This is a key point to allow autonomous work. *The students cannot skip an easy exercise.* When practical manipulations are proposed in the textbook, they are easily overlooked as too easy, and skipped. This can result is a false impression of having completed the work with the reasoning "I went through the textbook, that's all too easy for me, I didn't need to do the exercises". *The students cannot skip a hard exercise.* Some levels are purposely hard, and almost unfeasible by beginners without help. The rational is twofold: first, this encourages the students to help each other (the game itself is not graded, we ask the students not to give answers directly, but co-operation is welcome), and second, it force students to ask for help to the teacher. Autonomous work doesn't mean teacherless work: students go through the game at different speeds, but the teacher is indeed very active to answer questions. *Off course, this makes the sequence of exercises funnier than traditional ones.* Students are usually looking forward to reaching the last stage, and reading the textbook is a mandatory step to reach this. Not all students enjoy the fun of the game (at least, not all of them have as much fun playing the game than I had *creating* it!), but on average, the effect on motivation was very positive.

Note that these advantages come with a risk: students blocked at one level would miss the end of the game. It is the teacher's role to make sure this does not happen, by advising students, and sometimes by making surveys (who started the treasure hunt? Who went past level X?...).

4.2 Contents of Levels

The nature of the game requires the instructions for each levels to be hidden, and only discoverable by following instructions. We use essentially two tricks to achieve this:

- Instructions obfuscated with simple encryption schemes, typically variants of rot13. The text is easily available, but can be deciphered only with the instructions.
- Instructions in a file, in a non-listable directory. Files are either in the filesystem of a machine the students have access to (the Unix permission --x on directo-

ries allows giving access to files when user know their names), or on a website with directory listing disabled (so, students can easily access a level when they know its URL only).

The game follows the chapters of the textbook. Following are some examples of levels:

Internet: The game starts with a rot13-encoded piece of text. The player is told that rot13 is used, without being told it is. The expected solution is basically to search the web, and find, e.g. http://rot13.com, which allows online decyphering very quickly. As with many other levels, the solution of the level gives a few comments on the solution and the way to find it. In this case, the text insists on the need for students and future engineers to be able to quickly find the information.

Next steps include some navigation in the wiki, a script sending an email to the students, so that they are forced to read their email.

Basics: In this section, the students must copy a file from another user's directory. The file is an obfuscated Ada (the language taught in first year in the Ensimag) source-code that must be compiled and executed to provide instructions.

Useful Applications: This section consists in opening files made for various applications. Students have to compile a LaTeX file, open an OpenOffice.org file and a PNG image.

Text Editor: Again, students are provided Ada source code. This time, the file is very long, and contains a few syntax errors. Being familiar with a text editor (typically, being able to jump to a given line number) is almost mandatory. Then, another piece of code is given to the students, but split into 3 pieces, in a text file, within the instructions, and in an OpenOffice.org file, to force students to do inter-applications cut-and-paste.

Commands and Tools, and Bash: These two chapters are key ones, where students learn the essentials of the command-line. Players have to use a few commands like file, grep, find, sort, diff, tar, chmod, find hidden files, play with input/output redirects (|, < and >) and wildcards.

The hardest level consists in finding the biggest file within a directory (and its sub-directories). Students usually need the help of their teacher, which gives a good opportunity to explain or re-explain the concepts of pipe and the xargs command, with a solution along the lines of "find . -type f | xargs wc -c | sort -n | tail -n 2". Not all students really understand the complete command-line, but exposing them once to a complex command gives them a hint on what it's possible to do with Unix once they master it, and therefore what they would lose by not learning it.

Remote access: This chapter provide a few ways for the students to access a machine remotely, trying to answer the common question "how can I work with the Ensimag's machines and my personal laptop" with tools like SSH. Students have to fetch a file from a remote machine with sftp, and to execute remote commands with ssh -X.

Bonus Levels: This section is presented to students as non-mandatory. Beginners are not supposed to be able to solve all levels when they enter the school, but should be able to do so after a few months. Levels include finding information in HTTP headers of a webpage, basic shell-scripting, navigating in the history of a directory managed by the Git revision-control system,using strace or navigating in the /proc/ virtual filesystem, and using SSH private/public keys. The last level gives a pointer to the source code of the generation scripts. Students are encouraged to contribute new levels (but none actually did up to now).

4.3 Generation Library

The complete set of scripts used to generate the treasure hunt is available on the web, and is open-source. The instructions given to students are in french, but the source code is written and commented in english, with a relatively clean separation between library code and the actual code for each level, so it can easily be adapted to other schools, in other languages.

Technically, the library provides a few source code obfuscation functions (to generate unreadable LATEX, Ada or C code), and plain text encoding/decoding. For example, script generating the level about input/output redirects takes the instructions for the next level, encodes it, and provides the students a decoder that will read the encoded instructions on its standard input. It can be found online at the following URL: http://gitorious.org/unix-training

4.4 Students Feedback

The feedback from students completing the treasure hunt can be found on EnsiWiki (http://ensiwiki.ensimag.fr/index.php/Discussion:TP_Unix_-_Jeu_de_piste). Only 101 students out of 210 provided feedback. We have unfortunately no way to distinguish students who did not provide feedback because they didn't take the time to do it, and ones who didn't because they did not complete the game (the next version of the game will detect automatically when students reach some levels). The result is probably biased towards positive feedback.

Still, the majority of comments are *very* positive. For example, we can count 6 occurences of "thank you", which is in our experience seldom used in students feedback. The most frequently used words include "good", "friendly", "playfull", "instructive", ... Many students confirm that they did manage to complete the game without having prior knowledge about Unix.

Since the starting point of the game is public, 2nd year and 3rd year students have access to it too. We had several requests to install the necessary files on the servers they use, because they wanted to play, too! Some students even offered to host the game on their club's server.

5. LAB EXAM

Despite the very positive feedback we got from students actually completing the textbook and treasure hunt, this turned out to be insufficient to motivate *all* the students to actually complete the work. We have therefore set up an exam, designed to be very easy for anyone having done the work seriously, and very hard otherwise. Since the whole course is done in computer-rooms, it would make no sense to have a theoretical exam, so the exam is also done on computers, and consists of a set of technical manipulations.

5.1 Principle

The exam is made of a set of questions, highly inspired from the treasure hunt. The questions are independent: instead of giving access to the next level, the manipulation asked provide a key, that is used to answer questions on a web interface.

To fix the ideas, the first (simple) question is "The answer for this question is in the file c73df134.txt in your working directory (it is a text file).". The student's account contain a file named c73df134.txt, whose content is "The answer is 3d61f5e5", and the students must copy the string 3d61f5e5 in a web-interface to validate the answers.

The design was done with the following ideas in mind:

Automatic grading: the exam was set up to force the students' work, but should not overload the teachers. Setting up the exam was a rather large one-time effort, but grading should be as simple as executing a script to collect the answers.

Immediate feedback: the obvious problem with automatic grading is that automatic tools do not distinguish "almost correct answers" and "actually correct" ones. To solve this issue, the student get an immediate feedback: when giving a correct answer, the question is validated as correct, and otherwise, the students get an unlimited number of retries. This implies that the answers of the questions have to be impossible to find by trial-and-error.

Hard cheating: students are close to each others in the computer rooms. To avoid easy cheating, the exam is generated on a per-students basis. For almost all questions, the answer is different from a student to the next, even though the technical manipulation required to obtain it is the same. Questions are sorted in a pseudo-random order (which is possible since questions are independent). Also, during the exam, the machine's network is restricted with a firewall.

Simple technologies: since it is used for grading, the robustness of the exam infrastructure is critical. Also, we wanted the infrastructure to be re-usable outside the school. We have therefore chosen the simplest technologies to accomplish this, with a rather unix-ish design: shell-scripts generate the exam, and the web-interface used during the exam is simple PHP+SQL scripts (tested with both MySQL and PostgreSQL). No JavaScript, no external dependencies.

At the beginning of the exam session, the machines are initialized with an account containing only the files needed for the exam. During the exam, the students will have to perform manipulations on this set of files, and will validate the answers through a web-interface (a single web-page showing a text-box and a submit button for each question). The answers are stored in a database, and the grades are extracted from this database at the end of the exam.

To differentiate the answers for each students, the answers are pseudo-random (typically looking like 3d61f5e5). Actual random would be possible, but with the great drawback of being non-reproducible. Cryptographic hash functions [6] provide an elegant solution to this: we compute the answer to each question as the sha1 sum of the student's login concatenated with the name of the question, and a secret key for each exam. This way, regenerating the exam several times yields the same answers each time (which can be crucial if something goes wrong and the exam has to be regenerated at the last minute...).

5.2 Content of the Exam

The exam contains 28 questions where students are asked to compile Ada and LATEX code, to find files in a directory containing hundreds of subdirectories and files, to extract zip, tar and gz compressed files, to play with input/output redirects, find the size of a file, the destination of a symbolic link, to use sort, grep, diff, kill, to use Control-z to suspend a running executable, to download a file with sftp, to connect to an account with ssh, ... The exam is feasible in 30 minutes by an expert user, and we let 1 hour to the students, so that most of them do not have time to reach the end. This way, we test students on their speed as well as their skills.

5.3 Demo Mode

During the exam, users are identified with the IP address of their machine, and answers are recorded in a database. We made a variant of the generation scripts that do not use any authentication, and stores answers in PHP session variables (i.e. simple storage based on browser cookies). In this mode, the students can practice with a few questions, getting the same interface as the real one, but their answers are not transmitted to teachers. Such a demo was put online during the course, with trivial questions to get used to the web interface, and a few questions extracted from the actual exam. Some examples are available at `http://www-verimag.imag.fr/~moy/demos-unix-training/`. Next year, this demo will be integrated as one level of the treasure hunt.

5.4 Generation Library

As for the treasure hunt, the technical infrastructure behind the lab exam is published as Open Source. We did not publish the full set of questions, to avoid students finding it and publishing ready-made solutions, but this can be distributed in private upon request.

The generation library consists in a set of shell-scripts functions. The user defines two shell functions per questions. These functions will be called once per student. One gives the question, as will be displayed to the student (possibly depending on the student's login), and the other sets up the files as will they will be stored on the student's account. The first argument to this function is the expected answer. For example, the trivial question mentioned in 5.1 is implemented as:

```
desc_question_text () {
    echo "The answer for this question is in the file
<tt>$(hash textfile).txt</tt> in your working directory
(it is a text file)."
}

gen_question_text () {
    echo "The answer is $1" > $(hash textfile).txt
}
```

Notice the use of `hash` to compute the file name. It is provided in the generation library, and implements the pseudo-random based on `sha1sum` described in section 5.1. The same code-obfuscation library as the treasure-hunt is used.

The execution of this script will provide a directory containing one subdirectory per student, with the content of their account (then, other mechanisms have to be used to deploy it on students machine), and an SQL file to initialize the database with questions, and expected answers. We also provide the PHP files needed for the web interface during the exam.

The generation library, and a heavily commented example of exam that serves as documentation, can be found at the following URL: `http://gitorious.org/unix-training`

6. CONCLUSION

We presented the "introduction to Unix" class of the Ensimag. Starting from a relatively standard content based on a textbook, we introduced a wiki, and then two novel tools: the treasure hunt allows learning autonomously in a playful way, and the lab exam ensures the most recalcitrant find a motivation to complete the work.

In the past, we have already set up several lab exams, essentially in programming where the delivery is a program. This one differs from the others in that the skills tested are purely practical, and indeed relatively basic. Hence, we ask various small, independent manipulations. Previous exams have been very successful at motivating/forcing the students work. Prior to this, the practical skills were tested on team work, and many students were relying on their teammates. We believe to have made it much harder for them to fall through the cracks, and generally feel that students are becoming more comfortable with our computing environment.

We do not have students feedback other than their grades as far as the exam is concerned, but the treasure hunt received a very warm feedback. We could already feel the effect of the exam on the presence of students during the classes: the last two ones are non-mandatory, and only 10 to 15 students attended them last year, compared to about 100 (i.e. half) this year! The grades for the exam were surprisingly good. 18% of students got all answers correct, and the average grade was 15.2/20.

The technical infrastructure we developed can be compared to Linuxgym [4], which is based on a complete, modified, Linux server on which the students log in to get problems to solve. The focus of Linuxgym is scripting, while our goal is an introduction to day-to-day use of Unix. We believe the playful aspect of the treasure hunt, and the fact that the hunt is done directly on the student's machines makes it more motivating and more concrete for a first contact, but we will evaluate Linuxgym for the more advanced Unix courses in the school.

The content of the course was tailored for an introduction to Unix. The principle clearly does not apply to theoretical courses, and is probably not applicable as-is in programming courses: both the treasure hunt and the exam take advantage of the fact that each manipulation can be solved in a few minutes, while most interesting programming problems would take hour(s). Still, the concept can probably be adapted to other classes involving practical aspects (network courses would be nice candidates).

7. REFERENCES

[1] Ouverture facile, flash riddles. Web site. `http://ouverture-facile.com`.

[2] Ensimag. Introduction à Unix—l'environnement de travail à l'Ensimag. Student's textbook, 2008-2010. (english title: Introduction to Unix—Working environment in the Ensimag, France), `http://www-verimag.imag.fr/~moy/spip/?article74`.

[3] M. A. S. Hurtado and C. Vivaracho-Pascual. Learning unix in first year of computer engineering. In *ITiCSE*, page 392, 2005.

[4] A. Solomon. Linuxgym: software to automate formative assessment of unix command-line and scripting skills. In *ITiCSE*, page 353, 2007. Software available online from `http://linuxgym.com/`.

[5] Teachers and students in the Ensimag. Ensiwiki, 2008-2010. `http://ensiwiki.ensimag.fr/`.

[6] Wikipedia. Cryptographic hash function — wikipedia, the free encyclopedia, 2010.

Creativity Room 5555

Evoking Creativity in Game Design amongst CS Students

Timo Göttel
University of Hamburg
Department of Informatics
Hamburg, Germany
tgoettel@acm.org

Jonas Schild
Entertainment Computing
University of Duisburg-Essen
Duisburg, Germany
jonas.schild@uni-due.de

ABSTRACT

This paper highlights the importance of computer-free meeting places for Computer Science (CS) students participating in game design courses in the sense of learning spaces. Such environments have the potential of countering possible negative attitudes of CS students towards creative processes. During a game design course we offered a unique meeting room that offered playful and creative elements. Furthermore, the room had to be rearranged by the participants of the course. We describe the course and analyze it through observations and three formal surveys. Both the results and the quality of resulting prototypes indicate that CS students strongly benefit in their creative processes from working in individually arranged playful environments.

Categories and Subject Descriptors

K.3.2 [**Computing Milieux**]: Computers and Education— *Computer and Information Science Education*

General Terms

Design, Management

Keywords

Game Design Course, Creativity, Soft Skills

1. INTRODUCTION

Game design education is a highly interdisciplinary field that is increasingly encountered in Computer Science (CS) courses [13]. As the main audience usually consists of CS students, an interdisciplinary, creative approach, as emphasized in previous work [7], is often neglected. In general, due to common CS curricula the students' prior knowledge is focused on object-oriented programming and its underlying theories, which leads to structural and logical thinking skills. These play a very important role in game design, but we often observed discomfort amongst students when asking

them to realize their own ideas. This led to the assumption that our students were not well-trained in creative thinking and required soft skills. Some authors have already documented that CS students often encounter problems when confronted with creative tasks. They state that there is a lack of concepts to advance creativity where communication and discussions play an important role [1]. From a more general perspective, courses on game design should strengthen required skills for game programmer jobs as compiled by Brown et al. [4]. The authors identify a need to focus on people, processes, and planning. They propose a course design but do not go into detail on appropriate learning environments. In contrast, game design literature emphasizes three aspects for a creative game creation process: the importance of locating brainstorming sessions in playful environments, to actually play-test game design ideas, and to create physical prototypes that even allow play-testing at early project stages [5]. Yet, at CS faculties it is often very hard to find appropriate places that encourage creative activities. Mostly, brainstorming sessions in CS courses are held at ordinary seminar rooms and hence frequently appear to be very clinical, or—even worse—superimposed. Furthermore, play-testing requires a place where participants can play and/or talk about games and their underlying structures. Otherwise, students are forced to meet at private places, where important chance encounters or events rarely occur. The importance of physical prototypes at early project stages should remind participants to focus on creativity and play-testing instead of on underlying technical or programming issues. Yet such an approach might be questionable, i.e. letting CS students design their physical prototypes in rooms with readily available computers. Offering technology may increase the desire to actually use it. Therefore, it is astonishing that there are no recommendations for playful rooms at all project stages to strengthen the confidence in technology-free approaches.

In fact, there are many different promising approaches to enhance or redefine traditional computer labs in the CS community. All authors referenced below emphasize the need for communication and creativity in such rooms. However, it is clear that traditional workstation setups hinder collaborative work [14]. Thus, it seems appropriate to claim for sensible learning spaces that are built upon constructivist theory as proposed by Brown [2]. He says that learning has to provide a meaningful context for students, encourage students to play an active part, and to socialize. Hence, learning spaces should clearly represent these three principles. Furthermore, such rooms should explicitly aim at supporting

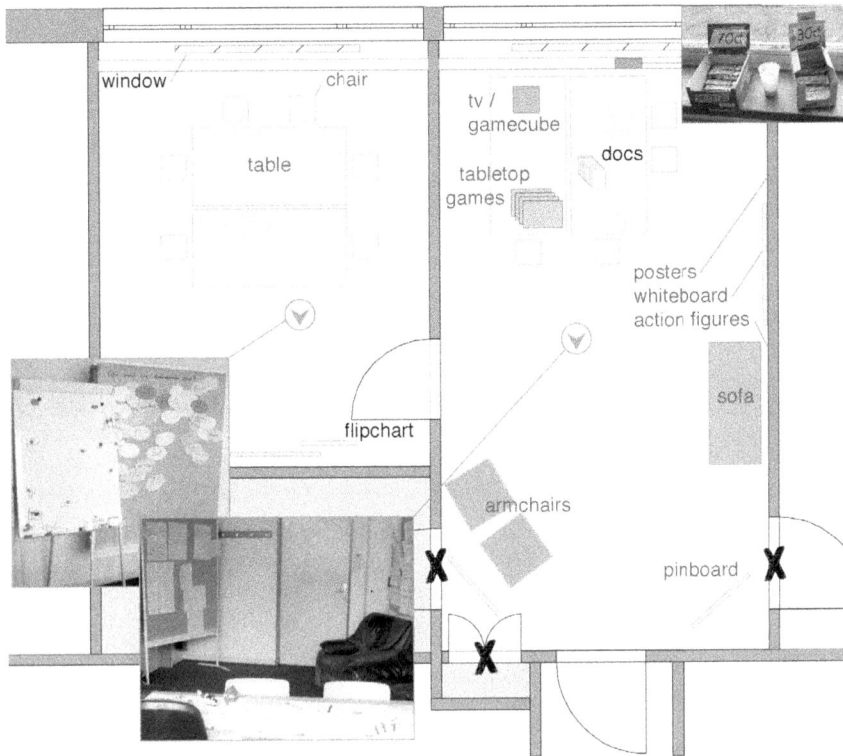

Figure 1: Final state of 5555

students in discovery, innovation, and scholarship [3]. Similar motives are visible in the idea to offer a studio-based teaching style that is more prevalent in architecture or the arts [10]. All of them highlight the need for open structures to foster cooperation. Previous case studies [11] propose to offer smaller sub-divided places that allow small teams to work together in front of workstations. However, none of these cases suggest technology-free spaces.

As shown, there are many ways to address these issues on fostering creativity. As a result, we propose to let students create their own creativity space by providing a room and certain infrastructure. The purpose was to create contexts that remind CS students of the creativity involved in game design as for example generating original gameplay ideas. In the following sections, we present our setting of Creativity Room 5555 and describe our observations in a student project about game creation. In our analysis we further assess the creativity aspects according to the students' perceptions and based on comments from visitors during a public presentation of the resulting games.

2. METHODOLOGY

We held a game design project in the winter semester 09/10 with 14 CS students that teamed up in three groups to create three individual games. In the first week, they were introduced to Creativity Room 5555[1] (short form: 5555). The room was exclusively booked for the project members. It was accessible on every working day. In addition, we

---

[1]The room was secured by a combination lock with these digits. The students' first task was to solve this *mystery* based on the name of the room...

booked two *traditional* PC labs that offered 6 workstations each.

Beforehand we had equipped the 5555 with three tables, 18 chairs, three portable pinboards, one flipchart and one whiteboard. We provided a box with training and workshop materials, such as felt pens, glue sticks, scissors, notepads and pins. To emphasize the playful ambiance of the room, we also supplied a remote-controlled mini-helicopter, two board games, two card games, six dice, modeling clay, a large set of Lego bricks, loudspeakers to connect audio devices and magazines on games and game design. The first homework was to bring individual cultural probes, as introduced by Gaver et al. [6], and anonymously arrange them in the creativity room. Conventionally, cultural probes are selected arbitrary private belongings provided by a target audience to give designers an insight on their individual characteristics. In our case, the cultural probes were meant to help the students to familiarize themselves with both the environment and the idea of using it as their private meeting place. The instructors did not review these cultural probes. We conducted exercises in which the students had to play games and modify the rules, as for example recommended by Lundgren [9], or the *GameGame* [8]. First, these games were of course played in the room and second, all resulting outcomes were documented on the display walls inside the room. We also introduced brainstorming techniques inside the room in the course of a hands-on session. Since we did not want to affect brainstorming sessions for particular game ideas, we focused this session on the room itself: We asked the students what a creative environment should look like. In addition, we asked them what 5555 was lacking. The following development process was structured into four mile-

Figure 2: One of many different Lego creations that appeared inside 5555.

stones for presenting progress of the prototypes. In these sessions, the fundamental playtesting took place in 5555.

3. OBSERVATIONS

The students started arranging the room by bringing cultural probes, such as posters, magazines, game action figures, game art books, a TV set and a video game console, as well as some games. After the brainstorming session on environments that promote creativity, the students strongly discussed whether a TV set plus a game console would impede or foster creativity. In the same breath, a vast majority agreed upon the idea of banishing desktop PCs. They argued that PC environments offer too many distractions, like checking mails, visiting social networks, and so forth. However, they were certain that at some point laptops would be necessary to implement the game prototypes hence should be allowed inside the room. Finally, it became apparent that all participants were very interested in places that promote creativity, and many told us that they do not like to work in computer labs as provided by the university.

The idea of bringing cultural probes alone did fill up the room, but did not improve coziness. Shortly after the brainstorming session, the participants realized that it would be very nice to rearrange the furniture and objects to develop a cozy and creative environment. They decorated the white walls with moderation paper to offer further alternatives for the visualization of ideas. They even acquired one used sofa and two armchairs to offer more cozy seating accommodations in 5555. They were put in the room in the fifth week which clearly shows that they were continuously rearranging 5555 according to their preferences and imagination. A final state of 5555 is outlined in Fig. 1.

One student bought a range of candy bars and made them freely available in the room, asking for a donation covering the purchase price. After some days he proudly told us that all candy bars had been eaten and that the sum donated covered the actual cost. He was happy about this outcome and bought new candy. As trivial as this example might sound, it exemplifies that students had started to adopt the room: They recognized and utilized it as a common ground for social interaction. After sofa and armchairs had been set up, the room truly became a meeting place. Almost every day of the week one could meet project members there. All teams had established regular meetings in the creativity

room. Additionally, many students worked there individually on their tasks at different days and times. Small groups often ordered pizza to the room or brought cakes to share them. Nearly every week new original Lego (Fig. 2) or modeling clay creations filled the room. It appeared to be a dynamic process of creating and sharing those artifacts among the visiting participants. It appeared to be a communication form that allowed the participants to overcome time differences in their visits. It has to be kept in mind that normally it is difficult motivating students to spend extra time at our facility.

The games created in the project (Fig. 3) were presented at a final event. Visitors and guests were invited, as were industry experts from game developers or publishers, and journalists. To get an understanding of the successful game development processes conducted inside the 5555, the resulting prototypes (developed using *iPhone SDK 2.2 / Cocos2D* and *Microsoft XNA 3.1* respectively) should be briefly described:

- *Baam-Bi* is a top view racer played on the *Apple iPhone*, where the player has to avoid or hit obstacles on the road. Yet, it provides constantly changing settings, e.g. cute deer become zombies by what the whole gameplay is inverted: The deer has to be hit by the car. At the presentation, the simple but addictive gameplay attracted many players who avidly fought for the best high-score.

- *VRacerPro* is a turn-based racer for up to four players on *Microsoft Windows* environments. In each turn phase, the players must quickly adjust the acceleration vector for the next move and trigger power ups or weapons. When a time limit is reached, all decisions are played out, with little chance of influence. At the event, the game was a big hit and people were enthusiastically shouting and screaming while playing it. Industry guests were impressed and recommended to participate in independent game festivals.

- *InkWars* is a real time strategy game for *Microsoft Windows* based on drawing units and their paths on exercise books. The key is that destroyed tanks provide new resources for creating new units, hence the balance is very dynamic. During the presentation, actual play suffered from network issues, but the concept was widely appreciated.

To conclude, all three games represent innovative extensions to their individual genres, *VRacerPro* may even define its own genre. *VRacerPro* was a nominee at the design competition of the Fun and Games Conference 2010. Furthermore, all artworks and sounds were self-made by the CS students.

4. SURVEY RESULTS

We conducted three surveys at the end of the semester, two amongst the 14 participants and one amongst 52 visitors of the final demo. We asked the participants on general topics in faculty wide periodic evaluation, and on the room itself in a separate form. The guests were asked to vote for their favorite game and to estimate individual elements, such as fun aspects, creativity, and social components visible in each game. All questions offered a four-point Likert scale from complete affirmation (1) to strong denial (4).

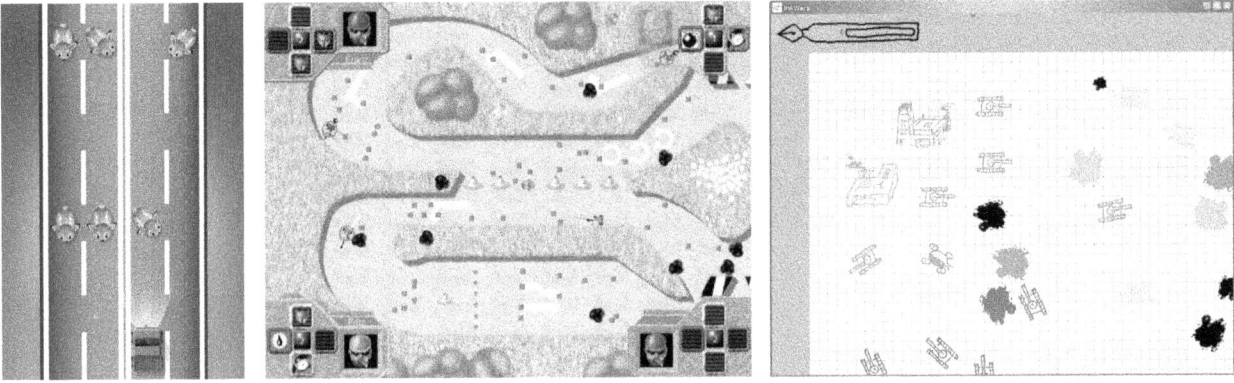

Figure 3: Resulting prototypes of the course. *Baam-Bi* (left), *VRacerPro* (center), *InkWars* (right).

Based on the periodic evaluation ($N = 13$), the project received a very good overall rating ($M = 1.2$; $MD = 1$; $SD = .4$). Considering ratings that can be related to an open-minded and creative learning environment, the students strongly affirmed that the instructors encouraged questions and designed the project to be interactive ($M = 1.2$; $MD = 1$; $SD = .4$) as well as interesting and agile ($M = 1.3$; $MD = 1$; $SD = .5$), and that the atmosphere was very pleasant ($M = 1.4$; $MD = 1$; $SD = .5$). Also, individual mentoring was rated as very good ($M = 1.6$; $MD = 1$; $SD = .9$). We should point out that on the negative side, students agreed that they did not learn much about the scientific method ($M = 2.7$; $MD = 3$; $SD = .7$).

Regarding the second questionnaire about the room, the students perceived a strong impact on communication. The room seemed to facilitate communication among the participants ($M = 1.5$; $MD = 1$; $SD = .5$), and with the instructor ($M = 2.2$; $MD = 2$; $SDs = .8$). As a result, it helped the participants a lot with organizing group processes ($M = 1.5$; $MD = 1$; $SD = .8$). Most students agree with an increasing awareness for the other group projects ($M = 2.5$; $MD = 2$; $SD = .9$), but not with a comparison of other teams' progresses ($M = 2.9$; $MD = 3$; $SD = 1.0$) on a competitive basis. The working atmosphere offered in 5555 was considered as very pleasant ($M = 1.4$; $MD = 1$; $SD = .5$) and overall the room provided an incentive for many students to stay longer at the faculty ($M = 2.4$; $MD = 2$; $SD = .8$) comparing to previous semesters.

In conclusion, for most students the 5555 contributed to their individual creative processes ($M = 2.1$; $MD = 2$; $SD = .5$). They wished more opportunities to arrange labs according to individual ideas ($M = 1.4$; $MD = 1$; $SD = .7$) and most regard the additional workload of creating a room as justified ($M = 1.7$; $MD = 2$; $SD = .8$).

At the final presentation *VRacerPro* was voted to be the best experience (69,2 %, $N = 52$). In *VRacerPro* the visitors clearly saw original elements ($M = 1.3$; $MD = 1$; $SD = .5$; $N = 50$), social aspects ($M = 1.3$; $MD = 1$; $SD = .5$; $N = 51$), and creativity ($M = 1.3$; $MD = 1$; $SD = .5$; $N = 52$). While those results are outstanding, the other two games were still good. For example, on creativity *InkWars* was slightly better rated ($M = 1.7$; $MD = 1$; $SD = .8$; $N = 50$) than *Baam-Bi* ($M = 2.4$; $MD = 2$; $SD = .1$; $N = 51$).

5. CONCLUSIONS

During a discussion, one student stated that he likes the idea of having a room as creativity environment, but that he dislikes the idea of being forced to program at computer labs afterwards. Therefore he would encourage the presence of desktop PCs in the 5555 as well. Many others disagreed by saying that there are enough rooms packed with PCs. In their opinion, not allowing PCs underlined the uniqueness of the creative environment. This was reassuring, since the topic was brought up by students themselves. Having said this, it becomes clear that CS students are aware of the issues described in this paper. This indicates a strong need for creative and playful meeting places, especially in a game design context which always highlights the importance of physical prototypes, playtests and communication. This becomes even more obvious considering that none of the PC labs was used during the course. The students decided to work on their own laptop PCs at home and inside 5555. Yet, laptop PCs were naturally packed away for creativity sessions, meetings, and discussions. During the brainstorming session on creativity rooms, it became apparent that students expect such places to be comfortable, individual, playful, and to allow for the unexpected. Moreover, it seemed to be very important to the students to take an active part in rearranging the 5555 according to their needs.

Even though it is hard measuring creativity, it was obvious that the resulting games contain unconventional features that contributes to attractive gameplay. Many game elements focus on social interactions as commonly seen in tabletop boardgames or card games. In our view, this clearly shows an impact of 5555 on the game designs. The observations are backed up by the results of the surveys conducted during the final presentation and after the course. Most visitors, especially industry professionals and journalists, recognized creative elements in the games. To further analyze creativity involved in the course we want to evaluate whether communication and discussions were encouraged during the course as proposed by Amoussou et al. [1]: Both questionnaires support the conclusion that the students appreciated the informal and pleasing atmosphere that let them exchange with the other participants. Furthermore, the questionnaires and many observations lead to the conclusion that 5555 was meaningful place to the participants where they could play an active part as claimed by M. Brown [2]. Of course, there is need for improvement to meet all three affordances highlighted by Q. Brown [4]: Especially team processes and planning decisions were poorly visible in 5555.

Subjectively, it was very easy to monitor project progress, group moods and behaviors by visiting the room occasionally. Furthermore, stopping by the room encouraged short informal conversations that account for an open, social, and creative context. As a result, all three game designs are well thought out and structured, extensively reviewed and focused on social interaction. With larger teams however, monitoring tools, e.g. logfiles of versioning systems, bug tracking software should be applied. One promising approach is using agile methods such as Scrum which provides backlogs and has recently shown to support students in managing their workflow [12].

To conclude, we strongly recommend to offer such creativity rooms as proposed with 5555. At best, the room should be arranged in collaboration with the participating students at the beginning of a course. Active discussions about using or abandoning technology help to establish a focus on creativity in game design. A very nice side-effect appears to be a strengthening of the group bond and a sense of responsibility for this room.

6. REFERENCES

[1] G. Amoussou, E. Cashman, and S. Steinberg. Ways to learn and teach creativity and design in computing science. In *Proceedings of the SoD'07*, pp.12–13, Arcata, California, USA, 2007. ACM.

[2] M. Brown. Learning Spaces. In D. G. Oblinger and J. L. Oblinger, editors, *Educating the Net Generation*, chapter 12, pp.174–195. Educause, Boulder, Colorado, USA, 2005.

[3] M. Brown and P. Long. Trends in Learning Spaces. In D. G. Oblinger, editor, *Learning Spaces*, chapter 9, pp.116–126. Educause, Boulder, Colorado, USA, 2006.

[4] Q. Brown, F. Lee, and S. Alejandre. Emphasizing soft skills and team development in an educational digital game design course. In *Proceedings of the FDG'09*, pp.240–247, Orlando, Florida, USA, 2009. ACM.

[5] T. Fullerton. *Game Design Workshop, Second Edition: A Playcentric Approach to Creating Innovative Games.* Morgan Kaufmann, 2008.

[6] B. Gaver, T. Dunne, and E. Pacenti. Design: cultural probes. *interactions*, 6(1):21–29, 1999. ACM.

[7] P. Gestwicki, F. Sun, and B. Dean. Teaching Game Design and Game Programming Through Interdisciplinary Courses. *Journal of Computing Sciences in Colleges*, 24:110–115, 2008.

[8] A. Järvinen. Theory as Game: Designing the Game Game. In *Changing Views: Worlds in Play: Proceedings of the DiGRA'05*, Vancouver, Can., 2005.

[9] S. Lundgren. Designing games: why and how. *interactions*, 15(6):6, 2008. ACM.

[10] K. Lynch, A. Carbone, D. Arnott, and P. Jamieson. A Studio-Based Approach to Teaching Information Technology. In *Proceedings of the WCCE'02*, pp.75–79, Copenhagen, Denmark, 2002.

[11] D. G. Oblinger, editor. *Learning Spaces*. Educause, Boulder, Colorado, USA, 2006.

[12] J. Schild, R. Walter, and M. Masuch. ABC-Sprints: Adapting Scrum to Academic Game Development Courses. In *Proceedings of the FDG'10*, pp. 187–194, Monterey, California, USA, 2010. ACM.

[13] K. Sung. Computer Games and Traditional CS Courses. *Communications of the ACM*, 52(12):74–78, 2009. ACM.

[14] B. Villanueva and L. Wong. Metamorphosis: from traditional computer labs to collaboratories. In *Proceedings of the ACM SIGUCCS'07*, pp.345–351, Orlando, Florida, USA, 2007. ACM.

Discovering Logic through Comics

Iliano Cervesato
Carnegie Mellon University — Qatar
iliano@cmu.edu

ABSTRACT

This paper describes a new experimental course introduced in the Spring of 2010 at Carnegie Mellon University in Qatar. *Discovering Logic* is an introduction to logic for Computer Science majors in their freshman year. It targets students who have had little or no exposure to logic and has the primary objective of 1) preparing them for sophomore classes which require proficiency with understanding formal statements expressed in English, elementary reasoning skills, and a sense of mathematical rigor. The course is structured as to achieve two additional objectives: 2) develop the students' communication skills, and 3) give them some historical depth into Computer Science and logic. This led to a somewhat unconventional approach that used a comic book, *Logicomix*, as the course textbook and that empowered the students to be active agents in the learning process through presentations and numerous open discussions. Preliminary analysis hints at an improved performance in follow-up courses, indicating that it may be achieving its primary objective.

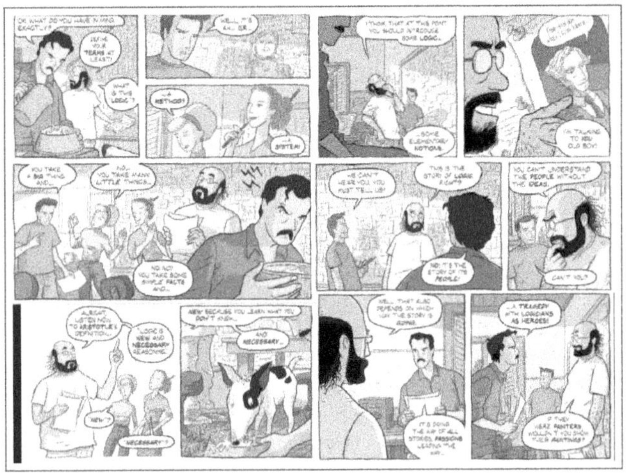

Categories and Subject Descriptors

K.3.2 [**Computers and Education**]: Computer and information science education—*Computer science education*; F.4.1 [**Mathematical Logic and Formal Languages**]: Mathematical logic; K.2 [**History of Computing**]: Theory

General Terms

Experimentation, Human Factors.

Keywords

Logic, first-year of college, comic books, *Logicomix*, computational thinking, communication skills, history of CS.

1. INTRODUCTION

Computer Science draws significantly from logic [4, 3] and therefore CS students need to master basic logic and develop

Figure 1: A sample page in *Logicomix* [5], where the authors portray themselves defining "logic".

good logical skills to succeed in their major and in their career [1]. This means not only getting some acquaintance with propositional and predicate logic, but also having developed fundamental skills at reading informal texts and extracting the logic they intend to convey. This is necessary for example to apply known theorems or other techniques to solve a problem, to write a program from specifications, and in general to engage in any reasoning task. In our institution (and many like it), these elementary logical skills are taught over a mere couple of hours as part of a busy discrete mathematics course in the freshman year. There are indications that this is insufficient to prepare students for the demanding sophomore and upper-division courses.

As an experimental remedy, we have introduced a dedicated half-term freshman logic elective, *Discovering Logic*, whose primary goal is to bridge this gap. To make it more appealing to students, we made the unusual choice of using a comic book, the much acclaimed *Logicomix* [5], as its textbook. This provided the opportunity to expand the scope of the course to developing the students' communication skills through presentations and essays, and to giving them some historical depth into logic, mathematics and Computer Science. Altogether, this set a fun, down-to-earth, class atmosphere that kept the students engaged — an end-of-semester survey confirmed that the course was well received. We monitored the students' performance throughout the sophomore year to assess whether it actually boosted their elementary logical aptitude compared with their peers who did not take the course — it apparently did.

This paper has two primary objectives: 1) to share an educational experiment with the community, and 2) to reflect on this experiment through the lens of recent research in CS education and related experiments.

This paper is organized as follows: we provide some context about logic in the CS curriculum and on the educational use of comic books in Section 2. We give a detailed description of *Discovering Logic* in Section 3 and of its learning objectives in Section 4. We report assessment results in Section 5.

2. BACKGROUND

We provide some context to the design of *Discovering Logic* by focusing on two characteristics of the course: the teaching of logic in the undergraduate CS curriculum and its use of comics in the classroom. We do not delve into other aspects, such as developing communication skills and student engagement, which deserve a much longer discussion.

2.1 Logic in CS

The ACM/IEEE 2001 Computing Curricula for Computer Science [1] and its 2008 interim revision [2] recommend that CS undergraduates be exposed to a minimum of 10 hours of "basic logic" (plus 12 hours on proof techniques) in their introductory courses, with additional logic taught as needed in courses such as databases, artificial intelligence and computability/complexity. These guidelines also leave the door open to students taking "advanced math electives such as logic" [1].

The initial exposure to logic is often confined to a busy discrete mathematics course in the freshman year which, at least in our program, is insufficient to provide students with the necessary logical skills for their subsequent CS courses. A fascinating recent survey of standalone introductory logic courses [12] indicates that they often mix a highly diverse population of students at all levels and from different majors (mainly philosophy). Based on an analysis of syllabi, they tend to focus on knowledge (definitions, properties, etc.) rather than skills (using logic as a learning tool, to solve problems, to engage in computational thinking).

Discovering Logic is designed to reinforce the discrete math exposure. It aims at building a solid foundation in those most elementary aspects of logic that are pervasively used throughout the CS curriculum: the basic skills that enable students to read a specification and translate it into a program, for example, or to read a problem statement and match it with known techniques to approach its solution. These skills quickly become second-nature, but acquiring them in the first place can be a struggle.

Many in the CS education community have advocated for more logic to be included in the CS curriculum [10, 3]. Paraphrasing [10] and [3], if logic is to Computer Science what calculus is to engineering, then it should be taught as such.[1] *Discovering Logic* is one concrete attempt to do so at the introductory level within the current system.

---

[1] Interestingly, Myers's passionate call for logic to take the place of calculus in CS is echoed in a milder way in [1, p.48] as "it is often more appropriate for computer science students to take less calculus and more courses in discrete mathematics or other material more directly relevant to the practice of computer science".

2.2 Teaching with Comics

In the last 30 years, many science topics taught at the college level have been given new colorful forms as comic books: Computer Science was penciled out in this way as early as 1983 [7] and several such books have been published in the last two years on subjects such as molecular biology [13], the theory of evolution [8] and now logic [5].

Surprisingly, we found little evidence of instructors using these and similar titles in their classes in the literature or on the Web, at least in science classes (comic books are occasionally used in K-12 humanities classes, and of course there are dedicated courses in graphic design curricula). The lone exception is Rota and Izquierdo's use of a purpose-made comic book to teach plant biotechnology in Brazil [11]. One other related attempt we are aware of is Yim et al's [14] use of cartoons hosted on the Web to illustrate CS concepts such as lists, etc. We strongly suspect however that more experiments have been attempted.

These graphic novels, comics and cartoons are an extreme form of the visual tools that are being used more and more frequently in teaching engineering and scientific subjects. In a recent multidisciplinary gathering [9], story telling and visual imagery were found to provide alternative ways to think about science and engineering, ways which promoted an effective form of visual learning. The benefits of visuals in engineering education were anticipated by Felder and Silverman [6] who observed that most people of college age have a predilection for visual information, while most college teaching has historically been verbal in these disciplines. The mentioned experiments narrow the gap between teaching and learning along this visual/verbal dimension.

3. COURSE ORGANIZATION

3.1 Origin and Motivations

Discovering Logic emerged from the confluence of a problem and an opportunity.

The *problem*, which had been pointed out repeatedly in our department over the years (but never really addressed), was that some students have difficulties working with formal statements in their sophomore year theory classes. Specifically, they have difficulties parsing English text and extracting the logical components (deep understanding) that allow them to solve problems and make the necessary connections to build up knowledge — this was observed both in the classroom, for example when students would have difficulties matching a theorem they knew well with a problem that paraphrased its hypotheses, and in exams or assignments where these parsing difficulties would cause them to spend a lot of time on a question. This problem was not universal, but a sufficient number of students manifested it as to elevate it to an issue of concern. Interestingly, once they extracted the logic, they rarely had difficulties applying formal rules or performing correct reasoning.

The *opportunity* was the publication in late 2009 of *Logicomix* [5], an intelligently crafted and beautifully illustrated comic book — the proper phrasing is "graphic novel" — which recounts the life of the logician Bertrand Russell as he witnessed and influenced the major developments of logic from the end of the 19th century to the eve of World War II. *Logicomix* is not a textbook, and indeed logic, although a pervasive theme, is never "taught" to the reader — as the authors say repeatedly, it is a story. The sample page of

Logicomix reproduced in Figure 1 exemplifies the rich multi-layered storytelling: there, it steps out of Russell's narration of his life to a group of protesters and shows the book's authors defining "logic".

In the context of the course, *Logicomix* was used for several purposes, none of which being the teaching of the technical aspects of logic.

- The first purpose was motivational: a course using a comic book fueled interest. All students who enrolled got drawn into the book and quickly started asking questions about characters, events and concepts.

- The second purpose was to enable some of the secondary objectives of the course: the book exposes students to a great deal of the history of logic, from references to Aristotle to the visual acquaintance with Georg Cantor, David Hilbert, Kurt Gödel, and several other major logicians of the pivotal period in the development of logic the book is about, and even a preview of the imminent rise of Computer Science through brief encounters with John von Neumann and Alan Turing.

- It also provided starting points for the selection of presentation topics and fed some of the in-class discussion about more technical content.

3.2   Position within the CS Curriculum

Carnegie Mellon University in Qatar is a satellite campus of Pittsburgh-based Carnegie Mellon University, a medium-size research-oriented American university: we follow the same model, just on a smaller scale. Enrollment in the CS program fluctuates between 20 and 30 students a year. In the Spring 2010, the freshman cohort numbered 27.

Like in many CS programs that follow a liberal education model, students at Carnegie Mellon University are enrolled in just a sprinkling of Computer Science classes in their first year (mostly programming classes) with the bulk of their time spent in math and humanities. Students get exposed to more substantial CS courses in their sophomore year. The transition to more abstract and theoretical topics is significant for all students and brutal for the weakest performers. By and large, students are left to their own devices to cope with this transition.

CS students at Carnegie Mellon University receive a minimal exposure to logic in their freshman year: their introduction to logic consists of two 50-minute lectures (plus graded assignment problems) in a discrete mathematics course they take in their second semester, much less than the 10 hours recommended in [1, 2]. Their next three years in the program depend on these two hours: this is insufficient. Many students learn the logic they need along the way, but a few stumble. *Discovering Logic* is an attempt at helping freshmen build up their proficiency with elementary logic as they ascend towards their sophomore year.

3.3   Course Structure

We offered *Discovering Logic* for the first time in the second half of the Spring of 2010 as a 7-week mini. It was an elective and accounted for 3 units (which roughly translates into an expected workload of 6 hours per week). The class met once a week for 80 minutes. Starting with the third lecture, this time was divided into a student presentation part which consisted of two 15-minute presentations plus 5-minute questions and feedback, and a 40 minute lecture.

The course instructor has significant expertise in logic in CS having done research in this area for years.

Enrollment was restricted to CS freshmen in order to keep the course focused on their needs — we had to turn down requests from non-CS and from non-freshmen. Nine students enrolled in the class, which is rather high for an elective — one third of the freshmen cohort. Only one dropped the class towards the end, in spite of good performance

3.4   Course Contents

The course contents fell into two broad categories: core material on which the instructor lectured, and a number of side topics that the students introduced to their classmates.

3.4.1   Core Material

The core material covered a discussion of what logic is, a brief history and why it matters to Computer Science, as well as the motivation for using formal/symbolic languages. The course then turned to propositional logic, with an initial emphasis on expressing natural language statements into logical formulas (and vice versa), followed by the study of truth tables which introduced elementary notions of model theory, and by a gentle presentation of propositional natural deduction and the question of the equivalence between validity and derivability. The next module of the course followed the same script with first-order logic: it introduced predicates, variables and quantifiers, putting a lot of emphasis on expressing informal statements as formulas, truth tables were then upgraded to a simplified form of Tarskian models and the natural deduction rules for the quantifiers were introduced. Originally, the schedule planned for discussing a few more topics, in particular logical paradoxes and logic programming, but we ran out of time.

Logicomix motivated some in-class discussions, but otherwise played a minimal role as far as this core content is concerned. The students relied on handouts provided by the instructor and on the notes they took in class.

We chose a highly interactive style of instruction for this course. Each lecture was peppered with discussions, at first triggered mostly by the instructor and later erupting spontaneously. The class atmosphere was intentionally kept light-hearted and fun. Humor was encouraged. We typically introduced a topic by posing a question to the class and guiding the discussion through the use of examples and counterexamples until the underlying notion or principle was made explicit. For instance, the concept of valid inference was introduced by the example "Alice is in Kansas and Kansas is the US so Alice is in the US" which was modified back and forth until consensus emerged that for an inference of this type to be valid, it cannot be that its premises are true and yet its conclusion is false. As suggested in [1], such Socratic dialogs can be seen as a form of the scientific method as the students are asked to inductively analyze instances of a phenomenon to then deduce a general principle or formulate a definition. By following this approach, we moved toward bridging another of the dichotomies Felder and Silverman originally found in engineering education [6]: students tend to learn material presented inductively (from the concrete to the abstract) more easily while teaching at the college level is most often deductive (from principles to applications). We used this approach extensively in *Discovering Logic*, from the most elementary concepts such as defining "inference" to complex issues such as nailing down the natural deduction rules for disjunction and quantifiers.

3.4.2 Student Presentations

The side topics were the subject of student presentations. At the beginning of the course, we asked each of them to select a topic from one of three broad categories (people, logic, and others). The presentations had multiple purposes: expanding the scope of the class beyond the core contents, developing the students' ability to research topics and organize ideas autonomously, developing their presentation skills, and analyzing constructively each other's work.

Because we had gone through relatively little core material by then, early presentations focused on the life of actual logicians: one student made a superb presentation about Christos Papadimitriou (one of the authors of *Logicomix* and a renowned complexity theorist) while another told the class about George Boole. By then, the students had read *Logicomix* and the presentation topics shifted to the historical context: students gave talks on illuminism and positivism, on mathematics in the 19th century, and on dadaism. The last batch of presentations transitioned to logic topics not covered in class, namely paradoxes, non-Euclidean geometry, fuzzy logic, temporal logic, and theorem proving.

Because each presentation lasted 15 minutes, there was no time to cover these topics at any depth. Yet, the class got some exposure to aspects of logic that rarely make it in the CS curriculum (especially the historical/contextual presentations). Maybe more importantly, this activity provided the students with a substantial opportunity to develop their communication skills: they had to research a topic to a sufficient depth to tell a compelling story, they had to organize what they found to share their newly acquired knowledge and make this story interesting, and they had to stand up in front of a picky audience. At the beginning of a session, all students were given a rubric with which to evaluate and comment on the presentations in that session. Each presentation session was followed by a debriefing where, rubric in hand, the students in the audience pointed to what the presenter did well and what he/she could have done better.

By and large, the student presenters did an outstanding job. A couple had difficulties in the research phase, coming back to us with keywords they did not understand rather than with an intuition of what their topic was about — in one case this took numerous iterations to correct. The presentations went from a highly creative PowerPoint comic book to duller bullet points with a few pictures thrown in.

3.5 Coursework

The student evaluation relied on their participation in class discussions (15% of the final grade), on the presentations we just examined (30%), on five homework assignments (40%) and one final paper (15%).

The first assignment asked the students to read *Logicomix* and to write an essay about it in the form of a letter to a friend or a review for Amazon.com; it also asked for three questions that the student would like to see answered in the course. For the final paper, they read the book again and wrote a second essay about it in the light of what they had learned in the course. They were also presented with a selection of their best questions from the first homework. These two essays had the purpose to develop another aspect of the students' communication skills: writing and specifically critical writing. The work they submitted provided a window on the writing abilities they had developed in high-school and on their attitude towards writing as CS majors:

one student's essays were sublime, the majority were what was expected of freshmen, and only two students submitted subpar work, betraying that they had not yet reached the developmental stage of their peers.

The remaining four homework assignments consisted of exercises that let the students practice their understanding of the core contents of the course and broaden their perspective about it. Extracting logic formulas from natural language was a recurrent theme, which we tried to contextualize to drive other points home (for example, giving them sentences in Italian or in Chinese with the only knowledge of how the propositional connectives were written had the dual purpose of demonstrating that logic deals with symbols, not meaning). Other exercises explored the connection between logic and Computer Science: they were asked to write about controlling search in Google and beyond, to get "if" statements to do the right thing, to develop a hypothetical three-valued logic for non-terminating programs, to annotate small programs with assertions, and so on. A minority of the exercises were logical in nature: do derivations, check validity, find counterexamples, etc. Student performance varied from acceptable to quite good, which indicates that the level of these exercises was neither to high or too low.

3.6 Student Feedback

Throughout the course, we provided students with numerous opportunities to give us feedback. In particular, on the last day of class, students were given a 3-question written survey ("What is working?", "What can be done better?" and "Any other suggestions?"). The one unanimous complaint was that 80 minutes once a week was not enough. Highlights included the presentations, the homeworks and the course contents. Suggestions ranged from discussing more topics to having a play at the beginning of each class.

4. LEARNING OBJECTIVES

4.1 Learn Elements of Logic

In our current curriculum, core "basic logic" accounts for less than two hours of instruction, against the 10 recommended by [1]. The students who elected to take *Discovering Logic* added another 10 hours (7 hours of instruction time and 3 hours of presentations). Our course covers all the topics and all the learning objectives for "basic logic" recommended in [1, 2]. It also embraces the less formalistic approach advocated in [2], although at a very basic level.

4.2 Nurture Researching, Presenting, Writing

When faced with a new word or a puzzling explanation, some students turn to the Web or other resources to quench their curiosity. Others turn the page. Clearly, the first attitude is much preferable and we would like to cultivate it in our students: this is a form of active learning [6]. *Discovering Logic* actively encourages students to overcome inertia in two main ways. First, *Logicomix* is full of these new words and alluded descriptions, but also has a gripping story line (actually multiple) that stimulates curiosity — and graded essays about the book can be pretty stimulating too. Second, while putting together their presentation, the students had to go out of their way and carry out this kind of research.

Autonomous curiosity, as well as effective written and oral communication skills, are some of the professional practice that CS students are expected to have acquired by the time they graduate [1]. This is further reinforced in [2]. These curricular guidelines state that "communication skills should not be seen as separate but should instead be fully incorporated into the computer science curriculum" [1, p.42]. Because they do not confine these skills to a standalone course (although many programs, like ours, do have a technical communication course), [1, 2] do not provide learning objectives for them. Yet they recommend that "students in computer science programs should be able to: communicate ideas effectively in written form; make effective oral presentations, both formally and informally; understand and offer constructive critiques of the presentations of other" [1. p.42]. *Discovering Logic* fully implements these recommendations.

4.3 Acquire Historical Depth

Students in physics, engineering and other experimental disciplines tend to be introduced to a good deal of historical anecdotes about their field. This is a lot less so in subjects like mathematics, logic and to a large extent Computer Science: ask a typical college student when limits came about and who defined the concept, and you are likely to get a blank stare back. We took advantage of *Logicomix*'s vivid description of the struggle of ideas that led to modern logic (and Computer Science) — the book's subtitle is *An Epic Search for Truth* — to help the students appreciate that many of the things they learn in their books, or that are now unquestioned in everyday life, took decades to be established, agreed upon, and accepted. "Proofs" are an example.

Here, *Discovering Logic* deviates from [1] which prescribes a single hour on the "history of computing" as part of the CS curriculum.

5. ASSESSMENT

As we said, the primary objective of the course was to give freshmen better logical skills in preparation for their more abstract sophomore courses. To assess whether *Discovering Logic* achieved this objective, we followed the entire freshman cohort through the first semester of their sophomore year and analyzed their academic performance. We focused on the one problem solving course, CS-251, that pervasively requires students to read formal statements and reason about them. We split the CS-251 students into those who took *Discovering Logic* (group A) and those who did not take it (group B). The idea was to compare both groups' average grade in CS-251 with the overall class average (group A+B). We tried to account for possible selection bias by first normalizing our data using each groups' performance in their first-semester freshmen CS and math classes (indeed, students who took *Discovering Logic* were on average better performers than students in group B — by normalizing, we canceled out this advantage). We then used this overall data to predict the CS-251 performance of the students in groups A and B and compared it with their actual performance in that course. The result is that the actual performance of the students in group A was 4% better than predicted (69.82 vs. 65.55) while the actual performance of the students in group B was slightly lower than predicted (60.77 vs. 60.93). Although encouraging, this analysis is not sufficient to conclude that *Discovering Logic* did achieve its primary goal: the sample sizes are too small for conclusive results (as indicated by other statistical tests we conducted). We plan to repeat this evaluation with future editions of the course.

6. CONCLUSIONS

In this paper, we have reported on a new experimental CS elective at Carnegie Mellon University in Qatar. *Discovering Logic* teaches basic logic at the freshman level while developing the students' communication skills and introducing them to the history of their discipline. The intentionally playful tone, engaging yet down-to-earth exercises, and the use of a comic book, *Logicomix* [5], kept the students motivated. Preliminary analysis indicates that students benefited academically from taking the course. We will repeat and expand *Discovering Logic* in the Spring of 2011, and continue monitoring the outcome.

7. REFERENCES

[1] Computing Curricula 2001: Computer Science, Final Report. Joint Task Force on Computing Curricula, IEEE/CS, ACM, 2001.

[2] Computer Science Curriculum 2008: An Interim Revision of CS 2001. Joint Task Force on Computing Curricula, IEEE/CS, ACM, 2008. Report from the Interim Review Task Force.

[3] K. B. Bruce, P. G. Kolaitis, D. M. Leivant, and M. Y. Vardi. Panel: Logic in the Computer Science Curriculum. In *SIGCSE'98*, pages 376–337, Atlanta, GA, 1998. ACM.

[4] M. Davis. Influences of Mathematical Logic on Computer Science. In *The universal Turing machine (2nd ed.): a half-century survey*, pages 289–299. Springer-Verlag, 1995.

[5] A. Doxiadis and C. H. Papadimitriou. *Logicomix: An Epic Search for Truth*. Bloomsbury, 2009.

[6] R. M. Felder and L. K. Silverman. Learning and Teaching Styles in Engineering Education. *Engineering Education*, 78(7):674–681, 1988.

[7] L. Gonick. *The Cartoon Guide to Computer Science*. Barnes and Noble, 1983.

[8] M. Keller and N. R. Fuller. *Charles Darwin's On the Origin of Species: A Graphic Adaptation*. Rodale Books, 2009.

[9] M. B. McGrath and J. R. Brown. Visual Learning for Science and Engineering. Tech. report, ACM, 2006.

[10] J. P. Myers. The Central Role of Mathematical Logic in Computer Science. *ACM SIGCSE Bulletin*, 22(1):22–26, 1990.

[11] G. Rota and J. Izquierdo. "Comics" as a tool for teaching biotechnology in primary schools. *Electronic Journal of Biotechnology*, 6(2), 2003.

[12] C. Schunn and M. Patchan. An Evaluation of Accelerated Learning in the CMU Open Learning Initiative Course "Logic & Proof". Report, Learning Research and Development Center, University of Pittsburgh, May 2009.

[13] M. Takemura. *The Manga Guide to Molecular Biology*. No Starch Press, 2009.

[14] K. Yim, S. Ahn, and D. Garcia. Computer Science Illustrated. http://csillustrated.berkeley.edu/.

Integrating Google Technology in Artificial Intelligence

Elena Sánchez-Nielsen
Dpto. E.I.O. y Computación Universidad de
La Laguna
38271, S/C de Tenerife, Spain
enielsen@ull.es

Stefan Klink
AIFB
Karlsruhe Institute of Technology
D-76128 Karlsruhe, Germany
stefan.klink@kit.edu

ABSTRACT
The use of Google technology in artificial intelligence courses gives new opportunities to focus the academic topics and learning objectives in order to meet the needs of students and computer science curricula. With the integration of Google developer toolkits, we can transform the class in order to use industry software tools as a motivating topic and as the domain for real-world software projects. This paper describes the methodology and motivating results using Google developer toolkits in teaching and practicing computer applications, which are based on artificial intelligence theory and techniques.

Categories and Subject Descriptors
K.3.2 [**Computer and Information Science Education**]: Computer Science Education.

General Terms
Algorithms.

Keywords
Artificial intelligence, Multiagent systems, Google technology.

1. MOTIVATION
The number of students enrolling on computer science programs in countries where computer science education had hitherto been expanding has begun to decline. This decline in student enrolment and the increase in demand have become so severe, that is now referred to as the *Computing crisis* [1]. One way of tackling the decrease in motivation is to seek innovative approaches that students find interesting and challenging, and yet motivating. Towards this end, the Review Task Force (RFT), conducted an interim review of the Computer Science Curriculum 2001 Volume (CS2001) [2] through consultation with both academia and industry. This process resulted in the Computer Science Curriculum 2008 report (CS2008) [1] which advises making certain changes such as finding new and better ways of teaching, and trying to place computing in a context that would serve to motivate and inspire students. At a broad level, the expected characteristics of computer science graduates can be expressed as follows: (1) system-level perspective, (2) appreciation of the interplay between theory and practice, (3) familiarity with common themes and principles, (4) significant project experience, (5) attention to rigorous thinking and, (6) adaptability. Also, expected capabilities and skills for computer science graduates related to cognitive, practical, and additional transferable capabilities are proposed.

Artificial intelligence (AI) topics are commonly referenced when computer science curricula are designed. There is a general consensus that AI provides a set of techniques for solving problems that are difficult or impractical to solve with other methods [3-5]. The student needs to be able to determine when an AI approach is appropriate for a given problem, and to be able to select and implement a suitable AI method. However, AI problem solving, planning, and communication mechanisms' has often focused on applying educational development tools to academic problems, distancing itself from real-world projects. As a consequence, a decrease in student motivation in AI topics has usually arisen.

This paper addresses how to integrate motivating real-life technology, based on Google developer toolkits, for students in teaching and practicing AI topics by means of combining academic goals and developing real-world software projects. We follow an instructional approach that first teaches basic topics, and then puts them into practice trough a team software project dealing with a real-life problem and delivering a working product. We also show our experience on how the Google technology has been successfully integrated into two graduate level AI courses at the La Laguna University (ULL).

The remainder of this paper is organized as follows. Section 2 introduces Google developer toolkits and programming languages to develop real-world software project for AI topics. Section 3 describes the teaching-learning methodology to combine academic goals with the development of real-world software projects in an AI context. Section 4 presents how we have used the Google developer toolkits in graduate level AI courses at ULL. Concluding remarks are provided in Section 5.

2. GOOGLE DEVELOPER TOOLKITS
It is widely accepted that designing, developing and implementing a software project to be applied to real-world problems provides students with valuable hands-on experience in the relevant topics of AI. An AI course that focuses on applying state-of-the art AI methodology to toy problems may meet scientific requirements, but cannot meet the actual problem of forming students with experienced real-world engineering as part of their formation as engineers. However, building a real-world software project from scratch is not something that every student will be able to complete in a few months. In addition, students should not invest too much time researching development tools, as this is not the

main focus of AI education. However, it is important for students to understand the use and value of tools within an AI project. Ideally, programming languages and developer tools should be simple and effective and run on a student's own PC without the need for complicated administration or tuning. The use of fairly modern tools accepted in industry contributes to enrollment and retention of students in AI courses. To this end, Google development toolkits and Java programming language are proposed as accessible and smart development tools to the students. Java provides modern applicative programming for delivering AI applications on personal computers, local networks, and the World Wide Web. The list of Google development toolkits includes social applications, mobile applications, geographical and maps applications, and AJAX/JavaScript applications.

In view of this, the use of Google technology and Java programming language in AI education provides an ideal and motivating playground for students to gain software experience and engineering skills in real-world application development and to experiment with AI topics they learn about in theory lectures. In order to develop a software project with AI topics, Google provides interesting developer tools and technical resources such as: AJAX APIs [6], App Engine [7], Google Web Toolkit [8] and open software programs [9]. Google's AJAX APIs are used to implement rich, dynamic Web sites entirely in JavaScript and HTML. The most widely used are the *Google Search API*, the *Google Maps API*, and the *Google Visualization API*. Other Google APIs of note for developing practical content are the *Google Earth API*, the *Google Book Search APIs*, the *YouTube API*, and the *Google Feed API*. By using the available APIs (application programming interfaces) to build applications with AI topics, students can improve their workflow and accelerate programming results.

The *Google AJAX Search API* enables developers to embed a simple, dynamic search box in a Web site in order to query all Web pages, YouTube videos, and Google Images and to display search results. The *Google Maps API* is a JavaScript API designed mainly for data representation purposes which can embed Google Maps in Web pages and allow the addition of content to the map. The *Google Visualization API* is a Google Chart tool which allows developers to embed visualizations directly on a Website.

The *Google App Engine* is the Google's Web infrastructure to run AJAX Web applications which include Java runtime, integration with Google Web Toolkit and a Google plug-in for Eclipse. The *Google Web Toolkit (GWT)* is a development toolkit for building and optimizing complex browser-based applications. The *Google open source programs* provide infrastructures with hosting services through *Project Hosting* and create new open source software through programs like the *Google Summer of Code* [10].

3. THE TEACHING-LEARNING METHODOLOGY

The design of a successful educational methodology to comprehend theoretical concepts and apply those concepts to real-world software projects must be supported by proven pedagogical theories. For this reason, a methodology to teach and practice AI topics which focuses on a social constructivism approach was applied. This approach focuses the responsibility of learning, on learners as an alternative to traditional "teaching by telling" approach (i.e., lecture-based approach) [11]. Furthermore, constructivism also promotes cooperative learning to reinforce the social dimension of education [12]. In cooperative learning, students work together in small groups on a structured activity. They are individually accountable for their work and the work of the group as a whole is also assessed.

A learning environment is designed and created to help students to acquire knowledge and understanding, as well as, practical experimentation with real-world projects. In order to meet these requirements, the practical course organization is based on the following principles:

- **Team working:** cooperative learning works best when group size is reduced [13]. The larger the group size the more difficult is to organize tasks, manage different skills, and reach a consensus. For this reason, teams of three are configured in order to participate in structured activities: lectures and a software development project.

- **Teaching and learning with social interaction:** interaction within student groups and with teaching staff is done through face-to-face (F2F) meetings and activities. F2F sessions are planned to introduce and discuss content and to guide and supervise students' activities. The following resources are used for the F2F activities: lectures on theory and problem solving, tutorial classes (to guide the student and answer questions), step-by-step tutorials, practical supervised laboratory activities, and seminar activities. Two types of seminar activities are offered: (i) lectures by teaching staff from other universities under the Erasmus teaching mobility framework [14], and (ii) lectures by industry professionals. The open source platform Moodle [15], a widely-used Content Management System (CMS), is employed to manage online resources. The use of the Moodle platform allows students to stay in touch and encourages cooperative work. Different resources are used between students and teaching staff: forums, chats, production of wikis, availability of lectures before class, step-by-step tutorials, and submission of student tasks.

- **Project organization:** distributing the work evenly among the team members prevents disproportionate individual workloads and team problems. An important focus for work distribution is to provide a clear responsibility profile for each team member. Two different roles are established in the software development project: (i) a software architect role, and (ii) a software developer role. Each team has a software architect and two software developers. The software architect is required to efficiently formulate the problem, design, evaluate and check the tasks while the software developers focus on coding and implementation. Any decision made by the software architect must be agreed upon by all team members. Students have two months to develop the software development project. Although students have basic programming skills, step-by-step tutorials on Java programming language and software engineering techniques are given during the first two weeks through the Moodle platform to ensure that the students have no difficulties in carrying out the software project. All the software development is organized and scheduled in different phases with delivery targets set per week. This procedure teaches students to manage their time in order to meet deadlines. The practical activities include step-by-step tutorials, a report on the requirements and the architecture solution, the implementation of each stage of the software project, and a final report. The lectures do not cover the technical details on Google developer toolkits because the different toolkits and APIs are introduced in the first laboratory session to convey basic knowledge of Google products. After the first two weeks of class, once students are familiar with Google developer tools and technical resources, they are required to submit via Moodle a report with the selected Google developer toolkits and APIs to be used to develop the software project. The remainder of the practical activity takes place over six weeks with a target delivery set per week.

- **Course assessment:** three types of ongoing assessment are carried out by the teaching staff: (i) problem solving, (ii) seminar activity lectures, and (iii) software development project. In order to evaluate the students' theoretical knowledge, an exam is given at the end of the course. The total course assessment is made up of 40% for theory, problem solving, and step-by-step tutorials; 20% for seminar activities; and the final 40% for the software development project. Theory topics, theoretical exercises and step-by-step tutorials are evaluated individually through quantitative methods (individual tests, exercises and Moodle tasks) while seminar activities and the software project development are evaluated in a cooperative way through both quantitative and qualitative methods.

4. APPLICATION
In this section, the teaching-learning methodology and the use of Google developer toolkits will be described on two artificial intelligent courses.

4.1 Search Strategies for Computer Problem Solving
A fundamental topic in teaching AI field is the search strategies course. This course at ULL includes the following features:

- Problem spaces; problem solving by search.
- Brute-force search.
- Heuristic search.
- Anytime search.
- Real-time search.
- Two-player games.

On completion of the course, the students will be able to:

- Formulate the problem space for a specific problem in terms of state spaces.
- Measure the complexity and performance of problems.
- Decide on the appropriate brute-force, and/or heuristic search algorithms for complex problem solving.
- Develop a software solution based on AI search algorithms for a real-life problem.

The course was designed to coordinate the timing of the lectures with the application of the lecture content to the software development project. The various seminars given by professionals in the industry and teaching staff from other universities gave the students insights into applying artificial search strategies to real-life problems.

The software development project required each group of students to create a Web application as a simulation tool in a volcanic scenario. The aim of this project was to use artificial search strategies to simulate the navigation of a helicopter on a grid in order to detect gaseous emissions in volcanic areas with unknown topology all the while avoiding areas with adverse meteorological conditions. The following tasks were to be carried out in the simulation: (1) choose and implement a brute-force search strategy to explore the whole map and detect all signs of gaseous emissions, (2) choose and implement an heuristic search to calculate the minimum path between two points of gaseous emissions, (3) choose and implement a real-time search strategy to explore the whole map, and (4) experimental evaluation.

After the first two weeks of class, once students are familiar with Google developer tools and technical resources, the practical activity was broken up into one assignment per week for a six week period (week three to week eight). The theoretical lectures were scheduled to coincide with the application of the relevant theory to the software development project.

Integrating Google technology in the AI software project was done in the following way: the *Google Web Toolkit (GWT)* was used to build the browser-based application. The *Google Maps API* was used to embed the input and output data on Google Maps (such as defining the geographical area where the search strategies are to be applied by clicking on the map, or by introducing the latitude and longitude coordinates; allowing flexibility in defining the position of the zones with marks of gaseous emissions and adverse weather conditions, both manually and randomly; and allowing user to view the trajectory viewing on the map according to search results). The *Google Visualization API* was employed to display the analytic results in an attractive way.

4.2 Multiagent Systems
Agents are autonomous entities which observe and act upon an environment and direct their activity toward achieving goals [4-5], [16-17]. The three-month multiagent systems course described here is taught in the last year of a graduate-level computer science program at the La Laguna University. The course is comprised of the following topics:

- Agent paradigm: foundations, applications and markets.
- Agent architectures.
- Communication, cooperation, and negotiation techniques.
- Software agents.
- Mobile agents and robotic agents.
- Agent Systems Development Life Cycle.
- Agents and Web Semantics.

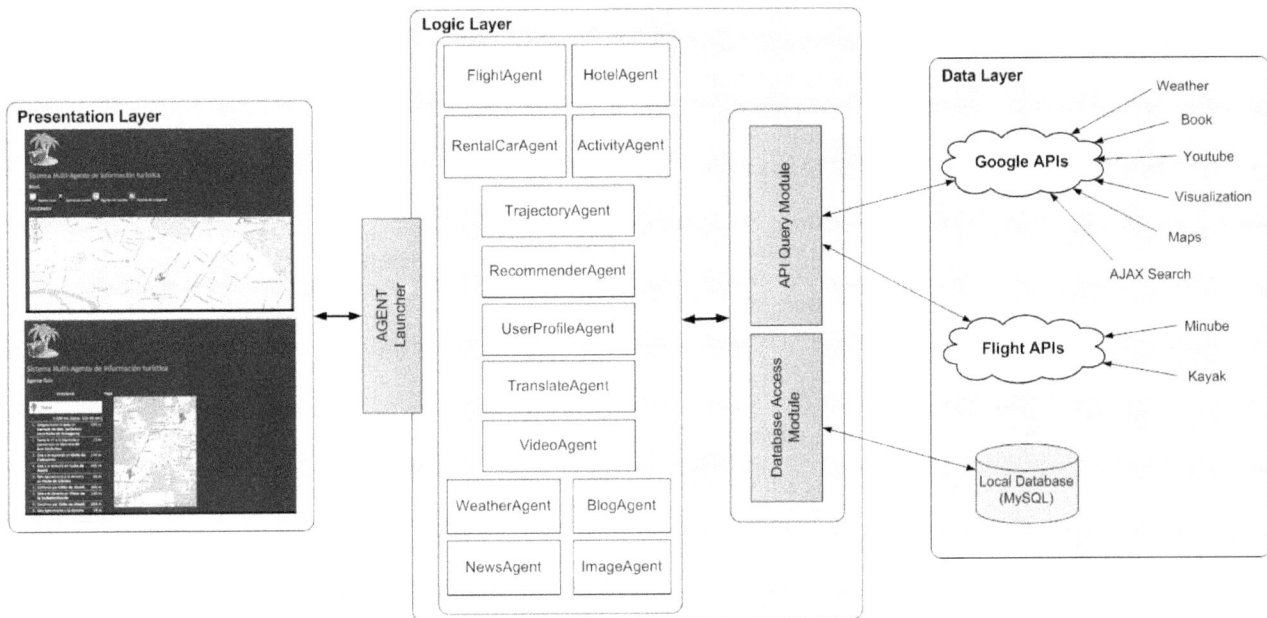

Figure 1. Multiagent information system

On completion of the course, the students will be able to:

- Understand the scope of application of multiagent systems;

- Design multi-agent systems in terms of agents, agent architecture, communication, cooperation and negotiation as a solution to concrete problems;

  - Develop a software project under the framework of multi-agent systems for a real-life problem.

The theory lectures were scheduled to coincide with seminar activities which applied lecture content to value-added applications in agent systems. The software development project included weekly tasks.

The software development project required each group of students to create a tourist Web application based on multi-agent system information. The application enabled users to plan a trip based on real-time information from various internet sources that was processed by software agents. The different software agents were: a *UserAgent* which requested users' travel requirements and showed the results; a *FlightAgent* that provided flight searches with different airlines according to the preferences of users; a *HotelAgent* that showed hotel availability according to users' profiles; a *RentalCarAgent* which delivers data describing rental car shopping results; a *TrajectoryAgent* that drawn a path from one point to another point of interest over the map for visiting specific places; a *TranslateAgent* which translates text between different language pairs; a *WeatherAgent* that showed weather forecasts for planned travel dates; an *ImageAgent* which provided destination images; a *VideoAgent* that showed videos related to the travel destination; an *ActivityAgent* which described possible activities; a *NewsAgent* which provided news about the destination; a *BlogAgent* that gave blog information, and a *RecommenderAgent* that provided recommendations in order to confirm or cancel the trip.

The tourist Web application consisted of a 3 tier architecture (see Figure 1). The bottom layer of the system was the data layer which included a local database to store users' preferences and

results. The system retrieved the data through Google's APIs and specific additional APIs related to flights, hotels, and rental cars (such as Kayak and Minube APIs). The Google AJAX Search API was used to search news and Google images on the internet; the Google Maps API was used to embed Google Maps with destination and hotel locations; the Google YouTube API was used to integrate YouTube videos of the destination, and the Google Weather API was used to access weather forecasts for the destination. The middle layer of the system was the logic layer, which was written in Java. The API query module was used by the different software agents to retrieve flight and hotel information, weather forecasts, news, images, videos, and blogs. This layer also contained a recommender agent that analyzed weather and news information to advise on possible cancellations caused by adverse meteorological conditions such as hurricanes, tornados or high temperatures.

The top layer of the system was the presentation layer. HTML, Java Server Page (JSP) and JavaScript were used to generate user-friendly and intuitive interfaces. The Google Web Toolkit (GWT) was used to build and optimize the browser-based application.

5. CONCLUSIONS

Change is an inevitable part of innovative teaching. With this in mind, an educational methodology based on the recognition of combining technology integration, and educational viewpoints has been presented in this paper. The aim of this approach is to improve the teaching and learning process in AI topics in computer science curricula and, familiarizing students with real-world engineering experience. This paper identifies the following guidelines as key to update AI courses and, better meets the needs and encouragement of students: (i) development of the practical activity focused on the practicing of software development projects applied to added-value applications using Google technology; (ii) interleaving academic topics from theory lectures with their application on the software development process; (iii) ongoing assessment for monitoring individual and class progress;

and (iv) the use of pedagogical methods which allows developing cognitive and practical capabilities.

Introducing Google technology in AI projects enables students to design smart Web applications. The students thus can focus on the use of academic topics to build value-added applications in real world projects. The use of Google developers toolkits allowed students to: (i) appreciation of the interplay between theory and practice; (ii) development of real-world software projects promoting teamwork and cooperative learning; (iii) acquisition of knowledge and hands-on experience in Web applications using AI topics; (iv) adaptability to computer science evolution; and, (v) the possibility of contribution to open source software projects.

An evaluation of the courses project based on teacher staff viewpoint, and feedback obtained from the students has been carried out of this methodology. The methodology was applied to two courses of about 30 students in their final year of a computer science degree at the La Laguna University. The interest was focused on two points: the global methodology and the use of Google developer toolkits as tool to develop real-world software projects. The results point that the students increasing their motivation on the academic topics, achieve industrial practices, present a high degree of satisfaction and get better results in exams and software development project.

From the evaluation of students' viewpoint, all of the students were able to apply what they learned from theory lectures to the software development projects. The use of Google developer toolkits and technical resources encouraged students' creativity and teamwork. Furthermore, five important observations were noted by the teaching staff: (i) a spirit of competition arose between the different groups of students to see who could achieve the best and most innovative software project. This situation led to the students' working, learning and experimenting cooperatively within the group; (ii) all of the software projects included more features than those requested by the teaching staff; (iii) the use of Google developer toolkits stimulated learning and motivation; and, (iv) exam results were better than those of previous courses where conventional methodologies were used. All the students indicated that the use of Google developer toolkits played an important role in the software development projects, allowing them to apply the theory to hands-on projects and to develop teamwork skills.

6. ACKNOWLEDGMENTS

The authors thank Google for making their developer toolkits and documentation available to the public. The authors thank all the students who took the courses and participated with their feedback.

This work has been supported by Projects TIN2008-06570-C04-03 and PIL2210901.

7. REFERENCES

[1] The Interim Review Task Force. 2008. "*Computer Science Curriculum 2008: An Interim Revision of CS 2001*". Report, Association for Computing Machinery, IEEE Computer Society. [Online].Available: http://www.acm.org//education/curricula/ComputerScience2008.pdf.

[2] The Joint Task Force on Computing Curricula. 2001. "*Computing Curricula 2001 Computer Science*". Final Report, IEEE Computer Society, Association for Computing Machinery. [Online]. Available: http://www.acm.org/education/education/education/curric_vols/cc2001.pdf.

[3] G. F. Luger. 2009. *Artificial Intelligence: Structures and Strategies for Complex Problem Solving*. Addison-Wesley Publishing Company Inc., Sixth Edition.

[4] S. Russell, P. Norving. 2010. *Artificial Intelligence: A Modern Approach*. Prentice Hall Press, Third Edition.

[5] N. J. Nilsson. 1998. *Artificial Intelligence: A New Synthesis*. Morgan Kaufmann Publishers, Inc.

[6] Google AJAX APIs, Google 2010, [Online]. Available: http://code.google.com/intl/en-ES/apis/ajax.

[7] Google App Engine, Google 2010 [Online]. Available: http://code.google.com/intl/en-ES/appengine/.

[8] Google Web Toolkit, Google 2010 [Online]. Available: http://code.google.com/intl/en-ES/webtoolkit/.

[9] Google and Open Source, Google 2010 [Online]. Available: http://code.google.com/intl/en-ES/opensource/.

[10] Google Summer of Code, Google 2010 [Online]. Available: http://code.google.com/intl/en-ES/soc/.

[11] C. Crook. 1994. *Computers and the Collaborative Experience of Learning*. New York: Routledge.

[12] L.S., Vygotsky. 1978. *Mind in Society: The Development of Higher Psychological Processes*. Cambridge, MA.: Harvard University Press.

[13] Bonwell, C.; Eison, J. 1991. *Active Learning: Creating Excitement in the Classroom AEHE-ERIC Higher Education Report No. 1*. Washington, D.C.: Jossey-Bas.

[14] Erasmus Staff Mobility, 2010 [Online] Available: http://ec.europa.eu/education/erasmus/doc1067_en.htm.

[15] Moodle. Modular Object Oriented Development Learning Environment, 2010 [Online] Available http://moodle.org/.

[16] G. Weiss. 2000. *MultiAgent Systems: A Modern Approach to Distributed Artificial Intelligence*. The MIT Press, Massachusetts.

[17] Wooldrige, M. 2000. Reasoning about rational agents. The MIT Press, Massachusetts.

Interactive Tools in the Graphics Classroom

Dino Schweitzer, Jeff Boleng, and Lauren Scharff
United States Air Force Academy
USAFA, CO 80840
+1-719-333-3945

dino.schweitzer@usafa.edu

ABSTRACT

Computer graphics is a fun course for both teachers and students. The topics are filled with interesting images and animations, there is a wealth of support material available, and students are motivated to express creativity in projects. There are also underlying math concepts and algorithms that some students find challenging to fully understand. At our institution, we teach a computer graphics course to junior and senior-level computer science majors as an elective. To assist their understanding of fundamental concepts and algorithms, we created and employed a collaborative learning approach using locally developed interactive tools during each lecture. The Think-Pair-Share model was used to facilitate collaborative interaction between students. The results of this approach were measured through in-class feedback questions and student performance on individual exam questions. Students enjoyed using the tools, highly rating them on the feedback forms, but were less enthusiastic about the classroom methodology used to present them. These results along with lessons learned will be addressed.

Categories and Subject Descriptors

K.3.2 [**Computer and Information Science Education**]: Computer Science education.

General Terms

Experimentation

Keywords

Collaborative Learning, Think-Pair-Share, Classroom Visualization, Computer Graphics Education

1. INTRODUCTION

Computer graphics is a popular course offered in many computer science programs as an elective. Different educators have proposed various approaches to teaching computer graphics such as an API approach [1], a tool-based approach [15], a web-based approach [10], a game-based approach [20], and a survey-based approach [2]. At our institution, we teach computer graphics bi-annually as an elective course in the computer science major. Different approaches have been used to teach it depending on the

preferences of the instructor. For the Spring 2010 offering, we took a "hybrid" approach: algorithms and underlying concepts were taught, but students did not implement low-level algorithms such as fill, line drawing, and rasterization. They did not use a high-level API either, but rather used the fundamental graphic capabilities built into the Java-based language and development environment, Processing [17]. To assist students in understanding the fundamental concepts and algorithms in computer graphics, we developed a set of interactive demonstrations as applets that can be used by students to explore ideas. Rather than just making them available, we employed a collaborative learning approach in the classroom, the Think-Pair-Share (TPS) model, to facilitate student-tool interaction and discussion. The goal of the approach was to increase student comprehension and enjoyment of fundamental computer graphic concepts. The focus of the project was not just on the tools, but on how to effectively incorporate them into the classroom setting.

1.1 Collaborative Learning

Many instructional models and experiences have been put forth in the educational literature to replace the traditional lecture form of instruction [11]. One of the primary premises of these non-lecture approaches is that students learn by actively participating in topic-related activities versus listening to a lecturer [6]. Many forms of active learning have been proposed and reported on within computer science under a variety of names [3,13,18].

One form of active learning is *collaborative learning*, in which students work together on problems and learn from interaction with their peers. Many variations of collaborative learning have been reported in many disciplines, including computer science [16]. It can include students working together on collaborative writing, joint problem solving, team debates, study groups, and joint programming efforts. There exists a large body of research in the educational literature which points to the positive effects of collaboration on student learning [7].

1.2 Think-Pair-Share

Collaborative learning happens naturally when students work together on class problems, homework, in study groups, and in group projects. For the purposes of this project we were interested in formalizing the process to put some structure around the student interaction. Such a structured approach uses a proscribed set of steps to enforce student interaction, as opposed to just "letting it happen" [9].

The specific form of structured collaborative learning that was used in this project was Lyman's *Think-Pair-Share* (TPS) model [12]. Many variations of TPS exist. The basic idea of TPS is that students are given a problem to work on their own and ponder the solution. After some period of time, students pair up with a peer to further discuss the solution to the problem. Finally, the pairs then share with the entire class their findings and have a formal discussion of the solution. This serves multiple purposes. First, when open-ended questions are asked as part of typical lectures, few students may respond, or the same students may respond all the time. If the question is directed at a student, even if randomly selected, all of the other students are "off the hook" and do not have to think about it. By asking all students to participate, first by themselves, and then with a partner, more students are engaged with thinking about the question and topic. Pairing with another student also adds a certain level of peer pressure to have something to contribute and not simply ignore the question. Finally, different students may have different points of views or backgrounds that enlighten a student's understanding beyond the instructor's lecture. The specifics of our approach are described below.

2. INTERACTIVE TOOLS

We implemented a structured TPS model to effectively utilize a set of locally-developed interactive, web-based tools that demonstrate many of the fundamental concepts of computer graphics. The structure of each tool was an applet with accompanying background information and instructions. The instructions included a set of interactive exploration questions and a challenge question which was used to stimulate individual thinking and problem solving (think), peer collaboration (pair), and finally, classroom discussion (share).

Interactive tools and demonstrations are widely used to teach and reinforce concepts in a variety of computer science classes such as algorithms, data structures, and architecture [4,5,14]. Computer graphics is an especially fertile topic to make use of tools and visualization as it is visual by nature and has several well-defined algorithms. A number of algorithms and concepts have been demonstrated with interactive tools and documented in the literature [8,10]. However, to our knowledge, there is not a complete set of tools for teaching computer graphics with a consistent presentation style and interactive look and feel. The tools discussed here were all developed with a uniform style and embedded in a web page with the following goals:

1. be highly interactive,
2. allow parametric changes in real time,
3. provide the ability to stop and reverse an operation,
4. focus on a single graphics concept,
5. be quick and easy to learn, and
6. be stand alone with no additional readings required.

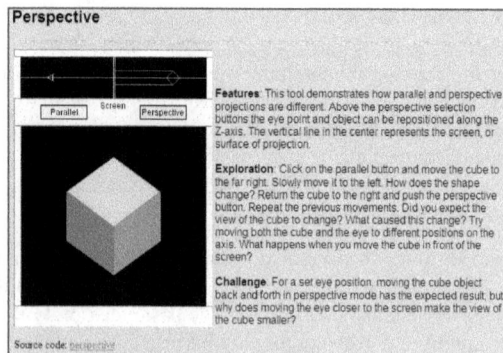

Figure 1: Example tool page and layout

Our approach to the instructional tools was to develop a java applet demonstrating the concept using the Processing language and embed it on an informational web page as shown in Figure 1. 32 interactive tools were developed to illustrate fundamental concepts and algorithms. Each of the tools focuses on a single topic that is central to the study of computer graphics. The topics of the implemented tools are shown in Table 1.

Table 1: Interactive tool topics

Sliding Selector Demo	Color Selection Demo
Color Lookup Tables	Pre-attentive/Post-attentive
RGB and HSV Colors	Graphical Primitives
Visual Sampling and Aliasing	Fill Algorithms
Interactions	Barycentric Coordinates
Graphical Transforms	Perspective
2D Viewing	3D Viewing
Quadtree Representations	Fractals
Particle Systems	Ray Tracing
Shading	2D Ray Tracing
Shadows	Frame Rates
Morphing	Phonemes
Image Formats	Seam Carving
Convolutions	Image Blending
Data Visualization	Toon Shading
Face Morphing	Line Warping

Each tool page was organized into three sections: Features, Exploration, and Challenge (see Figure 1). The feature section provided the student with a brief description and set of instructions for using the tool. This section allowed the students to quickly use and experiment with the tools without requiring extensive instructions or reference to other material, thus making them stand-alone. The next section, Exploration, contained a set of prescribed examples they could perform to experiment with the tool. These examples were designed to reinforce the concepts and tradeoffs inherent in varying input parameters and assumptions. Each tool showed the results of interactively changing the parameters in real time. The third section, Challenge, presented each student with a challenge question that required them to achieve a specific goal using the tools by varying the input values. These challenges were specifically designed to be non-trivial and encourage the students to demonstrate their understanding of the concept presented. In addition to the above, the page provides a link to the source code for every tool shown. This allows the students to examine the Processing code and use the algorithms or techniques as building blocks for their own, more advanced, graphics programming projects.

Figure 2 shows a sample tool without the surrounding web page and text sections (Features, Exploration, and Challenge). In this tool students were asked to experiment with different color tables as applied to different sample images. The challenge question for this tool is: "Why does the random table map make the teapot lose its three dimensional appearance?" This challenge requires some consideration beyond just color maps and makes the students think about what makes something appear three dimensional.

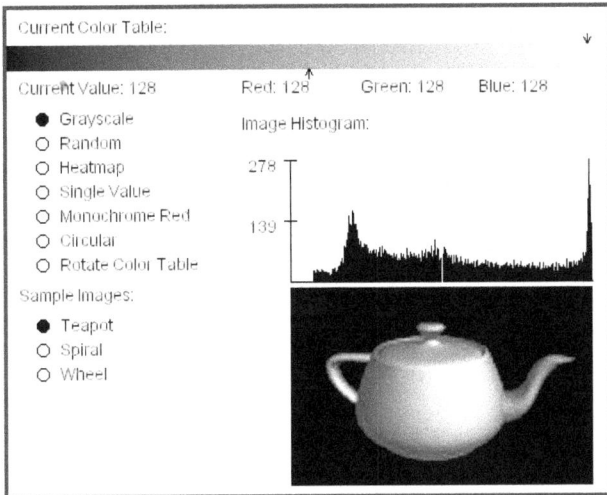

Figure 2: Color lookup tables

2.1 Tool Appeal and Aesthetics

The appeal of the tools and the corresponding instructions on each web page are an important component of motivating the students to use and explore them. Overall the tools were well received and quite popular (see section 4). A few stood out noticeably in terms of both enjoyment to use and usefulness in explaining difficult concepts. The most enjoyable tools, as rated by the students, were the fractal mountains demonstration (Figure 3), ray tracing demo, shading, and seam carving.

In addition to making the tools and encapsulating web pages visually appealing, we also strove to make them easy to learn and self-contained. These two goals at times are mutually exclusive, and balancing them proved challenging. We gathered constant feedback throughout the semester from the students. At times they would comment that the instructions to use a tool, or the exploratory examples were too long or unclear. In all cases we aimed to provide thorough enough instructions about the tool features so the students could use them for exploration and answer the challenge question posed, but not so detailed that students were bogged down reading about how to use the tool.

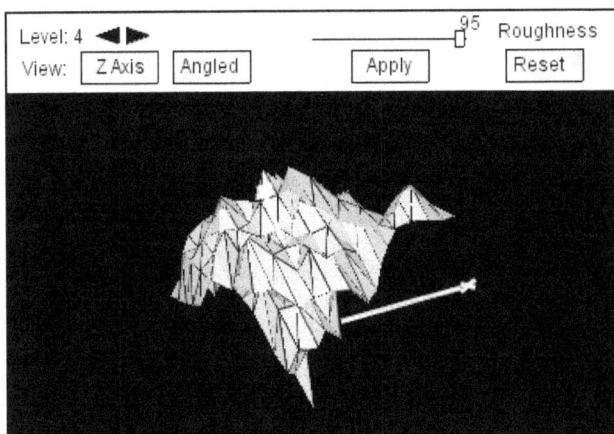

Figure 3: Fractal mountains tool

The appeal of the tools was apparent in that there was a strong propensity for the students to "jump right into" interacting with the graphical tool immediately and ignore the instructions and accompanying examples. We constantly reminded our students to read the instructions before rotating the shapes and changing the values. However, we often found the first several minutes of tool exposure were dedicated to unguided manipulation of the parameters with an accompanying comment similar to "hey, that's kind of neat, but what is it showing me?" Once the students took the time to read the instructions (always under two paragraphs), and work through the examples (also under two paragraphs), the concept being illustrated was recognized and reinforced quickly.

3. TOOLS IN THE CLASSROOM

In addition to creating the tools, we wanted to investigate how to effectively use them in the classroom to enhance student learning. The thought was that by using the tools in a formalized classroom setting, and using a well-defined methodology to guide tool exploration and discussion, students would gain more benefit in understanding the concepts. A version of the Think-Pair-Share (TPS) method described earlier was employed.

At the end of each lecture, the last 12-15 minutes of class were set aside as "Tool Time". Students were pointed to the tool of the day and given a one-page worksheet to fill out. The sheet contained survey questions on a scale of 1-5 (Strongly Disagree to Strongly Agree, respectively) for students to rate the tool:

- How easy was the tool to use
- Were the activities to accomplish clear
- Did the tool help clarify concepts
- Was the tool enjoyable to use
- Any problems encountered or suggestions

The worksheet also contained a place to write the answer to the "challenge question" for the tool. At the start of Tool Time, students were instructed to read through the features of the tool, follow the steps of the exploration section of the page, and play with the tool controls to understand how it worked. After 3-5 minutes, students were told to pair up with a partner and work on answering the challenge question together. After another 3-5 minutes, an open discussion in the classroom gave teams a chance to share in their discoveries. The instructor prepared a few additional challenges beyond the written challenge question to encourage further thought during the discussion. At the end of class, the instructor gathered the worksheets to collect feedback on the tools and as an added incentive for students to have completed the challenge question. Even though the worksheets were not graded, the fact that they were turned in seemed to encourage students to write something down and not just ignore the challenge. Many useful comments on suggestions for ways to improve the tools were often included.

Despite the success of the worksheet component, students initially tended to resist the interaction part of the TPS approach. The majority of students wanted to work on their own to figure out the challenge and then jump to the class discussion without first sharing and discussing with partners. Based on student comments and instructor reflection, we believe this response was due to the format of the earlier challenge questions: these questions tended to have specific correct answers rather than being ones that led to a variety of perspectives or approaches. Our students are often focused on achieving the "right" answer and seemed to want more immediate verification from the instructor that their response was correct. Later tools were modified to contain more in-depth challenges, and student engagement became higher across all aspects of the TPS approach.

4. EVALUATING IMPACT

One of the largest challenges in evaluating the effectiveness of the tools and their use in the classroom was the small class size (total of nine students). We could not run a control group and averages can be skewed by a single outlier. We present the results of our evaluation recognizing these limitations.

The daily worksheet surveys provided feedback on individual tools and students' perceptions of their usefulness in understanding the concepts. Figure 4 shows the range of response averages across all 32 tools. That is, the student responses for each question were averaged for the individual tools and the graph shows the low, high, first, and third quartile of averages for all tools. As shown in the graph, the majority of averages were in the 4-5 range, and all minimum averages were above 3. This indicated that students enjoyed using the tools and found them easy to use. The clarity of using the tools and whether the tools helped clarify concepts had slightly more spread distributions, but were still highly positive.

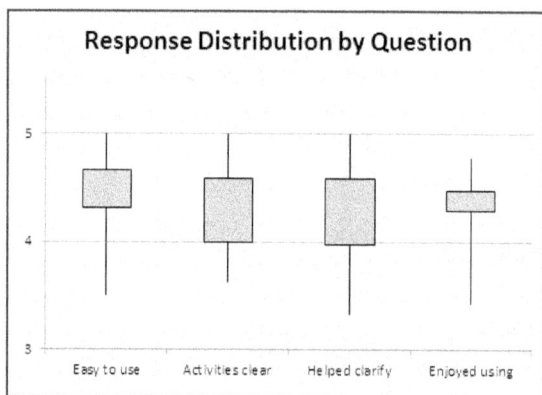

Figure 4. Distribution of survey responses.

To capture a more direct measure of the impact of the tools and the use of TPS on learning, we collected data on student performance on exam questions. Exams consisted of short answer questions on various concepts in the course. When developing exam questions, we tried to specifically identify concepts that were reinforced by the tools versus concepts that were just presented in readings or lecture. This was challenging, as described further below. Table 2 shows the median scores (to better control for outliers) for our identified tool and non-tool related questions.

Table 2. Median performance on exam questions.

	Exam 1		Exam 2	
	Num	Median	Num	Median
Non-tool	7	73.1%	10	92.6%
Tool	4	89.4%	5	92.8%

Of the 11 questions on Exam 1, four of them were determined to be associated with concepts that had been reinforced with the tools. As can be seen from the medians, students performed significantly better on tool-related questions than on non-tool questions, $t(8) = 2.49$, $p < .001$. The results from Exam 2 show no difference between tool and non-tool questions, $t(8) = 0.06$, $p = .48$. Review of the individual exam questions identified two factors that appear to affect our ability to discern the impact of the tools on student learning using the exam performance. First, it is very difficult to write short answer test questions at equal levels of difficulty. Thus, a "softball" question with essentially all correct scores, intentional or not, tends to skew the results. For Exam 1, there was one such question for both the tools- and non-tools-related categories, but for GR 2, there were two such questions for the non-tools-related category and only one such question for the tools-related category. This would tend to increase the relative performance on the non-tool related questions. Second, even when a test question is related to a tool concept, it is not always obvious that having used the tool specifically helped the student perform better on the question. It really depends on how the question is worded, how the student used the tool, and whether the answer to the question would have been just as easy (or hard) without the tool. Despite these challenges in writing questions that directly measure the tools' effects on student performance, the results appear to indicate a positive overall impact. More definitive results would require a larger sample size, a control group, and a better way of designing exam questions that were known to be directly impacted by tool use.

The final measure of evaluation was the end-of-course critique. Students were asked to rate the overall experience of using the tools and TPS and whether they felt it helped them learn the concepts of the course. To the question:

> *The daily tools helped explain concepts and were a useful part of learning the material*

the average response was 4.4 on a 5-point scale. Individual responses indicated they enjoyed using the tools, found them an entertaining and informative part of the course, and felt they demonstrated concepts. Conversely, to the question:

> *The Think/Pair/Share model was helpful in understanding the tools and concepts*

the average response was only 3. While the average was middle of the road, it was noticeably lower than the enthusiasm shown toward the tools themselves. Individual comments included that TPS did not add to the benefits of the tools and they should not be "forced" to do it.

5. LESSONS LEARNED

Interactive tools can be an effective active learning component for teaching computer graphics. Students are motivated by using the tools in an exploratory way and the tools can reinforce concepts to enhance the learning experience. However, exploratory learning can often be haphazard, and we wanted to be sure the students fully explored the tools and thought about the concepts. Therefore, we incorporated the TPS approach using dedicated time at the end of the class session. This decision did create some challenges. The cumulative amount of time required to go through the tools results in a loss of lecture time that is not insignificant. Students also seemed resistant to the structure. The neutral attitude toward the collaborative TPS approach could be the result of not "selling" it well enough to the students so that they could appreciate the benefits. Or, it could be the nature of the material such that students did not perceive any advantage of pairwise discussion over class-wide sharing. Our very small class size might also have been a factor in students' less enthusiastic attitudes toward the pairing part of the TPS approach: it was reasonable to have all students participate in the follow-up, whole-class discussion, unlike what happens with larger class sizes. As previously described, student attitudes about discussion improved after increasing the difficulty / scope of the challenge questions so that the benefit of having multiple perspectives during problem solving were more apparent. Adding an element of competition between pairs could also increase the motivation to work together collaboratively during the pair stage of the approach.

While our data suggest positive impact of the tools on learning, a larger case study using multiple sections is required to fully compare the effects of simply providing the tools versus the structured use of class time to explore and discuss them. Also, to more accurately measure the tools' impact on student performance, close attention needs to be made to the alignment of exam questions with the learning experience afforded by the tools.

Given the students' positive subjective feedback about the tools, we have made them publically available at <dinoonline.net/graphics_tools>. We would like to receive additional feedback from other institutions on their use of the tools, suggested additions, and experiences with how to effectively incorporate them into the class. Our hope is that a larger experience base with the tools and their incorporation into courses will provide insights for further development and implementation. Our plans for the next offering of the course are to continue using the tools, dedicate class time to them, but re-evaluate how TPS is used for student interaction.

6. REFERENCES

[1] Angel, E., Cunningham, S., Shirley, P., and Sung, K. 2006. Teaching computer graphics without raster-level algorithms. In *Proceedings of the 37th SIGCSE Technical Symposium on Computer Science Education*. SIGCSE '06. ACM, New York, NY, 266-267.

[2] Bresenham, J., Laxer, C., Lansdown, J., and Owen, G. S. 1994. Approaches to teaching introductory computer graphics. In *Proceedings of the 21st Annual Conference on Computer Graphics and interactive Techniques* SIGGRAPH '94. ACM, New York, NY, 479-480.

[3] Briggs, T. 2005. Techniques for active learning in CS courses. *J. Comput. Small Coll.* 21, 2, 156-165.

[4] Brown, M. H. 1988. Perspectives on algorithm animation. In *Proceedings of the SIGCHI Conference on Human Factors in Computing Systems*. J. J. O'Hare, Ed. CHI '88. ACM, New York, NY, 33-38.

[5] Budd, T. A. 2006. An active learning approach to teaching the data structures course. In *Proceedings of the 37th SIGCSE Technical Symposium on Computer Science Education*. SIGCSE '06. ACM, New York, NY, 143-147.

[6] Chickering, A. and Gamson, Z. 1987. Seven principles of good practice in undergraduate education. *AAHE Bulletin*, 39, 3-7.

[7] Dillenbourg, P. 1999. What do you mean by 'collaborative learning'?, In *Collaborative-learning: Cognitive and Computational Approaches*, 1-19, Oxford: Elsevier.

[8] Gary, J. and Crawford, R. 2003. Teaching parametric cubic curves with applets. *J. Comput. Small Coll.* 18, 4, 229-237.

[9] Kagan, S. 1989. The structural approach to cooperative learning, *Educational Leadership*, 47(4), 12-15.

[10] Klein, R., Hanisch, F., and Straßer, W. 1998. Web-based teaching of computer graphics: concepts and realization of an interactive online course. In *ACM SIGGRAPH 98 Conference Abstracts and Applications*. SIGGRAPH '98. ACM, New York, NY, 88-93.

[11] Lujan, H. and DiCarlo, S. 2006. Too much teaching, not enough learning: what is the solution? *Advances in Physiology Education*, 30, 17-22.

[12] Lyman F. 1981. The responsive classroom discussion. In: *Mainstreaming Digest*, edited by Anderson AS. College Park, MD: Univ. of Maryland College of Education.

[13] McConnell, J. J. 1996. Active learning and its use in computer science. In *Proceedings of the 1st Conference on integrating Technology into Computer Science Education*. ITiCSE '96. ACM, New York, NY, 52-54.

[14] Null, L. and Lobur, J. 2003. MarieSim: The MARIE computer simulator. *J. Educ. Resour. Comput.* 3, 1.

[15] Owen, G. S. 1992. Teaching computer graphics using RenderMan. In *Proceedings of the Twenty-Third SIGCSE Technical Symposium on Computer Science Education* (Kansas City, Missouri, United States, March 05 - 06, 1992). SIGCSE '92. ACM, New York, NY, 304-308.

[16] Sabin, R. E. and Sabin, E. P. 1994. Collaborative learning in an introductory computer science course. In *Proceedings of the Twenty-Fifth SIGCSE Symposium on Computer Science Education* (Phoenix, Arizona, United States, March 10 - 12, 1994). SIGCSE '94. ACM, New York, NY, 304-308.

[17] Schweitzer, D. and Boleng, J. 2010. Teaching introductory graphics with the Processing language. *J. Comput. Small Coll.*, (Dec. 2010).

[18] Schweitzer, D. and Brown, W. 2007. Interactive visualization for the active learning classroom. In *Proceedings of the 38th SIGCSE Technical Symposium on Computer Science Education* (Covington, Kentucky, USA, March 07 - 11, 2007). SIGCSE '07. ACM, New York, NY, 208-212

[19] Spalter, A. M. and Tenneson, D. K. 2006. The graphics teaching tool. In *ACM SIGGRAPH 2006 Educators Program*. SIGGRAPH '06. ACM, New York, NY, 41.

[20] Tori, R., Bernardes, J. L., and Nakamura, R. 2006. Teaching introductory computer graphics using java 3D, games and customized software: a Brazilian experience. In *ACM SIGGRAPH 2006 Educators Program*. SIGGRAPH '06. ACM, New York, NY.

Using the SCORE Software Package to Analyse Novice Computer Graphics Programming

Maximilian Wittmann
Macquarie University
Macquarie University NSW 2109
Australia
+61-2-9889-1305
mwittman@science.mq.edu.au

Dr. Matthew Bower
Macquarie University
Macquarie University NSW 2109
Australia
+61-2-9850-9572
matt.bower@mq.edu.au

Dr. Manolya Kavakli-Thorne
Macquarie University
Macquarie University NSW 2109
Australia
+61-2-9850-9572
manolya.kavakli@mq.edu.au

ABSTRACT

This paper presents the SCORE (Student Coding Observation and Recording Engine) software package designed to capture and analyse student coding processes. The package consists of an Eclipse [1] plug-in to gather observational data while students code a programming task, and an analysis tool that allows researchers to visualise, categorise and annotate changes in code. Because the SCORE package supports code text level analysis it enables more in-depth understanding of student programming and problem solving approaches than meta-data or program output analysis tools. SCORE also provides features to assist the analysis of Computer Graphics programs. An example analysis of a student's Computer Graphics assignments demonstrates how SCORE was used to reveal the dominant role of general programming issues in the early assignment, whereas spatial programming issues persisted throughout both assignments.

Categories and Subject Descriptors

K.3.2 [**Computer and Information Science Education**]: Computer Science Education;

General Terms

Measurement, Experimentation, Human Factors

Keywords

Computer Science Education, Computer Graphics Education, Program Analysis, Observational Research, Analysis Software

1. INTRODUCTION

In recent years, Computer Science Education (CSE) research has begun to utilise research approaches that utilise automatically gathered observational data on student programs. A range of systems (e.g. [2, 7, 10, 13]) have been used to gather and evaluate such data to gain a more detailed understanding of the

programming and problem-solving process than could be gathered via questionnaires or interviews. However, this approach has not yet been applied to Computer Graphics Education. Research into how students learn Computer Graphics is still sparse. A survey of existing Computer Graphics Education literature [3] revealed that while there has been research into learning tools to aid the teaching of Computer Graphics, there is little work investigating the programming and problem-solving process of Computer Graphics students.

The software package SCORE (Student Coding and Observation Recording Engine) presented in this paper supports code-level analysis of student programming processes and applies this approach to the domain of Computer Graphics Education. By supporting the analysing the student programming process at the level of text changes in code it may be possible to gain a better understanding of what strategies students use and what problems they face.

SCORE has been used in a research project with third-year students enrolled in Macquarie University's introductory Computer Graphics unit. While the main focus of this paper is to describe the SCORE software package and its functionality, outcomes of the research into introductory Computer Graphics programming will be used to illustrate the kind of analysis that is possible through the SCORE software package.

2. RELATED WORK

Approaches to analysing student programs can be categorised into three categories of approaches based on the level of detail at which the programming and problem-solving process is examined.

Meta-Data Approaches focus on code meta-data present a high-level view of the programming and problem-solving process. Examples include the mining of CVS meta-data [4] or of data from an automated grading and testing system [6] to identify performance indicators, the use of CVS meta-data to analyse student group work [5], the effectiveness of the Personal Software Process pedagogy in student programming [7] and the analysis of patterns of student CVS commit events [8].

Output Approaches collect data based on the output of programs. Such data may include the outcome of unit tests which measures correctness of the solution program, as well as data on error messages. Data on program results can correlate code metric data to programming success, as well as making it possible to gain an understanding of the frequency of errors that produce messages that can be automatically stored. Examples from the literature include the analysis of error messages [9, 10, 11] and the analysis of outcomes of unit tests performed by students [12].

Code Text Approaches investigate changes to the text of program code. Marmoset ([2], [13], [14]) captures code changes at this level, and an approach for tracking text changes to lines of code is outlined in [14]. However, research utilising Marmoset applies approaches of the second category and the proposal to analyse code text histories is not fleshed out in further papers.

The SCORE package presented in this paper allows examination of code text changes from compilation event to compilation event or analysis of line histories (the textual changes lines of code undergo). SCORE also provides tools to identify and categorise intensive segments of programming activity. This supports a very detailed analysis of student programming and makes it possible to identify errors and the context in which they occur, as well as the strategies students utilised during problem-solving. The application of this kind of program analysis to the domain of Computer Graphics Education is also novel and SCORE will support the better understanding of student problems and programming processes in Computer Graphics Education.

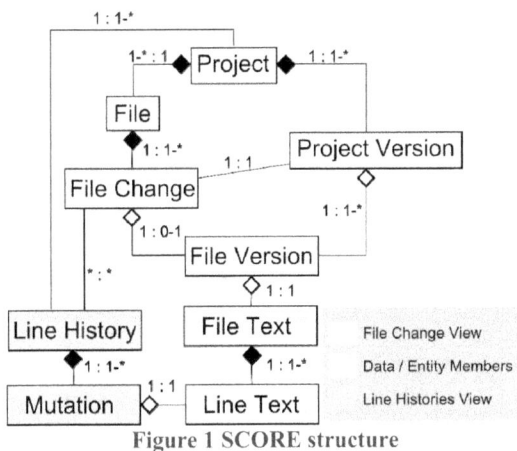
Figure 1 SCORE structure

3. SCORE PLUG-IN

The SCORE software package allows the gathering of observational data by creating a folder in each project where it will store a copy of the source file being edited each time a change is made. This allows data to be gathered for large student populations with the installation of one Eclipse plug-in. The SCORE plug-in is written for the Eclipse IDE. It is small (approximately 40kb) and can be installed via the Eclipse plug-in install feature or unzipped directly into the Eclipse plug-in directory. Currently the plug-in is configured to capture only C/C++ files but it could be extended to use with other programming languages available for use with the Eclipse platform.

The SCORE plug-in uses a local storage model instead of communicating with a server, with the versioned code automatically being submitted by the students with their assignments since it is stored in a sub-directory of the main project directory.

4. SCORE ANALYSER
4.1 Overview

The SCORE analyser provides facilities for browsing source code changes longitudinally and also provides features designed to facilitate analysis through the ability to execute and categorise each change. These features will be outlined in Section 4.2.

While comparing file changes using a traditional diff viewer as is included in many file versioning applications would be possible, such viewers are usually not designed to allow easy browsing of all code changes during the lifecycle of a project as developers are interested in comparing specific points of the development process rather than traversing code changes longitudinally.

The structure underlying SCORE is shown in Figure 1. The *Project* stores data for each *File* that was created during the lifecycle of the project. Each *File's* history during the *Project's* lifecycle is stored as a series of *File Changes*. *File Changes* that involve adding or modifying the file are associated with *File Versions*, which contain a reference to the *File's* code text at the associated *File Change*. Each *File Change* also gives rise to a *Project Version* which stores the *File Versions* for all *Files* that are in existence at the time of the *File Change*. These *Project Versions* can be used to compile the *Project* in the state that it was in at the associated *File Change*.

SCORE also stores information on each individual line of code created during the *Project's* life-cycle. It does so by creating a *Line History* for each unique line of code in the project. If a change is made to a line then the *Line History* will store this change as a new *Mutant*. The *Line History* will also store references to all the documents in which it occurs together with the line number at which they occur in that document. By analysing *Line Histories*, researchers can discover what lines were changed frequently and were thus likely involved in problems. (This feature is similar to the 'Tracking Lines and Equivalence Classes' feature described in [14]).

The SCORE application bundled with an example project can be downloaded from www.sourceforge.net/projects/score-package/.

4.2 Features

a) Change Analysis: The *File Change Analysis View* (Figure 2) provides a diff-style comparison view (Figure 2.1) displaying the compared file contents before and after the current *File Change*. Additions, deletions and mutations are also displayed in the *Changes view* (Figure 2.2). The *Project Version view* (not shown) displays all *File Versions* for the *Project Version* associated with the *File Change* being viewed. *File Changes* can be navigated in timestamp order over all *Files* or for only a single selected *File*.

b) Line History Analysis: The *Line History Analysis View* (Figure 3) displays a list of all *Line Histories*. For each *Line History*, a list of all mutants is displayed. Each mutant's text is displayed (Figure 3.1) along with a *Categorisation panel* (Figure 3.2) to allow for easy categorising of the *Mutation* by an educational researcher. *Line History* can be ordered by size, by total time taken for all of a *Line History's Mutations* or by time of occurrence, and can also be filtered using regular expressions.

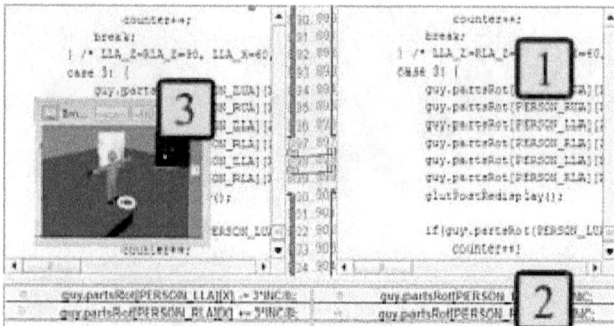

Figure 2 Main panels of the File Change Analysis View

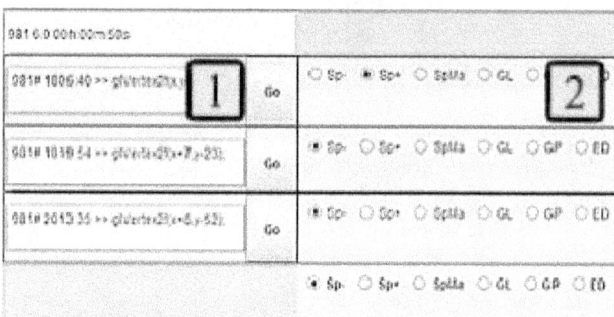

Figure 3 Main panels of the Line History Analysis View

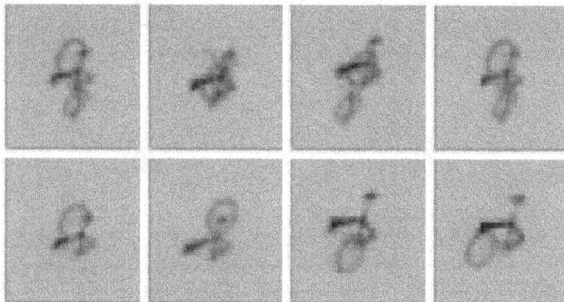

Figure 4: A sequence of screenshots from a student's

c) Visualisation tools: SCORE provides facilities for graphing the results of *Line History* and *Change Analysis* which allow the researcher to identify code segments with high activity in one of the categories which can aid in the detection of student problems.

d) Note-Taking and Categorisation of Changes and Mutations: Both the *File Change* and *Line History Analysis Views* provide a *Notes panel* that allows text notes to be taken for the current File Change or Mutation, for the File associated with the current *File Change*, or for the project overall. They also provide an *Annotation panel* that allows the current File Change or History Line to be categorised across a set of dimensions and categories that the educational researcher can define in a separate XML file. The annotation types currently in use will be discussed in Section 5.2.

e) Screen Captures, Editing and Execution: SCORE can automatically compile each *Project Version* and create a screen capture that will be displayed in the *Screenshot View* (Figure 2.3) for the *Project Version* associated with the *File Change* being viewed. Figure 4 shows a sequence of screen captures in which a

student is trying to assemble a bicycle model while making several spatial errors. Since it can be difficult to understand a Computer Graphics program by reading code only, SCORE also allows the *Project Version*'s executable to be run. SCORE can also open an editor that allows modification of all of a *Project Version*'s *File Versions*. Changes are made to copies of the original files and the resulting project can then be executed. This feature supports the analysis of complex changes to code when the combination of code text and program output from the executable do not facilitate a clear understanding of a *File Change* or *Mutation*.

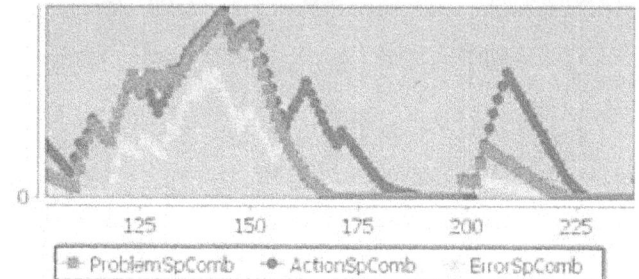

Figure 4: Section of a graph showing the rolling average for Spatial Actions/Errors/Problems

f) Analysis support:

- **Line History Generation:** *Line Histories* for *Line History Analysis View* are automatically generated by SCORE and include the File Change at which the line was added and deleted as well as Mutations of the line's text. By analysing those lines with the highest number of mutations, the analysis process can focus on those parts of the code the student modified the most.

  Mutations can be automatically categorised based on whether they match one of a hierarchy of regular expressions, for instance the expression 'glLightfv.*' can be used to categorise most lighting-related Mutations.

- **Visualisation of researcher coding:** The results of the researcher's coding of student programming (both Change and Mutant coding) can be used to generate charts (see Figure 4) that support identification of pertinent programming episodes.

g) Extensibility: When extending the SCORE analyser, new panels can be added to the *Additional Controls Panel* by implementing additional SCORE modules, or the *Additional Controls Panel* can be used to launch external applications which can be provided with SCORE data.

5. SCORE IN USE

5.1 Context

This section describes the purpose for which the SCORE software is currently being used. The core hypothesis under investigation is the role of spatial programming in Computer Graphics programming. The research project also aims to identify and analyse individual student programming problems.

The SCORE versioning plug-in has been used with students who completed an introductory Computer Graphics course at Macquarie University. Students were provided with an Eclipse

IDE package with the plug-in pre-installed. Students used this Eclipse package to complete their main two assignments.

Category / Dimension	Problem		Error		Task		Total Mutant		>=20% Mutants	
	A1	A2	A1	A2	A1	A2	A1	A2	A1	A2
General Programming	34.3	13.6	23.4	5.9	47.3	16.5	40.9	18.3	29.0	7.9
Spatial	27.1	16.6	5.2	12.2	33.3	49.7	18.8	45.0	46.2	81.6
Event-Driven Programming	8.1	X2	X2	X2	14.4	5.3	18	15.8	9.7	0
OpenGL Programming	X1	X1	6.3	1.7	X1	X1	14.2	4.5	10.8	10.5
Viewing	0	1.1	0	1.7	0	5.1	0	0	0	0
Lighting	0	1.3	0	1.6	0	8.2	0	4.9	0	0
Other	4.9	0.8	0.1	0	5	15.1 (Y1)	8.1	11.2	4.3	0
None	25.7	66.5	65	76.9	X3	X3	X3	X3	X3	X3

X1 – Category was initially only introduced for errors, pending recoding
X2 – Event-Driven Programming category was introduced to problem dimension during coding of A1, pending recoding
X3 – Category is not applicable to Error/Task dimension
Y1 – Clean-up/Maintenance items were assigned to Other instead of General Programming

Table 1 SCORE Example Coding results

5.2 Coding students' program changes

The coding categories for the analysis of student programs were created through the application of *Grounded Theory* [15]. A set of categories relevant to the Computer Graphics domain were created by investigating errors and resulting problems that occurred in student assignments. The categories form spanning sets that are able to uniquely code each Change or Mutant in a number of dimensions.

File Changes were coded in three dimensions; Task type, Error type and Problem type. The task coding identifies the primary programming task the student was working on during that File Change. An error is a student coding mistake; a problem is the resulting incorrect program output.

Mutants (belonging to *Line Histories*) were only coded in the task dimension due to the size of the dataset.

The same coding categories were used for all dimensions:

Spatial: Relating to coordinate changes or transformations

Viewing: Setting up a projection or view

Lighting: Performing OpenGL lighting or shading

General OpenGL Programming: OpenGL programming that doesn't fall into one of the more specific OpenGL categories

Event-Driven Programming: Implementing an event-driven program model

General Programming: Does not fall into one of the more specific programming categories

Other: Commenting and formatting.

None: Problems and Errors were categorised as *None* if there was no error or problem.

5.3 Example Results

This section presents an example of how the SCORE package was used to analyse one student's computer graphics programming processes based on two assessment tasks. The first assignment (A1) required students to implement an architectural/CAD-like tool using shapes such as rectangles and circles for furniture. The second assignment (A2) required students to assemble and create animations for a 3D human avatar model (a model importer was provided to students), and to enable the avatar to move in space.

5.3.1 Quantitative Analysis

Table 1 represents the results of the manual coding of the student's two assessment tasks along the Task, Error, Problem and Mutant dimensions. The fifth column lists the evaluation of the 'largest' (in terms of time taken) 20% of Line Histories from the Mutant dimension.

In each dimension, General Programming was the most significant category in A1 and became the second-most significant in A2, while Spatial Programming was the second-most significant category in A2 and became the most significant in A1 (excluding the None category which includes all File Changes that did not contain an Error/Problem). This suggests that OpenGL programming creates both traditional programming challenges and spatial programming challenges to a similar degree for this student. This supports the hypothesis that the challenge presented by spatial programming represents an important part of Computer Graphics programming ability.

Table 1 also shows how the relative time spent on general programming errors decreases from A1 to A2, while the time spent on coordinate errors increases. This may imply that in A2 the student overcame some of the general C++ programming problems she experienced in A1. General OpenGL programming is responsible for 6.3% of errors in A1, but only 1.7% of errors in A2. Also, 14.2% of A1 mutants involve OpenGL programming compared to only 4.5% of A2 mutants. This suggests that the ability to use OpenGL syntax and semantics developed during A1 and before A2 commenced.

The shift from General Programming tasks to Spatial tasks in the total Mutant and Task dimensions is even more pronounced than in the Error and Problem dimensions. This appears to indicate that while the student spent significantly more time fixing spatial errors in A2 than in A1, the student spent even more time tinkering with spatial aspects of the program when no error was present.

When comparing the results of coding all mutants there was a greater proportion of Spatial Mutants in the largest 20% of Mutants compared to Total Mutants, making up 46.2% of all of the largest 20% of Mutants in A1 and 81.6% in A2. This means that the lines that were changed most by a large margin involved spatial changes, suggesting that spatial problems were in fact the most time-consuming problems faced in both assignments. For the second assignment that involved programming in a three-dimensional environment, spatial problems made up almost all of the most time-consuming mutations of lines.

5.3.2 Qualitative Analysis

In-depth analysis of File Changes to identify the underlying problems provided qualitative insights that were not directly captured by the coding approach (though coding results can help identify such sequences). For instance, in A1 the student spent 90 minutes attempting to use the logical colour operation XOR. By stepping through the problem's File Changes and analysing the program code and executing and debugging the program when necessary, a range of inappropriate strategies such as the frequent superfluous use of glFlush, glutSwapBuffer and glutPostRedisplay were detected. This kind of qualitative analysis can contribute to a corpus of known problems in Computer Graphics Education.

6. CONCLUSION AND FUTURE WORK

The SCORE Plug-in and Analyser enable transparent capturing of student programming data and in-depth analysis of student programming processes. This moves beyond high-level analysis of the programming process provided by previous research to a detailed examination of all changes that occur during a student project's life cycle. SCORE specifically supports analysis of Computer Graphics programming by providing facilities for automatically taking and displaying screen captures as well as allowing for the execution and modification of any project state.

The analysis of a student's assignments reported to demonstrate the use of the SCORE system indicated that spatial programming aspects of the programming process were more difficult for the student than general programming aspects or OpenGL syntax and semantics. This theme has recurred during the analysis of other students' assignments (currently being performed). The analysis of the entire data corpus using SCORE will produce a body of problems faced by novice Computer Graphics students and will allow the comparison of different students' strategies and problem areas. Evaluation of these results will provide a better understanding of the role of spatial programming in Computer Graphics Education.

Several refinements are planned to enhance the SCORE system. Improvements to machine-based coding assistance will reduce time taken to analyse projects. Data-entry panels will be added to the Eclipse SCORE plug-in to allow students to comment on the work they are currently performing, with the comments stored along with other versioning data. This will enable researchers to validate their categorisation of student coding with the students' own description of their coding. The plug-in will be made compatible with Java coding (currently it works with C++ only).

Computer Graphics is a unique programming pursuit because it requires students to not only be proficient in the underlying programming language but also have the spatial understanding to solve spatial problems in two and three dimensions. Having tools and methodologies to support the analysis of students' programming allows computer science educators to better understand the effect of these requirements on students and their learning processes.

7. REFERENCES

[1] Foundation, T. E. (2011), 'Eclipse Integrated Programming Environment', The Eclipse Foundation, Electronic Resource.

[2] Spacco, J.; Hovemeyer, D.; Pugh, W.; Emad, F.; Hollingsworth, J. & Padua-Perez, N. (2006), 'Experiences with marmoset: designing and using an advanced submission and testing system for programming courses", *Proceedings of the 11th annual SIGCSE conference on Innovation and technology in computer science education*, ACM, 13-17.

[3] Maximilian Wittmann (2009), 'A survey of Computer Graphics Education literature'., *http://www.comp.mq.edu.au/~mwittman/Review_of_CGE_literature.pdf*, Retrieved 14.01.2011

[4] Mierle, K.; Laven, K.; Roweis, S. & Wilson, G. (2005), 'Mining student CVS repositories for performance indicators' *Proceedings of the 2005 international workshop on Mining software repositories*, ACM, 1-5.

[5] Liu, Y.; Stroulia, E.; Wong, K. & German, D. (2004), 'Using CVS historical information to understand how students develop software', *MSR 2004*, 32.

[6] Allevato, A.; Thornton, M.; Edwards, S. & Pérez-Quicones, M. (2008), 'Mining data from an automated grading and testing system by adding rich reporting capabilities', *Educational Data Mining 2008*, 167.

[7] Johnson, P.; Kou, H.; Agustin, J.; Chan, C.; Moore, C.; Miglani, J.; Zhen, S. & Doane, W. (2003), 'Beyond the Personal Software Process: Metrics collection and analysis for the differently disciplined' *Proceedings of the 25th International Conference on Software Engineering*, IEEE Computer Society, 641-646.

[8] Glassy, L. (2006), 'Using version control to observe student software development processes', *Journal of Computing Sciences in Colleges* **21**(3), 99-106.

[9] Jadud, M. (2005), 'A first look at novice compilation behaviour using BlueJ', *Computer Science Education* **15**(1), 25-40.

[10] Ahmadzadeh, M.; Elliman, D. & Higgins, C. (2005), 'An analysis of patterns of debugging among novice computer science students' *Proceedings of the 10th annual SIGCSE conference on Innovation and technology in computer science education*, ACM, 84-88.

[11] Murphy, C.; Kaiser, G.; Loveland, K. & Hasan, S. (2009), 'Retina: helping students and instructors based on observed programming activities', *ACM SIGCSE Bulletin* **41**(1), 178-182.

[12] Norris, C.; Barry, F.; Fenwick Jr, J.; Reid, K. & Rountree, J. (2008), 'ClockIt: collecting quantitative data on how beginning software developers really work' *Proceedings of the 13th annual conference on Innovation and technology in computer science education*, ACM, 37-41.

[13] Spacco, J. (2006), 'Marmoset: A programming project assignment framework to improve the feedback cycle for students, faculty and researchers', PhD Thesis, University of Maryland

[14] Spacco, J.; Strecker, J.; Hovemeyer, D. & Pugh, W. (2005), 'Software repository mining with Marmoset: an automated programming project snapshot and testing system', *ACM SIGSOFT Software Engineering Notes* **30**(4), 1-5.

[15] Strauss, A. & Corbin, J. (1994), 'Grounded Theory Methodology. An Overview Handbook of Qualitative Research', *Handbook of qualitative research*, 273-2

Evaluating a Web-Based Information System for Managing Master of Science Summer Projects

Till Rebenich
University of Southampton
Southampton
United Kingdom
tr08r@ecs.soton.ac.uk

Andrew M. Gravell
University of Southampton
Southampton
United Kingdom
amg@ecs.soton.ac.uk

Thanassis Tiropanis
University of Southampton
Southampton
United Kingdom
tt2@ecs.soton.ac.uk

ABSTRACT

We describe the design of a web-based information system for monitoring MSc summer projects in the School of Electronics and Computer Science at the University of Southampton, and a mixed method quasi-experimental study involving 290 MSc project students, 19 monitors, and 69 supervisors in electronics and computer science, using the system over a period of 17 weeks. Statistically significant results presented here are: Students making heavy use of the system achieved higher marks on their project dissertation, while no such correlation was found with marks for other parts of their MSc. Likewise, student's monitor activity is significantly correlated with their own activity and dissertation mark. These results suggest that educational information and project management systems positively affect student achievement and academic staff involvement is crucial for these systems to be successful. Future work includes a more detailed analysis of success factors and their impact on student performance.

Categories and Subject Descriptors

H.4 [**Information Systems Applications**]: Miscellaneous

General Terms

Design, Experimentation, Human Factors

Keywords

information systems, e-learning, project management, time management, impact study

1. INTRODUCTION

At the University of Southampton and at many other UK universities, the Master of Science (MSc) degree typically takes one calendar year to complete and is concluded by a three-month summer project during which students are expected to do independent research and practical work on a well-defined topic. At the end of the project, students must submit a dissertation which is marked independently by two or three examiners.

Normally, MSc students pursue their project under the supervision of at least one academic in the school. This concept is very much centred around project-based learning as students are required to work autonomously on a given task and are responsible for investigating a problem, making decisions, planning their work, and coming up with suitable solutions [9]. Due to the limited time available for this part of the MSc, good time management and project planning are crucial success factors.

In 2009/10, the school's MSc student intake significantly exceeded that of previous years. Numbers increased by 73.1%, from 171 in 2008 to 296 in 2009, posing additional challenges to academic staff. Our work focusses on organisational aspects of MSc project management, that is, on supporting project planning and monitoring using information technology. For this purpose, a web-based information system was developed and rolled out in the school in 2010. We did not use off-the-shelf (OTS) software since it either did not meet our requirements or was too difficult to customise and integrate. The system was used in a quasi-experimental mixed method study and served as a prototype for evaluating how similar systems can enhance teaching as part of a virtual learning environment. The aim of our system is to support project students in organising their work, report their progress, and plan meetings with their supervisor. Additionally, a monitoring scheme was introduced whereby each project student was allocated to a monitoring group led by a postgraduate research student. In total there were 39 groups, and each of them contained 6 students on average. Members of a group were told to meet once a week, raise problems, ask questions, and discuss their progress with peers typically working in the same topic area. These meetings do not replace supervision meetings but are a complementary measure to further support students. The information system supports this scheme by providing features for managing group meetings, interacting with its members, and recording meeting attendance. System use was compulsory for monitors, while supervisors were not required to use it in view of their high workload. It was expected that monitors spend approximately 1 hour per week on filing progress reports, subject to group size, and students could submit their report and manage their project tasks in no more than 30 minutes per week.

Both our system and the monitoring scheme are based on a small trial carried out in the summer of 2009 involving only two monitors and a subset of all MSc students. The outcomes of this trial were positive, but the monitors recommended the development of an information system supporting their work.

We also adopted some of the features used in previous work [8, 7] in the area of student time management. The positive relationship between good time management skills and academic performance has been emphasised in related work [1, 4]. In addition, we provided students with features increasing their progress awareness and motivation [5] by exposing certain progress statistics to the whole cohort, enabling students to compare their own progress with that of their peers (see Figure 1). Project monitors also had to report on the progress of each student and record their meeting attendance on the system.

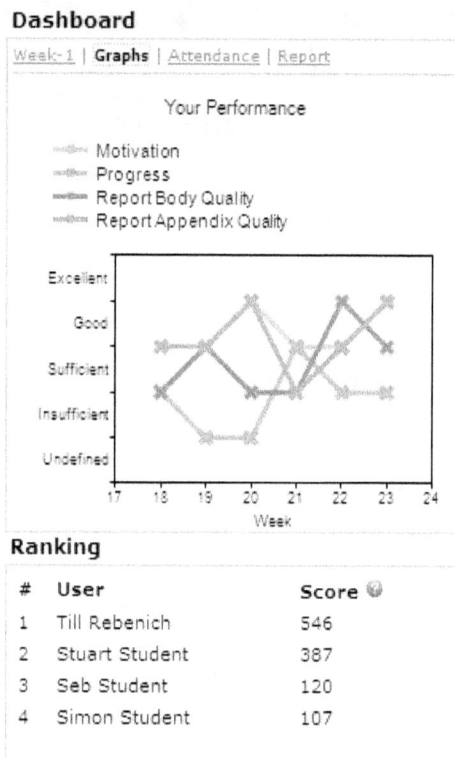

Figure 1: Example of dashboard and charts

2. SYSTEM DESIGN

The web-based information system used here was developed using ASP.NET MVC 2.0 and deployed on a virtual machine inside the school. It was released for general use on 14 June 2010, and workshops were provided to monitors and interested academic staff. It was also presented and explained to students as part of their project kick-off event. The current version is a stand-alone application available to all computer science and electronics MSc students. Users can log on using their school username and password. It consists of 5 components which are described in more detail in the following sections. They are: project management, meeting and event organisation, progress tracking, meeting attendance monitoring, and communication. To raise students' awareness of ongoing events, feedback submissions, and the activity of other users, email reminders were sent by the system.

Students can create lists of tasks with their interdependencies and prerequisites. For each task, basic metrics such as due date, planned duration, and current progress can be defined. Furthermore, four milestone tasks were pre-defined: submit dissertation brief, end practical work, submit first draft, and submit final report. Regular tasks can be assigned to one of these milestones. All task data can be exported and used with other project management client software such as Microsoft Project.

The system is based on a hierarchical structure of organisational units, namely degree, programme, group, and project. In this structure, the degree is the top-most unit, while a student project is a leaf unit. Multiple users can be associated with each unit. A project is pre-defined for each student, and each student is member of a monitoring group. Both single and recurring events or meetings can be defined in projects or groups. All students were asked to enter their supervision meetings into the system at the beginning of the summer project, and monitors were in charge of managing monitoring group meetings. All event data can be exported and used with other calendaring software, e.g. Google Calendar and others.

Every week, each student, their monitor, and their supervisor were asked to rate the student's overall progress, their motivation, and the quality of their written work on a scale from 0 (not seen) to 5 (outstanding). Ratings are also subject to an underlying ranking system, so that supervisor ratings take preference over monitor ratings, which again take preference over student ratings. Progress ratings were also aggregated and presented to all system users on graphs and charts, and a ranking table showed the performance of each student against their peers. All participants were able to view these statistics online at any time. Charts provided include (1) histograms showing current and last week's progress ratings for the programme cohort, (2) graphs of progress ratings over time, (3) attendance over time, (4) quantitative and qualitative report metrics over time, and (5) task statistics. Furthermore, all users were prompted for their meeting attendance feedback, that is, whether students had attended a particular event or not. Meeting attendance statistics were also used for ranking purposes and displayed graphically.

Users could interact on group pages using a thread-based messaging system, whereby members could comment on other users' threads in the same group. Furthermore, email addresses of all users were exposed to associated people.

3. STUDY DESIGN

As we did not have direct control over the organisation of MSc projects, we chose a quasi-experimental mixed method study design. In particular, it was required that all MSc students should be able to use the system. Hence we could not divide the student population into experimental groups. Furthermore, only students in the school were included: other disciplines and schools did not use the system. A total of 378 participants were involved in our study: 290 MSc students, 69 supervisors (academic staff), and 19 monitors (mostly postgraduate research students).

3.1 Method

We used a mixed method approach, whereby both quantitative and qualitative data was collected and analysed. The data comprises user activity logs on the system, progress

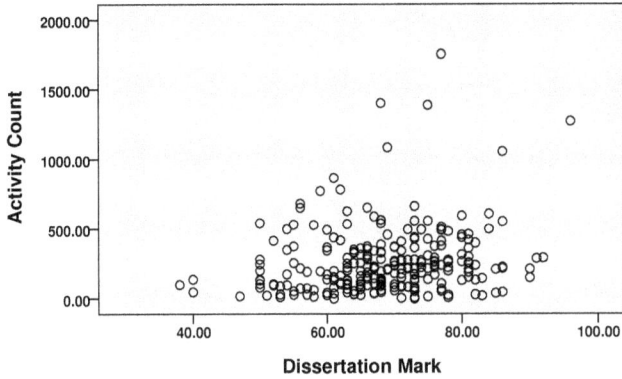

Figure 2: Scatter plot of activity count and dissertation mark

and event attendance feedback, and email notifications sent through the system, as well as subjective data gathered using an embedded online questionnaire, launched approximately one week before the final project submission deadline. Students and their monitors were asked to take this survey in which they were to rate the motivational impact of system features, their usefulness for project management, and their agreement with several general statements. The full version of the questionnaire can be found on our website[1].

3.2 Objectives

Our primary target was to test the effect of system use on student performance, that is, their final project mark. At this point, it is crucial to distinguish between project mark and the mark for other parts of the MSc. The former applies to the actual summer project only and is established based on the submitted dissertation, while the latter covers taught units completed *before* the start of the summer project, so we use the term "taught mark" for it in the remainder of this work.

Besides this primary objective, we were also interested in the effects of system use on student motivation, progress awareness, difficulty detection, user-to-user interaction, and peer support.

4. RESULTS

All results presented here are based on the analysis of the final data set made up by all data collected during the study. It contains 575 variables and was analysed using version 18 of the SPSS/PASW Statistics package. An outline of the types of variable used is given in Table 1.

We focussed on the main objective (see Section 3.2), that is, examining the effect of system use on student performance. System use in this context is the total number of user-system interactions. These interactions can be classified into categories, for example, the number of times a user accessed their project page, number of clicks made on the dashboard graphs, and so on. In the remainder of this paper, we shall refer to system use as the "activity count".

The most important outcome is a significant and positive correlation between students' system use and their dissertation mark ($r_s = 0.199$, $p = 0.002$). This relationship is depicted in Figure 2. We used a Spearman correlation test

---

[1]http://users.ecs.soton.ac.uk/tr08r/msctrial/survey.pdf

Table 1: Variables in the final data set

Content	Type
Quantitative report metrics	Scale
Qualitative report metrics	Ordinal
Overall student progress and motivation	Ordinal
User-system interaction counts	Scale
Questionnaire items	Ordinal
Late penalties on assignments in other parts of the MSc programme	Scale
Group and project meeting count	Scale
Score in ranking per week	Scale
Email notification count per user	Scale
Dissertation mark	Scale
Mark on other parts of MSc (taught)	Scale
Group note and reply count per user	Scale
User-system interaction count clusters	Ordinal

Table 2: System activity cluster correlations

		Taught Mark	Diss. Mark
Activity Count	r_s	0.064	0.199**
	p	0.314	0.002
Cluster 1	r_s	0.047	0.190**
	p	0.452	0.002
Cluster 2	r_s	0.079	0.258**
	p	0.212	0.000
Cluster 3	r_s	0.012	0.138*
	p	0.856	0.029
Cluster 4	r_s	0.028	0.170**
	p	0.656	0.007

because the activity count is not normally distributed and thus non-parametric, albeit Norman [6] suggests that parametric tests are robust enough to cope with such data. To rule out that only students who performed well before the start of their project heavily used the system, we examined the relationship between the taught mark and system activity, which is insignificant ($r_s = 0.064$, $p = 0.314$). However, students with a high taught mark usually also obtained a high mark on their dissertation ($r_s = 0.641$, $p = 0.000$).

We then performed a cluster analysis on the total interaction count, assigning subjects to low, medium, or high activity groups. Four different clustering algorithms were used: a cumulative activity count cluster (1), a single linkage nearest neighbour cluster (2), and two hierarchical clusters using the Ward method (3 and 4), one of them is based on Z-scores. The first algorithm uses the cumulative percentage of ordered activity count values, so that users are equally distributed over the three activity groups. The result of the correlation analysis using these clusters is shown in Table 2.

Drilling down into activity categories, we found that the number of views of the main entry page (contains statistics, ranking table, and monitoring group/project breakdown), the project page, and user profile pages correlates significantly with students' dissertation mark with $r_s = 0.216$, $r_s = 0.202$, and $r_s = 0.193$ at the 0.01 level ($p \leq 0.002$), respectively. The same was found for interactions with the statistics dashboard on the main page and with tasks on the project page ($r_s = 0.198$ and $r_s = 0.153$, $p \leq 0.015$).

We then looked at the relationship between total activity count and number of email notifications sent to students,

Table 3: Correlations with questionnaire items

		Student Activity	Diss. Mark
Perceived motivational effect			
Dashboard and statistics charts	r_s	0.222*	-0.032
	p	0.020	0.741
Student ranking table	r_s	0.285**	-0.091
	p	0.003	0.343
News feed	r_s	0.225*	-0.100
	p	0.018	0.297
Progress feedback by monitor	r_s	0.295**	-0.183
	p	0.002	0.055
Progress feedback by supervisor	r_s	0.281**	-0.011
	p	0.003	0.911
Event attendance feedback	r_s	0.237*	-0.163
	p	0.013	0.089
Helpfulness for project management			
Student ranking table	r_s	0.204*	-0.155
	p	0.038	0.118
Progress feedback by supervisor	r_s	0.256**	-0.058
	p	0.010	0.560
General feedback			
Enhanced project management	r_s	0.195*	-0.079
	p	0.042	0.409
Increased progress awareness	r_s	0.226*	-0.049
	p	0.018	0.609
Monitor/supervisor picked up on student feedback submitted through the system	r_s	0.203*	-0.145
	p	0.034	0.130

Table 4: Correlations of progress metrics

		Activity Count	Diss. Mark	Taught Mark
P1	r_s	0.195**	0.356**	0.238**
	p	0.003	0.000	0.000
P2	r_s	0.235**	0.158*	0.175*
	p	0.001	0.021	0.011
P3	r_s	0.253**	0.455**	0.348**
	p	0.006	0.000	0.000
M1	r_s	0.166*	0.322**	0.226**
	p	0.011	0.000	0.000
M2	r_s	0.236**	0.136*	0.147**
	p	0.001	0.047	0.032
M3	r_s	0.259**	0.503**	0.371**
	p	0.005	0.000	0.000
Attendance	r_s	0.293**	0.037	0.101
	p	0.000	0.598	0.152
Score	r_s	0.058	0.278**	0.231**
	p	0.369	0.000	0.000

Table 5: Descriptive statistics of project outcomes

	2008/9		2009/10	
Distinction	44	30.1%	68	24.8%
Pass	92	63.0%	199	72.6%
Fail	10	6.8%	7	2.6%
Total	146		274	

P1, P2, P3 Mean of self-reported, monitor-rated, and supervisor-rated overall weekly progress (value between 0 and 5)

M1, M2, M3 Mean of self-reported, monitor-rated, and supervisor-rated weekly student motivation (value between 0 and 5)

Attendance Total percentage of attended supervision and monitoring meetings

Score The mean of weekly scores in the student ranking table (includes previous metrics)

The results of the correlation analysis using these metrics is shown in Table 4. In summary, supervisors' ratings correlate most strongly with dissertation marks, while monitor feedback correlates least strongly. Surprisingly, student meeting attendance did not seem to affect marks at all.

In comparison with the previous year (2008/9), the analysis of project outcomes produces the statistics shown in Table 5. While the t-test does not show a significant difference between means ($t = 0.197$, $p = 0.844$), a slight downward trend in student failure rate is noticeable (from 6.5% in 2008/9 to 2.6% in 2009/10).

5. DISCUSSION

We briefly presented the design of a web-based information system for managing and monitoring MSc summer projects, and that of a quasi-experimental mixed method study carried out in the school using this system. Our statistical results are valid for the cohort because there are significant relationships between objective and subjective data. Although the strength of these results is encouraging, we would have to repeat the experiment in our own and other schools and institutions to verify that they generalise.

yielding a significant and strong correlation ($r_s = 0.978$, $p = 0.000$). In more detail, notifications about upcoming events ($r_s = 0.311$, $p = 0.000$) and other people's activity ($r_s = 1.000$, $p = 0.000$) on the system had the strongest positive effect on student activity.

We were also interested in the relationship between student activity and that of their project monitor and supervisor. The Spearman correlation test yields a positive and significant relationship between students' total activity count and that of their monitor ($r_s = 0.314$, $p = 0.000$). The parametric test (Pearson) also flags up a significant correlation with their supervisor's activity count ($r_p = 0.168$, $p = 0.009$), but no such relationship was found using the non-parametric correlation test.

As mentioned in section 3.1, we asked students to rate the motivational effect and helpfulness of system features on a Likert scale at the end of the project. We first tested the internal consistency reliability of these items using Cronbach's alpha: motivation-related items scored 0.925, helpfulness-related items 0.955, and general statements 0.858. The correlation analysis shows that student activity count correlates significantly with several items, as is outlined in Table 3. The table also shows that there is no significant relationship between feature ratings and dissertation mark.

Another important question was whether progress and motivation ratings submitted by students themselves, their monitor, or their supervisor are reflected in the final dissertation mark or student system use. For this purpose, we analysed the following metrics derived from data recorded on the system:

Our primary objective was to test the system's effect on student performance. We found a significant correlation between system use and students' final project mark, however, there is no such correlation with their taught mark. However, a strong correlation exists between taught and dissertation mark, in other words, students who performed well on the taught MSc part also performed well on their summer project. The missing relationship between taught mark and system use indicates that good performers did not necessarily use the system more frequently, but those who did performed better on their project. Our finding is important in light of project work being one of the most challenging areas of any degree programme.

The analysis of system feature usage shows that the use of the progress statistics dashboard, the ranking table, the project page, and task management on that page contributed significantly to project performance. This indicates that students who were aware of their own progress compared to that of their peers and who actively managed their project using system tools performed better than those who did not. Furthermore, the role of the monitor seems to be crucial for student engagement as the correlation between their activity counts suggests. One possible explanation is that the system explicitly supports the school's monitoring scheme, and that monitors and students used the system as a platform complementing their weekly meeting routine. Also, student system use is very strongly correlated with the number of email notifications sent out by the system. This goes in line with the findings reported in [3] and [2] who argue that this is because notifications make users aware of the existence of the system and the associated users' activity.

Regarding students' subjective feedback on the motivational effect of features and their usefulness for project management, our findings support the assumption that the statistics dashboard, the news feed, and feedback submitted by monitors and supervisors are crucial features. However, motivation and helpfulness ratings correlate with system use, meaning that only those students who used the system more frequently also gave high ratings. We are currently doing more detailed research on this issue.

Finally, the results on student progress and motivation ratings suggest that supervisors were most accurate in terms of their rating's reflection on the final project mark. Obviously, students with high taught marks also gained higher motivation and progress ratings compared to those with lower taught marks, suggesting that students were able to sustain their performance during the project. Since the ratings of all three roles are significantly correlated with both marks, all ratings accurately reflect student progress and motivation. However, there is no indication that event attendance affects performance whatsoever. This finding needs to be treated with care since not all students and groups managed their meetings on the system consistently.

5.1 Implications for System Design

From our findings, we can compile a set of recommendations for the design of similar educational information systems. First, the full support of all staff involved is crucial. In our case, monitor activity positively influenced student activity. Supervisors were not required to use the system, but it is likely that a higher activity on their part would have had a similar effect. Second, appropriate rating systems and data visualisation of aggregated metrics and user activity improve users' progress awareness and academic performance, provided that privacy issues are taken into account. This is supported by high helpfulness and motivation ratings provided by students on these features. Finally, push notifications and simple project management tools also positively affect user activity and progress awareness.

5.2 Future Work

Our next step is a more detailed analysis based on these general results and a shift of focus towards our secondary claims (see Section 3.2). More specifically, we need to evaluate which factors most accurately describe the positive effect on the final project mark using principal component analysis. Furthermore, subjective feedback submitted by users together with their progress and motivation ratings needs to be coded in order to be suitable for further analysis. In particular, we are interested in whether motivating comments by monitors/supervisors influenced student progress and motivation in the following weeks.

6. REFERENCES

[1] B. K. Britton and A. Tesser. Effects of time-management practices on college grades. *Journal of Educational Psychology*, 83(33):405–410, 1991.

[2] R. Farzan, J. M. DiMicco, D. R. Millen, B. Brownholtz, W. Geyer, and C. Dugan. When the experiment is over: deploying an incentive system to all users. In *Symposium on Persuasive Technology, In conjunction with the AISB 2008 Convention*, 2008.

[3] A. Girgensohn and A. Lee. Making web sites be places for social interaction. In *CSCW '02: Proceedings of the 2002 ACM conference on Computer supported cooperative work*, pages 136–145, New York, NY, USA, 2002. ACM.

[4] T. H. Macan. College students' time management: Correlations with academic performance and stress. *Journal of Educational Psychology*, 82(4):760–768, 1990.

[5] T. Mochizuki, K. Yaegashi, Y. Nagamori, H. Kato, and T. Nishimori. ProBoPortable: Development of cellular phone software to prompt learners to monitor and reorganize division of labor in project-based learning. In *Proceedings of EDMEDIA '08*, pages 5047–5055. AACE, 2008.

[6] G. Norman. Likert scales, levels of measurement and the "laws" of statistics. In *Advances in Health Sciences Education*, volume 15, pages 625–632. Springer, 2010.

[7] T. Rebenich, A. Gravell, and T. Tiropanis. Motivating university students using a location-aware time management system with social networking features. In *Proceedings of ED-MEDIA '10*, pages 3220–3224. AACE, 2010.

[8] T. Rebenich, A. Gravell, and T. Tiropanis. Survey of students' technology use for time management. In *Proceedings of ED-MEDIA '10*, pages 3134–3141, 2010.

[9] J. W. Thomas. A review of research on project-based learning. Technical report, The Autodesk Foundation, March 2000.

A Study of Video-based versus Text-based Labs for a Management Information Systems Course

Eric Breimer
Siena College
515 Loudon Road
Loudonville, NY 12211
USA
1-518-786-5084

ebreimer@siena.edu

Michelle Conway
Siena College
515 Loudon Road
Loudonville, NY 12211
USA
1-518-786-5084

mconway@siena.edu

Jami Cotler
Siena College
515 Loudon Road
Loudonville, NY 12211
USA
1-518-786-5088

jcotler@siena.edu

Robert Yoder
Siena College
515 Loudon Road
Loudonville, NY 12211
USA
1-518-783-4252

ryoder@siena.edu

ABSTRACT
In this paper we study key differences between video-based and text-based instructions by developing and testing an interactive website for delivering lab material in our Management Information Systems course. In a face-to-face lab setting, we tracked the performance and surveyed the impressions of 80 students where approximately half received video instructions while the other half received text instructions. The results indicate no statistically significant difference in students' correctness in answering lab questions, but slight differences in completion time and impression. We discuss our results and suggest ways to use video instruction effectively based on our results and observations.

Categories and Subject Descriptors
H.5.1 [**Information Interfaces and Presentation**]: Multimedia Information Systems – *video*; K.3.1 [**Computers and Education**]: Computer Uses in Education – *Computer-assisted instruction.*

General Terms
Performance, Design, Experimentation, Human Factors

Keywords
Video-based instruction, web-based labs, management information systems, computer lab activities, blended learning, automated feedback.

1. INTRODUCTION
Our introductory Management Information Systems (MIS) course includes weekly lab sessions (two-hour long) where students work in pairs on computer-based activities. Our lab activities have a "triad" structure that incorporates theory from lectures, practical case studies, and problem solving using computer applications such as Excel, Access, geographic information systems, and computer-mediated collaboration systems.

As a required course in the School of Business, approximately 240 students take our MIS course each semester. The instructions

for each lab are lengthy; the longest lab includes 35 pages with 44 embedded questions. In the past, the course would generate up to 3000 printed pages per week. To save paper, students now view the lab instructions (Word Document) on a dual-monitor PC and write their answers on a separate printed worksheet (2-4 pages).

While the worksheet reduces paper usage, it introduces a disorienting process where students must manage three very different information sources. First, the lab instructions guide students to complete tasks and answer questions. Second, application usage such as creating a pivot chart in Excel or a query in Access generates reports and data needed to answer the lab questions. Third, the question answers, which are recorded on the printed worksheet, are often referenced or needed in other parts of the instructions, which are viewed electronically.

Because of the complex lab process, students often lose track of where they are in the lab. Our goal is to make improvements to the lab process to make labs easier to follow, which we hope allows our students to concentrate on the higher-level, more compelling aspects of the labs. We believe this will create a more enjoyable lab experience. However, we also want the tasks and questions to remain challenging so we can differentiate student effort and preparedness.

2. OUR FIRST STEP: WEB-BASED LABS
Many of our labs include a series of tasks using spreadsheets or databases that build a solution progressively. If a student makes an early mistake, it often impedes their ability to complete subsequent tasks. When students detect a mistake too late, they often require substantial help and the instructor may not be immediately available. Students often spend significant lab time waiting for help, which has a very negative impact on learning and impressions.

While the instructor and students meet face-to-face in a computer lab setting, we have found many advantages to delivering lab material online in a style indicative of distance learning [1, 6, 8]. In our last study, we implemented the instructions for one lab session as an interactive website [2]. The questions are directly embedded in the instructions using *HTML* forms, and *jQuery* [5] is used to deliver immediate feedback after each question is answered. Students login to the system and each student's answers and a corresponding time stamp are recorded in a database. The system is implemented using an *AJAX*-framework and an underlying *MySQL* database.

This web-based approach creates numerous advantages in a face-to-face lab setting. First, it eliminates the worksheet so students do not have to switch between two documents (electronic instructions and paper worksheet). Second, it provides students with immediate feedback, so they can correct early problems and move through the lab with more independence. This allows the instructor to spend more time helping students who are struggling the most. Third, incorrect answers are recorded which helps instructors objectively differentiate student performance. Using worksheets, students can easily change an answer after receiving help. Fourth, by calculating the time difference between the answering of key questions, completion times can be measured for various parts of the lab activity. By tracking incorrect answers and completion times, we can better identify parts of the lab where students struggle or spend too much time, which can help us make targeted improvements.

Studies have demonstrated that online instruction has advantages in keeping students more engaged compared to other methods [4]. In our initial study, students had more favorable impressions of the lab session when using our web-based system rather than the paper-based approach [2]. The system enables us to investigate and evaluate different ways to present instructions to further improve the lab materials. In this study, we concentrate on the efficacy of video-based instructions to begin to ascertain what aspects of video-based instruction improve students' performance and engagement.

3. VIDEO-BASED INSTRUCTIONS

Instructions delivered on the web can include rich multimedia such as video, which may be a more effective way to present step-by-step instructions for using software or completing complex tasks or processes [1, 6, 8, 10]. Writing step-by-step instructions for using software applications often requires capturing images of the application interface being used. This process can be very tedious and when software versions change, instructions often have to be rewritten and images have to be recaptured.

As an alternative to text- and image-based instructions, video-capture software such as *Camtasia*, *ScreenFlow*, and *SnapZ* can be used to record a computer screen as an instructor narrates and performs activities. Some instructors may find video capture to be a more effective and efficient way to create step-by-step instructions [3]. Video capture software allows captions, callouts, and other visual enhancements to be added to recorded video. Free services such as *youTube* or *Vimeo* can be used to host videos, which can easily be incorporated into any webpage using the HTML *object* or *embed* tags.

Before embarking on an effort to create video instructions on a large scale, we first wanted to better understand the impact of video instructions on student impressions, the correctness of students' answers to questions, and the average time it takes students to complete activities.

4. EXPERIMENT

We created two versions of our sixth laboratory activity titled "Wagemart", which focuses on using Microsoft Access as a Decision Support Tool to help reduce payroll costs. The text-based version[1] is delivered using a website with 4400 words and 26 screenshots. The video-based version[2] replaces approximately

---

[1] **http://mis.sienacs.com/wagemart.php**

[2] **http://mis.sienacs.com/wagemart_video.php**

1600 words and 20 images with roughly 30 minutes of instructional video. The video was edited into short clips (1-6 minutes each) and appropriately embedded within the lab instructions using youTube.

The participants were distributed over six lab sections where three sections used the video-based lab while the other three used the text-based format. There were four different instructors where instructors #1 and #2 each supervised both a video- and text-based lab. Instructor #3 supervised a video-based lab and instructor #4 supervised a text-based lab. The text-based version was completed by 44 students (42 worked in pairs, while 2 worked individually) while the video-based version was completed by 47 students (42 worked in pairs, while 5 worked individually). For the video-based lab, students used headphones to listen to the audio/narration. Students working in pairs were encouraged to collaborate on answers and to take turns controlling the computer and using the applications.

5. RESULTS

In our experiment, we concentrated on three measures. First, we collected students' impressions through a post-lab survey. Second, we collected scores based on students' recorded answers for the 44 questions embedded in the instructions. Third, we collected the completion times of key tasks in the lab.

5.1 Impression Data

Immediately after the lab session, 35 of the 44 text-based participants and 34 of the 47 video-based participants completed a survey with the questions shown in Table 1.

Table 1. Post-lab Survey Questions

Q1.	How long did it take you to do this In Lab work? Rate 1 (very short) to 10 (very long)
Q2.	How difficult did you find the work for this Lab? Rate 1 (very easy) to 10 (very hard)
Q3.	How would you rate the level of feedback you received in lab? Rate 1 (no value) to 10 (great value)
Q4.	How easy was it to keep your place and follow Lab procedures using this lab format? Rate 1 (very easy) to 10 (very hard)
Q5.	How much did this Lab help you understand what is being studied in this course? Rate 1 (very little) to 10 (very much)
Q6.	How did the lab format affect how easy it was to keep your place and follow the lab procedures? Rate 1 (very easy) to 10 (very hard)
Q7.	How much did you enjoy the activities in this Lab? Rate 1 (very little) to 10 (very much)

Table 2 shows the mean values and standard deviations of the seven questions for both text and video participants. We also show the probability of the null hypothesis, i.e., no statistically significant difference, using an independent t-test (T) and the Mann-Whitney test (U). Note that while many researchers still use the t-test for Likert scale data, the Mann-Whitney statistic is more appropriate for ordinal (ranked) data [7]. For both T and U, a value below 0.05 (5%) is generally regarded as statistically significant.

Table 2. Survey responses (Likert Scale of 1 to 10)

	Text-Based Mean (STD) n = 35	Video-Based Mean (STD) n = 34	T	U
Q1.	7.00 (1.59)	6.56 (2.34)	0.36	0.45
Q2.	5.74 (1.84)	5.00 (2.20)	**0.13**	**0.13**
Q3.	7.31 (2.13)	7.15 (1.84)	0.73	0.50
Q4.	5.37 (2.90)	5.88 (3.10)	0.48	0.40
Q5.	6.80 (2.01)	6.79 (1.97)	0.99	0.81
Q6.	4.91 (2.82)	5.18 (3.16)	0.72	0.75
Q7.	5.60 (2.29)	6.71 (2.55)	**0.06**	**0.04**

Table 2 shows that the most significant difference (U = 0.04) was the level of enjoyment (Q7), where the video lab was considered more enjoyable. While the significance is not as strong (U = 0.13), the video participants found the lab to be less difficult (Q2). The video participants perceived the lab session to be slightly shorter (Q1), but the difference is not statistically significant as indicated by the T and U values. While participants found the text-based lab to have more valuable feedback (Q3), the difference was also insignificant. Questions 4 and 6 ask students about the ease of following the lab procedures. While the result is inconsistent, the high values for T and U indicate that the inconsistency likely arises because of the close similarity in impressions between the two groups. Finally, there was almost no measurable difference between the two groups in how the format helped students understand the course materials (Q5).

5.2 Student Score Data

Table 3 shows statistics for the number of correctly answered questions (out of 44 questions). The majority of students worked in pairs on one computer. We treat each pair of students as a single participant, which is why the value n is lower than the impression survey. Twenty-one student pairs and two individuals completed the text version while twenty-one student pairs and five individuals completed the video version. The text-based participants scored less than one point higher (out of 44), which is a highly insignificant difference (T = 0.76).

Table 3. Student Scores (out of 44 questions)

Text-Based Mean (STD) n = 23	Video-Based Mean (STD) n = 26	T
35.78 (8.47)	35.04 (8.16)	0.76

5.3 Completion Time Data

We measure the completion time of three distinct tasks and two key parts of the lab. Table 4 describes how the five different elapsed time intervals were obtained and their significance. While we could have analyzed the time intervals between all the questions, not all question intervals included video and explicit tasks. The intervals T1 to T3 (described in Table 4) are important because they each capture a non-trivial task and the corresponding video instructions that all participants were able to complete during the lab session. T4 captures the first two tasks along with 13 related questions. T5 captures all three tasks and 14 total questions.

Table 4. Description of elapsed time intervals

T1.	The elapsed time between question #9 and #10.
	Description: Immediately after question #9 students are instructed to create an Access query to calculate the number of employees available on a particular day. Question #10 asks students for the correct result of the query.
	Significance: This time interval captures a non-trivial task at a point where students should be comfortable with the lab process.
T2.	The elapsed time between question #17 and #18
	Description: Immediately after question #17 students are instructed to create an Access query to calculate the number of employees available given an overtime incentive raise. Question #18 asks for the correct result of the query.
	Significance: This interval captures a more complex task compared to T1.
T3.	The elapsed time between question #21 and #22
	Description: Immediately after question #21 students are instructed to create and execute three dependent queries that calculate the total labor cost of a hypothetical scenario. Question #22 asks for the total cost.
	Significance: This interval captures one of the most complex tasks that students are required to complete. Students often require help to complete this part of the lab and elapsed times could vary significantly.
T4.	The elapsed time between questions #9 and #21
	Description: This includes both the tasks in T1 and T2 as well as 13 related questions.
	Significance: This interval captures two related non-trivial tasks as well as questions that test students' understanding of tasks themselves.
T5.	The elapsed time between questions #9 and #22
	Description: This includes all the tasks in T1, T2, and T3 as well as 14 total questions.
	Significance: This interval captures three tasks that typically take students 30 minutes or more to complete.

Table 5. Completion Time in Seconds

	Text-Based Mean (STD) n = 23	Video-Based Mean (STD) n = 26	T
T1.	268.67 (143.84)	130.24 (100.45)	**0.00027**
T2.	136.31 (61.79)	170.74 (89.04)	0.12725
T3.	1157.45 (399.46)	969.80 (397.43)	0.12724
T4.	1043.57 (241.53)	1042.40 (300.13)	0.98815
T5.	2157.43 (488.76)	1976.16 (570.36)	0.26944

Table 5 shows the completion time in seconds among participants who completed the measured tasks (up to question #22) during the 2-hour lab session. In the first task we measured (T1), video-based participants required half as much time, which is a very significant difference. For the second, more complex task (T2), the text-based participants finished 34 seconds quicker on average, whereas for the third, most complex task (T3), the video-based participants finished almost one minute and 30 seconds faster on average. However, the differences for the more complex tasks (T2 and T3) are not as strongly significant as the difference in T1. The total completion time (T4) is almost identical between the two groups. And finally, the total completion time (T5) shows no statistically significant difference between the two groups.

6. ANALYSIS OF RESULTS

Typically, a considerable portion of the instructor's time during a lab session is spent guiding students through the more difficult tasks. While many students are comfortable and capable using Excel, a number of students have very limited experience using other applications, especially Microsoft Access. Oftentimes, unprepared students would rather have the instructor show them what to do rather than read the instructions, which are often characterized as tedious.

One of the goals in introducing video is to deliver instructions that "show" students exactly what to do, thus freeing the instructor to spend more time helping students with a concept or to reason through a solution. Overall, we expected the video participants to have a more positive impression of the lab experience. We also expected that video participants would perceive and actually experience shorter task completion. Our results are mixed and by no means conclusive but our observations and analysis in the next three sub-sections reveal some key reasons video did not produce overwhelmingly improved results.

6.1 Impression Analysis

We observed that students were able to carry out the video instruction with more independence compared to the text-based participants. In reducing the overall need for instructor support, the instructor was generally more available and responsive. The self-pacing and increased instructor responsiveness may be reasons why the video-based lab was perceived as being easier

and more enjoyable. However, students who might normally receive excessive instructor support might perceive the video lab as being more difficult to follow (Q4 and Q6) and might perceive decreased faculty contact as less feedback (Q3). At our institution, there is an expectation that lab sessions are a time to interact with the instructor. Video-based instruction may undermine some students' expectation of face-to-face lab sessions. The survey data indicates no difference in how the format helped students understand the material itself (Q5), which challenges assumptions that video is a superior format for delivering information.

6.2 Student Score Analysis

Among the text-based participants, the average number of questions answered correctly was 35.8 (out of 44 total questions) while the average among video-based participants was 35.0. This difference is not statistically significant as indicated by the T value shown in Table 3. In fact, the five questions that were most frequently answered incorrectly were the same for both text-based and video-based participants. The format of the instructions (video vs. text) appeared to have no measurable impact on students' ability to answer questions about the lab activity and the bigger problems being solved.

6.3 Completion Time Analysis

We observed students who would re-watch the video if they were unable to finish the task as the video was playing. Other students would pause the video to complete the task in synch with the video. While we expected that video would help accelerate completion times, we observed the opposite for complex tasks because students would often pause or rewind a video. This was most prevalent in T2 where the task in the video was completed quickly but included lengthy narrative explanations.

To accelerate their progress, students would fast-forward past explanations to the parts of the video where they believed the task was being demonstrated. Ironically, we observed that this fast-forwarding in fact slowed progress because students unknowingly skipped over audio explaining a task or concept. When a student encountered the related question or realized that they missed a task step, they would often replay the video, increasing task completion times. Rewinding and pausing possibly accounts for some of the longer completion times on more complex tasks (T2 and T3). Our videos include a mix of task instructions and concept explanations delivered through narration. It is likely more effective to separate and identify videos that are meant to be instructive (concrete concepts) versus videos that are meant to explain a concept or the output of a task (abstract concepts). This separation may decrease students' propensity for pausing and rewinding.

7. FUTURE WORK

In our next study, we will introduce students to our online delivery methods before they experience a video-based lab. In the experiment presented in this paper, the two groups of students (video and text) experienced the online delivery method for the first time in the semester. By familiarizing students with the online delivery system first, we will isolate the introduction of videos as the only new variable. We will also collect control data from instructors using the original paper-based method and use this data to compare impressions, scores, and completion times. But, we will also conduct an end of the semester assessment to measure student retention given the various methods of lab delivery. Finally, if feasible, we hope to experiment with students working exclusively in pairs or exclusively as individuals to help isolate additional variables that were present in this study.

If our next experiment continues to show the promise of video-based instructions, we hope to create a development environment where a team of instructors can collaboratively create and edit instructions and videos. We envision adding dynamic lab flow paths, so additional help or questions can be provided based on previous responses. We are also interested in adding functionality for students to become *prosumers* [9], where they can have a role in the development of the instructions or even the software. In the model envisioned, students will report problems and rate instructions and tasks to help us make targeted improvements.

Our continued challenge as a collaborative team of instructors is to formalize the concepts that each lab covers and to develop good tools to assess whether or not students truly learn the concept introduced. To this end, careful attention to lab design is important to ensure that material is presented in ways that improve student engagement and retention of concepts.

8. CONCLUSION

Advancing technology has made it easier than ever to create, edit, and disseminate instructional videos on the web. While video may not be a suitable replacement for a live lecture or demonstration, it has promising advantages as a substitute for step-by-step written instructions. While reading instructions may challenge students to more thoughtfully examine the task they are completing thus improving their understanding, our experiment showed no significant difference between text and video in students' ability to answer questions about the tasks and underlying problems being solved. However, our experiment is by no means comprehensive and there is great room to investigate the impact of video on student learning and retention, both short-term and long-term.

We were surprised that video did not significantly improve completion times. But, our experiment and results illuminate a common sense reason that is easy to overlook when developing a complex system. The inclusion or exclusion of video is obviously not the only factor that influences completion time. The quality and pacing of the video is greatly important. Instructors need to be cognizant of the speed at which students will likely complete the task. If the video is paced too fast, students will pause or rewind excessively which will naturally slow down progress. A video that is paced too slowly and includes extraneous details invites students to skip ahead. Just as poorly crafted instructions are problematic, poorly crafted video can impede students' progress.

Our impression survey shows that despite the potential problems that could have been introduced, students who experienced video instruction found the lab to be easier and more enjoyable. Increasing enjoyment is an important goal for us as instructors. When students enjoy the lab experience, they are more likely to become engaged in the case study or the broader problem being solved. Additionally, the video frees the instructor to spend more time helping students with concepts and reasoning instead of

spending the majority of lab showing a few struggling students exactly how to perform a task.

As a requirement in the School of Business, our MIS course is the first experience many students have in a Computer Science or Information Systems course at our institution. In creating a more enjoyable lab experience where students and instructors can concentrate on problem solving (instead of monotonous execution of instructions) we hope to inspire students to continue their study in the CS or IS fields.

9. REFERENCES

[1] Becvar, L. A. 2006. Video and image-based reflective learning tools for professional training environments. In *CHI '06 extended abstracts on Human factors in computing system*s (CHI '06). ACM, New York, NY, USA, 1735-1738. DOI=http://doi.acm.org/10.1145/1125451.1125776

[2] Breimer, E., Cotler, J., and Yoder, R. 2011. Towards an Innovative Web-based Lab Delivery System for a Management Information Systems. *Information Systems Education Journal*. Accepted, to appear in Volume 9 (Spring 2011).

[3] Charnigo. L., 2009. Lights! Camera! Action! Producing Library Instruction Video Tutorials Using Camtasia Studio. *Journal of Library and Information Services in Distance Learning*, 3, 1, 23-30.

[4] Elsenhiemer, J. 2003. Terms of Engagement: Keeping Learners Online. *Learning Circuits*, online: http://www.astd.org/LC/2003/0203_elsenheimer.htm.

[5] Garrett, J. J. 2005. Ajax: A New Approach to Web Applications, online: http://adaptivepath.com/ideas/essays/archives/000385.php

[6] Nicholson, J., Nicholoson, D. 2010. A Stream Runs through IT: Using Streaming Video to Teach Information Technology. *Campus-Wide Information Systems*, 27,1, 17-24-2010.

[7] Motulsky, H. 1995. *Intuitive Biostatistics*. Oxford University Press, New York, NY.

[8] Staman, M. 2009. Converged communications, video and innovation in pedagogic settings. In *Proceedings of the 10th ACM conference on SIG-information technology education* (SIGITE '09). ACM, New York, NY, USA, 205-206. DOI=http://doi.acm.org/10.1145/1631728.1631788

[9] Tapscott, D., Williams, A., 2006. *Wikinomics: How Mass Collaboration Changes Everything*. Penguin Group, New York, NY.

[10] Zahn, C., Hesse, F., Finke, M., Pea, R., Mills, M., and Rosen, J. 2005. Advanced digital video technologies to support collaborative learning in school education and beyond. In *Proceedings of the 2005 conference on Computer support for collaborative learning: learning 2005: the next 10 years!* (Taipei, Taiwan). CSCL '05. International Society of the Learning Sciences, 737-742.

Effects of Team-Based Learning on a CS1 Course

Lasserre Patricia
Computer Science, UBC Okanagan
3333 University Way
Kelowna, BC, V1V 1V7
(00) 1 250 807 9502

patricia.lasserre@ubc.ca

Carolyn Szostak
Psychology, UBC Okanagan
3333 University Way
Kelowna, BC, V1V 1V7
(00) 1 250 807 8736

carolyn.szostak@ubc.ca

ABSTRACT

Many active learning techniques have been used and described over the years, including team-based learning (TBL). While this technique is well established, it is only recently that analyses that compare it to other teaching techniques have been reported. In this paper, we evaluate the impact of team-based learning on two major concerns for computer science instructors: the drop/attrition rates, and students' success in CS1. The results show some major improvements both in terms of the drop rate and students' success, as measured by final exam grades. For example, the number of students obtaining 50% or more on the final exam has increased from 54% to 75.5%. Moreover, the drop rate has decreased from more than 30% to 6.4%.

Categories and Subject Descriptors

K.3.2 [**Computers and Education**]: Computer and Information Science Education – *Computer science education.* K.3.1 [**Computers and Education**]: Computer uses in education – *Collaborative learning.*

General Terms

Performance, Experimentation.

Keywords

Active learning, Team-based learning, CS1, Success rate, Drop rate

1. INTRODUCTION

The struggles of the computer science community to attract and maintain students in the discipline are well known and extensively studied problems [7,11,20]. The reported drop rate usually ranges between 30% and 50% [1,12]. Many have looked at how to solve this problem. Some have transformed their undergraduate courses to include hot topics, such as bio-informatics, or games in order to attract and retain students [2,6,10,15]. Collaborative work, active learning strategies and pair programming have also been tried as means to facilitate students' learning in CS1 [8,16]. Still others have been more radical and have argued that we must change our overall approach to teaching [9].

Team-based learning (TBL) is a teaching technique that has been used extensively in medicine since the 1980's. Larry Michaelson

and his colleagues have described in detail how to successfully implement TBL [17]. While there has been great interest in applying this teaching technique in other disciplines [14,19,22,23], evaluation of the effectiveness of TBL has been predominantly done within the health sector [4,5,13]. These studies have reported high levels of engagement, comparable to case-based learning, and better academic performance, especially for weaker students. In computer science, some instructors have used components of TBL [22], whereas others have implemented the full TBL protocol in their classes [14,23]. While an increase in the enthusiasm of the class has been consistently reported, very few attempts have been made to quantify the effectiveness of TBL. In this paper, we present the results of a 4-year study that compared the effectiveness of TBL with a traditional lecture format on the success of CS1 students. In addition, the effects of the teaching method on the drop rate in CS1, and the subsequent impact on CS2 enrollment was evaluated.

2. RESEARCH METHODS

Four years of CS1 classes were used to evaluate the effectiveness of TBL. During this time, the instructor (the first author) and the curriculum remained the same; only the teaching technique used to deliver the curriculum changed. The instructor had 7-years of experience in teaching CS1/2 with the traditional lecture format prior to 2006 and had received excellent feedback from students. In the first year of the study (2006), the course was delivered using a traditional lecture format. In the subsequent three years, a TBL approach was used. Data from years prior to 2006 were not included in this study either because the instructor was different, or because the instructor taught the course to a different population of students (e.g., not B.Sc. students).

2.1 Description of the lecture format

In the traditional model, the course was taught using lectures, group exercises, and home assignments. Students received guidance on how to best succeed in the course in several ways: posting of practice exercises (with possibility to visit the instructor for help), review practices prior to midterms, on-line access to lectures, summary notes for the major concepts taught in class, and quizzes including both multiple choice and programming questions for practice testing.

In preparation for the final exam, there were two midterms that followed the same format as the final (i.e., a combination of multiple-choice and programming questions). The first midterm was marked prior to the withdrawal deadline. The final grade of the course was based on the three components of the course: labs & home assignments, midterms, and final exam. The weighting of the three course components was determined by the instructor (see Table 1). In order to pass the course, students were required to pass all three components. The laboratory assignments and home assignments were marked by the teaching assistants (TAs). The formal examinations (midterm and final) were marked both by the instructor and the TAs using very detailed marking keys.

2.2 Description of TBL

The TBL strategy consists of using the class time for applying concepts instead of lecturing. The TBL technique used followed the format presented in [14]. The Readiness Assessment Process (RAP) ensures that students are ready to apply concepts. Students then work on exercises in teams. Those exercises must follow the 4 S's strategy: significant problem, same exercise for all, the result requires a specific choice, and there must be simultaneous report of the teams' result to the class. The TBL classes did not include midterm exams. These were replaced by RAP multiple-choice tests for each module. Students had completed three of these tests prior to the withdrawal date. Programming was part of routine exercises during class time but no formal examination of these skills happened prior to the withdrawal date. As with the lecture-based class, all course material, quizzes, summary notes, etc. were available on-line. An optional midterm two months after the start of term was offered to students. This optional midterm could be used to replace a missed or bad test, and to help students become familiar with the stressful demands of programming in the context of an exam. On this optional midterm, only programming questions were included, as students had already gained a lot of experience with multiple-choice tests (the test consisted of programming questions used previously in the midterms from the lecture classes). This opportunity was particularly important as a failing grade on the final exam resulted in failing the course. In this regard, students were warned that while they were learning in teams, each student still had to meet a minimum standard at the end of term in order to pass the course.

At the beginning of the semester, the instructor provided a possible range for the weight of each course component and the class determined the final weighting. The three components for the TBL format were the labs (range between 5% and 20%), the TBL component – which included individual tests, home assignments, as well as class group work – (range between 35% and 60%), and the final exam (range between 35% and 45%). Table 1 presents the class-determined weights for each year:

Table 1: Weighting of the course components

Year	Lab + Home / Lab*	Midterms / TBL*	Final Exam
2006 – Lecture	20%	40%	40%
2007 – TBL	18%	47%	35%
2008 – TBL	18%	47%	35%
2009 – TBL	11%	54%	35%

* Lecture class / TBL class components

It is important to emphasize that the nature of the course content did not change: the lab assignments remained the same; the exercises from the textbook previously recommended to students were done in class or as part of the home preparation; the major homework assignments that had previously been given to students in the lecture format became marked team work in the TBL classes. Importantly, the final exam was identical to the one administered in the lecture-based class.

The TBL classes included 6 modules that covered most of the typical CS1 topics. Two topics that covered 1.5 weeks in the course were moved to CS2 (i.e. recursion and exceptions). These two topics were not covered in the final exam used in this study.

The laboratory assignments, class preparatory assignments and group marks were marked by the TAs. The optional midterm and the final exam were marked both by the instructor and the TAs following the same very detailed marking keys.

2.3 The study

Two main questions were considered in evaluating the effectiveness of TBL. First, we wanted to determine whether TBL helped students to be more successful in the course. To this end, the same final exam was administered in CS1 for the four years. As previously indicated, the exam was marked in collaboration with TAs using a marking scheme previously prepared by the instructor. This ensured comparable marking every year. The final exam consisted of two parts worth 50% each. The first portion of the exam included multiple-choice questions at various levels of the Bloom taxonomy [3]; the second part included three programming questions that had not been previously solved either in class or in labs or assignments. Students were expected to solve the problems using the knowledge gained from previously presented and discussed examples.

Second, we wanted to determine if the change from the traditional lecture model to TBL influenced students' decision to remain in the course. An instructor can only impact a student's decision between the first day and last day of class. Hence, evaluating students' decision to remain in the course was accomplished by monitoring the drop rate of these courses over the four year period. Other measures were also examined, such as the number of students who registered in CS2, as well as the CS2 drop rates.

The second author, who had no instructional contact with the CS1 students, was responsible for explaining the study to the students, and for analyzing the data to minimize the potential influence of the dual roles of the first author (i.e., instructor and researcher). The instructor never spoke of the research study with the students.

3. RESULTS

3.1 Impact on students' performance in CS1

To evaluate the impact of the teaching method on students' success, the final grades of students who wrote the final exam and, as such, completed the course, were analyzed using a between-group analysis of variance. A significant, albeit weak, effect was obtained: $F(3,290) = 2.70$, $p < .05$.

Table 2: Means (standard deviation) of CS1 grades

Year	# students	Final grade	Grade on final exam
2006 – Lecture	49	67.2 (20.6)	58.1 (24.4)
2007 – TBL	62	72.5 (17.7)	63.2 (21.8)
2008 – TBL	85	73.5 (18.2)	64.0 (21.6)
2009 – TBL	98	76.4 (18.8)	64.1 (20.8)

As indicated in Table 2, there was a trend for the final grades to be higher in the TBL courses, relative to the lecture format. Pairwise comparisons using Dunnett's t-test indicated that the only reliable difference was between the 2006-Lecture class and the 2009-TBL class sections (p= .007). The difference between the 2006-Lecture and 2008-TBL classes approached significance (p =

.07). This result is not surprising: the TBL grades included team-work that is typically associated with greater success [18]. In the present study, marks for the team-work tended to be higher than the grades for individual assignments/tests. The overall grade for the TBL work, which is computed based on both individual and team-work, tended to be higher than grades on the lecture-based midterm exam. Moreover, the TBL work was weighted slightly more heavily than the midterm exams (see Table 1). The finding that the effect of the teaching method depended upon the specific TBL class is likely due to the instructor's differential experience with TBL: 2007 was the first time that the instructor had formally used TBL. With each successive course, the instructor was more familiar with the techniques and better able to implement them.

To further evaluate the nature of the effect of the teaching method, performance on the final exam that was common to the four classes was analyzed. Only students who attempted the exam were included in the analysis. While the average grade was somewhat greater in all 3 TBL classes, relative to the 2006-Lecture class (see Table 2), this effect was not statistically significant: F<1. The proportion of students who successfully passed the final exam (i.e., who received a grade greater or equal to 50%) was analyzed. This analysis yielded a significant difference: $\chi^2_{(3)} = 8.548$, p = .036. As indicated in Table 3, this difference reflects the fact that a substantially greater proportion of students in each of the 3 TBL classes passed the final exam, relative to students in the 2006-Lecture class.

Table 3: Performance on the final exam

Year	# students who wrote the final	Success rate	MCQ*	Prog. Q.*
2006 – Lecture	49	55.1%	32.9 (8.4)	22.3 (16.6)
2007 – TBL	62	75.8%	32.9 (7.9)	26.1 (14.9)
2008 – TBL	85	76.4%	32.9 (8.3)	28.0 (14.4)
2009 – TBL	98	74.5%	34.3 (7.4)	28.8 (14.2)

* mean (standard deviation) (marked out of 50)

In an attempt to better understand the effects of TBL on final exam performance, grades on the two separate components of the exam (i.e., multiple-choice questions vs. programming questions) were analyzed (see Table 3). Between-group ANOVA of the grades on the multiple-choice questions failed to yield a significant effect of teaching method: F <1. There was, however, a trend for TBL to be associated with better grades on the programming questions, relative to the lecture-based class: F(3, 290) = 2.364, p = .07.

Taken together, these results suggest that the benefit of TBL is in its potential to increase students' ability to answer programming questions. Indeed, the TBL technique emphasizes programming experience in a supportive environment as a fundamental part of the class work, both individually (as a class preparation) and as a team (in class). These practical experiences may have provided students with enough practice to understand how to approach this type of exercises, and/or increased their confidence. Together, they appear to have helped many students to gain enough to feel more comfortable and able during the final exam. In this regard, anecdotal inspection of the final exams suggested that TBL students were more willing to write programs. They seemed less

hesitant in writing the part of the code they knew (or at least thought they knew) how to do. For example, while they might not have been able to correctly extract the data as requested in the exercise, they were more likely to assume that the extraction had been done properly, and continued on with the code. In contrast, instead of making that assumption, students in the lecture-based class would just stop writing code.

3.2 CS1 drop rate

For the four years of the study, we closely monitored the fluctuations in registrations from the first day of class to the last day of term. It was anticipated that the CS1 drop/attrition rate would be less when the course was taught using TBL.

Students who officially dropped or withdrew from the course or who did not write the final exam were considered to have not completed the course. It should be noted that the drop rate obtained in the 2006-Lecture class (see Table 4) was comparable to rates reported in the literature [12]. Non-parametric analysis of these data demonstrated that the drop rate did, in fact, vary as a function of the teaching method: $\chi^2_{(3)} = 22.90$, p = .01. As depicted in Table 4, the percent of students who did not complete CS1 was substantially less in each of the TBL classes, relative to the 2006-Lecture class. It is important to acknowledge that an improvement in the attrition rates was also evident across the 3 TBL classes. This may reflect, at least in part, the acquired experience of the instructor in using the techniques of TBL.

Table 4: Drop rates for CS1

Year	Course completed	Course not completed	Drop rate (%)
2006 – Lecture	50	22	30.6%
2007 – TBL	64	14	17.9%
2008 – TBL	90	10	10.0%
2009 – TBL	103	7	6.4%

Taken together, it seems that TBL both increases the number of students remaining in the class, and at the same time, augments the number of students who successfully pass the final exam. The meaningfulness of these findings is demonstrated in the following example. Relative to the lecture version of CS1 (i.e., 2006), 24.2% more students completed the course in 2009 or approximately 25 students. Of these 25 students, it can be estimated that 75.5% successfully passed the final exam. That is, 19 students who would previously not have stayed in the course stayed and successfully passed the final (so passed the course). This suggests that students who previously felt they would not be successful were able to master enough of the topics covered to succeed.

While these data certainly suggest that the teaching method has an impact, it is important to acknowledge that other factors are, in all likelihood, also at play. For example, the absence of mid-term examinations in the TBL classes may have contributed to students' decisions to stay in the class. However, by the last date to officially withdraw from the class, students in all of the CS1 classes, regardless of teaching method, had received substantial feedback concerning their performance in the course.

3.3 Attrition and drop rate beyond CS1

Because the instructor was teaching both CS1 and CS2 every year (other than CS2 in the last year of this study), the enrollment in CS2 was also monitored. We examined the drop rate in CS2 to determine if there were any emerging patterns related to the method of instruction.

In 2006, students who completed CS1 and continued in CS2 were instructed using the lecture format. The students who completed CS1 with TBL continued in CS2 using a traditional lecture format. The major difference (other than the course topics) for those TBL students was the teaching technique. While TBL was not part of CS2, some of the most interesting tools such as the scratch test cards (see [14] for a sample card) were used in preparation for the midterm and final exams. The same methods described previously for the lecture format in CS1 were also used for this class. Finally, it should be noted that the instructor had taught CS2 for the same number of years as CS1 (i.e., 7 years experience prior to the start of the study).

Figure 1 shows the percentage of students who did not complete the course for the first three years of the study. The drop rate for the academic year 2009-2010 is not included as the course was taught by a sessional instructor.

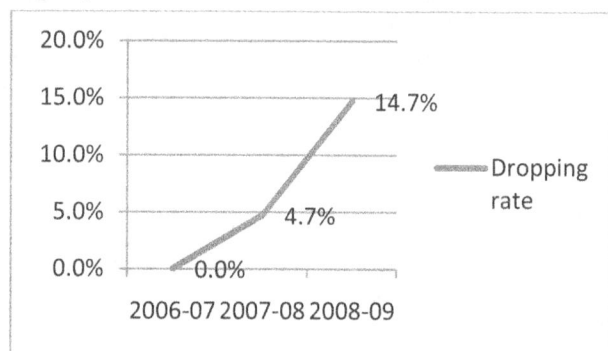

Figure 1: Drop rates in CS2

In 2006-07, when both courses were taught using the traditional lecture format, no students dropped the course after the first day of class. This might indicate that all students remaining in CS2 were planning to stay in that course for degree requirements. Somewhat surprisingly, since 2007, when TBL was introduced in CS1, the number of CS2 students who left after the class started, has increased, attaining a high of 14.7% in 2008-09. The reason for this change is unknown. It may be directly attributable to the change in the teaching technique. More likely, the reason is more complex, reflecting a combination of the interest and ability level of the students, as well as the teaching technique.

Anecdotal evidence suggests that students quickly reverted to a passive approach to learning as soon as the traditional lecture format re-appeared in the classroom: students did not come prepared to class even though readings were encouraged; assignments were left to the last minute; there was little interaction during class. Lots of difficulties in engaging the CS2 students were experienced by the instructor whereas in the TBL-based CS1 classes, a high level of participation had been the norm. It is important to reiterate that the instructor was the same for both CS1 and CS2. Moreover, the students in each CS2 class were a subset of the students who were in each of the CS1 classes. Both students and instructor in CS2 were frustrated at the lack of understanding evidenced by performance on the midterms, probably making students even more likely to withdraw. While acknowledging that the decision to withdraw is in all likelihood multifaceted, we strongly believe that the change in teaching technique from CS1 to CS2 had an impact on a student's decision

when the course was not required for the student's academic program (i.e s/he is not intending to major in CS or Math).

4. CONCLUSION

TBL has been described to be a powerful tool to engage students in the classroom, and improve students' success. It is a versatile technique that can be applied to any class level, with almost any size of class. However, as pointed out by Thompson and colleagues [21], success requires a full implementation and mastery of the technique, and a complete buy-in by the instructor.

In this paper, we demonstrated that TBL had a positive impact on CS1 students. Specifically, almost 20% more students completed the course when it was taught using TBL than when the traditional lecture format was used. In addition, approximately 20% more students passed the final exam when they had been taught using TBL instead of lectures. It appears that the greatest benefit of TBL was in terms of enhanced programming skills and students' confidence in their ability to program. These results are important as being able to write new programs is the most important skill to acquire from this course. Given the shortage of CS students, being able to retain students in our lower, introductory classes is crucial. Moreover, enhancing the success rate of those students without changing our standards of success is critical. TBL seems to meet these criteria.

While the present findings are very encouraging (and exciting), the effects were not always as strong as one would hope. It will be important to continue to investigate the nature of the benefits of using TBL to deliver CS curricula, and to determine if some techniques are more effective than others. In this regard, it is likely that TBL is more effective for some students than others. Future work will investigate the nature of individual differences in TBL effectiveness. For example, Koles et al. [13] argued that TBL had a more positive effect on the lower quartile students (better learning retention). It would be interesting to determine if, indeed, it is the lower quartile students who benefit the most from the TBL-based classes, and what kind of impact the teaching method has on the other quartiles. We are also evaluating the extent to which previous experience working in teams and attitudes about teamwork may influence their performance in CS1 when taught using TBL. If this is the case, then it may be important to provide students with preliminary information about how to work in a team and the benefits of this approach. In that regard, it may also be useful to determine if students, in fact, learn or acquire the right attributes for being a valuable team member; all valuable elements for CS1 students to learn.

While students did seem to benefit from TBL in CS1, there was evidence for negative effects in CS2 when the second course was offered using a traditional lecture format. That is, more students dropped the second course, relative to when both courses were lecture-based. In addition, students were less active and engaged. We are currently in the process of re-designing CS2 to be TBL-based. It will be interesting to evaluate the effects of this change on drop rates and also on students' performance.

5. ACKNOWLEDGMENTS

This work was financially supported by the Irving K. Barber Endowment Fund.

6. REFERENCES

[1] Beaubouef ,T., Mason J. 2005. Why the high attrition rate for computer science students: some thoughts and observations.

SIGCSE Bull., 37 (2), 103-106, ACM Press (2005). DOI = http://doi.acm.org/10.1145/1083431.1083474

[2] Beck, J., Buckner, B., and Nikolova, O. 2007. Using interdisciplinary bioinformatics undergraduate research to recruit and retain computer science students. In *Proceedings of the 38th SIGCSE Technical Symposium on Computer Science Education* (Covington, Kentucky, USA, March 07 - 11, 2007). SIGCSE '07. ACM, New York, NY, 358-361. DOI= http://doi.acm.org/10.1145/1227310.1227436

[3] Bloom B. S. (1956). Taxonomy of Educational Objectives, Handbook I: The Cognitive Domain. New York. David McKay Co Inc.
(http://www.nwlink.com/~donclark/hrd/bloom.html)

[4] Chung, E.K., Rhee, J.A., Baik Y.H., A O.S.. 2009. The effect of team-based learning in medical ethics education. *Med. Teach.* 31, 11 (Nov 2009), 1013-7.

[5] Clark, C.C., Nguyen, H.T., Bray, C., Levine R. E. 2008. Team-Based Learning in an Undergraduate Nursing Course. *J. Nursing Education.* 47/3 (March 2008).

[6] Eagle, M. and Barnes, T. 2008. Wu's castle: teaching arrays and loops in a game. In *Proceedings of the 13th Annual Conference on innovation and Technology in Computer Science Education* (Madrid, Spain, June 30 - July 02, 2008). ITiCSE '08. ACM, New York, NY, 245-249. DOI= http://doi.acm.org/10.1145/1384271.1384337

[7] Edmondson, C. 2008. Teaching tales: some student perceptions of computing education. *SIGCSE Bull.* 40, 4 (Nov. 2008), 103-106. DOI= http://doi.acm.org/10.1145/1473195.1473232

[8] Gonzalez, G. 2006. A systematic approach to active and cooperative learning in CS1 and its effects on CS2. In *Proceedings of the 37th SIGCSE Technical Symposium on Computer Science Education* (Houston, Texas, USA, March 03 - 05, 2006). SIGCSE '06. ACM, New York, NY, 133-137. DOI= http://doi.acm.org/10.1145/1121341.1121386

[9] Hamer, J., Cutts, Q., Jackova, J., Luxton-Reilly, A., McCartney, R., Purchase, H., Riedesel, C., Saeli, M., Sanders, K., and Sheard, J. 2008. Contributing student pedagogy. *SIGCSE Bull.* 40, 4 (Nov. 2008), 194-212. DOI= http://doi.acm.org/10.1145/1473195.1473242

[10] Hillyard, C., Angotti, R., Panitz, M., Sung, K., Nordlinger, J., and Goldstein, D. 2010. Game-themed programming assignments for faculty: a case study. In *Proceedings of the 41st ACM Technical Symposium on Computer Science Education* (Milwaukee, Wisconsin, USA, March 10 - 13, 2010). SIGCSE '10. ACM, New York, NY, 270-274. DOI= http://doi.acm.org/10.1145/1734263.1734358

[11] Howles, T. 2007. Preliminary results of a longitudinal study of computer science student trends, behaviors and preferences. *J. Comput. Small Coll.* 22, 6 (Jun. 2007), 18-27.

[12] Kinnunen, P. and Malmi, L. 2006. Why students drop out CS1 course?. In *Proceedings of the Second international Workshop on Computing Education Research* (Canterbury, United Kingdom, September 09 - 10, 2006). ICER '06.

ACM, New York, NY, 97-108. DOI= http://doi.acm.org/10.1145/1151588.1151604

[13] Koles, P., Nelson, S., Stolfi, A., Parmelee, D., Destephen, D. 2005. Active learning in a Year 2 pathology curriculum. *Med. Educ.* 39,10 (Oct 2005) 1045-55.

[14] Lasserre, P. 2009. Adaptation of team-based learning on a first term programming class. In *Proceedings of the 14th Annual ACM SIGCSE Conference on innovation and Technology in Computer Science Education* (Paris, France, July 06 - 09, 2009). ITiCSE '09. ACM, New York, NY, 186-190. DOI= http://doi.acm.org/10.1145/1562877.1562937

[15] Luxton-Reilly, A. and Denny, P. 2009. A simple framework for interactive games in CS1. In *Proceedings of the 40th ACM Technical Symposium on Computer Science Education* (Chattanooga, TN, USA, March 04 - 07, 2009). SIGCSE '09. ACM, New York, NY, 216-220. DOI= http://doi.acm.org/10.1145/1508865.1508947

[16] McKinney, D. and Denton, L. F. 2006. Developing collaborative skills early in the CS curriculum in a laboratory environment. In *Proceedings of the 37th SIGCSE Technical Symposium on Computer Science Education* (Houston, Texas, USA, March 03 - 05, 2006). SIGCSE '06. ACM, New York, NY, 138-142. DOI= http://doi.acm.org/10.1145/1121341.1121387

[17] Michaelsen, L. K., Knight A. B., and Fink D. L. 2004. Team-Based Learning: A Transformative Use of Small Groups in College Teaching. Stylus Publishing. Sterling VA.

[18] Michaelsen, L.K., Watson, W.E., Black, R.H. (1989) A realistic test of individual versus group consensus decision making . *Journal of Applied Psychology*, 74,5 (Oct. 1989) 834-839

[19] Ostafichuck P., Hodgson A. 2007. Standing on Our Heads: How Teaching Engineering Design Looks Different from a Team-based Learning Perspective. TBL Conference. Vancouver (June 2007)
(http://tbl.apsc.ubc.ca/conferences/2007/#h)

[20] Schulte, C. and Knobelsdorf, M. 2007. Attitudes towards computer science-computing experiences as a starting point and barrier to computer science. In *Proceedings of the Third international Workshop on Computing Education Research* (Atlanta, Georgia, USA, September 15 - 16, 2007). ICER '07. ACM, New York, NY, 27-38. DOI= http://doi.acm.org/10.1145/1288580.1288585

[21] Thompson, B.M., Schneider, P.H., Levine, R.E., McMahon, K.K., Perkowski, l.C., Richards, B.F. 2007. Team-based learning at ten medical schools: two years later. *Med. Educ.* 41,3 (March 2007) 250-257.

[22] Trytten D.A.. 2005. A design for team peer code review. *SIGCSE Bull.* 37, 1 (February 2005), 455-459. DOI=10.1145/1047124.1047492 http://doi.acm.org/10.1145/1047124.1047492

[23] Whittington K. J. 2007 Understanding the TBL divide; examining similarities and differences between writing and programming. TBL conference. Vancouver (June 2007) (http://tbl.apsc.ubc.ca/conferences/2007/#1)

Experience Report: A Multi-classroom Report on the Value of Peer Instruction

Leo Porter, Cynthia Bailey Lee, Beth Simon
Computer Science and Engr. Dept.
University of California, San Diego
La Jolla, CA USA
+1 858 534 5419

{leporter,clbailey,esimon}@ucsd.edu

Quintin Cutts
Sch. of Computing Science
University of Glasgow
Glasgow, Scotland
+44 141 330 5619

quintin@dcs.gla.ac.uk

Daniel Zingaro
Dept. of Computer Science
University of Toronto
Toronto, ON, Canada

daniel.zingaro@utoronto.ca

ABSTRACT

Peer Instruction (PI) has a significant following in physics, biology, and chemistry education. Although many CS educators are aware of PI as a pedagogy, the adoption rate in CS is low. This paper reports on four instructors with varying motivations and course contexts and the value they found in adopting PI. Although there are many documented benefits of PI for students (e.g. increased learning), here we describe the experience of the instructor by looking in detail at one particular question they posed in class. Through discussion of the instructors' experiences in their classrooms, we support educators in consideration of whether they would like to have similar classroom experiences. Our primary findings show instructors appreciate that PI assists students in addressing course concepts at a deep level, assists instructors in dynamically adapting their class to address student misunderstandings and, overall, that PI encourages students to be engaged in conversations which help build technical communication skills. We propose that using PI to engage students in these activities can effectively support training in analysis and teamwork skills.

Categories and Subject Descriptors

K.3.2 [**Computer Science Education**].

General Terms

Algorithms, Human Factors

Keywords

CS1, peer instruction, clickers, PRS, classroom response, active learning.

1. INTRODUCTION

Peer Instruction (PI) is a pedagogy that involves a conceptual shift away from a classroom dominated by one-way transmission of knowledge to a more collaborative, active learning environment [4]. For the past twenty years, PI has contributed to improvements in conceptual understanding among physics students [4], and is now being adopted by educators of other sciences [2,7]. Yet, adoption of PI in CS remains slow, with few reporting on its use in the last few years [5,9,10,13].

Traditionally, experience reports describe an instructor's experience with one course or tool—reporting their adoption experience. Here, rather than reporting on one course, we report the experience of adopting one *pedagogy* – across multiple instructors, institutions, and computing courses. Four instructors who adopted PI for varying reasons and in varying courses[1] each describe one question which was particularly compelling in their situation. From these experiences, we offer computing educators in many courses the opportunity to consider whether these reflect experiences they would like to have in their classrooms.

We do not report on the impact of PI on student learning here. Using a standardized concept inventory (CI) for comparison, PI has been shown to increase learning approximately twofold in large studies of physics courses [4,6]. It is difficult to make such claims in CS, where we have no accepted CIs available through which to measure learning gains. Instead, both the extensive documentation of PI's effect on learning in other disciplines and the clear basis of the pedagogy in constructivist learning models argue that it would be effective in computing.

Additionally, we do not fully document the process of developing and deploying a course using the PI pedagogy. There are numerous resources available that describe this process, for example, the video series and interdisciplinary handbook [12] and tactics for generating effective MCQs [1]. Closer to home, an experience report on adopting and adapting PI in a CS1 course can be found in [10]. We will provide discussion across the four experiences and describe how we believe PI naturally supports development of effective analysis, teamwork, and communication skills.

2. BACKGROUND & RELATED WORK

PI is a classroom pedagogy that makes use of clickers to enable all students in a class to respond or vote on multiple choice questions (MCQs) posed by the lecturer. A PI classroom session involves several iterations of a well-defined vote/discuss/re-vote procedure. Each PI iteration begins with an MCQ designed both to focus attention on and raise awareness of a key course concept. After individually thinking about and voting on the correct answer (the individual vote), students discuss the question in small groups, reach a consensus, and vote again on the same question (the group vote). The instructor can then make use of the results of both votes to lead a class-wide discussion to help review persistent misunderstandings. In the small groups, students are encouraged to discuss each answer option, verbalizing why it is correct or incorrect [10]. The discussion typically results in more students giving the correct answer, and there is evidence that this

---

[1] CS0, CS1, theory of computation, and computer architecture

improvement reflects gains in conceptual understanding rather than peer influence [11]. This process is often accompanied by quizzes of prior reading and mini-lectures during class. The reading quizzes, completed before class, prepare students to engage with in-class MCQs. The mini-lectures are given before particularly challenging PI questions to further prepare students.

The seminal work on PI reviewed learning gains achieved using PI in introductory physics over the span of 10 years [4]. Increases in conceptual understanding, measured using standardized tests applied before and after the courses, showed approximately a two-fold improvement over traditional methods.

In other disciplines, instructors have provided personal accounts of how the use of PI and clickers have changed their teaching [2,7]. In computing, [5,9,10,13] have discussed the process of integrating PI in their classrooms; [3] reports on brief uses of PI in an otherwise traditional course. Of these studies, [10] is the only one to include instructor reflections; for example, the instructor found that generating distracters for MCQs helped her make student misconceptions more explicit.

3. Theory of Computation
We next present and discuss four PI questions, one per section. The questions in this section and Section 4 demonstrate that students collectively learned via effective discussion. Sections 5 and 6 contain questions where student discussion helped the instructor identify problems and dynamically adjust course content to address misunderstandings.

Our first example comes from a Theory of Computation (Automata) course conducted in the summer of 2010 at a large R1 institution in the US. The course is limited to Computer Science majors, and is required for the major. The course seeks to develop an understanding of the mechanics of automata types (Discrete Finite Automata, Pushdown Automata, Turing Machines) and the properties of related language classes (Regular Languages, Context-Free Languages), as well as refine proof-writing skills.

Lectures were conducted almost entirely in PI format. A primary goal of using PI for this course was to give students as much practice as possible in the clear, concise, and convincing communication of theoretical concepts. Such communication is the essence of proof-writing, but is a fundamental challenge for many students. Proof-writing is not a new activity for students, but application of an understanding of what constitutes a proof is typically inconsistent. For example, even in this upper-division course, it was not uncommon for the instructor to observe students attempting to prove a universal statement by analyzing one specific example (a classically fallacious approach). Students can overcome these challenges with extensive practice and feedback. However, proofs are highly labor-intensive to read and assess, making it logistically difficult for course staff to provide adequate formative feedback to students.

PI provides an early, interactive environment for practicing communication of theoretical content, and, in some cases, even composing complete arguments. Compared to a traditional written assignment, classroom discussion is actually a more natural context for the act of proving. Proving is supposed to be convincing a peer, not merely producing a "correct" artifact in a vacuum or for a professor who one knows is already trivially convinced.

Many of the MCQs used in the course focused on automata mechanics and design. With these, PI develops essential skills in

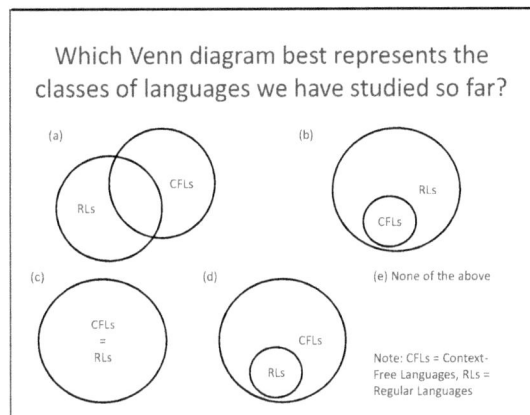

Figure 1: Language Classes MCQ

naming theoretical objects precisely, and analyzing their properties in words. These will be the building blocks for precise proof-writing. Other slides directly ask students to complete a proof, for example by selecting the correct missing sentence from a partially-completed proof. The MCQ presented here is one of a few from the course that does not directly ask students to construct a proof, yet induces spontaneous proof arguments during discussion.

3.1 Question: Language Classes
The question in Figure 1 is presented following PI slides introducing Pushdown Automata (PDA), which are associated with the class of Context-Free Languages (CFLs). Thus students are newly familiar with the mechanics of Pushdown Automata, but this is the first question on the properties of their class of languages, the CFLs. Students have previously studied the less-powerful Nondeterministic Finite Automata (NFA), and associated class of Regular Languages (RLs). The correct answer to this question is (d): the class of Regular Languages is a strict subset of the class of Context-Free Languages.

3.2 Results
The voting for this question was 26% (a), 67% (d), and 3% each of (b), (c), and (e). It would appear that most students began with the notion that some non-Regular languages are Context-Free, probably from experience with analyzing Pushdown Automata for languages that are clearly not Regular in the preceding slides. This understanding narrows the compatible choices to (a) and (d). So the key was to move students from (a) to (d).

Moving students from (a) to (d) involves proving that there is no RL that isn't also a CFL, in other words, that the class of RLs is a subset of the class of CFLs. To do this, we observe that, given an NFA, one can construct a PDA for the same language---simply copy the NFA's structure and ignore the additional stack feature of PDAs. Just as the instructor had hoped, she observed some students spontaneously invoking this argument in their group discussions.

In the whole-class discussion that followed, a few less rigorous explanations were offered along with the one above. It served as a good case study for how to identify arguments that are unambiguously convincing to people who are uncertain of the outcome, and motivated a review of a standard "toolkit" of approaches to proving different Venn diagram configurations. Peer Instruction was successful in inducing the exact kinds of natural context argumentation experiences and subsequent analysis that the instructor had desired for this course.

4. Computer Architecture

The following example appeared in an Introduction to Computer Architecture class in the summer of 2010 taught at a large R1 institution in the US. The class was taught using PI, clickers, and online reading quizzes before each class.

Computer Architecture poses particular challenges for the PI instructor. Similar to physics, many of the questions that appear in the text can be solved by applying a formula or basic algorithm to obtain the correct result. Examples of such problems include standard plug-and-chug problems using the performance equation, detailed decoding/encoding of MIPS assembly instructions, etc. However, these problems often fail to address core class concepts. For example, although encoding/decoding of MIPS instructions helps to clarify the role of an assembler, such questions may not drive at core concepts in Instruction Set Architecture design.

Although many of the PI questions from the class are interesting and many offer larger gains in student performance between individual and group votes, this particular question was chosen because of the discussion it fostered on core class concepts.

4.1 Question: Pipeline Design

Figure 2 is a question on pipeline design. When teaching pipelining in an undergraduate course, students often become so mired in the details of hazard detection logic, data forwarding, branch prediction logic, etc. that they lose sight of the big picture. This question was asked at the end of the section on pipelining to refocus students on the big picture.

In this question, splitting instruction fetch (IF) and memory (M) into two stages each will increase the impact of hazards on cycles-per-instruction (CPI). The students had worked with examples with a similar 7-stage pipeline so they had enough background that they could be capable of recognizing that longer pipelines tend to increase the impact of hazards on CPI. Similarly, they had worked examples in multi-cycle processors on the impact of properly balancing the amount of work done per cycle. In this problem, splitting IF and M into two stages better balances the time spent per stage of the pipeline and allows us to reduce cycle time (CT) by a factor of two. The correct answer for this question is (b).

4.2 Results

The initial voting for this question was 5% (a), 61% (b), 20% (c), and 7% each of (d) and (e). After the group vote, a larger number of students answered correctly (61% to 71%) but there were still 29% confused about the result. Of those confused about the correct result, 5% answered (c) and 12% answered each of (d) and (e). The complete opposite of the correct answer (increase in CT but decrease in CPI) was response (c). Considerably fewer students responded (c) after the group discussion. Both (d) and (e) were half correct in that (d) had the correct response for CT but the wrong response for CPI and (e) had the correct response for CPI but not CT. Thus, the improvement in their group response was not just in more students answering entirely correctly, but more students answering partially correctly.

Following the group vote, the instructor led a class-wide discussion addressing the correct response for CPI and CT indiv-

Selection	CPI	CT
A	Increase	Increase
B	Increase	Decrease
C	Decrease	Increase
D	Decrease	Decrease
E	Increase	No Change

Figure 2: Computer architecture question regarding the impact of longer (deeper) pipelines on CPI and CT.

idually. Finally, after discussing the correct response, the instructor used this example to segue into why deeper pipelines can be attractive and a longer explanation of tradeoffs involved in deciding on pipeline depth (namely its impact on CPI and CT).

What the instructor was most impressed about was that, led by a need to answer this question, students discussed high-level course content in a lively and intelligent manner. Having worked with students from prior classes for a number of years, the instructor had previously complained that students *rarely* have solid discussions on core course content. In prior years, students often focused on the aforementioned details of pipelining while missing the big picture (as demonstrated in exams and in conversations with the instructor). The few occasions where students were concerned about these tradeoffs seemed to only occur a few days (or even hours) before major exams. However, because of PI and the design of this question, students spent at least a significant period of class time engaging core concepts (in detail, with lively debate). Also, because this discussion occurred in class, the instructor was available to assist with their learning by guiding the resulting class-wide discussion. What had previously been an issue for "cram" sessions became an integral and vibrant part of the class experience.

5. CS0

This example comes from a large (~570 student) CS0 course, which was one pilot course for the AP CS Principles program in Fall 2010 at a large R1 institution in the US. The course is a required general education elective for some undergraduates, and seeks to develop computational thinking skills among students who may never take another computing course. The course focuses on developing technical analysis and communication skills through instruction in Alice and Excel. PI was a core feature of the instructional design of the course. We chose to use PI because it allowed a significant amount of students' time engaging in the course to be devoted to analysis and communication practice. Although we were "teaching" students to program in Alice, the real goal of the course was to affect students' confidence in using computers, positively impact their views of technology as a value in society, and develop their skills in "dealing" with computers and computation through analysis, communication, and organization skills. As such, most of the MCQs asked students to do one of the following:

- select a line of code to complete a given program to make it do a described task
- select a correct English description of what a code does
- identify the appropriate rationale for why a code works the way it does

5.1 Question: Dynamic Execution

Figure 4 shows an example of a "rationale" question asked in class. The question is referring to a line of code that students had just practiced evaluating (for specific values which resulted in 0.35) in the previous question. Up to this point, students had no specific experience in evaluating numerical expressions. Having just performed an evaluation given a specific set of objects, the concern that students do not recognize that the expression can evaluate to different values during different executions is raised. The core issue is to illuminate the key feature of the static code - dynamic execution model of programming.

Carl the Coder says:

This code will always cause the bee to move up 0.35 meters, no matter how you design your tulip and bee objects

```
bee move up ( subject = tulip 's height + ( subject = bee 's height / 2 ) )
```

A. Carl is Correct: The expression must always evaluate to 0.35 because that's the way we designed it

B. Carl is Crazy: The expression will evaluate to different values based on the heights of our tulip and bee objects

C. I don't know

Figure 4: Question on dynamic execution in CS0.

5.2 Results

When students considered this question individually, 89% answered correctly. After group discussion this increased to 98%. However, with this style of question, student correctness in voting is only the first step in valuable learning from the problem. The student-provided explanation during the class-wide discussion was "we didn't specify how tall the tulip and the bee are, and, yeah, it can change." This not-quite-satisfactory explanation both illuminated for the instructor students' interpretations of how dynamic execution happened and provided the opportunity for her to model her own way of thinking about the various ways in which the code could be called. This then led naturally into a demo of a situation where three tulips of different heights were used. We called the code three different times and it produced different values each time. The instructor was able to help students clarify and hopefully understand a more expert explanation – it is not that we do not specify a height, it is that the height can vary during various dynamic executions of the statement.

Again, the real value of this question cannot be summed up in the student voting record alone. The primary goal of the question was to engage students in discussions in their own words that can help them identify the static/dynamic execution concept. The issue is very abstract (yet core) and even though a demo where the steps through instructions are highlighted may help, here we use PI to help prepare students to learn a concept by having them engage in it first. The value of this approach in PI has been documented both in giving students appropriate time to consider an issue themselves and "try out" their understanding in discussions and in providing an impetus for students to want to focus and understand the following explanation and demonstration.

6. CS1

This section's example comes from a small (40 students), first-year, remedial CS1 course for engineering students at a large Canadian research university. All students in the course had been unsuccessful in taking the course the semester prior, and the course is required in order to continue in their program. PI was faithfully used: each class was structured around three or four MCQs, with reading quizzes graded for completion prior to each class. The course used C to teach standard introductory CS topics.

Consider the following code.

```
void recur (int i) {
  if (i == 0) {
    printf ("%d ", i);
    return;
  }
  for (int j = 0; j < 2; j++)
    recur (i - 1);
}
```

What is printed by the call recur (1)?

A. 0	D. 0 1
B. 0 0	E. None of the above
C. 0 0 0 ... infinitely	

Figure 5: Recursion question in a CS1 class.

In CS1, it is tempting to ask "factual recall" MCQs ("what is the C construct for creating a loop?"), as these are the concepts introduced in the course. Yet such questions can hardly be expected to generate animated discussion or student anticipation. Instead, many of our questions applied core constructs to determine whether students really understand how they work in practice.

6.1 Question: Recursion

We used the example here (Figure 5) in the third lecture on recursion. The first recursion lecture introduced the terminology and concepts of recursive flow, and the second provided several typical examples of recursion (reversing a number, finding the length of a string, etc.). We intended the example given in Figure 5 to be a quick warm-up that would lead directly into a discussion of recursive backtracking algorithms. As in any good PI question, the distracters target common misconceptions: answer (a) targets a looping mental model of recursion [8], (c) seeks a misunderstanding of the base case, etc. However, nothing in this question was meant to be tricky, or even particularly challenging.

6.2 Results

The supposed "warm-up" question showed that students were not yet ready to proceed further. The individual vote yielded a correctness of 50%; the group vote, hampered by this paucity of student understanding, yielded a correctness of 48%. Rather than proceed with recursive backtracking, undoubtedly further distancing at least half of the students, the instructor decided to spend the rest of lecture on questions similar to that given in Figure 5. It took two further MCQs, with careful discussion and tracing, until the instructor felt that students understood the concept well enough (69% correctness on a group vote) to proceed with backtracking in the next class. Without the use of this MCQ, the instructor would have proceeded to backtracking too early, being rather out of touch with students' level of understanding. PI often gets lauded for its ability to engage students in discussion and improve their conceptual understanding. We should also keep in mind its ability to help create flexible, demand-driven class meetings, where the demands come directly from student responses.

7. DISCUSSION

The examples discussed here show instructors finding value in PI in the ways that it:

- Enables instructors to dynamically adapt class to address student misunderstandings
- Engages students in exploration and analysis of deep course concepts
- Explores arguments through team discussions to build effective, appropriate communication skills

Through discussions among the authors, we identified experiences not reported in other disciplines. In many PI studies, deep understanding is the primary goal with student discussion a means to that goal. In computing, we believe PI both improves student understanding *and* fosters teamwork and communication skills. In our instructors' experience, the communication skills fostered through PI moved to the foreground.

Clearly, one of the benefits our instructors value is the *ability of PI to support students in explicit training of analysis and argumentation skills*. The focus of much of computing education is on producing: write a program, build a model, or develop a proof. One of the benefits of teaching computing is that we often rely on students' experiences with "programming projects" to foster deep understanding of concepts (hence OS simulators, processor design projects, etc.). However, common practice rewards the completion of (working) projects and products. It rarely evaluates the process and even more rarely assesses the analysis or understanding underlying those works. PI seems a natural model for embedding such desirable learning goals into existing coursework. While the classroom experience is a dramatic change from standard lecture formats, it is easy to implement in large scale, standard-seating arrangements, and does not require dramatic change to the course content.

Helping computing students develop teamwork skills is critical. *PI dramatically increases the emphasis on teamwork and communication skills.* Although different courses and instructors will vary, students in PI classrooms anecdotally spend 30-50% of lecture periods in small-group discussion, with additional time spent listening to the class-wide analysis and discussion. While we know of no examples where students doing PI are directly evaluated on their discussions in class, it is not challenging to imagine various ways it could be done.

Both of these findings lead to the single most important and simplest advice we have for instructors developing PI questions:

Create questions based around what you want students to be thinking and analyzing - if possible in ways that elucidate the process. For once in computing, getting the right output is of notably lesser importance.

8. CONCLUSIONS

This work seeks to encourage the adoption of PI in computer science classrooms by providing experience reports from PI instructors. Instructors reflect on the value of PI to monitor student understanding, engage them meaningfully with deep course concepts, and promote development of appropriate argument skills. We propose that widespread utilization of PI across the computing curriculum provides a fantastic opportunity to explicitly support student training in analysis, argumentation, communication, and teamwork skills.

9. ACKNOWLEDGEMENTS

This work was supported in part by the UK HEA-ICS.

10. REFERENCES

[1] Beatty, I. D., Gerace, W. J., Leonard, W.J., and Dufresne, R. J. Designing effective questions for classroom response system teaching. American Journal of Physics 74, 2006.

[2] Caldwell, J. E. Clickers in the large classroom: Current research and best-practice tips. CBE-Life Sciences Education 6, 2007.

[3] Carter, P. An experiment with online instruction and active learning in an introductory computing course for engineers: JiTT meets CS. 14th Western Canadian Conference on Computing Education, 2009.

[4] Crouch, C. H., and Mazur, E. Peer instruction: Ten years of experience and results. American Journal of Physics 69, 2001.

[5] Cutts, Q., Carbone, A., and van Haaster, K. Using an Electronic Voting System to Promote Active Reflection on Coursework Feedback. In Proceedings of Intl. Conf. on Computers in Education, Melbourne, Australia, 2004.

[6] Hake, R. R. Interactive-engagement vs. traditional methods: A six-thousand-student survey of mechanics test data for introductory physics courses. American Journal of Physics 66 (1), 1998.

[7] Knight, J. K. and Wood, W. B. Teaching more by lecturing less. Cell Biology Education 4, 2005.

[8] Ma, L., Ferguson, J., Roper, M., and Wood, M. Investigating the viability of mental models held by novice programmers. In Proceedings of the 38th SIGCSE technical symposium on computer science education, 2007.

[9] Pargas, R. P. and Shah, D. M. Things are clicking in computer science courses. In Proceedings of the 37th SIGCSE technical symposium on Computer science education, 2006.

[10] Simon, B., Kohanfars, M., Lee, J, Tamayo, K., and Cutts, Q. Experience report: Peer instruction in introductory computing. In Proceedings of the 41st SIGCSE technical symposium on computer science education, 2010.

[11] Smith, M., Wood, W., Adams, W., Wieman, C., Knight, J., Guild, N., Su, T. Why Peer Discussion Improves Student Performance on In-Class Concept Questions. Science 323, 2009.

[12] Wieman, C. and the staff of the CU and UBC Science Education Initiatives. Clicker Resource Guide, http://cwsei.ubc.ca.

[13] Zingaro, D. Experience report: Peer instruction in remedial computer science. In Proceedings of the 22nd World Conference on Educational Multimedia, Hypermedia & Telecommunications, 2010.

CoMoTo - the Collaboration Modeling Toolkit

Charlie Meyer, Cinda Heeren, Eric Shaffer, and Jon Tedesco
cemeyer2@illinois.edu, c-heeren@illinois.edu, shaffer1@illinois.edu, tedesco1@illinois.edu
University of Illinois at Urbana-Champaign

ABSTRACT

We are excited to introduce CoMoTo – the Collaboration Modeling Toolkit – a new, web-based application that expands and enhances well-known software similarity detection systems. CoMoTo is an end-to-end data management, analysis, and visualization system whose purpose is to assist instructors of courses requiring programming exercises to monitor and investigate the extent of student collaboration, both allowed and illicit. We describe CoMoTo's interface, which was designed to facilitate scrutiny of collaboration data projected along student, course, assignment, etc. attributes, and to allow for interactive visualization of pairwise similarity measures via a dynamic graph. We also elaborate on the details of CoMoTo's implementation. Finally, we briefly discuss two use cases that foreshadow CoMoTo's broad utility in student code analysis, not only for plagiarism detection, but also for investigating early student coding styles, and for evaluating software similarity detection systems, themselves.

Categories and Subject Descriptors: K.3.2 [Computer and Information Science Education]: Computer Science Education

General Terms: Reliability, Human Factors.

Keywords: Program Similarity, Pedagogy

1. INTRODUCTION

As educators, we spend countless hours adapting our interactions with students so as to maximize learning, and yet we still have very little insight into the way students work and the way they think when we are not there. In this paper we describe CoMoTo – the Collaboration Modeling Toolkit – a web-based software similarity visualization and analysis tool we have developed with the goal of adding value to the output from well-known source code similarity detection systems. Such systems have become an important tool in Computer Science education. While they are most commonly used in programming courses to detect plagiarism, a deeper analysis of code similarity reveals common programming styles among students, and even the sociology of how collaboration networks develop and function within a class. It is this richer understanding of student work that we achieve via CoMoTo.

The genesis of CoMoTo corresponds to our need to organize and understand software similarity system results when we applied it to student solutions to programming assignments. Course policy allowed constrained and cited collaboration, so we had an immediate need to assure that the course policy was being followed, and we wanted to avoid manual scrutiny in favor of a more complete and reliable evaluation. The output from the system gave us pairwise similarity measures for each pair of students in the class. We represented this output as a graph where each node was a student, and edges between pairs of students existed if their code similarity measure exceeded some reasonable threshold. This first, primitive implementation of a graphical visualization of software similarity results revealed that we had an opportunity to discover much more about student learning. The size of our course and many semesters of archived student code submissions provided us with an excellent and challenging testbed within which to develop our analytical tools. Since then, the software has been packaged into a end-to-end system that allows for simple student source code entry, flexible choice of software similarity detection system, many different projections of the similarity data, and interactive graphical visualizations.

This paper is organized as follows: Section 2 provides the background necessary to understand CoMoTo and describes related work, Section 3 is a tour of CoMoTo's interface and data flow, Section 4 is a technical description of CoMoTo's implementation, Section 5 briefly describes two use cases for CoMoTo's analysis, and Section 6 suggests future work.

2. BACKGROUND

Numerous similarity detection systems have been described in research literature. A good survey describing software similarity detection has been written by Roy and Cordy [11]. Most modern similarity detection systems begin by converting the source code into a token sequence. Similarity detection is then accomplished by measuring the similarity of sequences. How this measurement is performed is the main differentiator among these systems. YAP [15], JPlag [5] and the Measure of Similarity System (MOSS) [12] from Stanford all work in this manner. MOSS is perhaps the most widely used such system and is the tool we began using in our large introductory data structures course approximately 2 years ago.

There have been several studies published regarding the use of similarity detection to discover software plagiarism. Prechelt et al [4] report on their experience using JPlag. In this study, JPlag correctly identified more than 90 percent of the known plagiarism instances while demonstrating acceptable run-time efficiency. The authors also detail a taxonomy of plagiarism techniques they encountered and the relative success of each. In another recent study, Wise [14] compares the relative merits of Plague and YAP. While slower, YAP was seen as easier to use and arguably more accurate in detecting plagiarised code. To our knowledge, there has been no prior published study regarding the efficacy of MOSS. Moreover, our study differs from the others mentioned here because we are interested in explaining code similarity, whatever its cause, rather than focussing strictly on plagiarism.

MOSS employs a local document fingerprinting algorithm called *winnowing*, the details of which can be found in [12]. Offered as service on the Web, the input to MOSS is multiple sets of source code with each set corresponding to a distinct program (submitted by a student in our case). MOSS proceeds to measure the similarity between each program, generating a similarity score between 0 and 100 for each pair. In our usage, the top 500 most similar pairs are reported along with highlighting of the similar portions of code. As one would expect, MOSS is sophisticated and ignores whitespace and naming differences. It also allows for the blocking of certain parts of the code from comparison. This is useful if the submitted source code contains boilerplate or instructor-provided code.

We describe the primary course for which CoMoTo was designed because the use cases of Section 4 are motivated in part by the course structure. At our university, CS2 is composed of a mini-course in C++, followed by an intensive and classical treatment of data structures. Enrollment varies between 200 and 300 students per semester. Gender balance in the course is typically 15% female, and nearly all students are traditional aged. The course is required for Computer Science and Computer Engineering students, and as such, the enrollment is typically $\frac{1}{3}$ CS majors, $\frac{1}{3}$ Computer Engineering majors and $\frac{1}{3}$ other (though almost all are mathematical sciences or engineering).

In a typical semester, 30% of a student's grade is determined by his/her completion of programming assignments, of which 7 are assigned. In general, the assignments are considered challenging. Students are encouraged to work in small groups (policy varies across semesters), and they are required to cite their collaborators.

3. INTERFACE AND DATA FLOW

CoMoTo enhances the basic source code comparison features of Moss in several ways. A diagram summarizing the data flow of the system is found in Figure 1.

Through its web interface, CoMoTo facilitates simple data import from the Subversion [13] version control system, which we use to manage student programming assignment archiving and submission. This integration is a marked improvement from the original interface to MOSS, and it can easily be reconfigured to handle a variety of code collection mechanisms.

In CoMoTo, all data associated with MOSS analysis is accumulated, stored, and maintained in the tool. Code submissions are saved in CoMoTo until they are explicitly deleted, eliminating the need for repeated source code import over many analyses. This simplifies comparison of current student submissions for a given assignment with student submissions for a same or similar assignment from past semesters of a given course. Likewise, the pairwise similarity measures and highlighted code provided by MOSS are also saved in CoMoTo until deleted by the user, allowing for accurate record keeping across many offerings of a course.

CoMoTo projects and filters the MOSS analysis in many different ways. Initially, the tool parses the output of the MOSS engine partitioning the pairwise results into a report that indicates whether matching programs were submitted during the same semester, between different semesters, or optionally, whether a program matches an instructor supplied solution. These partitioned results can be filtered even farther. For example, users can limit the display to only show source code matches where at least one of the submissions comes from the current semester, limit the display to only show matches which meet a minimum threshold for similarity, or limit the display to only show a specific number of matches for any given student. In addition, CoMoTo can optionally parse student names from specific meta-data files which instruct the tool to regard certain groups of students as partners when running the analysis. This allows instructors to effectively monitor collaboration when limited group work is acceptable. Figure 2 shows the analysis page corresponding to a single student. Of particular interest is the list at the bottom of the screen of all significant similarity measures associated with that student. At a glance, an instructor can tell whether the student consistently works with the same partner(s) across multiple MPs, or whether he/she violates course policy, for example.

Finally, all CoMoTo's analyses are sent to an interactive graphical visualization that allows the instructor to navigate the data from many different perspectives and configurations. A rudimentary screenshot is given in Figure 3.

We require that student work be submitted in one of two possible formats, either via file archive or from a Subversion repository. In both cases, we prescribe that the student code must be arranged so that each student has a separate directory at the root of the archive or repository, and that within that student directory there is a directory for each programming assignment. Instructor-provided code should be formatted similarly. Beyond that, there are no restrictions on the structure of the student code.

4. IMPLEMENTATION

CoMoTo is a web-based tool, which makes it available to anyone with a web browser (in contrast to Moss which is

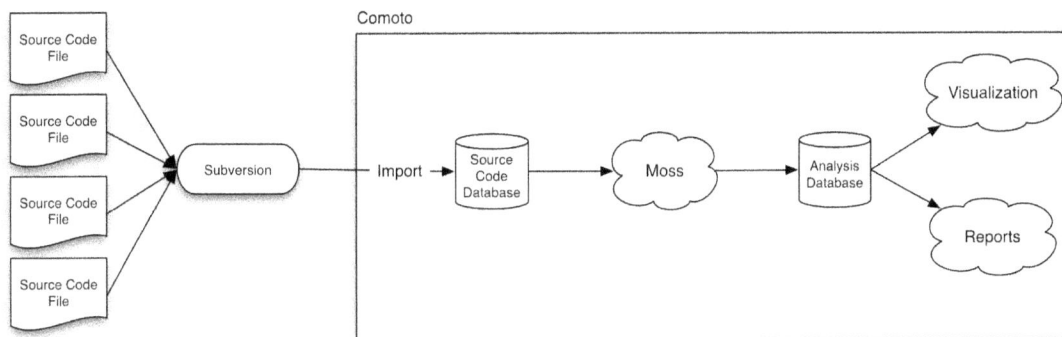

Figure 1: *CoMoTo data flow diagram.*

designed for terminal use). We built CoMoTo using the Pylons [8] MVC framework which allowed us to incorporate many other Python libraries into the tool to enhance its feature set. We utilize Pygments [6] for source code syntax highlighting, pygraphviz [7] for generating graphical visualizations of our analysis data, pysvn [9] for integration with Subversion , matplotlib [2] for generating statistical charts of our analysis data and python-ldap [10] for integration with the university directory. We utilize the MySQL [3] database engine to store and query data. For privacy reasons, we have chosen to license our own copy of Moss for use with CoMoTo so we can run all analysis locally and ameliorate concerns about confidential student information leaving university resources. Lastly, CoMoTo provides a XML-RPC based API allowing others to write their own tools or front-ends that utilize the CoMoTo functionality and/or data. We are currently developing an interactive Java-based visualization of the CoMoTo data which utilizes this API to interact with the tool.

In order to deploy a copy of CoMoTo, a dedicated server is recommended due to the high resource usage of the tool when performing analysis or generating visualizations of the data. We currently have our production copy of CoMoTo deployed on a virtual machine, configured with a four core Intel Xeon processor and four gigabytes of memory. During normal usage, the database back-end uses about a quarter of our system's main memory, and one of the four cores is at full utilization. Memory requirements are pushed when generating visualizations of our data using Graphviz. Our machine is running CentOS 5.5 and CoMoTo runs on top of the stock Python 2.4 distribution that comes bundled with the operating system. We installed several libraries as mentioned above to support the tool. We serve CoMoTo using a Paste HTTP server proxied behind a public facing Apache HTTP server. The Apache server is used to serve all static content and provide university-integrated authentication, while the Paste server serves up all the dynamic content and runs the core of the tool.

5. USE CASES

We anticipate that CoMoTo will be used to answer research questions about the form and extent of student collaboration in programming courses, and to investigate the *differences* between student code, but we would be remiss if we avoided

mentioning its utility in detecting and processing infractions of academic integrity. This section briefly discusses two case studies that begin to tell the story of the current and future value of the tool. These examples should be viewed as a reflective proof-of-concept, rather than rigorous research.

5.1 Plagiarism Detection

It is a sad truth that too many of our students do not follow our course and departmental policies on appropriate collaboration. In any given semester, approximately 25% of CS2 students are flagged by CoMoTo (via MOSS) for infractions of academic integrity due to plagiarism. Every flagged code submission is further scrutinized for some piece of convincing evidence, or a "tell", which invariably exists. (In the very rare case that a tell cannot be found, an accusation is not made–that is, we do not solely rely on CoMoTo to determine plagiarism.) In a class of 100s of students, this translates to dozens of accusations, which in turn translates into a similar number of 20 minute instructor-student conversations. It is in these conversations where CoMoTo has a profoundly positive effect on our course.

Early in a typical conversation, after explaining the charges of plagiarism, our CS2 instructor shows CoMoTo's graphical visualization of the similarity measures. Invariably, when a student identifies himself/herself with a node in the graph that is connected to others in a manner that is disallowed in course policy, a confession and explanation are forthcoming. Once that step is out of the way, the meeting moves past the infraction itself and the focus changes to advising and assisting the student toward a successful completion of the course. In the past four semesters, only 5 students (of over 100) have persisted in denying that they cheated, and of those 5, *none* have formally protested the penalty assessed against them (typically the loss of a letter grade in the course).

While it is unfortunate to speak with students in the context of cheating, anecdotally, the effect of the instructor-student interaction is very positive.

5.2 Coding Style

The very first time we applied CoMoTo to a student programming assignment in CS2, we were shocked at how *dissimilar* student code really is. The assignment in question was a

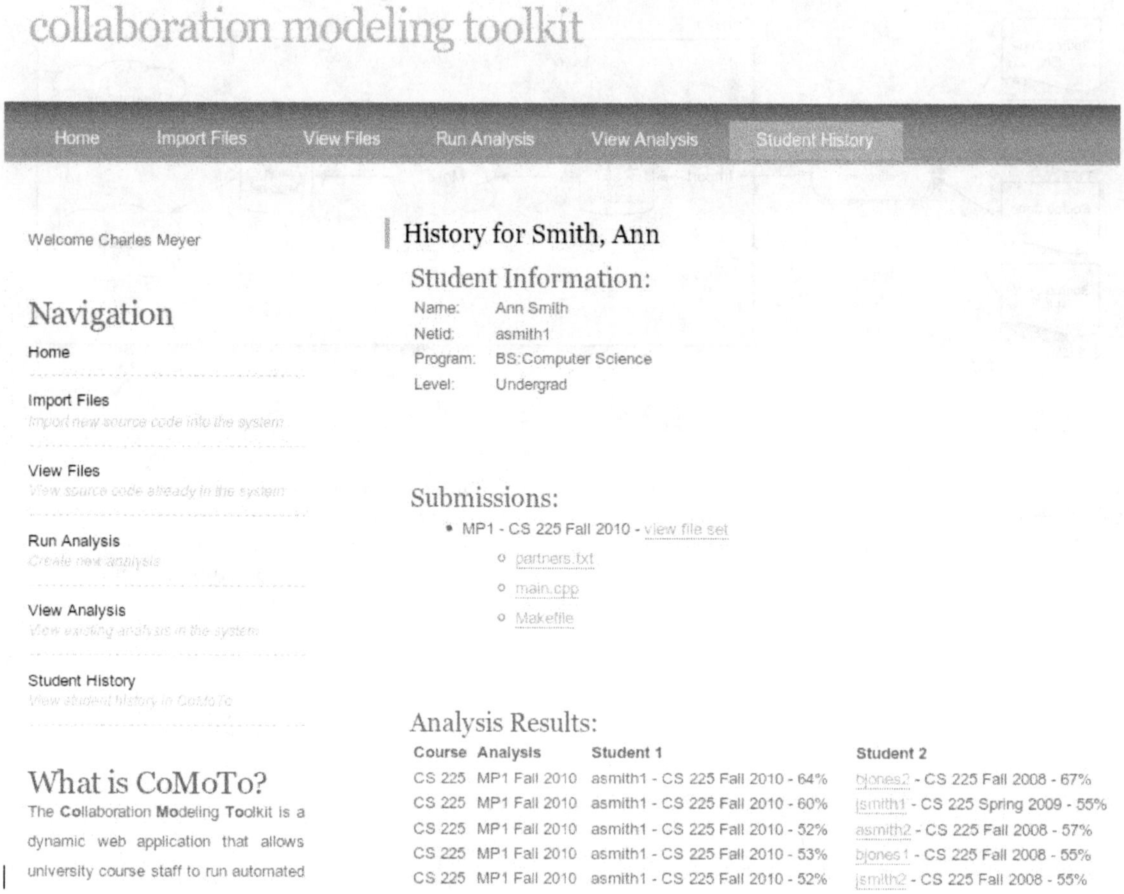

collaboration modeling toolkit

Home | Import Files | View Files | Run Analysis | View Analysis | Student History

Welcome Charles Meyer

Navigation

Home
Import new source code into the system

Import Files
Import new source code into the system

View Files
View source code already in the system

Run Analysis
Create new analysis

View Analysis
View existing analysis in the system

Student History
View student history in CoMoTo

What is CoMoTo?

The **Co**llaboration **Mo**deling **To**olkit is a dynamic web application that allows university course staff to run automated

History for Smith, Ann

Student Information:

Name:	Ann Smith
Netid:	asmith1
Program:	BS:Computer Science
Level:	Undergrad

Submissions:

- MP1 - CS 225 Fall 2010 - view file set
  - partners.txt
  - main.cpp
  - Makefile

Analysis Results:

Course	Analysis	Student 1	Student 2
CS 225	MP1 Fall 2010	asmith1 - CS 225 Fall 2010 - 64%	bjones2 - CS 225 Fall 2008 - 67%
CS 225	MP1 Fall 2010	asmith1 - CS 225 Fall 2010 - 60%	jsmith1 - CS 225 Spring 2009 - 55%
CS 225	MP1 Fall 2010	asmith1 - CS 225 Fall 2010 - 52%	asmith2 - CS 225 Fall 2008 - 57%
CS 225	MP1 Fall 2010	asmith1 - CS 225 Fall 2010 - 53%	bjones1 - CS 225 Fall 2008 - 55%
CS 225	MP1 Fall 2010	asmith1 - CS 225 Fall 2010 - 52%	jsmith2 - CS 225 Fall 2008 - 55%

Figure 2: *Screen shot of student data.*

very simple image manipulation task, wherein the students were asked to rotate an image by 180 degrees. They used an image library to read the bitmap data into a two dimensional array of pixels. Beyond that, the solution required a pair of nested `for` loops, some assignment statements to swap pixels, and a call to a library function to write the data into a new bitmap file. We expected the CoMoTo analysis to cluster all the students into a complete graph, because we were certain they would all write the same 20 lines of code. In fact that was not at all the case. Perhaps due to a fairly loose collaboration policy, there were a few small cliques in the graph, but most notably, there were very few edges in the graph at all, for a reasonable similarity measure (30%).

From a pedagogic standpoint, the lack of similarity among solutions indicates that even after taking CS1 the students did not produce idiomatic code in response to a common programming problem. It has been argued, by Kernighan and Ritchie [1] among others, that writing idiomatic code is important from a software engineering standpoint. Employing shared idioms makes source code more easily understood and maintained, increasing programmer efficiency and reducing the number of bugs introduced later in the software life-cycle. Even though our problem was simple and the code was short, very few students had significantly matched solutions. This result suggests an area ripe for improvement in our early courses, and in this case, CoMoTo would be a useful tool for assessing the effectiveness of new teaching strategies designed to give students a more common approach to writing fundamental constructs.

6. FUTURE WORK

CoMoTo is now tried and tested enough to be deployed broadly, and to be made available to others who may find it useful. We are ready to discuss the logistics of adapting the tool for a general audience and are excited about its potential.

Our next research objective is to prescribe an experimental methodology that employs CoMoTo to answer questions about student collaboration patterns with statistical reliability and validity. To do this we intend 1) to consult with statisticians so we understand the inferences we can reasonably make, and 2) to incorporate measures of student performance into the tool so we can measure the effectiveness of different collaboration models. Once the methodology is established, we will be in a position to pose and answer a host of questions about student code development and collaboration practices.

7. ACKNOWLEDGMENTS

We thank the previous members of the CoMoTo team, Alex Lambert, Michael Hines, Kevin Phillips, and Joe Gonzalez for their work on the project.

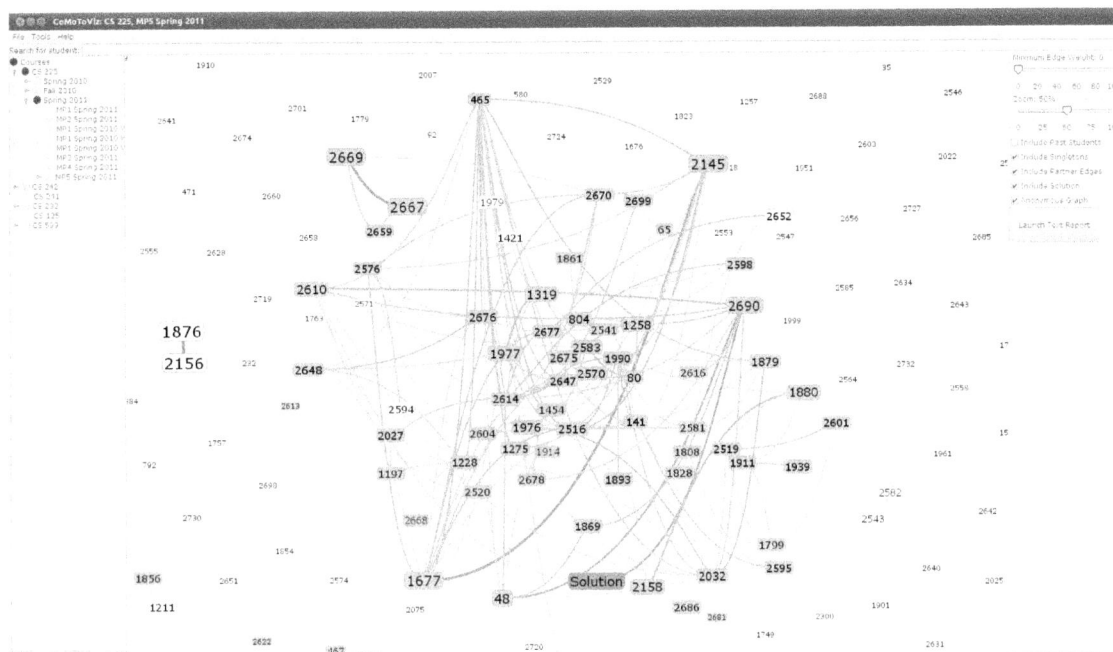

Figure 3: *Screen shot of interactive visualization page.*

8. REFERENCES

[1] B. W. Kernighan and R. Pike. *The Practice of Programming.* Addison-Wesley Inc, 1999.

[2] matplotlib. http://matplotlib.sourceforge.net/.

[3] MySQL. http://www.mysql.com/.

[4] L. Prechelt, G. Malpohl, and M. Philippsen. Finding plagiarisms among a set of programs with jplag. 8(11):1016–1038, 2002.

[5] L. Prechelt, G. Malpohl, and M. Phlippsen. Jplag: Finding plagiarisms among a set of programs. Technical report, 2000.

[6] Pygments. http://pygments.org/.

[7] pygraphviz. http://networkx.lanl.gov/pygraphviz/.

[8] Pylons. http://pylonshq.com/.

[9] pysvn. http://pysvn.tigris.org/.

[10] python ldap. http://www.python-ldap.org/.

[11] C. K. Roy and J. R. Cordy. A survey on software clone detection research. *SCHOOL OF COMPUTING TR 2007-541, QUEENÔS UNIVERSITY*, 115, 2007.

[12] S. Schleimer. Winnowing: Local algorithms for document fingerprinting. In *Proceedings of the 2003 ACM SIGMOD International Conference on Management of Data 2003*, pages 76–85. ACM Press, 2003.

[13] Subversion. http://subversion.apache.org/.

[14] M. J. Wise. Detection of similarities in student programs: Yap'ing may be preferable to plague'ing. In *SIGCSE '92: Proceedings of the twenty-third SIGCSE technical symposium on Computer science education*, pages 268–271, New York, NY, USA, 1992. ACM.

[15] M. J. Wise. Yap3: Improved detection of similarities in computer program and other texts. In *SIGCSEB: SIGCSE Bulletin (ACM Special Interest Group on Computer Science Education*, pages 130–134. ACM Press, 1996.

A Marking Language for the Oto Assignment Marking Tool

Guy Tremblay
Dépt. d'informatique, UQAM
C.P. 8888, Succ. Centre-Ville
Montréal, QC, Canada
H3C 3P8
tremblay.guy@uqam.ca

Paul Lessard
Dépt. d'informatique, UQAM
lessard.paul@courrier.uqam.ca

ABSTRACT

Marking programming assignments involves a lot of work, and with large classes, the feedback provided to students through marking is often rather limited and late.

Oto is a customizable and extensible marking tool that provides support for the submission and marking of assignments. Oto aims at reducing the marking workload and, also, at providing early feedback to students.

In this paper, we present Oto's new *marking language* and give an overview of its implementation as a Domain-Specific Language.

Categories and Subject Descriptors

K.3.1 [**Computer Uses in Education**]: Computer-assisted instruction

General Terms

Languages, Verification

Keywords

Educational Software, Automated Marking, Domain-Specific Language, Scripting

1. INTRODUCTION

Marking computer programs in programming courses requires a lot of work, as it involves dealing with many aspects: the program must be tested to ensure it exhibits the correct behavior; the text of the program and its documentation must be read to evaluate the program structure, style and adherence to standards, etc.

For large numbers of students, the feedback provided may be somewhat limited and, furthermore, may come late in the students' learning process. For instance, when a student finally receives his/her graded assignment, the topic dealt by this assignment may already be somewhat "outdated." Furthermore, feedback from marking does not help students

who misunderstood some key aspects of the problem: they will simply get low marks. In other words, the typical approach to marking programming assignments requires a lot of effort from the instructors (or teaching assistants), yet provides little timely feedback to students.

Various tools providing support for marking programming assignments are available: tools dealing with administrative aspects (submission and management of assignments) [2], metrics-based evaluation [11], testing of programs [3, 8], etc.—see [13, Sect. 2] for a more detailed presentation of these and other tools.

In a previous paper [13], we presented Oto, a tool providing support for the submission and marking of programming assignments. Oto can be used to provide early feedback to students, even *before* the final submission. Oto has also been designed to be *customizable*, *generic*, and *extensible*.

Customizability in Oto is supported through the use of *marking scripts*, allowing the instructor to specify the various steps required in marking a specific group of assignments. Since its initial release, Oto has been used in a number of programming courses. This experience led us to identify some of the weaknesses and shortcomings of our initial implementation. More precisely, the expressiveness of Oto's initial marking language—where marking scripts were somewhat similar to makefiles—was *too limited*, making it awkward to use Oto except for simple marking tasks. This led to the design and implementation of a new marking script language, implemented as a *Domain-Specific Language* (DSL). In this paper, we present this new marking script language.

Domain-specific language (DSL)

Fowler, in a recent book, defines a DSL as follows [4, p. 27]:

> *Domain-specific language* (noun): a computer programming language of limited expressiveness focused on a particular domain.

Thus, although a DSL is a programming language, it is not a general-purpose one. Rather, a DSL aims at solving a particular class of problems, supporting abstractions specific to the application domain.

There are two main types of DSL [4]:

- External DSL: Such a DSL possesses its own syntax, distinct from a specific host language.

- Internal DSL: Such a DSL is expressed within another host language, providing a language (or sub-language) with its own flavor, though it uses, and is constrained by, the host language's syntax.

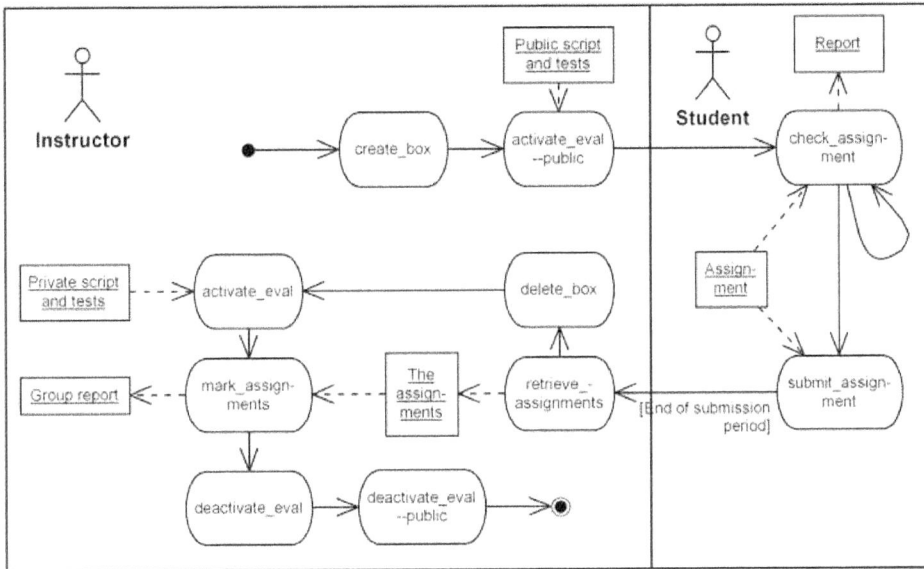

Figure 1: Activity diagram describing a typical use of Oto.

A DSL, whether external or internal, can be a complete and independent language. An internal DSL can also be *fragmentary*, where "little bits of DSL are used inside the host language code [thus] enhancing the host language with additional features" [4, p. 32]. Oto's new marking language is such a fragmentary internal DSL, expressed in Ruby. Thus, one must have a minimal understanding of Ruby to write marking scripts. However, this also implies that marking scripts can benefit from Ruby's expressiveness.

Outline of paper

The remainder of this paper is organized as follows. Section 2 presents Oto's key functionalities, including its support for program testing, It also describes how customizability and extensibility are attained, namely, with marking scripts expressed in Oto's *marking language* along with various *extension modules*. Section 3 then gives an overview of Oto's marking language implementation. Finally, Section 4 presents some preliminary experience report

2. OVERVIEW OF Oto AND ITS MARKING LANGUAGE

This section gives an overview of Oto's key functionalities and describes how Oto is made both customizable and extensible. For more details, see [13] (or http://oto.uqam.ca/).

2.1 High-level View

Fig. 1 presents an activity diagram describing a typical scenario for using Oto.[1] The instructor first creates a submission box (create_box) and defines appropriate *evaluations* (activate_eval):

- A public evaluation, used by students to perform a *preliminary verification* of their solutions. Such an evaluation provides students with early feedback, ensuring that they are "*on the right track.*"

- A private evaluation, available only to the instructor and used to mark the submitted assignments.

To each evaluation must be associated some tests as well as a *marking script*; the tests can be JUnit-like tests [1] or tests based on textual comparison (see Section 2.2).

When a student uses the public evaluation to obtain feedback on his/her program (check_assignment), the student's program is processed in the student's space and no trace is kept of that verification.[2] The student can also *submit* his/her assignment (submit_assignment) in the submission *box* created by the instructor (create_box).

Finally, the instructor can obtain the submitted assignments (retrieve_assignments) and mark them (mark_assignments) using the private evaluation. Once the due date is over, the submission box (delete_box) and the evaluations (deactivate_eval) can be removed.

An evaluation, private or public, generally consists of various elements, e.g., test programs, auxiliary files, and a *marking script* (activate_eval).

Oto is *generic*, *customizable*, and *extensible*. Generic means Oto can handle assignments written in various languages. Customizable means it is not tied to a specific marking procedure: given a library of marking *tasks*, one can specify how to mark a group of assignments using a marking script. Finally, extensible means that various kinds of tasks can be included in marking scripts by designing appropriate *extension modules*, for example, tasks to compile a program, to test it, etc. These characteristics are attained using two different mechanisms, *marking scripts* and *extension modules*, which we describe below. But before, we describe the ways in which Oto supports program testing, a key component of programming assignments marking.

2.2 Program Testing

Oto provides support for testing in two major ways, both defined through appropriate extension testing modules. First,

---

[1]Command names have been translated in English: Oto's commands are in French, although aliases can easily be defined.

[2]For debugging purposes, Oto logs the commands that are executed, but not the students' files themselves.

Oto provides modules for unit testing using specific *test frameworks*, for example, Java/JUnit [10], Haskell/HUnit [9].

Second, Oto provides modules for *system level tests* based on textual comparison of output. One such module (`test_pep8`) is language specific (Pep/8 assembler [14]), whereas the other (`test_filter`) applies to any executable *filter* program—a program that only uses the standard I/O streams. Each *test case* is specified using two text files—test data and expected result—and a *test suite* is composed of many such test cases. For each test case, the program is executed with the specified test data and the result is compared with the expected result using Unix's `diff` command.

2.3 Oto's Marking Language: Marking Scripts

A *marking script* describes the tasks that need to be performed to mark a group of assignments. Fig. 2 shows a marking script whose purpose is to mark a group of Java assignments: the student program (`Account.java`) is compiled and then tested using a JUnit test class provided by the instructor (`TestAccount`). Fig. 3 shows the output produced by the script execution for one specific assignment.

```
group.each do |a|
  compile = compile_javac(a) {
    :file >> "Account.java"      # Submitted by student
  }

  ensure compile.succeeded?, "*** Did not compile?!"

  test = test_junit(a) {
    :class >> "TestAccount"      # Provided by instructor
  }

  penalty = 100 / test[:nbtests]

  a["Final mark"] = 100 - penalty * test[:nbfailures]

  a["Test details"] = test[:details]
end

puts mk_complete_report(group)
```

Figure 2: A marking script for an `Account` Java class.

```
Team:      ANOJ
Deposit:   2010-11-17 at 08:25
Submitter: anon_jo
Name:      Joe Anonymous
Email:     anonymous.joe@courrier.uqam.ca

RESULTS:
  Final mark:
      100

  Test details:
      JUnit version 4.5
      ...
      Time: 0,008

      OK (3 tests)
```

Figure 3: Example report for one assignment.

A marking script expressed in Oto's new marking language is, in fact, a Ruby script [12] that uses a number of operations specific to Oto. For instance, the `group` identifier denotes the collection of assignments to be marked, whereas

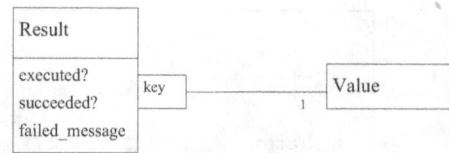

Figure 4: Partial description of a `Result` produced by a marking task (UML class diagram).

the `each` method allows to process, iteratively, each of the assignments from that group, where `a` denotes the current assignment being processed.

For each assignment, two tasks are performed: the first to compile the student program (`compile_javac(a)`), the second to test it (`test_junit(a)`). The second task, however, is executed only if an appropriate precondition (`ensure`) is satisfied, i.e., compilation succeeded without error.

The assignment handled by a task is specified as an explicit argument, e.g., `compile_javac(a)`, whereas additional arguments and options are specified using keyword parameters, e.g., `:file >> "Account.java"` indicates which file to compile from the student's submitted files.

The result produced by a task execution is an object modeled as in Fig. 4. Such a result has two different kinds of attributes: *i*) some that apply to *any task*, e.g., `compile.succeeded?`; *ii*) some that are specific to a task, accessed using Ruby's hash notation, e.g., `test[:nbtests]`.

The information to be included in the report for a specific assignment `a` is also specified using a hash, e.g., `a["Test details"] = test[:details]`. Finally, the report for all assignments is generated using `mk_complete_report(group)`—here, it is simply emitted on standard output (`puts`).

A marking script can use various predefined tasks to process an assignment; these are defined as *extension modules*.

2.4 Oto's Marking Tasks: Extension Modules

An extension module implements a marking task by playing a role of *proxy* between Oto and some external tools. For example, the `test_junit` extension module packages the information from the script (e.g., name of test class, optional classpath), executes the test class by running the `java` virtual machine, then analyzes the execution output to bind the task result attributes (Fig. 4) to the appropriate values.

Extension modules, as well as Oto itself, are written in Ruby [12]. Because Oto's initial target was introductory Java programming courses, it initially included only two modules [7]: `compile_javac` and `test_junit`. Since then, various other extension modules have been developed: see Figure 5. Most modules are *individual*, i.e., they process a single assignment, but other are *collective* modules, i.e., they process a whole group of assignments. *Reports*, although they do not generate structured results (only textual results or side-effects), are another kind of module.

3. IMPLEMENTATION OF OTO'S MARKING LANGUAGE

Implementing an external DSL requires building a parser to perform lexical and syntactic analysis, and to generate an appropriate intermediate representation that can be evaluated, through interpretation or code generation [4]. Implementing an internal DSL, however, is different: as the DSL

Individual modules	
compile_c	Compile C program.
compile_javac	Compile Java program.
test_filter	System-level test of *filter program*.
test_hunit	Test Haskell program using HUnit.
test_junit	Test Java program using JUnit.
test_pep8	Test Pep/8 assembler program.
Collective modules	
detect_plagiarism	Detect potential plagiarism between assignments (token stream similarity [6]).
generate_statistics	Compute various group statistics (e.g., average, distribution).
Report modules	
mk_complete_report	Generate complete and detailed (text) report for whole group.
send_email_report	Generate individual reports and email them to students.

Figure 5: Oto's extension modules and reports.

is *embedded* in a *host* language, it is analyzed and executed *through* that host language's processing.

Oto's marking language is a fragmentary internal DSL expressed in Ruby. Thus, an Oto marking script is a Ruby script. Such a marking script, however, is evaluated in a very specific context, called a *marking context*: Fig. 6 shows a (simplified) representation.

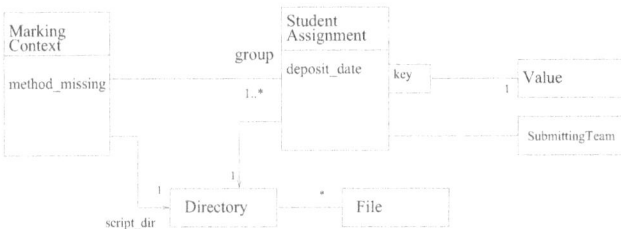

Figure 6: Marking context for an Oto script (UML class diagram).

Marking context

A marking context consists of a group of assignments to be marked, along with a directory (script_dir) containing various files provided by the instructor, e.g., marking script, test program, auxiliary files provided to the students, etc. To each student assignment is also associated a directory containing the files submitted by the student, along with information about the submitting team. The qualified association between StudentAssignment and Value (which could be any class) allows to keep track of information to be included in the report with respect to a specific student assignment.

Top-level command execution

Suppose we execute the following command,[3] where the content of file script.oto was shown in Fig. 2:

```
oto script.oto TestAccount.class *.tp_oto
```

The oto top-level program is essentially a dispatcher that recognizes the command to be executed, builds an appro-

---

³This command is shown in its Unix command line format. A Web interface is also available: http://oto.uqam.ca/

```
class CmdOtoMarkAssignments
def run( oto_script, aux_files, students_files )
  script ← Load script contained in oto_script file
  work_dir ← Create a temporary working directory
  Copy aux_files to work_dir
  Copy students_files to work_dir
  mc ← MarkingContext.new(...)
  mc.instance_eval(script)
  Clean up (remove work_dir)
end
```

Figure 7: Pseudocode for the run method from class CmdOtoMarkAssignments.

```
class MarkingContext
def method_missing( sym, *args, &block )
  if there exists an extension module named sym then
    student_files ← args[0]
    parameters ← evaluate parameters via block
    klass ← Get the class for extension sym
    ext ← Create a new instance of class klass
    res ← ext.execute( a, parameters, self )
    return res
  else if there is a report module named sym then
    ... Generate report ...
  else
    ... Evaluate sym as a Unix (bash) command ...
  end
end
```

Figure 8: Pseudocode for the method_missing **method from class** MarkingContext.

priate command object, then executes its run method (*command* pattern [5]). When the first argument to oto is a marking script instead of a command name, then this is interpreted as an invocation of the mark_assignments command. Thus, the run method shown in Fig. 7 is executed.

Setting the marking context

The key instruction in this run method is instance_eval [12]:

```
obj.instance_eval(aString) -> anObject
```

Evaluates a string containing Ruby source code [...] within the context of the receiver (obj). In order to set the context, the variable self is set to obj while the code is executing, giving the code access to obj's instance variables.

Here, this means the script from Fig. 2 *is evaluated in the context of* mc, the MarkingContext object for the assignments to be marked (*.tp_oto). The first expression to evaluate is then group.each do |a|...end, which iterates through the various student assignments.

Extensibility through dynamic invocation

Given a student submission bound to a, the next expression from the script compiles the Account.java file from a:

```
comp = compile_javac( a ) { :file >> "Account.java" }
```

To provide dynamic extensibility, extensions modules (such as compile_javac) are not known *a priori*. Instead, they are loaded at run-time by looking-up some specific directories. This behavior is obtained through *dynamic invocation*, using Ruby's method_missing mechanism, which allows to catch method invocations that are not found through regular method dispatch (class, super-class, etc.). In our case, method compile_javac is invoked on object mc. Since class

```
class OtoExtCompileJavac
def execute( a, parameters, marking_context )
  Set the arguments and options as specified
    by parameters and marking_context

  cmd ← "javac " + options + " " + a
  stdout, stderr ← Run cmd as a shell command

  res ← Create an appropriate Result object

  Analyze stdout/stderr and, among other things:
      res.succeeded? ← No fatal error encountered?
      res[:stdout] ← Information emitted on stdout

  return res
end
```

Figure 9: Pseudocode for the execute method from class OtoExtCompileJavac (proxy behavior).

MarkingContext and its super-classes do not define such a method, method_missing from mc is executed: see Fig. 8. In our example, it is called with the following arguments:

```
sym = :compile_javac
args = [ a ]
block = { :file >> "Account.java" }
```

The evaluation of the block object creates the proper bindings for the module parameters and options, as the ">>" operator has been defined to perform argument bindings.

Given a module name, canonical file and class names can be inferred, in this case, cmdoto_compile_javac.rb and CmdOto-CompileJavac. Fig. 9 shows the execute method from this latter class—called from ext.execute(...) in Fig. 8.

This latter method illustrates how an extension module acts as a proxy, here to the Java compiler: it builds and runs a shell command, creates a Result object, sets its various attributes by analyzing the results produced by the shell command execution, then returns that result—recall that a Result is modeled as in Fig. 4. Note that each student assignment is executed in a separate and clean environment, obtained through the work directory created in the run method from Fig. 7; a (configurable) time-out mechanism will also interrupt the student program if it consumes too much resources (CPU time or disk space).

Objects of class StudentAssignment (e.g., a) also have attributes that can be set within the script, for example:

```
a["Nb. errors"] = test[:nbfailures]
```

The information from the various student assignments can then be combined using a *report module*.

4. PRELIMINARY EXPERIENCE

Oto's new marking language was released in early fall 2010, although the first author used an early release during winter 2010. It has been in used in five courses (Assembly programming, Formal specification, Programming paradigms, Software construction, and Parallel programming) to handle assignments (groups of 30–50 students) written in seven different languages (Pep/8, OCL & Java, Haskell & Prolog, C, MPD).

The experience so far shows that the new language greatly eases the development of marking scripts: they are much more succinct and understandable, yet more expressive than the previous scripts (which were similar to simple makefiles). Furthermore, we also found that the DSL implementation makes it much easier to add new language features, a task which was quite complex in the previous implementation.

5. CONCLUSION AND FUTURE WORK

In this paper, we presented Oto's new marking language and described its implementation—as a fragmentary internal DSL in Ruby. This new release of Oto, as the earlier one, allows to provide early feedback to students and to reduce the marking workload. It is still generic, extensible as well as customizable. In fact, customizability is greatly enhanced, as Oto now provides a powerful and expressive scripting language, tailored to its specific application domain, namely, marking assignments.

As future work, we plan to expand Oto's marking language with new constructs, based on our experience in various courses and with various languages. Also, we already made available a number of script templates to help instructors define their own scripts, and we plan to add new templates as we develop them. We also intend to develop additional extension modules, for example, to evaluate *quality aspects* of programs (do they obey the required style guidelines or standards?), to evaluate the coverage of tests developed by students, etc. Again, the goal will not be to fully automate the marking process, but rather to provide support to instructors to help reduce the marking workload. Of course, these modules will also be made available to students, to provide them with early feedback on those other quality aspects.

6. REFERENCES

[1] K. Beck and E. Gamma. Test infected: Programmers love writing tests. *Java Report*, 3(7):37–50, 1998.

[2] K. Dawson-Howe. Automatic submission and administration of programming assignments. *SIGCSE Bulletin*, 28(2):40–42, 1996.

[3] D. Douce, D. Livingstone, and J. Orwell. Automatic test-based assessment of programming: A review. *ACM Journal on Educat. Resources in Comp.*, 5(3), Sept. 2005.

[4] M. Fowler. *Domain-Specific Languages*. Addison-Wesley, 2011.

[5] E. Gamma *et al*. *Design Patterns—Elements of Reusable Object-Oriented Software*. Addison-Wesley, 1995.

[6] D. Gitchell and N. Tran. Sim: A utility for detecting similarity in computer programs. *SIGCSE Bulletin*, 31(1):266–270, 1999.

[7] F. Guérin. Oto, un outil générique et extensible pour corriger les travaux de programmation. Master's thesis, Dép. d'Informatique, UQAM, oct. 2005.

[8] M. Joy, N. Griffiths, and R. Boyatt. The BOSS online submission and assessment system. *ACM Journal on Educat. Resources in Comp.*, 5(3), Sept. 2005.

[9] Hunit home page. http://hunit.sourceforge.net/, March 2011.

[10] Junit home page. http://www.junit.org/, March 2011.

[11] R. Leach. Using metrics to evaluate student programs. *SIGCSE Bulletin*, 27(2):41–48, 1995.

[12] D. Thomas and A. Hunt. *Programming Ruby: The Pragmatic Programmer's Guide*. Addison-Wesley, 2001.

[13] G. Tremblay, F. Guérin, A. Pons, and A. Salah. Oto, a generic and extensible tool for marking programming assignments. *Software—Practice and Experience*, 38(3):307–333, March 2008.

[14] J. Warford. *Computer Systems, fourth edition*. Jones & Bartlett, Publishers, 2010.

Supporting Student-generated Free-response Questions

Andrew Luxton-Reilly, Paul Denny, Beryl Plimmer, Daniel Bertinshaw
Department of Computer Science
The University of Auckland
Auckland, New Zealand
{andrew,paul,beryl}@cs.auckland.ac.nz | dber021@aucklanduni.ac.nz

ABSTRACT

Although a number of existing systems support student-generated multiple choice questions, such questions tend to focus on lower-order cognitive skills. Free response questions are frequently used to evaluate higher-order thinking, but supporting student-generated free-response questions is challenging. StudySieve is a web-based tool that extends student-generated questions to the free-response domain.

We report on the use of StudySieve for reviewing core content in three large undergraduate Computer Science courses. Students produce more content than required, provide feedback to their peers and report that they learn from question authoring, question answering, seeing the answers produced by their peers and evaluating those answers.

Categories and Subject Descriptors

K.3.2 [**Computers and Education**]: Computer and Information Science Education—*computer science education*

General Terms

Design, Human Factors

Keywords

StudySieve, question-generation, peer-review, free-response, student-generated, contributing student pedagogy, constructive evaluation

1. INTRODUCTION

Educators have long held the belief that students should not simply read (or listen) passively, but should instead be engaged in activities that encourage them to think about the content they are learning (e.g. [8]). One such activity is for students to generate questions that relate to the content they have learned.

A recent shift in the focus of education to student-centric practices [3] has seen a growing interest in use of technology to facilitate students contributing to the learning of their peers [9, 4]. Student-generated multiple-choice questions are supported by a number of web-based systems [2, 16, 15, 14, 6]. Studies of these systems have found a number of positive outcomes, including:

- students enjoy the experience of generating questions and using questions generated by their peers, they believe that it will help them learn, and they use the system more than required for assessment [6, 14];
- students who participate more frequently in question-generation and question-answering activities perform better in exams than those who engage less with the system, even when controlling for prior ability [2, 5];
- use of the system improves student confidence with content [16]; and,
- the repositories created by students are of a reasonable quality, that is, they contain questions that cover the course content adequately and vary in difficulty and complexity [7].

Although multiple choice questions can be an effective assessment and learning tool, particularly if students generate the questions [11], it is difficult to write multiple choice questions that address higher-order cognitive skills [12]. For example, it would be extremely difficult to create a multiple choice question that assessed the ability of a student to write programming code (a common task in CS1 courses). These kinds of questions require free-response answers.

StudySieve is a tool designed to extend the use of student-generated questions from the multiple-choice domain to *free response* questions. However, two central problems need to be addressed before student-generated free-response questions can be effectively supported.

1. Systems that support multiple choice questions can provide immediate feedback to a student answering a question, based on the alternative specified as correct by the author, and the aggregated responses of other students (i.e. students can see which are the most popular answers selected by other students). Feedback on the correctness and quality of answers to free-response questions must be provided by students themselves, and are difficult to automate.

2. Multiple choice questions that have the same solution can still be useful and valid questions within a single repository, as long as the alternatives differ. However, free-response questions that require the same solution in the same repository are redundant.

Previously, we investigated the feasibility of a tool that

supported student-generated free-response questions by tri-alling a prototype of StudySieve in a large introductory computing course. Although some students contributed more than required, we found that many students did not evaluate the content provided by peers. The repository was found to contain many duplicate questions, and students had difficulty finding appropriate questions to answer [10].

We have since reworked the interface and work-flow of StudySieve to address these problems. In this paper, we report on the revised interface, and we identify whether or not students in three large undergraduate courses value learning activities involving free response questions. Specifically, we answer the following questions:

- How do students feel about the use of student-generated *free-response* questions in undergraduate Computer Science courses?
- Do students use the questions generated by their peers for learning and revision?

2. SUPPORTING FREE-RESPONSE QUESTIONS

Based on observations of use during the first semester of 2010, StudySieve was redesigned to improve the work-flow, and the process of evaluation was structured to provide a greater degree of guidance. Additional functions were introduced to help students organize questions according to topics and to enable searching of the question content. Finally, a function to display questions with similar content was introduced to the question-authoring' page with the intention of reducing duplicate questions. The following subsections describe the revisions to StudySieve in more detail.

2.1 Creating a question

Guidelines have been introduced to remind students to check the quality of their question, and a preview of the question is displayed before submission is finalised. To help students find and organize relevant questions, the questions may be tagged with appropriate topics by the author. New tags may be entered if no suitable tag exists. At this stage only the author of a question may assign tags, but we plan to extend the system to allow other students to assign tags to a question during the evaluation phase.

To reduce the number of repeated questions, the question text is compared with existing questions in the database, and a list of similar questions is generated. Students can view any similar questions in a pop-up and may choose to alter their own question as a consequence. Figure 1 shows part of the new interface for adding a question.

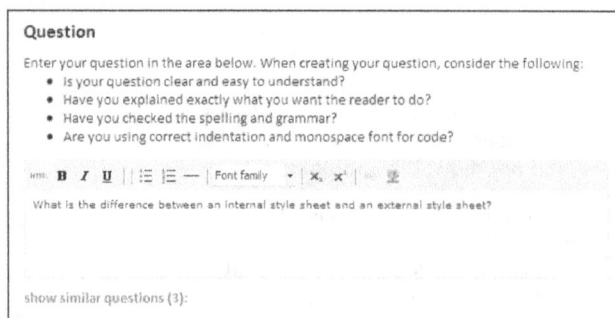

Figure 1: Adding a new question

2.2 Viewing all questions

To ensure that students can find relevant questions quickly, the questions contained in the repository are displayed in a single paginated list that can be sorted and filtered by various criteria. Students can choose to display only unanswered questions, questions they *have* answered, or all of the questions. In addition, the list can be filtered by the topics (tags) associated with each question, or a filtered list can be generated by searching the full text of each question for keywords.

The questions may be sorted according to the creation date, the number of answers, the ranking of the question (based on peer evaluations), or the difficulty of the question (based on peer evaluations). Figure 2 shows how the list of questions is displayed to students.

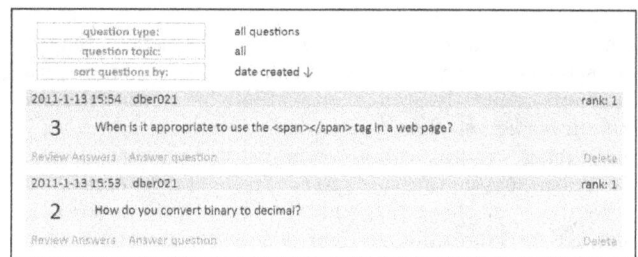

Figure 2: Viewing all questions

2.3 Answering questions and viewing peer answers

Commercial systems such as StackOverflow [1] that support user-generated questions and answers use peer review to identify the "best" answer by ensuring that all answers are visible. A user submitting an answer is able to view all current answers before they add their own contribution. However, in question-generation systems designed for educational purposes, students use the questions for drill and practice, and as such, any answers should remain hidden until the student attempts to answer the question. Only after an answer has been submitted should other answers be revealed.

2.4 Evaluating questions and answers

In the prototype, the process of evaluating questions and answers was optional. However, few students engaged with the evaluation phase. Systems that support multiple-choice questions can automatically generate feedback for students who answer questions, by reporting the correct option (as specified by the author of the question), and by aggregating responses of others. However, free-response questions are difficult to automatically evaluate, so students submitting an answer may obtain feedback by reflecting on the quality of their own answer with respect to peer answers, or must wait for peers to provide feedback to their own answer. It is therefore important to ensure that students are engaged with the evaluation process. In the revised interface, students are required to evaluate the question and three answers before they may return to the list of questions.

Whenever a student submits an answer to a question, they must evaluate the question by assigning a rating (on a 1–5 scale) to the usefulness of the question for studying the course material, and a second rating (on a 1–5 scale) to the difficulty level of the question. Once a rating is chosen, a histogram showing the ratings contributed by other students is revealed. Students have the opportunity to write some formative feedback to the question author, which is visible to all users, and can agree or disagree with other feedback provided by their peers.

Answers are evaluated by assigning a rating (on a 1–5 scale) to the correctness of the answer, and a second rating (also on a 1–5 scale) to how helpful the answer was. Similarly to the question evaluation, students may optionally provide formative feedback to the author of the answer and may agree or disagree with the feedback provided by their peers. Figure 3 shows the interface for evaluating an answer.

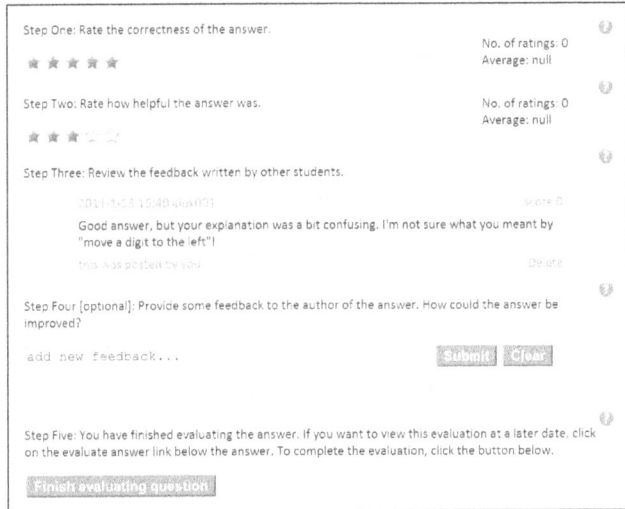

Figure 3: Evaluating an answer

3. METHODOLOGY

StudySieve was used in three large undergraduate courses (CS 111, CS 101 and CS 105) taught at The University of Auckland in the second semester of 2010. All students were provided with written information that explained the philosophy underlying student-generated content and a simple guide that outlined different kinds of questions. Students were required to submit questions and answers for a small portion (1%) of their final grade. Each course is briefly described here.

CS 111 A service course that provides non-majors with an introduction to computing concepts and their practical application.

CS 101 A standard introduction to programming in Java.

CS 105 A standard introduction to data structures and algorithms using Java. This course is normally taken by students who have completed CS 101.

During the last week of semester, a survey was distributed to students asking them to reflect on how the StudySieve tool impacted on their learning. Table 1 shows the survey questions. Questions 1–6 were rated on a 5-point Likert scale, while questions 7 and 8 were open-ended.

In addition to the student survey data, we analyse the logs of use, particularly with respect to non-assessed participation.

Q1	Writing questions helped me learn
Q2	Answering questions helped me learn
Q3	Viewing the answers of others helped me learn
Q4	Evaluating my questions and answers helped me learn
Q5	Evaluating others' questions and answers helped me learn
Q6	I would like to use the StudySieve tool in future courses
Q7	What was most helpful for your learning?
Q8	What improvements could be made?

Table 1: Survey questions used to evaluate student perceptions of StudySieve

4. RESULTS

In this section we report on the overall use of the system by students, and the survey results in each of the three courses.

For the purposes of this study, we define a student as being "active" in StudySieve if they have logged in and either created a question or answered a question. Table 2 shows the number of students enrolled in each course, the number of students who sat the final exam, the number of students who were active in StudySieve, and the number of students who completed the survey.

Students who dropped out of the course and failed to sit the final exam were removed from the analysis. The percentage of StudySieve users is calculated with respect to students who sat the final exam. The low response rate of the survey in the CS 101 course was a consequence of distributing the survey during lectures (which have a relatively low attendance rate), rather than during compulsory tutorials/labs as in the other two courses.

Course	Enrolled	Exam	StudySieve	Survey
CS 111	404	371	324 (87.3%)	264 (71.2%)
CS 101	256	208	173 (83.2%)	27 (15.6%)
CS 105	250	222	189 (85.1%)	106 (56.1%)

Table 2: Overall participation

4.1 Question contribution

The percentage of **active** students (i.e. those who contributed at least one question or answer) who contributed less than, equal to, or greater than the number of questions required for assessment is shown in Table 3. Very few of the students in CS 101 and CS 105 contributed fewer than the minimum required (i.e. authored no questions, but answered at least one question). The majority of students authored only the required number of questions, but in each course we observe numerous students voluntarily contributing more than required.

4.2 Answer contribution

The percentage of active students who contributed less than, equal to, or greater than the number of answers required for assessment is shown in Table 4. A substantial proportion of students in each course answered more than the minimum number of questions required, although in CS 111, the proportion of students contributing more than re-

Course	Req.	Mean	Fewer	Equal	Greater
CS 111	2	2.26	27%	46.1%	26.8%
CS 101	1	1.60	2%	67.0%	31.0%
CS 105	1	1.3	4%	82.0%	16.0%

Table 3: Question contribution of active users

quired is almost matched by the proportion contributing less than required.

Course	Req.	Mean	Fewer	Equal	Greater
CS 111	10	12.16	40.4%	15.4%	44.1%
CS 101	5	9.34	5.8%	34.7%	59.5%
CS 105	5	7.81	13%	34.4%	57.1%

Table 4: Answer contribution of active users

4.3 Feedback

It was not compulsory for students to provide feedback (i.e. write comments) to the authors of work they encountered during the evaluation process. However, in all three courses, we observed a substantial proportion of the class contributing feedback to their peers about the quality of questions or answers. Table 5 summarizes the percentage of students contributing feedback, and the average number of comments contributed per student.

Course	Students	Mean
CS 111	37.3%	3.09
CS 101	61.8%	2.36
CS 105	44.4%	2.28

Table 5: Feedback contribution of active users

4.4 Student perception

The results for the Likert scale questions are presented in Figures 4, 5 and 6 for the CS 111, CS 101 and CS 105 courses respectively. The bars showing the proportion of responses in each category (strongly disagree, disagree, neutral, agree and strongly agree) are centered on neutral, with negative responses to the left side and positive responses to the right side.

A one-sided t-test comparing the mean score for each question to a neutral response (3.0) showed a statistically significant difference from neutral ($p < 0.01$) in every case. In all three courses we observe a similar trend — students report that writing questions, answering questions and viewing the answers produced by their peers are all helpful to their learning. Students are still positive about the benefits of evaluating their own questions and answers, and those of their peers, but less so. The majority of students reported that they would like to use the StudySieve tool in future courses.

Given the low response rate in the CS 101 course, the survey data for that course should be treated cautiously. However, we note that the trends observed in the data are consistent with feedback obtained in the other courses.

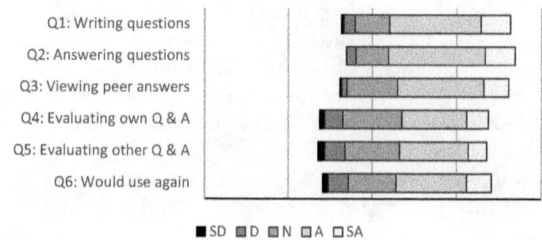

Figure 4: Student survey data from CS 111

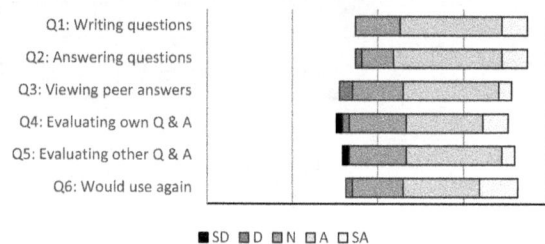

Figure 5: Student survey data from CS 101

5. DISCUSSION

Students in early stages of intellectual development typically expect instructors to be the source of knowledge, and may have concerns about learning from their peers [13]. In spite of the lack of authority, the majority of students report that participating in the question-generation, question-answering and evaluation process helped them learn. The Likert-scale responses are fairly consistent across all three courses, with question-generation, question-answering and viewing peer-generated solutions rated more highly than evaluation.

Students do not seem to write many questions beyond the minimum required, but they often answer more questions than required. This is consistent with findings in the domain of multiple-choice questions [6]. We note many students used the system more than the minimum required to satisfy the assessment criteria. This provides further evidence that students value the questions generated by their peers and find them useful for study.

We observed many students writing comments to their peers during the evaluation phase, even though qualitative (open-ended) feedback was not required nor assessed. In the trial of the prototype, only 23.9% of students contributed

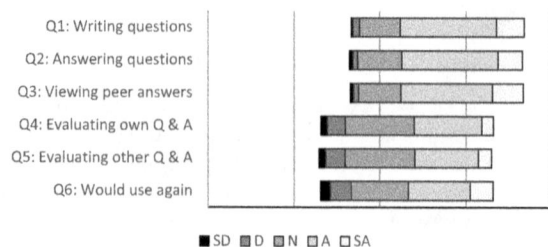

Figure 6: Student survey data from CS 105

feedback [10], whereas we see 37.3%–61.8% of students contributing feedback. Requiring students to work through a guided evaluation process involving compulsory steps (i.e. the ratings) and optional steps (i.e. open-ended feedback) appears to have increased the amount of feedback contributed by students.

6. CONCLUSIONS AND FUTURE WORK

This study shows that tools supporting student-generated free-response questions are feasible. Students use StudySieve more than required for assessment, and report that it is beneficial for their learning. Positive feedback from students, consistent with findings in the domain of multiple-choice questions is encouraging, particularly when considering the additional burden of reflecting on answers, and evaluating those answers, that is required by the free-response question domain. We now have strong evidence that StudySieve effectively supports student-generated free-response questions.

In future, we plan to evaluate the impact of the tool on performance and levels of confidence. We also intend to study the nature and quality of the artefacts (questions, answers and feedback) produced by students.

7. REFERENCES

[1] http://stackoverflow.com/.
[2] M. Barak and S. Rafaeli. On-line question-posing and peer-assessment as means for web-based knowledge sharing in learning. *International Journal of Human-Computer Studies*, 61:84–103, 2004.
[3] J. Biggs and C. Tang. *Teaching for Quality Learning at University*. Open University Press/McGraw Hill, 3rd edition, 2007.
[4] B. Collis. The contributing student: A blend of pedagogy and technology. In *EDUCAUSE Australasia*, Auckland, New Zealand, Apr. 2005.
[5] P. Denny, B. Hanks, and B. Simon. Peerwise: replication study of a student-collaborative self-testing web service in a U.S. setting. In *SIGCSE '10: Proceedings of the 41st ACM technical symposium on Computer science education*, pages 421–425, New York, NY, USA, 2010. ACM.
[6] P. Denny, A. Luxton-Reilly, and J. Hamer. Student use of the PeerWise system. In *ITiCSE '08: Proceedings of the 13th annual SIGCSE conference on Innovation and Technology in Computer Science Education*, pages 73–77, Madrid, Spain, 2008. ACM.
[7] P. Denny, A. Luxton-Reilly, J. Hamer, and H. Purchase. Coverage of course topics in a student generated MCQ repository. In *ITiCSE '09: Proceedings of the 14th annual ACM SIGCSE conference on Innovation and technology in computer science education*, pages 11–15, New York, NY, USA, 2009. ACM.
[8] J. Dewey. *Experience and education*. Macmillan, New York, 1952.
[9] J. Hamer, Q. Cutts, J. Jackova, A. Luxton-Reilly, R. McCartney, H. Purchase, C. Riedesel, M. Saeli, K. Sanders, and J. Sheard. Contributing student pedagogy. *SIGCSE Bull.*, 40(4):194–212, 2008.
[10] A. Luxton-Reilly, P. Denny, B. Plimmer, and R. Sheehan. StudySieve: supporting student-generated free-response questions. In S. Mann and M. Verhaart, editors, *1st Annual Conference of Computing and Information Technology, Education and Research in New Zealand (incorporating 23rd Annual NACCQ)*, pages 129–137, Dunedin, NZ, 6–9th July 2010.
[11] D. Nicol. E-assessment by design: using multiple-choice tests to good effect. *Journal of Further and Higher Education*, 31(1):53–64, 2007.
[12] E. J. Palmer and P. G. Devitt. Constructing multiple choice questions as a method for learning. *Annals of the Academy of Medicine*, 35(9):604–608, 2006.
[13] W. Perry. *Forms of Intellectual and Ethical Development in the College Years*. Holt, Rinehart, Winston, New York, 1970.
[14] E. V. Wilson. Examnet asynchronous learning network: augmenting face-to-face courses with student-developed exam questions. *Computers & Education*, 42(1):87 – 107, 2004.
[15] F.-Y. Yu. Scaffolding student-generated questions: Design and development of a customizable online learning system. *Computers in Human Behaviour*, 25:1129–1138, 2009.
[16] F.-Y. Yu, Y.-H. Liu, and T.-W. Chan. A web-based learning system for question-posing and peer assessment. *Innovations in Education and Teaching International*, 42(4):337–348, 2005.

Automated Assessment of Short Free-Text Responses in Computer Science using Latent Semantic Analysis

Richard Klein
School of Computer Science
University of the
Witwatersrand
Johannesburg, South Africa
kleinr@cs.wits.ac.za

Angelo Kyrilov
School of Computer Science
University of the
Witwatersrand
Johannesburg, South Africa
angelo@cs.wits.ac.za

Mayya Tokman
School of Natural Sciences
University of California
Merced, USA
mtokman@ucmerced.edu

ABSTRACT

In the last few decades, much research has focused on the evaluation and assessment of students' knowledge. The idea that computers can now be used to aid assessment is appealing. While implementing automatic marking of multiple choice questions is trivial, most educators agree that such form of assessment provides only limited insight into students' knowledge. Due to this limitation, teachers prefer to use unstructured questions in assessments. These questions, however, are much more complicated to mark as the semantic meaning of a response is more important than any of the individual keywords. Latent Semantic Analysis (LSA) has a remarkable ability to infer meaning from a text in this way. This paper describes the design, implementation and evaluation of an automatic marking system based on LSA and designed to grade paragraph responses to exam questions. In addition to presenting the algorithm and the theoretical basis of the system, we describe the tests that were conducted to test its efficacy. The tests included comparing the marks for several computer science courses exams generated by the system with the original grades awarded by a human examiner. The various settings of the system are studied to understand their effect on the accuracy. Using this understanding, along with trial and error, good configurations for each question are found. Under ideal configurations the system is capable of generating marks with correlations above 0.80 compared to the human examiner's grades. This is considered an acceptable variance. Generating these ideal configurations is nontrivial but possible by designing effective ways to extract appropriate settings from features of the data. If there is enough training data the system easily performs at rates that match the inter-correlation between human markers.

Categories and Subject Descriptors

K.3.1 [**Computer Uses in Education**]: Computer-assisted instructing (CAI)

General Terms

Algorithms, Experimentation, Theory, Measurement

Keywords

E-Learning, E-Assessment, Latent Semantic Analysis, Automated Grading, Automated Assessment

1. INTRODUCTION AND BACKGROUND

While assessment is a vital part of an educational process, time spent assessing students is time that is no longer spent instructing them. Administration and processing of students' assessments imposes a large toll on the instructor's time; [4] note that 30% of British teachers' time is spent on marking. As teaching is the most highly valued activity for teachers [4], assessments begin to seem counter productive as they take time away from students' learning and from teachers' teaching. Assessment, however, is a 'necessary evil' in the educational process since it is the only way to ensure that students are gaining necessary knowledge and skills.

As the advent of the computer has revolutionised so many aspects of life, one must consider how this powerful tool could be used to help solve the problems surrounding such a fundamental aspect of society as providing high quality education in the smartest possible way. As such, a large part of the research on assessment has been devoted to developing the capabilities of automatic marking systems.

While the automation of marking for structured forms of questioning, such as Column Matching, True/False or Multiple Choice Questions, is straightforward and easy to implement, many researchers consider objective-type questions to be inadequate when measuring aspects of complex achievement. For this reason, long and short essays are considered to be the most useful tool when assessing learning outcomes [2, 7, 8]. If e-Assessment systems are to succeed and be accepted by educators, they need to provide methods of reliably evaluating unstructured, free-text responses.

There exist a number of methods for the automatic assessment of free text responses. In-depth reviews of various systems can by found in [8] and [5]. The most popular methodologies on which these systems are based, include Latent Semantic Analysis (LSA), Natural Language Processing (NLP), Bayesian Networks and the extraction of Linguistic Features via Proxes. Most implementations employ one or several of these techniques to automatically mark texts. Comparing the efficacy of these systems, however, is difficult due to the lack of a large, standard corpus of test essays, as well as the absence of uniform and widely agreed upon comparison metrics. A review of the literature clearly indicates that we are far from resolving the question of which particular algorithm ensures the most effective marking. It appears, however, that ultimately the final solution will draw from a number of methods.

To address the challenges associated with essay marking our project focused on developing an automatic short essay marking feature for the online course management system already in existence and use at the School of Computer Science at the University of Witwatersrand. We are also looking at integration with Moodle, a widely used open source learning management system. The algorithm is based on a combination of Latent Semantic Analysis and clustering techniques. The system builds upon the ideas presented for automatic essay marking in [7]. The major difference, however, is that previous research used textbooks, the Internet and other general Computer Science information sources as master texts, while our method uses only the actual student submissions and processes them in a novel way to ensure accurate automatic marking. Our project also stretches LSA into a new application realm, using it to mark submissions that are considerably shorter than those tested in the surveyed literature.

The paper is organized as follows. In Section 2, we describe the theoretical rationale, the structure and the implementation of the developed system. Section 3, then presents the criteria used to evaluate the system as well as the results of these evaluations. These are drawn from comparisons of the automatically generated marks and those awarded by a human examiner. The effect of the various settings on the performance of the system is also explored. Finally, conclusions are presented in Section 4.

2. AUTOMATIC MARKING SYSTEM STRUCTURE AND IMPLEMENTATION

In order to be able to reduce the problem of assessment to a task that is narrow enough to enable automation, we need to focus the objectives of such a system and understand exactly what we expect the algorithm to accomplish. There are two major categories of assessment, namely *formative* and *summative*. Formative assessment "provides direction, focus and guidance" throughout some learning exercise, while summative assessment provides a summary mark that indicates the level of understanding has been achieved [7]. Computationally, these are very different problems with vastly differing needs. Formative assessment needs to be real-time to provide hints as they are relevant. These hints, however, do not need to be exact — knowing that the system is fallible forces students to evaluate the validity of the comments provided. This in itself serves as a useful learning tool. In contrast, summative assessment takes place off-line so efficiency is not as important, although the accuracy of the final marks becomes paramount. We present a summative assessment system focusing primarily on accuracy.

The next issue regards what should be assessed, *content* or *style*. Because of the precise, technical nature of the subject (Computer Science), as well as the relatively short length of the submissions, we chose to assess based on content only, rather than style. There are applications purely based on style assessment that achieve highly accurate results [8, 5].

As the system evolves we will consider including style assessment as a feature in our future work.

The specifications outlined above make Latent Semantic Analysis (LSA) an attractive approach to developing the system. As defined in one of the primary references on the subject [3, pg 259], LSA is a "method for extracting and representing the contextual-usage meaning of words by statistical computations applied to a large collection of texts." The LSA method constitutes one of the main components of our system and works as follows. Suppose that there are T terms identified in D different corpus documents, where "a term" can be defined as any semantic unit in which we are interested.

We treated individual words as terms. As LSA is invariant to word order, we find, unfortunately, that 'The left most node of the right subtree' and 'The right most node of the left subtree' are considered equivalent. Future work will consider $n-$grams, or strings of n consecutive words, as terms to avoid this problem.

A T by D, so called, *Term Frequency Matrix* X is then constructed with each entry $x_{ij} \in X$ equal to the frequency of the appearance of the $i-$th term in the j-th document. Next matrix X is weighted using the Term Frequency-Inverse Document Frequency (TFIDF) weighting scheme [6]. This results in the *Weighted Term Frequency Matrix*, X', with the entries x'_{ij}, where

$$x'_{ij} = \frac{x_{ij}}{N_j} \times \log\left(\frac{D}{D_i}\right), \qquad (1)$$

where N_j is the number of words in j-th document and D_i is the number of documents in which term i appears. Singular Value Decomposition (SVD) is then performed on the weighted term frequency matrix X' to produce the factorization

$$X' = U'S'V'^{T}, \qquad (2)$$

where U' is the matrix of left singular vectors, matrix S' contains singular values on the main diagonal and V' is the right singular vectors matrix. The singular values and vectors are reorganized, so that main diagonal of S' is decreasing. After the decomposition is performed, the dimensionality of the system is reduced by retaining only k singular values and vectors. Typically the k largest singular values are retained, along with their corresponding left and right singular vectors. This leaves us with the $k-$dimensional approximation to X'

$$X' \approx USV^{T}, \qquad (3)$$

where U is now $T \times k$, S is $k \times k$ and V^T is $k \times D$.

The reduced SVD provides us with a $k-$dimensional semantic space, where terms and documents are represented as points. Points representing documents/terms with similar semantic meanings occupy nearby areas within this space. The k co-ordinates of each point in the space come from the left and right singular matrices of the SVD.

Interestingly, the first dimension (the first co-ordinate) always corresponds to the length of the submission [6]. When dealing with long essays this dimension should not cause major differences in the analysis as the length of each essay relative to the others is unlikely to vary by much. When marking short paragraphs, however, this is very important. With each essay being quite short, the addition of even ten words could significantly change the relative length. This could ultimately cause drastic changes in the magnitude and direction of the first dimension. Thus for short submissions is it believed that the first dimension should be ignored. To test the validity of this omission we present tests to check its effect on the final scores in Section 3.

The co-ordinates of each term correspond to the T rows of U, i.e. the i-th co-ordinate of the j-th term is found in the i-th column of the j-th row of U (U_{ji}). The co-ordinates of each document correspond to the D columns of V^T, i.e. the i-th co-ordinate of the j-th document is found in the i-th row of the j-th column of V^T (V^T_{ij}).

This representation is the major distinguishing feature of our system compared to what was proposed before in [7]. In [7], the authors employ general information sources as the master texts used to form the semantic space. Student submissions are then projected onto this space to compare them with the information sources. Our system, rather, uses all the student submissions as the master texts. No projections need to be made as each student submission was part of the SVD, this allows the system to search for latent or hidden semantic structures within all the submissions as a whole. The user of the system then manually marks several submissions and based on these latent semantic structures, the system assigns marks to the remaining texts.

The student submissions are collected into the term frequency matrix and the method outlined above is used to decompose them into the necessary factors used to assign co-ordinates to each document. We then place some distance measure on the semantic space which allows us to compare the points in the space. This measure is referred to as the *similarity score* between two documents.

We used a linear combination of two distance functions to generate our similarity scores defined in Eqn. (6) with $\alpha \in [0, 1]$. The cosin similarity (Eqn. 4) measures the angle between vectors. The Euclidean distance d term in (6) (d defined in Eqn. 5) ensures that the points that are closer to each other have a higher score. Adjusting α allows us to weigh the combination in favour of the Euclidean distance or the cosin similarity.

$$\text{cosSim}(\vec{x}, \vec{y}) \quad = \quad \cos(\theta) = \frac{\vec{x} \cdot \vec{y}}{\|\vec{x}\|\|\vec{y}\|} \qquad (4)$$

$$d(\vec{x}, \vec{y}) \quad = \quad 1 - \sqrt{\sum_{i=1}^{k}(x_i - y_i)^2} \qquad (5)$$

$$\text{Sim}(\vec{x}, \vec{y}) \quad = \quad \alpha \cdot d(\vec{x}, \vec{y}) + (1 - \alpha)\text{cosSim}(\vec{x}, \vec{y}) \quad (6)$$

We now make the assumption that submissions with similar semantic meanings should be awarded similar marks. This is reasonable as we accepted that marking purely based on content was correct for technical fields. As the system is able to measure the similarity of submissions based on the latent semantic structures detected throughout all the submissions, we are able to assign grades for unmarked submissions based on the marks manually awarded to similar submissions. The system generates two marks per submission. The first mark, called the *Maximum Similarity Mark*, is based on a "winner-take-all" approach and is simply the same mark that was awarded to the most similar manually marked submission, with a similarity score above some threshold. The second method, *Average Similarity Score*, awards the mark based on a weighted average of the marks awarded to similar submissions above some similarity threshold.

The system will not assign a mark to a submission if it is not similar enough to any of the manually marked submissions. If there is no manually marked submission that has a similarity score above the set thresholds, then the current submission is said to be *non-comparable* and the system needs the user to mark more submissions manually before it is able to accurately assign a grade. The system will continue selecting submissions to be manually marked until it detects that all submissions are comparable.

By using the similarity thresholds, we force the system to maintain accuracy at the expense of requiring the user to mark more submissions manually. This is an important feature since the high correlation between the automatic and manually produced marks is desired. It means that the system is able to detect when it is unable to assign a mark with the required certainty and it requests help from the user. Thus users can trust that the marks awarded by the system are accurate up to the set thresholds. This trust is important as no system will be completely accepted unless the users trust the results.

The final aspect of the algorithm is the identification of a representative, but small, set of submissions to be marked manually. The system implements three methods to accomplish this task. The first is to select submissions for manual marking randomly until all submissions are comparable. The second method uses $k-$means clustering. Since the submissions form clusters of semantic meaning with high similarity scores, the system can detect these clusters. If a submission from each of the clusters is chosen to be marked manually, all of the remaining submissions will be comparable with at least one submission in the total set. Finally, the third method uses an adapted Min-Max algorithm. Let the set of manually marked submissions be M. The first submission for manual marking is selected randomly and added to M. Subsequent submissions are added to M by choosing the submission, $S_i \notin M$ with index i determined as $i = \arg\min_i\{\max_j Sim(S_i, M_j)\}$. Intuitively, this means that at each step we ask the user to manually mark the submission which is least similar to the closest submission already in M, i.e. the submission we are least sure about. In Section 3 we compare these three approaches. Note that it is also possible to devise an algorithm that uses several of such methods simultaneously, the system allows for such a composite approach as well.

In summary, our algorithm consists of the following steps:

1. All essays are pre-processed to standardize the texts by correcting the spelling and removing the stop words and punctuation (this step can be omitted if desired).

2. All essays are compiled into the term frequency matrix, X, and weighted to get X'.

3. SVD is performed and the singular decomposition space is reduced by selecting the k largest singular values and corresponding singular vectors to obtain factorization $X' \approx USV^T$.

4. A small master set M of essays is selected and graded manually.

5. All essays outside the set M are compared to the graded master essays in M using a pre-defined similarity function and marked.

Our system has been implemented in Python and used linear algebra functions from the `scipy` library. The source code and test data are available for academic purposes at http://www.cs.wits.ac.za/~kleinr/lsa/documents.php

3. TESTING AND RESULTS

In this section we describe the tests which demonstrate how various parameters affect the performance of the system. The effects of excluding the first dimension, weighting the term frequency matrix, the choice of k, the selection method for manual marking the similarity thresholds and the similarity measures are all investigated. Good choices for the various parameters were found manually, through trial and error, and the marks awarded by the system were compared with those awarded by the human examiner.

Our evaluation of the system is based on a subset of the seven metrics argued for in [5]. The primary measure is the Pearson correlation coefficient, ρ, which measures the similarity between two sets of scores. The correlation values of 0.8 are considered adequate [1]. The exact and adjacent agreement are also considered, along with the mean and standard deviation comparisons. To avoid artificial boosting of the results, the manually marked submissions are excluded when correlations are calculated.

In all 200 test runs of the system, the maximum similarity mark had a stronger correlation with the human examiner's marks than the average similarity mark. A one tail t-test with $p < 10^{-6}$ allows us to confidently reject the null hypothesis that the two methods are equally effective and we accept that the maximum similarity mark is more accurate. This means that it is better to award a mark based on the closest submission in M, rather than a weighted average of similar submissions in M. Because of this finding, the average similarity mark is not considered in the remainder of this paper.

To test how well the system can do given a good configuration, we marked seven questions from a 2007 first year Computer Science algorithms exam. Between 20 and 51 pseudo-random submissions were used per question totalling 282 submissions. Pearson correlations of 0.80 upwards were achieved in all questions except one. The question on which the system failed (Question 3) contained large amounts of mathematical notation in which terminology was not consistent among the submissions. Natural language processing techniques are not recommended for mathematical answers like this. This could be corrected by parsing formulae and labelling equivalent ones for the language processing section. In questions where the submissions did not contain much mathematical notation, or where the notation was highly consistent — for example order notation $O(n^2)$ — extremely high correlations of up to 1 were possible. Once a good configuration was found for each question, it was marked 10 times using different marking sets, M, to confirm the results. All correlations are calculated with significance of $p < 0.05$ or better.

With high similarity threshold values, the system is able to achieve high correlations. This comes at the cost of the user marking more of the submissions manually. As an example, the largest submission set (Question 4) had 51 submissions. With fairly high thresholds, the system required the user to mark 43 of the submissions manually. The system then automatically marked the remaining 8 submissions with 100% accuracy. In a second test, with lower thresholds,

the system required 37 submissions to be marked manually. It automatically marked the remaining 14 submissions with a correlation of 0.86 with the human examiner. In absolute terms, for Question 4 worth 3 points, 12 submissions were marked correctly, 1 was awarded 1.5 points too high and 1 was awarded 1 point too low. These results are consistently reproducible in all cases.

Table 1 shows the correlations of the system's marks with those of the human marker. It shows the question number, high or medium threshold value (Θ), the number of submissions manually marked, the number of submissions marked automatically and the correlation with the human examiner's marks. The threshold values (Θ) between different question numbers are not comparable as other settings, such as the number of dimensions (k) have changed as well. Rows with the same question number have identical settings other than the threshold value.

Table 1: Test results with a good configuration

#	Θ	Manual	Auto	ρ
1	0.85	44	5	1.00
1	0.80	40	9	0.85
2	0.85	30	10	0.92
2	0.80	30	10	0.92
3	0.85	49	0	-
3	0.65	41	8	-0.31
4	0.80	43	8	1.00
4	0.75	37	14	0.86
5	0.70	31	4	0.95
5	0.63	26	9	0.91
6	0.68	16	5	1.00
6	0.65	17	4	1.00
7	0.70	31	6	0.83
7	0.60	31	6	0.99

The most difficult decision when configuring the system is to what value of k the dimensionality of the semantic space should be reduced. Too small, and the system will be unable to represent the latent semantic structures in the texts; too large, and the system will be overly sensitive to noise introduced by different word choices used to present the same ideas. This remains an unsolved problem and automatic extraction of the value from features of the submissions will be the focus of future work. The problem is non-trivial as the dimensionality of the semantic space is a function of the structure of the input data; if there are large differences in the submissions, then the dimensionality is likely to be larger than if the differences are all fairly small. While there are examples of vastly differing values of k (between 5 and 30), we find that a good starting point is around 17.

The size of the threshold also depends on the number of dimensions k. If the semantic space is unable to accurately represent the submissions, then regardless of how high the thresholds are set, the system will perform poorly. If the space is to sensitive to the word choices used, then submissions will end up being compared based on word choice rather than meaning and the user will end up having to manually mark a large number of submissions.

The effect of excluding the first dimension, corresponding to the largest singular value, is not obvious. While the first dimension correlates strongly to the relative length of the submissions, it includes other data as well. We found that system generally needed more manually marked submissions when the first dimension was excluded. When run with different masters sets M, however, the variance of the correlations of marks with the human examiner's was lower. Both results are confirmed with a t-test with $p < 0.01$. This means that without the first dimension the system was less sensitive to the choice of the master set, although the set needed to be slightly larger. There were not obvious general differences in the strength of the correlations with or without the first dimension. On some questions the system was more accurate, on others less so. Whether the correlation of the marks increases or decreases is a function of the structure of the data.

The weighting of the term frequency matrix was a vital step. In all cases where the weighting function was deactivated, the system failed. This failure manifested, mostly, in requiring the user to manually mark the entire set of submissions. The TFIDF weighting method was highly successful, although no other weighting functions were tested.

As expected, of the three methods used to select the master set, M, of submissions for manual marking, the random method performed the worst. The differences were significant. The Min-Max algorithm worked the best, followed by the k-means clustering algorithm. The Min-Max algorithm generated the smallest set for manual marking which still spanned the semantic space. For example, on Question 1 with 49 submissions, the Min-Max algorithm consistently chose 35 submissions for manual marking. The k-means with 35 clusters did not span the space. When we allowed the Min-Max algorithm to continue after 35 submissions were chosen by k-means, the system needed 40 submissions. Finally using random selections, the system needed between 41 and 45 manually marked solutions. Over 10 runs each, the Min-Max algorithm consistently chose the smallest, most representative set. This is a consistent result verified by the analysis of variance (ANOVA) test with $p < 10^{-9}$.

The variance of the correlations achieved was $\sigma^2 = 0.02$, 0.05 and 0.14 for Min-Max, k-means and the random methods respectively. This indicates that while the Min-Max algorithm's first choice is random, the final set selected always covers the space correctly. The final selling point for the Min-Max algorithm over the k-means method is that it is non-parametric. The algorithm continues until all of the submissions are comparable. The k-means method needs a priori knowledge of the number of clusters. For these reasons the Min-Max algorithm is the recommended method of choosing the marking set.

Tests suggest that the number of submissions that need to be manually marked is based on the structure of the data, not on the overall size. In Table 1 above, we see that the Question 2 required 30 submissions to be manually marked. This indicates that 30 submissions were necessary to represent the entire spread of submissions in the semantic space. If more submissions are added, this value is unlikely to increase by much as most of the space is already spanned by M. Only outliers require user interaction. By collecting answers over time and using them as training data, the system can be trained to mark new submissions without extensive user intervention. This will be confirmed in future work.

The effect of varying α in the similarity function (Eqn. 6) was fairly obvious. For all values of $\alpha \in [0, 1)$ the threshold values could be adjusted to achieve comparable results. For $\alpha \approx 1$ the system was extremely sensitive to the threshold

values. In certain cases, a good configuration could not be found at all. The observation is that as long as the cosin similarity function is a large contributor to the overall similarity function, the system is usable. The closer we get to the Euclidean distance d-based score, the more unstable and difficult the system becomes. We recommend $\alpha = 0$.

4. CONCLUSIONS

In the paper we outlined the design and testing of an automated assessment tool based on the latent semantic analysis. Testing demonstrated that, given the right configuration, the system can be very effective, generating marks that strongly correlate with the grades assigned by a human examiner. Finding the right configuration, however, is a non-trivial task. Automatically extracting a configuration based on features of the data will be the focus of future work. Finding this configuration manually, without a target set of marks to work towards, is near impossible. If however there is a large set of training data, this data could be used to find optimal values for the dimensionality of the space, k, as well as the threshold value, Θ. With the correct configuration, correlations of 0.80 are easily achievable, often going as high as 0.95 upwards. If an adequate solution to the configuration problem can be found, the system has a high potential to significantly reduce the workload associated with the students' assessment. The ability to automatically grade free-text paragraph responses with high accuracy may become a reality.

5. REFERENCES

[1] D. Coniam. Experimenting with a computer essay-scoring program based on esl student writing scripts. *ReCALL*, 21(2):259–279, 2009.

[2] M. Feng, N. Heffernan, and K. Koedinger. Addressing the Testing Challenge with a Web-Based E-Assessment System that Tutors as it Assesses. In *WWW '06: Proceedings of the 15th international conference on World Wide Web*, pages 307–316. ACM, 2006.

[3] T. Landauer, P. Foltz, and D. Laham. An introduction to latent semantic analysis. *Discourse Processes*, 25(2):259–284, 1998.

[4] O. Mason and I. Grove-Stephensen. Automated free text marking with Paperless School. In *Proceedings of the 6th CAA Conference, Loughborough*. Loughborough University, 2002.

[5] D. Perez-Marin, I. Pascual-Nieto, and P. Rodriguez. Computer-assisted assessment of free-text answers. *The Knowledge Engineering Review*, 24(4):353–374, 2009.

[6] Puffinware. Latent semantic analysis (lsa) tutorial, 2010. http://www.puffinwarellc.com/index.php/news-and-articles/articles/33.html.

[7] P. Thomas, D. Haley, A. deRoeck deRoeck deRoeck deRoeck deRoeck deRoeck deRoeck deRoeck, and M. Petre. E–Assessment using Latent Semantic Analysis in the Computer Science Domain: A Pilot Study. In *eLearn '04: The Proceedings of the Workshop on eLearning for Computational Linguistics and Computational Linguistics for eLearning*, pages 38–44. Association for Computational Linguistics, 2004.

[8] S. Valenti, F. Neri, and A. Cucchiarelli. An Overview of Current Research on Automated Essay Grading. *Journal of Information Technology Education*, 2, 2003.

WeScheme:
The Browser Is Your Programming Environment

Danny Yoo
WPI
dyoo@cs.wpi.edu

Emmanuel Schanzer
Harvard University
schanzer@bootstrapworld.org

Shriram Krishnamurthi
Brown University
sk@cs.brown.edu

Kathi Fisler
WPI
kfisler@cs.wpi.edu

ABSTRACT

We present a programming environment called WeScheme
that runs in the Web browser and supports interactive development. WeScheme programmers can save programs directly on the Web, making them accessible from everywhere.
As a result, sharing of programs is a central focus that
WeScheme supports seamlessly. The environment also lever-
ages the existing presentation media and program run-time
support found in Web browsers, thus making these easily
accessible to students and leveraging their rapid engineering
improvements. WeScheme is being used successfully by students, and is especially valuable in schools that have prohi-
bitions on installing new software or lack the computational
demands of more intensive programming environments.

Categories and Subject Descriptors

D.3.4 [**PROGRAMMING LANGUAGES**]: Processors;
K.3.2 [**COMPUTERS AND EDUCATION**]: Computer
science education

General Terms

Design, Languages

Keywords

programming environments, Web

1. INTRODUCTION

A programming environment that runs entirely inside a
Web browser offers many benefits to educators and students:

- It is "zero-install", in that any user with a Web browser
  can use the environment without installing other tools.
  This is an advantage at institutions that have restrictions on what software can be installed.

- By using Web technologies like the *Document Object
  Model* (DOM) and *Cascading Style Sheets* (CSS), it
  can reuse the engineering effort of several companies
  who are competing to add features and performance.

- Giving the students access to the Web's display technology offers them an incremental path from Web authoring to programming, i.e., from statics to dynamics.

- It can allow for the development of *mashups*, programs
  composed of several Web applications working together.
  It offers the promise of deep interoperability with content and programs on the Web, like Flickr and Google
  Maps, and makes for interesting and novel programming exercises.

- It suggests storing programs in the Cloud, which enables easy global sharing. An important special case
  of "sharing" is with oneself: students can easily begin work at school, resume at home, continue again at
  school and so on, always having access to their "files".

We present WeScheme, a Web-based programming environment for the Scheme [11] and Racket [5] programming languages. It provides a syntax-highlighting program editor,
an interactive tool to run programs on-the-fly, and a hub for
sharing programs. Beneath the surface, WeScheme provides
a sophisticated runtime that enables interactive programs to
be written in a sequential, synchronous style, a model that
is particularly well-suited to beginners for its simplicity.

2. EDUCATIONAL CONTEXT

WeScheme is used primarily to support Bootstrap [10],
an educational program designed to help middle- and high-
school students see the ties between the mathematics they
are learning, and computation. At this stage students are
studying algebra, coordinate geometry, and simple modeling. The Bootstrap curriculum uses just these concepts to
create interactive animations and games [2]. This context
helps students find the mathematical concepts appealing and
thus more approachable. In turn, students eventually realize
that mathematics is not just a dry textbook discipline but
one that has direct application to topics they care about.

Because of this algebra-rich curricular context, we make
heavy use of *functional* programming. In functional programming, programmers write functions in the mathematical sense: a function consumes inputs, produces a value,
and is deterministic. It computes the value using algebraic

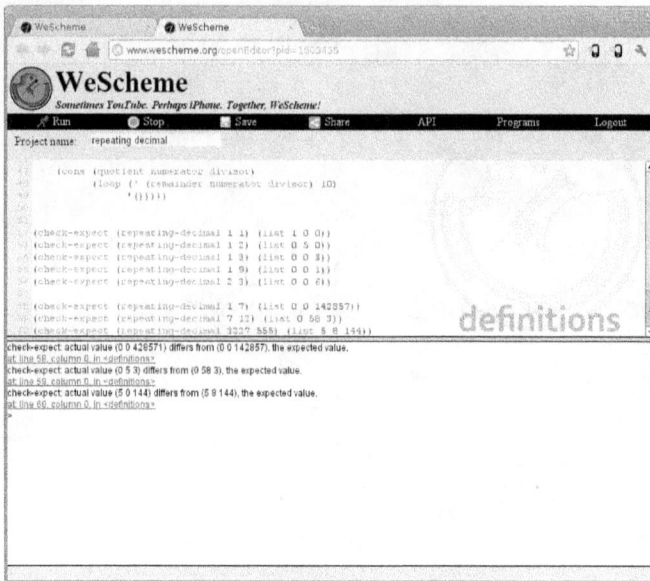

Figure 1: WeScheme

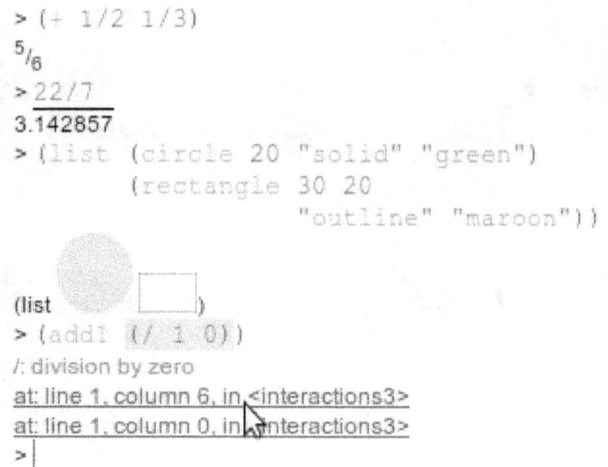

Figure 2: Examples in the REPL

substitution, as taught in schools. The kinds of values in WeScheme are much more compelling than those presented in a standard math textbook: rather than just numbers, they can be strings and booleans, but also images, sounds, and graphical animations. This combination of a simple computational model (functions and substitution) over rich values (strings, images, etc.) proves to be sufficient for writing quite sophisticated programs, including interactive games. A full discussion of the details of this curriculum is given in our textbooks [1] [3].

This educational mission has an impact on the design of WeScheme. Though the underlying virtual machine is very general and supports imperative programming, object-oriented programming, and more [5], many of the technical obstacles we have had to overcome have been to support the algebraic model. WeScheme can thus provide a simple programming interface for many Web programming tasks.

3. A QUICK TOUR OF WESCHEME

Figure 1 shows a screen-shot of WeScheme running inside the Google Chrome browser. (The environment looks essentially identical in other browsers.) The interface, which borrows heavily from DrRacket [4] (formerly DrScheme), is intentionally simple.

The toolbar at the top has the following commands:

- The Run button loads the program's definitions for use in the REPL.

- The Stop button interrupts the running program.

- The Save button saves the program onto the Cloud.

- The Share button allows the user to freeze the current program and produce a stable URL that refers to it. Accessing the URL presents an interface to look at the source code, if allowed by the owner, and to run the program outside the editing environment.

Below the toolbar is the *Definitions* pane which contains a rich-text program editor (currently a fork of CodeMirror).

The editor include a syntax highlighter with color-coding, parenthesis-matching, and context-sensitive indentation, all of which help users with the editing process.

The lower pane contains the REPL. A REPL presents a calculator-like interface to a program. A REPL allows a programmer to explore a program's definitions directly without having to create external binaries, etc. Instead, when the user enters an expression at the prompt, the REPL evaluates it, prints its value, and presents a fresh prompt. The use of a REPL allows for lightweight exploration of programs, and its interface can help cement the relationship between algebra and computation.

WeScheme's REPL makes heavy use of the browser's display and interaction technology. The screenshot in figure 2 shows four examples. In the first, the user is examining a fractional value; in the second, a repeated decimal. In both cases, WeScheme presents them using representations based on those of math textbooks. In the third example, the user evaluates an expression whose value is a list of images, which are all displayed in-line. In all three cases, WeScheme exploits the browser's display technology—JavaScript, canvases, and style-sheets—to present its output. The fourth example shows an error. Error messages are presented as hyperlinks, and clicking highlights the relevant region of code.

Users can browse through their list of programs, and edit, share, and delete them. Figure 3 shows such a listing. This list, which takes the place of a typical filesystem, resides on a cloud server, so the user sees the same list no matter where they log in. In the entry for "Baduk", the sharing icon is grey because that program has not yet been shared. When a user chooses to share a program, WeScheme shows the dialog in figure 6. This lets the author choose whether or not to divulge the program source. Once shared, WeScheme generates a stable link; hovering over the sharing link (now green) in the console, as shown in figure 4, provides this link, and also the ability to upload it to various social networking sites. Users who visit the shared URL will see the window in figure 5, where they can run the program and, if allowed, read the source code.

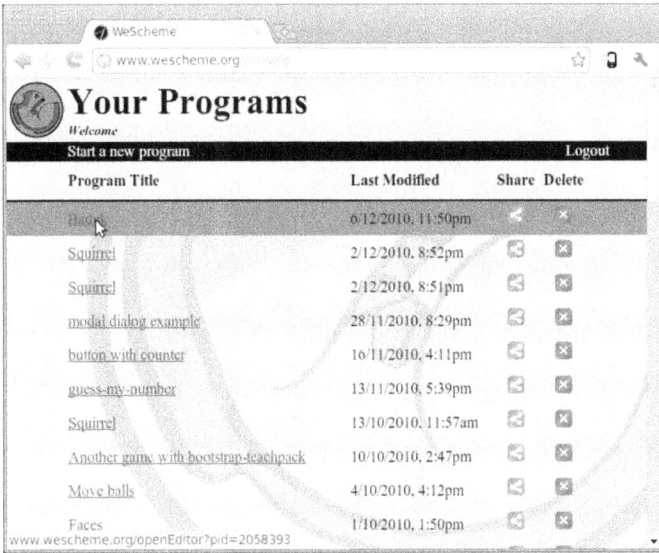

Figure 3: Program List

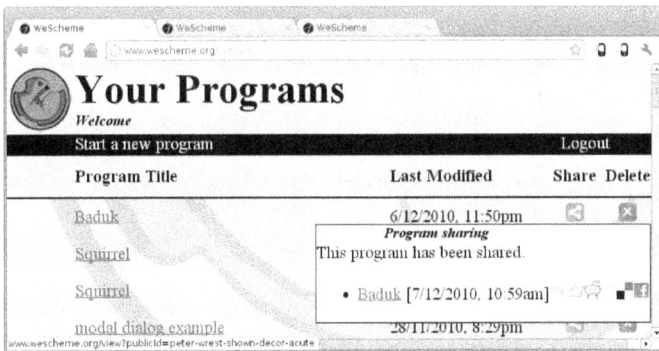

Figure 4: A Shared URL Link

Figure 5: Visiting a Shared Program URL

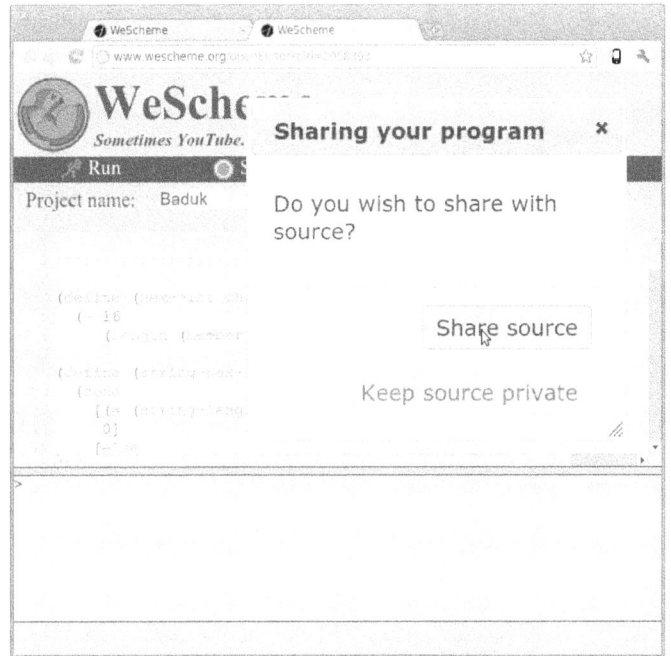

Figure 6: Sharing Dialog

4. IMPLEMENTATION TECHNOLOGY

WeScheme uses a compiler running on a cloud server. When the user clicks Run, the program is sent to the remote compiler, which converts the source into bytecodes. Likewise, every time the user types an expression at the REPL, it is sent to the server for compilation.

Of course, this architecture assumes continuous access to a server. This assumption is common in many contemporary Web-based systems such as Yahoo! Mail, Google Maps, etc. However, there is no difficulty in generating a binary that can be installed on the local host that provides access to the compiler without the need for networking support; we have simply not experienced demand for this yet. In this setup WeScheme would still run in the browser, but to initiate it the user would connect to a URL on the local machine rather than to www.wescheme.org. A launcher could automate this process by automatically feeding the URL to the browser, so that the details are sufficiently transparent to the user.

The bytecodes generated by the compiler are those of the Racket virtual machine [7]. The reader can think of this as analogous to the bytecodes of the Java Virtual Machine, though in fact the Racket language is richer in many ways and can thus support a host of other programming languages ranging from Java to Python (and the Racket project has even had experimental support for these other languages). We have implemented an interpreter in JavaScript for these bytecodes, relying on the threaded virtual machine technology [6] of most contemporary browser JavaScript implementations to optimize uses of the interpreter.

The programs that users write are similarly automatically backed up to and saved on the Cloud. We currently use Google's AppEngine for this purpose. When using a local compiler, we could save files to the local filesystem and periodically synchronize them on demand.

By virtue of exploiting the browser, we immediately and

automatically inherit improvements made by browser implementors. For instance, Web browsers recently added support for embedding videos inside Web pages in preparation for HTML 5. For a user to include a video in the output page (for instance, as a backdrop to a game) required no additional work from us at all. To make these videos programmatic objects—so that the user could, for instance, query the video or send it commands—required only a small amount of wrapping to make it an object in our virtual machine, on the order of about ten lines of code, most of which are boilerplate.

5. EXPERIENCE AND EVALUATION

WeScheme is in active use by students in Bootstrap, the program described in section 2. Students have created over 1000 programs in WeScheme, and over a quarter of these have been shared, most of them with the source made public. (These numbers naturally change on a daily basis.)

Many WeScheme users teach at schools with extremely limited computing infrastructure. In particular, they face two different kinds of limitations: limited computing power, and locked-down systems. When systems are locked down, it becomes impossible to install a programming environment like DrRacket. When the systems are weak, even if the instructors can install DrRacket, its resource consumption is so great that just starting and running it is virtually impossible. In contrast, these machines can still run Web browsers.

For instance, we recently had a school running Pentium III hardware and Windows 2000 software, on 256 Mb of RAM—a configuration over a decade old. On such a system today's DrRacket will barely start, but students were able to write and run modest programs in WeScheme. As browsers get leaner and more efficient, this gives WeScheme a significant engineering edge.

One of the factors driving improvement in browsers is the use of the same core browser engines in mobile platforms. Indeed, smartphone Web browsers are now sophisticated enough that one can run WeScheme directly in the phone—as we have, though of course using the editor is an exercise in masochism. However, while the phone is a poor *editing* medium, it is perfectly reasonable to *run* programs on phones. As phones are increasingly taken seriously as computing platforms, and browsers are recognized as an important component, our decision to target JavaScript, which may have seemed idiosyncratic, makes sense.[1] Indeed, the compiler underlying WeScheme has also been used in college-level courses that produce mobile phone applications.

The user interface of WeScheme is intentionally spartan, in contrast to the visual complexity of many contemporary programming environments. In this regard, and in many details, WeScheme mimics DrRacket. The differences, however, suggest ways in which DrRacket can improve. Beyond easy sharing, as mentioned earlier, we use hyperlinks to present error reports and also stack traces. DrRacket uses an icon, which users must click on, to represent stack traces. Many students have reported confusion about what that icon represents, and do not even know that it is clickable. In contrast, students have no difficulty understanding the visual metaphor of the hyperlink, and indeed it invites their exploration.

The limited space of this format makes it difficult to provide examples of program source and their output. However, because the programs are on the Web, readers can access them easily! Readers can both run, and view the source of (and thus easily modify and create their own versions of), the following programs: `tinyurl.com/2924s2s` presents a game, while `tinyurl.com/28jptyn` shows a use of the browser's display framework. We suggest trying these in Google Chrome.

6. RELATED WORK

WeScheme provides an on-line programming environment and a deployment platform that live entirely on the Web. Much of the related work in this area contain aspects of this, though often not in combination.

Lively Fabrik [8] is a programming language that runs entirely inside the browser without plugins. It is a simple, visual programming language consisting of components, pins, and connections with a dataflow semantics; these components are dragged and connected in a visual program editor. Yahoo Pipes (`pipes.yahoo.com`) is another specialized visual programming language for defining RSS feeds from data sources on the Web, using a similar set of tools to connect modules and operations together. Each component is implicitly an asynchronous event handler that listens to changes in their inputs. In contrast, WeScheme supports a general-purpose textual language with a strong tie to school mathematics. WeScheme provides synchronous interfaces to the Web's asynchronous programming style (which we have not discussed in the limited space of this paper), a feature that Lively Fabrik and Yahoo Pipes do not support.

Lively Fabrik runs atop the Lively Kernel [12], which is JavaScript augmented by an implementation of Morphic [9], a Smalltalk GUI interface. In contrast, instead of porting a different GUI library, we expose existing Web technology as the user interface platform—thus giving an incremental path from Web page authoring to programming, and also easily incorporating innovations in this rapidly growing field (such as the video example discussed in the paper).

Mozilla Skywriter (`mozillalabs.com/skywriter/`) (formerly known as Bespin) and CodeMirror (`codemirror.net`) are both text editor frameworks that work on the Web. Frameworks like these are needed because the plain `textarea` provided by HTML doesn't provide essential support for editing programs. Both these frameworks provide features such as syntax highlighting and indentation, though they use different rendering strategies: Skywriter uses a `canvas` element to render the editor, while CodeMirror uses nested DOM elements.

WeScheme's editor is based on CodeMirror, extended to support our environment's needs. We prefer CodeMirror's use of the DOM, as it allows a richer programmatic interface: individual elements can be addressed naturally, for both inspection and manipulation (including, for instance, styling with CSS). Using the DOM for a program editor also allows the intriguing possibility of allowing graphical elements to be used in program source code. WeScheme already allows REPL values to be represented as graphical DOM nodes; it should be technically possible to extend this graphical capability to program source as well, as found in DrRacket.

Web-accessible REPLs differ in how much of the work of

---

[1]For instance, though some phone manufacturers lock down application stores and place limits on choices of programming languages, they still allow the deployment of applications using JavaScript in browsers.

compilation and evaluation is done on the server versus the client. WeScheme takes a middle-of-the-road approach by compiling on the server-side, and evaluating the resulting bytecodes on the client. We compile on the server side so that we can reuse a well-tested, production-level compiler.

Non-interactive evaluators such as those on ideone (`ideone.com`) and REPLs such as those on Try Ruby (`tryruby.org`) or Try Haskell (`tryhaskell.org`) take the user's program, evaluate it entirely on the server side, and return the textual output back to the user's browser. This works well for textual output, but is impractical (due to bandwidth concerns) for richer data like images and videos, and obviously useless for interactive applications like games. Furthermore, these cannot provide the programmer access to the browser's own rich display facilities, such as the DOM.

A server-based REPL has additional problems. These evaluators have a choice of using session state on the server, or re-evaluating the entire sequence of interactions to reconstruct the state of bindings in the REPL. Using session state creates a resource management problem. However, re-evaluating expressions is even more problematic. First, if the definitions are computationally expensive, re-running all the expressions can become intractable. More subtly, re-running computations can produce surprising results. For instance, here is an actual interaction in Try Ruby:

```
>> x = rand(6)
>> x
3
>> x
2
```

That is, the value of x appears to have changed between uses even though x was not modified! This is because Try Ruby re-evaluates the assignment to x, and of course there is no guarantee that it will be bound to the same result. Needless to say, this is a rather confusing interaction. Therefore, this strategy can only be considered useful for toy programs.

In contrast to the strategy of running the program on a server, there are several virtual machine interpreters that run inside the browser, such as HotRuby (`hotruby.yukoba.jp`) and OBrowser (`www.pps.jussieu.fr/~canou/obrowser/tutorial/`). These use implementation techniques similar to those in WeScheme.

At the other extreme from running all computation on the server is the idea of performing all computation on the client. The REPL in wscheme (`wscheme.appspot.com`) (not to be confused with WeScheme) lies at the other end of the spectrum, by running entirely inside the user's browser. It accomplishes this by using the Google GWT compiler (`code.google.com/webtoolkit/`) to compile an existing Java implementation of Scheme (`jscheme.sourceforge.net/`) into JavaScript. While this strategy is attractive from the perspective of disconnected computation, wscheme's REPL has a major technical limitation relative to WeScheme: its evaluator does not implement cooperative multitasking (as required by JavaScript), so it is easy to starve the browser of cycles—thus, for instance, wscheme cannot implement a Stop button as found in WeScheme. In addition, its REPL doesn't produce stack traces with errors, and its error messages are not as informative as those of WeScheme.

Acknowledgements.
We thank Zhe Zhang, Brendan Hickey, Ethan Cecchetti, and Scott Newman for contributions to WeScheme, and Guillaume Marceau for comments on the paper. This work is partially funded by the US NSF and by Google.

7. REFERENCES

[1] M. Felleisen, R. B. Findler, K. Fisler, M. Flatt, and S. Krishnamurthi. *How to Design Worlds*. 2008. `world.cs.brown.edu`.

[2] M. Felleisen, R. B. Findler, M. Flatt, and S. Krishnamurthi. A Functional I/O System or, Fun for Freshman Kids. *International Conference on Functional Programming*, 2009.

[3] M. Felleisen, R. B. Findler, M. Flatt, and S. Krishnamurthi. *How to Design Programs*. second edition, 2010. `www.ccs.neu.edu/home/matthias/HtDP2e/`.

[4] R. B. Findler and PLT. DrRacket: Programming Environment. Technical Report PLT-TR-2010-2, PLT Inc., 2010. `racket-lang.org/tr2/`.

[5] M. Flatt and PLT. Reference: Racket. Technical Report PLT-TR-2010-1, PLT Inc., 2010. `racket-lang.org/tr1/`.

[6] A. Gal, B. Eich, M. Shaver, D. Anderson, D. Mandelin, M. R. Haghighat, B. Kaplan, G. Hoare, B. Zbarsky, J. Orendorff, J. Ruderman, E. Smith, R. Reitmaier, M. Bebenita, M. Chang, and M. Franz. Trace-based Just-in-Time Type Specialization for Dynamic Languages. *Programming Language Design and Implementation*, 2009.

[7] C. Klein, M. Flatt, and R. B. Findler. The Racket Virtual Machine and Randomized Testing. Technical report, Northwestern University, 2010. `plt.eecs.northwestern.edu/racket-machine/`.

[8] J. Lincke, R. Krahn, D. Ingalls, and R. Hirschfeld. Lively Fabrik: A Web-based End-user Programming Environment. In *Creating, Connecting and Collaborating through Computing*, 2009.

[9] J. H. Maloney and R. B. Smith. Directness and Liveness in the Morphic User Interface Construction Environment. *User Interface Software and Technology*, 1995.

[10] E. Schanzer. Bootstrap. `www.bootstrapworld.org`.

[11] M. Sperber, R. K. Dybvig, M. Flatt, A. van Straaten, R. Findler, and J. Matthews. *Revised^6 Report on the Algorithmic Language Scheme*. Cambridge University Press, 2010.

[12] A. Taivalsaari, T. Mikkonen, D. Ingalls, and K. Palacz. Web Browser as an Application Platform: The Lively Kernel Experience. Technical report, Oracle, 2008. `labs.oracle.com/techrep/2008/abstract-175.html`.

Habits of Programming in Scratch

Orni Meerbaum-Salant Michal Armoni Mordechai Ben-Ari

Department of Science Teaching
Weizmann Institute of Science
Rehovot 76100 Israel

{orni.meerbaum-salant,michal.armoni,moti.ben-ari}@weizmann.ac.il

ABSTRACT

Visual programming environments are widely used to introduce young people to computer science and programming; in particular, they encourage learning by exploration. During our research on teaching and learning computer science concepts with Scratch, we discovered that Scratch engenders certain *habits of programming*: (a) a totally bottom-up development process that starts with the individual Scratch blocks, and (b) a tendency to extremely fine-grained programming. Both these behaviors are at odds with accepted practice in computer science that encourages one: (a) to start by designing an algorithm to solve a problem, and (b) to use programming constructs to cleanly structure programs. Our results raise the question of whether exploratory learning with a visual programming environment might actually be detrimental to more advanced study.

Categories and Subject Descriptors

K.3.2 [**Computers & Education**]: Computer and Information Science Education - *Computer Science Education*.

General Terms

Human Factors.

Keywords

Scratch, middle schools, habits

1. INTRODUCTION

Scratch [11] is a visual programming environment that is widely used by young people. Scratch is used by individuals for self-study outside of any educational framework; it is used in informal settings like clubs and summer camps [8]; and, it is used in schools at all levels. Even lecturers at universities have taken to using Scratch in CS1 courses before plunging into programming in professional languages [7].

While the attractiveness of the Scratch environment and its ability to motivate young people are widely attested, we are interested in exploring whether Scratch can be used to teach *concepts* of computer science and programming. In previous work [6, 9], we showed that learning by middle-school students is uneven at best.

Contrary to the claim that open-ended exploration can achieve satisfactory learning outcomes [2], we found that concepts were only learned when students were explicitly taught the concepts while they created projects that use the concepts. This is not intended to denigrate Scratch in any way, but rather to emphasize that Scratch is just a tool, and that good teaching methods and learning materials are required to maximize potential learning with the tool.

During our research on learning concepts, we found incidentally that Scratch influenced not only the learning of concepts but also the *habits of programming* that the students develop. In this paper, we present the habits of programming that we found and we attempt to explain their development within the Scratch environment. Since these habits are very much at odds with the accepted practice, our research raises the possibility that learning with Scratch could be detrimental to successfully learning programming.

Section 2 contains a brief overview of Scratch and previous work on habits. Our research methodology is described in Section 3. Section 4 presents the two primary classes of programming habits that we found. Section 5 discusses the results and attempts to provide explanations for them. In the concluding Section 6, we reflect on the implications of our results and offer suggestions for further research.

2. BACKGROUND

2.1 The Scratch Environment

Scratch is a visual programming environment that was developed by the Lifelong Kindergarten group at the MIT Media Laboratory. Scratch is intended to foster creativity, increase motivation to engage with computers and reduce the anxiety that can result from the engagement. Like its predecessor LOGO, Scratch is based on constructionism [2, 5]. Programming is done by dragging and dropping blocks to form scripts that control the animation of two-dimensional sprites on a stage. The elimination of syntax errors makes Scratch accessible to young people, and most users create colorful games and stories. As reported in the literature, Scratch encourages self-directed learning: Many users learn Scratch as they go, trying commands from the blocks palette and using code from existing projects [8].

2.2 Habits and programming

Joni and Soloway [4] argued that educators cannot be satisfied when students produce programs that "just work." They found that students may write correct programs in the sense that they work (that is, they have correct I/O behavior for all input from the problem space), but cannot be considered as good since they are poorly structured. They recommended teaching students that readability (and therefore, good structure) is a criterion according to which programs are evaluated. Similarly, in mathematics, Cuoco et al. recommended that students be taught good habits of problem solving [1], and that these should even serve as a theme around which to organize the curriculum.

There are several websites that list good habits that programmers should have, in particular, ones that concern configuration management, testing and documentation:

http://web.mit.edu/~axch/www/programming_habits.html

http://drupal.technicat.com/writing/programming.html

HabiPro (Habits of Programming) is "a pedagogical and collaborative software designed to develop good programming habits. It doesn't try to teach programming but to develop in the novice student skills such as observation, reflection or structure, which are necessary to become good programmers" [13].

All this points out that an examination of teaching and learning processes in computer science should not neglect the aspect of programming habits.

3. RESEARCH METHODOLOGY

The phenomenon described in this paper arose during an investigation into the learning of computer science concepts in Scratch [8]. That research methodology was designed with certain goals in mind, but, serendipitously, during the data collection and its qualitative analysis, interesting findings arose, which we report on in this paper. In this section, we summarize those aspects of the research methodology of [8] that are relevant to this article.

We studied novices who used the Scratch environment in middle schools. Our subjects were drawn from two classes: one consisted of 18 students (11 boys and 7 girls), while the other consisted of 28 students (all boys, studying in a boys-only school). The students in both classes were 14–15 years old (ninth grade). Each class took place in one two-hour period a week for one semester.

The teacher of the first class taught mathematics in middle school and had no CS teaching experience, while the teacher of the second class had 15 years experience teaching CS. Both were encountering the Scratch environment for the first time.

A draft of a textbook written by the second and third authors was available to the teachers, but not to the students. This book emphasizes the process of developing a program by posing an algorithm, designing a solution and only then implementing the solution in the programming environment.

The investigation described here is based primarily on three sources of qualitative data:

- The first author was a non-participant observer in both classes, observing the students as they solved problems in class for two hours a week during the entire school year. The observations were documented in field notes.

- The students' work was collected and analyzed, including solutions to exams. In addition, 34 projects that they submitted for presentation at a public Scratch Day held at our institution were collected and analyzed.

- Interviews were conducted with ten students and two teachers. In addition, a discussion was held with a focus group consisting of two students from one class.

We emphasize that these tools were not designed to document the phenomena described in this paper; rather, these phenomena arose from the data, appearing repeatedly in different types of data.

4. HABITS OF PROGRAMMING

According to a dictionary (http://merriam-webster.com), a *habit* is "a settled tendency or usual manner of behavior" or "an acquired mode of behavior that has become nearly or completely involuntary." Our observations of students' behavior when programming with Scratch, together with our analyses of the programs they developed, led us to identify *habits of programming*, that is, habits used in the process of solving programming tasks.

The two characteristics we looked for in order to identify a habit were: (1) a behavior must be "settled" or "usual," in the sense that the behavior appeared in the work of many students, as well as on numerous occasions for an individual student; (2) the behavior must be "involuntary," in the sense that the students demonstrated the behavior unconsciously without attempting to justify it and without considering alternatives.

We identified two programming habits that were demonstrated over and over again during the students' work and in the resulting projects. The following subsections describe these two programming habits. To simplify the presentation and to stay within the limits of a conference paper, we will use a few concrete examples to exemplify the habits, although we found many more in our analysis of the data.

4.1 Bottom-up programming

In a bottom-up programming approach one starts with components, which are then linked together to form a larger subsystem, until a complete top-level system is formed. When used correctly, a bottom-up approach enables a programmer to design, implement and test logically-coherent components that can then be integrated to form a software system. In our case, students took this approach to its extreme, starting with the most basic elements of Scratch, the blocks with the instructions. During the observations and the interviews, we saw that when faced with a programming task, the students did not approach it by thinking on the algorithmic level and not even on the level of software design. Instead, they began to solve a problem by dragging all the blocks that seemed to be appropriate for solving the task, and then combining them into a script. This pattern of behavior can be characterized as programming by *bricolage*, as advocated by Turkle and Papert [12].

The Scratch environment fosters the development of this habit: All the instructions are given on the blocks palette that is visible at all times, so the users need not remember the instructions nor need they deliberate as to what instructions are needed. This is further exacerbated by the fact that individual instructions or fragments of scripts can be left in the script area without affecting the computation of the program that is executed. While this aids the interactive construction of scripts, it is obviously conducive to bricolage.

This habit was described by a student during an interview:

> When I need to solve a programming problem, first of all I choose which instructions to drag and drop to the script area, and then I try to see how all the instructions will fit together in the best way, what will be the simplest way to solve the problem without any interruption or difficulties.

4.2 Extremely Fine-Grained Programming

The second programming habit that we found complements the first one, in that it takes the top-down approach to its extreme. In a top-down approach [3], tasks are decomposed into smaller, more tractable subtasks. When used correctly for designing software, the decomposition is into logically coherent units that facilitate development and improve maintainability.

When analyzing the students' artifacts, we saw that they carried out the decomposition until the units (the scripts) became extremely small, and usually lacked logical coherency. We call this *extremely fine-grained programming (EFGP)*.

4.2.1 An example of EFGP

We will use the following example to demonstrate this habit: In a game, the player collects magical items by fighting their guards. Every time the player hits a guard (by touching him with his sword), he obtains the magical item that was watched over by the guard. When the player has collected six items, he can move to the next level.

A script to handle the event of the player winning a fight should be composed of the following steps: (a) move the item to the player's bag (by sending an appropriate message to the item); (b) update a counter of the items in the bag; (c) if the counter reaches six, move to the next level.

Here is an EFGP implementation of this sequence of steps:[1]

In Script1

In Script2

Although the three steps *as a whole* form a logically coherent unit, this student decomposed it further, creating a separate script for the third step of deciding whether to move to the next level. Furthermore, this script was for a *different* sprite, one that had nothing at all to do with the event of winning a fight!

As a result of the habit of EFGP, students' projects contained a very large number of scripts (occasionally hundreds).

---

[1] The examples we use are taken from students' projects, but have been simplified to obtain a concise and clear presentation.

Scratch is to be praised for its clear and convenient support of decomposition into multiple scripts for multiple sprites. However, it seems likely that this ease of decomposition fosters the habit of EFGP. The habit is closely related to habit of extreme bottom-up programming described in Section 4.2, in the sense that both demonstrate the lack of a design phase during the development.

In the following subsections, we analyze the habit of EFGP in more detail, relating it to specific concepts computer science.

4.2.2 EFGP and control structures

When the decomposition is very fine-grained, the use of control structures is affected in the sense that they are not always used as they should be and sometimes are not used at all. For example, the simplest implementation of the third step of the algorithm presented above uses a conditional statement::

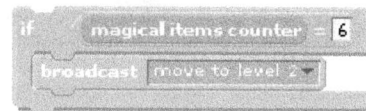

However, the student's solution used a conditional infinite loop, turning a simple conditional into a busy-wait loop. This phenomenon—the reduced use of if-blocks—was frequently found in the students' projects.

The reduced used of conditional execution in EFGP carried over to the more complex `if <cond> do <op1> else do <op2>` construct, which aggregates two subtasks together. Students tended to decompose this construct into the two smaller constructs, one for each subtask: `if <cond> do <op1>` and `if <not cond> do <op2>`.

The use of loop structures was similarly affected. A (finite) loop is a control structure that encapsulates two subtasks: repetition of a sequence of instructions and termination of the repetition when appropriate (after a certain number of times or when a certain condition holds). EFGP decomposes these two subtasks, resulting with an infinite loop that implements the repetition task, while another script handles the ending of the loop! Consider, for example, a game in which a missile moves until it touches a target. A simple control structure implementing this subtask might be:

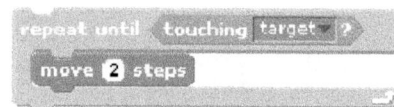

Here is an EFGP implementation:

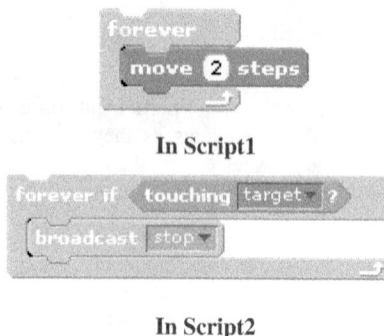

In Script1

In Script2

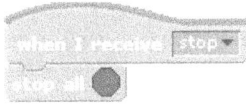

In Script3

The decomposition of the simple loop is into *three* subtasks: repeatedly executing the move instruction, checking the termination condition and then terminating the execution. We found this frequently: EFGP resulted in a reduced use of finite looping structures so that for-loops and repeat-until loops were replaced by forever-loops with external control of the execution.

4.2.3 EFGP and structured programming

Not only did EFGP result in a skewed use of the various control structures, but it also resulted in programs that we judged qualitatively to be poorly structured. A repeat-until loop is a coherent logical concept where the body of the loop and the condition for its termination are co-located and easy to understand. When these components of the loop construct are no longer co-located, it becomes very difficult to read and understand a program. This can be seen as analogous to objections to the goto-instruction, which can cause unstructured ("spaghetti") programs that have lost their logical coherence. Defenders of the goto-instruction claimed that the instruction was not at fault and that the instruction could be used in ways that were not detrimental to the structure of a program, but the consensus in modern language design and programming is that structured constructs like repeat-until loops should always be used *unless there is a special reason not to*. The students did not justify their choice of structures, though they are certainly too inexperienced to do so. Similarly, the forever-instruction should not be blamed for "spaghetti" code in Scratch; instead, one should look for reasons why the control structures were not used in the ways they were designed to be used.

4.2.4 EFGP and concurrency

The Scratch environment encourages the use of concurrency since all scripts of all sprites are executed at the same time. Extreme decomposition necessarily results in a highly concurrent program, but one in which the concurrency was *not consciously designed*. When actions are executed concurrently, understanding the execution is not simple since actions may be interleaved in various ways, leading sometimes to unexpected, even unwanted, results. Indeed, our students were frequently helpless when faced with unanticipated problems caused by concurrency issues.

For example, in the project described in Sction 4.2.1, the move to the next level might not happen when the student wanted it to happen. After the value of the counter became 6 in Script1, the player might touch the guard again, increasing the value of the counter to 7 before the condition in Script2 was checked. This would not have happened had the event of winning been handled in one script, containing the three-step sequence described above.

Since concurrent scripts (both within a single sprite and in separate sprites) are such an integral part of Scratch, one cannot avoid this issue when teaching Scratch. The textbook presented concurrency as early as in the second chapter, but in an informal manner. Synchronization of concurrent scripts is a very difficult concept, so a more formal and complete treatment was deferred to a chapter near the end of the textbook. Neither class had time to learn this material, and, in any case, it is unreasonable to assume that young novice students will easily develop the skills necessary to debug concurrent programs (even assuming that "debugging" is a viable concept in the context of concurrency).

Unfortunately, EFGP exacerbates the problem since the plethora of scripts makes problems more likely to occur. Given the very large number of scripts in the students' projects, race conditions were very common. The massive concurrency that results from EFGP made the programs difficult to debug and we believe that had the students developed programs using fewer, logically coherent, scripts, the programs would have been much easier to understand and debug.

5. DISCUSSION

We identified two habits of programming demonstrated by students who worked with the Scratch environment. Both of these habits are at odds with the accepted practice of computer science. Since habits tend to be persistent, this raises the possibility that they will be retained as students advance from an educational visual programming environment like Scratch to professional languages and environments.

The bottom-up programming habit is clearly encouraged by the characteristics of the Scratch environment and is in line with Papert's philosophy of constructionism [2] and with bricolage [12]. Normally, one would not be surprised that program design did not take place if no design is taught, but in our case, we did try to do so and still the results were not satisfactory from our point of view. As noted above, our textbook *does* emphasize analysis and design. Furthermore, one of the teachers was an experienced high-school teacher of computer science, who pays careful attention to teaching design in her courses at that level. Why, then, did she not emphasize program design in the context of this course, when clearly she was capable of doing so and had the support of the textbook?

When asked, the teacher agreed that she is fully familiar with the importance of program design. She claimed that her inexperience with Scratch was the reason that she did not engage the students in design during the teaching process. We believe that another factor may be relevant here: the colorful interface of Scratch and the fun of creating animated games can give the impression that Scratch is a toy or a video game; this has the potential to cause teachers to relax their vigilance concerning software design during teaching process. However, for all its glamour, Scratch is a sophisticated programming environment, and we believe that it should be treated like any other programming environment: as a tool with which to teach sound habits of programming. These sound habits do not develop by themselves; they can only develop if diligently instilled by the teacher.

The habit of EFGP is characterized by decomposition into very small, incoherent, modules. Modularity is a fundamental principle of software design, and indeed the textbook emphasizes decomposition into subtasks. However, the extreme to which this principle is taken results raises a few concerns.

First, we are concerned by the incorrect use of control structures. One major objective of an introductory course is to expose novice students to fundamental ideas such as algorithmic control structures. We are especially disturbed by the fact the students avoided the use of the most important structures: conditional execution and bounded loops. It is uncontroversial that these are difficult to learn, so it is unfortunate that students miss the opportunity to learn these structures in a fun environment.

We may be partly to blame because our textbook teaches the simpler if-statement before the if-then-else-statement and the simpler forever-loop before the repeat-until loop and the for-loop. This seems sound from a pedagogical point of view, but it does demand that the teaching process emphasize the more complex constructs and encourage their use in preference to the EFGP style of programming. A similar consideration applies not just to the individual control structures, but also to the inability of the students to write a well-structured program, a skill that is central to CS education.

An important advantage of the Scratch environment is that it lends itself naturally to projects such as games, which the students are able to implement themselves. But creating games by extremely fine-grained programming leads to projects with hundreds of concurrent scripts that are practically impossible for the students to debug and maintain. Paradoxically, the motivation that results from the ability to program interesting games can dissolve when the debugging process becomes difficult and frustrating!

6. CONCLUSION

While we are pleased with the willingness of students to engage in programming by using Scratch and with the technical skills that they develop, we are disturbed by the habits of programming that we uncovered. These habits are not at all what one expects as the outcome of learning computer science. Any habit, including a programming habit, tends to be persistent, so it is possible, even likely, that these bad habits will transfer to the students' further CS studies. On the other hand, perhaps they can outgrow these bad habits.

Our results can be framed as a dilemma: should we make things "easy" for students during their initial studies or should we teach them the "right way" from the beginning? This dilemma is extremely common in computer science education, because it arises any time an educational language, environment or technique is proposed. For example, even the "objects-first" controversy can be framed as a dilemma between learning what some consider as "the right way" initially vs. learning it later when the students have more experience and are ready to understand it.

This is not a question that can be answered by debate; instead, it is an empirical question that needs to be elucidated with further research (both qualitative and quantitative).

7. ACKNOWLEDGMENTS

This research was partially supported by the Israel Science Foundation grant 09/1277 and by a Sir Charles Clore Postdoctoral Fellowship.

8. REFERENCES

[1] Cuoco, A., Goldenberg, E.P., and Mark, J. 1997. Habits of mind: An organizing principle for mathematics curriculum. *Journal of Mathematical Behavior*, 15(4), 375-402.

[2] Harel, I., and Papert, S. (eds.). 1991. *Constructionism*. Ablex, Norwood, NJ.

[3] Hartman, J., 1991. Understanding natural programs using proper decomposition, *Proceedings of the 13th International Conference on Software Engineering* (Austin, Texas, May 13-17, 1991), 62-73.

[4] Joni, S. A., and Soloway, E., 1986. But my program runs! Discourse rules for novice programmers. *Journal of Educational Computing Research*, 2(1), 95-126.

[5] Kafai, Y., and Resnick, M., (eds.) 1996. *Constructionism in Practice: Designing, Thinking, and Learning in a Digital World*. Lawrence Erlbaum Associates, Mahwah, NJ.

[6] Kaloti-Hallak, F., 2010. *Learning Programming Concepts Using Scratch at the Middle-School Level*. Unpublished MSc Thesis, Weizmann Institute of Science.

[7] Malan, D. J., and Leitner, H. H., 2007. Scratch for budding computer scientists. In *Proceedings of the 38th SIGCSE Technical Symposium on Computer Science Education (SIGCSE '07)*. ACM, New York, 223-227.

[8] Maloney, J.H., Peppler, K., Kafai, Y., Resnick, M., and Rusk, N. 2008. Programming by choice: Urban youth learning programming with Scratch. *SIGCSE Bull.* 40, 1 (March 2008), 367-371.

[9] Meerbaum-Salant, O., Armoni, M., and Ben-Ari, M., 2010. Learning computer science concepts with Scratch. In *Proceedings of the Sixth International Workshop on Computing Education Research (ICER '10)*. ACM, New York, 69-76.

[10] Papert, S., 1980. *Mindstorms: Children, Computers, and Powerful Ideas*. Basic Books, New York.

[11] Resnick, M., Maloney, J., Monroy-Hernandez, A., Rusk, N., Eastmond, E., Brennan, K., Millner, A., Rosenbaum, E., Silver, J., Silverman, B., and Kafai, Y., 2009. Scratch: Programming for all. *Commun. ACM* 52, 11 (November 2009), 60-67.

[12] Turkle, S., and Papert, S., 1991. Epistemological pluralism and the revaluation of the concrete. In: Harel, I. and Papert, S. (eds.), Constructionism. Ablex, Norwood, MA, 161–192.

[13] Vizcaino, A., Contreras, J., Favela, J., and Prieto, M. 2000. An Adaptive, Collaborative Environment to Develop Good Habits in Programming. In *Proceedings of the 5th International Conference on Intelligent Tutoring Systems (ITS '00)*, Gilles Gauthier, Claude Frasson, and Kurt VanLehn (eds.). Springer-Verlag, London, UK, 262-271.

From Concrete to Abstract? Problem Domain in the Learning of Introductory Programming

Osvaldo Luiz de Oliveira
Faculty of Campo Limpo Paulista
Rua Guatemala, 167, Jardim América
Campo Limpo Paulista, SP, Brazil
55 11 4812-9407

osvaldo@faccamp.br

Ana Maria Monteiro
Faculty of Campo Limpo Paulista
Rua Guatemala, 167, Jardim América
Campo Limpo Paulista, SP, Brazil
55 11 4812-9400

anammont.per@gmail.com

Norton Trevisan Roman
University of São Paulo
Arlindo Béttio, 1000, Ermelino
Matarazzo, São Paulo, SP, Brazil
55 11 3091-1008

norton@usp.br

ABSTRACT

A good deal of research on learning introductory programming have been carried out along the past years based on a generalization to mature individuals of Piaget's theory which states that learning among childrens progresses from concrete to abstract. In this research, we set up two problem domains – a concrete and an abstract one – along with specific programming languages and compilers. We experimentally investigated how these domains were used by two groups of undergraduate students without previous programming knowledge. Results suggest that the type of domain (either concrete or abstract), when taken in and on itself, does not affect the learning of introductory programming. On the other hand, the previous knowledge students have about the domain does influence learning.

Categories and Subject Descriptors

K.3.2 [**Computers & Education**]: Computer & Information Science Education – computer science education.

General Terms

Human Factors, Languages, Experimentation.

Keywords

Introductory Programming, CS1, Empirical Research, Computer Programming Education, Languages.

1. INTRODUCTION

Problem domains may be concrete or abstract. In this paper, we take abstract domains to be those in which the constituting elements may be used to refer, at different moments, to different sets of objects and phenomena of the world. As such, ideas and abstractions of objects constitute the elements of an abstract domain. Concrete domains, on the other hand, are composed of elements that hold a direct relation to specific sets of objects and

phenomena of the world. Elements within this domains represent particular instances of objects and phenomena.

Algebra and Arithmetics are examples of abstract domains. In such domains, elements are generalizations of concepts and operations. The concept of an algebraic variable, for instance, may be used to model both temperature in thermodynamic systems and currency in economic systems. Operations, such as addition and multiplication, can be used to build up expressions and equations that deal both with temperature scale conversions and profit or tax calculation. At the other side of the scale, Karel's micro-world [7] is an example of a concrete problem space, to the extent that it refers to a board, graphically represented in the computer screen, constituting of a triangle (Karel robot), vertical and horizontal lines (representing walls), circles (beepers) and procedures the robot can execute, such as move forward and take a beeper, for example.

Focusing on introductory programming, i.e., the learning of sequences of sentences that express actions, conditions and repetitions, we carried out an experimental study with undergraduate students with no previous programming experience. The students were split up in two groups: the first one had to take part in a lecture of introductory programming in a concrete problem domain, whereas the second group had to work within an abstract domain. Along with setting up the domain, we have also developed different programming languages (and corresponding compilers) for the experiment, in order to hold constant some variables that were supposed to affect the learning of introductory programming, while varying only the type of domain (concrete or abstract) amongst groups. The investigated hypotheses are that (i) concrete domains and (ii) the previous knowledge about the domain make it easier for undergraduate students to learn introductory programming.

The rest of this paper is organized as follows. Section 2 presents the related work that motivated our research. Materials and methods used in the experiment are described in detail on Section 3. In special, we present the developed domains and programming languages, along with the subjects and the measures taken to isolate the type of problem domain from the remaining variables. Finally, Sections 4 and 5 present the results and our conclusions to this research.

2. RELATED WORK

Piaget, in his theory on cognitive development, sustains that the construction of intelligence proceeds in successive steps, with increasing complexity, chained to each other [8]. According to Piaget, children initially learn about tangible things, which are directly accessible to their visual, auditory, tactile and kinesthetic senses. Along the years, they gain the ability to understand more abstract concepts, manipulate symbols, logically reason and generalize over things. Particularly, the theory suggests that children development moves from the concrete operational stage, which occurs when they are 7 to 11 years old, approximately, to the abstract operational stage, when they are over 11. This classification has then fostered the development of a good number of pedagogic strategies based on the generalization, to mature individuals, of the idea that children's learning progression is usually from the concrete to the abstract.

Many concrete domains have been explored by studies about introductory programming: low-cost robot kits [11, 3], graphical interfaces that simulate robot inhabited micro-worlds [13, 7], image processing [12], computer networks [6], geometrical drawing [2], 3D [5, 4] and 2D [9] multimedia animation. Popular and real life applications are also used as a source of concrete problems for introductory programming courses. Particularly, Stevenson and Wagner describe a study in which the Internet is used as a source of problems such as, for example, spam classification and access to documents referenced in web pages links [10].

The idea of moving from concrete to abstract can also be found deeply rooted in the design of the Alice 3 programming environment, in which "the teacher can gradually lead students from the concrete context of animation to abstract data and structures in Java and a traditional context" [1]. Our work differs from existing research in that it proposes to separately investigate (i.e. holding constant other variables) how concrete and abstract domains, along with the previous knowledge students have about them, can influence the task of introductory programming learning by undergraduate students over 17 years old.

3. MATERIALS AND METHODS
3.1 World of the Robots and MRt Language
Inspired in Karel's micro-world [7], the World of the Robots constitutes a problem space involving a rectangular board, which represents the world, robots capable of moving across this world, walls and disks. In this world, which is possibly constituted of obstacles, represented by walls (Figure 1), one can both move the robot and manipulate objects (disks).

In this research, we developed a programming language, called MRt, containing those flow control structures which are traditional to programming languages under the imperative paradigm, along with statements such as "AndarFrente(r)" (MoveForward), "GirarEsquerda(r)" (TurnLeft), "PegarDisco(r)" (CatchDisk), and "SoltarDisco(r)" (DropDisk), responsible for, respectively, having the robot named "r" move one step forward, turn 90° left and take the disk at the robot's position. There are also statements that allow one to investigate whether the robot lies above some disk, "EstáSobreDisco (r)" (IsOnDisk), and if there is no wall before it, "FrenteEstáLivre (r)" (FrontIsClear). Figure 2 presents an algorithm to make "r" (the robot) collect all disks ahead, until it reaches a wall. A possible initial setup for this problem can be found in Figure 1.

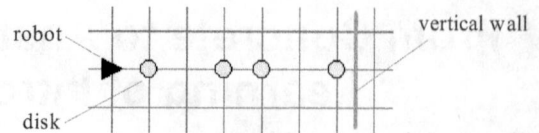

Figure 1. Initial configuration of a problem.

```
                                              while FrontIsClear (r) do
                                              begin
                                                 MoveForward (r);

                                                 if IsOnDisk (r)then
programa RecolherDiscos;                            CatchDisk (r);
usa r: Robô;
início                                         end

   enquanto FrenteEstáLivre (r) faça
   início
      AndarFrente (r);

      se EstaSobreDisco (r) então
         PegarDisco (r);

   fim

fim.
```

Figure 2. A program written in the MRt language.

3.2 Small Algebra and Pascalish Language
Traditional environments for learning introductory programming frequently use Algebra, with its sets, functions, expressions, equations and the like, as a source of problems. As such, languages from the imperative paradigm, such as Pascal or C, for example, are commonly used to implement algorithms that describe solutions to problems in this domain. For the purpose of this research, we used a subset of Algebra – Small Algebra – along with a subset of Pascal, with statements written in Portuguese, which we call Pascalish.

Small Algebra is a problem space composed of:

- Sets of integers and floats;

- Constants and variables (integer and floats);

- Algebraic expressions, involving constants, variables and arithmetic (+, -, *, /, REMAINDER), boolean (or, and, not) and relational (<, ≤, =, ≠, ≥, >) operators.

Pascalish was designed so that its primitives could directly reference elements in the Small Algebra domain, allowing for constants, variables and expressions to be used in a way that resembles real Algebra. Figure 3 shows an example of a program written in Pascalish. This program solves the problem of finding the highest value in a list of positive integers, taken one by one, and having as its stop condition the reading of a negative number.

3.3 Subjects
Twenty two first-year undergraduate students of a Brazilian private university took part in this experiment. Of these, 14 (64 %) were male and 9 (36 %) female, 11 (50%) of which coming from the exact sciences and 11 (50%) from the social sciences, with ages varying from 17 to 33, 22 being the mean and 20 the median. Also, none of the participants had any previous

programming experience, as determined by a questionnaire applied before the experiment began.

```
programa Maior;
var m, num: inteiro;
início
    m ← -1; num ← 0;

    enquanto num ≥ 0 faça
    início
        leia (num);

        se num > m então
            m ← num;

    fim;

    escreva ('Maior = ', m);
fim.
```

```
m ← -1; num ← 0;

while num ≥ 0 do
begin
    read (num);

    if num > m then
        m ← num;

end;

write ('Maior = ', m);
```

Figure 3. A program written in the Pascalish language.

3.4 Hypothesis

Tested hypotheses are:

H1: The use of a concrete domain (in this case, World of the Robots), as opposed to an abstract domain (Small Algebra), favors the learning of introductory programming concepts.

H2: The use of a problem domain previously known by students, as opposed to unknown domains, favors the learning of introductory programming concepts.

3.5 Experimental Setup

In order to test the set up hypotheses, participants were first randomly distributed among two groups.

- Group I: students that should learn introductory programming within the World of the Robots (concrete) problem domain.
- Group II: students that should learn introductory programming within the Small Algebra (abstract) domain.

The experiment was planned so that both groups would differ only in their problem domain, holding constant all other variables. It was run in two phases, designed to take place during the morning (phase 1) and afternoon (phase 2) of the same day, with a one and a half hour break for lunch between them.

During phase 1, each group was given a text describing in detail the lecture they would be attending. As such, all they had to do during the presentation was to take complementary notes about the subject. Next, they took part in the lecture for three hours and thirty minutes, with a fifteen-minute interval halfway through. In the lecture, students were presented the elements that constitute the problem domain they should deal with, along with the concepts of sequences of sentences that express actions, conditions and repetitions, present in each group's programming language.

Before the 15-minute break, participants carried out an exercise in which they had to deal with the presented concepts (sequences of sentences that describe actions and conditions). During this time, researchers (one per group) have individually interacted with the participants, presenting to all of them, at the end of the exercise, a possible solution.

After lunch, at Phase 2, participants had up to two hours to undertake an exam constituted of four questions, which presented some problems and asked the students to write down algorithms to solve them. Both groups were given basically the same exam, differing only in the problem domain and programming language. In these exams,

- Question 1 evaluated the use of sequences of imperative statements, and could be answered with such a sequence;
- Question 2 assessed the use of conditional statements, and could be answered with such statements;
- Question 3 evaluated the use of repetition statements, and could be answered with a single repetition of imperative statements;
- Question 4 assessed the use of imperative, conditional and repetitive statements altogether, and could be answered with a single repetition of a conditional statement with imperative statements inside.

Answers were then independently analyzed by two of the researchers. Each answer was then assigned a score, from 0 to 5. Disagreements were solved later on, by the researchers, who discussed them until agreement was reached.

3.6 Constant Factors and Other Precautions

In the experiments, some measures were taken as an attempt to reduce the influence of external factors other than the considered variables. First, both programming languages were grammatically and semantically identical, in terms of the flow control structures (sequences, conditions and repetitions) they present. Table 1 summarizes the concepts involved in the problem domains used in the experiment. In this table, one can see that the amount of concepts to be dealt with was comparable in both domains: both had three elements; the World of the Robots had four elementary operations and seven basic features to be used in comparisons (boolean expressions composed of conditional and repetitive statements), whereas Small Algebra had five and six, respectively. Finally, each language was designed so as to have their primitives directly reflect concepts of their respective domains.

Second, all problems presented to the experimental groups, during the lecture and exam phase (see Section 3.5), were made similar in terms of how hard it would be for students to solve them and how skilled should the student be to have them solved. To do so, the proposed problems were aligned, one by one, according to the linguistic structures needed to get to a solution for them. For example, a problem in the World of the Robots domain, whose solution demands the writing of a repetition statement, was correlated to another problem, within the Small Algebra domain, with the same characteristics.

Finally, additional measures were taken to avoid biasing the results of the experiment, such as:

- Having the experiment run in a single day (morning and afternoon), avoiding interference of external sources;
- Limiting the number of students in each group to 11, in order to reduce the natural difficulty in communication between the teacher and crowded classes;

- Having the programming languages deliver only statements in Portuguese (the students' native language), thereby reducing difficulties and misunderstandings that might be caused by the use of a foreign language; and

- Choosing domains with a small number of different concepts, reducing the cognitive load that assimilating the problem domain might pose to students.

Table 1. Concepts involved in each of the problem domains.

Domain of problems	Elements	Elementary operations	Comparisons
World of the Robots	robots, disks and walls	move forward, turn left, catch a disk and drop a disk	front is clear, is on disk, there are disks on the bag, point to north, south, east and west
Small Algebra	integer and real sets, constants, variables, expressions	+, -, *, / and remainder of integer division	=, ≠, <, ≤, >, ≥

4. RESULTS AND DISCUSSION

All students from group I claimed, in a questionnaire, to fully understand the concepts introduced in the World of the Robots, whereas not all students from group II have declared to understand the concepts presented in the Small Algebra domain. Hence, and having as our main goal the analysis of both results separately, we have divided group II into two subgroups:

- Group II-A: students that claimed, in the questionnaire, to fully understand the Small Algebra domain.

- Group II-B: Students that claimed to posses but a regular knowledge on the Small Algebra domain.

Table 2 presents, in a 0 to 5 scale, mean values and standard deviations for the scores obtained from groups I and II (this last group subdivided into its subgroups).

By comparing the scores from group I (those with a concrete problem domain) to those coming from group II (those with an abstract problem domain) one sees that, although group I had actually scored better than group II, this difference was not statistically significant ($t=1.88$, at the significance level of $p=0.07$), thereby not confirming hypothesis H1 (i.e. that the use of a concrete domain favors the learning of algorithmic concepts). This, in and on itself, presents enough evidence to state that H1 is, according to this study, inconclusive. When comparing the scores obtained by group I to those of group II-A (students within the Small Algebra domain that claimed to know this domain), one sees practically no difference whatsoever between them. In this case, mean values were almost identical (3.98 and 3.93, respectively, with $t=0.12$ at the significance level of $p=0.9$). Such results suggest that the type of domain used in the task of learning introductory programming, i.e., whether concrete or abstract, does not seem to affect the outcome of the task.

Table 2. Results (mean and standard deviation) of the scores obtained by the participants.

Group	n	Mean (0 – 5) ± SD
I	11	3.98 ± 0.82
II	11	3.07 ± 1.35
II-A	7	3.93 ± 0.80
II-B	4	1.59 ± 0.41

On the other hand, by comparing the scores by group I (participants with the concrete problem domain) to those of group II-B (those with an abstract problem domain that claimed to have only a regular understanding of it), one sees a considerably better performance by students from group I (mean 3.98 against 1.59 for group II-B). This is a statistically significant difference, ($t=5.46$ at the significance level of $p=0.0001$). A similar result can be obtained when comparing subgroups II-A (students with a fully understood abstract domain) and II-B (students with an abstract domain and a regular understanding of it). In this case, one observes a better performance of group II-A (means 3.93, for group II-A, and 1.59, for group II-B), this difference being statistically significant ($t=5.36$ at the significance level of $p=0.0005$). These results, in turn, confirm hypothesis H2 (i.e. that the use of a problem domain previously known by students favors the learning of introductory programming concepts). Thus, when it comes to learning introductory programming, the only feature, among the two analyzed variables, that seems to affect the performance of students is the knowledge the student has about the problem domain used in the learning environment.

5. CONCLUSION

Having as their fundamental concept, either deliberately declared or not, Piaget's theory on cognitive development and, specially, the generalization to a grown individual of the idea that children´s learning progression is usually from the concrete to the abstract, many efforts in introductory programming learning (the learning of a sequence of sentences that describe actions, conditions and repetitions) advocate for the use of concrete domains, based on the assumption that such domains facilitate learning in this field. In this research, we experimentally tested two questions associated with problem domains, to wit, (i) should concrete domains be preferred, in the teaching of introductory programming, over abstract domains? And (ii) would the previous knowledge students bring upon about the problem domain favor this kind of learning?

We have experimentally demonstrated that the students' previous knowledge about concepts present in a problem domain, be it concrete or abstract, does affect learning of introductory programming. We suspect that much of the performance gain reported in the literature about the learning of introductory programming, usually associated to the use of concrete domains (e.g. [4, 2, 6, 10, 12]), can be owed not to the fact that students were dealing with a concrete domain, but instead, to the previous knowledge they had about that domain. This previous knowledge, in turn, might have unintentionally slipped into the experiments by the fact that, frequently, concrete domains approached in the literature deal with highly intuitive concepts and, as such, are very well known by the students.

On the other hand, our experiments, along with the statistical analysis, do not allow us to advocate for the existence of statistically significant evidence for the type of domain (concrete or abstract) playing a major role in the learning of introductory programming. However inconclusive the results we obtained for this question, they still suggest that learning introductory programming, at least for undergraduate students (youngsters above 17 years old), does not seem to be affected by the type of problem domain taught. This is at the same time surprising and motivating. It is surprising because the very idea of concrete versus abstract lies in the heart of many research efforts (e.g. [1, 2, 5, 11, 13, 4]). It is also motivating because it makes us long for the search of a conclusive answer to this question, to whether the dichotomy between concrete and abstract domains do, in fact, play major roles (if any) in the learning of introductory programming, should one analyze bigger populations, at different geographical regions, universities and countries.

6. ACKNOWLEDGMENTS

We would like to thank all subjects that volunteered to the experiment for their invaluable contribution to this work.

7. REFERENCES

[1] Dann, W., Cooper, S. 2009. Alice 3: concrete to abstract. *Communications of the ACM* 52, 8 (Aug. 2009), 27-29. DOI=10.1145/1536616.1536628.

[2] Kordaki. M. 2010. A drawing and multi-representational computer environment for beginners' learning of programming using C: design and pilot formative evaluation. *Computers & Education* 54, 1 (Jan. 2010), 69-87. DOI=10.1016/j.compedu.2009.07.012.

[3] McWhorter, W. I. and O'Connor, B. C. 2009. Do LEGO® Mindstorms® motivate students in CS1?. In *Proceedings of the 40th ACM technical symposium on computer science education* (Chattanooga, Tenessee, USA, March 03 - 07, 2009). SIGCSE'09. ACM, New York, NY, 438-442. DOI=10.1145/1508865.1509019.

[4] Moskal, B., Lurie, D. and Cooper, S. 2004. Evaluating the effectiveness of a new instructional approach. In *Proceedings of the 35th SIGCSE technical symposium on computer science education* (Norfolk, Virginia, USA, March 03 - 04, 2004). SIGCSE'05. ACM, New York, NY, 75-79. DOI=10.1145/971300.971328.

[5] Mullins, P. M. and Conlon, M. 2008. Engaging Students in Programming Fundamentals Using Alice 2.0. In *Proceedings of the 9th ACM SIGITE conference on information technology education* (Cincinnati, Ohio, USA, October 16 - 18, 2008). ITICSE'08. ACM, New York, NY, 81-87. DOI=10.1145/1414558.1414584.

[6] Murtagh, T. P. 2007. Weaving CS into CS1: A Doubly Depthfirst Approach. In *Proceedings of the 38th SIGCSE technical symposium on computer science education* (Covington, Kentucky, USA, March 07 - 10, 2007). SIGCSE'07. ACM, New York, NY, 336-340. DOI=10.1145/1227310.1227429.

[7] Pattis, R., E. 1995. *Karel the Robot: a gentle introduction to the art of programming*. 2ª. ed.. John Wiley & Sons, New York, USA.

[8] Piaget, J. and Inhelder, B. 1972. *The Psychology of the Child*. Basic Books, New York, USA.

[9] Resnick, M. *et al*. 2009. Scratch: programming for all. *Communications of the ACM* 52, 11 (Nov. 2009), 60-67. DOI=10.1145/1592761.1592779.

[10] Stevenson, D. E., Wagner, P. J. 2006 Developing real-world programming assignments for CS1. In *Proceedings of the 11th annual SIGCSE conference on innovation and technology in computer science education* (Bologna, Italy, June 26 - 28, 2006). ITICSE'06. ACM, New York, NY, 158-162. DOI=10.1145/1140124.1140167.

[11] Summet, J., Kumar, D., O'Hara, K., Walker, D., Ni, L. Blank, D. and Balch, T. 2009. Personalizing CS1 with robots. In *Proceedings of the 40th ACM technical symposium on computer science education* (Chattanooga, Tenessee, USA, March 03 - 07, 2009). SIGCSE'09. ACM, New York, NY, 433-437. DOI=10.1145/1508865.1509018.

[12] Wicentowski, R. and Newhall, T. 2005. Using Image Processing Projects to Teach CS1 Topics. In *Proceedings of the 36th SIGCSE technical symposium on computer science education* (St. Louis, Missouri, USA, February 23 - 25, 2005). SIGCSE'05. ACM, New York, NY, 287-191. DOI=10.1145/1047344.1047445.

[13] Xinogalos, S., Satratzemi, M. and Dagdilelis, V. 2006. An introduction to object-oriented programming with a didactic microworld: objectKarel. *Computers & Education* 47, 2 (Sep. 2006), 148-171. DOI=10.1016/j.compedu.2004.09.005.

Draw a Social Network

Sarah Carruthers[*]
Departments of Computer
Science & Psychology
University of Victoria
Victoria, BC
scarruth@uvic.ca

Todd Milford
Department of Curriculum and
Instruction
University of Victoria
Victoria, BC
tmilford@uvic.ca

Timothy Pelton
Department of Curriculum and
Instruction
University of Victoria
Victoria, BC
tpelton@uvic.ca

Ulrike Stege
Department of Computer
Science
University of Victoria
Victoria, BC
stege@cs.uvic.ca

ABSTRACT

We investigate the effect of graph theory instruction on the representations of social networks by grade six students. In this quasi-experimental study, treatment groups participated in graph theory lessons as part of their mathematics class. In evaluating student responses to pre and posttests we observed that students shifted in their approach to representing a social network problem, from less to more abstract - starting with complex vertices (superfluous detail) and planar graphs (no crossed edges) toward simple vertices and non-planar graphs.

Categories and Subject Descriptors

K.3.2 [**Computer and Information Science Education**]: [computer science education, curriculum]

General Terms

Human Factors, Theory

Keywords

Teaching graph theory, social networks

1. INTRODUCTION

While computer science is sometimes a topic offered at high school, and more typically at post secondary, levels there is potential to begin introducing foundational computer science instruction earlier. Indeed, computer science

[*]Funded by an NSERC CGS Fellowship and an NSERC Pacific Crystal Fellowship

related skills such as problem solving, reasoning, representation and visualization are already important elements of elementary curricula such as science, math, art, and language arts.

For this study we chose to teach graph theory to grade six students (12 yr olds) and link it to the mathematics curriculum. Students in this grade are moving from the concrete operational to the formal operational stage of development and are ready to deal with abstractions and alternate representations needed to effectively learn graph theory [6]. In addition, they possess necessary reasoning skills to learn to apply graph theory in solving problems. In the curriculum at this level, students are already expected to be able to interpret information presented in bar graphs and charts, and analyze this data to solve problems [9]. While the British Columbia Ministry of Education's Mathematics K-7 Integrated Resource Package (IRP) does not refer specifically to graphs as they are used in graph theory, the types of reasoning and interpretation needed to represent information with graphs and interpret this information are similar to these expected abilities.

Graph theory provides a tool for representing and abstracting complex relationships and connections. Representation is an important skill in problem solving in general, and mathematical problem solving in particular. Abstracting information is an important step in organizing information when solving problems, and communicating mathematical ideas. Thus, the introduction of graph theory is in line with the mathematical processes identified in the IRP: communication, connections, mental math, problem solving, reasoning, technology and visualization [9]. Problem solving is an integral part of any mathematics classroom. In order to be effective problem solvers, students should be acquainted with a variety of problem solving strategies and means for abstracting problems. The IRP lists "draw a picture" as one of many problem solving strategies. Exposure to graph theory may expand student thinking with respect to their ability to apply abstraction in representing relationships visually and support them as they develop their problem solving skills.

Linking the teaching of foundational elements of graph theory to existing curriculum makes teaching a topic relevant to teachers, but it is equally important to make learning relevant to students. This can be done by finding links between subject matter being taught and experiences in learners' lives. In this study, graph theory was linked to familiar real-world concepts like: communication networks, roads and social networks.

Some surprising results emerged from the students' representation of social networks. Interestingly, even without graph theory instruction, students naturally tended to represent social networks with a graph. But it also appeared that there were differences in terms of the level of abstraction present in some students' graphs across the control and treatment groups, as well as across pre and post intervention in the treatment groups.

In response to the patterns that emerged, student graphs were analyzed with respect to students' representation of vertices, and the number of crossings present. This analysis can contribute to a better understanding of how students at this level learn to adopt and use graph theory. This has the potential to inform the education community and support the inclusion of computer science topics such as graph theory in elementary classrooms.

The graph theory interventions in this study were met with great enthusiasm on the part of both the teachers and the students. Prior to starting the lessons, the researcher was often approached by students and teachers with questions and queries about the upcoming lesson. Students were highly engaged during the lessons. Teachers in both treatment groups devoted a great deal of time and energy to making the lessons happen, and were eager to see how this, from their perspective, new topic could be integrated into their math class. This was augmented by support from both the District Principal, and local principals.

2. PRIOR RESEARCH

2.1 Social Networks

Social network theory has its beginnings in Germany in the 1930s. Pioneers like Moreno and Lewin described 'sociograms' in which points represented individuals, and lines represented relationships or causal sequences between individuals. The use of graphs to represent social networks might seem obvious today, but it was not until the 1950s that this model was formally linked to graph theory. This allowed for interpreting properties of social networks using mathematical analysis techniques from graph theory [10].

2.2 Graph Theory and Curriculum

Computer science (CS) is a broad subject, comprised of many different specialized areas of study. A first step any study of this type is to determine which of these many areas might be suitable for a middle school classroom and could support existing curriculum.

In 1975, Niman identified graph theory as a potential CS topic for elementary instruction, due to its versatility in visually representing ideas, and its application to puzzles [8]. Indeed, graph theory has the potential to support two key skills in mathematics learning: representation and abstraction. A graph is an abstraction of entities and connections, and details about these entities and connections are dropped. In a graph of a social network, people become points or simple geometrical shapes, and interhuman relationships become simple lines. Furthermore, the physical placement of these abstract representations do not

hold meaning. In a graph, edges may cross or not without changing the graphs meanings. Mathematical word problems are another abstraction, one which middle school students should be familiar with. According to the IRP, students should "draw to represent their thinking" when working on mathematical problems [9]. Relational graphs provide a natural way to visually represent relationships and connections between entities, and are a special case of this problem solving strategy. The CSTA Model Curriculum specifically identifies graphs as a CS learning goal for grades 6-8 [4].

In this study, we chose to integrate graph theory instruction to support mathematics curriculum in the classroom. Students were introduced to basic graph theory, properties of graphs and some applications of graph theory in problem solving. This paper focuses on a post-hoc analysis of the students' use of graphs with respect to the level of abstraction in their representation of social networks.

3. METHODOLOGY

3.1 Null Hypothesis

Student representations of social networks through graphs were explored and hypothesized to remain homogenous in regards to abstraction (i.e., simple vs. complex vertices, and whether or not the graphs contained crossings), for pre- and posttest across the control and treatment groupings.

3.2 Participants

The study took place at two public middle schools in a small town (population approximately 8000) in British Columbia, Canada. Four grade six classes participated in the study: two treatment and two control. The classes at one school will be identified as treatment one (T1) and control one (C1), and the classes at the other school will be identified as treatment two (T2) and control two (C2). Because the treatments took place as part of the regular math class, students were not randomly assigned to treatment or control groups. A total of 79 students participated in the study (45 male, 34 female). Class T2 and C2 each consisted of 30 students. Class T1 consisted of 27 students, and C1 of 26 students. Data was collected only for those students who gave informed consent, but all students were included in the activities. See Table 1.

Table 1: Participants by Group

Group	Male	Female	Total
C1	4	5	9
T1	8	12	20
C2	15	7	22
T2	18	10	28
Total	45	34	79

3.3 Graph Theory Activities

The study took place during the regularly scheduled mathematics class. All lessons were taught by the researcher, with assistance from the regular mathematics teacher. Students took part in five one-hour lessons (one per week) over a period of five weeks. The first two lessons covered necessary basics of graph theory, and the remaining three lessons covered applications of graph theory and problem solving with graphs.

These lessons included: instruction, class discussion and problem solving, individual worksheets and iClicker exercises. The iClicker activities where used to stimulate discussion and identify knowledge gaps [5, 7]. During the individual work periods, both the researcher and teacher were available for questions, and students were encouraged to discuss their work with their peers. The content of lessons addressed the following processes in the mathematics curriculum: Connections, Reasoning, Problem Solving and Visualization.

Lesson 1: Basic Graph Theory This lesson introduced the students to relational graphs. Students were given five rules for drawing relational graphs correctly: an edge must start and finish at a vertex; edges can be drawn as straight or curved lines; a vertex may be connected to another vertex by an edge, but doesn't have to be; vertices can be labelled (or named), as long as there are no vertices with the same name; and, if vertices in the graph are labelled, all vertices in the graph need to be labelled. Through class discussions, connections were made between relational graphs and other types of graphs, geometry, and real-world applications. Students were encouraged to discuss things in their lives that relational graphs could convey such as communication networks and family trees. After instruction and class discussion, students worked on individual worksheets. For five given graphs, students were asked to redraw them correctly if they were incorrect or indicate that if the graph was correct. Next they were asked to draw graphs according to given requirements (such as: 2 vertices and 3 edges). The lesson also consisted of iClicker activities in which participants were shown a series of graphs and asked to vote whether each was correct or incorrect. During the iClicker activity, anonymous student responses to each question were shown in a pie chart, once all participants had responded. This student data was used to initiate a discussion about the graphs and address knowledge gaps.

Lesson 2: Planarity and Isomorphism The first half of the lesson covered isomorphism. Students were shown techniques for identifying isomorphic graphs. After instruction and group discussion, students worked on individual worksheets. Students were asked to draw a graph that was isomorphic for each of four given graphs, to identify which graph was not isomorphic with a given set, to draw two graphs that were isomorphic, and identify pairs of graphs that were isomorphic. The topic of the second half of the lesson was planarity. Participants were taught the difference between plane, planar and non-planar graphs. Following group discussion and problem solving, students worked on individual worksheets in which they were asked to identify plane graphs, draw two plane graphs with 5 vertices and at least 4 edges, circle non-planar graphs, and draw a plane graph for given planar graphs. Students were given an additional challenge problem, called the Utility Problem. In this problem, students were asked if it was possible to connect three homes to three utilities such that none of the connections crossed. This is analogous to asking if there is a planar graph with three vertices, where each vertex is connected by an edge to each other vertex. Such a graph does not exist (in the plane).

Lesson 3: Minimum Spanning Trees This lesson offered an introduction to: trees, forests, cycles, connected components, and Minimum Spanning Trees (MSTs). Participants were shown an algorithm to find an MST for a given graph. This was the first lesson that focused explicitly on problem solving using graphs, and included discussion, group problem solving and individual practice sheet exercises. As part of this lesson, participants were shown a short video about relational graphs [2], and worked on individual worksheets consisted of questions in which students were asked to find a minimum spanning tree for given graphs. In some cases, students were given graphs for the problems, while in others they were given connection information in table format.

Lesson 4: Social Networks This lesson introduced: paths, shortest paths, clusters and social networks. This lesson included an iClicker exercise to lead a discussion about clusters, and individual practice sheet exercises. For the purpose of this lesson, a cluster is a set of connected vertices such that there is no path from any vertex in the cluster to a vertex outside the cluster. The class collaborated to draw a social network based on given friendships, and discuss relationships based on a given social network graph. Following this instruction and class discussion, participants worked on a worksheet. The first questions on the worksheet asked to identify clusters in a graph, and draw graphs with specific numbers of clusters. Students were also asked to draw a social network based on friendship information about a set of fictional people. Finally, participants identified the cost of minimum spanning trees for given graphs.

Lesson 5: Graph Colouring and Scheduling The final lesson introduced two concepts: graph colouring and using graphs to solve scheduling problems. As with all other lessons, it included an introduction to topics and terminology covered in previous lessons. The lesson included a discussion about minimum colouring of graphs, and individual practice sheet exercises, as well as an iClicker activity on graph colouring. The worksheet included minimum spanning tree questions (as a review), questions in which students were asked to find the minimum colouring for a graph, and a scheduling problem.

3.4 Instrument

Social Networking Question *On the first day of school, Mrs. Polly's math class did a survey of all the students' and their friendships in her new class. She found the following: Amy and Eva are friends. Matt had four friends: Carl, Stan, Dave and Peter. Stan and Nick are also friends, as are Carl and Dave. Beth is friends with Carl, Dave, Fergie, Stan and Laurie. a) Draw a picture of these connections:*

The responses to this question, were gathered as part of a four-question test used as a pretest and posttest in the larger study. Participants in the treatment groups completed a pretest prior to intervention, and two posttests following the five week intervention. The first posttest was administered immediately following the intervention. The second posttest was administered a few weeks later, following the winter break. Participants in the control groups completed a pretest at the same time as the treatment groups, and a single posttest after the treatment group completed the intervention. The lack of second posttest for the control groups is a result of problems with test administration in the control groups, and is fully addressed online thesis [1][1].

Student responses were coded in order to evaluate their ability to abstract using graphs. Vertices are typically represented by a point or simple geometric shape. However, in particular before graph theory instruction, it cannot be

---

[1]http://hdl.handle.net/1828/3193

assumed that students at this level would necessarily represent people in their depictions of social networks in this way. Student solutions were coded according to how they drew vertices: none (no drawing at edge intersections), simple (a simple geometrical shape) or complex (a drawing other such as a face or body). As a second measure, the number of crossings was counted as an index of their ability to abstract the relationships in a drawing.

4. RESULTS

In the following section, we present results for the abstraction present in students' representation of social networks using graphs. Data has been aggregated across the treatment and control groups, that is, data from T1 and T2 has been aggregated into one treatment data set, and similarly for C1 and C2. The total count of descriptive statistics is therefore higher than the number of participants, as the values in Table 2 represent the total number of responses in these aggregated groups on all tests, both pre and post. Data was analyzed with respect to changes across pretest and posttest(s) for both groups, as well as across control and treatment group.

4.1 Vertex Complexity

To investigate whether pre and post treatment groups differ in their drawing of vertices in their graphs, a chi-square statistic was used. Descriptive statistics of the data set are provided in Table 2. The Pearson's chi-square results indicate that for the treatment group, pre and post values are significantly different on whether or not they drew simple or complex vertices ($\chi^2 = 21.65$, $df = 2$, $p = .000$). This result highlights the differences between the type of vertices that the treatment groups drew pre and post treatment. Cramer's V, which indicates the strength of the association between the two variables, is .57; which is a moderate effect size [3]. As a second analysis, pre or post control groups did not differ on their abilities to draw vertices in their graphs ($\chi^2 = 2.48$, $df = 1$, $p = .116$, $\phi = -.321$). Fisher's Exact test reported $p = .179$. See Table 3. However, on this test, cell sizes were too low for any stable result.

We also wished to examine whether or not the treatment group differed in their abilities to draw vertices in their graphs on the posttest 1 and posttest 2 measures. However, as no members of the treatment group drew a complex vertex on either of the posttests, no viable chi-square statistic could be generated.

Table 2: Response Among Treatment and Control Groups

Grouping	Valid	Missing	Total
Treatment	67 (85%)	12 (15%)	79 (100%)
Control	24 (57%)	18 (43%)	42 (100%)

4.2 Crossings

To investigate whether pre or post treatment groups differed in their use of non-planar graphs (i.e., with edge crossings), a chi-square statistic was conducted. Descriptive statistics are provided in Table 2. Assumptions were checked and met. Pearson's chi-square results indicate that the treatment group on pret- and posttests are not significantly different

---

² There was no posttest 2 for the Control Group

Table 3: Simple vs Complex Vertices Drawn Among Treatment and Control Groups

Group	Var.	Pre	Post1	Post2	χ^2	p
Treat.	Simple	7	27	29	21.65	.000
	Complex	4	0	0		
	Total	11	27	29		
Contr.	Simple	3	17	NA^2	2.48	.116
	Complex	2	2	NA^2		
	Total	5	19	NA^2		

ferent on whether or not they crossed edges ($\chi^2 = 2.09$, $df = 2$, $p = .352$). Cramer's V, which indicates the strength of the association between the treatment variables is, .18. Chi-square was also used to determine whether pre or post control groups differed in their use of crossed edges in their graphs. Assumptions were again checked and met. Pearson's Chi-square results indicate that that pre and post are not significantly different ($\chi^2 = 0.51$, $df = 1$, $p = .475$). (See Table 4).

Table 4: Crossings vs. No Crossings Among Intervention and Control Groups

Group	Var.	Pre	Post1	Post2	χ^2	p
Treat.	No Cross.	6	10	9	2.09	.352
	Crossings	5	17	21		
	Total	11	27	30		
Contr.	No Cross.	2	11	NA^2	0.51	.475
	Cross.	3	8	NA^2		
	Total	5	19	NA^2		

5. DISCUSSION

When learning to adopt graphs in problem solving, students must shift from a concrete to an abstract representation of ideas and relationships: a picture of a person is not a person, but an abstraction of the idea of a person. This abstraction can be taken to different levels, but for the purpose of this analysis we looked at two features, each at two levels. These two indications of students' ability to apply abstraction when representing a social network with a graph are: the complexity of the vertices in their drawings, where these vertices represented people; and the students' ability to abstract the connections and relationships in the question in their drawings with respect the the number of crossings. In this way the complexity of the vertices is inversely related to the abstraction level, and the number of crossings is directly related.

There are different factors affecting the changes we have seen in the student responses. The treatment group was exposed to the use of graphs, and became more confident in using such to support their problem solving processes. Approximately half of all the students were exposed to the pretest and may have subsequently reflected on the questions used. This familiarity may have supported them in finding a more expedient and abstract process when the problem was presented a second time. Finally, some degree of fatigue when being asked to complete the test for a second time may have affected the time and effort that the students were willing to put into representing the problem.

5.1 Vertex Complexity

As a measure of abstraction in this study, we looked at student representation of vertices in a graph. Student depictions of the people in the question given to them varied, both across pretest and posttest(s), and across control and treatment groups. In some cases in both the treatment and control groups, students drew vertices that had human characteristics: bodies or faces. In the treatment group, no such representations were present on either of the posttests, where in the control group some students continued to represent the people in the question in this more complex manner.

Figure 1: Simple vs. Complex Vertices

In the treatment groups, student representation of people in their drawings of social networks shifted from complex to simple, (see Fig. 1), which suggests that students, upon receiving graph theory instruction, are able to learn to abstract further. This shift is not as evident in the control group. Although there appears to be a trend towards simplification of vertex representation, it is not statistically significant. Possible explanations for this shift are: increased familiarity with the problem after being introduced to it on the pretest, or cross contamination from the treatment group.

5.2 Crossings

A second index of abstraction is the incidence of crossings in student graphs. Edges in a graph of a social network represent connections between individuals, and are independent of the path that they take. Students in the treatment group were taught about graph isomorphism, and planarity. Both concepts are relevant in this level of abstraction of ideas in a graph. Our analysis of crossings in student graphs did not yield significant results. However, in the treatment group there was a trend towards an increased number students including crossings in their solutions. This trend is not evident in the control group, in fact the inverse is apparent.

6. LIMITATIONS

The small number of students who completed the pretest in this study is problematic. In addition, the imbalanced counts in pretest vs. posttest, as well as across control and treatment groups, coupled with the missing posttest 2 data for both control groups, reduce the strength of the analysis of the data collected in this study.

Replication is needed to strengthen the generalizability of these findings. In particular, a *repeated measures* design with larger number of participants would make it possible to determine if the trends suggested in this study are in fact indicative of grade six students' ability to learn to adopt graph theory and abstract the complex relationships in a social network in this way. Pairwise data would also indicate whether or not the trends seen here are evident on the individual level.

7. CONCLUSIONS

Graph theory instruction can support existing mathematics curriculum and provide novel problem solving strategies for students at the grade six level. Student and teacher willingness to participate actively during the graph theory lessons in this study indicates that graph theory may be a suitable computer science topic to integrate in classrooms at this level. Students were readily able to identify artifacts in their lives that could be represented with graphs, such as a communication network, a family tree, or a transportation network. This demonstrates that students are be able to make meaningful connections to graph theory.

Further study is needed to confirm the observations made in this study, and the extent to which graph theory instruction is responsible for the trends seen in the treatment groups. Other indices of the adoption of abstraction may also be feasible. However, our analysis of grade six students' representation of a social network indicates that students at this level are capable of abstracting relationship information into a graph to a greater extent following graph theory instruction. It is clear that even without graph theory instruction students at this level are capable of representing a social network using a graph structure. This, coupled with the students ability to relate graph theory to their lives, suggests that social networks are a suitable subject to use when introducing students of this level to graph theory.

8. REFERENCES

[1] S. Carruthers. *Grasping Graphs*. Master's Thesis, Departments of Computer Science and Curriculum & Instruction, University of Victoria, 2010.

[2] S. Carruthers. Relational Graphs: What are they? (video). In *Proceedings of the 41st SIGCSE Technical Symposium on Computer Science Education (SIGCSE'10)*, 2010.

[3] J. Cohen. *Statistical Power Analysis for the Behavioral Sciences*. Lawrence Erlbaum Associates, 1988.

[4] CSTA. A model curriculum for K-12 computer science: Final Report of the ACM task force curriculum committee. Technical report, Computer Science Teachers Associaton, 2003.

[5] iClicker. http://www.iclicker.com/dnn/.

[6] D. Kuhn. Formal operations from a twenty-first century perspective. *Human Development*, 51:48=55, 2008.

[7] M. E. Lantz. The use of 'clickers' in the classroom: Teaching innovation or merely an amusing novelty? *Computers in Human Behavior*, 25:556–561, 2010.

[8] J. Niman. Graph theory in the elementary school. *Educational Studies in Mathematics*, 6(2), 1975.

[9] B. C. M. of Education. *Mathematics K to 7: Integrated Resource Package 2007*. Queens Printer, Victoria, BC, 2007.

[10] J. Scott. *Social Network Analysis: a handbook*. Sage Publications, 2006.

CS Education Re-Kindles Creativity in Public Schools

Vicki Bennett
University of Colorado
Department of Communication
Boulder, CO 80303
(303) 492-7852, 001
Vicki.Bennett@colorado.edu

Kyu Han Koh
University of Colorado Boulder
Department of Computer Science
Boulder, CO 80303
(303) 495-0357, 001
kohkh@colorado.edu

Alexander Repenning
University of Colorado Boulder
Department of Computer Science
Boulder, CO 80303
(303) 492-1349, 001
ralex@cs.colorado.edu

ABSTRACT

Creativity is an important aspect of industry and education. The lack of creativity in current students has become a concern for educators. Through the process of implementing the Scalable Game Design project to teach computer science through game authoring, fostered/increased creativity occurred in public middle schools. Despite some structural limitations of the US educational system, creativity among the participating students was recognized. This paper describes a unique solution to fostering creativity while teaching game design in the limiting public school environment.

Categories and Subject Descriptors

K.3.2 Computer and Information Science Education

General Terms: Design, Experimentation, Human Factors.

Keywords: Middle School Programming, Game Design, Creativity, Computer Science Education, Scalable Game Design, Student Observation.

1. INTRODUCTION

According to popular press, the United States, as an individualistic culture, has been referred to as a creative capital. [1] But is it? Since 1990, a significant decline in the Torrence scores that measure creativity in American children, has many educators concerned. The Torrence creativity inventory (1958), is the "gold standard" in creative assessment [2]. Until 1990, the children's Torrence scores were steadily increasing. So, how can educators restore America's singular brand of creativity?

Increasing creativity in children would appear to be within the public school province. However, public schools have rarely been associated with a strong ability to foster creativity. Creativity is generally characterized as a natural human trait that is strongly developed in young kids. However, over time natural creativity can be eroded through the public school processes, due to the restrictive structure of the public school system. For instance, a forty-five minute class, two or three times a week, with 30-40 other children is the current norm in many public middle schools. Teachers have a difficult time addressing the required curriculum within this timeframe, much less inspiring creativity.

The reality of computer education within this public school structure can be even harsher. Teachers may not have the necessary computer science background, programming tools can be inadequate [3], and curriculum materials are often missing or not well integrated into emerging standards [4]. Making computer science education based on game design feasible can require teachers to explore pedagogical and presentation trade offs, which may compromise creativity. Presentation method can have a significant effect on the facilitation of creativity. The two extreme points of control in regard to teaching presentation are direct instruction [5] and discovery learning [6]. Direct instruction is described as teacher-dictated lessons with a step-by-step presentation and no allowed deviation from the students. On the one hand this is likely to get the students to finish the games. On the other hand, there is little potential for deep learning and creativity [7].

Conversely, discovery learning provides a lot of freedom to each individual student. In its most extreme form teachers would essentially instruct students "here is the tool, now make any game you want". Generally it is believed that this model fosters creativity, but, at the same time, the lack of scaffolding [5] can result in student frustration because of their inadequate skills for making a game from scratch. This model is normally employed by after-school, Friday Computer Clubs. Students attending these clubs are typically self-selected and are usually somewhat experienced in computer technology, so the discovery model works for them. These after school computer clubs also are able to give more time to individual students and the students can spend as much time as they wish on a given project. So naturally within this scenario game-authoring software inspires creativity.

Although educators have been working to introduce more computer science into lower level public schools [3], fostering creativity with the introduction of computer science was not a priority. So even if computer science education is to be a part of public education, fostering any kind of creativity at the same time would be difficult within the current structure? The Scalable Game Design (SGD) project [3, 8] has been quite successful getting computer science education into public schools. With a quickly growing number of sites including inner city schools, remote rural schools and Native American communities in Colorado, South Dakota, Alaska and Texas, a large pool of students is currently being reached. Some schools are instructing over 900 students per year in computer science through game design. Through the SGD project structural guidelines, computational thinking tools have been created [3], middle school students have been introduced to foundational computer science concepts through game design, and student creativity has been recognized.

Generally public school teachers lean towards the direct instruction approach. The commonly held assumption is that this approach is not conducive to fostering or enhancing creativity in students. Additionally, in the current educational climate, where the focus is on standardized testing, lack of creativity can seem like an acceptable cost [5, 6, 7].

The contribution of this paper is to highlight the SGD project approach to computer science education through game design. The benefit of fostering/increasing creativity in the participating student classes is unexpected because of the current public educational structure, which limits the teacher's ability to integrate creativity into curriculum. But despite the disadvantages of this limited structure, the SGD project model through loosely structured guidelines, Agentsheets software, and the use of examples in the Scalable Game Design Arcade (SGDA), has been able to show consistent creativity within the students' games.

2. METHODS

Over the course of the 2009/2010 school year the authors as members of the Scalable Game Design (SGD) Project research team, visited the participating middle school classrooms. Observations of these classrooms were written down as notes and in journal form, as well as the teacher interviews and comments. Participating classes also uploaded their self-created games to the Scalable Game Design Arcade (SGDA). Three representative classes (Abigail, Melvyn & Sheryle, all pseudonyms) were chosen for the purposes of this paper to demonstrate that despite the limitations of educational structure and observable diversity, creativity can still be fostered within a single curricular intervention model.

The three representative classrooms were chosen for their ethnic and gender diversity in comparison to each other, and because they represent different types of communities, urban, suburban and rural. Diversity within the range of technology experience of the classroom population, classroom size to student number ratio, the amount of actual classroom time, and teacher presentation method was also observed. Although the observations and comparisons for this paper are based on only three teachers, these three teachers represent most of the significant differences within the entire group of project participants. Consequently, the data from these three teachers is project representative.

Common factors for the project schools are as follows:

- All students are 6th/7th graders

- Teachers attended a week-long training before the implementation

- Frogger was the initial game taught to the students using Agentsheets software

- A trained Community College student is assigned to support the software implementation.

2.1 Creativity Dimensions in Game Design

Through the observation of the project classes and a set of the games produced by these classes, we could conceptualize the differences between these games as an indicator of creativity. The game design process allows variations along three main dimensions, where student creativity can be explored:

- **Characters:** Game characters, called agents in AgentSheets [8], are the objects of the game. In a game such as Frogger agent depictions include frogs, trucks, and alligators. Drawing these depictions can be a lot of fun for many students and even provides a sense of really making their game. Some teachers allow opportunities to change/create different agents. For instance, in a Frogger-like game the frog character may look entirely different, e.g., a monster, and not even be called a frog.

- **Levels:** Levels may vary enormously. Each game level, represented by a worksheet in AgentSheets, lays out the agents into a configuration that is likely to determine how hard the game will be. For example, a five-lane highway is much harder to cross in Frogger than a single lane highway.

- **Behavior:** The programming that students need to create determines the behavior of characters, and is by far the most complex aspect of a game. In AgentSheets the students use the rule-based Visual AgenTalk language to make behaviors with a drag and drop type interface [9].

Creativity can be expressed at all three dimensions. Despite public school limitations, within the participating schools we have many teachers using various combinations of interventions to foster creativity by dealing with ways to create characters, levels and behaviors within the parameters of the project's structural model.

2.2 Curriculum Interventions

Within this model, many curricular interventions are presented to the teachers during their training week. Each teacher can choose which ones suit their teaching style, while staying within these parameters. The required elements are that the first game taught is Frogger, Agentsheets software is used and a community college (CC) student is allowed to support the teacher in class. The different types of interventions include, but are not limited to:

- Use of online tutorial material by the teacher

- Use of online tutorial material by individual students with/without teacher direction

- Students gaining ideas from playing other student-created games on the SGDA

- Use of hand-outs for helping the students to remember all the required elements of the game and for peer review

- Integrating/separating the instruction on the agent design and programming in various and unique ways

- Specific time span allowed for the design and programming of individual agents

- Writing the required elements of the game on the board

2.3 Community College Student Support

The support of trained CC students in the participating classrooms is a unique element to this project. The students are trained to support the teachers as they teach the beginning game programming. These CC students also serve as mentors and role models for the middle school students. Each teacher may decide the kinds of roles/work they want their CC student to accomplish, as well as how often the CC student should attend. The types of roles include: 1) Basic design trouble shooting for the middle school students; 2) Various levels of paperwork, as needed; 3) Teaching implementation segments at the teacher's discretion; 4) Supporting substitute teachers; 5) Catching up absent students.

2.4 Classroom Descriptions

2.4.1 Abigail's Class (represents rural area)

Abigail's teaching style on the direct instruction/discovery learning continuum falls toward the direct instruction. Her class is comprised of 23-28 students, who view the Agentsheets programming lessons projected to the front of the classroom. Her classes are usually 50 minutes long. Abigail's class interventions include: 1) Students gaining ideas from playing other student-created game examples on the SGDA; 2) She teaches most of the agent depiction design first; 3) Most of the programming is taught after all the agents are designed; 4) Use of online tutorial material by the teacher when the games are uploaded to SGDA; and 5) Writing the required game elements on the blackboard for the students' reference. Abigail prefers for her CC student assistant to tutor the students who have missed portions of the lessons due to absence or other situations. During the lessons, students must pay attention to Abigail's explanations/demonstrations, but are free to experiment with their games within class time limits. When assessing the collection of the games from her class, a high degree of creativity in characters and behavior and a medium degree of creativity in levels were present.

2.4.2 Melvyn's Class (represents urban area)

Melvyn's teaching style falls into the direct instruction area. His current class has over 30 students, who are able to watch Melvyn's instruction on a Smartboard. Melvyn's students are seated closer together than Abigail's students because of space, and instruction time is less than 45 minutes after attendance-taking. Melvyn's interventions include: 1) Use of online tutorial material by the teacher; 2) Use of online tutorial material by individual students with/without teacher direction; 3) Students gaining ideas from playing other student-created game examples on the SGDA; 4) Use of hand-outs to help the students remember all the required elements of the game and for peer review; 5) Melvyn integrates the agent design with his programming instruction dependent on the class grade and time; and 6) Timed period for the design of individual agents. Melvyn prefers to have his CC student take a more active role in the teaching, such as presenting specific lesson segments and supporting substitute teachers when he is absent. Melvyn insists on a much stricter adherence to the lesson sequence and time restrictions. In the collection of the games from Melvin's class, a high degree of creativity in characters and levels and medium degree of creativity in behavior were found.

2.4.3 Sheryle's Class (represents suburban area)

Sheryle's teaching style falls more toward the discovery-learning end of the continuum, though she still maintains structure. Her classes range from 23-29 students, who learn Agentsheets from a Smartboard. Sheryle's students also have more space in their classroom and a large window. Sheryle's curricular interventions include: 1) Use of online tutorial material as the basis for her own tutorials; 2) Use of online tutorial material by individual students with/without teacher direction; 3) Students gaining ideas from playing other student-created games on the SGDA; 4) Sheryle tends to divide the agent design and the programming lessons in response to the particular class she is currently teaching; 5) Writing the required elements of the game on the Smartboard. Sheryle's teaching style could be characterized as more impromptu, because she can change the elements of the lesson to match the learning of the specific students she is teaching. Although her students usually complete the games within the same approximate time frame as the other teacher's classes.

3. FINDINGS: CREATIVE EMERGENCE

The creative process, described throughout research papers, usually has an identifiable outcome. Most of these descriptions involve an epiphany or evolution of a new thought or idea emerging from some sort of thought association. According to Herring, et al [10], creativity can be produced regularly through exposing yourself or team to visual examples. Examples can be similar to the sought-after outcome, or random artifacts with only marginal resemblance. Researchers agree that examples are one of the best ways to start the creative process [10, 11]. Observations of the project classes, show a large amount student creativity, especially in their agent and worksheet design (Figures 1 & 2).

Figure 1. Examples of the variety of "Frog" depictions created by the students

Although teacher comments and uploaded games supported this observation, the most significant commonality among the observed classes was the adherence to the project guidelines. Basically, these structured guidelines included the following protocols:

- Teaching Frogger as the first game
- Using AgentSheets software
- Uploading student games to the SGDA
- All other interventions were optional: Using SGDA as examples for inspiration was almost universal, though.

3.1 Observations: Creativity Begins

3.1.1 Abigail's Class

On the first day, the students began to play the Frogger games on SDGA. At first they just played the games without any direction. But since some of the uploaded games had errors or other problems, the students asked questions about the causes of these issues. Seeing the errors of previous students as well as the successes impressed on these students some of the intricacies of the game design process. Abigail instructed the students to write down any elements that they would want to use for their own game. The students thought about their own game design in regards to all the example games they had just played on SGDA. Eventually, the students were excitedly talking to each other about which game features they were going to use, based on the examples they had just experienced. Exposure to relevant examples is believed to lead a high degree of creativity in characters and behavior. The results of Abigail's class' game designs are shown below (Fig. 2).

3.1.2 Melvyn's Class

Melvyn takes role at the beginning of every class as required. Often this task takes a lot of class time. Melvyn keeps a tight rein on his class because there is never enough time to finish the lessons. He demonstrates the techniques of agent design for Frogger on his Smartboard. Because of time constraints (only 45 min.), a timer is used to keep his students on task when designing or programming each agent. Right before his class ended, Melvyn displayed all the frogs that all the students had designed during that class, on the

Smartboard. The students pointed out their specific frog to the other students, comparing them with the other frogs on the board. This generated increased enthusiasm and motivation for better agent quality. Melvyn's students were limited to a specific amount of time to design and program their agents, but still produced a high degree of creativity in characters and levels. His students' uploaded games are below (Fig. 2).

3.1.3 Sheryle's Class
Sheryle's teaching style is more flexible than most of our teacher-participants. She puts examples on her Smartboard and then circulates throughout her classroom, commenting on her students' work, and giving suggestions and help where needed. She regularly encourages her students to show each other their ongoing game designs for inspiration. The collection of the games from Sheryle's class shows high degrees of creativity in characters, levels, and behavior. During one of her classes, we saw her divide the agent design and the programming into two separate lessons, while during another observation of a different class, she instructed the class in the programming as each agent was designed. Sheryle says she believes in altering the protocols for each class based on the class time and abilities of her students. Sheryle's students' game designs are shown below (Fig. 2).

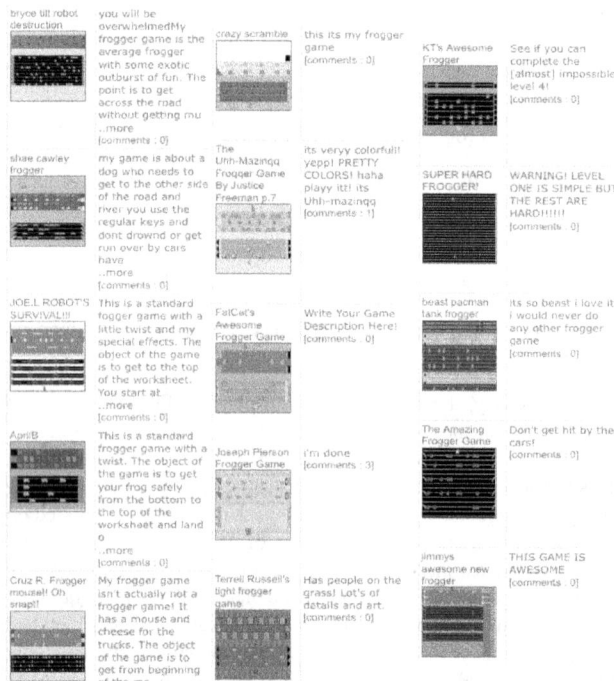

Figure 2. Screenshots and Descriptions of Frogger games collected from Abigail's (Two Left Columns), Melvyn's (Two Middle Columns), and Sheryle's class (Two Right Columns).

3.2 Teacher Comments
Throughout the classroom observations, some of the teachers made unsolicited comments about recognizing creativity during their project classes (*quotes in italics*). Others sent emails with descriptions of their student creativity. Some are listed below.

"I definitely witnessed more creativity within the confines of the project than I had seen through other projects."

Initially this creativity took the shape as outlandish and colorful agent depictions. Students used their ability to design their own

agents by making strange-looking frogs or other animals in the frog's place. They also created these agents in a rainbow of colors the original green frog would never recognize (email).

"After creating their basic Frogger game (Level 1), they went on to create additional levels with their own creative ideas which included unique characters, varied street directions & mystifying surprises along the Frog's path home."

I can't believe the unique game levels and versions from the students. Although these game versions were based on the Frogger game, only someone who knew the actual coding would be able to detect this similarity (email).

"They for sure want to change the agents to be their own styles, like soccer feet pushing soccer balls into goals rather than the normal Sokoban design with destinations ... or dogs running across the street to avoid dog catchers for Frogger."

As the teachers so aptly describe, their students are having a creativity field-day, throughout the game authoring classes.

3.3 SGDA Game Comparisons
When looking through all the Frogger games created by the project's participating middle school students, the variety of worksheet forms and agent color is apparent (Figure 1). The game agents and worksheets represent an outcome from the students' efforts to design something original within the designated parameters. In other words, the students played the games on SGDA, built on or expanded the previous students' designs to construct a unique and identifiable outcome, i.e. their own Frogger game. These new games are creative extrapolations of the Frogger examples the students originally played on SGDA, The project implementation structure seemed to increase the teacher's capability for fostering creativity in the students, in spite of the requirements normally placed on the average public school teacher. Some of these are listed below.

- Limited Class-time (less than an hour for a lesson)
- Role-Taking requirements (Class-time required)
- Increased disciplinary burden in the classroom (More class-time required)
- Compulsory curriculum with little flexibility for creativity
- Changing class periods & class frequency (no consistency)
- Increasing class size without restriction

So, given these difficulties and others currently placed on public school teachers, the expected range of creativity within the student participants was not expected to be as high as that expected from an after-school Computer Club [3, 4]. But since the student games uncharacteristically demonstrated creativity similar to Computer Club members, it was hypothesized that the project structure's elements could intrinsically foster creativity. So, the following sections further describe these possible elements that appear to have contributed to or fostered this outcome.

3.3.1 Creative Agent Depictions
Using Agentsheets software offers design flexibility for agents and worksheets that encourage creativity from the beginning of the learning process. Often other software parameters require the use of pre-designed agents. Within the project implementation structure, students are offered multiple examples of agent design and programming options from SGDA. The agent design skill is relatively simple to learn, so students are afforded the opportunity to

create exactly what they envision, to the extent of their learned ability (Figure 1). So, the uploaded games show a reasonably accurate representation of the students' creative abilities (Fig. 2).

3.3.2 Examples: Inspiring Creativity

Most project teachers chose to have their students play the games on SGDA before formal instruction. This intervention was usually viewed as a motivational tool to engender interest and encourage familiarity with a specific game, rather than a means of promoting creativity. But the teachers recognized a creative increase in their students' abilities in comparison to other creative project lessons.

Other ways that examples tend to be used in the SGD project to promote creativity are through peer-to-peer instruction and CC student mentoring. In both cases, a student is shown an example of the correct process and given the opportunity to ask questions before attempting the procedure on their own. From this process, students learn to see each other as creative resources.

4. CONCLUSIONS/DISCUSSION

Evidence presented in this paper suggests that the implementation structure of the SGD project has had a substantial role in increasing/fostering creativity within the participating schools. This structure, designed to promote interest in computer science (CS) through the design of games, using Agentsheets software, the multiple uses of examples (SGDA) and the subsequent uploading of these games to SGDA, resulted in a secondary effect of cultivating creativity. Since the participating schools offer a diverse student group (multiple locales, ethnicity, technology expertise, and class size), the SGD project structure constitutes the common factor in this equation. So, the authors believe that the characteristics of the SGD structure for introducing computer science to middle school students, which integrates the creative flexibility of Agentsheets, and teacher training and support, with the collaborative sharing and example resources of SGDA can be integrated to increase observed creativity while promoting CS.

SGDA is not unique in its function as a creative resource. But, the integral part it plays within the SGD project structure, coupled with the flexibility of the Agentsheets software, provides the students with a unique experience that appears to foster creativity. Throughout our observations, the students demonstrated creativity in the design of the game agents consistently. The teachers commented on this creativity within the project module. The indications from separate sources (uploaded games, observations, teacher comments) would tend to validate the SGD project structure and its guidelines as described, as a contributing to significant factor in promoting creativity.

5. FUTURE RESEARCH

Currently, the most obvious creative examples are represented by the agent depictions and worksheets. But all games must have programming and how creative the students have been with their programming is an aspect the authors hope to address in a future paper. As a relatively new curriculum, it will be interesting to track how the creativity aspect is affected as teachers continue to repeat the SGD lessons.

More investigation is warranted on the collection of student comments in comparison to, or supporting those of the teachers and the exploration of the elements within the SGD structure for use in other subject areas (geography, chemistry, etc.) for promoting creativity. Both could be valuable research areas.

The direct instruction/ discovery-learning continuum is another valuable research area. Public opinion holds that a freer discovery-learning approach is more conducive to fostering creativity, but most participating teachers favored a more scaffolded approach. Further research could help clarify this issue.

6. ACKNOWLEDGMENTS

This material is based in part upon work supported by the National Science Foundation under Grant Numbers No. DLR-0833612 and IIP-0848962. Any opinions, findings, and conclusions expressed in this material are those of the authors and do not necessarily reflect the views of the National Science Foundation.

7. REFERENCES

[1] Goncalo, J.A. & Staw, B.M., "Individualism-collectivism and group creativity", *Organizational Behavior &Human Decision Processes*, Vol. 100, 96-109, 2006.

[2] Bronson, P. & Merryman, A., "The Creativity Crisis", *Newsweek*, July 10, 2010.

[3] Repenning, A., Basawapatna, A., & Koh, K. H., Making university education more like middle school computer club: facilitating the flow of inspiration. In Proc. *14th WCCCE 2009*, Burnaby, British Columbia, Canada, 2009.

[4] Handler, M. G., & Strudler, N., The ISTE Foundation Standard: Issues of Implementation, *Journal of Computing in Teacher Education*, Vol. 13, N2, 16-23 Jan 1997.

[5] Adams, G. L., & Engelmann, S., Research on Direct Instruction: 25 Years beyond DISTAR, *Educational Achievement Systems*, 1996.

[6] Hammer, D., Discovery Learning and Discovery Teaching, *Cognition and Instruction*, Volume 15, Issue 4, 485-529, 1997.

[7] Peppler, K. & Kafai, Y. B., Collaboration, Computation, and Creativity: Media Arts Practices in Urban Youth Culture. In C. Hmelo- Silver & A. O'Donnell (Eds.), *In Proc. Computer Supported Collaborative Learning*, New Brunswick, NJ, 2007.

[8] Repenning, A., "AgentSheets®: an Interactive Simulation Environment with End-User Programmable Agents,"*In Proc. Interaction 2000*, Tokyo, Japan, 2000.

[9] Repenning, A., & Ambach, J.,"Visual AgenTalk: Anatomy of a Low Threshold, High Ceiling End User Programming Environment," *Department of Computer Science, University of Colorado Tech Report # CU-CS-802-96*, January, 1996.

[10] Herring, S.R., Chang, C.C., Krantzler, J. & Bailey, B.P. Getting inspired! Understanding how & why examples are used in creative design practice. *CHI2009*, 87-96, 2009.

[11] Squire, K., Video games in education. *International Journal of Intelligent Simulations and Gaming*, (2) 1. 2003

A Pre-College Professional Development Program

Stephen Cooper

Computer Science
Department
Stanford University
Stanford, CA 94305

coopers@stanford.edu

Wanda Dann

Computer Science Department
Carnegie Mellon University
Pittsburgh, PA 15213

wpdann@andrew.cmu.edu

Dan Lewis

Computer Engineering
Department
Santa Clara University
Santa Clara, CA 95053

dlewis@scu.edu

Pam Lawhead

Computer and Information
Science
University of Mississippi
University, MS 38677

lawhead@cs.olemiss.edu

Susan Rodger

Computer Science
Department
Duke University
Durham, NC 27708

rodger@cs.duke.edu

Madeleine Schep

Computer and Information
Science
Columbia College
Columbia, SC 29203

mschep@columbiasc.edu

RoxAnn Stalvey

Department of Computer
Science
College of Charleston
Charleston, SC 29401

stalveyr@cs.cofc.edu

ABSTRACT

In this paper, we describe the results of a four-year collaborative project conducted among six higher education institutions and their partner pre-college school systems across the US. The primary goal of the project was to offer professional development to middle and high school teachers to enable those teachers to create modules and courses to excite their students about computing. The project used Alice, a software program that utilizes 3-D visualization methods, as a medium to create a high-level of interest in computer graphics, animation, and storytelling among middle and high school students, to build understanding of object-based programming. More than 100 middle and high school teachers participated in the project, with approximately 80% of those reporting that they had used what they learned during summer workshops in their classrooms during the subsequent years.

Categories and Subject Descriptors

K.3.2 [**Computer and Information Science Education**]: Computer Science Education

General Terms: Measurement, Experimentation

Keywords: Alice, pre-college, professional development.

1. INTRODUCTION

Five years before Cuny's ambitious 10,000 teacher project [2], the authors had a more modest proposal: Would it be possible to offer sufficient professional development to 100 middle and high school teachers, to help them improve the quality of computing instruction the teachers were offering their students? Regardless

how well (or how poorly) computer science may be taught in college, college faculty cannot reach the students who are not sufficiently curious to at least take an introductory computing class. There is a second interest towards trying to expose more pre-college students to computing. Identified more than a decade ago by Snyder's NRC panel [6], and reiterated by many others, most recently in Rushkoff's new book [11], the reality is that all students need a certain competence with computing in general, and even with programming in particular.

We had good success using Alice in college [5]. Based on sales reports of Learning to Program with Alice [3], we were aware that Alice was being taught in pre-college (we guessed mainly in high school). So, it seemed natural to try to use Alice as part of a high and middle school program. In the US, middle school refers to students in grades 6-8 (ages 11-14), and high school typically refers to students in approximately grades 9-12 (ages 14-18).

We formed a team of interested college faculty and possible middle and high school teachers and school districts who were open to participating in this ambitious project. After a half-year of team-building, we identified the National Science Foundation's Information Technology Experiences for Students and Teachers (ITEST) program [13] as a potential funding source. The plan was to run a pilot program with the Virginia Beach School District (VBSD) starting in summer 2006, with implementation by the teachers during the 2006-2007 year. Modifications to the program would be made, with roll out to the Denver, Colorado, North Carolina, San Francisco Bay, California, and South Carolina areas during summer 2007 and to the Mississippi area in summer 2008 (with implementation by the teachers during the subsequent academic year). Participating colleges included Saint Joseph's University (working with VBSD), Colorado School of Mines (Denver), Duke (North Carolina), Santa Clara University (San Francisco), College of Charleston and Columbia College (South Carolina) and the University of Mississippi (Mississippi). Dann and Cooper were to work with each of the colleges in preparing for their parts of the project. The team received notification in summer 2006 that its proposal was going to be funded, and the pilot program was run. However, the actual award was not made until February 2007, and each of the 2007 sites pushed back plans to run teacher summer professional development until summer 2008, with planned teacher roll-out in the 2008-2009 year (and in the 2009-2010 year for teachers who were not able to get necessary approvals in place for the 2008-2009 year).

2. THE PROFESSIONAL DEVELOPMENT PROGRAM

2.1 Teacher Recruitment

Teacher recruitment was accomplished by using existing college outreach resources, communicating with the appropriate state Department of Education officials to make teachers aware of the existence of this program, presenting at state teacher conferences/workshops, and by individually contacting specific schools. In fact, teacher recruitment turned out not to be a challenge as there were far more teachers who wished to participate than there were available slots. Teachers who wished to participate needed to fill out an application, and most needed to include a letter of support from the school principal.

There was a significant challenge in identifying the "right" teachers for the project. There was a desire to include multiple teachers from the same school, or at least from neighboring schools, to provide a sense of community once the teachers returned to their schools. There was also the desire to reach out to a wider variety of schools (geographic as well as the demographic of the types of students served) and teacher backgrounds. Each site chose a different set of criteria for selecting teachers. For example, the Duke site focused on non-programming teachers and consisted of mostly middle school teachers or high school teachers that did not teach computer science.

2.2 Logistics

Teachers were expected to participate in three aspects of the project: attending and participating in three weeks of summer workshops, using Alice in one or more classes during the following academic year, and reporting back on their experiences the next summer. Teachers were paid a small stipend to attend each of the three weeks of summer workshops. (In the US, teachers often work second jobs in the summer, and the stipend helped to offset the loss of income for the three weeks in which they would be working with Alice.) They were paid a larger stipend upon reporting the following summer about their experiences (and sharing their curricular materials and collecting required data). During each of the first two weeks of summer workshops in the first summer, and for the wrap-up meeting the second summer, teachers were provided housing either at or near the college.

2.3 The Summer Program

As per the requirements of the ITEST program, comprehensive programs for students and teachers track, participating middle and high school teachers were required to receive 120 hours of summer professional development. The 120 contact hours were broken up into three week-long 40 hour activities. The first week was a workshop focusing on teaching the teachers Alice. The location was at the partner college, with either Cooper or Dann or Don Slater traveling to the site to co-run the workshop with the local college partner. Slater was not an original part of this project, but as a master Alice instructor, was called in to help co-run several of the workshops. The second week focused on curriculum development by the teachers. Again, Cooper or Dann

or Slater traveled to the site to co-lead the workshop (along with the college partner). The final summer activity was a one-week camp for students, led by the teachers who were trying out their curricular materials in a gentler environment (than in class), and observed by the college partner and by their peers.

There were a few differences across the summer program, most noticeably in North Carolina, where the focus was on middle school teachers who were not computing teachers. The focus of the first two workshops was for teachers to learn programming concepts and then have time to apply those concepts by working on Alice worlds related to their discipline. They would show their worlds during an animation fair and get feedback on them. There were two third weeks to split the teachers into two groups and to hold two one-week camps for middle school children.

2.4 Academic Year Support

The specific interaction between college and middle/high school teachers during the school year varied across sites. For example, in the VBSD pilot, Cooper traveled once a month to Virginia. Each month, he observed a different teacher teaching an Alice class. During each visit (which generally occurred when VBSD had in-service half-days), the team met in the afternoon to discuss various challenges they were facing, and innovative approaches individuals were using.

In North Carolina, Rodger visited one school. She also presented at the Durham Public School technical fair to show other teachers the work the team had been doing and also for recruiting teachers for additional workshops. Rodger had a few teachers visit her at Duke to show work and ask questions on worlds on which they were working. In South Carolina, Schep or Stalvey visited most teachers once a semester. Other sites made use of graduate and/or undergraduate students. Students were most frequently used to build specific virtual worlds to illustrate concepts for teachers, or to help teachers when they got stuck.

3. RESULTS

Results from the pilot project in Virginia Beach have been impressive. Four years later, Alice continues to be taught as the introductory computing class. There has been more than a tripling of students taking the introductory computing class (across the school district), with an analogous tripling of students taking the AP CS follow-on course. The increase in the number of women taking the AP CS class has gone from near 0% to almost 25%, and minorities also represent nearly 20% of the students. Further details are available in [1].

For the later sites where the professional development was run in summer 2008, with classroom implementation in either the 2008-2009 year or during the 2009-2010 year, it is still too soon to see the impact. The external evaluator's final report indicated that teachers who participated in the summer professional development sessions saw a statistically significant increase in their programming and programming in Alice knowledge as demonstrated by on a content exam administered as a pre- and post-test at the start and at the conclusion of the program (p = 0.000 for teachers of all sites combined, indicating significance at α=.025). The following remarks are drawn from the external evaluator analysis of several qualitative assessment instruments used in assessing our project. End of program (middle and high school) teacher evaluations showed that the teachers felt that the topics and instructional methods covered in the workshops were adequate for them to teach their students, and that interaction with partnering college faculty and college students met their needs. Teachers felt that Alice made programming fun and easier to teach their students. Teachers identified a myriad of benefits for classroom use of Alice. More than 90% of reporting teachers indicated plans to continue using Alice in their classrooms. There was a desire for additional follow-up (beyond the two-day wrap-up workshops) in future summers. There was also the desire primarily among middle school teachers to tailor Alice workshop instruction to specific individual subjects. In response to specific self-assessment questions, teachers believed that students enjoyed programming in Alice, students exhibited greater interest and spent more time on task and showed greater persistence in debugging programs, and were more likely to identify programming as a creative task. Teachers reported spending more time discussing objects and classes, as well as using more visual examples throughout their class. In summary, the evaluators concluded that there is evidence to support that significant advancement had been made towards the following goals: 1) providing and assessing teacher professional development, 2) enabling teachers to modify as appropriate, existing curricular materials, and 3) to establish partnerships as a network of K-12 teachers and local colleges at several locations throughout the US.

Perhaps one of the greatest impacts was not measured by the evaluators. This has been the continued excitement and enthusiasm by participating teachers. Not only are more than 80% of the participating teachers continuing to use Alice within their classes, they have been encouraging colleagues to adopt their materials, and going to local and statewide conferences to share what they have done. Another impact has been the surprising number of comments by teachers about their remarkable successes with special needs students, particularly with autistic children.

4. LESSONS LEARNED AND RECOMMENDATIONS

This section summarizes some of the items the team learned in working closely with middle and high school teachers over the past four years.

Difference in backgrounds among high school teachers: The absence of teacher certification for teaching secondary computer science is a challenge in the US. Depending on the state, mathematics, science, or business teachers are typically tasked with teaching a computing class. The teacher's field of study has a great deal to do with their previous programming experience. For example, mathematics teachers often are required to take a computing class as part of their undergraduate mathematics major. This is rarely the case for business teachers. Thus, teacher backgrounds (in terms of knowing how to program) vary greatly. As a result, it was a challenge to quickly and effectively instruct teachers of such varied backgrounds how to program using Alice (as the Alice content was taught over a one-week introduction). It was certainly possible to pair more experienced programming teachers with less experienced teachers, but it was quite a challenge to provide teachers who had little previous programming experience a sufficient exposure to programming in Alice in a week. While some of the workshop sites countered this challenge by including a non-trivial amount of Alice instruction in the second week (where the focus was intended to be curriculum development), the reality was that it probably would have been easier to have run the first week of Alice content in two separate

two to three day workshops, allowing some time for the teachers to practice what they had learned. Unfortunately, our budget did not allow for this, and the logistics of flying Cooper or Dann to a site an additional time was more than we could schedule/handle.

Differences in backgrounds between middle and high school teachers: We did not initially create a completely separate workshop of Alice instruction for the middle school teachers. We had (wrongly) assumed that the high school workshop could be covered (albeit at a slower pace) by the sites that had either a large number or exclusively middle school teachers. This was not a realistic assumption. The middle school teachers had no previous programming experience and frequently less comfort with computer use. They were also often generalists, rather than specialists, so were required to know less content about more subjects. In our case, this meant that they had less comfort with mathematics, so that teaching functions and their use in Alice was more of a challenge. We also needed to spend more time with the middle school teachers helping them identify where in their curriculum they could place an Alice unit.

Importance of involving school IT directors: While we required interested teachers to obtain a letter of support/commitment from the school principal (guaranteeing sufficient institutional support), we did not likewise require a letter of support from the IT director. In several cases, the IT director was unwilling to initially install Alice on school computers leading teachers to either need to provide students with memory sticks with which to run Alice (in the cases where they had permissions to run software in this manner) to the more extreme case of delaying their teaching of Alice by a year while convincing the IT director that Alice would not damage the machines.

Continued involvement throughout the school year: While the summer workshops were an important kick-off, to get the middle and high school teachers started, it was the continued involvement during the academic year that helped to ensure the project's success. While each site handled academic year involvement differently, each site did continue the partnership between college and middle/high schools.

Showcasing teacher work: An Alice Symposium was held at Duke University on June 17, 2009 with over 120 attendees. Twenty-five refereed papers on Alice topics were presented in two parallel tracks. Presenters included K-12 teachers from all levels (elementary school to high school) and college professors. We describe a few of the topics presented. An elementary school teacher and participant at the Duke ITEST site spoke about lessons learned in integrating Alice into a 5th grade enrichment class. Other topics included using Alice as games, integrating Alice with Robotics, and curricula for integrating Alice into different K-12 levels. Two two-day workshops were held prior to the Alice Symposium, one a follow-up workshop for Duke ITEST participants and the other an Alice 3.0 workshop.

Creating a community of practice: Ni [7, 8] explored reasons that teachers choose to adopt a new curricular approach. In particular, Ni identified the importance of "making the innovation fit and work in a local department." We believe that the continued partnership between Cooper and the teachers in the VBSD (and the frequent meetings throughout the school year) helped the VBSD team to make Alice work. In particular, the monthly meetings helped the team to develop what Fincher and Tenenberg [4] call a "Disciplinary Commons", a community where teachers teaching the same class can get together and improve upon each member's teaching.

A repository of teaching and training materials: Many teaching and training materials for using Alice 2.2 at the middle school level have been created as part of this ITEST project and made publicly available [10, 14]. This site includes tutorials, videos, and sample Alice worlds. The repository includes a variety of getting started tutorials from one hour to four hours of instruction, and over 40 tutorials on either computer science topics, animation topics or projects. Examples of computer science topics include functions, lists and variables. The titles of the tutorials try to appeal to middle school students, instead of using foreign-to-them computer science terms. For example, the title of the functions tutorial is "How tall are you?" Examples of animation topics include lighting, changing scenes and camera control. The videos and sample Alice worlds cover a variety of disciplines including science, language arts, mathematics, history, foreign language and music. Other materials available on this site are teacher participant lesson plans, schedules for using the tutorials in workshops, and sample worlds from teachers and students.

Teachers practicing their teaching of what they had learned: As part of the original ITEST grant, teachers were required to receive 120 contact hours. After the first two weeks of summer workshops (80 contact hours), the team decided that the remaining 40 hours would best be spent by having the teachers co-run (in partnership with the local college partners) a one-week "summer camp" for students, where the teacher would practice teaching with Alice. The impact of this 3rd week varied greatly. Some teachers felt it gave them the confidence to successfully teach with Alice during the next year, and that the feedback they received from their peers was valuable. (Teachers ran the camps in small groups, taking turns teaching and evaluating one another.) Others found this 3rd week to be less useful, and indicated that they felt they could have more productively used this time getting ready for their class. In North Carolina, during the third third week, the Duke team ran the kids camp. The teachers worked on lesson plans and observed the kids working. The teachers gained confidence in using Alice for their courses by seeing how easily the kids learned Alice and how excited they were to program in Alice.

Where computing fits in middle school: Middle schools already have a tight schedule and are unlikely to create a new course for computer science. Our approach is to integrate Alice into all disciplines. First, most middle schools have students create projects that might be a poster, an electronic presentation, or a physical model. Alice fits in nicely as another medium for a project in any discipline. An Alice world can tell a story, include interactive questions, or be a game. Middle school students can easily learn enough Alice to create a simple story. With further instruction, Alice can be used for more complicated tasks such as problem solving in science and math. For teachers, Alice can help them animate a topic and create fun quizzes. For example, one of our teachers created a funny story about school safety to show at the start of the year and a science teacher created a story on how hot spot volcanoes are formed, with a mad scientist going underground and a volcano being formed and bursting through the ocean. The paper [9] gives more detail on this approach for integrating Alice into the middle school level.

Where teaching computing fits in high school: Courses in computing found among US high schools include courses on office productivity applications (e.g., word processing, spreadsheets, presentation software), web and graphic design, robotics, and programming at introductory and advanced levels. In recent years, enrollment in Advanced Placement (AP) courses in computing has dropped, leading to elimination of the more advanced of the two AP tests in computer science.

Coupled with this is the absence of any certification program for teachers wishing to teach computing (resulting in computing classes being taught by business teachers, math teachers, as well as by teachers of other disciplines), and an absence of state-level standards for what computing and/or programming courses should entail in many states. (See [12] for greater detail about certification and standards.) There is also the widespread view among state educators that computing belongs as part of Career and Technical Education (CTE). CTE is largely a rebranding of the Vocational Education programs (auto mechanic training, woodworking, home economics, etc.), historically intended for those high school students who were not likely college-bound.

Computing teachers (who themselves have a varied computing background) face a wide range of student ability and interest in their classes. It is thus necessary to make computing an exciting class (as it is an elective course and competes with the other electives in the school), as well as a rigorous one. In addition, the current generation of students has grown up immersed in the media-rich content of the Web and computer games and expects more from a programming course than how to write the "text in, text out" applications of the past. Having to make sure that semicolons, parentheses and curly braces are properly placed only increases their frustration.

Alice has been shown to be an engaging and effective introduction to programming [5]. Running an Alice world produces a 3D animation that allows students to create visually appealing interactive games, simulations and stories, thus providing students the motivation to pursue more upper-level courses in programming and computer science. Alice prepares students for the transition to more advanced programming courses by providing mechanisms that support modular design, the object-orientated paradigm, and concurrent and event-driven programming.

5. FUTURE WORK AND CONCLUSIONS

Building on the success of the first ITEST project, we have proposed a scale-up ITEST grant expanding on the work described in this paper. The goal of this project is to provide state-wide training and support through a partnership with college faculty to middle and high school teachers to enable them to teach appropriate computer science concepts through the use of Alice. The project will be based in three states which were included in the first ITEST project: Mississippi, North Carolina, and South Carolina with the goal of attracting more students, particularly women and racial minorities, to computing.

At each institution, summer workshops will instruct middle and high school teachers in Alice. Teachers will develop curricular materials for the broader Alice community to be distributed online. In the following academic year, teachers will introduce Alice into their classrooms with the purpose of exciting students about computing, increasing student knowledge of fundamental computing and programming concepts, and growing the number of students who study in a computational field.

In North Carolina and South Carolina, two-week workshops will be held in the summer on college campuses to offer instruction in Alice and to develop curricular materials. A follow-up workshop (NC) and mini-conference (SC) will be held the next summer. Year-long support from college faculty, undergraduate students, or experienced high school teachers will be provided to teacher participants. The North Carolina site will target middle school teachers while the South Carolina site will target high school teachers. The Mississippi site follows a different model due to geographic constraints. The workshop organized by college faculty from Mississippi will train teachers to become master teacher trainers of Alice. Those teachers will then organize and run Alice workshops in their school districts for other teachers.

This project will have a special focus in building community throughout the tri-state region and sharing materials developed with teachers throughout the world. Teachers will present at local, statewide and national conferences. An online repository will be created that will house all curricular and instructional material developed during the pilot ITEST project and all instructional material created during this new phase. Wikis (or similar structures) will be created so teachers will easily communicate among each other. All three sites will run animation fairs where students will be able to display their work. Those fairs have been successful in generating interest among teachers and students.

We hope through our positive experiences with the ITEST grant working with middle and high school teachers in the United States, other faculty will be inspired to reach out within their own communities to encourage broadened participation in computer science. Through the collective efforts of faculty around the world, we can help prevent declining enrollments and retention in computer science and shape young people into computational thinkers.

In conclusion, we hope that faculty members interested in working with middle and high school teachers take advantage of what we have learned during our ITEST project.

6. ACKNOWLEDGMENTS
This material is partially based upon work supported by the National Science Foundation under Grant Numbers 0624654, 0624642, 0624528, 0623808, and 0624479. Any opinions, findings, and conclusions or recommendations expressed in this material are those of the author(s) and do not necessarily reflect the views of the National Science Foundation.

7. REFERENCES
[1] Cooper, S., Dann, W., and Harrison, J. 2010. A k-12 college partnership. In *Proceedings of the 41st ACM technical symposium on Computer science education* (SIGCSE '10). ACM, New York, NY, USA, 320-324.

[2] Cuny, J. 2010. Finding 10,000 teachers. *CSTA Voice*, 5, 6 (Jan. 2010), 1-2.

[3] Dann, W., Cooper, S., and Pausch, R. 2008. *Learning to Program with Alice* (2 ed.). Prentice Hall Press, Upper Saddle River, NJ, USA.

[4] Fincher, S. and Tenenberg, J. 2007. Warren's question. In *Proceedings of the third international workshop on Computing education research* (ICER '07). ACM, New York, NY, USA, 51-60

[5] Moskal, B., Lurie, D., and Cooper, S. 2004. Evaluating the effectiveness of a new instructional approach. In *Proceedings of the 35th SIGCSE technical symposium on Computer science education* (SIGCSE '04). ACM, New York, NY, USA, 75-79.

[6] National Research Council. 1999. *Being Fluent in Information Technology*. (Larry Snyder, Panel chair). National Academy Press.

[7] Ni, L. 2009. What makes CS teachers change?: factors influencing CS teachers' adoption of curriculum innovations. *SIGCSE Bull.* 41, 1 (March 2009), 544-548.

[8] Ni, L., McKlin, T., and Guzdial, M. 2010. How do computing faculty adopt curriculum innovations?: the story from instructors. In *Proceedings of the 41st ACM technical symposium on Computer Science Education* (SIGCSE '10). ACM, New York, NY, USA, 544-548.

[9] Rodger,S., Hayes, J., Lezin, G., Qin, H., Nelson, D., Tucker, R., Lopez, M., Cooper, C., Dann, W., and Slater, D. 2009. Engaging Middle School Teachers and Students with Alice in a Diverse Set of Subjects. In *Proceedings of the 40th SIGCSE Technical Symposium on Computer Science Education*, (SIGCSE '09), 271-275.

[10] Rodger, S., Bashford, M., Dyck, L., Hayes, J., Liang, L., Nelson, D., and Qin, H. 2010. Enhancing K-12 Education with Alice Programming Adventures. In *Proceedings of the 15th Annual Conference on Innovation and Technology in Computer Science Education* (ITiCSE 2010), Ankara, Turkey, 234-238.

[11] Rushkoff, D. 2010. Program or be Programmed: Ten Commands for a Digital Age. O/R Books.

[12] Wilson, C., Sudol, L., Stephenson, C., and Stehlik, M. 2010. *Running on empty: The failure to teach k–12 computer science in the digital age*. ACM. Available as: http://www.acm.org/runningonempty/fullreport.pdf

[13] NSF ITEST program solicitation. 2005. Available as: http://www.nsf.gov/pubs/2005/nsf05621/nsf05621.htm

[14] Alice repository of teaching materials. Available as: www.cs.duke.edu/csed/alice/aliceInSchool

GUIGraph – Editing Live Object Diagrams for GUI Generation Enables New Pedagogy in CS1/2

Duane Buck
Otterbein University
Westerville, Ohio
614-823-1793
dbuck@otterbein.edu

ABSTRACT

The GUIGraph software tool supports a new pedagogy, motivates students, and solves early user-interface issues. Regardless of the type of curriculum, it can provide an initial, intuitive introduction to object-oriented thinking, even before coding is discussed. By editing a UML-like object diagram, the student creates and links virtual Java Swing objects representing a user-interface, and can instantly view and manipulate its realization. GUIGraph is unique in that the student specifies an object structure to be created, equivalent to writing complex source code. When requested, GUIGraph generates the Java source code of an abstract class that constructs the object structure. The student then completes the coding of a concrete class that implements its application specific abstract methods. The functionality of the application is cleanly separated from its user-interface, which helps build design intuition, and iterative refinement of the user-interface is supported by regenerating the abstract class.

Categories and Subject Descriptors

D.1.7 [**Programming Techniques**]: Visual Programming

General Terms

Design, Human Factors, and Languages.

Keywords

Object-graph, User-interface, and Pedagogy.

1. INTRODUCTION

GUIGraph is a software tool supporting Java Swing development that is being made freely available by the author. While GUIGraph is intended for general use, its design was motivated by pedagogy. It utilizes a live object-graph editor that allows students to build a deep level of comprehension of object structures while synthesizing an application's interface.

Traditional curricula have relied on the student's imagination to visualize the object structure implied by source code. Recently, software tools (e.g., BlueJ [2], jGRASP [6] and others) have provided the capability for direct object visualization and manipulation, and the education community has recognized their importance. [7] Those tools are most applicable to objects-early curricula. GUIGraph is a very different tool, but it also provides opportunities for the student to benefit from experiences with live objects, and due to its intuitive nature it has the advantage of being applicable independently of the type of curriculum.

Permission to make digital or hard copies of all or part of this work for personal or classroom use is granted without fee provided that copies are not made or distributed for profit or commercial advantage and that copies bear this notice and the full citation on the first page. To copy otherwise, or republish, to post on servers or to redistribute to lists, requires prior specific permission and/or a fee.
ITiCSE'11, June 27–29, 2011, Darmstadt, Germany.
Copyright 2011 ACM 978-1-4503-0697-3/11/06...$10.00.

With GUIGraph, the student directly manipulates a UML-like object diagram to define a user-interface, and immediately sees its realization. Because the student does not write traditional source code, GUIGraph has the potential to provide new learning experiences early in the curriculum as students intuitively build object structures to create behaviors.

This paper is structured as follows: Section 2 discusses the potential impact of GUIGraph on pedagogy in the early curriculum. Section 3 describes technical aspects of GUIGraph and its design choices. Section 4 describes object-graph editing within GUIGraph. Section 5 gives examples of two object-graphs and their realizations. Section 6 discusses classroom experiences using GUIGraph. Section 7 compares GUIGraph to other user-interface generators and "object workbench" tools. Section 8 is devoted to how GUIGraph might evolve and makes a call to educators to help shape its direction. After the conclusion is presented in Section 9, Sections 10 and 11 provide acknowledgements and references.

2. PEDAGOGY

Copyright 2011 ACM 978-1-4503-0697-3/11/06...$10.00..Copyright 2011 ACM 978-1-4503-0697-3/11/06...$10.00..With GUIGraph, students specify the creation of object structures without writing traditional source code. They see the realization immediately, and can also extend the generated abstract class with their own methods in a concrete class. GUIGraph is applicable at the beginning of both control-structures-early and objects-early curricula. With an objects-early curriculum, the advantages of live object manipulation are obvious. With control-structures-early, the use of GUIGraph early-on provides an easier transition to objects and classes later. The students are doubly motivated because GUIGraph presents objects in an intuitive way and they are working within a familiar and interesting domain.

An additional benefit of using GUIGraph early in the curriculum is that students create realistic applications starting with their first assignment. There is no need for unrealistic dialog-based interfaces using static methods and console I/O or a series of dialog boxes. Using GUIGraph, the student naturally learns to separate the user-interface from the functionality of the application. In fact, a good source of assignments is to reimplement textbook examples using GUIGraph and cleanly separate those two aspects of the application.

GUIGraph has been under development for several years, and has been used extensively for the past two years. Our curriculum is "inside/out" [4] where the student first implements methods in the context of a class. The student sees a design and implements methods specified in the design. Originally, GUIGraph was seen as a tool for general use, including use by instructors to create shells for assignments. Its pedagogical importance was recognized later, and that is now its primary motivation.

In my courses a user-interface may evolve over multiple assignments, and GUIGraph has been designed with this in mind. When requested, GUIGraph generates the source code for an abstract Java class that constructs the diagram's object structure. Because the interface is fully defined in the GUIGraph file representing the object diagram, and the application specific code is contained in a Java concrete class extending the abstract class (and possibly in other application classes), there is never a need to edit the generated abstract file. It is safely regenerated whenever the interface is changed, so there is no need for additional tool support. GUIGraph works equally well with any integrated development environment or with a text editor and the command line. The separation of the user-interface from the implementation of the functionality also helps the student to build design intuition.

3. TECHNICAL OVERVIEW

GUIGraph presents the user with a graph editor with which they create a UML-like object diagram. The graph nodes are primarily virtual Java Swing objects. Directed edges connect the nodes to show aggregation. Some node types are shared and allow multiple impinging edges, although cycles are not possible. Graph manipulations are performed exclusively with the mouse. The left-button is used to select nodes and move them for visual appearance (having no relevance to their meaning). When a node is selected, configuration information for the node may be viewed and edited at the bottom of the window. The right-button brings up a context menu used to create and link nodes.

Although the coverage of the Java Swing library is not complete, a majority is supported. Fortunately, since the introduction of `BoxLayout` to the Java library, the complex and unintuitive `GridBagLayout` is no longer required for sophisticated layouts. It is not currently supported in GUIGraph.

An attempt has been made to make the virtual Swing objects and their structural hierarchy correspond as closely as possible to actual Swing objects and their structural hierarchy, as long as that does not interfere with making GUIGraph consistent and easy to learn. For much of Swing, the goals are consistent. The parts of Swing which are inconsistent, hard to learn, or tedious have been "virtualized" and appear to be consistent and simple in the graph. GUIGraph uses three object-graph abstractions from raw Swing, as described below. In reality, everything is done purely within Swing when the graph is realized. As a result, unlike some GUI generators, no special runtime library is required.

The first abstraction is the virtual object that is a component of a `JTabbedPane`. In raw Swing, there is only a tab index that is used to refer to a particular tab and manipulate its attributes, instead of having a "JTab" object. In GUIGraph the type of this "object" node is `int` with an annotation indicating it is the tab index. The tab's attributes are attached to the node, and the `int` may be given a Java identifier to use in the concrete class to identify the tab when `JTabbedPane` method invocations are required.

The second abstraction is that you may add any number of `JToolBar` objects directly to a virtual `JFrame` (or other top-level container) using the context menu command "Add JToolBar." In Swing, each `JToolBar` object must be added into its own `JPanel` with `BorderLayout`, which is then added into the Center of an enclosing `JPanel`. The ultimate content of the `JFrame` is added into the Center of the inner most `JPanel`. This complex structure is built automatically by GUIGraph when the interface is realized.

The third abstraction in GUIGraph is that `JPanel`s are unified with their layout manager into one object node. This is because the layout manager has an important influence on how the `JPanel` is used. The node's icon pictures the `JPanel`'s layout.

When a graph is constructed, it starts with a top-level container. Currently, the supported top-level containers are `JFrame`, `JDialog`, and `JPanel`. Note that `JPanel` is provided so that users can utilize GUIGraph to design part of a larger user-interface. The user can then add content to the container, and set its attributes. At any time, the user can display the current realization. There is also the option to have the realization updated after each graph edit, which works particularly well. The graph itself is saved for later editing: The GUIGraph file (with suffix "ggf") becomes one of the application's "source" files.

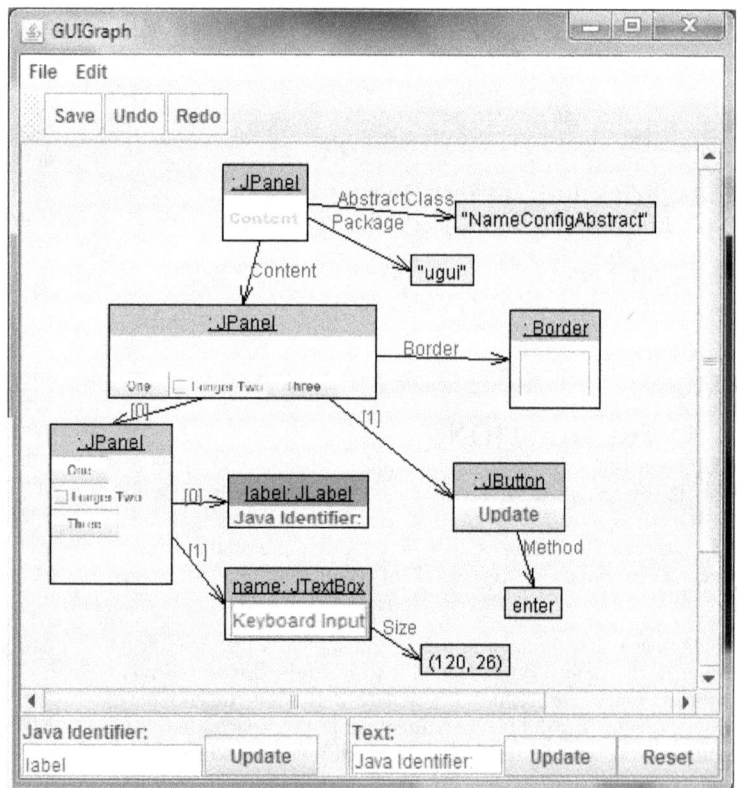

Figure 1: Diagram of `NameConfigAbstract`

Attributes of a top-level node include the name of its generated abstract class and its package (if any). This information is used when the user requests generation of the abstract class or an initial concrete class.

The user decides which Swing objects are made available to the concrete class by giving each of those object nodes a Java identifier. The user can also add a "Method" attribute to any Swing object that supports listeners. This causes the method to be declared as abstract, and code to be inserted into the constructor to make the connection. The initial generated concrete class has a stub for each method that displays a message dialog.

Because code generation is potentially confusing, care has been taken to minimize possible loss of work. Each generated source file begins with a date and time generated comment. When generating, if the file already exists, it is examined to see if it has been modified. If so, the user is advised of the possible conflict. The abstract class also begins with a comment warning that the file should not be edited because it may be regenerated.

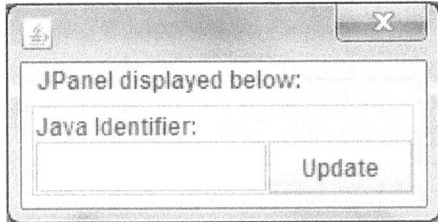

Figure 2: Realization of `NameConfigAbstract`

the window. The configuration data is specialized to the node type, and the node's icon visually reflects the configuration data. The icon changes whenever the configuration data is updated.

While configuration data applies only to one node type, attributes are not specialized to one node type. To reduce visual distraction, attributes are shown with nodes drawn as rectangles with one line of text, and they have incoming edges labeled with the name of the attribute. The type of an attribute is not shown explicitly, but may be deduced from the syntax of its text. Java identifiers are shown verbatim, `Strings` are shown with the text inside double-quotes, and `Dimension` objects are shown as ordered pairs.

When editing the diagram, everything is accomplished with the mouse. The left button is used to select a node or drag it to a new (visual) location in the diagram. The right button brings up a context menu. A context menu allows new nodes (virtual swing objects and attributes) to be created and linked to the identified node. It also provides the option of linking existing nodes by first selecting one of the nodes and then pointing to the other node while bringing up the context menu. In addition, one may unlink a node from incoming edges, duplicate or delete a single node, or its subtree. Right-dragging is like left-dragging, except that the node and its subtree are moved.

When developing a complex interface, the diagram can become busy, so the editor allows parts of the diagram to be collapsed and expanded when needed. The context menu has a "Frame Children" checkbox that when selected causes a frame to be drawn around the identified node and its children. If a child is itself framed or is a shared node, it is not included in the parent's frame. Double-clicking the frame will collapse it so that only the parent is shown and outgoing child edges are shown connecting to the parent. Double-clicking a collapsed frame expands it again. When a frame is selected, it is brought to the front. This scheme allows the user to utilize the available diagram area more efficiently while observing the overall structure.

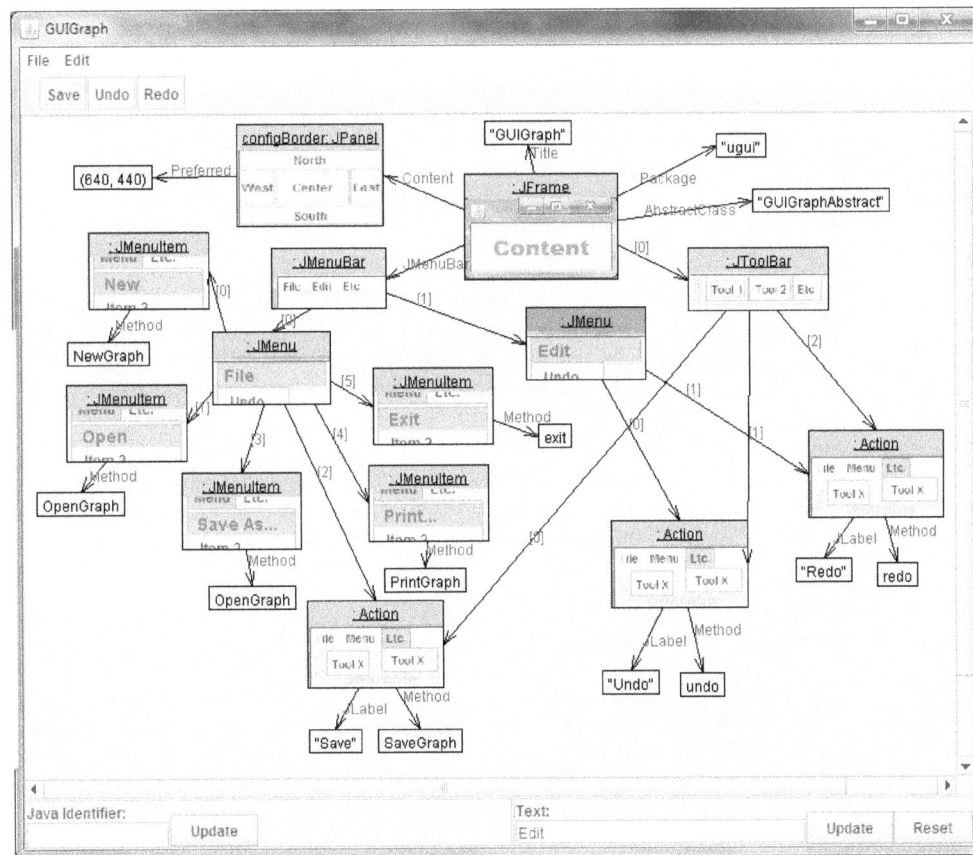

Figure 3: Diagram of `GUIGraphAbstract`

4. THE GRAPH DIAGRAM EDITOR

The graph editor was designed to be both robust and intuitive, and evolved with experience. Each node corresponding to a virtual Swing object is represented as rectangle. At the top of the rectangle, standard UML object diagram notation is shown including its type and (optional) Java identifier. Below it in the rectangle is an icon evocative of the object it represents. Often these are the bit-maps rendered by an actual Swing object. When a node is selected, its configuration data is shown at the bottom of

5. EXAMPLES

Parts of the GUIGraph interface were developed within GUIGraph itself. The examples shown below display GUIGraph diagrams ("ggf" files) used in generating GUIGraph's interface.

5.1 The Java Identifier `JPanel`

Figure 1 shows the GUIGraph application editing the object diagram corresponding to the `NameConfigAbstract` class. Figure 2 shows the realization provided while editing the graph.

At the lower left of Figures 1 and 3 can be seen the result, within the GUIGraph interface itself, of the generated abstract class.

5.2 The GUIGraph Application `JFrame`

Figure 3 shows the object diagram for the abstract class (`GUIGraphAbstract`) used to generate the GUIGraph application's `JFrame`. Note that the `Action` nodes are shareable within a GUIGraph diagram, like the actual Swing objects. Figure 4 shows the user-interface's realization while editing. The Edit menu is shown opened to demonstrate that the realization may be manipulated and that the same `Actions` are available from both the toolbar and menu. The generated abstract file is extended by the GUIGraph concrete class to produce the interface shown in Figures 1 and 3. The Center and South of the "Content" `JPanel` are added by the constructor of the GUIGraph concrete class by using the `configBorder` Java identifier.

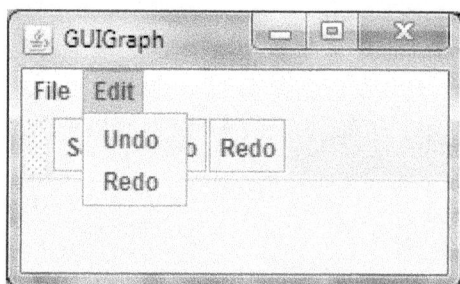

Figure 4: Realization of `GUIGraphAbstract`

6. CLASSROOM EXPERIENCES

GUIGraph has taken a central place in my courses for the past two years. I use it extensively in CS1 and CS2, as well as in other courses. In practice, it takes only minutes to create significant interfaces, even with the initial learning curve. As a project, one of my Practicum classes produced a video demonstrating the development of a Fahrenheit to Centigrade converter using GUIGraph. I have used this short video to introduce GUIGraph with success in CS1 and other courses.

It is liberating for students to be able to implement realistic applications. GUIGraph works so well that a question arises: Do we really need to devote much class time learning to hand-code GUIs? My tentative answer is no, unless it is motivated by another topic, like studying a design pattern. After using GUIGraph, hand-coding is like running in lead boots. It is analogous to the question of whether or not, and if so when, you should teach assembly or machine language. When studying textbook GUI chapters, I have the students implement the exercises in GUIGraph and examine the generated code, rather than write the code from scratch.

7. RELATED WORK
7.1 GUI Generation

User-interface generation is an area of intense interest. A detailed review is beyond the scope of this paper, so I summarize my observations here. Generators fit into three genres. The first utilizes a pictorial representation of the interface (referred to here as WYSIWYG, what you see is what you get). The second uses a textual representation of the user-interface elements and their relationships. Finally, research projects have implemented GUI generators based on higher level models of applications and their usage scenarios. It is interesting that popular CS1 Java textbooks do not utilize GUI generation. [3] This may be indicative of the

complexity of GUI generators, and/or that using them does not contribute to the course's curricular learning outcomes.

7.1.1 WYSIWYG Based Generation

With WYSIWYG based generation, user-interface components are placed onto a form. In some cases, positioning is absolute, which has very limited value for most applications because resizing of windows is expected. In more sophisticated systems, an attempt is made to deduce the relationships of the components and determine how they should be positioned as the window size changes. Some WYSIWYG generators (such as GLADE [1]) use a two-dimensional hierarchical containment structure.

WYSIWYG based generation is similar to GUIGraph in that it has an iconic representation of the widgets, and they can be given properties such as runtime identifiers and action methods. The explicit representation of the hierarchical containment structure can capture some of the meaning of GUIGraph's object-graph.

The fact that GUIGraph makes no pretense to be WYSIWYG gives it advantages over the WYSIWYG based systems. With WYSIWYG systems, the user must coordinate viewing the information in two or three windows, and shared components cannot be shown explicitly in a visual two-dimensional containment hierarchy. A GUIGraph object diagram shows the complete description in one view, and instantly displays the realization separately. This is superior because it displays the actual interface, not a simulation, the user can manipulate the interface and observe its behavior when resizing its window, and immediate feedback helps to reduce the learning curve.

7.1.2 XML Based Generation

With XML based generation, a user-interface specification is written conforming to a DTD definition defining the language. The user-interface code is generated by processing the XML file. In some cases, multiple platforms can be targeted with the same specification. Some examples of XML based generators are: SwiXml, Thinlet, XUL, XULUX, Jelly, and SwingML.

XML based generation is similar to GUIGraph in that the object structure is specified by the developer and is directly mapped to the generated code. It is dissimilar in that the object structure is not visual, and tedious text editing is required that is similar to writing source code.[1]

7.1.3 Model Based Generation

An example of this type is a generator that takes a description of the application data and lays out forms for data entry. These generators are based on research into models describing applications. For more about this research area, see the survey by Paulo Pinheiro da Silva [9]. He says model based generators "are often hard to learn and use" and talks about the need to overcome the complexity by "providing features such as graphical editors, assistants and design critics to support UI designers." It appears model based generators are targeting a sophisticated audience and are not applicable in the early computer science curriculum.

7.2 Object Visualization/Manipulation Tools

Below, GUIGraph is contrasted with important educational tools that overlap with it pedagogically. It is worth noting that the Scratch [10] tool, although very different, is in one fundamental

---

[1] Some WYSIWYG based systems output specifications that target text based generation.

way *more* similar to GUIGraph than those tools: The user creates objects (sprites) that become a permanent part of their application.

7.2.1 Blue and BlueJ
The Blue environment object workbench is the earliest example of an object visualization/manipulation tool. [8] At the ACM SIGCSE 2010 conference, Blue was referenced as one of the most influential tools in the history of computer science education. [7] The BlueJ environment is derived from Blue. Like Blue, it displays an object workbench and is intended to support an objects-early curriculum. [2]

Although both GUIGraph and BlueJ display and manipulate objects, they are not otherwise similar. The least significant difference is that while BlueJ uses UML-like notation for object nodes, it does not show the runtime structure by displaying the edges of an object-graph.[2] A more significant difference is that although a user could build a user-interface runtime structure in BlueJ by creating Swing objects and invoking their methods to connect them, it would be tedious and similar to writing code. The most significant difference is that nothing is remembered permanently: BlueJ's object workbench is useful for experimenting, not for implementing.

7.2.2 jGRASP
The jGRASP environment also has an object workbench. [6] Instead of being pictured as nodes in a UML-like object diagram, objects are shown textually in a list. However, an advantage of jGRASP over BlueJ is that it supports object structure visualization. When a parent object is opened, its children are displayed under it as indented sublists, showing a visual tree structure.[3] Otherwise, the jGRASP workbench is similar to BlueJ's and the more significant differences noted above apply, making it very different from GUIGraph.

Recently, an object-graph visualization capability was added to jGRASP [5], but it is intended to display and animate certain types of linked data structures, not to manipulate object structures.

8. FUTURE DIRECTIONS
It is possible to increase GUIGraph's coverage of the Java Swing framework, and I plan to do that, although there is not a pressing need for it. The constructor of a concrete class can easily extend the generated code with any missing feature.

Perhaps there is a greater need for similar support for other languages used in education. Because of its design, much of the GUIGraph code-base could be shared by generators for other platforms. Software similar to GUIGraph could be developed for another specific platform, such as Python's pyGTK. Another avenue is to develop software similar to GUIGraph that outputs a specification for an XML based generator. In that way, GUIGraph would support all the platforms supported by that code generator. I have yet to investigate the best approach and I solicit feedback from the community.

Although I believe GUIGraph is applicable in the workplace, my primary interest is in educational usage. I am interested in collaborating with educators to apply and refine GUIGraph.

---

[2] The object structure may be explored by opening viewers.

[3] If a node is shared, it appears multiple times in the tree. If the structure has cycles, the result is that the tree can be harmlessly opened to an unlimited depth as a cycle is traversed.

9. CONCLUSION
GUIGraph is a GUI generator that is motivated by pedagogy. It is easy to learn and utilize even before the student starts to write source code. Similar to the venerable "object workbench" tools, the student learns how object structures create behavior by direct experience. However, similar to Scratch, using GUIGraph the student may implement, rather than just experiment, because unlike runtime objects, the object-graph may be saved. With GUIGraph, there is no need to expose the student to dysfunctional user-interface coding early in the curriculum. GUIGraph separates the user-interface from the application's functionality, building design intuition. It turns a serious curricular difficulty, dealing with the user-interface, into an advantage, motivation for studying object structures. Because it is highly intuitive, GUIGraph provides new opportunities for enhanced learning outcomes in CS1 and CS2 regardless of the type of curriculum.

10. ACKNOWLEDGMENTS
The initial classroom version of GUIGraph was developed with the support of Otterbein University while I was on sabbatical leave during the autumn of 2008.

I thank my students for their enthusiastic support of GUIGraph. Their feedback proved to be invaluable as GUIGraph evolved. I particularly thank the students of my winter 2010 Practicum class for improving the code dealing with reading and writing the "ggf" file, developing icons, and producing an introductory video.

11. REFERENCES
[1] Aitel, D. A beginner's guide to using pyGTK and Glade. *Linux Journal*, Volume 2003 Issue 113, September 2003.

[2] Barnes, D., Kölling, M. *Objects First with Java: A Practical Introduction using BlueJ* (4th ed.), Prentice Hall 2008.

[3] Becker, B.W. "Pedagogies for CS1: A Survey of Java Textbooks" http://www.cs.uwaterloo.ca/~bwbecker/papers /javaTextbooks/.

[4] Buck, D., and Stucki, D.J. Design early considered harmful: graduated exposure to complexity and structure based on levels of cognitive development. In *Proc. 31st SIGCSE Tech. Sym.*, ACM, 2000, pp. 75-79.

[5] Cross II, J.H., Hendrix, T. D., Jhilmil, J., and Barowski, L.A. Dynamic object viewers for data structures. In *Proc. 38th SIGCSE Tech. Sym.*, ACM, 2007, pp. 4-8.

[6] jGRASP group. "The Workbench" http://www.jgrasp.org/tutorials187/09_Workbench.pdf.

[7] Kay, D.G. "SIGCSE 2010 Influential Papers" (report of the 41st ACM SIGCSE Tech. Sym. Special Session "Recognizing the Most Influential CS Education Papers"), http://www.ics.uci.edu/~kay/SIGCSE/influential.

[8] Kölling, M. and Rosenberg, J. An Object-Oriented Program Development Environment for the First Programming Course. In *Proc. 27th SIGCSE Tech. Sym.*, ACM, 1996, pp. 83-87.

[9] Pinheiro da Silva, P. User Interface Declarative Models and Development Environments: A Survey. In *Interactive Systems: Design, Specification and Verification* (7th International Workshop on Design, Specification and Verification of Interactive Systems), Limerick, Ireland. LNCS Vol.1946, Springer-Verlag, 2000, pp. 207-226.

[10] "Scratch|Home...," http://scratch.mit.edu/.

Toward Replicating Handmade Algorithm Visualization Behaviors in a Digital Environment: A Pre-Study

Ming-Han Lee   Guido Rößling

Department of Computer Science
Technische Universität Darmstadt
Hochschulstr. 10
64289 Darmstadt, Germany
{minghan, guido}@tk.informatik.tu-darmstadt.de

ABSTRACT

Low fidelity algorithm visualizations (AV) made manually using simple art supplies are believed to have several pedagogical advantages over high fidelity visualizations generated by computer. Our research thus aims to introduce the kind of paper-and-pen, handmade AV construction experience into a computer-based environment. We videotaped ten students constructing handmade visualizations of their chosen algorithms to determine user behaviors we need to translate into an AV system. Eight key operational behaviors are identified, which leads to further derived operational behaviors. Based on the pre-study, we propose three new lo-fi AV design requirements. Implementation of a browser-based AV system that supports these operational behaviors and meets these design requirements is underway.

Categories and Subject Descriptors

K.3.2 [**Computers and Education**]: Computer & Information Science Education – *Computer Science Education*

General Terms

Algorithms

Keywords

Algorithm Visualization, Computer Science Education, Low Fidelity AV, Pen-and-Paper AV, Effortlessness

1. INTRODUCTION

In the early days when the power of multimedia had begun to take hold in the CS education, algorithm visualization (AV) was nothing more than recorded animations shown to students in the classroom. After the initial enthusiasm waned and more studies were conducted, CS researchers concluded that students benefit little from passively viewing AVs prepared by their instructors [6].

Algorithm visualization has come a long way from yesteryear's mere display of instructor prepared computer animation to today's full-fledged systems, with which students not only view but also construct visualizations to help learning algorithms. As the didactic focus shifts from instructor prepared content to student constructed knowledge, how an AV system supports students constructing their own visualizations can be a pivotal factor in discerning its pedagogical value. The following findings have especially motivated our research.

Ihantola et al. [7] have characterized AV systems by their "effortlessness". One facet especially relevant to the construction of AV is the degree of its "on-the-fly" use, which is assessed by estimating the preparation time and effort needed for the creation of AV content. Ranking at the top are AV systems that do not require prior preparation at all, which, as the authors propose, is the direction future AV systems should go.

While conventional AV systems take the *high fidelity* approach, Hundhausen and Douglas have advocated for *low fidelity* algorithm visualizations [4, 5]. High fidelity visualizations may have a more polished appearance and are capable of accepting arbitrary input, but low fidelity visualizations enjoy several pedagogical advantages, as summarized in Table 1.

Table 1. Comparison of Visualization Fidelity Based on [4,5]

High Fidelity AV	Low Fidelity AV
Polished appearance	Sketched appearance
Capable of accepting arbitrary input of large amount of data	Takes a small, pre-selected data set
Time consuming	Less time consuming
Students tend to focus on low-level implementation details	Keeps students focusing on algorithm concepts
Student discussions tend to center around implementation details	Stimulate discussions on topics relevant to the algorithms
Not flexible in interactive presentations	More dynamic in interactive presentations
Institute a higher learning curve	Using art supplies, which users are comfortable and familiar with

In a related study, Hübscher-Younger and Narazanan have also found that students indeed learn from constructing and evaluating algorithm visualizations. Moreover, visualizations with complex media did not receive high ratings from students;

two textual visualizations received the highest pleasure ratings due to their humor and relevance to every day experiences [2].

The design requirements proposed by Hundhausen and Douglas [4] specify that users should be able to create and animate sketched graphics using direct manipulation and spatial relations; moreover, AV system should support a spatial execution model as well as interactive presentation. Based on these requirements, they have developed the SALSA language and the ALVIS system. Later, Hundhausen and Brown introduced ALVIS LIVE [3], a "what you see is what you code" programming environment.

Hundhausen and Douglas' vision of an "algorithms studio" [5] has inspired us to implement one of our own. Drawing on their findings on lo-fi visualization as our design space, and taking into consideration the "effortlessness" of AV content creation, we envision an AV system in which students construct lo-fi visualizations by direct sketching and manipulation without writing any code. The system would allow objects to be placed on the screen in any possible constellation without restrictions of a pre-defined grid, and sketched objects should be navigated or updated with a mouse, a stylus or even the tip of a finger.

Before we start the implementation of our AV system, we first need to collect data on user behaviors during the handmade AV construction process. The following sections will detail our pre-study and our findings.

2. THE PRE-STUDY

We modeled our pre-study after the study by Douglas, Hundhausen and McKeown [1] in which six study participants paired in twos were asked to use simple art supplies to construct visualizations of bubble sort. For our purpose, the following modifications were made:

(1) Participants worked alone instead of in pairs.

(2) A camera was used to record the construction process as students went along.

(3) Students could pick any algorithms or data structures they wanted to visualize, instead of having everyone work on bubble sort.

(4) Apart from the art materials we provided, students were free to bring and use their own items for the purpose of visualization.

(5) Study participants came individually to the lab at their convenience. The length of each session varied as needed.

2.1 Preparation

To recruit volunteer participants for the study, we put up ads on campus bulletin boards and online forums frequented by students. We had initially targeted our recruitment to CS students only, but decided later to open the study to all interested Mathematics and Psychology students to add to the scope and diversity of our pre-study. In order to provide more detailed information students could easily access, a website was set up[1]. To ensure that the study benefits from the heterogeneity of algorithms and real world examples students bring in, we set up an informal preliminary selection process in which we asked volunteer applicants to email us with an algorithm of their

choosing, the code of the algorithm if applicable, along with a brief description of how they would use a real world example to visually demonstrate the algorithm using art supplies. In our email exchange with the students, we made explicit to students that

(1) they should demonstrate how the algorithm works as they would to a classmate;

(2) the correctness of their demonstrating was not the subject of the study and would not be judged;

(3) they should pick an algorithm not already chosen and demonstrated, unless their proposed demonstration differed notably from the previous one.

2.2 Procedure

Once the camera started rolling, students were free to use art supplies to first create drawings or objects they needed for the visualization. They could also start their demonstration right away, sketching figures, cutting out paper objects, etc. as they went along. Each construction process automatically became a demonstration as students *showed* and *told* what they were doing and why. The camera only recorded participants' hand movement and their narration during the construction process and never their face. After the session, each participant received a ten euro Amazon Gift Card through email as a thank you, and their names were entered to a lucky draw for an additional 40 euro gift Card from Amazon when we have had a minimum of 10 participants to conclude the study. The winner has been announced on the aforementioned website.

3. THE RESULTS

Figure 1. Handmade Flood Fill in Action.

Eleven students have responded to the ad and contacted us through email; ten of them—four of undergraduate level and six in graduate school—have taken part in our pre-study. Except for one student from the department of Business Information Systems, all other students came from the CS department. Sorting algorithms were a popular choice for many of the applicants, so we made sure that the same sorting algorithm was not chosen twice. For a complete list of demonstrated algorithms

---

[1] http://iLearning.me

Table 2. Low Fidelity Algorithm Visualizations Demonstrated by Students

ID	Education Level	Algorithm / Data Structure	Short Description	Video Length (min.)
1	CS Graduate	Hash Table	Only static drawings of tables on a piece of paper are used to explain the concept and no animated objects.	7:49
2	CS Graduate	Bubble Sort	Weighted Bubbles of various sizes with numbers written on them are sorted vertically to visualize the bubble analogy.	2:43
3	BIS Undergraduate	Flood Fill	A circle is divided by parallel horizontal and vertical lines with each formed square or shape representing a pixel. Green paper cutouts are used to demonstrate the sequential color change of the circle.	26:38
4	CS Graduate	Towers of Hanoi	Three static rods drawn on a piece of paper and six rectangle paper cutouts of various lengths are used to visually solve the problem.	6:30
5	CS Graduate	Ford Fulkerson Algorithm	Water pipes made out of paper cutouts and color markings are used to demonstrate how the algorithm determines in how many ways water can flow from point s to point t.	18:00
6	CS Undergraduate	Quick Sort	13 pieces of playing cards brought by the student are laid out on the table to demonstrate the sorting algorithm.	4:35
7	CS Undergraduate	Gnome Sort	A Gnome assembled out of paper cutouts goes back and forth over an array of unsorted numbers to put them in order.	6:26
8	CS Undergraduate	Proxmap Sort	Six paper rectangle cutouts with book titles written on them plus 6 slots drawn on a piece of paper that represents a bookshelf are used for the demonstration.	12:07
9	CS Undergraduate	Skip List	Buckyballs brought by the student are used to form six units of a list, each unit with a number written on a piece of paper attached to it.	5:46
10	CS Undergraduate	Breadth First Search	A list of friends is jotted down on a piece of paper. Names of classmates are written on paper cutouts. A tree "grows" as student "calls" each of her friends, and then enquires further phone numbers of her classmates until she finds her MP3 player.	5:07

Table 3: Key Operational Behaviors Isolated from the Pre-Study

ID	Writing On Stage	Writing On Objects	Drawing On Stage	Drawing On Objects	Explaining orally	Cutting out paper objects	Moving objects around	Using different colors	Overlaying objects	Using external items
1	✓		✓		✓					
2			✓		✓	✓	✓	✓		
3	✓		✓		✓	✓	✓		✓	
4			✓		✓	✓	✓		✓	
5		✓		✓	✓	✓		✓		
6					✓		✓			✓
7		✓			✓	✓	✓		✓	
8		✓		✓	✓	✓	✓			
9		✓			✓	✓	✓			✓
10		✓			✓	✓	✓			

and a brief description of the demonstration, please refer to Table 2. The demonstrations varied in their degrees of details, and some contained a few minor errors. Let us look at both the longest and the shortest demonstrations as an example. The student demonstrating the flood fill algorithm (see Figure 1) has chosen to focus on the most important part of the algorithm, the *for*-loop. He wrote down the loop sequence along with a graphical representation. The student spent a fair amount of time to execute each step of the loop. Due to the complexity of the iterations, he lost track of the loop as the layers piled up and therefore failed to execute all possible loops even though he managed to traverse through each pixel.

The student who demonstrated bubble sort used an array of only four items, and a pair of open scissors was used to point to the pair of items being compared. No code was referenced, nor was there any explicit mention of variables or increment. The student seemed to think that, with each iteration, each sorted item would go into a second array until there is only one item left, thus ending the comparison loop (see Figure 2).

Figure 2. Handmade Bubble Sort in Action.

In order not to distract the students, we would only mention the errors after the demonstration if participants specifically asked for our feedback. We noted the duration of each demonstration for the sake of reference; this does not necessarily reflect the level of details students go into, nor does it directly correspond to the complexity of their chosen algorithm. For instance, some students simply spent more time making cutouts than others.

While we held the camera filming the AV construction process, we also played the role of these participants' classmates whom the participants were demonstrating the algorithms to. It appeared to us that most graduate school students tended to focus on the algorithmic operation as a whole and gloss over or completely ignore programming concepts underlying the code, whereas undergraduate students tended to take such details more into consideration. Although we have not conducted any formal interview with study participants, seven of them have explicitly expressed enthusiasm about the positive experience of constructing their own visualizations to assist learning. Four students have mentioned that it was their first time doing something like this. All have expressed an interest in taking part in further studies when a functional prototype of our AV system becomes available.

4. ANALYSIS AND DISCUSSION

In order to replicate as closely as possible the analog activities undertaken by users during lo-fi AV construction process in a computer-based environment, we need to concretize and quantify abstract, manifold user behaviors first. We carefully examined the collected video footage, listed all the activities each student had performed that were immediately observable and isolated eight actionable patterns, which we call key operational behaviors (see Table 3).

As can be expected, all study participants have performed a combination of the following tasks: writing down information, drawing graphics, making paper cutouts, and moving these objects around. Varied colors have been applied to differentiate or indicate state changes. Although writing and drawing in the real world may be regarded as the same thing behaviorally, in a digital environment, writing can be replicated simply by hitting a series of designated keys on the keyboard whereas drawing cannot, or at least not as elegantly.

We also differentiate between writing or drawing on a piece of paper (the static stage) and on the paper cutouts (the mobile objects). While the former can be easily realized in a digital environment, it is the latter that poses a greater challenge, since these objects need to keep listening for new events and updating themselves as students move them spatially or overlay them on top of one another.

Furthermore, we observe two very common and ordinary tasks that do not seem to have been explicitly reported on from previous studies: the use of oral explanation and the use of personal items. All students have explained *why* they were doing *what* as they construct lo-fi visualizations, turning the construction process into a demonstration, a combination of *show* and *tell*. One student has brought a set of playing cards in support of his quick sort visualization (which is probably easier and more fun than having to draw your own playing cards), and another has brought Buckyballs, which are little powerfully magnetic beads, to form tiny pyramids holding variables in a list to demonstrate the concept of skip list. In a computer-based environment, we can equate the analog introduction of foreign items to digital upload of external files, which is supported by many AV systems already. However, current AV systems that we are aware of have only support for the explicit *show* but not the *tell* part of the demonstration.

The missing oral explanations are usually compensated by on-screen explanations, by post-construction live presentations in front of the class, or sometimes nothing at all. For most CS educators, having each and every student presenting their AV construction is just not feasible due to resource constraint. Interpreting these mute computer animations without any explanations can sometimes be a very confusing task when the creator and the viewer do not share the same logic models, mental mappings, or cultural background. When presenting the results of our pre-study in the last section, we gave a couple of examples of logical errors made by the students during their AV demonstrations. It was their oral explanation that immediately provided us with the clues that something had gone awry during the demonstration. Without these audio cues, errors would be difficult to diagnose, if not downright impossible to detect.

While the actionable patterns discussed above were solicited by observation, we have noted further behavioral patterns that were not immediately apparent during the demonstrations, but would still play an important role in successfully replicating analog behaviors in a d igital environment. These we call derived operational behaviors. One such behavior we will need to implement is the fact that during the real-world, handmade AV construction process, students have almost unlimited space on the desktop at their disposal. On limited screen estate in a computer-based environment, students will need to be able to *extend* the stage when they run out of space. A second behavior that needs to be supported is the correction, deletion or removal of objects. On a piece of paper, students could simply cross out their mistakes or things they do not want. On a computer screen, a more elegant solution would be to actually erase unwanted objects. Not only does this save space and keep things tidy, it also does not require any effort on the part of the students.

Based on the analysis and discussions of our pre-study, we propose the following design requirements for implementing a lo-fi AV system in addition to the five requirements proposed by Hundhausen and Douglas [4]:

(1) To replicate the real-world, lo-fi AV construction experience in a co mputer-based environment, students should not have to write any code at all.

(2) AV can be more than a visual-only experience. Oral explanation should be integrated into the AV construction process. Audio support of capture and playback should be implemented.

(3) An AV system should be a networked environment so students can access and then assess each other's visualizations in order to ensure "socially negotiated correctness" [5].

5. SUMMARY AND FUTURE WORK

As the title indicates, our pre-study is just the beginning of a continuous effort to replicate the kind of lo-fi, handmade AV experience from the tabletop to the desktop, where the digital simulates the analog and the lo-fi rides on the high tech. In the pre-study, in which we videotaped students constructing algorithm visualizations using simple art supplies and their personal items, we have noted how the construction process itself is didactically demonstrative when combined with students' own oral explanations. We have identified a total of ten operational behaviors that we want to translate into the computerized environment. We have also proposed three additional design requirements for lo-fi algorithm visualization systems, extending the five proposed by Hundhausen and Douglas.

Based on these operational behaviors and design requirements along with the existing ones, we have begun working on a browser-based AV system to provide students with a networked environment that students can use to construct their algorithm visualizations effortlessly. Once a functional prototype is ready, the following iteration of studies will be carried out:

(1) The participants of our pre-study will be invited to a more formalized qualitative study in which they use our web-based system to try and replicate what they have done in the pre-study.

(2) Our original pre-study will be carried on indefinitely in order to discover new operational behaviors. As new

functional modules are implemented, these students will also be invited to participate in study (1).

(3) At some point we will begin to ask study participants to construct visualizations for less popular or more challenging algorithms that we have specified.

Making the AV construction process more natural and user-friendly is only one little step towards a more pedagogically effective algorithm visualization. Many more considerations, such as providing feedback for errors and correcting mistakes as part of the learning experience are of great pedagogical value as well. By supporting behaviors of the manual, analog AV construction process that is not only user-friendly but also pedagogically effective, and running them on the digital, browser-based technology that is widely available and future proof, we hope to bring the best of both worlds into the adoption of algorithm visualization in the CS curriculum.

6. ACKNOWLEDGMENTS

We are grateful for the funding provided by the German Research Foundation (DFG) in support of our research project.

7. REFERENCES

[1] Douglas, S. A., Hundhausen, C. D. and McKeown, D. 1996. Exploring Human Visualization of Computer Algorithms. In Proceedings 1996 Graphics Interface Conference. Toronto, CA. Canadian Graphics Society, 1996, pp. 9-16.

[2] Hübscher-Younger, T. and Narayanan, N. H.2003. Dancing Hamsters and Marble Statues: Characterizing Student Visualizations of Algorithms. In Proceedings of the 2003 ACM Symbosium on Software Visualization. pp. 95-104.

[3] Hundhausen, C. D. and Brown, J. L. 2007. What You See Is What You Code: A "Live" Algorithm Development and Visualization Environment for Novice Learners. In Journal of Visual Languages & Computing. Vol. 18, Issue 1. pp. 22-47. Elsevier Ltd, Amsterdam

[4] Hundhausen, C. D. and Douglas, S. A. 2001, A Language and System for Constructing and Presenting Low Fidelity Algorithm Visualizations. In Software Visualization, pp. 227-240. Springer-Verlag, Berlin.

[5] Hundhausen, C. D. and Douglas, S. A. 2002. Low-Fidelity Algorithm Visualization. In Journal of Visual Languages and Computing (2002) Vol. 13, Nr. 5, pp. 449-470. Elsevier Science, Amsterdam.

[6] Hundhausen, C. D., Douglas, S. A., and Stasko, J. T. 2002. A Meta-Study of Algorithm Visualization Effectiveness. In Journal of Visual Languages and Computing. Vol. 13, Issue, 3, June. pp. 259-90. Elsevier, Amsterdam.

[7] Ihantola, P., Karavirta, V., Korhonen, A. and Nikander, J. 2005. Taxonomy of Effortless Creation of Algorithm Visualizations. In ICER '05 Proceedings of the first international workshop on computing education research, pp. 123-133. ACM, New York.

Improving Compilers Education through Symbol Tables Animations

Jaime Urquiza-Fuentes, Francisco Manso, J. Ángel Velázquez-Iturbide,
Manuel Rubio-Sánchez
LITE - Laboratory of Information Technologies in Education, Rey Juan Carlos University
Madrid, Spain
jaime.urquiza@urjc.es, f.manso@alumnos.urjc.es, angel.velazquez@urjc.es,
manuel.rubio@urjc.es

ABSTRACT

This paper presents the evaluation of an educational tool focused on the visualization of the symbol table in the context of a compiler course. In a first evaluation we used simulation exercises and tested basic concepts of symbol tables. We detected efficiency improvements, students who used the tool completed the exercises with the same grading and significantly faster than the students who did not use the tool. In addition students' opinion was positive. In a second evaluation we used more active tasks, and tested students' skills on writing parser specifications regarding symbol table management. We have detected significant improvements. Students who used the tool outperformed those who did not use the tool in a 22%.

Categories and Subject Descriptors

D.3.4 [**Processors**]: Compilers; K.3.1 [**Computer Uses in Education**]: Computer-assisted instruction (CAI); K.3.2 [**Computer and Information Science Education**]: Computer science education

General Terms

Experimentation, Human Factors, Languages

Keywords

Evaluation, compiler visualization, symbol table

1. INTRODUCTION

Visualization has been widely used in computer science education. There are various surveys on using visualization as an aid for computer science education, e.g. [5]. At present there are tools which visualize program execution [10] or algorithms and data structures [2, 17].

There are also tools aimed at visualizing the relevant processes in compilers and language processors. It is a very common practice to divide a compiler construction course in two different parts. One of them involves the lexical and syntactical analysis of source code based on the formal languages theory techniques. Here many tools can be found in the literature as JFlap [13, 14] focused on authomata theory and formal languages, and VAST [1], CUPV [6], APA[1] [7] or GYacc [9] focused on parsing algorithms. The other part includes processes like syntax directed translation, with tools like as JACCIE[8], Lisa [11] or VCOCO [12], code generation and execution with tools like the PIPPIN Machine [3] and symbol table use or type checking for which we have not found any visualization tool aimed at education.

We have developed SOTA[2] [4] (SymbOl Table Animation), an educational tool aimed at visualizing, from a high level point of view, the working of a symbol table during the source code analysis. This paper reports on an experience about enhancing compilers teaching using the visualizations produced by this tool.

The rest of the paper is structured as follows. In the next section we describe the tool. In the section three we detail the experience used to evaluate the educational impact of the tool and its results. Finally, in the fourth section we address our conclusions and some future work.

2. SYMBOL TABLE VISUALIZATION WITH THE TOOL

In this section we describe our static and dynamic graphical representations of the symbol table concepts and the tool used to produce them. The main objective is to visualize the actual state of the symbol table, and the operations performed on it during the source code analysis. The tool has been designed for both, classroom and self study sessions.

The interface of the tool, see Fig. 1, is divided into three areas: the program area, the current state area and the messages area. The program area, on the left side of the interface, shows the source code of the program being analyzed. Currently, we work with a modification of the Pascal language called SimplePascal, its description is shown in the help of the tool. The current state area, on the upper right zone of the interface, shows the graphical representation of the current state of the symbol table, and the last opera-

---

[1]this tool has not name, APA is the title acronym of the paper where it is described
[2]http://www.escet.urjc.es/~jurquiza/research-iticse.html#sota

```
PROGRAM Example2;
VAR
  a,b: INTEGER;
  FUNCTION Fact(n: INTEGER): INTEGER;
  BEGIN
        if(n > 1) then Fact := n*Fact(n-1)
        else Fact := 1;
  END;
  FUNCTION Add(n1: INTEGER; n2: INTEGER): INTEGER;
  BEGIN
        Add := n1 + n2;
  END;
  PROCEDURE Proc(v: INTEGER);
  VAR
    b1, b2, b3: INTEGER;
  BEGIN
        VAR
              b21, b22 : INTEGER;
        BEGIN
              aux := a;
        END;
  END;
BEGIN
  b := Fact(4);
END.
```

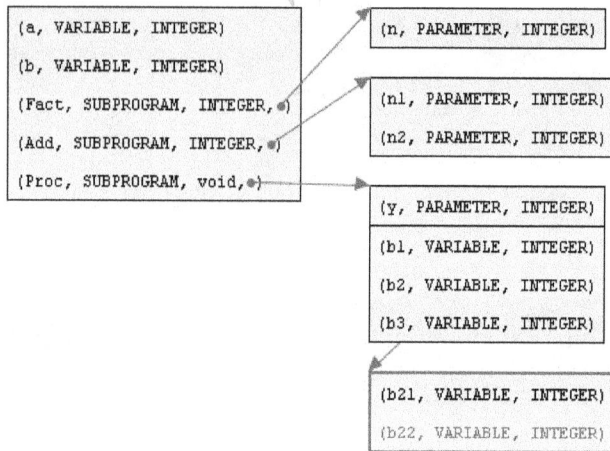

Figure 2: Source code and the corresponding tree structure of the symbol table

tions (identifier insertion, scope creation and successful or failed searches) performed on it. Finally, the messages area, at the bottom right zone of the interface, shows brief textual descriptions of all the operations performed on the symbol table until the current state has been reached.

The students can edit their own programs or use a set of predefined demonstration programs –with a name and a textual description– available via web. Teachers can contribute to these demonstrations with their own programs. Next we describe how the symbol table concepts are visualized, from both points of view static and dynamic.

2.1 Static visualization

When the symbol table structure is made up of different scopes, the most suitable visualization is the tree structure. In this tree, the nodes represent the scopes, and the arcs define the parent-children scope relations. The tree will grow to the right for new procedures and functions, and to the bottom for anonymous scopes. Fig. 2 shows a source code and its corresponding structure: the root scope with three children scopes corresponding to subprograms –Fact, Add and Proc–, and finally an anonymous scope in the subprogram Proc.

In addition to the structure of the symbol table, the tool

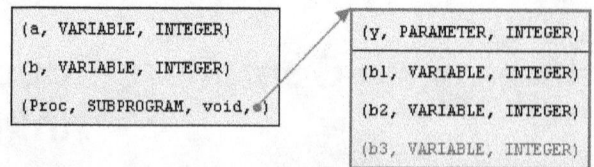

Figure 3: The last scope created and the last identifier inserted are highlighted in blue color.

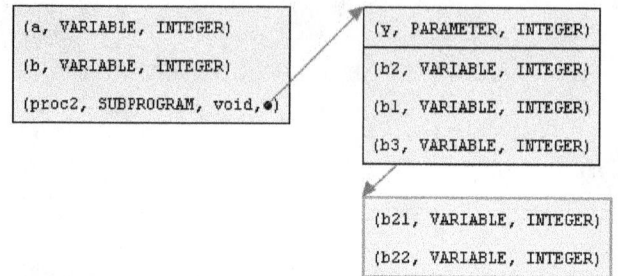

Figure 4: Entry search in an anonymous environment

highlights the last operations performed on the symbol table. On the one hand, there are operations that modify the symbol table structure, thus the last scope created and the last identifier inserted are highlighted. In Fig. 3, the last scope created corresponds to the procedure "Proc", and the last identifier inserted, corresponds to the variable "b3".

On the other hand, search operations and their results are highlighted: the current search scope, and the failed and successful search operations in the scopes. The scope where the compiler is searching the item is highlighted in red. If the search fails, the failed scope is marked with a diagonal line in red. If the search successes, the found item is highlighted in green. The following three figures show the three possibilities. In Fig. 4 the compiler is searching within the anonymous scope. In Fig. 5 a failed search in the anonymous scope is shown, but the search operation continues in the parent scope. Finally, in Fig. 6 is visualized a successful search, finishing in the root environment.

2.2 Symbol Table Animation

Animating the symbol table structure consists in a sequence of steps. Each step in the animation corresponds to an action performed on the symbol table during the pro-

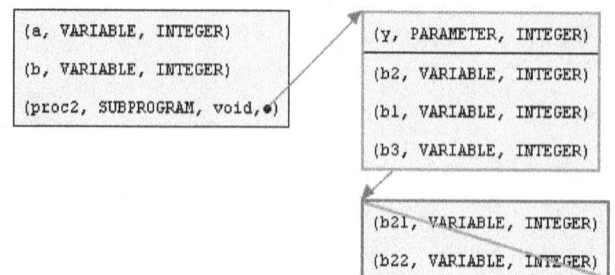

Figure 5: Failed search in the anonymous scope, the new search scope is the parent scope

204

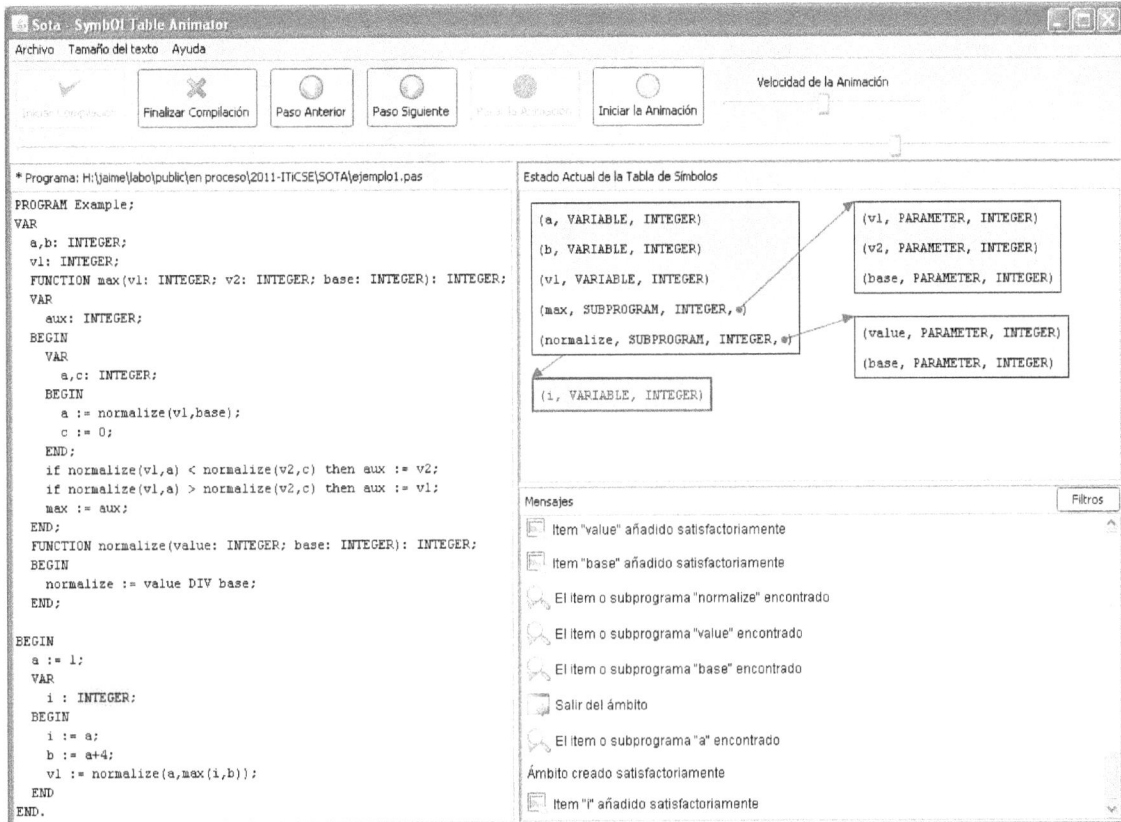

Figure 1: Graphical user interface of the tool

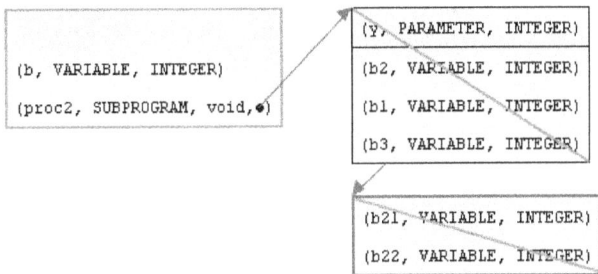

Figure 6: A successful search in the root scope

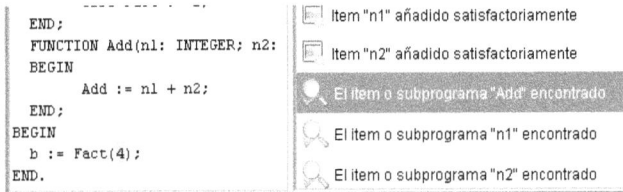

Figure 7: Highlighting the token in the source code related to the messages

gram compilation. In the case of search operations, each step is mapped to the search operations performed on the different scopes during the search process. The process begin at the current scope and ends when the searched item is found, or the root scope is reached. Animations can be controlled with typical VCR controls: begin, end, pause, play and speed selection. In addition, the tool allows to select the immediately previous or next animation step with the buttons "previous step" and "next step", or a concrete execution state, selected with the time bar.

To allow the user to have always accessible information about the performed actions at the moment, the tool provides a messages area. This area shows a message for each operation performed on the symbol table and its result: new scope creation, item insertion and search operations. In ad-

dition, the students can choose the kind of messages visible through a filter utility for the messages.

When a message is selected, the corresponding –the moment in which the action was performed– location in the source code is highlighted in yellow. E.g. in Fig. 7 it can be seen how when selecting a successful search message, the corresponding token in the source code is highlighted.

3. EDUCATIONAL EVALUATION

Visualizations can help students to understand concepts studied, but an evaluation is needed to know their actual educational impact. Next we describe the two evaluations performed with this tool.

3.1 First evaluation

This evaluation [16] was conducted as a controlled experiment with pre-post-test measurements. It was divided in two sessions, a theoretical session where concepts of the symbol table were explained and an exercises/laboratory session. The task performed by the treatment group consisted in mentally simulating how the symbol table structure would be built for a given source code, and assessing it with the tool.

We tested the effectiveness, efficiency and user's opinion about the tool. The effectiveness was measured with a knowledge test where, given a source code, the students had to draw the corresponding symbol table structure and answer questions about scopes and visibility errors. The efficiency was measured in terms of the time used to solve exercises during the exercises/laboratory session and to answer the knowledge test. Finally, students' opinion was collected with a questionnaire regarding ease of use, technical quality, usefulness and the support to the symbol table concepts.

The results of the experiment showed that there was no effectiveness improvement. But the treatment group performed significantly faster than the control group in completing the exercises (63,7%) and the test (32%), so there is efficiency improvement. Finally, the questionnaire about the tool showed that the students considered that the tool was easy to use, that its technical features had good quality, that its visualization features were very useful, and that the representation of the symbol table concepts was helpful. This acceptance of the tool by the students was also supported by actual use of the tool, 75% of the students used the tool to prepare the exam of the subject.

3.2 Second Evaluation

We have performed two changes with respect to the previous evaluation, see details at [15]. On the one hand, the difference between student's opinion and pedagogical effectiveness of the previous evaluation leaded us to question the design of the knowledge tests. In the previous evaluation we focused on how the symbol table works, some of these concepts are close to visibility and scope, both seen in most of structured programming courses. In this evaluation we add an exercise about the parser specification dedicated to the symbol table management.

On the other hand, following the Hundhausen et al's [5] conclusions, we focus the tasks on what students do with the tool, rather than what the tool shows to students.

3.2.1 Subjects

57 students enrolled in the evaluation, the participation was voluntary. We divided participants in two groups, the control group (n=34, called CG) and the treatment group (n=23, called TG). Groups formation were independent from the experiment. Students in the CG followed a typical methodology in symbol table teaching, while TG followed a methodology adapted with the tool.

3.2.2 Variables of the evaluation

We have used one independent variable, the use of the tool, and one dependent variable, pedagogical effectiveness. The measurement instrument is a knowledge test with questions regarding: the construction process of structure of the symbol table –given a source code the student has to draw the symbol table structure and answer questions about scopes, identifiers and errors, e.g. how many scopes (named and anonymous) have been created during the compiling process? – and the parser specification that builds the symbol table during compilation –given a grammar and the API

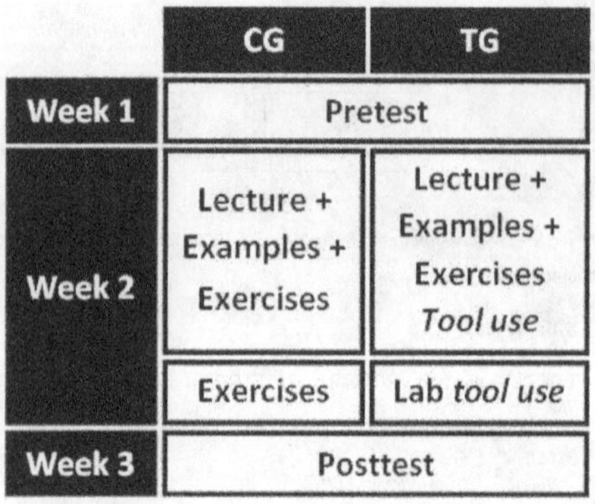

Figure 8: Protocol of the second evaluation

specification for building the symbol table structure, the student has to insert semantic actions into the grammar using the API to produce the parser specification that builds the symbol table structure.

3.2.3 Tasks and protocol

The protocol was divided in four steps, and lasted three weeks, see Fig. 8. At the beginning of the first week all the participants completed the pretest. During the second week each group attended to the theoretical (2 hours long) and lab (1 hours long) sessions. During the third week, again all the participants completed the post test.

The CG followed a typical teaching methodology without animations. The theoretical session consisted of teacher's explanations, examples and simple exercises. The tasks proposed in the exercises session were simulation exercises about the construction of the structure of the symbol table of given source codes. Students completed up to four exercises in this session.

The TG followed a teaching methodology adapted to the use of the animations generated by the tool. The theoretical session consisted of teacher's explanations, examples and simple exercises supported by the tool. The tasks proposed in the lab session were two kinds of exercises: simulation and coding. First, the teacher gives a source code to the students. While they mentally simulate the construction process of the corresponding symbol table they use the tool to assess themselves. The second kind of exercise, coding, ask students to reverse their mental process. The teacher provides a schema of a symbol table structure. This schema specifies child and anonymous scopes, and visibility errors. Fig. 9 shows an example of a coding exercise. The students have to write the source code that produces such structure. Again they can use the tool to assess their solution. Students of the TG completed one simulation exercise and up to eight coding exercises.

3.2.4 Results

We have studied students' scores in the post-test. Considering all the questions, we did not find post-test significant differences between both groups. Then we studied both kinds of questions separately. Regarding the construction process of the symbol table structure, we did not find post-test significant differences. But we found significant differences in the question regarding the parser specification ($t(39.84) = -2.8348$, $p < .01$). Learning improvements of

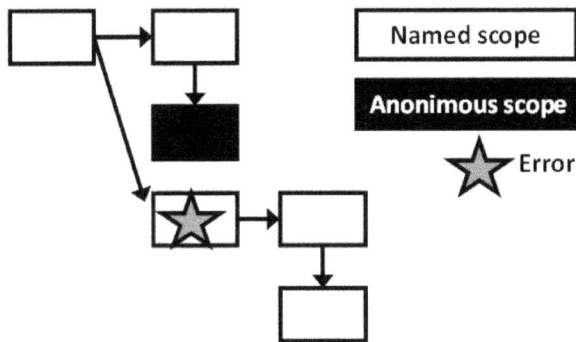

Figure 9: An example of coding exercise of the second evaluation

the CG were .1578, while those of the TG were .3817. Since the pre-test scores of both groups in this question were not significantly different $(t(50.588) = -1.8581, p > .05)$, TG outperformed CG in more than 22% regarding parser specification for symbol table structure building.

4. CONCLUSIONS

We have evaluated the use of symbol table animations in a compiler course. Animations are generated with a specialized software visualization tool, this tool has been designed to help in teaching and learning concepts of the symbol table. In the first evaluation we did not detected effectiveness improvements, but students who used the tool were faster completing exercises and knowledge test, and had a positive opinion about the tool: they believe that the tool helps in classroom and self-study and actually use the tool to prepare the exam.

In the second evaluation we used more active tasks and tested how students designed parser specifications for symbol table management. The tool allowed us to practice coding exercises. Although they could be solved without the tool, actually the amount of exercises would be drastically low, taking into account: the time used by students to think about the problem, write the solution (pen and paper) and the time used by the teacher assessing the different solutions proposed by the students. The students who used the tool produced significantly better parser specifications, they outperformed the students who followed a typical teaching methodology in a 22%.

Note that writing parser specifications is one of the most important objectives of a compiler course. With the tool we have improved students' skills on writing these specifications regarding the symbol table management.

We have designed effective symbol table visualizations and their effective educational use. Our future work consists in the development of an API that generates these visualizations. Thus students can visualize the symbol table management in their own parser specifications.

5. ACKNOWLEDGMENTS

This work was supported by project TIN2008-04103/TSI of the Spanish Ministry of Science and Innovation. Also, the authors thank to the former members of the research team, Micael Gallego and Francisco Gortázar, for the time and effort that they dedicated to this project.

6. REFERENCES

[1] F. Almeida-Martínez, J. Urquiza-Fuentes, and J. Velázquez-Iturbide. Visualization of syntax trees for language processing courses. *J. Univers. Comput. Sci.*, 15(7):1546–1561, 2009.

[2] T. Chen and T. Sobh. A tool for data structure visualization and user-defined algorithm animation. In *Frontiers in Education Conference, 2001. 31st Annual*, volume 1, pages TID –2–7 vol.1, Los Alamitos, CA, USA, 2001. IEEE Computer Society Press.

[3] R. Decker and S. Hirshfield. The pippin machine: simulations of language processing. *J. Educ. Resour. Comput.*, 1(4):4–17, December 2001.

[4] M. Gallego-Carrillo, F. Gortázar-Bellas, J. Urquiza-Fuentes, and J. A. Velázquez-Iturbide. Sota: a visualization tool for symbol tables. *SIGCSE Bull.*, 37(3):385–385, June 2005.

[5] C. Hundhausen, S. Douglas, and J. Stasko. A meta-study of algorithm visualization effectiveness. *J. Visual Lang. Comput.*, 13(3):259–290, 2002.

[6] A. Kaplan and D. Shoup. Cupv – a visualization tool for generated parsers. *SIGCSE Bull.*, 32(1):11–15, March 2000.

[7] S. Khuri and Y. Sugono. Animating parsing algorithms. *SIGCSE Bull.*, 30(1):232–236, March 1998.

[8] N. Krebs and L. Schmitz. Visual syntax tools. http://www2.cs.unibw.de/Tools/Syntax/english /index.hmtl, 2004.

[9] M. E. Lovato and M. F. Kleyn. Parser visualizations for developing grammars with yacc. *SIGCSE Bull.*, 27(1):345–349, March 1995.

[10] A. Moreno, N. Myller, E. Sutinen, and M. Ben-Ari. Visualizing programs with jeliot 3. In *AVI '04: Proc. of the Conf. on Advanced Visual Interfaces*, pages 373–376, New York, NY, USA, 2004. ACM Press.

[11] M. Mwernik and V. Zumer. An educational tool for teaching compiler construction. *IEEE Trans. Educ.*, 46(1):61–68, February 2003.

[12] R. D. Resler and D. M. Deaver. Vcoco: a visualisation tool for teaching compilers. *SIGCSE Bull.*, 30(3):199–202, August 1998.

[13] S. Rodger and T. Finley. *JFLAP - An Interactive Formal Languages and Automata Package*. Jones and Bartlett, Sudbury, MA, USA, 2006.

[14] S. H. Rodger, E. Wiebe, K. M. Lee, C. Morgan, K. Omar, and J. Su. Increasing engagement in automata theory with jflap. *SIGCSE Bull.*, 41(1):403–407, March 2009.

[15] J. Urquiza-Fuentes and F. Manso. DLSI1-URJC 2011-03: A second evaluation of SOTA. Technical report, Depto. de Lenguajes y Sistemas Informáticos I - Universidad Rey Juan Carlos, 2011.

[16] J. Urquiza-Fuentes, J. Velázquez-Iturbide, M. Gallego-Carrillo, and F. Gortázar-Bellas. An evaluation of a symbol table visualization tool. In *Proc. of 8th International Symposium on Computers in Education (SIIE 2006)*, pages 198–205, 2006.

[17] J. Velázquez-Iturbide, C. Pareja-Flores, and J. Urquiza-Fuentes. An approach to effortless construction of program animations. *Comput. Educ.*, 50(1):179–192, 2008.

Understanding the Syntax Barrier for Novices

Paul Denny, Andrew Luxton-Reilly, Ewan Tempero, Jacob Hendrickx
Department of Computer Science
The University of Auckland
Auckland, New Zealand
{paul,andrew,ewan}@cs.auckland.ac.nz,jhen095@aucklanduni.ac.nz

ABSTRACT

Mastering syntax is one of the earliest challenges facing the novice programmer. Problem solving and algorithms are the focus of many first year programming classes, leaving students to learn syntax on their own while they practice writing code. In this paper we investigate the frequency with which students encounter syntax errors during a drill and practice activity. We find that students struggle with syntax to a greater extent than we anticipated, even when writing short fragments of code.

Categories and Subject Descriptors

K.3.2 [**Computers and Education**]: Computer and Information Science Education—*computer science education*

General Terms

Design, Human Factors

Keywords

Syntax, Java, CodeWrite, drill and practice, assessment, constructive evaluation, student-generated exercises

1. INTRODUCTION

Writing syntactically correct code is a challenge that regularly confronts the novice programmer [5, 6, 7]. Despite this, CS1 courses tend to focus on algorithms and problem solving, and expect students to learn the "superficial" issues of syntax while working on programming assignments and lab exercises, which are a common form of assessment in introductory programming courses [3, 12, 10]. However, if students are struggling to understand syntax, they may have difficulty following presentations of algorithms and problem solving that are presented in the programming language. We therefore need to understand how much of a barrier syntax really is. In this paper, we present a study that investigates the degree to which syntax is causing problems for students learning to program in our Java-based CS1 courses. Our approach was to analyse the correctness of code submitted by students as part of a drill and practice activity, in which they attempt to solve short Java programming exercises. We examine the nature of the students' submissions and use this to inform our teaching practice.

2. RELATED WORK

Familiarity with syntax develops over time, through frequent practice and effort. Although not widely employed, the use of drill and practice activities can specifically help to focus the efforts of a novice on learning syntax. How well students perform on drill and practice exercises can provide a good indication of their understanding of syntax.

Palma [8] emphasises the importance of building confidence using drill and practice before requiring students to progress on to writing larger sections of code. An excellent web-based drill and practice framework is Parlante's CodingBat tool (previously named JavaBat) [9]. Students using CodingBat are presented with a description of a problem along with a corresponding method header. They may submit implementations of the method, which are then evaluated against a set of test cases. Edmonson's approach is to use *proglets* [2] to focus students' attention on a single aspect of a programming problem, highlighting fundamentals and helping students build confidence before being asked to produce "assignment quality" code.

The data reported in this paper was collected using a web-based drill and practice tool, CodeWrite, that provides students with a large bank of short Java exercises. What is unique about CodeWrite is that students create the bank of exercises that are available for practice. Each exercise created by a student consists of a description of the problem to be solved, along with the input types and output type for the problem expressed as a method header. The exercise author must also provide a set of test cases (input/output pairs) which are used to verify solutions to the problem. All exercises are solvable, as the exercise author must provide a working solution that satisfies the test cases. Students can attempt to answer any of the exercises authored by their peers by providing an implementation of the method that satisfies the test cases. A more complete description of the CodeWrite tool has previously been reported [1]. In this paper, we examine the answers submitted by students to the available exercises.

3. METHODOLOGY

3.1 Context of use

The COMPSCI101 course is an introductory Java programming course taught at the University of Auckland three times per year. We collected data from the Semester 1 (March-June) offering of this course in 2010. The 492 enrolled students were asked to make their contributions to CodeWrite outside of formal class time. Students were required to contribute one exercise, and to successfully answer 10 exercises (all test cases passing) to meet the participation requirements. Students were given four weeks to complete these requirements and, if successful, were rewarded with 1% credit towards their final grade. This period of participation spanned weeks 5-8 of the 12 week teaching semester. Prior to beginning the CodeWrite activity, students had already completed a programming assignment and attended 6 hours of supervised lab sessions.

In the following sections, we refer to a single answer submitted by a student to an exercise as a *submission*.

3.2 Research questions

Our study is framed around two research questions, focused on the submissions students made to CodeWrite when practicing writing code. These research questions, RQ1 and RQ2, are described below.

> RQ1: How frequent were syntax errors in student submissions, and was this frequency related to performance in the course overall?

Every submission a student makes when attempting to answer an exercise in CodeWrite can be classified into one of the three categories listed in Table 1.

Table 1: Submission categories

Type	Explanation
"P"	the submission compiles and passes all of the exercise test cases
"F"	the submission compiles but does not pass all of the exercise test cases
"X"	the submission does not compile

Students receive immediate feedback on each submission they make. In the case of an "X" submission, corresponding to a syntax error, the standard JDK compiler error message is shown. In the case of an "F" submission, corresponding to a logic error, a list of the failing test cases is displayed. A student may modify their code based on this feedback and resubmit as many times as they wish.

We expected that the better a student performed in the class overall, the fewer problems with syntax they would encounter during the activity. To measure student performance, we used the final mark achieved in the course (excluding the 1% participation mark for the CodeWrite activity). This mark is comprised of lab marks, assignment marks, a mid-term test mark and a final exam mark.

> RQ2: To what extent did problems with syntax prevent students from completing practice problems and receiving feedback on the logic of their code?

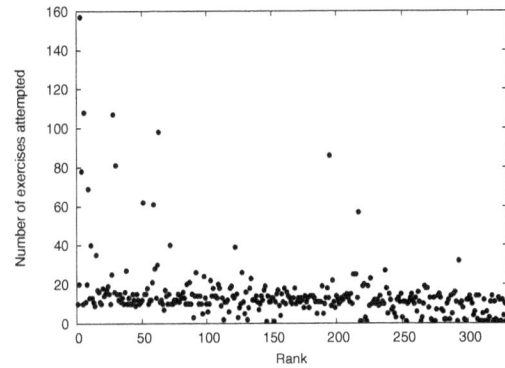

Figure 1: Total number of exercises attempted by student rank.

In our data, an individual student's attempt at answering a given exercise can be characterized by a string of "X", "F" and "P" characters, representing the results of each submission to that exercise. If a student is unable to produce code that compiles for a given exercise, it indicates they are struggling with syntax to such an extent that they do not receive feedback on the logic of their code. Such attempts, or abandoned exercises, would be represented by strings consisting entirely of "X"s. We examined how often this is the case for students of different ability levels.

4. RESULTS

In analysing our data, we have only included students who made at least one submission to CodeWrite and who sat the final exam for the course. Of the 492 students originally enrolled in the course, 437 sat the final exam, and of these 330 students attempted at least one CodeWrite exercise. The median number of exercises attempted by these 330 students was 12, marginally higher than the minimum requirements. We begin with an examination of student participation in the drill and practice activity with respect to overall course performance.

The final course marks (excluding the 1% CodeWrite participation mark) for these 330 students ranged from 98.6 to 5.0, with a median mark of 74.6 and an average mark of 69.2. Using these final course marks, students were assigned a rank from 1 to 330 (with 1 being the best performing student). Figure 1 is a plot of the number of exercises attempted against rank for every student in our analysis. Most of the data points are concentrated around the minimum required participation level of attempting 10 exercises, with only a few students attempting more than 20 exercises. With the exception of a number of students towards the lower end of the class attempting just one or two exercises, there is no obvious trend in this plot. The small number of students who have participated significantly beyond the requirements are primarily from the top end of the class.

The class was divided into quartiles of size 82.5, based on the final course marks, with Q1 being the top-performing quartile. Table 2 summarizes the number of exercises attempted and the number of submissions made (students may submit multiple times for each exercise) per quartile. The range of final course marks for each quartile is also included in the table.

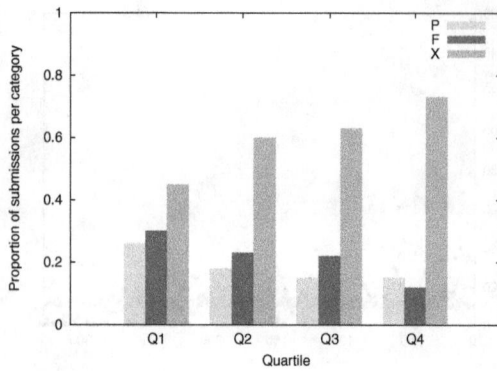

Figure 2: Proportion of submissions falling into each category by quartile.

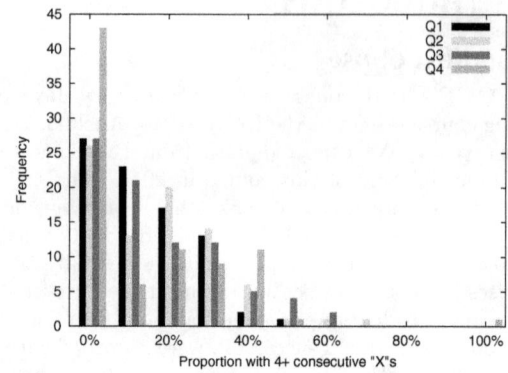

Figure 3: Frequency distribution of "syntax issues" by quartile.

It is worth emphasising that due to the nature of the drill and practice exercises, most submissions were relatively short fragments of code. The median number of lines of code over all compiling submissions was 8.

Table 2: Participation rates (exercises attempted and submissions made) of students by quartile

Quartile	Mark range	Total exs.	Median exs.	Total subs.	Median subs.
Q1	88.0–98.6	1908	14	7034	51
Q2	74.7–87.9	1071	13	4739	53
Q3	53.9–74.5	1122	12	5213	41
Q4	5.0–53.7	716	10	2943	25

4.1 Frequency of syntax and logic errors

Figure 2 illustrates the proportion of submissions that fall into the "P", "F" and "X" categories, averaged by quartile. In all quartiles, the most common type of submission was an "X". Students in the bottom quartile were submitting non-compiling code 73% of the time. Although a lower proportion of the code submitted by students in the top quartile was non-compiling, it still accounted for nearly half of their submissions and was higher than we anticipated.

We hypothesized that the high proportion of "X"s in Q1 was perhaps due to only a small number of students in that quartile making a large number of non-compiling submissions. To investigate this, we defined a student to have encountered a *syntax issue* if they made a sequence of at least 4 consecutive "X" submissions while working on any problem. The percentage of students in Q1, Q2, Q3 and Q4 experiencing a syntax issue was 67%, 68%, 67% and 46% respectively. It appears as though, even in the higher quartiles, the majority of students had experienced syntax issues. The lower percentage seen in Q4 may simply be a consequence of the relatively lower number of exercises attempted by these students (see Table 2).

To investigate further, we calculated for each student the proportion of questions for which they encountered a syntax issue (4 consecutive "X" submissions for any attempted exercise). This is presented as a frequency distribution for each quartile in Figure 3.

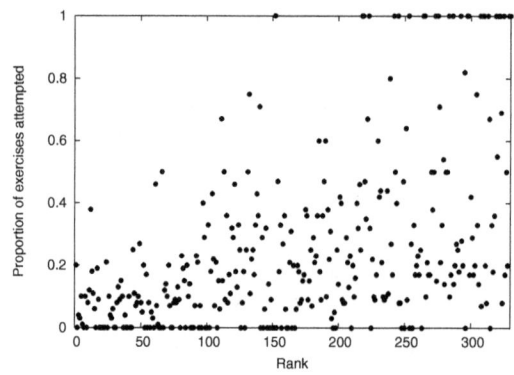

Figure 4: Percentage of exercises attempted with only non-compiling submissions by student rank.

4.2 Syntax difficulties preventing feedback

If a student is unable to produce compiling code for an exercise they are attempting, they will not receive any feedback on the logical correctness of their code. We calculated, for each student, the number of exercises they had attempted for which every one of their submissions was an "X". Dividing this by the total number of exercises attempted, we have the percentage of exercises attempted by a student for which they were not able to produce compiling code. This data is plotted, against student rank, in Figure 4. We see a concentration of data points scattered towards the left end of the horizontal axis at 0, and several outliers scattered towards the right end of the horizontal axis at 100. The trend clearly indicates that students who did not perform well in the course overall were more likely to have attempted exercises for which they were unable to produce compiling code.

4.3 Student attitudes

Given that students spent such a large proportion of their time wrestling with syntax errors, and were in many cases unable to produce compiling code at all, we were concerned that this may have a negative impact on their perceptions of the tool supporting the drill and practice activity. To investigate their attitudes, we conducted a survey consisting of the four Likert-scale questions (Q1-Q4) and the two open

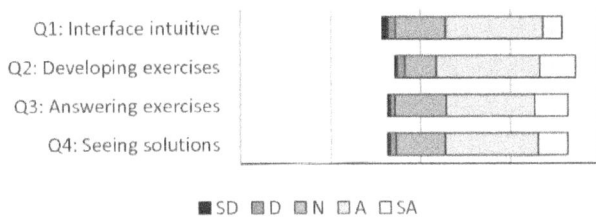

Figure 5: Attitude survey results.

response questions (Q5-Q6) shown in Table 3. Due to the fact our earlier analysis was not completed until after the end of Semester 1, the survey was conducted during the Semester 2 offering of the course. Participation requirements for the activity in Semester 2 were identical to those in Semester 1, with the only difference being that time was allocated during one of the students' scheduled lab sessions to work on their contributions to CodeWrite.

Table 3: Attitude survey questions

Q1	The interface was intuitive and easy to use
Q2	Developing new Java exercises helped me learn
Q3	Answering other student's Java exercises helped me learn
Q4	Seeing other student's solutions to exercises helped me learn
Q5	What did you find most useful about using CodeWrite?
Q6	What do you believe are the biggest problems with CodeWrite? Can you suggest possible solutions?

The attitude survey was conducted anonymously on paper towards the end of the Semester 2 course. As such, we are not able to provide a by-quartile breakdown of the responses. Of the 258 students enrolled in the course, 208 sat the final exam and 144 completed the attitude survey. Figure 5 summarises the student responses to the Likert-scale questions (each bar is centered on neutral, and shows the relative number of "strongly disagree", "disagree", "neutral", "agree" and "strongly agree" responses). Students' attitudes, with respect to these four survey questions, were mostly positive with at least 65% of students either "agreeing" or "strongly agreeing" with all four of the questions and less than 5% either "strongly disagreeing" or "disagreeing" with any of the questions. A one-sided t-test comparing the mean scores with neutral showed a statistically significant difference for each question ($p < 0.001$).

5. DISCUSSION

In the drill and practice activity described in this study, students of all ability levels have struggled with syntax to a greater extent than we anticipated. Students in the top quartile of the class were unable to write syntactically correct code nearly half of the time, even when tackling fairly simple problems (recall, the median number of lines of code was 8). Students in the lowest quartile often struggled to produce compiling code. As a consequence they received little feedback on the logic of the code they were writing.

Description:
Finding the largest integer between 50 and 100. You will be given 2 int values, you need to find the higher number between 50 and 100 (inclusive) and return it, returning -1 if neither number is in this range.

Method header:

public int returnLargest (**int** a, **int** b)

Test cases:

a	b	return
49	51	51
64	95	95
49	101	-1
83	251	83

Author's solution:

```
//finds which is bigger first
if (b > a) {
        int temp = a;
        a = b;
        b = temp;
}

// then checks if either is within range.
if (a >= 50 && a <= 100) return a;
if (b >= 50 && b <= 100) return b;
return −1;
```

Figure 6: Example student-authored question.

We see many examples of students making multiple, consecutive, non-compilable submissions to an exercise before making their first compilable submission. This may be a consequence of students being guided by the compiler and correcting one syntax error at a time. Consider the student-authored exercise shown in Figure 6. The exercise description, method header, test cases, and author's sample solution are shown. One student's first attempt at answering this exercise is shown in Figure 7 (the code is displayed as it was written, without indentation). There are a number of syntax errors in this initial submission:

- Outer parentheses are missing around all compound boolean expressions
- The keyword "else" is spelled "elsa" on both occasions
- Missing return statement

In addition, assuming the intended role of the "reInt" variable was to store the return value, there also exists the logic error that the smaller rather than the larger value will be returned when both values are in range.

Upon receiving the compilation error messages, this student made a single change to the code before making their next submission, 34 seconds after the first. The only modification was the addition of the statement "return reInt;" at the end of the code fragment. While this fixed one of the syntax errors, the modified code still would not compile, and at this point the student abandoned this exercise.

Despite the fact that students participating in this drill and practice exercise were so frequently confronted with negative feedback from the compiler, they appear to have had a generally positive attitude toward the activity. The results of the Likert-scale questions on the attitude survey were mostly positive (see Figure 5). In addition, some students

```
int reInt = -1;
if (a<=100)&&(a>=50){
if (b<=100)&&(b>=50){
if (b<=a){
reInt = b;
}elsa reInt =a;
}
reInt =a;
}elsa if (b<=100)&&(b>=50){
reInt = b;
}
```

Figure 7: One student's initial attempt at answering the exercise shown in Figure 6.

provided feedback on the open response questions. There was support for the fact that CodeWrite was easy to use as a practice tool, in comparison with setting up a new program in a development enviroment:

> "How simple it was to quickly answer problems, and get instant feedback on what you did wrong (if you did)"

> "No need to install JDK, directly write my code and run it"

> "There was no messing around with compiling and running programs"

When a student successfully solves an exercise, they are given access to all of the other solutions submitted to that exercise by their peers. This reveals to a student alternative techniques that may be more elegant or simpler to understand than their own. Chinn proposes that this type of sharing may enable students to recognize multiple correct solutions to a given problem exist [4], thus advancing them in Perry's scheme of intellectual development [11]. We note that several students commented directly on the benefits of seeing other students solutions:

> "Being able to see others code, and also errors others have made"

> "Seeing the different ways to write a program that gives the same output"

Of the problems identified by students, by far the most common was related to the clarity of the exercises developed by their peers. The exercises are student-authored, so certain quality issues are to be expected, however we would not expect these to contribute to the difficulties with syntax that students have exhibited. Survey comments representative of this theme are:

> "Questions from students are often vague and it can be hard to determine how they expect you to answer them"

> "The exercises done should be screened by someone who has the knowledge of these sort before letting others to answer it"

> "Students asking something other than what their code required. Their description did not always match their code. I don't think there is much you can do about that"

6. CONCLUSIONS AND FUTURE WORK

In this study we examined the frequency of syntax errors in student submissions to short drill and practice exercises. We found that students in all quartiles were writing code that does not compile, and that weaker students were often unable to solve their syntax problems. The number of syntax errors present in code authored by students in the top quartile was unexpected. We speculate that perhaps these students were attempting to solve more difficult problems and encountered different types of syntax errors than weaker students. We would like to continue this work with an investigation into the types of syntax errors that students are making, whether certain errors are more common for students of different abilities, and examine how we can apply these results to improve our teaching.

7. REFERENCES

[1] P. Denny, A. Luxton-Reilly, E. Tempero, and J. Hendrickx. CodeWrite: Supporting student-driven practice of java. In *Proceedings of the 42nd ACM technical symposium on Computer science education*, SIGCSE '11, pages 471–476, New York, NY, USA, 2011. ACM.

[2] C. Edmondson. Proglets for first-year programming in Java. *SIGCSE Bull.*, 41(2):108–112, 2009.

[3] S. H. Edwards, J. Börstler, L. N. Cassel, M. S. Hall, and J. Hollingsworth. Developing a common format for sharing programming assignments. *SIGCSE Bull.*, 40(4):167–182, 2008.

[4] E. F. Gehringer, D. D. Chinn, M. A. Pérez-Quiñones, and M. A. Ardis. Using peer review in teaching computing. In *SIGCSE '05*, pages 321–322, 2005.

[5] M. C. Jadud. A first look at novice compilation behaviour using BlueJ. In *Proceedings of the 16th Workshop of the Psychology of Programming Interest Group*, PPIG 16, pages 21–32, 2004.

[6] M. C. Jadud. Methods and tools for exploring novice compilation behaviour. In *Proceedings of the second international workshop on Computing education research*, ICER '06, pages 73–84, New York, NY, USA, 2006. ACM.

[7] M.-H. Nienaltowski, M. Pedroni, and B. Meyer. Compiler error messages: what can help novices? *SIGCSE Bull.*, 40:168–172, March 2008.

[8] P. D. Palma. Viewpoint: Why women avoid computer science. *Commun. ACM*, 44(6):27–30, 2001.

[9] N. Parlante. Nifty reflections. *SIGCSE Bull.*, 39(2):25–26, 2007.

[10] N. Parlante, J. Zelenski, Z. Dodds, W. Vonnegut, D. J. Malan, T. P. Murtagh, T. W. Neller, M. Sherriff, and D. Zingaro. Nifty assignments. In *Proceedings of the 41st ACM technical symposium on Computer science education*, SIGCSE '10, pages 478–479, New York, NY, USA, 2010. ACM.

[11] W. Perry. *Forms of Intellectual and Ethical Development in the College Years*. Holt, Rinehart, Winston, New York, 1970.

[12] D. E. Stevenson and P. J. Wagner. Developing real-world programming assignments for CS1. In *ITICSE '06*, pages 158–162, 2006.

Understanding Novice Programmer Difficulties via Guided Learning

Shuhaida Shuhidan
RMIT University
Melbourne, Australia
shuhaida.mohamedshuhidan
@rmit.edu.au

Margaret Hamilton
RMIT University
Melbourne, Australia
margaret.hamilton
@rmit.edu.au

Daryl D'Souza
RMIT University
Melbourne, Australia
daryl.dsouza
@rmit.edu.au

ABSTRACT

Learning to program is known to be problematic for a significant number of students as evidenced by high failure rates reported by Computer Science schools. Students either fail to comprehend a range of fundamental programming concepts or carry misunderstandings and misconceptions about programming well into the semester, leading to summative assessment failures. Multiple choice questions in summative assessments are a popular choice of instrument to test novice learners of programming, yet during their formative stages such questions are typically used in the traditional "practice" or "rote learning" contexts, leaving gaps in understanding of programming concepts. In this paper we report the use of multiple choice exercises in a guided learning approach, within the learning context of novice programmers who are typically first-time university students of a Computer Science program. In addition to the use of multiple choice questions for practice, we propose a guided learning tool to identify cognitive lapses in learning programming. We report results of a pilot study that uses a partially-completed guided learning tool, to prevent students at the outset from falling into the cognitive traps that often ensnare the novice programmer.

Categories and Subject Descriptors

K.3 [**Computer & Education**]: Computer & Information Science Education, Computer Science Education

General Terms

Human Factors, Languages, Measurement

Keywords

Programming, Novice programmer, Bloom's Taxonomy

1. INTRODUCTION

Students enrolled in Computer Science typically encounter their early challenges when learning programming for the

first time. Some often carry conceptual "baggage" that hinders their understanding of concepts to be learned in further study. Traditional delivery of course content is carried out via formal classes, including lectures, tutorials and laboratory sessions. Such a delivery model, whilst suited to some courses, is not ideal for learning programming, which is best absorbed in one-on-one contexts, such as individual practice, brainstorming with others, or indeed in face-to-face discussions with teachers and mentors [3]. Conceptual difficulties are better clarified with such latter examples of intensive interaction, during which many conceptual gaps are closed or clarified, enabling the learner to build confidence, and to do so at the early, critical stages of their learning experiences.

We are developing guided learning exercises with a dual purpose. One is to provide a "practice instrument" to allow students to explore and consolidate knowledge of programming. The other aim is to try to understand or probe the minds of the novice programmers, to enhance the practice environment with a learning emphasis that attempts to identify cognitive gaps. Our work aims to help students resolve some of their early misconceptions and improve their understanding of introductory programming concepts. Our guided learning exercises are based on some of more commonly known errors [8, 13] and misconceptions, identified through the experiences of teaching staff and in the existing literature from previous research. We realize that there exist many learning management systems that take care of the content of course materials.

Our approach is concerned with the student's engagement and the construction of a suitable mental model for learning programming. Our study is conducted in the context of a programming subject taken by novice programmers, who we classify as those learning programming for the first time at the university level. Our main idea is to propose a set of formative assessments, within our guided learning exercise environment in order to aid novice programmers and these exercises are based on levels of difficulty aligned with Bloom's Taxonomy. Specifically, we address the following research questions to allow us to capture two key elements, which are intended to help identify early learning difficulties in programming:

1. What is the appropriate level of exercises, questions and assessment to be given to novices?
2. How can we encourage novices to construct an appropriate mental model of the introductory programming concepts?

2. BACKGROUND

Many authors have written about the difficulties faced by novice programmers [4, 5, 7, 9, 10, 11, 13]. Many novices think that programming is difficult and requires too much knowledge and too many skills to be learned all at once and at the very beginning [15]. Other novices face difficulty in putting the pieces together to compose a valid program [17]. Students, in particular novices, put less effort into designing their program first, which can result in buggy programs that reveal misconceptions about a particular topic [5]. These misconceptions may be one of the causes of learning difficulties [6]. In related research Garner et al [4] reported that the top three common errors for novices are basic mechanics (which involve syntax errors in basic program structure including semicolons and curly braces as an example), being stuck on program design, and having problems with basic program structure [4].

Originally, Bloom's Taxonomy [2] had three domains of the learning outcomes, referred to as: Affective, Psychomotor, and Cognitive. Our study focuses on the Cognitive domain, which consists of six thinking levels: knowledge, comprehension, application, analysis, synthesis and evaluation. In 2001, the original Bloom's Taxonomy was revised and the keywords were changed to generate a more comprehensive taxonomy [1]. Figure 1 illustrates the cognitive process dimension of the revised version of Bloom's Taxonomy, which we have applied to the cognitive domain. The lowest level, "Remember" requires a learner to recall relevant knowledge from their own long term memory. Next, the "Understand" level requires a learner to construct meaning from the given information. In the "Apply" level, a learner needs to carry out the requested procedure in a particular specified situation. The higher levels, "Analyse", "Evaluate" and "Create" have been assigned to questions which are used to test novices in their assignments or projects. At the "Analyse" level, learners are required to break programs into parts and determine the connection between the parts and further determine the overall structure. In "Evaluation", students are required to look at others' works and make judgments about it. Finally, in the "Create" level, students reorganize elements to form a new pattern or structure and write new program code. Bloom's Taxonomy has long been introduced in the educational area but only as a hierarchical model for the cognitive domain. Only in the past ten years has Bloom's Taxonomy been applied to programming courses [9, 12, 16] and programming assessments [13, 14].

Assessments, including formative and summative assessments, are an important element in a student's learning. Students often do not examine the task given by instructors carefully enough [5]. This leads to erroneous programs that may not meet the program specification. In this study, we look at solely formative assessment used to aid student learning.

We adopt the idea of using guided learning exercises to encourage personalized learning, wherein novices may guide themselves through a set of exercises and find a balance between deep and surface learning approaches. Our ultimate aim is to develop a guided learning tool, to probe the mind of novice programmers, towards understanding and identifying their learning difficulties, and to assist them in the self-navigation learning approach.

Our research focuses on aiding novices who are having difficulty in program design, either via problems requiring translation of questions into valid programs or interpretation of programs. Our approach is to decompose the task based on keywords. This means, each keyword in a program will be linked to question(s) that may lead to aiding students' comprehension of a particular area. Similar approaches have suggested the use of pseudocode to aid novices to decompose or translate tasks into a program. Novices responded positively to the use of a tool that supports the pseudocode, to better understand a program and to help scaffold their problem [4].

3. METHODOLOGY

Our aim is to aid novices to construct their own mental models of a program. We consider that the first few weeks of the course represent the most crucial stage in learning programming. Therefore, we surveyed novice programmers, with little or no prior programming knowledge. We employed a bank of questions as guided learning exercises and an associated survey (Available at: www.cs.rmit.edu.au/~sshuhida/survey2010/survey.html), to coincide with the lower thinking levels of the cognitive domain of Bloom's Taxonomy. The students were able to access these resources anytime throughout the semester, making it convenient for them to use the exercises and also complete the survey.

3.1 Respondent Profile

Our work reported here represents a preliminary research study. In order to trial the use of our guided learning exercises, we approached first year students enrolled in our foundation programming course, Programming 1, which uses Java as the teaching language. We sent email via the Subject Coordinator, informing students about the survey. Participation was voluntary.

3.2 Learning Approach

We divided our formative assessment into two sections, which we labeled as the debugging question section and the multiple choice question section.

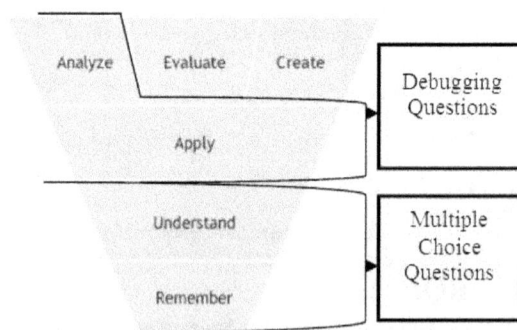

Figure 1: Applying Bloom's Taxonomy to Scale Programming Exercises Based on Cognitive Difficulty

Learning through debugging questions cover the higher levels of skill, "Apply" and "Analyse", whereas the multiple choice questions require the two lower levels of Bloom's Taxonomy, "Remember" and "Understand"(Refer Figure 1). We use a simple basic (common) first program introduced to students, the *Hello World* program. It is a program wherein students are required to print out "Hello World". As this is intended for a basic programming course, we do not see the need to test students on the highest levels of Bloom's Taxonomy, "Evaluate" and "Create".

3.2.1 Debugging Question Section

In this section, learners are required to detect the errors of the program and fix them. This section requires a high level of cognitive skill, as a person needs to be able to read code and analyse it to detect any errors in the code. As this tests the first basic program, the question only tests on syntax error. Once the errors are detected users may apply their knowledge to fix them. Users may require the "Analyse" skills to be able to detect the error and "Apply" their knowledge to write the correct program.

3.2.2 Multiple Choice Question Section

In this section the guided learning exercises highlight the main keywords associated with individual steps that may be built up to solve the problem. We aim to help novices to decompose the problem and guide the students by tackling each task one by one. We believe novices struggle to understand the jargon in Java. During the first few weeks there is a lot of terminology to learn from each word and symbol of a program. Hence the questions in this section require students to use the "Remember" and "Understand" skills of Bloom's Taxonomy. Although these are the two lowest levels in Bloom's Taxonomy, we cannot assume that it is easy. The questions in this section expose students to much of the jargon in the Java language and its usage. Figure 2 explains our thinking behind the questions tested. Each hyperlink chosen from the words in the program will be linked to multiple choice questions, which in turn are based on Bloom's Taxonomy. As an example, by clicking on the "import java.io.*;", users are linked to the question at the "Remember" and "Understand" levels.

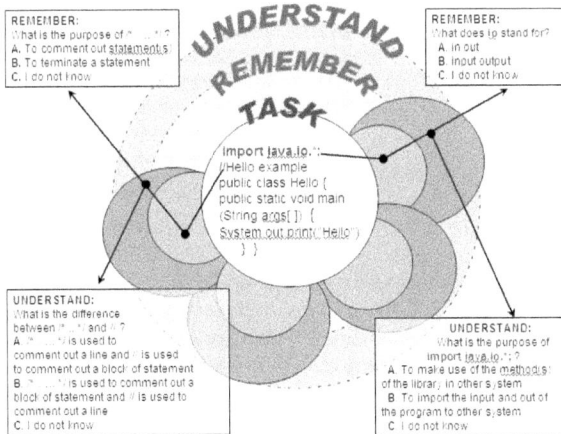

Figure 2: Rationale Behind the Design of the Guided Learning Tool

3.2.3 Survey

Once the learner has completed the exercises, they are asked to complete a survey. This survey extracts their opinions about the learning approach and their suggestions for improving it. The answers to the debugging questions and the multiple choice questions are provided to novices once the survey has been submitted.

4. RESULTS

The results of the survey are further discussed in this section. For this preliminary study, 11 students responded to the survey. There were 170 students enrolled in this course so we recognize that this is a low response rate representing only 6.47% of the class. However, we felt any responses were valuable to us in order to improve the tool for future use. Furthermore, the participation is voluntary, therefore these respondents' views were sincere and their willingness to contribute to the body of knowledge of computer science education should not be disregarded.

4.1 Debugging Question

In this section, students were presented with ten lines of code and required to identify the erroneous line and to subsequently fix the error(s). There are five syntactic errors in the program. Error number one (e1) required the student to place a "*" in line 4 or "//" to comment out the statement. Eight respondents detected and fixed this error. The second error (e2) required the student to add the missing "c" in "public". Nine respondents managed to detect and fix this error. There are two errors on line 7. The third error (e3), required the student to change the letter "s" to its capitalized equivalent "S", for the word "String". Two respondents detected and fixed this error. Eight respondents were able to detect and fix the fourth error (e4) by adding the word "args" on line 7. The fifth error (e5) is the missing semicolon (;) on line 9. Eight respondents managed to detect and fix this error. Overall, only one student (S8) detected and fixed all the errors in the program successfully.

4.2 Multiple Choice Questions

In this section, students were given a correct program, very similar to the one they attempted to correct in Section 4.1. There were 9 questions tested, students were given options in order to help them answer the questions. Note that *Num* in the first column denotes the question number.

Table 1: Responses to Multiple Choice Questions

Num	Number of response(s)			Correct
	A	B	C	Answer
1	1	10	0	B
2	6	5	0	A
3	11	0	0	A
4	0	10	1	B
6	1	10	0	B
7	11	0	0	A

For question 1, 2, 3, 4, 6 and 7, three options only were given, which were A, B or C. Questions 3 and 7 required respondents to recall basic knowledge of programming. In question 3, respondents were tested on the purpose of "/*..*/" whereas for question 7, on what "args" means. All respondents got the answer correct for these two questions. For each of questions 1, 4 and 6, only one respondent did not manage to find the correct answer. For question 4, one respondent admitted that they did not know the answer. Question 2 had six respondents that were correct and five

Table 2: Responses to survey (Part 1)

Questions	Number of response(s)				
	Strongly Disagree	Disagree	Neutral	Agree	Strongly Agree
a. These exercises help me learn programming	0	2	1	6	2
b. They are simply extra work for me	0	2	3	6	0
c. They are too hard	0	5	5	1	0
d. They help me to understand a basic structure of a program	0	1	1	7	2
e. They could help with any misunderstandings	0	1	2	8	0
f. They are too easy	0	2	6	3	0
g. They help me to recall the required information	0	1	2	8	0
h. I would like extra exercises like these to help me learn programming	1	1	1	5	3

chose option B, most probably because of the word "input-output". For question 8, two chose option A, one chose option B, one chose option E and nine chose option F. This means that more than half did not know the answer to this question. Only two respondents were able to answer this question correctly.

4.3 Survey

In this section, respondents give their views about the exercises. Their responses appear in Table 2. We received positive feedback from respondents that these exercises can help them to learn programming. We support this claim as two respondents strongly agree and six respondents agree with the proposition. More than half of the respondents agreed that these exercises amounted to extra work for them. Only two disagreed that they were extra work.

Almost half disagreed that the exercises were too hard for them and only three agreed that the exercises were too easy. We received five neutral responses to saying it was too hard and six neutral responses to saying it was too easy. We interpret this as approximately half of the respondents considered the questions to be neither too easy nor too hard. Next, two strongly agreed and seven agreed that the exercises helped them to understand the basic structure of a program, precisely the learning objective of the exercises. Furthermore, eight respondents agree that the exercises help them to recall the required information in learning programming. Eight agree that the exercises helped them with any misunderstanding. We also received positive feedback (three strongly agreed and five agreed) that they would like these exercises to help them to learn programming. Hence, the students consider this form of guided learning exercises can help them.

Referring to Table 3, respondents did not use help from the Internet or the textbook. However, one used a little and one used a lot of the course material to help them to answer the questions. Hence, they were relying on memory, which corresponds to the lowest level of Bloom's Taxonomy. Eight respondents chose exercises in both sections (debugging questions and multiple choice questions) to help them to learn programming. Two preferred multiple choice questions and one preferred debugging questions to help them to learn programming better.

In the final section, one respondent suggested that a question like *"What's the difference between System.out.println and System.out.print?"* to be included in the exercises. Other suggestions were:
- *"Teach students how to install JDK/JRE compiler on their*

own computers and not to hardly rely on Eclipse or any other programming software to train their programming skills"
- *"Add basic programming examples that are similar to the exam and assignments instead of complicating examples that are not related directly to the exam and assignments"*

5. DISCUSSION

We received a low number of responses to the survey. As participation was voluntary we nevertheless appreciated the responses received. They provided us with interesting and positive comments about the guided learning exercises, even though the sample size could not be considered as conclusive.

Novice programmers may think that there is too much information and too many skills to grasp in the first few weeks. For example, only two respondents managed to discover that Java is case sensitive and the program will terminate with an unhelpful error message, if this error is not fixed. Some students may overlook this, but we emphasize that the exercise here was to show how important it is that they be made aware of the entire set of basic rules, so that they will not carry on making these simple mistakes. Almost half of the respondents replied that the purpose of "import java.io.*;" is to import the input and output of the program to other systems, which means they were unable to understand the usage of the import statement.

We highlight these two questions here to show that what some assume as basic and simple may be complex and misunderstood by others. Moreover, such misunderstandings may be compounded with a significant negative impact if they are not addressed and corrected in the early stages. Most of the respondents scored better in the multiple choice questions section than in the debugging questions section. This is because multiple choice questions we set were associated with lower levels of Bloom's Taxonomy.

We hope that by questioning the students about multiple levels of Bloom's Taxonomy, we may invoke suitable mental models of learning programming. Almost half of the respondents disagreed that the questions were too hard, and approximately half gave a neutral response that the questions were too easy. Therefore, we can say that in the first few weeks of learning programming, students find it not too difficult, yet, they would not say that it is too easy either. Therefore, in this crucial time line (the first few weeks) students should be steered towards suitable questions to aid them to learn and to avoid misconceptions that may propagate further misunderstanding in later weeks.

Table 3: Responses to survey (Part 2)

Questions	Number of response(s)		
	Yes,a lot	Yes,a little	Not at all
i. I accessed the Internet to help me answer the above questions	0	0	11
j. I used the course materials to help me answer the above questions	1	1	9
k. I used a text book to help me answer the above questions	0	0	11

6. CONCLUSION

People make assumptions that basic knowledge is easy to learn. Most of the respondents in our survey agreed or strongly agreed that the questions based on the first few weeks of the syllabus were easy, but their responses to the questions did not support such claims. Our pilot study tested novice programmers on basic knowledge during their second week of learning programming to prove that some students were able to detect, fix basic programming errors and understand the basic jargon and its usage, others were not. Our guided learning exercises plan to aid those students to learn programming, by practicing exercises and learning through them. We categorize the questions using Bloom's Taxonomy to aid novices to decompose learning programming. We received positive feedback that more than half of the respondents second that the guided learning exercises help them to learn programming. Future work will address novice responses to multiple choice questions in a wider context, correlating such responses with a broader range of assessment instruments, such as assignments, tests and other assessments. It is hoped that, despite the complex challenges, such work will inform us about improvements to the guided learning exercises.

7. REFERENCES

[1] L. W. Anderson, D. R. Krathwohl, P. W. Airasian, B. S. Bloom, K. A. Cruikshank, P. R. Pintrich, and R. E. Mayer. *A Taxonomy for Learning, Teaching and Assessing*, pages 67–68. Addison Wesley Longman, Inc, complete edition edition, 2001.

[2] B. S. Bloom. *Taxonomy of Educational Objectives, Handbook I: The Cognitive Domain*, chapter Part II, pages 62–197. New York: David McKay Co Inc., 1956.

[3] D. D'Souza, M. Hamilton, J. Harland, P. Muir, C. Thevathayan, and C. Walker. Transforming learning of programming: A mentoring project. In *Proceedings of the tenth conference on Australasian computing education - Volume 78*, ACE '08, pages 75–84, Darlinghurst, Australia, 2008. Australian Computer Society, Inc.

[4] S. Garner, P. Haden, and A. Robins. My program is correct but it doesn't run: A preliminary investigation of novice programmers' problems. In *Proceedings of the 7th Australasian conference on Computing education - Volume 42*, ACE '05, pages 173–180, Darlinghurst, Australia, 2005. Australian Computer Society, Inc.

[5] D. Ginat, O. Astrachan, D. D. Garcia, and M. Guzdial. "but it looks right!": The bugs students don't see. In *Proceedings of the 35th SIGCSE technical symposium on Computer science education*, SIGCSE '04, pages 284–285, New York, NY, USA, 2004. ACM.

[6] D. Hammer. Tapping epistemological resources for learning physics. *Journal of the Learning Sciences*, 12:53–90, January 2003.

[7] J. Kim and F. J. Lerch. Why is programming (sometimes) so difficult? programming as scientific discovery in multiple problem spaces. *Information Systems Research*, 8(1):25–50, 1997.

[8] S. K. Kummerfeld and J. Kay. The neglected battle fields of syntax errors. In *Proceedings of the fifth Australasian conference on Computing education - Volume 20*, ACE '03, pages 105–111, Darlinghurst, Australia, 2003. Australian Computer Society, Inc.

[9] R. Lister and J. Leaney. Introductory programming, criterion-referencing, and bloom. *SIGCSE Bull.*, 35(1):143–147, 2003.

[10] M. McCracken, V. Almstrum, D. Diaz, M. Guzdial, D. Hagan, Y. B.-D. Kolikant, C. Laxer, L. Thomas, I. Utting, and T. Wilusz. A multi-national, multi-institutional study of assessment of programming skills of first-year cs students. *SIGCSE Bull.*, 33(4):125–180, 2001.

[11] I. Miliszewska and G. Tan. Befriending computer programming: A proposed approach to teaching introductory programming. *Issues in Informing Science and Information Technology*, 4:277–289, 2007.

[12] D. Oliver, T. Dobele, M. Greber, and T. Roberts. This course has a bloom rating of 3.9. In *ACE '04: Proceedings of the sixth conference on Australasian computing education*, pages 227–231, Darlinghurst, Australia, 2004. Australian Computer Society, Inc.

[13] S. Shuhidan, M. Hamilton, and D. D'Souza. A taxonomic study of novice programming summative assessment. In *Proceedings of the Eleventh Australasian Conference on Computing Education - Volume 95*, ACE '09, pages 147–156, Darlinghurst, Australia, 2009. Australian Computer Society, Inc.

[14] S. Shuhidan, M. Hamilton, and D. D'Souza. Instructor perspectives of multiple-choice questions in summative assessment for novice programmers. *Computer Science Education*, 20(3):229–259, 2010.

[15] J. C. Spohrer and E. Soloway. Novice mistakes: Are the folk wisdoms correct? *Commun. ACM*, 29(7):624–632, 1986.

[16] J. L. Whalley, R. Lister, E. Thompson, T. Clear, P. Robbins, P. K. A. Kumar, and C. Prasad. An australasian study of reading and comprehension skills in novice programmers, using the bloom and solo taxonomies. In *Proceedings of the 8th Austalian conference on Computing education - Volume 52*, ACE '06, pages 243–252, Darlinghurst, Australia, 2006. Australian Computer Society, Inc.

[17] L. E. Winslow. Programming pedagogy :a psychological overview. *SIGCSE Bull.*, 28:17–22, September 1996.

Continual and Explicit Comparison to Promote Proactive Facilitation During Second Computer Language Learning

Matt Bower
School of Education
Macquarie University
NSW, 2109, Australia
+61 2 9850 8626

matt.bower@mq.edu.au

Annabelle McIver
Department of Computing
Macquarie University
NSW, 2109, Australia
+61 2 9850 9579

annabelle.mciver@mq.edu.au

ABSTRACT

This paper describes a Continual And Explicit Comparison (CAEC) approach to overcoming proactive inhibition and amplifying proactive facilitation in a second year Java course. The approach utilizes continual and explicit comparison to students' prior learning (in this case C++ programming knowledge) in early stages of learning the new language in order to more rapidly build understanding and more definitively form concept boundaries between the two languages. The majority of students felt the approach supported learning of the second language (proactive facilitation) without causing any interference with second language learning (i.e. minimal proactive inhibition). Some students also indicated that the approach enhanced their understanding of the first language (retroactive facilitation) and overwhelmingly agreed that the approach did not interfere with their understanding of the first language (i.e. minimal retroactive inhibition). Students also indicated that their Java programming ability and their enjoyment of programming increased during the period that the continual and explicit comparison approach was applied.

Categories and Subject Descriptors

K.3.2 [**Computers and Education**]: Computer and Information Science Education - *Computer Science Education*

General Terms

Experimentation, Human Factors, Languages.

Keywords

Proactive Facilitation, Java, C++, Second Language, Pedagogy

1. SECOND LANGUAGE LEARNING

Moving from a first programming language to a second programming language is a significant point in a programmer's development. Only using one programming language risks stultifying students' development by undue concentration on one particular syntactic and paradigmatic approach [12]. Attempting to learn a second (or third or fourth) language provides students with a point of comparison that allows them to abstract programming concepts and move to more language-free approaches of thinking about computing [1]. Research in general language learning confirms that proficiency in more than one language results in higher levels of executive control and cognitive flexibility [6].

Second language courses need to be taught differently, because students already have an understanding of some key concepts [10]. As students encounter new knowledge they need to reorganise their understanding to assimilate the novel information within existing schema [12]. When students learn their second language they not only need to form strong concept boundaries for their newly acquired information, but also retain concept boundaries of previously learnt material.

There are suggestions (but little research evidence) about how second programming language capabilities can be effectively acquired. Some have argued for the greater use of language teaching principles when teaching computing [13]. It may be possible to leverage existing linguistic competence, in particular the ability to read code and extrapolate, in order to develop students' programming capabilities [13]. From the general educational literature, advanced organizers (information presented at the beginning of a learning episode to activate relevant prior knowledge) may be used to improve the acquisition of new knowledge [3].

However, none of these or other papers addressing second language acquisition (for instance [5]) apply an explicit pedagogical framework for overcoming proactive inhibition and leveraging proactive facilitation when learning a second programming language.

2. PROACTIVE FACILITATION AND ASSOCIATED AFFECTS

One of the main reasons that students forget information is 'interference'. Interference occurs when information is confused with or is suppressed by other information [14]. Interference can relate to either information that was learnt in the past or information that will be learnt in the future. 'Retroactive inhibition' occurs when previously learnt knowledge is lost because it is confused with new and somewhat similar information, and 'proactive inhibition' refers to circumstances where learning one set of information interferes with the learning of later information [14]. For example, in computer science education, learning C# may cause students to confuse or forget previously learnt Pascal knowledge (retroactive inhibition) and concurrently the previously learnt Pascal concepts may interfere with students' ability to acquire new C# concepts (proactive inhibition).

At the same time, prior and future information can work together to enhance learning. 'Proactive facilitation' occurs when previously learnt material supports the learning of new and somewhat similar information, and 'retroactive facilitation' refers to situations where newly learnt material improves students' understanding of previously learnt material [14]. For example, if taught correctly and depending on the student, some of the syntax and concepts learnt in Pascal may help students to learn C# (proactive facilitation), and learning C# may improve students' understanding of Pascal semantics and operations (retroactive facilitation). These effects and corresponding examples are summarized in Table 1.

Table 1 – Proactive and Retroactive Inhibition and Facilitation

	Retroactive	Proactive
Inhibition	Later learning causes interference with learning from the past. (Example: learning C# for-loop syntax causes students to forget Pascal for-loop syntax)	Prior learning interferes with the learning of something new. (Example: modularity in Pascal inhibits students from understanding modularity when learning C#)
Facilitation	Learning new concepts enhances understanding of previously learnt material. (Example: learning to program if-then-else blocks in C# helps students to program if-then-else blocks in Pascal)	Having previously learnt something supports the learning of new material. (Example: learning how to pass variables using Pascal supports students to pass variables in their C# programs).

The challenge then, for computer science educators, is to maximize proactive and retroactive facilitation while minimizing retroactive and proactive interference. There are several findings from the general educational psychology literature that inform this pursuit.

Research has found that the greater the amount of prior or future information, and the greater the amount of time between learning and examination, the greater the amount of retroactive or proactive interference [8]. This implies that it is important to not only minimize the time between learning the second programming language and applying it, but also the time between referencing the originally learnt language and the new language in order to minimize interference between the two languages.

Importantly in the context of understanding how students learn computer programming, interference does not just occur for rote-learnt material, but also for semantically learnt material [2]. However research has also found that 'deep-learning' [7] approaches that require students to think more intensely about the subject matter can result in greater proactive facilitation [9]. Thus having students actively apply and solve problems using the new language syntax and semantics may improve their transition from the first to the second language.

When students are learning a second programming language, any form of proactive inhibition will impede their progress. The degree of proactive inhibition that occurs depends on the quality of original learning; any errors or misconceptions in what was originally learnt will increase the proactive interference that occurs [11]. Proactive inhibition can affect the pace with which associations are made, as students need to spend more time deciding which item (for example language syntax) to select [11]. This implies that in order to effectively acquire a second programming language it is not only important that students are proficient in the first language, but it may be useful to explicitly focus on distinguishing between constructs in the first language and the second language and providing dedicated time for students to make automatic associations within the new language they are learning.

Factors that effect general cognition may also inhibit or facilitate learning. For instance, spatially and temporally collocating related material can improve concept acquisition by alleviating 'split attention' [4]. Excluding material that is irrelevant to the concepts being learnt reduces the possibility of cognitive overload [15].

3. A CONTINUAL AND EXPLICIT APPROACH TO TEACHING A SECOND PROGRAMMING LANGUAGE

The literature relating to proactive and retroactive interference and facilitation implies a range of principles for supporting the learning of a second (or third or fourth) programming language. On this basis, a Continual and Explicit Comparison (CAEC) approach to teaching second languages is proposed, that consists of the following elements:

a) Providing continual and explicit comparison of the new programming language to the previously learnt programming language in order to leverage prior understanding and form clear concept boundaries between the two languages

b) Minimising time to application of the newly learnt programming language to reduce proactive and retroactive interference [8]

c) Setting tasks that require problem solving in order to promote deep learning and in-situ application [9]

d) Providing ongoing opportunities to practice the new language so as to promote automaticity [11]

e) Minimising interference from extraneous sources that may impose unnecessary cognitive load [15].

This study investigated whether applying the CAEC approach during learning a second programming language supported learning of the new language and whether it interfered with understanding of the first language.

4. METHOD

The two research questions investigated in this study were:

1) Does learning of a second language by continually and explicitly focusing on the similarities and differences between the known and new language interfere with or facilitate learning of the second language?

2) Does learning of a second language by continually and explicitly focusing on the similarities and differences

between the known and new language interfere with or facilitate understanding of the first language?

The participants in the study were computing and IT students at Macquarie University learning Java for the first time as part of a second year programming subject conducted in Semester 2 of 2010. Students had already completed two 12-week units on basic programming in the C++ programming language during their first year of study. This meant they had some experience in using the various libraries and simple data structures available in C++, and some exposure to the concepts of classes, but no real experience in using inheritance nor any skill in working with the relationships between classes that inheritance supports. On completion of the second year unit students were expected to be able to write simple programs to implement algorithms such as sorting and searching and write applications based on that and similar functionality. There were 10 females and 73 males in the course. The majority of students were completing the degree directly following their high school studies, with approximately 15 mature age students aged up to 35 years old.

The Continual and Explicit Comparison (CAEC) approach was applied in practice using a range of mechanisms. In the initial three weeks of the unit all tasks and questions provided examples in the previously learnt language (C++). This enabled continual and explicit comparison to the new language (Java). A Java quiz engine was used directly within the learning management system (Moodle) so that students could attempt to apply their understanding as soon as the new concepts and language features were being taught (it was possible to attempt tasks via laptops during lectures). Because the tasks set were actual Java programming problems they encouraged deeper learning than if basic multiple choice or recognition tasks had been prescribed. The range of questions provided by the Java quiz engine meant that students had multiple opportunities to practice so as to develop their automaticity in the new language.

Both the questions (each comprising C++ examples) and solution space were provided through the learning management system, circumventing potential interference caused by having to learn an integrated development environment or by separation of the task and coding area. Students were also provided with a one-page "summary sheet" translator which set out the Java and C++ equivalents of the various basic syntactical elements. This provided a constant and accessible reference point for comparing and contrasting the two languages (for instance loop syntax and parameter passing in method calls). Students were exposed to the CAEC approach until the fourth week of semester, by which stage the concepts that had been covered in Java matched that of their previous experience in C++.

Students were surveyed before subject commencement in order to gauge their general programming ability and experience, Java programming ability and experience, and their enjoyment of programming. In order to evaluate student responses to the CAEC pedagogical approach, students were surveyed after week 4 and asked to indicate the extent to which the pedagogical approach that explicitly built upon on prior language knowledge (C++) inhibited or facilitated their acquisition of the second language (Java).

Of the 83 students enrolled in the unit, 58 responded to the pre-questionnaire and 43 responded to the post-questionnaire. The questionnaires were both anonymous and voluntary. Student responses consisted of Likert scale ratings (ordinal category

items) and open-ended responses to explain the rationale for their selection. While it would have been possible to attempt to measure proactive and retroactive facilitation and inhibition using assessment of first and second language programming ability, there are inherent difficulties in this approach relating to attribution. For instance, if students have improved their programming ability in a particular second language concept, it is difficult to determine whether that improvement is attributable to proactive facilitation (utilization of concepts learnt in the first language) or newly formed schema. Similar attribution difficulties exist for proactive inhibition and retroactive effects. For this reason the students, as adult learners, were asked to self-report the degree of proactive and retroactive facilitation and inhibition.

It should be noted that studies or retroactive and proactive inhibition and facilitation are typically conducted in laboratory conditions, use small-scale verbal knowledge sets (such as lists of words or passages of prose) and are often conducted often over short time periods of hours or days rather than weeks. To this extent they are one step removed from the real-life context of appropriately recalling and applying a complex knowledge base during authentic problem solving processes and in the longer term. This study focuses on detecting retroactive and proactive facilitation and inhibition in a naturalistic learning of a larger body of more scientific concepts over a period of several weeks.

5. RESULTS

Of the 58 respondents to the pre-questionnaire, 43 (78%) had not learnt Java before. On the other hand, all except one student indicated that they had learned at least one language previously.

Improvements in ability

Students provided a pre and post rating of their Java ability before and after the CAEC approach using a scale of none (0), basic (1) and confident (2). The results are shown in Figure 1.

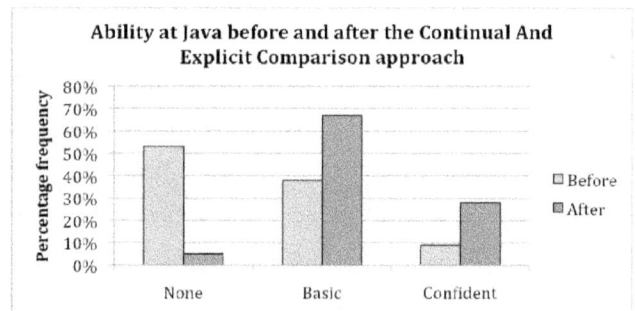

Figure 1 – Students' perceived ability at Java before and after the CAEC approach

As the pre ratings were not normally distributed a chi-square test was used to examine whether there was a difference in pre and post ratings. There was a significant difference in pre and post ratings ($\chi^2 = 27.7$, $p < 0.001$, d.f. = 2). The average student pre rating of Java programming ability ($\bar{x} = 0.55$, approximately half way between "none" and "basic") was considerably lower than the average student post rating ($\bar{x} = 1.23$, approximately a quarter of the way from "basic" to "confident").

Interactions between language understanding using CAEC

Student were also asked to rate how continually and explicitly drawing upon C++ examples to assisted their learning of Java (proactive facilitation). Responses were rated as "negative " (-1), "neutral" (0), "small positive effect" (1) or "strong positive effect"

(2). Student ratings are shown in Figure 2. A t-test of the data indicated a significant difference from zero effect ($t = 8.93$, d. f. = 42, $p < 0.001$), with the mean score of 1.05 indicating a perceived small positive effect.

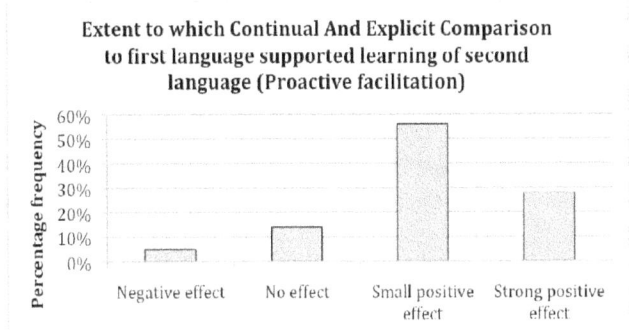

Extent to which Continual And Explicit Comparison to first language supported learning of second language (Proactive facilitation)

Figure 2 – Student perceptions of whether the CAEC approach supported proactive facilitation

On the other hand students were asked to rate the extent to which the continual and explicit comparison to C++ interfered with their understanding of Java using a scale of "interference" (-1), "neutral" (0), or "helpful" (1). The results (shown in Figure 3) indicate that generally students did not perceive any proactive interference by making continual and explicit comparison between the known language and the language being learnt.

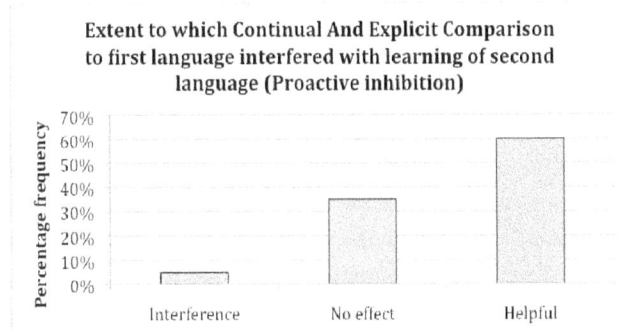

Extent to which Continual And Explicit Comparison to first language interfered with learning of second language (Proactive inhibition)

Figure 3 - Student perceptions of whether the CAEC approach caused proactive interference

Students were asked to indicate the extent to which the constant and explicit comparison to the language being learnt (Java) supported their understanding of the previously learnt C++ (retroactive facilitation). Results are shown in Figure 4.

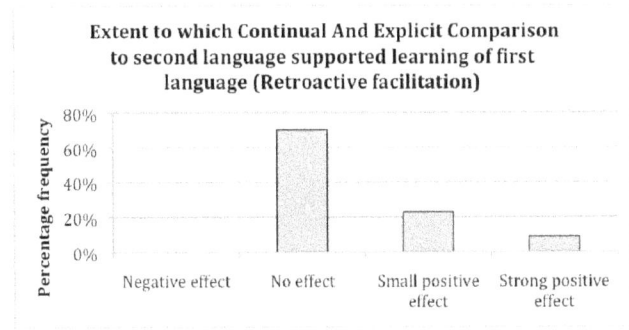

Extent to which Continual And Explicit Comparison to second language supported learning of first language (Retroactive facilitation)

Figure 4 – Student perceptions of whether the CAEC approach resulted in retroactive facilitation

Figure 4 indicates that all students either felt that the approach either had a positive or neutral effect on their understanding of the prior language (i.e. small retroactive facilitation effect).

Students were also asked to indicate whether the continual and explicit comparison to the language being learnt (Java) interfered with their understanding of the previously learnt language (C++). Figure 5 shows that all but one student indicated that it did not (i.e. very little perception of retroactive interference).

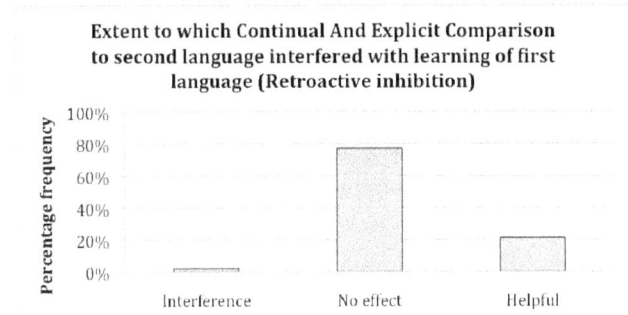

Extent to which Continual And Explicit Comparison to second language interfered with learning of first language (Retroactive inhibition)

Figure 5 – Student perceptions of whether the CAEC approach resulted in retroactive inhibition

Enjoyment of programming

Students were asked to rate their enjoyment of programming on a scale of "do not enjoy" (0), "mildly enjoy" (1), "enjoy" (2) and "highly enjoy" (3). The most significant change was observed at the extremities, with no respondents registering a post-treatment negative enjoyment and 6% more registering a very positive enjoyment.

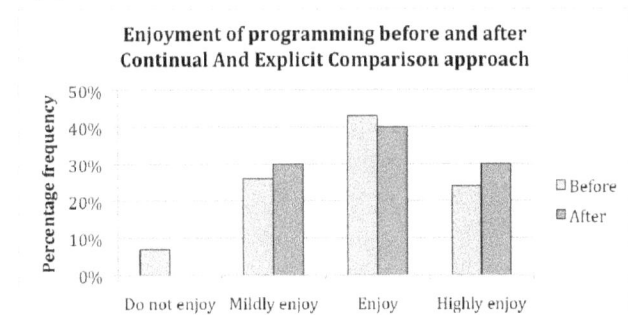

Enjoyment of programming before and after Continual And Explicit Comparison approach

Figure 6 – Enjoyment of programming before and after CAEC approach

Qualitative responses

Students' written responses to the open-ended survey questions also indicated that the CAEC approach enhanced their second language student learning experience:

- *I was able to apply my knowledge of C++ very quickly to Java without spending a long time reading books and looking up syntax;*
- *The C examples were good, [and] made learning the new Java [a] bit easier to remember because I could compare it to the C stuff I knew;*
- *It greatly helped my understanding: I could use pretty much anything on the reference sheet provided in the Week 1 lecture notes.*

Of all the responses to the open-ended questions, 41 were positive and only three were negative regarding the CAEC approach. This further supports the assertion that continually and explicitly building on an already-learnt programming language supports the learning of a second programming language.

Several students also indicated the online Moodle Java quiz engine supported directly supported their learning by removing extraneous cognitive load, for instance:

- *Overall the quiz was good because it saved me from having to figure out eclipse and Java simultaneously;*

In Likert scale responses 75% rated the use of the online Moodle checker as having a positive effect on their learning, with only 11% registering a negative response (in most cases relating to reliability of the system).

6. DISCUSSION & CONCLUSION

Based on the quantitative and qualitative results above the Continual and Explicit Comparison (CAEC) approach to developing programming ability in a new language by constantly drawing contrasts to an already known language appears to promote learning of the new language without interfering with the learning of the new language. That is to say, student feedback indicated that the CAEC approach resulted in proactive facilitation while minimizing proactive inhibition effects. Importantly, the CAEC approach was not perceived to have any substantial negative impact on the already known language and some students felt that it had a positive effect (i.e. little perceived retroactive inhibition and instances of perceived retroactive facilitation). These effects were all observed within a relatively short space of time (within the first few weeks of the second language course).

There were several limitations to this study. One limitation was that student perceptions were used to detect proactive and retroactive inhibition and facilitation. Although the participants were adult learners, using assessment of student ability has the potential to provide a more objective measure of effects (although attribution of performance to these affects has inherent difficulties, as described in the methodology section). Another limitation of this study was conducted using only one pair of programming languages; it is possible that other pairs of programming languages may result in different levels of inhibition and facilitation based on their underlying similarities and differences. Also the results relate to one class of students in one university; testing other classes and universities would inform the generalisability of findings from this study. Finally this study did not investigate in any depth the mechanisms underpinning the effects. It was conjectured that by drawing out the similarities and differences between the first and second language students are able to form more accurate mental models which in turn alleviates confusion (interference) between prior knowledge and the language being learnt. Further research would be required to validate this proposition.

When teaching a second language computer science educators must decide the extent to which they will draw upon the already known language to teach the new language. It would be feasible to assume that reference to the previous language may cause unnecessary confusion and it is better to only focus on the concepts and constructs in the new language. However the findings from this study indicate that an approach of Constant and Explicit Comparison to the previously learnt language not only facilitates learning of the new language but in some cases can improve understanding of the previously learnt language. It is intended that the outcomes of this study both inform the teaching of second language courses and encourages further research in this area.

REFERENCES

[1] Aharoni, D., Cogito, Ergo sum! cognitive processes of students dealing with data structures. *Proceedings of the thirty-first SIGCSE technical symposium on Computer science education*, (2000), 26-30.

[2] Anderson, R. C., and Carter, J. F., Retroactive Inhibition of Meaningfully-Learned Sentences. *American Education Research Journal*, *9*, 3 (1972), 443-448.

[3] Ausbubel, D. P., The Use of Advanced Organisers in the Learning and Retention of Meaningful Verbal Material. *Journal of Educational Psychology*, *51*, (1960), 267-272.

[4] Ayres, P., and Sweller, J., *The Split-Attention Principle in Multimedia Learning*, in *The Cambridge Handbook of Multimedia Learning*, R.E. Mayer, Editor. 2005, Cambridge University Press: New York, 135-146.

[5] Becker, K., Back to Pascal: Retro but not backwards. *Journal of Computing in Small Colleges*, *18*, 2 (2002), 17-27.

[6] Bialystok, E., and Feng, X., Language proficiency and executive control in proactive interference: Evidence from monolingual and bilingual children and adults. *Brain & Language*, *109*, (2009), 93-100.

[7] Craik, F. I. M., and Lockhart, R. S., Levels of processing: A framework for memory research. *Journal of Verbal Thinking and Verbal Behaviour*, *11*, (1972), 671-684.

[8] Kalbaugh, G. L., and Walls, R. T., Retroactive and proactive interference in prose learning of biographical and science materials. *Journal of Educational Psychology 65*, 2 (1973), 244-251.

[9] Kane, J. H., and Anderson, R. C., *Depth of processing and interference effects in the learning and remembering of sentences*. 1977, National Institute of Education. p. 2-28.

[10] Myers, W., Second language courses are different beasts. *SIGCSE Bull.*, *18*, 2 (1986), 48-50.

[11] Öztekin, I., and McElree, B., Proactive interference slows recognition by eliminating fast assessments of familiarity *Journal of Memory and Language*, *57*, (2007), 126-149.

[12] Piaget, J., *The Science of Education and the Psychology of the Child*. Grossman, NY, 1970.

[13] Robertson, S. A., and Lee, M. P., The application of second natural language acquisition pedagogy to the teaching of programming languages - a research agenda. *SIGCSE Bull.*, *27*, 4 (1995), 9-12.

[14] Slavin, R. E., *Educational Psychology - Theory and practice*. 9th ed., Pearson, Boston, 2009.

[15] van Merriënboer, J. J. G., and Ayres, P., Research on Cognitive Load Theory and Its Design Implications for E-Learning. *Educational Technology Research & Development*, *53*, 3 (2005), 5-13.

Computational Thinking
– What It Might Mean and What We Might Do About It

Chenglie Hu
Department of Computer Science, Carroll University
Waukesha, WI 53051, USA
1-262-524-7170
chu@carrollu.edu

ABSTRACT
Computational thinking has been promoted in recent years as a skill that is as fundamental as being able to read, write, and do arithmetic. However, what computational thinking really means remains speculative. While wonders, discussions and debates will likely continue, this article provides some analysis aimed to further the understanding of the notion. It argues that computational thinking is likely a hybrid thinking paradigm that must accommodate different thinking modes in terms of the way each would influence what we do in computation. Furthermore, the article makes an attempt to define computational thinking and connect the (potential) thinking elements to the known thinking paradigms. Finally, the author discusses some implications of the analysis.

Categories and Subject Descriptors
K.3.2 [Computer and Information Science Education]: Computer Science Education

General Terms
Theory

Keywords
Computational Thinking, Thinking Model, Computation, Computing Education

1. INTRODUCTION
Wing's influential article [18] suggested that computational thinking is a fundamental skill for us to gain understanding, live, and flourish in today's world. This promotion has been well received by the computing education community in the last few years, resulting in numerous workshops, conference panels and online discussions. Yet, the notion remains largely speculative today. Wing did not in fact define the term in her article. Indirectly, Wing described computational thinking to be involving solving problems, designing systems, and understanding human behavior by drawing on the concepts fundamental to computer

science and by including a range of mental tools that reflect the breadth of the field. In another article [19], Wing refined the meaning of computational thinking: "It's a kind of analytical thinking, and it shares with mathematical thinking for problem solving, with engineering for modeling and design constrained by the real world, and with scientific thinking for understanding computability, intelligence, the minds and human behavior. The essence of computational thinking is abstraction that can be automated, which is what computing is about." These descriptions, and various others the author has seen, do not explicitly attribute the thinking ability to the (potential) thinking elements, structures, or traits. Indirect and often abstract characterizations of computational thinking have made the notion diversely interpreted.

Often, fruitful discussions can be more valuable than finding definitive answers. However, if being able to think computationally is indeed as fundamental as being able to read, write, and do basic math, then an entire K-12 education could be at stake if educators fail to reach a consensus on the notion and ways to teach it. While speculations, discussions, and debates will likely continue, this article intends to provide some analysis to articulate the potential nature of computational thinking. It also indicates some philosophical difficulties we may face when searching for more accurate descriptions of the notion. The analysis suggests that computational thinking is likely a hybrid thinking ability that people gain through a variety of means. The article then makes an attempt to conjuncture what computational thinking may mean and link the (potential) thinking elements to the better known thinking paradigms. Finally, the article discusses some implications of what has been analyzed. The article begins, however, by providing a brief review of a collective public perception of the notion that the author has found and studied.

2. DIFFERENT PERCEPTIONS ABOUT COMPUTATIONAL THINKING
Educators have given various descriptions of computational thinking over the last few years, although many dodged a direct definition. Their views were diverse and from sometimes very different assumptions, perspectives, and personal experiences.

The Chartered Institute for IT, formerly known as British Computer Society (at http://www.bcs.org/), held a recent BCS Thought Leadership debate aimed to discuss what computational thinking is from attendees' own experiences and how it impacts upon our everyday lives. Some participants believed that computational thinking helps determine what it is that can be computed, deal with systems that generate large amount of data, and better understand the constraints to a problem, computational limits and complexity. Others thought that computing and computational thinking collectively has changed science forever as computational modeling becomes a widely used tool within all disciplines. This, however, also works in reverse as the other sciences direct the way in which computational thinking is going. The participants felt that it's time for the IT community to convince other subjects that computer science is a subject in its own right, and not just a facilitator for others. Computational thinking is a common language to explore possibilities of computing, and a means to address a declining "sense of wonder" among digital natives. Yet, questions remained. Some participants concerned about teach-ability of the notion if computational thinking is about abstraction. Some suspected that abstraction may not be universally useful, and in certain situations such as language processing it can actually hinder understanding. Many wondered how computational thinking differs from the study of the conventional computer science subjects that has been fundamental to computing for many years, and how it differs from mathematical thinking that, too, deals with abstractions and representations. Some believed that many who are not computer scientists are actually doing computational thinking unknowingly if computational thinking is just a way of describing the dynamics and the processing of computing. Interestingly, some even wondered whether computational thinking was related to the tension between empirical and theoretical investigations, as such tension exists in other scientific disciplines.

To respond to the question "What is Computational Thinking?" posted at the Website of the Computer Science Teachers Association, a reader wrote: "I like to think of Computational Thinking as the ability to see, comprehend and devise systems and processes. For me this includes dealing with abstractions. The ability to see a solution to a problem as a 'process' is what makes all computation possible. To put it another way, if you have some ingenious solution to a problem but can't explain it as a process then you don't have a computational solution." (http://blog.acm.org/archives/csta/2009/11/what_is_computa.html) Computational thinking is also understood as interpreting and transforming data, for which a clear definition was given at http://gasstationwithoutpumps. wordpress.com/2010/08/12/algorithmic-vs-computational-thinking/: "Computational thinking is thinking about data by using computers to summarize, massage, or transform data into a more easily understood form. Contrast to computational thinking that focuses on the data and the interpretation of the data, the algorithms are just tools available to help with that focus."

Computational thinking is also perceived in some researches as how we do mathematics computationally. It is viewed, for instance, as an aid to modeling, representing, and solving mathematics problems, and effectively using mathematics in all other disciplines [13]. A word frequency scale, termed Computational Math Scale to measure the level of problem-solving gestalt exhibited in textbooks about computational mathematics, is described in [12]. To develop such a scale, researchers used books and articles exclusively in computational mathematics as artifacts of computational thinking. They then examined word frequencies in research articles and compared them to those that form the Computational Math Scale. They concluded that the words frequencies seem to suggest that Mathematical, Abstract, and Computational (MAC) thinking

framework might integrate a wide range of topics relevant to computing.

Professionals at Google defined computational thinking to be thinking that involves a set of problem-solving skills and techniques that software engineers use to write programs that underlay the computer applications (http://www.google.com/edu/computational-thinking/what-is-ct.html). Meanwhile, notable computing educators also offered a rich set of opinions at a workshop organized by the National Research Council [14]. Collectively, they describe computational thinking as a form of procedural thinking; the study of the mechanisms of intelligence that can yield practical applications by magnifying human intelligence; the use of computation-related symbol systems to articulate explicit knowledge and manifest such knowledge in concrete computational forms; a way of formulating rigorous analysis and procedures for accomplishing a defined task efficiently; a meta-science to bridge between science and engineering; an open-ended and growing list of concepts that reflect the dynamic nature of technology and human learning; a careful reasoning about the methods of doing things, or thinking that complements mathematical or engineering thinking by combining the two.

The CPATH program of the National Science Foundation of the U.S. has supported endeavors aimed to promote computing education and foster computational thinking. Arguably, what people have done in CPATH-supported projects (the author has been involved in one such project) is not much different from what computing educators have done for years. Here is the dilemma. We seem confident that whatever we teach in computing promotes computational thinking. But why is this true? We struggle to answer this question. In fact, we don't seem to know the answers to some basic questions. Why is a separate promotion of computational thinking necessary given that it may share the thinking modes that are better known? To what extent would the notion really matter? Why would visual tools be the best way – or even a better way – to promote the learning of computational thinking and expect students to develop with the tools transferable skills of a higher order? And, what is computational thinking after all?

3. DIFFERENT THINKING MODES IN RELATION TO COMPUTING

A way of thinking conceivably consists of a set of thinking elements whether we realize or not. Foundation for Critical Thinking suggested one such collection of eight thinking traits that constitutes "critical thinking" at http://www.criticalthinking.org/courses/Elements_standards_model.cfm. To put them in a single sentence, whenever we think critically, we think with a purpose, raise questions, and embody a viewpoint by making assumptions and inferences and by using information and concepts, leading to implications. A person's critical thinking ability is applicable in any problem-solving context. Guided by the general principles of critical thinking, people in Computational X develop their own modes of thought commensurate with the kind of computation they do in the field X.

In computational physics, choosing a discrete model often requires a balanced consideration among physical constraints, numerical stability, accuracy, and computational cost. Physicists and numerical analysts contribute to finding a model by applying their distinctively different thinking modes. A physicist would ensure that an intended numerical model is relatively faithful to physics, whereas a numerical analyst would have to study the computational ramifications of the model. Indeed, collaboration across disciplines is common in Computational X.

A way of thinking at a higher order generally requires systematic training in a relevant field. For instance, in theory, anyone who understands the classical Schwarz-Christoffel conformal mapping between two singly connected regions in the complex plane can apply a standard numerical quadrature to numerically compute the mapping function. However, not until the early 1980s had the numerical computation of the mapping function become successful [17]. Generally speaking, only people who are systematically trained in numerical analysis would be able to recognize and overcome obstacles that may hinder a successful numerical computation.

A way of thinking may not appear "computational", yet have significant computational ramifications. For instance, by asking insightful questions, applied mathematicians had successfully made connections between cellular automata and nonlinear dynamic systems of some kind to explore various dynamic properties of cellular automata and new rules of their computation [2]. They were able to bring the existing computational models of neural networks under a purely mathematical framework to study. Their findings had, in turn, influenced computation profoundly in terms of discovering much improved algorithms, leading to more efficient cellular neural networks.

In summary, people who use application software, develop the software, or study the models and algorithms are equipped with domain knowledge of different kinds that plays a pivotal role in a critical thinking process. Thus, computational thinking is likely diverse in nature, affording an ever growing scope. Certain ways of thinking in computing may require extensive training. Certain ways of thinking may not appear "computational" despite the (potential) computational implications. However, in the end, what makes computing meaningful, insightful, and fruitful is our collective thinking ability fueled with our distinct domain expertise and thinking modes.

4. MATHEMATICAL THINKING IN RELATION TO COMPUTING

Computing is more mathematical than many think it is. Some aspects of computing, similarly in mathematics, are about recognizing and manipulating patterns. Some others, such as software development, may need a certain degree of accuracy to measure the quality of what we do in various development processes even though we often struggle to find effective measurements. Programming constructs such as classes and objects are essentially mathematical entities that most who use them do not realize. And, programming, a significant form of computing, is arguably a mathematical activity [7].

However, computing appears much less mathematical than many think it should. Each computing area has its own methodologies that people may understand and be able to use with little knowledge of the underpinning mathematics. Indeed, doing computing can be rather accommodating. Writing a correct loop requires only thinking in algebraic terms. Yet, one can instead stack a sequence of statements to do the same thing if practical. People rely on running unit tests, not conducting correctness proofs, to show whether functional modules are algorithmically correct. Today, application programming interfaces, library frameworks, and enterprise-level integrated development environments are enabling people to develop software with little formal training. Poor thinking ability in abstract terms may be the reason why people are unable to produce clear, elegant designs and programs [8]. Thus, improving our mathematical thinking ability seems a logical way to improve the quality of what we do in computing.

Thinking mathematically appears also better understood. It may suggest the following thinking abilities [16]:
1. Exemplifying and specializing (in order to find examples of what is generally stated)
2. Completing, deleting, and correcting (in order to allow, ensure, or contradict conclusions to be made)
3. Comparing, sorting, and organizing (in order to better understand the assumptions and hypotheses)
4. Changing, varying, revising, and altering (questions, assumptions, hypotheses, constraints, or solution routes)
5. Generalizing and conjecturing
6. Explaining, justifying, verifying, convincing, and refuting (with consequences, extrapolations, reformulations, counterexamples, etc.).

A mathematical thinking process is also analytical to break a task down, make assumptions, identify similar tasks, appropriate knowledge and skills, look for patterns or connections, select a strategy while considering alternatives, and assist thinking with examples, data, or visual aids. Arguably, one does computing by taking full advantage of his or her mathematical thinking ability and the ability to follow a mathematical thinking process with, perhaps, a different orientation. In particular, thinking to model or design a system is a mental process to decompose the system into subsystems, conceptualize and simulate design choices, and apply convergent-divergent thinking cycles [5]. This is very similar to doing mathematics. Thinking mathematically directly translates into thinking recursively, abstractly, logically, and procedurally – the essential thinking abilities for anyone to do computing effectively. As said, mathematicians and computer scientists share several modes of thought, particularly in representation of reality, reduction to simpler problems, abstract reasoning, information structures, and algorithms [9]. Thus, the inseparability between mathematics and computing makes many wonder whether computational thinking is a form of mathematical thinking. However, one may also suspect that computing differentiates itself from mathematics with its unique orientation and intricacy, and hence may require more than just mathematical thinking. But how much is there in computational thinking that is different from mathematical thinking? If there is, would other thinking paradigms address the difference? We struggle to answer these questions.

5. IS COMPUTATIONAL THINKING A MIXTURE, PERHAPS?

In a way, various thinking paradigms may be related to one another "hierarchically". Thinking paradigms lower in the "hierarchy" are useful precisely because of their specificity. For instance, one tackles problems in a step-by-step fashion with refinement iterations by applying algorithmic thinking, which is likely a form of analytical thinking or mathematical thinking. In light of critical thinking, all thinking paradigms may share some common attributes disconnected to in-depth domain knowledge. Thus, a simple question such as "How many months are there in a year that each has 28 days?" may be used to test one's logical, mathematical, and perhaps, computational thinking abilities. But evidently, it is the "high-order" computational thinking ability we are trying to understand.

It can, in fact, be rather philosophical to distinguish thinking paradigms when we engage in meaningful thinking. For instance, to improve performances of insertion and deletion operations of a sorted list, one wonders whether using a two-dimensional jagged array as storage might help (and it indeed will). Such thinking is clearly "computational". Can such thinking be labeled "analytical" or "mathematical" (and thus making "computational thinking" in such instances redundant)? It's difficult to argue it can't. Conversely, a philosophical undertaking, as described earlier, can impact computation profoundly, and yet may not appear "computational" at all. Arguably, one may apply essentially the same thinking process to produce possibly different mental products. For instance, mathematicians seek abstractions or representations to make mathematical structures richer, more predictable, or more complete. In contrast, computer scientists introduce abstractions or representations often for empirical reasons. However, they can be all using the same analytical thinking skill to create abstractions or representations and reason to seek them by exploring new ideas and approaches as they discard preconceived assumptions. In other words, one may acquire the very same thinking skill from a very different learning experience. Thus, it might be a philosophical challenge to stress the importance of computational thinking today while its products might have existed even before modern computers were born.

Nonetheless, "What might computational thinking be?" is at least philosophically interesting. To further the exploration, perhaps, we should have looked into the nature of computation in the first place. Classically, computation is an algorithmic process to produce output given input. Peter Denning describes computation as a process in which the transitions from one element of the sequence to the next are controlled by a representation [4]. Thus, he defines computational thinking to be an approach to problem solving that represents the problem as an information process and seeks an algorithmic solution. However, like many others, the definition might still be too broadly stated to be empirically helpful. What seems plausible however is the viewpoint that the essence of computation is to seek representations and models – the two intimately related yet subtly different concepts. Models, in a sense, are representations. However, a model – how entities in the model are represented – is a result of modeling, which is not simply how to represent things. Rather, modeling captures the dynamics of the entities based upon their representations. While a model can be abstract, a representation is most likely concrete. A model allows transforming data from one representation to another to make the data better understood or more "easily" manipulated. Models can be purely artificial, mathematically transformed, or algorithmically constructed by recognizing existing data patterns. With the above analysis, the author makes the following conjuncture of what computational thinking may mean in an operational sense.

Computational thinking is thinking to solve problems, automate systems, or transform data by constructing models and representations, concrete or abstract, to represent or to model the inner-working mechanism of what is being modeled or represented as an information process to be executed with appropriate computing agents. Such thinking is necessarily

o *logical, to capture what is essential to the models or representations;*

o *algorithmic, to step-wise define or refine operational processes;*

o *scientific, to gain understanding of models' capabilities, learn how to use them with maximum efficiency, and explore the effects of the computation in the original problem domain.*

o *mathematical, to be able to show the correctness of algorithms, specify precisely the functionality of a software system, measure the quality of what we do in a process of computation, and deal effectively with the complexity of the models and representations by exploring more effective and efficient alternatives;*

o *analytical, to model with purpose, assumptions and viewpoints, evaluate and adjust the models and representations by prototyping, and study their implications and consequences;*

o *engineering-oriented, to design the models and representations against known constraints and practical concerns, and to plan, execute, manage, and evaluate the process of computation in order to improve our capability and maturity level; and*

o *creative, to model the unthinkable.*

This definition is, in principle, consistent with the ones reviewed earlier. However, what makes this definition different is the linkage of the thinking elements to the better known thinking paradigms in terms of the relevance of each paradigm when applied to computation. Computation is diverse. Thus, it is hardly possible to describe computational thinking to encompass all possible thinking modes, their combinations and derivatives. The above definition should not preclude any thinking mode that can be more applicable in a specific area of computing with its focused characterization. For instance, software design needs "design thinking", thinking that enables a designer to tolerate ambiguity in an iteration of convergent-divergent thinking cycle, maintain sight of big picture, handle uncertainty, make sound decisions, and communicate in several design languages [5]. In the end, what matters is our ability to think critically, not the labeling of a thinking process.

Computing, as a discipline, has its well-established models of computation that we can still improve on. But perhaps, the perspectives drawn from other disciplines are really what makes computing full of wonders, challenges, and successes. Computation is unavoidable not only in the method of study, but in what is studied [3]. Likewise, computational thinking is present not only because of the nature of computation, but also because of the way how people think critically. We gain different kinds of critical thinking ability through a variety of means. These thinking skills, collectively, become a guiding force to enable us to do computation effectively. The more we do in computation, the more capable we are as computational thinkers. Thus, perhaps, it is not computational thinking we should promote, but computational doing at all levels of K-16 education in order for us to better understand the computational potential of the world in which we live. Therefore, whether or not we would be able to "accurately" define "computational thinking" might never be important.

6. IMPLICATIONS OF THE ANALYSIS

Colleges in the U.S. have faced years of declining enrollment in computing disciplines since the end of the dot-com era. The College Board of the U.S. has discontinued AP Computer Science AB Exam due to insufficient interests. Meanwhile, IT job markets remain strong in the U.S. and companies continue to seek IT talents overseas. The notion of computational thinking came in time to raise the level of urgency in promoting computing education across the entire spectrum of K-16 education.

Doing influences the way we think. A thinking paradigm means little to virtually anyone who hasn't had much experience in doing things with which the paradigm may help. We promote STEM education by having students solve STEM problems, not by advocating scientific, engineering, or mathematical thinking. There is inherently a C (Computing) in STEM. Learning STEM without learning computing is fundamentally inadequate. Learning computing while solving STEM problems, on the other hand, would inevitably foster one's computational thinking ability no matter how the notion is defined.

If the mainstream of computational thinking is thinking about process abstraction, then Jean Piaget's Stages of Cognitive Development [15] may suggest that this thinking skill cannot be effectively taught until adolescence age. Perhaps, what we need, instead, is a computational culture – a set of shared attitudes, values, goals, and practices that characterizes our education in which information processing and computation (in a variety of forms) are naturally integrated into what we teach. The authors of [11] proposed permeating the collective knowledge and lessons of computer science research into the discussion and development of all subjects that involve (information) processing. They also suggested some computational activities that can be naturally integrated into what we teach. In this way, students would be better prepared and more successful in learning programming as they progress computationally.

Fostering a computational culture is possible. When we ask students to search Web to find needed information, discuss how to do it effectively. When students are learning Excel software program, discuss ways to use it in solving perhaps optimization problems. When teaching students bisection method of finding roots of an equation, go a bit further to talk about binary search and other root-finding methods that can be potentially translated into more efficient search algorithms. When teaching polynomials, study the identity $a_nx^n + a_{n-1}x^{n-1} + \ldots + a_1x + a_0 = a_0 + x(a_1 + x(a_2 + \ldots + x(a_{n-1} + a_nx)\ldots))$ and its computational implications. Perhaps, students can learn how to design reasonably normalized databases as a modeling experience while still in high school. Students may possess commonsense computing abilities [10] that we should find ways to promote and build upon.

Yet, there are still serious obstacles. Studies have suggested that lack of or inadequate introduction of computer science at the high-school level, not the impact of the dot-com burst or IT overseas outsourcing, may have been a sustained major factor to prevent many capable high-school students from pursuing computing-related studies in colleges [1]. Meanwhile, teaching computer science is still an avocation, not exactly a hobby, but certainly not a primary job for many high-school computer science teachers [6]. As a result, few colleges have CS teacher education programs. To remove, or at least alleviate, the obstacles, educators have been promoting learning of CS in free environments (termed CS-unplugged at http://csunplugged.org/).

They are developing a new AP course: "CS: Principles" (http://csprinciples.org) aimed to broaden participation in computing. But, it might require a pervasive plug-in in our curricula at all levels to eventually make computing a fundamental part of our education.

In closing, our ability to think critically and innovatively when we engage in computation will continue to improve as digital technology advances whether we promote computational thinking or not. In contrast, we are searching for means to improve our ability to make computing an integral part of K-16 education if promoting computational thinking can indeed help.

7. ACKNOWLEDGMENTS

The author would like to acknowledge the support of the NSF CPATH program No. 0939032.

8. REFERENCES

[1] Carter, L. Why students with an apparent aptitude for computer science don't choose to major in computer science. *SIGCSE 2006*, Houston, pp. 27-31.

[2] Chen, F. et al. Realization of Boolean Functions via CNN: Mathematical Theory, LSBF and Template Design, *IEEE, TRANSACTIONS ON CIRCUITS AND SYSTEMS—I: REGULAR PAPERS*, 53, 10 (October 2006), 2203-2213.

[3] Denning, P. Beyond Computational Thinking, *Commun. ACM*, Vol. 5, No. 6, June 2009, 28-30

[4] Denning, P. Ubiquity Symposium 'What Is Computation?' Opening Statement, Nov. 2010, http://ubiquity.acm.org/article.cfm?id=1880067

[5] Dym C. et al. Engineering Design Thinking, Teaching, and Learning, *Journal of Engineering Education*, January, 2005, 103-120

[6] Harrison, J. Endings and Beginnings, at http://blog.acm.org/archives/csta/2009/05/

[7] Hu, C. It's Mathematical, After All – the Nature of Learning Computer Programming, *Education and Information Technologies* (Springer Netherlands), 11, 1 (January 2006), 83-92.

[8] Kramer J. Is Abstraction the Key to Computing? *Commun. ACM*, Vol. 50 No. 4, April 2007, 37-42

[9] Knuth, D. Algorithmic Thinking and Mathematical Thinking, *The American Mathematical Monthly*, Vol. 92, No. 3 (Mar., 1985), 170-181

[10] Lewandowski, G. et al. Commonsense Understanding of Concurrency: Computing Students and Concert Tickets, *Commun. ACM*, 53, 7 (July 2010), 60-70.

[11] Lu, J. & Fletcher, G. Thinking about Computational Thinking, SIGCSE 2009, Chattanooga, PP260-264

[12] McMaster K. et al. Integrating Mathematical Thinking, Abstract Thinking, and Computational Thinking, *Proceedings of ASEE/IEEE Frontiers in Education Conference*, October 27 - 30, 2010, Washington, DC

[13] Moursund, D. *Computational Thinking and Math Maturity: Improving Math Education in K-8 Schools* (Second Edition), 2007, retrieved at http://uoregon.edu/~moursund/Books/ElMath/ElMath.html.

[14] National Research Council, Report of a Workshop on The Scope and Nature of Computational Thinking Committee for the Workshops on Computational Thinking, retrieved at http://www.nap.edu/catalog/12840.html

[15] Piaget, J. *Studies in Reflecting Abstraction*, Hove, UK: Psychology Press, 2001.

[16] Watson, A. & Mason, J. *Questions and Prompts for Mathematical Thinking*, Association of Teachers of Mathematics, Derby, 1998.

[17] Trefethen, L. Numerical Computation of the Schwarz-Christoffel Transformation, *SIAM J. Sci. Stat. Comput.* 1 (1980), 82-102.

[18] Wing, J. Computational Thinking, *Commun. ACM*, 49, 3 (March 2006), 33-35.

[19] Wing, J. Computational thinking and thinking about computing, *Phil. Trans. R. Soc. A* (2008) 366, 3717-3725

Beyond Good and Evil Impacts: Rethinking the Social Issues Components in Our Computing Curricula

Randy Connolly
Dept. Computer Science & Information
Systems
Mount Royal University
4825 Mount Royal Gate SW, Calgary,
AB, Canada T3E 6K6
403-440-6061

rconnolly@mtroyal.ca

ABSTRACT

It is by now widely accepted that social and professional issues are an important part of any computer science curriculum. The approach taken in most social issues courses is to articulate the social impacts of different computer technologies and then apply macro-ethical theories to those impacts. This paper argues that this approach has a number of drawbacks. First, it is based on a technological deterministic style of social explanation that has been in disrepute in the academic social sciences for decades. Second, it uses an algorithmic approach to ethics that simplifies the social complexity and the uncertainty that is the reality of socio-technological change. It concludes by suggesting that the alternative to the ethical evaluation of impacts is to focus the course instead on the social context; that is, on clarifying and unpacking the complexity involved in the relationship between technology and society.

Categories and Subject Descriptors

K.3.2 [Computers and Education]: Computer & Information Science Education – computer science education.

K.4.2 [Computers and Society]: Social Issues.

General Terms

Design, Experimentation.

Keywords

CS Education, Computer Ethics, Social Issues, Impacts, Pedagogy.

1. INTRODUCTION

"Students need to be challenged to see the impact of computing from different perspectives, confronted with complexities that they have not considered previously, and engaged in situations having unexpected consequences or undesired behavior" [16]

One of the many breakthroughs in the teaching of computer science over the past two decades has been the relatively widespread recognition of the importance of social and professional issues in the education of computing professionals. The 1991 ACM/IEEE computing curricula report argued that students "need to understand the basic cultural, social, legal, and ethical issues inherent in the discipline of computing" [38]. Subsequent ACM curricula reports have maintained this claim. The current CS-2008 assigns sixteen core hours to Social and Professional Issues (SPI): five of those are to ethics, three to the social context of computing, and the remaining hours cover some key issue areas such as privacy, intellectual property, and security. The report also touches on the pedagogy of teaching this material. It recommends "a single required course along with short modules in other courses," [1] a recommendation that appears to have been widely accepted. A recent survey of American universities found 88% of computer science programs included ethics in their computer science curricula [36]. Another survey that also included non-American universities found a full 95% of their respondents included SPI content in their computer science programs [16]. When one examines the past decade of papers at SIGCSE, ITiCSE, and ICER, while there have by no means been an overwhelming number of papers about the teaching of SPI (only 21 or about 1% of the total), there certainly have been a number of interesting attempts at articulating the best ways of teaching these issues and integrating them into the computer science curriculum [6,7,13,23,25,30,32,33,36].

From the very beginning this concern over social and ethical issues has been dominated by a very specific analytic approach, namely, the articulation of the impacts of information and computing technology (ICT) and the ethical evaluation of those impacts. In the 1991 report, for instance, the authors argued that computing "practitioners must be able to articulate the impact of introducing a given product line to a given environment" [38]. The NSF-funded ImpactCS project [22] of the mid-1990s explicitly continued this focus on social impacts and through its analytic framework and its description of the main SPI content became an important resource for faculty in constructing their SPI courses. More recently, a working group at ITiCSE 2010 expressed concern that many computer science programs were "neglecting broader issues of societal impact" [16]. In each of these examples, the impact approach has a specific goal: the analysis of the outcomes or social practices created or strengthened by the technologies in question.

But the required social and professional issues course has always been about more than just awareness of social implications. A strong prescriptive element (under the categories of Analytic Tools and Professional Ethics in CS-2008) is required. That is, students are expected to apply existing moral theories to construct guidelines or even rules to correct or prevent the wrongs caused by a particular technology. Examining textbooks or published reports of these courses [2,7,25,31,32], one can see a very particular teaching approach. First provide the students with at least two substantive ethical theories, generally utilitarianism and a Kantian deontology. These two forms of ethical evaluation are then used to evaluate the impacts caused by computer technology in a paradigmatic impact area such as privacy, intellectual property, security, and access to information in order to both articulate and to ethically evaluate the effect various computing technologies have had on those areas.

The appeal of this approach for computer science faculty is not hard to see. It is attractive to us because it is so algorithmic. Most computer science faculty achieved their position through their knowledge and research in traditional computer science topics, and, as a consequence, the SPI course is often not in a computer science professor's primary knowledge area. As Grodzinsky has noted, the "many gray areas of computer ethics are often frightening … to professors who are worried about how to answer things of which they themselves are unsure." [17] Not surprisingly then, a clear-cut methodology for teaching this course has in fact been argued [25,32] to be the way to make this course less imposing for computer science faculty; this algorithmic approach is perhaps especially appealing since, as one survey found, the vast majority (84%) of all computer ethics courses are taught by computer science faculty [36].

Despite these attractions, this paper is going to argue that both this algorithmic approach and the understanding of the relationship between society and technology that it is grounded upon has some real limitations and may in fact give our students an impoverished understanding of the social issues of computation. It will argue that the way we teach this course needs to move away from the preoccupation with the ethical evaluation of ICT impacts and instead emphasize the social context aspects of the Social and Professional Issues knowledge area. In particular, the teaching of this material needs to integrate the decades-old insights of researchers in the philosophy, history, and sociology of technology which emphasizes the complex interaction and co-construction between the social environment and any given technology and the resulting radical uncertainty of technological change.

2. WHAT'S WROING WITH IMPACTS?

Perhaps the first step in recognizing the shortcomings of the ethical impacts approach is to realize the central flaw in the articulate social impacts step in our SPI courses. This flaw is predicated on what seems an obvious and common-sense belief, namely, the belief that technology is simply a tool available for us to achieve our ends. This belief encourages us to examine computer technology in a means-ends manner: that is, the SPI researcher identifies and observes what affect the means is going to have on the social environment. It generally assumes that the means are by and large clear and unproblematic and will always work in the same way for all people at all times. While the impacts approach sees ICT as a tool, it also sees it as a very special type of tool that can have large-scale impacts on society

and/or the people using it. That is, while ICT, like a hammer, is just a tool, its special general-purpose nature means it has far-reaching effects outside its tool domain, akin to a hammer that changes the weather or weakens the dollar every time it strikes a nail. This approach to technology is generally called technological determinism by those who study the history, philosophy, or sociology of technology [26,28]. In this approach, technological change is treated as very much the independent variable in societal change. According to this view (see [4] and [35] for a summary of the debates), technological inventions – especially key ones like the printing press, the steam engine, the computer, the internet, and social networking – have transformed the world and thus new technologies need to be subjected to analysis to understand the wide-ranging transformation they have had on us and the world. Or, in Langdon Winner's evocative analogy, studying technological impacts is the equivalent of picking ourselves up and carefully measuring the tread marks after the bulldozer has rolled over us. "Such is the impotent mission of technological 'impact' assessment" [41].

It is understandable why computer professionals find technological determinism attractive. After all, we are the people that are helping to invent some of these new technologies; it feeds our clear desire to be socially relevant [30] and to believe that we computer geeks are actually the driver of social change, and not politicians, business people, or celebrities. This view is so widespread among computer professionals that, for instance, this author's students and fellow department members find it difficult to believe that most current historians and sociologists of technology firmly reject technological determinism as being theoretically inconsistent as well as empirically under-supported. As one recent historian has noted, sweeping accounts "about machines that shape society remain popular, but they clash with the research of most professional historians of technology" [26]. The academic field of science, technology and society (STS) studies that began in the 1960s has time and time again found that when examined carefully, most technologies rarely have had the effect that was expected (see, for instance, [27] and [29]) and that the reason for this phenomenon is that "new technologies are shaped by social conditions, prices, traditions, popular attitudes, interest groups, class differences, and government policy" [26]. Notice the direction of agency in this quote: it is technology that is being shaped or impacted by society, not the reverse.

Most technological deterministic impact prognosticators do their work by looking at the functional capabilities of a given technology and then imagining the impact of those functions. For instance, internet search engines clearly make it easier to find knowledge; what then will the impact of increased knowledge? Household technologies make it quicker to do housework; what will be the social impact of all that spare time? Antilock disc brakes make it less likely to skid and get into accidents; what will be the social impact of fewer accidents? In all these cases – and practically any other set of prognostications and impact evaluations than begin from an unquestioned belief that the functional capabilities of a technology (i.e., the means) do what is promised (i.e., achieve their ends) – the expected social impacts ended up being wildly wrong because the prognosticators believed in a naïve technological determinism.

For instance, the introduction of household technology did not end up creating, in the words of Ruth Schwartz Cowan, less work for mother, but in fact more work because of a series of social changes that could not have been predicted if one limited one's analysis just to the functional capabilities of the household technologies. As Cowan demonstrated [11], household technologies created more housework due to changing expectations of what constitutes cleanliness (e.g., clothes changed daily instead of weekly), new unexpected technologies enabled by the technology (e.g., wall-to-wall carpets were unknown before vacuums), and the gradual displacement of household work done by external agents (e.g., laundry services, maids, nannies) to housewives partly as a consequence of household technologies and partly due to exogenous changes in the social and economic realm. Similarly, efficient internet search-engines have not resulted in people with too much knowledge; instead, unpredicted changes in how people interact with words (scanning replacing reading) and even possibly cognitive decline due to the brain's plasticity have arguably resulted in the exact opposite consequence [8,10]. And as is readily apparent to anyone who actually drives an automobile, the introduction of anti-lock disc brakes have not reduced accidents at all, partly because drivers tend to drive faster and tailgate more closely due to the improved braking technology and also partly because of increases in the intensity of traffic due to unexpected changes in urban geography [39].

The first step then we should take in our Social and Professional Issues course is to communicate how rarely technologies achieve their exact promise, and indeed, how many do the opposite. This so-called Revenge Effect is well-documented [37] and yet this author was unable to find it discussed at all in existing computer ethics textbooks or in published accounts of this course. As well, an equally important step we need to make in the teaching of the SPI course is to reject naïve technological determinism and help students understand the complex agency issues in the relationship between technology and society. One way to achieve this goal would be by beginning the SPI course with examples and readings in how certain vital technologies had little impact on some societies, or on how certain technologies were strongly modified and differently adapted in different cultures and countries. This more historically-nuanced (and significantly more empirically accurate) approach is what is generally called social constructivism [4,12,26,27,28,29]. In this approach, one looks at how technologies are researched, invented, financed, developed, adopted, marketed, and propagated within a very complex system generally referred to as society. If one carefully examines a given technology within the social system in which it is embedded, it becomes extremely difficult to maintain a belief in technological determinism. Instead one sees technologies much more strongly "impacted" by society rather than vice versa. Thus, the SPI course should integrate the historically-grounded insights of the STS research community. In other words, the SPI course should look more like a historical sociology course and a lot less like a philosophic ethics course.

3. IMPORTANCE OF UNCERTAINTY
The reason why revenge effects occur is due to the fact that "socio-technological transformation is a highly complex process which involves many uncertainties" [24]. While uncertainty is a key concept in fields like economics, management, medicine, environmental science, and a variety of other disciplines, within moral philosophy in general, and computer ethics in particular, it

is underappreciated [40]. This is an important problem because the substantive moral theories (such as deontology and utilitarianism) that are the bedrock of the usual computer ethics course require relatively clear and unambiguous information about effects in order to make judgments [14,15,40]. Typical problems or dilemmas for which macro-ethical approaches are applied are most often done in a context of complete knowledge (if you do action X, then Y people will be harmed, but Z people will be benefited). This is appealing for computer scientists, who often work with problems modeled by idealized abstractions for which complete knowledge is possible. The ethics of technology, by contrast, should be recognized as residing in a context of at least partial uncertainty or ambiguity. Furthermore, the degree of uncertainty is greater for emerging technologies, and the more complex the technology, the more uncertain we are as to the developmental trajectory of a technology [29]. As Collingridge noted in the context of ethically controlling technology, control (i.e., ethical evaluation) is difficult, "and not rarely impossible, because during its early stages, when it can be controlled, not enough can be known about its harmful social consequences to warrant controlling its development; but by the time these consequences are apparent, control has become costly and slow" [9].

There are many places where uncertainty intersects with the lifecycle of a technology. Following Sollie [34], we can visualize this as shown in Figure 1.

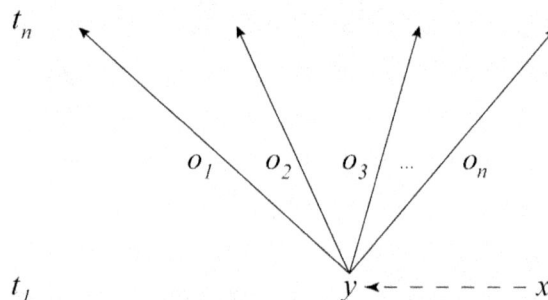

Figure 1. The Uncertainty of Technological Change

For the evaluating agent x (the professor or the student or the developer or the journalist) examining emerging technology y at time $t1$, the agent must have knowledge of the development trajectory in order to morally evaluate it. Unfortunately, as we have already seen, we very often cannot know the actual development trajectory and if we hypothesize one based purely on its functional capabilities, we more often than not will be woefully wrong. Thus, in reality, we need to recognize that technology y has multiple trajectories ($o1$, $o2$, $o3$, ...) and that it might be more important to attempt to understand which trajectories are more likely (by unpacking the web of interests and agents) than applying a prescriptive ethical judgment on a single trajectory.

4. BEYOND MORAL EVALUATION
One could argue that while uncertainty may be a feature of many aspects of life, we still manage to make practical and ethical decisions. That is, just because the arc of technological development is uncertain, that doesn't suddenly excuse us from making moral judgments. While this may be true, the argument

made in this paper is that moral evaluation in the uncertain realm of socio-technological change should perhaps be only tentative at best. That is, the ethical discussion in the SPI course should be purely descriptive ethics. As a consequence, it is this author's belief that the approach we should be taking in the SPI course is to expose the students to the many levels of uncertainty in the domain of technological evaluation, thereby allowing the students to achieve a level of critical awareness that weaves *some* ethical analysis into a richer understanding of the complex nature of socio-technological change.

As Brey has noted [5], the main problem with contemporary computer ethics is that the analytic effort is limited to evaluating well-recognized morally-controversial technological practices for which there is a policy or legal vacuum. While not unimportant certainly, the problem here, as discussed previously, is that it either depends on a level of epistemic certainty that may be unwarranted, or it may be evaluating a technological system that is so firmly established that its momentum has moved it beyond the effective reach of moral prescription. Furthermore, it tends to ignore the problems embedded in morally *non*transparent computer practices. The alternative approach offered here to the usual macro-ethical evaluation in SPI courses is sometimes referred to as disclosive ethics [5] and is more closely connected to a social constructivist understanding of technology. In this approach, rather than applying big ethical theories to well-known impacts, the focus is on disclosing the assumptions, values, and interests built into the design, implementation, and use of technology [20]. Thus, an alternative way of satisfying the Analytic Tools part of the CS-2008 SPI area would be to focus the SPI course on guiding the students in the unpacking of the normative assumptions of computer practice which in turn requires clarifying the complex web of social interactions that play a role in constructing the different trajectories a technology may take.

This approach is not about providing bright-line tests for evaluating the moral rightness and wrongness of technological practice but about opening up the black box of technological practice for understanding and to interrogate the assumptions, the embedded power relations, and the rhetorical and ideological contexts that we bring to those practices. While this may seem to some an abrogation of moral duty, it is perhaps the path that may end up being ultimately more socially responsible because it exposes our students to a more socially-nuanced understanding of their profession. Looking at the description of the core components in the SPI knowledge area in CS-2008 (and of the hours assigned to each), there is in fact recognition that it is equally important to have students appreciate the social and historical context of computing as it is to ethically evaluate it. We need to return our principal analytic focus in the SPI course back to this social context, and as the epigram that began this paper argued, focus the students' attention on different perspectives and on the complexities of socio-technological change.

5. CONCLUSION

Computer science has been immeasurably improved by the many dedicated scholars who have worked tirelessly to convince the rest of the field about the importance of social and professional issues. While most computer science programs do include a dedicated SPI course in their curriculum, there is often some anxiety associated with teaching this course due to a perceived lack of the appropriate knowledge by computer science faculty. As a consequence, there has been a convergence on a particular approach to teaching this course: articulate the impacts of different computer technologies and then apply a macro-ethical theory such as utilitarianism or deontology to those impacts. This paper argues that this approach is based on an old-fashioned social theory, namely technological determinism, which is both theoretically unsound and empirically under-supported. Furthermore, this paper also argues that the use of macro-ethical theories is inappropriate for domains in which there is a strong lack of epistemic certainty. Since the field of technological change is indeed characterized by substantial uncertainty, this paper concludes that we need to transform the way we teach the SPI course so that it is more closely allied with the insights of the broader science, technology and society research community. Doing so would make the SPI course much more focused on explicitly understanding the social contexts of computing and significantly less focused on its ethical evaluation.

6. ACKNOWLEDGMENTS

The author would like to thank Amber Settle for providing helpful feedback on earlier drafts of this paper.

7. REFERENCES

[1] ACM Interim Review Task Force. (2008). *Computer Science Curriculum 2008: An Interim Revision of CS 2001.* http://www.acm.org/education/curricula/ComputerScience2008.pdf.

[2] Baase, S. (2007). *A Gift of Fire: Social, Legal, and Ethical Issues for Computing and the Internet, Third Edition.* Prentice Hall.

[3] Barroso, P. and Melara, G. (2004). Teaching of Computer Ethics at the State of California's Universities and Other Countries. In *Proceedings ETHICOMP 2004.*

[4] Bijker, W.E. and Law, J., eds. (1992). *Shaping Technology/Building Society: Studies in Sociotechnical Change.* The MIT Press.

[5] Brey, P. (2000). Disclosive Computer Ethics. *Computers and Society* 30 (4).

[6] Califf, M.E. and Goodwin, M. (2005). Effective Incorporation of Ethics into Courses that Focus on Programming. In *SIGCSE'05.*

[7] Canosa, R. L. and Lucas, J.M. (2008). Mock Trials and Role-Playing in Computer Ethics Courses. In *SIGCSE'08.*

[8] Carr, N. (2010). *The Shallows: What the Internet is Doing to Our Brains.* Norton.

[9] Collingridge, D. (1980). *The Social Control of Technology.* St. Martin's Press.

[10] Connolly, R. (forthcoming). *What's Wrong with Online Reading.*

[11] Cowan, R.S. (1983). *Less Work for Mother.* Basic Books.

[12] Feenberg, A. (2000). From Essentialism to Constructivism: Philosophy of Technology at the Crossroads. *Technology and the Good Life?* Ed. Eric Higgs. The University of Chicago Press.

[13] Flieschman, W. M. (2006). Meta-Informatics and Ethical Issues in Computing. In *ITiCSE '06*.

[14] Floridi, L. (1999). Information ethics: On the philosophical foundation of computer ethics. *Ethics and Information Technology* 1 (1).

[15] Floridi, L. and Sanders, J.W. (2002). Mapping the foundationalist debate in computer ethics. *Ethics and Information Technology* 4 (1).

[16] Goldweber, M., *et al*. (2010). Enhancing the Social Issues Components in out Computing Curriculum: Computing for the Social Good. In *ITiCSE'10*.

[17] Grodzinsky, F. *et al*. (2004). Panel: Responding to the Challenges of Teaching Computer Ethics. In *SIGCSE'04*.

[18] Healy, T. The Unanticipated Consequences of Technology. http://www.scu.edu/ethics/publications/submitted/healy/cons equences.html.

[19] Himma, K. E. (2006). Foundational issues in information ethics. *Library Hi Tech* 25 (1).

[20] Introna, L. (2005). Phenomenological Approaches to Ethics and Information Technology. Stanford Encyclopedia of Philosophy. http://plato.stanford.edu/entries/ethics-it-phenomenology.

[21] Lawler, J. and Molluzzo, J. C. (2006). A Study of Data Mining and Information Ethics in Information Systems Curricula. *Information Systems Education Journal* 4 (34).

[22] Martin, C. D. and Weltz, E.Y. (1999). From Awareness to Action: Integrating Ethics and Social Responsibility into the Computer Science Curriculum. *Computers and Society* 29 (2).

[23] Martin, F.G. and Kuhn, S. (2006). Computing in Context: Integrating an Embedded Computing Project into a Course on Ethical and Societal Issues. In *SIGCSE'06*.

[24] Meijer, I., Hekkert, M., Faber, J. and Smits, R. (2006). Perceived uncertainties regarding socio-technological transformations: towards a framework. *International Journal of Foresight and Innovation Policy* 2 (2).

[25] Moskal, B., Miller, K., and King, L.A. (2002). Grading Essays in Computer Ethics: Rubrics Considered Helpful. In *SIGCSE'02*.

[26] Nye, D.E. (2007). *Technology Matters*. The MIT Press.

[27] Pacey, A. (1993). *The Maze of Ingenuity: Ideas and Idealism in the Development of Technology*. The MIT Press.

[28] Pinch, T. and Bijker, W.E. (1987). The Social Construction of Facts and Artifacts: Or How the Sociology of Science and the Sociology of Technology Might Benefit Each Other. *The Social Construction of Technological Systems: New Directions in the Sociology and History of Technology*. Ed. Bijker, E., Hughes, T.P. and Pinch, T. The MIT Press.

[29] Pool, R. (1997). *Beyond Engineering: How Society Shapes Technology*. Oxford University Press.

[30] Purewal, T.S., Bennett, C. and Maier, F. (2007). Embracing the Social Relevance: Computing, Ethics and the Community. In *SIGCSE'07*.

[31] Quinn, M.J. (2006). *Ethics for Information Age, Second Edition*. Addison-Wesley.

[32] Quinn, M.J. (2006). Case-Based Analysis: A Practical Tool for Teaching Computer Ethics. In *SIGCSE'06*.

[33] Sanders, A. F. (2005). A Discussion Format for Computer Ethics. In *SIGCSE'05*.

[34] Sollie, P. (2007). Ethics, technology development and uncertainty: an outline for any future ethics of technology. *Journal of Information, Communication & Ethics in Society* 5(4).

[35] Smith, M.R. and Marx, L., eds. (1994). *Does Technology Drive History? The Dilemma of Technological Determinism*. The MIT Press.

[36] Spradling, C. L., Soh, L., and Ansorge, C. (2008). Ethics Training and Decision-Making: Do Computer Science Programs Need Help? In *SIGCSE'08*.

[37] Tenner, E. (1997). *Why Things Bite Back: Technology and the Revenge of Unintended Consequences*. Vintage.

[38] Tucker, A.B., *et al*. (1991). Computing Curricula 1991. *Communications of the ACM* 34 (6).

[39] Vanderbilt, T. (2008). *Traffic: Why We Drive the Way We Do (and What It Says About Us)*. Knopf.

[40] Walker, W. *et al*. (2003). Defining uncertainty: a conceptual basis for uncertainty management in model-based decision support. *Integrated Assessment* 4 (1).

[41] Winner, L. (1986). Technologies as Forms of Life. *The Whale and the Reactor*. Chicago University Press.

Computing Student Practices of Cheating and Plagiarism: A Decade of Change

Judy Sheard
Faculty of Information Technology
Monash University
900 Dandenong Rd, Caulfield East, VIC
+61 3 9903 2701

judy.sheard@monash.edu

Martin Dick
School of Business Information Technology & Logistics
RMIT University
239 Bourke St, Melbourne, VIC
+61 3 9925 5976

martin.dick@rmit.edu.au

ABSTRACT

Cheating in undergraduate computing courses is an ongoing and widespread concern. In this paper we report an investigation of changes over the last decade in computing students' attitudes towards cheating practices, the extent of cheating behavior, and factors which influence cheating at an Australian university. A comparative analysis of data from surveys in 2000 and 2010 of undergraduate students in a School of Information Technology found that students in 2010 considered cheating less acceptable and the practice of cheating was reportedly lower. These results are discussed in terms of measures that have been taken to address this problem.

Categories and Subject Descriptors

K3.2 [**Computers and Education**]: Computer and Information Science Education – *computer science education*

General Terms

Human Factors

Keywords

Cheating, plagiarism, undergraduate students

1. INTRODUCTION

A common meme in debate at both the university and public level is that cheating and plagiarism are getting worse [18, 25]. This is hardly a new meme, one hundred years ago the Registrar of Stanford University wrote *"… and the freshman sees the game of cheating going on almost as a matter of course"* [9] (p.77). This current meme of increased cheating and plagiarism is built around a number of issues.

Firstly, the pressures of increasing class sizes and the shift towards on-line learning environments has meant a decline in face-to-face student-teacher contact. In addition, universities have emphasized collaborative learning with students encouraged to

work together. These factors are seen by some as lessening the influence and control of the teacher and allowing more opportunities for cheating to occur [7]. Secondly, new information and communication technologies have provided students with access to information in a form that is easily obtained and manipulated for their work. Thirdly, as technology has become an integral part of student learning environments the opportunities for students to cheat have increased [10]. Fourthly, ready-made or custom-made assignment solutions are available to download or be purchased to order on the Internet, affording new ways of cheating [4].

A variety of research has also suggested that student attitudes to these new avenues of cheating are more relaxed. A New Zealand study of 181 undergraduate students found that students viewed plagiarism from web sources as less serious than from other sources and will admit to plagiarism from web sources more than written sources [13]. However, a large USA and Canada web survey by McCabe held from 2002-2005 found that students showed slightly lower levels of reported plagiarism from the Internet than written sources. McCabe suggests this may be because students are turning to written sources which are not as easily detected by plagiarism detection software [14]. Of concern is that there is confusion about how information on the Internet should be used. As McCabe proposes "some students seem to view almost anything that they discover on the internet as general knowledge that does not require citation" (p.B7) [15].

Regardless, these are not new types of cheating or plagiarism as paper mills have been around from long before the Internet arrived and copying from books (as opposed to websites) is an almost ancient University tradition. The authors' earlier work in 2000 didn't identify students as seeing Internet and non-Internet cheating as significantly different [19-22]

In order to help understand the veracity of the meme, this paper examines the results of the same survey conducted in 2000 and 2010 at the same University in the same degree to determine the differences that exist between the two computing student populations. Has cheating and plagiarism increased? Is it more acceptable to current students than in the past? These are important questions that are necessary to be addressed to inform our teaching.

2. THE CHEATING PROBLEM

The literature on cheating and plagiarism in universities describe many ways that students may cheat, making it difficult to arrive at a simple definition of cheating. Whether a practice is cheating or not can depend on the rules set by an educator within a particular educational environment or for a particular task. We have defined a behavior to be *cheating* if it violates the rules that have been set for an assessment task or it violates the accepted standard of student behavior at the institution [22].

The literature on cheating in universities report alarmingly high rates of cheating practice and a problem that is widespread. For example, an early study of 5,422 North American undergraduate students in 1963 by Bowers [3] found that 75% admitted to having committed at least one of 13 specific cheating acts. These ranged from copying a few sentences of material without footnoting in a paper (43%) to admitting to taking an exam for another student (1%). A UK study by Newstead, Franklyn-Stokes and Armstead [17] found that 88% of 943 students admitted to cheating in at least 1 of 21 cheating behaviors, ranging from a form of plagiarism (54%) to sitting an exam for someone else (1%). Australian studies have reported similar high rates of cheating. For example, Marsden, Carroll and Neill [12] found that 81% of 954 students admitted to plagiarism and 41% to exam cheating on at least one occasion.

Cheating practice varies across disciplines, with computing students (along with engineering, science and business students) engaging in the highest rates of cheating [3, 5]. Focusing specifically on computing students, a study in 2000 by the authors [22] found that 79% of 504 undergraduate students admitted to at least 1 of 16 different cheating practices. Other studies have also reported high rates of cheating in computing courses, for example a study by Barrett and Malcolm [1].

Studies have identified a number of factors which influence cheating behavior. These may be due to personal characteristics, attitudinal or situational factors. Our study of computing students in 2000 [22] found time pressure and fear of failing as the main influences. Similar reasons have been found in other studies. For example, the studies by Newstead et al [17] and Wilkinson [26].

There are many suggestions for strategies to address the cheating problem. Bennett [2] proposes that strategies should be tailored according to the type of cheating. From results of an empirical study he determined that punishment could be a deterrent to major plagiarism; however, not necessarily effective against minor forms of plagiarism. McCabe [14] argues strongly that the emphasis should be on developing a culture of academic integrity. Honor codes have been used for this purpose with reported success, although these are not possible or appropriate for all contexts [16]. More recently, strategies have focused on education about the problems associated with cheating and possible consequences, and awareness of institutional policies. A study by the authors where we worked with a range of students identified a comprehensive list of strategies to address cheating and plagiarism [8]. A couple of examples of strategies devised for computing students are Barrett [1] who used an electronic plagiarism tool to educate students about correct use of source material. Joy [11] describes a resource to assess computing students' understanding of plagiarism and help them understand how it can be avoided.

Our study in 2000 showed concerning rates of cheating and impetuses for cheating within our School that were in line with other studies. This heightened awareness of this issue and prompted a range of measures to address the problem. These focused on education and prevention. Ten years on, we were keen to see whether these strategies had had any effect. With the changing learning environments and new educational practices over the last decade it was time to investigate whether attitudes towards and practice of cheating had changed within our School.

3. RESEARCH APPROACH

Students from selected courses in the School of Information Technology were surveyed near the end of second semesters in 2000 and 2010. Courses were chosen at each year level of the undergraduate degrees. A paper questionnaire was administered in tutorial classes by one of the authors not involved in teaching these classes. Participation was voluntary and, to encourage honest responses, the questionnaire was anonymous. Most students chose to participate and returned a completed questionnaire.

The questionnaire was developed by the authors for the first survey in 2000 and used again in 2010. A copy of the questionnaire is available from the authors. The questionnaire contained questions to determine:

- students' rating of acceptability of various questionable work practices described in 18 different scenarios;
- students' practice and knowledge of others' practice of each questionable work practice;
- factors which could cause or prevent cheating;
- students' responses to the cheating behavior of others; and
- students' perceptions of teaching staff and university attitudes to cheating.

The questionable work practices and factors which could influence cheating were situations which teaching staff had experienced or were sourced from other studies of cheating (e.g. [17]). To encourage discrimination in ratings of acceptability the scenarios ranged from practices that would generally not be considered cheating (e.g. showing assignment work to a lecturer for guidance) to serious forms of cheating (e.g. involving theft or fraud). The scenarios were referred to as "questionable" rather than "cheating" practices so as not to prejudice students' judgments of their acceptability. Scenarios to gauge student reactions have been used in other studies of cheating [23, 24].

4. RESULTS

The aim of this study was to investigate changes in attitudes and behavior in regards to cheating over the last decade. Reported in this paper is a comparative analysis of the undergraduate students' responses from the 2000 and 2010 surveys. Analyses of the 2000 survey data have been previously reported [20-22]. For the analysis reported here a subset of the 2000 dataset has been used. The 2000 survey was conducted at two metropolitan campuses. As the 2010 survey was only conducted one of these campuses (inner metropolitan), only the 2000 survey responses from this campus have been used.

A total of 415 questionnaires were returned from undergraduate students at the inner metropolitan campus (298 in 2000 and 117 in 2010). Seven questionnaires were removed from the dataset as the students appeared to have responded in an uncooperative way. For example, a couple of students gave a high rating of acceptability to and claimed to have practiced every scenario, which we considered unlikely.

Overall, 95% of the respondents were studying full time, 60% were local and the median course performance to-date was in the distinction range (70-79%). The profiles of the 2000 and 2010 groups were compared on these characteristics to establish any differences that could influence our interpretation of the results. Chi-squared tests on cross-tabulations of these characteristics found no differences. However, a difference was found in the gender profile between the 2000 and 2010 groups. The percentages of undergraduate male students was higher in 2010 (77%) than in 2000 (65%) and a chi-squared test showed this difference was significant (χ^2 (1, N = 396) = 5.23, p <0.05). As we had found a tendency by male students for higher levels of acceptance and practice of cheating in the 2000 study, the expected effect of this bias was that we would find an increase in acceptance of and levels of cheating in 2010.

4.1 Acceptability of cheating

The students were asked to consider 18 different scenarios, each describing a questionable work practice. For each scenario students were asked to rate how acceptable the practice was using a 5 point Likert scale, where 1 indicates *acceptable* and 5 indicates *not acceptable*. As this was ordinal scale data, Mann-Whitney U tests were used to determine differences between the 2000 and 2010 acceptability ratings. The results are shown in Table 1.

Comparisons between the 2000 and 2010 ratings showed that in 2010 students rated every scenario as less acceptable than in 2000 and for 10 scenarios this difference was significant according to Mann-Whitney U tests. Means of the acceptability ratings for 2000 and 2010 were calculated to give overall ratings of acceptability of cheating. Comparison of these showed a significant decrease in acceptability from 2000 (M=3.59, SD=0.59) to 2010 (M=3.89, SD=0.65) according to a t-test (t(406)=4.44, p < 0.05).

Table 1 Acceptability and practice of scenarios

Scenario	Acceptability			Practice		
	2000 (mean)	2010 (mean)	*Sig*	2000 %	2010 %	*Sig*
[a] Showing assignment work to a lecturer for guidance	2.07	2.21		37	42	
[a] Posting to an Internet newsgroup for assistance	2.07	2.28		27	34	
Two students collaborating on an assignment meant to be completed individually	2.54	3.20	***	44	36	
Resubmitting an assignment from a previous subject in a new subject	2.82	2.99		27	17	*
Submitting a friend's assignment from a past running of the subject	2.86	3.46	***	34	20	**
Copying the majority of an assignment from a friend's assignment, but doing a fair bit of work yourself	2.98	3.37	**	31	21	*
Not informing the tutor that an assignment has been given too high a mark	3.08	3.29		17	16	
Being given the answer to a tutorial exercise worth 5% by a class mate if the computer you used has problems	3.76	4.29	***	7	3	
Copying material for an essay from a text book	3.81	4.19	***	22	10	**
Copying material for an essay from the Internet	3.85	4.28	***	23	10	**
Obtaining a medical certificate from a doctor to get an extension when you are not sick	3.94	4.02		12	3	**
Swapping assignments with a friend, so that each does one assignment, instead of doing both	3.96	4.45	***	9	3	*
Copying another student's assignment from their computer without their knowledge and submitting it	4.18	4.62	***	7	3	
Copying all of an assignment given to you by a friend	4.30	4.62	**	10	3	**
Hiring a person to write your assignment for you	4.51	4.62	*	3	1	
Using a hidden sheet of paper with important facts during an exam	4.59	4.64		4	2	
Hiring someone to sit an exam for you	4.65	4.69		3	0	*
Taking a student's assignment from a lecturer's pigeonhole and copying it	4.72	4.72		4	2	

* = p < 0.05, ** = p < 0.01, *** = p < 0.001

[a] in accordance with School and University policies these scenarios are not considered cheating practices

4.2 Frequency of cheating practice

For each scenario the students nominated if they had practiced it personally. Cross tabulations were performed to determine any changes from 2000 to 2010. The results are shown in Table 1. To aid in the interpretation of the results, the scenarios are ordered from most to least acceptable based on the 2000 survey. There were decreases in practice for every scenario except the first two scenarios which are typically not considered cheating practices. For more than half the scenarios these changes were significant. Overall, the percentage of undergraduate students who claimed to have cheated in at least one practice (not including the first two) decreased from 78% in 2000 to 63% in 2010.

4.3 Reasons for cheating

The students were asked to consider 14 different reasons and asked to indicate the likelihood that each of these would cause them to cheat. A 5-point Likert scale was used, where 1 indicates *not at all* and 5 indicates *highly likely*. All except one reason were rated as less likely to cause students to cheat in 2010 and for five reasons the differences were significant according to Mann-Whitney U tests. These showed that time, workload and parental pressures were less likely to cause students to cheat in 2010. Also, students in 2010 were not as influenced by others cheating or motivated to cheat by monetary rewards. Means of the reasons for cheating ratings for 2000 and 2010 were calculated to give an overall rating. Comparison of these showed a significant decrease in likelihood of causing cheating from 2000 (M=2.54, SD=0.95) to 2010 (M=2.32, SD=0.96) according to a t-test (t(398)=3.14, p < 0.05).

4.4 Reasons for not cheating

The students were asked to consider 10 different reasons and asked to indicate the likelihood that each reason would prevent them from cheating. In contrast to the "reasons for cheating", these do not show any pattern of change from 2000 to 2010. The one significant increase was "Penalties if caught are too high", with two other reasons "Against your religious beliefs" and "Don't know how to" showing significant decreases according to Mann-Whitney U tests. Comparison of overall means of the reasons for not cheating ratings for 2000 and 2010 showed no change.

4.5 Responses to observed cheating

The students were asked what they would do if they had knowledge of another student cheating. Most claimed that they would do nothing if they observed someone cheating in an exam (80%) or if they knew someone who had plagiarized an assignment (82%). There was no change from 2000 to 2010 in these responses according to chi-squared tests.

4.6 Student perceptions of staff and University attitudes to cheating

The students were asked how strongly their teachers and the university felt about cheating. For these questions a 5-point Likert scale was used, where 1 indicates *not at all* and 5 indicates *very strongly*. Students considered that lecturers and tutors felt more strongly about preventing cheating in 2010 (M=4.09, SD=0.84) than in 2000 (M=3.75, SD=1.10). A Mann-Whitney U test showed this difference was significant (Z=-2.66). Furthermore, students considered that their university felt more strongly about

preventing cheating in 2010 (M=4.43, SD=0.84) than 2000 (M=3.89, SD=1.09). A Mann-Whitney U test showed this difference was significant (Z=-4.80). In 2010 students indicated strong awareness of University regulations on cheating (M=4.23, SD=0.84).

5. DISCUSSION

The initial research in 2000 was motivated by the authors' desire to test whether their personal experiences of cheating were being duplicated in other courses in the School. At that time, there was a strong view amongst a number of the School's academics, that cheating was not a significant problem and that few students were cheating and that most of those were caught. The 2000 results put paid to this point of view. Partly as a result of the 2000 research, the School and individual academics put in place a range of processes over the last decade to address the issue of cheating. These included:

1. a revised cheating and plagiarism policy that was much clearer and simpler to implement, resulting in increased use of the policy;

2. raising the issue of cheating at the start of every course;

3. stronger emphasis on an assignment cover sheet that students are required to sign, declaring that the work they are submitting is in compliance with University policies in regards to cheating and plagiarism;

4. introduction of a range of educational activities embedded in the curriculum of several individual courses in regards to cheating and plagiarism;

5. introduction of text and software plagiarism detection tools in many of the courses;

6. paying greater attention to the structure of assignment work to prevent cheating and plagiarism; and

7. courses using oral interviews to help reduce cheating [6].

The findings of this study research give an indication that such processes can have a positive impact on cheating. Overall the acceptability of cheating practices has gone down, with more than half significantly less acceptable in 2010. Even more positively, overall cheating practice has decreased, with more than half showing a significant reduction. In addition, student perceptions of the seriousness of the University and academics in regards to cheating and plagiarism have significantly increased.

All of the above findings make it clear that a positive change has occurred in the student body over the decade in regards to cheating awareness, acceptability and practice. Two aspects increase our confidence in the result, Firstly based on the relevant literature; the change in gender composition between 2000 and 2010 to a higher proportion of males would be likely to bias the results to a worse outcome as opposed to the actual improved outcome. Secondly, the reduction in student ignorance on how to cheat as a reason for not cheating would seem likely to result in an increase in cheating practice, not the overall decrease that we have seen.

One aspect that has not changed is the strong reluctance of students not to take action against the cheating practices of their peers; this might indicate that while students are taking more personal responsibility for their behavior, they do not see it as their role to maintain standards in this area.

Another interesting outcome from the findings is that in contrast to other research the computing students in 2000 and 2010 treat Internet and non-Internet plagiarism nearly identically in both practice and acceptability. This may be caused by the stronger knowledge of IT that the computing students have compared to students from other disciplines which leads them to be able to recognize that the plagiarized material's media is irrelevant to the acceptability of plagiarizing.

6. CONCLUSION

The results of the survey present us with a 'good news' story, the current student cohort on a range of measures finds cheating and plagiarism less acceptable and practice it less. While it is not possible to directly attribute causation to the processes implemented by the School and the efforts put in by individual academics, it seems unlikely that they have been irrelevant to the improved outcomes. That the relatively easy innovations have had a noticeable effect on cheating acceptability and practice indicates that the issue is both tractable and susceptible of hope for academics.

REFERENCES

[1] Barrett, R. and Malcolm, J. 2006. Embedding plagiarism education in the assessment process, *International Journal for Educational Integrity,* vol. 2.

[2] Bennett, R. 2005. Factors associated with student plagiarism in a post-1992 university, *Assessment & Evaluation in Higher Education,* vol. 30, pp. 137-162.

[3] Bowers, W.J. 1964. Student Dishonesty and its Control in College, Columbia University, New York CRP-1672.

[4] Clarke, R. and T. Lancaster 2008. Eliminating the successor to plagiarism? Identifying the usage of contract cheating sites, In proceedings of *2nd International Plagiarism Conference,* Gateshead, United Kingdom.

[5] Davis, S.F. and Ludvigson, H.W. 1995. Faculty Forum: Additional data on academic dishonesty and a proposal for remediation, *Teaching of Psychology,* vol. 22, pp. 119-121.

[6] Dick, M. 2005. Student interviews as a tool for assessment and learning ina systems analysis and design course, *SIGCSE Bulletin,* vol. 37, pp. 24-28.

[7] Dick, M., Sheard, J., Bareiss, C., Carter, J., Joyce, D., Harding, T., and Laxer, C. 2003. Addressing student cheating: Definitions and solutions, *ACM SIGCSE Bulletin,* vol. 35, pp. 172-184.

[8] Dick, M., Sheard, J., and Hasen, M. 2008. Prevention is better than cure: Addressing cheating and plaiarism based on the IT student perspective. In *Student Plagiarism in an Online World: Problems and Solutions,* T. S. Roberts, Ed. Hershey, PA, USA: Information Science Reference, pp. 160-182.

[9] Elliot, O.L. 1911. University Standards and Student Activities, *The Popular Science Quarterly,* vol. LXXIX, pp. 68-81.

[10] Jones, K., Reid, J., and Bartlett, R. 2008. Cyber cheating in an information technology age, *Digithum,* vol. 10, pp. 19-28.

[11] Joy, M., Cosma, G., Sinclair, J., and Yau, J.Y.-K. 2009. A taxonomy of plagiarism in computer science, In proceedings of *EDULEARN09,* Barcelona, Spain, pp. 3372-3379.

[12] Marsden, H., Carroll, M., and Neill, J. 2005. Who cheats at university? A self-report study of dishonest academic behaviours in a sample of Australian university students, *Australian Journal of Psychology,* vol. 57, pp. 1-10.

[13] Marshall, S. and Garry, M. 2005. NESB and ESB students' attitudes and perceptions of plagiarism, In proceedings of *2nd Asia-Pacific Educational Integrity Conference,* Newcastle, Australia, pp. 26-37.

[14] McCabe, D.L. 2005. Cheating among college and university students: A North American perspective, *International Journal for Educational Integrity,* vol. 1.

[15] McCabe, D.L. and Drinan, P. 1999. Toward a culture of academic integrity, *The Chronicle of Higher Education,* vol. 46, p. B7.

[16] McCabe, D.L. and Trevino, L.K. 1993. Academic dishonesty: Honor codes and other contextual influences, *Journal of Higher Education,* vol. 64, pp. 522-538.

[17] Newstead, S.E., Franklyn-Stokes, A., and Armstead, P. 1996. Individual differences in student cheating, *Journal of Educational Psychology,* vol. 88, pp. 229-241.

[18] Ross, M. 2010. Mired in a culture of cheating, In *The Boson Globe* Boston.

[19] Sheard, J., Carbone, A., and Dick, M. 2003. Determination of factors which impact on IT students' propensity to cheat, In proceedings of *Australasian Computing Education conference (ACE 2003),* Adelaide, Australia, pp. 119-126.

[20] Sheard, J. and Dick, M. 2003. Influences on cheating practice of IT students: What are the factors?, In proceedings of *Innovation and Technology in Computer Science Education (ITiCSE 2003),* Thessaloniki, Greece.

[21] Sheard, J., Dick, M., Markham, S., Macdonald, I., and Walsh, M. 2002. Cheating and plagiarism: Perceptions and practices of first year IT students, *ACM SIGCSE Bulletin, Proceedings of the 7th annual conference on Innovation and Technology in Computer Science Education (ITiCSE 2002),* vol. 34, pp. 183-187.

[22] Sheard, J., Markham, S., and Dick, M. 2003. Investigating differences in cheating behaviours of IT undergraduate and graduate students: The maturity and motivation factors, *Journal of Higher Education Research and Development,* vol. 22, pp. 91-108.

[23] Sierra, J. and Hyman, M. 2008. Ethical antecedents of cheating intentions: Evidence, *Journal of Academic Ethics,* vol. 51-55.

[24] Stepp, M. and Simon, B. 2010. Introductory computing students' conceptions of illegal student-student collaboration, In proceedings of *SIGCSE'10,* Milwaukee, Wisconsin, USA, pp. 295-299.

[25] Wenham, M. 2009. Cheats on the rise at our unis - Checks detect 2000, In *The Courier-Mail* Brisbane 2009.

[26] Wilkinson, J. 2009. Staff and student perceptions of plagiarism and cheating, *International Journal for Educational Integrity,* vol. 20, pp. 98-105.

"Computer Science and Nursery Rhymes"
A Learning Path for the Middle School

Doranna Di Vano
CSE Research Group of the Univ. of Udine
Scuola Media Statale "Via Petrarca"
via Petrarca, 19 – 33100 Udine (Italy)
doranna.divano@alice.it

Claudio Mirolo
Dept. of Mathematics and Computer Science
University of Udine
via delle Scienze, 206 – 33100 Udine (Italy)
claudio.mirolo@uniud.it

ABSTRACT

We have tried to introduce some ideas and way of thinking of computer science through a set of extra-curricular activities on nursery rhymes. In this paper we discuss our experience in an Italian middle school. The chosen subject is naturally connected to what the pupils see, or listen to, in the primary school as well as in their home. Starting from this material which is familiar to them, the pupils are guided to explore the "computational paradigm". This is accomplished through gradual steps, where they are solicited to observe, to analyze, to devise models and, eventually, to develop simple programs in Logo. Our work is an attempt to suggest a different perspective on computation, since most of the opportunities for the pupils to interact with the new technologies tend to reinforce a view that relegates all the computing sphere to a merely instrumental role.

Categories and Subject Descriptors

K.3.2 [**Computers and Education**]: Computer and Information Science Education — computer science education

General Terms

Human Factors

Keywords

K-12 curricula, control structures, variables, programming, interdisciplinarity, middle school.

1. INTRODUCTION

Informatics is a generic, all-encompassing term in Italy, which may mean *computer science*, *information technology*, or simply *ICTs*. This ambiguity is also present in the syllabi of the Italian Ministry of Education, as well as in the concrete implementations in the schools, and several teachers are scarcely aware of the actual nature of the activities that they propose under the hat of "informatics". In fact, we can distinguish three main interpretations of the term:

1. Informatics as an *instrument* in support of a variety of tasks outside its primary scope. The focus is on products and "the competences to be achieved by students are described in generic terms, [...] without instructional consistency and scrupulous planning of tasks" [2].

2. Informatics as a *technology*, addressing a large class of software artifacts. This approach nearly corresponds to the technological and social dimensions identified in [14]. The educational focus is on general patterns, cognitive invariants, structures and processes implied by the use of this kind of technology [2, 21].

3. Informatics as a *discipline* with its own identity, concepts and methodologies. It refers to the scientific dimension of [14]. The educational focus is on general principles to understand the computation processes and on problem-solving skills.

The problem of contrasting views of informatics, however, is also debated by the wider CS community, e.g. [1, 4]. Relative to the situation in their country, for instance, Clark and Boyle observe that computing "is being the victim of a terminological and political confusion that is to the detriment of education" [4]. In order to cope with a growing demand of dexterity with the ICTs, the secondary schools tend to offer computer literacy programs in the style of [8, 13], which do not give the students the opportunity to get a feel of the cultural and methodological aspects that characterize computer science as a rich and intellectually challenging discipline.

Unfortunately, the dominant image of informatics conveyed to most teenagers is that of a discipline about computing in its instrumental connotation, i.e. as mastering of technologies [20]. This may be one of the reasons why academic CS programs attract fewer bright students than other subjects, as attested by the statistics on the secondary school final grades of freshmen enrolled in the University of Udine.

To contrast the widespread stereotypical views of the discipline and to try to introduce in the middle school some of the ideas and way of thinking peculiar to computer science, we have developed a learning path around the theme of nursery rhymes. This path, which is specifically designed to "fit" into the Italian context, is built from a few extra-curricular units to be scheduled in each of the three years of the lower-secondary cycle. In particular, any feasible unit cannot be too ambitious in terms of time investment and should integrate as far as possible with the syllabi of other curricular school subjects. Ideally, we would also like to foster interdisciplinary work and give the teachers a chance to reflect on the nature of informatics and on its cultural role from a scientific perspective.

The pupils start working on raw material that they can retrieve from their everyday experience. To accomplish the proposed tasks, they are solicited to observe, to analyze, to model the phenomena under study and to re-elaborate the models in order to achieve new objectives. Through this work the students are gradually guided to explore the "computational paradigm" and eventually learn to carry out experiments with simple programs in Logo to generate the text of nursery rhymes. Following this path the pupils get exposed to programming, but it is worth noting that much work is meant to be done without using a computer, as suggested in [3], since important educational objectives can be better achieved through "old-fashioned" activities.

The rest of the paper is organized as follows. In section 2 informatics is set in the context of the Italian middle school. Section 3 outlines the learning path and illustrates the role of nursery rhymes in connection with computer science. In section 4 the experience is considered from a multidisciplinary perspective. Finally, section 5 summarizes the educational effects that the teachers have observed.

2. CS IN THE MIDDLE SCHOOL

Based on the framework of the Italian Ministry of Education for the lower-secondary cycle, *informatics* is not an autonomous subject, under the responsibility of a specific teacher, but each school is free to choose how to implement it as part of one or more other subjects. The *notions* and *competences* listed in the syllabi are broadly in line with the indications that can be found in the ACM/CSTA model curricula [19] for grades 6–8. Ordinarily, however, middle school informatics means ICT literacy and is just one of the topics of a course on technologies. In this context it would be important to enrich the learning experience with activities that allow to appreciate other, more interesting sides of informatics, as well as to take a more critical attitude toward computers, how they work, their potentials and limits.

A range of approaches can be adopted in order to design learning units specifically addressed to young students. In particular, the *CS Unplugged* [3] and *CS4FN* [5] projects are valuable models to introduce CS ideas through a variety of motivating activities. Other suggestions include: exploiting kinesthetic [22] or active learning [16] tasks, stimulating pupils' creativity within a multidisciplinary setting [18, 23], blending the procedural and narrative registers [11], working with more friendly programming environments, e.g. [17].

The teacher of "mathematics and science" is definitely the best qualified to take a computer scientist's viewpoint and to coordinate a project like that presented here. Furthermore, there is an interesting *interdisciplinary* section of the *mathematics* program, entitled "introduction to rational thinking", that lists a set of general abilities, in particular: (i) *observing and recognizing patterns*; (ii) *making conjectures to explain what is observed*; (iii) *reflecting on and verifying the conjectures*; (iv) *schematizing in various ways*. These are precisely the kinds of abilities that the pupils are expected to develop in order to analyze, to model and to create nursery rhymes.

3. CS AND NURSERY RHYMES

In this section we outline the learning path built around the recurring theme of nursery rhymes. This subject is naturally linked to the pupils' experiences in the primary school and in their home. While entering the secondary cycle of ed-

Figure 1: A "variable instantiation" mechanism based on gear wheels (in cardboard and wood).

ucation at the age of 10–11, the world of nursery rhymes is still able to inspire their imagination. Thus, their emotional engagement can be exploited to facilitate the achievement of educational objectives [10].

The analysis of nursery rhymes can profitably integrate the course of mathematics and science for its connections with the curricular topics: the key concepts of variable and function, the application of rules and the use of formal languages are naturally linked to the work of mathematicians; the ability to identify patterns and relationships, as well as to devise models constitute part of the repertoire of a scientist. Moreover, the material can be approached from the perspectives of other school subjects, such as literature, foreign languages, history, art and music.

First year (20 hours). To start, the pupils are invited to collect several examples of nursery rhymes, taken from their personal experiences. These small compositions are then analyzed in order to recognize repeats and, within each refrain, fixed and varying parts. Under the teacher's guidance, the students try to find hidden *structures*, discuss together and eventually reach an agreement about suitable criteria to classify the nursery rhymes on the basis of their structural properties. The main focus is on *syntactic* features, whereas the meaning and aims of the tiny stories may be considered in cooperation with the teachers of Italian and history.

The "mechanisms" that govern the simplest types of nursery rhymes are elaborated in playful activities. The pupils engage themselves in the construction of *concrete* models, toy *machines* like that shown in fig. 1, using cardboard and other cheap materials. Later, they can verify their ideas by trying out experiments on a larger set of examples with the aid of a small application, referred to as *ladybug*, that was specifically developed for this purpose by one of the authors, see fig. 2. Besides implementing a few traditional nursery rhymes, the pupils can also invent new ones of their own. While doing so, they are encouraged to figure out the actual inner working of the *ladybug* application and possible tasks it may fail to accomplish appropriately.

Second year (20 hours). The initial work is aimed at introducing the rudiments of programming in *Logo*. After teaching few basic language constructs and showing various examples, the leading theme is proposed again in a final task, when the students try to develop programs to automate the generation of simple nursery rhymes. Through this work they can gain a better understanding of what is going on "backstage" of the *ladybug* application and, more in general,

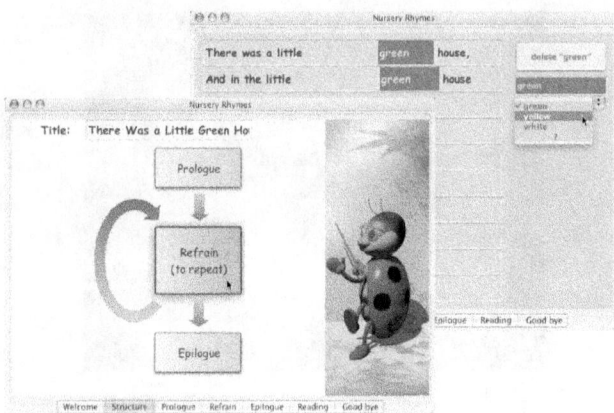

Figure 2: Screenshots of the *ladybug* application.

of other kinds of text-processing tools. We have chosen Logo as the programming medium because it seems an excellent tradeoff between expressiveness and ease of use, as well as between functional and imperative features.

Third year (10 hours). After some further work with Logo, the *ladybug* application is considered again at the end of the path. At that point, a more accurate account of what is going on can be grounded on the mental models developed through writing small pieces of software of their own. In particular, the students are invited to rethink and to discuss about the potentials and limits of this toy application in the light of what they have learnt from programming. The ability to reflect critically is most important to us, in order to induce the pupils to adopt a similar mental attitude towards the software tools they use in their everyday activities (word-processors, spreadsheets, etc.).

Most of the nursery rhymes that have been analyzed exhibit a simple cyclic structure, based on the repetition of a "refrain", possibly introduced by a short "prologue" and/or concluded by an "epilogue" — see the flow chart in fig. 2. Usually, the refrain is built up from some fixed text interleaved with one or more variable items (small pieces of text) which may be related to each other either syntactically or semantically. Here is a representative example:

There was a little green *house, / And in the little* green *house*
There was a little brown *house, / And in the little* brown *house*
. . . / There was a little heart.

A nursery rhyme of this kind can easily be "implemented" by writing the fixed text on a cardboard sheet and opening small windows for the variant parts. If the text layout is suitably designed, then a few specific instances of the variant parts can be drawn radially on a (cardboard) disk to be pinned underneath in such a way that different words are made visible through the windows when the disk is rotated. This rudimentary machine is also a useful device to introduce the concept of *variable*: the window hole plays the role of the variable, whereas the disk represents the range of its admissible values. Moreover, the fact that we can see just a value at a time through the window may be helpful to avoid the kind of misunderstanding observed by du Boulay in connection to the popular "box" metaphor [7], i.e. that "since a variable is like a box it can hold more than a single value".

Later on, the concept of variable is revisited during the work with the *ladybug* application, which allows to treat nursery rhymes with a simple iterative structure (*prologue*

```
to  refrain :color
    print (sentence [There was a little] :color [house,])
    print (sentence [And in the little] :color [house])
end

to  epilogue
    print [There was a little heart.]
end

to  there_was_a_little_green_house :colors
    foreach :colors "refrain
    epilogue
end
```

Figure 3: Logo program for the nursery rhyme "There was a little green house".

– *repeated refrain* – *epilogue*) and several variables. In the layout of the *refrain* the variables are visualized as colored fields and the values of variables of the same color are related to each other in some way. Some types of *syntactic* relations are automatically checked and processed by the application. The simplest case is that where the linked values are equal. In other situations simplified rules are applied to deal with varying suffixes (verb conjugations, singular vs. plural, etc.), articles, adjectives (possessive adjectives, demonstrative adjectives, etc.). There is also some limited support to check rhyming words, which is another interesting type of relation between variable values.

While considering these features of the *ladybug* application, the pupils are asked to figure out the structure of the implemented rules, as well as to test their conjectures by conceiving tricks to "fool" the machine. This kind of exercise gives them the opportunity to reflect about the concept of *rule*, to be understood as a merely *syntactic* manipulation of symbols, irrespective of the meaning they have for us.

As a final task, the students have to "translate" the structure of simple nursery rhymes into the structure of the programs that can generate them. Under the teacher's guide, special care is given to the procedural organization of the program, where the variables play again an important role. Fig. 3 illustrates a typical program structure. The main procedure receives as argument a list of words representing different colors. For instance:

```
there_was_a_little_green_house [green yellow white]
```

would produce the text of an instance of the nursery rhyme "There was a little green house" with three refrains.

Among other different types of structure, it is interesting to consider the following nursery rhyme which is well known by the Italian children. We provide a free translation in English meant to preserve some rhythmic feeling:

Once upon a time there was a king / Who sat on his throne
And said to the fool, / "Can you tell me a tale?"
And his witty jester did begin:

Once upon a time there was a king . . .

It is peculiar in that it can be analyzed from a twofold perspective. If we just look at the construction *syntax*, it can be seen as a piece of text that simply repeats itself over and over until you get bored. Its model is then the simplest form of *iteration* — repeat a given number of times:

```
repeat :times "refrain
```

where **refrain** is the name of a parameter-free procedure that prints the invariable text of the refrain.

```
to  the_jester_says :depth
    print [Once upon a time there was a king]
    print [who sat on his throne]
    print [and said to the fool,]
    print ["Can you tell me a tale?"]
    print [and his witty jester did begin:]
    ifelse (:depth = 1)
        [ epilogue ]
        [ the_jester_says (:depth - 1) ]
end

to  epilogue
    print [Once upon a time there was a king...]
end
```

Figure 4: Recursive interpretation of the nursery rhyme "Once upon a time there was a king."

If we look at its semantic content, on the other hand, we can realize an (unbound) *recursive* structure. An appropriate model in this respect is the Logo program reported in fig. 4, where the recursion depth is controlled by a conditional command — it may be worth noticing that similar tricks have also been used to introduce recursion at the college level, [6]. Another, more complex example that can be analyzed in terms of recursion is Branduardi's popular song "Highdown Fair", for which the pupils have proposed an "onion-skin" structure. Recursion is undoubtedly a difficult concept for middle-school ages, but it is also so because of the difficulty of finding concrete models to ground its understanding. Every concrete example offers at least the opportunity to develop and share an appropriate language to describe recursive phenomena and discuss about them [12].

As we have seen, the *structures* of nursery rhymes are initially introduced as conceptual schemes, useful to understand real world phenomena, and only later they are developed into *algorithmic* structures, ready to be translated into programs. Thus, the students should understand the underlying ideas in their broader sense, after being exposed to a variety of instantiations of them at several levels: initially through the analysis of the components of a nursery rhyme, then through the construction of a concrete, physical model (cardboard machine) and through the use of a specific application (*ladybug*), eventually through the design and experimentation of a program.

It may be worth observing that the analysis process aimed at classifying the structures of nursery rhymes, although very simple, is reminiscent of the analogous process carried out to identify useful *program* or *design patterns*. Similarly, when the pupils invent and implement new nursery rhymes of their own by exploiting the discussed models, they are essentially applying design/program patterns — see e.g. [15] for a discussion of program patterns in a CS1 context.

4. MULTIDISCIPLINARY CONTENTS

In line with the unitary view of knowledge that the new school programs recommend, the overall learning path offers a variety of opportunities to analyze and discuss the material from the perspectives of different disciplines. Since the first year the students could appreciate how any matter can be approached from different perspectives, and how different school subjects can contribute to a gain a deeper understanding of it. The multidisciplinary nature of the approach has been emphasized by the cooperation between the teachers of Italian and of mathematics and science, as well as by more sporadic contributions of other colleagues,

that resulted in a rich and varied learning experience with connections to several related topics such as:

- Observation, classification, modeling and empirical verification of hypotheses in science;
- Variables, functions, formalization and logical rigor in mathematics;
- Syntax and semantics of natural languages;
- Propp's functions in the fairy tales;
- Narrative structure of the ancient Myths in the literature, history and religions;
- Nursery rhymes in the foreign languages (specifically, English and German);
- Patterns and rules in music;
- Cyclic and recursive patterns in artwork (e.g., Escher's artwork).

The learning path is particularly synergic with the program of mathematics and science, both disciplines being under the responsibility of a same teacher in the Italian middle school. Being able to observe, to analyze, to contrast, to classify, to apply and infer rules, to recognize patterns, relationships and structures, to discern between variant and invariant features, to formalize through the use of appropriate languages, etc. are general competences that contribute to the achievement of cross-disciplinary objectives, most of which are *methodologically* relevant for computer science.

Much work has been organized in the form of "laboratory" activities to be carried out in groups. Thus, from a more general educational perspective, the pupils could get accustomed to working together, discussing with each other, taking into consideration different ideas, providing arguments in support of their opinions, and respecting each others' viewpoints. As a final remark, cooperating within a multidisciplinary project may also be beneficial to the teachers, who can become a little more aware of the implications of what they do with the information technologies from a computer science perspective.

5. DISCUSSION

In this section we summarize the main impressions and observations that the teachers reported from their experience with the class. To begin with, investigating *ladybug*'s rules to check rhymes has given the opportunity to discuss the potentials and the possible limitations of more general information processing technologies. Notably, the pupils themselves have been able to realize the analogy between rhyme checking with the *ladybug* application and spell/grammar checking with standard text-processing tools.

Through their engagement in programming tasks, it was expected that the pupils would move a step further to "demythicize" the computer capabilities. Interestingly enough, some feedback of the Logo environment, e.g., *"You don't say what to do with..."*, *"I don't know how to..."*, have prompted further discussion around the question of the computer intelligence. Although a few students experienced difficulties with programming tasks, others felt positively challenged: *"I feel smarter when I'm able to achieve the result."* All the pupils, however, could learn that the *computing* scope is wider than the numerical domains of mathematics and, perhaps surprisingly, that computational models can be applied to interpret what happens in the surrounding world.

241

The students could also see that the communication with machines and that between humans take place under different implicit assumptions, and so they could better understand the reasons of formal rigor in the former case. This is an important point according to Ferrari's interesting analysis of the role of languages in mathematics [9], where the lack of *concrete* motivations for the need of precise formal languages is identified as being one of the major causes that lead to disaffection. Besides this, in order to communicate their ideas about the structure of nursery rhymes, the pupils have been able to exploit set-oriented, flow charts and other sorts of graphical languages.

The teachers have also observed some learning transfer from the new experience to the curricular subjects in terms of methodological approach. After the "concrete" experience with the nursery rhymes, classifying the living beings in the natural sciences and the quadrilaterals in geometry, for instance, has been easier than it used to be. The understanding of some mathematical concepts, like the one-to-one and one-to-many relations in the first year, the concept of function in the second year, the general idea of *invariants*' of geometric transformations, seem to have improved because the pupils have previously been able to apply these concepts to simple, *concrete* situations. Moreover, the opportunity to approach a subjects of study from different perspectives has fostered the development of abstract thinking.

The learning experience seems to have also motivated the weaker students, who have been less reluctant to "take the risk" and engage themselves in the proposed tasks. Conceivably, they have perceived the proposed activities as independent of the school subjects which are sources of anxiety to them. Thus, they could gain in self-confidence and have been helped to cope with more difficult problems, especially in mathematics. Anecdotally, after interviewing a student who was weak in mathematics, a psychologist was impressed by her *deep* understanding of the concept of *variable*.

At the end of the experience, we asked the students about their subjective perception of these activities. More than three fourths of the class have considered the experience worth doing and would have liked to go deeper into the matter (one third would have liked *much* to). Incidentally, more than half of them also thought that the work done was really helpful to better learn mathematical concepts.

6. CONCLUSIONS

Despite the difficulties of scheduling the time slots for extra-curricular activities, especially in the third year, the overall experience seems to have been beneficial both to the students and to the teachers. All the (22) pupils, including those who have joined the class later, in the second or third year, have participated with interest in the wide variety of activities proposed to them and have been able to engage themselves to accomplish the assigned tasks.

Now, it would be interesting to replicate this experience and design appropriate instruments to assess the efficacy of the learning path from an educational research perspective. To this aim, it may be helpful to complement the written tests with individual interviews in order to gain a better understanding of the processes underlying pupils' answers.

Acknowledgments

Special thanks are due to Furio Honsell for providing valuable ideas and to Antonina Deotto for her enthusiastic cooperation.

7. REFERENCES

[1] J.-P. Archambault. Informatique et TIC: une vraie discipline? *Médialog*, 62:38–41, 2007.

[2] J. Baudé. Le développement de l'informatique et des TIC dans l'enseignement - et si la voie suivie n'était pas la bonne? EPI, 2007.

[3] T. Bell et al. Computer science unplugged: School students doing real computing without computers. *JACIT*, 13(1):20–29, 2009.

[4] M. A. C. Clark and R. D. Boyle. Computer science in english high schools: We lost the S, now the C is going. In *Proc. of the 2nd ISSEP*, volume 4226 of *LNCS*, pages 83–93, 2006.

[5] P. Curzon et al. cs4fn.org: Enthusing students about CS. In *Proc. of IEE IV*, pages 73–80, 2009.

[6] J. P. Dougherty. Using lyrics and music to reinforce concepts. *Journal of Computing Sciences in Colleges*, 23(3):106–113, 2008.

[7] B. du Boulay. Some difficulties of learning to program. *J. of Educational Comput. Research*, 2(1):57–73, 1986.

[8] European Computer Driving License Foundation. www.ecdl.com, 1997–2010.

[9] P. L. Ferrari. *Matematica e linguaggi. Quadro teorico e idee per la didattica*. Pitagora Editrice, 2004.

[10] D. Goleman. *Emotional intelligence*. Bantam Books, New York, 1995.

[11] C. Kelleher. Supporting storytelling in a programming environment for middle school children. In *Proc. of the 2nd ICIDS*, pages 1–4, 2009.

[12] D. Levy and T. Lapidot. Shared terminology, private syntax: the case of recursive descriptions. In *Proc. of the 7th ITiCSE*, pages 89–93, 2002.

[13] National Research Council. Being fluent with information technology, NAP, 1999.

[14] F. Paoletti. Épistémologie et technologie de l'informatique. *Le bulletin de l'EPI*, 71:175–182, 1993.

[15] V. K. Proulx. Programming patterns and design patterns in the introductory computer science course. In *Proc. of the 31st SIGCSE*, pages 80–84, 2000.

[16] M. Resnick and B. Silverman. Some reflections on designing construction kits for kids. In *Proc. of IDC'05*, pages 117–122, 2005.

[17] M. Resnick et al. Scratch: programming for all. *Communications of the ACM*, 52:60–67, 2009.

[18] E. Sendova. Handling the diversity of learners' interests by putting informatics content in various contexts. In *Proc. of the 2nd ISSEP*, volume 4226 of *LNCS*, pages 71–82, 2006.

[19] A. Tucker, Chair. A model curriculum for k-12 computer science: Final report of the k-12 task force curriculum committee. CSTA, 2003.

[20] J. van Leeuwen and L. Tanca. Student enrollment and image of the informatics discipline. Technical Report IE-2008-01, Informatics Europe, Oct. 2008.

[21] E. Vandeput. Milestones for teaching the spreadsheet program. CeFIS-DET-FUNDP, 2009.

[22] S. A. Wolfman and R. A. Bates. Kinesthetic learning in the classroom. *JCSC*, 21:203–206, 2005.

[23] B. Wursthorn. Fundamental concepts of CS in a Logo-environment. In *Proc. of EuroLogo*, 2005.

Experimental Evaluation of BeadLoom Game:
How Adding Game Elements to an Educational Tool Improves Motivation and Learning

Acey Boyce, Antoine Campbell, Shaun Pickford, Dustin Culler, and Tiffany Barnes

Department of Computer Science
University of North Carolina at Charlotte
9201 University City Blvd., Charlotte, NC, USA
1-704-687-8577

Tiffany.Barnes@uncc.edu

ABSTRACT

The Virtual Bead Loom (VBL) is a Culturally Situated Design Tool that successfully teaches students middle school math concepts while they learn about and create their own Native American bead artifacts. We developed BeadLoom Game to augment VBL with game elements that encourage players to apply the computational thinking skills of iteration and layering while optimizing the number of steps they take to solve a puzzle. In our prior work, we showed that BeadLoom Game is effective at teaching Cartesian coordinates, iteration, and layering. In this study, we use a switching replications experimental design to compare performance of BeadLoom Game with the VBL. Our results from two summer camps, one for middle school and one for college-bound high school students, show that through the addition of game based objectives, BeadLoom Game teaches Cartesian coordinates as well as the VBL but also teaches the computational thinking practices of iteration and layering.

Categories and Subject Descriptors

K.3.2 [**Computers and education**]: Computer and information science education. – computer science education.

General Terms: Design, Human Factors

Keywords: Game development, education, motivation, evaluation.

1. INTRODUCTION

Culturally Situated Design Tools (CSDTs) (csdt.rpi.edu) are a set of educational tools developed to teach students math and computer science through the creation of virtual cultural artifacts. Previous research has shown CSDTs to be effective at both motivating students to use the basic functions of the tools and at teaching the basic mathematic principles associated with those functions [6]. The Virtual Bead Loom (VBL) is a CSDT designed to teach students Cartesian coordinates, symmetry, and geometry through the creation of Native American bead art in a free-play environment. Its ease of use and its visually appealing cultural artifacts make it one of the most popular and successful CSDTs.

The VBL has been shown to produce positive results when teaching basic mathematical principles and students reported increased enjoyment from tool use when compared to traditional assignments [6]. However, as the VBL was used in extensive outreach [4], it was found that students often avoided using the more complicated functions of the VBL. These functions, including creative applications of iteration to make symmetric and aesthetic designs, were designed to reflect the rich cultural practices that Native Americans use to design their bead loom art and to show that algorithmic thinking is a natural part of Native American culture. We were disappointed that middle school students did not use and learn these interesting and intellectually rich concepts from the Virtual Bead Loom tool [2]. Iteration and looping are also important, but difficult to learn, computer science concepts. According to a survey of computing educators, iteration and looping are the third most difficult concept for novice computer science students to learn [3] making it even more important for students to not avoid these subjects.

In Spring 2009, we began designing a game to motivate students to learn the computational thinking practices of iteration, layering, and optimization from VBL. We first developed a paper version of the game that was played in conjunction with VBL, and later developed BeadLoom Game [2]. We chose to augment the VBL with game elements because of the inherent motivational properties games possess and their potential for improving educational applications [1,7]. We hypothesized that the increased motivation in BeadLoom Game would result in educational software that was both effective at teaching all the mathematical and computational thinking skills available in the VBL and would also be more fun and engaging.

Through a series of two experiments it was shown that BeadLoom Game did teach the advanced concepts of layering and iteration while providing stronger internal motivation and improving the replayability of the game. The first experiment was with a middle school summer camp that focused on CSDTs. Although no quantitative evidence was gathered on learning gains, it did show increased motivation to use the advanced functions. In the second experiment with a high school summer camp, students showed statistically significant learning increases from pre to post test in the areas of iteration and layering after playing the game [2]. However, these studies did not directly compare the learning gains of the VBL tool to that of BeadLoom Game, or test the ability of BeadLoom Game to teach middle school math or computational thinking skills. Here, we report on two studies to compare BeadLoom Game and the VBL for enjoyment and learning math and computational thinking practices within a middle school and a high school summer camp.

3. SOFTWARE DESIGNS

3.1 Original Virtual Bead Loom

Virtual Bead Loom is a Flash-based free-play tool that allows users to create their own Native American bead art by placing colored beads on a 41 by 41 Cartesian grid. To place the beads, users can choose from six different functions: Point, Line, Rectangle, Triangle, Linear Iteration, and Triangle Iteration. The Point function takes one point (e.g. x and y coordinates) as input and places a single bead at the specified location. This is the simplest function in the Virtual Bead Loom and also the least efficient for creating a full screen design. Students can and sometimes do create full screen designs using only the Point function, but this takes 1681 calls to completely fill the grid.

While it might seem unusual to talk about efficiency in creating art, it is important for several reasons. The VBL is often used in middle school classes and community organizations where time for each activity may be limited to 30 or perhaps 90 minutes. When students spend all of that time making a single design, they reinforce the learning for plotting Cartesian coordinates, an important middle school skill, but they do not learn the more interesting functions that could teach them about properties of lines, triangles, and rectangles, that could help them in developing geometry skills. Students also rarely appreciate the unique algorithmic thinking that Native Americans apply to design their hand-made bead patterns to be symmetric and beautiful.

If students instead learn to use all the rich functions provided by the VBL, they will increase efficiency, allowing more time to explore each tool and learn a variety of skills. The advanced functions place multiple beads each time they are called. For example, the Line and Rectangle functions each take two points as their input parameters and create a line or rectangle of beads based on these points. The Line function places beads along the two points given, while the Rectangle function fills in a rectangular region between the two specified points. These simple function calls can be used to illustrate that two points are enough to specify a line, and two points and a plane are enough to specify a rectangle. Similarly, the Triangle function takes three points for input, and uses them to create a triangle of beads. Although the Line, Rectangle and Triangle functions are slightly more complex, students tend to learn and use them quickly.

The Iteration functions are more advanced, and enable users to produce more complex patterns with a single call. As the name suggests, the Iteration functions use iteration to place beads in complex patterns onto the grid. These functions were not created randomly, but were designed to reflect how Native Americans achieve designs that demonstrate symmetry and aesthetically pleasing color changes in their art. Symmetry is an extremely important element of Native American bead art, reflecting balance and harmony. To make symmetric patterns, Native American bead artists developed algorithms to make diagonal lines and isosceles triangles. Since bead art is constructed one row at a time, these algorithms are based on creating a pattern in one row, and repeating and modifying it in subsequent rows.

The Linear Iteration function shown on the left in Figure 1 illustrates how wing-like patterns are achieved row by row. This function begins with a straight line of beads of a given length (A)

at a given point (B). In the next row in the specified direction (+x, -x, +y, or -y), the row is repeated in a graduated color, but may be shifted by adding or subtracting a given number of beads from each side of the line (C and D). This process is repeated, or iterated, for the given number of lines total (E). Using this function introduces students to a function much more complex than simply repeating a given process – this iterative algorithm repeats a process and modifies it at the same time!

The Triangle Iteration function shown on the right in Figure 1 demonstrates how isosceles triangles are made in bead art. A triangle begins with a single bead at a given point (F). Then, for G rows, the Triangle Iteration function copies the previous row. Once that is done, the function adds H beads to each side and copies the row G times. It does this for a given number of rows (I) and in a given direction. Writing a program to do this function is quite complex, requiring a nested loop. Students using this tool have a unique graphical demonstration of nested loops, a notoriously difficult concept for beginning programmers to understand. Although the students do not necessarily see use of this tool as a nested loop, we believe that it introduces nested loops in a fun and interesting way and can form the foundation of understanding and appreciating the computational thinking practice of using nested loops to create repeated patterns.

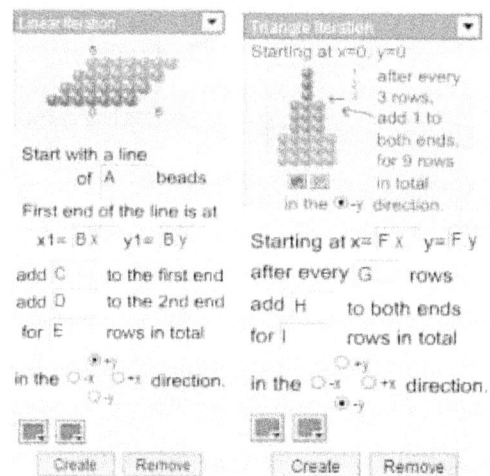

Figure 1: Linear and Triangle Iteration in the Virtual Bead Loom

All functions of the Virtual Bead Loom use layering: if you place one bead on top of another you will only see the top bead and no blending will occur. This is a simple implementation of the Painter's Algorithm, a key concept in three dimensional computer graphics. When rendering a scene using the Painters Algorithm, the object farthest away from the screen on the Z-axis is drawn first, and closer objects are drawn in descending distance to avoid calculating which objects occlude one another. The same technique can be applied to efficiently "paint" a pattern in VBL. For example, it is common in Native American bead art to build a pattern surrounded by a field of white beads. In the VBL, this is most effectively and efficiently achieved by first drawing a white rectangle before beginning to create other patterns. By thinking computationally and spatially, VBL users can make a pattern efficiently by imagining how different shapes can be layered to draw a desired pattern. Using layering is a powerful computational tool in many types of computer graphics applications – not just rendering but also in tools such as Adobe Photoshop® that use layers to achieve particular artistic effects.

Although the VBL provides these rich functions that allow opportunities to learn more about the Native American culture while also learning algorithms, iteration, and even layering, they are complex and students avoided them. Even when it would be much easier and faster to use an iterative function, students would add beads with the simpler Line and Point functions. There was simply no internal motivation to use these functions.

3.2 BeadLoom Game

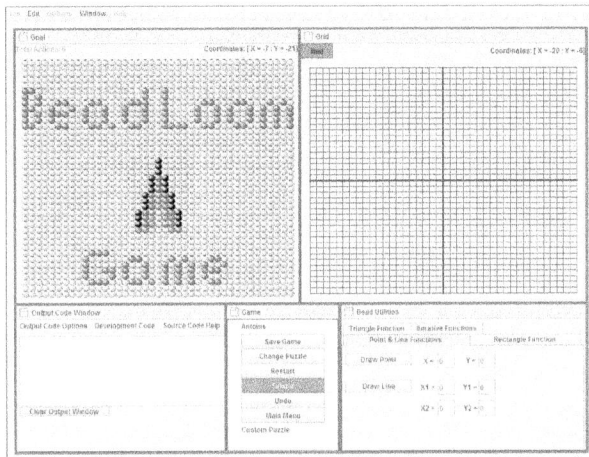

Figure 2: BeadLoom Game, with a target pattern on the left

In order to provide internal motivation to use the advanced functions of VBL, we created BeadLoom Game. The main goal of BeadLoom Game is to create a goal image using the minimal number of function calls, or "moves". Each time a player uses one of the six bead-placing functions it is considered one move. Whenever a player completes a puzzle they are awarded a medal based on their performance. Players can earn a platinum medal by finding the lowest number of moves needed to complete the puzzle, or the "ideal solution." Gold medals are awarded for solutions completed it in up to 1.5 times the ideal solution, and silver for up to 2 times the ideal solution. Players earn a bronze medal for completing the puzzle in any number of moves more than twice the ideal solution. BeadLoom Game puzzles encourage players to minimize the number of moves they make, reinforcing an important computational thinking practice of optimization. These puzzles were carefully designed to encourage the computational thinking practices of iteration and layering.

Players can earn bronze medals simply by using the Point function, but puzzles are designed so they must learn and master the skills of iteration and layering to earn platinum medals. The medal system also encourages players to replay completed puzzles to find better solutions. This is especially effective in encouraging competitive game play on the more advanced puzzles, where no one in a group has yet found the ideal solution.

Prior experiments have successfully proven that BeadLoom Game, through the game elements of player objectives, a medal system, and a competitive aspect, can impact student learning of the computational thinking skills of iteration and layering [2]. However, this study did not show if it did so better than the original tool or even if it worked with the original target audience: middle school students.

4. EXPERIMENTAL METHOD

We use a switching replications experimental design that compares the Virtual Bead Loom (Tool) with the BeadLoom Game (Game) first in a controlled study, then switches the control and experimental groups to test for ordering effects. This design is particularly effective for educational interventions, because it makes a beneficial intervention available to all students while holding the learning time constant for both groups. It also allows researchers to determine if the intervention has a long-term effect. Eagle and Barnes used this "crossover" experimental design to compare an educational game for teaching loops to a traditional programming assignment and found that their game was more effective, and also caused long-term learning effects [5].

We conducted experiments during two 5-day summer camps in 2010. The first camp, Exploring Technology through Culture and Art, engaged 21 middle school students (6 female) to create their own cultural artifacts while learning math and computing. The second camp, Aspire IT, engaged 20 college-bound high school students (7 female) to create games and explore computer forensics. The first day of each camp, students completed a 12-question pretest with 4 questions for each topic: Cartesian coordinates, iteration, and layering. We did not test for the computational thinking practice of optimization. For Cartesian coordinate questions, students plot given points on a graph. Figure 3 shows an iteration question where students fill in the missing numbers in an iterative function. Students also find the number of beads present after a given number of iterations in such a function. For layering questions students find the minimal number of shapes that can be layered to make a given image.

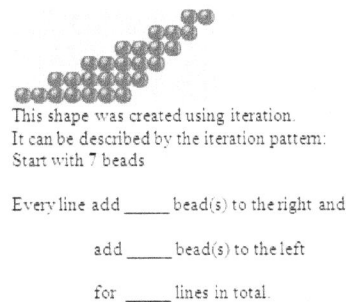

This shape was created using iteration.
It can be described by the iteration pattern:
Start with 7 beads

Every line add _____ bead(s) to the right and

add _____ bead(s) to the left

for _____ lines in total.

Figure 3: An example iteration question

Each camp was divided into two groups: the Game group played BeadLoom Game first and the Tool group used the original Virtual Bead Loom Tool first. Both groups were walked through a short demonstration of each of the six functions and then given 90 minutes to play BeadLoom Game or use the VBL Tool depending on their group. Afterwards, they were given an isomorphic mid test to evaluate their learning gains.

After using the Game and the Tool respectively, each group used the opposite software for another 90 minutes. Afterward, the middle school camp was introduced to other Culturally Situated Design Tools (CSDTs), while the high school camp learned how to use Game Maker game development software (available at yoyogames.com). Since none of the other CSDTs or Game Maker use iteration or layering, BLG would be the only source of learning in these areas. Each day started off with a 30-minute BLG Challenge where students competed to complete a given puzzle in the fewest number of moves. At the end of each day, students were given 30-60 minutes where they could choose from a selection of activities including BeadLoom Game, Virtual Bead Loom, and other tools. During this time students were able to more freely explore all areas of BeadLoom Game, including the custom puzzle creator. Once some custom puzzles were created, other students began attempting to find ideal solutions to their peers' work. At the end of each camp, students took an isomorphic post test to evaluate overall learning gains, and a short survey to determine how they felt about the game, what features they enjoyed most, and if they preferred the game or VBL.

5. RESULTS

5.1 Middle School Camp

For the middle school camp, we found that the game and the tool were equally effective at teaching Cartesian coordinates. This is not surprising, as BeadLoom Game and Virtual Bead Loom use the same basic functionality to plot Cartesian coordinates. The success of VBL for teaching Cartesian coordinates is one of its strongest features, so we made sure BeadLoom Game used the same interface.

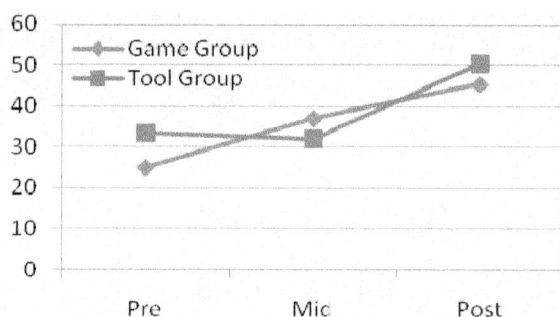

Figure 4: Middle school test results comparing Game & Tool groups

Figure 4 shows the middle school students' pre, mid, and post test scores on the remaining questions on iteration and layering. As the figure illustrates, the Game group showed increases in knowledge during the first session and continued to learn through the remainder of the summer camp. The Tool group showed no learning until after they began playing the game. Table 1 compares the learning differences for each group on these questions. There was a significant difference in the learning gains from pre to mid test, indicating that the Game group learned more from 90 minutes playing the Game than the Tool group learned from the same amount of time using Virtual Bead Loom. Since the Tool group accomplished the same overall learning gains as the Game group from pre to post, we believe that most of the learning gains for the week can be attributed to BeadLoom Game.

During the week, the middle school students were introduced to one to two additional CSDTs every day through Wednesday. At the end of each of these days, students were given free time where they could work with any of the CSDTs. As Table 2 shows, BeadLoom Game was the most popular selection every day.

Table 1: Learning differences between middle school groups

	N	Mid-Pre	Post-Mid	Post-Pre
Game	11	12.12	8.33	20.45
Tool	10	-1.67	18.75	17.08
Difference p value		0.019	0.27	0.70
t-stat		2.57	-1.12	0.38

When asked which they preferred, 16 selected BeadLoom Game and 5 chose Virtual Bead Loom. One student explained that he liked the game best "because we have to solve [puzzles] using our brains." Of the CSDTs, students ranked Virtual Bead Loom 4th most popular while BeadLoom Game was ranked 2nd. Over the 5 days, middle school students earned 183 platinum medals.

Table 2: Free time CSDT selection by day

	Monday	Tuesday	Wednesday
BeadLoom Game	16	19	13
Virtual Bead Loom	5	0	0
Other CSDTs	-	2	8

5.2 High School Camp

Similar to the middle school camp, there were no statistically significant differences between the high school Tool and Game groups for learning in Cartesian coordinates. These advanced high school students already had a strong working knowledge of Cartesian coordinates and showed very little change from pre to mid and on to post in either group. Figure 5 shows the high school students' pre, mid, and post test scores on the iteration and layering questions. The Tool group showed no learning gains by the mid test while the Game group saw learning gains from pre to mid test and mid to post test. Once again the Tool group achieved learning gains only after playing the game.

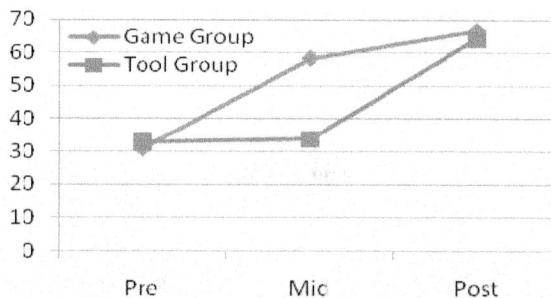

Figure 5: High school test results comparing Game and Tool groups

Table 3 compares the learning differences between the groups for the iteration and layering questions. There was a significant learning difference for the Game group from pre to mid test and for the tool group from mid to post test; in other words, after exposure to BeadLoom Game. As with the middle schoolers, the high school Tool group was able to overcome the initial learning gains difference and catch up to the game group by playing BLG.

When asked which they preferred, 13 chose BeadLoom Game and 7 chose Virtual Bead Loom. One high school student wrote of BeadLoom Game, "The game forces me to use more complicated iterations to improve my score which makes it a fun activity and a good learning tool." During their 5-day camp the high school students earned 215 Platinum medals.

246

Table 3: Learning differences between high school groups

	N	Mid-Pre	Post-Mid	Post-Pre
Game	10	27.50	8.33	35.83
Tool	10	0.83	30.42	31.25
Difference p value		.0012	.0031	.63
t-stat		2.57	-1.12	.49

We note that the middle school Game group outperformed the high school Tool group on the mid test, averaging 37.12% on iteration and layering while the high school Tool group averaged 31.67%. Although this was not a statistically significant margin, we were surprised that the middle school students outperformed the college-bound high schoolers after playing BeadLoom Game.

6. DISCUSSION

These two experiments show that BeadLoom Game is more effective than the Virtual Bead Loom at teaching the advanced concepts of iteration and layering to both middle and high school students. Anecdotally, we observed that the Virtual Bead Loom and BeadLoom Game complemented one another, as the original CSDT provides an easier environment to learn the basic concepts and experiment with the more advanced functions while the game motivates students to build stronger iteration and layering skills.

In our previous work, we showed that BeadLoom Game could teach high school students the same concepts as the Virtual Bead Loom educational tool while being fun and motivating [2]. However, that study did not compare BeadLoom Game with the VBL tool. It also lacked quantitative evidence that the tool worked with middle school students, the original target audience of the tool. Our study showed a positive comparison with the Virtual Bead Loom in learning gains for the important computational thinking skills of iteration and layering while teaching Cartesian coordinates just as effectively. We have shown statistically significant learning gains in iteration and layering for all students after exposure to BeadLoom Game.

The distinction between a piece of educational software and a new game derived from it was an important one to establish. We already knew games have a strong motivating force [1,7], but this study shows direct learning gain improvements resulting from the conversion of a successful educational tool into a game. We believe that our study shows that the addition of simple objectives and competitive aspects can increase students' internal motivation and enjoyment while also improving learning outcomes. Based on the success of the BLG we believe that this principle can be extended to many existing educational tool with similar results.

7. CONCLUSIONS AND FUTURE WORK

Our results show that BeadLoom Game not only taught the intended math and computational thinking concepts, but did so better than the original Virtual Bead Loom. The Game showed statistically significant learning differences in groups of middle and high school students who used it when compared to groups who used the Tool. By adding game elements we have been able to both increase student motivation and achieve higher learning gains than the tool in as little as 90 minutes. Our results show that incorporating game elements into educational software can increase learning gains through fun and challenging game objectives that directly correlate to learning objectives.

We plan to further investigate the importance that individual game elements have in converting educational software into games. For example, we plan to use feedback from users who prefer the Virtual Bead Loom to find what features they like best to determine how free play could be integrated into BeadLoom Game. We will also expand BeadLoom Game's online community and explore what effects the community aspects such as leaderboards and custom puzzles have on motivation and learning. We hope to repeat this process with other educational software, to eventually build a framework that educational software developers can use to choose game elements to improve the learning and motivation outcomes for their learning tools.

8. ACKNOWLEDGMENTS
We thank Kera Bell-Watkins' 2009 software engineering class for making a Java version of VBL, and Ron Eglash for developing the CSDTs. This work was partially supported by National Science Foundation grants CNS-0634342, CNS 0739216, CNS 0540523, IIS-0757521 and the UNCC Diversity in IT Institute.

9. REFERENCES
[1] Barnes, T., E. Powell, A. Chaffin, H. Lipford. Game2Learn: Improving the engagement and motivation of CS1 students. *ACM GDCSE* 2008.

[2] Boyce, A, and T. Barnes. BeadLoom Game: Using Game Elements to Increase Motivation and Learning. *ACM FDG 2010.* Monterey, CA, USA, June 19-21, 2010.

[3] Dale, N. B. Most difficult topics in CS1: results of an online survey of educators. *SIGCSE Bulletin* 38, 2 (2006), 49-53.

[4] Doran, K., A. Boyce, S. Finkelstein, T. Barnes. (2010). Short Paper: Reaching out with Game Design. *ACM FDG 2010.* Monterey, CA, USA, June 19-21, 2010.

[5] Eagle, M., T. Barnes. Experimental evaluation of an educational game for improved learning in introductory computing. In SIGCSE '09, PP. 321-325, 2009.

[6] Eglash, R., Bennett, A., O'Donnell, C., Jennings, S., and Cintorino, M. (2006). "Culturally Situated Design Tools: Ethnocomputing from Field Site to Classroom." American Anthropologist 108(2): 347-362.

[7] Garris, Ahlers, & Driskell. Games, motivation, and learning: a research and practice model. Simulation and Gaming, Vol. 33, No. 4, 2002, 441-467.

Teaching CS Unplugged in the High School (with Limited Success)

Yvon Feaster[†], Luke Segars[‡], Sally K. Wahba[†], and Jason O. Hallstrom[†]
† School of Computing, Clemson University, Clemson, SC 29634-0974 USA
‡ Computer Science, UC Berkeley, Berkeley, CA 94720-1776 USA
yfeaste@cs.clemson.edu, lukes@cs.berkeley.edu, {sallyw, jasonoh}@cs.clemson.edu

ABSTRACT

CS Unplugged is a set of active learning activities designed to introduce fundamental computer science principles without the use of computers. The program has gained significant momentum in recent years, with proponents citing deep engagement and enjoyment benefits. With these benefits in mind, we initiated a one-year outreach program involving a local high school, using the CS Unplugged program as the foundation. To our disappointment, the results were at odds with our enthusiasm — significantly. In this paper, we describe our approach to adapting the CS Unplugged materials for use at the high school level, present our experiences teaching it, and summarize the results of our evaluation.

Categories and Subject Descriptors

K.3.2 [**Computers and Education**]: Computer and Info. Science Education—*Comp. sci. education, Curriculum*

General Terms

Experimentation, Human Factors

Keywords

CS Unplugged, computer science outreach, high school curriculum, experimental evaluation

1. INTRODUCTION

According to the latest Taulbee Survey, the number of students majoring in undergraduate computer science degree programs rose for the second year in a row [10]. While the news is most welcome, the 14% cumulative increase is relatively modest when considered in context: In 2007, at the base of the enrollment decline in the U.S., computer science enrollment was approximately half of what it was in 2001 [9]. With the U.S. demand for computer scientists expected to increase by 24% over the next decade [3], there is a potential for a shortfall in the domestic labor market. To avoid this shortfall, computer science educators must find new ways to reach out to potential recruits.

One outreach program that is gaining momentum is *CS Unplugged* [4]. The program consists of a set of modules that introduce students to fundamental computer science principles using hands-on activities that are designed to be engaging and fun. The program is distinguished by two characteristics. First, the activities are largely designed to be completed without the use of computers. Instead, students are typically asked to complete kinesthetic tasks that reinforce the concept or algorithmic technique under study (e.g., placing physical objects, moving from one seat to another). Second, the activities are designed to support adaptation to suit a range of learning levels, from grade school students to high school students. Instructors can reveal progressively more detail as appropriate to the target audience.

CS Unplugged offers a compelling set of activities. They break the traditional mold of computer science education and open a new set of possibilities for energizing the K-12 curriculum. The program offers the promise of engagement, excitement, and meaningful learning — and ultimately, a deep supply of potential computer scientists.

With this in mind, we initiated a year long outreach program with a local high school based on the CS Unplugged activities. The program consisted of ten 40-minute sessions, repeated for two semesters in an introductory programming course. The evaluation objectives were two-fold. First, we sought to evaluate the impact of the program on student attitudes toward computer science. Second, we sought to evaluate the impact of the program on students' perceived content understanding. We expected the results would point to the obvious conclusion: The program would be a success.

This was not, however, the case. With only one exception, the program had no statistically significant impact on student attitudes or perceived content understanding. Indeed, in some cases, student attitudes moved in an undesirable direction (although these changes were not statistically significant). Given the inclusion of CS Unplugged activities in the ACM K-12 Model Curriculum [1], it is important for experience reports of this kind —both positive *and* negative— to be documented. Educators must not only understand how CS Unplugged can succeed, but also how it can fail.

Paper Organization. Section 2 presents key elements of related work. Section 3 summarizes the structure and content of the outreach program. Section 4 presents the pilot projects. Section 5 presents the results of our evaluation. Finally, Section 6 concludes with a discussion of the evaluation results and potential avenues of further exploration.

2. RELATED WORK

Our goals are shared by a number of other computer science outreach programs. Heersink and Moskal [5] study the attitudes of high school students toward computer science and information technology. The authors administered a pre-survey to 140 students attending computer science and information technology workshops across 5 states. In relation to the fields of computer science and information technology, the pre-survey measured students' interest level, perceived ability to learn the associated skills, perceived usefulness of the skills, gender issues, and attitudes toward a related professional career. The surveys were written in such a way that the terms "computer science" and "information technology" were interchangeable. Approximately one half of the students received the survey containing "computer science"; the other half received the "information technology" survey. The authors found that students could not distinguish between the two terms. They attributed this confusion to the broad use of educators who serve both as computer science and information technology teachers.

Mano et al. [7] introduce an outreach program at a local middle school, designed to increase student interest in computer science. Volunteers visited 4 classes for approximately 45 minutes each month. Some activities used in this program include disassembling and reassembling a computer, learning how to program with Alice, and using CS Unplugged activities. The authors state that the survey results and volunteers' observations suggest that the program had a positive impact on student interest in computer science.

Lambert et al. [6] similarly introduce a set of CS Unplugged activities to a group of fourth graders. The authors visited three classes once a week for 5 weeks; each session was approximately 30 minutes. They conducted pre- and post-evaluations to assess student interest in computer science and mathematics, and anxieties related to mathematics. One interesting result was that the students did not particularly favor the binary activity. This was the same response we received in our pilot, as we will discuss later.

Blum et al. [2] describe CS4HS (Computer Science for High Schools), an outreach program for high school teachers. The program was created to emphasize how computer science and computer science careers involve more than just programming. Workshop participants learned how to teach computer science concepts using CS Unplugged activities and other kinesthetic activities.

Closest to our work is that of Taub et al. [8], which focuses on analyzing the effect of CS Unplugged activities on participants' views of computer science. Their pilot program consisted of 13 seventh and eighth grade students. Eighteen CS Unplugged activities were presented. The evaluation consisted of a pre-survey focused on evaluating participants' views of computer science. (There was no mention of a post-survey.) Six students volunteered to participate in a structured post-interview. The interview involved viewing images and discussing students' thoughts on what the images represented with respect to computer science. The authors conclude that CS Unplugged activities had a positive effect on students' views of computer science, but their effectiveness could be improved. One suggested improvement was to strengthen students' weak connection between the activities and computer science concepts being taught. The authors also note that the activities do not adequately represent the career opportunities in computer science.

3. PROGRAM DESIGN

Our outreach program consists of ten activity modules, nine of which are based on CS Unplugged activities [4]. The tenth is a computer architecture activity. We adapted each CS Unplugged activity to suit our class length, as well as the high school age range. Below is a short summary of each lesson prepared for this program.

Lesson 1: Binary Numbers. The goal of this module is to introduce students to the binary number system. We discuss reasons why it is necessary to use binary instead of decimal numbers to store information on a computer. We then introduce students to the idea of converting between different numbering systems and give them several examples, as well as a few conversions for them to solve on the board.

Lesson 2: The Anatomy of a Computer. The goal of this module is to demystify the innerworkings of a computer by teaching students about the constituent hardware components and their functions. With assistance from the instructors, the students disassemble and reassemble desktop computers in small teams. (This is the only lesson not taken from the CS Unplugged activities.)

Lesson 3: Information Theory. The goal of this module is to demonstrate the role of context in assessing the importance of elements in a collection. We open the activity by presenting a paragraph that demonstrates how the brain processes words while reading ("Aoccdrnig to rscheearch at an Eligngsh uinervtisy,..."). We discuss how our brain uses context clues to interpret information. We then present activities that allow students to compare strategies for finding numbers in sorted and unsorted collections and explore the idea of finding data via binary search.

Lesson 4: Algorithms and Sorting. The goal of this module is to introduce students to algorithms and their importance to computer science. We explain the difference between two sorting algorithms (bubble sort and quicksort) using an activity involving sorting a group of students according to their height. We then discuss popular real-world applications of sorting, including iTunes track listings and Google's search results.

Lesson 5: Sorting Networks and Parallel Computing. The goal of this module is to introduce students to the idea of partitioning tasks to execute over multiple processing units. Using a job in a local grocery store, we draw a connection between having multiple employees at a job and multiple processors solving a computational problem. Next, we use the sorting network activity provided by CS Unplugged to demonstrate a parallelized sorting algorithm.

Lesson 6: Graphs and Minimum Spanning Trees. The goal of this module is to introduce students to the fundamentals of graph theory. We begin by drawing graphs describing airport routes and interstate maps between cities. We transition into the topic of minimum spanning trees and play a game using Prim's algorithm to find the cheapest way to tour Europe using a graph of major airports.

Lesson 7: Routing and Deadlock. The goal of this module is to introduce the concept of routing and the strengths and weaknesses of various network layouts. We discuss the need for redundancy, the possibility of deadlock when two cars come to a one-way bridge (with the CS Unplugged dining philosopher's activity), and the issue of privacy across networks (using a brief encryption/decryption exercise).

Lesson 8: Error Detection and Cryptography. The goal of this module is to introduce data corruption detection and encryption/decryption techniques. We use the CS Unplugged parity cards activity to explore how corrupted data could be detected and potentially fixed. We also share data encryption techniques designed to safeguard information streams.

Lesson 9: Public Key Encryption. The goal of this module is to demonstrate public and private key encryption. To explain these concepts we use two activities. The first uses a locked box passed from a "host" student to a "destination" student through several "malicious" students. In the second activity, we teach students how to send encrypted messages and how to decrypt these messages.

Lesson 10: Programming Languages. The goal of this module is to introduce students to the types of instructions required to program a computer. The class is broken into two teams. Each team appoints a designated "robot". After creating a set of instructions, each group is tasked with navigating their blindfolded robot through a maze.

4. PILOT PROJECT

The pilot program spanned two semesters, targeting two sections of an introductory programming class at a local high school. The grade levels of the students ranged from 9 to 12. Ten 40-minute activities were presented each semester. Most of the students in this class had limited knowledge of the concepts covered in these activities.

4.1 Semester 1

In the first semester, our pilot followed a quasi-experimental, nonequivalent control group design. We were not able to control participant selection or account for baseline differences in student attitudes and content understanding. The experimental section included 14 students. A second section of 15 students served as the control group. Prior to the first activity, a pre-survey was administered to both sections. On the last day of the program, an identical post-survey was administered. To receive feedback on the instruction and activities, the schools' Instructional Coach[1] was asked to observe one of the class presentations.

Upon completion of the first semester, the pre- and post-surveys were evaluated. Our analysis, detailed in Section 5, indicated that the activities were not having the impact we were anticipating. Specifically, gains in interest in computer science and content understanding were insignificant. In response, we consulted the Instructional Coach and class instructor; the decision was made to add accountability to the program to ensure the students were accountable for the lesson content.

4.2 Semester 2

In the second semester, the experimental group comprised the students that served as the control group in the first semester. For this reason, these students were not given another survey until the end of the semester. (Their post-survey from the first semester was considered as the pre-survey for the second semester.) These students were presented with the same activities as the first group. During each class, students were given a worksheet to complete containing 4 questions related to the lesson being taught. At the end of each lesson, the worksheets were collected, corrected, and returned to the students at the beginning of the following class. These worksheets had no impact on the students' grades. However, at the request of the instructor, two questions were provided each week to include in a weekly quiz.

---

[1] An *Instructional Coach* works with teachers to provide regular feedback related to course standards, classroom management, standardized testing, and curriculum strategies.

No.	Statement/Question
1	Computer science (CS) seems like it would be fun.
2	I might be interested in majoring in CS in college.
3	Working with computers is intimidating.
4	I think CS is useful in my daily life.
5	I can use a computer in math and science homework.
6	I am capable of doing well in a CS major in college.
7	CS is mostly about programming.
8	CS has a lot to do with math.
9	CS has a lot to do with problem solving.
10	CS would be useful to me even without a computer.
11	I think I understand how computers store information.
12	I would break something if I replaced a part in my computer.
13	I can guess a secret number between 1 and 100 in 10 guesses.
14	I think I understand how iTunes sorts songs.
15	I think I could explain what an "algorithm" is.
16	I think I basically understand how the Internet works.
17	I think I can find the tallest person among 16 in 3 minutes, with one comparison per minute.
18	In a list of 10 cities, I think it would be possible to reach the smallest city from every other city.
19	If you decided to pursue a CS degree in college, which topics or courses would you expect to study?
20	If you decided to pursue a CS degree in college, which high school classes do you think would be most important to prepare you?

Table 1: Student Survey

It was our hope that the addition of the worksheet and the quiz questions would add the layer of accountability needed for the program to be successful.

5. EVALUATION

The pre-/post-survey consisted of 18 Likert-style attitudinal and content understanding statements, as well as 2 free response questions. These questions were designed to evaluate the impact of the program on student attitudes toward computer science and impact on their perceived content understanding. Students were asked to rate their level of agreement with the statements, from *strongly disagree*, *disagree*, *moderately disagree*, *moderately agree*, *agree*, and *strongly agree*. Table 1 lists the survey statements and questions. Ratings of the statements were given the values from 1 to 6, for *strongly disagree* to *strongly agree*, respectively. When a statement had a negative connotation (i.e., statements 3, 7, 12), the values were inverted. Accordingly, an increase in the post-survey values indicates a desired result for all statements.

Rating Statements. A cursory review of each semester's survey results indicated little to no change in interest/confidence. To verify this, we performed a statistical analysis on the data from the first and second semester experimental groups. The analysis was to determine any significant change in the mean of the pre-/post- survey questions. First, for each question, a statistical F-test was performed to determine if the variance in the pre-/post- survey responses were equal. If the resulting p-value was greater than or equal to 0.05 (1 - confidence interval of 0.95), the variance was assumed to be equal. Second, for each question, a two-sample t-test was performed to determine if the pre-/post-surveys exhibited a significant change. Our original observations were verified in that only one question exhibited a significant change: Question 15 - "I think I could explain what an "algorithm" is." The first group had a pre-/post-survey mean of 2.73 and 4.72, respectively, with a variance

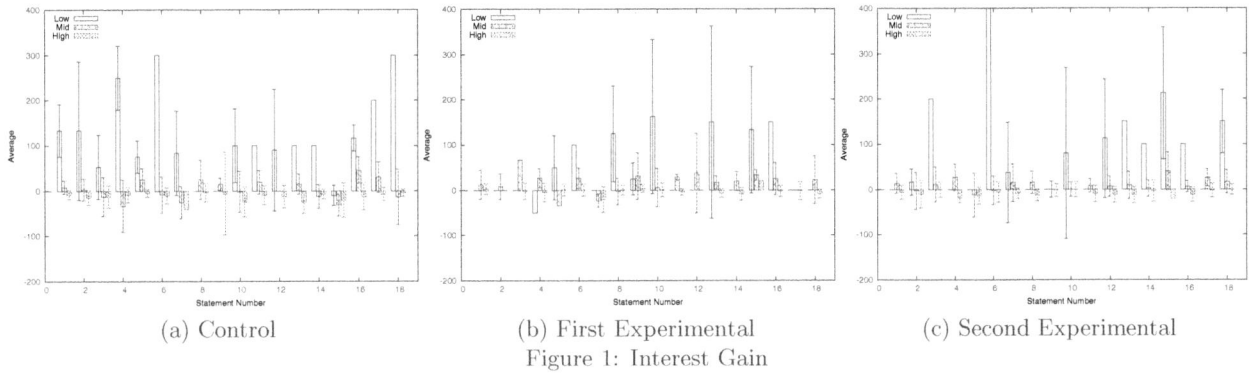

(a) Control   (b) First Experimental   (c) Second Experimental

Figure 1: Interest Gain

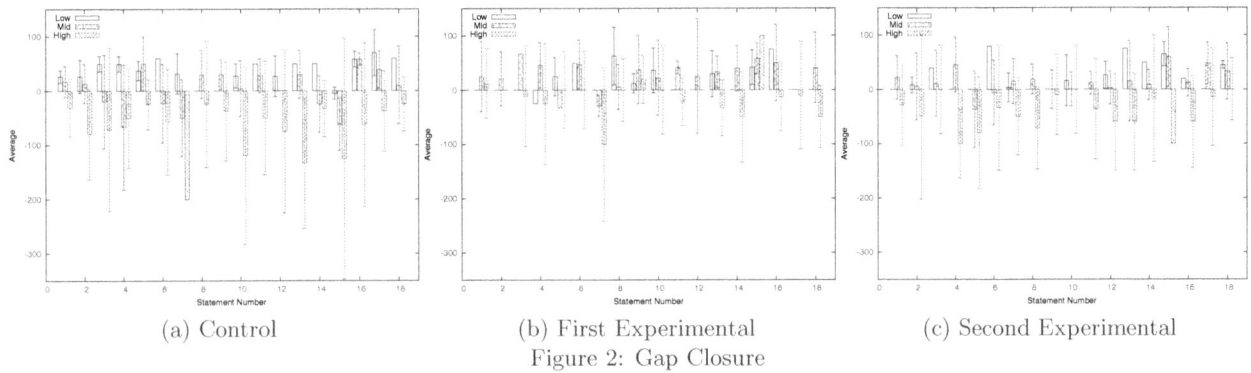

(a) Control   (b) First Experimental   (c) Second Experimental

Figure 2: Gap Closure

of 1.82 and 2.02, respectively. The F-test showed a p-value of 0.44, so a two-sample t-test with equal variance was performed. The p-value of the t-test was 0.01, indicating statistical significance. The second group showed similar results. The pre-/post- survey mean was 2.73 and 4.8, respectively, with a variance of 1.78 and 1.03, respectively. The F-test exhibited a p-value of 0.16, so again, a two sample t-test with equal variance was performed. The p-value of the t-test was 0.00005, indicating statistical significance. We hypothesize that this question showed significant change because the term "algorithm" was defined in an early module and revisited in many of the remaining modules. A worksheet with the complete data analysis can be found at: http://dsrg.cs.clemson.edu/PHSStatistics.xls.

Interest Gain and Gap Closure. We divided the student ratings for each Likert-style statement into three categories: *low* (1, 2), *mid* (3, 4), and *high* (5, 6) based on the pre-survey ratings. We wanted to study the effectiveness of our program on each group. For each group, we measured the percentage of interest/confidence gain using the following formula: [((post value - pre value) / pre value) * 100]. We also measured the interest/confidence gap closure in percent, measured using the following formula: [((post value - pre value) / (6 - pre value)) * 100]. A gap closure of -100 indicates a decrease of 1 point from a pre- to a post-survey value. Some categories have missing values, as no students rated the corresponding statements in these categories. Figures 1 and 2 summarize the average interest/confidence gain and average gap closure for each group, respectively. The x-axis represents the survey statement number; the y-axis indicates the average and standard deviation for the low, mid, and high groups. Notice that the averages for the *low* groups are consistently higher than the other groups. This indicates that we were more successful in increasing the level of interest/confidence among students in the low group than

we were among students in other groups. We postulate that it is easier to raise the level of interest among students who are not interested in the subject than it is to raise the level of interest among students with high pre-existing interest. Notice from Figure 2 that the gap for the *high* category increased significantly for the second experimental group. This indicates that students gave lower ratings in the post-survey than they did in the pre-survey, thus showing less interest/confidence. However, most of these results remained in the high category, where students who scored 6 in the pre-survey scored 5 in the post-survey. To our disappointment, when compared with the control group, there was not a significant interest/confidence gain or gap closure among the two experimental groups, and in many cases, the results were negative, especially among the mid and high groups.

Free Response Question 1. The free response questions ask the students to identify the classes they expect to study in an undergraduate computer science program, and the high school classes they feel would prepare them for the major. We grouped the classes identified by the students (i.e., *"binning"*) and counted the frequency of each response in the pre-/post-surveys. For the first question we noticed the presence of four new topics (i.e., robotics, computer science, binary numbers, networking) in the post-survey for the first group. These were topics covered in our modules, but were not necessarily covered in their class. For the second group, we also noticed the introduction of computer science as a subject in the post-survey that occurred three times. Further, computer engineering decreased from four occurrences to two. The students seem to have learned that computer science and computer engineering are different disciplines. Finally, the data in both groups indicates the students seem to believe that computer programming is an important subject to study in computer science. The occurrence of this subject did not change for the first group, with four occurrences. However, the occurrence count went up with the second group from eight to nine. This was surprising, as we were teaching the students computer science concepts *without* the use of a computer, and we never emphasized the importance of computer programming in computer science. We attribute this to the programming lessons they attended during the week. To our surprise, the control group seems to think that taking computer programming classes is not as important as they stated in their pre-survey. The occurrence count decreased from twelve to eight.

Free Response Question 2. As with the first question, we observed some interesting results concerning the second question ("...high school classes to prepare you for a computer science degree..."). We noticed that in the post-survey for the two experimental groups, the webpage design subject does not appear to be as important as students previously thought. For the first group, the occurrence count went down from one to zero, while it went down from three to one for the second group. Further, students seem to draw a stronger correlation between math and CS. The occurrence count went up from one to three, and from one to four for the first and second groups, respectively. This differs from the control group results. Finally, both groups seem to think that taking computer classes or computer-related courses will help prepare them for a computer science major in college. The control group appears to draw a stronger correlation between CS and programming than the experimental groups, who instead seem to emphasize mathematics.

Discussion. We have shown that the CS Unplugged program we presented had, on average, no impact on student attitudes toward computer science or their perceived content understanding. We believe there are several causes for this result. First, based on our experience with presenting CS Unplugged activities to other groups, we believe high school students do not find kinesthetic activities of this kind as exciting as middle or elementary school students, such as the groups participating in [6–8]. Although we attempted to modify the activities to be more suitable for high school participants, we observed that these students seemed less motivated to participate than we had hoped. Second, the selected students were already in a computer science programming class. We felt they would be more interested in the activities. However, after reviewing the data and reflecting on our experiences with these students, we believe most of the students perceived themselves as "experienced programmers" and so may have been less interested in spending time learning these concepts. Last, most successful CS Unplugged-based programs were either summer workshops or after school programs. Participants in these programs tend to be self-selected, with a strong pre-existing interest.

Threats to Validity. It is worth emphasizing that a number of experimental factors were outside of our control. In future pilots, several validity threats must be addressed. This includes increasing the population size, adjusting for preexisting differences in student attitudes and content understanding, adjusting for instructor-induced impacts, understanding the impact of computing lessons external to our program, and addressing data collection failures (i.e., missing student response data).

6. CONCLUSION

Like most computer science educators, we are looking for new ways to excite the next generation of undergraduates about pursuing a degree in computer science. The CS Unplugged program appears to offer a promising approach. The basic tenets resonate with our own attitudes about computer science and teaching effectiveness, and the program is gaining adoption fast. Indeed, we believed that success was a foregone conclusion.

Unfortunately, we were wrong. Using a quasi-experimental, nonequivalent control group design, we evaluated the impact of a semester-long outreach program based on CS Unplugged, repeated for two consecutive semesters. The results indicate, with only one exception, that the program had no statistically significant impact on student attitudes toward computer science or perceived content understanding. Indeed, in some cases, it appears as though the program had an undesirable effect (although these results were not statistically significant).

The purpose of this experience report is not to attribute failure to the CS Unplugged program. We have presented an unbiased report of our approach to adapting the program to a high school context and identified possible explanations for the poor results. The intent is to engage the community in a discussion of how CS Unplugged should be used — *and how it shouldn't*.

Acknowledgments

This work is supported by the National Science Foundation through awards CNS-0745846, DUE-1022941, and DUE-0633506. Yvon Feaster is an NSF Graduate Research Fellow. The authors would like to thank the local high school administration and Mr. George Rosser, the class instructor.

7. REFERENCES

[1] ACM K-12 Task Force Curriculum Committee. A model curriculum for K-12 computer science: Final report of the ACM K-12 task force curriculum committee. csta.acm.org/Curriculum/sub/CurrFiles/K-12ModelCurr2ndEd.pdf, 2006.

[2] L. Blum and T. Cortina. CS4HS: an outreach program for high school CS teachers. In *Proceedings of the 38th ACM Technical Symposium on Computer Science Education*, pages 19–23, New York, NY, USA, March 2007. ACM.

[3] Bureau of Labor Statistics, U.S. Department of Labor. Occupational outlook handbook, 2010-11 edition, computer scientists. www.bls.gov/oco/ocos304.htm, 2010. (*date of last access*).

[4] Computer Science Unplugged. Computer science unplugged. csunplugged.org/, 2010. (*date of last access*).

[5] D. Heersink and B. Moskal. Measuring high school students' attitudes toward computing. In *Proceedings of the 41st ACM Technical Symposium on Computer Science Education*, pages 446–450, New York, NY, USA, March 2010. ACM.

[6] L. Lambert and H. Guiffre. Computer science outreach in an elementary school. *Journal of Computing Sciences in colleges*, 24(3):118–124, 2009.

[7] C. Mano et al. Effective in-class activities for middle school outreach programs. In *Proceedings of the 40th ASEE/IEEE Frontiers in Education Conference*, pages F2E1–F2E6, Washington DC, USA, October 2010. IEEE.

[8] R. Taub et al. The effect of CS Unplugged on middle-school students' view of CS. In *Proceedings of the 14th ACM Annual Conference on Innovation and Technology in Computer Science Education*, pages 99–103, New York, NY, USA, July 2009. ACM.

[9] J. Vesgo. Enrollments and degree production in US CS departments drops further in 2006–2007. *Computing Research News*, 20(2):4, 2008.

[10] S. Zweben. Computing degree and enrollment trends from the 2008-2009 CRA Taulbee survey. www.cra.org/govaffairs/blog/wp-content/uploads/2010/03/CRATaulbee-2010-ComputingDegreeandEnrollmentTrends.pdf, 2010.

A Scheme for Improving ICT Units with Critically Low Student Satisfaction

Angela Carbone
Monash University
Caulfield, Victoria, Australia
+61 3 9903 4481
angela.carbone@monash.edu.au

Jessica Wong
Monash University
Caulfield, Victoria, Australia
+61 3 9903 4472
jessica.wong@monash.edu.au

Jason Ceddia
Monash University
Caulfield, Victoria, Australia
+61 3 9903 4472
jason.ceddia@monash.edu.au

ABSTRACT

Unit evaluations across many Australian universities indicate that close to 10% of units in Information and Communication Technology (ICT) and Engineering disciplines are flagged as needing critical attention, and as such these faculties often struggle to meet university and national targets on educational performance. Further, ICT and Engineering repeatedly have the highest student dropout rates. This paper reports on the efficacy of activities undertaken to improve teaching quality and student satisfaction. Specifically, this paper outlines a Peer Assisted Teaching Scheme (PATS) as a process that was embedded in the Faculty of Information Technology (FIT) at Monash University to build peer assistance capacity in the faculty to improve student satisfaction of units in need of critical attention.

Categories and Subject Descriptors

K.3.2 [**Computers and Education**]: Computer and Information Science Education - *Computer science education, Curriculum, Information systems education.*

General Terms

Human Factors, Design

Keywords

ICT Education, education quality in ICT, teaching strategy, action research

1. INTRODUCTION

A central theme in the Australian government's agenda for higher education is the quality of teaching and learning in universities [7]. Its importance is seen through three government initiatives: (a) the establishment of the Australian Learning and Teaching Council (ALTC) which is aimed at improving the student learning experience by supporting quality teaching and practice, (b) its recommendation that funding for institutions will be determined, in part, by the measurement of graduate satisfaction with teaching, [8] and (c) the establishment of the Tertiary Education Quality and Standards Agency (TEQSA) to ensure quality is monitored

and standards are set and met. As a result of these government measures there has been an increase in teaching quality initiatives, including the development of formal and informal programs aimed at improving teacher effectiveness [12].

Across Australian universities, teaching and unit quality are measured through student evaluations. One evaluation instrument used in this context is the Australian Graduate Survey [4] that comprises two components: the Course Experience Questionnaire (CEQ) and the Graduate Destination Survey (GDS). The CEQ is an annual survey in which universities gather data about graduates' perceptions of their higher education experience. Graduates rate their course in terms of three broad scales: the Generic Skills Scale, the Good Teaching Scale, and the Overall Satisfaction Item. The GDS collects data about the activities of graduates after the completion of their degrees, regarding their career and/or further study choices.

Many institutions also have their own survey instruments. For example, Monash University has the Monash Experience Questionnaire (MEQ) [15], which is used to identify major areas of the student experience that require attention by the University. At the unit and teacher level, surveys are used to measure unit and teaching quality respectively via the Student Evaluation of Teaching and Unit (SETU) instrument.

The impetus for this paper lies in the national results for the CEQ which indicate that disciplines such as ICT and Engineering do not perform as well as other discipline areas on the good teaching scale. MEQ 2009 data showed that ICT and Engineering were ranked second lowest and lowest respectively on the good teaching scale [16]. Generally these disciplines are rated lowest nationally and repeatedly have the highest student dropout rates. Unit evaluations across many Australian universities indicate that close to 10% of units in these disciplines are flagged as needing critical attention [3].

This paper reports on the Peer Assisted Teaching Scheme (PATS), a process that was embedded in the Faculty of Information Technology at Monash University to build teaching peer assistance capacity to improve student satisfaction of units. PATS was piloted in units that were in need of critical attention. The efficacy of PATS to improve student satisfaction and teaching quality is reported.

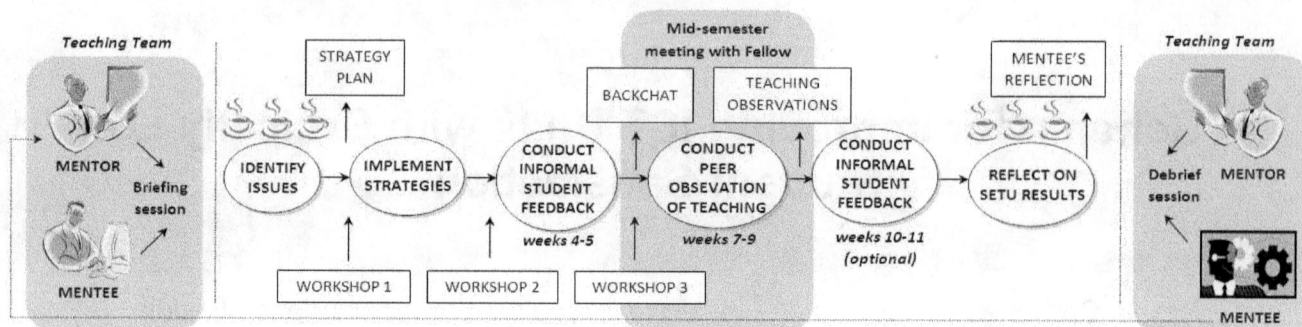

Figure 1. The Peer Assisted Teaching Scheme (PATS) process.

2. BACKGROUND

This section discusses how units in critical need of attention were identified and outlines the scheme piloted to improve them.

2.1 Student Evaluations of Teaching and Units

Evaluations of teaching and student experiences within units and courses are now standard practice in Australian universities. Monash University's unit survey contains the following five university-wide questions:

Item 1: The unit enabled me to achieve its learning objectives
Item 2: I found the unit to be intellectually stimulating
Item 3: The learning resources in this unit supported my studies
Item 4: The feedback I received in this unit was helpful
Item 5: Overall I was satisfied with the quality of this unit

Responses use a 5 point Likert scale ranging from Strongly Agree (5) to Strongly Disagree (1) with 3 representing "Neutral". Options for Not Applicable (6) and Don't Know (7) are also provided to respondents but are not counted in the means for questions. Any unit with a median value below 3.0 is flagged as needing critical attention. Any unit scoring above 4.7 indicates that the unit is outstanding.

Monash University has set a target that less than 5% of units should require critical attention. Figures from 2007 to 2009 unit evaluation surveys show that approximately 10% of units within the physical sciences (i.e. ICT, Engineering and Science) need critical attention [14]. This problem is a nationwide issue.

The scheme outlined in this paper aims to build peer assistance capacity in the faculty to improve student satisfaction of units. Peer assisted learning (PAL) involves participants facilitating the learning of other participants. [2] suggests that the role of the peer facilitator is more social than the traditional role of learner which is focused on self-learning. [17] defines peer assisted learning as the acquisition of knowledge and skill though active support among status equals or matched companions. [5] argues that PAL has the capacity to allow participants to articulate their understandings about a subject, to negotiate their new directions and to present their developing ideas and arguments. Furthermore, the social interactions and responsibilities associated with PAL programs have been shown to provide considerable potential for enhancing leadership skills among peer tutors [11].

PAL can be situated across the broad spectrum of the higher education system [13], [10], [6] and has been validated across a range of disciplines [1]. Given the positive outcomes reported on PAL for both instructors and participants, it seems reasonable that such a scheme and its positive results might be considered for teaching. Much of the research into improving teaching has been

via induction programs with mentors to ease the transition of beginning teachers into full-time teaching [9].

The version of the PAL program used in the pilot applies to academic teaching staff and uses currently recognized outstanding teachers or previous teaching awards winners as mentors.

2.2 The Peer Assisted Teaching Scheme

Figure 1 outlines the PATS process. The process begins with two academics from the same faculty being paired together – one taking on the role of the mentor and the other as the mentee. An initial briefing between the PATS facilitator and the participants takes place prior to the semester. During this briefing, roles and expectations of the mentor/mentee relationship are clarified.

During the semester, the partners meet to discuss and share ideas on how to improve the unit requiring critical attention. The meetings take place informally over coffee – six vouchers are provided to each participant. Participants are also encouraged to attend teaching workshops where they learn about strategies and methods to improve their teaching. As part of the scheme, participants are required to produce four deliverables: a strategy plan, a backchat session, a peer observation of teaching and a reflection of their end of semester results.

The *strategy plan* involves the partners identifying three to four key issues within the unit and devising strategies to address those issues. A *backchat session* occurs after the participants have collected informal feedback from their students. The feedback collection can be done via an online survey or handwritten during the class. At the following class, the lecturer (mentee) "feeds back" the information to the students and acknowledges how the key issues will be addressed. Both partners conduct a *peer observation of teaching* allowing them to reflect on each other's teaching styles. For the most effective outcome, both partners should take on the role of the observed and the observer. The *mentee's reflection* takes place at the end of the semester and involves reflecting on the unit evaluation results – both quantitative and qualitative, and students' results. These reflections are captured in a report. Finally, the PATS facilitator conducts a debriefing session where the participants discuss the process, their own experiences as participants and ways to improve it for future participants.

As a small incentive, if the partners are able to improve their unit evaluation result by 0.5 then both parties receive $500 towards the academic travel allowance.

3. IMPLEMENTATION

This section presents details of the project context and the data collected. The PATS pilot was conducted using only ICT units and ICT academics. The data measured changes in student unit evaluation results after PATS, and surveys to elicit participants' benefits and concerns.

3.1 Project Context

Eight ICT units (five units in 2009 and three in 2010) that were deemed to need critical attention were used. These units scored less than 3.0 on the university unit evaluation survey Item 5 "Overall I was satisfied with the quality of this unit". These units were taught into one of Monash's University four undergraduate ICT degrees and/or three postgraduate degrees of the Faculty of Information Technology (FIT). The academics were from three of Monash's six campuses.

PATS was piloted in 2009 with five units (i.e. five voluntary partnerships). In 2010 the project was supported by an Australian Learning and Teaching Fellowship grant and extended to all faculties in Monash's Physical Science cluster (this included ICT, Engineering and Science). Three ICT units (i.e. three partner pairs) were included in the scheme in 2010.

As comparisons were made from one year to the next, a requirement for participation for the mentee was that the mentee taught the unit in the following year.

The project was approved by the Monash University Standing Committee on Ethics in Research involving Humans (SCERH).

3.2 Data Collection

Three data collections used in this study were:

(a) Unit evaluation results in 2008, 2009 and 2010. These determine whether there were any changes in results after the PATS process was complete.

(b) Surveys of 2009 and 2010 participants. This explored the influence of PATS on staff's teaching practice. The participants were asked a variety of questions including the time spent with their partner, changes made to improve the unit, strategies and measures to improve the unit, and benefits and opportunities of the scheme.

(c) Focus group interviews of 2010 participants exploring the mentors' and mentees' perception of the scheme.

During the sessions, a number of topics were discussed including: the recruitment process into the scheme, the ease or difficulty in identifying issues with the units, approaches in gathering student feedback, conducting a peer observation of teaching, building a relationship with partners, positives and negatives of the scheme, and whether the PATS process would be suitable as a professional development component for new teaching staff.

Participants were also asked to write down their answers to the following eight questions:
1. Describe your impression of PATS.
2. How easy was it to identify issues with the unit using a scale of (easy) 1 to (hard) 5?
3. Did you gather informal student feedback during the semester?
4. Did you conduct a peer review of your partner's teaching?
5. Describe your relationship with your partner.
6. Identify something positive about the scheme.
7. Identify a weakness of the scheme.
8. Do you think this scheme would be suitable as part of the Graduate Certificate in Higher Education (GCHE)?

The focus group sessions were recorded and transcribed. The transcripts were sent to participants (after anonymising) to ensure this was an accurate reflection of the session.

The 2010 participants were also invited to draft a case study of their experience in PATS. These will be included in the production of a PATS guide, used as an information source for faculties wishing to embed the process in their faculty or institution.

4. RESULTS

The findings are presented in two general areas:
i) Changes to percentage of units needing critical attention over a three year period and the areas in units that students perceived as needing attention (sections 4.1 and 4.2)
ii) Participants perceptions of PATS (sections 4.3, 4.4, 4.5)

4.1 Percentage of Units Needing Critical Attention

Monash University has ten faculties. Past results show the Faculty of Information Technology ranked in the bottom half when compared to other university faculties (highest ranking 1, lowest 10). Table 1 shows results from semester 1 and Table 2 shows results from semester 2 over a three year period. It is important to note that comparisons can only be made for the same semester each year as units are typically only offered in one semester.

Table 1. Faculty of Information Technology (FIT)– Semester 1 % of units needing critical attention.

Year	%	Rank	FIT	University
2008	9%	9/10	Mean 3.61*	Mean 3.79*
2009	10%	6/10	Median 3.91	Median 3.94
2010	8%	7/10	Median 3.93	Median 3.96

Note * - in 2008 only mean values were reported, after that time median values were reported as the mean was deemed not an appropriate measure of central tendency.

Table 1 shows that there has been an improvement in the ranking of FIT from 9/10 in 2008 to 6/10 in 2009 as well as an improvement in median value unit satisfaction rating from 3.61 to 3.91. While the ranking decreased in 2010 to 7/10, the median satisfaction rating increased to 3.93.

Table 2. Faculty of Information Technology (FIT)– Semester 2 % of units needing critical attention.

Year	%	Rank	FIT	University
2008	10%	8/10	Mean 3.68*	Mean 3.78*
2009	8%	8/10	Median 3.90	Median 3.94
2010	NA	6/10	Median 3.95	Median 3.99

Table 2 shows similar trends to Table 1 for second semester units. In the first iteration of the scheme (in 2009) there were five partnerships participating. Two partners were involved in improving student satisfaction in two undergraduate units, and three partners focused on postgraduate units. In 2010, there were three partnerships focusing on unit improvement in undergraduate units.

4.2 Areas Students Perceived as Needing Attention

Comments on students' surveys showed areas that needed improvement. However, not all areas applied to every unit. PATS participants typically addressed one of those areas. From the participant surveys, two pairs addressed the lecture organization either through improving the content or linking the lecture to the tutorial material and three pairs addressed the clarity of assessment items. Common areas needing improvements were:

Lectures

The issues students raised in their qualitative comments concerned the content of the lectures, the structure, the use of slides, linking the lectures to the tutorials and the use of time during the lectures.

Content – students found there was too much content for each lecture. This created an information overload and students were unable to learn the content thoroughly for assessments.

Structure – the structure of the lecture was disorganized and disjointed therefore students found it difficult to follow the information being presented.

Slides – students raised issues with the presentation and content of the slides. They expressed concerns over the clarity of the information being unclear and not in enough detail.

Links to practical material – there seemed to be a significant content gap between the lectures and tutorials.

Use of time – students found the lectures were falling behind as time was not being used efficiently meaning important aspects were skimmed over and not properly covered before tests.

The Lecturers

Students were very critical about the way lecturers presented, the level of interaction with the class, students' consultations and the feedback provided on assessments.

Presentation – there were major concerns with not being able to understand what the lecturer was talking about due to language barriers. Also students commented on the lecturers simply "regurgitating" the content on the slides instead of elaborating and explaining the information. Due to a lack of interaction between the lecturer and the students during the class, student failed to feel motivated and excited about learning.

Consultation – lecturers did not have enough time to sufficiently consult with students.

Feedback – students did not find the feedback provided sufficient, in terms of detail.

Assessment

Students found the outline of assessments to be unclear.

Assignment specification – there was a lack of specification in regards to the assignments and students found this difficult in knowing the objectives and criteria of the assignment. Many students were stuck as what to do or where to start as a result. There was no clear outline at the beginning of the semester of the assessment tasks and some students struggled with being tested on something they had to learn completely on their own.

Resources

The resources, particularly the textbooks provided for students were inadequate and off-campus students had difficulty accessing the necessary resources.

Textbooks – students found the prescribed textbooks to be poorly written and difficult to understand. They were heavily worded but without enough useful or relevant information.

Notes – students relied heavily on notes provided by lecturers and found that the information given was not substantial in assisting in their learning.

Off-campus students – in the lectures, the lecturers discussed the topics with the use of diagrams on a whiteboard which cannot be seen by off-campus students in the online audio lectures. These students also stated that there is a vital need for an online discussion forum to aid in their learning due to lack of face-to-face learning.

4.3 Changes in Unit Performance

Table 3 shows the 2008 and 2009 unit evaluation results (overall unit satisfaction Item 5) for participants in the 2009 PATS. All units improved their ratings by at least 0.5 (note: unit codes have been anonymised).

Table 3. Changes in overall unit satisfaction Item 5

Unit	Semester	Median	#Enr	#Rsps
FIT1	S2, 2008	2.86	59	25
	S1, 2009	4.33	20	16
FIT2	S1, 2008	2.11	38	20
	S1, 2009	3.5	30	12
FIT3	S1, 2008	2.95	57	23
	S1, 2009	3.56	49	25
FIT4	S2, 2008	2.5	24	7
	S2, 2009	3.67	30	5
FIT5*	S1, 2009	4.36	25	16

* FIT5 was a new unit taught in 2009; while the lecturer had not taught the unit before he wanted to be involved in PATS because his previous unit was flagged as needing critical attention (Median: 2.95, Mean: 2.83 (112 students enrolled, 29 responses).

Three of the units (FIT1, FIT5, FIT4) moved out of the *critical attention* zone (median < 3.0) into *meeting aspirations* (median above 3.6) whilst the other two units (FIT2, FIT3) moved into the *needs improvement* zone (median greater than 3.0 but less than 3.6).

Table 4 shows the 2009 and 2010 unit evaluation results (overall unit satisfaction Item 5).

Table 4. Changes in overall unit satisfaction Item 5

Unit	Semester	Median	#Enr	#Rsps
FIT6	S1, 2009	3	48	8
	S1, 2010	2.92	40	17
FIT7	S1, 2009	3	167	64
	S1, 2010	3.28	131	46
FIT8	S1, 2009	2.5	70	16
	S1, 2010	4.3	40	10

One of the units (FIT8) moved out of the *critical attention* zone (median < 3.0) into *meeting aspirations* (median above 3.6), another unit (FIT7) moved into the *needs improvement* zone (median greater than 3.0 but less than 3.6) whilst the third unit (FIT6) remained in the *critical attention* zone (median < 3.0); this was thought to be because the partnership focused on one of several known issues with the unit.

4.4 Positive Benefits of PATS Partnership

Participants provided plenty of positive feedback about being in a PATS partnership. The most beneficial aspect was having the ability to discuss and share ideas in a non-threatening, friendly and relaxed environment. Other positive comments include:

- The scheme being beneficial to students as it aims to increase the quality of the unit for them.
- Providing academics with an opportunity to reflect on their own teaching that may not occur outside of the scheme.
- Providing an opportunity to engage with another colleague that may be from a different area of study/building, etc.
- Expanding professional network.

- Allowing for collaborative, mutual problem solving.

The mentors commented on:

- *'Gaining personal satisfaction in helping someone who really wants to improve, and makes the effort to do so.'*

The mentees mentioned the following positive benefits:

- *'Scheme is helpful in having someone to talk to, ask questions and seek advice from'.*
- *'Great having a mentor for support'.*
- *'Provides a chance to share ideas and receive feedback'.*

4.5 Concerns Raised by PATS Participants

The main concerns raised about PATS were in regards to being stigmatized as a *poor* or *bad* teacher. The majority of the mentees found a sense of stigma associated with being a participant in the scheme. They felt that if other academics found out about their participation, they would be perceived as "bad" teachers. Other concerns included:

- *'Takes up a lot of time - about 5 days of extra work'.*
- *'It relies on the goodwill of participants to keep the scheme going, otherwise there is no point in running it'.*
- *'There needs to be better communication in terms of choosing dates and times for meetings, etc'.*
- *'Tying the success of the scheme to the UE results and only giving money if there is at least a 0.5 improvement – there are other factors that are overlooked as contributors to success'.*

5. DISCUSSION AND CONCLUSION

PATS was proposed and piloted to address the increasing need by universities to reduce the unacceptably high number of units having critically low student satisfaction ratings. The scheme aims to assist academics in improving their unit by using peer support from those peers recognised as excellent. The academics work in partnership focusing on the students' qualitative comments to make improvements.

PATS raises the profile of learning and teaching in faculties and creates a level of prestige associated with the pursuit of improving student satisfaction of units. A critical success factor of PATS is the collegial partnership component to identify educational issues within units and facilitate approaches to address these issues. These approaches are facilitated via the sharing of experiences, innovation and good practice in learning and teaching.

It is expected that after the first year, PATS will continue as part of the normal practice for improving teaching and unit curricula across the university. The ultimate goal of PATS is to stimulate strategic change in higher education faculties which have a high percentage of units needing critical attention. Faculties have an opportunity to show leadership in enhancing teaching in their disciplines and provide academics with collegial support to explore new learning possibilities.

After receiving positive feedback from the PATS participants and achieving improvements to all five units in the 2009 pilot, the scheme was supported and funded by an ALTC Teaching Fellowship grant for university-wide implementation. The first phase of implementation covered the Physical Sciences cluster - a quarter of Monash's faculties, and the second phase (commenced in semester 1, 2011) will introduce PATS into the remaining

clusters ensuring coverage university-wide. This will also provide more data to demonstrate the effectiveness of the program.

6. ACKNOWLEDGMENTS

Our thanks to Australian Learning and Teaching Council Teaching Fellowship (ALTC) for funding to develop a process to build peer assistance capacity across all faculties of Monash University to improve student satisfaction of units.

7. REFERENCES

[1] Arendale, D. R. (2004). *Pathways of persistence: A review of postsecondary peer cooperative learning programs.* Center for Research on Developmental Education and Urban Literacy, General College, University of Minnesota, Minneapolis, MN.

[2] Ashwin, P. (2003). 'Peer facilitation and how it contributes to the development', *Research in Post-Compulsory Education*, 8, 1, 5-18.

[3] Australian Graduate Survey - Course Experience Questionnaire (CEQ) *National CEQ data - Survey Items Results: 2005-2009.* http://www.opq.monash.edu.au/us/pivot-table/, (Jan - 2011).

[4] Australian Graduate Survey. http://www.graduatecareers.com.au/ResearchandStatistics/Surveys/AustralianGraduateSurvey/index.htm, (Jan - 2011).

[5] Boud, D. (2001). *Introduction: making the move to peer learning.* Kogan Page, London.

[6] Cheng, D. and Walters, M. (2009). Peer-assisted learning in mathematics: an observational study of student success, *Australasian Journal of Peer Learning*, 2, 23-39.

[7] Commonwealth of Australia (2003). *Our universities: backing Australia's future.* Australian Government, City.

[8] DEEWR *Improving Quality in Australia's Higher Education - The last three decades.* http://www.deewr.gov.au/highereducation/programs/quality/qualityassurance/pages/improvingaustraliashe.aspx, (Jan - 2011).

[9] Gratch, A. (1998). Beginning Teacher and Mentor Relationships, *Journal of Teacher Education*, 49.

[10] Hodgson, Y. M. (2009). Students prefer lectures to peer teaching. In *Proceedings of the HERDSA* (Darwin, Australia).

[11] Jacobs, G., Hurley, M. and Unite, C. (2008). How learning creates a foundation for S1 leader training, *Australasian Journal of Peer Learning*, 1, 6-12.

[12] Ling, P. (2009). *Development of Academics and Higher Education Futures.* Australian Learning and Teaching Council, Sydney.

[13] Loke, A. J. T. and Chow, F. L. W. (2007). Learning partnership - the experience of peer tutoring amongst nursing students: A qualitative study, *International Journal of Nursing Studies*, 44, 237-244.

[14] Monash Unit Evaluation Data. https://emuapps.monash.edu.au/unitevaluations/wr/uewr_rp1_public_yearseme.jsp, (Jan - 2011).

[15] Monash University *Monash Experience Questionnaire.* http://www.opq.monash.edu.au/mqu/evaluations/meq/meq09/meq09_uni_college_questionnaire.pdf, (Jan - 2011).

[16] Monash University *Quantative results for MEQ 2009.* http://www.opq.monash.edu.au/mqu/evaluations/meq/meq09/meq-quantitative.html, (Jan - 2011).

[17] Topping, K. J. (2001). *Peer assisted learning: A practical guide for teachers* Brookline Books, Cambridge, MA.

Combining Multiple Pedagogies to Boost Learning and Enthusiasm *

Lori Pollock and Terry Harvey
Computer and Information Sciences
University of Delaware
Newark, DE 19360
{pollock, harvey}@cis.udel.edu

ABSTRACT

This paper describes the pedagogy we applied in a 5-week class, in which students taught themselves (and each other) a new language, new OS, GUI programming, and simple networking for collaborative games. They learned communication, negotiation, collaboration, presentation and teamwork skills; and project design and iterative development. We had four goals: increased learning, enthusiasm about CS, confidence in technical ability and communication skills. To achieve these goals, we decided to rely solely on the integration of teaching techniques that we believed would be highly effective: collaborative teams, student presentations, student critique of work, open-ended projects of student design, iterative process, journal reflection, and motivation through helping others. The students had to learn about each technique through discussion, modeling, and moderated practice. We focused on this process learning and trusted that the technical material would come from solving the (unspecified) assignments. This focus left no time for traditional teaching activities. We present quantitative and qualitative results from a student survey and the students' reflective journals. Students reported learning at a greater rate than in other CS courses while maintaining (and in some cases acquiring) a high level of enthusiasm and confidence.

Categories and Subject Descriptors

K.3.2 [**Computing Milieux**]: Computers and Education-Computer science education

General Terms

Human Factors

Keywords

collaborative learning, studio-based classroom, service learning, reflective journaling, problem-based learning

*This material is based on work supported by the National Science Foundation grant CNS-0940501.

1. INTRODUCTION

In Fall 2009, the authors decided to run an independent study together. We wanted 3 to 5 students to help us explore the development of software applications for the XO laptop [13], and for the Myro [2] robot. We believed that both topics had potential as classroom projects, and wanted to explore them with a small set of students before committing to a larger class. The only common ground was that both the XO laptop and Myro robot could be programmed using Python.

We were overwhelmed with 26 applications. Instead of selecting only 3-4 students, we viewed the challenge as an opportunity to experiment with integrating pedagogies that supported students managing and teaching each other. We had enough XOs and Myro robots for three teams of four students to have one of each per team.

The key challenge was how to design and execute a learning experience given these challenges: a large set of new concepts including programming language, hardware and operating system platform, and an event-based programming paradigm that neither instructors nor students knew at all; a 5-week session; 12 students, with a range of student backgrounds from sophomore (with two prior semesters of CS) through graduating seniors; and maintaining an independent study-like, exploratory learning environment.

Our primary goals were to increase overall learning, enthusiasm, confidence in technical abilities, and communication skills. Our secondary goal was that students develop an *awareness* of their learning and their ability to teach themselves and each other. To achieve these goals, we did not directly teach computer science, but instead taught students to work in teams, critique each others' work, design their own programming projects of increasing complexity, use iterative development, and to reflect on their learning in a personal journal.

The main contributions of this paper are:

- a description of how we integrated a set of pedagogies known individually to engage computer science students in learning, to create an independent study-like experience for a 12-student class, and

- evidence both quantitatively and qualitatively of the potential impacts of such a course design on student learning, attitudes, and perceptions.

2. INSTRUCTOR AS GUIDE

It was difficult for us to give up the teaching methods we had developed for so long: lectures, textbooks, and prescribed assignments. We were both excited by the possibilities of new methods, and wanted to try them in a short winter session where we would have time to collaborate, innovate, and support each other through the experiment.

We charged student teams with deciding how to learn the assigned concepts and how they taught it to each other. In this environment, the role of the instructor may not be immediately obvious. Establishing a safe and exciting learning environment was paramount. We led exercises to elicit and consolidate student knowledge on: what makes good teams work; tools and techniques to facilitate teamwork; what makes a good presentation; and how to offer kudos and critique on another team's presentation. We interleaved these exercises with other course work.

During such exercises, we tried to model what we wanted - enthusiasm, creativity, courtesy, and focus. In early classes, we would moderate and critique the student-driven process. For example, we might lighten a student critique by restating it and adding a compliment, or draw attention to some aspect of a presentation (good or bad) that we thought had been overlooked. In later classes, we frequently felt (wonderfully) superfluous as the students drove the classroom, with occasional reminders from us to move on to another topic.

2.1 Reflecting and Iterating

This course was our (and our department's) first use of reflective journaling with feedback. Reflection on learning is a pedagogical technique used to promote the higher order cognitive skills of analysis, synthesis, and evaluation, i.e., critical thinking [14]. We led discussion on what constitutes a good journal entry, and these reflective entries helped us monitor (and eventually evaluate) student experience, learning, and the quality of the environment. Giving brief feedback to entries provided another tool to guide students in their team relations and technical learning. Many students felt overwhelmed early on by the burden of discovering knowledge for themselves; while teams mitigated this burden, it was clearly a novel experience for many. Journal feedback gave us a way to acknowledge and support stressed individuals without having them feel exposed in the classroom setting.

This was the first course that these students had taken where they were given the opportunity to receive critiques of their ideas and projects as they were being developed and then revise their project based on the feedback. In this way, they watched their product take on new forms based on feedback of others and were then given the opportunity to show off their latest and greatest creation. They often commented on this iterative process and the feedback they received in their reflective journals.

2.2 Replacing Lectures and Textbooks

Our goal was for students to gain the desired knowledge and skills through discovery and collaboration. Class time was utilized for a number of active learning activities to foster discovery.

In a typical class, we began with progress reports from the teams on assignments. Teams would share successes and challenges, with other teams (and sometimes the instructors) offering kudos, suggestions and alternatives. Then a team would make a formal presentation of their learning from a previous assignment, and the class would 1) discuss the presentation, and 2) discuss the concepts. We found it was crucial to give discussion time to the presentation to establish high standards. Without such standards, other students could not be expected to learn from the presentation. (That said, since peer-teaching is highly effective [8], presentations below the standards of a professional teacher may produce learning when delivered by a peer.) Towards the end of class, a new assignment would be created, either through students deciding what knowledge they needed next (in the process of creating an activity for the XO) or the instructors providing a path.

While we had a general list of Python, the XO, and robot concepts that we wanted the students to learn, we did not plan in advance the ordering of topics or the specific assignments. The instructors met after every class to decide on scope and overall direction of the next stage. Students developed the actual assignment details. For example, in the first week, we moderated brainstorming of every feature of Python they would need to learn to program a networked, GUI game; then teams chose which features they would learn and present to the class and arranged the schedule of presentations. Sometimes all teams had the same assignment, while other times each had a separate topic.

This classroom environment integrated studio-based learning, problem-based learning, and reflective learning. It also developed communication skills, and team skills, and independent critical thinking. Preparing and giving presentations of concepts and ideas also reinforced the presenter's understanding of the concepts.

2.3 Student Choice and Helping Others

Research shows that students are engaged through choosing their own projects of interest to them [9]. We took this to the extreme, providing specifications in terms of each new concept they needed to explore. Students were then charged with demonstrating their knowledge and skills with respect to that concept. We left the means for their exploration open-ended. Each team decided how they wanted to gain that skill or knowledge, what program to write to demonstrate it, and how they would present it to the class.

Students were encouraged to find information on the Internet, in books, and especially from other teams. One assignment that turned out to be quite difficult was writing a game that used the XO's built-in mesh networking hardware. Online instructions worked only for simple examples. Two teams working at the same time realized the problem was far beyond what they had solved before, decided to join forces, and reconvened in one room until they started to make progress. All students agreed later that without team support, the frustration would have been overwhelming.

Since the available resources for students did not directly address many of their questions, a key task we set for students was to create a shared, living wiki document that would help future students learning how to program the XO laptops and robots. Many conversations surrounded thinking about how they could help future students by documenting some nugget of knowledge that they had learned through time-consuming exploration and experimentation.

Similarly, we directed students to think about how their knowledge could be used to help teach youth how to program a robot or how they could create a learning game for young children. They were concerned about how their final project, a learning game of their design, would be used

Table 1: Student evaluation of each course component in achieving course goals. Students used a four-point rating scale. The first number shown is the percentage of students who chose the highest rating; the second number is the percentage of students who chose either of the two positive ratings. For example, 89% of students said Collaborative Teamwork was *much more* effective at causing learning than previous course experiences; 100% of students said Collaborative Teamwork was either *much more* or *somewhat more* effective at causing learning.

Course Component	Course Goals							
	Learning		Enthusiasm		Technical Abilities		Communication Skills	
	highest	positive	highest	positive	highest	positive	highest	positive
Collaborative teamwork	89	100	100	100	44	88	67	100
Reflective journaling	22	78	11	55	11	67	44	100
Documentation	56	100	11	89	33	89	44	88
Continuous revision	89	100	100	100	78	100	44	77
Writing learning games	67	100	78	100	67	100	33	89
Open-ended project	89	100	100	100	78	100	44	88
Weekly presentations	78	100	33	100	56	100	67	100
Working with robots	56	100	56	100	33	100	44	77
Using Internet resources	56	100	56	100	44	100	33	66

by the young students and their teachers. This motivated many interesting discussions on how learning happens, giving these students their first taste of service learning[1].

Thus, students actively assisted others in four distinct ways: helping with tasks across teams; helping other teams through discussion and critique; helping peers taking the course in the future; and helping the intended client of their software (Service Learning). Students really enjoy making a contribution [3]. Each of these kinds of help was cited by students as a motivating factor and, we believe, contributed greatly to the success of the course.

3. EVALUATION

We evaluated the effectiveness of the course components through student post surveys and analysis of individual student journals.

3.1 Methodology

An assessment professional from University of Delaware Office of Education Assessment developed and implemented a student post survey with the goal of collecting the students' opinions of the impact of each novel course component on four course goals: increasing student learning, enthusiasm, confidence in technical abilities, and confidence in communication skills. Students rated the effectiveness of each component relative to their previous course experiences, using a four point scale (no middle) for each goal.

Three additional open-ended questions were directed towards gathering student opinion of the importance of a final, formal presentation to an audience of faculty, the effect of frustration on learning, and what the students would or would not change about the course.

The education assessment professional also developed a rubric for evaluating journal entries. The rubric measured the degree of reflective learning content and emotional content. For each student, the rubric was applied to 2-3 early

entries (called pre-data) and 2-3 late entries (called post-data), based on the volume of material.

Threats to Validity: The evaluation results are based on 9 respondents to the survey. The class had twelve students whom we hand-picked from 26 based on their application letters and their transcripts. Thus, the results here may not translate to a larger course, or to a course which admits all students[2].

3.2 Post-Survey Results

Table 1 shows data in response to the question "Compared to your previous experiences, how effective were the following components of the class in making you more X where X is indicated by the column title — Learning: helping you learn, Enthusiasm: enthusiasm about your program/field, Technical Abilities: confidence in your own technical abilities, and Communication Skills: confidence in your communication skills. The entries are the percent of student respondents who labeled each as *much more* and *somewhat more* effective than previous CS courses, respectively, for each course component.

Most importantly, all student respondents rated all 12 of the 13 pedagogical components as *much more* to *somewhat more* effective in helping them learn compared to previous experiences. The only exception was reflective journaling which received *much more* to *somewhat more* effective in 88% responses. Of particular note is that collaborative teamwork, opportunity for continuous revision, and open-ended project were ranked *much more* effective at helping students learn by 89% of respondents. These same three components had 100% respondents stating they were *much more* effective than prior experiences in making them more enthused about the program/field. All respondents ranked all components *much more* to *somewhat more* effective than

---

[1]The course has since morphed into a full service learning course.

[2]While these results are representative of only this selected class, we have since successfully used similar methods to teach an open version of the class.

previous experiences at increasing enthusiasm, except reflective journaling and documenting process during the project.

All students perceived all components except collaborative teamwork, reflective journaling, and documenting the process as increasing their confidence in their own technical abilities *very much* to *somewhat*. These three components were rated as increasing confidence *very little*. The components ranked as increasing confidence *very much* by the highest percent of students were opportunity for continuous revision and open-ended project. There were more mixed results for the components' effects on increasing confidence in communication skills. However, collaborative teamwork and weekly presentations had the most positive responses of *very much* impact by 67% of respondents. It is also noteworthy that 78% respondents ranked weekly presentations as *much more* effective at helping them learn compared to previous experiences.

Across course goals, the students placed the highest value on being able to continuously revise a project, having a project with an open-ended design, and working in teams. We had expected that students would love to design and extend their own projects, but were surprised at the value they placed on being able to iteratively improve the design and code as they learned new skills. Working in teams was slightly less highly-rated for generating enthusiasm, but more highly-rated for increasing communication skills.

Student ambivalence about weekly presentations is apparent, as most students rated it highly for learning, but few rated it highly for producing enthusiasm. It is interesting that students were able to separate their lack of enthusiasm from their judgement about the learning value.

Perhaps not surprisingly, reflective journaling and writing documentation were not highly valued by the students. However, we feel these were invaluable to the teachers as we monitored student and team progress. Furthermore, we suspect that writing about experiences helped students clarify their thinking; more than once we heard a student express an idea, opinion, or emotion in class that had first appeared in a journal. Also, while we responded to the journals, we are not trained in doing so, and better responses might increase student opinions of the journal process.

The open-ended questions in the post survey confirmed that students thought presentation was important. Overall, students enjoyed the final formal presentation to CS faculty, providing them an opportunity to summarize their experience and see how far they had come:

> It forced us to reflect on everything we learned and really analyze what worked and what didn't.

> It not only is a final goal to work towards but it actually makes you feel like you have done alot by filling up this presentation with your work.

> It ties up everything we did, as well as reflecting on what we spent our time on.

The second question was: "Working with unfamiliar tools like the Myro and OLPC can be frustrating. How do you think the frustration you met in this course affected your learning?" Many answers indicated that teams helped alleviate frustration:

> I think that when we got frustrated, it was nice to have other team members (and other teams)

who were there willing to help. And even if you were beyond your limit, and felt you had nothing left to give, knowing that your team needed you meant to just give it one more shot.

and that frustration could actually be valuable:

> The frustration is actually what helped us learn more. We had to go research and play around, trying different things to fix the problem instead of just breezing right through it. I feel I'm more likely to remember something I struggled on than something I just copied or read somewhere.

The final pair of open-ended questions asked what part of the course students would change/not change. No consistent answers appeared in what students would like changed, but two course components were consistently cited as "keepers": teams and the open-ended project design.

3.3   Results from Journal Analysis

The first rubric counted occurrences of student reflection about the learning process and/or connection between activities and learning versus merely listing activities and challenges without reflecting about the learning process. The post data shows 82% of the student journals exhibited evidence of reflection about the learning process beyond listing activities and challenges. While 36% of the early journal entries contained only listings of activities; this reduced to only 18% at the end of the semester.

The second rubric focused on how excited and curious about the project and/or confident the student sounds in his/her knowledge and abilities, based on their journal entries. The post data indicates that 91% of the student journals revealed the student was excited or somewhat excited and curious about the project and/or confident in his/her knowledge and abilities. The remaining 9% of students did not share challenges and successes in their journals. 27% of student journals at the start of the semester showed fear of the challenges in the project and/or appeared not confident in his/her knowledge and abilities. No student journals showed these fears in the later journal entries.

Some notable excerpts from the journal entries that show the student perspective about the pedagogical approach and their learning:

> Over the course of 5 weeks I was able to learn far more than I have before in a semester long course. I really enjoyed learning a language and information on my own. It was cool to try and look at online documentation and then internalize that knowledge to make something of my own.

> This course is unlike any other course I've taken, it is very different to have the professors treat the students as equals and expect to learn from the students. At the same time it is a very mature learning environment, I feel like a job in Computer Science would be a lot like this course in the sense that both superiors and employees would work together to tackle the problem presented.

> I feel that this course, as is, is a great aspect of my learning experience in regards to computer

science - especially software engineering. A professor can lecture all night and day over how you should code and why, but until you find yourself going back and trying to reapply your code to a new system, or trying to read someone else's code, you don't fully grasp the importance of software manageability.

4. RELATED WORK

Our course used techniques that have been demonstrated separately to provide successful learning outcomes in college courses. These include aspects of Problem-Based Learning [4], critiquing in Studio-Based Learning [7], and Active Learning [12]. The iterative approach to software engineering courses has been used by a variety of universities. Anewalt and Polack-Wahl [1] combined it with dynamic groups, showing that iterative development allows students to learn from previous iterations and incorporate feedback into the next iteration, while rotating the groups increased documentation quality and increased the project completion rate from 30% to 80% in a semester. Some of our course components, particularly iterative revision and team work, are inherent in extreme programming. In a study of MS students in a course project using the extreme programming model, Loftus and Ratcliffe [11] concluded that students' accuracy in estimating and planning were improved and students believed they learned new technologies faster.

A study of reflective journals in a computer science course by George [6] found that students who liked the reflective journal reported benefits to their learning, including understanding of concepts, identifying what they don't understand, problem solving in practical programming exercises and awareness of approach and attitude to learning. Perschbach [14] evaluation of student reflective journal blogging by community college computer science students showed that blogging effectively recorded critical thinking and provided the learner with a personal voice that created a sense of ownership of ideas, active participation and empowerment in personal learning, and a contribution to the collaborative learning effort.

Our course provides students opportunities to help others in several ways (section 2.3). The EPICS project at Purdue University is a well established example demonstrating the benefits of service learning in a computer science and software engineering education [10]. Others have more recently developed different models of service learning in CS courses [15, 5].

5. CONCLUSIONS

In the course of a 5-week class, our students taught themselves (and each other) a new language, new OS, GUI programming, and simple networking for collaborative games. They also learned communication, negotiation, collaboration, presentation and teamwork skills; and project design and iterative development. Students reported learning at a greater rate than in other CS courses while maintaining (and in some cases acquiring) a high level of enthusiasm and confidence in their abilities. They were motivated to achieve through their own desire to help each other, future students, and the children who would use their games. The instructors practiced a variety of techniques which they have since used in their regular semester courses.

6. ACKNOWLEDGMENTS

We thank Gordana Copic at University of Delaware Office of Educational Assessment for her efforts on evaluation.

7. REFERENCES

[1] K. Anewalt and J. A. Polack-Wahl. Teaching an Iterative Approach with Rotating Groups in an Undergraduate Software Engineering Course. *J. Comput. Small Coll.*, 25:144–151, June 2010.

[2] D. Blank. Robots Make Computer Science Personal. In *Communications of the ACM*, volume 49, pages 25–27, December 2006.

[3] D. Cone and S. Harris. Service-Learning Practice: Developing a Theoretical Framework. *Michigan Journal of Community Service Learning*, 3, 1996.

[4] B. J. Duch, S. E. Groh, and D. E. Allen, editors. *The Power of Problem-based Learning: A Practical 'How To' for teaching Undergraduate Courses in Any Discipline.* Stylus Publications, 2001.

[5] M. A. L. Egan and M. Johnson. Service Learning in Introductory Computer Science. In *Fifteenth Annual Conf on Innovation and Technology in Computer Science Dducation*, ITiCSE '10, pages 8–12, 2010.

[6] S. E. George. Learning and the Reflective Journal in Computer Science. In *Twenty-fifth Australasian Conference on Computer Science - Volume 4*, 2002.

[7] D. Hendrix, L. Myneni, H. Narayanan, and M. Ross. Implementing Studio-based Learning in CS2. In *SIGCSE '10: 41st ACM Technical Symposium on Computer Science Education*, pages 505–509, 2010.

[8] G. D. Kuh, J. Kinzie, J. A. Buckley, B. K. Bridges, and J. C. Hayek. What matters to student success: A review of the literature. Technical report, National Postsecondary Education Cooperative, July 2006.

[9] G. Lewandowski, E. Johnson, and M. Goldweber. Fostering a creative interest in computer science. In *Proceedings of the 36th SIGCSE technical symposium on Computer science education*, SIGCSE '05, 2005.

[10] P. K. Linos, S. Herman, and J. Lally. A Service-learning Program for Computer Science and Software Engineering. In *8th Annual Conference on Innovation and Technology in Computer Science Education*, ITiCSE '03, 2003.

[11] C. Loftus and M. Ratcliffe. Extreme Programming Promotes Extreme Learning? In *SIGCSE Conf on Innovation and Technology in Computer Science Education*, ITiCSE '05, 2005.

[12] S. Ludi, S. Natarajan, and T. Reichlmayr. An Introductory Software Engineering Course that Facilitates Active Learning. In *36th SIGCSE Technical Symp on Computer Science Education*, 2005.

[13] olpc Foundation. One laptop per child. http://one.laptop.org/.

[14] J. W. Perschbach. *Blogging: An Inquiry into the Efficacy of a Web-based Technology for Student Reflection in Community College Computer Science Programs.* PhD thesis, Nova Southeastern Univ, 2006.

[15] J. Tan and J. Phillips. Incorporating Service Learning into Computer Science Courses. *J. Comput. Small Coll.*, 20:57–62, April 2005.

A Cooperative Learning-based Strategy for Teaching Relational Algebra

Alexandra Martinez
alexandra.martinez@ecci.ucr.ac.cr

Arturo Camacho
arturo.camacho@ecci.ucr.ac.cr

Escuela de Ciencias de la Computación e Informática
Universidad de Costa Rica
San José, Costa Rica

ABSTRACT

This paper presents the design, implementation, and assessment of a cooperative learning-based teaching strategy to introduce relational algebra in an undergraduate database course. It has been implemented in four course sections across two semesters. The strategy was assessed from both students and teachers perspective. Assessment results show that between 78% and 92% of the students considered that the group work enriched their learning, providing support for the use of cooperative learning. Also, the results from a homework and an exam on the subject show an improvement on the students' learning of relational algebra.

Categories and Subject Descriptors

H.2.1 [**Database Management**]: Logical Design—*data models*; H.2.3 [**Database Management**]: Languages—*query languages*; K.3.2 [**Computers and Education**]: Computer and Information Science Education—*computer science education*

General Terms

Experimentation, Human Factors, Languages

Keywords

Database, active learning, cooperative learning, relational algebra, experience report

1. INTRODUCTION

The course Databases I is a 4-credit-hour mandatory course in the 3rd year of the Bachelor of Science's in the Department of Computer and Information Science at the Universidad de Costa Rica. This course provides students with the necessary concepts to design, implement, and manipulate relational databases. It also offers an introduction to object-relational databases.

The teaching methodology previously used in this course consisted on lecturing, with few opportunities for interaction among students (with the exception of laboratory practice sessions). The problem with such methodology was that students became bored in class and were eventually demotivated. This led us to question and rethink our approach to teaching, with one of the outcomes being the experiment hereby described. We designed, implemented and assessed a new teaching strategy based on cooperative learning (CL) for one of the course topics: relational algebra. The strategy divides the class in three *moments*, making use of formal and informal groups and the plenary group to foster student collaboration and learning.

We switched to CL as the basis of our teaching strategy for three main reasons: it was innovative within our course; it could potentially be applied to many other learning settings in the course; and there existed ample evidence on its effectiveness and benefits [1, 2, 3, 5, 6, 7, 8, 9, 10, 11], including some experiences in Engineering and Computer Science in particular.

2. THEORETICAL FRAMEWORK

The essence of CL, which lies in the formation of small groups for learning purposes, has a long history dating from the times of Socrates and Plato, and evolving with public-speaking masters such as Confucius, Buddha, and Jesus, who established guidelines for true teaching arising from human encounters [5]. Nowadays, in the context of school and university teaching, cooperative learning refers to the educational use of small groups that allow students to work together to improve their own learning and that of their peers [9]. Cooperative learning contrasts with traditional methodologies based on individualism and competition among students.

According to [5], teaching in small cooperative groups has three main goals: the development of communication strategies, the development of intellectual and professional competencies, and the personal growth of students. The teacher role is that of a mentor, guiding and facilitating learning. Johnson et al. [9] recommend that teachers structure five essential components in all educational activity: (*1*) positive interdependence, (*2*) promoter interaction, (*3*) individual responsibility, (*4*) interpersonal skills, and (*5*) group processing. Domingo [2] distinguishes two types of cooperative work groups that can be used in the classroom: informal and formal. Informal groups are formed to work for a short period of time, and serve to direct students attention to learning materials, while establishing a positive environment for learning. Formal groups are created to work on a specific task, and may span one or more classes. In formal groups, students work together to achieve their goals and each student is responsible for maximizing her learning and that of her peers [2].

CL has been extensively studied and increasingly applied in all levels of education and in many disciplines [7]. Research on the effects of CL have found that this methodology has both intellectual and attitudinal benefits for students. It has been shown that CL promotes cognitive achievement and academic performance, at least in comparison with the competitive and individualistic methods [7]. Other benefits of CL found in [2] are: it allows students to influence their own learning process, it facilitates the participation of all students, it offers a cozier and more friendly setting for learning, it increases student satisfaction with the learning experience, and it promotes positive attitudes towards the subject matter.

3. DESIGN OF THE STRATEGY

3.1 Learning Situation

The learning situation addressed by the strategy is that students understand the basics of relational algebra [4]. Such understanding can be built in three stages: first, introducing the topic of relational algebra; second, presenting the algebra operators, emphasizing in some of their key characteristics; and third, demonstrating how to use and combine these operators to solve queries in a relational database.

3.2 Rationale and Goals of the Strategy

In the past, the learning situation had been tackled primarily by lecturing, interspersed with a variation of problem-based learning where some example problems (i.e., translating user queries into relational algebra expressions) were solved by the teacher but students were not given the chance to attempt a solution by themselves in class. With this approach, students often confused operators and had difficulty to solve homework and test problems where they had to combine different operators in the same query.

The authors thought that one way in which students could gain a better grasp of relational operators was by leading the students to discover by themselves the most important characteristics of each operator so they could later discern when to use them. Cooperative Learning was considered a good fit for this purpose since it enables students to have an active role in building their knowledge and achieve learning through collaboration with their peers (guided by the teacher).

The goals of the teaching strategy were that students:

- Recognize the purpose of relational algebra.

- Be able to explain to their peers what some relational operators (that they study in depth) do.

- Be able to solve queries in a relational database using the relational operators.

- Respect and value the contributions of their peers when working on a group task.

- Collaborate in the construction and integration of knowledge, and in the generation of conclusions based on discussion and consensus.

- Assess their own learning as well as the group work and interaction.

3.3 Description of the Strategy

The strategy is designed to be applied in a session of 1 hour and 50 minutes in the regular classroom. It divides the class period in three *moments*, each having a corresponding activity which is specified in the form of a written *work guide* for the students.

First Moment.

In the first moment, informal groups of 3 to 5 students are created to introduce the topic of relational algebra. These initial groups are formed by the students themselves so that the activity begins with an atmosphere of trust and friendship. The activity consists in asking the groups to: (*i*) discuss their conception of relational algebra, (*ii*) make an analogy in terms of operands, operators and results, with other known algebra, and (*iii*) comment on the result of their work in the plenary group (consisting of all students plus the teacher). All groups are given the same work guide. The estimated time for this activity is 30 minutes, distributed as follows: 15 minutes for the initial discussion and analogy construction, plus 15 minutes for commenting in the plenary group.

Second Moment.

In the second moment, formal groups of 3 to 5 students are created for a detailed study of the relational operators. These groups are formed in advance by the teacher, seeking diversity of skills, personalities and gender in the groups. Every group receives a different work guide because each group is assigned a different set of relational operators. The activity consists in asking the students to: (*i*) read the material supplied on the assigned operators while trying to answer some given questions about the key characteristics of the operators, (*ii*) collaboratively solve the given exercises (as much as they can), and (*iii*) explain to the plenary group how the studied operators work and present the solution to relevant exercises. Along with the work guide, each group is given a reading, which is part of the assigned reading for the day, so students should be familiar with the subject (though they are not expected to master it). The estimated time for this activity is 1 hour and 10 minutes, distributed as follows: 35 minutes for studying the material and solving the exercises, plus 35 minutes for presenting to the plenary group.

Third Moment.

In the third and last moment, students keep working in the same groups created during the second moment. The activity consists in asking the students to: (*i*) perform an assessment of the teaching strategy, (*ii*) self-assess their learning, and (*iii*) assess the cooperative work performed by them and their group peers. All groups are given the same evaluation guide. The estimated time for this activity is 10 minutes.

3.3.1 Version 2: Variation of the Second Moment

A second version of the strategy was developed after experimenting one semester with the first version and analyzing students' feedback. The new version introduced two changes to the second moment. The first change was that the teacher did not explicitly provide students with reading material on the assigned operators because students were expected to have read the material prior to the class (pre-class readings were in use since the beginning of the semester), thus there was no need for students to read it again in class. However, they were free to consult the textbook at anytime. With this modification, more time could be devoted to peer discussion and exercise resolution. The second change was that instead of having one representative from each formal group present her operators to the plenary group, students were reorganized into new groups such that each group now had at least one member from each of the previous formal groups. In this new arrangement, each student became *the expert* on a set of operators within her group, and therefore was given the mission to convey to its peers its own knowledge about these operators (within a limited time). With this modification, all students had the opportunity to participate, they were highly motivated to understand their operators and be able to explain them to their peers.

4. IMPLEMENTATION

4.1 First Implementation

The original version of the strategy was implemented in two sections of the Database I course during the 7th week of the first semester of 2010, and it took the entire class session. A total of 24 students from Section 1 and 18 from Section 2 attended. This was the first of two classes devoted to the subject of relational algebra, thus, the strategy served to introduce the topic. The second class was used to work, in small groups, on a set of relational algebra exercises.

4.1.1 The Student Context

Section 1 was composed of 3 women and 21 men, while Section 2 was composed 3 women and 15 men. The entire course population was composed of young students in their third year of the B.S. program, most of whom were taking the course for the first time. By the time the strategy was applied, students were used to work in groups, since they were involved in several group activities (e.g., exercise solving and team competitions) during previous sessions. Therefore, students were prepared to take on the new teaching strategy based on CL.

4.1.2 The Place Context

Classes were taught in a small classroom located on the third (and top) floor of our Department building. This room has space for about 25 students; it has good lighting, a desktop computer and a video projector. The classroom poses some limitations for the learning and teaching process: (*i*) it gets hot, hence during summer time it is difficult to keep students' attention because of the high temperature inside the classroom, (*ii*) it does not isolate noise well, which essentially prevents from listening to the teacher or students in the presence of rain, (*iii*) it makes it difficult for students to mobilize (with their desks) within the classroom due to its small size.

4.1.3 The Time Context

The class met twice a week for 1 hour and 50 minutes. The class time for Section 1 was 1 p.m. to 2:50 p.m. and for Section 2 was 5 p.m. to 6:50 p.m. None of these times were particularly conducive to learning since fatigue and sleepiness normally worsened after lunch (class time of Section 1)

and towards the end of the labor day (class time of Section 2), which made even more necessary the use of teaching techniques that promote active student participation in class, minimizing the negative influence of the schedule.

4.2 Second Implementation

The second version of the strategy was implemented in two sections of the Database I course during the 7th week of the second semester of 2010, and it also lasted a class session. A total of 12 students from Section 1 and 9 from Section 2 attended. This was also the first of two classes devoted to the subject of relational algebra in the course.

4.2.1 The Student Context

Section 1 was composed of 2 women and 14 men, while Section 2 was composed of 3 women and 13 men. Like in the previous semester, most students were young and most were taking the course for the first time. They were also used to work in groups but students from Section 2 were particularly quiet and little participative, which posed a challenge for the application of the teaching strategy.

4.2.2 The Place Context

Classes were taught in a small classroom located on the third (and top) floor of our building, which presented similar conditions to the ones described in section 4.1.2.

4.2.3 The Time Context

The class met twice a week for an hour and fifty minutes. The class time for Section 1 was 11 a.m. to 12:50 p.m. and for Section 2 was 3 p.m. to 4:50 p.m. We considered that such schedules were more conducive to learning than the ones from the previous semester, where the strategy was first implemented.

5. ASSESSMENT RESULTS

5.1 Students' Perspective

During the third moment of the teaching strategy, each student was given an evaluation guide with ten questions. From these questions, four aimed to evaluate the teaching strategy, two aimed to assess students' own learning, and four aimed to assess the cooperative work performed by the groups. Answers were anonymous. In what follows we present only the more relevant questions and their results.

5.1.1 Self-assessment of Learning

Table 1 shows the students' assessment of their level of understanding regarding relational algebra (especially the operators). This table summarizes the responses to the multiple choice question "To what extent did you understand the concepts of relational algebra (especially the operators)?" across two implementations of the strategy and two sections in each implementation. In the first implementation, students asked if they could give two answers for this question: one for the relational operators they studied in detail in formal groups, and another for the operators presented by their peers to the plenary group. The teacher agreed, and this is why an extra column is shown for each section of the first implementation in Table 1; column labels F and P stand for formal group and plenary group. We can observe from Table 1 that in the first implementation, most students (79%

Table 1: Students' level of understanding.

	1st Implementation				2nd Implementation	
	Section 1		Section 2		Section 1	Section 2
	F	P	F	P	F	F
> 70%	19	4	16	6	6	7
30% to 70%	4	17	1	10	6	2
< 30%	1	3	1	2	0	0

Table 2: Learning enrichment through group work.

	1st Implementation		2nd Implementation	
	Section 1	Section 2	Section 1	Section 2
Yes	22	14	11	7
No	1	3	1	2
Blank	1	1	0	0

Table 3: Rating of group work.

	1st Implementation		2nd Implementation	
	Section 1	Section 2	Section 1	Section 2
Good	19	14	10	6
Fair	5	4	2	3
Poor	0	0	0	0

Table 4: Student satisfaction with the group interaction.

	1st Implementation		2nd Implementation	
	Section 1	Section 2	Section 1	Section 2
Yes	21	15	11	6
No	2	3	0	2
Partway	0	0	1	1
Blank	1	0	0	0

in Section 1 and 89% in Section 2) attained a level of understanding beyond 70% for the operators studied in formal groups, but for the operators that were presented in the plenary group, a large percentage of students (71% in Section 1 and 56% in Section 2) attained a level of understanding between 30% and 70%, and a non-negligible percentage of students (12% in Section 1 and 11% in Section 2) even attained an understanding of less than 30%.

In the second implementation, students did not request to give separate answers, which we attribute to the fact that the strategy was modified such that the plenary group activity was replaced by another formal group activity. Therefore, the results for the second implementation indicate the overall level of understanding (both for the operators studied in the first formal group and for the operators explained by their peers in the second formal group). We can see in Table 1 that in the second implementation all students considered that their level of understanding was at least 30%, and even a large portion of the students (50% in Section 1 and 78% in Section 2) considered that their level of understanding was higher than 70%. An interesting finding is that the overall level of understanding improved from the first implementation to the second, since no students chose the "less than 30%" option in either section, and only a few students wrote comments about not being able to understand what their peers explained (compared to the first implementation, where many students wrote such negative comments).

Table 2 summarizes the responses to the question "Do you think that the group work enriched your learning?" With this question, not only we assessed students' learning but also validated the choice of cooperative learning as the basis for the teaching strategy. In both implementations, the vast majority of students answered positively (between 78% and 92%, depending on the section). This provides evidence for cooperative group work being a positive and enriching factor for learning.

5.1.2 Assessment of Cooperative Group Work

Table 3 shows the responses to the multiple-choice question "How do you rate the work performed by your group?" For both implementations, the majority of the students (between 67% and 78%, depending on the section) rated the group work as *good*.

Table 4 shows the students' answers to the question "Did you like how the group interacted?" Since this was not a multiple choice question but a free-form one, student answers were classified in four categories: Yes, No, Partway, Blank. With the exception of Section 2 from the second implementation (where only 67% of the students responded positively), more than 82% of the students in all other sections said they liked the way in which the group interacted.

5.1.3 Assessment of the Strategy

Table 5 summarizes the students' responses to the question "Did you like the way in which the class was developed?" which provides an assessment of the student satisfaction with the teaching strategy. Answers were free-format hence they were classified in three categories (Yes, No, Partway) for the purpose of presentation. In the first implementation a large majority of students said they liked the way in which the class session was developed (92% in Section 1 and 78% in Section 2). However, in the second implementation the percent of positive answers decreased to 75% in Section 1 and 56% in Section 2.

5.2 Teacher's Perspective

We used two quantitative instruments to evaluate the students' learning on relational algebra: a homework and a midterm exam. However, the second semester that the strategy was used there was no homework on relational algebra, so we only have homework grades for one of the semesters where the strategy was used. We also have homework grades for the semester prior to the first use of the strategy (there were 18 students in Section 1 and 13 in Section 2 that semester). Table 6 shows the mean and standard deviation of the homework grades, combining students from both sections, for the semester where the strategy was not used and the first semester where the strategy was used. The last column shows the result (P-value) of a two-tailed t-test assuming unequal variances ($F = 1.88$, $P = 0.03$) over the homework grades for both semesters, $t(50) = 1.98$. A P-

Table 5: Student satisfaction with the teaching strategy.

	1st Implementation		2nd Implementation	
	Section 1	Section 2	Section 1	Section 2
Yes	22	14	9	5
No	1	2	2	2
Partway	1	2	1	2

Table 6: Homework results.

Strategy not used		Strategy used		t-test
Mean	Std. dev.	Mean	Std. dev.	P value
68	36	83	26	0.053

Table 7: Exam results.

1st Implementation		2nd Implementation	
Mean	Std. dev.	Mean	Std. dev.
88	16	80	23

value of 0.053 shows a moderate positive effect of the strategy over the students' understanding of relational algebra.

With respect to the midterm exam, it included one section of relational algebra. Table 7 shows the mean and standard deviation of the grades obtained by the students (from both sections) on the relational algebra section of the midterm exam for the two semesters where the strategy was applied. A mean of 80 or above is a good indicator of the high level of understanding achieved by the students through the teaching strategy. Unfortunately, we do not have comparative data from prior semesters where the strategy was not used. We have the overall exam grades, but comparing the overall grades would not lead to useful conclusions since several other topics were covered, and the topics covered in each exam varied across the semesters.

We also performed a qualitative assessment of the strategy based on the observed strengths and limitations. The main strengths of the strategy were that it (i) facilitated the interaction and collaboration among students; (ii) fostered the participation of all students; (iii) enabled students to construct their own knowledge based on readings, questions, exercises, and discussion with peers; and (iv) invited students to reflect on their own learning and the group work. On the other hand, a major limitation of the strategy was the large amount of time required to finish it, evidenced by complains of the students who said that they did not have enough time to complete all the exercises of the work guide. Using the traditional lecture approach, all the material was easily covered in a class session, but using the proposed strategy, a little more time was required, due to the increased student dynamism and participation. Another limitation came from the fact that not all students were effective communicators, meaning that it is possible that some students did not clearly explain their operators, leaving their peers confused or lacking some knowledge about them.

6. SUMMARY AND FUTURE WORK

A cooperative learning-based teaching strategy for relational algebra was presented. The design, implementation, and assessment of the strategy was described. Assessment of the strategy was performed from the students perspective through a survey-like evaluation guide, and from the teachers perspective through a midterm exam and a homework. Results from the students' assessment showed that the group work enriched their learning, providing support for the use of cooperative learning. Results from the teachers' assessment show an improvement on the students' learning of relational algebra.

In the future, we want to further improve the strategy in order to address some of its limitations, particularly the time aspect. We believe that by requiring students to read the material before class and enforcing it through a short online test, we will be able to reduce the amount of time needed for the *second moment* of the strategy. Additionally, we plan to explore the use of similar teaching strategies in other topics of the course, such as SQL, Entity-Relation model, and Relational model.

7. REFERENCES

[1] J. D. Chase and E. G. Okie. Combining cooperative learning and peer instruction in introductory computer science. *Proceedings of the thirty-first SIGCSE technical symposium on Computer science education*, 32:372–376, 2000.

[2] J. Domingo. El aprendizaje cooperativo. *Cuadernos de Trabajo Social*, 21:231–246, 2008.

[3] C. Echazarreta, F. Prados, J. Poch, and J. Soler. La competencia ńel trabajo colaborativoż: una oportunidad para incorporar las tic en la didáctica universitaria. descripción de la experiencia con la plataforma acme (udg). *UOC Papers*, 8, 2009.

[4] R. A. Elmasri and S. B. Navathe. *Fundamentos de Sistemas de Bases de Datos*. Pearson-Addison Wesley, 5 edition, 2007.

[5] A. Escribano. Aprendizaje cooperativo y autónomo en la enseñanza universitaria. *Enseñanza*, 13:89–102, 1995.

[6] D. Goelman. Databases, non-majors and collaborative learning: a ternary relationships. *Proceedings of the 13th annual conference on Innovation and technology in computer science education*, pages 27–31, 2008.

[7] E. Goikoetxea and G. Pascual. Aprendizaje cooperativo: Bases teóricas y hallazgos empíricos que explican su eficacia. *Educación XX1*, pages 227–247, 2002.

[8] G. González and L. D. Matajira. Aprendizaje colaborativo: una experiencia desde las aulasuniversitarias. *Educación y Educadores*, 8(0):21–44, 2005.

[9] D. W. Johnson, R. T. Johnson, and E. J. Holubec. *Los Nuevos Círculos del Aprendizaje: La cooperación en el aula y la escuela*. Aique, 1999.

[10] J. Muñoz, F. Álvarez, L. Garza, and F. Pinales. Modelo para el aprendizaje colaborativo del análisis y diseño orientado a objetos. *Apertura*, 5(1):73–82, 2005.

[11] M. Rodríguez and N. León. Estrategias de enseñanza-aprendizaje en ingeniería una experiencia de aprendizaje colaborativo y aprendizaje orientado a proyectos en cursos de sistemas de inteligencia para la innovación y análisis y diseño de productos. *PUZZLE Revista Hispana de Inteligencia Competitiva*, 3(12):10–15, 2004.

Open Source Contribution As An Effective Software Engineering Class Project

Robert Marmorstein
Department of Computer Science
Longwood University
Farmville, Virginia, USA
marmorsteinrm@longwood.edu

ABSTRACT

Software engineering courses often include a semester project designed to give students experience with real-world programming challenges and to expose them to phases of the software development cycle not covered in other classes. One means of engaging students in realistic programming challenges is to make participation in open source development a part of the semester project.

This paper describes an assignment in which students contribute to an open source project. The project is designed to immerse students in the open source community and expose them to the work flow and design strategies of a large project. Students work in small groups and decide both which open source community to contribute to and which specific contributions they will make. They can choose to focus on implementation of new features over software maintenance or can focus on documentation and design over both. The assignment contains a proposal phase that allows the instructor to ensure that students are exposed to a healthy cross section of the development cycle.

Categories and Subject Descriptors

K.3.2 [**Computers and Education**]: Computer Science and Information Science Education

General Terms

Design, Theory, Experimentation

Keywords

open source software, software engineering, real-world projects, team programming, software maintenance

1. INTRODUCTION

One of the goals of a software engineering course is to expose students to realistic programming challenges. It is a well-known problem[9, 1] that programming assignments in

Permission to make digital or hard copies of all or part of this work for personal or classroom use is granted without fee provided that copies are not made or distributed for profit or commercial advantage and that copies bear this notice and the full citation on the first page. To copy otherwise, to republish, to post on servers or to redistribute to lists, requires prior specific permission and/or a fee.
ITICSE'11, June 27–29, Darmstadt, Germany
Copyright 2011 ACM 978-1-4503-0697-3/11/06 ...$10.00.

academic courses are usually very different from programming tasks in industry. While most class projects focus heavily on design and implementation, real-world projects usually require manipulation of existing code.

A common solution to this problem has been to divide students into large groups and assign them a difficult project which they complete over the course of a semester. When the instructor designs the project, this approach suffers from many of the drawbacks that programming assignments in other courses do; it is very difficult to create an assignment which can be completed in a single semester and yet is complex enough to demonstrate the application of software engineering techniques.

Furthermore, these projects typically involve implementing code "from scratch" and focus most heavily on the first stages of the waterfall model: requirements analysis, design, and implementation, rather than on testing, software maintenance, and deployment. One novel approach to this problem is described in [7], where students were introduced to the *software change process model* using code that had been developed outside the course. While this project succeeded in making the code base more realistic, the development environment was still primarily academic. It is difficult to accurately simulate the work flow, communication model, and development guidelines of a real-world project in an academic setting.

In this work, we describe a project for a one-semester software engineering course in which small groups of students interact with developers from open source projects. A unique aspect of this project is that instead of implementing a project from start to finish, students are given freedom to contribute to the project in different ways. These contributions range from implementation of new features to software maintenance tasks such as fixing bugs, writing documentation, or packaging software for distribution. Students are required to familiarize themselves with the project and submit a proposal document that ensures their contributions will expose them to a broad cross-section of the development process.

2. BACKGROUND

There have been many attempts to incorporate realism into a software engineering class project. In [8], students at geographically separate universities were paired with each other to develop visualization software for the FAA. In [6], students were organized into "virtual corporations" which simulated the management hierarchy and development process of real-world corporations. In [10], students were assigned a project designed by the professor to imitate industry practices and work flow. At the University of Kentucky, students in a software engineering class developed software for tracking PKU medication for use by nurses at the medical school[3].

While most of these projects require students to produce code for real-world users, very few of them incorporate modification or maintenance of existing code. A possible explanation for this is that proprietary code is difficult to access and requires a significant time investment in the coordination between students and an industry partner.

In contrast, open source projects usually have very low barriers to entry and have well established code bases maintained by a team of experienced developers. This means that students can contribute in other ways than design and implementation of the project. Furthermore, many open source projects are sufficiently large that software engineering and project management techniques are required for their success.

Trinity University has made had success with a project that requires contributions to an open-source disaster relief application. They have incorporated open source development both into an introductory level class[5] and a software engineering course[2]. These projects were designed to engage students in service-learning and heavily emphasized the design and implementation phases of the development model, but engaged students in all phases of software production.

Faculty at North Carolina State University have had mixed success at incorporating open source into their software engineering classes[4]. In particular, they found that it is difficult to select a project that is well documented and suitable for completion in a single semester. To address some of the issues they have encountered, they established an online repository of open source projects suitable for use in the classroom. Using these projects has improved student success in their courses.

Most of these approaches require students to engage in a project selected or designed by the instructor. Since one of the most important advantages of open source is that it enables developers to "scratch their own itch", this is a serious limitation. Students are more likely to enjoy and become actively engaged in a project if they can choose something that matches their own interests. The more engaged students become in the project, the more likely they are to explore many different aspects of the design process. On the other hand, if given free reign, some students might abuse this freedom to avoid the more challenging aspects of software production. A hybrid approach, which gives students the freedom to design their own projects, but requires them to fulfill certain requirements can address both of these concerns.

3. PROJECT GOALS

Our institution's only software engineering course is a one-semester offering open to any undergraduate student who has completed the CS1 and CS2 courses. The object of the course is to introduce students to the software development processes and project management practices. The assignment of a large software project which the students work on in groups plays a large role in the accomplishment of this objective. In the past, the project has focused on the design and implementation from scratch of a web or database sys-

tem specified by the instructor. In Fall 2010, we decided to approach the software engineering project in a new way.

Instead of requiring students to create software from scratch or to modify code created by the instructor, we would require students to make contributions to an existing and active open-source project. The expected advantage of this approach was that it would expose students more directly to software engineering concerns and provide them opportunities to interact and network with programmers outside the academic environment. In particular, we hoped to achieve the following four outcomes:

- Students would experience the software life-cycle from design to maintenance.

- Students would develop proficiency in using the software tools and processes used to complete a large project.

- Students would master communication skills necessary for working in a large team.

- Students would learn the importance of internal and external documentation.

We also hoped to encourage students to become a part of the open source community and build relationships with open source developers.

4. PROJECT DESIGN

Students were allowed to work singly or in pairs. Each group could earn a total of 100 points toward the final grade. Twenty of those points were earned by completing a detailed project proposal. Another twenty points came from a six to eight paragraph summary of the available documentation and development resources for their project. The remaining 60 points were earned by successfully completing a set of contributions to the open-source project.

4.1 Proposal and Resource Summary

To ensure that projects contained a wide variety of tasks, each group was required to submit a short proposal that provided background information on the community to which they planned to contribute and included a detailed timeline of planned contributions. This allowed the instructor to reject proposals which did not have enough variety and to ensure that projects maintained a reasonable level of difficulty.

After acceptance of the proposal, students were required to submit a summary of the available development resources for their project. This served two purposes. One purpose was to familiarize students with the tools they would need in order to complete the assignment and to encourage them to initiate communication with the experienced developers already working on the project. A second purpose was to encourage students to begin looking at the source code for the project as early as possible.

4.2 Open Source Contributions

In order to earn the remaining sixty points for the assignment, students received credit for the following contributions:

- Writing, testing, and submitting code for a significant new feature earned the student all 60 points if the submission was accepted by the project developers and became part of the main source code repository. If the change was rejected by the project developers, students could still earn 30 points for a feature submission which worked correctly without crashes.

- Submitting a patch for a well-known bug earned 30 points if the patch was accepted into the source code, but only 10 points if not accepted (for coding style or other non-technical reasons).

- Reporting previously undiscovered bugs in the program and creating unit tests for known bugs earned 5 points each.

- Creating resources (such as icons, artwork, images, music, sound clips) or writing chapters of external documentation earned the student 5 points per resource.

Each group's proposal could incorporate any number of these contributions as long as the total added up to 60 points. If the initial proposal was concentrated too highly in a single area (for instance, if students wanted to only submit artwork), the professor rejected the proposal. After submitting a new, more balanced proposal, students were allowed to begin work on the resource report and the implementation of their project.

It is important to note that for most open source projects, the submission process for new features also involves working with tools for software maintenance, such as issue trackers and patch management systems. Some open source projects also require new contributions to be accompanied by unit tests. Submitting new features also exposes students to design concerns as the developers pick apart their code and uncover performance, style, and design flaws.

5. ANALYSIS AND RESULTS

Of the nine teams in the course, all but two completed the assignment with a passing grade. Five teams succeeded in getting their contributions accepted into the code base of their chosen project.

One team had particularly notable success. They completed the design and implementation of their project, a web browser plug-in for searching a music web site, very early in the semester and were able to focus on software maintenance tasks for most of the remaining time. Their software later won a best-in-class software award on a popular tech web site.

5.1 Assessment

To evaluate the success of this assignment and to assess how well we achieved the four outcomes listed previously, we performed an anonymous survey of the students. The survey consisted of sixteen statements. Students were instructed to mark 'Strongly Agree', 'Agree', 'Disagree', or 'Strongly Disagree' next to each statement. Students were also asked to approximate the total number of hours they spent working on the project.

Figure 1 shows the results of the questions used to evaluate the first outcome (students will experience the entire software life-cycle from design to maintenance).

Students almost universally perceived the project as instructive. They felt particularly strongly that they had learned about the design phase, but most of them also felt they had learned about implementation and maintenance.

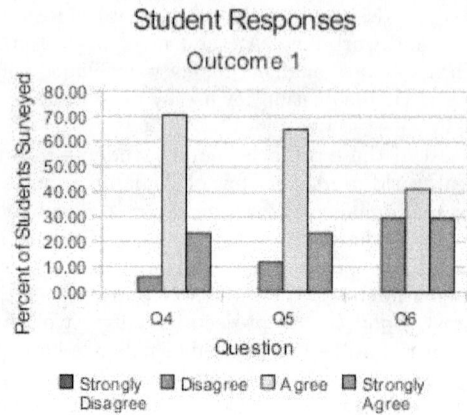

- Q4: This project taught me something about designing software

- Q5: This project taught me something about implementing software

- Q6: This project taught me something about maintaining/debugging software

Figure 1: Survey Results: Outcome 1

To assess the second outcome (students will develop proficiency in using software tools and processes), we used the questions in figure 2.

Every student surveyed indicated that the project had taught important lessons about software tools. However, a majority felt that they did not learn very much about working in a large team. This fact may be connected to the large number of students who indicated that the developers of the project they worked on were unhelpful (see figure 3).

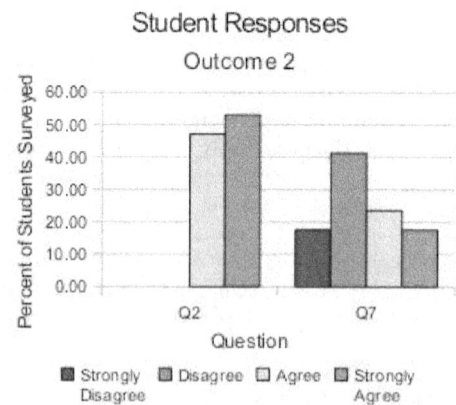

- Q2: This project taught me something about software development tools

- Q7: This project taught me something about working in a large team

Figure 2: Survey Results: Outcome 2

Student Responses
Outcome 3

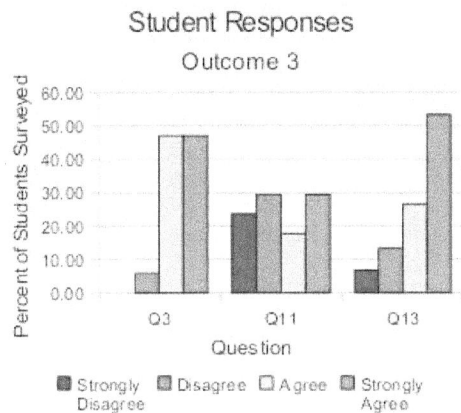

- Q3: This project taught me something about communicating with other developers

- Q11: The developers of the project I contributed to were helpful

- Q13: My partner and I worked well together

Figure 3: Survey Results: Outcome 3

It seems likely that many of these responses were from students who switched projects halfway through the semester. Better initial project selection and screening might have significantly improved this outcome.

Figure 3 shows the questions used to evaluate outcome three (students will master communication skills necessary for working in a large team). Two students, who worked without a local partner, refrained from answering question 13.

The survey results indicate that students felt they learned a lot about communicating with other developers, but that the developers of the project they contributed to were unhelpful. They were much more comfortable communicating with their peers. A wide majority felt that they had worked well with their partner on the project.

Some of the frustration with upstream developers may be due to unclear expectations. Several teams who had patches rejected felt that the developers they communicated with did not adequately explain their reasons for rejecting the patch or provide clear instructions on how to address those issues.

On the other hand, several teams had very positive experiences with upstream developers. One team extended a solitaire game to allow the user to provide custom artwork for the card decks. After their initial submission was rejected by the project maintainer, they were able to re-factor their code into a form that was accepted as a stand-alone companion application to the project.

The questions and results for the fourth outcome (students will learn the importance of external and internal documentation) are given in figure 4. Students universally agreed that they learned that good documentation was important. The fact that many of them found the code base they worked with difficult to understand may have contributed to this understanding, especially since a significant number of students also found the API documentation for their project lacking.

Student Responses
Outcome 4

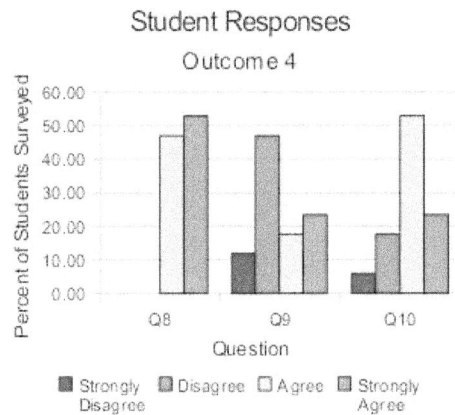

- Q8: This project taught me something about the importance of good documentation

- Q9: The code base I contributed to was easy to understand

- Q10: The API documentation for the project I contributed to was helpful

Figure 4: Survey Results: Outcome 4

In addition to questions about the four outcomes, students were asked general questions about their experience and perceptions of the project. These questions are listed in figure 5. Every student surveyed felt that they learned something from the project. A wide majority (82%) felt that they had done their best on the project, that they enjoyed the project (77%), and that the project would be helpful for finding employment (64%). However, only a few (55%) of students felt that they had started early enough on the project.

- Q1: I learned something from this project

- Q12: I did my best on this project

- Q14: I started early on this project

- Q15: The project was fun

- Q16: The project gave me experience that will help me find a job

Figure 5: Additional Survey Questions

5.2 Limitations and Future Work

One major limitation of this project is that there is very little exposure to the requirements analysis phase of software design. Students are working with established software and so their effort is heavily concentrated in the later phases of the rainfall model. Requirements analysis can be covered in other course material, but it would be nice if the project could better incorporate elements of all phases.

One way to incorporate this phase might be to require students to perform a usability study or interviews with users as part of the project proposal. The big drawback to this solution is that it extends the timeline — the students already have very limited time to complete a feature and get it accepted into the code base. Making the proposal step longer takes away valuable development time. However, this might be an appropriate improvement for a two-semester class or even for a one-semester course in which the students are organized into larger groups.

The results of the survey outline several additional limitations of the project. In particular, they highlight three major areas of concern that negatively impacted successful completion of the project: project time frame, poor communication with the open source developers, and poor documentation of the upstream project.

Many students felt that they did not have enough time to complete the project, but largely attributed that concern to not starting early enough. Groups who switched projects in the middle of the semester were particularly affected by this issue. Many of these teams finished with a passing grade, but did not get their final contributions accepted into the source code of the project. This problem strongly corroborates the experience in [4] that project selection plays a huge role in student success.

A more serious problem was that many students had difficulty communicating with upstream developers and understanding the project API documentation. Many of the teams who switched did so because of these issues. In particular, two teams of students initially attempted to work with the OpenOffice project, which had split into two competing projects (OpenOffice.org and LibreOffice). Both of these teams found communication with developers difficult, API documentation outdated, and the code base unintelligible. These teams switched to new projects, but lost several weeks of coding time.

These issues may stem partly from the students' inexperience with the technology open source projects use for communication. For example, many of the students had never used the Internet Relay Chat or subscribed to a listserv. Most large open source projects use these as their primary means of communication, blogs and social media have largely replaced these in the lives of the students. Assigning a short lab session on using these tools might be one way an instructor could facilitate better communication with the developers. Another way might be to require interviews with the project developers as part of the proposal process. The interview might include questions on project workflow and suggested coding style. The answers to the interview questions might help students be better participants in the project, but might also improve project selection in that it would "screen out" projects with a community that is unable or unwilling to take the time to interact with new developers.

The biggest drawback to these solutions is that they extend the amount of preparatory work, shorten the amount of time available for designing and implementing code, and make it harder for students to evaluate many projects. To give students more time at the end of the schedule, it might be desirable to combine the resource report with the project proposal. Merging these would eliminate a step in the preparation section of the project and get students to the implementation phase faster. Also, because the resource report requires students to take a close look at the project and initiate interaction with the project developers, this change might help students discover undesirable conditions earlier in the process.

Increasing group sizes might also make it easier for stu-

dents to finish their projects on time. While a team size of two is standard in the "extreme programming" paradigm, there is no reason to limit students exclusively to one development model. Adding a third member to the group might make it easier for students to successfully complete the project on time and would mitigate another issue observed in both projects that received failing grades: one student who was not willing to pull their own weight and resulting conflict between the partners.

6. REFERENCES

[1] D. Coppit and J. M. Haddox-Schatz. Large team projects in software engineering courses. In *Proceedings of the Special Interest Group on Computer Science Edcuation*, SIGCSE '05, pages 137–141, February 2005.

[2] H. J. C. Ellis, R. A. Morelli, T. R. d. Lanerolle, and G. W. Hislop. Holistic software engineering education based on a humanitarian open source project. In *Proceedings of the Conference on Software Engineering Education & Training*, pages 327–335. IEEE Computer Society, 2007.

[3] J. H. Hayes. Energizing software engineering education through real-world projects as experimental studies. In *Proceedings of the Conference on Software Engineering Education and Training*, CSEET '02, pages 192–207. IEEE Computer Society, 2002.

[4] A. Meneely, L. Williams, and E. F. Gehringer. Rose: A repository of education-friendly open-source projects. In *Proceedings of the Conference on Innovation and Technology in Computer Science Education*, ITICSE '08, pages 7–11, 2008.

[5] R. Morelli, T. de Lanerolle, and G. W. Hislop. Foss 101: Engaging introductory students in the open source movement. In *Proceedings of the Special Interest Group for Computer Science Education*, SIGCSE '09, pages 311–315, 2009.

[6] D. Petkovic, G. Thompson, and R. Todtenhoefer. Teaching practical software engineering and global software engineering: Evaluation and comparison. In *Proceedings of the Conference on Innovation and Technology in Computer Science Education*, ITiCSE '06, pages 294–298, June 2006.

[7] M. Petrenko, D. Poshyvanyk, V. Rajlich, and J. Buchta. Teaching software evolution in open source. *Computer*, 40:25–31, November 2007.

[8] A. Rusu, A. Rusu, R. Docimo, C. Santiago, and M. Paglione. Academia-academia-industry collaborations on software engineering projects using local-remote teams. In *Proceedings of the Special Interest Group on Computer Science Education*, SIGCSE '09, pages 301–305, March 2009.

[9] M. Shaw. Software engineering education: a roadmap. In *Proceedings of the Conference on The Future of Software Engineering*, ICSE '00, pages 371–380, June 2000.

[10] N. Tadayon. Software engineering based on the team software process with a real world project. *Journal of the Consortium for Computing Sciences in Colleges (JCSC)*, 19(4):294–298, April 2004.

Extreme Apprenticeship Method: Key Practices and Upward Scalability

Arto Vihavainen, Matti Paksula, Matti Luukkainen and Jaakko Kurhila
University of Helsinki
Department of Computer Science
P.O. Box 68 (Gustaf Hällströmin katu 2b)
Fi-00014 University of Helsinki
{ avihavai, paksula, mluukkai, kurhila }@cs.helsinki.f

ABSTRACT

Programming is a craft that can be efficiently learned from people who already master it. Our previous work introduced a teaching method we call *Extreme Apprenticeship* (XA), an extension to the cognitive apprenticeship model. XA is based on a set of values that emphasize doing and best programming practices, together with *continuous feedback* between the master and the apprentice. Most importantly, XA is individual instruction that can be applied even in large courses. Our initial experiments (n = 67 and 44) resulted in a significant increase in student achievement level compared to previous courses. In this paper, we reinforce the validity of XA by larger samples (n = 192 and 147) and a different lecturer. The results were similarly successful and show that the application of XA can easily suffer if the core values are not fully adhered to.

Categories and Subject Descriptors

K.3.2 [**Computers and Education**]: Computer and Information Science Education *Computer Science Education*

General Terms

Human Factors

Keywords

cognitive apprenticeship, continuous feedback, instructional design, programming education, best practices

1. INTRODUCTION

Arts *and* crafts are necessary components in programming excellence. Unfortunately, it is a "public secret" among many respected programming professionals that university programming courses can be counterproductive as non-optimal tools and old academic programming practices must be unlearned in order to develop competence in coding quality.

Part of the problem is that learning programming is hard (e.g. [3, 12, 11, 10]).

Although a long line of research [13, 16, 11] indicates that the problem is not in learning the syntax or semantics of individual language constructs, but in mastering the process on how to combine constructs into appropriate programs, lectures still tend to be structured according to the language constructs, rather than the more general application strategies.

Nowadays, many admit that lecturing is not the best way to support learning to program but even exercise sessions tend to remain as methods to just witness achieved learning results; typically, there is only minimal guidance to the students doing the exercises. Accumulation of applied knowledge in a student is assumed and expected. However, it is well-established in educational psychology (e.g. [7]) that, due to human cognition, a minimally-guided approach can be considered sub-optimal for novices learning tasks such as programming.

In a recent paper we presented a method that radically alters the traditional way to approach introductory programming (CS1) education in the context of formal higher education called *Extreme Apprenticeship* (XA) [14]. XA is based on a set of values and practices that emphasize *actual doing* of relevant work together with *continuous feedback* as the most efficient means for appropriate learning. Our previous experiments consisted of 67 and 44 students. The results were strongly encouraging, so we continued the experiment with significantly larger (n = 192 and 147) samples.

As the XA method strives to be as lecturer-independent as possible, this time the XA experiment was conducted with a separately recruited lecturer with extensive experience in traditional lecture-based courses but no involvement in the development of the XA method. In addition, as the XA method is by definition direct one-on-one interaction between the master and the apprentice, a question of scalability of the method becomes important. We briefly describe the tools and organizational approach used to scale up the XA method to larger courses.

2. EXTREME APPRENTICESHIP

The Cognitive Apprenticeship (CA) model [5, 6] has many applications in teaching programming (see e. g. [1, 2, 4, 8]). Extreme Apprenticeship (XA) builds on the Cognitive Apprenticeship model. Similarly, it emphasizes the process and consists of three phases: modeling, scaffolding and fading.

In modeling, the master, a teacher or an instructor, arms

the apprentice, a student, with a conceptual model of the process. An effective conceptual model is a set of *worked examples* [4], i.e. a detailed description of completing a programming task from start to finish. While completing the task, the master is thinking aloud all the time, explaining the decisions made during the process.

After acquiring the conceptual model, apprentices are exposed to tasks (i.e. exercises) to be completed under the guidance of a master. Scaffolding refers to supporting apprentices in a way that they are not given answers, rather, just enough hints to be able to discover the answers to their questions themselves. Scaffolding works especially well if apprentices are in the zone of proximal development as described by Vygotsky [15].

Fading of scaffolding occurs when the apprentice starts to master a task.

Even though XA builds upon CA, it differs significantly from many recent applications of CA in teaching programming (compared to e.g. [1, 2, 4, 8]). Our XA method is described by its core values that should be stressed in all course activities (paraphrasing differs slightly from the original description in [14]):

- The craft can only be mastered by actually practicing it. The skills to be learned are practiced as long as it takes for each individual.

- Continuous feedback flows in both directions. The apprentice receives feedback about his/her progress, and the master receives feedback by monitoring the successes and challenges of the apprentices.

The values above induce a set of practices to be applied in all courses:

1. Effectiveness of lectures in teaching programming is questionable; therefore, lecturing should cover only the minimum before starting with the exercises.
2. Topics covered in the lectures have to be relevant for the exercises.
3. Exercises start early, right after the first lecture of the course. During the first weeks of the course all the apprentices are already solving an extensive amount of simple exercises. This gives all the apprentices a strong routine in writing code and a motivational boost right at the start of the course.
4. Exercises are completed in a lab in the presence of masters scaffolding the instruction. There must be ample time to complete exercises while masters are present.
5. Exercises are split into small, achievable tasks. These small intermediate steps guarantee that apprentices can actually see that their learning is progressing.
6. Exercises are the driving force, so the majority of exercises are mandatory for all the apprentices.
7. The number of exercises should be high and to some extent repetitive in their nature.
8. Exercises have to provide clear guidelines, i.e. starting points and structures, e.g. on how to start solving the task and when a task is considered finished.
9. While doing the exercises apprentices are also encouraged to find out things that are not covered during the instruction provided.
10. Best up-to-date programming practices are emphasized throughout the scaffolding phase as they can be incorporated into instruction without any extra effort.

3. COURSES IN SPRING AND FALL 2010

Our semester-length (14 calender weeks) CS1-type introductory Java programming course consists of two separate parts: *Introduction to Programming* and *Advanced Programming*. Topics covered in Introduction to programming are assignment, expressions, terminal input and output, basic control structures, classes, objects, methods, arrays and strings. Advanced programming concentrates on advanced object-oriented features such as inheritance, interfaces and polymorphism, and discusses the most essential features of Java API, exceptions, file I/O and GUI.

Staffing

In Spring 2010, the lecturer was one of instructors in computer labs scaffolding students in XA-based exercises. Lecture material and exercises were aligned to suit scaffolding.

In Fall 2010, the lecturer was not a part of the XA team, in other words, he was not scaffolding students in the lab using XA method. Scaffolding was conducted solely by a group of instructors. All but one instructor were students themselves. In both courses, all instructors were compensated 17 Euros per hr, typically 2-6 hrs weekly.

There was an implicit hierarchy with the instructors, as a more experienced teacher acted as the instructor coordinator and was responsible for recruitment of additional instructors. A few instructors had significant programming experience (but limited teaching experience). Many of the instructors were in the early stages of their studies, their teaching experiences were limited to student tutoring at most. Some were truly novice programmers as they did not have any programming experience outside the few courses they had just passed at the university. The only common denominator among the instructors was the attitude: ready to confront the students in person and their challenges; active and eager to help.

Instructors were recruited "on the fly". As good atmosphere in the scaffolding sessions became a talking point within informal student communities, many students volunteered to be part of the XA-based course implementation.

Each instructor had the possibility to choose the most preferable time slots for him or her. Instructors were also able to call for more help on demand via IRC or text messaging, as some other instructors in the instructor pool were available to join in on short notice. We allowed double-teaming at the times we knew the labs were going to be full. We aimed for a 1 per 10 instructor per student ratio in the lab.

Study material and lectures

The study material (including lectures) play a key role in the modeling phase in teaching the skills to be learned. On the other hand, as programming is a craft, it requires plenty of practice. In Spring 2010, we reduced the number of lectures from the usual 5 hours per week to just 2 hours. In Fall 2010, the head lecturer reduced his lecture hours from 5 to 4 per week.

All the material shown in the lectures was available to students on-line as a web page, written in book-like format. The material followed the structure of exercises, allowing students to read the material as they proceeded.

Exercises

It is expected that students attending XA-based courses use most of the time they devote to the course in active solving of programming exercises. This trains the routine and gives a constant feeling of success by achieving small goals. Exercises especially in the beginning of the course were aimed to build up programming routine and confidence, as well as getting familiar with the environment and tools.

For each week we introduced a set of new exercises, an amount ranging from 15 to almost 40. Most of the initial exercises were small, especially at the start of the course, like "output numbers from 1 to 99". Sequential small exercises combined into bigger programs. Composing bigger programs showed students how to split a big task to sub-tasks – a vital skill in programming. Many of the sequentially done small exercises ended up as relatively large projects.

Exercise Sessions

All exercise sessions were organized in computer labs where students worked to solve the exercises. Help, in form of instructors, was continuously available during exercise sessions. Anyone could enter the lab without having to reserve a specific time slot. In Spring 2010, each week had 8 hours of exercise sessions; in Fall 2010, each week had 20 hours. Students were free to attend as many sessions as needed.

An important principle in our approach is that actual programming starts as early as possible. The first exercise session time was right after the starting lecture of the course. For the first week the students already had 30 small exercises to solve. Due to the guidance available, even those with no previous experience in programming managed well.

In order to enforce good programming habits such as principles of Clean Code [9], students had to have their finished solutions accepted by the instructors. If an instructor noticed a flaw in the approach (bad naming or indentation, too long methods, classes with to many responsibilities, too complex solution logic for the problem, etc.), he pointed it out, and the student had to redo parts of the exercise. In general, we allowed no compromises in the solutions of students. This way, each student refined their solutions to the point where the solutions could be regarded as "model answers".

Continuous Feedback

During the course we implemented continuous feedback to provide fast evaluation and a continuous feeling of progress for the students. During the exercise sessions students received positive reinforcement from the instructors.

If a student did not have specific questions during the exercise session, the instructors were active in making sure (in a non-intrusive fashion) that they were working towards the right direction with good working habits. If something to correct was noticed, the instructor nudged the student to the right direction by asking a question about the approach or by providing constructive feedback. This was the key continuous feedback as the hints received during the learning process are essential for acquiring good programming and problem-solving habits. Instructors were not allowed to give direct solutions to the exercises, and the key idea was to support the students so that they could figure out the solutions themselves.

In addition to instructor feedback, students had their com-

pleted exercises marked down to a check-list, allowing them to see the check-list filling with marked exercises. We feel that the list played an important role in feedback; every check was a small victory. Check-lists were also updated to the course web-page at the end of every day, allowing students to see the progress of other students as well.

The final exams both in Spring and Fall 2010 were constructed to be as similar as possible to the usual programming exams conducted at our university to provide meaningful comparison of the course results. The exams were programming on paper. A student had to get 50 % of the total maximum score in order to pass the course, regardless of the number of exercises finished in the XA scaffolding.

4. RESULTS

4.1 Incremental validation of Extreme Apprenticeship

The introductory programming courses at the Department of Computer Science, University of Helsinki are taught during both fall and spring semesters. Fall semesters consist mostly of CS majors, while Spring semesters consist mostly of CS minors.

Before Spring 2010 both the programming courses have followed very traditional teaching model based on lecturing and take-home exercises with weekly exercise sessions. The first course implementing Extreme Apprenticeship method was held during Spring semester 2010.

Next we will compare the outcome of the Extreme Apprenticeship-based courses to the previous course instances from past 8 years in terms of percentage of passed students. The results are reported separately in the tables below for Introduction to programming and Advanced programming. The XA-based implementations are highlighted in bold face. The column titled n denotes the number of students in each course. The numbers are comparable for all the course implementations as the exams have been alike.

Introduction to Programming

	n	passed
s02	92	38.0 %
f02	332	53.6 %
s03	98	39.8 %
f03	261	64.0 %
s04	84	61.9 %
f04	211	59.2 %
s05	112	46.4 %
f05	146	54.1 %
s06	105	41.9 %
f06	182	65.4 %
s07	84	53.6 %
f07	162	53.0 %
s08	72	58.3 %
f08	164	56.1 %
s09	53	47.7 %
f09	140	64.3 %
s10	**67**	**70.1 %**
f10	**192**	**71.3 %**

Advanced Programming

	n	passed
s02	88	26.1 %
f02	249	56.2 %
s03	65	30.8 %
f03	228	59.2 %
s04	66	43.9 %
f04	177	66.1 %
s05	70	57.1 %
f05	125	56.0 %
s06	52	44.2 %
f06	147	67.3 %
s07	53	58.5 %
f07	136	59.6 %
s08	29	51.7 %
f08	147	56.5 %
s09	22	50.0 %
f09	121	60.3 %
s10	**44**	**86.4 %**
f10	**147**	**77.6 %**

The long-term average (excluding Spring and Fall 2010) for passed students in Fall semesters is 58.5% and in Spring semesters 43.7%. In Spring terms, most of the participants are computer science minors. As can be seen, the result in Spring 2010 was higher than it has previously been, 70.1%, the second highest pass-rate being 65.4%. In Fall 2010 it was 71.3%, which was even better than the results from the first XA implementation in Spring 2010.

The pass-rate from Spring and Fall 2010 are approximately the same: 70.1% and 71.3%. Previous course instances have had a clear long-term difference in the failure rates between Fall and Spring semesters, which we do not observe in the XA-based courses. One explanation is the start-early approach: early success brings motivation.

The trend in the Advanced programming course is similar: the average passing percentage in Fall terms is 60.1% and Spring terms 45.3%, both marginally higher than the pass-percentages for the introductory course. This can be explained by the fact that students failing the Introductory course do not take part in Advanced programming.

The acceptance percentage in Spring 2010 was 86.4%, an all-time high in the department with a clear margin. The most natural explanation for the remarkably high passing rate is that the programming routine built during normal course implementations has been quite fragile for an average or below-average student. In an XA-based course, those students who survived from the initial shock of Introduction to Programming were improving all the time.

In Fall 2010, Advanced programming course pass-rate continued on a remarkably high level: 77.6%. Although not as high as expected, it is significantly higher than the average in previous, traditional Advanced programming courses. The reasons for less-than-expected increase in pass-rate are discussed in the next section.

4.2 Teacher-independence in Extreme Apprenticeship

Instructors spend a lot of time together in the labs and in informal interaction networks (mainly IRC and face-to-face discussions). In a way, this interaction means that instructors are mentoring each other. We observed that new instructors – invited to serve as instructors – were ready to scaffold without any training. Invitation was considered an honor.

Dynamic, on-demand allocation of instructors and the interaction between them brought implicit roles among them. This was evident during the courses when the responsibilities and time spent in the labs for less-experienced instructors faded towards the end, while more experienced stepped up. The same was true for all the courses in Spring 2010 and Fall 2010, even though the number of instructors was scaled up nearly threefold.

Although the result was very good (77.6%) when compared to the previous courses, it did not match our high expectations based on the experiences from Spring 2010 course (86.4%). The results were perplexing particularly since many of the instructors were the same for Spring and Fall 2010, thus having more experience in scaffolding. Moreover, in Fall 2010 the lecturer was one of the most lauded teachers at the whole university, having decades of experience in lecturing CS1-type programming courses.

This led to an investigation in the exercises and course material. The ultimate control (and thus the ultimate responsibility) over the course was handled by a lecturer not participating or involving himself in XA-style scaffolding in the computer labs. The lecturer's responsibilities covered generating the exercises as well. Even though the lecturer received the exercises and material from the Spring 2010 course, it seems that the importance of XA-style exercises was not fully conveyed to the lecturer – the exercises need to be relevant and there must be enough exercises for students to do. Introduction to Programming in Fall 2010 followed mostly the exercise sets from Spring 2010, but the exercises in Advanced programming in Fall 2010 converged towards a more traditional course implementation. The lecturer argued that the exercises and their contents are too demanding for the course. Therefore, he chose to use quite a bit of his old material instead, and reduced the number of mandatory exercises. For example, the first week of Advanced programming in Spring 2010 had 34 exercises, while the corresponding week in Fall had 11 exercises. The trend was similar throughout the whole Advanced programming course.

In Spring 2010, the number of required exercises was much higher than in Fall 2010. It is easy to see from the weekly accumulated data that the students stop challenging themselves if the course structures are not encouraging them continue.

When we reflect the activities during the Advanced programming course in Fall 2010, we can identify which XA practices were overlooked in: (2) Topics covered in the lectures were not always relevant for the exercises; (7) The number of required exercises was not high enough; (8) Exercises did not provide clear guidelines, i.e. starting points and structures. In short, part of the exercises were not XA.

As the effect of lecturing is small (many did skip the lectures), the problems with practices 7 and 8 are far more serious. Nevertheless, the sole reason for all the problems mentioned above was the lack of bi-directional flow of information between *every* participant in the process. Instructors scaffolding in computer labs received implicit and explicit feedback directly from the students and the challenges they faced. The lecturer, not present in scaffolding, did not receive explicit feedback from the labs. In this context, explicit feedback means that the lecturer did not *directly* observe how the students coped with the exercises, and their need for more meaningful and demanding exercises.

4.3 Scalability of Extreme Apprenticeship

XA-style instruction can potentially be overly expensive. We purposefully aimed not to spend more than in our traditional, lecture-driven, guidance-deprived teaching model. On-demand service was ensured by using IRC. On situations where there were too many students, the instructor could ask for extra assistance on-line. The communication tool worked also as a fast way to help and share information on problems that a specific instructor himself had faced earlier – similarly the instructors were able ask for tips on problems they could not help to solve. Self-organization and openness was important, as the mentors themselves handled the laboratories, and it was important to also share the problems with the group.

For bookkeeping of student exercises and allocation of instructors, we utilized online spreadsheets in Google Docs with our own macros. Each instructor was required to mark down the hours at the end of the day, which allowed us to keep track of the money spent so far and the demand for instructors during specific times. We extended our spreadsheet so that it created automatic predictions for the up-coming week based on the previous week. This allowed us to focus resource allocation for rush hours, and on the other hand we were also able to re-assign instructors from not-so-crowded hours. In the end, the price tag for the courses was indeed relatively the same as it has been over the past years.

5. CONCLUSIONS

Extreme Apprenticeship provides a solid structure for teaching skills that aim to build good routines and learning best practices from those who already master them. Emphasizing scaffolding in combination with the core values and the derived practices yields excellent learning results as was seen already in our initial implementations in Spring 2010. The excellent results were repeated in Fall 2010 with three-fold increase in student population.

XA strives to be a method for organizing teaching regardless of personal traits. We examined this aspect of XA by implementing the second cycle of programming courses with XA-style scaffolding under a traditional lecture course. The lecturer was informed about XA and its values and practices but chose not to be involved in scaffolding in the computer labs.

Even though the results for the latest course (Advanced programming) using XA were very good, they were clearly below what was expected. An inspection revealed that important XA-practices were overlooked, due to lack of observed feedback from the labs. Therefore, the approach used in Advanced programming course held in Fall 2010 is an example of an *Extreme Apprenticeship But* method, as in "We used Extreme Apprenticeship, but..". We believe that the ideas behind the Extreme Apprenticeship method – especially continuous bi-directional feedback and scaffolding – should be followed vigorously in order to provide enough support to help novices, struggling to learn programming, to become truly professional programmers.

Anonymous student feedback collected at the end of the courses showed clearly that the students truly valued the XA-style scaffolding. The most convincing evidence came from students that had tried to pass the course earlier in its traditional form, and now received the "XA-experience".

The outcomes from our initial experiments have led us to believe that the role of the lectures in a programming education clearly diminishes if the exercises are properly designed and there is personal support when trying to complete them. Personal support does not need to be overwhelming; instead, even few minutes spent well to nudge a student into right direction by an instructor who is not afraid to confront the student at his or her own level makes a huge difference.

6. ACKNOWLEDGMENTS

We acknowledge all the journeymen who have contributed to CS1 education at Helsinki University by helping out in labs and by spreading the good word on joy of programming. Especially, we would like to thank Thomas "Wilhelmsson" Vikberg, who has prototyped XA at the department of Mathematics and Statistics during Spring 2011, and shown that XA is applicable to other domains as well.

7. REFERENCES

[1] O. Astrachan and D. Reed. AAA and CS 1: the applied apprenticeship approach to CS 1. In *SIGCSE '95: Proceedings of the twenty-sixth SIGCSE technical symposium on Computer science education*, pages 1–5. ACM, 1995.

[2] T. R. Black. Helping novice programming students succeed. *J. Comput. Small Coll.*, 22(2):109 114, 2006.

[3] R. E. Bruhn and P. J. Burton. An approach to teaching java using computers. *SIGCSE Bull.*, 35(4):94–99, 2003.

[4] M. E. Caspersen and J. Bennedsen. Instructional design of a programming course: a learning theoretic approach. In *ICER '07: Proceedings of the third international workshop on Computing education research*, pages 111–122. ACM, 2007.

[5] A. Collins, J. Brown, and S. Newman. Cognitive apprenticeship: Teaching the craft of reading, writing and mathematics. In *Knowing, Learning and Instruction: Essays in honor of Robert Glaser*. Hillside, 1989.

[6] A. Collins, J. S. Brown, and A. Holum. Cognitive apprenticeship: making thinking visible. *American Educator*, 6:38–46, 1991.

[7] P. A. Kirschner, J. Sweller, and R. E. Clark. Why minimal guidance during instruction does not work: An analysis of the failure of constructivist, problem-based, experiental, and inquiry-based teaching. *Educational Psychologist*, 41(2):75–86, 2006.

[8] M. Kölling and D. J. Barnes. Enhancing apprentice-based learning of java. In *SIGCSE '04: Proceedings of the 35th SIGCSE technical symposium on Computer science education*, pages 286–290. ACM, 2004.

[9] R. Martin. *Clean Code: A Handbook of Agile Software Craftsmanship*. Prentice Hall, 2008.

[10] A. Pears, S. Seidman, L. Malmi, L. Mannila, E. Adams, J. Bennedsen, M. Devlin, and J. Paterson. A survey of literature on the teaching of introductory programming. In *ITiCSE-WGR '07: Working group reports on ITiCSE on Innovation and technology in computer science education*, pages 204–223. ACM, 2007.

[11] A. Robins, J. Rountree, and N. Rountree. Learning and teaching programming: A review and discussion. *Computer Science Education*, 13:137–172, 2003.

[12] H. Roumani. Design guidelines for the lab component of objects-first cs1. In *SIGCSE '02: Proceedings of the 33rd SIGCSE technical symposium on Computer science education*, pages 222–226. ACM, 2002.

[13] J. C. Spohrer and E. Soloway. Novice mistakes: are the folk wisdoms correct? *Commun. ACM*, 29(7):624–632, 1986.

[14] A. Vihavainen, M. Paksula, and M. Luukkainen. Extreme apprenticeship method in teaching programming for beginners. In *SIGCSE '11: Proceedings of the 42nd SIGCSE technical symposium on Computer science education*, 2011.

[15] L. S. Vygotsky. *Mind in Society: The Development of Higher Psychological Processes*. Harvard University Press, Cambridge, MA, 1978.

[16] L. Winslow. Programming psychology - a psychological overview. *SIGCSE Bulletin*, 27:17–22, 1996.

The Academic Enhancement Program in Introductory CS: A Workshop Framework Description and Evaluation

Rylan Egan
Instructional Development Office,
DELTS
Memorial University of Newfoundland
St. John's, NL, A1B 3X8
Canada
regan@mun.ca

Diana Cukierman
School of CS
Simon Fraser University
Burnaby, B.C. V5A 1S6
Canada
diana@cs.sfu.ca

Donna McGee Thompson
Student Learning Commons
Simon Fraser University
Burnaby, B.C. V5A 1S6
Canada
dmcthomp@sfu.ca

ABSTRACT

The Academic Enhancement Program (AEP) is a student focused proactive intervention initiated in 2006 by the School of Computing Science and the Student Learning Commons at Simon Fraser University to provide academic self-regulation skills. This program has been offered as a required component in selected first year courses since 2008. In this paper we provide a description and evaluation of AEP 101 - a two-hour workshop delivered in a first year programming course. The workshop material includes a proposed framework to address academic challenges in general, with specific emphasis on learning processes required for CS. Statistical evaluations provide evidence of students' interest and appreciation for the workshop. In addition, some statistically detectable correlations between workshop satisfaction, academic attitudes, and academic performance are described.

Categories and Subject Descriptors

K.3.2 [**Computer and Education**]: **Computer and Information Science Education** - *Computer Science Education*

General Terms: Human Factors, Experimentation.

Keywords: Study strategies, self-regulation, learning outcomes, learning taxonomies, experience report, CS education research.

1. INTRODUCTION

Educators and academic advisors find that many students have difficulty succeeding in first-year undergraduate Computer Science (CS) courses. For example, Biggers, Brauer and Yilmaz [2] report lower levels of success and retention in CS. Researchers have explored causes for poor performance and attrition in the discipline. For instance, Biggers et.al. [2] attribute leaving CS to low levels of student-faculty and peer-peer interaction. Also, in their review of literature on distinctions between successful and non-successful novice programmers, Robins, Rountree, and Rountree [16] concluded, "the most significant differences between effective and ineffective novices relate to strategies rather than knowledge" [p.165]. McCartney et al. [12] also found

that successful CS students apply a range of strategies for learning and understanding computing concepts. Looking from another angle, researchers found higher self-efficacy to be linked to better academic performance among computing science students [10].

Institutions, including our own university offer learning strategies workshops to support student success. By integrating learning strategies workshops into first year CS courses we hope to create a more disciplinary relevant experience for students. There have been several learning-strategy instruction models developed, such as supplemental instruction, adjunct courses, and discipline-based study skills courses [18, 6, 9]. In supplemental instruction (SI), for instance, optional weekly review sessions are offered to students in courses with a high risk for failure. These sessions are facilitated by trained successful previous students, who integrate course-relevant study skills [18]. In line with these objectives the Academic Enhancement Program, (AEP) focuses on "learning about learning" and potentially scaffolding the development of transferable self-regulation, study, and organizational skills relevant to CS courses. In addition, the program is administratively modest, potentially reaches all students in the course, and involves CS instructors in dialogues about learning.

1.2 The Academic Enhancement Program

To help students improve their performance in CS courses, we developed the Academic Enhancement Program [7]. The AEP is "a proactive model incorporating at least one required academic and learning strategies activity (suitable for CS topics) into each of several lower division CS core university courses" [7, p.171]. The AEP is "a collaborative program between the School of Computing Science and the Student Learning Commons (SLC) at Simon Fraser University. Our institution is a Canadian comprehensive university with [approximately 32,000] students across three campuses. The School of Computing Science offers undergraduate, masters and doctoral degrees with [over 750] undergraduate majors. The SLC is an academic learning centre mandated to assist and support students in their academic pursuits, providing writing and learning support" [7, p.171].

In the AEP program students are encouraged to reflect and discuss study strategies while engaging in metacognitive thinking, in courses that would not typically include such conversations. Students participate in the AEP as part of course requirements and receive course marks, which helps to ensure that the majority of students participate. Currently students may participate in three AEP activities in their studies, each tailored to a different core first year computing science course. One such activity is the 'AEP

101' workshop, which is tailored to, and delivered in, CS1 courses and is the focus of the current paper.

The AEP has been delivered since 2006, and preliminary data suggests that it has benefited students [7]. To more formally evaluate the effectiveness of the AEP, in 2009-2010, our team embarked on a project to identify the learning outcomes of AEP 101, and develop pre- and post-workshop survey instruments in alignment with those learning outcomes. As a result, we obtained more robust evidence regarding the positive impact of the program. We were also able to improve the AEP 101 workshop by more effectively targeting important factors of student success and retention, such as self-efficacy, study strategy development, and proactive help seeking.

In the next section we describe the current version of the AEP 101 workshop, focusing on the components of the workshop that were revised: the "Ladder to Success" framework and the "Range of Complexity" (ROC) model. Further we present results obtained from our analysis of the survey instruments.

2. THE AEP 101 WORKSHOP

The AEP 101 workshop has five key objectives. Specifically, we attempt to facilitate students' realization of, a) personal academic challenges, b) commonalties between self and peer challenges, c) the importance of developing valid study strategies, d) control over academic successes and failures, and e) implicit relationships between academic success and effective time management. The goal of AEP 101 is to empower students by creating awareness that student difficulties are controllable and predictable, as well as providing students with tools to manage the stress of first year CS.

AEP 101 is a two-hour intervention offered once per term in CS1 introductory computer programming courses. We aim to offer it at several different lab times and limit each session to a maximum of 30 participants. The workshop format is designed to elicit active, collaborative, and reflective participation from students. Workshop attendance and participation has been incorporated into the course grading scheme and accounts for up to 3% of the final grade.

2.1 Ladder to Success framework and the Range of Complexity (ROC) model

We begin AEP 101 by presenting students the *Ladder to Success,* a framework to guide learners through five steps for successively addressing academic barriers: (1) *'Identification'* of barriers and attribution of problems to controllable factors. This workshop component mainly consists of a participatory activity that gives students the opportunity to explore and share their current academic challenges. In this component, we emphasize a general strategy for addressing challenges - divide and conquer: distinguish which problems are controllable and which are not, and solve controllable problems one at a time [17]. Parallels between this process and problem solving techniques such as decomposition and divide and conquer, which are taught as seminal concepts in introductory computer programming courses is stressed in these discussions. (2) The next step in the Ladder to Success encourages study *'planning'*, in particular, adoption of time management strategies. Tools discussed include daily, weekly, and monthly schedules that can be used to organize academic and personal activities. (3) The *'study strategies'* component focuses on strategies organized around a paradigm that we developed for the workshop called *Range of Complexity (ROC),* described in detail below. (4) The proactive *'Help seeking'* step invites students to dialogue and share ideas to solve

concrete situations within the university context and identify other resources for help. (5) The *'Reflection'* step concludes the workshop, and invites students to visualize the whole *Ladder to Success* framework as adaptable to addressing challenges in general through successive iterations of the process.

The *Range of Complexity (ROC)* model presented in Step 3 in the Ladder to Success framework applies to computer programming specifically, and other disciplines requiring logical thinking, abstraction, creativity and problem solving. An essential aspect of this model is the representation of the learning process as a spiral broken into different sub areas (see Fig. 1). The spiral is superimposed onto a pie with each area of the pie corresponding to "stages" or "modalities" of learning: *Remember, Understand, Combine. Automatize, and Create.*

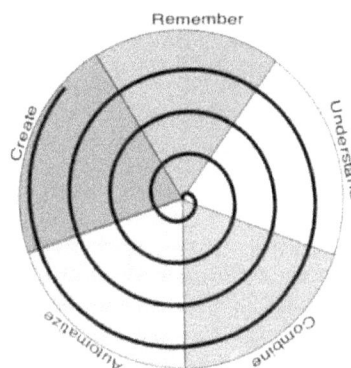

Fig 1. Visual representation: Range of Complexity (ROC)

These stages represent the sophistication that a learner would ideally apply when learning CS materials. The superimposed spiral reinforces the fact that these stages must be experienced by the learner reiteratively in increased *levels of complexity*. When learning more complex concepts, the spiral also indicates that previously learned information must be combined and adapted towards solving more complex problems. For example, at the most basic level of the spiral, the *Remember* stage might represent learning basic programming language statements and elements, such as integer numbers and the syntax of a For Loop. The *Understand* stage could include associating semantics to syntax of individual statements and expressions. In the *Combine* stage a learner will combine knowledge of basic statements to create more complex structures, such as combining a For Loop with printing statements for repetitive printing. Through practice the *Automatize* stage allows learners to apply complex structures intuitively as a whole. In analogy, the For Loop becomes more like a functional unit (a word) and less like a complex statement (ordered letters). Finally in the *Create* stage the learner begins to use functional units to develop novel solutions for problems. For example, at the Create stage the learner would come up with a way of calculating a running sum of integer numbers, combining a known construct (the For Loop) with the assignment statement. The next level in the spiral would start again with the remember stage, when new (possibly more complex) concepts are introduced, such as strings and concatenation, and further stages in the same spiral level would allow the learner to understand and then possibly combine the new concepts with concepts from the previous spiral level (For Loops with running sums) to again create new solutions to (more sophisticated) problems, such as running concatenation of strings.

The stages in this model were inspired by the revised version of Bloom's [4] taxonomy by Anderson et al. [1] who propose the categories Remember, Understand, Apply, Analyze, Evaluate, and Create. The model is also inspired by cognitive constructivist approaches to learning [e.g.14], literature in mathematical problem solving [e.g.15], and Bruner's notions of the spiral curriculum [5]. The concept of a reiterative learning cycle has also been documented in the computer science education literature with reference to learning taxonomies and how they influence learning in the CS setting [11]. Whereas Fuller et al. [11] proposed a taxonomy for instructors to assess a student's level of learning, our model is intended to introduce students to a series of processes for learning CS concepts. Notably, in CS it is vital to construct knowledge based on previously acquired knowledge. Many students attempt to learn new concepts as separate entities, instead of reaching an "extended abstract level" of learning as described in the SOLO taxonomy [3].

We present the ROC model in AEP 101 to increase students' awareness of the need to adapt to the complexity of learning in CS by using a broad range of study strategies. We stress, for example, that memorization alone will not help students learn how to program; instead students need to learn cumulatively by building on previous concepts. As developers and facilitators of the workshop we designed the ROC model to provide a succinct "easy to follow" layout that (we believe) allows students to better internalize the stages and the processes involved.

3. METHOD

To assess how students perceive AEP 101 and further guide us in polishing the workshop, we developed three surveys specifically tailored to workshop learning outcomes. A pre-post design for surveys 1 & 3, respectively, allowed us to investigate the evolution of students perceptions. The data presented here corresponds to the Spring (January – April) 2010 semester.

One hundred and eighty out of 207 students in a first-year CS1 Introduction to Programming course participated in the AEP 101 workshop, grouped in 8 sessions of 20 to 25 students each. One hundred and sixty seven, 183, and 158 students responded to surveys #1, #2 and #3, respectively. As our research required analysis across all three surveys, only students who attended the workshop and answered all three surveys were analyzed. Course bonus marks were given to students who completed all three surveys. In this group there were 106 undergraduate students (female=40), most of whom (102, or 96%) were either non-computer science or undeclared majors. Although depending on the semester this proportion can change noticeably, the demographics represented here are common to CS1 courses. The majority of students (96%) had not previously taken a computer programming course.

The three survey instruments used in this research were developed specifically for the goals and objectives of the AEP 101 workshop. All student responses were recorded on a 5-point Likert scale ranging from Strongly Disagree (1) to Strongly Agree (5). Responses were kept anonymous through a mechanism approved by the research ethics committee at our university.

The Statistical Package for the Social Sciences (SPSS) was used to conduct all statistical analysis. Two key tests were used: Exploratory Factor Analysis (EFA) and correlation. EFA is used to find common variance among multiple sources of data. In this case, a questionnaire was used with multiple items targeted at different aspects of each learning objective. EFA was used to determine if variance in student responses was highly correlated

with a latent (unobserved) variable composed of the shared variance between all factor items (i.e. items that "*loaded*," or correlated with the shared variance between variables) around one or more objectives. If so, a new variable or factor was created to represent multiple items. Correlations were also conducted between survey items and factors.

Survey #1 was administered prior to the AEP workshop. The intent of Survey #1 was to establish general demographic information, current academic regulation practices (attending TA/instructor office hours), and student opinions regarding the aforementioned workshop objectives. The 46 item questionnaire on workshop objectives proved to be satisfactorily reliable (ie. consistently measuring the same variables) ($\propto$ .83).

Survey #2 was administered and completed within 1 week of completing the AEP 101 workshop. The intent of survey #2 was to establish satisfaction ratings for each workshop activity, workshop facilitation, discussion, and usefulness for themselves and their peers. The 18 item questionnaire on workshop objectives proved to be satisfactorily reliable ($\propto$ .89).

Survey #3 was administered 6 weeks after completion of the AEP 101 workshop, the last week of the semester. The intent of survey #3 was to establish differences in ratings of workshop objectives. As a secondary goal we investigated relationships between factor ratings, and workshop satisfaction. The 46 item questionnaire on workshop objectives proved to be satisfactorily reliable ($\propto$ .87).

4. RESULTS

In this section we begin by providing descriptive statistics focused on students' perceptions of the AEP 101 workshop. Next, we describe a factor analysis that was conducted to find response trends. These trends or factors were then compared with outcome data including satisfaction, GPA, and course grades.

On average students agreed that facilitators were both knowledgeable about workshop topics (Number (N) =106, Mean (M) = 4.3, Standard Deviation (SD)=.69) and presented materials effectively (N=105, M= 4.2, SD=.72), where 5 indicates "strongly agree". Although slightly less enthusiastic, students indicated they would recommend the workshop to friends (N=106, M= 4, SD=.96) and that it was both engaging (N=106, M=3.9, SD=.89) and helpful (N=106, M= 3.7, SD=1.03). Forty-three percent of students indicated on survey #3 that they had made changes to their academic habits as a result of the AEP workshop.

To assess the variance among the questions in our surveys, exploratory factor analysis was conducted for the three surveys. All three surveys were tested for normality. Survey #1 had a large number of items that were found to be non-normal (standardized skewness and kurtosis statistics >3.0). Given the large positive skew, even dispersion of items across factor loadings, and the relatively large number of remaining questions it was determined that these items would not be included in the factor analysis. In contrast, survey #3 had only two items excluded due to high standardized skewness statistics.

Survey #1 factor analysis resulted in five logically irrelevant factors. Items loaded around superfluous question attributes such as person of reference (i.e., I am.... vs. Students are...) and positive or negative wording. In contrast, survey #3 factors formed loadings logically consistent with latent variables describing the nature and structure of workshop activities. Four factors were illuminated with eigenvalues ranging from 7.9 to 2.3. Eigenvalues above one are often used as criteria for extraction and use in analysis. A four factor model was chosen as a result of a recognizable 4 factor scree plot elbow and decreased variance below 5%. Cumulatively, 42.4% of variance in the data was explained by these 4 factors (see Table 1 for sample items). Detectable survey #3 factors included:

S3.F1. "Resource Problem Solving and Self-Efficacy",
S3.F2. "Awareness of Challenges and Peer Assistance (Self-Other Reflection)",
S3.F3. "Academic Planning and Scheduling", and
S3.F4. "Learned Helplessness"

Table 1. Partial list of questions from Survey #3, Factor 1, "Resource Problem Solving and Self Efficacy".

Questions as they appeared in Survey #3 in Factor 1	Loading
Incorporating enjoyable activities into my routine is important for my academic well-being.	.74
There are things I can do to positively influence my academic success.	.73
Good programmers have skills that include memorization, conceptual understanding, and creativity.	.68
I am ultimately in control of my academic success.	.61
Information can be understood in a variety of different ways	.60
I have the ability to develop positive study strategies	.55

Survey #2 factors formed loadings logically consistent with workshop activities. Four factors were illuminated with eigenvalues ranging from 6.9 to 1.1. A four factor model was chosen as a result of a recognizable 4 factor scree plot elbow. Cumulatively 64% of variance in the data was explained by these 4 factors. Detectable survey #2 factors included (see Table 2 for sample items):

S2.F1. "Effective and Well Run Workshop",
S2.F2. "Effective Activities (General)",
S2.F3. "Time Management", and
S2.F4. "Scenario Activities: Learning and Studying in CS"

Table 2. List of response items from Survey #2, Factor 4, "Scenario Activities about Learning and Studying in CS."

Items rated by value in Survey #2, Factor 4	Loading
Range of complexity (ROC)	.45
Scenario A: Too much gaming	.78
Scenario B: Running out of time during exams	.75
Scenario C: Getting stuck on assignments	.51
I would recommend this workshop to a friend	.51

An independent sample t-test indicated students who reported making changes to their academic habits as a result of the AEP workshop also reported a higher mean of "awareness of challenges and peer assistance" (n=94, t=3.145, d=.62, p < .001). In addition, small positive statistically detectable correlations were found between satisfaction levels about activities in the workshop (from survey #2) and factors from survey #3, see Table 3. For example, "Effective and Well Run Workshop" (S2.F1) and "Resource Problem Solving and Self-Efficacy" (S3.F1) are positively related with value .376, significant at the 0.01 level.

Table 3. Intercorrelations between Survey#2 and Survey#3 Factors.

Survey#. Factor#	S3.F1	S3.F2	S3.F3	S3.F4
S2.F1	**.376****	.195	-.068	-0.127
S2.F2	.017	**.266****	**.342****	**.221***
S2.F3	**.312****	.081	**.325****	.084
S2.F4	.207	-0.139	-0.171	-0.013

** Correlation is significant at the 0.01 level (2-tailed).
* Correlation is significant at the 0.05 level (2-tailed).

A small positive statistically detectable correlation was found between course grade (obtained by students at the end of the semester) and the factor S3.F1, "Resource problem solving and self-efficacy". In addition, small statistically detectable negative correlations were found between factor S3.F3, "Academic planning and scheduling," and both course grade and GPA, respectively (see Table 4).

Table 4. Intercorrelations between Survey#3 Factors and Course grade and GPA.

	S3.F1	S3.F2	S3.F3	S3.F4	Course Grade
Course Grade	**.418****	-0.148	**-.225***	.181	-
GPA	0.156	-0.157	**-.256***	**.318****	**.660****

** Correlation is significant at the 0.01 level (2-tailed).
* Correlation is significant at the 0.05 level (2-tailed).

5. DISCUSSION, FUTURE WORK

Our results provide statistical support for the demand for, and benefit of, an academic and personal self-regulation workshop for CS students. Although the workshop required additional work, the large majority of participants rated all aspects of the workshop highly. More importantly students reported changing academic strategies in response to new ideas provided in the workshop. Reflecting this change survey #3 (post-workshop) factors loaded on concepts explicitly targeted by the workshop. For example, in survey #3, factors reflecting problem solving and self-efficacy from across the curriculum (e.g., time management, stable/controllable attributions, and study strategies) loaded together. In contrast, survey #1 (pre-workshop) loadings were superfluous, suggesting that students did not have a clear understanding of the relationship between workshop topics. Importantly, students who reported greater engagement with the workshop *per se* and workshop activities generally were also statistically detectably more likely to report high self-efficacy, the ability to find resources to solve problems, the tendency to be aware of the challenges that lay ahead, and to plan to meet these challenges. Interestingly, these skills are similar to ones reported by Cukierman and McGee Thompson [7], Biggers, Brauer and Yilmaz [2], Robins, Rountree, and Rountree [16], and others to improve first year CS outcomes.

In our analysis we also found modest correlations between GPA and resource problem solving and self-efficacy. In contrast however, we found that time management (i.e. rating of how useful students found the time management activity in the workshop) and academic planning skills (i.e. rating of how useful students found the academic planning skills activity) were correlated with lower GPA. This may be a positive finding if it indicated that struggling students were taking proactive measures.

However, our data does not directly support this conclusion as our correlations are small and such a conclusion would risk the fundamental error of attributing cause to correlation.

Based on our representative sample of first year CS students we have support for the following conclusions; 1) students appreciate assistance regulating their personal and academic strategies, 2) positive engagement with our workshop was correlated with reports of positive study strategy, and 3) a correlation exists between students with positive study strategies and higher grades. It is clear that these findings do not represent any definitive support for a contention that the AEP workshop eliminates academic barriers for struggling first year CS students, nor can we contend that by adopting workshops such as the AEP universities can lower attrition from CS programs. However, we do contend that our results provide support for offering and further study of programs such as the AEP. Although statistically significant results in our study were modest, the intervention had a similarly modest scope. Of the many hours a typical first year CS student spends refining their craft, only two hours were dedicated specifically to AEP 101. Our results in combination with robust evidence of the importance of academic and personal self-regulation indicate that programs such as the AEP 101 should be offered and further studied.

Our preliminary analysis suggests that a large majority of students struggle with time management [7]. Further research is needed to more deeply explore the effect of workshops targeting time management strategies. In addition, we would like to extend our study to investigate the long term impact of the AEP program. We would also like to compare workshop participants with students who do not participate. Finally, the current study occurred in the Spring term, when most of the students in CS1 are typically not computing science majors and was taught by one of the authors of this paper. In the future, we would be interested in analyzing results in a term where the student population is mostly majoring in Computing Science and instructors are not directly involved with the AEP. This would refine results to students who intend to make CS their career. We are also considering applying the AEP model to STEM disciplines (science, technology, engineering, and mathematics.)

6. ACKNOWLEDGEMENTS

We would like to acknowledge the highly valuable contribution of research assistant, Maggie Karpilovsky-Aharon, a key member of the AEP research team, to the work described in this paper. We also thank Margo Leight for supporting the AEP from the start, as well as the School of CS, the Student Learning Commons and the Institute for the Study of Teaching and Learning in the Disciplines, for supporting the program expansion.

7. REFERENCES

[1] Anderson, L.W., Krathwohl, D.R., Airasian, P.W., Cruikshank, K.A., Mayer, R.E., Pintrich, P.R., Raths, J. and Wittrock, M.C., Eds. (2001). A taxonomy for learning and teaching and assessing: A revision of Bloom's taxonomy of educational objectives. Addison Wesley Longman, Inc.

[2] Biggers, M., Brauer, A., Yilmaz, T. (2008). Student perceptions of computer science: a retention study comparing graduating seniors with CS leavers. *ACM SIGCSE Bulletin, 40*(1), 402-406

[3] Biggs, J., and Collis, K. (1982). *Evaluating the Quality of Learning: the SOLO taxonomy* New York: Academic Press.

[4] Bloom B. S. (1956). Taxonomy of Educational Objectives, Handbook I: The Cognitive Domain. NY: D. McKay Co Inc.

[5] Bruner, J. S. (1960). *The process of education.* Cambridge: Harvard University Press.

[6] Commander, N. E., & Smith, B.D. (1995). Developing adjunct reading and learning courses that work. *Journal of Reading, 38*(5), 352-360.

[7] Cukierman D. and McGee Thompson D. (2009). The Academic Enhancement Program: Encouraging Students to Learn about Learning as Part of their Computing Science Courses, *ACM SIGCSE Bulletin, 41*(3), 171-175.

[8] Cukierman D. and McGee Thompson D. (2008). The Academic Enhancement Program in Computing Science: Helping Students Succeed in Post Secondary Studies; Listening to Students' Voices as We Expand. In *Proceedings of Western Canadian Conference on Computing Education*, (Victoria, BC, Canada, May 2008), 123-131.

[9] Durkin, K., & Main, A. (2002). Discipline-based study skills support for first-year undergraduate students. *Active Learning in Higher Education, 3*(1), 24-39.

[10] Emotional IQ Contributes to Computing Coursework Success, Virginia Tech Researchers Say. *Diverse: Issues in Higher Education, 22*(19), 32-32.

[11] Fuller U., Johnson C., Ahoniemi T., Cukierman D., Hernán-Losada I., Jackova J., Lahtinen E., Lewis T. L., McGee Thompson D., Riedesel C., Thompson E., (2007). Developing a Computer Science-Specific Learning Taxonomy, *ACM SIGCSE Bulletin, 39*(4), 152-170.

[12] McCartney, R., Eckerdal, A., Mostrom, J. E., Sanders, K., & Zander, C. (2007). Successful students' strategies for getting unstuck. *ACM SIGCSE Bulletin, 39*(3), 156-160.

[13] McGrath Cohoon, J., Wu, Z., & Luo L. (2008).Will they stay or will they go? *ACM SIGCSE Bulletin, 40*(1), 397-401.

[14] Piaget, J. (1985). *The equilibration of cognitive structures.* Chicago: University of Chicago Press.

[15] Polya G. "How to Solve It", 2nd ed., Princeton University Press, 1957.

[16] Robins, A., Rountree, J., and Rountree. N. Learning and teaching programming: A review and discussion. *Computer Science Education, 13*(2):137 – 172, 2003.

[17] Weiner, B. (1979). A theory of motivation for some classroom experiences. *Journal of Educational Psychology, 71*, 3-25.

[18] Widmar, G. E. (1994). Supplemental Instruction: From small beginnings to a national program. In D. C. Martin & Arendale, D. R. (Eds.), *Supplemental Instruction: Increasing achievement and retention.* Jossey-Bass, 3-10.

Getting CS Undergraduates to Communicate Effectively

Andreas Karatsolis, Iliano Cervesato,
Nael Abu-Ghazaleh, Yonina Cooper, Khaled Harras, Kemal Oflazer, Thierry Sans
Carnegie Mellon University – Qatar campus
PO Box 24866, Doha, Qatar
akaratsl@qatar.cmu.edu, iliano@cmu.edu, nabughaz@qatar.cmu.edu, yonina@cs.cmu.edu,
kharras@cs.cmu.edu, ko@cs.cmu.edu, tsans@qatar.cmu.edu

ABSTRACT

In the last decade or so, the ACM, the IEEE and other organizations have acknowledged that there is a problem with the way communication is taught in the Computer Science curriculum: the writing, speaking, and presentation skills students learn in the classroom do not match what is expected of them in the workplace. The proposed solution, adopted by many undergraduate colleges, was to add a technical communication course to the CS curriculum. This does not appear to be enough, as mainstream accreditation boards are still emphasizing the need for improvement of communication skills instruction in their recent reports and recommendations. For the last two years, we have experimented with a complementary transversal approach where many "traditional CS" courses in our program have added a communication component to their syllabus, while at the same time our technical communication course has been revamped to expose students to realistic practices as promoted by situated learning theory. The results, so far anecdotal, point to improved student performance and attitude across several communication dimensions, in particular writing and presentation. We plan to develop this experiment by spreading it across more classes and by starting to collect rigorous measurements of students' communication performance.

Categories and Subject Descriptors

K.3.2 Computer science education

General Terms

Professional practice; Curriculum issues; Communication Skills.

Keywords

Applied Communication, Situated Learning, Curriculum Alignment

1. INTRODUCTION

Professional organizations and accreditation boards supporting science-based curricula, such as ACM (Association for Computing Machinery) and ABET (Accreditation Board for Engineering and Technology) have been emphasizing for many years the importance of communication for the graduates of their programs. In many cases, the language used to describe desired student

outcomes in terms of communication skills (including written, oral and visual communication) points towards the direction of mastery, not mere ability, using adjectives such as "effective" or "excellent" to describe them [1-3]. These suggestions are in many cases driven by the demands of industry for well-rounded science professionals with advanced communication skills, as alumni and employee surveys show. In fact, more than a decade ago, Rensselaer conducted an alumni survey (for then recent graduates) which showed that communication skills were more important than the respondents felt they were prepared for, and that was true for every single one of the fourteen engineering departments [4]. We observed similar comments from surveying the employers of our own CS alumni. Even more recently, a task analysis of the ways junior software developers spend their day at Microsoft revealed that a significant percentage of their time, for some up to 50%, was dedicated to communication and documentation, skills they were expected to have mastered, but were not rigorously trained for [5].

Recently, several Computer Science faculty from various institutions have made the call for a renewed attention to language and technical writing skills, as General Education requirements do not seem to be sufficiently introducing students to professional communication practices [14]. At the same time, advanced discipline-specific courses expect that students should be able to perform at communicative events with the same (or similar) effectiveness that a professional would. To bridge that gap, most higher education science-based curricula in the United States have been requiring in the last decade sophomore or junior level coursework on professional communication, operating under the assumption that dedicated instruction for one semester will help students understand the basic principles of communication to apply them in later courses or their careers. The genres addressed in such courses are primarily academic (for definitions see [6]) with a strong emphasis on technical editing fundamentals, such as parallel structure, concision or coherence. While technical editing skills are useful, they are rarely sufficient in enabling students to carry out communication "performances" in a professional setting. To do so, they need to be exposed to the various forms of communication taking place in various settings, to practice them in mockup situations, and also to execute them in real situations, essentially placing rhetoric at the center of their efforts.

For a rhetorical model to be enacted, however, it is necessary to engage with real audiences within a context of a community of practice, not necessarily of academic practice. As we will explain in the next section in greater detail, developing technical expertise might be the basis to develop mastery, but students need opportunities to simulate the practice and perform in real contexts. And this is where the contributions of discipline-specific (CS) faculty can be critical, as most faculty might have little formal training in writing, but significant experience from their own professional practice.

Motivated by their understanding of professional practice and the desire to model it for students, several of our CS faculty began experimenting with incorporating opportunities for writing or speaking in their classrooms. These experiments started in an uncoordinated way, and were aimed at serving the objectives of individual courses. However, as this paper will reveal, if we look at these efforts through the lens of theories of learning, in particular theories of situated learning and distributed cognition [9,10] which capitalize on apprenticeship models, we can begin to develop a framework which can be used to design a more intentional, coordinated approach to incorporating communication/writing in CS courses. This paper, therefore, serves both as an experiential report of the efforts of our faculty, and as a position paper using primarily anecdotal evidence to delineate a framework for a communication across the curriculum model within CS programs.

2. BACKGROUND

Since the mid 1990s there has been a sustained interest in promoting student-centered curricula [16], especially in disciplines (such as Computer Science) where self-directed learning is critical, as the knowledge base and skills required to succeed evolve rapidly. In fact, the question no longer seems to be whether a student-centered curriculum is preferable, but rather which tools and technologies (multimedia modules, intelligent tutors, etc.) can be used to support such a curriculum, especially in terms of student engagement and active participation.

However, according to theories of situated learning, the distinction between a student-centered (or learning) curriculum and a teaching curriculum does not lie on student interest or engagement. A learning curriculum consists of situated opportunities for the development of new practice and evolves precisely out of participation in communities of practice [9]. This is not a novel idea for work done in the disciplines, as the joint ACM IEEE/CS Computing Curriculum from 2001 (and repeated in the 2008 interim report) states that "mastery of the discipline includes not only an understanding of basic subject matter, but also an understanding of the applicability of the concepts to real-world problems" [2]. For the purposes of developing effective communication skills, such a statement points directly to the need of engaging students with real audiences in real contexts through professional genres, a direction congruent with the rhetorical approach we discussed earlier.

Invoking theories of situated learning seems especially appropriate when we are considering practices that lend themselves to an apprenticeship model, such as medical doctors or tailors or butchers learning from more experienced, full participants of the practice. Enacting such an approach in the classroom, or for a whole curriculum, seems more complicated, mainly because the academic and the professional context are often at odds with each other. In the same way, however, that one learns how to play a sport or an instrument, we can think of a tripartite framework where one has to learn the technique (or acquire technical skills) first, then participate in simulated instances of the practice, and finally participate in real performances or authentic use. Pea points

out that the first step (practicing technique) can be a solitary activity, the second part (simulation) can be based on imitation of practice by others and the third part (performance) can be supported by guided participation in use by more knowledgeable others [10].

Previous efforts in incorporating communication skills within Computer Science curricula have been either focusing on the development of a single technical communication course for CS majors [11], or on the introduction of an aspect of communication (such as oral communication in several courses), although there is some evidence of the effectiveness of enacting a Communities of Practice approach for CS projects [15]. The results from such interventions are not definitive or clear, despite some evidence through reflective questionnaires of improvement of attitudes towards communication. However, a comprehensive model which can provide guidance and span the whole curriculum has not been proposed yet.

In the next section, we will describe our individual efforts to develop the communication skills of CS students in several courses in the curriculum.

3. CURRENT EFFORTS

For the last two years, a number of instructors at Carnegie Mellon Qatar have been independently experimenting with writing, speaking and visual communication assignments in several CS courses. This effort affected some 55% of the courses in the curriculum. At the heart of this effort was the revamping of a required sophomore-level applied communication course (CS-221) to incorporate elements of situated cognition theory. Moreover, several other instructors more or less independently incorporated communication and/or writing into their courses in a grass root, uncoordinated effort that currently spans about half of our CS curriculum.

Each one of the next three sub-sections will first present the ways CS-221 introduced each part of the model to students, thus providing them with a valuable framework, and then describe how other courses accommodated this model in their assignments.

3.1 Practicing technical skills

The development of expertise in most fields requires a certain degree of technical skill which can only come through sustained practice. In music or in sports, it takes months or years of practicing technical skills before one can perform in a concert or a game. Similarly, in revising CS-221, we decided that practicing technical writing and speaking skills was a critical step in enacting this model. Most technical communication courses make acquiring technical skills the focal point of the work that students do, but in our case we decided that recitation sessions or online modules would allow students practice without taking up classroom time. These practice sessions were directly related to the patterns they were encountering in classroom discussions of different genres. For example, when discussing the problem/opportunity section of proposals, which is most effective when presented as a detailed narrative, the technical skill practiced was nominalizations, in order to understand the placement of characters and actions in the subject and verb position respectively. Similarly, concision is practiced when discussing memos, or parallel structure is practiced alongside writing instruction manuals. More complex topics, such as principles of visual communication were practiced through interactive online modules (some courtesy of Carnegie Mellon's

Open Learning Initiative [18]), presenting content and exercises on topics like alignment, contrast or framing.

Such sustained engagement with the fundamentals of communication is also practiced before CS-221, in the freshman CS courses students have to take for their major. We will now describe how this is realized in two of them, CS-129 and CS-103.

In CS-129 (the first-semester computer science immigration course), the overall goal is to expose newly admitted students to the intricacies of being an effective computer science student at CMU. This includes building necessary skills for success in the program such as time management, patience, persistence, independence, and critical thinking. Finally, the course attempts to improve upon written communication and presentation skills.

To achieve the goals stated above, the class generally consists of the following components: (1) Weekly faculty talks given by experts in specific areas of computer science. (2) Weekly student presentations on other areas in computer science. Students conduct and receive peer evaluations for oral communication skills in these talks. (3) Several other requirements aimed at engaging with and contributing to the CMU community, including building their own webpage, interviewing faculty members, joining clubs, and attending talks/events.

The writing component is mainly related to the faculty presentations and independent research. Prior to every faculty talk, students are required to conduct background research and write a 500-word summary of the presenter's work, add references for their sources, and come up with at least three questions they would like to pose after the talk. There are several objectives behind these writing activities. First, students at this stage usually do not fully comprehend the difference between, say, software engineering, operating systems, and artificial intelligence. Listening to experts talking about the field, even when simplified, can lead to a negative experience for the students that have never been truly exposed to this area. However, surveying the area, independently picking sub-areas of interest to read about, and summarizing their findings, creates a framework for the in-class discussions and new levels of engagement during the faculty talks. Second, because grades are not assigned for the quality of writing, this can be seen as a writing-to-learn activity where we get to witness the students' "native" writing capacity with little effort placed on the mechanics, but with the focus on the exploration of concepts and growth as thinkers. This, combined with the multiple iterations of the activity, allows students to model "good" practice for maximizing the gain in CS content one might be exposed to.

This approach can apply with any activity from reading about an area before talking to someone you want to do research with, to reading about an author's work that you are about to meet and talk within a conference.

In the second freshman course, CS-103 (Principles of Computation), the instructors extend the work of the immigration course on communication skills. Students read texts or view videos with the specific intention to communicate a summary to their peers. Such sustained practice encourages students to read with a deep and critical understanding of the content. The readings are short texts on various aspects of computing such as what one would find in Scientific American: they are technical and are very relevant to their education in computer science, but the exposition is very accessible to a non-expert audience. Thus a

deep understanding of these texts will help them expand their horizons as part of this course and their education at CMU-Q. Then students are asked to present a summary of the text as, for instance, a Wikipedia article, in about 300 words, and post these on their web pages that they maintain as part of their immigration course. Students also watch again relevant presentations from, for example, the TED video series and do a similar summary for these. The summaries are then evaluated on both the content and the quality of writing. Academic Resource Center professionals give feedback on writing, while the instructor evaluates the quality of the content presentation. The students are then expected to update their web sites with a revised version of their summaries. Given the restriction of length for these summaries, concision in writing and precision in descriptions and analysis are practiced. Moreover, the introduction of an audience of lay people as the hypothetical intended audience, helps slowly transition to the second part of the model, simulating practice.

Overall, in the three first semesters students are required to engage in sustained practice in writing strategies and ways to summarize material in order to understand central CS concepts.

3.2 Simulating Practice

The second step towards developing expertise with communication skills is to begin simulating the practice. In the technical communication course (CS-221) students work on two projects where they have to simulate practice: first they have to develop job application materials in response to a job or internship advertisement, and then they have to write a proposal on a technical project in response to a request for proposals the instructors create for a real organization. Students, therefore, have to understand the affordances and constraints of real genres in the CS world and produce responses for real audiences, with the exception that these audiences do not receive the materials or act upon them.

These opportunities to simulate practice in CS-221 are framed by discussions and instruction on the ways the genre is enacted in the world. After analyzing the effectiveness of published examples, students can imitate the most effective strategies and apply them in their own projects. For example, for technical audiences the category of "Skills" in a resume is very important, so it has to be positioned appropriately or highlighted in their own resume. Similarly, an objectives section in a proposal can serve as a roadmap and a starting point to describe a methodology, especially for technically complex topics.

These simulations are evaluated both by peers assuming the position of the intended audience and by the instructor who requires students to explain in a separate, reflective document the design and writing decisions they made in consideration of the audience, the purpose and the context of this communicative event, in a similar manner to what Stone and Madigan have described [12]. This way the simulation becomes as close to the real experience as possible.

In Principles of Programming (CS-212), a functional programming course in which students are exposed to a new class of problems that requires a different programming paradigm to be solved, simulating practice is accomplished differently: students read about functional programming "in context." In each assignment,

20% of the grade is reserved for reading an essay, a blog article, a popular science paper or a light scientific paper that talks about the relevance of functional programming or a concrete problem that is related to the ones seen in class. To assess the reading, we ask two kinds of questions: The first is about understanding the content. We ask for a summary or responses to some technical questions. The second is about analyzing the content. We ask open questions that go beyond the topic or we ask for the students' opinion on something related. This way, they have to synthesize information and establish their position on a topic, much like a researcher involved in the current conversation in the field.

Not surprisingly, students have been taking this exercise seriously and consistently give feedback on the reading. Sometimes, the students came back with related articles that they found (and read) on their own. In the past, they had a negative opinion about the course and they were questioning its relevance. One of the reasons was that they did not see how these problems were related to "real life" problems. Indeed, we have always been trying to refer to concrete problems, but it has not always been possible nor desirable. Most of the time, we consider a simplified version of a problem to be able to focus on a very specific concept. However, after this activity where they could place larger disciplinary conversations in context, the course evaluation was very positive. There was a significant change in student opinion and the relevance of the course was no longer questioned.

3.3 Performing in Real Contexts

The last step of the model requires students to engage with real audiences (we will refer to them as "clients") and perform in communication events which are evaluated both by the instructors for the purposes of the course, but also by the clients.

The Technical Communication course (CS-221) introduces students to real communicative performance through a user guide assignment. As user manuals are rarely targeting specific audiences, it is critical for some clients to find people who can help them rewrite (most often condense) or develop from scratch user guides for their constituents. For example, in the Fall 2010 semester students in CS-221 developed user guides for tools and technologies intended to assist people with disabilities. Their client was MADA, the newly formed center for assistive technologies in Qatar, but their audience (who they will have to interact with for feedback and requirements specifications) was people with disabilities. Since students were already familiar with a rhetorical approach to communication, they were able to determine the requirements for their user guides based on information coming from users and the stakeholders. Interacting with real users of documents both in the requirements/drafting stage, and during their revisions makes students feel accountable for the quality of documentation they are producing. At the same time, the clients (MADA in this case), expect (and usually receive) artifacts they could utilize with little or no revision.

Besides the clear social benefit of providing MADA's clients with usable guides to support them in using the tools available to them, it is important to note that students get to see the "messiness" of authentic contexts outside the world of the course, where users and "clients" have real needs, change their minds or even are at odds with each other.

In the course Technology and Global Development (CS-502), students have an extended client project within the emerging field of TFDC (Technology for Developing Communities). One of the course objectives is to "enhance the students' writing and presentation skills." This is because it is important to be able to address many different audiences and not just those with a technology background. The course assignments reflect the kind of communication and writing required when working in TFDC. We find that students need extensive help in addressing assignment requirements, even with reading the assignment descriptions, which are lengthy because of the specificity of what is to be included in the write-up as well as the required focus or viewpoint of the writing. The course assignments are:

1. Research – research a proposed project
2. Campaign – design and implement plan to promote project
3. Capacity building – plan for given projects
4. Case study – critically read and analyze a case

During the early offerings of the course, simulated scenarios were used, sometimes even past real-life scenarios. Students did not seem overly motivated and complained to the course assistants and instructors when they received feedback on their inability to address the assignment requirements. Their comments reflected they were only interested in getting the assignment completed and not for the skill we were expecting them to acquire.

However, designing the same assignments to address a real-life project – one that would be carried out during an actual internship program the following summer, seemed to motivate and interest them in carrying out the assignments. This in turn made it easier from an instruction standpoint to have the students accept feedback and revise the assignments accordingly.

For the Technology Field Research in Developing Communities course (CS-302), the objectives and assignments are much the same as in the Technology and Global Development course except the course is tailored for the students who are the interns for the iSTEP (innovative Student Technology ExPerience) program [19]. The fact that the assignments address areas needed to be able to complete the field work in the upcoming summer aided the students in accepting feedback regarding their communication skills and making improvements in both written work as well as presentations. While it is not possible for the assignments (writing, reading, presentation) in all CS courses to have this real-life perspective, when this happens, it adds an understanding of the purpose for enhancing these skills.

4. DEVELOPING THE MODEL

Based on the previous discussion, it is evident that this grassroots effort by several of the CS faculty on our campus could be formalized into a Communication across the Curriculum (CAC) model, which will follow the tripartite model we described in section 3. We believe students will be able to see the relevance of practicing communication strategies or simulating practice without the evaluation of a real audience at stake.

The most important advantage of this model is that instruction and practice in communication skills is not limited to one course, but can be sustained throughout the curriculum. This approach is markedly different from previous attempts, where the recommendations were primarily centered around practical advice and the inclusion of clear tasks [17]. If students are introduced to the model early on, they will see from the beginning the relevance of all the classroom activities and assignments to professional CS practices, so the development of communication skills will not be viewed as a "distraction" by students (or faculty for that matter).

It is critical, however, that similar evaluation methods, or even the same assessment rubrics, apply for all instructors involved in this model, so as to avoid sending students mixed messages on what is important, correctness or rhetorical effectiveness. Since the sequence of courses is already known and fixed, and most instructors are positively predisposed to incorporating such elements in their courses, a curriculum sequencing exercise on communication skills can serve to make sure the model is sustained throughout the four years.

Finally, a larger assessment effort will have to be undertaken so as to evaluate the effectiveness of this model to support professional communication practices. Employer and alumni surveys can show if our CS graduates can enter the workplace adequately prepared to meet the challenges of rigorous writing and speaking projects.

5. CONCLUSIONS

In this paper, we have discussed a possible approach to incorporating technical communication skills, both written and oral, throughout the CS curriculum. This approach is articulated over three layers: technical practice in individual aspects of the communication act, exercise simulation of actual communication deliverables and performance of actual communication for a real-world audience. As a result of these modifications, we have observed changes in student attitude towards communication and in their performance. At this stage, these observations are purely anecdotal but we are designing a more formal study based on rigorous longitudinal measurements, both within the university as well as by following our students after they graduate. For now, we are observing diminished resistance to writing exercises from the students and better quality of writing and oral presentations.

A similar transformation of mindset is taking place among faculty: the pervasive resistance to incorporating writing and presentations in courses is rapidly vanishing, and in some cases it is enthusiastically being replaced with innovative approaches to fostering communication in their classes.

As our CS program is learning to appreciate the value of including communication in and across the curriculum, we are looking into making it more coordinated, intentional, integrated and pervasive. This will involve channeling our ad-hoc experiments into a more integrated and intentional design, so that different classes can build on each other. In essence, we are attempting to enact a pedagogical model based on aligned learning objectives and assessments in order to finally make instruction in communication skills in CS an activity that both students and faculty understand and willingly engage in.

6. REFERENCES

[1] Computing Curricula 2001: Computer Science, Final Report. Joint Task Force on Computing Curricula, IEEE Computer Society, Association for Computing Machinery, 2001.

[2] Computer Science Curriculum 2008: An Interim Revision of CS 2001, Joint Task Force on Computing Curricula, IEEE

Computer Society, Association for Computing Machinery, 2008. Report from the Interim Task Force.

[3] ABET (2009), Criteria for Accrediting Computing Programs.

[4] ABET Accreditation Self Study (2000), Rensselaer Polytechnic Institute, May 2003.

[5] A. Begel and B. Simon (2008). *Novice Software developers, all over again*, Proceedings of the fourth international workshop on Computing education research ICER 08 , 3-14.

[6] R. Dugan and S. Polanski (2006), "Writing for Computer Science: A Taxonomy of Writing Tasks and General Advice" *Journal of the Consortium of Computing Sciences,* 21:6, 191-203

[7] P. Gruba and R. Al-Mahmood (2004), "Strategies for Communication Skills Development" *Australian Computer Society,* 101-107

[8] R. Adams (2003), "Educating Effective Engineering Designers: the role of Reflective practice" *Design Studies*, 24:3, 275-294

[9] J. Lave and E. Wenger (1991), *Situated Learning: Legitimate Peripheral Participation*, Cambridge University Press, Cambridge UK.

[10] R. D. Pea (1993) "Distributed Intelligence and Designs for Education" in G. Salomon (ed.) *Distributed Cognitions: Psychological and educational considerations,* Cambridge University Press, Cambridge UK.

[11] E Giagrande (2009) "Communication Skills in the CS curriculum" Consortium for Computing Sciences in Colleges, 74-79

[12] J. Stone and E. M. Madigan (2007) "Integrating Reflective Writing in CS" Inroads: the SIGCSE bulletin, 39(2): 42-45.

[13] R. M. Felder and L. K. Silverman. Learning and Teaching Styles in Engineering Education. *Engineering Education*, 78(7):674-681, 1988.

[14] T. Beaubouef (2003). Why Computer Science Students Need Language. Inroads: the SIGCSE bulletin, 35(4): 51-55.

[15] P. Strazdins (2008). "Applying the Community of Practice Approach to Individual IT Projects" Proc. Tenth Australasian Computing Education Conference, Vol. 78: 136-146.

[16] C. Reynolds and C. Fox (2006). "Requirements for a Computer Science Curriculum emphasizing information technology: subject area curriculum issues" *Proceedings of the twenty-seventh SIGCSE technical symposium on Computer science education*, 28 (1): 247-251.

[17] R. Dugan and V. Polanski (2006). "Writing for Computer Science: A Taxonomy of Tasks and General Advice" Journal of the Consortium of Computing Sciences in Colleges, 21 (6): 191-203.

[18] Carnegie Mellon University Online Learning Initiative (April 2011) Available at: http://oli.web.cmu.edu/openlearning/

[19] Carnegie Mellon University, TechBridgeWorld iStep (April 2011), Available at: http://www.techbridgeworld.org

Undergraduate Research: A Case Study

Herman Koppelman
University of Twente
PO Box 217
7500AE Enschede, The Netherlands
+31534894650

H.Koppelman@utwente.nl

Betsy van Dijk
University of Twente
PO Box 217
7500AE Enschede, The Netherlands
+31534893781

E.M.A.G.vanDijk@utwente.nl

Gerrit van der Hoeven
University of Twente
PO Box 217
7500AE Enschede, The Netherlands
+31534893708

G.F.vanderHoeven@utwente.nl

ABSTRACT
This paper describes a one semester research course for undergraduates of computing programs. Students formulate a research proposal, conduct research and write a full paper. They present the results at a one-day student conference. On the one hand we offer the students a lot of structure and support; on the other hand an important feature of the course is that they are in control of their own research. A key aspect of the pedagogical approach is that the students are supervised in small teams by experienced staff. The results of evaluations show that the students are positive about the course. One of the main findings is that they feel well prepared to conduct research in the graduate program.

Categories and Subject Descriptors
K.3.2 [**Computers and Education**]: Computer and Information Science Education – *computer science education.*

General Terms
Human Factors.

Keywords
Undergraduate research.

1. INTRODUCTION
Including meaningful research in undergraduate curricula has several benefits, but it also proposes several challenges. Among the benefits are improved student retention and improved graduate recruitment in computing curricula [2, 3]. A major challenge is to develop a pedagogical approach that is appropriate for students who have no prior research experience and lack many relevant skills, and who therefore need a lot of support.

The benefits and challenges of undergraduate research in computing curricula have been discussed extensively in recent years. Panels have discussed attributes of successful undergraduate research projects [5] and explored ways to encourage and support research experiences for undergraduates

[2, 6]. A panel during ITiCSE 2009 took a global perspective and explored similarities and differences that instructors in different countries face when doing research with undergraduates [1]. Discussed topics were: Why do research with undergraduates? Are students required or encouraged to do research? What are pitfalls or drawbacks? A panel at SIGCSE 2010 focussed on the characteristics of relevant real-world undergraduate research projects [2].

There are several practitioners' reports discussing approaches and experiences with actual research courses in computing [7, 9, 10]. This paper reports the experiences of the department of Computer Science of the University of Twente with undergraduate research. We have been offering Computer Science and Business Information Technology students a research course for several years. A major motivation is that we like to position our university as a research university, with undergraduate research as one of its distinguishing features.

A key characteristic of the course is that it is mandatory. Students perform all activities that are involved in the life cycle of a scientific paper:

- they formulate a research proposal

- they conduct the proposed research and write a full paper

- they review proposals and papers written by fellow students

- they present their work at a student mini conference Twente Student Conference on IT (TSConIT).

Students learn a lot of skills that are needed for producing these deliverables. Accepted papers are included in the proceedings of the conference.

In this paper we describe the course in section 2, the support and structure we offer the students during the course in section 3, and the results and student experiences in section 4. In section 5 we discuss several issues that we feel have been critical for our approach to succeed.

2. DESCRIPTION OF THE COURSE
The course corresponds to 10 ECTS credits ('European credits'), which for students amounts to about 15 hours of study per week. It is a 20 week semester course and it is offered every semester. Usually we have 25-40 enrolments per semester.

Before the course starts, each student chooses one of the 5 or 6 tracks that are usually offered. Each track is related to one or more of the subdomains of computing, such as software engineering, security, information management, human-computer interaction, communication technology. Some students already have a specific problem in mind, but most of them still have to make up their mind.

During the first few weeks they orient themselves on possible research topics, which are suggested by the tracks. They search for and read relevant papers and discuss their findings with their supervisors and fellow students. After about four weeks they write a draft research proposal, which must include:

- a problem description and a few research questions

- a method of answering the research questions and a motivation for the chosen method

- the contribution of the research to the existing knowledge

- a plan for completing the work (conducting the research and writing the paper) on time.

This draft proposal is reviewed by 1 or 2 fellow students, and by the supervisor. Based upon the reviews the students write the final version of the proposal. The students are only allowed to continue the course and actually write the paper if the proposal is approved by the supervisor. If the proposal is rejected, the student has to start again in another semester.

In the second part of the course they conduct the research and write several drafts of the paper. The final draft is reviewed by a few fellow students and by the supervisor. Ultimately they submit a camera ready paper, using one of the prescribed ACM paper templates. The supervisor decides whether this paper is accepted or not for the one day student conference, which is organized as closing event of the course. If the paper is rejected, basically the student has to start again, with a new topic, in another semester. But in many cases, depending upon the circumstances, the student is allowed to finish the same topic in the subsequent semester.

Accepted papers are included in the printed conference proceedings and are presented at the conference. Every track has the possibility to award one paper as the best of the track. These best papers are presented in the plenary session of the student conference TSConIT; the other papers are presented in parallel sessions. Sometimes we invite a keynote speaker.

We give two examples of student research topics.

The first example is about the hidden energy cost of unsolicited ads on the web. Advertising on websites is an important source of income for some companies. But rendering and displaying ads on screen requires CPU-power, and therefore consumes energy. The goal of the research was to investigate this energy consumption. To do so, the researcher measured the difference in energy consumption, while surfing on the web with ads enabled, and with ads blocked. To consistently simulate web browsing, a browser-based tool was created, which periodically opened URLs. After measurements on several PCs with several browsers, it was found that on average the energy consumption caused by advertisements on websites is 2.5 W, which is 3.4 % of the total energy consumption while surfing.

The second example is from the domain of human-computer interaction. The goal of the research was to investigate how people experience an Embodied Conversational Agent (ECA) that uses beeping sounds as expressions of emotional states. The main research questions were: Which beeping sounds can be associated with particular emotions, and will the use of appropriate beeping sounds help in establishing an emotional relationship between an

ECA and the users? The research involved a user study with two groups of users. In one group the ECA communicated its emotions as response to events by sounding appropriate emotional beeps. In the other group the ECA communicated its emotions by random beeps. Qualitative evaluation of questionnaires showed that the ECA producing appropriate sounds was much more positively experienced by the users than the ECA producing random sounds.

3. SUPPORT FOR THE STUDENTS

An important aspect of our approach is the support we offer the students. We take into account that undergraduate students usually have to take considerable steps in the development of the many skills needed for writing a scientific paper. For example, they have yet to experience the problems of finding relevant papers, they have yet to learn to systematically search databases, they must learn how to check relevance, they must learn to read papers critically and to scan papers quickly for usefulness. Moreover, it is the first time students will be conducting research and writing a paper outside the context of a clear and limited assignment which has been carefully prepared for teaching purposes.

As a consequence they need a lot of support. The support we offer is aimed at structuring the *process* of writing a paper and the *products* to be delivered. A key element in structuring the process is a tight schedule, with deadlines for the main deliverables: the research proposal (draft and definite), peer reviews, paper (draft and camera-ready versions) and presentation. Key elements in structuring the products are outlines of the main deliverables: the proposal, the peer reviews and the paper.

This support is delivered in three ways. First, many aspects of research and writing a paper are taught in lectures. Second, the close supervision of students happens in track meetings, which are organized almost every week. Finally, we offer several documents that support the lectures and track meetings.

3.1 Lectures

We offer lectures dealing with:

- finding and processing information, with topics such as: which search tools are useful, how to find relevant papers efficiently and effectively, how to judge the quality of papers, how to reference papers?

- research methodology, with topics such as: which types of research are there, which research methods are there, how should research questions be formulated?

- writing a paper, with topics such as: which types of papers are there, what is the structure of papers, which sections does a paper have, which content does every section have, what is the role of the peer reviewing process in producing scientific knowledge, how to add to the chance of getting your paper accepted?

- the presentation of your paper at a conference, which stresses that preparing a presentation is more than producing slides, and that slides are meant to support the presentation; the students are advised only to start with producing slides after having decided what the presentation is about.

These lectures are supported by links to relevant sources.

3.2 Track Activities

By far the most important component of the structure we offer are the track meetings, which are held nearly every week. In these meetings the students learn about the skills needed for research, they present their experiences and products, and get feedback on them. The meetings are chaired by experienced researchers. The schedule in table 1 shows the main activities in the track meetings, and the main deliverables.

Table 1. Global schedule of activities and deliverables

Week	Main activities	Main deliverables
1	Searching papers Reading papers Formulating research questions Writing draft proposal	
2		
3		
4		
5		Draft proposal
6	Writing peer review Finishing proposal Starting research	Peer review proposal
7		Proposal
8		
9 - 10	No scheduled activities	
11	Conducting research Writing drafts	
12		
13		
14		
15		Draft paper
16	Finishing research Writing peer review Writing camera-ready paper Preparing presentation	Peer review paper
17		
18		Camera-ready paper
19	Attending conference	Presentation

During the first week the objective is to teach students to find relevant papers, using tools such as Scopus and Web of Science, and to 'scan' papers, in order to be able to quickly assess the relevance of sources for their own work. The students' experiences in finding papers and using tools are discussed. Another topic is how to assess the quality of sources. A usual assignment is to ask students to read and summarize papers, focussing upon identifying characteristic components, such as the research questions, the method used, the conclusions, and especially the relevance of the paper for their own work. After a few weeks of reading and orientation the students are asked to write the first drafts of their research proposal, focussing upon formulating the research questions and the method to answer these questions. These drafts are discussed within the track, with an emphasis on the research questions: are they operational, what is their contribution to the existing knowledge and are they specific enough to be answerable within the available time?

After 5 weeks a final draft proposal is submitted, which is reviewed by 1 or 2 other students, and by the supervisor. The reviews are discussed within the track. The students use this information to write the final version of the proposal, which is submitted for a go/no go decision by the supervisor.

In the second part of the semester the research is conducted and the paper is written. The progress of the work is discussed and monitored. If original ambitions appear to be too high, the scope of the work might be narrowed. Several drafts are submitted and discussed. It is discussed how to use a scientific style in writing (to support claims with evidence, to acknowledge other work, ..) and how to reference papers.

A final draft is submitted for a (peer) review by a few students, and the supervisor. These (peer) reviews are discussed, and the camera-ready version of the paper is submitted, to be accepted or rejected by the supervisor. After acceptance of the paper the students prepare a presentation, to be given at the conference.

3.3 Supporting Documents

Several documents are available, which support the lectures and the discussions in the tracks. The most important are:

- an outline of a research proposal, which shows the sections of a proposal

- a checklist for writing a review of a proposal, with the questions to answer in reviewing a proposal

- an outline of a paper, which shows the usual sections and topics (abstract, introduction, research questions, research method, review of literature, and so on) of a scientific paper and which also gives suggestions for the content of sections (for example, it suggests the kind of topics to be discussed in a section Discussion)

- a checklist for writing a review of a paper; this checklist gives the questions to answer in reviewing a paper.

4. EVALUATIONS AND RESULTS

The students evaluate the course by filling in questionnaires during the conference at the end of the semester. Tables 2 and 3 summarize some aggregate results from the last 2 conferences (N = 48, response rate is above 80 %). Table 2 gives results on questions and statements (5-point scale, 1 = not agree, 5 = agree)

Table 2. Evaluation results (5-point scale)

Question	Average score
Did you have enough previous knowledge to start this course?	4.1
I learned a lot about research skills.	4.1
I am confident I can now independently perform scientific research in the Masters courses.	4.0
The course was challenging.	4.3
The course had the appropriate level.	4.2
Track was well-organized.	3.9
If you needed supervision it was available.	4.2
The supervision was of high quality.	4.3

According to the students they have enough knowledge to start the course. They say they learn a lot about doing research and they are confident they will be able to do research in the Masters courses. They experience the course as challenging.

Table 3 gives scores on aspects of the course (10-point scale).

Table 3. Score on course aspects (10-point scale)

Aspect	Average
Conference	7.4
Proceedings	7.3
Track meetings	7.3
Overall score on course	7.2

About 85 % gave a score of 7 or higher (on a 10-point scale) for the overall score, with an average of 7.2. This overall score is similar to overall scores on other Computer Science courses. For example, in the last two terms the average of the evaluated courses was 7.1.

The students are positive about the proceedings. The score on this item is remarkable. Sometimes we have considered cancelling the paper proceedings in favour of electronic ones, but students do not like that idea. Although they belong to the 'internet generation', to be 'in print' is clearly an appealing idea for them.

Students are also positive about the one day conference. The procedure and the atmosphere during the conference resemble a 'real-world' conference. Talks are given with time constraints similar to typical conferences. After the end of each talk questions can be posed. The students pay serious attention to each presentation, and usually they pose relevant questions to the presenters.

The questionnaires also ask the students to mention some strong and weak points of the course. Some typical remarks are:

Strong points

- the freedom you have in choosing a topic and doing research

- supervisor was always willing to help

- I learned a lot about doing research.

Weak points:

- marking procedure is unclear

- I prefer less time for proposal, more for paper.

Most students finish the course within 1 semester. But some students experience serious problems, and drop out during a semester. We offer those students more guidance and support, but occasionally students only succeed after 3 or even more semesters. Some students find the course frightening. We try to identify those students so they can be offered more help.

The papers produced in the course are structured and formatted as would be any 'real world' conference paper. Indeed, it happens frequently that papers are sent to and accepted by external, peer reviewed conferences (usually after some 'polishing' of the paper).

5. DISCUSSION

Experienced faculty have to take into account continually that they have a lot of 'tacit' knowledge, which for students might be quite new. For example, some students might read a paper as a novel, or they might be inclined to present their results as if they are selling a commercial product. Also typical for novices in research is that many of them initially propose to research a problem with too broad a scope for the available amount of time. It takes time to realize that they can only research a minor issue. Supervisors have to realize that they have to be as explicit as possible about the entire process, and about the deliverables.

Several papers [1, 3, 10] discuss whether undergraduate research courses should be elective, or mandatory. Our course is a regular, mandatory course for all students. The experiences with this course have been largely positive. The students value the introduction to research skills. Only a small minority of the students experience real problems with the course.

As argued, we think it necessary to offer our students a lot of structure. But they also need some independence, to explore their own ideas, which might be motivating. Moreover, some independence is required to be able to conduct high-quality research.

When conducting research it is not always clear how to proceed next. One is likely to encounter unexpected problems and uncertainty about how to continue. One might be faced with dead-ends and detours. This is typical for doing research and we do not want to protect our students from such experiences.

The balance between structure and independence is a delicate issue. On the one hand we provide the students with a lot of structure: a tight schedule including many meetings and submission deadlines, a highly structured introduction to conducting research, and outlines of the deliverables. But when actually busy with their own research work, students should feel responsible and in charge of the involved research. We think that the student ownership is an important feature of the research, as is also stressed by others [7]. To achieve this, we give the students the possibility of choosing and formulating their own research. We want to avoid confining students to filling in gaps in existing research projects.

What are the benefits for students of having a research course in their undergraduate program? In literature many benefits are mentioned [2, 3], in the first place improved recruitment for the Masters in computing curricula and improved student retention. From our experience we notice as major benefits that:

- this course can help students understand what might await them in a Masters program, and hence it can support them to decide whether to apply for a Masters degree, or to refrain from doing so

- this course can provide the students with confidence that they can conduct research in Masters courses; indeed, we observed that Masters students are more comfortable conducting research since this course was introduced

- students learn many relevant skills. For example, information literary skills are nowadays very important, as the amount of information is growing explosively. Being able to find relevant sources, to critically and efficiently read sources, and to judge the quality of sources, are necessary skills. Not only (future) Masters students need those skills, but also students who will not apply for a Masters degree. Having some experience in the research process greatly enhances these skills. Our research course provides a natural context to learn these and other research skills.

What about the pedagogical approach of teaching research? Traditionally research has been taught above all in a one-to-one context, which has been called the master-apprentice model [8]. In this context one experienced researcher is guiding one student. Our approach is mainly a one-to-few model, where students are guided in small groups. This model can be seen as an extension of the master-apprentice model [8]. The benefits of this approach are:

- students benefit from the opportunity of seeing others at the same stage in the process; this can encourage students and help them stay on track

- the groups are usually small, so a lot of individual feedback is possible, not only from the supervisor, but also from fellow students

- teaching in small groups is more efficient for staff members than in a one-to-one context; all students are struggling with the same problems, discussions are useful for all students.

During the final stage students are mainly supervised individually, when supervisors are heavily involved in reviewing drafts.

It takes a lot of time for staff to supervise and guide students. But we have no problems in finding enough tracks and enough qualified staff members. In many cases they have a professional research interest in the topics researched, which makes it attractive to be a supervisor.

6. CONCLUSIONS

The research activities are necessarily constrained in scope, but they are genuine and they expose students to the entire process of writing a scientific paper. The resulting papers are of high quality, when one considers the level of the students and the available time.

The course is mandatory. We have largely positive experiences with this aspect. Most students are highly involved in the course and feel responsible for the outcome. The students' evaluations show positive results.

By doing the course students get a clearer picture of what they can expect in the Masters. Hence they are better prepared to decide whether to pursue a Masters degree or not. For some students the experience results in an understanding that they would do better to refrain from it.

7. REFERENCES

[1]   Lawrence D'Antonio, Roger Boyle, Amruth Kumar, Logan Muller, Claudia Roda, and Matti Tedre. 2009. Undergraduate research in CS: a global perspective. *SIGCSE Bull.* 41, 3 (July 2009), 139-140. DOI=10.1145/1595496.1562923 http://doi.acm.org/10.1145/1595496.1562923

[2]   Reynold Bailey, Guy-Alain Amoussou, Tiffany Barnes, Hans-Peter Bischof, and Thomas Naps. 2010. Relevant real-world undergraduate research problems: lessons from the nsf-reu trenches. In *Proceedings of the 41st ACM technical symposium on Computer science education* (SIGCSE '10). ACM, New York, NY, USA, 62-63. DOI=10.1145/1734263.1734283 http://doi.acm.org/10.1145/1734263.1734283

[3]   L. Barker. 2009. Student and Faculty Perceptions of Undergraduate Research Experiences in Computing. *Trans. Comput. Educ.* 9, 1, Article 5 (March 2009), 28 pages. DOI=10.1145/1513593.1513598 http://doi.acm.org/10.1145/1513593.1513598

[4]   Katrin Becker. 2005. Cutting-edge research by undergraduates on a shoestring?. *J. Comput. Small Coll.* 21, 1 (October 2005), 160-168.

[5]   Bhagyavati, Brenda Latka, Guy-Alain Amoussou, and Shivakant Mishra. 2006. Attributes of successful undergraduate research projects. *J. Comput. Small Coll.* 21, 5 (May 2006), 107-109.

[6]   Mary J. Granger, Guy-Alain Amoussou, Miguel A. Labrador, Sue Perry, and Kelly M. Van Busum. 2006. Research experience for undergraduates: successes and challenges. *SIGCSE Bull.* 38, 1 (March 2006), 558-559. DOI=10.1145/1124706.1121513 http://doi.acm.org/10.1145/1124706.1121513

[7]   Tony Greening and Judy Kay. 2002. Undergraduate research experience in computer science education. *SIGCSE Bull.* 34, 3 (June 2002), 151-155. DOI=10.1145/637610.544459 http://doi.acm.org/10.1145/637610.544459

[8]   Hilary J. Holz, Anne Applin, Bruria Haberman, Donald Joyce, Helen Purchase, and Catherine Reed. 2006. Research methods in computing: what are they, and how should we teach them?. *SIGCSE Bull.* 38, 4 (June 2006), 96-114. DOI=10.1145/1189136.1189180 http://doi.acm.org/10.1145/1189136.1189180

[9]   F. E. Sandnes, H-L. Jian, and Y-P. Huang. 2006. Involving Undergraduate Students in Research: Is it Possible?. In 9th International Conference on Engineering Education, 23-28 July, 2006, 1-6.

[10] Karen Ward. 2004. The fifty-four day thesis proposal: first experiences with a research course. *J. Comput. Small Coll.* 20, 2 (December 2004), 94-109.

Bringing Undergraduate Students Closer to a Real-World Information Retrieval Setting: Methodology and Resources

Julián Urbano, Mónica Marrero, Diego Martín and Jorge Morato
University Carlos III of Madrid
Department of Computer Science
Leganés, Madrid, Spain

{ jurbano, mmarrero, dmandres, jmorato }@inf.uc3m.es

ABSTRACT

We describe a pilot experiment to update the program of an Information Retrieval course for Computer Science undergraduates. We have engaged the students in the development of a search engine from scratch, and they have been involved in the elaboration, also from scratch, of a complete test collection to evaluate their systems. With this methodology they get a whole vision of the Information Retrieval process as they would find it in a real-world setting, and their direct involvement in the evaluation makes them realize the importance of these laboratory experiments in Computer Science. We show that this methodology is indeed reliable and feasible, and so we plan on improving and keep using it in the next years, leading to a public repository of resources for Information Retrieval courses.

Categories and Subject Descriptors

K.3.2 [**Computers and Education**]: Computer and Information Science Education – *information systems education*; H.3.4 [**Information Storage and Retrieval**]: Systems and Software – *performance evaluation (efficiency and effectiveness)*.

General Terms

Management, Performance, Experimentation.

Keywords

Information Retrieval, Education, Evaluation, Experiment.

1. INTRODUCTION

Information Retrieval (IR) is the discipline that studies the automatic search for documents and the information they contain in an effective and efficient manner. According to a recent market study, between 2009 and 2020 the amount of digital information in the world will grow by a factor of 44, and yet the staffing and investment to manage it will grow by a factor of just 1.4 [1]. Dealing with this rate difference is a real challenge, and the need for Computer Science (CS) experts with adequate IR knowledge is a clear necessity to alleviate the problem of managing the ever-growing information surrounding us. However, IR courses are not always part of the core program in Computer Science majors [2].

Many decisions in the Computer Science industry are taken on the basis of mere experience and bias towards or against certain technologies. Thus, it is imperative for CS professionals to have sufficient background on basic experimental methods and training

on critical analysis of experimental studies [3]. There are very few courses that can really show CS students how to run computer-related laboratory experiments and analyze their validity. Information Retrieval courses are very suitable for this purpose because it is a highly experimental discipline with a major focus on the evaluation of search engine effectiveness [4]. However, the experimental aspect of IR is not that common in IR courses [2].

In the University Carlos III of Madrid, the course on Information Retrieval is an elective course for senior CS undergraduates, where we discuss several aspects of IR with a special focus on the Web. In the Spring 2010 edition we incorporated many changes to assess the feasibility of a much more experimental-oriented program to resemble, as closely as possible, a real-world scenario where IR techniques are needed to manage relatively large amounts of digital information. This last year we have had 32 students and 5 faculty members available for the experiment, 2 of which are the course instructors. We developed with the students a brand new test collection of web documents, and a meta-analysis with well-established techniques shows that using such collections is indeed trustworthy for an IR course. In this paper we show how we adapted the methodology followed in TREC (Text Retrieval Conference) [5] and the results obtained with it.

The rest of the paper is organized as follows. Section 2 briefly revises other IR courses taught and analyzes critical factors missed. Next, we describe how we adapted our course to cover those factors, and in Section 4 we show that the collection created by students is indeed reliable for an IR course. Section 5 finishes with conclusions and lines for future work.

2. CURRENT IR COURSES

The development of IR systems from scratch or based on existing technology is a widely used method to teach IR in Computer Science. Some promote the use of frameworks or tools that can be customized and extended by students. The trouble in using these tools is variable, and some authors consider that these frameworks should be simple enough to use, for the students to focus on the course concepts rather than struggle with their intricacies [6]. For instance, IR Base [7] allows the integration of components, documentation and services so that prototypes can be quickly developed for research and educational purposes. Other free tools to build search engines are Alkaline, Greenstone and SpidersRUs, recently compared by students [8]. It is also frequent to find open source tools such as Lucene and Lemur for educational purposes.

But it is also possible to guide students through the development of an IR system from scratch. This approach is only possible in clearly technology-oriented majors, as it is necessary to have a good deal of experience on software development, algorithms, data structures, database management, etc. This need, obviously, has to be taken into account to evaluate the difficulty of the course assignments. In return, students get a much wider view of the techniques and processes explained in the lectures. Examples of this approach can be found in the "Build your search engine in 90 days" method [9] and others applied to Digital Libraries [10].

As to the evaluation of IR systems, the IEEE/ACM Computer Curricula establishes the importance of the Scientific Method in CS, and the necessity for students to learn it [3]. Some tools such as ONTAP [11] have been used to evaluate query performance in terms of classical precision and recall measures, but knowledge concerning evaluation methods is hardly found in IR curricula, let alone the design and analysis of experiments [2]. Students usually learn how to build an IR system, but they do not always learn how to evaluate it. Evaluation laboratory experiments are very useful in Computer Science to verify and tune tools being developed, and even in less technical majors like Library Science (LS) it is essential to choose the adequate tool on the basis of usability, effectiveness and efficiency. It is also interesting from the point of view of research, as these experiments tackle some issues widely studied by the IR research community and yet to be solved.

Furthermore, the solution of problems in CS demands capabilities with data analysis and experimentation, but for them to be meaningful they must be carried out under real-world conditions [12]. In the case of IR it is not always possible to freely access representative document collections and distribute them among the students. Some tools incorporate document collections and evaluation components. However, these resources are very limited and it is difficult to find diversity in terms of domain and documental types. It is therefore normal in IR courses to stick to the same test collection for several years.

Therefore, students should be able to use existing tools as long as they do not lose sight of the main purpose of their assignment; or develop their own as long as they are guided not to focus just on the implementation. Also, they should be involved in the evaluation of their systems to appreciate and understand the problems it bears. Finally, teaching resources are scarce in IR, and so it would be desirable that all resources elaborated by the students be somehow reused in the following years.

3. NEW TEACHING METHODOLOGY

3.1 Search Engine

The main lab assignment in our course consists in developing, from scratch, a complete IR system for web pages using C#. These systems are developed in 3 modules to hand in separately: a naïve retrieval system implementing some basic retrieval model; an extension to include query expansion; and the adaptation to identify named entities such as persons and localizations. To facilitate the development of their systems, we provided the students with the skeleton of a web crawler [13] and a framework to model the IR process their systems undergo, as well as to evaluate their effectiveness with the test collection. The development of the actual IR techniques has been guided by the course instructors, but no source code was provided in this case.

3.2 Test Collection

A test collection for Information Retrieval evaluation is made up of three basic components: a document collection, a set of information needs (usually called topics), and the relevance judgments (usually assessed by humans) telling what documents are relevant to the topics [4]. The systems to evaluate are run for each topic and return documents in the collection deemed relevant to the topic. Then, some effectiveness measures are used to assess, according to the relevance judgments, how well the systems actually answered the information needs.

The TREC conferences, organized by NIST, have traditionally followed a well-studied methodology to evaluate IR systems. In a typical TREC ad-hoc setting, the document collection is selected first, depending on the specific purpose and characteristics of the task [5]. Then, each relevance assessor available comes up with a set of candidate topics and estimates the difficulty and number of relevant documents with the help of a search engine. Out of all candidate topics, usually 50 of them are selected for the test collection. Both the document collection and the topic set are made public for the participants, who run their systems and submit a ranked list with the first 1,000 documents per topic. Then, NIST forms pools of documents for each topic, taking the first 100 documents (the pool depth) from each participating run. Depending on the particular topic complexity, the pool sizes vary significantly, as for some topics the systems tend to return the same results (leading to small pool sizes) and for others they differ greatly (leading to larger pools). The documents in these pools are the ones judged for relevance, and documents not in the pools are considered to be not relevant.

In our case, the methodology to create the test collection has to be different. First of all, the document collection cannot be as big as TREC's because undergraduate students do not have the appropriate level to handle that much information efficiently. Indexing and storing such collections requires a level of knowledge and expertise that these students do not have yet, restricting the size of the collection they can handle without much trouble. Because of this constraint, the election of topics has to be careful. We decided that all topics should have a common theme so that the document collection would not have to be too heterogeneous and hence be too large. We opted for all topics to be related to computing, as it sure is a theme attractive to Computer Science students. Thus, the test collection depends on the topics and not the other way around as usual.

The problem at this point is how to create the document collection assuring that at least some relevant material is included for every topic. We decided to issue queries to Google just as if we were trying to answer the information needs and find as much relevant material as possible (manually considering term proximity, query expansion, etc.). Doing so, we could discard topics apparently too difficult or for which there appeared to be no clearly relevant web pages. We narrowed down the topic set to 20 computing-related topics (plus 2 noisy topics, see below). Using a focused crawler [13], similar to the one developed by the students, we downloaded all results that Google returned for each topic. The union of these web pages was our complete document collection (see Table 1).

Now that we had documents and topics, we needed relevance judgments. There is another glaring difference here for us: it would not be safe to have the students judge documents once they have submitted their results, as some might try cheating and judge relevant all documents retrieved by their system. Therefore, we had to come up with a solution to create a reliable pool of documents and have the students judge them *before* they even start the development of their systems. We decided to create pools from the results of well-known and freely available IR tools such as Lemur and Lucene. These systems implement most of the techniques we regularly teach in our course, so it is fair to expect the student systems to retrieve similar documents. Thus, we configured 8 Lemur and 4 Lucene instances with different IR techniques (call these the pooling systems) and ran them with the documents and topics we developed. The pools formed with these systems are the ones the students judged and the ones they actually used for their systems (call this the biased collection).

Table 1. Summary of topics: documents contributed to the complete and biased collections, pool size and depth, and assessor agreement, when possible. * for topics judged by one faculty member, ** judged by two faculty members. † for the noisy topics.

Topic	Downloaded	Pool size	Pool depth	Kappa	Precision	Recall
001	328	100	28	0.362	0.811	0.545
002	417	100	26	0.243	0.233	1.000
003	616	100	30	0.517	0.906	0.829
004	220	102	25	0.470	0.769	0.638
005*	417	101	17	-	-	-
006**	768	102	19	0.468	0.622	0.821
007	547	100	25	0.456	0.889	0.429
008	729	100	23	0.096	0.818	0.164
009	374	100	37	0.625	1.000	0.550
010	609	101	26	0.217	1.000	0.111
011	218	100	56	0.192	0.250	0.500
012*	338	100	19	-	-	-
013	384	100	21	0.333	0.269	1.000
014	247	100	58	0.342	0.595	0.556
015	435	102	34	0.624	0.810	0.791
016	417	103	28	0.433	0.526	0.741
017	516	101	23	0.574	0.500	0.571
018	474	101	20	0.735	0.895	0.773
019*	488	100	15	-	-	-
020	459	105	20	0.395	0.278	0.833
021†	79	-	-	-	-	-
022†	689	-	-	-	-	-
Average	444	100.90	27.5	0.417	0.657	0.638
Total	9,769	1,967	-	-	-	-

But there is another difference with TREC here: if we took the first k documents (the pool depth) from the 12 pooling systems, the pool size could be very big for certain topics. Consider for instance topic 019, where each pooling system contributed only 15 documents to the pool. If we had taken around 27 documents, as the average resulted, the pool for topic 019 would have probably had around 200 documents to judge. If some students were assigned a pool this large, they could just stop judging or judge carelessly once they think they have done enough work compared to their classmates. To prevent this situation, we decided to pool documents until the pool had a minimum size of 100, making each topic's pool to have a different depth.

To measure the quality of the judgments made by students, we decided to include in those (at least) 100 documents 10 noisy documents not related to any topic, so that we could check afterwards whether students actually judged them non-relevant or not (we obtained these documents by issuing two queries to Google explicitly excluding the terms in the other 20 topics). Also, to be sure that the pools had some relevant documents, we added the first 10 results given by Google for each topic, as we checked before, when selecting topics, that some relevant material was found by Google. Therefore, all pools have 10 noisy documents, the first 10 documents retrieved by Google, and documents retrieved by the pooling systems up to a minimum of 100 documents altogether.

Documents for topic 006 were judged by two faculty members, topic 005 was judged by one faculty member, and topics 012 and 019 were judged by the two course instructors (one topic each). The other 16 topics were judged by the 32 students, two students per topic. Note that the two noisy topics needed not be judged. All documents were judged on a 3-point relevance scale (not relevant, somewhat relevant and highly relevant). Of all the 326 judgments on noisy documents, only once did a student judge the document as relevant. Therefore, we decided to trust the relevance judgments to some degree.

As can be seen in Table 1, the complete collection has 9,769 documents (735 MB) and 20 topics (plus the two noisy topics: 021 and 022). The biased collection (made up just by the pooled documents) has a total of 1,967 documents (161 MB). The pool sizes ranged from 100 to 105, so all students judged the same amount of documents (it took them about 2 hours to complete the task). However, the pool depths varied considerably, ranging from 15 (topic 019) to 58 (topic 014). This shows that the pooling systems tended to agree much more for some topics than others, which is to be expected considering the diversity in the topics purposes and difficulty, which agrees with current IR practice.

3.3 Search Engine Evaluation

While the students had a previous, much smaller collection to test their systems before submission, the evaluation of each of their three modules has been performed by the course instructors using the very test collection elaborated with the students. This evaluation followed well accepted criteria and effectiveness measures traditionally used in TREC [5]. In particular, we evaluated their effectiveness with NDCG (Normalized Discounted Cumulative Gain) [14]. This measure allows us to easily assess not only if the systems retrieve relevant material, but whether it is ranked properly, that is, with the most relevant documents before the less relevant ones. The measure ranges from 0 (no relevant information is retrieved at all) to 1 (all relevant information in the collection is retrieved at the best possible ranks).

We also evaluate the continuous learning process, as the development of the search engine is incremental and the students can further improve previous modules when submitting new ones, which they actually did. We also consider the difficulty of the IR techniques they decide to implement, their understanding and evaluation, which should be reflected in the reports they have to submit and present with each module. Also, the lab sessions are useful to assess the teamwork capabilities of the students.

4. RELIABILITY OF THE COLLECTION

The critical point of our methodology is the reliability of the test collection developed with the students. This type of IR evaluations has two main drawbacks: the inconsistency and incompleteness of relevance judgments [4][15][16]. Topical relevance is highly subjective, and some people might judge the same document differently, sometimes even the same person judges the same document differently over time. Therefore, the use of different judges to assess the relevance of documents could make the evaluation results inconsistent and little reliable, as some systems could benefit more from some judges than others. On the other hand, it is important to note that only the documents in the pools are judged for relevance, and every document outside the pool is considered non-relevant. As such, the judgments are incomplete, and if the student systems returned documents not included in the pool they would be penalized, even if some of them were actually relevant.

TREC test collections are generally considered reliable because they are built with many documents, topics and systems, and they have enough man-power to judge tens of thousands of documents. Inconsistency of judgments could be accentuated in our case because they are made by undergraduate students rather than trained IR experts, and the very small scale of our experiments could make the pools too incomplete to be reliable. The effect of these problems has been studied in TREC for over a decade with well accepted meta-evaluation techniques [15][16]. Next, we show the results of this meta-analysis in our collection to assess its reliability and hence the feasibility of the whole methodology.

4.1 Inconsistency of Judgments

4.1.1 Assessor Agreement

For 17 of the 20 topics we collected judgments from two different students (faculty members in the case of topic 006). We measured the agreement between each topic's two assessors using Cohen's Kappa (equal weights), resulting in an average score of 0.417 (see Table 1), which can be considered fairly high. We also measured the precision and recall of one student's judgments according to the other's, and the averages were 0.657 and 0.638. These results agree exceptionally well with Ellen Voorhees' finding that a practical upper bound on performance is 65% precision at 65% recall, as that is the level at which TREC's experts tended to agree with one another [15]. As such, the judgments from our students seem reliable compared to TREC's.

4.1.2 Effect on System Performance

Despite the students apparently tended to agree on the relevance judgments, the differences found could still have an impact on the evaluation of their systems. For 17 topics we have judgments from two assessors, and we can measure the effect of having used one or the other by randomly choosing one assessor per topic and then combining them all across topics.

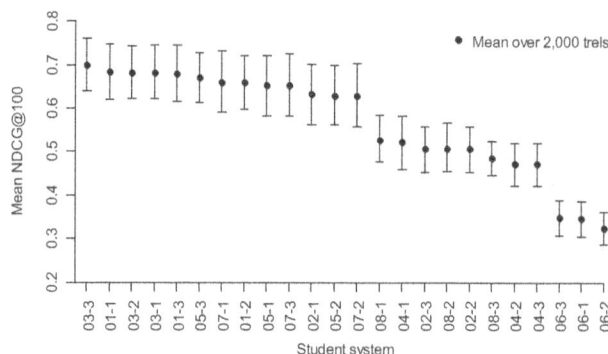

Figure 1. Mean, minimum and maximum NDCG@100 score for the student systems over a sample of 2,000 trels.

We made 2,000 such random combinations (call each of these a *trel* or topic relevance list) and used them to re-evaluate the student systems (see Figure 1). The differences between minimum and maximum NDCG@100 scores ranged from 0.075 and 0.146 across systems, which are about 1.5 times larger than those found for TREC data [15]. This is to be expected though, as our students have far less experience than TREC assessors, our judgments are inherently more variable because they are on a 3-point scale rather than the 2-point scale used in TREC, and the absolute effectiveness of the student systems was itself larger than those evaluated in TREC (about twice as much).

4.1.3 Effect on System Ranking

The interesting result of an IR evaluation experiment is not really how well the systems perform in absolute terms, as this highly depends on the particular test collection used, but rather what systems perform better; that is, their relative ranking. For example, in Figure 1 it can be seen that system 03-2 (module 2 by student group 03) performed much better than system 08-3. Because the actual effectiveness of the systems depend on the relevance judgments used, it is interesting to see how the final ranking of systems varies with one set of judgments or another. We measured this variation with Kendall's tau correlation coefficient between 2,000 random pairs of system rankings generated by random trels. The average correlation was 0.926, ranging from 0.811 to 1. This indicates that the final ranking of

systems is quite stable to variations in judgments, compared to Voorhees' findings with TREC data (an average coefficient of 0.938 [15]). Indeed, none of the ranking swaps between two systems were significant (Wilconxon, α=0.05).

4.2 Incompleteness of Judgments

4.2.1 Effect of Pool Size

Small pool sizes with incomplete relevance judgments are not reliable because many relevant documents could be left out of the pool. However, large pools are more expensive to evaluate, and because our assessors are the students themselves we need to find a reasonable midpoint for reliable pools at the minimum cost. We can assess the effect of progressively incrementing the pool size and re-evaluating the student systems to measure the differences in effectiveness that the pool size increment causes. We started with pools of just 20 documents (the 10 top results in Google and the 10 noisy documents), and re-evaluated the systems for average NDCG@100 score. Next, we incremented the pool sizes to 25 documents, and re-evaluated again. The increment in NDCG@100 score ranged between 14.55% and 37.13%. We kept doing this with increments of 5 documents up until the last increment from pool sizes 95 to 100 documents (see Figure 2). The increment in NDCG@100 performance here ranged from 0.4% to 1.63%, with an average of just 1%.

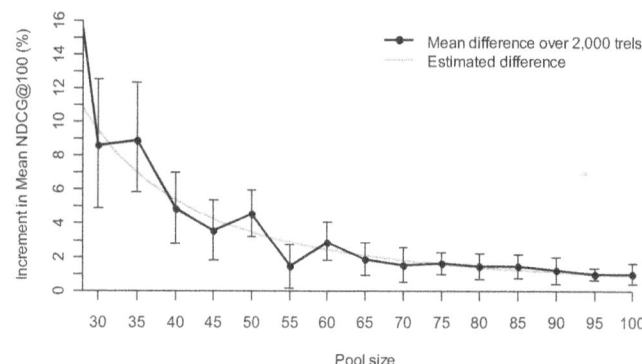

Figure 2. Mean, minimum and maximum increment in NDCG@100 score for the student systems evaluated with 2,000 trels, for different pool size increments (20 and 25 omitted for clarity). Estimation is plotted in grey.

As the figure shows, differences in performance decrease as pool size increases, because as the pools get larger there are fewer relevant documents yet to be discovered. Average performance differences were found between 0.5% and 3.5% in TREC data, with some observations of up to 19% [16]. In our case, differences in this range can be found for pool sizes of about 60-65 documents and more, so our collection is fairly reliable despite the small pool sizes and the fact that none of the student systems contributed directly to the pools.

4.2.2 Extrapolation from Pool Size

Using the points in Figure 2, we can extrapolate the average increment in NDCG@100 scores for pools over 100 documents. If the increments decreased considerably for small additions to the pools, we could consider having a few more documents to judge for the sake of completeness and stability of results. We fitted a non-linear regression model (see gray curve in Figure 2), according to which we would need to have about 135 documents per pool to have average increments in NDCG@100 below 0.5%. Therefore, it does not seem reasonable to increment the pool sizes that much, considering that the average increment is just 1% for pools with 100 documents and 35 more are just too many for such a small improvement.

5. CONCLUSIONS AND FUTURE WORK

Information Retrieval courses do not always pay much attention to the IR process as a whole. We believe, though, that it is very important for students to be involved in the process from the very beginning, not using any data or tool as given. In particular, it is of major importance for undergraduate students to focus on the actual techniques learned in class rather than on particular technologies, as well as getting used to laboratory experimental settings. In IR courses, these evaluations usually take place with small test collections that are maintained from year to year, with the students facing always the same documents, the same topics and the same relevance judgments beforehand. Therefore, we updated the program of our IR course to give more importance to evaluation experiments, involving the students in the development and use of a brand new test collection.

We have described how to adapt TREC's ad-hoc methodology to build such collections for an IR course. The first main difference is that the documents in the collection are gathered after selecting the topics, and not the other way around as usual. The second main difference is related to the pools of documents to judge. The systems developed by the students cannot contribute directly to the pools to prevent cheating, and the judging effort is limited because the students cannot be asked to judge as many documents as we would want. Due to this limitation, the pools are formed differently, with the help of freely available IR tools. With typical meta-analysis techniques we measured the reliability of this methodology in terms of judgments inconsistency and incompleteness. We observed high agreement scores between students, and very high correlations between their systems when using different sets of relevance judgments. In terms of pool reliability, we estimated that pools of size 100 and different depths are quite reliable and do not seem to affect the evaluation significantly. We conclude that the judgments made by students can be trusted, and that the pooling method proposed seems to work reasonably well for these small-scale evaluations.

Having students participate in the whole process of building a test collection helps them realize the complexities and limitations of IR evaluations, especially regarding the concept of relevance and the scale of the evaluation itself, and gives them a good sense of empirical experiments for computer-related tasks. The results in our pilot experiment have been satisfactory both in terms of reliability of the collection and response by the students. Their reviews by the end of the semester show that apparently they had more technical problems this year (the score dropped from 3.27 to 2.82, over 5), unveiling possible gaps in the CS program, especially in terms of database technology and big data management. Nonetheless, they showed the same satisfaction levels as previous years, which is very appealing for us given that this year they had to work significantly more than previous students, and carrying out a pilot study like this always bears daily, intangible logistics problems both for them and for us.

We plan on improving the methodology and build one new collection each year. A clear benefit of this is that each year the students will have more and more small test collections to train and tune their systems, which helps them in the development and improvement phases. Moreover, beginning the next year we will have considerably more students, and so more collaborative methodologies can be explored to build larger collections, or maybe two different ones with different purposes. We are also planning the coordination of this course with another CS course where students have to develop a large application based on already available components, and a Library Science course where students are more focused on the user side of the IR process. The idea is that the students in the development course could develop better tools and frameworks for the IR students to build their search engines, and the LS students to contribute to the test collections for them to be more realistic and reliable.

The collection and frameworks described in this paper are publicly available for research and educational purposes at http://ir.kr.inf.uc3m.es. All forthcoming collections will be freely available as well, with reports commenting on their development.

ACKNOWLEDGEMENTS

We would like to thank the students that participated in this pilot experiment for their effort and understanding, as well as Sonia Sánchez-Cuadrado. We would also like to thank Ellen Voorhees for her comments on the inconsistency analysis.

REFERENCES

[1] J. Gantz and D. Reinsel. *The Digital Universe Decade, Are You Ready?* IDC iView, 2010.

[2] J.M. Fernández-Luna, J.F. Huete, A. MacFarlane, and E.N. Efthimiadis. Teaching and Learning in Information Retrieval. *Journal of Information Retrieval.* 12(2): 201-226, 2009.

[3] IEEE/ACM. Computing Curricula 2001. http://www.acm.org/education/curricula-recommendations.

[4] E.M. Voorhees. The Philosophy of Information Retrieval Evaluation. In *CLEF Workshop*, pages 355-370, 2002.

[5] E.M. Voorhees and D.K. Harman. *TREC: Experiment and Evaluation in Information Retrieval.* MIT Press, 2005.

[6] N. Madnani and B.J. Dorr. Combining Open-Source with Research to Re-Engineer a Hands-On Introductory NLP Course. In *Workshop on Issues in Teaching Computational Linguistics*, pages 71-79, 2008.

[7] P. Calado, A. Cardoso-Cachopo, and A.L. Oliveira. IR-BASE: An Integrated Framework for the Research and Teaching of Information Retrieval Technologies. In *Int. Workshop on Teaching and Learning of Inf. Retrieval*, 2007.

[8] M. Chau, C.H. Wong, Y. Zhou, J. Qin, and H. Chen. Evaluating the Use of Search Engine Development Tools in IT Education. *JASIST.* 61(2): 288-299, 2010.

[9] M. Chau, Z. Huang, and H. Chen. Teaching Key Topics in Computer Science and Information Systems Through a Web Search Engine Project. *ACM Journal on Educational Resources in Computing.* 3(3), 2003.

[10] D.G. Hendry. History Places: A Case Study for Relational Database and Information Retrieval System Design. *ACM Journal on Educational Resources in Computing.* 7(1), 2007.

[11] K. Markey and P. Atherton. *ONTAP: Online Training and Practice Manual for ERIC Data Base Searchers*, 1978.

[12] G. Braught, C.S. Miller, and D. Reed. Core Empirical Concepts and Skills for Computer Science. *ACM SIGCSE Bulletin.* 36(1): 245-249, 2004.

[13] J. Urbano, J. Lloréns, Y. Andreadakis, and M. Marrero. Crawling the Web for Structured Documents. In *ACM International CIKM Conference*, pages 1939-1940, 2010.

[14] K. Järvelin and J. Kekäläinen. Cumulated Gain-Based Evaluation of IR Techniques. *ACM Transactions on Information Systems.* 20(4): 422-446, 2002.

[15] E.M. Voorhees. Variations in Relevance Judgments and the Measurement of Retrieval Effectiveness. *Information Processing and Management.* 36(5): 697-716, 2000.

[16] J. Zobel. How Reliable are the Results of Large-Scale Information Retrieval Experiments? In *International ACM SIGIR Conference*, pages 307-314, 1998.

AnimalSense: Combining Automated Exercise Evaluations with Algorithm Animations

Guido Rößling
Technische Universität
Darmstadt
Dept. of Computer Science
64289 Darmstadt, Germany
roessling@acm.org

Mihail Mihaylov
Technische Universität
Darmstadt
Dept. of Computer Science
64289 Darmstadt, Germany
mistemi@gmail.com

Jerome Saltmarsh
Queensland University of
Technology
IT Department
Brisbane QLD 4001, Australia
jerome_saltmarsh@hotmail.com

ABSTRACT

Exercises with an automatic evaluation can be helpful for students, if they cover meaningful tasks and are sufficiently challenging. We have designed an exercise system that combines exercise tasks with automatic evaluation and integrated algorithm animation. The paper describes the current status and sample tasks our system can handle.

Categories and Subject Descriptors

K.3.2 [**Computers and Education**]: Computer & Information Science Education - *Computer Science Education*

General Terms

Management

Keywords

CS1, exercise, support, automatic evaluation, animation

1. INTRODUCTION

Algorithms and data structures play a central role in many areas of computing education, especially in the first few semesters. Students typically need to become familiar with a large number of different algorithms and data structures. To ensure that they have understood these materials, they may be asked to implement some algorithms or answer questions, often in the form of homework assignments.

While the type of "submission" for such problems can be in many different forms or media, we will consistently use the (simplifying) term "exercise" for all such problems given to students for the remainder of this paper. This lets us abstract from homework or programming assignments, voluntary tasks, tasks in textbooks, hand-written solutions, sub-' mission of source (or compiled) code in some programming language, and other forms of (potentially digital) content.

In this paper, we will first define the type of exercises we are targetting. We will then examine the state of art in related exercise support systems. In Section 4, we present the design for our exercise support system, followed by a brief description of how the system works. Section 6 provides some illustrative examples of exercise tasks that our system can currently handle. We conclude the paper with a summary and areas of further research in Section 7.

2. TARGETED EXERCISE TASKS

A typical exercise for sorting algorithms is to "manually execute" the given algorithm. While students should be able to do so, we think that there are more interesting—and at least partially more advanced—tasks that could be given. We provide a short list of such questions here, all selected for a given array and an specific implementation of Quicksort and the associated pivot choice strategy:

- What is the total number of swaps for this array?

- What will be the third pivot element?

- What will be the final position of the value initially at position 2?

- How often will the value 5 change its position during the execution of Quicksort?

- In which recursive call will 6 be the pivot element (please enter 0 for "never", otherwise 1...n)?

- With which element will value 4 be swapped in its first swap (please enter 0 if 4 is never swapped)?

- What value should be used for -100 in the array so that this element does not change its position?

- Provide an input array of at least length 10 so that the second pivot element chosen will be at position 5.

We believe that all of these questions are valid and that a good student should be able to work out correct or almost correct answers for them. Some of the questions may require the student to either manually trace the algorithm until "the right point", or to apply a deeper understanding of the algorithm to reach the correct answer. Of course, we usually hope for the latter, but also appreciate the possible learning gained from the former approach.

We are not interested in providing these questions as a multiple choice quiz, where students may easily "determine" the correct answer by simply trying out all possible (predefined and visible) answers in any order. Additionally, we do not want to hard-code the correct answer, although this would make automated evaluation very easy. Each of the above questions would work equally well with *any* array that contains (at least) the values referrred to in the question. Accordingly, we want to be able to provide a broad range of related exercises, perhaps even with almost identical questions, but where the input arrays are different. This allows students who have solved a given question correctly to try the same question on a different array, in order to validate if they have really understood the algorithm and can thus transfer their answer. At the same time, the system should avoid creating a huge workload for the student.

Based on the *Engagement Taxonomy* [9], we want students to be more actively involved than merely copying answers from mostly a passively viewed visualization. Thus, tracing the execution of Quicksort is out of scope for this paper: the student only has to open a visualization of Quicksort on the given parameter, "fast forward" to the proper positions, and write down the state of the array at these positions. Conversely, while the answer to some of the above questions can also be found in a visualization of the algorithm, extracting it (e.g., by going through it step by step and counting the number of swaps) may actually cause more effort than trying to manually determine the answer!

To raise the attractivity of the system for educators, the amount of work needed to transfer one exercise set to another by changing concrete variable or parameter values should be as low as possible. Apart from editing the inpt parameters, the educator should *not have to determine the (changed) correct answer*, since this can result in much work for some of the above questions. Instead, the system shall be able to automatically determine the correct answer, so that the educator has to replace *only* the input parameters and modify their occurrence in the questions, where applicable.

Our desired system should thus be able to:

1. Support "interesting" questions that ask about details in the algorithm's behavior.

2. Allow the student to specify input parameters which shall cause a certain behavior; for example, see the last example in the above list.

3. Provide automated feedback on whether the student's answer was correct or not.

4. Support creating new exercises from existing ones by simply replacing the input parameters and/or the question text, without having to manually determine the correct (changed) answer.

5. Reduce the student's manual workload by visualizing the behavior of the algorithm on request.

6. Integrate the visualization of the algorithm on both the given parameters and on student-provided parameters for reflection and further exploration.

3. RELATED WORK

Several approaches have been developed to support the grading of exercise tasks. For example, students can submit their work digitally in a learning platform, such as *Moodle*

[3]. There are also initiatives to augment learning management systems to better address computing education requirements [13]. Depending on the type of tasks, the answer may be graded automatically or wait for a human grader.

Other systems visualize algorithms to help students understand how they behave. Such "algorithm/program visualization" systems have been very well documented [7, 8, 12]. Some systems already combine visualization with learning materials, often in so-called hypertextbooks [10, 14, 15] which directly include the visualizations inside the page or start the tool using Java WebStart once the user clicks on the associated link. Alternatively, the visualization system can be started within a learning management system [7, 15]. Visualization systems typically do not support questions or are restricted to multiple-choice questions, and cannot handle questions such as outlined in Section 2.

Some visualization systems can also visualize the algorithm based on user-provided input data, for example JHAVÉ [8] and ANIMAL [11]. Other systems like Trakla2 [6], Matrix2 (which is also used in Trakla2) [5], and the recently introduced Jype [4], provide "algorithm simulation exercises". Here, the student has to manually perform a given algorithm, typically by dragging elements to their new or target position or clicking on buttons to cause a certain function, e.g., a rotation in an AVL tree. While this can be very helpful for students, the focus of this approach is not suited for our intentions.

Since none of the established tools could support the operations that we wanted, we set out to design our own system, which we will describe in the next Section.

4. SYSTEM DESIGN

Based on the requirements described in the previous Sections, students shall be able to select an exercise in the system, answer the exercise questions and submit their answers. After submission, they shall receive an almost instanteous feedback on whether the answer was correct. Additionally, the system shall prepare an animation of the algorithm and allow students to access this animation. The animation shall help students in seeing what actually happened and thus pinpoint where and what they may have misunderstood.

This system requires a number of different functionalities:

1. The system must be able to simulate or execute the selected algorithm.

2. It must be able to visualize the selected algorithm.

3. It must be able to evaluate the student's answer.

4. Writing a new exercise should not require changing any existing (Java) code.

We decided to base the implementation of our system on the established ANIMAL system, since this system already supports the ad-hoc generation of animation content based on user-provided data [11]. It therefore directly fulfills requirements 1 and 2. Generating a visualization based on user input does not require any special effort from the educator, assuming that a suitable generator already exists.

We wanted to ensure that the system is also usable by educators with limited or no Java programming experience. The determination whether the answer was correct should thus not occur in the generator or in the underlying algorithm, as this would require programming and code modifications whenever a new exercise question was implemented.

Instead, we have decided to use checkpoints, similarly to the "interesting events" used in several algorithm visualization systems since the 1980s [2]. This means that at the places where something "interesting" happens, the educator inserts an API call similar to the one shown in Figure 3 to store all relevant attributes and local variables into the checkpoint. Since this API call always has the same essential form, doing so does not require much programming skill. Based on the checkpoint data, the system will use a sequence of operations to determine if the question was answered correctly. The student then receives appropriate feedback. The student can also click on a button to see the animation of the concrete execution.

The execution proceeds as follows:

1. The student selects an exercise file, written in XML.

2. The XML specification is deserialized into concrete exercise-related objects.

3. The exercise is displayed to the student together with the associated exercise tasks.

4. The student provides input data, usually parameter values or answers to questions.

5. The algorithm is run on the input specified by educator and/or student. While the algorithm is running, relevant data is collected for use in the next step.

6. A script determines if the student's input led to the expected result. It retrieves data entries from the checkpoints based on the logic implemented in the script. More information on this script is given in the next section. Based on the result of this process, appropriate feedback is generated and shown to the student.

   The student can also click on a "Show me" button to see an animation of the algorithm, which may highlight the parts of the process relevant to the current task.

An example of the student view, together with a graded answer submission, is shown in Figure 1.

5. A BRIEF LOOK BEHIND THE SCENES

This Section provides an overview of the system for determining if a student answer was correct. We first look at the evaluation scripts and then examine how a given code needs to be modified to dump the relevant data.

5.1 Evaluation Script

An evaluation script is used to determine if the user's answer was correct. The goal of designing this script notation was to make it easy to use for educators. The evaluation script uses JXPath [1], a W3C-standardized notation used for navigating and querying graphs. The "graph" to be navigated in our case is the data gathered from the checkpoints.

Scripts can use variables to store results of any type, such as int values or complete lists of events. Currently, only ten functions are available, as follows:

Animate(x) processes a list of checkpoints or events x and ensures that the associated animation steps are indicated in the table of contents for this animation.

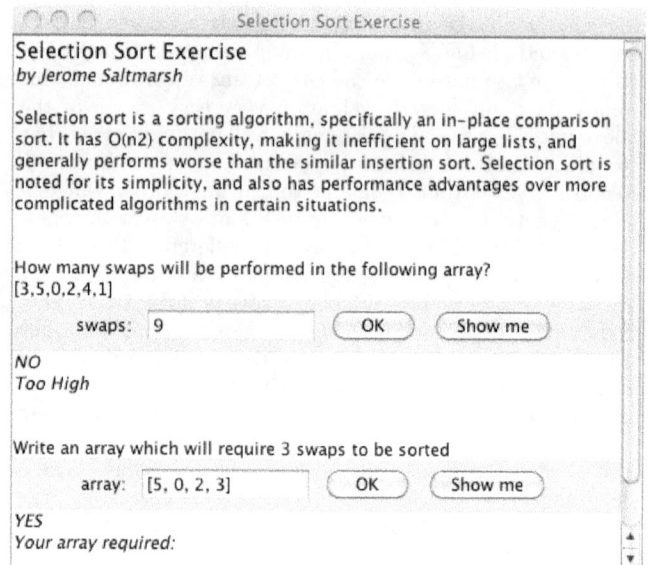

Figure 1: A task with a validated student answer

Check(cond) checks if the condition passed in in JXPath notation is correct. If this is not the case, the execution of the script ends. The user can also provide an optional comment as a second parameter which is shown if the condition is evaluated to false.

Comment(s) shows the comment s to the student.

CommentIf(cond, s) shows the comment s if the condition *cond* (given in JXPath notation) evaluates to true.

Debug() works like the *Dump()* command in *debug* mode, but is ignored otherwise.

Dump() dumps the list of all variables and their values as a comment. If variable names are passed in, only the names and values of these variables are dumped.

Equals(a, b) tests if both parameters are equal.

Max(a, b, ...) returns the maximum of all parameters.

Ok(...) assigns a result to the exercise and ends the execution. Without parameters, the query is regarded as successful. A JXPath condition can also be passed in to determine the result. If two parameters are passed in, the exercise will be regarded as successful if they are equal.

Retrieve(exp) executes the JXPath expression *exp*. The result is typically a list of data or a single piece of information. If a second parameter is provided, the query uses this object as the source for retrieving data; otherwise, the complete pool of knowledge is used.

Figure 2 shows a script that checks if the user provided an array *array* in which the second pivot element chosen by Quicksort will be 5. Line 1 uses a JXPath expression to retrieve the second interesting event labelled "pivotChange", providing direct access to all associated variables at this point of the algorithm's execution. The "sequence number" is incremented during the simulation of the algorithm whenever a new iteration of the outer loop or a new recursion starts. Thus, the query in line 1 refers to all *pivotChange* events with a sequence number of 2. The resulting checkpoint data is stored in the internal variable *s*. Line 2 retrieves the field "pivotValue" from the object stored in line 1. Thus, *piv* holds the value of the second pivot element.

```
1   s = Retrieve("events/pivotChange[seqnr = 2]");
2   piv = Retrieve("/pivotValue", s);
3   Debug();
4   Check("$piv = 5", "Incorrect");
5   Ok();
```

Figure 2: Example Evaluation Script for an Exercise

Line 3 provides debug data visible only for educators. Line 4 checks—using JXPath notation—whether the retrieved value *piv* is equal to 5, and if not, marks the solution as incorrect. Otherwise, line 5 marks the solution as correct.

After a short familiarization, the evaluation script allows even complex queries to be performed easily.

5.2 How to Modify Existing Generators

As mentioned in Section 4, the implementation of the visualizations is based on the ANIMAL system [11]. The visualizations will be generated on-demand by so-called "generators". A generator is a Java class that implements a special interface and contains (among others) a *generate* method that is responsible for creating the visualization. Of course, the actual work may also be delegated to service methods.

A given generator uses the same variables as any other implementation of the algorithm to faithfully execute the algorithm. Thus, all values are present in the generator in the form of local variables or object attributes. By using the *checkpointEvent* method, the educator can generate a simple checkpoint, as shown in Figure 3.

```
1   CheckpointUtils.checkpointEvent(this,
2       "pivotChange",
3       new Variable("pivotValue", pivot),
4       new Variable("pivotIndex", r),
5       new Variable("leftIndex", l),
6       new Variable("rightIndex", r),
7       new Variable("animstep",lang.getStep()));
```

Figure 3: Dumping Relevant Data to a Checkpoint

6. EXAMPLE EXERCISE TASKS

Table 1 lists some of the tasks that we have implemented. All of these tasks work on data that the educator has specified, for example a concrete array of values to be sorted. The educator only has to copy a given exercise specification, say for CombSort, and enter a different base array to generate a new "exercise sheet" with the same tasks, but working on a different basic input. Nothing in the exercise logic has to be changed, so that most computing educators should be able to create a new exercise sheet from an existing one.

The scripts (as described in Section 5.1) to evaluate the

correctness of the student's answer typically have only 3-5 lines (not counting comments and debug information).

Figure 4 shows an example animation, started by clicking on the "Show me" button in Figure 1. The "table of contents" shows the interesting events in this animation, and draws attention to the swap events by prepending them with ">>".

Algorithm	Task	User input
Graph Algorithms		
Bellman-Ford	Give the weight of the shortest path from the source vertex A to vertex D.	`int x`
Breadth-First Search	Start at node S. Give the distance from S to V, S to T, and S to X.	`int sv, st, sx`
Breadth-First Search	Give the sorted order.	`char n1 - n7`
Kruskal	Sort all edges in increasing order of length and give the fourth edge.	`char from, to`
Kruskal	Give your third chosen edge.	`char from, to`
Searching Algorithms		
Interpolated Search	How many iterations are needed to find the value 2?	`int x`
Sorting Algorithms		
CombSort	Which values are swapped when the gap size is 2?	`int a, b`
CombSort	Provide an array that will be sorted by three swap operations.	`int[] x`
GnomeSort	How often is the value 1 swapped?	`int x`
Quicksort	Provide an array which uses 4 pivots to be sorted.	`int[] array`
ShakerSort	How many "shakes" are required to sort the array?	`int x`
ShakerSort	On the first "up" shake (from left to right), which will be the first indices to be swapped?	`int a, b`
ShakerSort	Which elements are swapped in the 11th swap operation?	`int a, b`
Shellsort	Provide an array in which the first values swapped are 7 and 3 with a distance of 4.	`int[] array`
Selection Sort	How many swaps will be performed in the following array [3, 5, 0, 2, 4, 1]?	`int swaps`

Table 1: Example Tasks in the Exercise System

7. SUMMARY AND CONCLUSIONS

In this paper, we have presented a system for automatically evaluating student-submitted exercise solutions. The system supports the creation of new exercise sheets based on existing exercise sheets by simply replacing the input parameter, e.g., the array to be sorted. This therefore does not require any programming skills. The correct solution does not have to be given, since the system can automatically determine this based on short evaluation scripts.

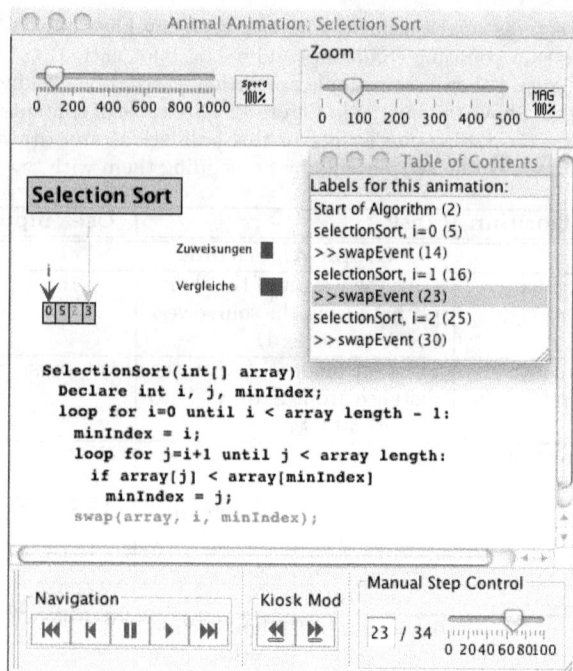

Figure 4: Generated animation with relevant events

Currently, the system covers only selected algorithms and exercise sheets. We are working on further exercise sheets for other algorithms. Most exercises were implemented—regarding both questions and evaluation scripts—by undergraduates, illustrating that the system is easy to use.

We cannot yet provide a formal evaluation of the system: the first exercises were only begun in November 2010, and our targetted lecture is scheduled for the summer term. Anecdotal evidence from students who have experimented with the system and our own experience indicates that the system can be very helpful. The integration of an animation of the algorithm means that students are not forced to manually "trace" the algorithm, considerably reducing the workload even for tasks that require multiple executions of an algorithm with "trial and error" input variations. This allows us to ask questions that we would not normally expect students to answer correctly, as shown in Table 1.

8. REFERENCES

[1] Apache Foundation. Jxpath home page. WWW: http://commons.apache.org/jxpath/.

[2] Marc H. Brown and Robert Sedgewick. Interesting Events. In John Stasko, John Domingue, Marc H. Brown, and Blaine A. Price, editors, *Software Visualization*, chapter 12, pages 155–172. MIT Press, 1998.

[3] Mary Cooch. *Moodle 2.0 First Look*. Packt Publishing, 2010.

[4] Juha Helminen and Lauri Malmi. Jype - a program visualization and programming exercise tool for python. In *Proceedings of the 5th international symposium on Software visualization*, SOFTVIS '10, pages 153–162. ACM Press, New York, NY, USA, 2010.

[5] Ville Karavirta, Ari Korhonen, Lauri Malmi, and Kimmo Stålnacke. MatrixPro - A Tool for Ex Tempore Demonstration of Data Structures and Algorithms. In *Proceedings of the Third Program Visualization Workshop, University of Warwick, UK*, pages 27–33, July 2004.

[6] Lauri Malmi, Ville Karavirta, Ari Korhonen, Jussi Nikander, Otto Seppälä, and Panu Silvasti. Visual Algorithm Simulation Exercise System with Automatic Assessment: TRAKLA2. *Informatics in Education*, 3(2):267–288, 2004. http://www.vtex.lt/informatics_in_education/htm/INFE048.htm.

[7] Andrés Moreno. Program Animation Activities in Moodle. In *Proceedings of the 13th Annual SIGCSE Conference on Innovation and Technology in Computer Science Education (ITiCSE 2008), Madrid, Spain*, page 361. ACM Press, New York, NY, 2008.

[8] Thomas Naps. JHAVÉ – Addressing the Need to Support Algorithm Visualization with Tools for Active Engagement. *IEEE Computer Graphics and Applications*, 25(6):49–55, December 2005.

[9] Thomas L. Naps, Guido Rößling, Vicki Almstrum, Wanda Dann, Rudolf Fleischer, Chris Hundhausen, Ari Korhonen, Lauri Malmi, Myles McNally, Susan Rodger, and J. Ángel Velázquez-Iturbide. Exploring the Role of Visualization and Engagement in Computer Science Education. *ACM SIGCSE Bulletin*, 35(2):131–152, June 2003.

[10] Rockford J. Ross and Michael T. Grinder. Hypertextbooks: Animated, Active Learning, Comprehensive Teaching and Learning Resources for the Web. In Stephan Diehl, editor, *Software Visualization*, number 2269 in Lecture Notes in Computer Science, pages 269–284. Springer, 2002.

[11] Guido Rößling and Tobias Ackermann. A Framework for Generating AV Content on-the-fly. In Guido Rößling, editor, *Proceedings of the Fourth Program Visualization Workshop, Florence, Italy*, pages 106–111, June 2006.

[12] Guido Rößling and Bernd Freisleben. Animal: A System for Supporting Multiple Roles in Algorithm Animation. *Journal of Visual Languages and Computing*, 13(2):341–354, 2002.

[13] Guido Rößling, Lauri Malmi, Michael Clancy, Mike Joy, Andreas Kerren, Ari Korhonen, Andrés Moreno, Thomas Naps, Rainer Oechsle, Atanas Radenski, Rockford J. Ross, and J. Ángel Velázquez Iturbide. Enhancing Learning Management Systems to Better Suppoert Computer Science Education. *SIGCSE Bulletin inroads*, 40.4:142–166, December 2008.

[14] Guido Rößling, Thomas Naps, Mark S. Hall, Ville Karavirta, Andreas Kerren, Charles Leska, Andrés Moreno, Rainer Oechsle, Susan H. Rodger, Jaime Urquiza-Fuentes, and J. Ángel Velázquez-Iturbide. Merging Interactive Visualizations with Hypertextbooks and Course Management. *SIGCSE Bulletin inroads*, 38(4):166–181, December 2006.

[15] Guido Rößling and Teena Vellaramkalayil. A Visualization-Based Computer Science Hypertextbook Prototype. *ACM Transactions on Computing Education*, 9(2):1–13, June 2009.

Using Run Time Traces in Automated Programming Tutoring

Michael Striewe
Paluno – The Ruhr Insitute for Software
Technology
University of Duisburg-Essen
Essen, Germany
michael.striewe@paluno.uni-due.de

Michael Goedicke
Paluno – The Ruhr Insitute for Software
Technology
University of Duisburg-Essen
Essen, Germany
michael.goedicke@paluno.uni-due.de

ABSTRACT

Running test cases against a student's solution of a programming assignment is one of the easiest ways to generate feedback. If black-box tests are used, students may have difficulties to retrace the complete system behaviour and to find erroneous programming statements. This paper discusses the use of automated trace generation for assisting students in this task. Both manual and automated trace interpretation is discussed and evaluated by examples.

Categories and Subject Descriptors

D.2.5 [**Software Engineering**]: Testing and Debugging—*Tracing*; K.3.1 [**Computers and Education**]: Computer Uses in Education—*Computer-assisted instruction (CAI)*

General Terms

Verification

Keywords

Intelligent Tutoring Systems, Automated Tutoring, Trace Analysis

1. INTRODUCTION

Using run time tests for automated grading of programming assignments is as old as automated grading itself. Running test cases against a student's solution is one of the easiest ways to generate feedback on the solution, both for grading and tutoring. It can be assumed that systems using this way of automation exist for virtually any programming language used for teaching programming. Most of these test systems employ black-box tests, providing input to the program under test and comparing the output to the expected output for a correct program. While this is the typical way of unit testing also in industrial projects it may have some limitations in tutoring scenarios: Students may have difficulties to deduce the erroneous programming statement if they just know the input and the final output. They are most probably not experienced in thinking in system states and thus not able to retrace the program behaviour completely in their mind. Teaching the use of debugging tools may be an appropiate solution, but increases the cognitive load for the students. Especially the less proficient students that make many mistakes may also have the most problems in using additional tools. In the worst case, they may not even be able to reproduce the errors revealed by the automated tutoring system on their own with a debugging tool.

This paper discusses the use of automated trace generation in this context. It argues why trace generation integrated into automated tutoring systems may help to overcome the limitations of black-box tests and external tools named above. The considerations are motivated by the fact that the positive effects of trace visualization on program comprehension have succesfully been studied in depth for industrial size applications during the last years [1]. However, industrial size tools are out of the scope of introductory courses. In addition, they may be not appropiate for small programming exercises. Thus this paper elaborates on a simpler and more lightwight approach. Furthermore, it discusses advanced options of automated feedback that are available through automated trace analysis and are not solely focussed on program comprehension.

The remainder of this paper is organized as follows: Section 2 gives an overview of the general use of traces in programming education. Section 3 elaborates on special use cases where automated analysis of traces is involved. Section 4 provides evaluation of the concepts explained before based on the experiences made so far and names important future work. The paper is wrapped up with related work in section 5 and conclusions in section 6.

1.1 Technical Notes

Any implementations discussed in this paper are related to Java (version 1.6). This is no general limitation, since the underlying concepts are likely to apply to many other programming languages. The only requirement is to have a possibility to observe the program execution, e.g. by using the debugging hook of a run time environment. This subsection provides technical information on how trace recording is realized in Java to give a better understanding of possible limitations. Readers who are not interested in technical details can skip to the next section. The actual implementation this paper is based on has been realized as an extension for the automated grading and tutoring system JACK [10].

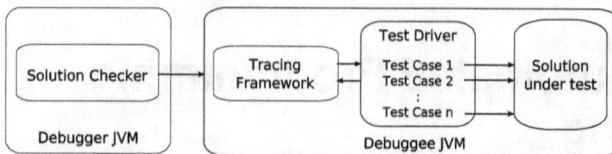

Figure 1: Architecture for trace generation with Java. The solution checker starts the tracing framework on the debuggee JVM, which in turn invokes the test driver. The test driver makes calls to the solution under test.

Recording of run time traces in Java can be realized through the Java Debugging Interface [6]. It allows to start a Java Virtual Machine (JVM) from another already runing JVM and attach to this new JVM as a listening debugger. The debugger has full control of the debugged JVM. In particular, it can suspend and resume the JVM, read objects from the stack frame and the object heap and can force an early return from a method execution. Trace recording happens by suspending the JVM after each single step execution, reading any available variable values from the stack frame and the object heap and resuming the JVM for the next step execution.

The overall concept is depicted in figure 1 and consists of three steps: First, the solution checker running on the debugger JVM starts the tracing framework on the debuggee JVM. Second, the tracing framework invokes the test driver, which is a special java class where the test cases are defined. Third, the test driver makes calls to the student's program under test. Debugger JVM and tracing framework are reusable components, while test drivers have to be written for each exercise to be checked. The debugger JVM is able to force an early return from a running test case and to instruct the tracing framework to invoke the next test case from the test driver. The test driver is allowed to make explicit calls to the tracing framework, e.g. for setting markers to the recorded trace. However, the actual work in tracing is done by the solution checker, which observes any operation on the debuggee JVM and writes them into the trace.

Solutions for programming exercises are typically small in the number of variables used and objects created during run time. However, reading any available variable values from the stack frame and the object heap produces a significant time overhead. Execution can be slowed down to less than 100 single step executions per second (on a typical desktop PC) in contrast to thousands of single step executions per second without trace recording. Thus mass validation of exercises using trace recording require the use of powerful servers or even several servers in parallel, since the execution of a single test case may require minutes instead of seconds.

In addition, storing all recorded data for thousands of single execution steps may consume a significant amount of memory in the debugger. Thus it may be necessary to limit the number of steps that are recorded in a trace.

2. GENERAL USE OF TRACES

A trace of a program execution is a list of each single execution step accompanied by a description of the related system state in terms of variable values. Reading this trace from beginning to end, a student can follow the complete program run and understand how the system state evolved from the given input to the final state. If the student has an idea of a correct system behaviour in his or her mind (which is a necessary prerequisite to solve an assignment at all), he or she can read the trace and try to identify where the actual system behaviour differs from the intended one.

However, it is not necessary to read a trace completely from beginning to end in every case, which may be a longsome and tedious task. Instead, reading the trace can be started from the end, searching for program steps that directly affected the final erroneous output. This way, students can try to identify the reasons for the erroneous output and correct the related program statements.

Reading traces is not only useful for locating erroneous statements. It can also be used by students to check whether program behaviour or complexity is as expected. For example, a student may have planned that a recursive operation calls itself for not more than three times. The student can use the trace to check this property for the tests run by the tutoring system. This way students can not only verify their program to be correct in terms of the relation between input and output, but also in terms of the relation between expected execution steps and actually performed execution steps. This can be beneficial to gain a deeper understanding of programs and programming.

Since automated tutoring systems are intended to help students to evolve a correct solution, it is the nature of these systems that students submit more than one solution. In general, each subsequent solution of the student will have some differences in contrast to the previous one and will ideally be more complete. During this process of changing a solution, students might be interested in comparing the behaviour of different solutions. However, even students that are able to retrace the complete program behaviour manually without automated aids will hardly be able to keep different traces in their mind. In this case, automated trace generation saves at least the burden of writing down traces manually in order to reuse them in future comparison steps.

2.1 A Simple Example

Listing 1 shows a part of the source code written by a student for a programming assignment. The task was to write a Java method that takes a quadratic array as an input and returns the arithmetic mean of the minimum values for both diagonals of the array. The source code in listing 1 is obviously wrong, since it returns a value that is calculated from some variable value plus 1 (see line 53), which is no valid way to determine an arithmetic mean of two values.

Table 1 shows the trace generated for this solution using the array {{10,2,1},{4,3,2},{2,2,7}} as input parameter. The trace easily reveals that there are two more major problems in the source code: First, it is easy to see that variables i and j are intended to be index variables for row and column of the array, but that they are running just from 0 to 1 and not from 0 to 2 as necessary for a 3x3 array. Second, it is easy to see that variable minSecond is never changed.

Of course both mistakes can also be noticed from the source code by careful reading. However, the trace offers an alternative representation which is based on a concrete run. This alternative representation allows to see possible errors e.g. by just inspecting one column instead of studying several or even all lines of code.

The source code and the trace in the example discussed so far are quite short and easy to analyze. This analysis can

File and line	i	j	mat	minMain	minSecond	meanValue	Line of code to be executed
Testat3:42			{{10,2,1},{4,3,2},{2,2,7}}				`float meanValue = 0.0f;`
Testat3:43			{{10,2,1},{4,3,2},{2,2,7}}			0.0	`float minMain=0, minSecond=0;`
Testat3:44			{{10,2,1},{4,3,2},{2,2,7}}	0.0	0.0	0.0	`for(int i=0; i<mat.length-1; i++){`
Testat3:45	0		{{10,2,1},{4,3,2},{2,2,7}}	0.0	0.0	0.0	`for(int j=0; j<mat.length-1; j++){`
Testat3:46	0	0	{{10,2,1},{4,3,2},{2,2,7}}	0.0	0.0	0.0	`if(mat[i][j]>mat[i+1][j+1]){`
Testat3:47	0	0	{{10,2,1},{4,3,2},{2,2,7}}	0.0	0.0	0.0	`minMain=mat[i+1][j+1];`
Testat3:45	0	0	{{10,2,1},{4,3,2},{2,2,7}}	3.0	0.0	0.0	`for(int j=0; j<mat.length-1; j++){`
Testat3:46	0	1	{{10,2,1},{4,3,2},{2,2,7}}	3.0	0.0	0.0	`if(mat[i][j]>mat[i+1][j+1]){`
Testat3:45	0	1	{{10,2,1},{4,3,2},{2,2,7}}	3.0	0.0	0.0	`for(int j=0; j<mat.length-1; j++){`
Testat3:44	0		{{10,2,1},{4,3,2},{2,2,7}}	3.0	0.0	0.0	`for(int i=0; i<mat.length-1; i++){`
Testat3:45	1		{{10,2,1},{4,3,2},{2,2,7}}	3.0	0.0	0.0	`for(int j=0; j<mat.length-1; j++){`
Testat3:46	1	0	{{10,2,1},{4,3,2},{2,2,7}}	3.0	0.0	0.0	`if(mat[i][j]>mat[i+1][j+1]){`
Testat3:47	1	0	{{10,2,1},{4,3,2},{2,2,7}}	3.0	0.0	0.0	`minMain=mat[i+1][j+1];`
Testat3:45	1	0	{{10,2,1},{4,3,2},{2,2,7}}	2.0	0.0	0.0	`for(int j=0; j<mat.length-1; j++){`
Testat3:46	1	1	{{10,2,1},{4,3,2},{2,2,7}}	2.0	0.0	0.0	`if(mat[i][j]>mat[i+1][j+1]){`
Testat3:45	1	1	{{10,2,1},{4,3,2},{2,2,7}}	2.0	0.0	0.0	`for(int j=0; j<mat.length-1; j++){`
Testat3:44	1		{{10,2,1},{4,3,2},{2,2,7}}	2.0	0.0	0.0	`for(int i=0; i<mat.length-1; i++){`
Testat3:52			{{10,2,1},{4,3,2},{2,2,7}}	2.0	0.0	0.0	`meanValue=minMain+1;`
Testat3:53			{{10,2,1},{4,3,2},{2,2,7}}	2.0	0.0	3.0	`return meanValue;`

Table 1: Trace generated for the source code shown in listing 1, when invoked for the array {{10,2,1},{4,3,2},{2,2,7}}.

```
41      public float minDiagonal(int[][] mat){
42          float meanValue = 0.0f;
43          float minMain=0, minSecond=0;
44          for(int i=0; i<mat.length-1; i++){
45              for(int j=0; j<mat.length-1; j++){
46                  if(mat[i][j]>mat[i+1][j+1]){
47                      minMain=mat[i+1][j+1];
48                  }
49              }
50          }
51
52          meanValue=minMain+1;
53          return meanValue;
54      }
```

Listing 1: Piece of source code cut out from a student's solution. The method is supposed to return the arithmetic mean of the minimum values on the diagonals of an quadratic array.

be done manually. Larger programs and traces may raise desire for automated help in trace analysis, which will be discussed in the next section.

3. SPECIAL USE CASES

In this section, four special use cases are discussed in which traces are not only generated at run time, but also analyzed automatically. The first one involves on-the-fly analysis of traces and may cause early termination of a test run. The second use case focusses on trace analysis after termination. The third use case involves comparison of traces. The last one comes back to on-the-fly analysis, but related to the more generic problem of infinite loop detection.

3.1 Assertion Checking

As mentioned in the introduction, typical run time tests handle the program under test as black-boxes. Thus feedback can only be given to return values of method calls or object fields that are visible from outside the system. Contrary, data stored in private fields is not accessible. Since it is good coding practice to use private fields whenever a field represents the internal state of an object, it is not acceptable to use public fields in teaching just for the benefit of automated testing. However, it may be beneficial to consider both public and private fields for more detailed feedback.

Tracing solves this problem, since it makes use of the debugging interface and is thus able to check the contents of private fields. Hence it is sufficient to add a method to the tracing framework which can be called by the test driver during test case execution. The method takes the variable name and the expected value as parameters and compares this value to the latested recorded value in the trace.

This way of assertion checking can be used in the following example: A method call to the tested program is executed that creates a new object. Assertion checking is used to check whether private fields of this new object are set correctly, i.e. whether the constructor of this object's class works as expected. If some assertion is violated, the test can be aborted with a detailed feedback message. If aborting the test is not desirable, the spotted violation can at least be marked in the trace. Regardless of the way choosen, students are informed about the location where an error happens and not just about the malicious effects this error causes in the results of subsequent operations. Of course, students can also locate the error manually reading the trace, but assertion checking can help them in this task.

It is not necessary to limit assertion checking to the last observed step in the trace or to private fields. Instead, also permanent checks for a given field or local variable can be performed. For this purpose the tracing framework needs methods to switch on and off assertion checking for a given field or variable name for all subsequent program steps. This can be used for example to check invariants of sorting algorithms. In this case, first some method calls to the student's program can be performed to fill an array with data. Afterwards checking of assertions ensuring data consistency is switched on and a sort algorithm implemented by the student is invoked. If the algorithms does not perform correctly, the test run can be aborted immediately after the program step that violated an assertion or a marker in the trace can be set. This way the student gets a precise hint on the location of an error instead of just being informed that the overall result of the algorithm is wrong.

In any case it is obviously necessary to know the names of the private fields or variables to be checked. In teaching scenarios it is possible to provide code templates to the students, which incorporate at least all necessary field declarations. However, this does not solve the problem with local variables. A more complex technique suitable both for private fields and local variables is to apply static code analysis to the programs written by students [7]. For example, this can be used to identify all variables used in the termination condition of a `while`-loop, allowing to apply assertion checking to them for checking some loop invariant.

3.2 Extended Assertion Checking

Not all propositions about a correct program can be made in a way that allows for on-the-fly checking of assertions. For example, the correct implementation of an search algorithm may require to eventually set a boolean flag to `true`. If it is allowed to set the flag back to `false` at some later point in time, this constraint can neither be checked by permanent assertion checks nor by an assertion check for the last observed step before program termination. Instead, it is necessary to check this constraint by analyzing the complete trace after program termination.

The general procedure of assertion checking in this case is similar to manually reading the trace from start to end, but less tedious, since it is automated. Assertions to be checked can be specified using a temporal logic for programs, which is defined over traces of distinct system states [9]. Results from evaluating such logical formulae can be used either to add additonal information to a failed test case or to spot additional errors not revealed by black-box tests and simple assertion checks.

3.3 Trace Alignment

In section 2 two use cases where mentioned in which traces are compared manually: Comparison of actual trace and theoretical idea of system behaviour and comparison of different traces from different solution variants. In both cases, the student compares the trace with behaviour or changes that he or she expected. This task can obviously not be automated. However, automated trace comparison can be performed, if the trace of a student's solution is compared to the trace of a sample solution. In this case, algorithms known from string or sequence alignment [4] can be used to align the trace of the sample solution with the actual solution. Two major patterns can be expected:

- The traces are almost similar in the beginning but from some point on there is hardly any possible alignment. In this case, the actual solution seems to do something wrong that leads into the wrong direction. The region of the last reliable alignment marks the region of program code where the responsible erroneous statement is most likely to be located.

- There are sections with good alignment between sample solution and actual solution all over the trace, which cover almost the complete sample solution trace, but only parts of the (consequently longer) trace of the actual solution. In this case, the solution seems to be unnecessarily complicated. The code executed during the trace steps without alingment are consequently most likely superflous. Of course, the same may also happen the other way round, if

a student finds a solution more compact than the sample solution used for comparison.

In both cases, trace alignment cannot be used for direct error responses, since results are vague. Sequence alignment is based on propabilities and thus this kind of analysis can only sketch regions of program code that are worth a closer manual inspection. However this can guide students to get a deeper understanding of their program code more easily.

3.4 Infinite Loop Detection

A typical mistake made by students learning programming is the incorrect use of loop statements, resulting in infinite loops at run time. Since these loops would block the automated tutoring system, it is usual to cancel running solutions after a certain amount of time. With tracing, the number of execution steps can serve as an additional simple criterion.

A more complex technique is to analyze the trace to check for duplicate states. If a running program has entered a certain state, i.e. a certain line in the program code and a certain variable assignment, it can be checked whether the same state has already been entered before. If the state has been entered before and any execution step in between these to states did only contain deterministic statements, the program will reach this state infinitely often in the future. Hence, the lines of code executed between the two occurences of the state form an infinite loop and the program execution can be terminated with an adequate feedback message.

It is important to notice that this technique of infinite loop detection only covers a small subset of all possible types on infinite loops. Situations not covered by this technique particularly include code sections which use non-deterministic statements and infinite loops that result from the infinite creation of new system states. Techniques for covering these types of loops can also be based on traces, but are out of the scope of this paper.

4. EVALUATION AND FUTURE WORK

A software component that is able to generate traces of Java programs has been used in an introductory course on Java programming for about 400 first year students in winter term 2010/2011 at the University of Duisburg-Essen. In 16 different exercises a total amount of several thousand solutions have been submitted to the tutoring and assessment system. Traces were presented to the students anytime a test case failed. This way, a total amount of 20'660 traces has been generated during the first 10 weeks of the course. No assertion checking or trace alignment has been applied to the traces. In some exercises, program runs have been aborted when they took more than 50'000 execution steps, assuming that they were stuck in an infinite loop in these cases. Due to technical limitations, the feedback shown to the students did only contain the first 150-200 lines of the trace.

The automated tutoring system in use can be accessed from everywhere over the internet, but designated tutoring hours where offered in which students could come to a computer pool and discuss their solutions and the automated feedback with human tutors. Regarding the traces, the following positive and negative reactions could be observed:

- Students and tutors got quickly used to use the traces at least for a short glance when reading the feedback messages created by the tutoring system.

- Students got interested in a more detailed step-by-step analysis of their solutions, which in turn encouraged the tutors to give spontanious introductory sessions on the use of debugging tools, although this was not a planned content of the lecture.

- The truncation of traces after 150-200 lines was seen as a major drawback, since these lines did just cover some initialization in more complex solutions, while the really interesting lines got lost. Hence only in few cases the reason for an erroneous output could be deduced directly from the traces.

- Students did not just read the traces in order to get a better understanding of their own code, but also to get to know which input parameters for black-box tests were used by the tutoring system, since the test cases used on this system where not public available.

- Graphical presentation of traces turned out to be an important issue, because it was reported to be very annoying to have both vertical and horizontal scroll bars when viewing a trace in the browser window.

- The limit of 50'000 execution steps turned out to be too low for complex exercises, in which larger data structures had to be traversed by nested loops.

In summary, the negative reactions did cover solely technical issues, which can be solved by an improved implementation of the tracing component. The fact that issues like bad layout and truncation have been reported as negative feedback also show that students and tutors were interested in using the traces actively, but got disappointed by these technical obstacles. Thus on the conceptual level an overall positive feedback remains, in which traces easily encourage a deeper interest in a step-by-step analysis of program behaviour.

Consequently, future work includes to solve technical problems and remove obstacles. Afterwards, more studies can be conducted to get a clearer view of the correlation between the use of automated trace generation and the depth of understanding students have about their own solutions.

5. RELATED WORK

Automated generation and analysis of traces is a commonly used technique in several fields of software engineering, e.g. model recovery [8], adaptive systems [11], run time model checking [12] and of course debugging. While the use of debugging tools is frequently taught in introductory courses, integration of debugging aids and tutoring or assessment systems is much less common. The very old system Assyst uses a simple form of tracing for counting execution steps to gather performance measurements [5], but do not provide full traces or even deeper analysis of traces.

Run time analysis without explicit tracing but based on symbolic execution, invariant generation and theorem proving is used in industrial approaches for inifite loop detection [2, 3]. However, assimilable approaches are currently not in use in automated tutoring systems.

6. CONCLUSIONS

This paper discussed the use of run time traces in automated tutoring systems for programming exercises. It could be shown that traces can be used both for manual and automated analysis in tutoring scenarios. Automated analysis is able to add benefits to an automated tutoring system because it allows to provide feedback that cannot be generated without tracing. The evaluation focussed on the manual interpretation of traces and showed an overall positive effect, but also much space for improvements.

Acknowledgments: The authors would like to thank all tutors who provided their experiences and observations from the tutoring hours for the evaluation section of this paper.

7. REFERENCES

[1] A. v. D. Bas Cornelissen, Andy Zaidman. A controlled experiment for program comprehension through trace visualization. Technical Report TUD-SERG-2009-001, Delft University of Technology, 2009.

[2] J. Burnim, N. Jalbert, C. Stergiou, and K. Sen. Looper: Lightweight detection of infinite loops at runtime. In *Automated Software Engineering, 2009. ASE '09. 24th IEEE/ACM International Conference on*, pages 161 –169, 2009.

[3] A. Gupta, T. A. Henzinger, R. Majumdar, A. Rybalchenko, and R.-G. Xu. Proving non-termination. In *POPL '08: Proceedings of the 35th annual ACM SIGPLAN-SIGACT symposium on Principles of programming languages*, pages 147–158, New York, NY, USA, 2008. ACM.

[4] D. Gusfield. *Algorithms on strings, trees, and sequences: computer science and computational biology.* Cambridge University Press, New York, NY, USA, 1997.

[5] D. Jackson and M. Usher. Grading student programs using assyst. *SIGCSE Bull.*, 29(1):335–339, 1997.

[6] Java^{TM}Debug Interface API. http://java.sun.com/javase/6/docs/jdk/api/jpda/jdi/index.html.

[7] C. Köllmann and M. Goedicke. A Specification Language for Static Analysis of Student Exercises. In *Proceedings of the International Conference on Automated Software Engineering*, 2008.

[8] S. Maoz. Using model-based traces as runtime models. *Computer*, 42(10):28–36, 2009.

[9] A. Pnueli. The temporal logic of programs. In *Proceedings of the 18th Annual Symposium on Foundations of Computer Science*, pages 46–57, Washington, DC, USA, 1977. IEEE Computer Society.

[10] M. Striewe, M. Balz, and M. Goedicke. A flexible and modular software architecture for computer aided assessments and automated marking. In *Proceedings of the First International Conference on Computer Supported Eductation (CSEDU), 23 - 26 March 2009, Lisboa, Portugal*, volume 2, pages 54–61. INSTICC, 2009.

[11] P. Ulam, A. Goel, and J. Jones. Reflection in action: Model-based self-adaptation in game playing agents. In *Challenges in Game Artificial Intelligence: Papers from the AAAI Workshop*. AAAI Press, 2004.

[12] W. Visser, K. Havelund, G. Brat, S. Park, and F. Lerda. Model Checking Programs. *Automated Software Engineering Journal*, 10(2), 2003.

A Proposal for Automatic Evaluation in a Compiler Construction Course

Emilio Julio Lorenzo
LTCS group at UNED
C/ Juan del Rosal, 16
28040 Madrid Spain
+34 91 398 8652

emiliojulio@lsi.uned.es

Javier Vélez
LTCS group at UNED
C/ Juan del Rosal, 16
28040 Madrid Spain
+34 91 398 4976

jvelez@lsi.uned.es

Anselmo Peñas
NLP & IR group at UNED
C/ Juan del Rosal, 16
28040 Madrid Spain
+34 91 398 4976

anselmo@lsi.uned.es

ABSTRACT

Experience in teaching the subject of Language Processors within the degree for Technical Engineering Computer Science, highlights the difficulties developing a compiler, for both students and instructors. The former because they are often disoriented when they are unable to get some feedback on their work and the latter because of the amount of effort and time involved to perform the evaluation. This paper presents a system for assisting evaluation using test cases, aligned with the trends of European Higher Education Area ongoing evaluation methodology. This approach is implemented in four phases where different problems are faced. The first phase consists of designing a test case set, accurate enough to discern whether the student successfully absorbed the different concepts and contents of the subject. The second phase involves the implementation of a runtime environment for the designed tests, so that many of the tasks required by the teaching staff can be automated. In the third phase, automatic assessment, according to different criteria is implemented. The fourth phase is the report of the results of the previous execution like straightforward feedback for both students and teachers.

Categories and Subject Descriptors

K.3.2 [**Computers and Education**]: Computer and Information ScienceEducation – *Computer science education*; *Curriculum*

K.3.1 [**Computer Uses in Education**]: Computer-assisted instruction(CAI), Distance learning

D.3.4 [**Programming Languages**]: Processors – *Compiler, Code generation*

General Terms

Management, Measurement, Languages, Human Factors

Keywords

Compiler automatic assessment feedback

1. INTRODUCTION

Adaptation to EHEA (European Higher Education Area) [1] methodologies requires the inclusion of practical exercises, as well as ongoing evaluation throughout the academic year. This trend includes project-based learning (PjBL)[2], which is based in the use of in-depth projects to facilitate learning and assess student competence. This approach fits with Language Processors course, eminently practical, where students have to design and implement a full compiler for a programming language proposed by the instructors. The main problem here is: How do instructors manage to evaluate student's work using ongoing methodology? In situations with hundreds of students, teachers have several problems related to time and effort for the assessment and feedback of the student improvements. These problems are compounded in the case of distance learning, where teacher-student communication is usually performed only by email.

There are several limitations to traditional evaluation systems in case of compilers, like in [3]. Firstly, the kind of work that students have to perform, changes every year. Adding and removing functionalities and concepts, and not only a mere change in the instructions. Secondly, the main issue is to evaluate the compiler itself. However, the traditional systems are focused in the final code, but not in the processes to create it. Finally, the compiler has to check source code errors. That means "erroneous programs" should be marked as correct, if the error is detected.

There is a lot of work related to building compilers like [4] [5], but the aim of this work is to assist in the evaluation independently of the compiler tools used. For this evaluation, the chosen method is based on test cases, comparing the final and partial outcomes of the compiler in order to grade students and give feedback. Several approaches propose automatic generation of test cases [6] [7] [8], but they do not usually deal with automatic grading and feedback. Other problems are the complexity of the systems, which make them difficult to use, and the dependency of certain architecture.

In this paper, we propose an automatic evaluation system that: 1. indicates the state of the compiler; 2. helps to grade it and 3. provides convenient feedback about their mistakes and successes.

Our proposal involves several recommendations to design test cases and an easy-to-use automatic evaluation system, independently of the compiler tools used. We use 'evaluation' instead of 'grading' because our goals are not only to assess but also to give feedback to students and teachers. This system has been implemented in order to evaluate the stage of development of a full compiler, which includes the usual phases: lexical analyzer, syntax analyzer, semantic analyzer and intermediate and target-machine (final) code generation. Each part will be evaluated separately, so one of the prerequisites is that they have to be implemented in different conceptual modules.

In the following sections we discuss how teachers must design the test cases, how the system runtime environment was implemented, what kind of automatic assessment we propose, the report generation and technical issues of our system. To finalize we will present the system tested in a real scenario and conclusions.

2. THE SYSTEM ARCHITECTURE

Figure 1 shows the system architecture. Our system manages the flow-control of the compiler architecture, giving test cases as inputs, collecting outputs and giving final code to the emulator.

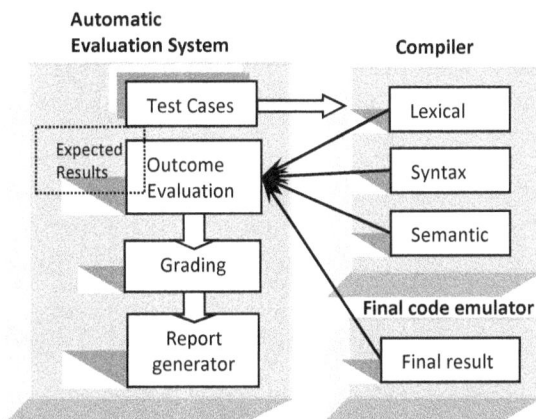

Figure 1. System Architecture

We use blackbox evaluation for checking the outcomes of each phase. Therefore, the different modules must be able to inform the system about several events, basically writing messages in log files, which will be compared with the expected results. Finally, the execution of final code has to generate a text format outcome as a result of this execution. In the rest of the paper, final code is referred to be assembly language, but this is not always necessary.

3. DESIGNING TEST CASES

Instructors must design the test cases for the evaluation of student knowledge. This includes checking if they have assimilated the theoretical concepts, by putting them into practice building the compiler. This task has to be redefined annually by adapting tests to the proposed programming language. Along with the implementation of the source code files, the expected results must be also written. For instance, one year the proposed language contains records as data structure and the next year arrays are required. The expected result files will be compared with the result of the compilers.

3.1 Defining Basic Functionalities

The design must be exhaustive with respect to the tasks that make up the subject. For this reason, a generic test suite, which includes the basic features that every compiler should fulfil, is designed. There are several approaches to create test cases that could be used [6] [7] [8]. Following, a set of basic concepts, to check with the test cases, are proposed. According to our teaching experience and [9]:

- Main subprogram without body

- Basic I/O operations
- Constants declaration
- Variables declaration
- Basic Arithmetic
- Advance Arithmetic
- Logical variables declaration
- Logical operators
- Precedence of operators
- Type expressions and data structures
- Subprograms (functions, procedures and methods) declaration
- Flow-of-control statements
- Recursive subprograms

Designing the test cases as atomic as possible is a useful method. That is, we must avoid, as far as possible, to include additional functionalities in a specific case, because it could be misleading when the test fails. For example, in most test cases it is necessary to add a variable declaration, and if that functionality is not correctly supported by the compiler, the test will fail, but does not mean that the concept being evaluated does not work. For this reason, test cases are designed with increasing difficulty. If the first set of test cases fails, there is no point in further evaluation. Another consideration to take into account is the fact that we have to check the different phases of a compiler, which are divided into lexical, syntactic, semantic, code generation, intermediate and final code.

3.2 Erroneous Programs

An important set of tests is related to detect coding errors in each stage or phase. This means that the compiler works properly when detecting the errors in "erroneous programs". To face the problem of how to identify the error and in which phase it happens, we define a standard error messages that students have to emit as output of their compilers. In [10] is showed that, although there are a large number of different error types, several categories are prevalent. In our system, the main errors are the following:

- *Lexical errors*: Non-closed comments, erroneous nested comments, bad symbols.
- *Syntax errors*: Incoherent patterns, types or variables declaration, block construction.
- *Semantic errors*: Type or variable value assignation, procedures when expecting functions, return in functions and special language characteristics.

This information, with the line and column number, is also useful in case of a normal test case, because it will show what kind of unexpected error is detected by the compiler and in which phase of development is located. This is an important feature in order to provide debugging information to students. Experience shows that in many cases it is difficult to determine the error, looking at the output of the tools used to develop the compiler. For example, the addition symbol "+" is not allowed, in the case the language to compile accepts only subtraction "-". Examples of error messages that the students' compilers should emit are the following ones:

```
[LEXICAL ERROR]-Token[29]['+', 12, 11]- Bad Symbol

[SYNTAX ERROR]-Token[34]['}', 10, 13]- Block Error

[SEMANTIC ERROR]-Token[56]['b', 20, 14]- Type Error
```

4. RUNTIME ENVIRONMENT

The evaluation system automates all necessary steps to generate the compiler and runs it with the previously designed test cases as inputs. The first step is to prepare the environment where compilers will be evaluated. To do this, each student has their own directory, which contains test cases and results. In this sense, the test case suite is collected from a specific general directory and then copied to each student's. This solution allows instructors to modify test case set in two easy ways: 1) all students, changing the general test case, or 2) a single one, changing the student directory. This distinction is important to adapt the test cases to a specific compiler. In so manner, if the compiler has a little mistake, instructors can go on just by changing the test to avoid it, and giving more feedback about other functionalities. Once the environment is ready, the steps that the automatic evaluation system carries out are the following:

1. *Compiling the compiler.* The compiler is also a program that must be compiled and executed. This step is only performed once for each student and if it fails, the evaluation stops here.

2. *Compiling the test case.* The compiler compiles the test cases. The different phases of a compiler will be checked in this step. If they are successful, the result will be a final assembly code file.

3. *Running the final code.* An emulator, to execute the final assembly code created in the previous step, is used. If this step is successful, the outcome will be a text file with the result of the execution.

4. *Evaluating the outcome.* In this step, the previous text file is compared with the expected result. For example, if the source code contains the expression 2 + 2, the result should be 4. We have to assure the compiler works and that it works correctly.

5. *Reporting generation and grading.* Steps 2 to 4 have to be repeated for each case of the test case set. Once all cases have been checked, relevant reports are generated and a provisional student assessment is also calculated.

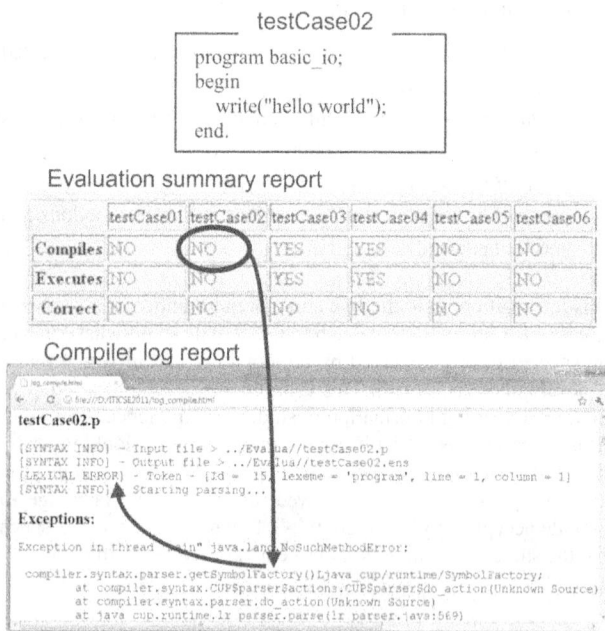

Figure 2. Evaluation example

To illustrate all these steps, Figure 2 shows an example where test case number 2 fails in the compilation phase. This case is related to i/o functions and seeing the compilation report instructors can find out that the error is an exception in the method "getSymbolFactory". That is related to make a new symbol table and it causes a false lexical error. Those reports will be explained in report generation section.

5. AUTOMATIC ASSESSMENT

Multiple proposals provide automatic assessment for a programing course [3] [11], but the goals of a Language Processors course are different. It is not necessary to check the code for being well formatted; the result of that code is the important issue. For instance, the Symbol Table must do what it is expected, but its implementation is not too important. Besides, the complexity of the compiler and the variety of implementation techniques make us discard a deeper code style evaluation.

A simple approach for the grading method follows the classical formula:

$$mark = \frac{Success\ test\ cases}{Total\ test\ cases}$$

In this approach, a test case is considered success if the execution succeeds and returns the expected value. This is carried out by comparing the outputs generated with the expected. [12] points out that a success is determined in two dimensions: correct behaviour and user-friendliness, where the latter is largely determined by the helpfulness of error messages. We can check this dimension due to the standard vocabulary for errors described previously.

Although the emulator outcome (final result) format is described by the assembly emulator, there are many instances in which students are unable to follow, either by neglect or inability. For example, the output should be lowercase, but many practices use capitals. A text filter is used, prior to the result matching, to avoid generating false errors in those cases.

Our proposal allows a more sophisticated method, using the features when compiling and running the student compilers for a more accurate assessment. Specifically, the assessment is divided into three distinct parts:

- *Compilation.* The student compiler compiles the source code of a test case correctly. This means that there are no errors on the lexical, syntax and semantic phases. This part corresponds with step 2 of section 4.
- *Execution.* The compiler generates intermediate code and final code in the form of text files containing the program in assembly language. This part corresponds with step 3 of section 4.
- *Correction.* The assembly code runs on an emulator and produces the expected result. This part corresponds with step 4 of section 4.

With these changes, the grading method may be more complex. An example of the new calculation is as follows:

$$mark = \frac{\sum_{i=1}^{N} C_i * H_i}{N} \quad C_i \in \{0, 0.25, 0.4, 1\}\ H_i \in [0..1]$$

Being N the total number of test cases, C_i the numerical result of evaluating a test case and H_i the weight of the case. C_i can take four values: 0 if it does not compile 0.25 if it only compiles, 0.4 if it compiles and executes, and 1 if the outcome is correct. H_i depends on the test importance, therefore important or advanced concepts can improve the final marks more than initial building compilers concepts.

This formula could be improved to be more specific, for instance, by adding lexical, syntax and semantic phases, or by considering the kind of errors. Another easy way to implement weights is to add more test cases related with the functionalities that are more important for the final mark.

Concerning 'erroneous programs', if one of those tests fails, it is considered right compilation, execution and correction, without checking the last two assessment parts. For helping instructors, it is possible to configure the system to indicate what kind of error is expected. This task is done in a declarative way by using the standard error messages described previously.

6. REPORT GENERATION

An important part of this project is the automatic report generation for both students and instructors. These reports are made by analyzing the logs generated at each assessment phase (compilation, execution, correction). The report format is based on HTML web pages, so that visual comprehension is improved. For instructors, a comprehensive report is generated, with the identifier of students and their proposed marks. The rest of the reports are for each student personalized monitoring. In particular, four of them are generated:

- *Compilation of the compiler.* This report shows whether the student compiler can be built correctly or not, showing potential programming errors committed.

- *Compilation log.* This report shows the log generated by the compiler during the compilation phase of each test case. In case of error, there is a text indicating its type and location (lexical, syntax or sematic phase). This is possible through the use of a standard error vocabulary (see Figure 2).

- *Final code log.* This report aggregates the results of running each test case final code by the assembly emulator. These results will be compared with those expected and it will determine if the case is "correct".

- *Evaluation summary.* This report shows, in a table format, the results of each part of the assessment (compilation, execution, correction) in each test case (see Figure 2).

The compilation and final code log reports, along with the test cases, are very for students. They can be consulted for an in-depth checking, as well as for finding the concepts students need to further improve in order to carry out their practice.

Not only are these reports used for debugging but they are also used to exchange them with other students and instructors. Using a common vocabulary messages and reports, it is easy to ask for helping and hints, when developing the compiler. According [5] good outcomes promote collaboration among students. Moreover, reports help instructors in their communication with students. A complete written report, including errors and clarification, is a hard task and the EHEA ongoing evaluation makes it even more difficult. Our experience shows that sending standardized reports is enough feedback in most cases.

7. TECHNICAL ISSUES

Two prototypes were built incrementally in order to implement the runtime environment. The first prototype was programmed using an operating system scripting language for automation. The run and evaluation phases were implemented by two separate Java programs, called from the script file. This first prototype had several important problems: First, blocked execution. When the compilation or execution generated an error or exception and blocked the automation. Second, little flexibility. It is difficult to change the behaviour of automation. This is interesting because students make unexpected changes in their compilers that can hinder or prevent their evaluation. Finally, system dependency. Because of operating system scripts.

To solve these problems, a second prototype was developed. It replaced the operating system scripting language and Java programs by Groovy [13], a Java-based scripting language. With this change flexibility was achieved to treat easily particular cases and all steps are unified in a single program to facilitate maintainability. Thanks to the new environment, it is possible to avoid blocking practices. In this way, all compilers can be evaluated at once, adding a new level of automation. Not only is a practice evaluated but all of them are also in a batch process. The processes of compiling the compiler and running its test cases is carried out using tasks programmed in ANT [14]. We defined a task for each phase to check.

Using those technologies the system is able to be run in a web container, so it can be used as an online evaluation server service. Students can submit their work and get almost instant feedback.

8. TESTING THE PROPOSAL

This automatic evaluation proposal was tested in the context of a Technical Engineering in Computer Science distance degree, in a Language Processors course with about two hundred students. Two different statements were developed to discourage plagiarism. The system helped grading student compilers and gave feedback to students who wanted a review. JFlex [15] and CUP [16] were used as lexical and syntax generators, along with our own compiler development architecture. To check the final code an assembly emulator was chosen, which allowed windows and console running. The latter is important for automation, because accepts text inputs and generates text outputs, what it is necessary for matching them with the expected results.

The testing results were interpreted from a qualitative and quantitative point of view. The former shows how students and instructors see the new work environment and the latter presents some data to support these findings.

8.1 Qualitative

The evaluation and further communication with the students was simplified and reinforced by the student emails. They showed their positive evaluation of the test case set and associated reports tailored to the idiosyncrasies of the subject. This was also exposed in the forums posts, where students interacted with each other more fruitfully. It seemed that they were able to understand better their classmate's problems and dialog with the same vocabulary, what improve collaborative learning. The practice instructions become also more comprehensible. The questions about the functionalities that the proposed language had to implement were usually answered just looking at the test cases. In this manner, the students' questions were focused in the concepts about building compilers more than in "what they had to do". Concerning instructors, they had the same advantages about their communication with students; furthermore, they were able to follow easily the student improvements, just checking the historical of evaluations.

8.2 Quantitative
It is estimated that in the case of practices with errors, the evaluation and reporting time is reduced almost entirely. In previous years the teacher had to test practices one by one and answer individually to each student.

An indicator that can be used to measure the usefulness of the reports, when reviewing, is the number of messages sent by students and instructors. In the case of students who were not sent the reports, it showed an average of eight sent messages until the student understood and accepted the evaluation. In the case of those who were sent them, the average was two. It was noted that students accepted their marks and needed less interaction to understand their mistakes. The consequence was a reduction of debugging time by both students and instructors, so communication between them is more direct, clear and concise.

9. CONCLUSIONS AND FUTURE WORK
This paper has presented a proposal for automatic evaluation of the practical part of a Language Processors course within a distant course computer science degree and focused on the trends of EHEA ongoing evaluation methodology. The approach used to assess students' knowledge is the realization of a practice throughout the course, following the project-based learning philosophy. Practice to do is to implement a full compiler for the programming language proposed by the teaching staff each year.

It has seen that this sort of practice is quite complex to implement and therefore, to assess. Our system helps to automate all processes and phases involving compiler evaluation. In order to help instructors to test compiler functionalities, a basic test cases set has been defined. This framework along with common compiler messages vocabulary allows instructors to reduce time consuming and improve feedback and communication to students. Finally, the proposal was tested in a real distance course, showing that both students and instructors agree with it.

There are several topics that can be tackled in the future. Firstly, we should try other ways to automatic assessment, plagiarism detection mechanism and make it available online. Secondly, for a complete evaluation, our system must be tested with other compiler tools and architectures.

Finally, the system should be integrated in a virtual community environment. So, a metamodel approach will be used to wrap student outcomes and reports as learning objects with automatically generated metadata [17]. These objects will be also stored in a learning object repository in order to improve accessibility and reusability. This way, other pedagogical activities can be made, with pedagogical tools which allow learning objects as inputs.

10. ACKNOWLEDGMENTS
Our thanks to UNED for the support of III educational innovation network. MCINN for the support of Project TIN-2009-14317-C03-03, Madrid Region for the support of S2009 TIC-1650. Thanks to Sergio Galvez for previous work and Alvaro Rodrigo for his review and comments.

11. REFERENCES
[1] EHEA 2011. http://www.ehea.info/ January 2011

[2] Savery, J., and Thomas, D. 1996. Problem based learning. An instructional model and its constructionist framework. In *Constructivist learning environments: Case studies in instructional design* Ed. B.Wilson, 135-148 ISBN= 0877782903.

[3] Malmi, L., Korhonen, A., and Saikkonen R. 2002. Experiences in automatic assessment on mass courses and issues for designing virtual courses. In *Proc. of ITiCSE '02*, NY, 55-59 DOI=10.1145/544414.544433.

[4] Demaille, A., Levillain, R. and Perrot, B. 2008. A set of tools to teach compiler construction. In *Proc. of ITiCSE '08* NY, 68-72 DOI=10.1145/1384271.1384291.

[5] Waite, W. M., Jarrahian, A., Jackson M.H., and Diwan A. 2006. Design and implementation of a modern compiler course. *SIGCSE Bull.* 38, 3 (June 2006), 18-22. DOI=10.1145/1140123.1140132.

[6] Boujarwah, A. S. and Saleh, K. 1993. Compiler test case generation methods: a survey and assessment. Information and Software Technology, 39, 9, 617-625, DOI= 10.1016/S0950-5849(97)00017-7.

[7] Sturmer, I. and Conrad, M. 2003. Test suite design for code generation tools. *In Proc. 18th IEEE International Conference on Automated Software Engineering, (Oct 2003)*, 286- 290, 6-10 DOI= 10.1109/ASE.2003.1240322.

[8] Salmela, L., Tarhio J. and Montonen T. 2009. Towards automated management of compiler assignments. *In Proc. CSEDU 2009, INSTICC 2009* Vol. 2, 243–249.

[9] Computing Curricula 2001: Computer Science. The Joint Task Force on Computing Curricula, IEEE Computer Society, ACM, 2001. Available: http://www.acm.org/education/education/education/curric_vols/cc2001.pdf. January 2011.

[10] Lewis S. and Mulley G. 1998. A comparison between novice and experienced compiler users in a learning environment. *SIGCSE Bull.* 30, 3 (August 1998), 157-161. DOI=10.1145/290320.283106.

[11] Douce C., Livingstone D., and Orwell J. 2005. Automatic test-based assessment of programming: A review. *J. Educ. Resour. Comput.* 5, 3, Article 4 (September 2005). DOI=10.1145/1163405.1163409.

[12] Griswold, W.G. 2002. Teaching Software Engineering in a Compiler Project Course. *J. Educ. Resour. Comput.* 2, 4, 2002, DOI= http://doi.acm.org/10.1145/949257.949260.

[13] Groovy 2011. http://groovy.codehaus.org/ January 2011.

[14] Ant 2011. http://ant.apache.org/ January 2011.

[15] JFlex. 2011. http://jflex.de/ January 2011.

[16] CUP. http://www2.cs.tum.edu/projects/cup/ January 2011.

[17] Lorenzo, E.J., and Verdejo M.F. 2010, CARDS: A Metamodel Approach to Aggregate Outcomes of Learning Tools, In *Proc. ICALT 2010*, 5-7 (July 2010) pp.156-157 DOI= 10.1109/ICALT.2010

Evaluation Framework Underpinning the Digital Divas Programme

Annemieke Craig
Deakin University
Victoria, Australia
+61 3 5227 2172
acraig@deakin.edu.au

Julie Fisher, Helen Forgasz
Monash University
Victoria, Australia
+61 3 9903 2621
julie.fisher@monash.edu
helen.forgasz@monash.edu

Catherine Lang
Swinburne University of Technology
Victoria, Australia
+61 3 9214 5884
clang@swin.edu.au

ABSTRACT

In Australia, as elsewhere, women's participation rates in Information Technology (IT) have been low. IT is the generic term used to refer to the many courses in the Computer Science, and Information Systems disciplines. While there have been a number of intervention programmes implemented aimed at encouraging women into IT and retaining them once there, few have included evaluations of the efficacy of the intervention. Thus little is known about the factors contributing to the success, or lack of success, of the interventions, or of the medium and longer term impacts for the participants. In this paper we briefly describe an intervention programme implemented with girls in the high school years. We present an evaluation framework providing a detailed overview of the aims and processes involved in the evaluation of the programme. Data for the evaluation were embedded within the data gathering methods associated with the research on the intervention itself.

Categories and Subject Descriptors

K.3.2 [**Computers and Education**]: Computer and Information Science Education - *Computer science education, Curriculum, Information systems education.*

General Terms

Human Factors

Keywords

Evaluation, Intervention, Gender and diversity; Students attitudes; K-12 education

1. INTRODUCTION

Australian statistics, consistent with those from other western developed nations, indicate that participation levels by women in IT education and training have been low since the 1980s [1]. To attract girls to computing, and retain women once in the field requires intervention programmes to specifically address the factors discouraging participation [2]. Over the last twenty years in Australia and elsewhere [3] many intervention programmes have been implemented. Evaluation helps us identify the most effective programmes as well as to learn from programmes which

are not having the desired consequences. Few detailed programme evaluations of interventions for women and computing were found in the literature. Evaluation of programmes, particularly to help understand why they are not sustainable, is lacking from the literature [4]. Australian research focused specifically on females moving into non-traditional areas of work, including computing, suggests that evaluation of current strategies 'is generally lacking or piecemeal' [5, p.3].

Given the number and frequency of implemented intervention programmes, why are reports of evaluation lacking? It has been argued that one possible reason for the paucity of published evaluations is that if interventions are evaluated quantitatively and there is no significant change, then the evaluations are not considered worth reporting [6]. Alternatively, it may be that evaluation was not formally undertaken due to a deliberate decision, or lack of expertise and/or resources. Intervention programmes for women in computing are difficult to evaluate, and limited resources frequently hinder deep analysis of programme outcomes [7]. Various authors therefore argue for greater focus on evaluation [5, 8, 9].

To improve our understanding of which programmes are best, for whom, and in what context, a cumulative information base must be created [10]. Not only do programme evaluations need to be conducted, but they need to be used and the results shared.

A framework specifically created for the evaluation of women and IT intervention programmes [11] was adopted for the Digital Divas programme upon its inception. In this paper we report on the implementation of the evaluation framework to provide information which will enable informed decisions to be made regarding the success, or otherwise, of the Digital Divas programme.

2. DIGITAL DIVAS

This first section of the paper provides a brief overview of the Digital Divas Programme. Digital Divas is the result of over 20 years of research [12] into women and IT and, in particular, intervention programmes. Our aim was to develop a sustainable, long term intervention programme focusing on 12-15 year old girls. The underlying assumption of Digital Divas is that if girls are provided with exciting learning materials this will stimulate their interest in IT, leading to careers in IT. The development of the programme was the result of collaboration between a number of partner organisations involved in IT, women and IT, an education authority, and high schools. The programme was first run in one school in 2008 and is currently running in six Australian high schools.

Table 1 describes the strategic approach behind Digital Divas and the relative advantages of each aspect of the programme:

Table 1. Approach to Digital Divas

Curriculum	Focus on what interests girls (e.g., image, fashion, diet), THEN introduce programming through storytelling (Alice). Group and collaborative projects are encouraged. The programme is embedded in the school timetable, not an add-on or a one-day event and is not run at lunch time.
Informal role models	At least one IT under-graduate female student is in the classroom with the teacher each week. She serves as an informal role-model, showing by example that girls do choose computing in university. Invited female guest speakers, with a focus on recent graduates, are brought in to show the breadth of technical, creative and business IT-related careers.
Showcase / Celebration	Students create, print and display colourful posters, and produce an item or logo (e.g. key-ring or lanyard) to identify as their own. An end of semester celebration with principal, media and, of course, parents is held.

The authors examined previous research investigating school-based girls and IT intervention programmes. It was found that the vast majority of the programmes were not formally evaluated. The reasons included a lack of confidence in conducting evaluations, lack of resources including the time of a programme champion, and a lack of awareness as to why evaluation was important. Where programme evaluations were conducted, it was often the case that evaluations measured activities (number of events, number of participants) or response by participants, rather than results of the interventions (ie. the programmes' effects on participants in the longer term). Parker [9] advises that for change to take place, written reports on intervention programmes need to be more precise, not just about the research itself but about the actual practice in the area of IT.

Many intervention programmes reported in the literature also fail to mention longer term outcomes of the intervention with few, if any, reporting that formal evaluations were conducted. In the process of developing the Digital Divas programme the need to conduct a formal evaluation was considered essential in order to: understand what did or did not work so that others would have the opportunity to learn from what was done; and to execute an evaluation framework that could be easily used by others.

3. THE EVALUATION FRAMEWORK

Programme evaluation is 'the task of studying social interventions so that sound judgements can be drawn about the social problems addressed, and the design, implementation, impact, and efficiency of programs that address those problems' [13, p.2]. Evaluation helps identify the most effective programmes as well as to learn from programmes which are not having the desired consequences.

The essence of any social programme is its expected impact. According to Chen [14, p.43], a programme's theory is 'a specification of what must be done to achieve the desired goals, and what other important aspects may also be anticipated and how these goals and impacts may be generated'. If the assumptions embodied in the theory of a particular programme are incorrect, the intended social benefits will not be realised [15]. Without

appropriate evaluation the assumptions on which a programme is built will not be identified, and measuring success will be difficult.

There is no basis for developing intervention programmes unless programme initiators use causal thinking [16]. We argue that effective evaluation begins with the development of a programme's theory. A programme-theory driven evaluation is one in which the evaluator constructs a theory of how the programme is expected to work, and uses this theory to guide the evaluation process.

The literature provides a number of models and frameworks to assist in the process of evaluation. A framework built around the logical model (see Figure 1) and guidelines (see Table 2), and specifically created for the evaluation of women and IT intervention programmes [17], was adopted for the evaluation of the Digital Divas programme.

Adopting a formal evaluation framework will still not guarantee effective evaluation. The evaluation instruments developed and used, such as surveys or interviews, must be appropriate and the questions asked must measure what they are intended to measure and, to be practical, provide useful answers [14]. The guidelines will also not alleviate the necessity to work within the constraints of a particular programme, such as the lack of resources and time limitations.

Figure 1. Evaluation Framework

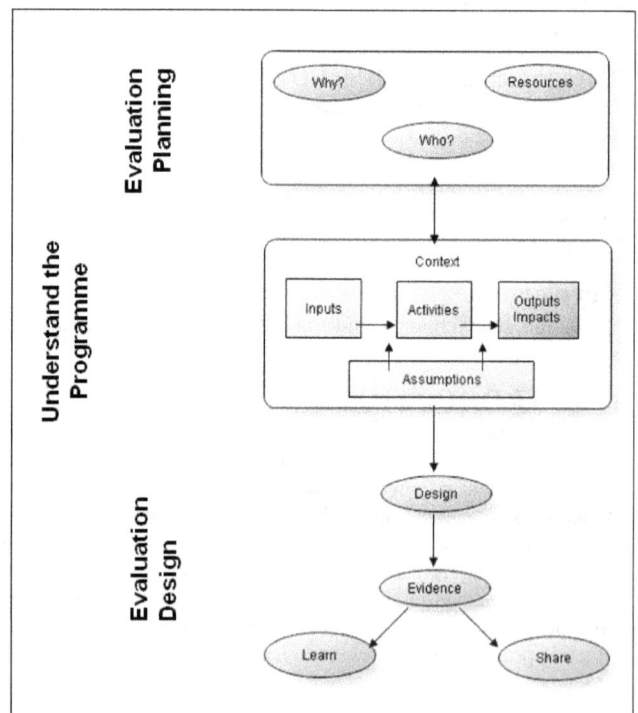

Table 2: Guidelines for evaluating intervention programmes

Phase	Description
Evaluation Planning:	
Why	At the start of designing an intervention programme consider the need to undertake evaluation of the programme: Why evaluate the proposed programme?
Who	Who requires the outcomes of any evaluation? Who will be the evaluation team? Will all stakeholders including multiple team members be involved?
Resources	What resources are available for the evaluation (e.g., volunteers, expertise, time, money, equipment)?
Understand the Programme:	
Context	What is the problem the programme sets out to solve? What change is expected after the implementation of the programme? Create a logic model showing the programme inputs, activities and expected outcomes/impacts. What are the assumptions (or theories) that will lead from the programme activities to the outcomes/impacts? Are the assumptions realistic? Over what time period are changes expected to occur? What level of change is required to define success?
Evaluation Design:	
Design	Describe how the evaluation will be conducted and the evaluation activities in the context of why the intervention programme is needed. Design the evaluation activities. What is being measured, how and when? For example: • The participants - who will be involved. • The results of the programme; the short and medium term outcomes in participants' knowledge, skills or behaviour. • The longer term outputs/impacts. • How the link between change and theory will be evaluated?
Evidence	How will the data be analysed? What evidence is needed and is it credible for assessing change? On what basis will conclusions be drawn and recommendations made?
Learn	How will the results be used in future? How will the lessons learned be shared?
Share	How will evaluation results contribute to the gender and IT literature and theory?

4. THE APPLICATION OF THE FRAMEWORK

The next section describes how the framework has been implemented for the Digital Divas programme. The three sections and their components are each discussed in terms of how the evaluation has been conducted to date.

4.1 Evaluation Planning:

Why: The purpose of our evaluation is to check the programme's theory of change - the change expected from the implementation of the Digital Divas programme, how it will come about, and to inform the wider community of the results. The evaluation is deemed to be important for the stakeholders: the students, the parents, the participating schools, the organisations who partnered with us as well as the broader women in computing community.

Who: All project team members (six researchers) to be involved in the design and analysis of the evaluation. It was decided that the evaluation would be carried out by two particular members of the team.

Resources: We were able to budget for sufficient resources: expertise, access, finance and time.

4.2 Understand the Programme:

Context: By implementing the Digital Divas programme, the problem we set out to address was the lack of senior high school girls choosing IT courses at university. The goals of the Digital Divas programme are to:

• design material that will engage the girls as part of the middle school curriculum
• raise awareness and ignite girls' interest in IT and IT careers
• increase girls' confidence and attitudes towards IT
• identify what factors influence the programme's implementation
• create sustainable programmes for schools

The change expected after the implementation of the programme is an increase in the number of girls considering to undertake computing subjects in later years at the participating high schools (and then ultimately in higher education).

These aims of the programme were refined and confirmed with the major stakeholders in the programme. Then the way the programme was expected to work, from the inputs required to run the activities to generate the outputs anticipated, and the embedded assumptions were discussed and agreed upon.

Inputs required

• A Teacher who is motivated, committed, creative, skilled in IT and passionate.
• A School that is supportive: Champion at the management level who is knowledgeable about IT, innovative /creative environment, flexible timetable, appropriate IT resources available (ie. appropriate technology which is relatively up-to-date, works well, and there is good network access).
• Expert Divas: Undergraduate female IT students, who are committed and motivated, have good IT skills, have empathy with the students, and are good role models.
• Guest Speakers: who are appropriate female role models.
• Appropriate Curriculum Modules which are engaging for the participants.

Activities to be conducted

• Digital Divas Programme, of one semester duration, to be delivered as an elective to girls at the pertinent grade level who (select to) participate.
• At least one guest speaker per semester to present to the girls.
• An Expert Diva to attend at least one classroom session every week of the semester.

Outputs anticipated

Short term outputs:

• The girls are excited about the Digital Divas Programme which translates into them being more excited about IT.
• The girls have a more positive attitude towards IT.
• They are more confident about using IT.
• They are more knowledgeable and aware of IT careers and jobs for computing professionals.

- They see the relevance of IT studies.
- They don't dismiss IT as something they cannot do.

Medium term
- The girls seek further information about IT options.
- They consider selecting IT at higher year levels within their school.

Longer term outputs/impact
- The participants can see themselves in IT careers.
- The girls are self sufficient with technology.
- They consider selecting an appropriate higher education course.
- The Digital Divas programme is sustainable within the school.

Assumptions

The assumptions (or theories) that underpin this programme include:

- The curriculum modules will excite the participants and deliver positive messages about IT.
- By participating in Digital Divas the girls will learn skills based on curriculum topics that challenge the prevailing stereotypes/myths within society that computing is boring, technical and involves working alone.
- That the IT Career range presented involves the analysis, development, programming, designing, and the problem solving aspects of IT, not just the use of computers as tools.
- That the teacher delivering the programme has brought to the attention of the girls (or made explicit) the links between the activities the girls are undertaking and their real world significance (e.g., Alice is not just a game but is an example of programming and why this is important).
- The role models present accessible choices of computing careers.
- That any increase in motivation/enthusiasm for IT is maintained from the time that the Digital Divas programme ends, to the time for the girls to make further subject selection.
- The wider community (school, parents, other teachers, other students not participating in Digital Divas) are supportive.
- Girls who undertake IT-based subjects in later years at high school will be more likely to consider a higher education course in IT.

4.3 Evaluation Design

Design: The framework and guidelines described above were used as tools for the development of the programme, the construction of the theory underlying it, and then to guide the design of the evaluation. What was to be measured and when it needed to be done had to be considered.

Evidence: The appropriate and credible evidence to be gathered and analysed includes the following:

Schools

Collect appropriate information regarding the schools (through document collection, web site search and observation).

- To capture the school in context: size of school, gender-ratio, ethnic makeup, type of school (public/private, co-ed/single-sex, year levels offered), socio economic status of the families, specialities of the school – music, science etc.
- Past academic performance as measured by student results.

- How/what/quantity of technology available in the school (lab setting/ laptop programme etc. physical set up of computer labs).
- Computer per student ratio.
- Technical support available in the school.
- The perceived status of computing within the school, the blocking of IT subjects, current school offerings of IT subjects and cross curriculum activities at all levels.
- Number of teachers who have formal qualifications in teaching IT.
- Any IT training / support programs offered for school staff.
- The school's history of girls selecting IT classes at senior level or going to higher IT courses.
- The technology available for conducting the Digital Divas programme. Confirm impressions of school in context with school leadership.

Teachers
- Pre-Survey teacher prior to the commencement of the programme (their background in IT, their perception of computers in their school, their knowledge of the Digital Divas programme)
- Post-Survey teacher at the end of each semester regarding any inhibitors or enablers of the delivery of the programme and their perceptions of the girls' engagement with the materials. Their perceptions of the guest speakers and value of the Expert Divas. What worked and what did not? What improvements could be made?
- Interview some of the teachers at the end of each semester to gather more in depth information regarding any inhibitors or enablers of the delivery of the programme, what worked and what did not, and what improvements could be made.

Participating girls
- Pre- and Post-surveys of all the participants. Girls complete surveys at the commencement and at the end of each semester. Measure changes in attitude, confidence, motivation, their perception of their skills, engagement with IT, awareness of IT careers, and what messages about IT that are coming through.
- Focus group interviews with some participants or individual interviews. Interviews to be conducted at the end of the semester as well as focus groups 12 months later to collect reflections about the programme and look at medium term outcomes.

Expert Divas
- Ongoing reflections by Expert Divas collected at three points throughout the semester: weeks 3 and 12, and at end of semester.
- Focus Groups with all Expert Divas at the end of the semester regarding the interaction they established with the girls, the type of support the girls asked for from them e.g., Did they ask about the Expert Divas's university studies or ideal career? Did they ask questions about possible careers in IT? About being a geek? From the Expert Divas' perspectives, what inhibited or enabled the delivery of the programme? What was their perception of the girls' engagement with the materials? What worked and what did not? What improvements could be made? Did they feel that they added value to the girls' experience of Digital Divas? In what way/s? What support (if any) did they provide for the class room teacher?

Other

- Was the wider environment supportive? A graduate student was recruited to look into this area. (Parents, other teachers, other students in the year level not in the Digital Divas programme).

Learn/Share: It was planned that the lessons learnt from the Digital Divas Programme would be shared within relevant IT research contexts and professional organisations:

- Articulate the lessons learnt and share – this paper aims to begin this process
- Justify the interpretation, judgment, conclusions or recommendations made.
- Use the results to inform new iterations of the programme.
- Use the results from multiple implementations within different schools to inform policy, guidelines, and professional development.

5. CONCLUSION

Although data gathering has commenced we have yet to analyse the results. However, designing the evaluation framework early has ensured that from the start the important elements for an effective evaluation were put in place. Together the framework used in conjunction with the guiding questions enabled the planning of the evaluation of the Digital Divas programme. The framework encompasses a logic model for articulating the theory of how the Digital Divas programme is expected to work and guided the evaluation design. Questions could be asked such as: Is the model meaningful? Are the assumptions reasonable? Is the intervention within our capabilities and is it testable? The guidelines then directed the design of the evaluation instruments, the evidence gathering, as well as ensuring that the critical elements of using and sharing the results were considered. It also enabled the design of the evaluation instruments and identification of the types of evidence that should be gathered. The result was a detailed evaluation plan.

We believe that the evaluation framework described in this paper could be used for a variety of intervention programmes. It does not require extensive resources, it can be carried out by those implementing any intervention and more importantly, will encourage effective evaluations to be conducted and outcomes shared. This in turn will enable the programmes that fail to have much impact be learnt from. While those that actually make a difference be further replicated.

6. REFERENCES

[1] DEST: Department Of Education Science and Training. (2002). *Australian selected higher education statistics*, Table 2: All students with user specified field of study by gender, 1989 to 2000. Commonwealth of Australia.

[2] Wasburn, M. and S. Miller (2006). Still a Chilly Climate for Women Students in Technology: A Case Study. *Women, Gender, and Technology*. M. F. Fox, D. G. Johnson and S. V. Rosser, Board of Trustees of the University of Illinois: 60 - 79.

[3] Suriya, M. and A. Craig (2003). Gender Issues in the Career Development of IT Professionals: A Global Perspective. *AusWIT 2003 - Participation, Progress and Potential*, Hobart, Australia, University of Tasmania.

[4] Lang, C. (2007). Twenty-first Century Australian Women and IT: Exercising the power of choice. *Computer Science Education*, **17**(3): 215 - 226.

[5] Lyon, A. (2003). *Broadening Pathways for Young Women through VET: A report to the Victorian Office of Training and Tertiary Education* Collingwood, Equity Research Centre, State of Victoria.

[6] Teague, J. (1999). *Perceptions and misperceptions of computing careers.* Geelong, Deakin University, School of Management Information Systems, Australia.

[7] von Hellens, L., Beekhuyzen, J., and S. Neilsen (2005). Thought and Action: The WinIT Perspective Strategies for Increasing Female Participation in IT. *Proceedings of Women, Work and IT, Contemporary perspectives on the reproduction of gender inequality in employment*, School of Political Science and International Studies, University of Queensland.

[8] Darke, K., Clewell B., and R. Sevo (2002). Meeting the Challenge: The impact of the National Science Foundation's Program for women and girls. *Journal of Women and Minorities in Science and Engineering* 8: 285-303.

[9] Parker, L. (2004). Gender and Technology in the Information Society: Networking to Influence Information and Communications Technology in Education. In *GIST - Gender Perspectives Opening Diversity for Information Society Technology, Bremen, Germany*.

[10] Weiss, C. H. (1998). *Evaluation: Methods for studying programs and policies.* Englewood Cliffs, NJ:Prentice-Hall.

[11] Craig, A. (2010). *Attracting women to computing: A framework for evaluating intervention programmes* Saarbrücken, Germany, VDM Verlag Dr Muller Aktiengesellschaft & Co. KG.

[12] Lang, C., Craig, A., Fisher, J., and H. Forgasz (2010). Creating digital divas-scaffolding perception change through secondary school and university alliances. *Proceedings of the 15th Annual Conference on Innovation and Technology in Computer Science Education*. Bilkent, Ankara, Turkey, ACM:38-42

[13] Rossi, P., Lipsey, M. and H. Freeman (2004). *Evaluation: A Systematic Approach*. California, Sage Publications Inc.

[14] Chen, H. T. (1990). *Theory driven evaluations: A comprehensive perspective*. Newbury Park, California: Sage.

[15] Rossi, P., Freeman, H. and M. Lipsey (1999). *Evaluation: A Systematic Approach*. California, Sage Publications Inc.

[16] Owen, J. and P. Rogers (1999). *Program Evaluation: forms and approaches.* Sydney, Allen & Unwin.

[17] Craig, A. Fisher, J. and Dawson, L (2011) Women in ICT: Guidelines for evaluating intervention programmes. *Proceedings of The 19th European Conference on Information Systems – ICT and Sustainable Service Development (ECIS 2011)* Helsinki, Finland. (in press).

The Impact of IMPACT: Assessing Students' Perceptions After a Day of Computer Exploration

Mary Anne L. Egan
Siena College
Computer Science Department
515 Loudon Rd.
Loudonville, NY 12211
(518)782-6546
maegan@siena.edu

Tim Lederman
Siena College
Computer Science Department
515 Loudon Rd.
Loudonville, NY 12211
(518)783-4197
lederman@siena.edu

ABSTRACT

Declining enrollments in computer science are a cause of great concern. There has been a 30% decline in enrollments in US computer science bachelor programs over the previous decade and more than a 50% decline in the enrollment of women in computer science [20]. Some research suggests this is due to the negative perceptions high school students hold of computer science [6,16]. IMPACT is a unique way of attracting excellent students to the major by inviting students and their teachers to a day of exploration and competition hosted by our college. The aim of our research is to investigate how the students' attitudes change and to assess the impact of this daylong event. This paper will demonstrate that IMPACT increases awareness of computer science and changes the perceptions of the students who attend the event.

Categories and Subject Descriptors

K.3.0 [**Computers and Education**]: General

General Terms

Human Factors

Keywords

Recruitment, gender studies, IMPACT, preconceptions, perceptions of computer science

1. INTRODUCTION

This paper describes research into changes in high school students' perceptions of and attitudes about computer science after attending a daylong event at our college. According to Galpin and Sanders [7], experience and research have shown that students often have a narrow understanding of the nature of computer science and that they often make a strong link between computer science and programming, to the exclusion of other aspects of the discipline. This is most likely due to the lack of career counseling, and an introduction to computing at the high school level that focuses on applications, such as word processing, and programming. Another possible explanation for lack of understanding is the diversity of the discipline, since it contains aspects of science, engineering and mathematics [5] and because

it is not well-defined [15]. Other research has identified incorrect perceptions such as computing careers only involve programming, there are limited career opportunities, there is little interaction with people, and that computing careers are linked to administration or secretarial work [8,4,3].

Our research investigates students' attitudes before and after participation in our program. The methodology used in this research involved comparing responses from questionnaires completed at the beginning of the day and at the end of the day.

The results show that the students became more aware of the computer science climate and the skills needed to succeed. They also learned aspects about the computer science profession – what it is and isn't, what computer scientists do and the positive job outlook.

The structure of this paper is as follows: the next section will give a brief overview of the IMPACT program. Then we present perceptions that have been identified as problematic to the study of computer science. Next we describe the methodology and the results found in the surveys. Finally, we discuss ways to incorporate our findings into future offerings of IMPACT.

2. IMPACT

Student IMPACT (Students Interested in Mathematics and Problem-solving unAware of Computing Talent) is a one day program in career exploration and competition for Computer Science and Information Systems (CS/IS). The program is designed to provide high school students with demonstrated academic talent, especially in mathematics and problem-solving, an opportunity to explore some of the ways that college students and professionals think and work in CS/IS. This opportunity is made available for students who have not yet experienced a computer science course and are undecided about their academic and career goals. It gives participating students the chance to investigate areas in which they have potential talent.

2.1 Purpose

The program grew out of the need to recruit more computer science majors. Recent U.S. Department of Labor surveys indicate that the areas set to experience the most growth from now until 2016 include computer technology, health services and social services. The computer related industry is expected to experience rapid growth, adding 489,000 jobs between 2006 and 2016 [19]. These statistics, coupled with the declining enrollments, puts the United States in a precarious technological position with not enough talent to fill the available jobs. Unfortunately, the United States is not the only country experiencing this disparity between jobs and talent.

Furthermore, many students indicate that they never considered computer science as a major because they were unsure what computer scientists did for a living. Or if they did have an idea, it typically wasn't a very appealing image. Additionally, exposure to computer science during high school is a deciding factor in 33% of girls' decision to major in computer science [11]. Programming contests exist for those students who already are exposed to and have experience with computer science. This alternative contest gives the same competitive spirit to the exploration of various areas of the computer science field.

2.2 Participants
The program was originally designed for high school juniors and seniors (ages 17 and 18) enrolled in or having completed Pre-Calculus, with no computer programming courses. We have since targeted the program for high school juniors as it seems that seniors may have already decided on their course of study for college.

Additionally, participating high schools are instructed that perspective students in IMPACT should be strong in mathematics and problem solving, should be "people persons" and possess good communication skills. The teams are required to include at least two female students in their team of four.

We invite all high schools from the four counties surrounding Siena College. The invitations are addressed to a math teacher at each school. Through previous outreach programs, our secondary mathematics education program and personal contacts, we are able to send personalized invitations. We believe this was an important factor in running a well-attended inaugural program. Subsequent programs have also been well attended based on the success of the previous programs.

2.3 Outline
IMPACT consists of a set of short (25 minute) instructional sessions where students learn about CS/IS topics. These sessions are followed by slightly longer (40 to 45 minute) activity periods where students work on some task(s) or solve problems related to the material of the instructional sessions. Past topics have been drawn from areas such as computer graphics, software development, geographic information systems, finite automata, security and database systems. Almost all activities require students to work together. Once the activity time is complete, scores are computed for each team and they proceed to their next instructional session.

The program for students also includes advice from faculty members about academic and career opportunities in CS/IS. In addition, there are CS/IS professionals who describe their careers and the type of academic preparation needed for success in these careers. College students are also available throughout the program to provide general help to the groups, sign off on the achieved objectives and generally act as role models for the high school students.

3. PERCEPTIONS
Computer science research identifies several misconceptions about computer science that preclude many high school students from considering a major or a career in computer science. Sands et al. [18] outlined common misconceptions about the field of computer science and what computer scientists do. Some of these misconceptions are that:

- Computer scientists lead "solitary, antisocial" lives [1]
- Computer science is about hardware [8]
- Mathematical ability is essential for writing programs [8,11]
- Computer science is all programming [8].

Additionally we wanted to test the perception of computer science as a primarily "male" field from the viewpoint of a high school student [14].

3.1 Changes in attitude
As shown above, computer science is often construed as a difficult, solitary pursuit done by nerdy boys for hours at a time. High school students, their parents and teachers often hold this perception. To determine if this is true and the impact of our program on these perceptions, we surveyed the students before and after IMPACT, asking questions about teamwork, communication skills, work day length, difficulty and gender ability (i.e., can a girl do computer science). We were hopeful that our program could change these perceptions in the minds of high school students and their teachers and guidance counselors.

3.2 Perception of computer science
Other common misconceptions arise about the computer science curriculum and the type of student who will succeed. It is commonly thought to be all programming and that only good math students will do well. One of the ways in which IMPACT addresses this issue is to specifically limit the number of programming sessions and invite high school math teachers. It is just as important that the high school teachers and guidance counselors understand that there is more to computer science than programming and that students of varying abilities can succeed. The pre and post surveys ask the students for their perceptions in these two areas. We were hopeful that we could demonstrate that there is more to computer science than programming, but unsure whether we would affect a change on the math perceptions as we had pre-selected the students based on math ability.

3.3 Perceptions of computing careers
Different than the previous sections, perceptions in this area cover some more general ideas about computing careers. For example, do the students have an idea about what computer scientists do? How about the job prospects? Do they know that there are ways to benefit society with a computer science degree? By incorporating this information into the opening talk, each session and the meeting with alumni, we hoped that the students would show a greater understanding of some of these topics.

3.4 Gender differences in attitudes
Finally, because of the lack of females in computer science, we were curious as to which of the perception changes was more noticeable among girls than boys. In other words, what aspects of IMPACT affected more change in the girls and was it beneficial or detrimental?

4. METHODOLOGY

4.1 Questionnaires
Upon arrival, as part of the registration process, the high school student-participants completed a questionnaire. The questionnaire obtained demographic, educational, and advisement background of each student, and a two-page 19-question survey. The 19 questions covered a wide variety of topics related to perceptions about computer science as a subject-area, computing-related

jobs/careers, skills and interests needed to be a successful computing professional, and types of people who would be best suited to pursue a career in computing. At the end of the day's activities, each student was again asked to complete the same questionnaire. The students could not see their previous answers, and the students had not been informed earlier that there would be an exit questionnaire.

4.2 Analysis

The 19 questions were treated as Likert-type items having a 7-point scale: 1="strongest No"; 7="strongest Yes"; 4="neutral" or "no opinion". The pre-IMPACT and post-IMPACT data were tabulated and analyzed to assess: (1) the students' initial perceptions; (2) any changes in perceptions which might have taken place over the day of activities; and, (3) gender differences in initial perceptions and in changes in perceptions.

A paired t-test (pre vs post data) was performed for each student, for all questions (44 students). This test requires that the data be normally distributed and have equal variances; and, the measurement data should be continuous variables. These results are shown in Table 1. Since the data have ordinal values, we decided not to pursue other variants of t-tests (such as a t-test for populations with unequal variances); however, we performed a non-parametric analysis more appropriate for ordinal data, a Wilcoxon signed-rank tests for paired ("before" and "after") samples [12]. Since our data sets has fewer than 100 samples, a range of P values was provided by the analysis tool.

t-tests were also performed on female/male grouping of pre-IMPACT data and on female/male grouping of post-IMPACT data (27 female and 17 male). More appropriate non-parametric analysis was also carried out using a Mann-Whitney U test for the significance of the difference between the sample-distributions [10]. The results of both of these analyses are shown only for questions for which there was a significant difference (either in the Pre-IMPACT data and/or in the Post-IMPACT data).

5. RESULTS AND DISCUSSION

At least three general considerations should be kept in mind regarding interpreting the data for each survey question. First: was the initial (pre-IMPACT) average on the side of the range that we expected (the "No" side or the "Yes" side). Second: how much change in average response took place by the end of the day (this is the "impact", which ranged from a change of 0.6 to 2.6). Third: was a change statistically significant (14 out of 19 changes were statistically significant). While all changes were in the "right" direction, we will primarily discuss statistically significant changes. All results are shown in Table 1, while Table 2 shows only the statistically significant results.

5.1 Perceptions of computer science

Questions 1, 2, 6, 9, 12 and 15 are related to computer science as an area of study, how computer scientists go about their work, and what types of activities computer scientists do. Referring to Table 1, the greatest change in perception can be seen in Question 9 (a positive change of 2.6), "I know what Computer Scientists do." This change in perception represents a change from the "No" side to the "Yes" side of the scale. This means that the students generally did not know what computer scientists do for a living, but had a better understanding after IMPACT.

It is interesting to note that students arrived with a very strong perception that computer science involves creativity and left with

this perception enhanced almost to the maximum. The students arrived with the perception that computer science mostly involves solitary programming, but these perceptions were significantly diminished by the end of the day. One of our intentions was to impress upon the students that while most computer scientists are accomplished programmers, programming is not necessarily the primary activity of many computer scientists.

Questions 4, 10 and 16 are related to being good listeners, communicators and team-members. The day's activities significantly reinforced these "social-skills" perceptions as evidenced by the data.

Table 1: IMPACT Survey Results

Comparison of Pre-IMPACT & Post-IMPACT Survey Data Less than 5% is considered to indicate a significant difference				
Post-Survey Avg	Diff Pre-Post	Paired t-test value	Wilcoxon signed-rank test	Question #. Survey question
6.0	+2.6	0.0%	< 0.1%	9. I know what kind of work CStists do
5.8	+2.1	0.0%	< 0.1%	19. I know what jobs CS grads will lead to
1.7	-2.0	0.0%	< 0.1%	1. CS is solitary - always in front of computer
6.6	+1.5	0.0%	< 0.1%	10. CStists need to be good communicators
2.2	-1.3	0.0%	< 0.1%	12. CStists work alone most of the time
5.6	+1.2	0.0%	< 0.1%	16. CStists usually work in teams
6.4	+1.0	0.0%	< 0.1%	4. CStists need to be good listeners
3.0	-0.9	0.4%	< 1%	2. CS is about hardware
2.8	-0.9	0.0%	< 0.1%	6. CStists spend most of time programming
6.3	+0.8	0.1%	< 0.5%	14. Career prospects in CS are good
3.0	-0.8	0.0%	< 0.1%	5. Learn CS in courses in Excel, PPT, Word
3.1	-0.8	0.0%	<0.1%	18. CStists work 18 hour days (60+ hr weeks)
2.1	-0.7	0.5%	< 1%	8. Girls more inclined to study CS than boys
6.5	+0.7	0.3%	< 0.5%	15. CS provides opportunities for creativity
2.2	-0.6	0.6%	< 10%	13. CS in college will be too difficult for me
2.8	-0.5	7.7%	< 10%	7. Only the best math/sci students will excel in CS
1.9	-0.4	9.1%	< 20%	17. Only gamers will like CS
6.4	+0.3	12.5%	<20%	3. CS provides opportunities to help people/societies
6.6	+0.1	52.1%	> 20%	11. CStists can have a normal family life

5.2 Perceptions of computing careers

Continuing with Table 1, questions 14 and 19 are related to the types of jobs for computer scientists and the job outlook. Both of these perceptions were significantly reinforced. It was surprising to see that the students arrived for the day with the perception that the job market was quite good. *We* know this to be true, but it is not necessarily the message in the popular media.

5.3 Other perceptions that changed

Also in Table 1, questions 5, 8 and 18 are all perceptions that did not experience as significant a change by the end of the day as the previously discussed questions. During IMPACT sessions, we did not specifically address the fact that Microsoft Office courses were not CS courses (Question 5), nor did we address the hours computer scientists work in their jobs (Question 18). The change observed in question 8 ("girls are more inclined towards CS") was low in the pre-IMPACT response (meaning "No") and became more "No" in the post responses. We are unsure as to what this change can be attributed and we will consider a better-stated question and/or an additional question on this topic in the future.

5.4 Perceptions that did not change

According to the data in Table 1, questions 3, 7, 11, 13 and 17 did not experience any statistically significant changes. It should be noted that in all cases, the responses were on the "correct" end of the range at the start of the day. Three of the questions were in the low end ("No") of the scale both pre- and post-IMPACT – computer science being too difficult in college, the importance of math to computer science ability, and only gamers will like computer science. The two questions related to computer scientists having a normal family life and being able to help society were both very high in the "Yes" category in the pre-IMPACT survey (over 6, increasing to about 6.5).

5.5 Gender differences in perceptions

Table 2 highlights the statistically significant differences in responses based on gender. More females believe that one learns computer science through courses in Office, that computer science in college will be to difficult for them and that computer scientists spend most of their time programming. The remaining questions showed no statistical significance in their difference.

The post-IMPACT results show that perceptions showing significant differences all decreased, indicating a stronger "No" answer, which is good. For example, the girls in the pre-survey had a mean of 3.2 and the boys a mean of 2.0 for the question about computer science being too difficult for them in college. This mean dropped to a 2.3 for girls and 2.1 for boys at the conclusion of the program, which is not statistically significant anymore.

After IMPACT, only one of the questions still indicated a significant difference between genders, the question about how one learns computer science. It seems that we still need to work towards educating the students, especially girls, on what constitutes a computer science course. It may also be worth investigating why there remains a gender difference on this question.

6. CONCLUSION

The IMPACT program has been in existence for four years and has plenty of anecdotal evidence of its success. The smiling, happy faces of students learning about computer science, the engagement of their faculty advisors, the return of schools year after year, and enrollment in our major are indicators of a successful program. This research attempts to quantify the success of one aspect of the program – altering the perceptions of computer science among high school students.

The small sample size of our data limits the power of our findings. However, it captures the transformations we have observed and that the teachers have reported. In the future, administering the pre and post surveys every time we run the program will augment our data.

Table 2: Selected Survey Results separated by gender

Pre-IMPACT & Post-IMPACT Differences of less than 10% Between Male and Female responses Less than 5% is considered to indicate a significant difference				
Pre-IMPACT Survey Data				
Pre-Survey Female Mean	Difference Compared to Male	Paired t-test value	Mann-Whitney U	Question #. Gist of the survey question
4.4	+1.6	0.0%	< 0.0%	5. Learn CS in courses in Excel, PPT, Word
3.2	+1.2	0.5%	< 0.9%	13. CS in college will be too difficult for me
4.0	+0.8	1.6%	< 1.9%	6. CStists spend most of time programming
Post-IMPACT Survey Data **Significant Differences Between Male and Female responses**				
Post-Survey Female Mean	Difference Compared to Male	Paired t-test value	Mann-Whitney U	Question #. Gist of the survey question
3.5	+1.5	0.1%	< 1%	5. Learn CS in courses in Office
2.9	+0.6	20.4%	< 36%	6. CStists spend most of time programming
2.3	+0.2	64.4%	< 35%	13. CS in college will be too difficult for me

The results give us important feedback and insight into what we believe is an opportunity for us to improve the program. Any of the questions that scored above 6 in the pre-IMPACT survey are not areas on which we need to focus. The questions that scored in the 1 to 6 range are areas where we can improve and should direct our efforts.

While this study measured the short-term impact of IMPACT, future plans for this project include contacting past participants and measuring the long-term impact.

This paper has shown the effects of a daylong event exposing high school students to the area of computer science. It demonstrated measurable changes in their attitudes about and perceptions of computer science.

7. REFERENCES

[1] American Association of University Women Educational Foundation Commission on Technology and Teacher Education. "Tech-Savvy: Educating girls in the new computer age." 2000.

[2] Beyer, S., DeKuester, M., Walter, K., Colar, M., and Holcomb, C. "Changes in CS students' attitudes towards CS over time: an examination of gender differences." *SIGCSE '05: Proceedings of the 36th SIGCSE technical symposium on computer science education.* St. Louis, MO, 2005. 392-396.

[3] Clarke, V. and Teague, J. "Characterizations of computing careers: Students and professionals disagree." *Computers & Education* 26, no. 4 (1996): 241-246.

[4] Craig, A., Paradis, R., and Turner, E. "A gendered view of computer professionals: preliminary results of a survey." *ACM SIGCSE Bulletin* 34, no. 2 (2002): 101-104.

[5] Denning, P., Comer, D., Gries, D., Mulder, M., Tucker, A., Turner, A., and Young, P. "Computing as a discipline." *Communications of the ACM* 32, no. 1 (1989): 9-23.

[6] Fisher, A., Margolis, J. and Miller, F. "Undergraduate women in computer science: experience, motivation and culture." *SIGCSE Bulletin* 29, no. 1 (March 1997): 106-110.

[7] Galpin, V.C., and I.D. Sanders. "Perceptions of Computer Science at a South African University." *Computers & Education* 49, no. 4 (December 2007): 1330-1356.

[8] Greening, T. "Computer Science: Through the eyes of potential students." *Proceedings of the Third Australasian Conference on Computer Science Education.* Brisbane, Queensland, Australia, 1998. 145-154.

[9] Liao, Y. "A meta-analysis of gender differences on attitudes toward computers for studies using Loyd and Gressards' CAS." *World Conference on Educational Multimedia, Hypermedia and Telecommunications.* 2000. 605-611.

[10] Lowry, R. *VassarStats: Website for Statistical Computation, 2011, Procedures Applicable to Ordinal Data, Mann-Whitney Test.* Vassar College, Poughkeepsie, NY. 2011. http://faculty.vassar.edu/lowry/VassarStats.html (accessed 2011 йил 10-January).

[11] Margolis, J., Fisher, A., Miller, F. "Caring about connection: gender and computing." *IEEE Technology and Society,* December 1999.

[12] McDonald, J.H. *The Handbook of Biological Statistics, 2009, Wilcoxon Signed-Rank Test.* 2009. http://udel.edu/~mcdonald/statsignedrank.html (accessed 2011 йил 10-January).

[13] Moore, C. "Attitudes towards computers, the influence of sex stereotypes, experience, ownership and mathematics." *Unisa Psychologia* 21, no. 2 (1994): 20-27.

[14] Moorman, P. & Johnson, E. "Still a stranger here: Attitudes among secondary school students towards computer science." *ACM SIGCSE Bulletin* 35, no. 3 (2003): 193-197.

[15] Nielsen, S., von Hellens, L., Greenhill, A., and Pringle, R. "Conceptualising the influence of cultural and gender factors on students' perceptions of IT studies and careers." *SIGCPR '98: Proceedings of the 1998 ACM SIGCPR Conference on Computer Personnel Research.* Boston, Massachusetts, 1998. 86-95.

[16] Olivieri, L. "High school environments and girls' interest in computer science." *SIGCSE Bulletin* 37, no. 2 (June 2005): 85-88.

[17] Pike, N., Hofer, A., and Erlank, S. "Effect of gender and occupational aspirations on attitudes towards computers." *South African Journal of Education* 13, no. 1 (1993): 25-29.

[18] Sands, M., Evans, J., Blank, G. "Widening the K-12 Pipeline at a Critical Juncture with Flash." *J. Comput. Small Colleges* 25, no. 6 (June 2010): 181-190.

[19] U.S. Department of Labor. 2011. http://www.bls.gov (accessed 2011 йил 5-January).

[20] Zweben, S. "CRA Taulbee surveys." *Computing Research News*, May 2003-2010.

Female Students' Experiences of Programming: It's Not *All* Bad!

Reena Pau
University of Southampton
School of Education
Southampton
+44 (0)2380 599 356
Rp302@soton.ac.uk

Wendy Hall
University of Southampton
School of Electronics and Computer Science
Southampton
+44 (0)23 8059 2388
wh@ecs.soton.ac.uk

Marcus Grace
University of Southampton
School of Education
Southampton
+44 (0)23 8059 3213
Mmg1@southampton.ac.uk

John Woollard
University of Southampton
School of Education

ABSTRACT
Programming has been cited as a barrier for female students to enjoy and pursue computing as a career or at higher education. However, there are examples of good practice, which demonstrate that programming can act as a bridge rather than a barrier. As a result of surveying 103 students and interviewing 60 students from 3 different UK higher education institutions and this paper demonstrates that female students can enjoy programming and take it further for their careers.

Categories and Subject Descriptors
K.3.2 [**Computer and Information Science Education**]: Computer Science Education; K.4.2 [**Computer and Society**]: Social Issues

General Terms
Human Factors

Keywords
Gender, Computing, Programming, Coding and Student experience.

1. INTRODUCTION AND BACKGROUND
The declining numbers of women in the IT industry is a cause for concern in industry and education alike. Those in the IT industry are developing life changing tools such as applications for health, education and other areas. The concern is that women are not able to contribute and influence the way in which the tools are created [1]. The shortage of women has been especially noticeable in the last five years durings which, there has been a significant decline of women in technological roles [2]. As it stands the percentage of women in the IT industry has fallen by 4% since 2004 meaning that only 21% of the IT workforce is female [3]. This has contributed to a skills shortage in the Information Technology sector, which is prominent both in the UK [4].

Higher education in the UK is also experiencing a decline in numbers of female students opting to study computing. With UCAS giving this figure at 7%. Nevertheless, enrolments on mathematics degrees are up by 8% and engineering subjects are up by 6.4% [5].

Programming in undergraduate computing lessons is cited as a reason for female students to be dissuaded from careers in computing. This is due to it being perceived as difficult and 'nerdy' and they report their experiences of programming as lonely, difficult and unsatisfying for them [6].

However, learning to program is a fundamental part of any computing course and is seen to be essential when applying for jobs in computing [7]. It is part of the day to day routine for computing undergraduate students. Those who are currently on a computing course have varied experiences of computing. For instance, Murphy, Richards, McCauley, Morrison and Westbrook (2006) have described programming little or no impact upon female interest in computing [8]. In contrast, Margolis and Fisher (2002) reported that females found programming modules to be the hardest to get through. Once they had 'battled' through these, they felt that they could manage the rest of the course [6]. This is also demonstrated by Lahtinene, Ala-Mukta and Jarvinen (2005), where 500 students were asked to rank computing subjects to their difficulty and students ranked programming as difficult, more specifically ranking arrays seen to be difficult [9]. To expand, Guzadial and Soloway (2002) argue that those who teach computer science are using a 'outdated' view of computing and its students, which therefore provide an outdated experience of computing [10].

It has been noted in the literature that it is also common for female students to lack confidence in computing, specifically programming. Cooper and Weaver (2003), suggest that low self-confidence in computing is to do with computer-anxiety. In the sense that female students find it difficult to use the computer in front of others in case they make a mistake and feel embarrassed [11]. Lab work in undergraduate computing courses involves using the computer in front of others or in groups, which could bring about anxiety. An approach to addressing this is

Permission to make digital or hard copies of all or part of this work for personal or classroom use is granted without fee provided that copies are not made or distributed for profit or commercial advantage and that copies bear this notice and the full citation on the first page. To copy otherwise, or republish, to post on servers or to redistribute to lists, requires prior specific permission and/or a fee.
ITiCSE'11, June 27–29, 2011, Darmstadt, Germany.
Copyright 2011 ACM 978-1-4503-0697-3/11/06...$10.00.

demonstrated by Williams, who suggests that pair programming could help put female students at ease in lab work. Pair programming is a good support mechanism as it teaches students to work together and support each other [12].

Females have mentioned feeling isolated on computing courses and felt that they needed to prove themselves against the males. Women in industry felt that once they got through the initial hurdles, they enjoyed being with people who could program and felt a sense of 'camaraderie' on the course [13].

The way in which the IT industry is perceived is that it is 'only' about programming [14]. Programming is portrayed as difficult because it is unfamiliar to a number of students when they start their computing course. This is linked to the low confidence levels of which female students have, as they assume it is something impossible. A study by Leveson (1990) demonstrates this, whereby a group of male students who had not studied computing had perceived themselves to be knowledgeable in it, whereas female computing students did not rate themselves so highly in this category [15]. As well as a negative self-views in computing there are also negative perceptions of those who work in computing and work with code. A common perception of the type of person who works in the IT industry is the 'IT Geek'. It is a colloquial term used to describe someone who understands and works with the technical side of computers but has limited social understanding. The term 'geek' is defined in the Oxford English Dictionary as: '1. an unfashionable or socially inept person. 2. a knowledgeable and obsessive enthusiast [16]. It is the geeky image that is putting women off a career in IT. The next section describes the methods used to conduct a study looking into experiences of computing.

The main focus of this paper is to report the positive aspects, by exploring factors that influence interest and enjoyment in their courses.

2. RESEARCH DESIGN

Qualitative and quantitative data collection methods were used. We surveyed 103 participants from 3 different institutions and then interviewed 60 from the same three institutions. 60 of these participants opted to be interviewed.

The interviews added context to the questionnaires and bought the responses 'to life', as there was the opportunity to probe and therefore add more depth to the data. All participants were at different stages of their undergraduate course in computing. Table 1 provides the interview sample.

University	Number of Interviewees
A	30
B	15
C	15

Table 1 Interview Sample

The questionnaire elicited information in the following topic areas:

1. Experiences of the computer at university.

2. Experience of computers at home.

The questionnaires helped to provide numerical information to understand how young people used technology in university and at home. Without these, it would have been difficult to probe into this further at the interview stage. In essence, the need to do

these questionnaires was to confirm that there were differences and what these differences were.

Interviews were then used to delve deeper into these differences, so as to understand the feelings and motivations behind why young people felt a certain way. The script for the interview was based on the results of the questionnaire and helped narrow what needed to be asked. At this stage the impact that programming made on the student experience was clear. The interviews focused on obtaining a further understanding of how programming affected participants plans for the future, how it impacted perceptions of IT careers, and its influence in IT careers.

3. RESULTS

There were obviously some negative comments but this analysis focuses upon the positive factors. We would like to highlight the positive good practice around UK universities to encourage tutors and female students to make programming a more positive experience. The questionnaire results demonstrated some apathy towards programming among female undergraduate students. However during the interviews, it was very clear that programming is both a positive and satisfying experience. It was apparent that it was the support and perceptions surrounding computing which proved problematic. These results will focus on the positive experiences participants had of programming. We have found through our data collection that programming can act as a 'hook' into computing careers. We have identified examples of good practice and case studies, which demonstrate that programming, can act as an enabler into higher education and beyond.

Our data analysis and review of the literature indicates that the issues with programming are not to do with the act of programming specifically but rather the way it is taught, the support given and the way in which it is perceived.

Within our survey, programming as an activity on the computer was given a negative rating in comparison to other activities in our survey. It was evident that although programming was not the least preferred activity, it certainly wasn't very high in the rankings. See Table 2.

Rank	Activity	I like it	OK	I really don't like it	I hate it
1	Email	45	5	2	0
2	Social Networking	41	5	6	0
3	Website Design	25	10	15	2
3	Surfing the Web	25	12	15	0
4	Computer Games	21	10	9	10
5	Blogging	15	21	12	2
6	Graphic Design	12	15	13	8
6	**Programming**	**12**	**15**	**20**	**3**
7	Homework	5	16	25	6

Table 2 what people liked to do on the computer at UG level (Rankings constructed from the average of outcomes).

Email and Social networking were the most popular. Doing the interviews, it was expected that coding would have negative responses due to the literature survey and the questionnaire data. However, it was surprising to receive positive comments about it and enough to be able to analyze positive aspects of it. The next sections demonstrate these in more depth, using qualitative evidence to show these findings.

3.1 Interview Results: Positive experiences

There were different ways in how participants found programming to be a satisfying experience. 48 out of the 60 female students interviewed, mentioned how programming was enjoyable and how it helped them to understand their subject further. There were obviously negative comments; however this analysis focused upon the positive factors. We would like to highlight the positive good practice around UK universities and through highlighting these; we may be able to make programming a more positive experience for female students. Table 3 demonstrates how many participants mentioned each category of positive experience; there maybe some overlap as participants may have mentioned more than one category.

Category	Number of participants
1.Real life context to programming	31
2. Programming support	39
3. Parental Influence	47
4. Mathematics as a pre-course	30

Table 3 shows the different positive categories participants mentioned.

The following sections provide examples using qualitative data from the interviews.

3.1.1 Providing a real life context to programming.

Female participants said that they enjoyed programming the most when it was applied to a real life context. This was suggested by 31 participants (13 first year and 18 second year). Participants said that during the first year when they were learning how to program, they seldom understood the point of it, as they were 'generic tasks' to do in order to get the grade they needed. However when they got to the second year and were asked to program to solve a problem, in other words creating a real solution to a real problem, they then understood the relevance and 'beauty' of what they were doing. The quote below by a third year female studying computing, specializing in artificial intelligence:

'I came in with no programming experience... I didn't know what it was. I just knew it was going to be difficult. The thing is in the first year I just did not see why we had to spend ages coding things, I kept on thinking 'why am I here... this really sucks'. Then we got to the second year: It all fell into place; I suddenly understood and suddenly loved it. I found myself staying up until 3am trying to debug something. I was hooked when we had to solve a problem on flight simulations. It sounds boyish... but I love flying and I got to decide what buttons did

what, what color did what - I was the pilot of this particular plane and everything else to do with programming. I love it'.

Relating coursework / assignments to real life was a real hook into programming for the female student quoted above. This type of assignment bridged the gap between a task being difficult and the task being challenging but satisfying. This also enabled her to learn experientially. In other words, she learnt through doing without realizing as she had a task to complete by the end of it.

3.1.2 Programming support

The quote above mentioned that the participant was working on her assignment until early in the morning. Enabling students to do this was a factor in developing students' passion for programming. Female students did not react well to the time pressure of coding in seminar sessions and preferred either working in the lab at their own pace or working from home. One example was how female participants from University A (29 students) mentioned that at the beginning of the year they were given a CD with all the resources they needed to work from home so they could work at their own pace. The quote below demonstrates how doing this enabled a female student to develop her programming skills so she didn't feel intimidated in seminars.

'I could sit down with my laptop on my bed, had my music on and I opened my C book and just worked through it at my own pace. I didn't have to worry about people being a head of me. I felt that if I stayed a chapter a head of the seminar sessions then I was able to handle the computer lab. It sounds geeky but it saved me and it now means that I am not scared in lessons anymore. Sometimes I forget to read before hand but I am confident enough in my ability to just 'pick it up'.'

This was a popular technique with female students, reading ahead meant they were able to understand the work at their own pace. Working in the computer lab was a popular location for completing work and the environment of the lab proved to be a positive impact on female students. Table 4 shows that that from the survey, working from home was popular. Working from home was prominent in the interviews.

	Home	Library	Computer Lab	Friend or Family House
Percentages (%)	67	11	22	0

Table 4 Location of computer use preference

Female students from all year groups mentioned that in between lectures they enjoyed hanging around the lab to get on with work or to just surf the web. They said it was a comfortable atmosphere, where they could eat food, talk and get help with work. The quote below describes how a female student felt about the lab.

'Oh the lab is cool. I go there sometimes, it's like base camp. Theres always a good computer in the lab to do work. I do code in the lab sometimes cos I can eat and things there. Its cool we had a group coding project and we ordered pizza. It meant we weren't interrupted and we could work quite late together. It

also means I can work with my friend until late and we can both go home and get the bus together. I guess it's just where all the action happens!'

Female participants above mentioned above being able to work late into the lab, but they also worried about walking home alone. University A had a safety bus for student union clubbers, which coders also made use of. This was something, which that particular group of students felt liberated by.

All 60 students commented on the positives and negatives of group work. The positives for every female student was having at least one other female in the group to talk to. They said that it was more likely than not that they knew all the female students on the course so having another female in the group would be less intimidating than having a group full of male students. The quote below demonstrates this point.

'I would have died if I was in a group with a bunch of guys on my own. Don't get me wrong, they are really helpful but I know for a fact that if [female student] was not there then I would get stuck doing tasks I did not want to like written work. At least with the two of us it's easier to stick up for our opinions and workload.'

It is interesting that the points above are not to do with programming but rather the support involved. Within University B and A, female students had a lot of support during their first year. They felt that it stopped them from wanting to quit their computing course as programming was difficult, but with the right support they were able to enjoy programming and treat it as a challenge rather than an impossible task. They were assigned study groups where they regularly met with the same classmates and were given the help of a postgraduate student who assisted with any issues. This postgraduate was not there as someone to do the work for them but just to support them. The students found that during the first couple weeks they really needed the help, but they then learnt to solve problems and realized that debugging and feeling challenged was part of programming. Once they had accepted this, they were able to enjoy programming. This quote from a second year student demonstrates this:

'We thought it was strange that the postgraduate student couldn't solve our programming queries instantly. She had to go through various processes to solve the problem. I think that she taught us that programming is exploratory and that's where the satisfaction comes from. Its very frustrating but seeing that an expert also has problems, kinds of helps!'

In general all year groups found that they instinctively formed study groups and places like labs, *Facebook* and tutor groups enable this to happen. Even though the number of females on the degree courses was small, they had formed their own support network where they were able to call on each other for help if needed.

Researcher: 'So when did you feel part of your course, like when did you think – yes, this is great I really like it.'

DegreeComputingSolentF17: 'Honestly?'

Researcher: 'Yep!'

DegreeComputingSolentF17: 'After about a year and a half. I always felt that I shouldn't have been here ... that everyone knows a lot more than me. But they don't, everyone else is just too scared to show they are struggling as well. But I think it took me a while but now I am going for it!'

The experiences young people have of programming vary, however we need to remember as a community that it is not programming which puts students off computing but rather the support around it.

3.1.3 Parental Influence on course decisions

All female participants who decided to study Computing or IT said they did so because of the positive influences and encouragement they had encountered from out of school and at school. However, there were fears about learning how to program. Those who decided to do computing said they were supported by their parents who told them that learning to program would not be their biggest barrier.

Female participants studying for computing degree level courses at all three universities indicated that their parents had been the main driving force behind them deciding to study computing at university. In particular it was fathers who encouraged their daughters.

'I was really scared about doing a computing course and I was going to go for maths. My dad asked what I was scared about and I said it was programming. He said that everyone is scared of programming but its OK and that not everyone will be expert programmers when they first start. I think this reassured me. Yes I think it did.'

There were two groups of students, female participants who had taken mathematics at A-level and were influenced a lot later to take computing at degree level and participants whose fathers had been an ongoing influence to them to take computing.

'My dad works at IBM and he always liked to explain technical concepts to me. So I got the other side of computing as well as the user side'.

Fathers had exerted influence through playing computer games, introducing them to new things on the computer, encouraging their daughter to help set up a computer and encouraging their daughter to think about computer careers. In some cases, it was fathers who had a computing/technical job, which influenced female participants to study the subject as their fathers often bought their work home with them.

3.1.4 Positive impact of Mathematics

The majority of female participants (29 out of 34) who decided to study computing had done so because of their interest in mathematics. This is indicated in Table 5 which shows that 85% of female participants studied mathematics before deciding to study computing. These were female participants who enjoyed mathematics but were not sure about carrying it on at degree level, but were told that they could use their mathematics and apply it to computing. Interestingly, programming was something that bought these students in as they said they understood it due to the logical thinking.

'I dunno, I wanted a more practical application and computing seemed to fit! The programming wasn't a huge issue as it seemed to be liked logic'.

These female participants had not taken computing before and were not wary of it but curious about the degree.

Female Participants	Computing A-level	IT A-level	Mathematics A-level
Percentage (%)	9	6	85

Table 5 Participants who had taken mathematics previously.

It may be that computing at A-level is putting people off but mathematics and the curiosity about its relation to computers is bringing people in. All female participants who were doing computing because of mathematics had been introduced to computing by either a parent or teacher.

4. REFLECTIONS AND CONCLUSIONS

The samples in this study are not necessary representative of the population and no attempt has been made to make population estimates in this study. The aim of this paper is not to document or assume that every female is of a certain opinion. However, the trends are an indicator of what is happening with regards to female students' experiences of IT and computing. We do believe that this study has demonstrated that programming can be an enriching experience if students are supported in the right way.

We read about examples of bad practice; however we feel that this paper demonstrates that we need to focus on how programming can help open doors for female students. It is clear from the interviews with different female students that support and raising confidence is a factor in increasing the enjoyment of programming. We should make sure that students are aware that it is challenging but it is also possible. Initially it seemed that programming was detrimental to female students enjoying computing, however through further probing we found that this was not the case, and it might be that female students may not know themselves that they enjoy programming and may rely on their first instinct, which is that it is difficult and not enjoyable.

This study has shown that programming itself on undergraduate courses is not the sole reason for female students for not taking up computing as a career but there are other factors, which have been highlighted. Instead, we need to focus as much as possible to enhance the programming experience, and from the data we have, we feel that taking into account the categories above can assist with this.

Through applying programming to real life situations, we have seen that students were able to understand the virtues of knowing how to program and thus gained satisfaction from doing so. It was clear that once they had grasped the underlying purpose of what they had to do, they felt less alienated when programming.

Support given in institutions was a factor in encouraging female students to pursue programming further. Support came in the form of providing students with CD's to take software to work from home or providing them with access to a postgraduate student to help them out on programming aspects they felt they needed support on. This type of support was important to raise the confidence female students had in programming.

Female students had suggested that programming had been something which put them off studying computing at university. It was positive that their parents had put their fears at ease by explaining that not everyone on the course would know how to program during the first year. Within this study, parental influence seems to have helped female students to choose computing at university.

Mathematics acted as a 'hook' into programming and it was the students who had studied mathematics previously, who felt confident about applying on a computing course at university.

This paper began with the premise that programming is frustrating and difficult. However, we have found through our data collection that programming can enable female students to enjoy programming. We have identified examples of good practice that demonstrate that programming can act as a bridge into higher education and beyond.

5. REFERENCES

[1] Greenfield, Peters, Lane, Rees and Samuels Set Fair: A Report on Women in Science, Engineering and Technology *London: Department of Trade and Industry*2002).

[2] Faulkner, W. and Lie, M. Gender in the Information Society. *Gender, Technology and Development*, 11, 2 2007), 157-177.

[3] BCS, BERR, Intellect and UK, e.-s. *Women in IT Scorecard.* 2009.

[4] NCC. *NCC: Benchmark Results 2009*. National Centre for Computing, 2009.

[5] UCAS *University and Colleges Admissions Service: Subject Search* City, 2006.

[6] Fisher, A., Margolis, J. and Miller, F. Undergraduate women in computer science: experience, motivation and culture. *SIGCSE Bull.*, 29, 1 1997), 106-110.

[7] QCA *ICT National Curriculum Scheme of Work*. Department of Skills and Education City, 2005.

[8] Murphy, M., Westbrook, Richards, Morrison, Fossum. Women Catch Up: Gender Differences in Learning Programming Concepts. In *Proceedings of the SIGCSE* (Texas, 2006). ACM,]

[9] Lahtinen, A.-M., Jarvinen *A study of the difficulties of novice programmers.* . ACM, City, 2005.

[10] Guzdial, M. and Soloway, E. Teaching the Nintendo generation to program. *Commun. ACM*, 45, 4 2002), 17-21.

[11] Cooper, W. *Gender and Computers: Understanding the Digital Divide* 2003.

[12] Werner, L. L., Hanks, B. and McDowell, C. Pair-programming helps female computer science students. *J. Educ. Resour. Comput.*, 4, 1 2004), 4.

[13] Clarke and Teague Characterizations of computing careers: Students and professionals disagree. *Computers & Education*, 26, 4 1996), 241-246.

[14] Kinzie, M., Delcourt, M. and Powers, S. Computer technologies: Attitudes and self-efficacy across undergraduate disciplines. *Research in higher eduation*, 34, 6 1994), 745-768.

[15] Leveson Educational Pipeline Issues for Women. *Comput Res News*1991).

[16] OED *Oxford English Dictionary*. Oxford, City, 2006.

A Medical Motif for Teaching Computer Graphics in Context

James Wolfer
Indiana University South Bend
South Bend, IN, USA
jwolfer@iusb.edu

ABSTRACT

In conjunction with Eurographics 2009 and SIGGRAPH, a working group explored the nature and role of teaching computer graphics in context. One issue identified in that forum was acquiring the resources necessary to embed a real-world context into a computer graphics course. This work describes an infrastructure subset for embedding a medical motif into a senior-level computer graphics course.

Categories and Subject Descriptors

K.3.2 [**Computers and Education**]: Computer Science Education

General Terms

Human Factors

Keywords

Education, Computer Graphics, Medical

1. INTRODUCTION

Introducing a systematic context to act as a topical scaffold for computing classes has garnered increasing attention recently. Examples include the Case-Cunningham hosted Eurographics 2009 workshop to explore teaching computer graphics in context [1], a Cooper-Cunningham paper which provides a defensible intellectual framework supporting contextual instruction [2], and a Guzdial response [3]. Informed by recent literature, along with work teaching Artificial Intelligence in context [5], this paper describes an infrastructure for establishing a medical motif for a CS introduction to computer graphics elective.

The course covers topics ranging from pixel representation and geometric transformations to rendering. The first motif-related student activity is to manually construct a model of their own hand to provide students with insight into the impact of model representation for subsequent computation, such as polygon normal orientation. A sample hand is shown in Figure 1.

Later assignments use instructor provided anatomical models created from Osirix DICOM CT datasets [4]. These models contain between 40 thousand and 1.5 million triangles.

Figure 1: Models and Images

Examples are shown in Figure 1. The skull in Figure 1 is actually composed of a skull-top and a separate mandible. Students use OpenGL to generate an animation which rotates the skull around the transverse axis while simultaneously rotating the mandible through a local axis, thus introducing compound transformations and animation.

Additional motif-illustrated concepts include using haptics to explore mammograms and vascular structures such as the aorta and carotid arteries, stereographic rendering, arterial fly-through, and basic image processing. All of medical infrastructure reported here was accomplished using open-source tools and publicly available data.

While we do not yet have a quantitative assessment of the learning impact, anecdotally the embedded medical motif has provided motivation and inspiration as evidenced in post-course projects including CT analysis for cardiology, mammogram processing, and GPU-accelerated image analysis.

2. REFERENCES

[1] C. Case and S. Cunningham. Teaching computer graphics in context. In *Report of Computer Graphics 2009 Workshop*. Eurographics, ACM, March 2009.

[2] S. Cooper and S. Cunningham. Teaching computer science in context. *ACM Inroads*, 1(1):5–8, March 2010.

[3] M. Guzdial. Does contextualized computing education help? *ACM Inroads*, 1(4):4–6, December 2010.

[4] Osirix. Open-source dicom viewer. http://http://www.osirix-viewer.com/.

[5] J. Wolfer. Work in progress - a biomedical motif for teaching artificial intelligence in context. In *Frontiers in Education Conference Proceedings*. ASEE/IEEE, October 2010.

Courseware: Student Learning via FOSS Field Trips

Heidi J. C. Ellis
Western New England College
1215 Wilbraham Rd.
Springfield, MA 01119
011-413-782-1748

hellis@wnec.edu

Gregory W. Hislop
Drexel University
3141 Chestnut St.
Philadelphia, PA 19104
011-215-895-2179

hislop@drexel.edu

ABSTRACT
Many faculty members understand the potential for computing students to learn via participation in Free and Open Source Software (FOSS) projects. However, there are few resources for introducing students (and faculty members) to FOSS projects. This tip presents several "FOSS field trip" assignments that allow students to explore and learn about FOSS projects.

Categories and Subject Descriptors
K.3.2 [**Computers and Education**]: Computer and Information Science Education – *Computer Science Education.*

General Terms
Human Factors.

Keywords
Open source software, student learning, computing education.

1. EXAMPLE FIELD TRIPS
"Field trips" are exploratory assignments intended to introduce students to various aspects of open source software. These assignments may be customized depending on student background and may be used for introductory students as well as experienced computing majors. Additional field trips may be found on the SoftHum site: http://www.xcitegroup.org/softhum

1.1 Exploring a Forge
One activity that provides students with a perspective on the size and longevity of the open source software world is to have them explore a "forge" (e.g., SourceForge) and report on their discoveries. Students begin by browsing the forge based on category of FOSS project. Questions to guide student investigation include:

- How many projects are there in this category?

- Which ones are the leading projects?

- Browse the category of "humanitarian" FOSS projects such as Mifos, Sahana and OpenMRS.

- List several other examples of humanitarian FOSS projects.

- Pick one humanitarian FOSS and look at the available data.

- How would you decide whether it was worth using?

- How would you decide whether it was worth contributing to as an IT professional?

The results of the "field trips" can be discussed and compared as a class. One alternative is to allocate different students to different forges and compare the results.

1.2 Assessing a Project
The goal of this assignment is to help students develop some skills at approaching and assessing a larger project. The goal isn't for students to understand the project in detail, but rather that they get some feel for the scale of the project, and a bit of understanding about how the project operates from a developer's perspective.

The instructor selects two projects that are of interest that are somewhat different (e.g., VUFind and Mifos). Students spend about an hour looking over each of the projects. They are instructed to try to approach the project as someone interested in helping with the project (as a developer, documenter, tester, etc).

Students provide a written summary discussing what they found and what they thought about the projects. Some questions to try to answer about either or both projects include:

- How many people are working on the project?

- How active is the project?

- Are there clear starting points for someone interested in helping with the project?

- Are there usable technical documents that describe the project?

- How are bugs and feature requests tracked? Are there a lot of open items? Are they being worked on?

- Do you think you could download and install this product?

- How do the developers communicate with each other?

- What has been the most interesting thing you learned through this exercise?

Students then can compare results in class. The idea is that not all of the questions above are answered, but the questions are used to guide the exploration of the project.

2. ACKNOWLEDGMENTS
This material is based on work supported by the National Science Foundation under Grant Nos. DUE-0958204 and DUE- 0940925. Any opinions, findings and conclusions or recommendations expressed in this material are those of the author(s) and do not necessarily reflect the views of the National Science Foundation (NSF).

Infandango: Automated Grading for Student Programming

Mike Hull
School of Informatics
University of Edinburgh, UK
m.j.hull@sms.ed.ac.uk

Dan Powell
School of Informatics
University of Edinburgh, UK
d.c.powell@sms.ed.ac.uk

Ewan Klein
School of Informatics
University of Edinburgh, UK
ewan@inf.ed.ac.uk

ABSTRACT

Infandango[1] is an open source web-based system for automated grading of Java code submitted by students. Uploaded Java files are compiled and run against a set of unit tests on a central server, with results being stored in a database. Students gain near-instant feedback on the correctness of their code, and instructors are able to monitor the progress of students in the class.

Categories and Subject Descriptors: K.3.2 Computer and Information Science Education:Computer Science Education

General Terms: Human factors, Measurement

Keywords: Automatic grading, Java, Django, reStructuredText, Sphinx

1. OVERVIEW

Like many other educational institutions, we run an introductory course in Java programming for undergraduates, and face the problem of giving students feedback on their answers to practical exercises in the lab. Although this work is, in the main, formatively assessed, we have found that students appreciate receiving a numerical grade for their work; the obvious mechanism for achieving this is to run relatively fine-grained JUnit[2] tests over the code. In developing our own software for automatic assessment, we focussed on the following requirements: **modularity**, **security**, and **ease of use** for both students and instructors. We based our software on the Django[3] web framework because of its excellent support for agile development.

Figure 1 shows the architecture of infandango. Communication between the web frontend and Jester, our Junit testing daemon, is mediated by a PostgresSQL[4] database. The database holds information about files that have been submitted by users and the results that they receive from Jester. User access to the system is protected by CoSign[5] authentication. In addition, there is a set of Python tools for uploading question sheets, batch uploading code for testing by Jester, and for generating reports.

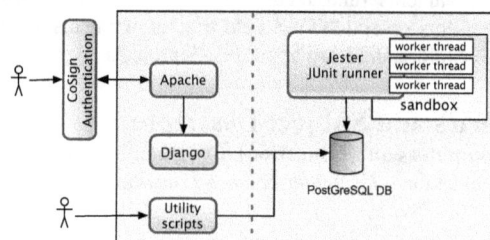

Figure 1. The infandango server

When a Java source file is submitted, Jester compiles it, executes it in a sandbox and runs the unit tests. If the tests succeed, the student is awarded marks in the database; if not, they are informed about which tests failed.

Lab exercise are written using the Sphinx[6] extensions of reStructuredText.[7] This provides excellent support for syntax highlighting of code blocks, and made it very easy to produce standalone versions of the lab exercises in addition to those served *via* infandango.

2. DEPLOYMENT

Infandango was first deployed in January 2011 for our introductory Java programming course. Exercises were written on a weekly basis and merged into the live system, resulting in a total of 45 exercises marked by over 150 JUnit tests. Over 100 students used the system, submitting close to 5,500 Java source files, and to date, over 20,000 unit tests have been executed on student code.

3. CONCLUSION

The most notable features of infandango are its modularity and extensibility. Components of the system are loosely coupled: standalone modules for authentication, web frontend and unit testing interact with each other only where necessary. Since the CoSign authentication uses standard HTTP headers, it can easily be replaced by another method. The frontend could be replaced or further customised without affecting the tester in any way, and in principle, different test components could replace Jester. Finally, there is little dependence on PostgreSQL, and switching to another database manager would take very little effort.

---

[1] https://bitbucket.org/ewan/infandango
[2] http://www.junit.org/
[3] http://www.djangoproject.com/
[4] http://www.postgresql.org/
[5] http://cosign.sourceforge.net/

[6] http://sphinx.pocoo.org/
[7] http://docutils.sourceforge.net/rst.html

Scheduling and Student Performance

Clifford A. Shaffer
Department of Computer Science
Virginia Tech
shaffer@cs.vt.edu

Stephen H. Edwards
Department of Computer Science
Virginia Tech
edwards@cs.vt.edu

ABSTRACT

We present data showing strong correlation between students' time management and a successful outcome on programming assignments. Students who spread their work over more time will produce a better result without additional expenditure of total effort. We examined performance of students who sometimes did well and sometimes did poorly, and found that their good performance occurred on the projects where they displayed better time management. While these results will not surprise most instructors, hard data is more compelling than intuition when trying to train students to use good time management.

Categories and Subject Descriptors

K.3.2 [**Computers and Education**]: Computer and Information Science Education

General Terms

Experimentation

Keywords

Scheduling, student performance, time management

1. SUMMARY

A persistent problem for students in programming classes is poor performance due to poor time management on multiweek programming projects. Procrastination is always a concern for students, but computer programs are especially unforgiving to those who delay engaging the work. While instructors often tell students to start programming projects early and spread the workload over time, admonishments alone do not affect student behavior. Our data show strong evidence that starting early on projects and spreading the work over time correlates with a successful outcome on programming assignments. While this will not surprise most instructors, hard data is more compelling than intuition when trying to train students to use good time management.

Since Fall, 2006, we require students to submit weekly schedule sheets in our Sophomore-level data structures and algorithms course. The programming projects have a three to four week life cycle. Student enter their own list of tasks required to complete the project, list the number of hours they predict will be required for each task, and their own intermediate deadlines. Each week they update the schedule

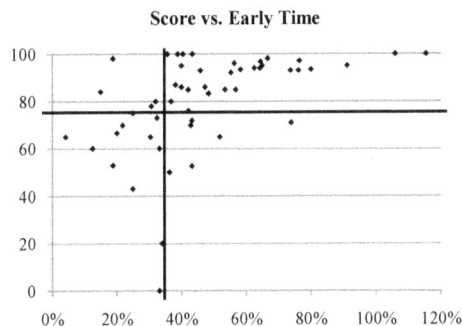

Score vs. Early Time

to indicate hours actually worked, and new time estimates and completion dates. Many students report that they do not like to do the scheduling sheets, though a significant minority report that they find that it improves their performance, and anecdotal evidence indicates that many students have concluded in retrospect that scheduling is beneficial.

The amount of time put in "early" was analyzed. The figure shows project score (vertical axis) vs. % of original estimated time students completed about a week before the due date. Time (horizontal axis) can be greater than 100% since students might spend more time than originally estimated. The horizontal line is the mean across all four projects. The vertical line is the optimal partition, 36.8% of initially estimated time completed before the last week. Most submissions are grouped into the upper right (good) and lower left (bad) quadrants. In the vast majority of projects that scored below the class mean, students put in fewer than 50% of initially estimated hours before the final week. The vast majority of students scoring above the mean completed more than 36.8% of the estimated time in advance.

These results do not necessarily mean that starting early causes good performance. To investigate this issue, an evaluation was made of five years of data collected in the first three programming courses at Virginia Tech through the Web-CAT grading system. Since students submit partial programs for automated testing to assess program correctness, these data provide good estimates of student progress during program development. Project results were split into A/B vs. C/D/F categories. Only students with scores in both categories were evaluated, and a within-subjects comparison of these scores was performed. The data show that when students received A/B scores, they started earlier and finished earlier than when they received C/D/F scores. They did not spend more time on their work, so it is clearly in a student's best interest to begin projects early. Unfortunately, getting students to do so still seems difficult.

Try a Little History

John Impagliazzo
Emeritus, Hofstra University
Department of Computer Science
Hempstead, New York 11549 USA
+1 631 513 2833

John.Impagliazzo@Hofstra.edu

ABSTRACT

This presentation describes ways in which teachers could use computing history to enrich topics in their courses. Computing history can be a very effective tool to teach computing courses. Using history as a pedagogical technique contributes to students' understanding and their life-long learning experiences. History also encourages students to appreciate better the subject at hand and enables them to gain a better sense of the nature of inquiry surrounding their area of study that includes the human dimension.

Categories and Subject Descriptors

K.2 [History of Computing]; K.3.2 [Computer and Information Science Education]: Computer science education

General Terms

Human Factors

Keywords

Computing history, computing education, course enhancement

SUMMARY

The inclusion of historical elements in a course has the advantage of making students think beyond the immediate computing topics. History has a way of encouraging students to look beyond the machine and broadens their outlook on the social implications of computing. Historical interludes might simply include a recitation of anecdotes to perk student interest or they might include extensive undertakings to engage students in critical thinking about a computing topic. Unlike some other fields of study, computing professionals tend not to promote and preserve their own history in a broad and consistent manner. As a result, teachers may be reluctant to include even elements of the subject in their teachings.

This presentation suggests ways in which teachers could include history in their courses. The approach is a result of a project conducted at Hofstra University that addressed the use of history in computing courses. The project attempted to change the way students learn by incorporating history as a theme used within existing courses. The approach encouraged students to explore computing history through various methods including virtual museums such as the Computer History Museum in California, the Charles Babbage Institute in Minnesota, the IEEE History Center and its Virtual Museum, the American Computer Museum in Montana, and other virtual museums worldwide.

In support of the history theme for the Hofstra project was (and still is) the website <www.CompHist.org> containing many historical resources and ancillary historical tools to help teachers prepare classes. The website contains links to historical resources such as chronologies, computing museums, corporate links, history courses, and allows users to search history by name or by period. The site even contains a history "puzzle" encouraging users to guess the identification of some principal contributors to the evolution of computing. The website contains some excerpts from the History of Programming Languages conferences, emulators for Turing machines and other theoretical computing machines, and other items of interest useful for a course in computing. The website also allows users to generate mini-history chronologies by topic. These historical "slices" correspond to knowledge areas that appear in recommended computing curricular reports. In addition, the project developed other focused areas related to computing history such as a discussion on DNA and quantum computing described in an elementary manner.

The website is a smart starting point for instructors who wish to explore the use of computing history in their courses. The embedded chronologies offer a good first step. History clusters show how a one could assemble a lesson plan to create a class experience on a particular history topic. It would not take long for teachers to familiarize themselves with history to develop a more effective learning experience for students.

Bridging storytelling with technical content could form a unique opportunity to connect technical material to real life. All teachers of computing should try this history approach. The rewards derived from the experience could certainly offset any preparation needed to present it. So, *try a little history*. You just might enjoy it while making your courses more exciting, more informative, and more relevant to today's world.

Best Practices in Teaching Mobile Application Development

Qusay H. Mahmoud

School of Computer Science, University of Guelph, Guelph, ON, N1G 2W1, Canada

ABSTRACT

This paper presents best practices for teaching mobile application development across the Computing curricula. While the focus is on the BlackBerry smartphone, the best practices can be used when teaching application development for other mobile platforms. The best practices are supported by the freely available CMER Academic Kit for integrating mobile devices into the Computer Science Curriculum.

Categories and Subject Descriptors: K.3.2 [**Computing Milieux**]: Computer and Information Science Education – *computer science education, curriculum, human factors, literacy.*

General Terms: Algorithms, Design, Experimentation, Languages.

Keywords: Mobile application development, mobile devices, BlackBerry, programming for fun, teaching computer programming, teaching tools.

1. Introduction

Developing mobile applications is quite challenging because such applications are developed on platforms such as Microsoft Windows or Linux but deployed on a totally different platform such as a BlackBerry Smartphone [1]. Teaching students how to develop mobile applications can be a rewarding experience or a nightmare. This paper presents best practices for teaching mobile application.

2. Best Practices

The following best practices contribute to effective and satisfying teaching and learning experience to both, faculty and students.

2.1 Start Early, But It is Never Too Late

Teaching mobile application development can be done as early as the first introductory programming course (or even earlier) or late in the curriculum in a specialized mobile computing course, a software engineering course, or even in the capstone project. I have taught across the curriculum [2]. The unique characteristics of mobile devices and the considerations that need to be taken into account will assist students to look at traditional application development on desktop platforms from a different perspective and apply some of the strategies in mobile application development to developing applications for other platforms.

2.2 Setup a Virtual Environment

Some of the mobile platforms require several software packages to be installed, and if you're going to teaching mobile application development at the introductory level then setting up a working

environment can be challenging. For such situations, create a virtual machine with a working development environment so that students could just download the virtual machine and run it on their desktops or laptops. Other platforms, such as the BlackBerry, require a single software install such as the all-inclusive Eclipse Plugin for Java and Web development. However, students still need to download and install simulators and other packages, and hence it is recommended to setup a working development environment into a virtual machine.

2.3 Provide Students with Mobile Devices

While running applications in an emulated or simulated environment provides a good framework for testing, we believe that allowing students to experiment with the physical devices themselves provides a totally different and better experience. If students happen to have mobile devices running the platform you're teaching on then you could ask them to do that. Otherwise, most vendors have an academic program, such as the BlackBerry Academic Program (www.blackberry.com/academic) that provides devices (free of charge) to academic institutions interested in integrating mobile devices and mobile application development into their curriculum.

3. Instructor Resources

The CMER Academic Kit [3] has been created to facilitate the integration of mobile devices into the Computing curricula. The kit, which is available free of charge, takes a mobile approach to teaching Computing content with a focus on Java ME, BlackBerry application development, and Web-based Mobile Apps. The academic kit contains 30 weeks worth of teaching material including lesson slides, labs, tutorials, quizzes and assignments. The topics covered feature Java ME, BlackBerry, GUI, event handling, multimedia, security, and networking, and widgets.

4. Conclusion

The popularity of mobile devices among students is inspiring faculty to look for ways to teach students how to develop mobile applications. The best practices presented in this paper are supported by the CMER Academic Kit that is available free of charge for academic use.

5. References

[1] Mahmoud, Q.H., and Dyer, A., "Integrating BlackBerry Wireless Devices into Computing Programming and Literacy Courses", *Proceedings of the 45th Southeast Conference*, Winston-Salem, NC, USA, March 2007, pp. 495-500.

[2] Mahmoud, Q.H., "Integrating Mobile Devices into the Computer Science Curriculum". The 38th Annual Frontiers in Education Conference (FIE 2008), Saratoga Springs, NY, USA, October 22-25, 2008., pp. S3E-17-S3E-22.

[3] CMER Academic Kit: CMER.cis.uoguelph.ca, last accessed on March 10, 2011.

A Mobile Web-based Approach to Introductory Programming

Qusay H. Mahmoud

School of Computer Science, University of Guelph, Guelph, ON, N1G 2W1, Canada

ABSTRACT

In this paper an approach for teaching introductory programming courses using mobile web-based technologies is introduced. This approach focuses on using standard Web technologies, such as HTML, JavaScript, and Cascading Style Sheets to make teaching computer programming fun, especially for users of mobile devices. This approach is supported by the CMER Academic Kit for integrating mobile devices into the Computer Science Curriculum.

Categories and Subject Descriptors: K.3.2 [**Computing Milieux**]: Computer and Information Science Education – *computer science education, curriculum, human factors, literacy.*

General Terms: Algorithms, Design, Experimentation, Languages.

Keywords: Mobile application development, mobile devices, BlackBerry, programming for fun, teaching computer programming, teaching tools.

1. Introduction

With the widespread use of mobile devices such as smartphones and pocket personal computers, there is a great need for innovation in Computing education to reflect today's reality [2]. For example, students in introductory programming courses usually develop and test their programming assignments on a platform similar to the one on which they will be tested by the instructor or teaching assistant. However, this is not the case for mobile applications which are developed on one platform such as Microsoft Windows or Linux and deployed on a totally different platform such as a BlackBerry smartphone [1]. A great opportunity exists for introducing students to different programming models which will not only be very practical but can also inspire students to be excited about learning. Those students, equipped with the most current training in this field, may play a key role in driving innovations in the mobile space.

This paper presents a mobile web-centric approach for teaching introductory programming courses.

2. The Approach

Several papers have been publishing describing approaches for teaching introductory programming, that have ranged from using computing games, to robotics, to special environments such as Alive, Scratch, and Greenfoot. Each approach has its pros and cons, but I believe the context in which programming is taught is important and relevant for student learning. I believe that the use of the Web and Mobile Devices as a context is particularly interesting as these technologies provide a medium that the students are familiar with and could easily relate to. The approach focuses on using HTML, Cascading Style Sheets (CSS), and

JavaScript for developing simple Web applications, and later to use the same technologies for developing mobile applications that will run on their own devices. This approach is attractive as student use simple tools to build powerful applications, and students do not need to worry about cryptic error messages as the applications they develop run in browsers which are forgiving.

3. Software Tools

The software tools needed depend on which mobile platform you wish to target. For BlackBerry smartphones for example, you'll need the BlackBerry Widget SDK (or WebWorks) which is a free open source project. This tool, which is an Eclipse Plugin, comes with all the necessary utilities for developing, compiling, and running mobile applications on the BlackBerry simulators. These simulators, which are available free to charge, provide a low-barrier entry to get started with mobile application development. However, for some applications that make use of the camera or GPS, it is best to test the applications on a real device and students are also excited about this. However, in order to run Widgets on devices, they need to be signed and the instructor and/or students need to apply for signing keys from RIM (www.blackberry.com/SignedKeys). There is a $20 cost, and given the low cost, it is recommend that each student obtains his/her own signing keys.

4. Instructor Resources

The CMER Academic Kit [3] has been created to facilitate the integration of mobile devices into the Computing curricula. The kit, which is available free of charge, takes a mobile approach to teaching Computing content with a focus on Java ME, BlackBerry application development, and Web-based Mobile Apps. The academic kit contains 30 weeks worth of teaching material including lesson slides, labs, tutorials, quizzes and assignments.

5. Conclusion

The popularity of mobile devices among students is inspiring faculty to look for ways to teach students how to develop mobile applications, and the use of HTML and JavaScript present a powerful opportunity for teaching introductory programming for mobile devices. This approach is supported by the CMER Academic Kit which is available free of charge for academic use.

6. References

[1] Mahmoud, Q.H., Dobosiewicz, W., and Swayne, D. "Redesigning Introductory Computer Programming with HTML, JavaScript, and Java." In Proc. of the 35th SIGCSE Technical Symposium on Computer Science Education (SIGCSE2004), Northfolk, VA, USA, pp. 120-124.

[2] Mahmoud, Q.H., and Dyer, A., "Integrating BlackBerry Wireless Devices into Computing Programming and Literacy Courses", *Proceedings of the 45th Southeast Conference*, Winston-Salem, NC, USA, March 2007, pp. 495-500.

[3] CMER Academic Kit, http://CMER.cis.uoguelph.ca. Last accessed on March 10, 2011.

Two Kinesthetic Learning Activities: Turing Machines and Basic Computer Organization

Michael Goldweber
Xavier University
mikeyg@cs.xu.edu

ABSTRACT

Kinesthetic learning "is a learning style in which learning takes place by the student actually carrying out a physical activity, rather than listening to a lecture or merely watching a demonstration."[2] Activities that incorporate kinesthetic learning are called KLAs. There is a rich set of opportunities for using KLAs in computer science education[3]. This report describes two KLAs; one which is used to convey basic computer organization/stored-program architectures, and the other to convey the basics of Turing machines.

Categories and Subject Descriptors

K.3.2 [**Computer and Information Science Education**]: [Computer Science Education]

General Terms

Design, Experimentation

Keywords

Kinesthetic Learning Activities, In-class Exercises

1. BASIC MACHINE ORGANIZATION

Many introductory computing classes include a module on basic computer organization. A difficult concept for introductory students is the stored-program concept. This KLA is designed to assist students in understanding this concept.

The KLA is based on the Simple Computer[1] model; a base 10 computer with 100 memory cells, a ten instruction ISA and a 3-digit "word-size." Instead of simply working through the operation of one of the available emulators, one can employ a KLA. Initially, one declares the ISA and describes the semantics of each instruction. To keep complexity down, only input, output, load, store and addition are needed. $n-3$ students are employed to represent the first $n-3$ memory cells. The remaining three students are assigned the task of PC, IR, and ACCUMULATOR.

Position the the memory cells in a circle around the cpu registers. Using notecards that have been pre-filled, hand out the instructions for a simple introductory program. (e.g. Input two values, add them together and output the result.) Load the PC with the address of the first instruction and "run" the program. In this KLA, the PC actually *fetches* the targeted instruction (notecard held by the named memory cell), hands it off to the IR, and updates its own value (PC = PC+1). The IR register *decodes* the instruction handed to it and *executes* the indicated operation.

2. TURING MACHINES

In a Theory of Computation or Formal Languages course one introduces Turing machines (TM) sometime after the halfway point. With luck, this will correspond to tolerable outdoor temperatures, as this KLA takes place outdoors. Using sidewalk chalk, any sufficiently long sidewalk will perfectly represent a TMs tape.

The initial preparation is to create a simple TM program. (e.g. A TM to recognize a non-context free language or one that will compute a simple function.) Using notecards (the staple of any KLA practitioner) write down each state's transitions; all of state q_i's transitions on card i. Distribute the notecards to students and designate one other student as the read/write (R/W) head.

Using the chalk, place the input string on the "tape." Physically place the R/W head at the start square and inform the R/W head what their start state is. The TM operates by having the R/W head shouting out what state they are in and what symbol they are standing on. For a deterministic TM, only one student transition should answer with directions: new state, new symbol, and a left/right move command. Using the chalk, the R/W head follows the shouted out directions and repeats.

After students get some facility with creating their own TMs one can return to the outdoors to test student written TMs. Its always instructive to have TMs with infinite loops or TMs that send the R/W head off down the tape infinitely.

3. REFERENCES

[1] Decimal computer emulator. http://emulator.decimalcomputer.com/.
[2] Kinesthetic learning. http://en.wikipedia.org/wiki/Kinesthetic_learning.
[3] A. Begel, D. Garcia, and S. Wolfman. Kinesthetic learning in the classroom. In *Proc. of the 35th SIGCSE Technical Symposium on Computer Science Education*, 2004.

Stimulating Learning and Engagement: An Integrated System Simulator for Computer Architecture

Besim Mustafa

Business School
Edge Hill University
Ormskirk, UK.
+44 (0)1695 657640

mustafab@edgehill.ac.uk

ABSTRACT

An educational system simulator integrating several specialized simulators in one software package supporting the students of computer architectures and operating systems is described. The highly interactive and visual simulators demonstrate the important principles of modern CPU architectures, optimizing compilers and multi-threading operating systems. The simulations enable the students to understand the layered architecture of modern computers and to study in detail the ways in which the CPU hardware, the CPU instruction set architecture supported by the optimizing compiler and the operating system services interact and cooperate to maximize system performance.

Categories and Subject Descriptors

K.3.1 [**Computers Uses in Education**]: Computer-assisted instruction (CAI); K.3.2 [**Computers and Information Science Education**]: Computer Science Education --- *CPU architecture, operating system.*

General Terms

Algorithms, Experimentation.

Keywords

CPU architecture, CPU instructions, operating system, compiler, visualization, simulation, education, pedagogy.

1. INTRODUCTION

A unique integrated set of simulators collectively identified as the system simulator [2] has been designed and implemented to support lectures and tutorials in undergraduate computer architecture courses. The system simulator closely adheres to modern principles of pedagogy by facilitating student engagement and enhancing student learning experiences [1, 3].

2. INTEGRATED SYSTEM SIMULATOR

The system simulator captures the three important and key aspects of computer architecture: generation of CPU instructions by high-level language compilers; the CPU as the instruction processor; the operating system (OS) facilitating multiprogramming and multi-threading of CPU instructions. The system simulator demonstrates and explores the interplay between these areas. All simulations are highly configurable, interactive and visual. The simulator is freely available for educational purposes from www.teach-sim.com.

2.1 THE CPU SIMULATOR

The CPU simulator simulates RISC type architecture with a large register set, minimal addressing modes and a small register-based instruction set. It incorporates a 5-stage pipeline simulator and Harvard style separate data and instruction cache simulators. Multiple processors are supported to explore parallel processing.

2.2 THE OS SIMULATOR

The OS simulator is designed to support the two key aspects of resource management: process management and memory management. It simulates multi-threading and incorporates a deadlock simulator; it explores areas such as process states and scheduling, paging and virtual memory, synchronization, critical regions, deadlock detection, avoidance and prevention methods, dynamic library support and inter-process communication.

2.3 THE INBUILT COMPILER

The inbuilt assembler and compiler are used to experiment with CPU instruction set architecture, low-level code generation, addressing modes and compiler optimizations. The high-level language includes features designed to support and drive the CPU and the OS simulations. The compiler generates both assembly code and byte-code. A virtual machine is designed to run the byte-code on Windows and Linux operating systems.

3. REFERENCES

[1] Bloom, B. S., Krathwohl, D. R. 1956. Taxonomy of Educational Objectives; the Classification of Educational Goals, Handbook I: Cognitive Domain. Addison-Wesley.

[2] Mustafa, B. 2009. YASS: A System Simulator for Operating System and Computer Architecture Teaching and Learning. FISER'09 Conference, Famagusta, North Cyprus, Mar 22-24, 451-460.

[3] Naps, T.L., et al. 2003. Exploring the Role of Visualization and Engagement in Computer Science Education. ACM SIGCSE Bulletin 35(2), June 2003, 131-152.

Teaching Computer Architecture with a Graphical PC Simulator

Michael Black
American University
mblack@american.edu

Manoj Franklin
University of Maryland
manoj@umd.edu

ABSTRACT
We have developed a full system x86 simulator for teaching computer architecture, with graphical interfaces allowing the internal components of the simulated computer to be observed and modified at runtime, and utilities for designing and simulating custom processors. In this presentation we show how we used the simulator in our computer organization and computer architecture classes to teach assembly programming, I/O, and processor design.

Categories and Subject Descriptors
C.0. [**Computer Systems Organization**]: General

General Terms
Design, Experimentation

Keywords: Simulator, x86

1. INTRODUCTION
Computer simulators are widely used in computer architecture classes to allow students to visualize computer internals, test and troubleshoot low-level programs, and learn how processors work. We have developed a graphical teaching simulator that faithfully models a complete personal computer, including a i386 processor, physical memory, I/O ports, disks, interrupts, timers, and ports. The simulator can run preexisting software such as FreeDOS, Windows, and Minix. It includes graphical user interfaces to allow students to view and modify the processor, memory, disks, and devices at runtime. It also includes a processor development utility that allows students to design their own custom processor, including datapath and control, and test it alongside the x86 processor.

During this last year we developed lessons, labs, and projects using our simulator and incorporated them into our classes. In a beginning computer organization course, students used the simulator to learn assembly programming, device drivers, and instruction set design. In a second-level computer architecture course, students used the simulator to construct and model their own pipelined processors.

2. PROJECTS
In our presentation we discuss our labs and demonstrate sample work using the simulator, as well as student feedback. The following projects are described:

Assembly Language A disk image is provided containing FreeDOS, Turbo C, and Turbo Assembler. Students are given several drill problems to write in x86 assembly, and use the simulator to single-step and troubleshoot their programs.

I/O Students write a simple Pacman-like game where they use the arrow keys to move an icon around the screen and eat dots. This project requires students to implement several low-level functions. Their programs must poll and reset the keyboard controller, initialize the interval timer, handle timer interrupts, and write directly to video memory. Because the simulator accurately models a PC, students run their completed games directly on their own laptops.

Datapath In a three-part project, students develop and simulate their own processor. In the first part, students develop their own RISC instruction set and encoding. They then use the simulator's datapath design utility to draw the registers, ALUs, multiplexors, and buses that make up their processor. Students use the simulator's control design utility to build the state machine to implement their instruction set. They finally simulate their processor and verify that it works correctly on sample programs.

Pipeline Students are given a small instruction set and design a 5-stage pipeline processor. They use the simulator's datapath and control design utilities to wire together the pipeline, input its control state machine, and simulate it. Students load benchmark programs into the simulator's memory, and run these programs on their processor to measure its performance.

Figure 1. Simulator main window screenshot

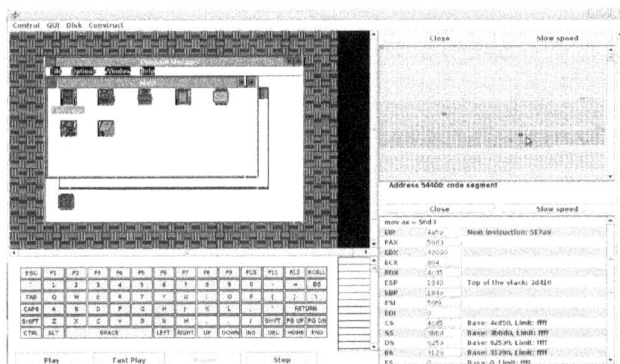

The simulator, its Java source code, and sample disk images is freely available online at 147.9.80.65/mblack/simulator.html (also linked to at blackware.org), and may be downloaded as a stand-alone application, or run directly from the website as an applet. Our paper [1] describes the simulator itself in more detail.

3. ACKNOWLEDGEMENTS
This work was made possible by NSF CCLI grant 0941057.

4. REFERENCE
[1] Black, M., Komala, P. 2011. A full system x86 simulator for teaching computer organization. SIGCSE Technical Symposium on Computer Science Education, 2011.

A Java Implementation of the Myro API for Using Personal Robots in CS1

Douglas Harms
DePauw University
Department of Computer Science
Greencastle, Indiana 46135, USA
+1 765 658 4727

dharms@depauw.edu

ABSTRACT

Myro is popular Python-based API for controlling personal robots used in many CS1 courses around the world. This paper describes the author's implementation of the Myro API in Java.

Categories and Subject Descriptors

K.3.2 [**Computers and Education**]: Computer and Information Science Education – *computer science education.*

General Terms

Design, Languages

Keywords

Personal Robots, CS1 Curricula, Java, IPRE

1. INTRODUCTION

Many schools are using personal robots (where each student has his or her own robot on which to work, both in and out of class) in their CS1 course because they are tangible, fun to program, and provide immediate feedback to students [4]. The curricular materials developed by the Institute for Personal Robots in Education (IPRE) [1,3] are used at many of these institutions.

IPRE defines an API called Myro (for *My Ro*bot) that allows students to write programs that interact with and control a personal robot. Myro was originally defined in the Python programming language. This paper briefly describes the author's implementation of the Myro API in Java, a popular programming language taught in CS1.

2. SCRIBBLER/FLUKE ROBOT

The Scribbler robot and IPRE Fluke add-on board are shown in Figure 1. The Scribbler is a rugged and small (188 x 158.8 x 81 mm) robot with two independently controlled wheels, three light sensors, two IR obstacle sensors, two line sensors, a speaker that can produce simple tones, and several programmable LED lights. The IPRE Fluke add-on board attaches to the Scribbler's serial port; it has a low-resolution (256 x 192) color camera, three IR obstacle sensors, a Bluetooth adapter for wireless communication with the host computer, and the ability to communicate with other Scribbler/Fluke robots via IR signals. The cost of the Scribbler/Fluke robot is approximately US$220.

3. MYRO/JAVA OVERVIEW

The Scribbler class defines over 50 methods for controlling and interacting with an attached robot. For example, the following

Figure 1. The Scribbler Robot with IPRE Fluke Add-on.

code connects to a Scribbler connected wirelessly to Bluetooth port COM5, then instructs it to move forward at ¾ speed until the motor stalls (i.e., it hits a wall and stops moving):

```
Scribbler robot=new Scribbler( "COM5" );
robot.forward( 0.75 );
while( !robot.getStall() )
    MyroUtils.sleep( 0.1 ); // wait .1 sec
robot.stop();
```

Methods are defined for movement (e.g., `forward`, `backward`, `turnLeft`, `turnRight`), sensing (e.g., `getLight`, `getObstacle`), imaging (e.g., `takePicture`, `getPixel`, `setPixel`), and sound/light control (e.g., `beep`, `setLED`).

In spring 2011 the author developed Myro/Java a lab assignment for students enrolled in CS1 at DePauw University. These students had no prior experience with robots and minimal Java programming experience. Using the BlueJ environment [2] and Myro/Java these students were able to develop and understand non-trivial Java programs to control a robot. The author will teach sections of CS1 in 2011-2012 based entirely on Myro/Java.

Myro/Java download, demos, and tutorials are available at:

```
http://wiki.roboteducation.org/Myro_in_Java
```

4. REFERENCES

[1] Blank, D. 2006. Robots Make Computer Science Personal. *Communications of the ACM.* 49, (Dec. 2006), 25–27.

[2] BlueJ - Teaching Java - Learning Java. *http://www.bluej.org/.* Accessed: 03-17-2011.

[3] Institute for Personal Robots in Education. *http://www.roboteducation.org/.* Accessed: 03-17-2011.

[4] Markham, S.A. and King, K.N. 2010. Using Personal Robots in CS1: Experiences, Outcomes, and Attitudinal Influences. *Proceedings of the Fifteenth Annual Conference on Innovation and Technology in Computer Science Education - ITiCSE'10* (2010), 204–208.

Changes to JFLAP to Increase its Use in Courses [*]

Susan H. Rodger
Duke University
Durham, NC USA
rodger@cs.duke.edu

Henry Qin
Duke University
Durham, NC USA
hq6@cs.duke.edu

Jonathan Su
Duke University
Durham, NC USA
jws36@cs.duke.edu

ABSTRACT

JFLAP is software for experimenting with formal languages and automata theory. In this Tips and Techniques session we describe the recent changes to JFLAP to make it more usable in an automata theory course.

Categories and Subject Descriptors

F.4.3 [**Theory of Computation**]: Mathematical Logic and Formal Languages Formal Languages; D.1.7 [**Software**]: Programming Techniques Visual Programming

General Terms

Theory

Keywords

JFLAP, automata, formal languages, pumping lemma, CYK parser

1. DESCRIPTION OF JFLAP

JFLAP[2, 3] is software for creating and experimenting with several types of automata and grammars, and for experimenting with related construction-type proofs. With JFLAP one can build an NFA, then go through the steps in converting it to a DFA, then convert it to a minimal state DFA, then convert it to a regular grammar or a regular expression. With JFLAP one can also experiment with l-systems, the simulation of the growth of plants and fractals, and parsing, such as brute force parsing, LL(1) and SLR(1) parsing. JFLAP is available for free on www.jflap.org[1].

2. ADDITIONS TO JFLAP

In this session we will demo new features of JFLAP to make it easier to use in lecture and to make it fit more definitions of automata. Probably the most useful feature added in the editing panes are UNDO and REDO buttons.

After creating an automaton in JFLAP, one can now save it in an image file in the formats: png, jpg, gif or bmp, or export to svg format. These images could then be placed easily into a PowerPoint presentation for a lecture.

When using JFLAP in a large lecture hall, it would be useful to make the tool display in a larger size. We have added a zoom functionality with slider bars to many of the panes such as the editor pane for finite state machines, and to many of the panes in the construction proofs.

In displaying an automaton, previously we allow users to move states around, but arcs would be set. If there were two arcs between two states in different directions the arcs would automatically curve. We have extended the arc capability by allowing one to change the shape of an arc by forcing it to curve.

To allow for more real life examples, we have extended the label capability for finite automata to accept a regular expression form. We define [1-9] on an arc to define $1+2+3+4+5+6+7+8+9$ (1 or 2 or 3 or 4 or 5 or 6 or 7 or 8 or 9) and similar notation for [a-z] and [A-Z].

The acceptance of pushdown automata have been extended to include accepting by empty stack. Before acceptance was always by final state. Now when you enter an input string you must select the type of acceptance.

Several additions were added to JFLAP to allow users to match an automaton more formally. For example in the DFA, you can add or take away a trap state by a selection item to make the automaton complete. When creating an NPDA, one can now select the definition of the NPDA. The default definition is to make the NPDA more general, so multiple symbols can be popped from the stack in one step. To restrict this the user can select "single character input" to restrict that only a single character at a time can be popped from the stack.

3. REFERENCES

[1] S. H. Rodger. Jflap web site and tutorial, 2011. www.jflap.org.

[2] S. H. Rodger and T. W. Finley. *JFLAP - An Interactive Formal Languages and Automata Package.* Jones and Bartlett, Sudbury, MA, 2006.

[3] S. H. Rodger, E. Wiebe, K. M. Lee, C. Morgan, K. Omar, and J. Su. Increasing engagement in automata theory with jflap. In *Fourtieth SIGCSE Technical Symposium on Computer Science Education*, pages 403–407. SIGCSE, March 2009.

---

[*]The work of all the authors was supported in part by the National Science Foundation through NSF grant DUE-0442513.

Merlin-Mo, an Interactions Analysis System for Moodle

Raquel Hijón-Neira and Ángel Velázquez Iturbide
Departamento de Lenguajes y Sistemas Informáticos I
Universidad Rey Juan Carlos
C/ Tulipán s/n, 28933 Móstoles, Madrid, Spain
raquel.hijon@urjc.es, angel.velazquez@urjc.es

ABSTRACT

We present Merlin-Mo, a complete interactions analysis system that fits into any running Moodle LMS and provides teachers with all the information they need about how their students are working within the course. The system provides with both: self configured interfaces, for easy data gathering, and a wide variety of data representations, including statistical and interactive visualizations.

Categories and Subject Descriptors

K.3.2 [**Computers and Education**]: Computer and Information Science Education - Computer science education, self-assessment.

General Terms

Performance.

Keywords

Interactions Analysis, Visualization, e-Learning, Moodle, LMS.

1. INTRODUCTION

Teachers increasingly need electronic feedback about how students are performing in blended or e-learning courses. Due to its importance new tracking systems have been emerged, like GISMO [1] and eLAT [2] to be used in LMS. One of the most extended LMS is Moodle [3], however, it lacks guided interfaces or even visual representation of the data to be shown that would engage and encourage its use.

2. MERLIN-MO

Merlin-Mo, a system of tracking and visualization of interaction for the Moodle LMS largely improves the original analysis capacities of Moodle. The system is offered free to the academic community. Its main objective is offering teachers a wider perspective about how their students are working towards enhancing the teaching-learning pace. Therefore a partial objective is the enhancement of the interactions analysis functionality Moodle offers through open queries interfaces, allowing a higher precision degree. Another one is offering several birds' view of the classroom to its teachers. Furthermore attractive interactive and motivating visualizations that would get a higher teacher engagement and willingness to "want to get more". Last but not least, it offers statistical visualizations of the query results, which can also be either downloaded or easily printed. Other functionality the system fulfills are: detailed information about what students are doing within a course and time period; different representations of students' work throughout the year; visualization of how students are accessing different resources; students' actions analysis on each resource type; easy identifications of "not popular parts/resources" and/or lurkers/proactive students; students' collaborative activities analysis in web 2.0 resources; dynamic and personalized interfaces. Moreover, the system uses Moodle security, allowing only course teachers access to student data; and language and other user settings inherited from the Moodle host. Merlin-Mo interfaces and query results are shown in Figure 1.

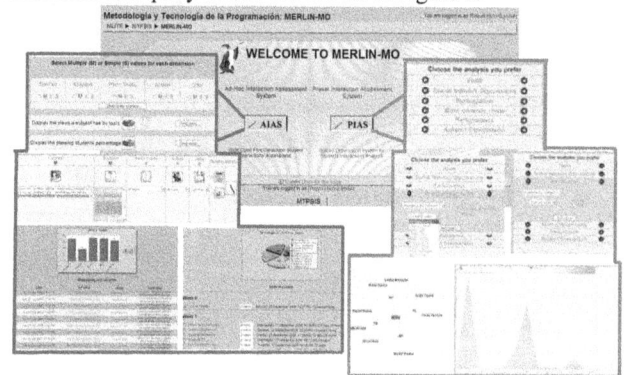

Figure 2. Merlin-Mo system, left AIAS, right PIAS

The system is easily reached by a new menu option that now appears into Moodle. Once there, users has two main systems; on the left hand side the Ad-Hoc Interaction Assessment System, AIAS, and on the right hand side the Preset Interaction Assessment System, PIAS. The former, offers a wide open query interface teachers can use to get to know how students are working, furthermore, it is also possible to select a representation type for the data. The latter, offers a complete and more guided analysis, since guided interfaces are offered under different domain knowledge that provide with the best visualization type for each case. The system has been monitoring students participating in 9 courses of Computer Science and Telecommunications degree in our university for over 3 years.

3. REFERENCES

[1] Mazza, R. & Botturi, L. (2007). Monitoring an Online Course With the GISMO Tool: A Case Study, Journal of Interactive Learning Research, 18(2), 251-265. Chesapeake, VA: AACE

[2] O. Petropoulou; I. Altanis; S. Retalis; C. A. Nicolaou; C. Kannas; M. Vasiliadou; Ireneos Pattis (201), Building a tool to help teachers analyse learners' interactions in a networked learning environment , Educational Media International, Volume 47, Issue 3 September 2010, pages 231 – 246

[3] Open Source Learning Management Systems http://www.scribd.com/doc/404896/Open-Source-LMS accessed March 2011

UWA Java Tools: Harnessing Software Metrics to Support Novice Programmers

Rachel Cardell-Oliver and Patrick Doran Wu
School of Computer Science and Software Engineering
The University of Western Australia, M002, 35 Stirling Highway, Crawley, 6009, Australia
rachel.cardell-oliver@uwa.edu.au

ABSTRACT

Many attributes of program quality can be measured automatically. UWA Java Tools is a collection of automatic software measurement tools configured for novice Java programmers. Measurement tools are used in industry to increase productivity and improve software quality. Our research demonstrates how such tools can benefit teaching and learning in programming courses.

Categories and Subject Descriptors

K.3.2 [**Computers and Education**]: [Computer and Information Science Education - self-assessment]; D.2.3 [**Software Engineering**]: [Software/Program Verification]

General Terms

Measurement

Overview

UWA Java Tools is a collection of automatic software measurement tools configured for novice Java programmers. JUnit4, Checkstyle and PMD are the measurement tools currently used. JUnit4 is used to create and execute unit test cases for Java classes. Following a Test Driven Development methodology, students are taught how to read the test code as a contract for the code they are to produce. Checkstyle and PMD perform static analysis of Java programs. Configurable rules are used to test for code layout and naming conventions; complete Javadoc documentation; code complexity; and common coding and design errors. Java utilities are used to report lines of code (with and without comments) and measure the structure of a Java class (using the Reflection library) in order to identify unusual student submissions for further inspection.

UWA Java Tools can be used with many integrated development environments (IDEs) because the open-source tools used are widely available as plug-ins. We have taught courses using UWA Java Tools with both the BlueJ and Eclipse IDEs. BlueJ is a system for novice Java programmers. The standard release of BlueJ is integrated with the JUnit3 system. We have built a new version of BlueJ with JUnit4 support. JUnit4 offers simpler specification of test cases, timeouts, and exceptions than its predecessor JUnit3.

Applications

Students use UWA Java Tools for *formative assessment* while they are working on programming assignments. In each programming laboratory, students are provided with method signatures and Javadoc documentation, a JUnit test suite(s) and a Checkstyle or PMD rule set appropriate to their experience. These artefacts provide the acceptance criteria for each programming exercise and they are used by the students for self-assessment of their work.

Instructors use UWA Java Tools for *diagnostic assessment* and *computing education research*. The toolset can be used to generate a vector of metrics for each student submission. These can be used to identify outlier submissions and unusual patterns in the cohort. *Summative assessment* criteria can be evaluated automatically using UWA Java Tools metrics. Assessment criteria functions are typically evaluated using several attributes: for example passing a specific set of test cases, together with code structure and style constraints.

Results

UWAJavaTools have been used and improved over 4 years in two different first year programming courses, taught by 4 different instructors and with cohorts of 80 to 250 students. Weaker students using UWA Java Tools may give up because they are overwhelmed with the pragmatics of tool use or with long error reports. This form of cognitive overload can be minimised by configuring measurement tools and assignments so that only a manageable amount of feedback is offered at any time. Students have reported that they appreciate the clear criteria and instant feedback of tool-supported programming by contract. Besides improving their productivity, students are motivated by using industry standard tools that prepare them for entering the software and IT industry. Qualitative analysis of student submissions demonstrates software quality improvement in that students' conformance to programming assignment "contracts" with UWA Java Tools is higher than for assignments with prose specifications only.

UWA Java Tools and the JUnit4 version of BlueJ are available from http://www.csse.uwa.edu.au/UWAJavaTools.

Acknowledgments

This research is supported by a Teaching Fellowship grant from the University of Western Australia.

Using Greenfoot in Teaching Inheritance in CS1

Tamar Vilner
The Open University of Israel
Computer Science Dept.
1 University Road
Raanana, Israel

tami@openu.ac.il

Ela Zur
The Open University of Israel
Computer Science Dept
1 University Road
Raanana, Israel

ela@openu.ac.il

Shay Tavor
The Open University of Israel
Computer Science Dept
1 University Road
Raanana, Israel

shay.tavor@gmail.com

ABSTRACT
In the Open University of Israel CS1 course, there are eight assignments contributing various percentages to the overall course assessment. The concepts of inheritance and polymorphism are covered in assignment 5. In the fall semester of 2009, assignment 5 was changed to demonstrate these topics using the Greenfoot environment. Here we describe this assignment and its rationale.

Categories and Subject Descriptors
K.3.2 [**COMPUTERS AND EDUCATION**]: Computer and Information Science Education.

General Terms
Human Factors.

Keywords
CS1, Visualization, Games, Inheritance and Polymorphism.

1. INTEGRATING GREENFOOT IN CS1
One of the main topics in the course is inheritance. Usually, when teaching this subject, simple examples like shapes or animals are demonstrated. When further practice is needed, more complex examples, rather than "toy" problems, are preferable. Greenfoot enables the use of scenarios and the creation of complex examples without dealing with the details of GUI, so that students can concentrate on the main topic – inheritance, but still have nice visual effects.

Assignment 5 deals with the concepts of inheritance and polymorphism.

The following paragraphs describe the assignment we gave to the students; after each question we present its rationale.

The assignment was based on the Balloons scenario supplied with the standard Greenfoot package [1]. The assignment had two parts. In the first part, there was an explanation about the Greenfoot environment and installation, and the students had to familiarize themselves with the Balloons scenario and explore its features and capabilities.

The second part of the assignment included four questions:

1. In question 1 the students were asked to read the APIs for the *World* and *Actor* classes and the code for all of the other classes included in this scenario, and to answer questions that make sure that the students read and get to know the scenario code. This will help them with later sections.

2. In question 2 the students were asked to add some new classes which should inherit from the class *Balloon* and to change some existing classes. They had to consider carefully which inherited methods from the *Balloon* class should be used and which should be overridden. The rationale behind this question is that students should make new inherited classes, a new abstract class, and understand which methods should be made abstract, which need to be overridden and which inherited.

3. In question 3 the students were asked to create a new *Ball* class that inherits from the *Actor* class. They had to make the necessary changes in code such that the program will now include balls in the game, which should move across the screen in certain speed and proportion vs. the balloons. The rationale for this question was to force the student to make changes and understand the code in the Dart, Bomb and Explosion classes, and use inheritance related subjects such as polymorphism, instanceof, casting, etc., by making the Ball class inherit from Actor, even though it would have been more "correct" to have made a "target" class from which all targets (balloons and ball) would inherit.

4. In question 4 the students were asked to create their own new and original dimension for the game. They also had to describe the elements that they added to the game. The rationale for this question was to allow the students to be creative and to challenge them to investigate the Greenfoot environment and the topics of inheritance and polymorphism, by inventing a new dimension for the game. Since the Greenfoot system supports the customized addition of classes, attributes and methods, and lets developers use graphics without writing their own, it is easy to implement interesting ideas and see how they behave.

2. RESULTS
The solutions students submitted to the fourth question showed that they indeed enjoyed the assignment. The students were asked to create their own new and original dimension to the game. Of course, many of them added expected elements, but some students created some beautiful extensions to the game.

For example, one student added hot air balloons and magnets. Hot air balloons appear one at a time and move five times as fast as regular balloons. When a hot air balloon is popped, a magnet appears in its place. The magnet spins round and round gathering speed and pulls all the balloons and balls in the vicinity towards it. When the magnet reaches a certain speed it blows up all nearby balloons and balls.

3. REFERENCE
[1]   Greenfoot Website: http://www.greenfoot.org

ITICSE'11, June 27–29, 2011, Darmstadt, Germany.
ACM 978-1-4503-0697-3/11/06.

Animation Projects in CS1 from Scheme to Java

Mirela Djordjević
Associate Professor
Manhattanville College, Purchase
NY 10577, USA
01-914-323-1923
djordjevicm@mville.edu

ABSTRACT

Scheme animation projects are transformed into Java projects.

Categories and Subject Descriptors

D.3.2 [**Software**]: Programming Languages – *Object-oriented.*

General Terms: Languages.

Keywords: Java Programming, Introductory Programming Course, Computer Science for Liberal Arts

1. INTRODUCTION

Recently, Manhattanville adjusted the introductory Java course to start with the Program Design methodology. This paper proposes that animation projects in Scheme are transformed into Java animation projects. Our intention is to teach two thirds of the semester Design Programs in Scheme and then switch to Java. This transition has to be done very carefully and precisely, having all projects easily translated into Java projects. We also want to keep our students motivated by using graphic examples. Picturing Programs[1] follows this path for Scheme. How to Design Classes[2] develops same projects with different topics. Viera Proulx[4] teaches Java a separate course that has a prerequisite Design Programs course. We want to use Design Program methodology and also to prepare students with basic programming in Java. What can be covered in a course? How to follow textbooks? We propose to teach this introductory course as a parallel model: each project in Scheme is also shown in Java.

2. PARALLEL MODEL

The parallel model makes a transition very carefully: by using same projects and repeating purpose statements, contracts, and examples. The following topics are included from Scheme: variables, functions, animations, conditionals, animations with conditionals, structures, self-referential structures (following textbook Picturing Programs). Transition to Java includes: classes, unions of classes, methods, self-referential structures, abstract classes, animations (following textbook How to Design Classes). Suggestion is to have the same projects in Scheme. In preparing the course, work in the opposite direction: set up projects in Java, and then re-work those in Scheme.

The UFO game project in Java, given in [3] is gradually explained with different topics throughout the textbook. In order to follow the parallel model, we use the same project in Scheme. This project introduces structures, functions for structures, and finally combines everything into the animation. Similarly, the project in Java defines all classes, methods for the classes and the final animation.

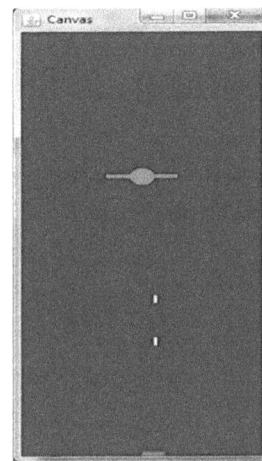

Figure 1. UFO project

3. CONCLUSION

We manage to reach lists and trees, abstract classes and interfaces in Java, but we do not cover assignment statements, circular structures which are left for Java 2 course.

4. REFERENCES

[1] Bloch, S., Picturing Programs, College Publications, (August, 2010.)

[2] Felleisen, M.,et. How to Design Classes (draft), http://www.ccs.neu.edu/home/matthias/HtDC/htdc.pdf

[3] Felleisen, M.et. How to Design Programs, http://www.htdp.org/

[4] Proulx, V. http://www.ccs.neu/home/vkp/index.html

Outreach Programs to Promote Computer Science and ICT to High School and Middle School Students

Mary Anne L. Egan (moderator)
Siena College
Computer Science Department
515 Loudon Rd.
Loudonville, NY 12211
+1 518 782 6546
maegan@siena.edu

Catherine Lang
Swinburne University of Technology
Information and Communication Technologies
Australia
+61 3 9214 5884
clang@swin.edu.au

Reyyan Ayfer
Bilkent University
Ankara, Turkey
+90 312 290 5065
ayfer@bilkent.edu.tr

Annemieke Craig
Deakin University
School of Information Systems
Deakin University, Australia
+61 3 5227 2152
acraig@deakin.edu.au

Jane Chu Prey
Microsoft Corporation
Microsoft Research
Redmond, WA
+11392145884
jprey@microsoft.com

Categories and Subject Descriptors

K.3.0 [**Computers and Education**]: General

General Terms

Human Factors

Keywords

Recruitment, gender studies, outreach programs

SUMMARY

Can hands-on computing programs for high school and middle school students create interest in Information and Communication Technology (ICT)? Which outreach program is appropriate for your school or company? We will explore several established programs with a view of sharing resources and ideas. We will begin a conversation to determine if current workshops do enough to engender student desire to act by committing to a higher degree in ICT. We will be presenting information on existing programs in different countries, such as the Digital Divas program (Australia), the Digigirlz program (various countries) and project IMPACT (US).

Attendees of this panel will be exposed to details of each of the named programs with the objective of enabling them to be able to organize and present a suitable outreach program of their own.

This panel is timely and necessary because the 'shrinking pipeline' of women and men in ICT is a problem in many countries and has dwindled to a trickle with students often making poor decisions due to misinformation and stereotypes. These ICT programs aimed at middle school and high school students expose them to the potential for exciting careers in ICT and increase awareness that technical innovation plays a critical role in virtually every sector of the global economy. As academics and industry professionals, we are concerned that a shrinking talent pool leads to reduced innovation and competitiveness. Current trends indicate that we need to act now to encourage more young people into ICT to meet future employment and creativity demands.

The materials presented will include sample activities, sample agendas, coding exercises, etc which will be available to all attendees.

Mary Anne Egan

Mary Anne will introduce Student IMPACT (Students Interested in Mathematics and Problem-solving unAware of Computing Talent), a one day program in career exploration and competition for Computer Science and Information Systems (CS/IS). This program is designed to provide high school students with demonstrated academic talent, especially in mathematics and problem-solving, an opportunity to explore some of the ways that college students and professionals think and work in CS/IS. This opportunity is made available for students who have not yet experienced a computer science course and are undecided about their academic and career goals. It gives participating students the chance to investigate areas in which they have potential talent.

Research has shown that many students indicate that they never considered computer science as a major because they were unsure what computer scientists did for a living. Or if they did have an idea, it typically wasn't a very appealing image [1]. Additionally, exposure to computer science during high school is a deciding factor in 33% of girls' decision to major in computer science [1] Programming contests exist for those students who already are exposed to and are experienced in computer science. This alternative contest gives the same competitive spirit to the exploration of various areas of the computer science field.

Project IMPACT has been running for four years and has measurably changed common student misconceptions about the field of computer science and what computer scientists do. Some of the more significant changes occur in the areas of knowing what computer scientists do, realizing that it will not be a solitary career and understanding that communication skills are necessary.

Annemieke Craig

Annemieke's research interests include issues of gender and computing, online learning and website usability. Annemieke has been involved in numerous research investigations concerning the attraction, retention and advancement of women in the ICT area. She is currently involved in the Digital Divas program and the Go Girl Go for IT event, with a focus on evaluation of the impact of each program on changing students perceptions, attitudes and confidence in ICT. Both programs are developed to enthuse female students through engaging curriculum, accessible role models as well as connections to the ICT profession.

Catherine Lang

Catherine has been researching factors to account for the under-representation of women in IT since 1996. Her strong interest in ICT pedagogies led to the current research project "Digital Divas", a curriculum initiative running in secondary schools in Australia. In 2010 she was awarded Australian Learning and Teaching Council Citation for her sustained leadership in building a student "Women in ICT" community at Swinburne that promotes engagement and leadership by recruiting university students to regularly participate in middle and high school IT classrooms alongside the teacher. This outreach program aims to encourage school students to consider an IT degree in the future by providing informal role models and mentoring. The program is now in its fourth year.

Jane Prey

Jane is Senior Program Manager for Microsoft Research External Research and leads the MSR Gender Diversity Strategy and Implementation Initiative. Microsoft's DigiGirlz programs give high school girls the opportunity to learn about careers in technology, learn about some cool technologies and participate in hands-on activities.

Reyyan Ayfer

Reyyan Ayfer is working at Bilkent University in Ankara, Turkey and currently holds a multitude of titles including: Department Chair at the Department of Computer Technology and Programming, where she also teaches courses in Programming, Data Structures, System Analysis and Design; Assistant Chair at the Department of Computer and Instructional Technology Teacher Education; General Coordinator of BETS (Bilkent Educational Technology Support Team) and the Director of the Institutional Relations and History Unit. In addition to her current work, she also contributes her time to international committees in the field of computer education. She undertook responsibilities in the organization committees of ACM SIGCSE's ITiCSE conferences in the years 2008 and 2009 and she co-chaired ITiCSE 2010, the 15th Annual Conference on Innovation and Technology in Computer Science Education, which was held at Bilkent, Ankara, Turkey.

Additionally, Reyyan Ayfer is leading a community of students at Bilkent University since 2005, who have come together to form the first international ACM-W Student Chapter. She was the Turkish Ambassador of ACM-W between 2002-2010. She received the Anita Borg Change Agent Award in 2008 and ACM Recognition of Service Award in 2010.

REFERENCES

[1] Margolis, J. and Fisher, A. *Unlocking the Clubhouse: Women in Computing.* Cambridge, MA: The MIT Press, 2002.

Using Video Games to Teach Security

Mario A.M. Guimaraes
College of Information
Technology
Zayed University
United Arab Emirates
mario.guimaraes@zu.ac.ae
(on leave from KSU)

Huwida Said
College of Information
Technology
Zayed University
United Arab Emirates
huwida.said@zu.ac.ae

Richard Austin
Southern Polytechnic State
University
Marietta, GA
raustin2@spsu.edu

ABSTRACT

This paper describes a project to design educational video games as an aid to teaching security. The first section describes the need to create practical hands on security examples where the student is an active learner. This section explains why video games are a natural fit for educational software, particularly in the field of information security and assurance. The second section examines existing videogame software and provides links to download them. The third section describes the three videogame development environments adopted at our university. In the last section we describe the videogame prototypes developed for teaching security as well as the ones under construction.

Categories and Subject Descriptors

K.3.2 [**Computer and Information Science Education**]:
Computer science education, Curriculum

General Terms

Security, Videogame

Keywords

Game Engine, Game Maker, Unity, Forensics, Network, Pedagogy, Phising, SDLC.

1. MOTIVATION

Traditional security classes are often professor-centered lectures where students learn basic threats and defense mechanisms, without applying this knowledge. Video games offer the possibility to create simulations that bridge the gap between theory and practice by creating a scenario where the user has to react to a series of events and verify the results within a limited time frame.

2. EXISTING VIDEO GAMES

Many existing security-related games are complicated and do not have a friendly user interface [1-2]. Also, most games depend on thrill and suspense to deliver the goals of the game, which may make them unsuitable for all ages. Moreover, these games were designed for advanced users who already have basic knowledge about security.

Most games don't provide awareness about security and how to deal with it. They teach users to be hackers and ignore ethics.

3. GAME DEVELOPMENT

Three game development platforms were chosen: Game Maker, Flash and Unity Pro. Game Maker is suitable for quick prototypes. Flash is the natural choice for web-based games and Unity is for serious gamers to develop and deploy their products to a multitude of platforms.

4. PROPOSED SYSTEM

The proposed system is being implemented with two levels or type of games. Since we are in the prototyping phase, Gamemaker is used. At level 1, several prototypes are built where students gain background and apply basic security knowledge. At level 2, the system attempts to simulate a real world environment with the knowledge gained from level 1.

4.1 Level 1

Figure 1 displays the network diagram at the beginning of the game. The user drags the text in yellow to the corresponding image on the diagram.

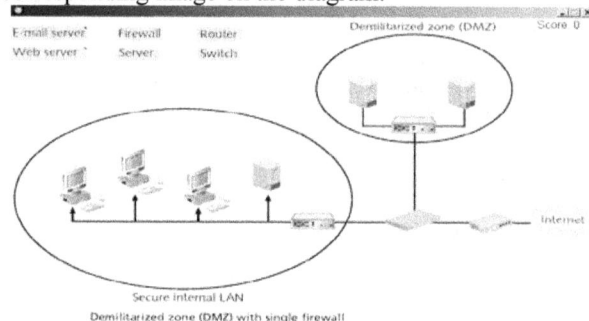

Figure 1 – Network Diagram – Start of Game

4.2) Level 2

In level 2, the user must defend his/her system. The goal of the game is to survive the attacks. Every 10 seconds that the user lasts, he receives 50 points. If the user survives all the attacks, the user will advance to the next level. There is a **Help** Menu, an **Accounts** Menu, an **Application** Menu and an **E-Mail** Menu. Level 2 is currently under construction and the first prototype should be concluded and tested prior to May of 2011.

REFERENCES

[1] Uplink, Retrieved Jan 6, 2011, from http://www.introversion.co.uk/uplink/about.html

[2] Portsign Hacking 2, Retrieved Jan 6, 2011 from http://download.cnet.com/PortSign-Hacking/3000-7551_410728340.html

A System for Usable Unification of Interfaces of Learning Objects in M-Learning

Eva García, Luis de-Marcos, Antonio García, José-Ramón Hilera
Computer Science Department, University of Alcalá, Spain

{eva.garcial, luis.demarcos, a.garciac, jose.hilera}@uah.es

ABSTRACT

This article proposes a system for unification of interfaces of learning objects in m-learning, and it explains the part which is currently being developed in a doctoral dissertation.

Categories and Subject Descriptors

K.3.1 [**Computers and Education**]: Computer Uses in Education – *Distance learning*.

General Terms

Design, Theory.

Keywords

Interfaces, m-learning, guidelines, usability.

1. INTRODUCTION

Although progress has been made in technological innovations, there are still obvious limitations of the interfaces of mobile devices due to their characteristics, i.e. small screens, low resolution of them, non-traditional input methods and navigation difficulties [1]. In addition, due to the proliferation of models of mobile devices from different manufacturers in recent years there is a great diversity of them, with consequent differences in input mode (pointer, keyboard, finger), in processing power, in size and resolution of the screen, etc. Therefore, each manufacturer has its own interface. The same occurs when dealing with learning objects used by m-learning systems, since each of those has a different interface, and it would be desirable to unify to make them more visually pleasing to the learner.

The system here proposed will design the interfaces of learning objects in a usable and unified way so that all may look alike being easy to use and intuitive for learners.

2. ARCHITECTURE OF THE SYSTEM

The system (see Figure 1) detects the mobile device's features and searches in a federated and semantic search system [2] the course that best fits it. After selecting the course, it searches in a repository of guidelines (specifically designed for m-learning by an expert) the most appropriate for the specific case, and then the course will be converted, according to these guidelines, to the learner's mobile device. If there is no course in the LMS that fits

the features of the mobile device, it will also be saved for future use so that it will not be necessary to re-convert it again.

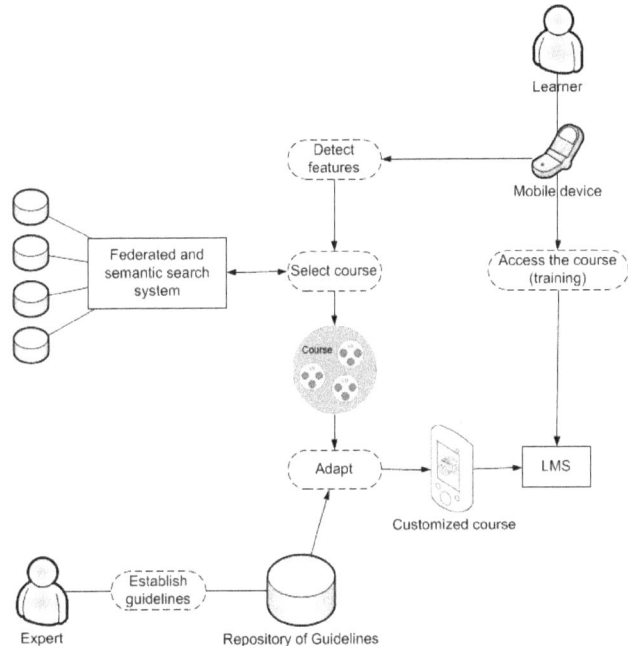

Figure 1. System for usable unification of interfaces of learning objects

The system presented here is currently under development. We have begun with the establishment of usability guidelines specific for m-learning. These guidelines are being developed in a doctoral dissertation taking into account the ISO 9241-151 [3].

3. REFERENCES

[1] Nah, F. F., Siau, K. and Sheng, H. 2005. The Value of Mobile Applications: A Utility Company Study. *Communications of the ACM*. 48, 2 (Feb. 2005), 85-90. DOI= http://dx.doi.org/10.1145/1042091.1042095

[2] Otón, S., Ortiz, A., Hilera, J.R., Barchino, R., Gutiérrez, J.M., Martínez, J.J., Gutiérrez, J.A., de Marcos, L. and Jiménez, M.L. 2010. Service Oriented Architecture for the Implementation of Distributed Repositories of Learning Objects. *International Journal of Innovative Computing Information and Control*. 6, 3(A) (Mar. 2010), 843-854.

[3] International Organization for Standardization. *Ergonomics of human-system interaction. Part 151: Guidance on World Wide Web user interfaces*. International standard ISO 9241-151: 2008. Switzerland.

Best Practices for Peer Feedback in Interdisciplinary Research Groups

Sebastian Harrach
Department of Philosophy
Darmstadt University of Technology
Darmstadt, Germany
harrach@phil.tu-darmstadt.de

ABSTRACT

This paper describes the successful development and implementation of an approach to peer feedback and collaborative writing within extensively interdisciplinary research groups likely to be formed in research projects concerning computer science education and e-learning.

Categories and Subject Descriptors

K.6.1 [**Management of Computing & Information Systems**]: Project and People – *Training*

General Terms

Management, Human Factors

Keywords

Best practice, interdisciplinarity, feedback, peer groups

1. INTRODUCTION

One of the challenges within a research group focusing on computer science and education, and in particular on e-learning, is that technology supported learning does not belong to a single field of study - for further reference, see[1]. Therefore, research groups concerned with this topic will tend to be extensively interdisciplinary. This favors the group's tendency to fragmentize into different subgroups of graduate students from the same field/discipline – at least concerning peer feedback on each other's work and collaborative publishing. Even if this problem is dealt with explicitly, the communication channels used are typically those that are used for the regular research of the biggest subgroup. Communication problems occurring because of this will be tackled here.

2. DEVELOPMENT OF THE APPROACH

To reduce the fragmentation mentioned above, the research group e-learning at the Darmstadt University of Technology supported the graduate students in establishing informal teams for peer feedback. The corresponding method has been improved consistently throughout the five years of work within the research group.

At first, classical peer feedback was realized by forming „tandems" - teams of two starting graduate students - which were meant to meet regularly to offer feedback on current progress or obstacles. This eventually enabled both participants to develop an additional perspective on the topic of the respective research or even to cooperate on publications.

This approach was then improved by some graduates (Franz, Rose & Schuchart; Universität Hamburg) into a format later named "triadic intervision". In this format, three students from different fields but with related research topics – who would not work together otherwise – form a group which meets every two weeks. The group dynamics of this three-participant approach allow for very constructive peer feedback, while at the same time avoiding the deadlocks or the lack of commitment appearing within tandems.

Each member of the group is allowed to put one of their texts or one problem up for discussion in each meeting. Each of these meetings takes at least four hours (!), following a preset timetable. The structure of these meetings and the methods within each time slot were optimized and re-simplified for several years by the first groups using the approach. Today, triadic intervision contains a conclusive collection of methods for constructive peer feedback on technical and on personal topics with the main focus on keeping the graduate students "operational".

Figure 1 gives an overview of the deliberately simple structure of each meeting with breaks (marked in grey). In the first quarter of the meeting the participants first take some time to "arrive" mentally, then (marked with an "?") the three topics which are to be discussed are presented by the participants and assorted in order of urgency.

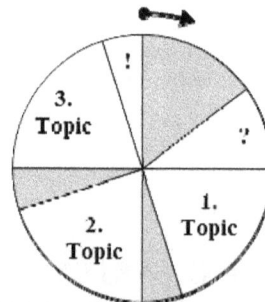

Figure 1. Timeframe

The three quarters left consist of the discussion of each topic. They are separated by short breaks to focus on the upcoming topics and are concluded in a short summary (marked with an "!") of the results and feedback on the meeting as a whole. Practical experience shows that the extensive timeframe is necessary and useful.

3. REFERENCES

[1] Kaminski, A.; Mühlhäuser, M.; Sesink, W.; Steimle, J. (Ed.) 2011: Interdisciplinary Approaches to Technology Enhanced Learning. Münster: Waxmann.

Programming in Secondary Education: Benefits and Perspectives

Michail N. Giannakos
Ionian University, Corfu, Greece
mgiannak@ionio.gr

Spyros Doukakis
University of the Aegean, Rhodes, Greece
sdoukakis@rhodes.aegean.gr

Panayiotis Vlamos
Ionian University, Corfu, Greece
vlamos@ionio.gr

Christos Koilias
Technological Educational Institution of Athens, Greece
ckoilias@teiath.gr

ABSTRACT

In this study, we present results of a research that investigates the impact of attending programming courses at Lyceum (15-18 years old students), on students' confidence and behavioral intention towards algorithmic logic. In particular, we measured students' behavioral intention for programming and students' confidence regarding data structures, problem solving and programming commands (Conditional - Loop). Responses from 81 graduate students, whose curriculum included programming courses at Lyceum were used to examine the benefits of programming in secondary education. The results indicate that students with prior attendance of programming courses exhibit high levels of confidence and acceptance regarding structured logic.

Categories and Subject Descriptors

K.3.2 [**Computers and Education**]: Computer and Information Science Education - Computer science education, Curriculum.

General Terms

Human Factors, Standardization.

Keywords

Informatics in Secondary Education, Programming Skills, Curriculum.

1. INTRODUCTION

For many years, in many different countries computing has been included in the curriculum as a distinct discipline in secondary education. Computing focuses on how computers work (hardware) and how to program them (programming and software development), whereas ICT (Information and Communication Technology) is focused on how to use computers. Specifically, programming with an emphasis on algorithms as a methodology of thought seems to be an important objective in students' education, aiming, among other things, to their preparation for tertiary education.

In addition, the content of the curriculum largely defines the

knowledge that students are expected to gain from a course in algorithms and programming. According to various curricula, the purpose of a course in algorithms and programming is to foster analytical and synthetic thought in students, to develop their creativity and imagination in design, to foster their austerity and clarity of formulation, to develop their methodology skills and, finally, to enable them to proceed to problem solving using programming knowledge.

2. OVERVIEW

In Greece, the course of Development of Application in a Programming Environment has been taught in secondary education and students have been assessed on it since 1999. However, no research has been conducted to draw conclusions contributing to the study of possible benefits from algorithmic courses, as well as on the confidence of students graduating from secondary education.

3. RESEARCH APPROACH

Our research methodology included a survey composed by questions on the demographics of the sample and on four principal constructs which are: 1) Behavioral Intention for Programming (BI), 2) Problem Solving Confidence (PSC), 3) Confidence for using Programming Commands (Conditional - Loop) (CPC) and 4) Confidence for using Data Structures (CDS). The sample of respondents consisted of 81 graduate students (2010 graduation year) of Lyceum, whose curriculum included the programming course. All constructs were measured using 5-point Likert scales.

4. RESEARCH FINDINGS-CONCLUSIONS

In this empirical study, we measured students' acceptance and confidence regarding the courses of programming. The levels of acceptance (BI=4.25/5) and confidence (PSC=3.91/5; CPC=4.34/5; CDS=3.92/5) are relatively high amongst students. Results show the advantage gained by tertiary education students, whose curriculum includes programming course. On the basis of the above, one could argue that attending relevant courses in secondary education is beneficial and contributes to the establishment of a higher level of courses in tertiary education.

Integrating Greenfoot into CS1 – A Case Study

Tamar Vilner
The Open University of Israel
Computer Science Dept.
Raanana, Israel
tami@openu.ac.il

Ela Zur
The Open University of Israel
Computer Science Dept
Raanana, Israel
ela@openu.ac.il

Shay Tavor
The Open University of Israel
Computer Science Dept
Raanana, Israel
shay.tavor@gmail.com

ABSTRACT

In the Open University of Israel CS1 course, there are eight assignments contributing various percentages to the overall course assessment. The concepts of inheritance and polymorphism are covered in assignment 5. In the fall semester of 2009, assignment 5 was changed to demonstrate these topics using the Greenfoot environment. The change was accompanied by study to examine students' attitudes toward the Greenfoot environment and how they cope with it, both in terms of technical operation and from the point of view of learning.

Categories and Subject Descriptors

K.3.2 [**COMPUTERS AND EDUCATION**]: Computer and Information Science Education.

General Terms

Human Factors.

Keywords

CS1, Visualization, Games, Inheritance and Polymorphism.

1. INTEGRATING GREENFOOT IN CS1

In recent years, a number of studies examined the use of visual environments to help the students cope with the CS1 course In order to simplify the programming of complex examples, and to increase students' motivation, we looked for an educational environment that enables presentation of visual examples. We decided to use Greenfoot. Greenfoot is an Interactive Development Environment (IDE). It provides a visual environment in which the programmer can create objects and manipulate them, and immediately see the changes in properties and behavior on the screen [2].

In our CS1 course we teach Java, using the BlueJ environment [1]. There are eight assignments contributing various percentages to the total course assessment. Each assignment deals with Java code writing and other theoretical subjects.

One of the main topics in the course is inheritance. Usually, when teaching this subject, simple examples are demonstrated. When further practice is needed, more complex examples, rather than "toy" problems, are preferable. Greenfoot enables the use of scenarios and the creation of complex examples without dealing with the details of GUI, so that students can concentrate on the main topic – inheritance, but still have nice visual effects.

Assignment 5 deals with the concepts of inheritance and polymorphism. In the past, we used to ask a question that presents a hierarchical structure of classes, and the students were usually

asked to implement the classes. In the fall semester of 2009, assignment 5 was changed. As before, the purpose of the assignment was to demonstrate the topics of inheritance and polymorphism, but this time by using the Greenfoot environment. The change was accompanied by a study.

2. METHODOLOGY

The questions of the study were: 1) **Pedagogical aspects** – What were the students' attitudes toward working with Greenfoot? 2) **Technical aspects** – To what extent were students satisfied with the technical aspects.

The tools we used were a specially designed questionnaire comprising four questions and the university database.

The research population consisted of 634 students who took the course in the fall semester of 2009. The findings are based on a sample of the 325 students (51%) who returned the questionnaire.

3. RESULTS

The students reported enjoying the work with Greenfoot very much. Most of them reported that the assignment was challenging. The fact that they had to be creative caused them to make an extra effort when answering the questions. The solutions students submitted showed that they indeed enjoyed the assignment. The students were asked to create their own new and original dimension to the game. Of course, many of them added expected elements, but some students created some beautiful extensions to the game.

About half of the students said that working with Greenfoot helped them understand the concept of inheritance much better. When checking whether this fact was supported statistically in the final course grades, we found no significant changes between this semester and previous ones. This result didn't surprise us since we added Greenfoot only in the middle of the semester and only in one assignment. However, the fact that this was the students' feeling is meaningful in itself.

It is clear from the results of the questionnaire that the installation of the Greenfoot environment was very easy for the students. Since we see that integrating Greenfoot into our CS1 course was very successful, we have decided to continue integrating it in the following semesters.

4. REFERENCES

[1] BlueJ Website: http://www.bluej.org

[2] Kolling, M. and Henriksen P., Game Programming in Introductory Courses with Direct State Manipulation, *Proceedings of the 10th annual SIGCSE conference on innovation and technology in computer science education*, 2005, pp. 59-63.

GLMP for Automatic Assessment of DFS Algorithm Learning[1]

Gloria Sánchez-Torrubia

gsanchez@fi.upm.es

School of Computing, Universidad Politécnica de Madrid, Boadilla del Monte, 28660 Madrid, Spain

Carmen Torres-Blanc

ctorres@fi.upm.es

Gracian Trivino

gracian.trivino@softcomputing.es

European Centre of Soft Computing
Mieres, Asturias, Spain

ABSTRACT

We describe how to use a Granular Linguistic Model of a Phenomenon (GLMP) to assess e-learning processes. We apply this technique to evaluate algorithm learning using the GRAPHs learning environment.

Categories and Subject Descriptors

I.2.3 [**Artificial Intelligence**]: Deduction and Theorem Proving - *Answer/reason extraction; Deduction (e.g., natural, rule-based); Inference engines.* K.3.2 [**Computers and Education**]: Computer and Information Science Education – *computer science education.*

General Terms

Design.

Keywords

Granular Linguistic Model, Computing with Words and Perceptions, Automatic Assessment, Fuzzy Inference.

1. INTRODUCTION

Through the use of e-learning environments huge amounts of data can be output about a learning process. Nevertheless, this information has to be interpreted and represented in a practical way to arrive at a sound assessment that is not confined to merely counting mistakes. This includes establishing relationships between the available data and also providing instructive linguistic descriptions about learning evolution. Currently, only human experts are capable of making such assessments. Also, as e-learning sessions grow in complexity, it becomes more necessary, but also harder, to automate this assessment task. Our goal is to create a computational model that simulates the instructor's reasoning and generates an enlightening learning evolution report in natural language.

2. DESIGN OF A GLMP

Here, we have used a GLMP [2] to model the learning process of the depth-first search (DFS) algorithm. GLMPs are hierarchical structures used to organize and process data. In GLMPs, each of the elements in one level, which we call computational perceptions, will be a summary of a number of elements from lower levels. The information will be expressed in more or less detail depending on its position in the structure, where the bottom level will represent the finer-grained information. A GLMP aims to manage large quantities of information, which is grouped and summarized by means of computing with words techniques to extract the most important points.

In this GLMP, the input data are the correct and incorrect response rates in each algorithm step. These data are extracted from the interaction log generated by GRAPHs [1]. Figure 1 is a

diagram of the GLMP that linguistically describes the proficiency level acquired by a student in the DFS algorithm learning process. This diagram shows the design of how information about the learning of key aspects of the algorithm is extracted from the available data. These partial summaries will be used to find out the final proficiency level acquired. The GLMP will output a numerical grade explained by a natural language report containing both the partial summaries and the final summary.

Each of the level-1 perceptions is composed of a numerical input variable and a linguistic output variable, represented by a vector that denotes the fuzzyfication of the input with respect to a number of linguistic labels.

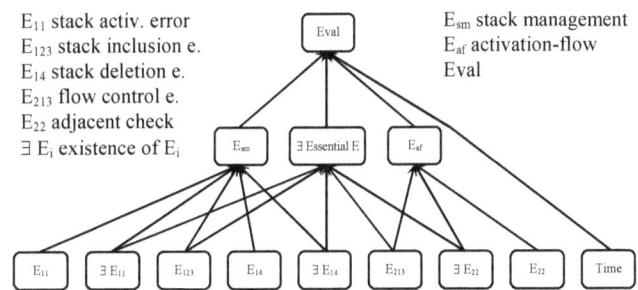

E_{11} stack activ. error
E_{123} stack inclusion e.
E_{14} stack deletion e.
E_{213} flow control e.
E_{22} adjacent check
$\exists E_i$ existence of E_i

E_{sm} stack management
E_{af} activation-flow
Eval

Figure 1. GLMP of the level of proficiency acquired by the student

Higher-level perceptions, output by a fuzzy inference engine, summarize the information from the lower levels. *Eval* perception is defuzzyfied using a weighted average to produce the numerical grade, and linguistic templates are enabled to express the summaries in natural language. For example, *in this simulation, the stack activation error is small..., the flow control error is acceptable..., the adjacent management error is low, the error in essential steps is not null... and the algorithm simulation time is adequate. Thus, the correctness level acquired by the student is very good and the grade attained is 7.4.*

3. CONCLUSION

Using computing with words and perceptions, the designed GLMP is able to emulate an expert instructor and automatically generates a natural language assessment report.

4. REFERENCES

[1] M. G. Sánchez-Torrubia, C. Torres-Blanc and S. Escribano-Blanco. 2010. GRAPHs: a learning environment for graph algorithm simulation primed for automatic fuzzy assessment. In *Proc. Koli Calling'10*, 62-67.

[2] G. Trivino, A. Sanchez, A. S. Montemayor, J. J. Pantrigo, R. Cabido and E. G. Pardo. 2010. Linguistic description of traffic in a roundabout. In *Proc. IEEE Fuzzy'10*, 1-8.

[1] This work has been partially supported by CICYT (Spain) project TIN2008-06890-C02-01

An Innovative Teaching Tool Based on Semantic Tableaux for Verification and Debugging of Programs *

Rafael del Vado Vírseda
rdelvado@sip.ucm.es

Fernando Pérez Morente
fperezmo@fdi.ucm.es

Departamento de Sistemas Informáticos y Computación
Universidad Complutense de Madrid, Spain
C/ Prof. José García Santesmases s/n, 28040 Madrid

ABSTRACT

In this paper, we propose a new methodology based on a logic teaching tool on semantic tableaux that has been developed to help students to use logic as a formal proof technique in advanced topics of Computer Science, such as the formal verification of algorithms and the algorithmic debugging of imperative programs.

Categories and Subject Descriptors

F.3.1 [**Specifying and Verifying and Reasoning about Programs**]: Logic of programs.

General Terms

Algorithms, Design, Theory, Verification.

Keywords

Semantic Tableaux, Verification, Debugging.

1. INTRODUCTION

Computational Logic is a subject that is taught in the first courses of almost all the Computer Science (CS) departments around the world. However, most of the educational software developed for teaching logic[1] ignores their application in a number of subjects of the CS education domain [1]. The aim of this work is to describe an innovative methodology based on a logic teaching tool, named TABLEAUX[2], that uses semantic tableaux to visualize formal proofs of advanced topics in CS, such as the design of correct and efficient algorithms from logical specifications. A semantic tableau is a semantic but systematic method of finding a model for a given set of formulas Γ, usually classified as a refutation system because a theorem φ is proved from Γ by getting its negation $\Gamma \vdash \neg \varphi$. The tool is based on propositional and first-order semantic tableaux and helps students to learn how to build semantic tableaux and to understand the philosophy of this proof device for verification and debugging purposes. Our major contribution is the development and implementation of new tableau methods that provide semantically reach feedback to the students in order to help them to understand the formal reasoning performed in the design and analysis of correct and efficient imperative programs.

---

*This work has been supported by the project PIMCD 2010/97 for the Innovation and Improvement of the Educational Quality.

[1]http://www.ucalgary.ca/aslcle/logic-courseware
[2]gpd.sip.ucm.es/TABLEAUX

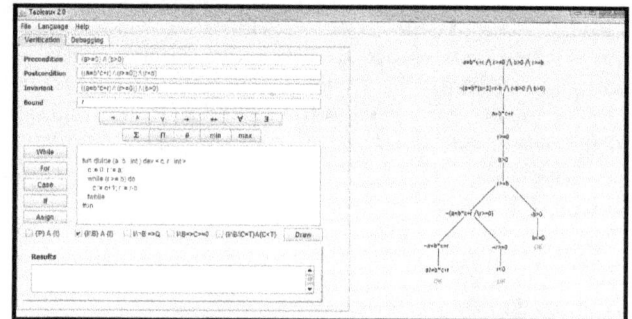

Figure 1: The logic teaching tool TABLEAUX.

2. VERIFICATION OF ALGORITHMS

The main novelty of the TABLEAUX tool is to train students in the art and science of specifying correctness properties of algorithms and proving them correct. To be sure of the correctness of an algorithm A one has to prove that it meets its specification $\{P\} A \{Q\}$, given by a precondition P and a postcondition Q, both predicates expressing properties of the values of variables in A. An algorithm together with its specification is viewed as a theorem. The theorem expresses that the algorithm satisfies the specification. Hence, all algorithms require proofs (as theorems do). The TABLEAUX tool verifies algorithms according to their specifications in a constructive way based on semantic tableaux $P \vdash \neg wp(A,Q)$, where $wp(A,Q)$ is the weakest precondition of A with respect to Q, which is the 'weakest' predicate that ensures that if a state satisfies it then after executing A the predicate Q holds (see **Figure 1**).

3. ALGORITHMIC DEBUGGING

We have successfully applied the TABLEAUX tool for the algorithmic debugging of programs to show how one can reason about the results of the execution of a program only considering the meaning of the program itself, provided by its specification, and ignoring complex operational details. Algorithmic debugging proposes to replace computation traces by computation trees with program fragments attached to their nodes. As a novelty, in this work we propose using semantic tableaux as computation trees. During the academic year 2009/2010, we have applied the TABLEAUX tool to design illustrative classes of problems to provide a training in the reasoning needed for designing correct and efficient software.

4. REFERENCES

[1] B. P. Lancho, E. Jorge, A. de la Viuda, and R. Sanchez. Software Tools in Logic Education: Some Examples. *Logic Journal of the IGPL 15(4)*, pages 347–357, 2007.

Moodle-Integrated Open Source Synchronous Teaching

J. Mark Pullen
Department of Computer Science
George Mason University
Fairfax, VA 22030
+1.703.993.1538

mpullen@netlab.gmu.edu

Nicholas K. Clark
C4I Center
George Mason University
Fairfax, VA 22030
+1.703.993.1743

nclark1@netlab.gmu.edu

ABSTRACT

It is well understood that the two prevalent approaches to distance education, synchronous and asynchronous, can be combined to good effect. However, existing open source software generally is separated into these two categories. This paper introduces an open source capability that combines the popular Moodle asynchronous learning management system with a new synchronous online teaching/conferencing system called MIST/C. This combination is supporting online delivery of the Master's programs in our Computer Science Department effectively. This paper describes the design and implementation of MIST/C and our experience using it to support Computer Science MS programs.

Categories and Subject Descriptors

K.3.1 [**Computing Milieux**]: Computer Uses in Education – distance learning

General Terms

Management, Performance, Human Factors

Keywords

Internet distance education, synchronous, asynchronous

1. MOTIVATION

Distance Education (DE) often is lumped into two major categories: synchronous DE, where student and instructor communicate electronically in real time, and asynchronous DE, where the instructor commits the learning materials to some medium, from which the student receives them afterward. It is recognized that these two approaches are complementary and can enable better effect together than either achieves individually [1]. However, the open source educational software community has been slow to produce systems combining these capabilities.

We share the observation of [1] that synchronous and asynchronous modes are more effective when combined. Therefore, when we discovered the software integration facilities in the Modular Object-Oriented Dynamic Learning Environment (Moodle), we were motivated to rework our previous product into the Moodle environment. Moodle is widely recognized as a high-quality Learning Management System (LMS) supporting asynchronous DE [2], This paper is about the result: Moodle Integrated Synchronous Teaching/Conferencing (MIST/C) [3].

2. DISCUSSION

MIST/C provides audio, video, and whiteboard interfaces, a floor control/chat panel, a recorder, and a playback unit, all under control of a master client. The system can function well (absent video) over a 56 kilobit/second modem, and even better (including video) over a good Internet connection. It runs on Windows, Linux and MacOSX platforms. The following additional open-source features have been provided as part of Moodle integration:

- Auto-reconnect, so that ongoing class is not disrupted in case of network problems

- Server-side recording, to provide a backup to client recording

- Integrated control panel for all functions, with full student names

- Whiteboard functions for window capture and PDF slide format

We have used MIST/C extensively to teach Master's level Computer Science courses, blending classroom participation with on-line attendance. Both lecture and seminar styles have worked well in this mode, including cases where students made their project presentations remotely. A total of 24 courses taught by our Computer Science department have been presented. Student and faculty feedback has been positive, and has been used to improve MIST/C further.

Our latest work on MIST/C is aimed at the ability to scale operations from tens of courses to hundreds, in a cloud environment. Managing such a large collection of MIST/C servers effectively on a scheduled basis would be very difficult; a much better arrangement is *dynamic load balancing*: when a MIST/C session starts, a scheduling process will choose the available server platform with the lightest load and designate that platform to support the session. We have prototyped a MIST/C server in the Amazon Elastic Cloud and determined that a straightforward implementation of dynamic load balancing is possible. A byproduct of this work was a test client implementation that makes it easier to do a distributed load test of the MIST/C server. During this process we produced the largest configuration of MIST/C (or NEW) clients ever tested, confirming that the MIST/C server will support over 200 clients in a session with no performance degradation, using a typical server platform. We intend to include the dynamic load balancing feature as a standard MIST/C deployment option.

3. REFERENCES

[1] Hrastinski, S. Asynchronous and Synchronous E-Learning, *EDUCAUSE Quarterly*, vol. 31, no. 4, Oct–Dec 2008

[2] Moodle Modules and Plugins, http://moodle.org/mod/data/view.php?id=6009

[3] MIST/C website, http://netlab.gmu.edu/MISTC

Teaching with CEOHP

Vicki Almstrum
Computing Educators Oral History Project
Austin, TX 78756 USA
almstrum@acm.org

Deepa Muralidhar
North View High School
John's Creek, GA 30022 USA
deepa.muralidhar@gmail.com

Mary Last
Computing Educators Oral History Project
Fort Mill, SC 29707 USA
mary.last@gmail.com

Barbara Boucher Owens
Southwestern University
1001 East University
Georgetown, TX 78628 USA
1-512-863-1513
owensb@southwestern.edu

ABSTRACT

The Computing Educators Oral History Project (CEOHP) is a collection of interviews with computing educators. During 2010, evaluation efforts guided major updates of the CEOHP website (ceohp.org) and the addition of new sections with activities appropriate for use in secondary and post-secondary classes. This poster introduces the CEOHP project, describes the pedagogical aspects of the site, and suggests uses for the educational materials.

Categories and Subject Descriptors

K..2 [Computer and History] K.3 [Computing and Education], K.7 [The Computing Profession]

General Terms: Human Factors

Keywords

Gender, Equity, Careers, Oral History, Life Stories, Evaluation, Pedagogy, Lesson Plans, Curriculum

1. BACKGROUND

The Computing Educators Oral History Project (CEOHP) has grown steadily since 2003 as the project was formalized and project members began to collect interviews both during conferences and through specially arranged visits. In addition to challenges such as learning how to conduct oral history interviews and properly process the materials, project members had to explore reasonable approaches to presenting the interviews, determine legal procedures, and arrange to permanently archive the materials. As of March 2011, the collection includes 25 approved interviews with educators from around the world.

2. EVALUATION AND UPGRADING

During 2010, two rounds of formal evaluation sought feedback from educators with a variety of backgrounds. The first round of evaluation included one-on-one semi-structured interviews with four professors and two graduate students. The format of the interviews allowed each participant to delve more deeply into areas of personal interest. This round of evaluation led to greater consistency and improved quality across the interviews.

During the second round of evaluation, ten pre-college computing teachers from three different states (Georgia, Indiana, and Texas)

focused on how to make the website more attractive and usable in pre-college settings. The upgraded website debuted on December 8, 2010, in time for Computing Education Week in the USA.

3. PEDAGOCAL MATERIALS

While the interviews in the CEOHP collection contribute to the historical record by capturing life stories from a variety of computing educators, if leveraged appropriately these materials can encourage students to consider careers in STEM fields and, in particular, can provide role models and inspiration for female students. For example, the interview overview page is designed to give key information about the interviewee (brief background description, links to relevant external resources) in addition to the interview audio and transcript. Literary references mentioned in the interviews are collected on a reference page, a resource that includes ideas for how to incorporate outside literature when teaching computing topics. In late 2010, two Computer Science and Technology educators from American high schools developed the framework for three lesson plans that provide meaningful contexts for students to explore the CEOHP materials during one or more class meetings. These materials are now featured on the CEOHP website and are being cataloged in the CSTA Source, an on-line repository of teaching and learning materials (csta.villanova.edu).

4. PLAN FOR THE POSTER

While the poster will introduce CEOHP and describe the evaluation and upgrade work during 2010, the emphasis will be on the teaching materials. We will design the poster to encourage attendees to suggest ideas for additional lesson plans, techniques for incorporating the interviews into the secondary and post-secondary computing curricula, and how to best showcase the project for Computing Education Week.

5. ACKNOWLEDGMENTS

Thank you to the Institute of Oral History at Baylor University, SIGCSE, and NCWIT for their support of this project. CEOHP is a special project of ACM-W and has received grants from the National Science Foundation (NSF 0710536) and the Sam Taylor Fellowship Fund. During 2011, all interview materials will be permanently archived at the Charles Babbage Institute at the University of Minnesota.

Facilitating Learning Dynamic Programming Through a Previous Introduction of Exhaustive Search

Arturo Camacho
arturo.camacho@ecci.ucr.ac.cr

Alexandra Martinez
alexandra.martinez@ecci.ucr.ac.cr

Escuela de Ciencias de la Computación e Informática
Universidad de Costa Rica
San José, Costa Rica

ABSTRACT

A strategy to facilitate learning Dynamic Programming (DP) is presented. The strategy consists in introducing Exhaustive Search (ES) before DP. The foundations of the strategy are the following hypothesis: (1) knowing ES can be a contributing factor in learning DP; (2) ES is easier to understand than DP; and (3) having an ES solution can help to find a DP solution. Based on the implementation of the strategy during one semester, we conclude that it was effective, since the students were able to understand DP more easily than in the previous semester, where the strategy was not applied.

Categories and Subject Descriptors

F.2.0 [**Analysis of Algorithms and Problem Complexity**]: General; E.1.0 [**Data Structures**]; K.3.2 [**Computers and Education**]: Computer and Information Science Education—*computer science education*

General Terms

Algorithms

Keywords

Dynamic Programming, Exhaustive Search

1. INTRODUCTION

We propose a strategy to facilitate learning dynamic programming (DP). The strategy consists in switching the order in which Exhaustive Search (ES) and DP are usually taught (DP is usually taught before ES [1, 2, 3, 4]). The rationale behind the strategy is based on the following assumptions:

1. Prior knowledge of ES can facilitate learning DP.

2. Learning ES is easier than learning DP.

3. Having an ES solution can contribute in creating a DP solution.

2. DESCRIPTION OF THE STRATEGY

The strategy consists of two stages: learning ES, and learning DP.

2.1 Learning ES

In this stage students are introduced to ES. First, the teacher shows how to use ES to solve a couple of problems that cannot be solved efficiently using DP (to avoid students discovering DP too early). Then, the technique is improved by introducing the concepts of *branch-and-bound* and *backtracking*, which bring in the philosophy of DP: eliminating redundant calculations.

2.2 Learning DP

In this stage students are introduced to DP. First, the teacher formulates a problem that can be solved efficiently using DP (e.g., the 0/1 knapsack problem). Then, students are asked to brainstorm an ES solution to the problem. After that, students are asked to enhance the proposed solutions by using branch-and-bound and backtracking (if applicable), and analyze the improvements in efficiency. Finally, the teacher shows that, even after using branch-and-bound or backtracking, there is still redundant work in the solution, and proceeds to show how DP may contribute to reduce redundant work.

3. APPLICATION OF THE STRATEGY

The strategy was applied during one semester, and it was observed that students were able to understand DP more easily than in the previous semester, in which the strategy was not applied. This observation was confirmed by results of exams and homework.

4. REFERENCES

[1] A. V. Aho, J. D. Ullman, and J. E. Hopcroft. *Estructuras de Datos y Algoritmos*. Addison-Wesley Iberoamericana, 1988.

[2] W. H. Ford and W. R. Topp. *Data Structures with C++ Using STL*. Prentice Hall, 2 edition, 2001.

[3] E. Horowitz, S. Sahni, and S. Rajasekaran. *Computer Algorithms*. Silicon Press, 2 edition, 2007.

[4] S. Sahni. *Data Structures, Algorithms, and Applications in Java*. Silicon Press, 2 edition, 2004.

A Bioinformatics E-learning Lab for Undergraduate Students

Feng Lu[1]
lufeng@hust.edu.cn

Hui Liu[1]
huiliu.mail@gmail.com

Yi Jian[1]
hiyijian@gmail.com

Yanhong Zhou[2]
yhzhou@hust.edu.cn

Zhenran Jiang[3]
jiangzhenran@163.com

[1] Serv Comp Technol & Syst Lab, Cluster & Grid Comp Lab, Huazhong Univ Sci & Technol, Wuhan, China.
[2] Sch Life Sci & Technol, Huazhong Univ Sci & Technol, Wuhan, China.
[3] Dept Comp Sci & Technol, East China Normal Univ, Shanghai, China

ABSTRACT

Bioinformatics has become an important subject in computer science (CS). While it is an active research area, bioinformatics is still of infancy in CS education. E-learning labs are emerging as important educational tools for bioinformatics. We consider that it can be improved with case study and simulated virtual environment. In this study we present a dedicated case-study e-learning lab for bioinformatics (CELB). It is publicly accessible at http://bioinfo.hust.edu.cn:8080/blast4/. The evaluation results reveal that this e-learning lab is suitable for training students' problem-solving ability in bioinformatics.

Categories & Subject Descriptors

K.3.2 [**Computers and Education**]: Computer and Information Science Education

General Terms

Design, Experimentation, Human Factors.

Keywords

Bioinformatics, E-learning, Exercise development, Case-study

1. THE SYSTEM

The web-based e-learning labs have the potential to provide valuable complements to face-to-face training and become a research hotspot in bioinformatics education. Most of the e-learning labs emphasize training in "tool use", deviating from the training goal--answering fundamental questions of biology and medicine with the aid of computer science. In this research, we have developed a dedicated case-study e-learning lab for bioinformatics (CELB) (figure 1), which adopted "blast for gene discovery" as our training case. Being a basic and common problem in biology, gene discovery is suitable for bioinformatics problem-solving training. Another benefit of this case is that it requires students to actively use the most famous bioinformatics tool--the Basic Local Alignment Search Tool (BLAST) to specific situations, including parameters setting and results analysis. Besides, students can learn to grasp the principles of database searching and sequence analysis under certain principles.

CELB offers features as following: 1) step-by-step guidance for beginners, 2) "one stop" service with an intuitive web interface that students can complete the case smoothly, 3) automatic aided analysis that guide students to interpret the results correctly and critically. In this way, novice trainees can do the exercise at their own pace.

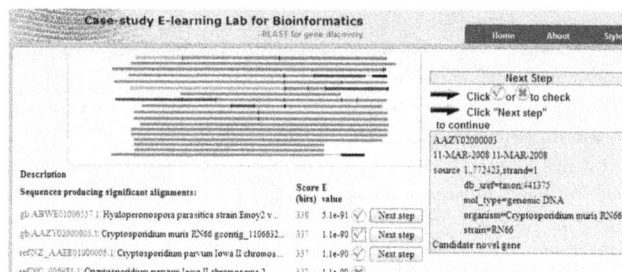

Figure 1. CELB screenshot. The automatic aided analysis marked as '√' or '×' (separately representing candidate 'novel' gene and annotated gene).

2. RESULTS

A quasi-experimental study was used in this study. Students were assigned to complete the case when they were taking the course "Introduction to Bioinformatics" in the first semester of their junior year (2009-2010) at Huazhong University of Science and Technology. The evaluation results reveal that, in contrast with the existing e-learning labs, such as NCBI Education, EBI e-learning, Bioinformatics Education Online at University of Manchester, Expasy e-proxemis, SADR, Bioinformatics Information Resource and eLearning Center (BIREC), BioManager and ADP, CELB: 1) shows real-world examples providing concrete illustrations of analysis principles, that is not only 'how' but also 'why' must do so, 2) simulates real environment designed to promote student aware of both tool use and analysis skills, 3) provides a dedicated web portal for beginners.

3. ACKNOWLEDGMENTS

This research was supported by 2008 Innovational Experimental Area Program for Talented Person Raise Pattern by the Ministry of Education of China (DHE-Doc[2009], No.4, SN.71), the National Key Technology R&D Program (2008BAH29B05), the Educational Reform Program of Hubei Educational Committee, and the College Student Innovation Experiment Plan of Huazhong University of Science & Technology (2010131).

A Model for Visualizing Sentence Complexity

Stefanie A. Markham
Department of Computer Science,
Georgia State University, Atlanta, GA 30303
smarkham@gsu.edu

Ying Zhu
Department of Computer Science,
Georgia State University, Atlanta, GA 30303
yzhu@cs.gsu.edu

ABSTRACT

Learning how write and communicate effectively is a common challenge that spans most academic disciplines. "Can a model be developed that visually captures the structural and linguistic complexity of text?" This paper proposes a model for visualizing sentence complexity.

Categories and Subject Descriptors

H.1.[**Models and Principles**]: 1.System and Information Theory – *Information theory;* 2. User/Machine Sys – *Human information processing* H.5.2.[**Information Interfaces and Presentation**]: User Interfaces – *Natural Language*

General Terms

Design, Human Factors, Languages, Theory

Keywords

Visualization, Linguistic Complexity, Education

1. INTRODUCTION

Learning how to write and communicate effectively is a common challenge that spans most academic disciplines. Why do some speakers or writers confuse the audience while others are easy and enjoyable to follow? Analyzing the complexity of text can give us insight into this puzzling question.

The field of linguistics contributes the theoretical basis for the complexity of text. While there is not one standard definition of text complexity, several aspects can be integrated to give an insightful picture of the complexity. Once writers see where and why their writing is complex, they can learn how to write more clearly. Readers can also benefit by evaluating the complexity of a document before reading it. Existing work include statistical analysis of text that results in a single number representing an entire document, which is very limiting. What is the granular complexity of text and how can we visualize it in such a way that gives us knowledge about where the problems are? This paper begins at the sentence level. Once we see the complexity of a sentence, we can zoom out and in on a document to see varying resolution. The work in progress is developing an integrated model for visualizing the complexity and structure of text using a linguistic theoretical basis. Thus the research question is: *"Can a model be developed that visually captures the structural and linguistic complexity of text?"* This paper proposes a model for visualizing sentence complexity.

2. BACKGROUND

Theoretical basis includes classic readability models as well as structural analysis of text. Syntactic complexity measures are computed on the sentence level, and semantic properties focus on

the complexity of words. Structural complexity is based on clause analysis and relationship. Types of sentences include simple, compound, complex, and compound-complex. According to Kemper, et al., left-branching clauses require more working memory than right-branching clauses.

Example: After going to the movies, the student, who is a senior, stayed up all night to study for her math test.

One of 69 possible Kellogg diagrams generated by online tool (1aiway.com/nlp4net/services/enparser/):

Output from the Stanford Parser (nlp.stanford.edu/software/lex-parser.shtml):

3. THE PROPOSED MODEL

Our model for sentence complexity will preserve the sentence length including readability features, preserve the sentence structure incorporating branching, preserve word order, match the feature with most natural visualization component, and make it simple and meaningful enough to expand into a discourse analysis.

The example sentence used above in section 2 has no complex words (words with >= three syllables). There are 21 words in the sentence which is borderline complex (>20 words). The sentence type is complex (at least one dependent clause), and it begins with a left branching clause (After going to the movies).

Statistical analysis of text is averaged over an entire document. We are working toward a picture that displays a more granular view of complexity and requires little training to understand. Our plan is to analyze the complexity of text from the sentence level to the document level, use a large display visualization wall to analyze large texts, perform user studies, and gather independent expert opinion on the usability and accuracy of the results.

4. REFERENCES

[1] Chall, J. S. & Dale, E. 1995. *Readability Revisited: The New Dale-Chall Readability Formula,* Cambridge, MA, Brookline Books, May 1995.

[2] Cheung, H., & Kemper, S. 1992. Competing Complexity Metrics and Adults' Production of Complex Sentences. *Applied Psycholinguistics,* 13:53-76, Mar 1992.

[3] Flesch, R. F. 1948. A New Readability Yardstick. *Journal of Applied Psychology,* 32(3):221–233, June 1948.

[4] Oelke, D., et al. 2010. Visual Readability Analysis: How to Make Your Writings Easier to Read. *In Proceedings of the IEEE Conference on Visual Analytics and Technology, VAST'10,* 2010.

Do Educational Software Systems Provide Satisfactory Learning Opportunities for 'Multi-Sensory Learning' Methodology?

Peter Chan
Student, Faculty of Business
Australian Catholic University
40 Edward St
North Sydney, NSW2060, Australia
61425567328
gm.peter@gmail.com

Girija Krishnaswamy
Lecturer, Faculty of Business
Australian Catholic University
40 Edward St.
North Sydney, NSW2060, Australia
61402823871
girija.krishnaswamy@acu.edu.au

ABSTRACT
'Multi-sensory' learning approach accelerates the learning process; aided by the use of educational software. This paper attempts to identify an educational software system that truly supports a 'multi-sensory' learning approach.

Categories and Subject Descriptors
K.3.1 [**Computer uses in education**]: Computer-assisted instruction – Collaborative learning

General Terms
Performance, Design, Human Factors

Keywords
Multiple Intelligences, Split-Brain, Computer Based Training, Mind Mapping, Multi-sensory learning

1. INTRODUCTION
A number of studies have concluded that one of the best approaches to accelerate the learning process is to apply a 'multi-sensory' learning approach, in which learners are provided with as many different learning styles as possible, facilitating the flow of information to the learners' brains simultaneously and holistically. This approach is aided by the use of educational software [1]. Are there any educational software systems that satisfactory provide 'multi-sensory' learning opportunities? The data required to answer this question has been compiled from the exploration of 41 publications, retrieved from various sources.

To adequately cover and facilitate the understanding of the roles of these multimedia/interactive features in stimulating learning styles, two architecture models of the human brain, namely the 'Split-Brain' [4] and 'Multiple Intelligences' models [2,3], have been utilized in this paper. Two educational software systems, namely Computer Based Training (CBT) and Mind Mapping (MM) software systems have been found to be able to be programmed to implement a vast variety of multimedia/interactive features. However, one or more of the available multimedia/interactive features that were found capable of being programmed into one system were found to be not capable in the other.

Accordingly, multimedia/interactive features can be categorised into three groups: - Multimedia/interactive features that can be implemented in both CBT and MM software packages (Group01);

- those that can be implemented only in CBT (Group02); and - those that can be implemented only in MM (Group03).

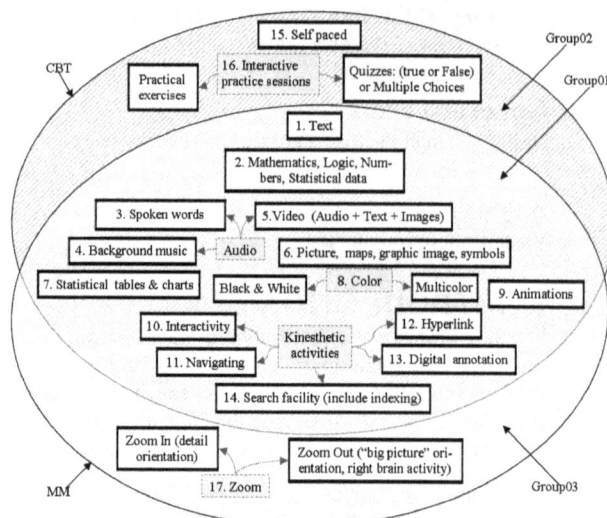

Multimedia and Interactive features applicable in CBT and MM

There is enough evidence to suggest that those multimedia/interactive features that were present in CBT, but absent in MM programs, and vice versa, do play a significant role in stimulating certain learning pathways. In conclusion, therefore, neither CBT nor MM software systems on their own have the ability to provide learners with a truly 'multi-sensory' learning capability.

2. REFERENCES
[1] Franco, C. (2007). E-learning and multiple intelligences: Catering for different needs and learning styles. *Revista Eletrônica Do Instituto De Humanidades*, VI(XXIII).

[2] Gardner, H. (1983). Frames of Mind. New York: Basic Books Inc.

[3] McKenzie, W. (2002). Multiple Intelligences and Instructional Technology. (2nd Ed.) ISTE Publications.

[4] Sperry, R. (1982). Science and Moral Priority: Merging Mind, Brain, and Human Values. In Convergence, Vol. 4 New York: Columbia University Press.

Adaptation of Educational Contents to Mobile Devices

Antonio García, Eva García, Luis de-Marcos, José-Antonio Gutiérrez
Computer Science Departament. University of Alcalá. Spain.

{a.garciac, eva.garcial, luis.demarcos, jantonio.gutierrez}@uah.es

ABSTRACT

In this paper, we propose a system for adaptation of educational contents to mobile devices, taking into account the skills of the learner, his context and the characteristics of his device.

Categories and Subject Descriptors

K.3.1 [Computers and Education]: Computer Uses in Education – Distance learning.

General Terms

Algorithms, Design

Keywords

m-learning, adaptation, mobile devices, skills

1. INTRODUCTION

E-learning has brought a revolution in training methods, as well as support to traditional learning or as new training system. However the main feature of these systems (independence in the student's location) is not completely fulfilled, since the minimum hardware requirement is a personal computer (PC). A true independence in time and place means learning where and when a person wants access to learning materials [1]. Mobile learning (m-learning) is an evolution of e-learning and is based on the use of mobile devices.

Because mobile devices, by their nature, are usually used by one person at the same time, we propose a system capable of adapting educational contents to learners who are performing the training through their mobile device.

2. SYSTEM OF ADAPTATION

The system (Figure 1) aims are to produce educational contents adapted to the needs of the learner (skills), its context and the characteristics of his mobile device. This system has as inputs learning objects (LOs), skills of the learner and features of the mobile device. As output the system will generate an adapted and customized course to the learner. The system is divided in subprocesses that are listed below:

• Selection: It is the process responsible for selecting the components (learning objects, skills and features of mobile device).

• Sequencing: This is the process that sorts the learning objects so that training is conducted according to the constraints involved in the process of learning [2].

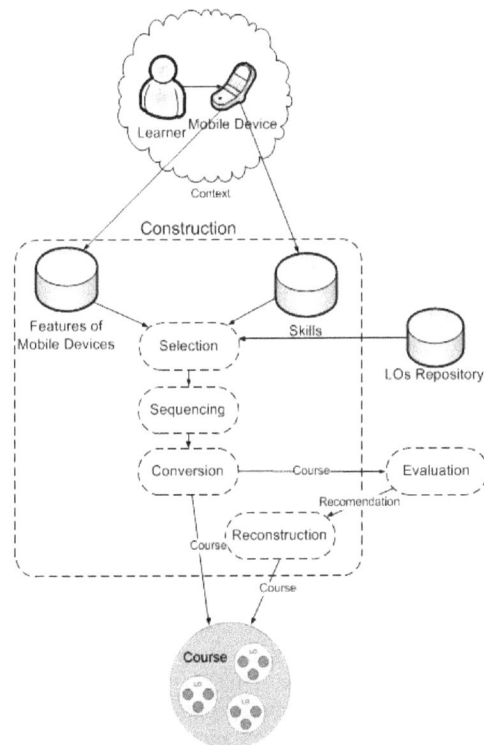

Figure 1. System of adaptation of learning objects.

• Conversion: It is the process that performs the conversion and adaptation of learning contents, taking into account the limitations of the mobile device (screen, operating system, etc.).

• Evaluation: An external expert can make further improvements or suggestions to re-adapt a learning object or course.

• Reconstruction: If the expert has suggested or made changes on any content, this process will rebuild the course.

3. REFERENCES

[1] Motiwalla, L. F. Mobile learning: A framework and evaluation. Computers & Education, 49, 2007), 581–596.

[2] de Marcos, L., Barchino, R., Martínez, J.J., & Gutiérrez, J.A. A New Method for Domain Independent Curriculum Sequencing: A Case Study in a Web Engineering Master Program. International Journal of Engineering Education, 25, 5 (2009 2009), 632-645.

A Comparison of Software Engineering Knowledge Gained from Student Participation in Humanitarian FOSS Projects

Heidi J. C. Ellis
Western New England College
1215 Wilbraham Rd.
Springfield, MA 01119
011-413-782-1748
hellis@wnec.edu

Gregory W. Hislop
Drexel University
3141 Chestnut St.
Philadelphia, PA 19104
011-215-895-2179
hislop@drexel.edu

Ralph A. Morelli
Trinity College
300 Summit St.
Hartford, CT 06106
011- 860-297-2220
ralph.morelli@trincoll.edu

ABSTRACT

This poster reports on student opinion of the Software Engineering knowledge gained by students exploring a Humanitarian Free and Open Source Software project. Eight students in a non-majors class and eleven more-advanced software development students were surveyed pre- and post-course on their opinions of technical and professional knowledge gained.

Categories and Subject Descriptors

K.3.2 [**Computers and Education**]: Computer and Information Science Education – *Computer Science Education.*

General Terms

Human Factors.

Keywords

Open source software, software engineering, computing education.

1. INTRODUCTION

Instructors have long been using software projects to convey software engineering knowledge to students. In fact, the CC 2005 guidelines [1] suggest project courses as one way of conveying technical and professional skills to students. Humanitarian Free and Open Source Software (HFOSS) projects have been demonstrated as being useful for attracting students to computing majors [2,3]. However less attention has been paid to the actual knowledge gained by students. This poster provides some insight into the software engineering knowledge gained by students involved in an HFOSS project.

2. THE STUDY AND RESULTS

A small study was conducted to compare the knowledge gained by a class of eight non-computing majors to the knowledge gained by eleven students in a more advanced software development class. The projects used ranged from Sahana (disaster management application) to GNOME accessibility projects. The same pre- and post-survey combination was used for both groups. The survey used a 5 point Likert scale that ranged from "strongly disagree" to "strongly agree". Student opinion was solicited in two areas: a) knowledge of software development; b) professional skills.

Copyright is held by the author/owner(s).
ITiCSE'11, June 27–29, 2011, Darmstadt, Germany.
ACM 978-1-4503-0697-3/11/06.

Results indicated that both groups felt that they had increased their understanding of technical skills from the beginning to the end of the courses. As might be expected, the more advanced group of students indicated that they had a better grasp of software engineering knowledge overall.

The results for professional knowledge gained were more mixed with the introductory students indicating less confidence in their professional skills at the end of the course than the beginning and the more advanced students indicating a generally positive gain in professional skills. Both groups indicated an increase in confidence in being able to "identify when peers in an H-FOSS project are behaving in an unprofessional manner." However, both groups showed a decline in "Participation in an H-FOSS project has improved my understanding of how to behave like a computing professional." Interestingly, both groups indicated a decline in the area of "gained some confidence in collaborating with professionals from a variety of locations and cultures."

These results may arise from this being students' first in-depth exposure to a professional environment. Students may have gained a much clearer picture of the scope and complexity involved in professional software development and therefore may be more conservative in their opinions of their abilities to interact in such an environment.

3. ACKNOWLEDGMENTS

This material is based on work supported by the National Science Foundation under Grant No. 0958204. Any opinions, findings and conclusions or recommendations expressed in this material are those of the author(s) and do not necessarily reflect the views of the National Science Foundation (NSF).

4. REFERENCES

[1] Computing Curricula 2005: Computer Science. The Overview Report. IEEE CS and ACM 2005.

[2] Morelli, R.A., Tucker, A.L., Danner, N., de Lanerolle, T.R., Ellis, H.J.C., Izmirli, O., Krizanc, D., and Parker, G. 2009. Revitalizing Computing Education by Building Free and Open Source Software for Humanity, *Communications of the ACM*, 52, 8, (August 2009), pp. 67-75.

[3] Hislop, G.W., Ellis, H.J.C., and Morelli, R.A. 2009. Evaluating Student Experiences in Developing Software for Humanity, In *Proceedings of the Fourteenth Annual ITiCSE,* Paris, Jul. 2009.

CROKODIL – A Platform Supporting the Collaborative Management of Web Resources for Learning Purposes

Mojisola Anjorin
Mojisola.Anjorin@kom.tu-darmstadt.de

Renato Domínguez García
Renato@kom.tu-darmstadt.de

Christoph Rensing
Christoph.Rensing@kom.tu-darmstadt.de

Multimedia Communications Lab
Darmstadt University of Technology
64283 Darmstadt, Germany

ABSTRACT

CROKODIL is an ongoing project at the Darmstadt University of Technology. The aim of the project is to implement a platform for collaborative knowledge acquisition based on web resources. In this paper, we analyze according to a social search model, how CROKODIL provides support for all stages of the search process which is an important and integrated part in today's learning process.

Categories and Subject Descriptors

K.3.1 [**Computer Uses in Education**]: Collaborative learning.

General Terms

Human Factors.

Keywords

Collaborative learning, recommender systems, web resources, social networks, social search, knowledge networks

1. INTRODUCTION

These days, it is almost impossible to imagine learning without searching in Google, checking up a topic in Wikipedia, or looking for something in a forum or blog. Searching for learning resources on the Internet has become such an integrated part of today's learning process that it is nearly taken for granted. According to an evaluation of search behavior and a resulting social search model [2], social interactions play an important role in all stages of search: before, during and after search. Therefore, this form of learning with resources found on the Web, is not an individual activity but rather a collaborative one and deserves more technical and pedagogical support. CROKODIL is an online collaborative learning platform providing a holistic solution offering diverse forms of support during all three phases of the search process.

During all phases, CROKODIL offers learners the means to communicate with others on the platform via a chat or by sending messages. Learners are encouraged to build friendship relations and to work collaboratively in groups.

Initially, in the before search stage, it is important for the learner to define activities or goals needed to attain the knowledge required to solve a certain task [1]. This didactical concept of constructing an activity structure helps the learners to better reflect and plan their learning process, thereby explicitly preparing for and improving the search process. CROKODIL supports this stage by offering the learner the means to create such an activity tree via a plugin [1] in the web browser.

Thereafter, during the research or searching phase, the learner now looks for adequate resources on the internet for these activities. CROKODIL supports the learner here via the aforementioned plugin which allows snippets of the web resource to be stored and attached to activities. These resources can also be semantically tagged [1] with key words and tag types describing the resource. The underlying backend structure storing the users, resources and tags is based on a semantic network structure, called knowledge network [1]. This representation offers the advantage of being able to browse through the network and perform semantic searches along the relations between the elements of the network [1]. A future planned enhancement will be the relevance ranking of these resources to support the effective retrieval of important and relevant resources.

Learners are able through all phases to view the resources collected by other learners as well as the other users' tags. To enhance this form of collaborative learning, CROKODIL provides recommendations suggesting related or interesting resources from fellow learners on the platform. Tag recommendations are also offered to unify the tagging concepts and choices of tags. Automated tag type identification [1] is also planned as a future feature in the platform.

Finally, after search, the learner commences the learning phase, where the resources stored in the above steps are retrieved. An important pedagogical step for the learners is reflecting on their learning experiences. In CROKODIL, learners can document their learning experiences by writing posts attached to the activities in the activity tree. These posts are shared with others on the platform, who can also post their feedback.

Future project goals are planned to offer recommendations based on the relevance ranking of resources in a social context. Such filtering, ranking and matching algorithms will therefore be implemented taking into consideration the social network structure of the platform. A usability evaluation is also planned to evaluate the acceptance and quality of the platform.

2. REFERENCES

[1] Böhnstedt, D., Scholl, P., Rensing, C., Steinmetz, R. 2010. Enhancing an Environment for Knowledge Acquisition based on Web Resources by Automatic Tag Type Identification. In: *Proc. of International Conference. on Computer-aided Learning* (ICL 2010), p. 380-389.

[2] Evans, B. M. and Chi, E. H. 2009. An elaborated model of social search. *Information Processing and Management*, (2009), doi:10.1016/j.ipm.2009.10.012.

Is Iteration Really Easier to Master than Recursion? An Investigation in a Functional-First CS1 Context

Claudio Mirolo

Dept. of Mathematics and Computer Science – University of Udine
via delle Scienze, 206 – 33100 Udine (Italy)
claudio.mirolo@uniud.it

ABSTRACT

Despite a general consensus on the difficulties faced to master recursion, a two-year investigation on the achievements in a *functional-first* introductory course does not corroborate the hypothesis that students are more at ease with iteration than they are with recursion.

Categories and Subject Descriptors

K.3.2 [**Computers and Education**]: Computer and Information Science Education — computer science education

General Terms

Human Factors

Keywords

programming learning, iteration, recursion.

1. SUMMARY OF THE WORK

We often tend to take for granted that *iteration* is easier to learn than *recursion*. However, wide-ranging comparisons of students' mastery of recursive vs. iterative structures are scarcely addressed in the educational literature. This raises questions about the extent to which iteration may facilitate the learning of programming, as opposed to recursion, particularly in relation to the development of higher-level competences. I have attempted to gain some insight into these questions by investigating three *learning dimensions*: (i) the understanding of the computation model, (ii) the ability to establish relations with the problem domain, and (iii) the ability to deal with program structures.

The introductory CS course at the University of Udine first teaches functional programming using Scheme, before approaching the imperative paradigm with Java. My analysis is based on the results of two related questionnaires: a mid-course *recursion test*, that was the subject of a previous paper [2], and an end-of-course *iteration test*. Each questionnaire was administered in a two-hour session to volunteers attending the course in the a.y. 2008-09 and 2009-10. Overall, 54 students took part in both tests.

Rationale. To address dimension (i), the students were asked to trace the computations of short programs: a linear and a tree recursion in the first test; a simple and a nested iteration in the second. Questions of this type pertain the

intermediate *application* level of Bloom's scale and the *multistructural* level of the SOLO taxonomy, see e.g. [3, 1]. The tasks for dimension (ii) were to formulate appropriate recursive relations (Bloom's *synthesis* level) in the first test; to recognize the function of the traced code (Bloom's *analysis* level) and to apply iteration to solve an easy problem (*synthesis*) in the second test. Relative to dimension (iii), in the first test the students had to describe the recursive structure of a fractal drawing (*analysis*) and to write a program for building a recursive structure (*synthesis*); in the second test they had to describe the iterative structure of a tessellation (*analysis*) and to write code to fill a matrix with integers following a given pattern (*synthesis*). From a SOLO viewpoint, dimensions (ii) and (iii) refer to the *relational* level.

Results. Here is a brief summary of the main findings. (i) From the program traces it appears that nested loops are as challenging to students as tree recursion. Viable computation models can be inferred from 87% of the answers for liner recursion, 81% for tree recursion, 94% for simple iteration, and 74% for nested iteration. (ii) In the *synthesis* tasks that require to relate the program and problem domains, the percentage of success turns out to be about 60%, both for recursion and iteration. (iii) Dealing with structures seems to be the most demanding kind of task. Students' *analysis* is consistent, without missing important features, in 52% of the cases for the recursive structure; in 56% for the iterative structure. The (structure) *synthesis* problems are solved by 59% of the subjects in the recursive case; by 50% in the iterative (matrix-filling) case. Moreover, if we compare the *best-* and *worst*-performance quartiles, we can see that the relative deviations from the average item scores are most enhanced for the items about *structures*.

Conclusions. The outlined results cast some doubt on the assumption that it is easier for a learner to master iteration than recursion. The investigation was carried out in the context of a functional-first course, but the indication may be of more general validity, since most students were exposed to imperative programming in secondary school.

2. REFERENCES

[1] R. Lister et al. Not seeing the forest for the trees: novice programmers and the SOLO taxonomy. In *Proc. 11th ITiCSE*, 2006.

[2] C. Mirolo. Learning (through) recursion: a multidimensional analysis of the competences achieved by CS1 students. In *Proc. 15th ITiCSE*, 2010.

[3] C. Starr et al. Bloom's taxonomy revisited: specifying assessable learning... In *Proc. 39th SIGCSE*, 2008.

Natural Language in Introductory Programming: An Experimental Study

Osvaldo Luiz de Oliveira
Faculty of Campo Limpo Paulista
Rua Guatemala, 167, Jardim América
Campo Limpo Paulista, SP, Brazil
55 11 4812-9407

osvaldo@faccamp.br

Ana Maria Monteiro
Faculty of Campo Limpo Paulista
Rua Guatemala, 167, Jardim América
Campo Limpo Paulista, SP, Brazil
55 11 4812-9400

anammont.per@gmail.com

Norton Trevisan Roman
University of São Paulo
Arlindo Béttio, 1000, Ermelino
Matarazzo, São Paulo, SP, Brazil
55 11 3091-1008

norton@usp.br

ABSTRACT

Although characterized as being "high level", classical programming languages such as Pascal and C have a grammar that is very different from natural language. In this research field, two main streams are noteworthy, one of them is characterized by an attempt to facilitate the understanding of the grammar of classic programming languages [1] and the other investigates how one may design languages for novices which are in line with their natural way of thinking about programming [2]. Focusing in the learning of concepts such as sequence of sentences that express actions, conditions and repetitions, we conducted an experimental study to investigate the hypothesis that the use of natural language can facilitate learning introductory programming.

Categories and Subject Descriptors

K.3.2 [**Computers & Education**]: Computer & Information Science Education – computer science education.

General Terms

Human Factors, Languages, Experimentation.

Keywords

Natural Language Programming, Introductory Programming, CS1, Empirical Research, Computer Programming Education.

1. THE EXPERIMENT

In our experiments, we used a microworld comprising robots, walls and disks as our problem domain. We developed two languages (and corresponding compilers), one following a classical context-free grammar notation (MRt) and the other defined by a grammar that allows for the generation of sentences similar to those of the Portuguese language (MRp). We experimentally investigated the learning of introductory programming in two groups of undergraduate students with no previous experience on programming. The first group used the MRp language (treatment), while the other the MRt language (control). The students were first taught about the language they should be using. Next, both groups received the same exam, consisting of four questions. The questions answered by the participants were independently reviewed by two of the researchers, having been assigned a score from 0 to 5. The experiment was carefully designed so that all other variables that might affect learning remained constant, so that the type of grammar was the only measured variable.

2. RESULTS

Table 1 shows the mean and standard deviation scores for both groups, on a 1 to 5 scale. Means and standard deviations were almost identical for both groups with no statistically significant difference between these averages ($t = 0.20$ at the significance level of $p = 0.85$), which means that the proposed hypothesis could not be confirmed.

Table 1. Results (mean and standard deviation) of the test

Group	n	Mean (1 – 5) ± SD
I (treatment)	11	3.91 ± 0.79
II (control)	11	3.98 ± 0.82

This result is somewhat surprising because it suggests that, in and on itself, the type of grammar used by novices (whether classical or natural) does not affect the learning of introductory programming. In the future, we shall try to perform the experiment described with more participants, in order to obtain a broader coverage, in geographical and social terms

3. REFERENCES

[1] Villalobos, J. A., Calderon, N. A., and Jiménez, C. H. 2009. Developing programming skills by using interactive learning objects. *ACM SIGCSE Bulletin* 41, 3 (Sep. 2009), 151-155. DOI=10.1145/1562877.1562927.

[2] Guzdial, M. 2008. Paving the Way for Computational Thinking. *Communications of the ACM* 51, 8 (Aug. 2008), 25-27. DOI=10.1145/1378704.1378713.

ITiCSE'11, June 27–29, 2011, Darmstadt, Germany.
ACM 978-1-4503-0697-3/11/06.

A First Step Mapping IMS Learning Design and Merlin-Mo

Raquel Hijón-Neira and Ángel Velázquez Iturbide
Departamento de Lenguajes y Sistemas Informáticos I
Universidad Rey Juan Carlos
C/ Tulipán s/n, 28933 Móstoles, Madrid, Spain
raquel.hijon@urjc.es, angel.velazquez@urjc.es

ABSTRACT

Mapping the specification IMS Learning Design and the tracking system we have developed and have been using for several years, called Merlin-Mo, is a logical step forward on interoperability between e-Learning tracking systems and specifications. In order to increase the best acceptance of the specifications into the widespread world of e-Learning systems and to ensure the standardization of the outputs from the systems to be used in others.

Categories and Subject Descriptors

K.3.2 [**Computers and Education**]: Computer and Information Science Education - Computer science education, self-assessment.
D.2.12 [**Software Engineering**]: Interoperability – Data Mapping.

General Terms

Standardization

Keywords

IMS Learning Design, Interactions Analysis, Moodle, Mapping.

1. INTRODUCTION

What the mapping of Merlin-Mo and IMS-LD aims to is the re-usability of an analysis plan/course/UoL of Merlin-Mo into an IMS-LD compliant tool, or the other way around; this re-usable information package could be used as a base for a further development or as they are actually defined. Furthermore, this mapping is focused on the interoperability and the reusability of an information package/UoL, no matter the original platform that is used for it.

2. BASIC APPROACH ON MAPPING IMS-LD AND MERLIN-MO

In order to achieve the best understanding between IMS-LD and Moodle, Burgos et al. [1] define a three step process: To realize these three steps we need to establish a general framework, with some restrictions. Since both parts are different in essence (Merlin-Mo is a tracking system for a CMS, while IMS-LD is a specification) a constraints list is required in order to find a common agreement which the understanding could be built upon (see Table 1). The first step in the integration process is focused on the export of a Merlin-Mo analysis to an IMS-LD UoL. IMS-LD is defined as a metaphor built around a theater using roles, plays and acts. In Figure 1, there are several couples of elements IMS-LD and Merlin-Mo defined in the most basic structure of Merlin-Mo analysis:

Table 1: Elements in an IMS-LD UoL mapped to Merlin-Mo

Issue	Merlin-Mo feature-comp	IMS-LD structure	Remarks
0	AIAS / PIAS	1UoL,1play,1act,1AS	
1.1	Setting:Analysis' Name	Title of Learn.Design	
1.2	Setting:Query Descripti.	Title of Play	
1.3	Setting:word for teachers	Roles:teachers:title	
1.4	Setting:word for adminis.	Roles:adminis.:title	
2.0	Type of Analysis	Learning activity	* (1)
2.1	Type of Analysis 0	Learning activity (1st)	
2.2	Descrip. of Analysis	Activity Description	
2.3	Activity: Chat	Synchron. conference	Services
2.4	Activity: Forum	Asynchr. conference (conference-type)	Services
2.5	Activity: Quiz	-	
2.6	Activity: Survey	External	Level B
2.7	Activity: Wiki		
3.0	Resource	Learning Object	*(2)
3.2	Resource: Label	Learning Object	*(3)
3.3	Resour.: Link to a file	Learning Object	*(4)
3.4	Reso.:Link to website	Learning object	*(5)

*(1) If a resource or an activity is defined there will be an environment
*(2) All resources ended as learning objects except Directory and Link
*(3) Could map to a title of environment if needed
*(4) File should be included in content pack
*(5) Link should be an absolute URL

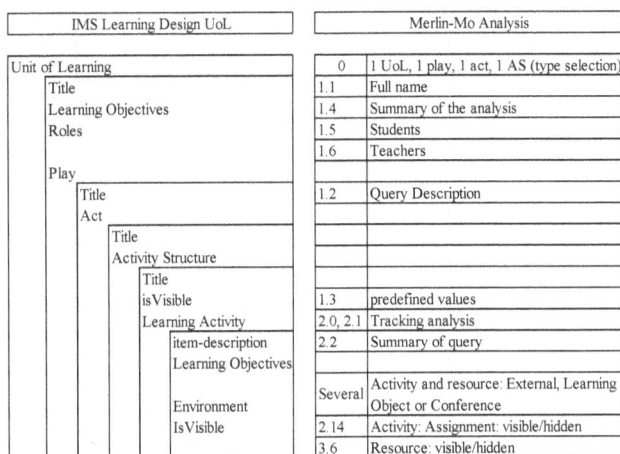

IMS Learning Design UoL		Merlin-Mo Analysis	
Unit of Learning		0	1 UoL, 1 play, 1 act, 1 AS (type selection)
Title		1.1	Full name
Learning Objectives		1.4	Summary of the analysis
Roles		1.5	Students
		1.6	Teachers
Play			
Title		1.2	Query Description
Act			
Title			
Activity Structure			
Title			
isVisible		1.3	predefined values
Learning Activity		2.0, 2.1	Tracking analysis
item-description		2.2	Summary of query
Learning Objectives			
		Several	Activity and resource: External, Learning Object or Conference
Environment		2.14	Activity: Assignment: visible/hidden
IsVisible		3.6	Resource: visible/hidden

Figure 1. Basic match between an IMS-LD UoL & Merlin-Mo

3. REFERENCES

[1] Burgos D., Tattersall C., Dougiamas M., Vogten H., Koper R.: A First Step Mapping IMS Learning Design and Moodle. Journal of Universal Computer Science, vol. 13, no.7 (2007), 924-931 submitted: 7/3/07, accepted: 25/7/07, appeared: 28/7/07 @ J.UCS

Using Student Blogs for Documentation in Software Development Projects

Robert Law
Glasgow Caledonian University
70 Cowcaddens Road
Glasgow
+441413313921

Robert.law@gcal.ac.uk

ABSTRACT
This poster will describe an ongoing attempt to encourage students to engage with the process of documentation and design within software development through the use of blogs.

Categories and Subject Descriptors
K.3.2 [Computer and Information Science Education]: Computer Science Education:

General Terms
Documentation.

Keywords
Blogs, Software Development.

1. INTRODUCTION
Over a number of years there has been a noticeable deterioration in the depth and quality of documentation submitted within my institution by students attempting programming projects. It appears that the compartmentalization of subject areas within the curriculum leads students to assume that analysis/design, and programming, which are typically taught in separate modules, are not interrelated. Students undertaking programming modules often focus largely on coding, and some will happily submit a development project with no or little documentary evidence of the design and development process.

The rise of blogging has led to many academics across a number of disciplines, including CS, incorporating the use of blogs into their teaching [1]. A broader aim of the blog in this context is to encourage reflection, allowing students to become active learners [2]. With this in mind the common blog was enlisted to encourage students to record and reflect on their process during the course of the development of a software product. This somewhat informal medium would hopefully create a relaxed environment for the student to communicate their design and thought processes. The ability provided within this medium of the lecturer to comment on the student's blog posts allows progress to be monitored and constructive feedback given.

The multimedia rich blogging environment should provide the students with the platform to develop and showcase their design and documentation skills by creating an online portfolio of their work.

2. THE DEVELOPMENT BLOG
Blogs have been introduced into two Game Programming modules, at years 2 and 4 (the final year of an Honours programme). The numbers of students participating in these modules were 25 and 9 respectively. The coursework for both modules involved the students creating a game of their own design. The open nature of the coursework means that it is imperative that the students analyze, plan and design their games before typing any code. Applying a "think, then do" attitude to software development will increase productivity and reduce debugging of error strewn code.

The submission was split into three main sections: coding (40 marks), documentation (40 marks) and extension work (20 marks). The blog was worth 10 of the 40 marks available in the documentation section. Students were expected to make regular blog postings to build a reflective log, with date and time stamps allowing students to trace the development of their software. This should give them a better overview of the time and effort expended developing the product and the iterative nature of software development should become apparent. Material from the blog postings could then be incorporated into the final submitted documentation.

Results showed that the Y2 students outperformed the final year students, averaging a mark of 6.4 out of 10 for the blogging component compared with 5.0. In general a low blog mark corresponded to a low overall mark for documentation.

3. CONCLUSION
It is perhaps surprising that the final year students put far less effort into their blog postings than students at an earlier stage in their studies. Further study will be carried out to establish whether engagement with the blogging activity can be traced clearly into the final submission, and to explore the reasons for the apparent lack of engagement in the more mature students.

4. REFERENCES
[1] McDermott, R., Brindley, G., and Eccleston, G. 2010. Developing Tools to Encourage Reflection in First Year Students Blogs. *ACM ITiCSE'10*, 26-30 (Jun. 2010), DOI= http://dx.doi.org/10.1145/1822090.1822132.

[2] Safran, C. 2008. Blogging in Higher Education Programming Lectures: An Empirical Study. *ACM MindTrek'08*, 7-9 (Oct. 2008), DOI= http://dx.doi.org/10.1145/1457199.1457228.

How Educators Find Educational Resources Online

Monika Akbar
Dept. of Computer Science
Virginia Tech, Blacksburg, VA
amonika@vt.edu

Weiguo Fan
Dept. of Computer Science
Virginia Tech, Blacksburg, VA
wfan@vt.edu

Lillian Cassel
Dept. of Computing Sciences
Villanova Univ., Villanova, PA
lillian.cassel@villanova.edu

Lois Delcambre
Dept. of Computer Science
Portland State, Portland, OR
lmd@cs.pdx.edu

Clifford A. Shaffer
Dept. of Computer Science
Virginia Tech, Blacksburg, VA
shaffer@vt.edu

Edward A. Fox
Dept. of Computer Science
Virginia Tech, Blacksburg, VA
fox@vt.edu

ABSTRACT

Search engines are mostly targeted toward the generic user but educators have specific information needs with specialized information-seeking behaviors. When designing a course, educators may create a syllabus, lecture slides, and use tools as lecture aides. These resources are scattered across a large number of websites and require time and effort in finding them. To design a useful system for educators we must understand the problems they face when they seek, use, and re-use online resources. With that in mind, the Ensemble team[1] conducted focus groups to identify current practices and problems in locating online resources for educational purposes. The data provides better understanding of the information-seeking process of educators that can lead to better educational resource sites.

Categories and Subject Descriptors

H.4 [**Information Systems Applications**]: Miscellaneous; H.1.2 [**Information Systems**]: MODELS AND PRINCIPLES User/Machine Systems

General Terms

Design, Experimentation, Human Factors

Keywords

Educational resources, Ensemble, Computing portal

1. INTRODUCTION

The abundance of educational resources in scattered and mostly unstructured forms throughout the Internet makes it difficult for educators to locate and use quality materials. A number of approaches have been devised to address the issue. As a result, educators use sites like MIT Open-CourseWare [3], Merlot [2], and Connexions [1]. Each of sites has specialized collection, resides at different locations,

has its own browsing and navigation schema, making it time-consuming for educators to locate the right material at the right time.

To serve the information needs of educators, we must better understand current practices that are prevalent there. The Ensemble team conducted focus groups at Virginia Tech. In this poster we present the results obtained from two focus group sessions. Our questions to participants were split across two broad topics: (i) How do they search for educational materials; and (ii) feedback on the Ensemble portal. The results indicate that educators use a number of ways to seek resources, and there is a great need for improvement in existing systems if we want to support the overall information needs of this audience.

2. DATA AND ANALYSIS

The responses can be summarized in three broad categories: Resource Seeking, Reusing Course Materials, and Collections and Online Communities.

Educators usually depend on Web searches and personal connections to acquire materials. They look at different university sites for course material, use publishers' sites to some extent, borrow course material from others, frequently visit sites that provide various educational tools such as video clips, receive newsfeeds from other sites and so on.

Recycling course material is a common practice among educators who teach the same courses in different semesters. Thus, while they build on existing course material, they tend to stick to what they have been using. Even with material in place, the process for updating content is not efficient.

The importance of having an online community for educators was vastly recognized by the participants who prefer to join a community that already has a large group of members. Presence of experts in the community is another motivating factor for joining online communities.

3. ADDITIONAL AUTHORS

Yinlin Chen (Dept. of CS, Virginia Tech, Blacksburg, VA, email: ylchen@vt.edu)

4. REFERENCES

[1] Connexions, http://cnx.org/.
[2] Merlot, http://www.merlot.org.
[3] MIT OpenCourseWare, http://ocw.mit.edu/.

[1]This research is funded by NSF Grants DUE-0840713, 0840715, 0840719, 0840721, 0840668, 0840597, 0836940, 0937863.

A Contextualized Project-based Approach for Improving Student Engagement and Learning in AI Courses

Ingrid Russell	Zdravko Markov	Joy Dagher
University of Hartford	Central CT State University	University of Hartford
200 Bloomfield Ave	1615 Stanley Street, New	200 Bloomfield Ave
West Hartford, CT 06117, USA	Britain, CT 06050, USA	West Hartford, CT. 06117, USA
1 860 768 4191	1 860 832 2711	1 860 768 4444
irussell@hartford.edu	markovz@ccsu.edu	dagher@hartford.edu

ABSTRACT

The goal of Project MLeXAI, Machine Learning Experiences in Artificial Intelligence, is to develop a project-based framework for teaching core AI topics with a unifying theme of machine learning. In this paper, we provide an overview of Project MLeXAI and the curricular material being developed. We present experiences during the second phase of the project that involves its implementation at several diverse institutions involving twenty instructors.

Categories and Subject Descriptors

K.3.2 [**Computers and Education**]: Computer Science Education

General Terms

Experimentation

Keywords

Artificial Intelligence, Projects

1. PROJECT MLEXAI

The goal of Project MLeXAI, Machine Learning Experiences in Artificial Intelligence, is to develop a project-based framework for teaching core AI topics with a unifying theme of machine learning. We build on the success of our smaller-scale Phase 1 work. The objectives are to enhance student learning experiences in the AI course by implementing a unifying theme of machine learning to tie together the diverse and seemingly disconnected topics in the AI course, to increase student interest and motivation to learn AI, and to introduce students to an increasingly important research area. To that end, a suite of hands-on term-long projects have been developed. Each project involves the design and implementation of a learning system which enhances a particular commonly-deployed AI application. In addition, the projects provide students with an opportunity to address not only core AI topics but also many of the issues central to computer science, including algorithmic complexity and scalability problems.

Phase 1 involved the development of six modules and the implementation of these modules at three institutions: a small liberal arts college, a medium-sized comprehensive university, and a state university. The goal of phase 2 is to increase the number of modules and expand the implementation to include a larger and more diverse set of colleges and universities. A total of 26 projects were developed for use in the introductory AI courses. The rich set of applications that students can choose from spans several areas including recommender systems, web document classification, pattern recognition, data mining, and games. In keeping with the project goal, between the fall of 2007 and spring of 2010 semesters, the material was implemented and taught at a total of 14 diverse institutions involving 20 different instructors. Participating colleges and universities spanned a diverse group ranging from small to large, public to private, and include a number of institutions with a diverse student body including underrepresented groups.

The effectiveness of this project in achieving each of the goals listed earlier is being evaluated through a multi-tier evaluation system involving the students taking the AI course, members of the advisory board, and the two PIs and 18 participating faculty on this project who are teaching introductory AI courses. Students were asked to evaluate the student projects which were an integral part of the course by completing a survey comprised of 22 ranked questions and two open-ended questions. In addition, either individual students or small groups of students were interviewed at multiple locations to gather more qualitative data on the student experience.

In previous publications we reported on assessment results of Phase 1 [1, 2]. In this paper, we provide an overview of Project MLeXAI and present experiences of the PIs and participating faculty during phase 2 of the project, along with preliminary results of assessment of phase 2.

ACKNOWLEDGEMENTS

This work is supported in part by the National Science Foundation under grant number DUE- 0409497 and DUE- 0716338.

REFERENCES

[1] Russell, I., Markov, Z., Neller, T., Coleman, S., MLeXAI: A Project-Based Application-Oriented Model, *The ACM Transactions on Computing Education*, 10(3), August 2010.

[2] Wallace, S., McCartney, R., Russell, I., Games and Machine Learning: A Powerful Combination in an Artificial Intelligence Course, *Computer Science Education*, 20(1), pages 17-36, January 2010.

Java2Sequence – A Tool for the Visualization of Object-Oriented Programs in Introductory Programming

João Paulo Barros*+, Luís Biscaia*, and Miguel Vitória*
*LabSI2 & ESTIG, Instituto Politécnico de Beja, R. Pedro Soares, Beja, Portugal
+UNINOVA - CTS, Portugal
joao.barros@ipbeja.pt, lcds.biscaia@gmail.com, migueljvt@hotmail.com

ABSTRACT

This poster presents a Java™ based visualization tool for introductory object-oriented courses. The tool generates UML Sequence Diagrams from the execution of Java™ programs. The generated diagrams are enriched with a set of textual annotations that facilitate comprehension as they "connect" code and the respective diagrammatic representation.

Categories and Subject Descriptors

K.3.2 [**Computers and Education**]: Computer and Information Science Education—*Computer science education*; D.2.5 [**Software Engineering**]: Testing and Debugging—*Debugging aids*

General Terms

Languages, Design, Documentation.

Keywords

Java™, object-oriented, sequence diagram, UML, visual, diagram, program comprehension, visualization.

1. INTRODUCTION

The teaching of introductory object-oriented programming faces several challenges. A significant one resides on the difficulty to visualize the inherent additional levels of abstraction, namely the concepts of class, object, method calling, and the associated interdependencies. UML Sequence Diagrams [2] provide a readable graphical representation for the dynamics of simple programs, especially the ones that students usually build in introductory programming courses.

We present a tool that allows the generation of sequence diagrams from the execution of Java™ programs.

2. EXAMPLE

Fig. 1 shows an example sequence diagram for the following code, showing four popups for the respective arrows. Besides the minimal UML sequence diagram syntax defined in the UML specification, the tool adds several annotations that are associated to the arrows. To avoid cluttering the diagram, those additional annotations are only visible on demand: putting the mouse over the respective plus sign, the

user can see additional data associated to each arrow. Fig. 1 shows those annotations for four call arrows.

```
public class Dispenser {
    private List<Product> products; // products in machine
    private MoneyBox moneyBox; // handles money

    public static void main(String[] args) {
        Dispenser dispenser = new Dispenser();
        dispenser.addProduct(new Product("cookies", 100));
        dispenser.insertCoin(20);
    }
    // ...
}
```

3. FUTURE WORK

As future work, the tool should allow step by step construction of each diagram and should be possible to use it as an extension to BlueJ [1].

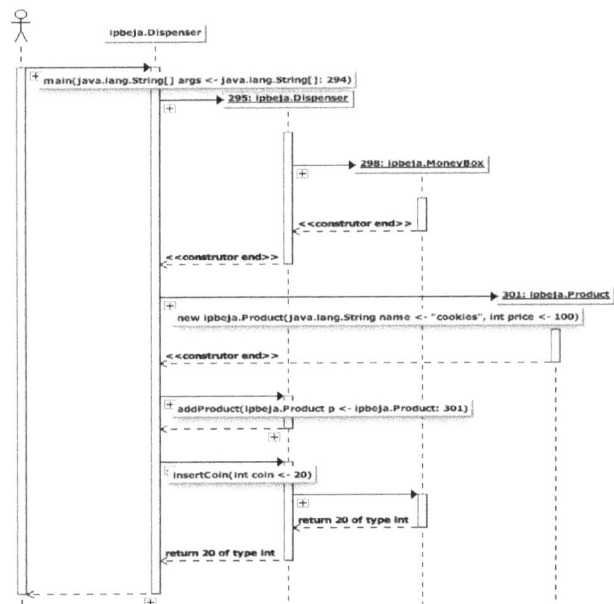

Figure 1: Generated sequence diagram.

4. REFERENCES

[1] M. Kölling. BlueJ – The interactive Java environment. http://www.bluej.org/. Accessed on 2011/04/07.
[2] OMG. UML 2.3. http://www.omg.org/spec/UML/2.3/. Accessed on 2011/04/17.

An Initial Look at Prospective Student Mentoring

Amber Settle
DePaul University
243 S. Wabash Ave
Chicago, IL 60604
(312) 362-5324
asettle@cdm.depaul.edu

Sarah Pieczynski
DePaul University
243 S. Wabash Ave
Chicago, IL 60604
(312) 362-5846
sarah@cdm.depaul.edu

Liz Friedman
DePaul University
243 S. Wabash Ave
Chicago, IL 60604
(312) 362-5384
efriedm2@cdm.depaul.edu

Mary Jo Davidson
DePaul University
243 S. Wabash Ave
Chicago, IL 60604
(312) 362-8239
mdavidson@cdm.depaul.ed

ABSTRACT

Effective student recruitment is an important issue for computing educators. We describe a mentoring program designed for prospective students at DePaul University and begin to understand the effectiveness of such a program. The program has been in place since 2004, and an initial analysis of survey data has led to changes in the way the program will be run and in how data will be collected for the next phase of the study.

Categories and Subject Descriptors

K.3.0 [**Computing Milieux**]: Computers and Education – *general*

General Terms

Design, Management, Performance.

Keywords

Prospective student mentoring, student retention, outreach

1. SIGNIFICANCE AND RELEVANCE

Effective student recruitment has long been of interest to educators (Chapman, D., 1981. A Model of Student College Choice. In *The Journal of Higher Education*, 52:5, 490-505), and such interest is not restricted to U.S.-based institutions (Binsardi, A. and Ekwulugo, F., 2003. International Marketing of British Education: Research on the Students' Perception and the UK Market Penetration. In *Marketing Intelligence & Planning*, 21:5, 318-237 and Cubillo, J.M., Sánchez, J., and Cervino J., 2006. International Students' Decision-Making Process. In *International Journal of Educational Management*, 20:2, 101-115). This is particularly true in computing because despite favorable job projections, the numbers of students enrolling in programs in computer science, information systems, and information technology programs in recent years is only beginning to recover from the precipitous decline seen in the past decade. One approach to retaining students is to use mentoring programs, but mentoring programs are often not implemented until the student has enrolled at an institution. In this work we describe and begin to evaluate a mentoring program for prospective students.

2. CONTENT

Since 2004, the College of Computing and Digital Media at DePaul University (CDM) has had a mentoring program that pairs faculty members with prospective students applying to CDM. The goal of the faculty mentoring program is to allow students early access to faculty, with the hope that such access will provide them with academic information that they would not otherwise receive from contacts with advising staff and improve the enrollment rate among prospective students. The CDM undergraduate services staff assign students to volunteer faculty within a few weeks of their admittance. Students are sent the contact information for faculty, and faculty receive a spreadsheet with mentees' information. Faculty are expected to initiate at least one contact with the student and to answer any questions.

Some initial data about the program was gathered during the 2009-2010 academic year and includes surveys of participating faculty members, surveys of current CDM students who are alumni of the program, and surveys of prospective students. The response rate for the current student survey was only 18% (64 out of 355), which was lower than hoped. The prospective student survey response was also poor with a 20% (66 out of 325) and 12% (31 out of 245) response rate to the first and second surveys. Such a low response rate is not likely to produce useful information. The faculty survey, however, produced some usable results with a 54% response rate (13 out of 24). Faculty survey respondents could choose more than one option, so the percentages may sum to more than 100. Ten faculty (77%) reported contacting students within 30 days of the students being assigned to them, two (15%) reported contacting students monthly, and one (7%) reported never contacting students. Five faculty (38%) answered prospective student questions at least once, three faculty (23%) answered questions monthly, five faculty (38%) answered questions weekly, and one faculty (7%) was not contacted by students. When asked about the benefits of the program, faculty indicated the uniqueness of the program and the access to curricular experts. Improvements suggested by faculty included encouraging students to contact their faculty member, making it more salient in faculty merit reviews, and easing the burden on faculty by providing administrative support.

The 2010-2011 program will involve a broader call for faculty and an opt-in rather than an opt-out method in an effort to recruit faculty who are more enthusiastic about the goals of the program. A different approach to data gathering is also planned. Faculty will be surveyed as in the previous year, but no current students will be surveyed as it appears that their recall about the program is insufficient to produce usable information. The prospective students will be surveyed at their summer orientation rather than by e-mail, with the hopes that this will produce an improved response rate. We will also gather retention data for first-year students who have completed the program.

ITiCSE'11, June 27–29, 2011, Darmstadt, Germany.
ACM 978-1-4503-0697-3/11/06

IR²gT: A Report Generation Tool for Institutional Repository

Jayan C. Kurian
RMIT International University
HCMC, Vietnam
(+848) 3776 1300

Jayan.kurian@rmit.edu.vn

Ashly Markose
National University of Singapore
Singapore
(+65) 9132 1765

ashly@comp.nus.edu.sg

Blooma Mohan John
RMIT International University
HCMC, Vietnam
(+848) 3776 1300

Blooma.John@rmit.edu.vn

ABSTRACT

"Report Generation" in general brings added value to Information Management Systems with no exception to Institutional repositories. In this paper, we describe IR²gT, a report generation tool for Institutional repositories. Taken from an academic perspective, one of the main reasons for this development was to generate reports based on individual authors and contribution period in an Institutional repository. Our plan was to achieve this report generation based on data extracted from DSpace [1] Institutional repository and present this grouped by various custom filter options such as author, contribution period, and summarized reports. The motivation for this project was based on feedback received from the academic community at Nanyang Technological University (NTU), Singapore during an Institutional repository presentation. In-addition, this project proposal was accepted and completed as part of Google Summer of Code (GSOC) program and was released under open source policy norms [2].

Categories and Subject Descriptors

H.2.3 [**Database Management**]: Languages – *Report writers.*

General Terms

Management.

Keywords

Report generation, Institutional repository, Open source tool.

1. INTRODUCTION

An institutional repository is defined as a central reference base for an organization's intellectual output. DSpace is an open source digital repository system offering a practical and cost-effective means for preserving and disseminating an Institution's intellectual output. One of the motivating factors that would facilitate usage of Institutional repositories by academic communities and repository stakeholders would be the capability

to generate reports based on data extracted from a repository database. To further extend the potential of this work, we sought feedback from the DSpace user community through an online survey and this is discussed in the next section.

2. SURVEY ANALYSIS

The survey was responded by 64 participants registered with the DSpace mailing list. From the survey, it was evident that majority (84%) of respondents have not used third-party reporting tools for generating Institutional repository reports. Only 2% used existing report generation tools. Some respondents (15%) used analytical tools for statistical information (e.g. page views) rather than general reports (e.g. Author/Publication report). All participants (100%) agreed that they are interested in using an open source reporting tool for DSpace. In general, respondents were globally spread with 31% from North America, followed by Europe with 29%, Asia with 20%, and 5% from Africa.

3. REPORT GENERATION SYSTEM

The workflow for report generation is given below in Figure 1. We use JasperReports [3] on a Java environment to develop this tool. Further information regarding this and the complete source code with documentation for this tool is available at [2].

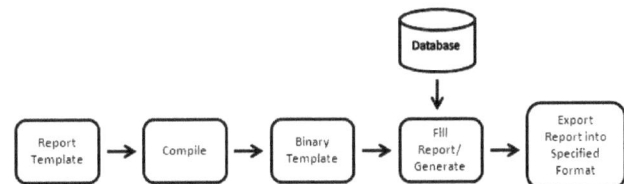

Figure 1. Report generation workflow

4. REFERENCES

[1] Tansley, R.,Bass, M., and Smith, M. 2003. DSpace as an open archival information system: current status and future directions. In: Koch, T., Solvberg, I.T. (eds.): Research and Advanced Technology for Digital Libraries. LNCS. Springer. Vol 2769, NY, 446-460.

[2] GSOC, Google summer of code program, project wiki accessible at
https://wiki.duraspace.org/display/GSOC/Google+Summer+of+Code+2009+Report+Generation+Tool

[3] JasperReports, Open source Reporting Engine accessible at
http://jasperforge.org/projects/jasperreports

An Update on the Use of Community-Based Non-Profit Organizations in Capstone Projects

David K. Lange
Grand Valley State University
Allendale, MI USA 49401
1.616.331.2060
langed@gvsu.edu

Roger C. Ferguson
Grand Valley State University
Allendale, MI USA 49401
1.616.331.2060
ferguson@gvsu.edu

Paul M. Leidig
Grand Valley State University
Allendale, MI USA 49401
1.616.331.2060
leidig@gvsu.edu

ABSTRACT

This poster updates a paper [3] presented at ITiCSE 2006 and re-examines a ten-year effort of our institution's use of community-based non-profit organizations (NPOs) in the information systems capstone course. Computer science or information systems majors often have adequate technical skills but lack an understanding of organizational processes, team project experience, and the ability to integrate information technology into an organizational setting. To bridge this gap, we use service-learning group projects that leverage local organizations. We document this effort to provide recommendations for successfully implementing similar courses.

Categories and Subject Descriptors

K.3.2 [**Computers and Education**]: Computer and Information Science Education - *Curriculum*

General Terms: Documentation

Keywords: Capstone projects, non-profit organizations, community-based projects

1. INTRODUCTION

As described in a paper [1] on 'socially-relevant' projects, Buckley et al. recommend students work on *actual projects for real customers*. We focused their recommendations to have our capstone class work on projects that serve the greater good of the community, replacing instructor-developed projects. There are additional benefits for students working with an actual local company in their capstone project [1,2]. This paper revisits the efforts our institution has taken using community-based NPOs in information systems capstone projects, and updates a paper [3] presented at ITiCSE in 2006. We present recommendations for successfully implementing similar capstone courses at your institution based on our ten-year experience.

2. THE PROBLEM

Educators have utilized group projects for years. Those who have taught using team projects know they often present challenges, including motivating students, unclear initial specifications, determining appropriate work given the size of the group. In 2002, we instituted an NPO-based project capstone course to address some of these issues with significant success.

3. OUR ORIGINAL SOLUTION

Our first step identified possible community NPOs that would benefit from students projects. The second step defined the project with the NPO prior to assigning students. The next step presented project options for student selection. Step four involved students working on development and testing. In the last step, students deliver the product to the NPO with a final presentation.

4. LESSONS LEARNED

In managing student teams, the following are four lessons learned: 1) Students underestimate time required for projects. Use project management software with a Gantt chart with short deadlines, continually updating the status. 2) Student success involves individual achievement. As in industry, these projects involve teamwork and are difficult for students to adapt. Use collaboration software to manage projects and develop team skills. 3) Require students to monitor projects and update the NPOs via weekly status reports. 4) Team members hold each other accountable through challenging overstated weekly individual effort reports.

Using NPOs has benefits to the community; however there are challenges: 1) Many NPOs use volunteers for IT support, often with questionable results. 2) Students learn to provide advice, and educate the NPO on the use of technology standards and protocols. 3) NPOs with limited budgets, frequently solicit universities for hardware or software donations. Universities typically do not have sufficient funding to support donations to NPOs. Helping obtain infrastructure funding from other sources is often part of the project. 4) Software licensing issues can be educational for NPOs. Many NPOs do not understand licensing models, and explaining them is often difficult for students, as well as purchasing necessary software with limited financial resources. 5) While NPOs sign agreements to eliminate recourse against the university and students, and limit time frame commitments, many NPOs expect ongoing "tech support" from the professor after the project is completed, and this must be addressed in the agreement.

5. CONCLUSION

With careful planning and well-defined requirements, community based capstone projects provide many benefits to computing students, and help develop university/industry relationships.

6. REFERENCES

[1] Buckley M., Kershner H., Schindler K., Alphonce C, Braswell J., Benefits of using socially-relevant projects in computer science and engineering education, *Proceedings of the 35th SIGCSE technical symposium on computer science education*, March 03-07, 2004, Norfolk, Virginia, USA

[2] Hoxmeier, J., Lenk, M.L. Service-learning in information systems courses: Community projects that make a difference. *Journal of Information Systems Education*, 14 (1). 91-100.

[3] Leidig, P., Ferguson, R., Leidig, J. The use of community-based non-profit organizations in information systems capstone projects. *Proceedings of the 11th annual SIGCSE conference on Innovation and technology in computer science education* (ITICSE '06). ACM, New York, NY.

Findings from an ACM Strategic Summit on Computing Education in Community Colleges

Elizabeth K. Hawthorne
Union County College
Senior Prof. Computer Science
Cranford, NJ USA
+1 908 497 4232
hawthorne@ucc.edu

Karl J. Klee
Alfred State College
Ret. Prof. Information Technology
Alfred, NY USA
+1 607 587 3413
kleekj@alfredstate.edu

Robert D. Campbell
CUNY Graduate Center
V.P. Information Technology
New York, NY USA
+1 212 817 7350
rcampbell@gc.cuny.edu

ABSTRACT

At the request of and funded by the US National Science Foundation, the ACM Committee for Computing Education at Community Colleges (www.acmccecc.org) conducted the *Strategic Summit on the Computing Education Challenges at Community Colleges*. The *Report of Findings* from the Summit will provide the impetus for future grant proposals to available funding sources. The objective is to share the *Report of Findings*, including those elements that are most relevant to faculty at four-year colleges and universities. The presenters will facilitate a discussion on an individual basis with computer science educators on topics from the report centered on the major challenges and associated opportunities. Attendees should come away from the session with ideas for crafting future funding proposals.

Categories and Subject Descriptors:

A.0 [Conference Proceedings]
K.3.2 [Computer and Information Science Education]

General Terms:

Standardization, Management

Keywords:

Summit, Challenges, Opportunities, Community, College, Two-Year, Education.

1. BACKGROUND

The *Report of Findings* titled "Digitally Enhancing America's Community Colleges: Strategic Opportunities for Computing Education" details the findings from the *Strategic Summit on the Computing Education Challenges at Community Colleges*. To ensure a broad view, a diverse group of thirty-three professionals from two-year colleges, four-year colleges, high schools, industry and government were invited to participate in the *Summit*. These experts engaged in spirited discourse framed by three themes: Perceptions, Preparation and Environments. To seed the breakout discussions, designated panelists delivered succinct presentations from three perspectives, Employer, Faculty and Student, after which the participants assembled into small groups for extended periods of focused interaction and exchange of ideas. All presentations and breakout discussions were digitally recorded and served as the foundation for producing the final report.

2. FINDINGS

The *Report of Findings*, elucidated by actual quotes captured during *Summit* deliberations, identifies twenty specific challenges and associated opportunities for post-secondary education with the express intent of providing a foundation and impetus for future grant proposals, initiatives and partnerships led by community college computing faculty and academic administrators. Many of the findings are applicable to baccalaureate-granting colleges and universities, especially those accepting transfer students from associate-degree granting institutions. A reading of this report reveals the following overarching themes:

- Active collaboration is required among the various sectors of education (high school, two-year colleges, four-year colleges and universities), together with business and industry, to address the challenges identified and achieve the opportunities noted.
- Well-defined computing nomenclature, curricula, assessment techniques and educational pathways are required to position the computing disciplines as first choice career options for two-year college students and to facilitate student achievement.
- The unique characteristics of computing education in community colleges require approaches and solutions specifically tailored to this field of study.

A few of the findings include:

- Embedding Computing Education in Our Changing Society
- Embracing Anytime, Anywhere Computing Education
- Applying Learning Research to Computing Education
- Actualizing Pathways in Computing Education
- Demystifying Computing Disciplines and Professions

3. FOLLOW-UP OPPORTUNITIES

The presenters will discuss appropriate findings and suggest possible follow-up opportunities with interested computer science educators. Attendees will come away from the poster session with ideas for crafting grant proposals and other initiatives at their colleges and universities. Although the *Summit* has ended, the discussion continues via an interactive blog. Feel free to join the ongoing conversation at www.acmccecc.org/capspaceforums/.

Printed copies of the *Summit Report of Findings* and the accompanying strategic planning materials will be provided at the poster session. These materials may also be obtained from the Committee's website, www.acmccecc.org/summitreport/.

A Problem Solving Teaching Guide based on a Procedure Intertwined with a Teaching Model

Ronit Ben-Bassat Levy*
University of Rey Juan Carlos
Mostoles, Madrid
Spain
ntronit@gmail.com

J. Ángel Velázquez Iturbide
University of Rey Juan Carlos
Mostoles, Madrid
Spain
angel.velazquez@urjc.es

ABSTRACT

The difficulties Computer Science (CS) students encounter with solving problems have been documented extensively. The literature in CS education (CSE) provides many successful ways to enhance students' performance in problem-solving. Nevertheless, those difficulties have been reported to persist. This has prompted us to develop a Problem-Solving Teaching Guide (PSTG) that emphasizes a structured teaching model. This PSTG was used by our undergraduate university instructors. We investigated its effect on students' performance and documented students' attitudes towards the PSTG.

Categories and Subject Descriptors

K.3.2 [**Computers and Education**]: Computer and Information Science Education – *computer science education.*

General Terms

Human Factors

Keywords

Problem solving, learning styles.

1. INTRODUCTION

Solving a problem is one of the most studied subjects in the area of CSE. It is a process that each of our students should be able to handle well. Extensive efforts have been invested to improve problem-solving skills. Nevertheless, it appears that the students have difficulties to accomplish this process. For example [3] documented difficulties in using patterns.

We believe that one of the reasons for the persistence of such difficulties is that the instructors at university level are not familiar with pedagogical issues. To fill this gap, we developed a teaching guide based upon [4]. Subsequently, we trained four university instructors to use our PSTG.

2. THE PSTG

The PSTG provides the user with a procedure intertwined with unique pedagogical instructions in order to properly use the guide in class. The pedagogical instructions are based on the taxonomy of Bloom [1] as well as on the Learning Styles [2]. The procedural part of the PSTG is described in the following Table-1.

*Current address: The Weizmann Institute of Science, Israel

Instruction	Meaning
1. Read the question carefully	A careful reading will prevent misunderstanding of the problem.
2. Inputs and outputs	The students should provide the outputs for the inputs according to their understanding of the problem.
3. Look for similar problems solved in class.	The students should search in their notes for a similar problem in order to enable them to relate to it during the "Adaptation stage."
4. Adaptation: introduce changes	The students should be able to introduce changes in the solution of the "similar problem" so that their problem will be solved properly.
5. Check the solution	The students should check the solution using their inputs and outputs as defined in the "Inputs and outputs stage."

Table 1 – The procedural part of PSTG

3. THE STUDY AND RESULTS

The PSTG was introduced to the instructors during a lecture. The PSTG was used at undergraduate courses only at the second half of the semester, so that the differences in performance could be compared. The results of the first half of the course (prior to using the PSTG) were compared to the results of the second half (after using the PSTG). The results show an improvement in the students' grades as well as positive attitudes towards the use of PSTG. Based on these results, we recommend training students to use the PSTG in class.

4. ACKNOWLEDGMENTS

This work was partially supported by research grant TIN2008-04103 of Spanish Ministry of Science and Innovation.

5. REFERENCES

[1] Bloom, B.S., Englehart, M.D., Furst, E.J., Hill, W.H., Krathwohl, D.R. (1956). *Taxonomy of Educational Objectives, Handbook. I: Cognitive Domain*. New York: David Mackay.

[2] Felder, R.M., Silverman, L.K. (1998). Learning and teaching styles. *Engr. Education 78*(7), 674–681.

[3] Ginat, D. (2009). Interleaved pattern composition and scaffolded learning. *ACM SIGCSE Bulletin 41*(3), 109–113.

[4] Polya, G. (1957). How to Solve It. Princeton University Press, Second Edition.

A Normative Competence Structure Model for "Embedded Micro- and Nanosystems" Development

André Schäfer
Rainer Brück

Institute of Microsystems Technology
University of Siegen,
Germany
+49-271-7402378

andre.schaefer@uni-siegen.de

Steffen Jaschke
Sigrid Schubert

Didactics of Informatics and
E-Learning, University of Siegen,
Germany
+49-271-7403233

steffen.jaschke@uni-siegen.de

Dietmar Fey
Bruno Kleinert
Harald Schmidt

Chair of Computer Science 3
University of Erlangen-Nürnberg,
Germany
+49-9131-8527003

dietmar.fey@informatik.uni-erlangen.de

Categories and Subject Descriptors

K.3.2 [**Computers and Education**]: Computer and Information Science Education – Computer Science Education.

General Terms

Human Factors, Theory, Experimentation, Design.

Keywords

Competence model research, embedded micro- and nanosystems development, higher education didactics.

ABSTRACT

In our poster, we present the research project "competence development with embedded micro- and nanosystems (KOMINA)" promoted by the German Research Foundation (GRF) and mainly its first step, the development of a normative competence structure model (NCSM.) This kind of competence model is necessary progressing from a subjective and content oriented design of courses and tests to traceable and outcome oriented courses. The importance and the regular procedure of defining competencies in a model and the associated tests are shown in [2]. Up to now, most research projects in the field of competence development are limited to learning and teaching in lower education. In contrast, KOMINA focuses on computer engineering in higher education and in particular embedded micro- and nanosystems (EMNS). Our aim is to make a contribution to the system oriented didactics of computer engineering which includes skill-building experiments for practical courses. In addition, for mastering the development of future EMNS, especially those based on highly parallel and redundant nanostructures, a paradigm shift to a Bottom-Up approach is required and also a consideration of physical constraints on even high levels of abstraction.

Since there is neither a competence model for EMNS nor for computer engineering we will introduce a model to support the development of EMNS considering the paradigm shift. According to [2], we developed the competence structure model in a normative way by analyzing the module descriptions of several excellent rated universities in the field of computer engineering and embedded systems. In addition, we analyzed the modules of the project members' universities and the curricula recommendations of the Association for Computing Machinery (ACM) [1]. As a result, we clustered competencies in four dimensions.

C1: Competencies as preconditions (Basis)

This dimension includes the basics of mathematics, physics, computer science, electrical engineering, materials science, English, scientific work and learning process.

C2: Development competencies (EMNS)

Obviously we need this dimension which includes the competencies of the development process (requirements analysis, system design, implementation, optimization and test) and the organization of the process itself.

C3: Competencies for multi-level development of EMNS

To develop EMNSs, it is necessary to be able to work on one abstraction level and to consider constraints of the other levels at the same time.

C4: Non-cognitive competencies

The non-cognitive competencies include the attitudes, social-communicative, motivational and volitional skills of the students.

Proposal for sub dimensions: While we chose a purely thematic division for breaking down C1 and C2 to sub dimensions, we recommend dividing C3 into solution approaches. It is important that the students are able to use different solution approaches (more precisely, to consider constraints at any lower/higher step of the selected approach) dependent on the concrete problems. So we defined the sub dimensions: C3.1 Top-Down, C3.2 Bottom-Up and C3.3 Meet in the Middle. In further work, this model will be empirically refined by experts of computer engineering.

From sub dimensions to practical courses: We exemplify the deduction from a sub dimension to a concrete task of a practical course and therefore the usefulness of the NCSM for the training of developers with C3.2. Performance tests to assess student learning outcomes have to assign their cognitive abilities to a level of taxonomy. This is possible e.g. during a design experiment of a mobile robot. In general mobile robots include sensors, actuators, and control electronics. If a concrete hardware for a Bottom-Up approach is given (e.g. LEGO Mindstorms) the task could be: Implement the control electronics so that the mobile robot finds a driving route autonomously. On the one hand this task is an implementation task (C2.4) but on the other hand it requires hardware knowledge of the sensors and actuators (C3.2). Finding the right route implies the competence C3.2 because the students have to take into account the accuracy of the motors and IR sensors.

REFERENCES

[1] ACM & IEEE (eds.): Computer Science Curriculum 2008: An Interim Revision of CS 2001. www.acm.org/education/curricula/ComputerScience2008.pdf

[2] Leutner, D.; Klieme, E.: Competence Models for Assessing Individual Learning Outcomes and Evaluating Educational Processes. Priority Programme of DFG,2007-2013, URL: http://kompetenzmodelle.dipf.de/en?set_language=en

Identifying the Predictors of Educational Webcasts' Adoption

Michail N. Giannakos
Ionian University, Corfu, Greece
mgiannak@ionio.gr

Panayiotis Vlamos
Ionian University, Corfu, Greece
vlamos@ionio.gr

ABSTRACT

In this study, we extended the Unified Theory of Acceptance and Use of Technology (UTAUT) [3] to include key variables from Social Cognitive Theory (SCT) [2] and Theory of Planed Behavior (TPB) [1]. We used this hybrid framework to clarify several issues regarding the adoption of the educational webcasts' and to investigate the effects of the key variables. Responses from 292 webcast based learners were used to examine the adoption of the educational webcast.

Categories and Subject Descriptors

K.3.2 [**Computers and Education**]: Computer and Information Science Education. H.1.1 [**Information Systems**]: Models and Principles – *systems and information theory.*

General Terms

Human Factors, Measurement, Theory.

Keywords

Educational Webcast, UTAUT, Technology Acceptance, Adoption Factors.

1. INTRODUCTION

The introduction of e-learning tools in teaching is often complex and learners do not always use ICT as expected. For instance, beliefs, social influence and difficulties in technology are some of the most widespread barriers for effective ICT integration. Despite efforts to position ICT as a central principle of education, the fact that many learners make limited use of ICT tools reduce the overall interest.

In the context of educational webcasts, the usage for learning purposes has been increased last years. More and more institutions and business organizations provide their content using webcasts. Furthermore, there are many video search engines where one can find learning videos (youtube.com), and there are even video search engines exclusive for learning videos (my learningtube.com).

In this study, we propose a hybrid framework based on the integration of UTAUT, SCT and TPB, to investigate the factors that affect learners' acceptance of webcasting. Another research

query is whether the webcast adoption exhibits any differentiation based on the learners' level of experience.

2. BACKGROUND AND HYPOTHESES

Several models and theories have been used to address the issues of e-learning and to identify the cause and the effect of different factors in the adoption of e-learning tools. For instance, UTAUT, SCT and TPB are some of the most widely used theories and Effort Expectancy (EE), Performance Expectancy (PE), Social Norm (SN), Computer Self Efficacy (CSEF) and Perceive Behavioral Control (PBC) are some of the most commonly used factors affecting the learners' intention to use an e-learning tool.

3. METHODOLOGY AND FINDINGS

Our research methodology included a survey composed by questions on the demographics of the sample and on the six principal constructs. A number of different methods were recruited for attracting respondents; questionnaires distributed in various places (universities, public areas) and e-mails were sent to different mailing lists. All constructs were measured using 7-point Likert scales.

In this empirical study, we analyzed learners' acceptance of educational webcasts. Our research has demonstrated that the three theoretical models UTAUT, SCT and TPB, and their key variables exhibit a high degree of reliability and credibility in the context of educational webcasts.

The findings indicate that EE, PE and SN display a highly significant impact on learners' Behavioral Intention. Moreover, CSEF and PBC influence learners' behavioral intention, however, the findings showed that this effect is less significant than the effect of the previous three key variables.

4. REFERENCES

[1] Ajzen, I. 1985. From intentions to actions: a theory of planned behavior. *In: J. Kuhl and J. Beckmann,* Editors, Action control: From cognition to behavior, Springer, New York, 11–39.

[2] Bandura, A. 1986. *Social foundations of thought and action: a social cognitive theory.* Englewood Cliffs, NJ: Prentice-Hall.

[3] Venkatesh, V., Morris, M. G., Davis, G. B. & Davis, F. D. 2003. User acceptance of information technology: toward a unified view. *MIS Quarterly 27*(3), 425-478

Investigating Cognitive Structures
of Object Oriented Programming

Peter Hubwieser
Technische Universität München
Boltzmannstr. 3
D-85748 Garching, Germany
+49 (89) 289 17350
peter.hubwieser@tum.de

Andreas Mühling
Technische Universität München
Boltzmannstr. 3
D-85748 Garching, Germany
+49 (89) 289 17350
muehling@in.tum.de

ABSTRACT

We present first results of an ongoing research that investigates the learning progress of students in a CS course, using concept maps. We aim to indentify knowledge elements that are prerequisites for basic competencies in object oriented programming.

Categories and Subject Descriptors

K.3.2 [**Computers and Education**]: Computer and Information Science Education, *Computer science education.*

General Terms

Measurement, Human Factors, Languages.

Keywords

Learning, mental model, concept-maps, object orientation, objects first.

1. INTRODUCTION

Usually students attend lectures in order to acquire certain competencies (e.g. programming a computer), but most competencies require some specific knowledge (e.g. syntax elements of a programming language). By drawing concept maps, students externalize some of their declarative knowledge, hereby disclosing it to a certain extent [1].

In order to explore cognitive structures as necessary preconditions for competencies and to develop suitable research instruments, we closely evaluated a CS1 course for students of engineering. Our teaching concept follows a quite radical "objects-first" approach.

2. METHODOLOGY

At first we identified the declarative knowledge that was taught during the course. We started with the textbook and the slides that were used in the course and removed all irrelevant information from that. The result was a list of about 300 statements ("knowledge elements") without any examples or explanations, e.g.: *If an attribute is marked as private, only objects of the same class are allowed to read or write its value.* From this, we extracted a list of 40 core concepts (e.g. *object, class, attribute*) by applying a standardized process of qualitative text analysis. The students were asked to draw their concept maps using these core concepts as nodes and labeling all their edges (associations) with a suitable denominator of their own choice (see [2]). The students were asked to draw maps at four different times: before the first lesson, after 4 weeks, both on paper, after 7 weeks and after the last lesson using the graph editor *yEd*. Additionally, a small exam was taken, allowing us to investigate how the concept maps correspond to their competencies (i.e. the application of their knowledge).

3. ANALYSIS AND RESULTS

We started by normalizing the labels of the edges and classified them into 40 categories. This allowed a consistent scoring by the lecturer concerning the correctness of the associations connecting two concepts, each. The sequence of the average number of (meaningful) associations per student in combination with the proportions of the *totally correct* edges (in parentheses) proves that the students have really gained some relevant knowledge: 9,7 (31,1%); 13,8 (37,1%); 18,2 (58,0%); 21,3 (53,2%).

More surprisingly, the ruggedness of the maps has been increasing as well over the course. This might indicate that students are learning in a way that favors creating clusters of new knowledge instead of integrating it into an existing model, confirming the *knowledge-as-elements* perspective of the Conceptual Change theory.

Additionally we investigated the evolution of certain combinations of single student maps ("average" or "consensus" maps) over the course. When correlating the number of occurences of a concept in the knowledge elements (between two tests) with a number reflecting the changes in edges connected to that concept, we found a strong positive correlation.

Ultimately, we hope for a methodology allowing a mostly objective and systematic extraction of concepts from given course material as well as an empirically proven measure of how well those concepts are reflected in the concept maps of students. This would allow a close monitoring of the progresses students make (or the lack thereof) and, in return, allow for a better designed course material or structure.

4. REFERENCES

[1] Albert, D., Steiner, C.M.: Empirical Validation of Concept Maps: Preliminary Methodological Considerations. In: Proceedings of the Fifth IEEE International Conference on Advanced Learning Technologies (ICALT'05) (2005).

[2] Kate Sanders, et al. 2008. Student understanding of object-oriented programming as expressed in concept maps. In *Proceedings of the 39th SIGCSE technical symposium on Computer science education.* ACM, New York, NY, USA, 332-336

The Beaver Contest - Attracting Youngsters to Study Computing

Bruria Haberman
Computer Science Department,
Holon Institute of Technology, Holon,
Israel, and Davidson Institute of
Science Education, Weizmann
Institute of Science,
Rehovot 76100, Israel
bruria.haberman@weizmann.ac.il

Avi Cohen
The Ministry of Education,
2 Hashlosha str.
Yad-Eliahu, Tel-Aviv 61092,
Israel
Avi@CSIT.org.il

Valentina Dagiene
Vilnius University
Vilnius, LT-08663 Lithuania
+370 698 05448
valentina.dagiene@mii.vu.lt

ABSTRACT

Attracting young students to computer science studies has always been a challenge. We present a unique outreach program: the Beaver international contest on informatics and computer fluency that was established with the goal to convey computing concepts to as many youngsters as possible in a way that can motivate them to be more interested in computing. For the last few years the contest has been operating in several countries in Europe (http://www.bebras.org). Recently, in order to attract youngsters to study computer science, the Beaver project was initiated in Israel by adapting its framework to the requirements of the national educational system.

Categories and Subject Descriptors

K.3.2 [**Computer and Information Science Education**]: Computer Science Education

General Terms

Human factors

Keywords

Computer science education, outreach, computational thinking.

1. THE BEAVER CONTEST

Contests play an important role as a source of inspiration and innovation and can attract students to be interested in the contest's related domain. The Beaver International Contest on informatics and computer fluency was established with the goal to convey computing concepts to as many youngsters as possible in an attractive way. The main goals of the Beaver project are to promote students' interest in computing from the very beginning at school and to motivate students to learn and master computers [2,3]. The key idea is to pose to students interesting problems that do not require specific pre-knowledge in a way that leads to explorative learning regarding how to deal with problem solving tasks as well as informally familiarizing the students with core concepts and principles of the domain. Specifically, the idea is to encourage students to attain a deeper understanding of computers and to use computational thinking [4] and modern technologies more intensively and creatively. The International Beaver Contest addresses all lower and upper secondary school pupils, who are divided into three age groups: Benjamin (age 11-14), Junior (age 15-16), and Senior (for upper secondary level). Students who enter this annual competition are challenged to solve a variety of tasks from a broad range of computing areas without using programming. By using a computer, students have to solve 15 to 21 tasks on different levels within 45 minutes. The contest is composed of interactive tasks and multiple-choice tasks that can be classified by content regarding the CS/ICT themes and concepts presented in the task. An additional area on ICT and Society gets them to think about the wider issues of computing.

For the last few years the contest has been operating in several countries in Europe [1]. A fruitful collaboration between the involved countries has been established regarding task development and organizational aspects. Recently, in order to attract youngsters to study computer science, plans have been made to initiate the Beaver project in Israel, while adapting its framework to the requirements of the national educational system. Since January 2011 over 800 students (age 12-16) participated in a pilot implementation of the project in Israel.

The poster will describe and discuss the following: (a) The implementation of the Beaver contest in Europe with emphasis on collaboration between participating countries; (b) Challenges in developing attractive tasks; (c) Sample tasks; and (d) The pilot implementation of the project in Israel, its preliminary evaluation and further assimilation plans.

2. REFERENCES

[1] Bebras. International Contest on Informatics and Computer Fluency. http://www.bebras.org/en/facts, accessed 10 Oct. 2010.

[2] Dagiene, V. 2006. Information Technology Contests – Introduction to Computer Science in an Attractive Way. *Informatics in Education*, 2006, 5(1), 37-46.

[3] Dagiene, V., Futschek, G. 2008. Bebras International Contest on Informatics and Computer Literacy: Criteria for Good Tasks. In: R. T. Mittermeir, M. M. Syslo (Eds.), *Lect. Notes in Computer Science*, 5090. Informatics Education – Supporting Computational Thinking, Springer, Heidelberg, 19–30.

[4] Wing, J.M. 2006. Computational thinking. *Communications of the ACM*, 49(3), 33-35.

Computing for the Social Good: A Service Learning Project

Michael Goldweber
Xavier University
mikeyg@cs.xu.edu

ABSTRACT

"Computing for the Social Good[2]" is an umbrella term for any activity which strives to focus students to consider the following fundamental question; "Instead of using computers to make money or do basic scientific research, how can one use computing to do good in the world?" Since computing students rarely study abroad, let alone undertake a service learning semester, the development of an overseas service learning experience in computing would serve a double purpose.

Categories and Subject Descriptors

K.3.2 [**Computer and Information Science Education**]: [Computer Science Education]

General Terms

Design, Experimentation

Keywords

Service Learning, Study Abroad

1. SERVICE LEARNING EXPERIENCE IN COMPUTING - A RATIONALE

While there is no hard data to present, anecdotal evidence suggests that computing majors rarely study abroad or undertake a service learning semester. Again, there are many influencing factors in addition to the ubiquitous issue of cost. Course density in the major is also a major factor. Essentially none of the traditional international study experiences allow computing students to make forward progress in the major. Since most required courses are offered no more frequent than once a year, managing a semester abroad without lengthening one's undergraduate career is, while doable with sufficient advance planning, tricky at best.

Furthermore, the vast majority of computing majors spend their summers in one of two ways. The first is as interns/entry-level employees/Co-ops in computing. The other is in an undergraduate research capacity. (e.g. National Science Foundation sponsored Summer Research Experiences for Undergraduates.) This option is for those students either committed to or simply considering graduate studies to have an authentic post-graduate experience.

Universities in general and (American) liberal arts colleges in particular were created for the purpose of educating students to serve the common good. A liberal or liberating education was meant to instill qualifications for leadership in a theocratic society. In contemplating who we wish our students to become professionally, it seems obvious that unless we explicitly connect disciplinary experiences with both service to others and the promotion of justice, we will never fully achieve our aspirations.

Therefore, it is imperative that we attempt to get computer science students to address the following fundamental question: "Instead of using computers to make money or do basic scientific research, how can one use computing to do good in the world?" Consider the potential if for these future professional problem solvers their role models were not just Bill Gates or Sergey Brin but also included Paul Farmer and Greg Mortenson. Even more ambitious would be the goal that students might initially explore computing as a major because they see it as a vehicle for positive impact/change in the world - much like students who dream of finding a cure for AIDS are attracted to Biology/Medicine.

Consider the impact that the successful development of a service learning experience in computing would have on this goal. Furthermore, this project, which is currently under development, has other ancillary goals; increased attraction and retention of students overall and women and under-represented minorities in particular. Recent research suggests that students select their major based on a desire to have a positive societal impact.[1]

2. REFERENCES

[1] M. Buckley, J. Nordlinger, and D. Subramanian. Socially relevant computing. In *Proc. of the 39th SIGCSE Technical Symposium on Computer Science Education*, 2008.
[2] M. Goldweber, J. C. Little, G. Cross, R. Davoli, C. Riedesel, B. von Konsky, and H. Walker. Enhancing the social issues components in our computing curriculum: Computing for the social good. *ACM Inroads*, 2(1), 2011.

A Collaborative Linked Learning Space

Kai Michael Höver
Department of CS
TU Darmstadt
Germany
hoever@acm.org

Michael Hartle
Department of CS
TU Darmstadt
Germany
mhartle@tk.informatik.tu-darmstadt.de

Guido Rößling
Department of CS
TU Darmstadt
Germany
roessling@acm.org

ABSTRACT

Current learning systems typically do not allow students to combine learning materials with additional content, for example materials found on the web. We present a system that enables both educators and students to augment learning resources by creating meaningful links between them. In this way, both students and educators can benefit from the augmentations of others, and relate them to personal knowledge.

Categories and Subject Descriptors

K.3.1 [**Computer Uses in Education**]: Collaborative learning; K.3.2 [**Computer and Information Science Education**]: Computer science education

General Terms

Design, Experimentation

Keywords

CLLS, Linked Data, Web-based learning

1. COLLABORATIVE LINKED LEARNING SPACE

Students often use information resources either created by themselves or found on the Web in addition to provided learning material to bridge existing knowledge gaps or to get more suitable explanations. Many learning systems allow students and educators to add only text or digital ink annotations to learning material. Thus, it is hardly possible to augment provided learning materials with other learning resources.

Educators and students are rarely able to share learning resources they appreciate with other learners while preserving the semantic relations, e.g., a Web page that gives an example to the content of a slide. In this paper, we present a web-based system called *Collaborative Linked Learning Space (CLLS)* that provides access to learning materials, and enables learners to both create and share their personal knowledge graphs composed of different learning resources.

CLLS is a learning tool that supports learners in actively constructing knowledge graphs. It also provides a player for

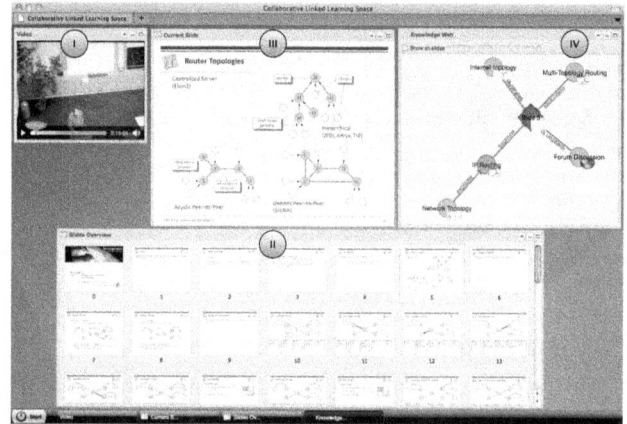

Figure 1: Graphical User Interface of CLLS

lecture recordings that can be used to bootstrap the construction. Figure 1 shows a lecture recording and the corresponding knowledge graph that is collaboratively created by the users. The lecture replay function provides a video of the lecturer (I), a slide overview (II), and the currently selected slide (III). The knowledge graph panel (IV) depicts a graphical representation of the knowledge graph. Nodes in the knowledge graph represent learning resources such as slides, PDF documents, and images. Edges represent the semantic relationship between the learning resources, e.g., "illustrates", "contradicts", or "exemplifies".

To link a slide to a figure from a web page, for example, the user drops the figure on the slide in area III or on the corresponding node of the knowledge graph in area IV. In principle, all information resources with an Uniform Resource Identifier (URI) can be linked with each other. After the user has chosen the label for the relation, the knowledge graph updates automatically. The new information is also sent to the messaging server, which distributes it to both the central storage and the currently connected clients.

Learners can use the system in an exploratory way and in a constructive way. When using the system in an exploratory way, learners navigate through the public knowledge graph compiled by public elements of each personal knowledge graph led by their aims and interests. In constructive use, learners create a personal knowledge graph by interlinking and arranging different knowledge resources, either from the web or other learners' knowledge graphs.

STEM and ICT Instructional Worlds: The 3D Experience

Katherine Ross
Clemson University
Professional Communication
Clemson, SC 29631
kross@g.clemson.edu

Yvon Feaster
Clemson University
School of Computing
Clemson, SC 29631
yfeaste@g.clemson.edu

ABSTRACT

North and South Carolina state agencies and universities, local school districts, and various businesses are working together to teach Science, Technology, Engineering and Math (STEM) to middle school students through the use of 3 dimensional (3D) immersive virtual technologies. The project is being implemented over a three-year period during summer sessions. Results indicate that the project is producing positive results for both students and teachers.

Categories and Subject Descriptors

K.3.1 [**Computer and Education**]: Computer uses in education—*Computer-assisted instruction*

General Terms

Experimentation, Human Factors

Keywords

Virtual Reality,3D modelling, middle school curriculum, experimental evaluation

1. INTRODUCTION

The STEM and information communication technologies (ICT) Instructional Worlds: The 3D Experience (STEM-ICT 3D) project is funded by the National Science Foundation Innovative Technology Experiences for Students and Teachers (ITEST) program and is a joint effort between Clemson University and Appalachian State University. The intent of the project is to motivate and provide the skills necessary for diverse, under-represented middle grade students who are interested in pursuing studies and careers in STEM disciplines. The purpose of this strategies project is to engage teachers in continuous STEM learning, interest students in pursuing STEM careers, and prepare students with the skills necessary to succeed in STEM by promoting the use of 3D technologies in middle schools. These goals are being accomplished utilizing summer academies being provided over a three year period. Each summer, rising seventh grade students and teachers from their respective schools, team up to plan and create lesson modules that are implemented during the proceeding school year. Two of the three summer academies have been held with evidence indicating a positive impact on the students as well as the teachers.

2. SUMMER ACADEMY

For the first two summers, instruction at the academy was provided over a period of two weeks. During the third summer academy, a two-day conference will be held in which middle school educators from all over both North and South Carolinas will be invited to attend. The summer academies are held at each of the two universities. Participants consist of twelve rising seventh grade students along with twelve teachers from local school districts. During the first week of the two-week academy, the students learn about 3D modeling and designing virtual worlds. They are taught how to plan and create objects for a virtual world. During this week the students use virtual world technology to collaborate with students from other states. Teams are formed using students from both universities. Working as a team in the immersive environment, the students decide on a theme and plan and create a virtual world. The teachers join the students during the second week of the summer academy to learn about 3D technologies and how they can be implemented in their curriculum. Also during the second week of the academy, the student's role shifts to "technical expert". The students work with their school's teachers to plan and create a virtual world to use in teaching a lesson module. These modules are then implemented in the classroom in the following school year. In this following year, the students continue in their role as "technical expert", in that they continue to assist the teachers during the implementation phase.

3. PROJECT IMPACT

This project has had a positive impact on many of the students and teachers alike. The results show that students have expressed an interest in pursuing STEM careers while creating an environment in which they are motivated to help others, their peers and teachers. More than half of the teachers have implemented their lessons during the first year resulting in students having increased expertise and a desire to share their knowledge in the classroom. Teachers are presenting their experiences at state and national level conferences. This poster will present information and qualitative research data along with pictures of the multiple summer academies and the virtual worlds made by both teachers and students.

4. ACKNOWLEDGMENT

This work is supported by the National Science Foundation (NSF) ITEST Program (Grant No.0833552). Yvon Feaster is supported by an NSF Graduate Research Fellowship Program.

Collaborating Across International Boundaries … Using Twitter as a Tool in the Classroom

Stefanie A. Markham
Department of Computer Science,
Georgia State University, Atlanta, GA 30303
smarkham@gsu.edu

Saeid Belkasim
Department of Computer Science,
Georgia State University, Atlanta, GA 30303
sbelkasim@cs.gsu.edu

ABSTRACT

A problem in education today is being able to reach out to the students in innovative ways. While making it relevant and important for the students, we used twitter as a tool for student collaboration. A class in the USA and a class in Australia used twitter as a tool to collaborate within their courses as well as with each other for one semester. While this study did not find twitter to be the ideal tool for social education, it has opened up a new way to collaborate across boundaries. Humans are social beings and as educators, we can use the success of social web technologies to help educate the world.

Categories and Subject Descriptors

K.3 [**Computers and Education**]: 1. Computer Uses in Education – *Collaborative learning* 2. Computer and Information Science Education – *Computer science and Information systems education*

General Terms: Experimentation, Human Factors

Keywords: Education, Motivation, Microblogging, Twitter

1. INTRODUCTION

A problem in education today is being able to reach out to the students in innovative ways. Often technology is blamed for students' inability to concentrate, while others argue that it is a way to reach out to students. A recent article in the New York Times titled 'Growing Up Digital, Wired for Distraction', highlights this. Technology is pervasive and relevant to most disciplines and we can use our experiences, not only to help each other find the most effective tools, but also to enlighten the others about the power and usefulness of these tools. We can do this across many boundaries, not only geographical, but disciplinary boundaries as well. The youtube video 'A Vision of Students Today' by Michael Wesch gives a real look into what is important to modern students. It underscores the pervasiveness of technology in their lives, shows off their interests, and gives a glimpse into some of the problems they see with education. It is our hope that if educators can reach out to students for everyone's benefit. In this paper we focus on using twitter as tool in the classroom, and the potential it has for student communication and collaboration across international boundaries.

2. OUR APPROACH

Many people view twitter as best suited for keeping up with their favorite celebrity. While that is a popular use, we argue that is extremely limited and there are many worthy, important uses. One in particular is to look for a job, a concern for students, and

we saw a need for students to be familiar with the technology. While making it relevant and important for the students, we wanted to use twitter as a tool for student collaboration. The goal was not only communication within the same class, but with students in a different class, and even across oceans. We used twitter as part of our weekly assignments within our course, as well as a tool to communicate with students in another country.

3. RESULTS / EXPERIENCES

Sample:

tweeterUSA1 USA One
Is outsourcing/offshoring work ethical? #csXXX

aussietweeter Aus One
RT @tweeterUSA1:outsourcing/offshoring work ethical?#csXXX#itXX.interesting question when every1 will'b looking only @ economic benefits

tweeterUSA1 USA Two
@tweeterUSA1 It depends. E.g.: If, outsourcing causes a decline in QoS then it would likely be unethical. #csXXX #itXX

Twitter advantages – open, public, and some people already using it. Disadvantages – hard to follow threads, limited number of characters, search (in)capabilities, very restricted history

Because of the disadvantages listed above, twitter is probably not the ideal tool for social education. However it has opened up a new area of possibility in collaborating across boundaries. One of the largest advantages of twitter for this purpose is its openness. We need to be innovative. Many universities use iTunesU, google groups (interestingly now defunct), and facebook groups; I wonder if google wave will swell? The actual technology doesn't matter. Sometimes educators waste time arguing over particular tools and technologies. It is important, however, to spend the time necessary to find the best, most effective tools and make convincing arguments why they are the best. But it is also crucial to be flexible and open, and willing to try new technologies. We were hoping to report that twitter is the answer. It is not, there are pros and cons to all technologies, and we must pick the best one for the task at hand. We can also learn from others' experiences. Humans are social beings and as educators, we can use the success of social web technologies to help educate the world.

4. REFERENCES

[1] Grosseck, G., Holotescu, C. 2008. "Can We Use Twitter for Educational Activities?" 4th Int'l Scientific Conf, eLSE - *eLearning and Software for Education*, Bucharest, April 17-18, 2008.

[2] Miners, Z. 2010. "Twitter Goes to College", US News and World Report on Education.

[3] Parry, B. 2008. "Twitter for Academia." Retrieved January 1, 2011, from http://academhack.outsidethetext.com/home/2008/twitter-for-academia/

[4] Richtel, M. 2010. "Growing up Digital, Wired for Distraction", *New York Times*. Nov21, 2010

[5] Wesch, M. 2008. *A Vision of Students Today (& What Teachers Must Do)* , Oct 21, 2011. Youtube/Encyclopedia Britannica Blog

Enhancing Learner Capability: Success of IT@School Project, Kerala, Region of India

Girija Krishnaswamy
Lecturer, Faculty of Business,
Australian Catholic University and
PhD Student, Curtin University
40 Edward St., North Sydney, NSW2060, Australia
61402823871
girija.krishnaswamy@acu.edu.au

V.Sasi Kumar
Free Software Foundation of India
32 NCC Nagar Peroorkada
Thiruvananthapuram 695005
Kerala India
919895465365
v.sasi.personal@gmail.com

ABSTRACT

IT@School is termed the single largest simultaneous deployment of Free and Open Source Software (FOSS) based Information and Communication Technology (ICT) educational Project in the world. Capacity Building is one of the prime objectives of IT@School Project; it also integrates diverse activities such as content development, infrastructure deployment, satellite based education and e-Governance initiatives in a holistic manner.

Categories and Subject Descriptors

K.3.1 [**Computer uses in education**]: Computer-assisted instruction – Collaborative learning

General Terms

Performance, Design, Human Factors

Keywords

IT Education, IT Enabled Education, IT Embedded Education, FOSS, Public Action

1. INTRODUCTION

The development experience of Kerala, the southernmost State of India has attracted considerable academic and political attention over the last few decades. The consistently high Physical Quality of Life Index (PQLI) and Human Development Indicator (HDI) scores, despite economic constraints of the State has resulted in the term 'Kerala Model of Development'. As development experience all over the world show, none of the 'Models' can be replicated as such, but there are lessons to be learnt from Kerala development scenario. Development scholars attribute 'Public Action' as a significant causative factor for the high social development of Kerala. The IT education in Kerala features certain unique characteristics driven by Public Action, and facilitated by government.

IT@School is a project of the Department of General Education, Government of Kerala, set up in 2001, to foster IT education in schools and to facilitate ICT enabled education in the long term. The Teacher empowerment programme started in 2002 with assistance from 'Intel Teach' program using Microsoft (MS) Windows and MS Office. IT became a compulsory subject in the state curriculum in 2003. Soon after, the Free Software community in the state protested that the government was promoting Intel and Microsoft products. It emphasised that training should be given in generic applications (word processor, spreadsheet, etc.) and not in proprietary software. As the protests

mounted with the largest association of school teachers behind it, the government was forced to change the curriculum to include Free Software. However, many schools continued to use MS Windows and several groups pointed out that schools should not be using unlicenced copies of software and demanded teachers be trained in Free Software. Several schools started migrating to Free Software in 2005 and eventually, succumbing to pressure from various sources, the government decided to completely shift to Free Software in 2006. The Project developed its own Operating System-IT@School GNU/Linux, now used in all the schools in the state.

The 2nd phase - ICT Enabled Education - started in 2010 on 'close to completion' of the first phase – IT Education. Students' performance in competitions like painting using computers, creating multimedia presentations, conducted regularly at local, district and state levels improved. Students who have computers at home install Free Software and contribute to localized content development. 'SchoolWiki', a customized version of WIKI provides a comprehensive knowledge database of all schools in the state, and includes collaborative content from student and teacher groups. Educational free software such as Dr. Geo, Rasmol, K-Tech lab, Geogebra, Chemtool, Kalcium are customised in developing teacher friendly applications to facilitate ICT enabled education. Use of FOSS platforms has resulted in educational outcomes that appear superior to those of outsourced models [1] and savings of 2.5 Million US$ a year. IT@School Project has implemented several e-Governance initiatives for the General Education Department of the Government of Kerala-Single Window admission system for Plus One admissions, Noon meal distribution computerization, Total Physical Fitness Programme software etc. The impact of IT@Project has been assessed as 'very high' in Learner Capabilities Enhancement, Infrastructure Creation for IT Education and creation of Organisational Structure to support faster implementation [3]. The Project has received recognition at the Stockholm Challenge [2] as it looks forward to progressing towards the final phase of IT Embedded Learning.

2. REFERENCES

[1] Kasinathan, G. (2009). ICTs in School Education - Outsourced vs Integrated Approach, in *IT for Change*.

[2] Stockholm Challenge (2010). IT@School Project - programme for ICT interventions in schools in Kerala, India.

[3] T.A.Pai Management Institute (2010). IT@School - Excellence and Quality in Education - No Exceptions No Excuses, *Impact Study Report*.

Deconstructing VLEs to Create Customized PLEs

Salvador Ros[1], Agustín C. Caminero[1], Antonio Robles-Gómez[1], Roberto Hernández[1],
Rafael Pastor[1], Timothy Read[1], Alberto Pesquera[1], Raúl Muñoz[2]

[1]Universidad Nacional de educación a Distancia (UNED). 28040 – Madrid, Spain

sros@scc.uned.es

[2]IBM. Advisory IT specialist on WebSphere Portal

ABSTRACT

Personal Learning Environments (PLEs) have gained importance over recent years thanks to the wide use of the Web 2.0. An interesting functionality is the creation of customized PLEs, to improve the learning process. This work proposes a new paradigm to create customized PLEs by deconstructing a Virtual Learning Environment (VLE).

Categories and Subject Descriptors

K.3.2 [**Computer and Information Science Education**]: Information systems education. K.3.1 [**Computer Uses in Education**]: Distance learning.

General Terms

Management, Design, Experimentation, Standardization.

Keywords

VLEs, PLEs, customization, versatility.

1. INTRODUCTION

In recent years, there has been an increasing interest for the development of Personal Learning Environments (PLEs) [1]. This interest can be understood since institutions reluctant to changes, and normally under tight restrictions, may harness the possibilities offered by Web 2.0. One of the possible ways to reach this target is by means of using Mashups [2], which allow easy generation of customized environments.

The design of customized environments and gadgets must consist of external elements/applications, such as Google, Facebook, GoogleDocs, etc. In addition, elements that allow the institution to keep some control must also be included. This control is aimed at two main aspects, namely (1) students enrolment, meaning *"who belongs to the institution?"*, and (2) tracking of the progress of the enrolled students. These tasks are normally centralized in the institutional Virtual Learning Environment (VLE).

To accomplish the aforementioned goals, we propose the deconstruction of the VLE. This new paradigm allows (1) the addition of new tools, (2) new uses of the Internet in the institutional spaces, and (3) keeping control over the users.

2. DECONSTRUCTION OF VLEs

Deconstructing a VLE means that its building blocks can be split and presented separately. Thus, the deconstruction of the VLE aims at allowing institutions to be capable of having some institutional control over the existing PLEs. This way, the VLE will still be the center of the learning systems of the institution, though certain clearly defined services can be extracted from it, hence permitting their access from different platforms. This allows the creation of customized learning spaces where institutional gadgets will cohabitate together with other gadgets through the adequate containers.

In order to accomplish this goal, UNED has developed a set of gadgets based on OpenSocial that allow the query of VLE's information from any Mashup platform compatible with the standard. As first step, authors considered the development of gadgets to access the different UNED's Learning Management System (LMS) services. These services are considered as fundamental parts for the implementation of the European High Education Area (EHEA), according to the methodology of UNED. Thus, these services will permit the access to different types of information on courses and communities hosted in the VLE to the users registered in the institutional information system. The access to the institutional LMS platform, called aLF, is by means of a communication protocol based on the interchange of text messages using a standard format.

3. ACKNOWLEDGEMENT

The authors would like to acknowledge European Union Leonardo Project 142788-2008-BG-LEONARDO-LMP, mPSS – mobile Performance Support for Vocational Education and Training Project, and Spanish Ministry of Science and Innovation for the Project TIN2008-06083-C03/TSI "s-Labs – Integración de Servicios Abiertos para Laboratorios Remotos y Virtuales Distribuidos". We also thank Community of Madrid for the support of E-Madrid Network of Excellence S2009 TIC-1650.

4. REFERENCES

[1] D. Gillet, E.L-C. Law, A. Chatterjee. "Personal Learning Environments in a Global Higher Engineering Education Web 2.0 Realm". Proc. of the Engineering Education Conference (EDUCON). 2010. Madrid, Spain.

[2] Ebner, M. & Taraghi, B. "Personal Learning Environment for Higher Education – A First Prototype". In Proc. of World Conference on Educational Multimedia, Hypermedia Telecommunications. 2010. Chesapeake, USA.

What Matters Most When Teaching CS1?

Ana Paula Ambrosio
Instituto de Informatica (INF)
Universidade Federal de Goiás
Campus II, Goiânia/GO - Brazil
+55 62 3521 1181

apaula@inf.ufg.br

Scheila W. Martins
Centre for Informatics and Systems of the University
of Coimbra (CISUC)
Pólo II, Pinhal de Marrocos, Coimbra - Portugal
+351 239 790 000

scheila@dei.uc.pt

ABSTRACT

The objective of research and proposals related to the domain of computer science and education is to offer resources and contexts that help teachers and students to increase learning effectiveness. Algorithms and Programming courses present an obstacle to an increasing number of first year students worldwide, and has become the object of study of many researchers and faculty members worried with the consequences this difficulty entails, such as high dropout and failure rates, and lack of motivation [1].

Several proposals have been made, using different programming languages and paradigms, as well as different methodologies, including the development of tools and environments that help students to develop their programming abilities. Most of these proposals are concerned with the motivational aspect of the course, and try to involve the students in the discipline, leading them to persist and not give up in spite of its natural difficulty [2].

In many cases there have been reports of success. Often the credits of success are given to the new approaches, methodologies and environments adopted in the experiment. However, an important variable is often disregarded: the teacher's quality and motivation. It should be observed that most of these experiments are undertaken by high quality teachers that are also motivated researchers in the domain of Computer Science education. Their enthusiasm and dedication to the course is undeniable. The question is: to what extent does the teacher's motivation and enthusiasm contribute to the success of the experiment? Most reports do not discuss this issue and often they are limited to the application of the new approach to groups taught by the researcher himself or by members of the research team, equally motivated.

Many reports have established that the human factor is key to the success of an educational system [3]. In all educational levels, from kindergarten to the university, there are examples of brilliant pedagogical proposals that fail. Some of them, apparently due to how they were executed [4]. More, some government and specialists are rethinking the essential factors that may influence the schooling outcome and produce more effective results in educational reforms, specially since despite the massive increases in spending, the performance of many school systems has barely improved in decades [5,6].

Experiences of top school systems suggest that three things matter most to good quality schooling: 1) getting the right people to become teachers, 2) developing them into effective instructors and, 3) ensuring that the system is able to deliver the best possible instruction for every student [6].

If this is true for schools, can't we suppose that this is also true in teaching CS1? If so, can we deduce that the teacher is determinant in the outcome of the teaching experience? And that the new methodologies, tools and environments are efficient support for these teachers?

Categories and Subject Descriptors
K.3.2 [**Computer and Education**]: Computer and Information Science Education – *Computer science education*

General Terms
Human Factors

Keywords
Programming learning, Human factors, Teacher motivation.

REFERENCES

[1] Guzdial, M. 2011. From science to engineering. *Commun. ACM* 54, 2 (Feb. 2011), pp. 37-39. DOI=10.1145/1897816.1897831, http://doi.acm.org/10.1145/1897816.1897831

[2] Hamza, M. K., Alhalabi, B. and Marcovitz, D. M. 2000. Creative pedagogy for computer learning: eight effective tactics. *SIGCSE Bull.*, 32, 4,(Dez. 2000), pp. 70-73. DOI=10.1145/369295.369335, http://doi.acm.org/10.1145/369295.369335

[3] Thompson, T. G. and Barnes, R. E. (Eds.). 2009. *The Engine of Successful Education Reform: Effective Teachers and Principals.* Commission on No Child Left Behind. The Aspen Institute. Denver, (Oct. 2009).

[4] Kirschner, P. A., Sweller, J. and Clark, R. E. 2006. Why minimal guidance during instruction does not work: an analysis of the failure of constructivist, discovery, problem-based, experiential, and inquiry-based teaching. *Educational Psychologist*, 41(2), pp. 75-86, 2006. doi:10.1207/s15326985ep4102_1

[5] Hingel, A., Saltelli, A. and Mercy, J. (Eds.). 2008. *Progress Towards the Lisbon Objectives in Education And Training: Indicators and Benchmarks 2008*, Commission Of The European Communities, Tech. Rep. SEC (2008) 2293.

[6] McKinsey & Company. 2007. *How the World's Best-Performing School Systems Come Out on Top*. Technical Report. September 2007

Combining Memory Management and Filesystems in an Operating Systems Course

Hans-Georg Eßer
University of Erlangen-Nuremberg
Chair for IT Security Infrastructures
Martensstr. 3, D-91058 Erlangen, Germany
h.g.esser@informatik.uni-erlangen.de

ABSTRACT

Teaching memory management aligned with filesystems in an Operating Systems course instead of treating them as separate topics can increase students' understanding and improve their grades in end-of-term examinations. In a survey they also state that they like this method.

Categories and Subject Descriptors

K.3.2 [**Computer and Information Science Education**]: Computer science education; D.4 [**Operating Systems**]: Storage Management; D.4 [**Operating Systems**]: File Systems Management

General Terms

Design, Experimentation

Keywords

Didactics, Memory Management

1. INTRODUCTION

Treating Memory Management (MM) and Filesystems (FS) separately in an OS course introduces a certain redundancy. For example, in simple allocation schemes, such as fixed size partitioning, where each process is given a fixed amount of memory or a file can use a fixed amount of disk space, students have to see identical concepts twice. The same is true for internal and external fragmentation which can occur in both areas. When we gave an Introduction to Operating Systems (OS) course in summer 2009, we tested the parallel treatment of the two topics and evaluated the effects on the students: We compared exam results with those of a traditional course from 2008 and also asked the students of their opinions.

The goal was to test whether this change could improve the students' understanding while repurposing redundant lecture time.

In a traditional OS course students will also note that some concepts from MM reappear in FS (or the other way round), while some concepts do not. However, the modifications we made and tested make this affinity explicit. The similarity of MM and FS in some areas becomes obvious and lets students focus on overall concepts instead of details (while not neglecting the details but letting students put them into the whole picture more easily).

This should make students more capable of transferring knowledge from one area to another.

2. EVALUATION

We evaluated the results of our modification with two methods:

(1) Class results in the end-of-term exam were compared, for this purpose each question in the tests was classified as MM related, FS related, or other, and students' marks on each question were recorded separately. Since it is not helpful to compare students' successes from two different academic years, it makes sense to look at relative success: we compared how well students handled MM and FS questions with their overall performance by calculating quotients such as P_{FM}/P_T (where P_{FM} is the average percentage of FS and MM points gained in the exams and P_T is the average overall percentage of points). We observed an increase from 87.9 % to 97.8 % in this ratio.

(2) Students voiced their opinions about the combined treatment in a survey. Its results are positive, too, but weaker since students could not base their assessments on knowing both types of teaching OS concepts, but only the new combined approach. Also, only ten students participated in this survey. 90 % stated that the combined treatment made sense, and 80 % said that the frequent changes between FS and MM did not cause confusions. All participants said, the combination made it easy to understand that many concepts from one topic translate to the other. However, they were sceptical about combining more topics in a similar fashion (30 % approval).

3. CONCLUSIONS AND FURTHER WORK

Results from the double evaluation motivate further research in this area: Since students performed better in the exam and also valued the combined treatment, it makes sense to identify further OS topics that are typically treated separately but might also benefit from being combined. It would also be helpful to repeat this comparison with larger groups of students, ideally with a class large enough that it could be split by pretesting and forming two equally strong groups which then attend lectures that are identical except for the presentation of FS and MM topics.

More generally, it would be interesting to identify further Computer Science topics which are traditionally taught separately but share many concepts, and apply the same approach. The overall idea behind this is a shift of focus from concrete topics to general concepts.

An extended version with detailed descriptions of the modifications and the evaluations' results is available as a technical report [1].

4. REFERENCES

[1] Eßer, H.-G., *Treating Memory Management and Filesystems as One Topic*, University of Erlangen, Dept. of Computer Science, Technical Reports, CS-2011-04, April 2011.

SyntaxTrain: Relieving the Pain of Learning Syntax

Andreas Leon Aagaard
Moth
DTU Informatics
Tech. Univ. of Denmark
DK-2800 Lyngby, Denmark
s051608@student.dtu.dk

Jørgen Villadsen
DTU Informatics
Tech. Univ. of Denmark
DK-2800 Lyngby, Denmark
jv@imm.dtu.dk

Mordechai Ben-Ari
Dept. of Science Teaching
Weizmann Institute of Science
Rehovot 76100 Israel
moti.ben-ari@
weizmann.ac.il

ABSTRACT

SyntaxTrain parses a Java program and displays the syntax diagrams associated with a syntax error.

Categories and Subject Descriptors

K.3.2 [**Computer and Information Science Education**]: Computer science education

General Terms

Human Factors

Keywords

syntax, syntax diagram, learning programming

1. INTRODUCTION

In introductory courses, too much time must be devoted to developing proficiency with the difficult syntax of languages like Java and C++. The formal description of the syntax of a language is presented in BNF, but BNF is difficult for students to use.

An alternative presentation of syntax is available: the *syntax diagrams* used in the first published book on Pascal [1]. Here is a fragment of the syntax diagram for the nonterminal `statement`:

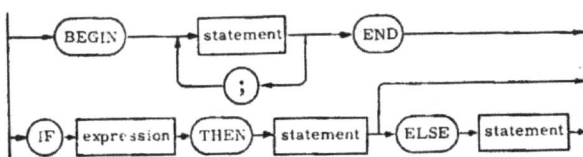

We can clearly see, for example, the use of a semicolon as a separator, rather than as a terminator. One need not give an ad hoc rule: don't place a semicolon before an `else`.

Strangely, these easy-to-read diagrams are almost non-existent in current textbooks! Furthermore, students are no longer interested in using printed documentation. We designed and developed the software package **SyntaxTrain** to display syntax diagrams for Java. The software is built upon a parser so that when a syntax error is encountered, the diagram for the offending construct is displayed, together with a trace of the containing constructs.

2. USER INTERFACE

SyntaxTrain parses source code in Java. When an error is detected, the syntax diagrams of the relevant constructs are shown in a stack, starting with the construct containing the error, then its parent, grandparent, etc. In each diagram, the path taken by the compiler is highlighted in blue and the part in error is highlighted in red.

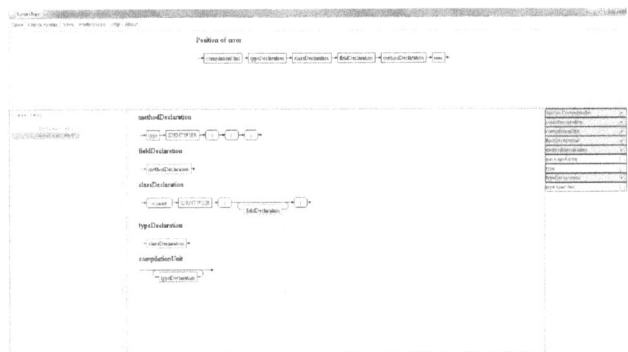

SyntaxTrain also displays the source code with the error highlighted and a diagram showing the constructs relevant to the error. Unused syntax rules can also be shown; this enables the user to browse through the diagrams in order to understand the grammar of the language.

3. IMPLEMENTATION

SyntaxTrain consists of a command-line tool and a graphical tool. The former uses a parser built using ANTLR to read a BNF file for a language and convert it into a parser for use by the graphical tool. The output of the parser is a table of which rules failed and which components inside each rule were successfully matched. An XML file is created along with the parser to supply a simple specification of the BNF structure and to facilitate the translation of the output of the parser. The graphical interface uses the XML file to generate syntax diagrams and calls the parser with a reference to the source code that should be checked. The output of the parser is used to highlight the rules that failed, along with which subrules were successfully matched inside the generated diagrams.

SyntaxTrain is an open-source project available at `http://code.google.com/p/syntaxtrain/`.

4. REFERENCES

[1] K. Jensen and N. Wirth. *PASCAL User Manual and Report*, volume 18 of *LNCS*. Springer-Verlag, 1975.

The Impact of Memory Transfer Language (MTL) on Reducing Misconceptions in Teaching Programming to Novices

Leonard J. Mselle
The University of Dodoma
mselel@yahoo.com

Raphael Mmassy
Tanzania Commission for Science and Technology
rmmasi@yahoo.com

Categories and Subject Descriptors: D.3.m Miscellaneous

General Terms: Languages

Keywords: Learning programming, Memory Transfer Language (MTL)

1. INTRODUCTION TO MEMORY TRANSFER LANGUAGE (MTL)

Memory Transfer Language (MTL) is a paper-and-pencil device that mimics computer memory (RAM). It is used to aid novice programmers to understand their codes. Functionally, MTL is used by the programmer to interpret his/her code the way the machine uses compilers/interpreters to understand codes. The relationship between compilers and MTL is depicted in Figure 1.

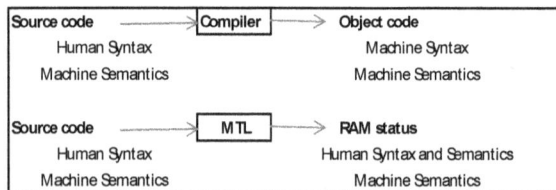

Figure 1. Comparison between MTL and compiler

From Figure 1, we deduce that;

- The machine uses Compiler/Interpreter to understand the code. The produced object code is in machine- language syntax which is only readable and meaningful (semantics) to the machine.
- The programmer uses MTL to interpret the source code. The produced **Memory (RAM) status** is readable to programmers (human syntax). At the same time, RAM status conveys the meaning of the source code from machine point of view (machine semantics) as well as in human semantics (visual RAM status).

2. DESCRIPTION OF MTL

MTL is used to illustrate all elementary programming concepts such as variable declarations, data feeding, assignments, data operations and outputting. MTL is used to illustrate flow of control mechanisms such as selections and loops. Other programming concepts such as arrays, functions and file

handling are best described by MTL. Program interpretation using MTL is partially illustrated using Figures 2 and 3 where a program (Figure 2) is interpreted through MTL (Figure 3).

```
//Program 2
#include <iostream>
main()
{
    int sum=0;
    int i=1;
    while (i<4){
        sum=sum+i;
        i=i+1;
    }
}
```

Figure 2. Loop implementation in C++

With MTL, Program 2 (the source code) is interpreted as shown in Figure 3.

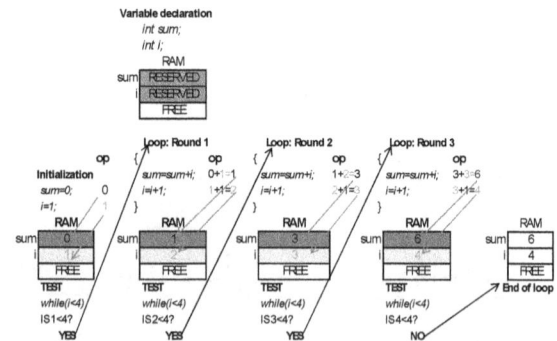

Figure 3. Demonstration of MTL. (Description of Program 2- flow of control with a while-loop)

3. THE EXPERIMENT, RESULTS AND CONCLUSION

A class experiment was carried out to evaluate the impact of MTL in reducing common misconceptions which culminate in programming errors by novices. Based on the results, it is concluded that the use of MTL by novice programmers increases comprehension, and reduces the number of errors committed.

Optimizing Collaborative Learning Processes by Using Recommendation Systems

Sebastian Harrach
Department of Philosophy
Darmstadt University of Technology
Darmstadt, Germany
harrach@phil.tu-darmstadt.de

Mojisola Anjorin
Multimedia Communications Lab
Darmstadt University of Technology
Darmstadt, Germany
mojisola.anjorin@kom.tu-darmstadt.de

ABSTRACT

In this paper, we present the work of the research group e-learning at the Darmstadt University of Technology by describing a paradigmatic research cooperation between the departments of philosophy and computer science. Here, the perspective of Parallelkommunikation from the philosophy of technology is used to increase the transparency of recommendation systems used in certain learning scenarios. This is achieved by providing explanations to allow a better understanding of the reasons behind recommendations. With this enhanced understanding, users can give more relevant feedback, thereby actively influencing the ranking of resources.

Categories and Subject Descriptors

K.3.1 [**Computers and Education**]: Computer Uses in Education – *Collaborative learning*

General Terms

Human Factors

Keywords

Machine learning, semantic network, Parallelkommunikation

1. INTRODUCTION

We apply the perspective of Parallelkommunikation [1] to a general learning scenario (where a group of learners are working collaboratively within a semantic network) and thereby exemplify the interconnectivity and interdisciplinary character of the projects of the research group e-learning.

We then focus on one paradigmatic subproject: the task of improving recommendation systems [2] based on ranking algorithms.

2. RECOMMENDATION FEEDBACK

The perspective of Parallelkommunikation [1] calls for three additional communication levels in any user/system interaction:

1. User/Developer communication regarding the developer's perceptions on user stereotypes

2. Community based meta-communication regarding the general requirement about system communication

3. On demand transparency within the user/system communication while the system is active

These three communication levels have been investigated by the research group e-learning:

(1) Currently, a research group member of the department of pedagogy is in the initial stages of investigating dynamic modification of user stereotypes by analysing formative assessments.

(2) A meta-discussion of collaborative learning practices in online communities from the point of view of educational theory was part of a completed dissertation of a research group member of the department of pedagogy [3].

(3) Concerning this third level of communication, we present here a more detailed description of the work in progress currently being conducted on a paradigmatic project within the research group. This will give an impression of the daily work within the group and what research questions arise as a result:

Providing explanations and thereby supporting the transparency of recommendations is an important field in computer science and particularly in recommendation systems [2]. Explanations provide additional details so the user can better understand the reasoning of the system and why specific recommendations are generated. This transparency helps the user to better influence the ranking algorithms which calculate the relevance of resources in the network. Examples of ranking algorithms are FolkRank, TrustRank or Interestingness Ranking [4]. Some ranking algorithms use machine learning algorithms to generate recommendations based on the textual content of the resource, the structure of the network, the user's activities or a combination of these.

The user can actively take part in improving the ranking of resources by explicitly giving relevance feedback [4]. This can be implemented when the learner accepts or ignores (implicitly rejects) the recommendations made by the system. The relevance feedback can then be used to improve the selection of resources to be recommended once again. However, learners should be able to switch off these complex ranking algorithms [4] to avoid over-specifying the individual rankings and recommendations.

3. REFERENCES

[1] Hubig, C. 2006: Die Kunst des Möglichen (pages 190f). Bielefeld: transcript Verlag.

[2] Jannach, D., Zanker, M., Felfernig, A., and Friedrich, G.: 2010: Recommender Systems - An Introduction, 143-165. Cambridge University Press (CUP).

[3] Koenig, C. *To Appear*: Bildung im Netz. Münster: Ph.D. Thesis, TU Darmstadt.

[4] Peters, I. 2009: Folksonomies. Indexing and Retrieval in Web 2.0, 339-362. Walter de Gruyter. Sauer.

The Use of Mediating Artifacts in Embedding Problem Solving Processes in an E-Learning Environment

Orry Messer
School of Computer Science
University of the Witwatersrand
Johannesburg, South Africa
messero@cs.wits.ac.za

Angelo Kyrilov
School of Computer Science
University of the Witwatersrand
Johannesburg, South Africa
angelo@cs.wits.ac.za

Categories and Subject Descriptors

K.3.1 [**Computer Uses in Education**]: Computer-assisted instruction (CAI)

General Terms

Measurement, Design, Human Factors

Keywords

E-Learning, Cognitive Theory, Mediating Artifacts

ABSTRACT

In this poster we report on the design, implementation, testing and evaluation of an e-learning tool which helps students learn how to solve recursion problems in the first year computer science courses at the University of the Witwatersrand, Johannesburg, South Africa. The aim of this project was to create a tool that interactively helps students learn rather than just displays information on a computer screen. The design is based on distributed cognition theory and Polya's problem solving framework. The problem solving framework is broken up into four dynamic stages:

1. Understanding the problem

2. Making a plan

3. Carrying out the plan

4. Looking back (evaluating the outcome)

The process is dynamic, since at any stage the user can either move forward, to the next stage, if she is satisfied with the outcome of that stage, or the user can move backward, to the previous stage, if she is unable to complete that stage to her satisfaction. Several of the stages were broken up into sub-stages. The tool, whose main purpose was to instil good problem solving practices while keeping the students motivated, was implemented as a web interface, using HTML and PHP with database support from MySQL. In order to implement the tool in a manner consistent with the framework delineated above, at each stage the tool led the user to complete the stage at a level that required more than a surface level understanding of the problem. For example, in stage one, the user was asked questions about the problem,

in order to promote a deeper level of understanding about the problem.

To test the tool's effectiveness, volunteers from an undergraduate Computer Science class were split up into two groups. Over the course of two weeks both groups were asked to implement four recursion problems in a programming context. The programming language used was Python. One group (test group) had access to our tool, while the other (control group) did not. The following are two of the four initial problems the students were asked to solve:

1. write a program in Python which will calculate the nth Fibonacci number.

2. write a program in Python which will find the greatest common divisor of 2 positive integers using Euclid's Algorithm.

At the end of the experiment both groups were given a final problem. Neither group used the tool in this final evaluation. The purpose of this test was to see whether the students who used the tool had developed better problem solving approaches. The problem given for the final evaluation was as follows:

final problem: write a program in Python which will calculate the nth Catalan Number, $cat(n)$.

The results of the experiment were analysed using a series of t-tests at a 5% significance level. The analysis revealed that at worst, the test group performed at least as well as the control group and otherwise the test group performed significantly better when attempting the first four problems. It was also revealed that the test group performed significantly better in attempting the final evaluation. This led us to conclude that the tool is a useful addition to the current set of instruments for teaching Computer Science.

1. REFERENCES

[1] M. Morgan, G. Brickell, and B. Harper. Applying Distributed Cognition Theory to the Redesign of the 'Copy and Paste' Function in Order to Promote Appropriate Learning Outcomes. Technical report, Elsevier, 2008.

[2] A. H. Schoenfeld. *Learning to think mathematically: Problem solving, metacognition, and sense making in mathematics. In D. Grouws (Ed.), Handbook for Research on Mathematics Teaching and Learning (pp. 334-370).* MacMillan, 1992.

Introducing Students to Computer Science With Programmes That Don't Emphasise Programming

Tim Bell
Computer Science and Software Engineering
University of Canterbury
Christchurch, NZ
+64 3 364-2987
tim.bell@canterbury.ac.nz

Paul Curzon
School of Electronic Engineering and Computer Science
Queen Mary University of London
London, E1 4NS, UK
+44 (0)20 7882 5212
paul.curzon@eecs.qmul.ac.uk

Quintin Cutts
School of Computing Science
University of Glasgow
Glasgow, G12 8RZ, Scotland
+44 (0)141 330 5619
quintin.cutts@glasgow.ac.uk

Valentina Dagiene
Vilnius University
Vilnius, LT-08663 Lithuania
+370 698 05448
valentina.dagiene@mii.vu.lt

Bruria Haberman
Computer Science Department,
Holon Institute of Technology, Holon, Israel,
and Davidson Inst. of Science Education,
Weizmann Inst. of Science,
Rehovot 76100, Israel
bruria.haberman@weizmann.ac.il

ABSTRACT

We examine five outreach programmes that introduce school students to Computer Science. All downplay programming as a pre-requisite skill for engaging with Computer Science, yet they use a wide variety of formats for reaching students, including contests, shows, magazine articles, and resources for teachers. We classify these different approaches, identifying the different ways they have been adapted to their target audience, and drawing out the common elements to provide guidance for similar initiatives.

Categories and Subject Descriptors

K.3.2 [**Computer and Information Science Education**]: Computer Science Education

General Terms

Human factors

Keywords

K-12 outreach, computational thinking.

1. OUTREACH PROGRAMMES

We compare five outreach approaches with the common goal of attracting students to study Computer Science (CS). The approaches enable students to engage with concepts from CS without having to first learn how to program and present practical ways to engage students in Computational Thinking [5]:

(a) The Bebras competition, which is based around CS concepts [4]. Students who enter this annual competition are challenged to solve a variety of tasks from a broad range of computing areas without using programming. An additional area on ICT and Society gets them to think about the wider issues of computing;

(b) CS Unplugged, a series of activities originally designed as an outreach resource for engaging students with meaningful games, magic tricks and challenges that involve a broad range of concepts from CS without using a computer at all [1];

(c) The cs4fn (CS for Fun) project presents shows in schools and at science festivals, and produces free magazines, online articles and books [2]. Its aim is to present advanced CS topics and research in offbeat ways to high school students to enthuse them about interdisciplinary CS, science and engineering;

(d) The CS Inside project, a series of lessons primarily aimed at teachers, providing engaging ideas for introducing CS concepts in the classroom situation [3]. The activities are intended to bring out some of the CS to be found inside the technology that is part of students' everyday lives.

(e) The CS, Academia and Industry programme is intended to bridge the gap between school and the "real world" of computing by enabling students to meet with experts from academia and industry [6]. It includes enrichment meetings, field trips and software development projects under the supervision of experts.

Our aim is to suggest a classification tool for: (a) evaluating existing approaches of this kind, examining how they can be adapted to a target population, and (b) suggesting new approaches aiming at attracting specific target populations to study computer science in a novel way. Drawing out the common features and themes of these successful programmes provides guidelines for the design of future initiatives. The tool may enable those designing outreach to evaluate approaches, to choose the most suitable approach for their students, and to adapt the approaches to the target population and context. The approaches described here have all had widespread adoption and influence. We conclude that programmes that downplay or avoid programming provides an effective and scalable way to introduce CS.

2. REFERENCES

[1] Bell, T Alexander, J., Freeman, I. and Grimley, M. 2009. Computer Science Unplugged: School Students Doing Real Computing Without Computers. In *The New Zealand Journal of Applied Computing and Information Technology*, 13(1), 20-29.

[2] Curzon, P. and McOwan P.W. 2008. Engaging with Computer Science through Magic Shows, *ACM SIGCSE Bulletin*, 40 (3), 179-183.

[3] Cutts, Q., Brown, M., Kemp, L. and Matheson, C. 2007. Enthusing and informing potential computer science students and their teachers. *ACM SIGCSE Bulletin*, 39(3), 196-200.

[4] Dagiené V. 2006. Information technology contests– introduction to computer science in an attractive way. *Informatics in Education*, 5 (1), 37-46.

[5] Wing, J.M. 2006. Computational thinking. *Communications of the ACM*, 49(3), 33-35.

[6] Yehezkel, C., and Haberman, B. 2006. Bridging the gap between school computing and the "real world". *Lecture Notes in Computer Science*, 4226, 38-47.

Integrating Scholarly Articles Within E-Learning Courses: A Framework

Bee Bee Chua, Danilo Valeros Bernardo II
University of Technology, Sydney
1 Broadway P O Box 123
New South Wales, Australia
bbchua@it.uts.edu.au and bernardan@gmail.com

ABSTRACT

Most e-learning courses do not include research as part of teaching materials for learners. A framework SOAR (**Sch**olarly **ar**ticles) based on an educational theory can foster a circle of educational knowledge building and sharing between educators and learners that emphasizes a better understanding of scholarly articles. This framework has been validated in several courses and its results demonstrate that it has a positive impact on students' learning, which has shown a significant improvement as well as an increase in both creativity and innovation skills.

Categories and Subject Descriptors

H.0 Scholarly Articles, E-Learning

General Terms

Theory, Experimentation, Measurement

Keywords

Student learning, educators, learners, scholarly articles

1. E-LEARNING CHALLENGES

Two challenges faced by learners while using E-learning systems are: 1) Uninteresting course materials fail to promote deep learning, and 2) learning approaches are insufficient to increase knowledge that extends beyond theories and concepts.

2. INTRODUCTION OF SOAR FRAMEWORK

SOAR (Scholarly Articles) — a framework we developed — can help to guide educators through the process of integrating a research component into their courses and create a learning environment that is more conducive and meaningful to students.

Our framework allows learners a thinking space in which to develop creativity and apply it by enabling them to build their problem solving and research skills. The design of this framework is based on Brown et al.'s [1] educational theory and framework, which aims to foster a circle of educational knowledge building and sharing. Our framework (SOAR) in Figure 1 requires a subject as an input. Scholarly articles are picked because past, present and future works in each field are clearly presented.

This *creates* an educator's thinking space in which to decide whether to *use* scholarly articles [2] as a 1) class activity, 2) a test assessment or 3) whether to integrate it and *remix* into a

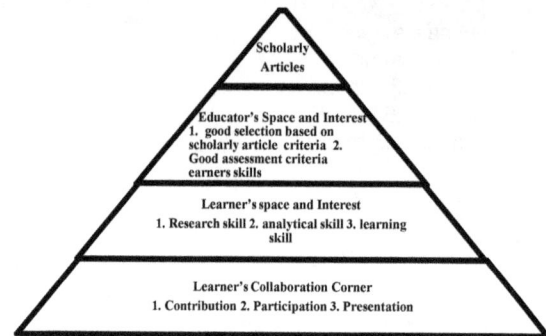

Figure 1 SOAR Framework.

tutorial. The e-learning interface acts as a middle process or agent to facilitate open discussion via social networking and as a process to promote a learner's space which will encourage more collaboration, participation and presentation.

3. METHOD

INPUT: Course materials and scholarly articles uploaded on an e-learning system.

PROCESS: Students must read each scholarly article and relate it to its concept and apply it in the context of a case study. Students must contribute their discussions or answers on a discussion board questions being asked by presenters.

OUPUT: Group presenters summarize their findings including the outcome of student discussions and present their talk (an overview of the paper, research questions and a summary of participants' comments) in a class or a video conference.

4. RESULTS

The results of the learning outcome show that students in groups understand scholarly articles and the concepts they have learned in the class. Students surveyed about the framework say that they find it very useful, because it helps them sharpen their critical thinking skills. The results (evidences from screenshots of an e-learning system) further imply that the framework gives students a better opportunity to learn that help improves their analytical skills, and enables them to contribute innovative ideas.

5. REFERENCES

1. J.S.Brown and R.P.Alder.Minds of Fire: Open Education, the Long Tail and Learning 2.0, EDUCAUSE Review, Vol 43. No 1.Pp1632 http://educause.edu/ir/library/pdf/ERM0811.pdf
2. B.B.Chua, and D.V.Bernardo,. Introducing Scholarly Articles: A Way for Attaining Educational Sustainability. In Proceedings of the Second International Conference on Mobile, Hybrid, and On-Line Learning. 2010

Supporting Peer Learning with Ad-Hoc Communities

Johannes Konert[1], Kristina Richter[2], Stefan Göbel[1], Ralf Steinmetz[1], Regina Bruder[2]

[1]Department of Electrical Engineering and Information Technology, Multimedia Communication Lab, Working Group Serious Gaming, Rundeturmstraße 10, 64283 Darmstadt, Germany
{johannes.konert, stefan.goebel, ralf.steinmetz}@KOM.tu-darmstadt.de

[2]Department of Mathematics, Working Group Didactics of Mathematics, Schloßgartenstraße 7, 64289 Darmstadt, Germany
{richter, bruder}@mathematik.tu-darmstadt.de

ABSTRACT
Research in learning and competence development shows the benefits of peer support and access to peers' solutions for learning and understanding[1]. We propose a concept for task-focused knowledge exchange in a learner network using a digital learning environment that supports creation of ad-hoc (sub)communities by matching learning opportunities. Structural results from Social Network Analysis (SNA) are incorporated in the derived models of community-based learning in (sub)communities. The approach, research questions and the planned evaluation setup are described.

Categories and Subject Descriptors
K.3.1 [**Computer Uses in Education**]: Computer-Assisted Instruction (CAI)

General Terms
Algorithms, Measurement, Design, Experimentation, Human Factors.

Keywords
Learning communities, peer reviews, knowledge sharing, ERGM.

1. MOTIVATION
As learning is a highly individual process, learning opportunities need to be provided appropriately. Computer technology may support this process, but cannot replace human interpretation and assessment – especially of open format questions[2], because here manifold strategic approaches and argumentations are possible. Learning opportunities arise here from two sides: First, assessment of such (existing) solutions can support consolidation of one's own understanding of the topic. Second, consuming the feedback that a second peer left on one's own solution can reveal (new) strategic knowledge and concepts for understanding[1]. Supporting this knowledge sharing in a computer-based learning environment opens new possibilities for the quality of blended learning. Especially for freshmen lectures of computer science (e.g. those dealing with maths) this approach provides loosely connected students with broad access to their fellows' knowledge - independent from time and place. With diagnostic design behind[2], and SNA[3] individual learning opportunities can be optimized and sub-clusters of the existing network can be formed (for learning).

2. APPROACH
Accompanying lectures, the software PEDALE consists of an authoring tool and an independent player tool, both connected to a central content database. Without any programming skills, lecturers or educational professionals can setup the learning environments with test questions provided to students for practicing, diagnosis of their understanding and their solitary learning processes. The player component allows access to tasks and their solutions, which can be assessed. Assessment of one's own solutions from peers can be rated. The environment matches previous learning results (internal learner model) to learning opportunities (next tasks matching possible deficits). Solving similar tasks repeatedly allows the system to analyze the significant attributes of nodes in the underlying social network and multi-entity networks of existing knowledge (skill profile), accessed tasks, solutions and accomplished actions for maximization of learning efficiency.

3. RESEARCH THESES, EVALUATION
(1) The access to peer heuristics in ad-hoc learning communities with PEDALE enhances learning processes.
(2) PEDALE supports learners in becoming aware of their status of knowledge and abilities.
(3) The establishing of (sub)-groups of learners with more effective learning outcomes in PEDALE using a peer matching algorithm based on relevant measures from the underlying (social) network structures leads to better learning outcomes.

The evaluation setup is planned to comprise interviews, pre- and posttests and continuous activity measuring (content access/provision, test question results) in order to generate exponential random graph models (ERGM or p*) based on the significant attributes calculated with social network analysis (SNA). The accuracy of the models can then be shown by simulation.

4. REFERENCES
[1] W. Damon, "Peer education: The untapped potential," *Journal of Applied Developmental Psychology*, vol. 5, Dec. 1984, pp. 331-343.
[2] M. Bayrhuber, T. Leuders, R. Bruder, and M. Wirtz, *pedocs - Repräsentationswechsel beim Umgang mit Funktionen – Identifikation von Kompetenzprofilen auf der Basis eines Kompetenzstrukturmodells. Projekt HEUREKO*, BELTZ Pädagogik, 2010.
[3] G. Robins, P. Pattison, Y. Kalish, and D. Lusher, "An introduction to exponential random graph (p) models for social networks," *Social Networks*, vol. 29, May. 2007, pp. 173-191.

Exploring Flow in Novice Programming Environments

Mark Zarb
School of Computing
University of Dundee
markzarb@computing.dundee.ac.uk

Dr Janet Hughes
School of Computing
University of Dundee
jhughes@computing.dundee.ac.uk

ABSTRACT

Flow theory describes a way of gauging happiness and motivation. The flow experience has been widely researched within several contexts, such as work and education. There are opportunities to explore the occurrence of flow within the context of novice programming. What can help students achieve flow? Can flow affect programming success?

Categories and Subject Descriptors

K.3.2 [**Computers and Education**]: Computer and Information Science Education – *computer science education.*

General Terms

Measurement, Performance, Human Factors

Keywords

Flow, cognition, novices, programming, learning, teaching.

1. BACKGROUND RESEARCH

Flow is a state of mind where people are so involved in an activity that they strive to achieve their fullest potential. They do this simply for the sake of experiencing the activity itself, rather than because it is required of them. Flow occurs when the individual experiences an optimal balance between challenge and skill, and is characterised by several qualities, including an intense concentration, transformed sense of time, and a merging of their action and awareness [1]. Essentially, flow equates with a strong sense of self-motivation, which is considered the best way to learn. This theory has been used as a way of guiding students in various areas of education, which increases their overall success [2]. Research ranges from applying key concepts to system design to inspire flow in the users [3], to focusing on how students achieve flow through a re-structuring of their learning process [4].

Programming has been taught for several decades. The idea of looking at improving techniques for teaching programming is not a new one – research typically deals with improving the way novices are introduced to programming. It is normally the case that successful students are not challenged by the subject, whilst weak students find it difficult to grasp complex concepts. These concepts become increasingly difficult and challenging, effectively leaving weaker students behind [5].

2. MEASURING FLOW

In other contexts, such as sport, flow has been researched extensively and has been linked to the individual's success on several occasions. This has led to the creation of the Flow State Scales (FSS), which are a set of items that can be used to measure the nine dimensions of flow in a physical activity setting [6]. The scales have recently been revised to provide some conceptual and statistical perspectives. To date, the Flow State Scales are arguably the only multidimensional measure of flow that can be used without disrupting the individual's performance [7].

This research involves looking at the different means of measuring flow in a programming environment. Initially, the FSS shall be slightly edited to be in context within this environment. A range of ways for applying them shall then be explored. Paper-based and tablet-based forms shall be considered in various environments such as during lab assignments, and group-work

3. FUTURE WORK

The identification of a metric to measure flow in a programming environment would allow exploration of the differences in flow duration and achievement between successful and weaker students. This would contribute to an understanding of whether flow has an impact on the students' overall success. Similarly, any distractions of flow, and the effect these have on the students, would also be explored in the context of this work.

4. ACKNOWLEDGEMENTS

The research work disclosed in this publication is partially funded by the Strategic Educational Pathways Scholarship Scheme (Malta). The Scholarship is part-financed by the European Union – European Social Fund.

5. REFERENCES

[1] Csikszentmihalyi, M. *Flow.* Rider, London, 2002.
[2] Malone, T. W. and Lepper, M. R. Making learning fun: A taxonomy of intrinsic motivations for learning. *Aptitude, learning and instruction*, 3 (1987), 223-253.
[3] Storey, M. A. D. Improving Flow in Software Development through Graphical Representations. In *Proceedings of the IEEE Symposium on Visual Languages and Human Centric Computing* (30 Sept, 2004).
[4] Bakker, A. B. Flow among music teachers and their students: The crossover of peak experiences. *Journal of Vocational Behaviour*, 66 (2005), 26-44.
[5] Lister, R. and Leaney, J. First Year Programming: Let All the Flowers Bloom. In *Proceedings of the 5th Australasian Computer Education Conference* (Adelaide, 2003). Australian Computer Society, Adelaide.
[6] Jackson, S. and Marsh, H. W. Development and validation of a scale to measure optimal experience: The Flow State Scale. *Journal of Sport and Exercise Psychology*, 18, 1 (1996), 17-35.
[7] Jackson, S. A. and Eklund, R. C. *The Flow Scales Manual.* Fitness Information Technology, US, 2004.

Muddy Hill Games

Jessica Blevins
jessica.k.blevins@gmail.com

Andy Kearney
kearneyandy@gmail.com

Eric Mullen
emullen@hmc.edu

Emily Myers-Stanhope
Emily_Myers-Stanhope@hmc.edu

Z Sweedyk
z@cs.hmc.ed@hmc.edu

Harvey Mudd College
301 Platt Blvd.
Claremont, CA 91711
U.S.A.

ABSTRACT

Computer games are widely used as pedagogical tools in the classroom. In recent years, the use of game projects in Computer Science (CS) curriculum has grown in popularity. The Muddy Hill Games project marries these ideas by engaging CS students in the design and development of educational games for middle school students. This approach enhances the game projects by providing a real customer and users. It results in free educational software that serves middle school learning objectives. Finally, it informs middle school students' understanding of Computer Science and motivates interest in the field. Here we describe four games that have come out of the project.

Categories and Subject Descriptors

K.3.2. [**Computer and Information Science Education**]: Computer Science Education, Curriculum

General Terms: Design, Experimentation

Keywords

Games, Broadening Participation, K12, Software Engineering Education

1. INTRODUCTION

Muddy Hill Games is a collaborative project between Harvey Mudd College (HMC) and Hillside Middle School (HMS), Kalamazoo, MI. Social science teachers Greg Orr and Josh Yavor at HMS are customers for educational computer game projects carried out by HMC students as part of the software development course. This collaboration benefits all parties. The software development projects are enhanced by having real customers and users. The middle school teachers acquire free educational software that is designed specifically for their needs. The project also serves to inform middle school students' understanding of Computer Science and motivates interest in the field.

Four of the most promising games developed over the 2009-2010 academic year were refined by the authors for use in HMS classrooms. These games are currently being assessed as pedagogical tools.

2. The Games

In *Hectare*, the player manages the weather and other environmental factors in order to help computer-controlled agricultural settlements flourish.

The player in *Energy Empire* is charged with running a power company and must balance economic and environmental factors when choosing the types of power plants to build.

Village Defense teaches students about the agricultural revolution. The player delegates villagers to various tasks, such as hunting, farming, and village defense, in order to ensure their continued survival.

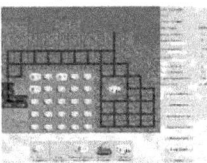

In *Time Mystery Mischief*, the player's friends have been trapped in the past by a villain with a time machine. The player must discover clues in historical artifacts in order to pinpoint when in time each friend is located.

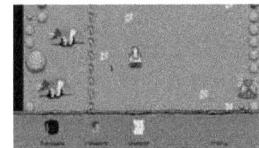

3. Acknowledgements

Thanks to Greg Orr, Josh Yavor and their students at Hillside. Thanks to all of the CS121 students who contributed to these games including B. Fish, C. Loncaric, A.Novak, and A. Yodipinyanee for *Hectare*; D. Huie, S. Pernsteiner, and A. Zuckerberg for *Energy Empire*, E. Carlson, J. DeBlasio, K. Ewing, E. Fujimoto, K. Gragg, S. Lakhani, A. Lawrence, and L. Vasserman for *Time Mystery Mischief*.

Author Index